W9-BMD-243

Modern American Women Writers

Modern American Women Writers

ELAINE SHOWALTER
CONSULTING EDITOR

LEA BAECHLER
A. WALTON LITZ
GENERAL EDITORS

CHARLES SCRIBNER'S SONS / NEW YORK

COLLIER MACMILLAN CANADA / TORONTO
MAXWELL MACMILLAN INTERNATIONAL / NEW YORK OXFORD SINGAPORE SYDNEY

Library of Congress Cataloging-in-Publication Data

Modern American women writers / Elaine Showalter, consulting editor,
Lea Baechler, A. Walton Litz, general editors.
p. cm.
Includes bibliographical references and index.
ISBN 0-684-19057-5
1. American fiction—Women authors—Dictionaries. 2. Women authors. American—Biography—Dictionaries. 3. American literature—Women authors—Bio-bibliography. 4. Women and literature—United States—History—20th century—Dictionaries. 5. American literature—20th century—Bio-bibliography. 6. American literature—20th century—Dictionaries. I. Showalter, Elaine. II. Baechler, Lea. III. Litz, A. Walton.
PS151.M54 1991
810.9'9287'03—dc20 90-52917
CIP

Charles Scribner's Sons
Macmillan Publishing Company
866 Third Avenue
New York, New York 10022

Collier Macmillan Canada, Inc.
1200 Eglinton Avenue East
Suite 200
Don Mills, Ontario M3C 3N1

Impression

4 5 6 7 8 9 10

PRINTED IN THE UNITED STATES OF AMERICA

ACKNOWLEDGMENTS

ELIZABETH BISHOP Excerpts from *The Collected Prose* by Elizabeth Bishop, copyright © 1984 by Alice Methfessel; excerpts from the *The Complete Poems, 1927–1979* by Elizabeth Bishop, copyright © 1979, 1983 by Alice Helen Methfessel; excerpts from *The Diary of "Helena Morley"* translated by Elizabeth Bishop, copyright © 1957 by Elizabeth Bishop. Reprinted by permission of Farrar, Straus and Giroux, Inc. Excerpts from the letters of Elizabeth Bishop are used with the permission of her Estate, copyright © 1989 by Alice Helen Methfessel. Excerpt from *Writers at Work*, 6th Series, edited by George Plimpton. Copyright © 1984 by the Paris Review, Inc. Reprinted by permission of Viking Penguin, a division of Penguin Books USA Inc.

LOUISE BOGAN "Medusa" and "Night" from *The Blue Estuaries* by Louise Bogan. Copyright © 1968 by Louise Bogan. Reprinted by permission of Farrar, Straus and Giroux, Inc.

GWENDOLYN BROOKS Excerpt from *Report from Part One* by Gwendolyn Brooks, Broadside Press, 1972. Reprinted by permission.

EMILY DICKINSON From *The Complete Poems of Emily Dickinson*, edited by Thomas H. Johnson. Copyright 1914, 1929,

1935, 1942 by Martha Dickinson Bianchi; © renewed 1957, 1963 by Mary L. Hampson. By permission of Little, Brown and Company. And reprinted by permission of the publishers and the Trustees of Amherst College from *The Poems of Emily Dickinson,* Thomas H. Johnson, ed., Cambridge, Mass.: The Belknap Press of Harvard University Press, Copyright 1951, © 1955, 1979, 1983 by the President and Fellows of Harvard College. Quotations from Letters of Emily Dickinson reprinted by permission of the publishers from *The Letters of Emily Dickinson,* edited by Thomas H. Johnson, Cambridge, Mass.: The Belknap Press of Harvard University Press, Copyright © 1958, 1986 by the President and Fellows of Harvard College.

HILDA DOOLITTLE Excerpts from materials in the Hilda Doolittle papers at the Beinecke Rare Book and Manuscript Library, Yale University, are quoted by permission of Perdita Schaffner and New Directions Publishing Corp., agents.

MARY E. WILKINS FREEMAN Quotations from letters collected in *The Infant Sphinx: Collected Letters of Mary E. Wilkins Freeman,* edited by Brent L. Kendrick, Scarecrow Press, Inc., 1985.

CHARLOTTE PERKINS GILMAN Permission has been granted by the Schlesinger Library, Radcliffe College, for use of material from Collection 177 of the Charlotte Perkins Gilman Papers. Quotations from letters by Charlotte Anna Perkins to Martha Luther [Lane], dated August 15, 1881, and September 6, 1881, have been reprinted from the Charlotte Perkins Gilman Papers, Rhode Island Historical Society, Manuscript Division.

MAXINE HONG KINGSTON Excerpts from "At the Winter Palace" and "A Song for a Barbarian" from *The Woman Warrior* by Maxine Hong Kingston. Copyright © 1976 Maxine Hong Kingston; and excerpts from "Great Grandfather of the Sandalwood Mountains" from *China Men* by Maxine Hong Kingston. Copyright © 1980 Maxine Hong Kingston. Reprinted by permission.

AMY LOWELL From "Venus Transiens," "The Taxi," "The Weather-Cock Points South," and "The Sisters," from *The Complete Poetical Works of Amy Lowell* by Amy Lowell. Copyright © 1955 by Houghton Mifflin Co. Copyright © 1983 renewed by Houghton Mifflin Co., Brinton P. Roberts, and G. D'Andelot Belin, Esquire. Reprinted by permission of Houghton Mifflin Co.

EDNA ST. VINCENT MILLAY All quotations from Edna St. Vincent Millay's poetry and letters are reprinted by permission of Elizabeth Barnett, Literary Executor for the Estate of Edna St. Vincent Millay/Norma Millay Ellis.

MARIANNE MOORE Excerpts from "To Military Progress," "The Fish," "England," "New York," and "Marriage," copyright 1935 by Marianne Moore, renewed 1963 by Marianne Moore and T. S. Eliot; excerpt from "Virginia Britannia," copyright 1941 and renewed 1969 by Marianne Moore. Reprinted with permission of Macmillan Publishing Company and Faber and Faber Ltd from *Collected Poems* by Marianne Moore. Excerpts from *The Complete Prose of Marianne Moore* by Marianne Moore. Copyright © Clive E. Driver, Literary Executor of the Estate of Marianne C. Moore, 1959, 1960, 1961, 1962, 1963, 1964, 1965, 1986. Introduction copyright © Patricia C. Willis, 1986. Copyright © Marianne Moore, 1941, 1942, 1944, 1946, 1948, 1955, 1958, 1959, 1960, 1961, 1962, 1963, 1964, 1965, 1966, 1967, 1968. Copyright renewed Marianne Moore, 1969, 1970, 1972. Copyright renewed Lawrence E. Brinn, 1974, 1976. Copyright renewed Lawrence E. Brinn and Louise Crane, 1983, 1985, 1986. All rights reserved. Reprinted by permission of Viking Penguin, a division of Penguin Books USA, Inc. Excerpt from T. S. Eliot, reprinted by permission of Mrs. Valerie Eliot and Faber and Faber Ltd from *Dial* LXXV.6 (December 1923). Excerpt from "Efforts of Affection: A Memoir of Marianne Moore" from *The Complete Prose* by Elizabeth Bishop. Copyright © 1984 by Alice Methfessel. Reprinted by permission of Farrar, Straus and Giroux, Inc. Excerpts from Louise Bogan, *A Poet's Alphabet* and *What the Woman Lived,* reprinted by permission of Ruth Limmer. All rights reserved. Quotations from *The Selected Letters of Ezra Pound 1907–1941,* edited by D. D. Paige (Copyright 1950 by Ezra Pound) and from *Selected Essays of William Carlos Williams* (Copyright 1931 by William Carlos Williams) are used by permission of New Directions Publishing Corporation. Photo caption from "Remarkable American Women: 1776–1976" in *Life,* 1976, Special Issue. *Life* Magazine © Time Warner.

JOYCE CAROL OATES All quotations copyright Ontario Review, Inc.

GRACE PALEY Excerpts reprinted by permission of Grace Paley. Copyright 1974 from *Enormous Changes at the Last Minute,* Farrar, Straus and Giroux, Inc.; and copyright 1956 from *The Little Disturbances of Man,* Viking Press.

DOROTHY PARKER Excerpts from "Partial Comfort," "Resume," "Testament," and "Far from Well" from *The Portable Dorothy Parker.* Copyright 1925, 1926, 1928, copyright © renewed 1954 and 1956 by Dorothy Parker. Excerpts from "Lady with a Lamp" and "The Lovely Leave" from *The Portable Dorothy Parker.* Copyright 1932, 1943 by Dorothy Parker. Reprinted by permission of Viking Penguin, a division of Penguin Books USA Inc., and Gerald Duckworth and Co. Inc. Excerpt from "To a Tragic Poetess" by Ernest Hemingway in *88 Poems,* © 1979 by The Ernest Hemingway Foundation and Nicholas Georgiannis, reprinted by permission of Harcourt Brace Jovanovich, Inc.

SYLVIA PLATH From "Female Author," "Winter Landscape, with Rooks," "Pursuit," "Electra on Azalea Path," "In Plaster," "Blackberrying," "The Bee Meeting," "The Swarm," "Ariel," "Nick and the Candlestick," "Tulips" (Copyright © 1962 by Ted Hughes), "The Moon and the Yew Tree" (Copyright © 1963 by Ted Hughes), "Daddy" (Copyright © 1963 by Ted Hughes), "Lady Lazarus" (Copyright © 1963 by Ted Hughes) from *The Collected Poems of Sylvia Plath,* edited by Ted Hughes. Copyright © 1981 by Ted Hughes. Reprinted by permission of Harper & Row, Publishers, Inc. and Olwyn Hughes. Excerpts from "The Thin People," "All the Dead Dears," "The Disquieting Muses," "Full Fathom Five," "The Beekeeper's Daughter," "The Colossus," and "The Stones." Copyright © 1960, 1961, 1962,

INTRODUCTION

In the preface to her anthology *American Female Poets* (1848), the novelist Caroline Kirkland explained that the biographical notes were disappointingly brief because the women writers were too constrained by feminine decorum to say very much about themselves. "To say where they were born seems quite enough while they are alive," Kirkland noted apologetically. "Thus, several of our correspondents declared their fancies to be their only facts; others that they had done nothing all their lives; and some—with a modesty most extreme—that they had not lived at all." Happily, American women writers are no longer so self-effacing, nor critics so reluctant to investigate their lives, whether they led what Ellen Glasgow called "a sheltered life," or a life of travel, adventure, romance, and fame. Feminist criticism in the 1970s and 1980s has established the importance of women's personal experience in relation to their artistic opportunities and choices. Childhood, relationships with mothers and fathers, sexuality, decisions about marriage and maternity, friendships with other women, the aging process—all of these aspects of women's creative lives affected the way they were able to shape their literary careers.

This book brings together critical and biographical essays about forty-one representative women writers who have published in the United States since the 1870s. In its range and depth, it is the most extensive study of American women's writing to date. The writers begin chronologically with Frances Ellen Watkins Harper, born in 1825, and end with Alice Walker, born in 1944. They span a wide range of regions, races, and genres; there are poets, playwrights, short story writers, autobiographers, and novelists, as well as intellectuals such as Charlotte Perkins Gilman, Maya Angelou, Elizabeth Hardwick, and Susan Sontag, who can best be seen as American women of letters. Each essay combines a detailed account of the writer's life with a thorough and original analysis of her work, and a substantial bibliography. While in most literary histories women authors are still excluded, treated as minor, or bundled with other minorities, this book offers an opportunity to see the diversity and power of American women's writing on its own terms and, in the words of Adrienne Rich, "on its own premises."

Reading about these very different lives, we discover first of all that there is no single pattern that distinguishes American women's literary careers; they are no more alike than their male counterparts. Women writers came from all kinds of class, ethnic, and regional backgrounds; they found a wide variety of solutions to the problem of combining love and work; they located themselves at every point along the axis from feminist activism to political indifference. Some writers explicitly repudiated the idea of a feminine voice in literature, or even dissociated themselves from the work of their female predecessors. In 1895, Willa

Cather asked whether "Women have any place in poetry at all"; and as an aspiring young playwright, Lillian Hellman expressed her contempt for "ladywriter" stories. Describing the gap between the writer's self-image and her critical reception, Joyce Carol Oates observed, "A woman writer is a writer by her own definition, but she is a *woman* writer by others' definitions." Yet in every generation there have also been American women writers who have defined themselves centrally in terms of their gender, and have attempted to express feminine difference in the language, images, structures, and themes of their work.

Do these writers, then, have anything in common as women? I think we can identify a few important issues and concerns. First of all, there is the question of self-naming. Women's names carry a special significance, both because they are assumed to be temporary and contingent, and because in most instances, as literary signatures, they disclose and emphasize the author's gender. American women writers named themselves differently from their European counterparts. In the nineteenth century, it became almost standard for serious women writers in England and Europe, such as the Brontës, George Eliot, and George Sand, to publish their work under male pseudonyms, in order to gain artistic freedom, receive fair treatment from the critics, and assert their literary ambition beyond stereotypes of domesticity and femininity. These celebrated authors were revered by American women; Sarah Orne Jewett was one of many nineteenth-century admirers of the Brontë sisters who made a pilgrimage to Haworth parsonage. In her early writing, Jewett called herself "A. C. Eliot," in homage, Marilee Lindemann suggests, to the pseudonyms of the Brontës (Acton, Currer, and Ellis Bell) and George Eliot. But while the male pseudonym swept England and Europe from Norway to Spain, it never caught on in the United States. Here pseudonyms were feminine or even hyperfeminine: Fanny Fern or Grace Greenwood. Jewett was soon calling herself "Sarah O. Sweet," and before long she dropped that pseudonym to publish under her own name. In a young country, there was both more pride of female authorship and more confidence that it would find a fair hearing and an audience.

Yet self-naming has been important for American women writers in other respects. For Hilda Doolittle, the literary signature "H.D." became an iconic emblem of purely poetic identity, a "pattern of letters" rather than a man or a woman. Mary Flannery O'Connor and Lula Carson McCullers dropped their girlish first names when they began to write. Even early in the twentieth century, a surprising number of women writers did not take their husband's names. These choices signal an awareness of the conflict between traditional images of women and the writer's identity.

Second, while women were rarely prevented from writing, they had to deal with social expectations that biological and literary creativity were antithetical for women. We first hear of women writers in America in 1645, when the governor of Hartford, Edward Hopkins, brought his wife, Anne, to Boston, seeking medical help. "A godly young woman of social parts," Anne Hopkins had lost her wits, her husband believed, "by occasion of her giving herself wholly to reading and writing and hath written many books" (John Winthrop, *History of New England*). When Anne Bradstreet published a book of poems, *The Tenth Muse, Lately Sprung Up in America,* in 1650, her brother-in-law explained that the poems were "but the fruit of some few hours, curtailed from her sleep and other refreshments," not an interruption of her domestic work or religious devotions. Such assumptions affected modern women as well. Charlotte Perkins Gilman was subjected to a rest cure in which she was not allowed to read or write; Ellen Glasgow was told to go home and have babies; Anaïs Nin's psychoanalyst believed that when she was cured of her neuroses, she would "become a woman" and stop writing.

Critically, women's writing was often categorized as sentimental or intellectually limited. Since the period after the Civil War, many American women writers have been dismissed under the label of "regionalist," with the implicit assumption that the literature of a particular community, especially a rural community, cannot be universal or meaningful in an urbanized, postindustrial age. Setting out to write *O Pioneers!*, Willa Cather wryly acknowledged that "Nebraska is distinctly déclassé as a literary background; its very name throws the delicately attuned critic into a clammy shiver of embarrassment." Yet, as Jewett wrote, "One may travel at home in a most literal sense." To those gifted with imagination and perception, no place can be too small to yield a rich diversity of human experience. Eudora Welty, who has such gifts, has been one of the most eloquent contemporary defenders of "place in fiction." When Welty went away to Mississippi State College for Women, only two hundred miles from her home, she was struck by the astonishingly "different voices" of the girls from across the state, from the Delta to the cities. Mississippi and the South have been a region that, she writes, "endows me and enables me." While many of the most celebrated American male writers, from Thoreau to Faulkner, have also been regionalists, the label was used more against women, who were thought of as conservative and immobilized. In reading these essays, we need to remember that the writers here were the survivors, the strongest and most determined, who persisted in the face of pychological obstacles, personal difficulties, and often periods of critical rejection.

While individually these essays explore a diversity of experiences and triumphs, together they constitute a history of American women's writing since the 1870s. The American female tradition is the product of literary exchanges. There is nothing essentially feminine in women's imagination determined by their biology, bodies, or psyches that leads them to write about particular subjects in particular ways. Rather, as Henry Louis Gates, Jr., has argued in the introduction to his edition of nineteenth-century black women writers, a tradition develops "because writers read other writers and *ground* their representations of experience in models of language provided largely by other writers to whom they feel akin. It is through this process of literary revision, amply evident in the *texts* themselves—in formal echoes, recast metaphors, even in parody—that a 'tradition' emerges and defines itself." Clearly, American women writers read and revised each other's work across generations, regions, and even races. Sarah Orne Jewett drew inspiration from Harriet Beecher Stowe, Willa Cather from Jewett, Toni Morrison from Cather. Alice Walker was influenced by both Flannery O'Connor and Zora Neale Hurston. Louise Bogan studied the work of such forgotten predecessors as Louise Imogen Guiney and Lizette Woodworth Reese, as well as Emily Dickinson.

In order to understand the historical and cultural contexts of American women's writing since the 1870s, we need to know something about its early history. After the Revolution, American attitudes toward women and literature were in fact more progressive than those of England and Europe. Americans took patriotic pride in the country's female genius, seeing the development of women's abilities as a testimonial to the democratic ideal. In 1800 a critic declared his pleasure that "female literary merit hath presented so brilliant an addition to our national glory." The Declaration of Independence was an important literary document for women, to whom it signified their freedom to speak out. Harriet Beecher Stowe was one American girl who heard it read aloud on the Fourth of July and vowed someday "to make some declaration on my own account." In 1848, at the first American women's rights convention in Seneca Falls, New York, Elizabeth Cady Stanton wrote the feminist "Declaration of Rights and Sentiments," which demanded for women "all the rights and privileges which belong to them as citizens of the United States."

Writing was one of these privileges, and also one of the few professions, apart from teaching, in which women could earn money and prestige. Margaret Fuller's *Woman in the Nineteenth Century* (1845) saluted "the triumphs of Female Authorship" as a "sign of the times." In *Female Poets of America*, one of several anthologies of American women's writing that appeared during this period, the editor, Rufus Griswold, boasted of "the increased degree in which women among us are taking a leading part in literature. . . . The proportion of female writers at this moment in America far exceeds that which the present or any other age in England exhibits."

By the 1850s, women were the best-selling American authors, far surpassing in popularity all the famous male writers of the American Renaissance. Judith Fetterley argues persuasively in her book *Provisions* (1986) that during the mid nineteenth century, women were indeed "more comfortable with writing than their male counterparts," who were expected to enter more stable and lucrative professions. Women writers were welcome as long as they confined themselves to feminine subjects and verse for the ladies' magazines. But as women became serious competitors in the literary market, especially as novelists, critical attitudes toward their work became much harsher. Hawthorne's famous remark of 1855, that "America is now wholly given over to a damned mob of scribbling women," reflects this change.

Thus, by the 1870s, even as women's writing was becoming ever more sophisticated, diverse, and artful, critics had established a two-tier system of high art and popular fiction, in which women's books were seen as the trashy best-sellers that drove male genius out of the market.

In much American literature of this period, women stand for bad poetry, prayer meetings, and genteel refinement. In most literary histories of American literature there has been a tacit division of aesthetic labor that has relegated women's writing to an inferior plane of the popular, the regional, or the sentimental.

After the Civil War, the separate world of women's culture began to dissolve as American women demanded entrance to higher education, the professions, and the political world. The female "local colorists" who began to publish short stories of American regional life in the 1870s, such as Jewett and Freeman, were attracted to the masculine worlds of high art and prestige opening up to women. Claiming both male and female artistic models and precursors, they openly spoke of themselves as artists. Frances Harper was influenced by Whittier and Longfellow; Kate Chopin read Maupassant; Jewett kept a motto from Flaubert above her desk. The New Women writers of the 1890s did not grieve for the female bonds and sanctuaries of the past, and challenged puritanical beliefs about female sexuality as well. In both the form and the content of their work, they sought freedom and innovation, introducing fantasy and allegorical modes into the novel, as well as experimenting with impressionistic narratives that attempted to explore a hitherto unrecorded female consciousness. By the turn of the century, women writers were creating new narrative forms and endings for women's stories. This was a period of intense aesthetic development for both fiction and poetry.

With the success of such writers as Willa Cather and Edith Wharton, and with the momentum of the suffrage movement, a golden age of American women's writing seemed to have dawned. In *The Man-Made World* (1911), Charlotte Perkins Gilman predicted that "the humanizing of woman" would lead to new subjects and plots in fiction: "The position of the young woman who is called upon to give up her 'career' . . . for marriage and objects to it; . . . the middle-aged woman who at last discovers that . . . it is not more love she wants but more business in life; . . . the inter-relation of women with women . . . the [lifelong] interaction between mothers and children, and the new attitude of the full-grown woman." The fiction of Zora Neale Hurston, Tillie Olsen, Katherine Anne Porter, Toni Morrison, and Joyce Carol Oates, among many others, fulfilled her prophecy.

But after World War I, the critical contexts of women's writing changed. With the passage of the Nineteenth Amendment, feminism waned, as if all the solutions to women's problems had been found. With the rise of American academic literary history, women were written out of the national canon. In *The Cambridge History of American Literature* (1917), a critic noted that "acquaintance with the written record of these two centuries should enlarge the spirit of American literary criticism and render it more energetic and masculine." Whether criticism became more energetic may be open to debate, but there can be no doubt that in the years after World War I it became more masculine. While before the war, most American textbooks and anthologies included a substantial representation of women writers, after the war the women were rapidly dropped. By 1935, *Major American Writers*, the standard college textbook edited by Howard Mumford Jones, included no women writers at all. The critical reputations of Cather and Wharton continued to decline in the 1930s and 1940s.

Whether in Greenwich Village bohemia, in the Left, or in the Harlem renaissance, women writers were marginalized and patronized by the exponents of modernism, communism, or "the race." The austere tenets of modernism espoused by T. S. Eliot and Ezra Pound created difficulties for women lyric poets such as Edna St. Vincent Millay and Louise Bogan. Some women writers, among them Gertrude Stein and H.D., became expatriates, finding more supportive artistic communities in Paris and London. While, as Harriet Chessman comments, Stein's daring and playful work "throws other modernist literature into a more conservative light," during her lifetime she was often ridiculed and misunderstood. The poems of H.D. and Marianne Moore that entered the modernist canon were those, as Celeste Goodridge points out, which were "recognizably 'feminine,' and thus either patronized or pathologized." Black women writers, including Jessie Fauset, Zora Neale Hurston, and Gwendolyn Brooks, continued to explore the personal disappointments and sexual dilemmas of black women in their fiction despite pressure to conform to uplifting racial ideologies.

The low point for American women writers during the twentieth century was the 1950s, when Freudians preached in the medical and the popular press about the tragedy of American women, and when postwar domestic values urged them to return to their kitchens and nurseries. In college-level textbooks and anthologies of American literature, women averaged only about 3 percent of the writers represented. For talented girls growing up female in the 1940s and 1950s, such as Sylvia Plath and Anne Sexton, the lack of female role models was intensely discouraging. Their main ambition was to distinguish themselves from other women writers who had failed. In 1958, Anne Sexton wrote to her mentor, the poet W. D. Snodgrass, "I wish I were a man—I would rather write the way a man writes." This was the generation that all too often seemed to pay for its literary achievements in depression, alcoholism, and suicide.

But in the late 1960s, the second wave of American feminism brought with it a renewed interest in women's writing. Lost women writers were rediscovered, their works brought once more into print, to be read, taught, and discussed. Fueled by the attention and devotion of feminist criticism, and by the burgeoning market for their work, American women writers entered a renaissance. One of its most significant aspects has been the encouragement of writers from many ethnic and racial backgrounds, and the opportunity for black and Asian-American writers to reach wide audiences. "For a serious American writer, especially a woman writer," Joyce Carol Oates has said, "this has been by far the best era in which to live."

With the addition of women's writing, we can now begin to rethink what Joan deJean and Nancy K. Miller call "the categories and vocabulary of literary history itself—period, genre, value, masterpiece, classic, major, minor, all of which have been at work in the displacement and elimination of 'women's writing' from the national canon.'' Women have revised the fundamental themes and conventions of American literature, including its myths of individuality, community, language, and the frontier. Feminine imagination and feminine energy are part of our cultural heritage, and any history of American literature that excludes women's contribution cannot be complete. Today, Wai-chee Dimock confidently claims in her essay on Kate Chopin, ''a college student is as likely to have read *The Awakening* as *Moby-Dick*.'' This may be too optimistic an assertion, but this book will surely be an important contribution to the knowledgeable appreciation of American women's writing that is long overdue.

ELAINE SHOWALTER

CHRONOLOGY

1640– Anne Bradstreet, first woman author in the United States, publishes her *Several Poems.*

1756 In Uxbridge, Massachusetts, the widow of Josiah Taft becomes the first woman in the United States to have her vote recorded.

1776 New Jersey is the first colony to grant the vote to women; woman suffrage is repealed in 1807.

1784 Hannah Adams, probably the first professional woman writer in the United States, publishes *Alphabetical Compendium of the Various Sects. . . .*

1796 Sarah W. A. Morton is coauthor (with William H. Brown) of the first novel published in the United States, *The Power of Sympathy.*

1797 Isabella Graham founds the Society for the Relief of Poor Widows with Small Children, believed to be the first benevolent association in the United States managed by women.

1809 Elizabeth Bayley Seton establishes the Sisters of St. Joseph, the first religious order founded in the United States.

1824 The first strike by women takes place in Pawtucket, Rhode Island.

1825 Frances Wright establishes Nashoba, a cooperative settlement of slaves meant to prepare them for freedom, near Memphis.

1825–1911 Frances Ellen Watkins Harper

1829 Frances Wright begins publication of *The Free Enquirer,* a newspaper dedicated to examining social, political, and religious issues.

1830–1886 Emily Dickinson

1834 The American Female Moral Reform Society is formed.

1835 *The Advocate,* written and edited by women of the American Female Moral Reform Society, begins publication.

1836 Wesleyan College, in Macon, Georgia, the first chartered women's college, is opened.

1840 Catherine E. Brewer is the first woman college graduate in the United States.

1845 Margaret Fuller's *Woman in the Nineteenth Century* is published.

1846 Mount Union College, in Alliance, Ohio, is the first college in the United States to grant absolutely equal rights to female students.

1848 Elizabeth Cady Stanton and Lucretia Mott organize the Seneca Falls Convention, the first women's rights convention in the United States.

The Seneca Falls Declaration of Rights and Sentiments is delivered and published.

1849 Elizabeth Blackwell is the first woman in the United States to receive the M.D. degree.

1849–1909 Sarah Orne Jewett

1850 The first national convention of women advocating woman suffrage is held in Worcester, Massachusetts.

Lucy Ann Stanton is the first black woman college graduate in the United States.

1850–1904 Kate Chopin

1852–1930 Mary E. Wilkins Freeman

1853 Antoinette Brown Blackwell is ordained a minister in the Congregational Church, the first woman in the United States to be ordained in a regularly constituted religious denomination.

Elizabeth Blackwell, Emily Blackwell, and Marie Zakrzewska establish the New York Infirmary for Women and Children, the first such institution in the United States to be staffed entirely by women.

Paulina Davis begins publishing *Una,* the first distinctly women's rights newspaper in the United States.

1855 Lucy Stone is the first woman in the United States to retain her maiden name after marriage, as a symbol of equality.

1860–1935 Charlotte Perkins Gilman

1862–1937 Edith Wharton

1863 Clemence Lozier founds the New York Medical College and Hospital for Women.

1866 The American Equal Rights Association is organized by Lucretia Mott and Susan B. Anthony.

1867 Virginia Minor leads in the organization of the Woman Suffrage Association of Missouri, the first organization to have the exclusive aim of enfranchising women.

1868 Susan B. Anthony and Elizabeth Cady Stanton publish *The Revolution*, a radical weekly newspaper.

1869 Belle Mansfield becomes the first practicing female attorney in the United States.

Elizabeth Cady Stanton and Susan B. Anthony found the National Woman Suffrage Association.

Lucy Stone and Julia Ward Howe found the American Woman Suffrage Association.

Wyoming (territory) grants women the vote.

1871 Charlotte Ray is the first black woman in the United States to earn a law degree.

1872 Victoria Claflin Woodhull runs for president of the United States as a candidate of the Equal Rights Party.

Susan B. Anthony and fifteen other women are arrested in Rochester, New York, for attempting to vote in the presidential election.

1873 The Comstock laws, prohibiting dissemination of information on contraception and prescription of contraceptive devices, are enacted.

1873–1947 Willa Cather

1873–1945 Ellen Glasgow

1874 Women's Christian Temperence Union formally established.

1874–1925 Amy Lowell

1874–1946 Gertrude Stein

1876–1948 Susan Glaspell

1877 Helen Magill is the first woman to receive the Ph.D. degree in the United States.

1879 Mary Baker Eddy founds Christian Science.

1881 Clara Barton founds the National Society of the Red Cross.

1881–1886 Elizabeth Cady Stanton, Susan B. Anthony, and Matilda Joslyn Gage compile and publish the six-volume *History of Woman Suffrage.*

1882–1961 Jessie Fauset

1886–1961 Hilda Doolittle

1887–1972 Marianne Moore

1889 Jane Addams and Ellen Gates Starr found Hull-House in Chicago.

1890 The National Woman Suffrage Association and the American Woman Suffrage Association merge to form the National American Woman Suffrage Association, with Elizabeth Cady Stanton as president.

1890–1980 Katherine Anne Porter

1891–1960 Zora Neale Hurston

1892–1950 Edna St. Vincent Millay

1893–1967 Dorothy Parker

1895 Elizabeth Cady Stanton's *Woman's Bible* is published.

1896 The National Association of Colored Women, headed by Mary Church Terrell, is formed.

1897–1970 Louise Bogan

1898 Charlotte Perkins Gilman's *Women and Economics* is published.

1901 The Army Nurse Corps is created, thereby opening the armed services to women.

1902 Martha Washington is the first American woman to be depicted on a U.S. postage stamp.

1903 The Women's Trade Union League is established.

1903–1977 Anaïs Nin

1905–1984 Lillian Hellman

1909– Eudora Welty

1911–1979 Elizabeth Bishop

1912 Juliette Low founds the Girl Scouts of America.

1912–1989 Mary McCarthy

1913 The Woman's Peace Party of New York is organized.

1915 The Woman's Peace Party becomes a national organization; Jane Addams is the first national president.

1916 Janette Rankin is the first woman elected to the U.S. House of Representatives.

Margaret Sanger opens the first birth control clinic in the United States.

1916– Elizabeth Hardwick

1917 The National Birth Control League is founded by Margaret Sanger.

Laura E. Richards and Maude Howe Elliott are the first women to win the Pulitzer Prize, for the biography *Julia Ward Howe.*

1917–1967 Carson McCullers

1917– Gwendolyn Brooks

1919 Jane Addams is a founder of the Women's International League for Peace and Freedom.

1920 The Nineteenth Amendment, giving women the vote, is ratified.

The League of Women Voters is organized by Carrie Chapman Catt.

Ethelda Bleibtrey is the first American woman to win a gold medal in the Olympic Games.

1921 Edith Wharton wins a Pulitzer Prize for *The Age of Innocence.*

1922 Rebecca Latimer Felton is the first woman appointed to the U.S. Senate.

1922– Grace Paley

1923 The Equal Rights Amendment is presented to Congress by Alice Paul.

Willa Cather wins a Pulitzer Prize for *One of Ours.*

Edna St. Vincent Millay wins a Pulitzer Prize for *The Ballad of the Harp-Weaver, A Few Figs from Thistles,* and eight sonnets in *American Poetry, 1922, a Miscellany.*

1925 Nellie Tayloe Ross is the first American woman to be elected governor of a state.

1925–1964 Flannery O'Connor

1926 Amy Lowell wins a Pulitzer Prize for *What's O'Clock.*

1928–1974 Anne Sexton

1928– Maya Angelou

1929 Janet Gaynor is the first woman to win an Oscar.

1929– Adrienne Rich

1931 Susan Glaspell wins a Pulitzer Prize for *Alison's House.*

Jane Addams shares the Nobel Prize for peace with Nicholas Murray Butler.

1931– Toni Morrison

1932–1963 Sylvia Plath

1933 Frances Perkins is named secretary of labor, the first woman to hold a cabinet post.

1933– Susan Sontag

1934 Florence E. Allen is the first woman appointed to the Federal Court of Appeals.

Hattie W. Carraway is the first woman elected to the U.S. Senate.

1934– Joan Didion

1936 Physicians win the right to dispense birth control information and devices.

1938 Pearl S. Buck is the first American woman to win the Nobel Prize for literature.

1938– Joyce Carol Oates

1940 Hattie McDaniel is the first black woman to win an Oscar.

1940– Maxine Hong Kingston

1941– Anne Tyler

1942 Ellen Glasgow wins a Pulitzer Prize for *In This Our Life.*

1944– Alice Walker

1947 Dr. Gerty T. Cori is the first woman awarded the Nobel Prize in medicine or physiology.

1948 The Women's Armed Forces Integration Act provides permanent status for women in the U.S. armed forces.

1949 Eugenie Moore is appointed the first U.S. woman ambassador.

1950 Gwendolyn Brooks wins a Pulitzer Prize for *Annie Allen.*

1952 Marianne Moore wins a National Book Award and a Pulitzer Prize for *Collected Poems.*

1955 Rosa Parks, a black woman in Montgomery, Alabama, refuses to yield her seat in the front of a bus to a white man. The resulting confrontation leads to a boycott by blacks of the Montgomery bus system—the beginning of the civil rights movement in the United States.

1956 Elizabeth Bishop wins a Pulitzer Prize for *Poems—North & South.*

1963 The Equal Pay for Women Act, which requires equal wages and salaries for men and women doing equal work, becomes law.

Betty Friedan publishes *The Feminine Mystique.*

1964 Title VII of the Equal Rights Act prohibits discrimination based on sex by employers of twenty-five or more employees, employment agencies, and labor unions with twenty-five or more members; educational institutions are exempted.

1966 Betty Friedan founds the National Organization for Women.

Katherine Anne Porter wins a National Book Award and a Pulitzer Prize for *Collected Stories.*

1967 Anne Sexton wins a Pulitzer Prize for *Live or Die.*

1968 Shirley Chisholm is the first black woman elected to the U.S. House of Representatives.

1969 The First Congress to Unite Women convenes in New York City.

1970 Elizabeth P. Hoisington, director of the Women's Army Corps, and Anna Mae Hays, chief of the Army Nurse Corps, are the first women to be promoted to the rank of brigadier general in the U.S. Army.

New York State law permits abortion on demand; only the consent of a woman and her physician is required.

Kate Millett publishes *Sexual Politics.*

Joyce Carol Oates wins a National Book Award for *Them.*

Elizabeth Bishop wins a National Book Award for *The Complete Poems.*

Lillian Hellman wins a National Book Award for *An Unfinished Woman.*

1971 The National Woman's Political Caucus is organized by Gloria Steinem, Bella Abzug, Shirley Chisholm, and Betty Friedan.

1972 The Equal Rights Amendment passes Congress and is sent to the states for ratification.

Shirley Chisholm is the first black woman to run for president of the United States.

Gloria Steinem and Patricia Carbine found *Ms.* magazine.

Sally Preisand is the first woman rabbi to be ordained in the United States.

Flannery O'Connor wins a National Book Award for *The Complete Stories.*

1973 In *Roe* v. *Wade,* the Supreme Court rules that a state may not prevent a woman from having an abortion during the first six months of pregnancy.

Eudora Welty wins a Pulitzer Prize for *The Optimist's Daughter.*

The National Black Feminist Organization is founded.

Bonnie Tiburi is hired as the first female pilot to fly for a major airline.

1974 Adrienne Rich wins a National Book Award for *Diving into the Wreck.*

The first American female Episcopal priests are ordained.

The U.S. Merchant Marine Academy is the first service academy to admit women. Little League baseball teams are opened to girls.

Janet Gray Hayes is the first woman to be elected mayor of a major U.S. city (San Jose, California).

1975 The First Women's Bank opens in New York City.

The Army, Navy, Air Force, and Coast Guard academies admit women.

Elizabeth Bayley Seton is the first American-born woman to be canonized a saint in the Roman Catholic Church.

1981 Sandra Day O'Connor is the first woman justice of the Supreme Court.

1982 Sylvia Plath wins a Pulitzer Prize for *The Collected Poems.*

The Equal Rights Amendment fails to be ratified by thirty-eight states by the 30 June deadline.

1983 Sally Ride is the first American female astronaut in space.

Alice Walker wins an American Book award and a Pulitzer Prize for *The Color Purple.*

1984 Geraldine Ferraro, a New York congresswoman, is the first woman to be nominated for vice president by a major political party.

1985 Montana is the first state to forbid insurance companies to discriminate against women in terms of premium paid and policy conditions.

1987 The Supreme Court requires Rotary International to admit women as members.

1988 Toni Morrison wins a Pulitzer Prize for *Beloved.*

1989 Kristen M. Baker is named first captain of the corps of cadets at West Point.

Barbara Harris is consecrated the first woman bishop of the Episcopal Church in the United States.

In *Webster* v. *Reproductive Health Services,* the Supreme Court reverses Missouri state court ruling that had held unconstitutional a state statute which stated life begins at conception, limited use of public funds for abortion, and prohibited abortions after twenty weeks of pregnancy.

1990 Marianne Moore is honored on a U.S. postage stamp.

EDITORIAL STAFF

CONTENTS

Modern American Women Writers

MAYA ANGELOU

1928–

THROUGH HER LIFE and work, Maya Angelou has triumphantly created and re-created the self, endowing her life story with symbolic significance and raising it to mythic proportions. How many people could master so many careers: streetcar conductor, madam, dancer, actress, autobiographer, director, screenwriter, journalist, poet, and playwright? "I love life," says Angelou in an interview with Robert Chrisman in *The Black Scholar*. "I love living life and I love the art of living, so I try to live my life as a poetic adventure, everything I do. . . ."

Angelou has written five volumes of autobiography, including the widely celebrated *I Know Why the Caged Bird Sings* (1970), *Gather Together in My Name* (1974), *Singin' and Swingin' and Gettin' Merry Like Christmas* (1976), *The Heart of a Woman* (1981), and *All God's Children Need Traveling Shoes* (1986). She is also the author of four volumes of poetry, including *Just Give Me a Cool Drink of Water 'fore I Diiie* (1971), *Oh Pray My Wings Are Gonna Fit Me Well* (1975), *And Still I Rise* (1978), and *Shaker, Why Don't You Sing?* (1983), as well as plays, screenplays, and numerous periodical articles.

Maya Angelou was born Marguerite Johnson on 4 April 1928 in St. Louis, Missouri, the only daughter of Bailey and Vivian (Baxter) Johnson. Educated in public schools in Arkansas and California, Angelou later studied music privately and dance with Martha Graham, among others. Her long and varied career as an author, playwright, professional stage and screen performer, and singer has included appearances in *Porgy and Bess* (a twenty-two-nation tour sponsored by the United States State Department in 1954–1955), Off-Broadway performances and a Broadway debut in *Look Away* (1973), and the direction of the film *All Day Long* (1974) and her own play *And Still I Rise* (1976).

A member of the Directors' Guild of America, she has also served on the board of trustees of the American Film Institute. Angelou, who speaks numerous languages fluently, has traveled extensively in Europe, the Middle East, and Africa; worked as a journalist for foreign publications (the *Arab Observer*, 1961–1962, and the *Ghanaian Times*, 1963–1965); and been honored by the academic world, receiving a Yale University Fellowship (1970) and being named a Rockefeller Foundation Scholar in Italy (1975). She has taught at the University of Ghana, the University of California (Los Angeles), and the University of Kansas (as writer-in-residence), and currently holds a lifetime chair as Z. Smith Reynolds Professor of American Studies at Wake Forest University. Included among her many awards are the Woman of the Year Award in Communications of the *Ladies' Home Journal*, and her nominations for the Pulitzer Prize and Tony Award. Maya Angelou is much sought after on the lecture circuit.

Lynn Z. Bloom describes Angelou's poetic adventure as an "odyssey" encompassing parallel psychological, spiritual, literary, and geographical movement, beginning with what is probably Angelou's best-known work, *I Know Why the Caged Bird Sings*. In addition to her volumes of autobiography, Angelou's verse collections of address similar themes, images, and rhythms. Poems like "When I Think About Myself" and "Times-Square-Shoeshine-Composition" (in *Just Give Me A Cool Drink*) echo the blues/protest poetry of Langston Hughes, but they are also grounded in Angelou's experience as a black woman. Poems like "Woman Me," "Phenomenal Woman," and "And Still I Rise" celebrate this experience as exemplary and symbolic of a spirit that refuses to be crushed. "I speak to the black experience," Angelou once said, "but I am always talking about the human condition—about what we can endure, dream, fail at, and still survive." In this sense, she faithfully depicts her home ground as a version of the universal human experience.

I Know Why the Caged Bird Sings distills the essence of her autobiographical impulse, turning it into lyric imagery touched by poignant realism. The title of this work is taken from the poem "Sympathy" by the great black poet Paul Laurence Dunbar. The sentiment of Dunbar's poem suggests the tone of Angelou's autobiography, and her struggle to overcome the restrictions of a hostile environment. Angelou is in "sympathy" with the bleeding bird behind the mask, and it seems likely that Dunbar would have been in sympathy with Angelou as well. Like the Dunbar poem and the spirituals sung by Southern blacks, *I Know Why the Caged Bird Sings* displays an impulse toward transcendence. Like the song of the caged bird, the autobiography represents a prayer sent from "the heart's deep core," from a depth of emotion. The author prays that the bird be released from its cage of oppression so that it may fly free from the definitions and limitations imposed by a hostile world.

The work is perhaps the most aesthetically satisfying autobiography written by a black woman in the years immediately following the civil rights era. As a creative autobiographer—one who borrows techniques from fiction but writes in the first person and asserts the truth—Angelou focuses entirely on the inner spaces of her emotional and personal life. The mature woman looks back on her bittersweet childhood, yet her authorial voice retains the power of the child's vision. The child's point of view governs Angelou's principle of selection, and when the mature narrator steps in her tone is purely personal. Myra K. McMurry calls *Caged Bird* "an affirmation, . . . Maya Angelou's answer to the question of how a Black girl can grow up in a repressive system without being maimed by it."

Angelou does not progress only from a state of semi-orphanhood to one of motherhood; she develops through various stages of self-awareness. The Johnson family moved from St. Louis to Long Beach, California, where Angelou's "parents . . . put an end to their calamitous marriage." This action occurs off camera in Angelou's graphic autobiography. Her own story begins with an image that embodies the sense of displacement that Marguerite, the heroine of *Caged Bird,* strives to overcome—the image of two children, aged three and four, arriving in Stamps, Arkansas, as "tagged orphans." Young Marguerite Johnson would remain in Stamps with her paternal grandmother, Mrs. Annie Henderson, whose "deep-brooding love hung over everything she touched."

Religion, an important theme throughout *Caged Bird,* represents a sustaining force in the life of Mrs. Henderson, who derives spiritual sustenance and fortitude from "the Bread of Heaven." When threatened, Momma (as Marguerite calls her grandmother) turns to her faith, which is clearly a source of her personal power. Respecting her grandmother's homespun teaching, Marguerite embraces both the literary and the folk influences of her culture, through observation, study, and loving imitation. Marguerite faces the threat of lynching and other frequent intrusions of "white reality" by following her grandmother's example. She learns the virtue of courage, which the mature writer regards as "the most important virtue of all."

One of the important early turning points in the autobiography centers on Marguerite and her brother's move to St. Louis, which comes after the children have lived happily with their grandmother for about five years. Initially more of a change in geographic location than a change in consciousness, the move eventually precipitates profound problems of identity. In

St. Louis, Marguerite endures the most shattering experience of her childhood when she is raped by her mother's boyfriend, Mr. Freeman. She feels physical and psychological guilt as a result of the rape, but also the guilt of having exposed Freeman, who meets a violent death at the hands of "persons unknown" (presumably Marguerite's tough St. Louis uncles). The rape marks a new period of intense crisis for Marguerite, who after Freeman's death decides, voluntarily, not to speak to anyone except her brother Bailey.

Marguerite loses much of her innocence during this "perilous passage," which cuts her childhood painfully short. Soon Marguerite and Bailey find themselves on the train going back to Stamps, a place that provides the obscurity the eight-year-old girl craves "without will or consciousness." After a year of voluntary muteness, Marguerite meets Mrs. Bertha Flowers, "the aristocrat of Black Stamps." Flowers fulfills the role of teacher and healer, providing the traumatized youngster with a process through which to tap internal creative sources for self-healing. Because of the loving protection, encouragement, and direction given to Marguerite by her mother, her grandmother, and Mrs. Flowers, she is better able to survive later confrontations with white racism.

A specific encounter with racial violence motivates Momma to send her grandchildren back to California. When whites force Marguerite's brother to help recover the sexually mutilated body of a lynching victim accused of "messing with" a white woman, Momma can no longer avoid two topics long forbidden to Marguerite and Bailey: white folks and "doing it." Soon Marguerite and Bailey are back in California, under the primary care of their mother, a woman of great personal power, resourcefulness, and hypnotic beauty.

The motif of flight captures the spirit of Marguerite's adventurous attempts to transcend the limitations imposed on her. Caught between her father's indifference and his girlfriend's jealousy when she visits them in southern California one summer, Marguerite runs away and lives in an abandoned junkyard with a financially independent and racially mixed group of young runaways. In another identity-building experience, Marguerite breaks the color barrier by getting a job as the first black "conductorette" on the San Francisco streetcars.

The most significant challenge facing Marguerite is also the most intimate—that of self-image and sexuality. Marguerite begins to fear that she is a lesbian after reading Radclyffe Hall's *The Well of Loneliness.* She decides that what she needs to counter her fear is a boyfriend. Marguerite's irrational fear of lesbianism leads her to seduce a handsome young man from the neighborhood. She becomes pregnant but manages to conceal the pregnancy from her family for over eight months, enough time for her to finish high school. Like her mother and grandmothers before her, Marguerite relies on her ingenuity to support her son, Guy. Sidonie Smith points out that Marguerite "has succeeded in freeing herself from the natural and social bars imprisoning her in the cage of her own diminished self-image by assuming control of her life and fully accepting her black womanhood."

The patterns established in *Caged Bird* continue in Angelou's subsequent autobiographies. The narrator adapts herself to each new situation creatively, replenishing her sense of self in difficult circumstances, discovering the fullness of her sexuality, and learning to nurture and protect. The events of *I Know Why the Caged Bird Sings* become a touchstone for Angelou's later narratives. For example, in *Gather Together in My Name* grandmother Annie Henderson looks back on her decision to send Marguerite and Bailey to California again, revealing a point of view Angelou withheld in *Caged Bird:* "I never did want you children to go to California. Too fast that life up yonder."

Gather Together in My Name and *Singin' and Swingin' and Gettin' Merry Like Christmas* are transitional volumes that cover the period from Angelou's later teen years through her mid twenties. Bloom notes that in *Gather Together* Angelou's "bold headstrong self-assurance and confidence lead her to "bluff" her way into dangerous situations. Sometimes "she cannot learn enough quickly enough to escape" before becoming dependent on others who exploit her. At other times, Bloom suggests, it is Angelou who does the exploiting. In describing Angelou's roguish trajectory and her mode of narration in *Gather Together*, Bloom goes on to suggest that Angelou's comic-lyric narrative style prevents her picaresque tale from becoming confessional. And yet the volume has confessional qualities. Angelou describes an affair with a customer at a restaurant where she works as a Creole chef; her initiation into prostitution; her brief career as madam to a pair of lesbian lovers who double as heterosexual prostitutes; a brief visit to Stamps that turns sour when she talks back to a white store clerk; and her experimentation with marijuana. She concludes *Gather Together* with an appeal to her audience for forgiveness: "I was as pure as moonlight and had only begun to live. My escapades were the fumblings of youth and to be forgiven as such."

Singin' and Swingin', the next installment of Angelou's odyssey, is actually more of a memoir than an autobiography; it covers a mere five years of Angelou's life, from the ages of about twenty-two to twenty-seven. This volume treats her marriage to Tosh Angelos, the white former sailor who was temporarily a source of stability for Marguerite and her young son. Unsuited to the institution of marriage as she knew it with Angelos, she returned to her career as a dancer and divorced him within three years. Soon after, she joined the European touring production of *Porgy and Bess*, another important turning point.

Gather Together and *Singin' and Swingin'* set the stage for *The Heart of a Woman*, wherein Angelou recounts seven years (1957–1963) of her coming of age and her involvement with the civil rights movement and the women's movement. Displacement and the search for a place of one's own in which to redefine and re-create the self are once again a central theme as Angelou recounts her career as an entertainer, writer, and freedom fighter.

The Heart of a Woman—the title is taken from a poem by the Harlem Renaissance–era poet Georgia Douglas Johnson—treats Angelou's commitments to her son, Guy, the civil rights movement, marriage, and her own writing. Now in her thirties, the heroine of *The Heart of a Woman* is once again in search of an identity and a place. She has come to New York City from California seeking a career as a writer, and begins her involvement with the Southern Christian Leadership Conference (of which she later becomes Northern coordinator) as co-author of a successful theatrical fund-raiser, *Cabaret for Freedom*. In New York she meets Bayard Rustin, Martin Luther King, Jr., and Malcolm X, and leads a protest at the United Nations over the assassination of Patrice Lumumba. Her friends include John O. Killens, Rosa Guy, Paule Marshall, Abbey Lincoln, and Max Roach.

In New York City, Maya also meets South African freedom fighter Vusumzi Make, who proposes marriage to her while she is still engaged to Tom, a lackluster bail bondsman who provides Maya and Guy with a margin of security and stability, though he offers no understanding of or sympathy for her commitment to writing or to civil rights. ("At home, Guy watched the television and Thomas read the sports pages while I cooked dinner. I knew that but for my shocking plans, we were acting out the tableau of our future. Into eternity.") Make, on the other hand, stands for more exciting prospects, and when he invites Maya to follow him to London, where he is to attend a conference of international freedom fighters, she accepts, and is known thereafter as Mrs. Vusumzi Make. They are never "married" in the traditional sense, yet they are acknowledged and accepted as husband and wife.

In Egypt with her husband, she later discovers that she has only shed one kind of entrapment for another, as she comes to learn the restrictions of being "an African wife"—the kind who will never question her husband or seek work outside the home, who will speak only when spoken to, and who will dutifully keep up appearances. In spite of her husband's wishes, she becomes the associate editor of Cairo's *Arab Observer* when she discovers that Make's creditors are seeking to collect for the extravagant household furnishings that he himself could not afford with his modest income. Eventually the marriage sours when Make becomes sexually involved with other women. She leaves him and Egypt and goes to Ghana, during the time of President Kwame Nkrumah, to enroll her son at the University of Ghana—at that time the best institution of higher education on the African continent.

An introspective passage records Angelou's reaction upon leaving Egypt. She looks out the window of the airplane in which she and Guy are flying:

> I made no attempt to explain that I was not crying because of a lack of love, or certainly not the loss of Vus's affection. I was mourning all my ancestors. I had never felt that Egypt was really Africa, but now that our route had taken us across the Sahara, I could look down from my window seat and see trees, and bushes, rivers and dense forest. It all began here. The jumble of poverty-stricken children sleeping in rat-infested tenements or abandoned cars. The terrifying moan of my grandmother, "Bread of Heaven, Bread of Heaven, feed me till I want no more." The drugged days and alcoholic nights of men for whom hope had not been born. The loneliness of women who would never know appreciation or a mite's share of honor. Here, there, along the banks of that river, someone was taken, tied with ropes, shackled with chains, forced to march for weeks carrying the double burden of neck irons and abysmal fear. In that large clump of trees, looking like wood moss from the plane's great height, boys and girls had been hunted like beasts, caught and tethered together. Sacrificial lambs on the altar of greed. America's period of orgiastic lynchings had begun on yonder broad savannah.
>
> (*The Heart of a Woman*, p. 257)

This passage looks back to *I Know Why the Caged Bird Sings*, when Momma Henderson stands singing "Bread of Heaven, feed me till I want no more" while she is being insulted by a group of "poor white trash" adolescent girls. It also looks forward to *All God's Children Need Traveling Shoes*, where Angelou discovers an even greater sense of connectedness with the African past.

Having arrived in Accra, Ghana, just before he is scheduled to enroll at the University of Ghana, Guy is severely injured in an automobile accident. He requires a full-body cast, but nevertheless he is able to matriculate. Parting is difficult for both mother and son. Angelou reflects, "Sometimes we lived with others or they lived with us, but he had always been the powerful axle of my life." As Guy prepares to leave, Angelou cautions him to remember his injuries and not to lift a heavy trunk: "Mom, I know I'm your only child and you love me. . . . But there's something I want you to remember. It is my neck and my life. I will live it whole or not at all. I love you, Mom." He goes on to say, "Maybe now you'll have a chance to grow up." A mother since she was sixteen, Angelou now faces life on her own as the powerful axle of her life seeks his own maturity and his manhood.

"I was soon swept into an adoration for Ghana as a young girl falls in love," she writes in *All God's Children Need Traveling Shoes*, the most recent volume of her odyssey, "heedless and with slight chance to find the emotion requited." The dedication and epigraph for *All God's Children* reveal the central motif of this volume, the search for a symbolic home. Angelou dedicates the book to "Julian and Malcolm and all the fallen ones who were passionately and earnestly looking for a home." The epigraph is taken from the African American spiritual "Swing Low, Sweet Chariot." Symbolically Angelou's quest is the quest of Julian Mayfield, Malcolm X, and all African American people, her homecoming the homecoming of African people born on American soil:

> Our people had always longed for home. . . . In the yearning, heaven and Africa were inextricably combined. . . . So I had finally come home.

> The prodigal child, having strayed, been stolen or sold from the land of her fathers, having squandered her mother's gifts and having laid down in cruel gutters, had at last arisen and directed herself back to the welcoming arms of the family where she would be bathed, clothed with fine raiment and seated at the welcoming table.
> (pp. 19, 20, 21)

In Accra, Angelou finds an administrative post at the University of Ghana and shares an attractive home with African American women friends drawn to Ghana by the excitement of Kwame Nkrumah, known by his people as "man who surpasses man, iron which cuts iron." Nkrumah had thrown off British rule; his revolution was both cultural and economic. He had been educated in the United States at Lincoln University, and he welcomed Americans like W. E. B. Du Bois and others who were prepared to make a contribution to the black African destiny. Nkrumah's presence was like a magnet for the questing African Americans. When Angelou sits down at the welcoming table, the reader, especially if that reader happens to be an American of African descent, sits down with her. But her homecoming is not completely untroubled.

The climax of this narrative comes near its end when Angelou visits the seaside village of Keta, which had been "hit very hard by the slave trade." In Keta, Angelou is accosted by a woman who seems to know her and will not believe that she cannot speak Ewe. The woman's resemblance to Angelou's grandmother, Momma Henderson, is startling: "When she raised her head, I nearly fell back down the steps: she had the wide face and slanted eyes of my grandmother. Her lips were large and beautifully shaped like my grandmother's, and her cheekbones were high like those of my grandmother." The woman, finally persuaded that Angelou is "an American Negro," "lifted both arms and lacing her fingers together put them on top of her head" and moaned in a gesture of mourning. Angelou is introduced to others from the village, who adopt the same gesture. She is told that the people mourn because they are sure that she is descended from mothers and fathers stolen long ago

> Here in my last days in Africa, descendants of a pillaged past saw their history in my face and heard their ancestors speak through my voice. . . . This second leave-taking would not be so onerous, for now I knew my people had never completely left Africa. We had sung it in our blues, shouted it in our gospel and danced the continent in our breakdowns. . . . It was Africa which rode in the bulges of our high calves, shook in our protruding behinds and crackled in our wide open laughter.
> (pp. 207, 208)

For Angelou, Africa, and the welcome table, will forever be within.

The life and work of Maya Angelou are fully intertwined; the poetic adventure of her life, her personal odyssey, is representative of all Americans of African descent. Angelou's poetry and personal narratives form a larger mosaic wherein the symbolic Maya Angelou rises to become a point of consciousness for African American people, and especially for black women seeking to survive what Angelou has called "the tri-partite crossfire of masculine prejudice, white illogical hate and Black lack of power." Angelou's personal narratives, poems, and screenplays all trace this path as Marguerite Johnson, "tagged orphan," becomes Maya Angelos, becomes Mrs. Vusumzi Make, becomes Maya Angelou Make, becomes Maya Angelou the prodigal daughter, coming home from her long journey to the Africa within.

Maya Angelou's place in the canon depends, in part, on whose canon one is talking about. She established her place in the American autobiographical canon with *I Know Why the Caged Bird Sings,* a volume that generated a wealth of critical literature as well as a solid recognition for Maya Angelou not only as a black woman writer but also as an American autobiographer. Each ensuing volume extends the stature attained with *Caged Bird,* although some, like *The Heart of a Woman,* have received more critical acclaim than others. In any case, all of

Angelou's autobiographical volumes are widely read and taught, and they continue to inspire lively critical responses.

Angelou's poetry and screenplays are less well known and critics, generally speaking, have been less generous in criticizing them. Some have even referred to her poetry as "too simple," a suggestion that, in their minds, it is unworthy of inclusion in the "established" canon of American poetry, a body of literature written largely by whites and men. But Angelou's audience, composed largely of women and blacks, isn't really affected by what white and/or male critics of the dominant literary tradition have to say about her work. This audience does not read literary critics; it does read Maya Angelou. Readers of her poetry appreciate its rhythm, lyric imagery, and realism. Angelou has become, in effect, the progenitor of her own mini-canon, as reflected in both the sales of her books and her popularity on the lecture circuit.

Anyone who has been present at one of Angelou's readings and/or lectures knows the almost hypnotic effect she can have on an audience. Indeed, many respond to the towering (six feet plus) grandmother figure almost as they would to a rock star; she performs, lectures, scolds, and teaches, providing direction and further enhancing her place. The people who read Angelou's work include both critics and lay readers, many of them wildly devoted to her, and she has achieved a measure of true sainthood in their eyes by transcending brutal racism, sexual abuse, and poverty to become one of America's most celebrated contemporary writers. Her work has been translated into many languages. She is loved, moreover, not only for her work but also as a symbol of what a woman may become as she sings her sassy song of herself, and for the encouragement and support she has given to so many. She is a strong black woman and an artist, not an ivory tower marionette.

Regarding her reception by critics of the dominant tradition, Angelou might seem to say, "If that canon, that body of literature written largely by whites and men, acknowledges my work, then well and good. I accept this honor." On the other hand, lack of praise from those in the literary establishment does not seem to have much effect on Angelou's work, which presents its own challenge to the "mainstream." It is this body of work that extends her character to almost mythic proportions, for Maya Angelou and her canon are alive and well, and they are helping to change the course of the so-called mainstream. Angelou's life and work will continue to be a force to be contended with wherever they are found.

Selected Bibliography

PRIMARY WORKS

AUTOBIOGRAPHIES

I Know Why the Caged Bird Sings. New York: Random House, 1970.

Gather Together in My Name. New York: Random House, 1974.

Singin' and Swingin' and Gettin' Merry Like Christmas. New York: Randon House, 1976.

The Heart of a Woman. New York: Random House, 1981.

All God's Children Need Traveling Shoes. New York: Random House, 1986.

POETRY

Just Give Me a Cool Drink of Water 'fore I Diiie: The Poetry of Maya Angelou. New York: Random House, 1971.

Oh Pray My Wings Are Gonna Fit Me Well. New York: Random House, 1975.

And Still I Rise. New York: Random House, 1978.

Shaker, Why Don't You Sing? New York: Random House, 1983.

DRAMA

Cabaret for Freedom. New York: Village Gate Theatre, 1960. Written with Godfrey Cambridge.

The Least of These. Los Angeles, 1966. Two-act drama.

Ajax. Los Angeles: Mark Taper Forum, 1974. Two act drama adapted from Sophocles.

And Still I Rise. Oakland, Calif.: Ensemble Theatre, 1976.

SCREENPLAYS

Georgia, Georgia. Independent-Cinerama, 1972.

All Day Long. American Film Institute, 1974.

RECORDINGS

Miss Calypso. Liberty Records, 1957. Songs.

The Poetry of Maya Angelou. GWP Records, 1969.

An Evening with Maya Angelou. Pacific Tape Library (BC 2660), 1975.

SECONDARY WORKS

BIOGRAPHICAL AND CRITICAL STUDIES

Arensberg, Liliane K. "Death as a Metaphor of Self in *I Know Why the Caged Bird Sings.*" *CLA Journal* 20:273–291 (1976).

Bailey, Paul. "Black Ordeal. *Observer,* 1 April 1984, p. 22.

Bloom, Lynn Z. "Maya Angelou." In *Dictionary of Literary Biography.* Vol. 38. Edited by Thadious M. Davis and Trudier Harris. Detroit: Gale Research, 1985. Pp. 3–12.

Braxton, Joanne M. "A Song of Transcendence: Maya Angelou." In her *Black Women Writing Autobiography: A Tradition Within a Tradition.* Philadelphia: Temple University Press, 1989. Pp. 181–201.

Chrisman, Robert. "The *Black Scholar* Interviews Maya Angelou." *Black Scholar* 8:44–53 (1977).

Demetrakopoulos, Stephanie A. "The Metaphysics of Matrilinearism in Women's Autobiography." In *Women's Autobiography: Essays in Criticism.* Edited by Estelle Jelinek. Bloomington: Indiana University Press, 1980. Pp. 180–205.

Elliot, Jeffrey M., ed. *Conversations with Maya Angelou.* Jackson: University Press of Mississippi, 1989.

Kent, George E. "Maya Angelou's *I Know Why the Caged Bird Sings* and Black Autobiographical Tradition." *Kansas Quarterly* 7:72–78 (Summer 1975).

McMurry, Myra K. "Role Playing as Art in Maya Angelou's *Caged Bird.*" *South Atlantic Bulletin* 41:106–111 (1976).

Smith, Sidonie Ann. "The Song of a Caged Bird: Maya Angelou's Quest After Self-Acceptance." *Southern Humanities Review* 7:365–375 (1973).

Stepto, R. B. "The Phenomenal Woman and the Severed Daughter." Review of *And Still I Rise* and *The Black Unicorn,* by Audre Lorde. *Parnassus: Poetry in Review* 8:312–320 (1979).

BIBLIOGRAPHY

Cameron, Dee Birch. "A Maya Angelou Bibliography." *Bulletin of Bibliography* 36:50–52 (1979).

JOANNE M. BRAXTON

ELIZABETH BISHOP

1911–1979

THOUGH SHE TRAVELED a great deal—born in Massachusetts; raised in Canada and Massachusetts; living for short periods of time in Mexico, France, England, and elsewhere; coming of age in Key West, growing older in Brazil—Elizabeth Bishop was not a tourist, a poet on holiday in foreign countries. "We'd rather have the iceberg than the ship," she writes in "The Imaginary Iceberg" (*North & South*, 1946), "although it meant the end of travel." Her travels were departures, a constant leave-taking of people and places, of the past and of houses. An underlying sadness seems commonplace to such departures, as a secular predestination is very much common to Bishop's poetry. Still, perseverance triumphs (though never completely) over sadness:

> Good-bye, we say, good-bye, the ship steers off
> where waves give in to one another's waves
> and clouds run in a warmer sky.
> Icebergs behoove the soul
> (both being self-made from elements least
> visible)
> to see them so: fleshed, fair, erected indivisible.

Witness the pun on "waves" in the lines above: waves of water implying—and becoming—gestures of farewell.

Becoming Elizabeth Bishop, poet and traveler, was an effort of strength and perhaps even of wit for Elizabeth Bishop, orphan and migrant. In an interview with Elizabeth Spires conducted in 1978, she spoke of her life with brevity:

> My father died, my mother went crazy when I was four or five years old. My relatives, I think they all felt so sorry for this child that they tried to do their very best. And I think they did. I lived with my grandparents in Nova Scotia. Then I lived with the ones in Worcester, Massachusetts, very briefly, and got terribly sick. . . . Then I lived with my mother's older sister in Boston. I used to go to Nova Scotia for the summer. When I was twelve or thirteen I was improved enough to go to summer camp at Wellfleet until I went away to school when I was fifteen or sixteen. . . . But my relationship with my relatives—I was always a sort of a guest, and I think I've always felt like that.
>
> (*Paris Review* [1981], pp. 74–75)

Bishop never made a secret of her past troubles, but neither did she make them the stuff of biographical notes, of explanations. She never trumpeted her early (or late) misfortunes.

Born on 8 February 1911 in Worcester, Massachusetts, Elizabeth Bishop was the only child of Canadian-American parents. Her father, William Thomas Bishop, died when she was eight months old; her mother, Gertrude Bulmer, was hospitalized in sanatoriums for most of Bishop's childhood. Passed from family member to family member, suffering one childhood illness after another, Bishop eventually settled (albeit temporarily) as an undergraduate at Vassar College in the early 1930s. She began her studies as a music major, intending to become a composer. A fear of public performance, however, led her to abandon music for writing. Her schoolmates included the poet Muriel Rukeyser and the novelists Eleanor Clark and Mary McCarthy. Bishop's poetic vocation was furthered and confirmed in 1934, when, as a senior, she was introduced to Marianne Moore, who became the younger poet's first champion and lifelong friend. (Their friendship is recounted in "Efforts of Affection," a memoir included in Bishop's *The Collected Prose* [1984].) In 1935 Moore introduced Bishop to the American public in an anthology entitled *Trial Balances*. Bishop's contributions included "The Reprimand" and "Three Valentines" (reprinted in *The Com-*

plete Poems, 1927–1979 [1983]) and "The Map," the opening poem in *North & South,* her first published collection. Surely Bishop held on to "The Map" those eleven years between *Trial Balances* and *North & South* because, in some prescient way, she knew the poem addressed concerns that would be always central to her work.

The form of "The Map" reflects topography's concern for boundaries and interiors. Bounded by two rhymed stanzas (having the scheme abbacddc), the poem's interior is an unrhymed, eleven-line, free-verse stanza, roughly iambic pentameter. Even the boundary stanzas are hemmed in, not by rhyme but by repetition, so that lines a1 and a2 and c1 and c2, repeat their end word (or words) exactly:

> Land lies in water; it is shadowed green.
> Shadows, or are they shallows, at its edges
> showing the line of long sea-weeded ledges
> where weeds hang to the simple blue from
> green.
> Or does the land lean down to lift the sea from
> under,
> drawing it unperturbed around itself?
> Along the fine tan sandy shelf
> is the land tugging at the sea from under?

This homemade scheme seems at once simple and complicated; it also shows just how much Bishop learned from those poets she studied and admired. George Herbert comes to mind, and how the shapes of his poems often made flesh of their subjects: "The Altar" is shaped like a church altar; his "Easter Wings," like pinions.

"The Map," of course, is not shaped like a map. That would mean the poem resembled a given country and, despite the occasional place-name, Bishop is concerned not so much with *site* as with what is revealed by *sight,* and even by touch. "We can stroke these lovely bays," she writes, "under a glass as if they were expected to blossom, / or as if to provide a clean cage for invisible fish." Sight and touch grow closer:

> the names of seashore towns run out to sea,
> the names of cities cross the neighboring
> mountains
> —the printer here experiencing the same
> excitement
> as when emotion too far exceeds its cause.

We could argue that Bishop's "printer," the one writing the names of towns and cities on the actual map, is a figure for the poet herself. Emotion that "too far exceeds its cause" seems a knowing parody of Wordsworth's claim that "poetry is the spontaneous overflow of powerful feelings: it takes its origin from emotion recollected in tranquillity." From the emotional we move, almost abruptly, to the tactile: "These peninsulas take the water between thumb and forefinger / like women feeling for the smoothness of yard-goods."

"The Map" concludes, "Are they assigned, or can the countries pick their colors?" Bishop never quite answers the question posed; or, rather, she answers the question but with a third possibility. Color is neither assigned nor selected but is in some very real sense original. We might say that yellow *is* the only possible color for Labrador, that Newfoundland *is* a gray shadow: "Topography displays no favorites." No one country is rewarded with green while another suffers with black, and yet, "more delicate than the historian's are the map-makers' colors." The colors are a given, but their shades—how deep the blue, how pale the red—are left to the topographer's discretion. It is not so much a matter of choice as it is a matter of what we do with the givens: how delicately, how precisely, we manage the world.

Like "The Map" and "The Imaginary Iceberg," many of the poems in *North & South* lean toward the allegorical. "The Man-Moth" and "The Weed" are two examples. "The Man-Moth" takes as its point of departure a newspaper misprint for "mammoth." The poem investigates this neocreature who lives underground and "scale[s] the faces of buildings." Although one of Bishop's great strengths lies in description, in accurate but fanciful detail, nowhere in the poem does she tell us just what the man-moth looks like. He becomes a sort of everycreature. We know him by his actions and thoughts rather than by his appearance. The man-moth "must investigate" the facades he climbs, and he "must" climb if he wishes to get anywhere. The climb, the investigation, are as original to him as the various colors are to "The Map," original and inescapable.

At poem's end there is a moment characteristic of Bishop's work: the tear that is the man-moth's "only possession," his only offspring:

> If you catch him,
> hold up a flashlight to his eye. It's all dark pupil,
> an entire night itself, whose haired horizon tightens
> as he stares back, and closes up the eye. Then from the lids
> one tear, his only possession, like the bee's sting, slips.
> Slyly he palms it, and if you're not paying attention
> he'll swallow it. However, if you watch, he'll hand it over,
> cool as from underground springs and pure enough to drink.

The distorted eye also appears, slightly altered, at the end of "Love Lies Sleeping," the poem that follows "The Man-Moth" in *North & South.* The tears reappear in "Sestina," a poem from *Questions of Travel* (1965), and in "The Weed."

In "The Weed," a poem that Bishop once acknowledged as modeled after George Herbert's "Love Unknown," the poet dreams that a "slight young weed" has grown up through her heart and broken the surface of her breast. The heart breaks open, and water pours forth:

> A few drops fell upon my face
> and in my eyes, so I could see
> . . . .
> that each drop contained a light,
> a small, illuminated scene.

These tears are, and are not, the poet's own. The weed, she writes, "lifted its head all dripping wet / (with my own thoughts?)." The weed seems a pregnancy of sorts, a dream's revelation of divided loyalties, though we can only presume to know to whom, or to what, those loyalties are pledged.

"The Weed" begins Bishop's explorations of violence and redemption, a theme echoed in several poems in *North & South.* "Roosters," thought by many to be a war poem (it was first published in the *New Republic* in April 1941), begins with an ardent dismissal of nature's violence (sunrise and sunset) and concludes with the biblical story of Peter, who thrice denied Christ. What better figure could there be for the inescapable, for the man (or woman) predestined to some particular action (or place)? Christ told Peter of his impending denial. Indeed, the penultimate line from "Roosters" is borrowed from the Gospel according to Matthew (26:58), which recounts Peter's following the guards who have taken Christ, "to see the end"—that is, to find out whether Christ's prophecy will come true—but also to see Christ's end, the bloody but ultimately spiritual violence of His crucifixion.

Violence and redemption are also integral to "The Fish." Had Bishop ever decided to write directly about the Crucifixion, the result might have been a poem as sanguine as "The Fish" with its "five big hooks / grown firmly in his mouth," like a misplaced crown of thorns or the five wounds of Christ. The fish is an age-old symbol for Christ; perhaps this is a poem about the Crucifixion after all. What redemption we find in "The Fish," however, lies in the narrator's ultimately releasing her catch. The iridescence of the fish suddenly resembles "rainbow, rainbow, rainbow!"—a symbol, as told in the story of Noah's ark, of God's promise never again to unleash a flood on earth, an outward and visible sign of His renewed covenant with man. If God can never again destroy the earth, how can Bishop destroy the fish? She has to let it go, and she does.

All in all, *North & South* seems, for all its surface beauty, for all its guidebook splendor, a dark, reticent collection: dark in its concerns, reticent in its narration. How much is the poet willing to locate herself within the poems? An omniscient, nearly ubiquitous "we" is Bishop's favored personal pronoun, the narrator's eye more common (more important?) than the narrator's "I." We would be wrong, though, to see the distance as a disservice to the poems; it seems a means of self-protection, allowing Bishop to slip out of herself and, with greater concentration, into the world. More intimate poems come later in her career, when (or so we might conjecture) the risks of revelation are fewer, are less severe or less threatening.

In the years between *North & South* and Bishop's second collection, *A Cold Spring* (1955), her literary circle grew. Marianne Moore became less of an influence, personally and poetically. Bishop met, among others, Randall Jarrell and Robert Lowell; she and Lowell became fast friends, exchanging letters and drafts of poems. Soon after, she was appointed consultant in poetry to the Library of Congress (1949–1950) and received a Guggenheim Fellowship (1947) and other awards. Still, Bishop never really saw herself as a member of "the old-boy school" of American letters, preferring the company of friends who were not writers or poets.

The title poem of *A Cold Spring* is one of renewal, of spring rising from the snows of winter, although this is a reading that a number of recent critics have thought too literal. Instead, they have discussed "A Cold Spring" as a love poem or as a poem of sexual awakening. (Not coincidentally, the volume closes with "The Shampoo," a less guarded expression of affection—a cold spring become a warm spring.) In this poem the sexual subverts the pastoral; or, rather, the pastoral *is* the sexual and, also, the sacred. The poem is a catalog of verdant life, each detail chosen for a specific reason:

> Greenish-white dogwood infiltrated the wood,
> each petal burned, apparently, by a cigarette
>   butt;
> and the blurred redbud stood
> beside it, motionless, but almost more
> like movement than any placeable color.

According to Christian legend, the dogwood is the tree from which Christ's cross was made; and the redbud is also known as the Judas tree. While some recent theological speculation has centered on the idea that Jesus, not God, chose Judas as the disciple who should identify Him to the soldiers in Gethsemane as the one to betray Him—as He chose Peter—traditional theology argues that all of these acts were preordained, that no free choice existed. Although "A Cold Spring" gives no clues, it seems safe to say that Bishop aligns herself with traditional theology, if only by virtue of faith's role in her earlier poems, and that she selected the dogwood and the redbud because of their associations with Gethsemane. Although we cannot be certain that either tree grew in the biblical garden, we can make the leap of faith to see Bishop's pastures as a modern Gethsemane, and to see Judas' kiss, itself a somewhat sexual act, not as betrayal but as a portent of resurrection. Indeed, a secular resurrection closes the poem:

> Now, from the thick grass, the fireflies
> begin to rise:
> up, then down, then up again:
> lit on the ascending flight,
> drifting simultaneously to the same height,
> —exactly like the bubbles in champagne.
> —Later on they rise much higher.

If, in "A Cold Spring," the sexual undercuts the religious, the obverse is true of "Over 2,000 Illustrations and a Complete Concordance." The poem presents sexuality not as renewal but as a chamber of horrors. To view that chamber, Bishop takes us on a pilgrimage through the Bible, "the heavy book" from which the title derives. "Thus should have been our travels: / serious, engravable," the poem begins—as though "our" travels had been anything but serious and engravable. ("*Our* travels"? There is no direct mention of another in the poem.) "Our travels" do not begin for thirty-two lines, lines that make of the biblical illustrations a sacred photo album. The shift from religious allusion to real geography is quiet. Bishop provides us with place-names, but as they are also the names of two disciples (St. John and St. Peter), it takes a moment before we realize that she has led us from the Holy Land to Canada. (St. John's is located in Newfoundland, and St. Peter's in Quebec.) We are next led to Mexico, England, Marrakesh, and elsewhere. As the travels proceed, they grow more and more bizarre. In Marrakesh, "little pockmarked prostitutes" dance naked and "fling themselves . . . giggling against our knees, / asking for cigarettes." Bishop's New England–bred self-possession breaks down. Something about the dancing girls—their nakedness, their scarred faces—prompts Bishop to directness and to confession:

> It was somewhere near there
> I saw what frightened me most of all:
> A holy grave, not looking particularly holy.

Fear overpowers self-possession. "I" becomes the only possible vehicle for speaking about the fear.

The grave, the "trough," is personified as a mouth, "yellowed / as scattered cattle teeth; / half-filled with dust." It is a decaying body. The dancers lead Bishop to consider the body's mortality and the deterioration of the flesh. Do the "pockmarked prostitutes" prefigure the scars of decomposition? The memory of the grave leads Bishop back to the Bible, to an illustration of the manger:

> Everything only connected by "and" and
> "and."
> Open the book. (The gilt rubs off the edges
> of the pages and pollinates the fingertips.)
> Open the heavy book. Why couldn't we have
> seen
> this old Nativity while we were at it?
> —the dark ajar, the rocks breaking with light,
> an undisturbed, unbreathing flame,
> colorless, sparkless, freely fed on straw,
> and, lulled within, a family with pets,
> —and looked and looked our infant sight
> away.

The four lines describing the Nativity interrupt a single question: "Why couldn't we have seen / this old Nativity while we were at it? / . . . and looked and looked our infant sight away?" One answer might be that we never see what we should while we are "at it," that our infant sight (by which Bishop sees the Holy Family as merely "a family with pets") is with us always, a blessing and a curse, an unalterable given.

"The Bight" presents another sort of nativity; its dedication reads, "on my birthday." Which particular birthday Bishop meant, we cannot be sure, although the poem was first published in the *New Yorker* in 1949, when Bishop was in her late thirties. The locale would seem to be Key West, where Bishop lived from the late 1930s until the early 1950s.

Although, typically, "The Bight" contains no personal pronouns, it is decidedly personal, delicate, and humorous. It is not, however, an easy or a peaceful poem. "The Bight" is filled with tiny, violent gestures: the pelicans who "crash" into the water "like pickaxes," and the threat of flame from "pilings dry as matches," for instance. The scene is at once "awful" and "cheerful." These two characteristics—violence and an infrequent but steadfast "I"—can also be found in "At the Fishhouses."

In "At the Fishhouses," the setting appears to be either Nova Scotia or Massachusetts, certainly a landscape from Bishop's childhood. The poem recounts a visit with an elderly fisherman who, Bishop writes, "was a friend of my fathers":

> There are sequins on his vest and on his
> thumb.
> He has scraped the scales, the principal beauty,
> from unnumbered fish with that black old
> knife,
> the blade of which is almost worn away.

The violence here is an everyday one: the violence of making a living from the sea. The sight of the silver tree trunks at "water's edge" leads Bishop down to the water itself: "Cold dark deep and absolutely clear, / element bearable to no mortal, / to fish and to seals. . . ." A curious phrasing: that water cannot sustain mortals. Aren't fish and seals mortal? Bishop equates mortality with human memory, human life. She and the fisherman have talked of "the decline in the population," the death of contemporaries. So far, they have beaten fate. The water will eventually prove them mortal.

She goes on to recall one seal in particular to whom she sang "Baptist hymns," with both Bishop and the seal "believer[s] in total immersion"—a lovely pun on the ritual of river baptisms. The loveliness of the moment and of the surrounding scenery give way to a violence that is anything but everyday—the violence of the past and of knowledge:

> If you should dip your hand in,
> your wrist would ache immediately,
> your bones would begin to ache and your hand
> would burn
> as if the water were a transmutation of fire
> that feeds on stones and burns with a dark
> gray flame.
> If you tasted it, it would taste bitter,
> then briny, then surely burn your tongue.
> It is like what we imagine knowledge to be.

These lines recall the flame ("an undisturbed, unbreathing flame") that burns at the close of "Over 2,000 Illustrations and a Complete Concordance." In a sense the poems in *A Cold Spring* record the progress from "infant sight" to knowledge. Or perhaps these are one and the same, measured in differing degrees; one is reminded of a newborn's first contact with light.

We would do well to talk for a moment of *A Cold Spring* as a whole. *A Cold Spring* was never published as a separate volume. With a reissued *North & South,* it was included in a volume entitled *Poems: North & South—A Cold Spring.* The idea of a dual volume was not wholly favored by Bishop, as letters to her publisher reveal, yet *Poems* went on to receive the Pulitzer Prize for poetry for 1956. Bishop apparently had other difficulties with the collection. After two printings one poem ("The Mountain") was dropped and the order of the final poems rearranged. "The Mountain" is by no means one of Bishop's better poems; it is curious and charming, though, and we can only wonder why she made the decision never to reprint it. ("The Mountain" reappears in the posthumous *Complete Poems.*) The new closing sequence more clearly illustrates the female nature of these last poems. Two poems are expressly dedicated to women friends, "Letter to N.Y." (for Louise Crane) and "Invitation to Miss Marianne Moore." Two others, "Argument" and "The Shampoo," seem implicitly addressed to women. Interestingly, "Four Poems," which precedes this final sequence, was originally called (by Bishop in a letter to her publisher) "Love Poems." The change in titles is not at all surprising; it is one example of Bishop's seeming reluctance to fully declare herself before the public.

It is fairly common knowledge, though exterior to many of the poems, that Bishop was a lesbian. Midcentury America was not at all the country it is today, and openly revealing one's sexual preference was then much less socially acceptable; one had almost no choice but to keep such matters private. The reasons for Bishop's reticence are clear in the final four lines of "Conversation," the first of "Four Poems":

> And then there is no choice,
> and then there is no sense;
>
> until a name
> and all its connotation are the same

The lines seem to address, as openly as Bishop herself felt, her sexuality. "O Breath," the last of "Four Poems," makes Bishop's sexuality less a cage (a frequent metaphor in her work) than an eventual promise of release:

> something that maybe I could bargain with
> and make a separate peace beneath
> within if never with

Ultimately, Bishop's sexuality does not diminish but subtly amplifies "Four Poems," as it does "The Shampoo," playing not an overt but a latent role—tellingly in accord with her natural reserve.

Nor was Bishop comfortable with the sometimes pejorative title "woman poet." In a letter partially reprinted in *The Norton Anthology of Literature by Women,* Bishop protests, "Undoubtedly gender does play an important part in the making of any art, but art is art and to separate writings, paintings, musical compositions, etc., into two sexes is to emphasize values in them that are *not* art."

In the years following the publication of *Poems*, Bishop's life changed greatly. On a trip to Brazil, she became temporarily ill and settled in to recover. She remained in South America for nearly twenty years, living with a Brazilian architect, Lota de Macedo Soares. In 1956 she received the Pulitzer Prize for *Poems*. In a late interview she tells how, after learning the news and eager to share it with someone, she went into town and met the local grocer, who of course had little idea what such an award meant. He and Bishop celebrated by eating cookies.

Bishop began a translation of *Minha vida de menina*, first published in English in 1957 as *The Diary of "Helena Morley."* "In English, the title means 'My Life as a Little Girl,' or 'Young Girl,' " she writes in the introduction, "and that is exactly what the book is about, but it is not reminiscences; it is a diary . . . actually kept by a girl between the ages of twelve and fifteen, in the far-off town of Diamantina, in 1893–1895." Translating *Minha vida de menina* prompted Bishop to think more decidedly about her own life as a young girl. Shortly afterward she wrote two remarkable prose memoirs, "Primer Class" and "The Country Mouse," as well as a number of poems that originated in recollections of childhood.

About this time she was hired to write a book about Brazil for Time-Life Books. Bishop and her editors at Time-Life never fully agreed on how the book should be done, and at one point she refused to rewrite certain chapters. Candace MacMahon, in her extensive bibliography of Bishop's work, tells how the poet inscribed one copy of the book, correcting the title page to "some by Elizabeth Bishop and more by The Editors of *Life*." *Brazil* was published in 1962, but even in 1978 Bishop still seemed unnerved by the experience. "Could you say that ALL of the chapters headings were concocted by *Life*?" she implored MacMahon. "Not one of my original chapter headings was used."

Certainly Bishop's translation of a young Brazilian's diary and her travel writing contributed to the structure and theme of her third volume of poems, *Questions of Travel* (1965). The book is divided into two sections, "Brazil" and "Elsewhere." *Questions of Travel* also includes "In the Village," an autobiographical short story of a young girl witnessing her mother's descent into madness. (Very probably Bishop took the idea of a prose interlude from Robert Lowell's *Life Studies* and its prose memoir, "91 Revere Street.") "In the Village" possesses, as does all of Bishop's prose, a clarity and a precision that were hers alone:

> There are the tops of all the elm trees in the village and there, beyond them, the long green marshes, so fresh, so salt. Then the Minas Basin, with the tide halfway in or out, the wet red mud glazed with sky blue until it meets the creeping lavender-red water. In the middle of the view, like one hand of a clock pointing straight up, is the steeple of the Presbyterian church. We are in the "Maritimes," but all that means is that we live by the sea.

Questions of Travel continues Bishop's explorations of choice and necessity, of travels taken out of necessity. The book opens with "Arrival at Santos," as notable for its light comic touch—Miss Breen, the "retired police lieutenant," whose skirt catches on a boat hook—as for its modest resignation:

> Here is a coast; here is a harbor;
> here, after a meager diet of horizon, is some
> scenery:
> impractically shaped and—who knows?—self-
> pitying mountains,
> sad and harsh beneath their frivolous
> greenery,
> . . . .
> Oh, tourist,
> is this how this country is going to answer you
> and your immodest demands for a different
> world,
> and a better life, and complete comprehension
> of both at last, and immediately,
> after eighteen days of suspension?

The implied answer is "Yes, of course." The actual answer, the one provided, is "Finish your breakfast"—the sort of reply one gives a child who has asked too many questions for which no answers, or disappointing ones, come. Yet Bishop, whatever guilelessness she adopts, is anything but childlike. She is, rather, too much aware of the absurdity of adulthood, and chooses instead the wonders of "infant sight." "There. We are settled," she writes. But we are not yet settled. The poem concludes: "We leave Santos at once; / we are driving to the interior."

The traveler's queries continue in the collection's title poem, "Questions of Travel," one of Bishop's most heartbreaking poems—if "heartbreaking" is a word applicable to a poet who shunned such melodrama. Santos' "meager diet of horizon" here becomes an overabundance of "too many waterfalls" and "so many clouds." The lush interior prompts not contentment but doubt: "Should we have stayed at home and thought of here? / Where should we be today?" The adult's absurdity is, once more, played out in children's terms: "What childishness is it that while there's a breath of life / in our bodies, we are determined to rush / to see the sun the other way around?" Typically, Bishop answers a question with a question: "Oh, must we dream our dreams / and have them, too?" Then, suddenly, the questions turn to protests in favor of travel, we might even say of tourism. Protest follows upon protest, as question followed question. "But surely it would have been a pity / not to have seen the trees along this road." Ultimately, the questions win: *"Is it lack of imagination that makes us come / to imagined places, not just stay at home?"*

One answer to these interrogations can be found in the poems immediately following "Questions of Travel," a series of Brazilian poems in which the country comes to life through its inhabitants. For whatever reason, these are poems that, by and large, have been overlooked in surveys of Bishop's work (as have her translations from the Portuguese of Carlos Drummond de Andrade and from the Spanish of Octavio Paz, among others). The Brazilian poems occupy an important place in Bishop's body of work. They portray the poet's concern for outsiders, for exiles, for burglars and "squatters' children," as did "Cootchie" and "Songs for a Colored Singer" (reportedly written with Billie Holiday in mind) in *North & South.* Strongest among the Brazilian poems is "Manuelzinho," a dramatic monologue. As a brief note explains, someone clearly other than the poet is speaking. "Manuelzinho" tells the story of a rather inept gardener whose produce seems prone to accidents of nature: "You bring me / a mystic three-legged carrot, / or a pumpkin 'bigger than the baby.' " Inept at even simple accounting, shoddily clothed, Manuelzinho is, until the poem's surprising and lovely final stanza, treated with an exasperation this side of contempt. He is "the world's worst gardener since Cain." The brief, final stanza is thus surprising in its declaration of affection for Manuelzinho:

> You helpless, foolish man,
> I love you all I can,
> I think, Or do I?
> I take off my hat, unpainted
> and figurative, to you.

"Brazil," the first section of *Questions of Travel,* closes with "The Burglar of Babylon," a ballad recounting the escapades of an incompetent burglar. (Also published separately as a children's book, complete with illustrations, the ballad is based on a story that Bishop once acknowledged as true.) The children's-literature simplicity of its construction better prepares the reader for the dramatic change in time and location that follows.

Leaving South America for North America, the present for the past, Bishop returns us to her childhood. What is most startling about the poems in the section titled "Elsewhere" is their candor, their steady gaze at the "child of 1918"—a child who has lost her father to death and her mother to madness. Bishop's extended and makeshift family occupies the wide gap left by her parents' absence; they serve to complete the poems. "Sestina," for instance, is a marvel of absence and presence:

> September rain falls on the house.
> In the failing light, the old grandmother
> sits in the kitchen with the child
> beside the Little Marvel Stove,
> reading the jokes from the almanac,
> laughing and talking to hide her tears.

House, grandmother, child, stove, almanac, tears these six words repeat themselves throughout the poem in a preordained form, a form at which poets of lesser accomplishment have often failed. What makes Bishop's "Sestina" succeed, aside from its sad good nature, is that following each of these end words, a verb often begins the successive line. These verbs, in effect, become subtle distractions from the grandmother, the child, and their "inscrutable house."

> Birdlike, the almanac
> hovers half open above the child,
> hovers above the old grandmother
> and her teacup full of dark brown tears.
> She shivers and says she thinks the house
> feels chilly, and puts more wood in the stove.

But these are impossible distractions. In 1956 Bishop wrote to Marianne Moore, "What I'm really up to is recreating a sort of deluxe Nova Scotia all over again in Brazil. And now I'm my own grandmother." Brazil was very much home, and the idea of home always always seemed to transport Bishop back to her childhood.

In "Manners," "Sestina," and "First Death in Nova Scotia," we once more meet the child narrator of "In the Village," the young girl who has transformed misfortune into the stuff of poems. The transformation is possible because in these poems, as elsewhere, self-possession guides Bishop's fictionalized autobiography. Unlike Lowell's *Life Studies,* which she read in manuscript and greatly admired, *Questions of Travel* intends to place the self not in history but in a smaller, more tangible (if lost) world. In "Sestina," "With crayons the child draws a rigid house / and a winding pathway," the drawing a visual twin to the poems Bishop was writing, and beginning to write, in the early 1960s.

"First Death in Nova Scotia" continues Bishop's verse autobiography, recounting the death of her young cousin Arthur. Her mother hovers over the poem, which modulates from queer humor and fantasy to quiet terror, like death itself. The mother invites, commands, the young Elizabeth to "say good-bye / to your little cousin Arthur," who lies in state watched over by chromographs of the Royal Family and by a stuffed loon, "shot and stuffed by Uncle / Arthur, Arthur's father." The child transposes death into something less threatening:

> Arthur's coffin was
> a little frosted cake. . . . He was all white, like
> a doll
> that hadn't been painted yet.

Death becomes small, unreal but manageable, a landscape of reds and whites: Arthur's white face, the white loon with the desirable red glass eyes, Jack Frost painting "the Maple Leaf (Forever)," the red and ermine furs of the royal couples in the chromographs. The child's escape into fantasy resonates with adult knowledge. It is clearly the adult Elizabeth recalling the funeral scene. Again we encounter the difficult passage, never fully undertaken, from "infant sight" to "knowledge." Knowledge is always and only tempered by innocence; as innocence is broken, though not dismissed, by knowledge. Never a poet one could comfortably call a moralist, Bishop nontheless means for us to know the impossibility of escape. We can no more escape back to childhood than Arthur can go with the Royal Family to court, "with his eyes shut up so tight / and the roads deep in snow."

Although "First Death in Nova Scotia" is the only poem in which Bishop's mother actually appears, the mother's presence can be felt in several other poems. With "Visits to St. Elizabeths," Bishop's tribute to Ezra Pound, incarcerated in a Washington, D.C., psychiatric hospital ("the house of Bedlam"), it seems safe to say that Pound's hospitalization might have reminded Bishop of her mother's own prolonged stay, and her eventual death, in such an institution. From 1916, the year she was committed, until her death in 1934, Bishop never again saw her mother. A mother figure (if not Bishop's own) also hovers over "Filling Station." In this poem "somebody" has decorated, domesticated an otherwise dank, if serviceable, filling station. But these are poor attempts at making a home. "Some comic books provide / the only note of color— / of certain color." "Filling Station" seems to argue that escape—into the family, here—is possible though somewhat pathetic. Certainly the station provides no more than a "meager diet" of what might constitute a family: a father in an "oil-soaked monkey suit," "several quick and saucy / and greasy sons," "a dirty dog, quite comfy." Who is missing? A mother. But she must be the one who has decorated the station with "grease- / impregnated wickerwork" and a "big hirsute begonia." (That the furniture is *impregnated* with grease seems confirmation of the absent but present mother.) She must be the one who "arranges the rows of cans / so that they softly say: / ESSO—SO—SO—SO / to high-strung automobiles." Against the "rigid house," the "inscrutable house" of "Sestina," this odd, "dirty" home seems a comfort. Clearly, there is affection here for the "oil-permeated" family. "Somebody loves us all," Bishop concludes, as though any small sign, any gesture of familial tenderness could prompt such far-reaching conclusions. Does somebody love us all? No. But someone loves this family, and we take—Bishop takes—love where love is found.

Two years after *Questions of Travel* was published in 1965, Bishop's lover, Lota de Macedo Soares, committed suicide while on a visit with Bishop to New York. Not only did Bishop lose one of the more stabilizing influences in her life, she also lost the house where she and Lota had lived together for so many years. In 1970 Bishop wrote to Robert Lowell, "I miss her more every day of my life. This is one of the reasons why I want to leave Brazil (forgive me)." A few months later, in another letter to Lowell, she wrote, "It is all too much like my early days"; and later still, "I lost my mother, and Lota, and others, too." Behind these pained remarks we can see Bishop's characteristic resolve and resilience, qualities that lie just beneath the surface of "One Art," the famous villanelle from her fourth collection, *Geography III:*

> I lost two cities, lovely ones. And, vaster,
> some realms I owned, two rivers, a continent.
> I miss them, but it wasn't a disaster.

To lose something—or someone—in some way creates a situation in which we are most helpless, in which we least have a choice: "So many things seem filled with the intent / to be lost that their loss is no disaster." Bishop's stoic calm wavers and cracks, slightly, in the final stanza.

> —Even losing you (the joking voice, a gesture
> I love) I shan't have lied. It's evident
> the art of losing's not too hard to master
> though it may look like (*Write* it!) like disaster.

"The art of losing" is no longer "not hard to master," but "not too hard to master."

The parenthetical asides in the final stanza give the poem a tremendous power. The first aside seems to have two possible meanings: that "the joking voice" belongs to the "you" Bishop addresses, and that she is attempting to set down a loved trait. It can also be seen as self-reflexive, that "Even losing you . . . I shan't have lied" is *told* in a "joking voice," the voice of pathos, of loss masquerading as black comedy. One argument in favor of the latter reading is that the second aside ("*Write* it!") is quite clearly addressed by Bishop to herself. Why not the first as well?

The second aside is the more famous. One criticism sometimes wrongly leveled at Bishop is that her tone, her voice, never modulates;

that it is too often quiet and introspective, more observant than otherwise. A specious criticism, at best—and here the variance is unmistakable. There is something so unlikely about the force and the sheer will of this one admonition that makes it stand out, an open wound, from the body of Bishop's work. "*Write* it!" The aside has all the clarity and emphasis of a stage direction; in a sense it *is* a stage direction. Self-possession lies here not in reserve or concealment but in what Octavio Paz has called "the power of reticence," in confession that loss may only *look* "like disaster." (Note the use of simile, not metaphor, to convey the poem's fiercest moment.) The only way we can overcome loss is to concede helplessness—but that concession *is* a choice.

Before "One Art" was written, Bishop had left Brazil, begun a teaching career at Harvard, and published *The Complete Poems.* The latter title, as Robert Hemenway points out, can be read as a pun describing the poems themselves and not the whole volume; individual poems are complete, finished, whole. Of these three events, the most important, perhaps the most devastating, was leaving Brazil. "There are so many places I'll never go back to," she wrote near the end of her life. "I change, the places change."

The parallels between Bishop's later life and the life of Robinson Crusoe are many. Even a cursory awareness of Bishop's biography makes "Crusoe in England," her poem about Defoe's shipwrecked sailor, resound with other, often deeper meanings. Nonetheless, "Crusoe in England" at once resists and redefines autobiography; it is an autobiography of the spirit. Like Bishop, who returned to Massachusetts after living for years south of the equator. Crusoe returns to England after years on his "un-rediscovered, un-renamable" island. Remembering those years, he laments:

> I often gave way to self-pity.
> "Do I deserve this? I suppose I must.
> I wouldn't be here otherwise. Was there
> a moment I actually chose this?
> I don't remember, but there could have been."
> What's wrong about self-pity, anyway?
> With my legs dangling down familiarly
> over a crater's edge, I told myself
> "Pity should begin at home." So the more
> pity I felt, the more I felt at home.

Shipwrecked and left to himself, Crusoe had only the "same odd sun," numerous goats, and turtles for company. At one point, reciting remembered poetry to "iris-beds" of snail shells, he cannot remember the final words of Wordsworth's "They flash upon that inward eye, / which is the bliss . . ." The missing words, of course, are "of solitude." Crusoe's solitude is broken when Friday appears: "Friday was nice, and we were friends. / If only he had been a woman! / I wanted to propagate my kind . . ./ —Pretty to watch; he had a pretty body."

Crusoe's paradise—or seeming paradise—comes to an end with his rescue: "Now I live here, another island, / that doesn't seem like one, but who decides." As Bishop's Massachusetts residence was decorated with souvenirs of her travels, so is Crusoe's: a "homemade" flute, a pair of "shedding goatskin trousers," the makeshift parasol that "folded up, / looks like a plucked and skinny fowl." And, of course, that knife so reminiscent of the knife in "At the Fishhouses":

> The knife there on the shelf—
> it reeked of meaning, like a crucifix.
> It lived. How many years did I
> beg it, implore it, not to break?
> I knew each nick and scratch by heart,
> the bluish blade, the broken tip,
> the lines of wood-grain on the handle . . .
> Now it won't look at me at all.
> The living soul had dribbled away.
> My eyes rest on it and pass on.

Another artifact haunts "In the Waiting Room": a 1918 issue of *National Geographic* magazine. At the dentist with her aunt, the young Elizabeth reads quietly, as a well-mannered child will, repelled and fascinated by the photos of

> babies with pointed heads
> wound round and round with string;
> black, naked women with necks
> wound round and round with wire
> like the necks of light bulbs.
> Their breasts were horrifying.

(In many ways these lines recall the "pock-marked prostitutes" of "Over 2,000 Illustrations and a Complete Concordance," and the horror with which they are observed.) Too ashamed, too curious to lift her eyes from the page, young Elizabeth is startled from her reading by "an *oh!* of pain" from behind the dentist's office door. Is it her aunt's voice? Her own? Is it an echo of her mother's scream, so painfully detailed in "In the Village"? These questions—explicitly addressed in the poem, or implied—prompt the child's first real self-knowledge: "You are an *I*, / you are an *Elizabeth*, / you are one of *them*." She comes to realize how very much she lives in the world, the world of adults, and that the fate of her "foolish aunt" could well be her own. In "In the Waiting Room," Bishop places her younger self very much in the midst of the disorienting confusion that is life: sex, death, pain.

Along with "The Moose" and "Poem," "In the Waiting Room" forms part of a trilogy of poems in *Geography III* that examine ideas of placement and displacement. They are poems in which identity is bound up with a given, remembered place and its inhabitants.

In "The Moose," a poem that recalls a long bus ride west after a visit to Bishop's childhood Nova Scotia, she places herself in the world by leaving the past and its poor enchantments behind: "Good-bye to the elms, / to the farm, to the dog." (The elms reappear at the close of "Poem.") From the back of the bus, she overhears "an old conversation / —not concerning us, / but recognizable. . . ." The commonplace tragedies she hears recounted are familiar, too much so, perhaps; and then someone replies—Is it Bishop or those she listens to?—"Yes."

> "Yes . . ." that peculiar
> affirmative. "Yes . . ."
> A sharp, indrawn breath,
> half groan, half acceptance,
> that means "Life's like that.
> We know *it* (also death).

From the passing woods, a female moose appears on the road ahead. Somehow the "curious creature" offers the travelers a benediction:

> Taking her time,
> she looks the bus over,
> grand, otherworldly.
> Why, why do we feel
> (we all feel) this sweet
> sensation of joy?

The joy is a release from pain. It is sweet to be let go from memory's burdens and responsibilities. Then the moose steps aside and the bus goes on, her benison now vanished in "an acrid / smell of gasoline."

"Poem" seems Bishop's effort to reconcile past and present, childhood and the memory of childhood, landscape and the memory of landscape, and to find a home for herself in the process. The subject of the poem is a small painting, "about the size of an old-style dollar bill," painted by the same uncle whose artwork figures in the earlier "Large Bad Picture." The painting is a Nova Scotia landscape, of which Bishop writes with the same great care her ancestor took in creating the work: "In the foreground / a water meadow with some tiny cows, / two brushstrokes each, but confidently cows." Grays pervade the scenery: "gray greens," "steel grays," "gray-blue"; whites, too—the colors of early spring, before green returns to the country, to the eye. The eye viewing the painting gives way to an inner eye, so that little is truly what it seems: "A specklike bird is flying to the left. / Or is it a flyspeck looking like a bird?" The question breaks Bishop's reverie; then, all of a sudden, she has gone through the painting, like Alice through the looking glass, into her past:

> Heavens, I recognize the place, I know it!
> It's behind—I can almost remember the
> farmer's name.

> His barn backed on that meadow. There it is,
> titanium white, one dab. The hint of steeple,
> filaments of brush-hairs, barely there,
> must be the Presbyterian church.
> Would that be Miss Gillespie's house?
> Those particular geese and cows
> are naturally before my time.

As several critics have pointed out, any poem so baldly entitled "Poem" must somehow be self-reflexive; it must say something about the nature of poetry. Bishop's "Poem" addresses a past that is "still loved / or its memory is." What is remembered is not the scene itself but how the scene appeared to the observer, first her uncle and then Bishop herself:

> Our visions coincided—"visions" is
> too serious a word—our looks, two looks:
> art "copying from life" and life itself,
> life and the memory of it so compressed
> they've turned into each other.

It is art—and by extension poetry—that helps us to see "the little that we get for free, the little of our earthly trust. Not much." Bishop's "Poem" helps her to recognize, and to place in perspective the deterioration of landscapes, the loss of loved ones. "Our abidance" is mortal as well: "the munching cows, / the iris, crisp and shivering, . . . the geese" have all died since the painting was first made. And yet, "the water / [is] still standing from spring freshets," the elms (which figure here and in "The Moose") are "yet-to-be-dismantled." The past, for little more than an instant, for "one breath," has been perfected. It has been made into a home that, although impossible to occupy, is no longer inscrutable or rigid but welcoming.

In the last years of Bishop's life she met with even greater critical and public acceptance. Shortly after the publication of *Geography III* she was awarded the *Books Abroad*/Neustadt International Prize for Literature (1976), the first time that prestigious award had been given to an American; it was also the first time the award had been given to a woman. Although she published few poems in her last years, they were poems in which she seemed more comfortable with open expressions of sadness and, by turns, of elation. "Pink Dog," a poem in triplets, despairs for South American poverty *and* celebrates the carnival season in Brazil; and "North Haven," an elegy for Robert Lowell (who died in 1977), seems prescient with Bishop's knowledge of her own mortality. She died of a stroke in Boston on 6 October 1979.

In an essay on life in the Galápagos Islands, where Bishop visited later in life, Annie Dillard writes, "Geography is the key, the crucial accident of birth." The same could be said of, perhaps even said by, Bishop. Much has been made of her transience, and of the fact that for her books she chose titles reflecting climate and place, geography and travel. Book titles are, of course, conscious decisions; residence, though, is often a crucial accident. It's not so much that we elect to live in one town, in one country or another, but that often we can do little more than decide whether to stay on or to leave. Home, address, residence: these occupy our imaginations, our hearts. Still and always, there comes a time when it seems we must decide to sink our roots farther in or to pry them loose. Then, maybe only then, do we see just how accidental our domestic lives have been, how random and uncertain they might always be—"Everything only connected by 'and' and 'and.' "

Selected Bibliography

PRIMARY WORKS

POETRY

North & South. Boston. Houghton Mifflin, 1946.

Poems: North & South—A Cold Spring. Boston: Houghton Mifflin, 1955.

Questions of Travel. New York: Farrar, Straus & Giroux, 1965.

Geography III. New York: Farrar, Straus & Giroux, 1976.

"It is marvelous. . . ." In *The Best American Poetry 1989*. Edited by Donald Hall. New York: Macmillan, 1989.

NONFICTION

Brazil. With the editors of *Life*. New York: Time, Inc., 1962.

TRANSLATIONS

An Anthology of Twentieth-Century Brazilian Poetry. Edited and with an introduction by Elizabeth Bishop and Emanuel Brasil. Middletown, Conn.: Wesleyan University Press, 1972.

The Diary of "Helena Morley" (Minha vida de menina). New York: Ecco Press, 1977.

The Collected Poems of Octavio Paz, 1957–1987. Edited and translated by Eliot Weinberger. With additional translations by Elizabeth Bishop and others. New York: New Directions, 1987.

Travelling in the Family. Translated by Elizabeth Bishop and others. New York: Random House, 1987. Poems by Carlos Drummond de Andrade.

COLLECTED WORKS

The Complete Poems, 1927–1979. New York: Farrar, Straus & Giroux, 1983.

The Collected Prose. Edited and with an introduction by Robert Giroux. New York: Farrar, Straus & Giroux, 1984.

SECONDARY WORKS

BIOGRAPHICAL AND CRITICAL STUDIES

Corn, Alfred. "Elizabeth Bishop's Nativities" and "God's Spies: Elizabeth Bishop and John Hollander." In his *The Metamorphoses of Metaphor*. New York: Viking Press, 1987.

Estes, Sybil P., and Lloyd Schwartz, eds. *Elizabeth Bishop and Her Art*. With a foreword by Harold Bloom. Ann Arbor: University of Michigan Press, 1983. Includes previously uncollected prose by Bishop and a bibliography.

Goldensohm, Lorrie. "Elizabeth Bishop: An Unpublished, Untitled Poem." *American Poetry Review*, January–February 1988.

Kalstone, David. "Elizabeth Bishop: Questions of Memory, Questions of Travel." In his *Five Temperaments: Elizabeth Bishop, Robert Lowell, James Merrill, Adrienne Rich, John Ashbery*. New York: Oxford University Press, 1977.

———. *Becoming a Poet: Elizabeth Bishop with Marianne Moore and Robert Lowell*. Edited by Robert Hemenway. New York: Farrar, Straus & Giroux, 1989. Includes some of Bishop's letters.

McClatchy, J. D. "Elizabeth Bishop: Some Notes on 'One Art.' " In *White Paper*. New York: Columbia University Press, 1989.

Merrill, James. "Elizabeth Bishop (1911–1979)" and "The Transparent Eye." In *Recitative Prose*. Edited by J. D. McClatchy. San Francisco: North Point Press, 1986.

Moss, Howard. "All Praise," "The Canada–Brazil Connection," and "The Long Voyage Home." In his *Minor Monuments*. New York: Ecco Press, 1986.

Parker, Robert Dale. *The Unbeliever: The Poetry of Elizabeth Bishop*. Urbana: University of Illinois Press, 1988.

Stevenson, Anne. *Elizabeth Bishop*. New York: Twayne, 1966.

Vendler, Helen. "Elizabeth Bishop." In her *Part of Nature, Part of Us: Modern American Poets*. Cambridge, Mass.: Harvard University Press, 1980.

———. "Elizabeth Bishop." In her *The Music of What Happens: Poems, Poets, Critics*. Cambridge, Mass.: Harvard University Press, 1988.

INTERVIEWS

Brown, Ashley. *Shenandoah*, Winter 1966.

Spires, Elizabeth. *Vassar Quarterly*, Winter 1979. Reprinted, with slightly different text, as "The Art of Poetry XXVII: Elizabeth Bishop." *Paris Review* 23:56–83 (Summer 1981).

Starbuck, George. " 'The Work!': A Conversation with Elizabeth Bishop." *Ploughshares* 3, nos. 3 and 4:11–29 (1977).

BIBLIOGRAPHY

MacMahon, Candace W. *Elizabeth Bishop: A Bibliography, 1927–1979*. Charlottesville: University of Virginia Press, 1980.

DAVID CRAIG AUSTIN

LOUISE BOGAN

(1897–1970)

"BEING WITH LOUISE, the most life-enhancing person imaginable, gave everything a zany charm, even disaster," May Sarton wrote, recalling "small occasions"—one involving a near-collision with a horse in Brooklyn—that she and Louise Bogan shared in the mid 1950s. Their friendship, which came relatively late in Bogan's life, survived Sarton's wish for greater intimacy than Bogan would allow. Bogan explained that she had a "psychic flaw" resulting from her relationship with her mother that would make closeness to another woman traumatic. Sarton appreciated this explanation, regarding it as tactful and generous; it is also a Freudian account of emotional illness boiled down to its conventional basics. "Except for a certain saving *humor*," Bogan wrote to Sarton of her demonic obsessiveness during her second marriage, "I should have indeed been a full *monster*." Survival—emotional overlaid on economic—required lifelong struggle for Bogan. Psychiatry was a refuge in which she placed unquestioning faith. It also supplied the outline of a rigorous spiritual journey toward mature detachment that informed Bogan's poetry, her criticism, and the shape of her life as she and others saw it.

That life was a private one. Bogan shunned publicity, did not join political movements, and kept distant from literary cliques. Her poetry is not confessional. "Actually, I have written down my experience in the closest detail," she noted in a journal. But the "outright narrative" is repressed; "the rough and vulgar facts are not there." The first published version of that narrative was *What the Woman Lived: Selected Letters of Louise Bogan, 1920–1970* (1973), edited by her literary executor, Ruth Limmer. The task of compiling, annotating, and selectively cutting nearly four hundred pages of correspondence was completed as quickly as possible after Bogan's death in 1970. Limmer cautiously justified risking a posthumous violation of Bogan's privacy: the letters had literary importance and were a joy to read—though her annotations revealed a sometimes baffling minimum of "vulgar facts."

The first letter in the collection, to William Carlos Williams, was written when Bogan was almost twenty-three; it concerns John Coffey, a thief and dubious cause célèbre. A successful shoplifter, he claimed, when he was caught with furs, that he was stealing to publicize the plight of the poor, and he enlisted the support of artists and writers. We do not learn from Limmer that Coffey was briefly Bogan's lover, an exploitative liaison that haunted her for many years. But as Bogan's friendships with such literary figures as Edmund Wilson, Morton Zabel, and Rolfe Humphries unfold, Limmer's justifications for publishing the letters become increasingly convincing: they are a particular record of the development of American modernism over half a century, and contemporary rewritings of the story of modernism should include Louise Bogan.

W. H. Auden, whose friendship with Bogan began in 1941, told her he could not understand why her work was so little known. Other poets admired her poetry, and Auden considered her the finest poetry critic in America. Her explanation was that she was not respectable. Whether she believed the reputation of being a gangster's moll still lingered from her involvement with John Coffey twenty years earlier, or whether she saw her lower-middle-class Irish Catholic origins and her lack of a college education as the blots on her respectability, Bogan continued to regard herself as a literary outsider even after years as an influential reviewer for the *New Yorker.* When honors came to her later in her life, she would quip to friends, "Not bad for a little Irish girl from Maine." "I never was a member of a 'lost generation,' " Bogan wrote to Morton Zabel on 11 June 1937:

> I was the highly charged and neurotically inclined product of an extraordinary childhood and an unfortunate early marriage, into which last state I had rushed to escape the first. . . . I had no relations whatever with the world about me; I lived in a dream, populated by figures out of Maeterlinck and Pater and Arthur Symons and Compton Mackenzie . . . and H. G. Wells and Francis Thompson and Alice Meynell and Swinburne and John Masefield and other oddly assorted authors. What I did and what I felt was, I assure you, *sui generis.*

No further version of the narrative of Bogan's life appeared until seven years after the letters, although a small press brought her final collection of poems, *The Blue Estuaries,* back into print in 1977. In *Journey Around My Room: The Autobiography of Louise Bogan* (1980), Limmer pieced together published and unpublished writings—stories, journal entries, letters, and poems—to create a mosaic of fragments of Bogan's voice, more satisfying as a still mysterious, emotionally charged reclamation of meaning than as a source of information about events.

In the introduction Limmer again emphasizes Bogan's privateness, quoting at length a letter Bogan wrote but never sent when she was asked asked in 1939 to supply biographical data for a reference volume. "My dislike of telling future research students anything about myself is intense and profound," she began. "If they know everything to begin with, how in hell can they go on eating up their tidy little fellowships researching? And I believe the less authentic records are, the more 'interesting' they automatically become." The letter serves the additional purpose of correcting what Limmer believed was the one distortion in her piecemeal "autobiography": the shortage of examples of Bogan's rapier wit. "I used to lie in confession regularly," Bogan warned, "from the time I first confessed, at the ripe moral age of about nine."

Nevertheless, Bogan's account of her literary apprenticeship, her immersion as an adolescent in the writings of late-Victorian precursors of modernism, seems at least partly authentic.

> My great gifts of imagination always took the form of lies, in fact, up to my entrance into puberty, when I became a radical and a Fabian, and discovered Bernard Shaw, Aubrey Beardsley, Arthur Symons, Nietzsche, Wagner, Max Stirner and Walter Pater. My first literary exercises were strongly influenced by William Morris and D. G. Rossetti and I wrote a long poem, or a sonnet sequence, every day, for about four years, after coming home from school.
>
> (*Journey,* p. xvii)

She rakishly insisted on her lack of respectability:

> That I have no criminal records is entirely due to the kindness of several members of the legal and psychiatric professions, who, I am sure, put me down as nuts, and just let me go on thinking that a stay in the booby-hatch, now and again, would not run into so much money as a stay in jail.
>
> (*Journey,* p. xviii)

Under "Influences" she wrote, "I think alcohol comes in here." Her list of "Dislikes" shows the anti-academicism of Bogan the autodidact and her antipathy toward the upper classes: "well-bred accents, loud talk, the professional literati of all ages, other women poets (jealousy!), other men poets, English accents, Yale graduates and bad writing and bad writers."

Several books on Bogan appeared in the mid 1980s. The first of these were two books of criticism, a collection of essays edited by Martha Collins and a volume written by Jaqueline Ridgeway, both published in 1984. Ridgeway dates a revival of interest in Bogan to the publication of her letters in 1973, and attributes Bogan's previous obscurity to limitations in the culture that were yielding to new feminist insights about the position of women artists. Yet for many readers of the long, painstaking, scholarly biography of Bogan that was finally published in 1985, she continues to be a new discovery. Reviewing Elizabeth Frank's *Louise Bogan: A Portrait,* Gloria Bowles notes that feminist criticism has contributed little to a Bogan revival. One reason for this neglect is the apparent misogyny of her often-anthologized poem "Women." A powerful feminist project of the 1970s was to supply positive models of women to counteract the reduced, sexist images produced abundantly in male-dominated culture. Bogan could be included in such a project only with difficulty. A decade later, feminist scholarship was reconstructing a more complete women's literary history, with all its anguish, and feminist critics, according to Bowles, are now able to understand Bogan's poem "for its social accuracy and its record of a woman writer's ambivalent relationship to her own sex."

In her book, Frank discusses Bogan's poetry biographically, volume by volume. Of "Women," published in Bogan's first collection, *Body of This Death* (1923), Frank notes that it is a highly specific list of women's shortcomings, full of an envy of men's superior abilities to perceive, imagine, and act. Yet the poem contradicts its own judgments. Bogan the woman invented the very sights, sounds, and thoughts the poem claims women cannot attend to. The poem itself becomes a way of setting up and defeating a fear, a limited female poetic persona. In this poem and in her critical writings, Bogan refers to women as "they." Who, then, is speaking? Is this an ironic, nonfemale mask, and can we really say whether Bogan the woman owned these opinions? In either case the voice that frames the attack receives destructive treatment nearly equivalent to the anger directed against "women"; and yet, in spite of the impossibility of a point of view, a poem is made.

In her 1987 book *Louise Bogan's Aesthetic of Limitation,* Bowles points out the complexity of Bogan's ambivalence in "Women." She urges that the poem be read in relation to Bogan's critical writings about her female predecessors and contemporaries, as part of a "lifelong quest for expression" from the precarious position of a woman caught between a male tradition and a female tradition against which the stringent aesthetics of male modernism were often pointedly directed. "Women have no wilderness in them" is the first complaint in "Women." Yet in a lecture on women writers that Bogan delivered at Bennington College in 1962, she quoted a passage from Dorothy Richardson that plays on some of the same meanings as "no wilderness," except that they unequivocally represented to Bogan "a woman's perceptions, in full upward flight, a woman's sense of the worth of her womanhood, richly displayed." The passage is from *Deadlock,* the sixth volume of Richardson's *Pilgrimage:* "Women do not need civilization. It is apt to bore them. They keep it back. That does not matter, to themselves. But it matters to men. . . . There isn't any 'chaos.' . . . It's the principal masculine delusion. It is not a truth to say that women must be civilized."

Although Bogan scrupulously referred to her work as minor—lyric poetry being classically considered a minor mode—Bowles's premise is that Bogan was a major American modernist. The question she must struggle with is one that also troubled Limmer and Frank: why didn't Bogan write more poetry? Bowles found the answer in a restrictive, perfectionist poetics. She cites a passage from a 1961 review of Bogan's poetry by Theodore Roethke that has weighed heavily on discussions of Bogan in several major feminist books on women's poetry, including Gilbert and Gubar's *No Man's Land* and Ostriker's *Stealing the Language.* Roethke took the opportunity to make a witty list of the flaws of women's poetry that Bogan happily escaped:

> the spinning-out; the embroidering of trivial themes; a concern with the mere surfaces of life—that special province of the feminine talent in prose—hiding from the real agonies of the spirit; refusing to face up to what existence is; lyric or religious posturing; running between the boudoir and the altar, stamping a tiny foot against God; or lapsing into a sententiousness that implies the author has re-invented integrity; carrying on excessively about Fate, about time; lamenting the lot of the woman; caterwauling; writing the same poem about fifty times, and so on.
>
> (Bowles, p. 35)

Bowles points out that far from being simply male ridicule of women's writing in the guise of literary standards, the passage represents tastes that Bogan encouraged in Roethke. The strategy of praising a poet's work for its freedom from fashionable errors was one she often used in her *New Yorker* reviews, and she, too, deployed sarcasm against women's verse. Bogan and Roethke had a brief, playful affair in 1935, when Roethke was twenty-six—he was twelve years her junior—and a promising apprentice poet, and after their separation Bogan in her correspondence with him continued to serve as his mentor. Her list of rules for women poets in her 1962 lecture echoes Roethke's, but is also consistent with the critical viewpoint she had developed in her years as a reviewer:

> First, in literature (or in any other art) women must not lie. Second, they must not whine. Third, they must not attitudinize (in the role of the *femme fatale* least of all). And they must neither theatricalize nor coarsen their truths. They must not be vain, and they must not flight or kite in any witch-like way. Nor, on the other hand, go in for little girlishness and false naïveté. Nor "stamp a tiny foot at the universe."
>
> (*Journey*, p. 156)

It seems unlikely that the question of why she did not write more poetry will continue to be productive for explorations of Bogan's writings. It is a question that was pressed on Bogan by some of her greatest admirers, including Auden, and that Bogan herself raised; but, from her knowledge of earlier lyric poets such as Emily Dickinson, she believed the lyric career to be necessarily brief. Bogan's work lies at the troubled crux of the tradition of nineteenth-century women poets with tightly circumscribed lives writing emotionally flooded poetry, and of the male modernist tradition, reaching back through romanticism to a tense metaphysical masking of feeling in form; and for the alienations of class, gender, and ethnicity Bogan brought with her to big-city literary life, psychiatric modernism made available powerful interventions that, for better or worse, shaped her relationship to her poetry.

The broadening of the canon of American literary modernism—still often centralized around the accomplishments of a few male giants—to include a figure such as Bogan requires students of poetry to move past grieving for what was not written, a critical stance that risks drawing her as a poet minus poetry. There are, after all, more than a hundred poems in *The Blue Estuaries,* few likely to be quickly used up by repeated discussion in classrooms and critical literature. At least a score of the poems have been considered by critics, particularly other poets, to be among the finest lyrics in English. There are also her letters and her criticism, as significant to the cultural history of literature as is her poetry.

Critics of Bogan's poetry, Martha Collins writes in her introduction to *Critical Essays on Louise Bogan,* have belonged to two camps: the formalists, who are fascinated by her great technical skill, and the feminists, committed to placing her in women's literary traditions through biographical and cultural criticism. New Criticism, as a modern version of formalist approaches, earned a reputation for obscuring the part that social forces play in literary production; and Bogan herself hated the elitist authority that New Critical academics developed. Yet poetry as formally adept as Bogan's demands its match, some kind of formalist sophistication, in its readers. Formalism and feminism need not be mutually exclusive, however, and several critics have found ways to combine them.

An often directly stated goal of Bogan's critics has been to locate a new audience for her work, to send the reader to *The Blue Estuaries* (1968). Published two years before her death, it includes most of the poems that appeared in the five earlier books. Ridgeway and Frank both thoroughly discuss poems never published in any of the volumes and account for Bogan's later judgment against ones that she at first included. The following list covers often-anthologized poems as well as those frequently singled out in critical discussions; its aim is to send the reader both to Bogan's poetry as a whole and to critics, such as Ridgeway, Frank, and Bowles, who have supplied extensive biographical and contextual discussions of her work: from *Body of This Death* (1923), reprinted in Section I of *The Blue Estuaries:* "Medusa," "The Frightened Man," "The Crows," "Women," "Last Hill in a Vista," and "The Alchemist"; from *Dark Summer* (1929) and Part II, "The Crossed Apple," "Cassandra," "I Saw Eternity," "Simple Autumnal," and "Late"; from *The Sleeping Fury* (1937) and Part III, the title poem, "Roman Fountain," and "Henceforth, from the Mind"; added in *Poems and New Poems* (1941) and included in Part IV of *The Blue Estuaries,* "Several Voices out of a Cloud," "To Be Sung on the Water," and "Zone"; from the new section of *Collected Poems 1923–1953* (1954) and Part V, "The Dream," "Evening in the Sanitarium," "Song for the Last Act," and "After the Persian"; and Part VI, from the latest poems in *The Blue Estuaries,* "Night" and "Three Songs."

Bogan wrote lyric poetry when the lyric mode was losing popularity, and the Bogan revival has occurred at a time when classroom attention to poetry has been low or segregated into creative writing programs. Literary theories since structuralism have been applied at much greater length to fiction than to poetry. Historical and cultural approaches face the difficulty with lyrics of wresting material and temporal meanings from a mode purged of such referents. Literary theory has been seen as actually hostile to poetry—for example, directed toward exposing the falseness in so central a theme as the self's striving toward transcendence. Yet scrutiny of the position of the poetic subject also turns up insights into the ways poems criticize, question, and revise the traditions of what is needed to make a poem.

Bogan repeatedly made poems out of subject positions from which utterance would seem to be virtually impossible. In "Medusa," for example, the speaker is frozen in place in a frozen scene. Ridgeway mingles quotes from Bogan's prose reminiscences of her childhood in a discussion of "Medusa," showing that the disabling paralysis of the subject had to do with Bogan's conflicted relationship with her mother. Roethke saw the poem as a struggle with the Anima, the Medusa being a kind of masculine mother "welling up" from the unconscious—a Jungian reading with which Bogan would have agreed, although she would likely have been uneasy if the exposed unconscious processes were taken as an excuse for her small poetic output. "We must not bring back and describe 'the bad mother'—'the Dragon mother'—in order to justify ourselves. Only to understand," she wrote in a journal in 1960.

As an account of its own source, "Medusa" tells of an encounter with a muse whose monstrosity serves to objectify the "I" as part of the poetic scenery, caught in the reification that occurs when an aesthetic object is made:

> I had come to the house, in a cave of trees,
> Facing a sheer sky.
> Everything moved,—a bell hung ready to
>   strike,
> Sun and reflection wheeled by.
>
> When the bare eyes were before me
> And the hissing hair,

Held up at a window, seen through a door.
The stiff bald eyes, the serpents on the
forehead
Formed in the air.

This is a dead scene forever now.
Nothing will ever stir.
The end will never brighten it more than this,
Nor the rain blur.

The water will always fall, and will not fall,
And the tipped bell make no sound.
The grass will always be growing for hay
Deep on the ground.

And I shall stand here like a shadow
Under the great balanced day,
My eyes on the yellow dust, that was lifting in
the wind,
And does not drift away.

What the shadow "I" has left to look at is dust that does not blow away: mortality frozen into permanence, an almost mocking revision of the "striving toward transcendence" theme. That this "I" is made by a woman writer is important. A woman reading male lyric poetry would find her gender not in the subject position but as the object of scrutiny. Bogan's Medusa, overrepresenting the presence and power of the lyric eye, is the male gaze and the maternal muse made one. There is also the curious twist that Bogan's horrific vision is "Held up at a window"; what if, instead of a whole Gorgon, a Perseus is in the house holding up the severed head of female monstrosity to stop a woman poet in her tracks? An idea Bogan adopted from T. S. Eliot—that poetic originality is "merely development," doing "the next thing"—leads to a further question: Finding that lyric poetry has been made out of severely undermined subject positions, do we hope for a sturdier ego base for women writers, or do we take the instability of the self as a critical position generating questions that point to directions in which poetry by writers of either sex might go?

"To separate the work of women writers from the work of men is, naturally, a highly unfeminist action," Bogan wrote rather defiantly in a 1963 review of May Swenson and Anne Sexton. "But beneath surface likenesses, women's poetry continues to be unlike men's, all feminist statements to the contrary notwithstanding." Ever the nonjoiner, Bogan in her criticism stood against generalized "feminist" positions. That she rarely discussed social conditions in her criticism makes her special treatment of women writers often stark, as if she expected them to perform to their utmost within limits that were essential to their nature rather than culturally bound.

But she did recognize the brevity of the tradition of women's poetry and the constraints under which it developed. She was impatient for it to grow up. "But is there any reason to believe that a woman's spiritual fibre is less sturdy than a man's?" she wrote in an exasperated 1939 review of Edna St. Vincent Millay, whom she thought was wasting her talent. "Is it not possible for a woman to come to terms with herself, if not with the world; to withdraw more and more, as time goes on, her own personality from her productions, to stop childish fears of death and eschew charming rebellions against facts?" As the outline of a standard of spiritual maturity, the question turns back on Bogan herself. "I have been *forced* to find a way of loving my destiny," she wrote to May Sarton in 1954, referring to her psychological crises in the early 1930s, "of not opposing it too much with my will. I have been *forced* 'to forgive life' in order to get through existence at all." Whether or not stoic detachment was a just standard for her to apply to the literary careers of others, it was the saving adjustment she gained from psychiatric treatment and served Bogan the critic as a criterion of spiritual strength.

Two books of Bogan's criticism, *Achievement in American Poetry, 1900–1950* (1951) and *Selected Criticism: Prose, Poetry* (1955), were published during her life and one, *A Poet's Alphabet: Reflection on the Literary Art and Vocation* (1970), after her death. The title of the last volume identifies Bogan's criticism—the content of the three books overlaps—as one poet's canon, comparable with the canons that the early modernist poet-critics put together out of readings that influenced their own writings. Bogan's canon is unusual in several ways. It was published not in small, avant-garde literary journals but largely in the *New Yorker,* a magazine appealing to a literate, liberal, urbane readership, mediating taste to middle-class consumers of culture.

That Bogan's criticism was journalistic no doubt contributed to the importance she gave nineteenth-century newspapermen as forerunners of twentieth-century American poetry. In her first book of criticism, the only one arranged historically, she highlighted James Gibbon Huneker, a columnist who used "living ideas" from Europe to critique the narrowly moralizing, conventional tastes associated with New England's intellectual tradition. Modernism began with the French symbolists; William Butler Yeats was the greatest poet of the era; Ezra Pound, Robert Frost, Gertrude Stein, Wallace Stevens, Marianne Moore, and T. S. Eliot were key Americans in the poetic renaissance just before and after World War I; by the 1940s Auden had replaced Eliot as the single most influential figure. These features of Bogan's account are standard, although her discussion of Pound is specially weighted. She served on the committee that awarded the first Bollingen Prize to Pound in 1948, a choice that was highly controversial because of his wartime involvement with Italian Fascism. Attacks on the committee were published, and its members defended their decision. Bogan's careful accounting of Pound's influence in her book extended that defense, although years later she agreed with Karl Shapiro that Pound should not have received the prize, that his anti-Semitism spoiled the quality of his art.

What is most distinctive about Bogan's critical canon is her consideration of women writers. "The American literary tradition, from the time of seventeenth-century Ann Bradstreet, . . . had never been without an outstanding American woman 'singer,' " she wrote in *Achievement in American Poetry,* in a half-chapter on female predecessors of twentieth-century verse. Even if separate attention to women were considered nonfeminist in the early 1950s, Bogan's discussions of the special place of such forgotten poets as Louise Imogen Guiney and Lizette Woodworth Reese proved valuable to later feminist scholars engaged in reconstructing women's literary history. Cheryl Walker's *The Nightingale's Burden: Women Poets and American Culture Before 1900* (1982) is one study that makes use of Bogan's participation as a poet-critic in the female tradition. Popular verse by women, Bogan wrote, "reflected with deadly accuracy every change in the nation's sentimental tendencies." Much of this verse made her howl, but she ascribed to women poets the revivifying of emotion: "the line of poetic intensity which wavers and fades out and often completely fails in poetry written by men, on the feminine side moves on unbroken."

Though Bogan believed an intuitive, feeling nature better suited to lyric poetry than to long forms or experimental styles, she did not consider sustaining the "line of feeling" to be a small contribution. "All art," she insisted in a lecture in the 1960s, "in spite of the struggles of some critics to prove otherwise, is based on emotion and projects emotion." Continually at odds with Virginia Woolf's feminism, which she regarded as narrowly upper-class and Anglo-Saxon, Bogan criticized Woolf's worrying the question of whether a woman would ever write a work comparable to Shakespeare's plays. That test of a poet's powers was "a little old-fashioned," Bogan wrote in "The Heart and the Lyre" (1947). "Can it be that there is no basic reason for women to excel in the art of poetry by producing the same sort of poetic structures as men? Men, as a matter of fact, stayed with the five-act poetic tragedy far too long. Perhaps women have more sense than to linger over an obsessing form of this kind."

What civilization needed from poetry had changed and, in the twentieth century, standards of greatness drawn from the canon of male writers no longer applied. The achievements of women poets served for Bogan as one indication of "the next thing" to come from modernism, or the direction of development that would continue to generate originality in poetry by both women and men. In a 1943 essay, "Some Notes on Popular and Unpopular Poetry," Bogan predicted this future direction: "The only really usable and incontrovertible modern discoveries are in the spiritual field"—always for Bogan associated with emotion and its conversion into symbol—"and these have their everyday diagnostic and therapeutic uses." For Bogan, modern spirituality was tied up with psychiatry. Her description of this truth-telling poetry cleared of the nineteenth century proceeds, a familiar strategy, by negatives:

> No more rhetoric; no more verbalizing; no more exhortations or elegies or eulogies. No more conscious and affected investigations of dark corridors and deserted strands; no more use of the universe as a backdrop against which one acts out hope or despair. No more dejected sitting about. No more searching nature for an answering mood. . . .

To "the rough and vulgar facts": Louise Marie Bogan was born on 11 August 1897 to Daniel Joseph and May Murphy Shields Bogan, who had an older child, Charles Joseph, born in 1884. "Birthplace: Livermore Falls, Maine, a town on the Androscoggin River, run by a paper mill," Bogan wrote in her unsent satirical response to a 1939 research questionnaire. "My father has often told me about the excellent hard cider made by Billy Bean, the proprietor of the town's combination brothel and saloon. B. Bean used to add all sorts of things to the original apple juice, including ground up sirloin steak, and the results of drinking this nectar, when it was ripe, were terrific." A prose book called *Laura Daly's Story,* which she began writing in the mid 1930s but never finished, was to have borne this epigraph from La Rochefoucauld: "The accent and character of one's native region live in the mind and heart just as in one's speech." What does exist of this autobiographical project, three stories published in the *New Yorker* in the 1930s and some journal entries from the 1950s and 1960s, is woven into *Journey Around My Room,* and evokes the unstable, sometimes violent tone of Bogan's growing up, which she described to Sarton as "Micawberish."

Daniel Bogan worked his way up through the ranks of a Livermore Falls paper mill from clerk to superintendent. In 1901 the family moved to Milton, New Hampshire, where they lived in two rooms of a hotel called Bodwell's. Bogan dated her consciousness of her surroundings to this time. She became aware of "secret family angers and secret disruption." Verbal and physical battles would break out between her parents in which May Bogan, taller than her husband by five inches and adept with invective, would usually gain the upper hand. A lively woman raised by her adoptive mother to marry well, May was bored by her husband and their small-town life. Louise observed hushed, conspiratorial discussions between May and her confidantes, and sometimes May took her daughter along to assignations with lovers, leaving her to wait outside the room. Once May went off with a lover for several weeks.

In 1904 the Bogans moved to Ballardvale, Massachusetts, where Daniel and Charles both worked for a bottling company. The family lived at first in a boarding house, then in a series of homes of their own. In 1906 Louise was sent to a convent school in New Hampshire. May spent much of the next year traveling across the country with two companions, a woman friend and a lover.

Ethnicity and class were always issues in the mill towns, where workers were French-Canadian and Italian and the management class usually Anglo-Saxon "Yankees"; in boarding school, Louise became aware of the nuns' favoritism toward her blond schoolmates. Although lonely, she did so well in school that she skipped a grade.

In 1909 the family moved again, this time to Boston. Her parents kept Louise out of school for a year (1908–1909), but in 1910 May enrolled her in Girls' Latin School, a public high school that offered a classical education to superior students. Besides the classics and nineteenth-century writers, Louise read *Poetry: A Magazine of Verse* from issue one at the Boston Public Library. "I began to write verse from about fourteen on," she remembered fifty years later. "The life-saving process then began. By the age of 18 I had a thick pile of manuscript, in a drawer in the dining room—and had learned every essential of my trade." Early poems of hers were published in the school's literary journal, *The Jabberwock,* and the *Boston Evening Transcript.* She went on to Boston University but left after a year and turned down a scholarship to Radcliffe. She married an army officer instead—her escape from home.

Louise and Curt Alexander were married in September 1916. The following spring, when war was declared, he was sent to Panama. Louise, four months pregnant, followed him. Their daughter, Mathilde, called Maidie, was born in October. Bogan hated Panama, and the marriage was troubled. "All we had in common was sex," she later told Ruth Limmer. She returned to America with Maidie in May 1918. In October, near the end of the war, her brother, Charles, was killed in battle in France. Curt was stationed at Fort Dix, New Jersey, to assist in the demobilization of soldiers in 1919, and Louise and Maidie lived with him in Hoboken. Louise had begun to establish literary contacts in New York—two poems of hers were published in *Others,* an avant-garde magazine, while she was in Panama. From Hoboken she would take the ferry to Greenwich Village, where she found a lively literary scene that welcomed her. By summer, she had left Alexander, taken Maidie to live with her parents in Farley, Massachusetts, and moved to New York alone. Alexander died of pneumonia in 1920, leaving his widow a small army pension.

Louise's literary life at first centered on the people involved with *Others* but soon expanded. She met William Carlos Williams, Lola Ridge, Malcolm Cowley, Mina Loy, John Reed, Louise Bryant, Conrad Aiken, Edmund Wilson, and Rolfe Humphries soon after moving to New York. Wilson and Humphries became her close lifelong friends. In 1921 *Poetry* accepted five of her poems, and by the end of that year her poetry was appearing in many prestigious journals. Bogan's first book of poems, *Body of This Death,* published in 1923, was dedicated to her mother and her daughter. The October 1923 issue of *Vanity Fair* placed her photograph among those of seven other women, including Amy Lowell, Edna St. Vincent Millay, and Sara Teasdale, in a spread captioned "Distinguished American Women Poets Who Have Made the Lyric Verse Written by Women in America More Interesting Than That of the Men." The *New Republic* published Bogan's first piece of critical prose, "The Springs of Poetry," in a poets' symposium ("Views of American Poetry") on 5 December. She was assisting with editorial work on the *Measure,* a journal that favored well-made lyrics over avant-garde free verse, and in 1924 served as its acting managing editor. At Edmund Wilson's urging, Bogan began to write reviews; her first was published in the *New Republic* in March 1924.

Bogan had fallen in love with Raymond Holden, an independently wealthy poet whose worship of Robert Frost had led him to buy a farm from Frost and live near him, somewhat unsatisfactorily, for a time. Wilson, himself half in love with Bogan, declared Holden "an amiable mediocrity." Holden was separated from his wife, and he and Bogan lived together until his divorce was final, then married in July 1925. They moved from New York City to Boston to Santa Fe, back to New York, then to a house in the country in upstate New York. Maidie came to live with them. *The Dark Summer,* Bogan's second book, was published in 1929. Its theme of betrayal reflects the gathering unhappiness in her marriage. Holden adored Bogan, but she saw in him—accurately, it seems—an adolescent "Shelleyan" who had to be in love.

On the day after Christmas in 1929, their house burned down. Bogan lost all her work in progress, along with furniture and books. Holden's financial assets had fallen with the coming of the Great Depression. They moved back to Manhattan, where Holden became managing editor of the *New Yorker.* The magazine had just begun to publish serious verse, and the editors wanted to run poetry reviews as well. Bogan's first review in the *New Yorker* appeared in March 1931; she wrote omnibus reviews called "The Season's Verse" twice a year for the next thirty-eight years.

Starting in 1930, Bogan was plagued by anger, resentment, fear, and self-hatred. She drank excessively and fought openly with Holden. In the spring of 1931 she was hospitalized for two months of psychiatric treatment and left the hospital aware that she was still unwell. Late in 1932, at the urging of Morton Zabel, Bogan applied for a Guggenheim grant to travel in Europe. Zabel was an associate editor of *Poetry;* their friendship, carried on by mail, began in 1930 after he reviewed *The Dark Summer.* At first Bogan mocked him for his stuffiness: he was fanatically devoted to high culture. But as more of her friends, including Wilson and Humphries, subordinated their artistic commitments to leftist politics—a trend Bogan regarded as a betrayal of aesthetic standards—she increasingly relied on Zabel for his support of her position.

Bogan's self-confidence was low, but to her surprise she received the Guggenheim. Leaving in April 1933, she traveled in Italy, France, and Austria. The value of the dollar was falling, and the Guggenheim Foundation urged Bogan to come home and take the rest of her grant at a more economically stable time. Her correspondence with Holden was tortured: she suspected him of having affairs; his denials left room for suspicion, and he criticized her neurotic doubts. She returned home in September, emotionally shattered. In November she again entered a psychiatric hospital, this time determined to stay until she felt well. She was in treatment for six months. By May 1935 she and Holden had separated; they divorced in 1937.

Holden was to send Bogan support payments of $40 a week, but the money at times came irregularly. Bogan's eviction from her apartment in September 1935 scarcely fazed her; she wrote to Zabel, "I have been very much at peace, since the roof fell in; in fact, I haven't felt so peaceful in my life as now." It was a productive year. In spite of their differences over politics, Bogan and Wilson were close and met often to translate German poetry. Bogan discovered the poetry of Rilke, a new major influence on what she wanted her lyrics to achieve, and her boisterous affair with Roethke inspired poems. She also was reading and taking notes on psychoanalytic theory. A passage she copied from Jung's *Psychology of the Unconscious* gives as the goal of psychoanalysis the detachment Bogan had very nearly achieved: a mature personality "who does willingly and without complaint everything required by necessity."

Toward the end of 1936, when Bogan was preparing her third volume of poetry, her mother died. Poems in *The Sleeping Fury* show Bogan's struggle to face "the dragon mother." Much of the old conflict was resolved, and Bogan was able to remember her mother as a loving woman with a gift for language, the source of her own talent. In 1937 Bogan used the balance of her Guggenheim to go to Ireland. In Dublin paranoid anxiety struck her, but on the boat train, as she was leaving for home, another passenger, a working-class Irish New Yorker, nursed and teased her out of her anxiety. None of Bogan's friends ever met this man, though their relationship lasted eight years. To Sarton she described the affair as "utterly different from anything that had gone before; perfect freedom, perfect detachment, no *jealousy* at all—an emphasis on *joy*. . . ." In 1939 she began preparing *Poems and New Poems,* but inspiration—which she required—was becoming infrequent. The volume was finished in 1941. Over the next thirteen years she published only three poems.

Bogan had recoiled from the genteel literary circle in whose center Holden's *New Yorker* position placed them during the last years of their marriage. She thrived better among a few close friends. With Wilson and Humphries, she could battle out class and political differences one on one, within a background of intimacy. By 1939 she began to be less withdrawn from the poetry world. She surprised herself by contributing to the *Partisan Review*'s forum "The Situation in American Writing," seriously answering questions that she had mocked in the unsent questionnaire earlier that same year. It was a time of leftist disillusionment with Stalin and communism, and Bogan took the opportunity to present her view of the spiritual malaise behind the political enthusiasms of the 1930s.

In the 1940s Bogan's belief that she was not respectable was challenged by a progression of honors. She was elected a fellow in American letters of the Library of Congress (1944) and appointed a consultant on poetry for a year (1945). She served Doubleday as a consultant on belles-lettres (1946–1947). She became a judge for the Guggenheim poetry fellowships, a role she filled for twenty years. She was invited to universities as a visiting lecturer and won the Harriet Monroe Award from the University of Chicago (1948). In 1951 she received a grant of one thousand dollars from the National Institute of Arts and Letters, which the next year elected her a member.

Through the 1950s and 1960s Bogan was a busy woman of letters. She made new friends, Sarton and Limmer among them. Her correspondence was filled with literary gossip. Two books of criticism and *Collected Poems 1923–1953* were published. She took on special writing projects—an essay on contemporary American poetry for the *Times Literary Supplement,* introductions to reprints of classic novels, translations of poetry and prose, a biographical essay on Frost. Lecturing and teaching assignments took her all over the United States and to Europe. Honors continued to come. In 1955 she shared the Bollingen Prize with Léonie Adams; in 1956 Western College for Women awarded her an honorary doctorate. The Academy of American Poets gave he a prize of five thousand dollars in 1959. She received a Senior Creative Arts Award from Brandeis University in 1962 and in 1964 returned to Boston for a year as visiting professor at Brandeis.

In June 1965 Bogan was hospitalized again. "This depressed state began last fall, I think—with the return to the scenes of my childhood—or adolescence," she wrote to Ruth Limmer. "Boston is really filled with sorrowful memories of my family, and my early self.—I thought, because I had 'insight' into it all, that I could rise above it." She was treated at first with Librium, a new "miracle" psychotropic drug that became available in the early 1960s. The medication's side effects drained her, but she blamed herself for her psychic collapse:

> Surely I have acted in a consistently *optimistic* fashion, ever since the 1933 breakdown.—I have surmounted one difficulty after another; I have *worked* for life and "creativity"; I have cast off all the anxieties and fears I could; I have helped others to work and hold on. . . . Why can't I refuel—recover?
>
> (*Journey,* p. 175)

When her condition deteriorated in September, she was given electroshock therapy, from which she sustained the common long-term effect of memory impairment.

Nevertheless, by 1967 Bogan was teaching and traveling again, and in November she took her first public political action, reading "To My Brother" at a Poets for Peace rally protesting the Vietnam War. There were more honors: a grant of ten thousand dollars from the National Endowment for the Arts in 1967 and election to the American Academy of Arts and Letters in 1969. *The Blue Estuaries* received few reviews and no awards. She was still taking Librium, had diabetes and eye trouble, and was allowed no more than two drinks a day. Often anxious, fatigued, and mentally scattered, she found it difficult to keep up with new trends in poetry. In September 1969, she resigned as reviewer for the *New Yorker*.

In her creative writing classes Bogan would ask her students where they encountered rhythms in their everyday lives. Often, to her dismay, they could think of only breath and the heartbeat. "Night," one of her last poems, seems to draw directly on this exercise. The voice comes from an elemental landscape to remind itself that its brief, hushed rhythms take part in movement that goes on everywhere. Where is the poetic subject? Barely present or impossibly spread on the personless scene; fading as it finds universality in its craft; preaching, teaching, or admonishing itself to let go of its last claim on desire, on human separateness:

> The cold remote islands
> And the blue estuaries
> Where what breathes, breathes
> The restless wind of the inlets
> And what drinks, drinks
> The incoming tide;
>
> Where shell and weed
> Wait upon the salt wash of the sea,
> And the clear nights of stars
> Swing their lights westward
> To set behind the land;
>
> Where the pulse clinging to the rocks
> Renews itself forever;
> Where, again on cloudless nights,
> The water reflects
> The firmament's partial setting;
>
> —O remember
> In your narrowing dark hours
> That more things move
> Than blood in the heart.

Louise Bogan died of a coronary occlusion on 4 February 1970.

Selected Bibliography

PRIMARY WORKS

POETRY

Body of This Death: Poems. New York: Robert M. McBride, 1923.

Dark Summer: Poems. New York: Scribners, 1929.

The Sleeping Fury: Poems. New York: Scribners, 1937.

Poems and New Poems. New York: Scribners, 1941.

Collected Poems, 1923–1953. New York: Noonday Press, 1954.

The Blue Estuaries: Poems, 1923–1968. New York: Farrar, Straus & Giroux, 1968. Repr. New York: Ecco Press, 1977.

CRITICISM

Achievement in American Poetry, 1900–1950. Chicago: Henry Regnery, 1951.

Selected Criticism: Prose, Poetry. New York: Noonday Press, 1955.

A Poet's Alphabet: Reflections on the Literary Art and Vocation. Edited by Robert Phelps and Ruth Limmer. New York: McGraw-Hill, 1970.

LETTERS

What the Woman Lived: Selected Letters of Louise Bogan, 1920–1970. Edited by Ruth Limmer. New York: Harcourt Brace Jovanovich, 1973.

AUTOBIOGRAPHY

Journey Around My Room: The Autobiography of Louise Bogan—A Mosaic. Edited by Ruth Limmer. New York: Viking Press, 1980.

TRANSLATIONS BY BOGAN

The Glass Bees. By Ernst Jünger. New York: Noonday Press, 1960. With Elizabeth Mayer.

Elective Affinities. By Johann Wolfgang von Goethe. Chicago: Henry Regnery, 1963. With Elizabeth Mayer.

The Journal of Jules Renard. New York: George Braziller, 1964. With Elizabeth Roget.

"The Sorrows of Young Werther" and "Novella." By Johann Wolfgang von Goethe. New York: Random House, 1971. With Elizabeth Mayer.

ANTHOLOGY

The Golden Journey: Poems for Young People. Chicago: Reilly and Lee, 1965. Compiled with William Jay Smith.

RECORDING

"Louise Bogan Reads Her Works." Yale Series of Recorded Poets. Carillon Records YP 308 (1961). Critical notes by Harold Bloom.

LETTERS, MANUSCRIPTS, AND PAPERS

Letters to May Sarton are held at the New York Public Library, Berg Collection.

The Louise Bogan papers are at the Amherst College Library.

Manuscripts and papers at the Princeton University Library are: Louise Bogan papers (1936–1954), archives of Charles Scribner's Sons (author files I), Allen Tate papers, Sylvia Beach papers, general manuscripts, Ridgely Torrence papers, and R. P. Blackmur papers.

Poetry magazine papers (1912–1936) are held at the University of Chicago.

SECONDARY WORKS

BIOGRAPHICAL AND CRITICAL STUDIES

Bowles, Gloria. "The Pursuit of Perfection." *Women's Review of Books* 2, no. 10:8–9 (July 1985).

———. *Louise Bogan's Aesthetic of Limitation.* Bloomington: Indiana University Press, 1987.

Collins, Martha, ed. *Critical Essays on Louise Bogan.* Boston: G. K. Hall, 1984.

Drake, William. *The First Wave: Women Poets in America 1915–1945.* New York: Macmillan, 1987.

Frank, Elizabeth P. *Louise Bogan: A Portrait.* New York: Knopf, 1985.

Gilbert, Sandra M., and Susan Gubar. *The Madwoman in the Attic: The Woman Writer and the Nineteenth-Century Literary Imagination.* New Haven: Yale University Press, 1979, 1984.

———. *No Man's Land: The Place of the Woman Writer in the Twentieth Century.* 2 vols. New Haven: Yale University Press, 1988.

Middlebrook, Diane. "Liberation: Poetry of William Butler Yeats and Louise Bogan." In her *Worlds into Words: Understanding Modern Poems.* Stanford, Cal.: Stanford Alumni Association, 1978. Pp. 47–63.

Muller, John. "Light and the Wisdom of the Dark: Aging and the Language of Desire in the Texts of Louise Bogan." *Memory and Desire: Aging—Literature—Psychoanalysis.* Edited by Kathleen Woodward and Murray M. Schwartz. Bloomington: Indiana University Press, 1986. Pp. 76–96.

Ostriker, Alicia Suskin. *Stealing the Language: The Emergence of Women's Poetry in America.* Boston: Beacon Press, 1986.

Pope, Deborah. "Music in the Granite Hill: The Poetry of Louise Bogan." In her *A Separate Vision: Isolation in Contemporary Women's Poetry.* Baton Rouge: Louisiana State University Press, 1984. Pp. 14–53.

Ridgeway, Jacqueline. *Louise Bogan.* Boston: Twayne, 1984.

Roethke, Theodore. "The Poetry of Louise Bogan." *Michigan Quarterly Review* 6:246–251 (Autumn 1967).

Sarton, May. "Louise Bogan." In her *A World of Light: Portraits and Celebrations.* New York: Norton, 1976. Pp. 215–237.

Smith, William Jay. "Louise Bogan: A Woman's Words." In his *The Streaks of the Tulip: Selected Criticism.* New York: Delacorte Press/Seymour Lawrence, 1972. Pp. 31–56.

Walker, Cheryl. *The Nightingale's Burden: Women Poets and American Culture Before 1900.* Bloomington: Indiana University Press, 1982.

BIBLIOGRAPHY

Couchman, Jane. "Louise Bogan: A Bibliography of Primary and Secondary Materials, 1915–1975." *Bulletin of Bibliography* 33, no. 2:73–77, 104 (February–March 1976); 33, no 3:111–126, 247 (April–June 1976); 33, no. 4:178–181 (July–September 1976).

JANET GRAY

GWENDOLYN BROOKS

(1917–)

The Black woman must remember, through all the prattle about walking or not walking three or twelve steps behind or ahead of "her" male, that her personhood precedes her femalehood; that, sweet as sex may be, she cannot endlessly brood on Black Man's blondes, blues, blunders. She is a person in the world—with wrongs to right, stupidities to outwit, *with* her man when possible, on her own when not. And she is also here to enjoy. She will be here, like any other, once only. Therefore she must, in the midst of tragedy and hatred and neglect, . . . mightily enjoy the readily enjoyable: sunshine and pets and children and conversation and games and travel (tiny or large) and books and walks and chocolate cake. . . .

(Report from Part One)

GWENDOLYN BROOKS, a major contemporary American poet, was the first Afro-American to win a Pulitzer Prize. Yet in spite of national and international prestige, Brooks remains closely connected to such common realities and concerns of everyday life as the emotional well-being of the masses of black women in America. She was fifty-five years old, with prize-winning books and well-deserved honors behind her, when the words above were published in her autobiography (1972). Such sentiments expressed the most essential aspects of her consciousness, and she knew of what she spoke. Fame had come to her, perhaps more easily than to others equally deserving, but she had also lived as a black woman in this country for all of her life, and she knew firsthand the frustrations which assaulted that group at every turn, inside and outside of the racial community. In spite of them, she had gone beyond survival and created for herself a life with rich meanings—one that gave her joy and self-fulfillment. She had taken firm hold of those "tiny and large" things that even black women can have for their own satisfaction. Her injunction—a message to the Sisterhood, old and young—was a challenge to each to eschew the victimization of intra- and interracial sexual oppression, and instead to take control of and responsibility for the direction of her life.

Gwendolyn Brooks, the daughter and elder child of Keziah Corine Wims and David Anderson Brooks, was born in Topeka, Kansas, on 7 June 1917. Her father, son of a runaway slave, came from a family that moved first to Kansas, where he was born, then to Oklahoma City. David Brooks was the only one of his twelve brothers and sisters (several of whom died early in their lives) to graduate from high school. Following that, he attended Fisk University for a year with hopes of becoming a doctor. A move to Chicago undermined his educational plans. Full-time employment, a necessity for his physical survival, and school work were not compatible. In 1914, in Kansas, he met Keziah Wims, a schoolteacher and a native of Topeka. They married in 1916 and settled in Chicago. Leaving her husband in their new home, Keziah returned to Topeka for the birth of her first child, and remained there until Gwendolyn was five weeks old. A second child, a son named Raymond, was born sixteen months later.

At first the family lived in an apartment in Hyde Park. Although some of the residents had small plots of land for gardening, and there were afternoon walks in Jackson Park, it was not ideal. The inconveniences of the neighborhood included a lack of sufficient playmates for the children and the inadequate size of the apartment for the needs of the family. That situation changed by the time Gwendolyn was four years old. Then they moved to a house on Champlain Avenue, where she and her brother had more playmates, a front and back yard, a porch, a hammock, and a sandbox of their own. Here the family lived modestly, in what the poet characterized as "genteel poverty."

David Brooks represented proud selfhood, security, and love to his children. He seldom spoke of his inner feelings, but after his death his daughter remembered him warmly for his cheerfulness, kindness, and industry. A good mechanic, he could make anything work, she reported, including a lasting fire in the furnace. At the same time, his family background offered the children a profile in courage. Gwendolyn Brooks and her brother grew up listening to their father's stories of their freedom-loving paternal grandfather, Lucas Brooks. He, having braved the dangers of white men and nature to leave slavery behind, fought in the Civil War, but later lost the struggle against racism in his attempt to establish a decent livelihood for his family. He died of pneumonia before David was five.

David Brooks inherited his father's drive for success and set lofty educational goals for himself. Although he never realized his medical ambitions, and spent most of his working life in janitorial service, in his daughter's words, he "revered books and education" and nurtured this love in his children, to whom he read or told wonderful stories. In addition, he enjoyed singing and reciting poetry to them in his robust baritone voice, and fully supported their goals for academic achievement.

When she was thirteen years old, David Brooks gave Gwendolyn one of her best-loved childhood treasures: an old desk, made up of "many little compartments, with long drawers at the bottom, and a removable glass-protected shelf at the top, for books." It came from the music firm for which he worked as a janitor. His appreciative daughter wrote much of her early poetry at this desk, even as she dreamed a future for herself. In her autobiography, Gwendolyn Brooks paid eloquent tribute to her father: "I think that his in-life, before he came to know Keziah and Gwendolyn and Raymond and cages nice and belts all tidy and snug, was of cinerama proportions, . . . suffused with wild organ music deep-centered." Unfortunately, having met only one of his sisters and two of his brothers, and only twice in her life, she knew no more of his family than her quiet father revealed.

There were no such barriers to information in Brooks's mother's family. Luvenia and Moses Wims, her grandparents, had ten children, five of whom were daughters. Among the sisters, only Keziah had children of her own, but this had no effect on the family's cohesiveness and unity. Brooks describes her mother as "a quick-walking, careful, Duty-Loving" woman who sang in a high soprano that complemented her husband's voice. In addition, "she played the piano, made fudge, made cocoa and prune whip and apricot pie, drew tidy cows and trees and expert houses with chimneys and chimney smoke." Having been a teacher before her marriage, she assisted her children with their school work.

One of Brooks's aunts lived with her husband and three adopted children on a fourteen-acre farm in Michigan. The rest of the Wims clan took advantage of the welcome that always awaited them there and visited frequently. Another aunt, with a liking for dancing and "the juice of the grape," was the jolliest of the sisters and taught her niece to do the Charleston. In later years, a third, a buoyantly happy woman who loved to cook, saved pennies, nickels, dimes, and quarters in jelly jars until there were sufficient coins to buy a savings bond for Gwendolyn's (future) son.

The fourth, an adept seamstress who taught that trade to high school students, took care of her young niece's wardrobe. Although this aunt alone of the sisters remained unmarried, Brooks describes her as "the Queen of my family." Among other things, she rose to the top of her profession, becoming the head of the sewing department of Tulsa's Booker T. Washington High School. Not only did she make a good living for herself, she was financially able to make the lives of her parents (the Wimses) comfortable in their old age. The young Gwendolyn was duly impressed by her aunt's stylish clothes, her "fancy *poudres* and rouges and creams," and her generosity toward her nieces and nephews. In the summertime, this aunt attended the University of Chicago, where, in time, she received a degree.

In addition to her aunts, Brooks refers to three of her mother's brothers in her autobiography: the first, she remarks cryptically, became "a citizen of Milwaukee"; the second she calls a miser who remained in Topeka all of his life; and the third, a chiropractor, had a wife who was famous for her pies, coconut cakes, and hot rolls.

Life in the Brooks household and with her mother's family gave Gwendolyn a rich and happy childhood within that group. Money was sometimes a problem, especially during the Depression, for her father was the sole breadwinner in his house, and often the people for whom he worked could not afford to pay him his full earnings. But love within the nuclear and extended families was mostly bountiful. Home for the Brooks children meant playing games with each other and their parents, listening to the radio, and celebrating Christmas, birthdays, and other holidays with great festivity that included surprises, relatives, gifts, and tables that groaned under the weight of food that had been weeks in preparation. From these gatherings and celebrations, Brooks learned early in her life that ordinary black people could lead meaningful lives, secure in the love and caring they felt for each other. These, she felt, were the most important ingredients for happiness.

According to Keziah Wims Brooks, Gwendolyn began to write poetry at age seven, and the mother predicted then that her daughter would become "the *lady* Paul Laurence Dunbar." The daughter's poetry notebooks begin when she was eleven years old, but she also recalls that she was writing all the time, even before the notebooks began. She dreamed through childhood and adolescence—of colors she saw in the sky from the step of her back porch, of little girls, and angels, and heroes and gods. As a teenager, she dreamed of boys as well.

In 1930, when she was thirteen years old, two significant things occurred in the life of Gwendolyn Brooks. For one, she discovered *Writer's Digest* and immediately felt a kinship with all others in the world of writers—imagining a community of souls like herself. For the other, she published her first poem, "Eventide," in *American Childhood* magazine. If, as she notes, she had always known that she *"was"* a poet (after all, she wrote, "Didn't I write a poem every day? Sometimes *two* poems?"), now she had the proof. Thus began her publishing career. By 1934 she was a regular poetry contributor to the *Chicago Defender*'s variety column "Lights and Shadows," where seventy-five of her pieces appeared in two years.

In these early years of her life, Brooks's poetic talent brought her personal satisfaction and adult approbation. At the same time, she developed almost no positive social relationships with her peers. She had discovered, almost as soon as she entered elementary school, that she did not possess the principal requisites for popularity. By age eight, she quietly resigned herself to the role of the outsider. Thanks to her seamstress aunt, she was always well dressed, but her skin was too dark and her hair too short and kinky for membership in the group of the "socially successful" girls from upwardly mobile families. She notes that these negative attributes could have been offset were her hair long and hot-comb straight, and had her parents been better situated financially—had her father been a doctor, or lawyer, a City Hall employee, or even a postman; or had her mother been a schoolteacher. True, the latter had taught in Kansas before her marriage, but that did not qualify her for inclusion within the current elite.

Nor was Brooks eligible for membership among the blacks of "lesser quality." To that group, her neat and well-kept clothes were a personal affront to their lack of the same. Nor could/did she behave as they did. She could not "fight brilliantly, or at all," or excel in the gym, ride a bicycle, play jacks, or whisper about her boyfriends, of whom she had none. Meanwhile, the boys paid no attention to her except to name her "Ol' Black Gal."

Consequently, as a teenager, Brooks went to few parties and felt uncomfortable at those she attended. She was timid and shy around her peers and did not participate in their fun and games. Instead she turned to collecting paper dolls. At age fourteen, she said, she "owned great numbers of them," around which she "organized governments, theaters, tournaments—planned wardrobes, coiffures, planned feasts." At that age, too, school presented her with other trying difficulties. First she attended the predominantly white Hyde Park High School, where she felt ignored by everyone. After transferring to the all-black Phillips High, her lack of social skills such as dancing made her feel as alienated from that student body as she had at Hyde Park. A second transfer took her to Englewood High, which, in spite of its predominantly white student body and lack of black teachers, had a larger representation of black students than Hyde Park.

Remarkably, during this crucial stage of her emotional and psychological development, in spite of her negative experiences in various schools, Brooks never resorted to self-hate. She seems always to have believed in her own capacity to fulfill her ambitions. Her autobiography begins:

> When I was a child, it did not occur to me, even once, that the black in which I was encased (I called it brown in those days) would be considered, one day, beautiful. Considered beautiful and called beautiful by great groups.
>
> I had always considered it beautiful. I would stick out my arm, examine it, and smile. Charming! And convenient, for mud on my leg was not as annunciatory as was mud on the leg of light Rose Hurd.

This love of self (later reinforced by the events of the 1960s and 1970s), which she extended to all people, especially to those of African heritage, has guided the life of Gwendolyn Brooks.

At age sixteen Brooks had her first encounter with famous living Afro-American poets when James Weldon Johnson and Langston Hughes visited Chicago. Before that, she had written to Johnson, who had responded with enthusiasm, suggesting that she read modern poets like Ezra Pound, T. S. Eliot, and e. e. cummings. Still, when she met him, he seemed not to recognize her, which left Keziah Brooks disgruntled with him. Hughes, on the other hand, was gracious and warm toward the young Gwendolyn, and the two later became good friends. "Langston Hughes," a poetic tribute to him, appears in her third collection of verse, *The Bean Eaters,* and in *Report from Part One* she calls him "the noble poet, the efficient essayist, the adventurous dramatist." His work was extremely influential on her own.

Brooks graduated from Englewood High School in 1934 and from Wilson Junior College in 1936. By then she was making great progress toward mastery of traditional poetic forms. In high school special teachers nurtured her artistic potential, and she was familiar with the writings of many black poets. In 1938 she joined the NAACP's Youth Council, where she met, for the first time, peers who accepted her and valued her talents, and she began to take an interest in social, political, and racial events. Through her involvement with the Council she met Henry L. Blakey II, another aspiring young writer, whom she married in 1939.

The 1940s were significant years for Gwendolyn Brooks. First her marriage took her out of the comfortable if modest home of her parents to the crowded and bleak existence of kitchenette apartment living shared by many of Chicago's poor. Out of this experience came the powerful poems of her first volume, *A Street in Bronzeville* (1945). But life was more than the depressing aspects of poverty and overcrowding. An early joy for the young couple was the birth of their son, Henry L. Blakey III, in 1940. As happy as this made her, it did not deter Gwendolyn Brooks from the search for poetic satisfaction and reward. In 1941, she and her husband joined a workshop led by Inez Cunningham Stark, a wealthy white writer, scholar, and reader for *Poetry* magazine. Stark lived on Chicago's North Side "Gold Coast," and against the advice of her friends, she went to the South Side to instruct young black would-be poets in their craft. In the group were others who later became famous, including Margaret Burroughs, Margaret Danner, and William Couch.

Brooks first enjoyed public recognition in 1943, when she won the Midwestern Writers' Conference Poetry Award. In 1945 Harper's published her first book. This was a momentous occasion for Gwendolyn Brooks, made even more so by splendid reviews like that of Iowa poet Paul Engle, in the *Chicago Tribune*. Praise for the new poet poured in from many other sources. All paid tribute to her mastery of technique. She valued most the praise from other black poets—Claude McKay, Countee Cullen, and James Weldon Johnson among them. Also in 1945 she received the *Mademoiselle* Merit Award and, following that, the American Academy of Letters Award (1946) as well as Guggenheim Fellowships for 1947 and 1948. Brooks was now a poet of national stature, and by 1948 her book reviews appeared in the *Chicago Sun-Times*, the *New York Times*, and *Negro Digest*. Her second book, *Annie Allen*, appeared in 1949. For that publication she received the Eunice Tietjens Memorial Award for poetry (1949), and in 1950, the Pulitzer Prize for literature.

Gwendolyn Brooks called her first major publication *A Street in Bronzeville*, locating the book in the black ghetto area on Chicago's South Side, where she lived. Bronzeville, so named by the *Chicago Defender*, gained prominence in a 1945 sociological study, *Black Metropolis*, by St. Clair Drake and Horace R. Cayton. Drake and Cayton focused their analysis on the harmful effects of racism and segregation on the community, and prescribed racial integration as the most effective mechanism to combat the evils of the situation. Brooks, mindful of the line separating art and polemic, nevertheless achieved a sophisticated social criticism in her presentation of a cross section of life on a street in this part of town. *Bronzeville* was well received. Advance sales were more than 2,500 copies, and in September, a month after its release, a second printing appeared.

A Street in Bronzeville takes a panoramic view of a slice of life among the Afro-American poor. The volume is divided into three sections. The first, "A Street in Bronzeville," has twenty vignettes that focus on common experiences within the racial community. Such highly unlikely topics for poetry as "the old-marrieds," which describes the death-in-life daily existence of an elderly couple who are alienated from each other, and "kitchenette building," which focuses on the hopelessness of those who live in substandard housing, find their way onto the pages of this book. More likely subjects for poetry, such as "the mother," undergo radical transformation under the pen of Gwendolyn Brooks. Removed from her traditional place of infinite love and personal sacrifice for others in black literature, the mother in Brooks's poem bemoans the abortion deaths of her children. Another painful reality for black people, intraracial prejudice, surfaces in "the ballad of chocolate Mabbie."

The second part of *Bronzeville* is a set of longer poems consisting of five individual portraits. Of these, "The Sundays of Satin-Legs Smith," the longest poem in the book (158 lines), is one of the most memorable. "Satin-

Legs Smith" describes a man's futile struggles to gain fulfillment in the ghetto. Brooks exposes the emptiness of his efforts by revealing the pathos in his illusions of false grandeur. While she does not cast blame for his condition on Satin-Legs, she also does not exonerate him, for he takes no reasonable action to alter the conditions of his life. Satin-Legs, too, is responsible.

In the first two sections of this book Brooks makes use of a number of poetic techniques that include the ballad and the blues, and she borrows from classical, modern, spiritual, and secular as well as uniquely African American traditions in poetic composition. The final section of the book, called "Gay Chaps at the Bar," is a Petrarchan and Shakespearean sonnet sequence of twelve poems that is dedicated to "Staff Sergeant Raymond Brooks and every other soldier," and contemplates the situation of American servicemen, particularly black soldiers, during World War II. The poems focus on death, and include the unpreparedness of young men to die, and the bitterness of those who survive the ordeal of war.

Annie Allen, the poetic life of a young black woman, is dedicated to and contains a memorial poem to Edward Bland, a black soldier killed in Germany in 1945, who had been a member of the Inez Cunningham Stark poetry workshop that Gwendolyn Brooks and her husband attended in 1941. This collection also has three parts: "Notes from the Childhood and the Girlhood," with eleven poems; "The Anniad," with forty-three stanzas and three "Appendix" poems; and "The Womanhood," with fifteen poems. Although well received at the time of its publication, *Annie Allen* has often been cited for its difficult and complicated structure. Such criticism is especially made of "The Anniad" section. On the other hand, while critics like Claudia Tate recognize the book as "a collection of rigorously technical poems, replete with lofty diction, intricate wordplay, and complicated concatenations of phrases" (Tate, p. 140), they do not consider it incomprehensible. Brooks responded to comments on the work's difficulty by explaining that it was her fascination with what words can do and her interest "in the mysteries and magic of technique" that led her to write it. Few people would disagree that *Annie Allen* is Brooks at her technical best.

"The birth in a narrow room," which opens the collection, sets the tone of Annie Allen's life. The room is so small that it inhibits her breathing, offers her "not anything," and leaves her "not anything to do." Nevertheless, it is years before Annie Allen realizes how "pinchy" is the space that life bequeathes to her. The section proceeds through the passivity of Annie's parents; her responses to racism, killing, and death; and her unfulfilled dreams. The final poems foreshadow disappointments that await her in womanhood.

The 304-line "The Anniad" is a mock-heroic, episodic narrative poem that conforms to epic conventions. The problems of eroding relationships between men and women, including those precipitated by war, are the poem's concerns. Annie's anticipation of marriage, her courtship, marriage, separation from her husband by war, his infidelity, their reconciliation, and his final desertion and death constitute the narrative action. The movement is from innocence and optimistic idealism to the loss of faith in the face of harsh reality. At the same time, Annie accepts her experiences passively, and acts consciously only in her daydreams. The "Appendix" poems, which elaborate on themes within "The Anniad," make the whole an experimental project in which Brooks uses an old conventional form in conjunction with modern language to examine the effects of action or lack of it, and of human love and sacrifice, on ordinary life.

"The Womanhood," meditations of the mature Annie, opens with a sequence of poems entitled "the children of the poor." These are five meditative and heroic sonnets that examine postwar society, church, and state from a mother's perspective. Her children, born into a world torn apart by war, must come to terms with faith and death. Religion will help, but they must also learn to challenge social injustices around them. A variety of other topics occupy the mother's reflections in the remainder of the poems in this section of the book. Most notably, the inert Annie of the earlier parts of the book is now a woman who wants to reform the world. As in her earlier book, her ability to manipulate style, language, and form links Brooks's accomplishments in *Annie Allen* to other significant American poets, including Emily Dickinson. This work encompasses lyric, elegiac, irregular rhymes, and free verse, in a diversity that one critic notes "reflects maturely upon life." *Annie Allen* won Brooks the Pulitzer Prize.

But the 1940s were important to Gwendolyn Brooks for reasons other than the progress of her literary career and the joys of family life. During this time, as she flourished professionally, the shy, retiring teenager blossomed into a socially engaged and popular woman. Her emergence in this light was assisted by the phenomenon of the Chicago Renaissance, when the South Side became a version of what Harlem had been to blacks in the 1920s. At the center of this artistic activity were the weekend parties. In Brooks's words, at these gatherings, conversation was "rich" and "fantastic," and talk often went on until dawn over cheap red wine, tea, coffee, black bread, cheese, or spaghetti, depending on the economic situation of the host or hostess. Although these gatherings were often racially integrated, unlike equivalent activities in New York during the 1920s, they seem not to have attracted whites in search of black exotics, or to have spawned the white patronage system that has made some contemporary critics cynical of the true successes of the New York Harlem Renaissance. Brooks and her husband knew most of the people who were active in Chicago's artistic black world of the 1940s: the writers Margaret Walker and Frank Marshall Davis; the artists Elizabeth Catlett and Charles White; the sculptor Marion Perkins; musicians; dancers; actors; photographers; and famous visitors to the city, such as Paul Robeson and Langston Hughes.

The 1950s were also exciting years for Gwendolyn Brooks. Daughter Nora was born in 1951. In 1953, Brooks published her first major prose work, *Maud Martha,* a poetic novel of a young black woman in the ghetto; and in 1956, *Bronzeville Boys and Girls,* children's poetry with illustrations, dedicated to her son and daughter, appeared. In 1953 the family moved from the crowded apartment in which they had lived for many years to the house on the South Side that is still Brooks's home. Without diminishing the importance of such a move, in her autobiography, Brooks recalls, with fondness, her years in the kitchenette buildings:

> As for my husband and myself, our own best parties were given at 623 East 63rd Street, our most exciting kitchenette. 623 was right on the corner, the corner of 63rd and Champlain, above a real estate agency. If you wanted a poem, you had only to look out of a window. There was material always, walking or running, fighting or screaming or singing. We gave a party for Langston Hughes.

The poetic *Maud Martha* is Gwendolyn Brooks's only novel. Although initial reviews in Chicago and in the *New York Times* and some California newspapers were "overwhelmingly good," among her major works, *Maud Martha* has received the least critical attention. Yet this novel is the earliest attempt by a black writer to portray the everyday experiences of an ordinary black women in fiction without characterizing the protagonist as "tragic." Barbara Christian, responding to the critical neglect of *Maud Martha,* notes that it is a book in which Brooks "replaced intense drama or pedestrian portrayal of character with a careful rendering of the rituals, the patterns, of the ordinary life, where racism is experienced in sharp nibbles rather than screams and where making do is continually juxtaposed with small but significant dreams."

Maud Martha's life is presented in thirty-four short, impressionistic chapters (vignettes) that detail her early childhood, school years, adolescence, courtship, work, marriage, motherhood, and reactions to the Depression and the war. Always she struggles with those elements which seek to diminish her existence, but also there are times that are joyful and fulfilling. Readers are aware of these levels of Maud Martha's life through Brooks's exploration of the inner life of her protagonist. In fact, Brooks notes that the unity within the narrative is "the central point of view of Maud Martha herself as she grows up." Unlike Annie Allen, she is not wholly made by the world in which she lives. She also creates her world, striving to answer the question within herself that permeates the action of the entire book: "What, *what* am I to do with all this life?" Considering the limitations on the lives of poor black girls growing up in America in the 1940s, such a question raises Maud Martha's ordinary life to a level of dignity few people would otherwise accord her. Neither heroic nor pathetic, Maud Martha's awareness of her own value makes her life story worthy of literary appraisal.

Bronzeville Boys and Girls (1956) is a collection of thirty-four poems that portray the lives of children in Bronzeville from their own perspectives. This is the first of Brooks's three books for children. Each poem in the Bronzeville collection examines the life of a child in a particular time and place. Thus the pieces carry such titles as "Beulah at Church" and "Eunice in the Evening." *Bronzeville Boys and Girls* is the world of children where innocence and youth transcend the problems and disappointments that most black children face.

The 1960s were momentous years for most black Americans, and no less so for Gwendolyn Brooks. *The Bean Eaters,* her fourth book of poetry, appeared in 1960. Nationally, she was highly visible, and invitations for readings on white and black college campuses came to her from all across the country. In 1962 President John F. Kennedy invited her to read at a Library of Congress poetry festival. Younger black writers saw her as a spiritual mother. In 1963 she published *Selected Poems* and began teaching at Columbia College in Chicago, from which she received her first honorary degree in 1964. Until then, Brooks had held fairly rigid traditional ideas on writing poetry; now, contact with younger African American writers began to influence her thinking. Instead of "the New Negro" of the 1920s, she was meeting "the New Black" of the 1960s and having to reconsider her old ways. Initial evidence of changes in her work shows up in *The Bean Eaters* and in *Selected Poems.*

The Bean Eaters opens with an elegiac ballad honoring David Anderson Brooks, Gwendolyn's father, who died while the collection was in preparation. This poem, an attempt to express the meaning of a black man's life, sets the stage for the heroic quality of the whole collection.

Excluding the opening poem, *The Bean Eaters* contains thirty-five poems that range over several subjects, most of them political in nature. Although the civil rights movement was nearing the peak of its momentum when the collection appeared, the shift in emphasis in her work was a significant departure for Brooks. *The Bean Eaters* contains such poems as "A Bronzeville Mother Loiters in Mississippi. Meanwhile, a Mississippi Mother Burns Bacon," a dramatization with bloody imagery of the murder of Emmett Till; and "The *Chicago Defender* Sends a Man to Little Rock," a poem about school integration. Other poems address issues of class, race, and gender, while scattered throughout are poems on romance, aging, children, nature, and various other topics.

Predictably, this change in Brooks's work troubled critics who disapproved of what they perceived as her rejection of lyric for polemic. Yet, in spite of the overt protest in this work, she remained committed to the techniques in which she had been trained, a stance that disturbed more radical critics. Those sympathetic to her pointed to the book as evidence of the power of her skill in combining her poetic gift with conventional form. Some of Brooks's most powerful political poetry is in *The Bean Eaters.*

In the early 1960's Gwendolyn Brooks and her publisher decided to release a collection of her work as *Selected Poems* (1963), which contained what they considered the best of the early work and some additional new poems. Like the books that preceded it, this volume was critically acclaimed and went through several printings in hard- and soft-cover editions.

The climax of radical change toward which she had been moving in her writing since the early 1960s occurred for Brooks in 1967, when, as she describes it, her blackness confronted her "with a shrill spelling of itself." It happened at the Black Writers' Conference at Fisk University in Nashville, Tennessee, at the end of a tour that had taken her to several states, including South Dakota. At Fisk she compared the "cold respect" that greeted her with the reverence she experienced on white college campuses. She also observed that the younger writers present, a group that included Carolyn Rodgers, Nikki Giovanni, John O. Killens, Imamu Amiri Baraka, and Ron Milner, spokespersons for "the New Black Literature," were extremely angry and fervent in their protest against the social conditions of black people in America. Furthermore, they integrated their social protest into their art, not only into the content of their materials but into its form as well.

Brooks had always written about the black experience and been critical of the status quo, but she had done so politely and within the confines of conventional poetic style and diction. These new writers were rejecting traditional Western forms and techniques in writing, and adapting their poetry to emulate the rhythms and nuances of black language and black music. At first their irreverence for the old forms shocked Brooks, but she listened and awakened to a new consciousness of the meaning of her work as a black woman poet. "The energy [and] electricity, in look, walk, speech, [and] *gesture* of the young blackness" captivated her. It was a turning point for her. She had always thought of herself as a Negro; now, for the first time, she realized what it meant to be black. Since then, she has devoted her energies to promoting the work of young black writers who strive for a black idiom, and writing poetry that in form and content speaks to her status as an African American woman.

Artistically, the results of this awakening on Brooks's work appears in full bloom in *In the Mecca,* a revolutionary volume in which she finally breaks with traditional poetic techniques in favor of black form and content in her work. Published in 1968, this book was nominated for the National Book Award. Also in that year Brooks was appointed poet laureate of Illinois. Much of the attention given to *In the Mecca* focuses on the title poem, named for the four-story gray brick building (in which Brooks once worked) that serves as the microcosm of the pain that dominates the world of poor black people. The narrative framwork is simple. Mrs. Sallie Smith, a domestic servant and mother of nine children, returns home to the Mecca at the end of a day to find one of the children missing. Her frantic search for the child, who was murdered, provides the backdrop for a cinematic view of the evils and hopes that reside in the Mecca. Other poems in the collection are memorials to such real-life black figures as Malcolm X and Medgar Evers.

A well-received volume, *In the Mecca* went through three printings in the first six months of its existence. Although some of her early white literary supporters criticized Brooks for her change from lyric to political poet, the poet laureate appointment indicated the respect in which she was held by large numbers of people. She used this position to assist young would-be writers, whites and blacks, in elementary and high schools, by sponsoring writing contests, offering scholarships, and financing trips to Africa.

Through the publication of *In the Mecca,* Gwendolyn Brooks's books appeared from Harper and Row in New York, in a mutually satisfying arrangement between writer and publisher. After 1967, however, she decided to turn her allegiances toward promoting black publishing houses, and informed Harper's of this in 1969. The immediate results were a number of small volumes of poetry—*Riot* (1969), *Family Pictures (1970), Aloneness* (1971), and *Beckonings* (1975)— produced by Broadside Press, a black publishing company in Detroit. *Riot,* whose opening highlights events in the aftermath of the assassination of Martin Luther King, Jr., contains three poems; *Family Pictures,* eight; *Aloneness,* a children's book on solitude, a single reflective piece; and *Beckonings,* twelve poems. In 1974 Brooks published *The Tiger Who Wore White Gloves; or, What You Are You Are,* a beast fable for children, with Chicago's black Third World Press. In 1981, *To Disembark,* an anthology that pulls together her work from the 1960s to the 1980s, dedicated to Dudley Randall, appeared from Third World Press as well. Her own imprint, Brooks Press, came into being in 1980 with *Young Poet's Primer,* a ten-page manual with thirty-three rules for high school and college students, followed in 1983 by *Very Young Poets,* twenty practical lessons on reading, writing, and subject matter. In 1980, she printed *Primer for Blacks,* a chapbook of "Three Preachments," under the name of Black Position Press, her magazine. In 1987, *Blacks,* comprising *A Street in Bronzeville, Annie Allen, The Bean Eaters,* "New Poems," *In the Mecca, Maud Martha,* and selections from *To Disembark* and *The Near-Johannesburg Boy and Other Poems,* were published by the David Company of Chicago.

Although the greater literary value of Gwendolyn Brooks's work will always rest on her poetry, in recent times black feminists, in particular, have called a good deal of attention to her novel. One important aspect of this criticism notes the poetic qualities that Brooks transferred into a work of prose. Similarly, Brooks's autobiography, *Report from Part One* (1972), published by Broadside, bears the marks of its author's poetic sensibilities. *Report from Part One* marked a new milestone in Brooks's writing career, and especially in her manner of manipulating long-standing conventions in Afro-American autobiography to create a form to suit the image of herself she projects.

Report has four sections. The first follows such traditional autobiographical elements as chronological order and the physical and emotional growth and development of the author. She writes about her life as a whole, from early childhood through her conversion to heightened racial consciousness in the late 1960s. The second section, "African Fragment," owes its existence to a trip that Brooks took to Kenya and Tanzania in 1971. Making the journey was an accomplishment worth noting, since fear of flying had previously confined her within the United States. The section focuses on her expanded conception and understanding of her black identity. The third section of the book contains three interviews, two given to white men and the third to a black woman. These are closely associated with the mature writer's political philosophy and clarify the process of her journey toward full black selfhood through writing and action. The final section of the book, "Appendix," serves to provide footnotes on the earlier sections and to give the writer an opportunity to reflect aloud on the earlier parts.

Report from Part One, uniquely the story of a black woman's life, draws from the spiritual, prophetic, and *Bildungsroman* traditions in autobiography to make an impress of Brooks's connectedness to her family, to all black Americans, and to Africans and descendants of Africans in the diaspora. In taking large liberties with form and structure she empowers herself and all black women to take authority for self-definition. Like her poetry, her language is rich, full, and complex, unfolding the spiritual journey that is her life as an African American woman.

Selected Bibliography

PRIMARY WORKS

POETRY

A Street in Bronzeville. New York and London: Harper, 1945.

Annie Allen. New York: Harper, 1949.

Bronzeville Boys and Girls. New York: Harper, 1956.

The Bean Eaters. New York: Harper, 1960.

Selected Poems. New York: Harper & Row, 1963.

In the Mecca. New York: Harper & Row, 1968.

Riot. Detroit: Broadside Press, 1969.

Family Pictures. Detroit: Broadside Press, 1970.

Aloneness. Detroit: Broadside Press, 1971.

The Tiger Who Wore Gloves; or, What You Are You Are. Chicago: Third World Press, 1974.

Beckonings. Detroit: Broadside Press, 1975.

To Disembark. Chicago: Third World Press, 1981.

Blacks. Chicago: David, 1987.

PROSE

Maud Martha. New York: Harper, 1953.

Report from Part One. Detroit: Broadside Press, 1972.

Primer for Blacks. Chicago: Black Position Press, 1980.

Young Poet's Primer. Chicago: Brooks Press, 1980.

Very Young Poets. Chicago: Brooks Press, 1983.

ANTHOLOGY

The World of Gwendolyn Brooks. New York: Harper & Row, 1971. Contains *A Street in Bronzeville, Annie Allen, Maud Martha, The Bean Eaters*, and *In the Mecca*.

SECONDARY WORKS

BIOGRAPHICAL AND CRITICAL STUDIES

Andrews, Larry R. "Ambivalent Clothes Imagery in Gwendolyn Brooks' 'The Sundays of Satin-Legs Smith.' " *CLA Journal* 24:150–163 (December 1980).

Bird, Leonard G. "Gwendolyn Brooks: Educator Extraordinaire." *Discourse* 12:158–166 (Spring 1969).

Christian, Barbara. "Nuance and the Novella: A Study of Gwendolyn Brooks's *Maud Martha*." In *A Life Distilled: Gwendolyn Brooks—Her Poetry and Fiction*. Edited by Maria K. Moofry and Gary Smith. Urbana and Chicago: University of Illinois Press, 1987. Pp. 239–253.

Davis, Arthur P. "The Black-and-Tan Motif in the Poetry of Gwendolyn Brooks." *CLA Journal* 6:90–97 (December 1962).

Furman, Marva R. "Gwendolyn Brooks: The 'Unconditioned' Poet." *CLA Journal* 17:1–10 (September 1973).

Gayle, Addison, Jr. "Gwendolyn Brooks: Poet of the Whirlwind." In *Black Women Writers (1950–1980): A Critical Evaluation*. Edited by Mari Evans. Garden City, N.Y.: Anchor/Doubleday, 1984. Pp. 79–87.

Hansell, William H. "Gwendolyn Brooks's 'In the Mecca': A Rebirth into Blackness." *Negro American Literature Forum* 8:199–207 (Summer 1974).

Kent, George E. "Gwendolyn Brooks' Poetic Realism: A Developmental Survey." In *Black Women Writers (1950–1980): A Critical Evaluation*. Edited by Mari Evans. Garden City, N.Y.: Anchor/Doubleday, 1984. Pp. 88–105.

———. "Gwendolyn Brooks: Portrait, in Part, of the Artist as a Young Girl and Apprentice Writer." *Callaloo* 2:74–83 (October 1979).

Lattin, Patricia H., and Vernon E. Lattin. "Dual Vision in Gwendolyn Brooks's *Maud Martha*." *Critique* 25:180–188 (Summer 1984).

Melhem, D. H. *Gwendolyn Brooks: Poetry and the Heroic Voice*. Lexington: University Press of Kentucky, 1987.

Miller, R. Baxter. "Define . . . the Whirlwind: *In the Mecca*—Urban Setting, Shifting Narrator, and Redemptive Vision." *Obsidian* 4:19–31 (Spring 1978).

Miller, Jean-Marie A. "Gwendolyn Brooks: Poet Laureate of Bronzeville, U.S.A." *Freedomways* 10:63–75 (First Quarter 1970).

Mootry, Maria K., and Gary Smith, eds. *A Life Distilled: Gwendolyn Brooks—Her Poetry and Fiction*. Urbana and Chicago: University of Illinois Press, 1987.

Redmond, Eugene B. *Drumvoices: The Mission of Afro-American Poetry*. Garden City, N.Y.: Anchor/Doubleday, 1976. Pp. 270–284.

Shaw, Harry B. *Gwendolyn Brooks*. Boston: Twayne, 1980.

Smith, Gary. "Gwendolyn Brooks's *A Street in Bronzeville*, the Harlem Renaissance, and the Mythologies of Black Women." *Melus* 10:33–46 (Fall 1983).

Tate, Claudia. "Anger So Flat: Gwendolyn Brooks's *Annie Allen*." In *A Life Distilled: Gwendolyn Brooks—Her Poetry and Fiction*. Edited by Marie K. Mootry and Gary Smith. Urbana and Chicago: University of Illinois Press, 1987. Pp. 140–152.

Washington, Mary H. " 'Taming All the Anger Down': Rage and Silence in Gwendolyn Brooks' *Maud Martha*." *Massachusetts Review* 24:453–466 (Summer 1983).

Werner, Craig. "Gwendolyn Brooks: Tradition in Black and White." *Minority Voices* 1:27–38 (Fall 1977).

Williams, Gladys M. "Gwendolyn Brooks's Way with the Sonnet." *CLA Journal* 26:215–240 (December 1982).

BIBLIOGRAPHIES

Loff, Jon N. "Gwendolyn Brooks: A Bibliography." *CLA Journal* 17:21–32 (September 1973).

Mahoney, Heidi L. "Selected Checklist of Material by and About Gwendolyn Brooks." *Negro American Literature Forum* 8:210–211 (Summer 1974).

Miller, R. Baxter. *Langston Hughes and Gwendolyn Brooks: A Reference Guide*. Boston: G. K. Hall, 1978.

NELLIE MCKAY

WILLA CATHER

1873–1947

WILLA CATHER REMAINS an anomaly in American literature. Her novels have been embraced by the general public, both in her time and in ours. She has appeared on best-seller lists, been awarded the Pulitzer Prize (in 1923, for *One of Ours*), and generally received positive, frequently laudatory, reviews of her fiction in periodical literature such as the *Saturday Review of Literature* and *Commonweal*. Both her friend Elizabeth Sergeant and her presumed lover Edith Lewis have written fond memoirs of Cather's determined, energetic, and occasionally overbearing personality. Truman Capote recalled Cather as the person who most impressed him. And it is not uncommon to hear Willa Cather proclaimed as someone's favorite writer, an opinion expressed with equal frequency by professors, contemporary American fiction writers, general readers of novels, and students alike. Something in Cather's lucid, accessible, and seamless prose continues to draw readers into the elusive, yet essentially American, world of her fiction. This quality of readability Cather referred to elliptically as that which "is felt upon the page without being specifically named there, . . . the emotional aura of the fact or the thing or the deed, that gives high quality to the novel or the drama, as well as to poetry itself."

Despite such widespread and sustained popular acceptance of her work, Cather has fared less well in critical studies and in the American literary canon. While her fiction is perceived to be significant in some vague way, she has never been accorded the status of a "major" twentieth-century writer along the lines of William Faulkner or F. Scott Fitzgerald. In part this is because she is difficult to place. Neither a realist nor a modernist, Cather wrote novels that confound easy categorization and, by extension, canonization. Those works which have been embraced by critics—*O, Pioneers!* (1913), *The Song of the Lark* (1915), *My Ántonia* (1918), and *Death Comes for the Archbishop* (1927)—celebrate the pioneer spirit so essential to our mythic notions of an ordained, manifest American destiny. Although critics have generally praised these books as vigorous expressions of an authentic American voice, they have been less accepting of Cather's other fiction, those novels which explore the increasing social restrictions brought to bear on American society and on women in particular. Cather's literary reputation, as Sharon O'Brien has documented, suffered in the 1930s and 1940s, when critics defined her work solely in terms of nostalgia, elegy, escape, and a rejection of the modern world.

As a consequence, half of Cather's oeuvre remains unread. Her critical reputation is defined by region, in the best and, paradoxically, most limiting senses of that term. Cather is, on the one hand, still considered to be the great muse of the Midwest, a role most eloquently alluded to in the line from Vergil's *Georgics* that so impresses Jim Burden in *My Ántonia:* "Primus ego in patriam mecum . . . deducam Musas" (For I shall be the first, if I live, to bring the Muse into my country). At the same time, however, the label of "regionalism" has confined Cather to that ambiguous and marginal group of women writers (including her literary mentor, Sarah Orne Jewett) who hold a distinctly "minor" position in the canon of American literature. It is both curious and ironic that a writer who is so difficult to place in the canon is finally relegated to a specific regional place which then becomes the prevailing "meaning" of her work.

It might instead be more accurate to understand Cather not by specific geographical place but by those strategies which the child, girl, woman, and writer adopted in order to create places of possibility, of self-expression, and of self-definition within the spheres of family, work, and nation. And for Cather, much like her critical reputation, these are places of ambiguity, of ambivalence, and even of anomaly.

Named after an aunt who had died of diphtheria, Wilella Cather was born on 7 December 1873 in Back Creek, Virginia. Called "Willie" by her family and oldest friends, Cather, the eldest child of seven, thrived in the extended familial and social network that characterized this rural community. Living on her grandfather William Cather's sheep farm, Willow Shade, in her childhood Cather experienced the pleasures of both physical activity and the imagination. Allowed to accompany her father when he herded and drove the sheep into their folds in the evening, she had the run of the farm, and explored the neighboring hills and fields at will. She was taught to read at an early age by her maternal grandmother, Rachel Boak, in whose lap Cather first encountered stories from the Bible, *Pilgrim's Progress*, and *Peter Parley's Universal History*. Stories soon came to occupy an important, if not primary, place in her life. The young Willa Cather expanded her repertoire of histories to include the oral as well as the written. She listened attentively to the stories recounted by local women in Back Creek, especially those of Mary Ann Anderson (the figure on whom Mrs. Ringer in *Sapphira and the Slave Girl* is modeled), reputedly the best tale-teller in the community.

An anecdote often recounted by the young "Willie" Cather illustrates the ambivalence with which the adult Cather was to approach gender throughout her life. Directed by her mother to appear in the parlor and say "Howdy do" to a visiting elderly judge, Cather instead shocked the assembled company by announcing, "I'se a dang'ous nigger, I is!" Edith Lewis classifies this moment of rebellion as "an attempt to break through the smooth, unreal conventions about little girls," conventions Cather would later explore in such novels as *A Lost Lady, My Mortal Enemy*, and *Lucy Gayheart*.

But of Cather's childhood undoubtedly the most traumatic, as well as influential, event was the family's move to the Nebraska Divide after their sheep barn burned down in 1883. The nine-year-old Willa was at first terrified by the vast emptiness of the prairie, feeling that the exposed landscape would swallow and even obliterate her. This terror recurred periodically throughout Cather's life. In later years she told Elizabeth Sergeant that she always beat a hasty retreat from the state after visiting her parents, "for fear of dying in a cornfield." When Sergeant expressed sincere confusion at this declaration, Cather retorted, "You could not understand. You have not seen those miles of fields. There is no place to hide in Nebraska. You can't hide under a windmill."

Despite Cather's insistence on needing a place to hide, her childhood on the Nebraska Divide and in the prairie town of Red Cloud (where her family finally settled in 1884) afforded her an open and undefined space through which she was able to fashion a decidedly unconventional identity. Cather's initial identification in Nebraska was with the immigrant settlers from Bohemia, Germany, Scandinavia, Russia, and France whose homesteads she visited while she lived on her grandfather's farm. The young girl soon established friendships with the pioneer farm women, who told their rapt listener stories about the old country, many of which made their way into *My Ántonia* when Cather re-created her early childhood experiences in that novel. Later, when her family moved to Red Cloud, Cather's friendships with older people who introduced her to the canon of Western literature enabled her to escape, at least imaginatively, the provincial life of a Midwestern prairie town. With Will Ducker, an English shopkeeper, she advanced her studies in Greek and Latin; together they pored over Vergil, Homer, and Ovid. Cather also encamped in the home of the Wieners (on whom the Rosens in "Old Mrs. Harris" are based), a relatively cosmopolitan couple who spoke both German and French, and who lent Cather numerous classics of European literature.

If imaginative literature afforded Willa Cather a kind of escape from small-town life, it also complicated the issue of identity in subtle and telling ways. Cather's favorite literature during her high school and college years was romantic adventure fiction typified by Robert Louis Stevenson and Rudyard Kipling, stories in which female heroism simply did not exist. And as Sharon O'Brien has argued in her influential biography, *Willa Cather: The Emerging Voice* (1987), Cather rejected the version of conventional female behavior she saw in her mother, in popular women's romance fiction (such as the novels of Marie Corelli), and in society at large. What the young girl adopted instead was a persona constructed exclusively through male identification; around 1888 Cather cut off her long hair, began to wear masculine clothes, and referred to herself as "William Cather, M.D." and "William Cather, Jr." Her four-year experiment in cross-dressing was not the only behavior that singled her out as an iconoclast in Red Cloud. Determined to become a doctor, Cather performed numerous experiments on and dissections of animals, a practice that was frowned upon and drew vocal criticism from her neighbors. In her 1890 high school commencement speech, "Superstition Versus Investigation," she retaliated by accusing her critics of provincialism, backwardness, and an ignorant fear of scientific progress. On this note she left Red Cloud for the larger world of Lincoln and the University of Nebraska.

Willa Cather happened upon the first of her two vocations early in her college career. Intending to devote herself entirely to science when she arrived, she soon discovered the lure of journalism when an English professor submitted what was to become her first published essay, "Concerning Thomas Carlyle." Seeing her work in print in the *Nebraska State Journal* had an intoxicating effect. She began intensive course work in Greek, Latin, English, and French literature; became the literary editor (and later managing editor) of the university publication *Hesperian;* and regularly wrote columns and drama reviews for the *Nebraska State Journal* and the *Lincoln Courier*. Able to support herself as a regular columnist, Cather attained the reputation of a professional, though frequently scathing, critic through her college journalism, beginning a career that would last for fifteen years.

Cather considered her early work in journalism to be one long apprenticeship to the elevated realm of art. In her columns on literature, opera, and drama, what singles out her journalism is its obsession with defining what does or does not constitute art. Frequently her critical prescriptions exposed her own ambivalence about the possibility of being both a woman and an artist. Especially vituperative was her 1895 assessment of Christina Rossetti and of women poets in general:

> It is a very grave question whether women have any place in poetry at all. Certainly they have only been successful in poetry of the most highly subjective nature. If a woman writes any poetry at all worth reading it must be emotional in the extreme, self-centered, self-absorbed, centrifugal. . . . Learned literary women have such an unfortunate tendency to instruct the world. They must learn abandon. The women of the stage know that to feel greatly is genius and to make others feel is art. The women of literature have still to realize that.

Many of Cather's early short stories, written while she was still cutting her literary teeth in journalism, reflect her ambivalence about becoming a woman of literature, and demonstrate her attempt to locate an appropriate voice and subject for her fiction. A number of her early pieces, including "Peter" (1892), her first published story, draw on her Nebraska memories of immigrant pioneers and describe the pain of isolation and of living, literally, at the edge of town society. "Lou, the Prophet" (1892), Serge Povolitchky from "The Clemency of the Court" (1893), Canute Canuteson in "On the Divide" (1896), and Peter Sadeleck in "Peter" all embody inarticulate desires and sorrows that their respective stories attempt to present sympathetically. The motifs of these immigrant tales, sometimes even the stories themselves, later appeared in more mature works like *My Ántonia* and *O, Pioneers!* Murder, suicide, romance, and an inability to adapt to the harsh, aggressive life of the Nebraska farm and to American capitalism appear as central elements in these stories, and prefigure the tragedies of Mr. Shimerda *(My Ántonia)*, Emil Bergson *(O, Pioneers!)*, and Frank and Marie Shabata *(O, Pioneers!)*.

Other early works betray the tension that Cather must have felt between her pronouncement that women writers express emotion "in the extreme" and her realization that her own extreme emotion toward other women, her lesbianism, must be concealed, contained, or displaced. The results of this conundrum are stories such as "On the Gulls' Road" (1908), in which Cather experiments with a first-person narrative in the male voice. Narrated by a man who sketches and falls in love with the older, married Alexandra Ebbling, the tale, subtitled "The Ambassador's Story," describes both the woman and her portrait. The self-conscious play of representation in the tale—the artist cannot possess his desired object, so he re-creates her as art—is a technique Cather adopted later in the novels *My Ántonia* and *A Lost Lady* (1923), each narrated by a man in love with a woman who is unavailable to him. Another story that reveals Cather's attempt to render artistically her emotional attachments to women is "Tommy, the Unsentimental" (1896). Tommy, née Theodosia, is a fresh-faced farm girl who returns from school with a female companion. The older men of the town note that "it was a bad sign when a rebellious girl like Tommy took to being sweet and gentle to one of her own sex, the worst sign in the world." Later, when a young man with whom Tommy has grown up takes a fancy to her friend, the men remark that this attachment is "right and proper and in accordance with the eternal fitness of things. But there's this other girl who has the blindness that may not be cured, and she gets all the rub of it." While Tommy's "blindness" is never really "cured," she partially resolves the sexual ambiguity of the story by facilitating the relationship between her two friends. Casting herself as "odd man out," so to speak, Tommy is left alone and notes, fatalistically and ambiguously, that though men are "awful idiots . . . we do like 'em!" Though Cather treated male homoeroticism in such later novels as *My Ántonia* and *Lucy Gayheart* (1935), she was never again as open about lesbianism.

Living in Pittsburgh and editing the *Home Monthly*, a women's magazine that became a competitor of the *Ladies' Home Journal*, Cather continued to produce columns and to work on her own stories. When the magazine changed ownership, she resigned but stayed in Pittsburgh, writing for the *Leader* and making extra money for her drama criticism. She attended operas and plays, and began to form friendships with such popular actresses as Lizzie Collier and Helena Modjeska. It was in Lizzie Collier's dressing room, in fact, that Cather encountered the second great impetus of her career. The childhood move from Virginia to Nebraska had given her the essential subject of her art; her lifelong friendship with Isabelle McClung provided her with the support and self-confidence necessary to produce that art.

When they were introduced in 1899, Cather was immediately taken with the twenty-one-year-old Isabelle, daughter of a wealthy and socially respected Pittsburgh judge. Drawn to Isabelle by their mutual interest in music, theater, and literature, Cather learned from her a more "feminine" taste in clothes. Cather's preference ran to silks, deep though flashy colors, and the rich velvets that characterized her dress forever after. She became a frequent visitor to the McClungs' posh Murray Hill Avenue home, and resigned from the *Leader* the next year. Soon Cather began one of the most prolific periods of writing in her young career, contributing stories, poems, and an occasional article to the *Library*, a new literary weekly magazine in Pittsburgh. In 1901 she was installed as a permanent guest in the McClung household, sharing an upstairs bedroom with Isabelle and provided with her own study on the third floor. To support herself Cather began teaching high school Latin and, later, English and American literature. She and McClung traveled together to Europe in 1902, the first trip abroad for Cather, and in 1903 *April Twilights*, a collection of thirty-seven poems, was published. Cather had finally found both the space and the time to begin her literary career in earnest.

The year 1903 was a watershed for Cather in other respects as well. She had sent several stories to S. S. McClure, who promptly invited her to come to New York. At their initial meeting he promised to publish her stories in *McClure's* magazine, and intimated that he would consider issuing them as a book. Cather worked on this collection for another two years, and in 1905 *The Troll Garden* was released. Like much of her early fiction, this collection of seven stories dealt with life in the Midwest. But instead of returning to the struggles of immigrant pioneers, the *Troll Garden* stories seemed to launch an all-out attack on the provincialism, small-mindedness, and cultural aridity of Nebraska life. Stories like "A Wagner Matinée" and "The Sculptor's Funeral" depicted Midwestern farm and town life as unequivocally antithetical to art and, perhaps more important, to the sensibilities of the artist. Cather's most anthologized tale, "Paul's Case," demonstrates the consequences of an environment in which artistic inclinations can find no outlet. Other stories, including "A Death in the Desert" and "Flavia and Her Artist," explore the effects of artistic aspiration on those who are, or have been, real artists, and upon those who are merely pretenders to the title. As a volume, *The Troll Garden* suggests another stage of Cather's internal debate about whether she had the talent and power necessary to enter the potentially dangerous world of art.

During this time Cather met the woman who was to become her lifelong companion and chief protector from the outside world. On a summer trip to Nebraska in 1903, she encountered Edith Lewis, who had recently graduated from Smith College and was soon to enter the publishing field. Cather visited Lewis in New York the next two summers, and in 1906 accepted a job at *McClure's* magazine. She moved into Lewis's Greenwich Village apartment and took up what was to be a semi-permament lifelong residence in New York. In later years she spent summers in Jaffrey, New Hampshire, and on the isle of Grand Manan.

Cather's arrival at *McClure's* coincided with the abrupt departure of Lincoln Steffens, Ida Tarbell, John Phillips, and other staff members who left to found the *American* magazine. Cather began as an associate editor and became managing editor in 1908. Lewis, employed at *McClure's* as a proofreader, described the experience as "working in a high wind, sometimes of cyclone magnitude." In her first year Cather was sent on assignment to Boston to research and essentially rewrite Georgine Milmine's *The Life of Mary Baker G. Eddy and the History of Christian Science.* While in Boston she met Ferris Greenslet, an editor at Houghton Mifflin, which published her first four novels. She also was taken by the wife of the noted attorney Louis Brandeis to the home of Annie Fields (widow of the powerful publisher James T. Fields), where she met yet another woman who was to direct the course of her artistic life, the novelist Sarah Orne Jewett.

Cather had long admired Jewett's work,

and the two exchanged correspondence that was later included in *Letters of Sarah Orne Jewett* (1911), edited by Annie Fields. One exchange in particular was to have a profound influence on Cather's career. Writing to Jewett in 1908, the year she became managing editor of *McClure's*, Cather complained of extreme mental and emotional fatigue, and expressed anxiety that her literary skills were simply not developing. Jewett's reply suggested to Cather that she could not manage two careers at once, leaving Cather with a choice that she alone could make:

> My Dear Willa,—I have been thinking about you and hoping that things are going well. I cannot help saying what I think about your writing and its being hindered by such incessant, important, responsible work as you have in your hands now. I do think that it is impossible for you to work so hard and yet have your gifts mature as they should—when one's first working power has spent itself nothing ever brings it back just the same, and I do wish in my heart that the force of this very year could have gone into three or four stories. . . . If you don't keep and guard and mature your force, and above all, have time and quiet to perfect your work, you will be writing things not much better than you did five years ago. . . . Your vivid, exciting companionship in the office must not be your audience, you must find your own quiet centre of life, and write from that to the world. . . . To work in silence and with all one's heart, that is the writer's lot; he is the only artist who must be solitary, and yet needs the widest outlook upon the world.
>
> (*Letters of Sarah Orne Jewett*, ed. Annie Fields [Boston: Houghton Mifflin, 1911], pp. 247–248)

When Sarah Orne Jewett died in June 1909, the devastated Cather continued to manage *McClure's,* even assuming sole responsibility for the magazine when McClure went to Europe. By 1911, however, she had reached the bottom of her reservoirs of energy. She spent weeks in the hospital, recovering from an attack of mastoiditis, and made frequent visits to Annie Fields in Boston and to Jewett's sister, Mary, in South Berwick, Maine. Over that summer she had begun her first novel, *Alexander's Bridge,* and in October she took a formal leave of absence from *McClure's,* an act that signified her permanent separation from both the magazine and the world of journalism. Cather was ready, finally, to embark on her second career, as an American novelist. She was thirty-seven years old.

In 1931 Cather wrote a short essay for *Colophon* entitled "My First Novels (There Were Two)," in which she described *Alexander's Bridge* (1912) as "very like what painters call a studio picture." Cather's allusion here is to what she would insist in hindsight was the Jamesian imitation upon which the novel depended. Her engineer hero, Bartley Alexander, designs and builds an enormous bridge over the St. Lawrence River. But the bridge, and his affair with a former lover, Hilda Burgoyne, ultimately collapse, sending Bartley plunging to his death in the cold waters of the St. Lawrence. Cather's somewhat awkward dialogue and the drawing-room settings in Boston and London make *Alexander's Bridge* different from her subsequent productions, and in the library edition of her collected work she exiled it, along with *April Twilights,* to the third volume of her apprenticeship pieces. In her creative chronology, she placed *O, Pioneers!* as her first novel.

Cather had been working on two short pieces with Western settings, "The Bohemian Girl" and "Alexandra," as she was finishing *Alexander's Bridge.* In the spring of 1912 she traveled with her brother Douglass in the Southwest, and explored the region's canyons, cliff dwellings, and Indian ruins from April to June, beginning an attachment to this region that would persist throughout her life. She returned to Pittsburgh in July or August and, while staying with the McClungs, began "The White Mulberry Tree," a story she eventually combined with "Alexandra" to form the foundation for *O, Pioneers!* (1913).

In looking back on her early work in the essay "My First Novels (There Were Two)," Cather emphasized both place and setting as the elements that signaled her artistic coming of age:

> When I got back to Pittsburgh I began to write a book entirely for myself; a story about some Scandinavians and Bohemians who had been

> neighbours of ours when I lived on a ranch in Nebraska, when I was eight or nine years old. I found it a much more absorbing occupation than writing *Alexander's Bridge;* a different process altogether. Here there was no arranging or "inventing"; everything was spontaneous and took its own place, right or wrong. . . . But I did not in the least expect that other people would see anything in a slow-moving story, without "action," without "humour," without a "hero"; a story concerned entirely with heavy farming people, with cornfields and pasture lands and pig yards,—set in Nebraska, of all places! As everyone knows, Nebraska is distinctly déclassé as a literary background; its very name throws the delicately attuned critic into a clammy shiver of embarrassment.
>
> ("My First Novels . . . ," in *Willa Cather on Writing,* pp. 92, 94)

Cather's giving herself over to her material, something she would later argue is a requisite attitude for the production of art, is paralleled by her heroine, Alexandra, who works in and with the land, reaping the rewards from what *it* yields. This stance suggests a movement from Bartley Alexander to Alexandra Bergson, from an artist who tries to dominate the landscape by erecting an enormous bridge to one who conceives of her relationship with the environment as a partnership, an integration. Moreover, in Alexandra, Cather created an epic heroine whose story does not follow the conventional trajectories of marriage or death. Contrasted with Marie Shabata, who is murdered by her husband for having an adulterous relationship with Alexandra's brother, Emil, Alexandra combines both power and beauty, authority and submission. Indeed, the novel itself consciously creates a new and different version of American pioneer experience. Taking its title from Whitman's epic vision of subduing the land ("Pioneers! O Pioneers!"), it is dedicated to Sarah Orne Jewett, whose *The Country of the Pointed Firs* (1896) offers a pastoral vision of female power and of female community. In *O, Pioneers!* Cather was finally able to envision a world in which both artistry and female identification are possible, and in this respect *O, Pioneers!* may very well be, as she believed, her first novel.

Cather followed the critical success of *O, Pioneers!* with a veiled autobiographical novel about female artistic power, *The Song of the Lark* (1915). In 1913 Cather had met and interviewed for *McClure's* the Swedish soprano Olive Fremstad. What impressed Cather particularly about Fremstad was the singer's insistence on the power of her own voice, a belief that enabled her to extend her range from contralto to soprano. Cather, who had recently discovered her own "voice" in *O, Pioneers!*, fashioned *The Song of the Lark* into the *Künstlerroman* of Thea Kronborg, whose Midwestern childhood mirrors that of Cather herself. As with Cather, it is after a trip to the Southwest that Thea locates the power of her own voice and launches a remarkably successful operatic career. In later assessments of the novel, Cather felt that it was entirely too long; she should not, she argued, have described the mature life of the artist, since the struggle toward success was infinitely more interesting. Nor was she entirely comfortable with the narrative method that such a chronological telling of a life entailed. "Too much detail is apt," she concluded, "like any other form of extravagance, to become slightly vulgar; and it quite destroys in a book a very satisfying element analogous to what painters call 'composition.' "

Though Cather believed that *My Ántonia* (1918) "took the road of *O, Pioneers!*—not the road of *The Song of the Lark*"—her most famous and canonized novel does not, in actuality, conform to either of her previous narrative forms. Instead, it marks Cather's conscious experimentation with narratives and with conventional expectations of how novels tell stories. The text is, more than anything else, a collection of sketches, remembered vignettes, and repeated stories that are loosely tied together and represented as Jim Burden's written composition, originally titled "Ántonia," to which he appends the possessive adjective "My." *My Ántonia* is also the work that inaugurates Cather's use of first-person address as the controlling voice and consciousness in a novel, a technique she would later employ in both *A Lost Lady* (1923) and *My Mortal Enemy* (1926). As in all of these works, the subject of the narrator's tale is a woman, an object either of desire or of veneration, or both. What constitutes the particular appeal of Jim Burden's narrative is its amalgamation of unfulfilled desire, a deep reverence for the Nebraska landscape, and a pervasive nostalgia for those lost days of unfettered youth. Its fluid structure of artfully condensed tales is a technique that Cather employed and further refined in her late, "historical" novels, *Death Comes for the Archbishop* (1927), *Shadows on the Rock* (1931), and *Sapphira and the Slave Girl* (1940).

The narrative experimentation that characterizes *My Ántonia,* especially condensing tales to their immutable essence, is perhaps the prevailing concern of Cather's novels throughout the 1920s. In 1920 Cather published a short piece, "On the Art of Fiction," in the *Borzoi,* in which she summarized what was to be her special contribution to narrative technique in American fiction:

> Art, it seems to me, should simplify. That, indeed, is very nearly the whole of the higher artistic process; finding what conventions of form and what detail one can do without and yet preserve the spirit of the whole—so that all that one has suppressed and cut away is there to the reader's consciousness as much as if it were in type on the page.
>
> (*Willa Cather on Writing,* p. 102)

Cather's interest in the "conventions of form" appeared during the decade as revisions of particular novelistic genres, including both the novel of romance and the historical novel. In 1920 *Youth and the Bright Medusa* was released, a collection of eight stories, four of which are revised and edited versions of tales that had been included in *The Troll Garden.* But at the beginning of the decade Cather was in a period of transition. She had recently changed publishers, moving from Houghton Mifflin to Alfred A. Knopf out of dissatisfaction with the former's business practices and what she felt was less than aggressive marketing. She had also begun a novel, *Claude,* about a young farm boy who escapes the deadening Midwest for a more literal, triumphant death on the battlefields of France. Though it drew considerable criticism, Cather's novel, retitled *One of Ours* (1922) by Knopf, was not a novel about war. Rather, it was a novel about escape and maturity, a journey that led inevitably to Europe and to France as the sacred wellsprings of culture in Cather's universe. Though critics accused Cather of romanticizing the war and ignoring the more gruesome aspects of life in the trenches, the novel was her biggest popular success to date. In 1923 she was awarded the Pulitzer Prize for fiction.

But it was with *A Lost Lady* and *My Mortal Enemy* that Cather's artistic credo of simplification was demonstrated most startlingly. Her essay "The Novel Démeublé" (1922) had appeared in the *New Republic,* and its insistence on "unfurnishing" the house of realistic fiction made itself manifest as a narrative technique in these two novels. Adopting yet again a first-person narrator, Niel Herbert and Nellie Birdseye, respectively, *A Lost Lady* and *My Mortal Enemy* analyze the fictions of "romance" that their protagonists attempt to affix, without success, to older women. Honing all description, sensation, and reflection to revelatory glimpses of the narrators' psyches, these novels explore as well the distorting power of "romance" as a script for women's lives and for their stories. Niel and Nellie attempt to fit Marian Forrester and Myra Henshawe into conventional categories of female behavior and mortality, and both young narrators suffer severe disillusionment. Though Cather ends each novel with the death of the romanticized older woman, there is a sense that the women, as subjects, have escaped the limitations of their narrators. Their essence, as women and as characters, remains a mystery both to the young narrators and to us as readers. In paring down her fictions to that which is implied but not articulated, Cather implicitly criticizes the conventions of categorization and of meaning we are drawn to in an attempt to "place" troublesome and unconventional women.

A number of painful occurrences throughout the 1920s may have impelled Cather toward the considerations of time and of history that dominate *The Professor's House* (1925), *Death Comes for the Archbishop* (1927), and *Shadows on the Rock* (1931). Cather made two trips to Red Cloud in the 1920s: to celebrate her parents' fiftieth wedding anniversary in 1922, and in 1928 to bury her father, who had died of a heart attack. In 1927 the Bank Street building where she had shared an apartment with Edith Lewis was demolished, and the two women took up residence at the Grosvenor Hotel on Fifth Avenue. Feeling herself homeless and uprooted, Cather also spent much of the decade traveling—to the Southwest, to Quebec, to the isle of Grand Manan (where she and Lewis later built their own cabin), and to France to visit Isabelle McClung, who in 1916 had married the violinist Jan Hambourg. The decade ended with acclamation—Cather was elected to the National Institute of Arts and Letters and was awarded an honorary degree from Yale—and also with heartache, when Cather's mother was confined to a Pasadena, California, sanatorium, partially paralyzed and unable to speak.

Critics have frequently read the historical situations of *The Professor's House, Death Comes for the Archbishop,* and *Shadows on the Rock* as escapist, emblematic of Cather's retreat from personal pain as well as from the harsher realities of America during the Great Depression. Yet such a reductively biographical explanation obscures the radical narrative experimentation in which Cather is engaged in these novels, all of which are self-reflexive insofar as they incorporate and even address the act of tale-telling as both their subject and their structure. In her explanatory essays in *Willa Cather on Writing* (1949), Cather is explicit about the fact that her historical fictions not only contain different kinds of stories but also engage in a dialogue with other written and oral texts.

In *The Professor's House* (1925), for example, tale-telling is essential. In her essay "On *The Professor's House,*" Cather notes that her primary source for that novel lay in an oral history:

> I myself had the good fortune to hear the story of it from a very old man, brother of Dick Wetherell. Dick Wetherell as a young boy forded the Mancos River and rode into the Mesa after lost cattle. I followed the real story [about the discovery of the Mesa Verde cliff dwellings] very closely in Tom Outland's narrative.
>
> (*Willa Cather on Writing,* p. 32)

Formally, tale-telling also composes the novel's structure. Cather remarked that with "Tom Outland's Story," the middle section of the novel, she had inserted "the *Nouvelle* into the *Roman*"—placing a potentially autonomous tale or story into a novel—and Tom's story is itself introduced in the text as a tale he tells "on one of those rainy nights, before the fire in the dining-room." Equally significant is the fact that Godfrey St. Peter is a historian who has just completed his eight-volume *Spanish Adventures in North America,* in which "he was trying to do something quite different" in the genre of historical narration. The novel suggests that it is engaged in a certain kind of experimentation with formal structures of both fiction and history while thematically examining issues of material appropriation, familial disaffection, and the search for a dwelling in which the mind can feel at rest.

Similarly, Cather's fictive account of Archbishop Lamy's struggle to establish the Roman Catholic Church in the American Southwest in *Death Comes for the Archbishop* (1927) was suggested to her through "a great many interesting stories . . . from very old Mexicans and traders who still remembered him." Drawing on William Howlett's *The Life of Right Reverend Joseph P. Machbeuf* as the principal source for her novel, Cather reconstructed history through a self-conscious attention to tales and stories as the agents of history. A variety of characters in *Death Comes for the Archbishop* contribute different stories to the narrative: tales of greed, of betrayal, of miracles and legends, of human endurance, and of human frailty. All of these tales, the novel seems to suggest, form the tapestry that we know as history and represent the way history is passed down to us as a kind of story.

Of these three novels, *Shadows on the Rock* (1931) is perhaps Cather's most radically experimental. Writing a seemingly conservative and domestic novel about the establishment of seventeenth-century French culture on Canadian soil, Cather called this text "anacoluthon," a term that signifies the shift from one construction, left incomplete, to another; and the narrative incorporates this sense of discontinuity and rupture. Remembered and recounted stories construct the skeleton of the narrative, each drawn from different story genres: legends, hagiography, personal histories, miracles, adventure stories, dreams, visions, and historical vignettes. Moreover, one of the ostensible subjects of the novel seems to be the documentation of how cultures are created, revivified, and then re-created by the tales that are passed down both in the individual imagination and in the collective historical memory of a given society. What *Shadow on the Rock* does so brilliantly is to dramatize how fictions determine what is recorded as history—those tales which are retold by and about a society—while it simultaneously presents history as a composition of different tales or fictions.

Cather's output in the 1930s slowed considerably, owing to the death of her mother in 1931 and to chronic inflammation in both her wrists, a condition that seriously affected her writing because she found dictating impossible. Besides *Shadows,* she produced only two books during this decade, both seemingly more conventional than her experimental fiction of the 1920s. The first of these, *Obscure Destinies* (1932), is a collection of three stories that return to her early life in Nebraska: "Neighbour Rosicky," "Old Mrs. Harris," and "Two Friends." Simple, concise, and emotionally subdued, the stories distill carefully rendered aspects of Nebraska character—self-reliance, generosity, stubbornness, and a quiet stoicism toward the vagaries of life. Of these stories, "Old Mrs. Harris" stands as Cather's most autobiographical work of fiction. Based on her grandmother Boak, her mother, and herself, it explores how individual women compete for the space (both physical and emotional) they so desperately need to articulate their desires and their identities. Employing a shifting narrative perspective, "Old Mrs. Harris" also examines the limitations of knowledge and of judgment; the reader is encouraged to make judgments about the characters, only to have them undercut by new information and a different angle of vision in successive paragraphs. It is perhaps Cather's best evocation of the family tensions and pleasures that she explored in much of her fiction.

Cather's other major fiction of the decade, *Lucy Gayheart* (1935), is *the* Cather novel critics love to hate. Dismissed as sentimental, gushingly romantic, and trite, it has never enjoyed a wide readership though it remains in print. *Lucy Gayheart,* however, is a novel in which Cather returns to some of the aesthetic, sexual, and gender issues raised in her earlier fiction. In one way, *Lucy Gayheart* corrects the problem of length Cather perceived in *The Song of the Lark,* since it kills off its heroine just as she has reached the end of her psychological struggle to identify and then create a rich and fulfilling life for herself. In its depiction of Clement Sebastian, the middle-aged opera singer with whom Lucy imagines herself in love, the novel also plays ambiguously with homosexuality and homoeroticism. Sebastian's relationships with a young man he "adopts" (and of whom his wife becomes jealous) and with his accompanist, the lurid and potentially dangerous James Mockford, are the darkest and most seamy representations of homosexuality in all of Cather's fictions. Finally, the novel also addresses the complex problem of how women are frequently killed off in fiction so that they can become a story, be remade as art. The last long section of *Lucy Gayheart* does precisely this: Lucy's story is taken over and narrated by Harry Gordon, the man she had refused to marry, who is inadvertently responsible for her death. Seemingly the most conventional novel Cather wrote, *Lucy Gayheart* is actually a strange and even perverse reworking of the conventions that both dictate and shape stories about women.

In the year following *Lucy Gayheart*, Cather published her collection of essays *Not Under Forty*, with her now famous comment that "the world broke in two in 1922 or thereabouts." Indicating her dissatisfaction with and alienation from American life after World War I, this comment has come to symbolize what many critics read as Cather's failing talent in her late career and her inability to produce fiction of merit equal to *My Ántonia* or *O, Pioneers!* Yet her last novel, *Sapphira and the Slave Girl* (1940), is a tour de force of narrative, returning once again to history as a series of tales told and tales remembered. A pre–Civil War novel set in the Virginia of Cather's early childhood, *Sapphira and the Slave Girl* intertwines the escape narrative of Nancy, an enslaved African American, with that of Sapphira Dodderidge Colbert, the imperious, proud, and vengeful mistress of the house. Though undeniably racist in its characterization of African Americans, the novel's real power lies in its evocation of narrative remembrance. Especially interesting is the "Epilogue," in which the authorial voice is introduced as that of a young child who has listened to, internalized, and then imaginatively transformed these actual stories into fiction. Ironically, this personal and historical return to the stories that made her a writer was Cather's last work of long fiction.

Cather spent her remaining years assessing the primary relationships of her life and forging new and fruitful friendships with young people just coming into their own. She survived the deaths of her brother Douglass in 1938 and of her brother Roscoe in 1945. Isabelle Hambourg's death in 1938 brought a profound emptiness that never left her. Yet in these years Cather developed a strong relationship with the young Menuhins—Yehudi, Hephzibah, and Yaltah—that sustained her through devastating personal loss. The children referred to her as "Aunt Willa," and she accompanied them frequently on walks in Central Park and spent afternoons reading Shakespeare with them. Cather's last story, "The Best Years" (1945), incorporates both the sense of loss and the sense of pleasure she felt in relationships with her younger brothers and the Menuhin children, and takes stock of life with the comment that "our best years are when we're working hardest and going right ahead, when we can hardly see our way out." On 24 April 1947, while taking an afternoon nap, Willa Cather died of a cerebral hemorrhage.

The inscription on Cather's tombstone in Jaffrey, New Hampshire, is a quote from *My Ántonia:* "That is happiness; to be dissolved into something complete and great." Edith Lewis, who survived Cather, facilitated her lover's wish to be "dissolved." Consigning the bulk of Cather's correspondence to the fire, she protected Cather's privacy to the end. As a consequence, Willa Cather, the woman and lesbian, remains a character only approximated, a purposefully veiled personality who left only her complex and ambiguous fiction as explicable texts. "The stupid," Cather wrote in *The Song of the Lark,* "believe that to be truthful is easy; only the artist, the great artist, knows how difficult it is."

Selected Bibliography

PRIMARY WORKS

POETRY

April Twilights. Boston: Richard G. Badger, 1903.
April Twilights and Other Poems. New York: Knopf, 1923.

FICTION

The Troll Garden. New York: McClure, Phillips, 1905.

Alexander's Bridge. Boston: Houghton Mifflin, 1912.

O, Pioneers! Boston: Houghton Mifflin, 1913.

The Song of the Lark. Boston: Houghton Mifflin, 1915.

My Ántonia. Boston: Houghton Mifflin, 1918.

Youth and the Bright Medusa. New York: Knopf, 1920.

One of Ours. New York: Knopf, 1922.

A Lost Lady. New York: Knopf, 1923.

The Professor's House. New York: Knopf, 1925.

My Mortal Enemy. New York: Knopf, 1926.

Death Comes for the Archbishop. New York: Knopf, 1927.

Shadows on the Rock. New York: Knopf, 1931.

Obscure Destinies. New York: Knopf, 1932.

Lucy Gayheart. New York: Knopf, 1935.

Sapphira and the Slave Girl. New York: Knopf, 1940.

The Old Beauty, and Others. New York: Knopf, 1948.

CRITICAL AND MISCELLANEOUS WRITINGS

Not Under Forty. New York: Knopf, 1936.

Willa Cather on Writing. New York: Knopf, 1949.

Writings from Willa Cather's Campus Years. Edited by James R. Shively. Lincoln: University of Nebraska Press, 1950.

Willa Cather in Europe: Her Own Story of the First Journey. New York: Knopf, 1956.

The Kingdom of Art: Willa Cather's First Principles and Critical Statements, 1893–1896. Edited by Bernice Slote. Lincoln: University of Nebraska, 1966.

The World and the Parish: Willa Cather's Articles and Reviews, 1893–1902. Edited by William M. Curtin. 2 vols. Lincoln: University of Nebraska Press, 1970.

Willa Cather in Person: Interviews, Speeches and Letters. Edited by L. Brent Bohlke. Lincoln: University of Nebraska Press, 1986.

ANTHOLOGIES

Five Stories. New York: Random House, 1956. With an essay by George N. Kates on Cather's Avignon novel fragment begun in 1941.

Early Stories of Willa Cather. Compiled by Mildred Bennett. New York: Dodd, Mead, 1957.

Willa Cather's Collected Short Fiction, 1892–1912. Edited by Virginia Faulkner. Lincoln: University of Nebraska Press, 1965.

Uncle Valentine and Other Stories: Willa Cather's Uncollected Short Fiction, 1915–1929. Edited by Bernice Slote. Lincoln: University of Nebraska Press, 1973.

Willa Cather: Early Novels and Stories. Edited by Sharon O'Brien. New York: Library of America, 1987.

24 Stories. Edited by Sharon O'Brien. New York: New American Library, 1988.

Willa Cather: Later Novels. Edited by Sharon O'Brien. New York: Library of America, 1990.

SECONDARY WORKS

BIOGRAPHICAL AND CRITICAL STUDIES

Adams, Timothy Dow. "My Gay Antonia: The Politics of Willa Cather's Lesbianism." In *Historical, Literary, and Erotic Aspects of Lesbianism*. Edited by Monika Kehoe. New York: Harrington Park Press, 1986. Pp. 89–98.

Arnold, Marilyn. *Willa Cather's Short Fiction*. Athens: Ohio University Press, 1984.

Bennett, Mildred. *The World of Willa Cather*. New York: Dodd, Mead, 1951; Lincoln: University of Nebraska Press, 1961.

Bloom, Edward A., and Lillian D. Bloom. *Willa Cather's Gift of Sympathy*. Carbondale: Southern Illinois University Press, 1962.

Brown, Edward K., and Leon Edel. *Willa Cather: A Critical Biography*. New York: Knopf, 1953; Lincoln: University of Nebraska Press, 1987.

Brown, Marion Marsh. *Only One Point of the Compass: Willa Cather in the Northeast*. Danbury, Conn.: Archer Editions, 1980.

Byrne, Kathleen D., and Richard C. Snyder. *Chrysalis: Willa Cather in Pittsburgh, 1896–1906*. Pittsburgh: Historical Society of Western Pennsylvania, 1980.

Daiches, David. *Willa Cather: A Critical Introduction*. Ithaca, N.Y.: Cornell University Press, 1951.

Fryer, Judith. *Felicitous Space: The Imaginative Structures of Edith Wharton and Willa Cather*. Chapel Hill: University of North Carolina Press, 1986.

Gelfant, Blanche. "The Forgotten Reaping-Hook: Sex in *My Ántonia*" and "Movement and Melody: The Disembodiment of Lucy Gayheart." In her *Women Writing in America: Voices in Collage*. Hanover, N.H.: University Press of New England, 1984. Pp. 93–143.

Gerber, Philip. *Willa Cather*. Boston: Twayne, 1975.

Giannone, Richard. *Music in Willa Cather's Fiction*. Lincoln: University of Nebraska Press, 1968.

Gilbert, Sandra M., and Susan Gubar. "Lighting out for the Territories: Willa Cather's Lost Horizons." In their *No Man's Land: The Place of the Woman Writer in the Twentieth Century*. Vol. 2, *Sexchanges*. New Haven: Yale University Press, 1989. Pp. 169–212.

Jessup, Josephine Lurie. *The Faith of Our Feminists: A*

Study in the Novels of Edith Wharton, Ellen Glasgow, Willa Cather. New York: R. R. Smith, 1950.

Lee, Hermione. *Willa Cather: Double Lives*. London: Virago, 1989; New York: Pantheon, 1990.

Lewis, Edith. *Willa Cather Living: A Personal Record*. New York: Knopf, 1953, 1976.

Lilienfeld, Jane. "Reentering Paradise: Cather, Colette, Woolf, and Their Mothers." In *The Lost Tradition: Mothers and Daughters in Literature*. Edited by Cathy N. Davidson and E. M. Broner. New York: Frederick Ungar, 1980. Pp. 160–175.

McFarland, Dorothy Tuck. *Willa Cather*. New York: Frederick Ungar, 1972.

Moorhead [Vermorcken], Elizabeth. "The Novelist: Willa Cather." In her *These Two Were Here: Louise Homer and Willa Cather*. Pittsburgh: University of Pittsburgh Press, 1950. Reprinted Folcroft, Pa.: Folcroft Press, 1969; and Philadelphia: R. West, 1978.

Murphy, John J., ed. *Five Essays on Willa Cather: The Merrimack Symposium*. North Andover, Mass.: Merrimack College, 1974.

———. *Critical Essays on Willa Cather*. Boston: G. K. Hall, 1984.

Nelson, Robert James. *Willa Cather and France: In Search of the Lost Language*. Urbana: University of Illinois Press, 1988.

O'Brien, Sharon. " 'The Thing Not Named': Willa Cather as a Lesbian Writer." *Signs: Journal of Women in Culture and Society* 9:576–599 (1984).

———. *Willa Cather: The Emerging Voice*. New York: Oxford University Press, 1987.

———. "Becoming Noncanonical: The Case Against Willa Cather." *American Quarterly* 40:110–126 (1988).

Pers, Mona. *Willa Cather's Children*. Stockholm: Almqvist & Wiksell, 1975.

Randall, John H., III. *The Landscape and the Looking Glass: Willa Cather's Search for Value*. Boston: Houghton Mifflin, 1960.

Rapin, René. *Willa Cather*. New York: Robert M. McBride, 1930.

Robinson, Phyllis C. *Willa: The Life of Willa Cather*. Garden City, N.Y.: Doubleday, 1983.

Rose, Phyllis. "Willa Cather" and "The Case of Willa Cather." In her *Writing of Women: Essays in a Renaissance*. Middletown, Conn.: Wesleyan University Press, 1985. Pp. 17–20, 136–152.

Rosowski, Susan J. *The Voyage Perilous: Willa Cather's Romanticism*. Lincoln: University of Nebraska Press, 1986.

Rule, Jane. "Willa Cather." In her *Lesbian Images*. Garden City, N.Y.: Doubleday, 1975. Pp. 74–87. Also New York: Pocket Books, 1976. Pp. 79–91.

Russ, Joanna. "To Write 'like a Woman': Transformations of Identity in the Work of Willa Cather." In *Historical, Literary, and Erotic Aspects of Lesbianism*. Edited by Monika Kehoe. New York: Harrington Park Press, 1986. Pp. 77–87.

Sacken, Jeannée P. *"A Certain Slant of Light": Aesthetics of First-Person Narration in Gide and Cather*. New York: Garland, 1985.

Schroeter, James, ed. *Willa Cather and Her Critics*. Ithaca, N.Y.: Cornell University Press, 1967.

Sergeant, Elizabeth Shepley. *Willa Cather: A Memoir*. Philadelphia: J. B. Lippincott, 1953; Lincoln: University of Nebraska Press, 1963.

Slote, Bernice, and Virginia Faulkner, eds. *The Art of Willa Cather*. Lincoln: University of Nebraska Press, 1973.

Slote, Bernice, and Lucia Woods. *Willa Cather: A Pictorial Memoir*. Lincoln: University of Nebraska Press, 1973.

Stouck, David. *Willa Cather's Imagination*. Lincoln: University of Nebraska Press, 1975.

Van Ghent, Dorothy. *Willa Cather*. New York: Frederick Ungar, 1964.

Welsch, Roger L., and Linda K. Welsch. *Cather's Kitchens: Foodways in Literature and Life*. Lincoln: University of Nebraska Press, 1987.

Woodress, James L. *Willa Cather: A Literary Life*. Lincoln: University of Nebraska Press, 1987.

BIBLIOGRAPHIES

Arnold, Marilyn. *Willa Cather: A Reference Guide*. Boston: G. K. Hall, 1986.

Crane, Joan. *Willa Cather: A Bibliography*. Lincoln: University of Nebraska Press, 1982.

Lathrop, JoAnna. *Willa Cather: A Checklist of Her Published Writing*. Lincoln: University of Nebraska Press, 1975.

DEBORAH CARLIN

KATE CHOPIN

1850–1904

IN APRIL 1899, when *The Awakening* was published, Kate Chopin was an author with a national reputation. She had written more than a hundred short stories, many of which had appeared in magazines such as *Vogue, Century,* and the *Atlantic*. Her two collections of short stories, *Bayou Folk* (1894) and *A Night in Acadie* (1897), had been widely reviewed and had been praised for their "force" and "charm." "There is not a weak line" in these stories, the *St. Louis Post-Dispatch* had rhapsodized, "or a page which will not improve with every new reading." Chopin was, moreover, something of a literary lioness in St. Louis. She had numerous admirers, both intellectual and amorous, her gracious home and salon having attracted some of the city's best-known writers and artists.

Within weeks after the publication of *The Awakening,* however, this social and literary landscape that had seemed so serenely comfortable became anything but serene and anything but comfortable. The flood of reviews that greeted *The Awakening*—and it was a veritable flood—all paid grudging respect to the novel's "consummate art," but they were also emphatically censorious, detailing their repugnance in physical, medical, and olfactory terms. "One dislikes to acknowledge a wish that [Chopin] had not written her novel," the *Mirror* confessed, but confessed as well to "a sick feeling" upon finishing the book. This sick feeling was evidently shared by the *St. Louis Daily Globe-Democrat,* which said, quite simply, that *The Awakening* was "not a healthy book."

The *Providence Sunday Journal* could not agree more. "We are fain to believe that Miss Chopin did not herself realize what she was doing when she wrote it," this publication speculated, adding that "it is nauseating to remember that those who object to the bluntness of our older writers will excuse and justify the gilded dirt of these latter days." Along the same lines the *Los Angeles Sunday Times* lamented that "the evident powers of the author are employed on a subject that is unworthy of them, and when she writes another book it is to be hoped that she will choose a theme more healthful and sweeter of smell." The *St. Louis Republic* thought that something as dangerous as *The Awakening* "should be labeled 'poison.' "

These and other hostile reviews (including one by Willa Cather for the *Pittsburgh Leader*) eventually led to the removal of *The Awakening* from the Public Library and the Mercantile Library of St. Louis. Chopin was shunned by many of her former associates and was refused membership in the Fine Arts Club. She tried to make light of this uproar and, seemingly undaunted, offered a tongue-in-cheek "retraction" in the July 1899 *Book News,* where her unfortunate heroine was made to shoulder all the blame:

> Having a group of people at my disposal, I thought it might be entertaining (to myself) to throw them together and see what would happen. I never dreamed of Mrs. Pontellier making such a mess of things and working out her own damnation as she did. If I had had the slightest intimation of such a thing I would have excluded her from the company. But when I found out what she was up to, the play was half over and it was then too late.
>
> (p. 612)

Chopin's pluckiness is much in evidence in this disclaimer. And yet, despite this brave show of irreverence, the harsh reception of *The Awakening,* together with her diminished stature as a writer, seems to have affected her more than she cared to admit. After the publication of the novel she wrote very little—only seven short stories between 1900 and 1904. Her health began to fail, even though she was only in her early fifties. She now had trouble publishing her work; her short story "Ti Démon" was rejected by the *Atlantic* (on the ground that it was "too somber"), and her third collection of stories, tentatively called "A Vocation and a Voice," was returned by Herbert S. Stone. Fortunately, her large and affectionate family sustained her spirits. She suffered a stroke while visiting the St. Louis World's Fair, and died soon afterward, on 22 August 1904.

After her death, Chopin's work was virtually forgotten and all but impossible to obtain. In 1932 Father Daniel S. Rankin published *Kate Chopin and Her Creole Stories,* an anecdotal biography that presented Chopin primarily as a local colorist. The major reinterpretation of her work did not begin until 1952; appropriately enough, it gathered momentum in France with Cyrille Arnavon's 1953 translation of *The Awakening* (under the title *Edna*) and his championship of it as a neglected masterpiece. American critics came to the same conclusion. Van Wyck Brooks praised the work in *The Confident Years* (1952) as "one novel of the nineties in the South that should have been remembered, one small perfect book that mattered more than the whole life-work of many a prolific writer." In *Patriotic Gore* (1962) Edmund Wilson similarly found the novel "quite uninhibited and beautifully written, [one] which anticipates D. H. Lawrence in its treatment of infidelity." In 1956 Kenneth Eble published "A Forgotten Novel: Kate Chopin's *The Awakening,*" an important reappraisal, and in 1969 the Norwegian scholar Per Seyersted (who had studied with Arnavon at Harvard) published a critical biography of Chopin as well as a two-volume collection of her complete works, including her hitherto unavailable first novel, *At Fault* (1890), and the bulk of her short stories. Half a century after her death, Chopin was finally accorded the canonical status that had so sorely eluded her during her life.

This initial burst of critical interest, however, turned out to be only the barest intimation of what was to come. The 1970s and 1980s saw something of "a Chopin revival"—a revival to which many influential critics contributed—and *The Awakening* increasingly appeared as a logical choice in survey courses. Today a college student is as likely to have read *The Awakening* as *Moby-Dick.* Like Melville, Chopin is fortunate to have been granted a second life; and, also like Melville, her critical rebirth dramatizes the extent to which literature is an institution—a contingent and to some degree arbitrary phenomenon—shaped not only by authorial creativity but also by readerly receptivity, not only by individual genius but also by the cultural dispositions at work in an interpretive community.

Certainly *The Awakening* as we now know it is very much a joint achievement: the achievement of Chopin, to be sure, but in addition, the achievement of critics like Cynthia Griffin Wolff, Emily Toth, Elizabeth Fox-Genovese, and, more recently, Sandra Gilbert and Elaine Showalter, as well as such younger critics as Patricia Yaeger and Margit Stange. Not surprisingly, feminist readers are especially drawn to the novel, seeing it as variously exemplary of the women's tradition. For Sandra Gilbert the novel belongs to "a regenerative and revisionary genre, a genre that intends to propose new realities for women by providing new mythic paradigms through which women's lives can be understood." For Elaine Showalter it represents "the transitional female fiction of the fin-de-siècle, a narrative of and about the passage from the homosocial women's culture and literature of the nineteenth century to the heterosexual fiction of modernism." For Patricia Yaeger the novel exemplifies the challenge as well as the difficulty of devising "emancipatory strategies" in women's fiction.

In this context it is worth remembering that *The Awakening* was written during a period when feminism was emerging as a vital force in American public life. By 1890 the "New

Woman" was a phenomenon no one could ignore. Upper-class women gained visibility by attending college, entering the professions, and demanding the vote. Lower-class women made themselves heard by unionizing and combating unfavorable working conditions. In spite of these efforts, however, gender inequality remained a glaring fact at the turn of the century. In New Orleans, for instance, the Napoleonic Code still formed the basis for the marriage contract. The wife and all her "accumulations" after marriage were the property of her husband, and she was legally bound to live with him and to follow him wherever he chose to go. As stipulated by Article 1591 of the laws of Louisiana, four groups of people were deemed "absolutely incapable of being witness to testaments": children not yet sixteen; persons who were insane, deaf, dumb, or blind; criminals; and "women of any age soever."

To get a sense of the social climate—and social ferment—amid which Chopin wrote, it is useful to read her in the company of her contemporaries, both male and female, both ardent and bemused, who had made it their business to comment on the condition of women at the turn of the century. Charlotte Perkins Gilman comes to mind—not just the Gilman of *The Yellow Wallpaper* but also the Gilman of *Women and Economics* (where she discusses such topics as "Women as Mothers," "Modification to Maternity," and "The Mother's Duty"). Thorstein Veblen, not noted for his feminism, nonetheless has much to tell us about the plight of wives in an age of compulsory leisure and conspicuous consumption. Dorothy Dix, the first woman to become the editor of a major American newspaper, published a provocative column in the New Orleans *Daily Picayune* just a year or two before Chopin published her even more provocative novel. As collected in the Norton Critical Edition of *The Awakening*, this column included items such as "Are Women Growing Selfish?" "The American Wife," "A Strike for Liberty," and "Women and Suicide." Thus suggestively presented, they offer a valuable background as well as a valuable contrast to *The Awakening*.

The contrast is worth emphasizing, because, while Chopin was undoubtedly sensitive to "the woman question," she was neither an activist nor an advocate. Earlier in her life (during her honeymoon, no less), she had crossed paths with Victoria Claflin, the noted feminist, and what she recorded of that encounter says something about her interest—in both senses of the word. She was genuinely fascinated, but also not a little bemused:

> We had the honor and pleasure of making the acquaintance of Miss Clafflin [*sic*], the notorious "female broker" of New York—a fussy, pretty, talkative little woman, who discussed business extensively with Oscar, and entreated me not to fall into the useless degrading life of most married ladies—but to elevate my mind and turn my attention to politics, commerce, questions of state, etc., etc. I assured her I would do so—which assurance satisfied her quite.
>
> (quoted in Seyersted, p. 33)

In this unguarded and yet not quite guileless passage, with its alternate play of mockery and edification, we get more than a hint of the tonally ambiguous Chopin that readers of *The Awakening* would come to know both so well and so little. Like Walt Whitman, whose presence is so palpable in her work, Chopin might have described herself in the following terms, from "Song of Myself":

> Apart from the pulling and hauling stands what I am,
> Stands amused, complacent, compassionating, idle, unitary
> . . . Looking with side-curved head curious what will come next,
> Both in and out of the game and watching and wondering at it.

Even though, in its bare outline, *The Awakening* would seem to be the archetypal story of a New Woman—Edna Pontellier begins the story as a wife and mother and ends up leaving her husband to live in a house of her own—that story is hardly unqualified and hardly unattended by irony. As several critics have pointed out, it is surely paradoxical, if not downright bedeviling, that in a novel called *The Awakening* the protagonist should spend so much time being so soundly asleep. To what extent is Edna "awakened" at the end of the book? To what extent is she lulled into a more fateful kind of sleep? Has she progressed at all in the course of the book? Or has she simply regressed (as Cynthia Griffin Wolff has argued) into a kind of primordial babyhood?

It is surely a tribute to the rhetorical agility of *The Awakening* that critics should disagree so thoroughly both about the specifics of its ending and, more generally, about the character and virtues of Edna Pontellier. Had Chopin been able to foresee such critical controversies, she would no doubt have been delighted. She was an author, after all, who dwelled in the realm of the momentary and the evanescent, who eschewed anything like a singleness of purpose. In her capacity as critic and judge, she had more than once expressed annoyance with those authors who had made their meaning too unmistakable. She found Thomas Hardy's *Jude the Obscure,* for instance, "detestably bad" and "unpardonably dull" because "the characters are so plainly constructed with the intention of illustrating the purposes of the author, that they do not for a moment convey any impression of reality." Similarly, she complained about Émile Zola's "glaringly" didactic presence in *Lourdes:* "Not for an instant, from first to last, do we lose sight of the author and his note-book and of the disagreeable fact that his design is to instruct us."

Chopin herself certainly cannot be accused of that design in *The Awakening.* Indeed, in her refusal to instruct, she would seem not only to be dissenting from the novelistic tradition of Hardy and Zola but also to be honoring a kind of family tradition—one of suspending judgment—that appears to have been instilled in her from her earliest childhood. Chopin's remarkable openness of mind did not come quite unheralded. She was fortunate to have grown up under the influence of women who, in their lack of prudery and their judgmental restraint, were perhaps as remarkable as she was.

Katherine O'Flaherty Chopin was born on 8 February 1850 to an Irish father and a Creole mother. Her father, Thomas O'Flaherty, had come to America from County Galway in 1823 and, after a few years in New York, had moved to St. Louis, becoming in time one of its most prominent citizens. After his first wife died, he married Eliza Faris, who came from an aristocratic if impoverished French family. Thomas O'Flaherty owned a wholesale grocery business, a boat store, and a commission house. In time he also became a director of the Pacific Railroad of Missouri. With other local leaders he took the inaugural train across the Gasconade River in 1855, and when the bridge collapsed, he was one of the twenty-nine killed.

Thomas O'Flaherty left his family financially well off. His death also transformed it into a practical matriarchy, with four generations of women living under the same roof. Eliza Faris was not yet sixteen when she married in 1844; she was only twenty-seven when she became a widow. Since women in her traditional Creole family had always married young, she was able to welcome into her household not only her widowed mother, Athénaïse Charleville Faris, but also Kate's great-grandmother Victoria Verdon Charleville.

Madame Charleville spoke French better than English, and legend had it that she had never been able to pronounce the outlandish O'Flaherty name. She made a point, in any case, of speaking only French to her great-granddaughter. She also made a point of telling her "stories of questionable nature" (as Daniel S. Rankin calls them), to which the young Kate "listened with astonished attention." Foremost among these was a story about the colorful Madame Chouteau, who was said to have left her husband after the birth of their son, and who later became the consort of Pierre Laclède, the founder of St. Louis, living with him and bearing his four children but not marrying him. This story, "repeated over and over," according to Rankin, "stirred Katherine O'Flaherty's interest in the intimacy of people's lives and minds and morals." It was obviously told in the spirit of Madame Charleville's favorite saying: "One may know a great deal about people without judging them. God does that." The young Kate must have been impressed. Three decades later, when she came to do her own storytelling, she would continue to leave judgment entirely to God.

Enlightened as it was, however, Chopin's childhood was not without its limitations and prejudices. St. Louis in the 1850s was a city bitterly divided over the question of slavery. In 1836 the well-known newspaper editor Elijah P. Lovejoy had been driven out of the city; a year later he was killed in nearby Alton, Illinois, by a mob incensed by his abolitionist activities. The city also gained national attention as the scene of the Dred Scott trial. The O'Flahertys were slaveholders and rebel supporters in a Union city. Kate's best friend at the Sacred Heart Academy, Kitty Garesché, came from a similar background, and Kate was inconsolable when Kitty's family was banished from the city because of their pro-slavery politics. When the Civil War broke out, Kate's half brother, George, then in his early twenties, joined the Confederate army, and he seems to have carried with him all of Kate's sympathies. She became "the littlest rebel" of St. Louis and, years later, would recall the dramatic moment when she "tore down the Union flag from the front porch when the Yanks tied it up there."

Kate's Confederate sentiments were undoubtedly the impulses of a young girl, and should hardly be exaggerated. But neither should they be completely dismissed. Indeed, some remnants of those sentiments seem to have survived into her adulthood: as a young wife, Kate was quite comfortable with her husband's racial politics. Oscar Chopin supported the repressive measures of the postbellum South, was a member of the White League (an armed organization using violence to restore white supremacy), and even took part in the famous Battle of Liberty Place (14 September 1874), in which thirty-five hundred White Leaguers, under the command of Confederate general James Longstreet, overwhelmed an equal number of black militiamen and metropolitan police, and occupied the city hall, statehouse, and arsenal in New Orleans.

Chopin's amoral stance—her indifference to reform and impatience with "preaching"—must be understood in this context as well. And it should not surprise us that in much of her work, beginning with her first novel, *At Fault*, and continuing through such stories as "For Marse Chouchoute," "The Bênitous' Slave," and "Tante Cat'rinette," the black characters are portrayed as simple, childlike, and mindlessly devoted to their masters—not unlike those portrayed by authors such as Thomas Nelson Page. Even in "Désirée's Baby" (perhaps her best-known short work) racial injustice is, in some sense, only a necessary background against which Chopin stages her deadly dramatic irony. Armand Aubigny, the proud aristocrat who accuses his wife of having contaminated their child with black blood, is miraculously revealed, on the last page, to be the guilty party. (He comes upon a letter written by his mother that contains a reference to her membership in "the race that is cursed with the brand of slavery.") The injustice here is not the injustice of racial oppression but the injustice of a wrongly attributed racial identity.

If the national trauma of the Civil War—and the causes behind the Civil War—remained relatively unimportant to Chopin, her life was nonetheless darkened by a series of personal traumas. She was hardly six when her father died. Having learned to cope with that tragedy, she would often have occasion, later in life, to make painful use of what she had learned. In 1863 the two people dearest to her died within a month of each other. Her half brother, George, whom she adored, was captured and imprisoned in 1862; later released in a prisoner exchange, he died of typhoid in February while returning to his regiment. A month earlier, Madame Charleville had also died, leaving Kate and her young mother quite disconsolate.

When Kate recovered from these terrible losses, she went on to become a popular young belle, attending fashionable events, playing music (she was an accomplished pianist with an exceptional musical memory, as Kitty Garesché recalled), learning to smoke in New Orleans (a rather daring thing for young ladies in those days), and, above all, reading voraciously. She read not only Sir Walter Scott, Dickens, Jane Austen, and Charlotte and Emily Brontë but also Dante, Cervantes, Pierre Corneille, Jean Racine, Molière, Madame de Staël, Chateaubriand, and Goethe. Being bilingual, she had an easy familiarity with, as well as a special affinity for, French literature.

This French connection would evolve in realms other than literature. Soon Kate met and fell in love with twenty-five-year-old Oscar Chopin, a French-Creole businessman. In 1870, at the age of nineteen, she married him. In October the couple moved to New Orleans.

Oscar Chopin had grown up in Natchitoches Parish, Louisiana. His father, Dr. Victor Chopin, had left his native France to settle in America in the 1840s and had married Julia Benoist of Cloutierville, a woman of distinguished French lineage. In 1852 they bought the McAlpin plantation, which had 4,367 acres and ninety-four slaves. Robert McAlpin, who had owned the plantation until his death in that year, was reputed to have been the model for Simon Legree in Harriet Beecher Stowe's *Uncle Tom's Cabin*. (Chopin makes use of this interesting information in *At Fault*, where she changes McAlpin's name to McFarlane and has a character remark, "He's the person that Mrs. W'at's her name wrote about in *Uncle Tom's Cabin*.")

Victor Chopin was apparently something of a Simon Legree himself. His cruelty to slaves was legendary: for the sake of efficiency he had them all chained in a row to work in one field at a time. Not surprisingly, his slaves were always trying to run away. He attempted to make Oscar the overseer of the plantation, and, also not surprisingly, the boy ran away as well, choosing to live with relatives. Victor's wife could not stand his meanness, and for some years in the 1850s, when Oscar was still young, she lived apart from her husband. Kate Chopin no doubt had the old doctor in mind when she suggested in *The Awakening* that the heroine's father might have "coerced his own wife into her grave."

In any case, this unusual parental influence had the fortunate effect of making Oscar Chopin a highly unusual husband. He respected his young wife as an intellectual equal, accepted her unconventional attire, put up with her cigarette smoking and beer drinking, and laughed it off when anxious relatives rebuked him for allowing her to forget her "duty." Chopin, on her part, was "very much in love with her Oscar," as everyone reported. Although the couple spoke French to each other, they lived on the American side of town, outside the Vieux Carré.

New Orleans fascinated Chopin. Here she encountered aristocratic Creoles, unpretentious Cajuns (or Acadians: French pioneers who in 1755 had chosen to leave Nova Scotia rather than live under the British), Redbones (part Indian, part white), "free mulattoes" (so called because they had never been slaves), blacks, and a cosmopolitan assortment of Germans, Italians, Irish, and Americans. She developed a habit of roaming the city, sometimes in a streetcar and sometimes on foot, often unaccompanied. She and Oscar had a busy social life, including a weekly reception day when (like Edna Pontellier) she had to stay home and entertain.

Chopin was frequently pregnant. By the time she was twenty-eight, she had given birth to five sons. With her children she took frequent trips to St. Louis, and spent long summers on Grand Isle, an idyllic Creole retreat in the Gulf of Mexico, no doubt to avoid the yellow fever epidemic that afflicted New Orleans every year.

Oscar Chopin was a cotton factor at this time. In an environment hostile to trade, the cotton factor, with established family connections and gentlemanly habits, was a much-needed intermediary between the world of the plantation and the world of modern finance. He handled the planter's money, sold his cotton, and provided him with all the necessary farm equipment and supplies. Oscar prospered for a while, but in 1878 and 1879 excessive rain ruined the cotton; Oscar, who had made large advances to the planters, suffered heavy losses. He closed his business and moved with his family to Cloutierville.

In this tiny French village, which later became the setting of many of Chopin's stories, Oscar opened a general store, and the family continued to live in style and comfort. Here, Kate gave birth to Lélia, her last child and only daughter. Here, too, she found herself living for the first time in a small town, with its many charms and frustrations. The longtime residents were shocked by "the fantastic affair" that was her riding habit, and tut-tutted when she smoked Cuban cigarettes and lifted her skirts to reveal her ankles when crossing the town's one street. But her kindness and charm soon won them over. In 1880 the new Cane River packet was named after her newborn daughter, surely an eloquent testimony to her popularity.

In December 1882 Oscar Chopin came down with a severe case of swamp fever, and within days he was dead. Kate now became "a handsome, inconsolable . . . Creole widow "—not unlike Thérèse Lafirme, the heroine of her first novel. Unlike Thérèse, however, she had six children to care for. She took over Oscar's business for more than a year, managing the Chopin plantations and dealing with cotton factors in New Orleans, and was pursued by an attractive but married local planter. In 1884 she sold her belongings and moved to St. Louis to join her mother, a reunion that lasted for only a year. In June 1885 Mrs. O'Flaherty died, and Kate was left once again to mourn her dead. In later years her daughter described the effect of these personal tragedies on her mother:

> When I speak of my mother's keen sense of humor and of her habit of looking on the amusing side of everything, I don't want to give you the impression of her being joyous, for she was on the contrary rather a sad nature. . . . I think the tragic death of her father early in her life, of her much loved brothers, the loss of her young husband and her mother, left a stamp of sadness on her which was never lost.
>
> (quoted in Rankin, p. 35)

How that "stamp of sadness" registers itself in Chopin's fiction is a question that critics have yet to explore. In any case, during this period of great personal sorrow, Chopin turned increasingly to Dr. Frederick Kolbenheyer, who had been her obstetrician and was now her family doctor as well as close friend. He was very much an intellectual of the European stripe. His radical ideas had made it necessary for him to leave his native Austria. Settling in St. Louis in 1870, he soon became friends with the city's leading journalists, including Joseph Pulitzer, who later made him vice president of his *St. Louis Post-Dispatch*. He was a determined agnostic, and his influence on Chopin was such that she was soon prevailed upon to question (and later to reject) her Catholic faith. He encouraged her to explore the new studies of science, and soon she was reading Darwin, Huxley, and Spencer. At the same time—and perhaps even more significantly—she was read *to* as well. Her own letters, sent to Kolbenheyer from Louisiana, were now recited aloud by him, so that she might notice their literary merits. With such earnest promptings, she finally took up writing when she was thirty-eight years old and a mother of six.

The publication of the love poem "If It Might Be" in January 1889 marked Chopin's first appearance in print. By the end of the year, two of her short stories had been published as well: "Wiser Than a God" in the *Philadelphia Musical Journal* and "A Point at Issue!" in the *St. Louis Post-Dispatch*. In 1890 her first novel, *At Fault*, was published at her own expense; it garnered a great deal of attention, including a mixed review in the *Nation*. By 1894 Chopin was a familiar figure in the nation's most prestigious literary magazines. In January of that year, "A No-Account Creole" appeared in the *Century*, and "La Belle Zoraïde" appeared in *Vogue*; in February, *Vogue* printed another of her stories, "A Respectable Woman"; in March her first collection of short stories, *Bayou Folk*, was published by Houghton Mifflin of Boston; in September, "Tante Cat'rinette" appeared in the *Atlantic*.

Significantly, it was in mid April 1894, when Chopin was luxuriating in her literary success and, more specifically, in the glowing reviews of *Bayou Folk*, that she wrote what is surely one of her most unforgettable stories, "The Story of an Hour." This now-celebrated tale opens with the gingerly care taken by friends and relatives before they proceed to tell Mrs. Louise Mallard about the sudden death of her husband, Brently, in a railroad accident, knowing that she has a heart ailment. The stricken woman "wept at once, with sudden, wild abandonment." Presently, however, she notices that the trees before her house are "all aquiver with new spring life," and by and by "a monstrous joy" comes to possess her:

> She knew that she would weep again when she saw the kind, tender hands folded in death; the face that had never looked save with love upon her, fixed and gray and dead. But she saw beyond that bitter moment a long procession of years to come that would belong to her absolutely. And she opened and spread her arms to them in welcome.
>
> There would be no one to live for her during those coming years; she would live for herself. There would be no powerful will bending her in that blind persistence. . . . "Free! Body and soul free!" she kept whispering.
>
> (*Complete Works* 1:353–354)

At that moment of joyous liberation, however, "some one was opening the front door with a latchkey." Brently Mallard turns out not to have been in the railroad accident at all. But, having avoided one disaster, he has now come home to another. The last paragraph of the story contains only one terse line: "When the doctors came they said she had died of heart disease—of joy that kills."

Chopin herself, of course, had never complained about any "powerful will bending hers in blind persistence," but it is surely significant that this story about the fantasized freedom of a woman should come to her in the flush of her literary success, when the advantages of achieved freedom were so gratifyingly demonstrated in her own person. Her diary entry on 22 May 1894 is equally suggestive:

> How curiously the past effaces itself for me! I sometimes regret that it is so, for there must be a certain pleasure in retrospection. . . . If it were possible for my husband and my mother to come back to earth, I feel that I would unhesitatingly give up every thing that has come into my life since they left it and join my existence again with theirs. To do that, I would have to forget the past ten years of my growth—my real growth. But I would take back a little wisdom with me; it would be the spirit of perfect acquiescence.
>
> (quoted in Seyersted, pp. 58–59)

Modern readers are entitled to be a bit skeptical about "the spirit of perfect acquiescence" that Chopin claimed to feel. But it would be wrong simply to dismiss her fond profession as an empty gesture. If "The Story of an Hour" hauntingly recounts the lethal effects of a husband's return, other stories by her tell of reunions between husbands and wives that are transformative rather than regressive, life-giving rather than life-shattering.

"Athénaïse," an impressive and, for Chopin, an unusually long short story, was completed in April 1895 (just one year after "The Story of an Hour"). It begins with the heroine's return to her parents and her avowed wish never to go back to her husband.

> No, I don't hate him. It's jus' being married that I detes' an' despise. I hate being Mrs. Cazeau, an' would want to be Athénaïse Miché again. I

> can't stan' to live with a man; to have him always there; his coats an' pantaloons hanging in my room; his ugly bare feet—washing them in my tub, befo' my very eyes, ugh!

Cazeau comes and fetches her home, but Athénaïse, with her brother Montéclin as an accomplice, runs away again, this time to New Orleans. There she captivates the heart of Gouvernail, a gentleman who lives in the same boardinghouse (and who remains her principled friend and caretaker). And there, too, she is initiated into the ecstatic knowledge that she is pregnant with Cazeau's child. She returns to him, a changed woman:

> Her husband lifted her out of the buggy, and neither said a word until they stood together within the shelter of the gallery. Even then they did not speak at first. But Athénaïse turned to him with an appealing gesture. As he clasped her in his arms, he felt the yielding of her whole body against him. He felt her lips for the first time respond to the passion of his own.
>
> (*Complete Works,* 1:454)

In the silence between husband and wife, so erotically charged, so literally pregnant with meaning, and so intimately understood by both of them, we see a reunion that is the very antithesis of the one in "The Story of an Hour," which, not inappropriately, is marked by "a piercing cry." "Athénaïse," of course, is a more complicated story than its precursor. It is complicated not only by the hint of incest between Athénaïse and Montéclin—and not only by the prospect of adultery between Athénaïse and Gouvernail—but, above all, by the fact that the story is not just Athénaïse's story, but Cazeau's as well. Cazeau has a voice and a subjectivity of his own—as Brently Mallard most assuredly does not and his pain is both more immediately present and more deeply felt than Athénaïse's petty complaint:

> He knew that he could again compel her return as he had done once before,—compel her to return to the shelter of his roof, compel her cold and unwilling submission to his love and passionate transports; but the loss of self-respect seemed to him too dear a price to pay for a wife. . . . The great sense of loss came from the realization of having missed a chance for happiness,—a chance that would come his way again only through a miracle. He could not think of himself loving any other woman, and could not think of Athénaïse ever—even at some remote date—caring for him.
>
> (*Complete Works* 1:438–439)

Cazeau is not a simple villain, not a typical specimen of the tyrannical husband, because the reader is able to see—because Chopin is determined to make us see—his proud vulnerability, his capacity for sorrow, injury, and despair. Like the husband of "Her Letters," who is charged by his dead wife to destroy, unread, a mysterious package of letters and is driven to suicide by that unbearable mystery, and like the young boy in "A Vocation and a Voice," alternately bewitched and repelled by the bold Suzima, Cazeau exemplifies a kind of male subjectivity that is not at all uncommon in Chopin: one that makes itself felt not only in its dominion but also in its fragility and hurt.

In accommodating that subjectivity—and, more obviously, in the outcome of its plot—"Athénaïse" stands both as a response and as a complement to "The Story of an Hour." Together they illustrate the range of emotional possibilities in Chopin's fiction, its variety of affective experience. It is almost as if, for every dramatic situation, Chopin can develop two equally vital sequences of events and two equally compelling conclusions. Between the two stories we can imagine some kind of implicit dialogue, with Chopin shuttling back and forth between them taking stock of each, bouncing one against the other, and holding both in a perpetual and deliberate mutuality.

Within this context, Chopin's first novel, *At Fault,* would seem to have incorporated, within the compass of a single work, the same double perspectives—the same cross-references and even cross-examinations—that make "The Story of an Hour" and "Athénaïse" joint commentaries. Even without this structural complexity, however, the novel is fascinating enough in its subject matter. It is one of the few late-nineteenth-century American novels about divorce (the other and better-known one being *A Modern Instance* [1882] by William Dean Howells, to whom Chopin sent a copy of her book).

Thérèse Lafirme, a thirty-year-old widow and mistress of a Louisiana plantation, finds herself in love with a newcomer from St. Louis, David Hosmer, but learns, to her dismay, that he has been married and divorced. She makes him go back to his wife, Fanny, a confirmed alcoholic. The remarried David and Fanny now live on Thérèse's plantation, and this high-minded lady has the pleasure of watching the man she loves living in constant and accusatory misery. All is not lost, however. A flood comes along, Fanny is miraculously swept off and drowned, and Thérèse and David are finally free to marry—which they do, in a happy ending that is as shamelessly contrived as any in American literature.

The contrived ending, of course, points to a not-so-artfully concealed and largely unresolved question at the heart of *At Fault*, a question having to do with the boundaries and limits of moral obligation. The importance of such a question, of course, extended well beyond *At Fault*. Indeed, according to social historians such as Thomas Haskell, this was arguably the most pressing question in the nineteenth century, a period characterized not only by rapid social change but also by attendant changes in ideas about causality, connectedness, and responsibility. In *At Fault* such meditations take on a romantic urgency. To what extent is David Hosmer responsible for his alcoholic wife? Having once been married to her, does he have a continual obligation for her welfare? He has the legal freedom, of course, to marry again, but is that the same as moral freedom? And what sort of obligation does Thérèse have? Is she in turn compelled to make David "do the right thing"—insofar as she can interpret that right thing? Or is she "at fault" for having taken on that unnecessary obligation?

The deus ex machina of the flood effectively silences these questions, making them immaterial as well as seemingly gratuitous. And yet, we should not forget that it is these questions which animate the plot in the first place. Chopin's refusal to confront these issues has something to do, of course, with the weightiness of the subject, but it has something to do as well, it would seem, with her commitment to what Willa Cather calls "a flexible, iridescent style," a style resistant not only to the pressures of advocacy but also (to some extent) to the pressures of argument. In *The Awakening* we see the irresistible charm of such a style; in *At Fault* we see something of its cost.

Like Ralph Waldo Emerson, then (who actually figures in *The Awakening*, in the curious detail that, after her husband's departure, "Edna sat in the library after dinner and read Emerson until she grew sleepy"), Chopin herself might be said to have elevated "whim" to a literary virtue. Her work habits confirm this. She customarily wrote at a rapid pace. The idea of a story would come to her almost fully formed, and she would write it down in just that fashion, with no revisions afterward. The whole process would often take no more than a couple of hours. As Chopin herself explained: "I am completely at the mercy of unconscious selection. To such an extent is this true, that what is called the polishing up process has always proved disastrous to my work, and I avoid it, preferring the integrity of crudities to artificialities." Indeed, for her, storytelling was simply "the spontaneous expression of impressions gathered goodness knows where."

In this context, it is useful to consider Chopin's tribute to Guy de Maupassant, a tribute perhaps as unambiguous as she is ever capable of. She had come upon his work rather late in her life. Having once discovered him, however, she not only read him with devotion but also translated some of his stories, including the two significantly called "Solitude" and "Suicide" (now collected in Thomas Bonner, Jr., ed., *The Kate Chopin Companion*). In "Confidences," an autobiographical piece that she wrote at the invitation of the *Atlantic Monthly*, she had this to say about her favorite author:

> I had been in the woods, in the fields, groping around; looking for something big, satisfying, convincing, and finding nothing but—myself; a something neither big nor satisfying but wholly convincing. It was at this period of my emerging from the vast solitude in which I had been making my own acquaintance, that I stumbled upon Maupassant. I read his stories and marvelled at them. Here was life, not fiction; for where were the plots, the old fashioned mechanism and stage trapping that in a vague, unthinking way I had fancied were essential to the art of story making. Here was a man who had escaped from tradition and authority, who had entered into himself and looked out upon life through his own being and with his own eyes; and who, in a direct and simple way, told us what he saw. When a man does this, he gives us the best that he can; something valuable for it is genuine and spontaneous. He gives us his impressions.
>
> (*Complete Works* 2:700–701)

Oddly, what Chopin deems most valuable in Maupassant is something other readers will no doubt find quite trivial, his "impressions." These, according to Chopin, are "the best" that any writer has to offer. They are the opposite of the received, obligatory, and didactic—the opposite, that is, of "tradition and authority"—and, as such, they represent for her the highest literary ideal.

Indeed, Chopin's own work might be read as a collage of impressions. As Michael Gilmore points out, her writings invite comparison with the paintings of the French impressionists because, in their work as well as in hers, "the spontaneous is preferred to the static, the momentary accorded a higher value than the permanent." In both, "shapes tend to lose their solid form as they change and blur in accordance with the shifting position or feelings of the observer."

For Chopin, one of the practical consequences of this impressionist aesthetics is the trope of surprise that concludes so many of her stories. Since things are transitory in her writings—nothing is fixed, irrevocable, or predetermined—the endings, too, come with a certain freedom. They sometimes echo the preceding story and sometimes do not. Like a passing mood or a fitful glance, they embody no unerring logic, only an oblique, perhaps capricious, but in any case unpredicted set of possibilities—as if they were the beginning of a story and not the end. What will Mildred in "A Shameful Affair" say to the man who has so rudely kissed her when she runs into him again? What will Mrs. Baroda (who is "a respectable woman," as the title of the story tells us) say to her husband when he congratulates her on having "overcome" her dislike for the man to whom she is madly attracted? And what sort of last word might we expect in a story like "The Storm," with its explosive and unashamed adultery? In that story, the literal last word turns out to be an improbable one-liner: "So the storm passed and every one was happy." But, speaking less literally, we might also say that there is no last word in Chopin. Light and shadows play in her fiction; moods come and go. Nothing stands still, and everything could have been otherwise.

Selected Bibliography

PRIMARY WORKS

NOVELS

At Fault. St. Louis: Nixon-Jones, 1890.

The Awakening. Chicago: Herbert S. Stone, 1899.

SHORT STORIES

Bayou Folk. Boston: Houghton Mifflin, 1894.

A Night in Acadie. Chicago: Way & Williams, 1897.

COLLECTED WORKS

The Complete Works of Kate Chopin. 2 vols. Edited by Per Seyersted. Baton Rouge: Louisiana State University Press, 1969.

A Kate Chopin Miscellany. Edited by Per Seyersted and Emily Toth. Natchitoches, La.: Northwestern State University Press, 1979.

SECONDARY WORKS

BIOGRAPHICAL AND CRITICAL STUDIES

Allen, Priscilla. "Old Critics and New: The Treatment of Chopin's *The Awakening*." In *The Authority of Experience: Essays in Feminist Criticism*. Edited by Arlyn Diamond and Lee R. Edwards. Amherst: University of Massachusetts Press, 1977.

Arms, George. "Kate Chopin's *The Awakening* in the Perspective of Her Literary Career." In *Essays on American Literature in Honor of Jay B. Hubbell*. Edited by Clarence Gohdes. Durham, N.C.: Duke University Press, 1967.

Arner, Robert. "Kate Chopin." *Louisiana Studies* 14:11–139 (1975).

Bonner, Thomas, Jr., ed. *The Kate Chopin Companion, with Chopin's Translations from French Fiction*. Westport, Conn.: Greenwood Press, 1988.

Cantwell, Robert. "*The Awakening* by Kate Chopin." *Georgia Review* 10:489–494 (1956).

Culley, Margaret. "Edna Pontellier: 'A Solitary Soul.' " In *"The Awakening": A Norton Critical Edition*. Edited by Margaret Culley. New York: W.W. Norton, 1976.

Davidson, Cathy N. "Chopin and Atwood: Woman Drowning, Woman Surfacing." *Kate Chopin Newsletter* 1:6–10 (1975–1976).

Dyer, Joyce. "Kate Chopin's Sleeping Bruties." *Markham Review* 10:10–15 (1980).

———. "Night Images in the Work of Kate Chopin." *American Literary Realism* 14:216–230 (1981).

Eble, Kenneth. "A Forgotten Novel: Kate Chopin's *The Awakening*." *Western Humanities Review* 10:261–269 (1956).

Ewell, Barbara C. *Kate Chopin*. New York: Frederick Ungar, 1986.

Fletcher, Marie. "The Southern Woman in the Fiction of Kate Chopin." *Louisiana History* 7:117–132 (1966).

Flück, Winfried. "Tentative Transgressions: Kate Chopin's Fiction as a Mode of Symbolic Action." *Studies in American Fiction* 10:151–171 (1982).

Fox-Genovese, Elizabeth. "Kate Chopin's Awakening." *Southern Studies* 18:261–290 (1979).

Franklin, Rosemary F. "*The Awakening* and the Failure of Psyche." *American Literature* 56:510–526 (1984).

Gilbert, Sandra M. "The Second Coming of Aphrodite: Kate Chopin's Fantasy of Desire." *Kenyon Review* 5:42–66 (Summer 1983).

Jasenas, Elaine. "The French Influence in Kate Chopin's *The Awakening*." *Nineteenth-Century French Studies* 4:312–322 (1976).

Jones, Anne Goodwyn. "Kate Chopin: The Life Behind the Mask." In *Tomorrow Is Another Day: The Woman Writer in the South, 1859–1936*. Baton Rouge: Louisiana State University Press, 1981.

Jones, Suzanne W. "Place, Perception, and Identity in *The Awakening*." *Southern Quarterly* 25:108–119 (Winter 1987).

Justus, James H. "The Unawakening of Edna Pontellier." *Southern Literary Journal* 10:107–122 (Spring 1978).

Koloski, Bernard, ed. *Approaches to Teaching Chopin's "The Awakening."* New York: Modern Language Association of America, 1988.

Lattin, Patricia Hopkins. "Kate Chopin's Repeating Characters." *Mississippi Quarterly* 33:19–37 (1979–1980).

Leary, Lewis. "Kate Chopin and Walt Whitman." *Walt Whitman Review* 16:120–121 (1970).

Martin, Wendy, ed. *New Essays on "The Awakening."* Cambridge and New York: Cambridge University Press, 1988. Includes Elaine Showalter, "Tradition and the Female Talent: *The Awakening* as a Solitary Book"; Michael T. Gilmore, "Revolt Against Nature: The Problematic Modernism of *The Awakening*"; Andrew Delbanco, "The Half-Life of Edna Pontellier"; and Christina Giorcelli, "Edna's Wisdom: A Transitional and Numinous Merging."

May, John R. "Local Color in *The Awakening*." *Southern Review* 6:1031–1040 (1970).

O'Brien, Sharon. "Sentiment, Local Color, and the New Woman Writer: Kate Chopin and Willa Cather." *Kate Chopin Newsletter* 2:16–24 (1976–1977).

Potter, Richard H. "Kate Chopin and Her Critics: An Annotated Checklist." *Missouri Historical Society Bulletin* 24:306–317 (1970).

Rankin, Daniel S. *Kate Chopin and Her Creole Stories*. Philadelphia: University of Pennsylvania Press, 1932.

Ringe, Donald. "Romantic Imagery in Kate Chopin's *The Awakening*." *American Literature* 43:580–588.

Rocks, James E. "Kate Chopin's Ironic Vision." *Louisiana Review* 1:110–120 (1972).

Rosen, Kenneth M. "Kate's Chopin's *The Awakening:* Ambiguity as Art." *Journal of American Studies* 5:197–199 (1971).

Rosowski, Susan J. "The Novel of Awakening." *Genre* 12:313–332 (1979).

Seyersted, Per. *Kate Chopin: A Critical Biography.* Baton Rouge: Louisiana State University Press, 1969.

Skaggs, Peggy. "Three Tragic Figures in Kate Chopin's *The Awakening.*" *Louisiana Studies* 13:345–364 (1974).

Spangler, George M. "Kate Chopin's *The Awakening:* A Partial Dissent." *Novel* 3:249–255 (1970).

Stange, Margit. "Personal Property: Exchange Value and the Female Self in *The Awakening.*" *Genders* 5:106–119 (1989).

Sullivan, Ruth, and Stewart Smith. "Narrative Stance in Kate Chopin's *The Awakening.*" *Studies in American Fiction* 1:62–75 (1973).

Thornton, Lawrence. "*The Awakening:* A Political Romance." *American Literature* 52:50–66 (1980).

Tompkins, Jane P. "*The Awakening:* An Evaluation." *Feminist Studies* 3:22–29 (1976).

Toth, Emily. "The Independent Woman and 'Free' Love." *Massachusetts Review* 16:647–664 (1975).

———. "Kate Chopin's *The Awakening* as Feminist Criticism." *Louisiana Studies* 15:241–251 (1976).

———. "Timely and Timeless: The Treatment of Time in *The Awakening* and *Sister Carrie.*" *Southern Studies* 16:271–276 (1977).

———. *Kate Chopin: A Solitary Soul.* New York: Atheneum, 1989.

Treichler, Paula A. "The Construction of Ambiguity in *The Awakening:* A Linguistic Analysis." In *Woman and Language in Literature and Society.* Edited by Sally McConnell-Ginet, Ruth Borker, and Nelly Furman. New York: Praeger, 1980.

Walker, Nancy. "Feminist or Naturalist: The Social Context of Kate Chopin's *The Awakening.*" *Southern Quarterly* 17:95–103 (1979).

Wheeler, Otis B. "The Five Awakenings of Edna Pontellier." *Southern Review* 11:118–128 (1975).

Wolff, Cynthia Griffin. "Thanatos and Eros: Kate Chopin's *The Awakening.*" *American Quarterly* 25: 449–471 (1973).

———. "Kate Chopin and the Fiction of Limits: 'Désirée's Baby.' " *Southern Literary Journal* 10:123–133. (Spring 1978).

Yaeger, Patricia S. " 'A Language Which Nobody Understood': Emancipatory Strategies in *The Awakening.*" *Novel* 20:197–219 (1987).

Ziff, Larzer. "An Abyss of Inequality: Sarah Orne Jewett, Mary Wilkins Freeman, Kate Chopin." In *The American 1890s: The Life and Times of a Lost Generation.* New York: Viking Press, 1966.

Zlotnick, Joan. "A Woman's Will: Kate Chopin on Selfhood, Wifehood, and Motherhood." *Markham Review* 3:1–5 (1968).

BIBLIOGRAPHIES

Bonner, Thomas, Jr. "Kate Chopin: An Annotated Bibliography." *Bulletin of Bibliography* 32:101–105 (1975).

Springer, Marlene. *Kate Chopin and Edith Wharton: An Annotated Bibliographical Guide to Secondary Materials.* Boston: G. K. Hall, 1976.

———. "Kate Chopin: A Reference Guide Updated." *Resources for American Literary Study* 11:280–303 (1981).

WAI-CHEE DIMOCK

EMILY DICKINSON

1830–1886

EMILY DICKINSON IS at once the most intimate of poets, and the most guarded. The most self-sufficient, and the neediest. The proudest, and the most vulnerable. These contradictions, which we as her readers encounter repeatedly in her poems, are understandable, not paradoxical, for they result from the tension between the life to which she was born and the one to which she aspired. Language was where she both expressed this tension and sought to mediate it, using words to create her own identity. Language was Dickinson's salvation and her surrogate, as it gave her a place in which to come alive and a way in which to encounter the world outside her self. Language was undoubtedly power for Emily Dickinson; but it was not, nor could it be, *everything.* A life invented in words is real, but it lives only in the imaginations of the one who writes it and those who read it into existence.

Emily Dickinson's greatness, as both poet and person (for they are inexorably linked), has to do with the creation of such a life—a life of purpose, authority, and achievement—in the teeth of everything that her culture put in her way to deny it to her. Her significance has to do with the creation of 1,775 poems—brilliant, extraordinary, endlessly rewarding poems—that represent her life, there to be read by that same world. Emily Dickinson's misfortune is that her words were used as a substitute, not a supplement, for another sort of life, one for which she always yearned even as she protected herself from it: that of personal closeness, literal intimacy. Not sex so much as love. Neither of these statements cancels out the other. Taken together, they tell us something about who Dickinson was and what she means to us.

Dickinson's construction of a self was particularly focused on issues connected with power, authority, and control. In fact, we could say that for Dickinson, identity was consistent with authority, to the extent that having a self meant being able to define, to interpret, to construct meaning. The most fundamental way in which she understood gender identity as an aspect of the self, and the difference that it confers in all social relationships, was that being male equaled possession of this authority, and being female equaled its lack. Consequently, her own intelligence, articulateness, and ambition presented a difficulty regarding identity, since these qualities signified "male," not "female," in the culture into which she was born.

Dickinson's attempts to create herself, therefore, have to do with finding a way to be a woman who has authority and authenticity in relation to all that is external to her: the world. Someone who can define it, know it. But there are grounds for much conflict and ambiguity in this ambition. On the one hand, Dickinson finds herself attracted to those already in possession of that power: to strong male figures like fathers, husbands, judges, generals, editors, clergymen, and, of course, God. Their love and admiration would give her power by proxy, or so a part of her (a part she has in common with many women, both before and since) believes. On the other hand, she understands full well that their power negates and denies her own. She can have no separate identity if she gives herself over to them. And so she struggles to make a new space for herself. That struggle usually results in denying them access: keeping herself inviolate.

But the self needs something more than authority, which constitutes a form of control over experience. It needs as well the connection to experience: relationship, on all levels of existence. As a woman trained from birth to value connection rather than separation, a woman who was, however, denied that most basic connection of all—the nurture of a mother who loves her for being exactly who she is (in this case, an intelligent, articulate, ambitious female)—Dickinson sought this kind of fulfillment as well. She sought it repeatedly and hungrily all her life, even while it was at odds with her battle for control. These two apparently contradictory impulses determined the kind of self she would create, one neither traditionally "female" nor traditionally "male." Unlike a traditional woman, she did not marry, bear children, or satisfy affiliative needs in the social world of her community. Unlike a traditional man, she did not seek or achieve power over others in the public world of professional enterprise. Instead she sought to create herself, in private, as a writer whose words would reach out for her and do the deeds she yearned to do, deeds that included both taking charge of experience and connecting herself to it: belonging.

Language was Dickinson's means for accomplishing these ends. In 1,775 poems, as well as in the letters she sent with unflagging energy to the people she wanted for her own, she defined herself and her world. Endlessly exploring the meaning of emotional, intellectual, and spiritual existence, she found words that would bring into being what she thought, saw, and knew. Hers is a language that not only tells but also invites, so that we cannot understand its meanings unless we participate in it. Join her, in other words, where she herself is: located in this very space of words. The features of Dickinson's distinctive language—its startling metaphors and images, its strange ambiguities and missing parts (deletions both recoverable and not), its singular precision and eager haste, its general applicability and peculiar idiosyncrasy, the chances it takes with syntax and diction that are so pronounced and so characteristically her own—all work to accomplish these ends. These are poems that alert us to the presence of an intelligence and a passion unsurpassed in literature, poems that cause us, in turn, to feel intensely for the person who comes alive in them. And these are poems that tease us, escape us, distance us from that person, that consciousness, both frustrating and challenging us. In its complexity, richness, and volatility, Dickinson's language creates her poetry and her self.

Emily Elizabeth Dickinson was born on 10 December 1830, the middle child of Emily Norcross Dickinson and Edward Dickinson. Her older brother, Austin, was born in 1829; her younger sister, Lavinia (Vinnie), in 1833. Hers was one of the leading families in Amherst, Massachusetts. Her father was a prominent lawyer and the treasurer of Amherst College, which her grandfather, Samuel Fowler Dickinson, had been instrumental in founding. Her mother, as was customary, centered her world on her devotion to husband and children.

It is not surprising that Dickinson first recognized the patriarchal power to which she was so drawn in her strong-willed father, and that she extrapolated from this relationship the one in which she would find herself over and over again with other men, with God, and with all institutionalized authority. "His heart was pure and terrible, and I think no other like it exists," she sums him up in a letter to Thomas Wentworth Higginson. Both her father's absolute power over the household and his aloofness contributed to her attraction: "Father, too busy with his Briefs—to notice what we do." Along with the appeal, however, comes a spirit of rebellion that is, significantly, couched in terms of language, writing, and books "My father only reads on Sunday—he reads *lonely & rigorous* books." "He buys me many Books—But begs me not to read them—because he fears they joggle the Mind." "We do not have much poetry, father having made up his mind that its pretty much all *real life.* Fathers real life and *mine* sometimes come into collision, but as yet, escape unhurt!"

Language is associated with her father, not her mother, a woman who "does not care for thought," as Dickinson predates the Lacanian notion of language as "Name-of-the-Father": the form in which culture reifies itself. But at the same time, she sees language as something she can wrest from him and revise to suit herself. If Father is real life, Emily is poetry. She could not be a lawyer to get him to take notice; but she could, she thought, be a writer.

Dickinson's relations with other men in her life were similar to the one with her father: a tense combination of adoration and competition. With Higginson, the editor to whom she sent her poems for criticism (and recognition), she is at once obsequious and proud. "Would you have time to be the 'friend' you should think I need? I have a little shape—it would not crowd your Desk—nor make much Racket as the Mouse, the dents your Galleries." However, when her requests for "improvement" are met with suggestions that are well meant but all-too-conservative, she simply refrains from following his directives: "You say I confess the little mistake, and omit the large." In a series of love letters to a mysterious person addressed as "Master," she is at her most subservient. "Master—open your life wide, and take me in forever, I will never be tired—I will never be noisy when you want to be still. I will be your best little girl—nobody else will see me, but you—but that is enough—I shall not want any more." At the same time, she challenges the way he abuses the power he possesses by virtue of his gender: "If I had the Beard on my cheek—like you—and you—had Daisy's petals—and you cared so for me—what would become of you? Could you forgive me in fight, or flight—or the foreign land?" For Dickinson, love for men, on patriarchal terms, always brought suffering and loss, but it also occasioned her attempts to renegotiate those terms so that she might acquire some of the power, and with it, the love.

In her weakness and inarticulateness, Emily Norcross Dickinson could not be a model of authority for her daughter. But the need and blame that Dickinson directed at her mother were for something else entirely: for the love and nurture that her mother, she believed, never gave her. "I never had a mother. I suppose a mother is one to whom you hurry when you are troubled," she told Higginson. "I always ran home to Awe when a child, if anything befell me. He was an awful Mother, but I liked him better than none." Instead of a real mother, she depicts herself with the abstract idea of a parent who is gendered male—that is, a father—with qualities of grandeur but not of care. In the place of Mother there is nothing, a gap or hole.

Later in her life Dickinson described the reconciliation that came while she nursed Mrs. Dickinson through her final illness. "We were never intimate Mother and Children while she was our Mother—but Mines in the same Ground meet by tunneling and when she became our Child, the Affection came." The daughter can become close to her mother by reversing their roles, but when the never-nurtured child becomes "Mother," it is her authority, not her dependence and vulnerability, that gives her access to a situation of care. This does not replace the missing mothering, and it is clear from Dickinson's letters and poems that her yearning for the unconditional love of the mother-child relationship remained powerful throughout her life: "Could you tell me what home is?"

Dickinson's friendships with women, especially with Susan Gilbert, who later became her brother's wife, are characterized by her demand for such love. Against the trajectory of their lives away from Amherst, as they moved toward schooling (and sometimes work), courtship, and marriage, she sought to hold them and keep them in the bonds of her affection—to remain the most important, the most desirable one. That it was a losing battle only increased the deep and dreaded sense of loss that love always provoked in her. These words to

Susan are echoed over and over in her letters and poems to women:

> I need you more and more, and the great world grows wider, and dear ones fewer and fewer, and every day that you stay away—I miss my biggest heart; my own goes wandering round, and calls for Susie—Friends are too dear to sunder, Oh they are far too few, and how soon they will go away where you and I cannot find them, *dont* let us forget these things.
>
> (Letter 94, 11 June 1852, *Letters*, vol. 1, p. 211)

With female friends Dickinson seems to have been acting over and over the drama of her relationship with her mother: asking for and never getting the support and recognition of being first and always in the affection of a warm and loving woman.

Some women, however, did serve as models for Dickinson, women she identified with the power of language if not with the comfort of unconditional love. Dickinson was a great reader, and among her favorite writers the Englishwomen Elizabeth Barrett Browning, the Brontës, and George Eliot stand out. "What do I think of *Middlemarch?*" she wrote, "What do I think of glory—except that in a few instances 'this mortal has already put on immortality.' George Eliot is one." Dickinson idolized these "women, now, queens, now," as her frequent tributes to them attest; and that intense appreciation and affection had much to do with the way in which each represented a self defined in relation to language. "The look of the words as they lay in the print I shall never forget" is how she memorialized George Eliot. These are women who prove that a life in literature is possible. They are not traditional women like her mother; instead they represent a power and significance toward which she herself strives. Her relationship with them is important and compelling, for it is a connection created entirely in the imagination and by means of language, the kind of connection that she will try to establish for herself with other people.

From 1840 to 1847 Dickinson attended Amherst Academy, where she received an education as demanding as that of many colleges today. Amherst Academy was closely connected with Amherst College; many of its teachers were professors at the college, and students of the academy often attended lectures there. Dickinson studied languages, philosophy, and science. Under the aegis of Edward Hitchcock, professor of geology and moral theology, she received a thorough grounding not only in the most modern scientific thought of the day but also in its direct connection with religion, for Hitchcock believed that truth in every branch of learning manifested God's nature and will as revealed in the Bible. He encouraged revivals, as did Mary Lyons, the founder of Mount Holyoke Female Seminary in nearby South Hadley, which Dickinson attended for two terms, for moral instruction and secular learning were not viewed as separate categories.

Dickinson, however, found herself incapable of the commitment to Christ that her friends and family were making. Although conversion was necessary in order to become an "established Christian," she never did make a profession of faith. Her strong religious interest took the form, rather, of constant challenges to a patriarchal God whom she could believe in but never obey. In her poetry she contends with God and what he stands for, seeking a space for her independent identity and inquiry: "The name They dropped upon my face / With water, in the country church / Is finished using, now" (Poem 508). Dickinson's many poems about the issues that concerned the most dedicated theologians—from the purpose and role of faith to the existence of immortality—endlessly tease received doctrine to see what truths it might hold or conceal, and what different or "slant" truths might be wrested from it.

With the exception of three trips to Boston (in 1851, 1863, and 1864) and a visit to Washington, D.C., with stops in Baltimore and Philadelphia (in 1855), Dickinson never left Amherst and its environs. Her life was centered on her home and family—father, mother, and sister,

Vinnie, who also never married. Vinnie served as Emily's practical and loyal helpmeet, taking the largest responsibility for household affairs. (Dickinson gardened and baked—"people must have puddings"—and wrote, though few realized it, many poems.) Her adored brother, Austin, a lawyer like his father, settled next door with his wife, Susan.

Dickinson's status as a recluse—"I do not cross my Father's ground to any House or town"—was gradual but effective. Seeing fewer and fewer people within the confines of her own home except her immediate family, eliminating the wider world of visits, church, and social events, gave her in their stead an intense and resonant private life. In her relationships with only those with whom she was truly intimate, in her richly mined relationship with her own mind and soul, Dickinson explored with both passion and discipline the emotional, psychological, and spiritual facets of existence lived at its most fervent. Her extreme privacy was at once protective and liberating. It gave her control over her experience, especially beneficial to someone so sensitive to every nuance of every event, and it freed her to experiment with and invent that existence along lines that would not have been possible in a more public arena. It gave her the time and the opportunity to write: to find the words that could express a self at odds with the culture that had bred her.

Aside from her immediate family, Dickinson developed friendships of an ardent nature with people with whom she did not as a rule come into personal contact. Instead, she used letters both to create these relationships and to regulate them. She corresponded with girlhood friends like Abiah Root Strong and Kate Turner Anthon; relatives like her cousin Lavinia Norcross and her daughters, Louise and Frances; and friends from public life—the editor and writer Josiah Gilbert Holland and his wife, Elizabeth; the editor Thomas Wentworth Higginson; the writer Helen Hunt Jackson; the editor Samuel Bowles and his wife, Mary; the Reverend Charles Wadsworth; and Judge Otis Lord. She also engaged in extensive correspondence with her brother, Austin, before he settled in Amherst, and with her sister-in-law, Susan, both before she married Austin and even after she lived in the house next door. Her attachment to all of these people was strong, and she loved many of them, women and men, romantically and fervently. Bowles, Wadsworth, and Lord, as well as Susan Gilbert and Kate Anthon, have been proposed by one or another advocate as Dickinson's lovers. Lovers they clearly were, but these relationships probably did not extend to any sort of physical consummation. Both from preference and from situation, Dickinson kept her erotics in the mind and on the page. When Judge Lord actually proposed marriage to Dickinson after the death of his wife, she refused him: "Dont you know that 'No' is the wildest word we consign to Language?"

In language Dickinson sought and often won the affection of people who became the recipients of her words for all occasions—words as pungent, precise, cryptic, and seductive as her poems. Dickinson's letters are in fact very like her poems, their elliptical phrasing and excessive figuration growing more and more condensed over the years, their hymn rhythms forming sentences that, punctuated by dashes, are prose only insofar as they are not divided into verse lines. (Because she both enclosed poems with and appended poems to her letters, it is easy to understand why editors have always had trouble determining exactly which parts of the letters are prose and which are poetry.) Not only do her letters look like her poems, but they function like her poems, those "letter[s] to the World": they create herself to the audience she is imagining, they engage that audience with all the attractiveness of her wit and wisdom (as well as the lure of her need), and they draw that audience into intimacy, to the best of her ability.

Although her family and friends knew that Dickinson wrote poetry, no one had any idea of the extent of her writing. Ten of her poems appeared in print during her lifetime, but the poet who sought out Higginson to tell her if her poems were "alive," to teach her "how to grow," ultimately did not try for, and even refused, publication, it was "so foul a thing" (Poem 709). There is a real contradiction between her statement that "Publication—is the Auction / of the Mind of Man" (Poem 709) and her concern to "find the rare Ear / not too dull" (Poem 842). Higginson's conservative response to her work and the editing of the few published poems to fit conventional standards must have affected the poet who resolutely hung on to her own language, no matter how "wayward." If it were necessary for the fox to fit the hound, as she put it in Poem 842, this hound soon discovered that there were not that many foxes to be found.

After Dickinson died of Bright's disease on 15 May 1886, her sister discovered hundreds of poems in her desk drawers, many of them carefully copied and sewn together into small booklets, or fascicles. Others were less systematically organized, written on scraps of paper, the backs of recipes—on anything, it seems, that had been at hand. Although Dickinson had stipulated that her letters and papers be burned after her death, Vinnie decided that the poems were exempt from this mandate. Subsequently she made it her business and her life's goal to have them published. The history of the publication of Dickinson's poetry is worth an essay in itself, for it is the story of a war between women that continued, through their daughters, well into the twentieth century.

When Susan Dickinson turned down Vinnie's request for help, Vinnie approached Mabel Loomis Todd, the wife of David Peck Todd, an astronomer at Amherst College. Mabel Todd was a woman of literary aspirations whose longstanding love affair with Austin Dickinson was an ill-kept Amherst secret. In turn, Mrs. Todd enlisted the aid of Higginson. The project, which involved transcribing the poems from Dickinson's difficult handwriting, along with making editorial decisions about punctuation, line arrangement, and even word choice (for Dickinson preferred to provide alternatives for words and phrases), took several years. *Poems by Emily Dickinson* was published in 1890. Thereafter, for over fifty years, subsequent volumes of poems and then letters were published not only by Mrs. Todd and Higginson and Mrs. Todd's daughter, Millicent Todd Bingham, but also by Susan Dickinson's daughter Martha Dickinson Bianchi, for Susan had in her possession hundreds of poems and letters that she would never relinquish to Vinnie. In this way the women who were her heirs competed to present *their* Emily Dickinson to the world that she had coveted as much as avoided.

In 1955 the scholar Thomas H. Johnson published, in approximately chronological order, a complete edition of Dickinson's poems that seeks to replicate, at last, the form in which they were originally written. Johnson also published the collected letters in 1958. In 1981 R. W. Franklin published *The Manuscript Books of Emily Dickinson,* a manuscript edition that arranges the poems in fascicle order. Today even greater attention is being paid to the manuscripts, the form in which Dickinson achieved her particular version of "self-publication."

To read in the volume that contains Dickinson's 1,775 poems is to be constantly delighted and surprised. There is no way to remember each and every poem. Rather, every reader finds the ones that speak most powerfully to her one day, one year—and often an entirely different set that speak in similar personal and enlightening terms at the next reading. In this essay a few of the many poems have been selected for discussion in some detail because the close look that follows the original response is what is most rewarding about reading Dickinson. On closer reading the poems become more, not less, complicated; but in that complexity lies the richness of Dickinson. A Dickinson poem cannot be skimmed: it must be entered, and the reader must be prepared for an extended visit. Yet no one poem determines or summarizes the poet's position about anything. Rather, the poems approach and surround a theme like points on a circle, a circumference, offering complements and alternatives. Reference to other poems demonstrates how singularity is embedded in the content that the rest of the poems comprise. The poems chosen here show Dickinson in relation first to another person; then to the world outside her, to nature; and then, of course, to us, her readers, a relationship created through our own interactions with the words with which she engages us.

Dickinson characteristically understands love as a relationship about power. As the lover she is often all too ready to find that power in the one she loves:

> You constituted Time—
> I deemed Eternity
> A Revelation of Yourself—
> 'Twas therefore Diety
>
> The Absolute—removed
> The Relative away—
> That I unto Himself adjust
> My slow idolatry—
> (Poem 765)

This poem is addressed to an unidentified "You," conceived of as so all-encompassingly powerful that everything else becomes an aspect of him. As Time can be understood as the force in which all existence operates, the space in which everything exists, so the "You" can be understood as "constituting" time. Eternity and even God are a part of time; thus they are included within this person, the poetic conceit maintains. Such power becomes the idea of power itself, its absolute, and everything else is therefore relative to it and accordingly less significant. The "You" turns into "Himself" by the end of the poem, the capital *H* that is usually reserved for God now allotted to the one to whom love has given the superior or, rather, the ultimate power. In a case such as this, "love" constitutes "idolatry," as even the lover understands. Many of Dickinson's poems express this attitude, which, as it offers the most hyperbolic of compliments to the beloved, may be understood as a form of courtship. Subsuming her identity in his is flattery in accordance with cultural conventions. He is the absolute to her tiny relative: "Least Rivers—docile to some sea. / My Caspian—thee" (Poem 212).

The docility is not, however, the whole story. For Dickinson cannot give up her identity, however much she thinks she ought to or says she will. The very act of saying so in a carefully structured poem attests to the energy of a self-consciousness that undermines the willingness to lose it. Many of her poems are about the struggle to maintain that identity at all costs:

> It might be lonelier
> Without the Loneliness—
> I'm so accustomed to my Fate—
> Perhaps the Other—Peace—
>
> Would interrupt the Dark—
> And crowd the little Room—
> Too scant—by Cubits—to contain
> The Sacrament—of Him—
>
> I am not used to Hope—
> It might intrude upon—
> Its sweet parade—blaspheme the place—
> Ordained to Suffering—
>
> It might be easier
> To fail—with Land in Sight—
> Than gain—My Blue Peninsula—
> To perish—of Delight—
> (Poem 405)

"The Sacrament of Him" could be a reference to God, so that this poem, with its vocabulary of "blaspheme" and "ordained," could be read as addressing the speaker's struggle with religious authority. Or it could be, as in Poem 765, about her relationship with a person she has deified, out of love. The point is that these relationships are profoundly similar, so that Dickinson's "religious poems" and her "love poems" not only overlap but also are variations on the same theme. Reading this one as a love poem or, rather, an anti-love poem, does not annul our awareness of its other connotations.

The contrast between "lonelier" and "loneliness" with which this poem begins turns out to be a contrast between "delight" and "loneliness," or psychic death versus psychic life. Self-appointed loneliness, the self alone, or solitude is not as *lonely* as the closeness of relationship, that delight—for one can die of the latter. The poem is about the unraveling of this paradox, for paradox it is, antisocial and antitraditional: that a person would choose solitude over relationship, especially when that person happens to be a woman. In a succession of parallel images that accumulate to explain, describe, and expand the opening statement (Dickinson's poems tend to develop not chronologically or narratively, but according to a principle of accrual, like snowballs rolling through the snow, growing fatter and denser), the poem defines the meaning of both "loneliness" and "lonelier."

Loneliness is "my Fate," "the Dark," "the little Room," and "the place—Ordained to Suffering." If loneliness is a mental condition, it is imaged as a physical space: a tiny room in which this soul is living. Lonelier, on the other hand, is equivalent to "the Other," "Peace," "The Sacrament—of Him," "Hope," and a "sweet parade." For the first three stanzas of the poem the contrast seems to be between something attractive and appealing—peace, hope, and sweet parade—and something restricting, constricted, and negative—dark, scant, and suffering.

However, as we look more closely, especially at the verbs of the poem, the action as it is being imagined (for the whole poem is set in the subjunctive mood, as a hypothetical or imaginary event), we get a different sense of the contrast. "Interrupt," "crowd," "intrude," and "blaspheme": we understand that something is happening in the little room, something valued by its occupant, no matter the pain of it; that, in fact, the pain is a part of its significance. If an other—bigger, grander, more powerful—entered, it would suck the life of the little room away. The second stanza shows this happening in physical terms, as he takes up all the air in her small space. The phrase "interrupt the Dark" changes "Dark" from a condition into an activity: in the dark, we assume, something is going on. The third stanza shifts to an emotional plane. Hope is out of place in the emotional environment of suffering. Now we understand that a challenge is being mounted between his sanctity and *hers,* for his sacrament turns into blasphemy when encountering her "ordination." The religious vocabulary heightens the sense of spiritual significance in these choices. It is this contrast of identities that prepares us for the startling final stanza.

Suddenly, the image pattern shifts. We are out of the little room—suffocatingly small or liberatingly private, as we choose to think of it—and in the world, on the seashore. The change in locale is disconcerting, even confusing. In what way is the small room of the soul equivalent to the outside world? Yet there is clearly parallelism with the opening stanza: "It might be lonelier" and "It might be easier." The stanzas stand back to back, like bookends buttressing the rest of the poem, balancing one another. But how?

One way to read the stanza is to say that if his presence would be lonelier than the loneliness of her solitude, lonelier in that she would be cut off from her self, then by the same token, "failure" might be preferable to "gain," or success. Success is winning him, the "Blue Peninsula" that is contrasted to "Land in Sight," the beckoning, faraway, beautiful promontory out there on the horizon, as contrasted with what is known and close by. The blue peninsula is equivalent, as well, to delight; and delight resonates with all the other words of pleasure that have accumulated during the poem, like "peace" and "hope."

Gaining delight means, however, death: death by drowning. Pleasure is frequently aquatic in Dickinson's canon. "Rowing in Eden— / Ah, the Sea!" begins the last stanza of one of her best-known love poems (Poem 249); but we remember the Caspian Sea of Poem 212 that will consume a small river, an image that recurs in these lines: "The Drop, that wrestles in the Sea— / Forgets her own locality— / As I— toward Thee" (Poem 284).

Clearly delight is *dangerous.* Why, then, is its opposite, failing with land in sight, such a failure? It is failure in exactly the same terms that solitude is deemed loneliness: because society says so. Why would a woman give up the sacrament of him, that romantic and exciting blue peninsula? Giving him up is failure in societal terms. But the poem has taken great pains to show us why there is danger in this kind of love. Thus, the so-called failure is really success, because it is keeping her—her own self—alive.

On the other hand, the ambiguity in the imagery as well as the parallel structure of this stanza and its indeterminate dashes make it possible to read it, and therefore the rest of the poem, differently. "Easier to fail": there is so much fear, timidity, and even masochism in this poem. The speaker could easily be accused of cowardice and a failure of nerve, of wanting to keep things safe and small, and of being hopeless, afraid to confront the marvelous totality of "perishing" of delight. If the final stanza opposes "fail" to "gain," why shouldn't we take it literally? She starts out on her quest for the blue peninsula, but she can't reach it. She drowns before, not when, she gets there. Her life in the little room is the living death; "the Sacrament of Him," a salvation that she will not, cannot accept.

Although the first reading is the more attractive, the second one is altogether possible— not only because there are readers who cannot understand the need to save the self from greater powers, who cannot imagine any felicity to life in a tiny, dark room ordained to suffering, but also because the language itself, in significant moments, is ambiguous. The last stanza, in particular, can be read as accepting cultural norms or as challenging them. Which is right? Maybe both are. That is, if both readings are based on what is *there,* then what is there is Dickinson's tension around these very issues and her need to say it both ways, at the same time. This not only protects her rebellion but also contains it in the same layers of social conformity that surround her own private life in her own private room in Amherst. The doubleness ought not be overlooked or simplified. It is an aspect of Dickinson's language, as it is an aspect of her self.

Interpersonal relationships are one arena for the encounter with authority and culturally designated power. Encounter with the external world is but another version of it. In Dickinson's struggle for the power to grant meaning to experience, language again becomes the agent and the answer. The world may have a name for it, but language is infinitely flexible; as poet, she can name it differently. She can especially do so with metaphor and figurative language, which counters the literal, the norm, with words that tell lies in order to come closer to the truth—the emotional as well as the analytic, subjective as well as objective components of experience:

> They called me to the Window, for
> " 'Twas Sunset"—Some one said—
> I only saw a Sapphire Farm—
> And just a Single Herd—
>
> Of Opal Cattle—feeding far
> Upon so vain a Hill—
> As even while I looked—dissolved—
> Nor Cattle were—nor Soil—
>
> But in their stead—a Sea—displayed—
> And Ships—of such a size
> As Crew of Mountains—could afford—
> And Decks—to seat the skies—
>
> This—too—the Showman rubbed away—
> And when I looked again—
> Nor Farm—nor Opal Herd—was there—
> Nor Mediterranean—
>
> (Poem 628)

This whimsical treatise on the meaning of the word "sunset" is not a particularly complex poem, so it is a good way to begin our look at Dickinson's nature poems. Culture's word "sunset" does not suffice, in this speaker's opinion, for her experience. It is abstract and general, while the event is particular, synesthetic, and dynamic. Against abstraction she poses metaphor, bringing out her words with a flourish, showing off her skill at creating meaning. A sapphire farm, a herd of opal cattle grazing—the image is simple but spectacular, as colors and shapes take on recognizable identities that exist in the imagination. Soon this vision dissolves into another: an enormous sea, sailed by ships so immense that mountains serve for crew and skies for passengers. This is one way to incarnate verbally the feeling of grandeur we get from the evening sky: its colors, shapes, and movement.

However, this poem concludes with a reminder not of her own power but of the struggle that underlies it. For her verbal performance is suddenly outclassed by another, that of the "Showman" who rubs away her farm and cows and seas like a teacher erasing a student's efforts on the blackboard. *He* is in control, not she. She may have named the shapes, but he put them there—and he can take them away. Yes, this is a clever way for her poem to announce the coming of night, the end of sunset's fireworks display, but her words reveal her awareness of an antagonist other than ordinary language. Is the Showman God? Nature? The poem does not say. But it does show how, for Dickinson, the quest for authority informs even her most "universal" or "humanistic" poems—the nature poems. As they seek to define external phenomena (so many of her poems begin with a definition, like "Presentiment—is that long Shadow—on the Lawn" [Poem 764]), they often send up the brilliance of her own flamboyant imagery in the context, the teeth of, another power that got there first and is supposed to take precedence:

The name—of it—is "Autumn"—
The hue—of it—is Blood—
An Artery—upon the Hill—
A Vein—along the Road—

Great Globules—in the Alleys—
And Oh, the Shower of Stain—
When Winds—upset the Basin—
And spill the Scarlet Rain—

It sprinkles Bonnets—far below—
It gathers ruddy Pools—
Then—eddies like a Rose—away—
Upon Vermilion Wheels—
(Poem 656)

Such a tour de force is this definition of "Autumn," which, as does Poem 628, offers metaphor, a growing crescendo of it, in place of the abstract term. Dickinson replaces "Autumn" with "Blood" to invoke the feeling of the season, and blood starts her on a series of synesthetic associations that result in a macabre landscape where the inside of a body is splayed upon the New England hills and roads. Blood is color (red) and it is substance (wet). In veins and arteries blood begins to turn into rain and stain, a storm that inundates the world with brilliance and death and then departs, like a great red wheel of a flower, for roses are also red. Dickinson's rendition of the seasonal confrontation between life and death is like a painting by Van Gogh, a swirling palette of intensity that reveals not only the potency of the season but also her own somewhat histrionic skill. Some people have a terrible time with this poem, as the images overlap one another in a way that is as illogical as it is startling and disturbing. However, what Dickinson demonstrates here is that emotion is not particularly reasonable or logical, and that there is an autumn which we feel within as well as the one in the weather report. Nonetheless, what she is also doing in this poem is showing off, pitting her skill against the Showman's:

I send Two Sunsets—
Day and I—in competition ran—
I finished Two—and several Stars—
While He—was making One—

His own ampler—but as I
Was saying to a friend—
Mine—is the more convenient
To Carry in the Hand—
(Poem 308)

Here Dickinson's subjects are her "competition" with the Showman and, because they are integrally associated, the power of poetry. However, this little poem manifests a different spirit and a different resolution from the other nature poems discussed here: a concern for connection and belonging rather than for control. It is so charming because, while admitting to the presence and power of a force outside her, here identified as "Day," it allows for different but equal authority. Reality need not be either/or; it can be relational. Day's sunsets are real enough, but so are hers, created in the words of her poem, exactly as we have watched her do in Poem 628. His are ampler, true; but hers are convenient. The *comfort* of relationship is at the heart of this valorization of relative experience—not only the poet's with nature but also the poet's with her reader.

"I send two sunsets," her poem begins: sunsets we can hold in the hand, sunsets that come to life only in the relationship between her words and our reading them. From her hand to ours: the imagery of touch is poignant. Perhaps day is that much less of an antagonist here because the reader is that much more acknowledged. When the poet sends her words, and we hold them, so convenient, in our hand, the poet is aware of the electricity and the care produced by her words as they form a conduit between us. In this poem the words function less as protection or as challenge than as bridge. They validate connection rather than conquest, so that the poem actually revises the word "competition," with which it began to establish a different manner of relating, more "maternal" in its spirit than "paternal." This is not physical touch, but the words come close to it:

Good to hide, and hear 'em hunt!
Better, to be found,
If one care to, that is,
The Fox fits the Hound—
Good to know, and not tell,
Best, to know and tell,
Can one find the rare Ear
Not too dull—
(Poem 842)

This is a quintessential Dickinson poem, as it refers to her relationship with others. The Dickinson who hides and hears them hunt, knows and does not tell, is the person in the little room too scant by cubits; the person who has to cut herself off and protect herself from a hound that does not fit, that seeks out the fox to *kill* it. Solitude is good because it gives power as well as life to the self, inasmuch as it provides a space that may be literally small but is nonetheless conceptually large: the space of the imagination, where words and poems can come into being. But solitude is a response to the problem of a world that would negate the existence of one self for the authority of another, all in the name of love.

"Best, to know *and* tell" (italics added). This would be possible if there were another, less like a father and more like a mother, who would "fit" and therefore be able to hear the words, to recognize and understand. If no one like that comes along—a mother, a friend, a lover, an editor, a reader—well, one can get along without her or him. "If one cares to, that is." This vulnerability can be controlled. There is self-protection and self-defense: words can be veil as well as window. But words can be an invitation as well as a barricade. A rare ear: this poem does not give up the hope and the search, even as Emily Dickinson probably never did.

It is telling that the other is imaged here as an ear and in the sunset poem as a hand: a hand to hold the poems, an ear to hear the words. Only through language could the connection be made. Dickinson did not count on there being a real person, in the flesh, in the room. In this way the pressures of her culture in all its manifestations—from a father who could not admire her for who she was, and a mother who could not love her for who she was, to editors who did not want her words the way she wrote them, to a society that did not want her alone in the room and writing—hurt her irrevocably. But by the same token, those pressures brought out the best in her, the genius in her—her ability to defend and to fight for her right to have a self and to send it forth into the world for posterity. "If fame belonged to me, I could not escape her," she told Higginson when he advised her not to publish. To take the language, the words for reifying normative values and behavior, and turn them into a vision of the world and a vision of herself—that was something. If today the best we can give her is an ear, many ears, that, too, is something: something remarkable, to be with her in this way.

Selected Bibliography

PRIMARY WORKS

POETRY

Poems of Emily Dickinson. Edited by Thomas H. Johnson. 3 vols. Cambridge, Mass.: Harvard University Press, 1955. Variorum edition.

The Complete Poems of Emily Dickinson. Edited by Thomas H. Johnson. Boston: Little, Brown, 1957.

The Manuscript Books of Emily Dickinson. Edited by R. W. Franklin. 2 vols. Cambridge, Mass.: Harvard University Press, 1981.

LETTERS

The Letters of Emily Dickinson. Edited by Thomas H. Johnson. 3 vols. Cambridge, Mass.: Harvard University Press, 1958.

The Master Letters of Emily Dickinson. Edited by R. W. Franklin. Amherst, Mass.: Amherst College Press, 1986.

SECONDARY WORKS

BIOGRAPHICAL AND CRITICAL STUDIES

Anderson, Charles R. *Emily Dickinson's Poetry: Stairway of Surprise.* New York: Holt, Rinehart, and Winston, 1960.

Benfrey, Christopher E. G. *Emily Dickinson and the Problem of Others.* Amherst: University of Massachusetts Press, 1985.

Bianchi, Martha Dickinson. *Emily Dickinson Face to Face: Unpublished Letters with Notes and Reminiscences.* Boston: Houghton Mifflin, 1932.

Bingham, Millicent Todd. *Ancestors' Brocades: The Literary Discovery of Emily Dickinson.* New York: Harper, 1945.

Cody, John. *After Great Pain: The Inner Life of Emily Dickinson.* Cambridge, Mass.: Harvard University Press, 1971.

Diehl, Joanne Feit. *Dickinson and the Romantic Imagination.* Princeton: Princeton University Press, 1981.

Eberwein, Jane. *Dickinson: Strategies of Limitation.* Amherst: University of Massachusetts Press, 1985.

Frankling, R. W. *The Editing of Emily Dickinson.* Madison: University of Wisconsin Press, 1967.

Gelpi, Albert J. *Emily Dickinson: The Mind of the Poet.* Cambridge, Mass.: Harvard University Press, 1965.

Juhasz, Suzanne. *The Undiscovered Continent: Emily Dickinson and the Space of the Mind.* Bloomington: Indiana University Press, 1983.

Johnson, Thomas H. *Emily Dickinson: An Interpretative Biography.* Cambridge, Mass.: Harvard University Press, 1955.

Keller, Karl. *The Only Kangaroo Among the Beauty: Emily Dickinson and America.* Baltimore: Johns Hopkins University Press, 1979.

Leyda, Jay. *The Years and Hours of Emily Dickinson.* 2 vols. New Haven: Yale University Press, 1960.

Lindberg-Seyersted, Brita. *The Voice of the Poet: Aspects of Style in the Poetry of Emily Dickinson.* Cambridge, Mass.: Harvard University Press, 1968.

Longsworth, Polly. *Austin and Mabel: The Amherst Affair and Love Letters of Austin Dickinson and Mabel Loomis Todd.* New York: Farrar, Straus & Giroux, 1984.

Martin, Wendy. *An American Triptych: Anne Bradstreet, Emily Dickinson, Adrienne Rich.* Chapel Hill: University of North Carolina Press, 1984.

Miller, Cristanne. *Emily Dickinson: A Poet's Grammar.* Cambridge, Mass.: Harvard University Press, 1987.

Mossberg, Barbara. *Emily Dickinson: When a Writer Is a Daughter.* Bloomington: Indiana University Press, 1982.

Pollack, Vivian R. *Dickinson: The Anxiety of Gender.* Ithaca, N.Y.: Cornell University Press, 1984.

———, ed. *A Poet's Parents: The Courtship Letters of Emily Norcross and Edward Dickinson.* Chapel Hill: University of North Carolina Press, 1988.

Porter, David T. *The Art of Emily Dickinson's Early Poetry.* Cambridge, Mass.: Harvard University Press, 1966.

St. Armand, Barton Levi. *Emily Dickinson and Her Culture: The Soul's Society.* New York: Cambridge University Press, 1984.

Sewall, Richard B. *The Life of Emily Dickinson.* 2 vols. New York: Farrar, Straus & Giroux, 1974.

Weisbuch, Robert. *Emily Dickinson's Poetry.* Chicago: University of Chicago Press, 1975.

Wolff, Cynthia Griffin. *Emily Dickinson.* New York: Knopf, 1986.

BIBLIOGRAPHIES

Buckingham, Willis J., ed. *Emily Dickinson: An Annotated Bibliography.* Bloomington: Indiana University Press, 1970. Covers over 2,600 items through 1968.

Clendenning, Sheila T., ed. *Emily Dickinson: A Bibliography.* Kent, Ohio: Kent State University Press, 1968. Includes an essay on the history of Dickinson scholarship.

SUZANNE JUHASZ

JOAN DIDION

1934–

JOAN DIDION CAME out of the West, a storyteller born in the sixth generation of a family who laid claim to having traveled with the Donner party, experienced terror, seen the worst. She came from California, once the frontier, a place of endless possibility, and went to New York a writer who understood that "endless possibility" was a dangerous belief. Still she wanted to write about the believers. Some of them were real, and some were her invention.

"We tell ourselves stories in order to live," she writes in *The White Album* (1979), her second collection of stories that happen to be true. "We live entirely, especially if we are writers, by the imposition of a narrative line upon disparate images, by the 'ideas' with which we have learned to freeze the shifting phantasmagoria which is our actual experience." Regarded by many as less a novelist than a journalist, Didion has written wonderful essays on a vast range of subjects and some of the most compelling political journalism of the 1980s. She has also written four accomplished novels that bespeak a firm grounding in the narratives of Joseph Conrad and Henry James, and that can be as passionate as William Faulkner's, and as romantic as F. Scott Fitzgerald's. All her writing—fiction or essay, what she knows and what she thinks about it—shows us not just the characters but Didion as well, and her opinions are stunning and final. In the end the essays and novels have a lot in common. They are all stories.

Joan Didion was born 5 December 1934, the first of two children, to Frank Reese and Eduene Jerrett Didion of Sacramento. Her father was an Army Air Corps officer, her mother a housewife, and the family moved often. By the time she was five she had written her first story, about a woman who dreamt she was freezing to death in the Arctic only to wake and discover herself dying in the hot Sahara sun.

She discovered literature by reading Hemingway and Conrad and, later, Henry James, examining their writing and determining how their sentences worked, and she developed a perspective on grammar that seems to have served her very well indeed:

> Grammar is a piano I play by ear. . . . All I know about grammar is its infinite power. To shift the structure of a sentence alters the meaning of that sentence, as definitely and inflexibly as the position of a camera alters the meaning of the object photographed.
>
> ("Why I Write")

After graduating from Berkeley in 1956 Didion moved to New York, the recipient of first prize in a contest sponsored by *Vogue* magazine for her essay on California architect William Wilson Wurster. Offered the choice between a trip to France and a job at *Vogue*, she took the job, intending to learn what she could writing copy, expecting to stay in New York six months; she stayed nine years. She had met the writer John Gregory Dunne, who had become a good friend. After Didion's unhappy breakup with another writer, she and Dunne began to live together. They married in 1964 and adopted a daughter, Quintana Roo, in 1966. In 1985 they bought an apartment in New York to be closer to Quintana, then a student at Barnard, and began to divide their time between East Coast and West.

Didion and Dunne have written about each other and about their life together, and they read each other's work. They alternated as columnist for "The Coast" in *Esquire* (1976–1977) and for a column in *New West* (1979–1980). Didion herself wrote a column for *Life* (1969–1970) in addition to the work she did at *Vogue*. She frequently reviewed films in the early years, and to this day reviews books. She and Dunne have lived in Brentwood and in Trancas, on the California coast, and for a while in 1968 and 1969, after a day when Dunne reportedly left home to buy a loaf of bread and didn't stop driving until he reached Las Vegas, spent some time apart. Their reporting has taken them to Central and South America and the Far East. Together they have written many screenplays, five of which have been made into films, including one based on Didion's second novel, *Play It As It Lays* (1970; screenplay, 1972), and one based on Dunne's first, *True Confessions* (1978; screenplay, 1981). Didion's novel *Democracy* (1984) has been optioned by director Tony Richardson.

Didion has said that she "came late to the apprehension that there is a void at the center of experience" and that her early novels were a way of dealing with this. "I write in order to find out who I am and what I fear," she begins the essay "Why I Write," and she spares no suspicion about what is beneath any story, retains few illusions about how the world has changed since she was the child of a family of pioneers and certain things—home, family, tradition, and reward for a life well lived—could be relied on. Still she seems, in her novels at least, to love the characters who are most deluded.

Her writing has been termed desolate and even nihilist, and her hard-won, spare, cultivated style has brought out a wave of touchy criticism, some of it oddly angry. Two prominent critics, Barbara Grizzuti Harrison and Susan Lardner, have gone so far as to parody her style in their reviews to make the point that it seems needlessly extreme. She has also been called, by John Leonard, "the best woman prose stylist in America."

There are those who say she is a women's writer; there are those who say she "writes like a man." There is a firm consensus, especially, that she writes a better essay than she does fiction. In fact her best fiction is easily as compelling as her best essays, though perhaps less often understood. By her own admission her novels have been steered by her splendid reporting, and echoes of what she has discovered as a journalist resonate in the stories that are hers alone. Thus the "People-to-People" programs of the Jaycees and the "fresh wind from the sea" used by the organization to describe its Operation Brotherhood in the essay "Good Citizens," written in the 1960s, reappear in Didion's imaginary Boca Grande in *A Book of Common Prayer* (1977). That novel also mentions a city strung with a web of colored lights as a specific against cholera. As it happens, such a string of lights was used to ward off typhus, in another country, and subsequently appears in the nonfictional *Salvador* (1983). Didion is a seasoned hunter-gatherer of real ironies, and they nourish her tales in a way that invented ones could never do. That they are somewhat arcane as subject matter makes them all the more memorable.

Didion's first two collections of essays, *Slouching Towards Bethlehem* (1968) and *The White Album*, were compiled from essays she first published in the *Saturday Evening Post*, *Esquire*, *Life*, *Travel & Leisure*, the *New York Times Book Review*, the *New York Review of Books*, the *Los Angeles Review of Books*, *Holiday*, the *American Scholar*, and *New West*. One of her best subjects is Hollywood, referred to in *The White Album* as "the last extant stable society":

> At midwinter in the survivors' big houses off Benedict Canyon the fireplaces blaze all day with scrub oak and eucalyptus, the French windows are opened wide to the subtropical sun. . . . Dinner guests pick with vermeil forks at broiled fish and limestone lettuce *vinaigrette*, decline dessert, adjourn to the screening room, and settle down to *The Heartbreak Kid* with a little seltzer in a Baccarat glass.
>
> (pp. 152–153)

On ironies such as the blazing fireplace in the warm climate Didion builds a case for "automization, the proof that things fall apart" (*Slouching Towards Bethlehem,* p. 11). This entropic dissolution is one of the darker threads in her earliest work, and it is pervasive.

"In the Islands," collected in *The White Album,* follows Didion as a tourist on sojourn *en famille* to save her marriage, but the lush surroundings of the Royal Hawaiian Hotel prove a less than perfect respite from the dull thud of the ordinary: one cannot even enjoy the beach, because there has been an earthquake in the Aleutians and a tidal wave is expected. Tradition at the Royal has undergone a sea change as well. The mildly exotic "pink palace of the Pacific . . . [that once] made Honolulu a place to go," a bastion of tradition, seems the perfect environment for the renewal of a marriage, but it is not, as Didion soon discovers:

> I . . . talk to a pretty young woman who has honeymooned at the Royal, because honeymoons at the Royal are a custom in her family, with each of her three husbands. My daughter makes friends . . . with another four-year old, Jill, from Fairbanks, Alaska, and it is taken for granted by Jill's mother and aunt that the two children will meet again, year after year, in the immutable pleasant rhythms of a life that used to be, and at the Royal Hawaiian seems still to be. I sit in my voile beach robe and watch the children and wish, against all the evidence I know, that it might be so.
>
> (p. 140)

The extraordinary array of dislocations in the everyday often move Didion to seek out and report on the fastidiously well ordered, such as the painstaking process whereby orchids are mated and crossed ("Quiet Days in Malibu"), or the new Los Angeles freeway lane designed to carry thousands of cars and improve traffic ("Bureaucrats"; both essays collected in *The White Album*). But neither order nor planning offers any real guarantees: the new freeway system, extended at a cost of forty-two million dollars, does not work, and even causes many more highway accidents, and the greenhouse containing the orchid crosses, and a decade's labor, is all but completely destroyed by one of the raging brushfires that are a commonplace in California.

Didion's tracking of dislocation is at its best in her book-length essays *Salvador* and *Miami* (1987). Nominated for a Pulitzer Prize in 1983 and one of her best-acclaimed works, *Salvador* signaled the beginning of Didion's changing persona as essayist. Now she wrote fuller, more compelling works that, like *Salvador,* traced the history of an incredible metastasis of disorder. (Though Conrad's influence is more obvious in Didion's fiction, it is no accident that *Salvador*'s epigraph is from *Heart of Darkness,* where one man's ambitious vision is the skeleton on which to hang a tale of terror.)

What ironies there are to be savored in the mythical American dream pale beside the realities of life in volatile El Salvador, where inch-thick Plexiglas seems a standard fixture of the Cherokee Chiefs people prefer to drive, and where Didion's innocent act of fishing in her handbag for an address causes rifles to click up and down the street. In El Salvador the danger is immediate and never ending:

> On an evening when rain or sabotage or habit had blacked out the city . . . I became abruptly aware, in the light cast by a passing car, of two human shadows. . . . It seemed to me unencouraging that my husband and I were the only people seated on the porch. In the absence of the headlights the candle on our table provided the only light, and I fought the impulse to blow it out. We continued talking, carefully. Nothing came of this, but I did not forget the sensation of having been in a single instant demoralized, undone, humiliated by fear. . . . I came to understand in El Salvador the mechanism of terror.
>
> (p. 26)

Somehow Didion manages to remain a master of dark laughter: even as she and her husband are passing through immigration, "negotiated in a thicket of automatic weapons [though] by whose authority the weapons are brandished is a blurred point," she notices that "documents are scrutinized upside down."

Not long after, a visit to the Metrocenter, "Central America's largest shopping mall," transforms Didion. The journalist sees cocktail glasses packaged with bottles of Russian vodka and other signs of a view toward "progress," and begins taking notes as she might for any other story. But El Salvador has already left its mark on her:

> This was a shopping center that embodied the future for which El Salvador was presumably being saved, and I wrote it down dutifully, this being the kind of "color" I knew how to interpret, the kind of inductive irony, the detail that was supposed to illuminate the story. As I wrote it down I realized I was no longer much interested in this kind of irony, that this was a story that would not be illuminated by such details, that this was a story that would perhaps not be illuminated at all. . . .
>
> (p. 36)

On her way out of the mall, Didion is faced with the obscene truth of random murder—and with her own powerlessness—and it all but paralyzes her: "As I waited to cross back over the Boulevard de los Heroes to the Camino Real I noticed soldiers herding a young civilian into a van, their guns at the boy's back, and I walked straight ahead, not wanting to see anything at all." The place has changed everyone she knows who has been there; it has changed Didion to the point where she averts her eyes (something we have come to expect from her characters, but hardly what we would expect of her). Later, after an impasse in which the car carrying Didion risks knocking over the motorcycles of two uniformed men and a friend of theirs, a "pointless confrontation with aimless authority," exacerbated this time by the touchy anger of the people holding the weapons, she concludes that terror is in the everyday, and leaves the country without looking back, rigid in her seat. She completed the book eight months later, about the time the administration of President Ronald Reagan was quoted as believing "that it had 'turned the corner' in its campaign for political stability in Central America."

In *Miami*, which recounts the history of relations between the United States and Cuba, notably under the administrations of John F. Kennedy and Reagan, Didion paints the city's relationships in triptych: Miami's blacks and whites, Washington and Cuba, and Cubans and Anglo Miamians, who view the Hispanic 56 percent of the city's population as little more than an interesting minority. The writer's search for patterns of meaning in any event turns up the political style of *el exilio*, with its common belief that individuals "affect events directly," that "revolutions . . . are framed in the private sector." This outlook, "indigenous to the Caribbean and to Central America," makes Miami what it is:

> a tropical capital: long on rumor, short on memory, overbuilt on the chimera of runaway money and referring not to New York or Boston or Los Angeles or Atlanta but to Caracas and Mexico, to Havana and to Bogotá and to Paris and Madrid . . . since 1959 connected only to Washington, which is the peculiarity of both places, and increasingly the warp.
>
> (pp. 13–14)

Another place where anything can happen, Miami provides a visual metaphor for the fluid politics of a tropical capital:

> A certain liquidity suffused everything about the place. Causeways and bridges and even Brickell Avenue did not stay put but rose and fell, allowing the masts of ships to glide among the marble and glass facades of the unleased office buildings. The buildings themselves seemed to swim free against the sky: there had grown up in Miami during the recent money years an architecture which appeared to have slipped its moorings, a not inappropriate style for a terrain with only a provisional claim on being land at all.
>
> (p. 31)

This "liquidity" clearly is meant to apply to much else besides. Arcane goings-on involving the purchase and transfer of weapons and point-blank shootings of the purchasers are details that shock, and leave the reader wondering, "What next?" "In this mood," Didion writes, "Miami seemed not a city at all but a tale, a romance of the tropics, a kind of waking dream in which any possibility could and would be accommodated." Here the locals cannot even comprehend the need to know a little Spanish, the language not only of the two mayoral candidates (both Cuban), but of more than half the population, a people betrayed by Washington for three decades, a people who would not be there at all but for that betrayal.

And those who, like Didion, write about what they see, well, they do not clarify anything at all, but just make matters worse, if one is to listen to the experts. " 'The search for conspiracy,' Anthony Lewis had written in the *New York Times* in September of 1975, 'only increases the elements of morbidity and paranoia and fantasy in this country. It romanticizes crimes that are terrible because of their lack of purpose. It obscures our necessary understanding, all of us, that in this life there is often tragedy without reason' " (quoted on p. 203).

The denials spin on, nothing changes. *Miami* is, finally, proof of the thesis that enough lies from the rich and powerful can cover over anything, no matter how compelling the argument against whatever distortions someone is attempting to promote. There is nothing random about the violence: a situation has exploded because somewhere behind the scenes of an intense conflict, someone with a match has decided to light a fuse.

Didion the journalist went further afield as she grew, beginning with essays on California and the Sacramento Valley, then covering the rest of the continental United States and Hawaii and making brief sojourns to Mexico, Colombia, and later El Salvador. So her fiction traveled slowly away from her beginnings.

Her first novel takes place in California. *Run River* (1963), written while Didion was still working in New York but longed for the West, is a very different kind of writing from the dreamy fictional chants that followed, a more traditional storytelling, the history of the marriage of Lily Knight to Everett McClellan, told in flashback, from the moment Lily hears him kill Ryder Channing, her lover, to the moment she hears Everett kill himself. It is an extended reflection framed between two gunshots, and within it are the threads that bind three generations and two prominent families in the Sacramento Valley.

The landscape of the valley is an Eden complete with a snake to haunt each of the three protagonists, all of whom yearn for an innocence, the time before knowledge when everything was simpler. Forced to confront the present, they destroy themselves by adultery, abortion, murder, and suicide.

Because of the tight symbolism, the reiterated myth, *Run River* is a work separate and distinct from her later novels: it now seems less characteristic of Didion than those fictional works in which she relies on a spare, focused style that capitalizes on flashes of knowing dialogue and indisputable detail. Still it nicely conveys the sadness of finally confronting the inevitability of change, and the dangers of believing, naively, that one can know how things will turn out when that is impossible.

Play It As It Lays (1970), nominated for a National Book Award, is stylistically the most controlled of her novels: there is no word or phrase that does not tell. How uniquely clean this style must have seemed at the time can only be guessed at, but it seems to have had its admirers and detractors; this is one book reviewers like to parody. Many critics expressed dissatisfaction with the nihilist tone of the work, which seems to have distracted them from its virtues: a keen structure, a precise, cinematic laying-out of events scene by scene, a brilliant fix on the priorities of the Hollywood film community, and a clear view of the pervasiveness of quotidian disorder as seen through the eyes of the anomic Maria Wyeth:

> For days during the rain she did not speak out loud or read a newspaper. She could not read newspapers because certain stories leapt at her from the page: the four-year-olds in the abandoned refrigerator, the tea party with Purex, the infant in the driveway, the rattlesnake in the playpen, the peril, the unspeakable peril, in the everyday.
>
> (pp. 98–99)

In this story, Maria's husband has left, and her brain-damaged daughter, Kate, has been institutionalized. To bring some sense of order to her days she drives the freeway, until it begins to appear in her dreams:

> She drove it as a riverman runs a river, every day more attuned to its currents, its deceptions, and just as a riverman feels the pull of the rapids in the lull between sleeping and waking, so Maria lay at night in the still of Beverly Hills and saw the great signs soar overhead at seventy miles an hour. . . .
>
> (p. 14)

After she discovers she is pregnant (perhaps by her married lover, Les Goodwin) Maria's husband, Carter Lang, arranges an abortion, though it is not what she wants: Maria agrees only because it may enable her to gain custody of Kate. The bond between mothers and daughters figures strongly in this novel, but Maria finds only unconnectedness. Her own mother is dead, having run her car off the road in the desert; her daughter Kate is emotionally dead; and the baby she could have had has been aborted.

Maria's attempts to break out of her anomie by returning to her career do nothing but subject her to humiliation and reinforce her belief that it is perhaps simpler not to try at all. Everywhere she turns Maria finds evidence that effort does not seem to pay off. Out in the desert, where Carter is filming, she strikes up a conversation with a local woman and is invited to visit. The woman's house is surrounded by sand, which blows onto the concrete that serves as a yard: "The woman picked up a broom and began sweeping the sand into small piles, then edging the piles back to the fence. New sand blew in as she swept." The futility of such an effort is readily apparent to Maria, but the woman goes on sweeping, explaining that she once "made a decision," declared her faith in a prayer meeting, which has enabled her to keep on as she does, and even to endure the betrayals of a deserting husband.

While Maria has no such ordered faith, the lessons of her father—to "play it as it lays," and "not do it the hard way," lessons from the craps table—are her method, her prayer. It seems an almost Taoist approach to life, especially for a woman who has difficulty differentiating between herself and everything else:

> By the end of a week she was thinking constantly about where her body stopped and the air began, about the exact point in space that was the difference between *Maria* and *other.* She had the sense that if she could get that in her mind and hold it for even one micro-second she would have what she had come to get.
>
> (pp. 169–170)

The only character sympathetic to Maria is the filmmaker BZ. She and he both seem to know what others do not: they have arrived at the same place. But BZ does not want to go on. Lying with him, holding his hand while he takes a fatal dose of barbiturates, Maria becomes the girl on the edge escorting her psychic twin to the other side. It is at first a peaceful scene, but then the lights blaze on and Maria is left to face the otherness of the world—the horrified Carter and Helene (BZ's wife)—all by herself. But that in itself is pretty remarkable. *"One thing in my defense,"* Maria says, *"not that it matters: I know something Carter never knew, or Helene, or maybe you. I know what 'nothing' means, and keep on playing."*

If Maria Wyeth is pained by her knowing, Charlotte Havemeyer, the heroine of the critically acclaimed *A Book of Common Prayer,* is undone by her delusions.

Inspired by a 1972 trip with Dunne to a film festival in Cartagena, Colombia, *Prayer* begins in the imagined Boca Grande (intentionally "big mouth"), a cousin to Conrad's Costaguana. In this banana republic, terminally ill Grace Strasser-Mendana lives out the last of her days, experimenting with biochemistry and watching and writing about Charlotte.

As with Didion's fictional heroes—Milly Theale in James's *The Wings of the Dove* (1902), Axel Heyst in Conrad's *Victory* (1915), and the young Charlotte Rittenmeyer in Faulkner's *The Wild Palms* (1939)—Charlotte Havemeyer is given to "extreme and doomed commitments," and like her Faulknerian namesake she is in love with love, traveling anywhere it can be found. This pursuit eventually takes her south, making *Prayer* the first of Didion's books to leave North America. The California-born-and-bred Charlotte and her lover and ex-husband, Warren Bogart, journey through the South and pass through New Orleans, where Faulkner's lovers, Harry Wilbourne and Charlotte Rittenmeyer, first meet—and Charlotte dies.

Didion's earlier novels exhibited more than one point of view, but *Prayer* belongs to the dying Grace, whose existence is etched alongside Charlotte's, for better or worse: "Unlike Charlotte I do not dream my life. . . . I will die (and rather soon, of pancreatic cancer) neither hopeful nor its opposite. I am interested in Charlotte Douglas only insofar . . . as the meaning of that sojourn continues to elude me." Didion's chant echoes Faulkner's, whose Charlotte, once gone, survives in memory only through her companion, Harry, who lives to tell the tale. Imprisoned for having performed the botched abortion that killed her, Harry returns to his cell after being sentenced to fifty years' hard labor and rejects suicide in the form of a cyanide pill offered him by Charlotte's husband, Rat. It is only in choosing to endure the pain of his sentence that he can keep Charlotte's memory alive. In Faulkner's words, *"When she became not then half of memory became not and if I become not then all of remembering will cease to be,—Yes,* he thought, *between grief and nothing I will take grief."* In their respective stories, Grace and Harry each tell the beads of a mystery, record a passion as plainly as the offertory to a mass. Their purpose as narrators is to recount the events that lead up to a death.

Charlotte Havemeyer Douglas's passion concerns her daughter, Marin, a self-styled revolutionary wanted by the FBI for the hijacking of a plane. Charlotte and her second husband, Leonard, a defense lawyer, are visited just after Marin's indictment by Warren, Charlotte's first husband, a romantic rogue-scholar who is arguably the first of Didion's male characters to be as emotionally complex and well developed as her women. Remembering herself at eighteen, and "how lonely she was until Warren came to her door," Charlotte resists the dying man's advances for a time, then gives in. Pregnant with Leonard's child (though the pregnancy "didn't happen in time": Warren was still able to get to her), she and Warren travel through the South until Charlotte has the baby in New Orleans. Discovering that the baby is too sick to live, Charlotte leaves Warren in New Orleans and takes the child to Mérida to die. "Maintain[ing] that blind course south" in her efforts to reunite with Marin, Charlotte visits Antigua and Guadeloupe and finally Boca Grande, "the cervix of the world through which a child lost to history must eventually pass."

But mother and child will never cross paths, let alone learn to understand each other. Charlotte will succumb, through carelessness and bad luck, to the whim of the revolution, such as it is, another innocent bystander lost to someone else's cause. Her innocence is fatal.

It is only in Boca Grande that Grace can begin to experience the life of Charlotte firsthand and be witness to the last year of it. What she sees is a woman "innocent of history," oblivious enough to the dangerous connections in life that her carelessness brings her to her death.

The anarchy of Boca Grande is typical of Didion, and, unlikely as it seems, Charlotte becomes the center of intrigue there. Leonard, it turns out, has financed those who provided hardware to the last coup; in return they have given him the conspicuous emerald that Charlotte wears as a wedding ring. It is as if she is married to chance itself.

She dismisses her connection to Leonard (and all others—she has had an affair with Victor Strasser, head of the ruling family, and another with his nephew Gerardo) as irrelevant, but because of whom she happens to know, word that she is in Boca Grande soon gets out and is brought to the attention of the Strassers. It is now only a matter of time before she will risk being targeted by one side or another as someone whose presence is "inconvenient."

The troika of witnesses—Charlotte "watching" Marin, Grace observing Charlotte, and Didion (and the reader) observing Grace—create the narrative. Didion affirms the purpose of Grace's last days even as Grace affirms the meaning of Charlotte's. Just as Lily Knight watched and held the dying Everett in *Run River* and Maria held BZ's hand in *Play It As It Lays,* Leonard will be there to bury Warren in New Orleans, and Grace will see Charlotte's coffin loaded into the hold of a plane bound for America. It is a plangent ballad of the frontier: we stay with our dead; it is the moral thing to do.

And even if we cannot find out every truth ("I have not been the witness I wanted to be," Grace writes at the end of her story), and even if we misperceive one another as Charlotte does Marin (she was thinking of "some pretty baby, not me," Marin says), the consecrated act of remembering is what redeems us.

In *Democracy* (1984) Didion the writer becomes Didion the character, blurring the distinction between journalistic subject and protagonist (a distinction one has been able to blur with Didion all along). Even more to the point, that character is the omniscient narrator-witness (like Grace, like Marlow in *Heart of Darkness*), but more credible because she is real. And Didion seems to embrace narrative in this novel, openly and without apology (unlike earlier writing, where she frequently admitted to "resisting narrative").

In his essay "On Writing a Novel" (1987), John Gregory Dunne makes a point about plot being something like "the queen died, the king died," and narrative being more like "the queen died, the king died of a broken heart." While Dunne's is by his own admission a very free translation of E. M. Forster's definition in *Aspects of the Novel* (1927), it is a key to Didion's struggle with narrative, and her insistence that she is merely stating the facts. But the sensibility and timbre of her narrative are important clues to the intensity of her fiction.

Didion has said that her work on *Miami* prompted some of the elements in *Democracy,* in which she sends her characters even farther afield (Honolulu, Saigon, Kwajalein, Kuala Lumpur) even as she herself becomes more specific and direct about her motives and method. Her presence in the book may confound her critics, but it serves to authenticate the tale—the stories a journalist tells, if we can accept the limits of narrative, are true. That some of Didion's characters are not unlike real people—many have noted the resemblance of Harry Victor to one Kennedy or another, for example—underscores this credibility.

Two families are at the heart of *Democracy,* the Christians and the Victors, and each is a house divided. Inez Christian Victor, born into the first, married into the second, has come a long way from the Didion heroines who have pledged their lives to futile passions; already she can clearly see in her husband, Harry, the tragedy of expecting things to turn out. She has made her peace with the random, the unpredictable, and will, through her resourcefulness, come to transcend quotidian entropic dissolution.

Although she and Harry, a congressman and onetime presidential hopeful, have a son and daughter and have managed to stay together, for some twenty years Inez has maintained a watch on one Jack Lovett, an "information specialist" and "consultant in international development," and he on her. He sees Inez every time her husband makes the nightly news, usually on Harry's arm. They are rarely together. Inez remembers that her mother once suggested, "When a man avoids a woman, it means he wants to keep their love alive"—a pretty thought, though circumstances would have kept him far from her no matter what.

There is little for them to do but watch each other from afar, but just before the fall of Saigon in 1975, when Inez discovers that her daughter, Jessie, has run off to Vietnam to look for work, she realizes Jack may be the only person she knows who can do something about finding Jessie and bringing her back.

The Victor family is disintegrating: Inez's sister Janet is the comatose victim of a shooting; Inez's father, arrested for that shooting, is emotionally disturbed; and Jessie, Inez's daughter, is in terrible peril. Jack has the connections needed to help her. He has waited twenty years for Inez. On the day he rescues her daughter, saves her from being a casualty of the fall of Saigon, he and Inez leave together, never to return.

In Inez, Didion builds a resilient heroine who, rather than maintaining "a doomed commitment," searches for a way out of her unfortunate marriage, for love with someone who cares about her more than her husband does, someone she can respect. The character Inez is an evolved Maria Lang, a woman who finds herself and finds purpose in her life (even after her lover dies of a heart attack).

The character Joan Didion, who visits Inez several months after Jack's death, learns that after escorting the body back to be buried at Schofield, Inez has returned to the Far East to work in a refugee camp in Kuala Lumpur, doing what she can to be of some use to someone (as Jack had done while he was alive). Inez will not leave until the last refugee is gone ("presumably never," Didion the character says): she has broken her marriage vows to take a lover, and now that he is gone, will live a life of duty. But her ideals are sound—unlike the wishful causes of such Conrad heroes as Axel Heyst, unlike the blind strivings of Didion's earlier protagonist Charlotte Havemeyer, and unlike the acquiescing of Maria Wyeth, who has learned to accept things but survives restrained in an institution. Jack lives on in Inez through what she does, not just through her remembering.

Didion says she writes because she does not know herself, "to find out what I'm thinking, . . . what I fear and what it means." Her novels have their antecedents in Conrad especially, yet they are hers alone: her narrative style and the investigative skills she has mastered set them apart. Her ability to build a story from incisive details and invest it with meaning is rare, and so is her very personal voice. It is not any journalist who can write a novel. It is not any journalist who can tell a story. Perhaps, like her character Inez, she has come to believe that a different road is the only solution, sometimes.

But Didion always knew as much. In 1966, in the essay "Going Home," she wrote a birthday wish for her one-year-old daughter as she lay sleeping:

> *I would like to promise her that she will grow up with a sense of her cousins and of rivers and of her grandmother's teacups. . . . I would like to give her* home

for her birthday, but we live differently now. I give her a xylophone and a sundress from Madeira, and promise to tell her a funny story.

A daughter of Scheherazade could not dream a better gift. It is more than eight thousand and one nights since then.

Selected Bibliography

PRIMARY WORKS

FICTION

Run River. New York: Ivan Obolensky, 1963.

Play It As It Lays. New York: Farrar, Straus & Giroux, 1970.

A Book of Common Prayer. New York: Simon & Schuster, 1977.

Telling Stories. Berkeley, Calif.: Bancroft Library, 1978.

Democracy: A Novel. New York: Simon & Schuster, 1984.

NONFICTION

Slouching Towards Bethlehem. New York: Farrar, Straus & Giroux, 1968.

The White Album. New York: Simon & Schuster, 1979.

Salvador. New York: Simon & Schuster, 1983.

Miami. New York: Simon & Schuster, 1987.

UNCOLLECTED PROSE

For works published prior to 1979, see the listings under "Bibliographies."

"Meditation on a Life." *New York Times Book Review*, 29 April 1979. Review of Elizabeth Hardwick's *Sleepless Nights*.

"Letter from Manhattan." *New York Review of Books*, 16 August 1979, pp. 18–19. Review of Woody Allen's films *Manhattan, Interiors*, and *Annie Hall*.

"Without Regret or Hope." *New York Review of Books*, 12 June 1980, p. 20. Review of V. S. Naipaul's *The Return of Eva Peron with the Killings in Trinidad*.

"Boat People." *New West* 5 (14 July 1980).

"Honolulu Days." *New West* 5 (14 July 1980).

"Making Up Stories." In *The Writer's Craft*. Edited by Robert A. Martin. Ann Arbor: University of Michigan Press, 1982.

"Why I Write." In *Joan Didion: Essays and Conversations*. Edited by Ellen G. Friedman. Princeton, N.J.: Ontario Review Press, 1984.

"Letter from Los Angeles." *New Yorker*, 4 September 1987. On the Democratic National Convention and journalism.

"Insider Baseball." *New York Review of Books*, 27 October 1988. Reprinted in *The Best American Essays, 1989*. Edited by Robert Atwan. New York: Ticknor & Fields, 1989.

"Introduction" to *Some Women*, by Robert Mapplethorpe. Boston: Bullfinch/Little, Brown, 1989.

"Life at Court." *New York Review of Books*, 21 December 1989. Review of six books of the Reagan era.

"Letter from Los Angeles." *New Yorker*, 26 February 1990.

SCREENPLAYS (WITH JOHN GREGORY DUNNE)

The Panic in Needle Park (1971).

Play It As It Lays (1972).

A Star Is Born (remake; 1976).

True Confessions (1981).

Democracy (1987).

The Deer Park (1989).

Hills Like White Elephants (from the story by Ernest Hemingway: part 3 of the anthology film *Men and Women: Stories of Seduction;* 1990).

UNCOLLECTED INTERVIEWS

Atlas, James. "Slouching in Miami." *Vanity Fair*, October 1987.

Daley, M. "PW Interviews." *Publishers Weekly* 202:26–27 (9 October 1982).

Garis, Leslie. "Didion and Dunne: The Rewards of a Literary Marriage." *New York Times Magazine*, 8 February 1987, p. 18.

Kazin, Alfred. "Joan Didion: Portrait of a Professional." *Harper's*, December 1971, pp. 112–122.

Kuehl, Linda. "The Art of Fiction." In *Writers at Work: The Paris Review Interviews*. Edited by George Plimpton. New York: Viking, 1981. Pp. 339–357.

Torgoff, Martin. "Joan Didion." *Interview*, June 1983, p. 36.

Zusy, Anne. "Kennedy, Reagan, and After: Joan Didion Discusses *Miami*." *New York Times Book Review*, 25 October 1987, p. 3.

SECONDARY WORKS

BIOGRAPHICAL AND CRITICAL STUDIES

Dunne, John Gregory. *Vegas: Memoir of a Dark Season*. New York: Simon & Schuster, 1976.

———. *Quintana and Friends.* New York: Simon & Schuster, 1980.

———. *Harp.* New York: Simon & Schuster, 1989.

———. "Enter the Muse: In Praise of the Literary Wife." *Esquire,* June 1990, p. 142.

Friedman, Ellen G., ed. *Joan Didion: Essays and Conversations.* Princeton, N.J.: Ontario Review Press, 1984. Includes "Why I Write," two interviews, and eight critical essays.

Henderson, Katherine Usher. *Joan Didion.* New York: Frederick Ungar, 1981.

———. "Joan Didion." In *American Women Writing Fiction: Memory, Identity, Family, Space.* Edited by Mickey Pearlman. Lexington: University Press of Kentucky, 1989. Pp. 69–93.

Hinchman, Sandra K. "Making Sense and Making Stories: Problems of Cognition and Narration in Joan Didion's *Play It As It Lays.*" *Centennial Review* 29:457–473 (1985).

Hollowell, John. "Against Interpretation: Narrative Strategy in *A Book of Common Prayer.*" In *Joan Didion: Essays and Conversations.* Edited by Ellen G. Friedman. Princeton, NJ.: Ontario Review Press, 1984. Pp. 164–176.

Kazin, Alfred. *Bright Book of Life: American Novelists and Storytellers from Hemingway to Mailer.* Boston: Little, Brown, 1973. Pp. 189–198.

Loris, Michelle Carbone. *Innocence, Loss, and Recovery in the Art of Joan Didion.* New York: Peter Lang, 1989.

McCarthy, Mary. "Love and Death in the Pacific." *New York Times Book Review,* 22 April 1984.

Winchell, Mark Royden. *Joan Didion.* New York: Twayne, 1980; rev. ed., 1989.

BIBLIOGRAPHIES

An annotated international bibliography of works published between 1981 and 1990 is available on-line from the Modern Language Association (fifty-five entries as of this writing).

Jacobs, Fred Rue. *Joan Didion: A Bibliography.* Keene, Calif.: Loop Press, 1977.

Olendorf, Donna. "Joan Didion: A Checklist, 1955–1980." *Bulletin of Bibliography* 32:32–44 (January–March 1981).

JOAN ZSELECZKY

HILDA DOOLITTLE

1886–1961

LIKE HER BEST poems, H.D.'s signature is an energy bundle: a seed, a cocoon, a wrapped mystery. Its two letters condense the birthname Hilda Doolittle, given her on 10 September 1886 in Bethlehem, Pennsylvania, by her parents, Helen Wolle Doolittle, a member of one of Bethlehem's most prominent Moravian families, and Charles Leander Doolittle, professor of mathematics and astronomy at Lehigh University. In September 1912, in the British Museum tearoom, these initials became her official "writing signet or sign-manual" when her friend Ezra Pound cast his eye across a draft of three poems, exclaimed, "But . . . this is poetry," appended the adjective *Imagiste* to the initials, and sped the manuscript off to Harriet Monroe's *Poetry*. Throughout H.D.'s long public career as a poet, translator, novelist, autobiographer, and cultural critic, until her death on 27 September 1961, the initials "H.D." not only signed volume after volume of her poetry but also suggested titles for her books and poems, names for her characters, and pseudonyms for the title pages of her novels and the credits of her films

"H.D." was more than a nom de plume: it was, as Susan Stanford Friedman has pointed out, a name to be performed. In her texts H.D.'s initials generate embodiments that do not so much mirror her life within the world as extend and elaborate it on the page. "H.D." thus becomes "Helga Dart," the name on the typescript of her first novel, "Paint It To-Day," and "Helga Doorn," the name that signs the novel *Her* and scrolls up on the credits for her feature-length film *Borderline*. In her novel *Hedylus* (1928) the initials split and double to produce both Hedyle, the mother, and Hedylus, her son. In "Heliodora," the title poem of one of her first collections, and *Hermetic Definition*, the title of her last poem, the initials reach out to implicate the gods H.D. invoked to guide her writing: Helios, the Greek sun "who is light, who is song, who is music, is mantic, is prophetic," and Hermes, the Greek scribe who conveyed the messages of the gods. Helga, Hedyle, Hedylus, Helios, Hermes: this series of multiple and overlapping identifications spans the distance between the feminine, Victorian, slightly whimsical resonance of the name "Hilda Doolittle" and the hermetic authority of the poet whose late long epics take on the task of reshaping a world in crisis.

The spin of H.D.'s signature has both exhilarated and exasperated her readers. Not only does it all but erase the staid femininity of her birthname; it also enables both the writer and her critics to construct in its place an "I" constituted in, by, and through language, a subject that travels with the ease of Virginia Woolf's Orlando through time, across space, and between genders. "H.D." was less a woman of letters or a man of letters than a pattern of letters. "H.D. is *H.D.*," she reminded her friend and literary adviser Norman Holmes Pearson, not a person but a "literary personality," one of an array that stretched from "Edith Gray," who signed her earliest pieces, through "J. Beran," "Rhoda Peters," "John Helforth," and "D. A. Hill," to "Delia Alton," the "personality" who not only signed much of her late work but in 1949 composed an overview of her foresister's productions, a survey she called, wonderfully, *H.D. by Delia Alton* (1986). It is largely for consistency and convenience, then, that we continue to call this multiple and mysterious being "H.D."

But, still, *who* is H.D.? The elusiveness of this writer can be exasperating for readers eager to understand the conditions of her creativity, readers who want to know not just how Hilda Doolittle became H.D. but how her bold, fresh, and startling vision managed to unfold and flousish in a world inimical to many of its most basic intuitions. In *A Room of One's Own* (1929), Virginia Woolf imagines Shakespeare's "extraordinarily gifted" sister Judith, a girl who is as adventurous, imaginative, and wild to see the world as her brother but whose attempts to develop her gifts are relentlessly blighted. It was H.D.'s habit to imagine herself the sister, twin, or companion of such writers as Ezra Pound and D. H. Lawrence—for she was certainly as adventurous, imaginative, and wild to see the world as they—but despite liabilities similiar to those Woolf envisions for Shakespeare's sister, H.D. was able not only to bring her extraordinary gifts to expression but to point a way across some of the most perilous crossroads of the modernist era.

During her lifetime H.D. witnessed the collapse of Victorian certainties; the coalescence of technology, materialism, and power politics in a multinational "death-culture"; the convulsion of that culture in two great world wars; and the development of a bomb powerful enough to destroy humankind many times over. To press back against these intolerable pressures, H.D. and her confederates developed imagism, avant-garde narrative, and the modernist epic; they inaugurated experimental cinema, disseminated the discoveries of psychoanalysis, and struggled against racism, masculinism, and materialism. After her departure for Europe in 1911, during almost a decade in London, she worked with Pound, Lawrence, and Eliot; corresponded with William Carlos Williams and Amy Lowell; and shared a larger literary milieu with such figures as William Butler Yeats, Ford Madox Ford, James Joyce, and Woolf. In the mid decades of her life, circulating between residences in London and Switzerland with stops in Paris and Berlin, she came to know Dorothy Richardson, Gertrude Stein, Sylvia Beach, Norman Douglas, and the filmmaker G. W. Pabst. The generosity, exuberance, and stamina one companion called H.D.'s "genius for friendship" also sustained her lifelong alliance with Marianne Moore and her late creative relationships with E. M. Butler, Erich Heydt, and Norman Holmes Pearson.

Because of her presence at so many of modernism's crucial junctures and because of the ambition and complexity of her writings, H.D. has been one of very few women to be celebrated or criticized, loved or despised, by the makers of the modernist canon. To her earliest reviewers, she was the exemplary imagist, author of the poems Pound promoted as "Objective—no slither— . . . straight talk—straight as the Greek!" As her writing opened into longer, more overtly personal, political, and visionary dimensions, however, the same critics who admired the dilations of Pound and Williams held H.D. tightly to her "crystalline" concision and editors continued to anthologize the same few brilliantly compact poems written between 1913 and 1917.

H.D.'s imagist poems may have seemed "perfect," at least in part, because by the clichés of the time they were predictable: as brief, bright, and bristling as Emily Dickinson's, as "objective" as Marianne Moore's, they were recognizably "feminine" and therefore easily patronized or pathologized. In the years when Dickinson was thought to be a lovelorn recluse and Moore a spunky spinster, Hugh Kenner bemoaned H.D.'s self-destructive constraint, Douglas Bush deplored her escapism, and Randall Jarrell found her simply high-strung and silly.

Aside from the chapters of Robert Duncan's *The H.D. Book,* which started to appear in countercultural journals of the early 1960s, the prelude to H.D.'s re-emergence as a serious poet was a special H.D. issue of *Contemporary Literature* assembled by L. S. Dembo in 1969. In addition to unpublished letters and manuscripts, an interview with Pearson, and new readings of H.D.'s novels and epics, however, this collection contained two essays that pathologized H.D. anew by pegging their readings to the concept of penis envy, the longing for a male organ, which Norman Holland identified as the basis of H.D.'s interactions with Freud, and Joseph Riddel identified as the source of all her creative endeavors. Like Kenner, Bush, and Jarrell, Holland and Riddel seemed to assume that any woman who would succeed as a poet must overcome, destroy, or transcend her femininity in order to write like a man. This assumption—exposed by Susan Stanford Friedman in an essay provocatively entitled "Who Buried H.D.? A Poet, Her Critics, and Her Place in 'The Literary Tradition' "(1975)—is the opposite of the assumptions that have most recently constructed H.D.'s life and work, assumptions that emerge from cultural and post-structuralist feminism.

If masculinist readings of H.D. probed what they seemed to perceive as a feminine pathology, early feminist readings retrieved and celebrated what they understood to be a female nature. Taking off from the thinking of Mary Daly and Adrienne Rich, these readings defined a female essence, identified patriarchy as its subjugator, and set about finding ways to release and redeem it. In "The Echoing Spell of *Trilogy*" (1978), perhaps the single most influential essay on H.D.'s World War II epic, Susan Gubar argues that *Trilogy* uses a vision of the goddess to re-establish the primacy of what masculinist culture has rendered secondary. Arguments like this echo through the many subsequent readings of H.D. that identify her project as the discovery of an authentic or archetypal female identity located outside culture and beyond or behind language.

In the period since Gubar's essay, feminist critics have grown increasingly edgy about the intellectual and political implications of this conception of "woman" and have preferred instead to emphasize H.D.'s embeddedness in history, her complicity with as well as her resistance against the ideologies of her time, the problematic nature and status of the "I" in her texts, and, most happily, the intricate processes of her writing. Feminist readings of her work that draw on one or another element of post-structuralism celebrate the play of her language, its indeterminancy, and its ability to disrupt notions like "authentic" identity without at the same time eradicating the marks of her gendered subjectivity.

Like Pound, H.D. read the work of literary scholars with partisan zeal. Despising critics who merely haggled over dates or annotated terms, she passionately admired those who enriched and disseminated the visions that inspired them. Two of H.D.'s major creative endeavors—her "translations" and her "tributes"—engaged and directly challenged the work of contemporary scholars: her renderings of parts of Homer's epics, Sappho's lyrics, and Euripides' plays and her homages to Shakespeare, Pound, and Freud all set out to promote materials she believed contemporary scholars had scanted or scorned.

H.D. set herself into rivalry with some of the most powerful scholars of her day not only because as a creator she felt vulnerable to their reductions but also, more importantly, because as a "research worker" she shared their dedication to knowledge. Her extensive collection of books—now split between Yale University's Beinecke Rare Book and Manuscript Library and the Long Island home of her daughter, Perdita Schaffner—includes dictionaries, encyclopedias, and scientific expositions of astronomy, botany, and biology, as well as tomes on anthropology, comparative religion, classical history and literature, psychoanalysis, mythology, folktales, and magic. Each period of H.D.'s life is marked by at least one major research project, whether on her ancestral Moravians, the Native American tribes of Pennsylvania, ancient Egyptian mythology, Greek and Roman hermetic traditions, medieval alchemy, or the writings of Dante, Shakespeare, or Dante Gabriel Rossetti. Clearly what sustained H.D. was, at least in part, an indefatigable curiosity, intelligence, and hard work.

In charting the sources of her creativity, H.D. positioned herself at the confluence of two kinds of intelligence: the practical and aesthetic, the secular and sacred, the Yankee and European strains she liked to call "my father's science and my mother's art." Her mother's family, the Wolles, were ministers, schoolmasters, scholars, and musicians, learned and genteel people who were prominent in the Bethlehem Moravian community. The Moravian Church was a marginal, visionary group founded in 1457 by followers of the Bohemian reformer and martyr Jan Hus. Centuries later a Moravian group founded a small Pennsylvanian settlement, given the name Bethlehem when Nikolaus Ludwig, Count Zinzendorf, joined the group on Christmas Eve 1741. Deeply stirred by Moravian history, H.D. re-created scenes from it in her novel *The Mystery* (1976), her short story "The Death of Martin Presser" (1965), and her autobiography, *The Gift* (1982), exploring in each the group's visionary perspective, its generous and flexible faith, and its ability to survive harassment and persecution.

Like the Switzerland of H.D.'s final decades, Bethlehem was a peace-loving, cultured, international community. H.D.'s grandfather, the Reverend Francis Wolle, was a first-generation American and, like other early Americans, distinguished himself with a graceful versatility: he invented a machine that made paper bags, formed the Union Paper Bag Machine Company, became vice-principal and then principal of the Young Ladies' Seminary, was ordained a presbyter of the Moravian Church, and finished his life as a microscopist internationally known for his catalogs of freshwater algae.

When H.D. identified her art with the Wolles, though, she was thinking back, as Woolf said women writers do, through her mothers. Her matrilineage passed from her great-grandmother Mary Weiss, to whom family tradition ascribed psychic powers, through her mother's mother, Elizabeth, presented in *The Gift* as a visionary who retrieves through music a repressed portion of ecstatic Moravian history, to her mother, Helen, who taught music and painting at the Reverend Wolle's seminary but was, H.D. explained to Freud, "morbidly self-effacing." This matrilineage proves that women can have the combination of art and vision H.D. called "the gift" and that they can pass it on, but it does not guarantee that they can glory in it. The question Helen Wolle Doolittle posed for H.D. is the same question Judith Shakespeare posed for Woolf: What happens to a gifted women in a culture that cannot honor her creativity?

H.D. opens *The Gift* with a horrifying scene in which Helen as a tiny child watches a girl burn to death inside her elaborate hoopskirts at the Reverend Wolle's seminary. This scene initiates a sequence in which the young Hilda recites to herself the names of all the dead girls in her family: Elizabeth's daughter Fanny; Helen's daughter Edith; Alice, her father's daughter by his first wife; and Elizabeth Caroline, the only daughter of an aunt and uncle whose five boys flourished along with H.D.'s three brothers, two half brothers, and three additional boy cousins. "Why was it always," the little girl asks, "a girl who had died?" This was not a question with an easy answer, nor was it a question that vanished, for at the age of seventy, H.D. recorded a dream in which, like her mother before her, she watched helplessly as another woman suffered. The woman in this dream was Helen herself, who was about to be raped. " 'My mother, my mother,' I cry," H.D. reports, "I sob violently . . . [but] she was passive. . . . I have never had such a terrible dream."

The hoops that held Helen Doolittle were the Victorian conventions that constricted the roles of daughter, sister, wife, and mother. Unlike her mother and grandmother, Helen chose to emphasize the domestic rather than the visionary or artistic in her life, a choice that meant—at least in the eyes of her talented daughter—that she passively allowed her gifts to be dispersed. Her musical ability went to her brother, J. Fred Wolle, the organist who founded the famous Bethelehem Bach Festivals; her young life went to her father and his seminary; her daily devotion went to the astronomer she married at twenty-eight and served thereafter, hushing the company when he wished to speak and rising toward dawn on winter nights to thaw the hairs of his whiskers that had frozen tight to his telescope.

H.D.'s father, Professor Charles Leander Doolittle, was a decade older than her mother. Esteemed by his colleagues as a genial and precise scientist, he was remembered by his daughter as a remote, abrupt, and compelling "outsider": a pathfinder, an explorer, a man who eluded the known world of the domestic by going out at night—" 'like a thief or an astronomer,' as he would say"—to gaze at the heavens. In *The Gift*, he repeatedly emerges from the night as if "from another world, another country," the cold and darkness clinging to him, to take her hand, to tell her "his one girl was worth all his five boys put together." Besides making "a terrible responsibility," this alliance bound H.D. to a harsher set of ancestors, for the Doolittles were English Puritans who over several generations had emigrated to Connecticut and then had moved inland to Indiana, where Charles was born. In 1895, after twenty years on the faculty at Lehigh University, Doolittle accepted an appointment at the University of Pennsylvania as professor of astronomy and mathematics and director of the newly established Flower Observatory, thereby precipitating the first great break in H.D.'s life: the move from the Bethlehem Moravian community to a bare new house on the observatory grounds outside Philadelphia.

When in *The Gift* H.D. tries to explain just what was different about her new public school, she emphasizes not the loneliness or the strange children but "the way the clock ticks on the wall." This was public, secular time—not the Moravian time that aligns a frontier outpost with the town of Christ's birth, but the linear time that counts achievements and expects progress, a time associated with the father who "wanted eventually (he even said so) to make a higher mathematician of me or research worker or scientist like (he even said) Madame Curie." Perhaps in pursuit of such a plan, H.D. enrolled in 1902 at Friends' Central School in Philadelphia, a preparatory school highly respected by the elite colleges that welcomed many of its students after graduation. Here, as Emily Mitchell Wallace has shown, H.D. distinguished herself as one of ten girls in the academically demanding Classical Section, where, in the kind of "research work" that would occupy the rest of her life, she read Greek, Latin, German, and French, studied ancient history, and composed an essay titled "The Poet's Influence" that she delivered at her commencement in June 1905.

The next tick propelled H.D. to Bryn Mawr, the college that prepared the era's "new women" to excel in fields previously reserved for men; but here her success clock first slowed and then abruptly stopped. With hindsight H.D.'s "entire failure to conform to expections" might seem, as the narrator of one of her autobiographical novels suggests, "some subtle form of courage," but at the time it meant anguish, estrangement, and negativity: she would not be Marie Curie, as her father had wished, nor a schoolteacher, as her mother had been, nor even one of the "English gentlemen" that Bryn Mawr's formidable president, M. Carey Thomas, was rumored to make of her graduates. If Marianne Moore, who was in H.D.'s class, barely passed Bryn Mawr English, H.D. flunked it outright, along with elocution, Latin prose composition, and various key tests in spelling, trigonometry, and analytical conics.

Sometime during the fall or winter of 1906, H.D. withdrew from Bryn Mawr without completing her third semester. Except for a brief enrollment during 1908–1909 in the University of Pennsylvania's College Course for Teachers, her formal education was over.

"Writing," H.D. muses in *HER,* the novel that scripts the next period of her life. "Love is writing." This equation has many meanings, most of which circulate through H.D.'s accounts of the years between her exit from Bryn Mawr in 1906 and her departure from the United States in 1911. In these years H.D., like a Shakespearean in exile, created an academy on the observatory grounds where she explored with two suitors—first a man, then a woman—a love of writing, a writing created through love, a love understood through writing. Her erotic entanglements with Ezra Pound and Frances Josepha Gregg taught H.D. the interdependence between desire and creativity that she theorized in *Notes on Thought and Vision* (1982) and enacted throughout her life. Everywhere in H.D.'s work, the mysteries of vision are tied to the mysteries of eros. In "research work" she could not possibly have carried on at Bryn Mawr, she discovered a cycle of sexual desire, mutual creation, interruption, betrayal, and endurance that she would re-experience throughout her life with men and women, older and younger, white and black, close and remote, human and, in H.D.'s eyes, by incarnation or evocation, divine.

It seems appropriate that two people who played so many roles in the dramas of each other's lives first met at a Halloween fancy dress ball. In 1901 H.D. was barely fifteen and not yet enrolled at Friends' Central, while Pound, himself only sixteen, was a freshman at the University of Pennsylvania. Both were avid readers, opinionated talkers, and incipient poets: "He danced badly," H.D. remembered, but "one would dance with him for what he might say." He sported lurid socks and an "immensely sophisticated, immensely superior, immensely rough-and-ready" wit; and when he returned in 1905 from a two-year sojourn at Hamilton College, they moved quickly toward the first of a number of "engagements." Between 1905 and 1907, when Pound departed for Wabash College, they read and discussed such writers as Shakespeare, Balzac, Swedenborg, Swinburne, Ibsen, Shaw, and William Morris; Pound wrote a series of ornate poems that addressed her as "Is-Hilda" or "Ysolt"; and, licensed by their "engagement," they experienced erotic transports that left her, in the words of her late poem *Winter Love,* "*Virgo,* unravaged, / but knowing the thirst."

To sustain the volatile mix of sexuality, vision, and art that composed H.D.'s creativity, it was important that desire be interrupted, that she remain "virginal"—"Virgo"—a trope she, like the Greeks, understood to signal not so much the sexually intact as the unowned woman. What is expressed in *HER* as a fear of being sexually "smudged out" reappears in *End to Torment* (1979) as the conviction that "Ezra would have destroyed me and the center they call 'Air and Crystal' of my poetry": had the engagement proceeded to marriage, both texts imply, Pound would have made her into a muse like Poe's "Helen" or a wife like her father's Helen, a Helen Do-little, but not a poet like her own visionary Helen of Egypt. Perhaps fortunately, then, their passion was interrupted by many elements: by her father's intrusions, by her mother's reservations, by the scandal that ejected Pound from Wabash College in February 1908 and propelled him in March to Europe, and, around the time of his return to Pennsylvania in June 1910, by a new element altogether, the presence of Frances Josepha Gregg.

Just as H.D.'s love for Pound took its shape from texts by Shakespeare and Morris, her desire for Gregg drew on the writings of Sappho, Swinburne, Wilde, and Pater. Her fiction presents Gregg as a startling, staring creature called "Fayne." Compounded from words like "fay," "fey," "fain," "feign," and "flame," this name captures an elfin unpredictability in Gregg that H.D. found at once compelling and cruel. Seemingly immune from social conventions, Gregg inhabited a shabby part of Philadelphia with her mother, read Freud, and had visions that—as they are re-created in *HER*—transport the two women from the hierarchical, heterosexual, domestic world of manners into a classical landscape not unlike the terrain of H.D.'s first imagist poems, a place where they lean together, "prophetess to prophetess on some Delphic headland," and labor to see. The exaltation they feel is the desire to live, love, and write differently, to be something and somewhere "else."

Deeply in love, H.D. wrote her first poems for Gregg, poems modeled on translations from Theocritus that Pound had given her. In a pattern that would recur throughout H.D.'s erotic life, this love that issues from and in writing moves in a triangular circuit. Just as the poems Pound gave H.D. passed with alterations from H.D. to Gregg, sometime in 1910, in a shift registered both in H.D.'s fiction and in Gregg's journals, Gregg fell in love with Pound. Although it set the participants spinning, this affair did not definitively break either H.D.'s brittle "engagement" to Pound or her more tensile connection with Gregg. In February 1911, Pound sailed for Europe, followed, in July, by Gregg, her mother, and H.D.

When Gregg returned to Philadelphia with her mother in late October or early November 1911, H.D. remained in London by herself but near enough to Pound for him to squire her around the literary scene, monitor her poems, and intervene, "glowering and savage," when Gregg abruptly married, returned to Europe, and invited H.D. on her honeymoon. By the end of 1912, however, when H.D. was writing steadily, and on her own, Gregg had vanished and Pound appeared only sporadically—to enter "pounding *(Pounding)*," as H.D. put it, and then, as quickly, disappear. Although they had withdrawn, H.D. never fully released these two figures with whom her creativity had been forged, for she understood them to re-enter her life again and again through the agency of others: by her reckoning, Pound's place as "initiator" would be taken up again by such figures as Richard Aldington, D. H. Lawrence, Kenneth Macpherson, Lord Hugh Dowding, and Erich Heydt, while Bryher (Annie Ellerman) would take up and settle into the place occupied by Gregg.

H.D.'s early poems swept across the literary landscape like gusts of salt air. "Whirl up, sea—," "Oread" starts, "whirl your pointed pines, / splash your great pines / on our rocks." Brief, bright, urgent, and arresting, these poems oppose both the misty symbolic vagaries and the patriotic vigor of late Victorian poetry. The thinking that informs them is concrete rather than abstract, spatial rather than narrative or logical, investigative rather than oratorical, "scientific," in Pound's terminology, rather than "subjective." It is pointless to ask whether the pine tree-waves in "Oread" are pines seen in terms of waves or waves seen in terms of pines, for the poem dissolves conventional categories in order to make visible an energy that surges through all forms of matter. In F. S. Flint's apt oxymoron, the effect is "accurate mystery": hard, sharp-edged, and stingingly precise, the poem is also radiant and elusive, for the world the "oread" or mountain nymph evokes is a place of prophecy and epiphany that the poem reconstructs—"o read"—for its readers. H.D.'s imagism is art crossed with vision and charged with desire, the first amazing coalescence of her creativity.

During the years around World War I, the business of poetry was largely conducted by groups of writers who constituted themselves as "schools," formulated "doctrines," and published sectarian anthologies. From the moment Pound attached the adjective *Imagiste* to her initials, H.D.'s poems both exemplified and justified a movement whose prohibitions against "indirection," verbiage, and fixed metrical form were designed to oppose *Symbolisme*. Imagism drew heavily on the thinking of Henri Bergson and T. E. Hulme, but, as Cyrena N. Pondrom has argued, its immediate models were the poems H.D. began to compose soon after she arrived in London. At the center of the group Pound put together in his 1914 anthology, *Des Imagistes*, were H.D., Richard Aldington, F. S. Flint, and himself; at its periphery were Joyce, Williams, Ford, Amy Lowell, John Cournos, and Skipwith Cannell. When Pound dropped imagism for vorticism, Amy Lowell stepped in as impresario, propagandist, and financier and with the help of H.D. and Aldington assembled three more imagist anthologies.

The poems of "the early H.D." were published in little magazines, quoted in manifestos, featured in anthologies, singled out in reviews, and collected in *Sea Garden* (1916), her first volume of poems; but "H.D." remained a vague and hieratic figure, recognized rather than known. The anonymous coastline, androgynous voice, suspended time, and constitutive brevity of the *Sea Garden* poems held them for the most part outside the events that swirled around imagism and soon broke it asunder. In August 1914, only a few months after the appearance of *Des Imagistes*, World War I erupted across Europe and in its turmoil scattered H.D.'s poetic companions, swept away her marriage, her brother, and her father, and all but annihilated her in its last epidemic before it finally released her in 1919 with a newborn daughter, Frances Perdita; a new partner, Bryher; and a newly forged meditative practice that boldly linked two forces she came to call "vision of the womb and vision of the brain."

H.D. met Richard Aldington in 1912. Six years younger than H.D. and equally new to the London literary scene, he was—in Woolf's not entirely kind description—a "nice downright man": bluff, vigorous, hardworking, a bit blunt, perhaps, and blustering. Educated at the University of London and currently a free-lance writer with literary ambitions, he found in H.D. a fellow aspirant to the life of truth and beauty. They took rooms, one above the other, across a "courtyard" from Pound, haunted the British Museum Reading Room and Elgin Marbles, and traveled to Paris with Pound and to Rome, Capri, and Venice with the Doolittles. Their "research work" was "Greek," a topic that seemed to signify two things: on the one hand, the enigmatic but exhilarating verse from the Greek Anthology that they translated, analyzed, and imitated, and, on the other, a playful, poetry-laden eroticism to which Pound alluded when he reported to Dorothy Shakespear that "the Dryad" and her "faun" were "submerged in . . . hellenism." When they married on 18 October 1913, they became the Aldingtons, two increasingly recognized and controversial writers linked, like the Brownings, through their commitment to art and the day-to-day writing, reviewing, translating, and editing that make up a life in letters.

Perhaps because of her Moravian sense that grand patterns work through many planes at once, H.D. never divided the public from the private, the political from the personal: the great catastrophes of her century were for her at once external and internal. Her "Autobiographical Notes" juxtapose a memory of standing outside Buckingham Palace on the night World War I began with her memory of a pregnancy that started in the summer of 1914 and ended with the stillbirth of a daughter in May 1915. The novel *Asphodel* places the blame succinctly on the shock of war: "Khaki killed it." Warned not to conceive again while medical personnel were needed for fighting men, H.D. withdrew from Aldington, the eroticism drained from their marriage, and—as *Bid Me to Live* (1960) puts it—"the Brownings" turned into "Punch and Judy." Within a year Aldington had launched the first of several affairs and enlisted in a war from which he would return with the taint of gas in his lungs and a heart full of desperation and desire. As H.D.'s fiction again and again tells the story, the young poet in love with Greece turned into a heavy, hearty, oversexed officer. When Aldington committed himself to an extended affair with Dorothy Yorke, the marriage was effectively over.

After her marriage bed had become a "deathbed," H.D. yielded first to a cerebral passion for Lawrence, who consoled her after the stillbirth and continued to kindle her creativity, then to companionship with the composer and music critic Cecil Gray, with whom she went to Cornwall in the spring of 1918. The coalescence of art, vision, and eroticism that occurred in Cornwall was largely solitary: she worked on poems, translations, and a novel; roamed the ancient, stony landscape; and, in the summer of 1918, conceived a child. Unwilling to marry Gray and unable, despite efforts on both sides, to get back together with Aldington, H.D.—with the help of her friends Margaret Snively and Brigit Patmore, after the death in action of her brother Gilbert in September 1918 and the death in grief of her father in March 1919, in spite of her own near fatal "war-pneumonia," and just after a "pounding" from Pound ("My only real criticism," he said, "is that this is not my child")—at noon on 31 March 1919 delivered a baby girl to whom she gave the name Frances Perdita.

"Names are in people," H.D. declared in *HER*, "people are in names." The name "Frances Perdita" restored to H.D. both a matrilineage and a lost female community. In the palimpsestic overlays H.D. loved, Homer's Helen is the mother of Hermione, the name H.D. selected for herself in *Asphodel* and *HER*, and Hermione is the mother of Perdita, the "lost" daughter Shakespeare restores to her mother at the end of *The Winter's Tale*. The "lost one" is, then, H.D.'s stillborn child restored, but it is also "Frances," her lost lover, returned through a woman H.D. met soon after the child's conception on a day they would celebrate the rest of their lives. "It was July 17, 1918," Bryher recalled. Having memorized *Sea Garden*, located its author, and screwed up her courage, she knocked at the door of the cottage in Cornwall and found her own loss restored. "The door opened," Bryher continued, "and I started in surprise. I had seen the face before, on a Greek statue or in some indefinable territory of the mind. We were meeting again after a long absence but not for the first time."

Born Annie Winifred Ellerman in 1894, Bryher was the daughter of Sir John Ellerman, a poor boy from Hull who built one of England's great fortunes in shipping and publishing. An active, intelligent, rebellious child who found or forged her personality through boys' adventure stories, Bryher chafed at being a girl and fell into a suicidal depression at the thought of becoming a "woman." To H.D., who had spent her own early twenties trying to write in the confines of a family eager to see her married, Bryher's anguish was familiar. Throughout the fall and early spring, in letters that started "Dear Miss Ellerman" and "Dear Mrs. Aldington," they traded books, manuscripts, and advice, proposed trips to Greece and America, and broached the subject of what H.D. termed "women who are more than women, or different from what is ordinarily accepted as such" and what Bryher thought of more bluntly as being, at heart, "boys." Precipitated by the pneumonia that almost killed H.D. and her unborn baby, the pledge both women understood to be a lifelong commitment came in March 1919. "If I got well," H.D. remembered, "she would herself see that the baby was protected and cherished and she would take me to a new world, a new life, to the land, spiritually of my predilection, geographically of my dreams. We would go to Greece."

If we understand "Greece" to mean, as it did for many early-twentieth-century lesbians, the fused art and eros of Sappho's Mitylene, H.D. also took Bryher to a "land . . . of [her] predilection." The exchange was mutual:

Bryher gave H.D. emotional, practical, and financial support; H.D. gave Bryher a reason to be "strong and wise," the tutelage of an established writer, an apparently respectable companionship that finally freed her from her family's clutches, and a fey erotic playfulness that lingered well into the 1920s. "I will comfort you," H.D. wrote Bryher in 1924, enticing her back from Paris with an appropriately fauve fantasy, "and buy some green corsets and lie on the bed done up in magenta scarves. I will perhaps have my hair carroted as a nice little surprise—." In the early years, H.D. and Bryher traveled, fussed over Perdita, fumed at each other, wrote furiously, and, in the autumn of 1921, set up residence together in Territet, Switzerland, where they maintained a tenuous respectability through Bryher's marriage of convenience to Robert McAlmon in 1921 and the calm presence of Helen Doolittle, who lived with H.D., Bryher, and Perdita until her return to America in 1925.

Once again for H.D. art, vision, and eros had coalesced. The war years had produced longer, more explosive, more explicitly gendered and historically nuanced poems, poems such as "Eurydice," which railed against masculinist privilege, and "The Tribute," which assailed militaristic "squalor" and commercialism. Now, in *Notes on Thought and Vision* (written in 1919), H.D. began to develop an aesthetic that privileged her experiences as a woman and a visionary. Perhaps because her partner was female, perhaps because she had just given birth, perhaps because this birth seemed to return her lost daughter, H.D. based her poetic on the mysteries that re-enacted Demeter's search for Persephone. In their celebration of eros, community, vision, and rebirth, the Eleusinian Mysteries proposed an alternative to death-centered and divisive materialism of war. Like initiates in the mysteries, H.D. argues, artists come to vision in stages: first, an erotic arousal "not dissipated in physical relation"; second, the development of a consciousness H.D. calls the "womb-brain or love-brain," a state in which the body thinks and the mind feels; and, finally, an intense, meditative concentration that gives the artist access to "the whole world of vision."

In this Eleusinian poetic, thought and vision are not isolate but communal. "We must be 'in love' before we can understand the mysteries of vision," H.D. maintains, not only because love stirs desire but also because when the minds of artists merge, their visionary capacities intensify. H.D. supports this thesis with examples from ancient Italy and Greece, but its antecedents were more immediate: on her July 1919 trip with Bryher to the Scilly Isles, H.D. had her " 'jelly-fish' experience," the first of a series of visions that "would not have happened," she insisted, ". . . if I had been alone." Three subsequent visionary moments marked the promised trip to Greece in the spring of 1920—the appearance of a figure H.D. called the Man on the Boat, a series of dance scenes, and a sequence of light pictures projected onto the wall of a hotel room in Corfu—all either produced for or cocreated with Bryher. As if fulfilling the mandate of *Notes,* these visions generated the themes H.D. would pursue across the following decades, confirmed her abilities as a seer, and reinforced her determination to dedicate her art to "the mysteries of vision."

Schooled by Moravian history to expect antagonism, H.D. did not hesitate to use her visionary consciousness to oppose the conventions of her culture. Many of her best poems of the 1920s and 1930s emerged from this oppositional or "revisionary" seeing: the practice of "perceiving the other-side of everything." The most powerful examples of this practice are H.D.'s mythological poems, for, as Susan Stanford Friedman, Rachel Blau DuPlessis, and Alicia Ostriker have shown, to surface "the other-side" of a myth is to contest the arrangements a culture assumes to be universal, natural, or archetypal. Everyone knows the dominant side—the story of Odysseus, Achilles, or Orpheus—but what of Calypso, Helen, or Eurydice? When

H.D. re-enters a myth and gives voice to the characters who have been "muted," the meaning of events is not just destabilized but, as DuPlessis suggests, also potentially delegitimized. The act of speaking from "the otherside" breaks the silence or partial speech that has constructed our notions of gender and forces a renegotiation of the rules we have agreed to live by.

The pressure that poems like "Eurydice," "Calypso," and "Helen" exerted on mythology, H.D.'s prose applied to her personal life. As she explained in *H.D. by Delia Alton,* her novels, shorter fiction, memoirs, and journals provided an occasion for "a very subtle emotional exercise" in which she went "over and over the ground" of her life searching for "relationships or parallels" between temporal events and eternal patterns. Only when events "came true" by fitting a timeless "formula" did H.D. allow her texts to pass out of her hands and enter into the world through publication or, more frequently, into the Yale University Library through Pearson, who maintained a shelf there for her unpublished manuscripts. Unlike her poetry, most of which appeared in her lifetime, the bulk of H.D.'s prose remained unpublished. As Friedman points out, the great service of Pearson's manuscript collection was to provide an intermediate stage, a way for H.D. to release her finished but as yet unpublished texts and move on.

Although she continues to be known primarily as a poet, H.D.'s first productions were prose sketches written sometime after 1907 and published in newspapers between 1909 and 1913. During the years in which she was establishing herself as an imagist, she probably wrote little or no prose, but for the rest of her life she labored with pride and persistence over fiction, autobiography, essays, and journals. The "research work" of H.D.'s first full-length fiction was the interpretation of the overlapping personal, political, and spiritual crises surrounding World War I. A lifelong project, this "novel," started in Cornwall in 1918, was not completed until the manuscript she called "Madrigal" was shelved with Pearson in 1949 and finally published as *Bid Me to Live* in 1960. Its three full drafts—"Paint It To-Day" (1921), "Asphodel" (1921–1922), and "Madrigal"—form a kind of composite text that moves back toward her childhood and forward through 1919, experiments with Jamesian, Joycean, cinematic, and poetic styles, and thinks its way through the various subject positions available to a bisexual binational, visionary woman writer caught in "the cosmic, comic, crucifying times" of modernism.

Looking back on the two other clusters of fiction she composed in the 1920s and 1930s, H.D. found them unnerving and "weedy." "Pilate's Wife" (1924), *Hedylus* (1928), and "Hipparchia," the first story in *Palimpsest* (1926), were romans à clef that played out the events of her life in ancient Palestine, fictions nonetheless hewed closer to a realistic surface than the second cluster, a series of magic and mercurial "booklets" published in limited editions "for the author's friends." Written between her mother's death in 1927 and her psychoanalysis with Freud in 1933–1934, the two best novellas of this series—*Kora and Ka* (1934) and *Nights* (1935)—record the vagaries of H.D.'s alliance with the fey, fascinating man who became her next co-creator.

When Frances Gregg introduced them in 1926, H.D. was forty and Kenneth Macpherson twenty-four, a graceful, talented knockabout who quickly became H.D.'s lover and Bryher's companion. After negotiating a settlement handsome enough to turn McAlmon into "McAlimony," Bryher divorced her first husband and in September 1927 married Macpherson. For large parts of the next five years, H.D., Bryher, and Kenneth maintained a household in Switzerland, together with Perdita in intervals between English schools, housekeepers and gardeners in and out of favor, flocks of visiting writers, filmmakers, actors, and analysts, and even, for a while, a band of pet dourocouli monkeys. The nicknames this ménage made up for themselves—H.D. was "Cat"; Bryher, "Fido"; Macpherson, "Rover"; and Perdita, "Pup"—reflect the warmth and tenor of their alliance: H.D. scratched and purred, Bryher remained staunch and steadfast, Macpherson strayed but stayed, and Perdita struggled to grow up.

H.D.'s next "research work" was a creative adventure that began with a camera Bryher gave to Macpherson and Macpherson used to make three Dadaist or expressionist home movies—*Wingbeat* (1927), *Foothills* (1928–1929), and *Monkey's Moon* (1929)—and then, in 1930, a feature-length film called *Borderline*, starring H.D. and Paul Robeson, and featuring Bryher in a cameo role as a cigar-smoking innkeeper. Evoking G. W. Pabst's psychoanalytic films and employing Eisenstein's "overtonal montage," the film was a co-creation: written, directed, and shot by Macpherson, edited by H.D. and Bryher, theorized and publicized by H.D., it used a story of interracial desire to test a series of social, psychic, and artistic borderlines. In addition to starring in three of Macpherson's four films and learning to use the cinematic equipment, H.D. wrote eleven articles and a series of poems for *Close Up*, a journal edited by Bryher and Macpherson as a forum for writers, filmmakers, and psychoanalysts on such topics as spectator manipulation and the politics of representation. In the spring of 1929, responding to a survey conducted by the *Little Review*, H.D. expressed her delight in all these activities. "I should like for the moment," she concluded, "to be what I am."

The contentment of this period faltered in the next year when Macpherson's roving led to a passionate attachment to Toni Slocum, a black man he had met in Monte Carlo. Well before July 1931, when they moved into Kenwin, their specially built cube of a house above Lake Geneva, their bond had begun to dissolve. The house contained a projection room, a series of cabin-sized bedrooms, and enough decks to make it look like a stately ship, but the life it had been designed to forward now seemed to have run aground: Macpherson was increasingly absent, Bryher increasingly reserved, H.D. increasingly agitated. The abrupt, lonely, disoriented poems of *Red Roses for Bronze* (1931) express a yearning for "a lost measure" that is not just classical metrics but a general sense of life's proportion and beauty. Once again H.D.'s erotic arrangements and creative alignments had begun to dissolve; once again, ominously, war was approaching.

In her "Autobiographical Notes," H.D. dates her next research project from 1932, but her immersion in Freud's thought, begun with Gregg in Philadelphia, had continued with Bryher, an early student and advocate of psychoanalysis and, after November 1928, an analysand of Freud's disciple Hanns Sachs. After two false starts in 1931, first with Mary Chadwick and then with Sachs, H.D. turned to the master himself and on 1 March 1933 began two series of sessions with Freud. The first lasted until mid June, when the Nazi presence made it too dangerous to linger any longer in Vienna; the second, lasting from 31 October to 2 December 1934, followed her collapse at the news of the sudden death of Dr. J. J. van der Leeuw, a scholar, theosophist, and fellow analysand whom H.D. had expected to spiritualize and disseminate Freud's teachings. "I came back to Vienna," H.D. told Freud, "to tell you how sorry I am." "You have come," Freud replied, "to take his place."

H.D.'s reasons for entering analysis had much to do with war. Like most of Freud's late analysands, she considered herself as much his student as his patient, for she planned not only to disseminate his teachings through her writings but to enact them through the practice of lay analysis. Both in order to write freshly and forcefully and in order to work effectively with those about to be shocked and shattered by war, she knew she had to return to her own World War I traumas and, like a trench soldier, "dig down and dig out . . . strengthen my purpose, reaffirm my beliefs, canalize my energies." Because it seemed at once to reaffirm her vocation and to suggest a way out of war, it was especially important for her to return to and reread with Freud "the writing on the wall," the vision at Corfu that had positioned her as a seer, predicted the conflict now imminent, and promised that at the end of this war she would be free to "go on in another, a winged dimension."

H.D. recorded her interactions with Freud in detailed daily letters to Bryher; in her poem "The Master," which she held back from publication; in her Vienna journals, which she edited and entitled *Advent* (1974); in the tribute to Freud she called *Writing on the Wall* (1945–1946); and, finally, in her epic poem *Helen in Egypt* (1961). The initial event of the analysis and spark of the creative work to come was, once again, a surge of erotic energy: the transference that began the analysis proper. For Freud, this event positioned him as her mother; for H.D., it turned him into "Papa," "the Professor," the possessor of an arcane, all-powerful knowledge they explored throughout their sessions. Because it rejoined art and science, love and knowledge, "mother" and "father," the hard work of analysis was for H.D. an ecstatic labor. Throughout its long weeks she remained, as she reported to Bryher, "well, happy, sane, sobbing."

Analysis with Freud taught H.D. ways of pursuing wisdom that mark all the work that follows: from him she learned to follow out associative chains of memories, to use her childhood experiences to understand the myths that record the childhood of the race, and to accept or even anticipate the unending conflict between eros and thanatos, the drive to life and the drive to death. Freud's brilliant, stubborn self-analysis gave H.D. the courage to pursue her own reveries, dreams, and visions to "the other-side of everything," the source Freud identified as the unconscious but H.D. understood more broadly as the wisdom that generates all great and sacred writing. Unlike the American analysts who would turn his theories to the task of "normalizing" their analysands, Freud affirmed H.D.'s differences from him and from her culture and reinforced the eros, art, and vision that constituted her creativity: she was, Freud told her, "that all-but-extinct phenomena [*sic*], the perfect bi-[sexual]"; "you are," he affirmed and again, "a poet"; "the secret," he said, "lies with you."

The war that marked H.D.'s next flare-up of creativity broke out in September 1939. By November, H.D. had moved from Kenwin to the Lowndes Square flat she maintained in London, where in September 1940 she was joined by Bryher. In these cramped quarters close to the anti-aircraft batteries in Hyde Park, and thus constantly in the target range of German bombers, H.D. and Bryher sustained each other through the terror and tedium of the London blitz. The creative group they formed around them included Edith and Osbert Sitwell, Robert Herring, George Plank, Silvia Dobson, Gerald and Cole Henderson, and, most crucially for H.D., Norman Holmes Pearson, whom she had first met on a trip to the United States in 1937. Now assigned to a wartime post in London, Pearson joined her for long Sunday-afternoon teas during which he became not only a confidant but a literary consultant who would henceforth not only stimulate and steady her writing but guide it gently toward publication.

During the years between the end of her analysis and the outbreak of war, H.D. had worked on a variety of short stories and novels, completed her translation of Euripides' *Ion*, (1937), and composed most of "Madrigal," but her most intense creative burst occurred between 1941 and 1946. A vignette from Pearson's notes captures the sustained call and response between H.D.'s typewriter and the German bombs: "tap, tap, tap on the machine when the explosion came & Mrs. Ashe [the charwoman] saying 'But, Madame' and H. saying—'Go away! Go away! Let me type!' " Driven by recurrent spells of memory, dream, and vision, H.D. wrote furiously and brilliantly, composing the sketches from *Within the Walls* (1990), the novel "Majic Ring," her "autobiographical fantasy" *The Gift* (1982), her tribute to Freud in *Writing on the Wall* (1945–1946), and the poems published in *What Do I Love?* (1944) and *Trilogy* (1973).

Like *Helen in Egypt* (1961), the three-part poem H.D. composed in Switzerland between 1952 and 1955, *Trilogy* is a poem of epic reach and design. Composed in the midst of crisis, drawing on knowledge amassed in lifelong "research," it is the work of a writer assuming authority as a culture-shaper. Like all epics, this poem narrates the audience's historical and mythic heritage, provides models of exemplary conduct by which we can regulate our lives, and speaks for values the writer holds crucial to our collective well-being. The readers of this poem are positioned not as solitary, inward individuals but as citizens responsible for the continuance of our social and spiritual heritage.

If, as H.D. informed Pearson, "this book is 'philosophy,' " it teaches not a dogma but a process of thinking that undermines all fixities: rejecting materialism, utilitarianism, nationalism, and the rigidities of a masculinist monotheism, the poem guides its readers backward through Christian, Greek, Hebrew, and Egyptian mythologies; draws on dream, vision, and alchemical wisdom; and reaffirms the rhythms of breakdown and metamorphosis, blight and blossom, death and resurrection. At the poem's center is H.D.'s vision of a woman who incarnates the fused erotic, spiritual, and artistic energies crucial not just to personal but also to cultural creativity: "we have seen her / the world over," H.D. writes, but now, portending, perhaps, our release from repetition, she appears to us as a Lady carrying "the blank pages / of the unwritten volume of the new."

Like many who held up stoically throughout the blitz, H.D. broke down, shocked and shattered, at the end of the war. Malnourished, overstressed, rubbed raw by Bryher's "state of permanent rush," and exhausted by her own exaltations, she was, finally, tipped over the edge by a rebuff from the spiritualist Lord Hugh Dowding, the former chief air marshal of the British Royal Air Force, to whom she had tried to convey messages she felt she had received from his dead pilots. Tormented by visions of an imminent third world war, H.D. collapsed completely and in May 1946 was flown to the Brunner clinic, at Küsnacht, near Zürich. This flight marked the transition into the final, creatively rich decades of her life.

"Indeed," H.D. wrote in one of her late journals, "Ellen Glasgow is right, our lives begin, some of them, when we are 60." In late 1946, after recovering from her breakdown, H.D. began a creative push that lasted until her final stroke in 1961. In addition to completing old manuscripts, she researched and wrote four long novels: "The Sword Went Out to Sea," a narrative of the visionary events of World War II; "White Rose and the Red," the story of Rossetti and his circle; "The Mystery," a fictionalized episode from Moravian history; and "Magic Mirror," an account of life in the Swiss clinic where she spent long stretches of her last years. In addition to editing her Freud journals and writing book-length tributes to Pound and Shakespeare, she composed "Delia Altons's" analysis of "H.D.," completed a set of "Autobiographical Notes," wrote three long journal-essays, and finished her last great poems: the magisterial and mysterious *Helen in Egypt* (1961) and the long, arcane meditations she called *Vale Ave* (1982), *Sagesse* (1972), *Winter Love* (1972), and *Hermetic Definition* (1972).

Although they never lived far apart, after their years in London H.D. and Bryher never again lived together: Bryher continued to inhabit Kenwin, H.D. moved back and forth between clinics in Küsnacht and various hotels in

Lausanne and Lugano. In June 1950, Perdita married John Schaffner, and in 1951 she produced the first of four grandchildren, each of whom H.D. crossed the ocean to greet. She continued her correspondence with Pearson, developed an epistolary conversation with the scholar Eliza M. Butler, and continued exchanging friendly letters with Aldington, from whom she had been formally divorced in 1938. Her most intense relationships in these years, however, were her encounters with a series of men who rekindled the erotic energies that always sparked her creativity: Erich Heydt, an analyst at Küsnacht who revived her memories of Pound and brought forth *End to Torment* and *Winter Love;* Lionel Durand, a Haitian journalist who interviewed her on the publication of *Bid Me to Live,* reminded her of Paul Robeson, and elicited the passion that produced parts of *Hermetic Definition;* and St.-John Perse, whom she met when she received the Award of Merit Medal from the American Academy of Arts and Letters (1960) and who sparked yet another part of *Hermetic Definition.*

In her last years H.D. suffered a number of physical ailments without losing either her beauty or her flair. She had, Bryher recalled from the midst of her own old age, "a face that came directly from a Greek statue and, almost to the end, the body of an athlete." In addition to her intensity and seriousness, she possessed, Heydt recalls, a comic and lovable extravagance, an exuberance that her friend the composer Eric Walter White catches in his account of tea with her during her recovery from a broken hip. "With Bryher and myself sitting down cautiously at opposite ends of the table," White remembers, "H.D. stomped to her chair and then hurled her aluminium crutches over her shoulders with a gesture worthy of Long John Silver." Writing from her bed after intense, prolonged daily meditation, H.D. continued, almost to the end, to produce poems that are, like the late poems of Yeats and Stevens, at once alert and attenuated, attuned to fierce but unearthly music.

"It requires more bravery to overcome the weariness and lassitude of old age than to go into the battlefield," H.D. wrote, but at the end she held on through a stroke, aphasia, a heart attack, and flu until on 27 September 1961, hours after the first copy of *Helen in Egypt* had been placed in her hands, she passed quietly away. Her ashes were interred in the Moravian cemetery in Bethlehem, but her words continue to inhabit "the winged dimension" predicted by the writing on the wall in Corfu and celebrated in a speech she delivered as she accepted her Award of Merit in 1960. In words that catch both the expansiveness and the humility of her best texts, H.D. wrote: "Winged words make their own spiral; caught up in them, we are lost, or found. . . . This winged victory belongs to the poem, not the poet. But to share in the making of a poem is the privilege of a poet."

Selected Bibliography

PRIMARY WORKS

POETRY

Sea Garden. London: Constable, 1916; Boston: Houghton Mifflin, 1916.

The Tribute and Circe: Two Poems. Cleveland: Clerk's Private Press, 1917.

Hymen. London: Egoist Press, 1921; New York: Henry Holt, 1921.

Heliodora and Other Poems. Boston: Houghton Mifflin, 1924.

Hippolytus Temporizes. Boston: Houghton Mifflin, 1927; Redding Ridge, Conn.: Black Swan, 1985.

Red Roses for Bronze. London: Chatto & Windus, 1931; Boston and New York: Houghton Mifflin, 1931.

The Walls Do Not Fall. London and New York: Oxford University Press, 1944.

What Do I Love? London: Brendin, 1944.

Tribute to the Angels. London and New York: Oxford University Press, 1945.

The Flowering of the Rod. London and New York: Oxford University Press, 1946.

By Avon River. New York: Macmillan, 1949; Redding Ridge, Conn.: Black Swan, 1989.

Helen in Egypt. New York: Grove Press, 1961.

Hermetic Definition. New York: New Directions, 1972.

Trilogy. New York: New Directions, 1973. Contains *The Walls Do Not Fall, Tribute to the Angels,* and *The Flowering of the Rod*.

"Vale Ave." In *New Directions in Prose and Poetry 44*. Edited by James Laughlin et al. New York: New Directions, 1982. Pp. 18–68.

FICTION

Palimpsest. Paris: Contact, 1926; Boston: Houghton Mifflin, 1926; rev. ed. Carbondale: Southern Illinois University Press, 1968.

Hedylus. Boston: Houghton Mifflin, 1928; rev. ed. Redding Ridge, Conn.: Black Swan, 1980.

"Narthex." In *Second American Caravan*. Edited by Alfred Kreymborg, Lewis Mumford, and Paul Rosenfeld. New York: Macaulay, 1928. Pp. 225–284.

Kora and Ka. Dijon: Darantière, 1934. Contains *Kora and Ka* and *Mira-Mare*.

The Usual Star. Dijon: Darantière, 1934. Contains "The Usual Star" and "Two Americans."

Nights. Dijon: Darantière, 1935; New York: New Directions, 1986. By "John Helforth."

The Hedgehog. London: Brendin, 1936; New York: New Directions, 1988.

Bid Me to Live (a Madrigal). New York: Grove Press, 1960; New York: Dial Press; Redding Ridge, Conn.: Black Swan, 1983.

The Mystery. In Eric W. White, *Images of H.D.* London: Enitharmon, 1976. White publishes chs. 3, 14–19 of *The Mystery*.

HERmione. New York: New Directions, 1981. Reprinted as *HER*. London: Virago, 1984.

Within the Walls. Iowa City: Windhover, 1990.

Asphodel. Durham, N.C.: Duke University Press, 1990.

TRANSLATIONS

Choruses from Iphigenia in Aulis. London: Egoist Press, 1916; Cleveland: Clerk's Private Press, 1916.

Choruses from the Iphigenia in Aulis and the Hippolytus of Euripides. London: Egoist Press, 1919.

Euripides' Ion. London: Chatto & Windus, 1937; Boston: Houghton Mifflin, 1937. Reprinted as *Ion: A Play After Euripides*. Redding Ridge, Conn.: Black Swan, 1986.

NONFICTION

Borderline: A Pool Film with Paul Robeson. London: Mercury, 1930. Also in *Sagetrieb* 6, no. 2: 29–49 (Fall 1987).

"Writing on the Wall." *Life and Letters To-Day* 45:67–98, 137–154 (April–June 1945); 46:72–89, 136–151 (July–September 1945); 48:33–45 (January–March 1946). Published in book form as *Writing on the Wall*. New York: Pantheon, 1956. Reprinted as *Tribute to Freud*. Boston: David R. Godine, 1974. The 1974 edition also includes "Advent."

End to Torment: A Memoir of Ezra Pound. Edited by Norman Holmes Pearson and Michael King. New York: New Directions, 1979. Includes Pound's *Hilda's Book*.

The Gift. New York: New Directions, 1982. Abridged version. Unabridged portions as follows: ch. 1, "The Dark Room," *Montemora* 8:57–76 (1981); ch. 2, "The Fortune Teller," *Iowa Review* 16:14–41 (Fall 1986); ch. 3, "The Dream," *Contemporary Literature* 10:605–626 (1969).

Notes on Thought and Vision and The Wise Sappho. San Francisco: City Lights, 1982.

"H.D. by *Delia Alton*." *Iowa Review* 16:174–221 (Fall 1986).

"Paint It To-Day." *Contemporary Literature* 27:444–474 (Winter 1986). Chs. 1–4.

SELECTED AND COLLECTED EDITIONS

Collected Poems of H.D. New York: Boni & Liveright, 1925, 1940.

Selected Poems of H.D. New York: Grove Press, 1957.

Collected Poems, 1912–1944. Edited by Louis L. Martz. New York: New Directions, 1983.

Selected Poems. Edited by Louis L. Martz. New York: New Directions, 1988.

MANUSCRIPT PAPERS

The Collection of American Literature, Beinecke Rare Book and Manuscript Library, Yale University, houses manuscripts of unpublished and some published works, correspondence, and an index file of books H.D. left to Norman Holmes Pearson. Additional letters are at the Houghton Library (Harvard University), the Berg Collection (the New York Public Library), the Lilly Library (Indiana University), the Lockwood Library (the State University of New York–Buffalo), the Rosenbach Collection (the Rosenbach Foundation, Philadelphia), the Huntington Library (San Marino, Calif.), and the libraries of the

University of Texas–Austin, Southern Illinois University, the University of Arkansas, UCLA, Temple University, and Bryn Mawr College.

SECONDARY WORKS

BIOGRAPHICAL AND CRITICAL STUDIES

Burnett, Gary. *H.D. Between Image and Epic: The Mysteries of Her Poetics.* Ann Arbor: UMI Research Press, 1989

DuPlessis, Rachel Blau. *H.D.: The Career of That Struggle.* Brighton: Harvester, 1986; Bloomington: Indiana University Press, 1986.

Friedman, Susan Stanford. *Psyche Reborn: The Emergence of H.D.* Bloomington: Indiana University Press, 1981.

———. *Penelope's Web: H.D.'s Fictions and the Engendering of Modernism.* Cambridge and New York: Cambridge University Press, 1991.

Friedman, Susan Stanford, and Rachel Blau DuPlessis, eds. *Signets: Reading H.D.*. Madison: University of Wisconsin Press, 1990.

Fritz, Angela DiPace. *Thought and Vision: A Critical Reading of H.D.'s Poetry.* Washington, D.C.: Catholic University Press, 1988.

Guest, Barbara. *Herself Defined: The Poet H.D. and Her World.* Garden City, N.Y.: Doubleday, 1984.

King, Michael, ed. *H.D.: Woman and Poet.* Orono, Me.: National Poetry Foundation, 1986.

Kloepfer, Deborah Kelly. *The Unspeakable Mother: Forbidden Discourse in Jean Rhys and H.D.* Ithaca, N.Y.: Cornell University Press, 1989.

Laity, Cassandra. *H.D. and the Turn-of-the-Century: Gender, Modernism and Romantic Influence.* Princeton, N.J.: Princeton University Press, 1990.

Swann, Thomas Burnett. *The Classical World of H.D.*. Lincoln: University of Nebraska Press, 1962.

SPECIAL JOURNAL ISSUES ON H.D.

Agenda 25, no. 3–4 (1987–1988). Edited by Diana Collecott.

Contemporary Literature 10 (Autumn 1969). Edited by L. S. Dembo.

Contemporary Literature 27 (Winter 1986). Edited by Susan Stanford Friedman and Rachel Blau DuPlessis.

H.D. Newsletter (1987–). Edited by Eileen Gregory.

HOW(ever) 3 (October 1986). Edited by Kathleen Fraser.

Poesis 6 (Winter 1985). Edited by Thomas H. Jackson.

Sagetrieb 6 (Fall 1987). Edited by Rachel Blau DuPlessis.

San Jose Studies 13 (Fall 1987). Issue on Emily Dickinson and H.D.

Iowa Review 16 (Fall 1986). Edited by Adalaide Morris.

ARTICLES, ESSAYS, AND BOOK CHAPTERS

Arthur, Marilyn. "Psycho-Mythology: The Case of H.D." *Bucknell Review* 28, no. 2:65–79 (1983).

Boughn, Michael. "Elements of Sounding: H.D. and the Origins of Modernist Prosodies." *Sagetrieb* 6:101–122 (Fall 1987).

Buck, Claire. "Freud and H.D.: Bisexuality and a Feminine Discourse." *M/F* 8:53–65 (1983).

Collecott, Diana. "Remembering Oneself: The Reputation and Later Poetry of H.D." *Critical Quarterly* 27:7–22 (Spring 1985).

———. "Images at the Crossroads: The 'H.D. Scrapbook.' " In King, pp. 319–367. Revised version in Friedman and DuPlessis, *Signets.*

Drake, William. *The First Wave: Women Poets in America, 1915–1945.* New York: Macmillan, 1987. Ch. 5.

Duncan, Robert. "The H.D. Book: Outline and Chronology." *Ironwood* 22:65 (1983). This lists the seventeen chapters and chapter parts of Duncan's important "H.D. Book" published as of 1983.

———. "From the H.D. Book, Part II, Chapter 5." *Sagetrieb* 4: 39–85 (Fall–Winter 1985).

———. "The H.D. Book: Part II, Chapter 6." *Southern Review* n.s. 21:26–48 (January 1985).

———. "H.D.'s Challenge." *Poesis* 6:21–34 (Winter 1985).

DuPlessis, Rachel Blau. "Romantic Thralldom in H.D." *Contemporary Literature* 20:178–203 (Spring 1979).

———. "A Note on the State of H.D.'s *The Gift.*" *Sulfur* 9:178–182 (1984).

Writing Beyond the Ending: Narrative Strategies of Twentieth-Century Women Writers. Bloomington: Indiana University Press, 1985. Pp. 66–83, 116–121.

———. "Language Acquisition." *Iowa Review* 16:252–283 (Fall 1986).

DuPlessis, Rachel Blau, and Susan Stanford Friedman. " 'Woman Is Perfect': H.D.'s Debate with Freud." *Feminist Studies* 7:417–430 (Fall 1981).

Firchow, Peter. "Hilda Doolittle." In *American Writers,* supp. 1, pt. 1. Edited by Leonard Ungar. New York: Scribners, 1979. Pp. 253–275.

Friedberg, Anne. "Approaching *Borderline.*" *Millen-*

nium Film Journal 7–9:130–139 (Fall–Winter 1980–1981). Expanded version in King, pp. 369–390.

Friedman, Susan Stanford. "Who Buried H.D.? A Poet, Her Critics, and Her Place in 'the Literary Tradition.' " *College English* 36:801–814 (March 1975).

———. " 'I Go Where I Love: An Intertextual Study of H.D. and Adrienne Rich." *Signs* 9:228–245 (Winter 1983). Expanded version, "Adrienne Rich and H.D.: An Intertextual Study." In *Reading Adrienne Rich: Reviews and Re-Vision, 1951–1981.* Edited by Jane Roberta Cooper. Ann Arbor: University of Michigan Press, 1984. Pp. 171–206.

———. " 'Remembering Shakespeare Always, but Remembering Him Differently': H.D.'s *By Avon River.*" *Sagetrieb* 2:45–70 (Summer–Fall 1983).

———. "Palimpsest of Origins in H.D.'s Career." *Poesis* 6:56–73 (Winter 1985).

———. "Hilda Doolittle (H.D.)" In *Dictionary of Literary Biography.* Vol. 45, *American Poets, 1880–1945, First Series.* Edited by Peter Quartermain. Detroit: Gale Research, 1986. Pp. 115–149.

———. "H.D. Chronology: Composition and Publication of Volumes." *Sagetrieb* 6:51–55 (Fall 1987). Revised version in Friedman and DuPlessis, *Signets.*

———. "The Return of the Repressed in Women's Narrative." *Journal of Narrative Technique* 19:141–156 (January 1989). Expanded version in Friedman and DuPlessis, *Signets.*

Friedman, Susan Stanford, and Rachel Blau DuPlessis. " 'I Had Two Loves Separate': The Sexualities of H.D.'s *Her.*" *Montemora* 8:7–30 (1981).

Gelpi, Albert. "Re-membering the Mother: A Reading of H.D.'s *Trilogy.*" In King, pp. 173–190.

Grahn, Judy. *The Highest Apple: Sappho and the Lesbian Literary Tradition.* San Francisco: Spinsters, Ink, 1985. Pp. 49–57, 101–109, 135.

Gregory, Eileen. "Rose Cut in Rock: Sappho and H.D.'s *Sea Garden.*" *Contemporary Literature* 27:525–552 (Winter 1986).

———. "Scarlet Experience: H.D.'s *Hymen.*" *Sagetrieb* 6:77–100 (Fall 1987).

Gubar, Susan. "The Echoing Spell of H.D.'s *Trilogy.*" *Contemporary Literature* 19:196–218 (Spring 1978).

———. "Sapphistries." *Signs* 10:43–62 (Autumn 1984).

Hatlen, Burton. "Recovering the Human Equation: H.D.'s 'Hermetic Definition.' " *Sagetrieb* 6:141–169 (Fall 1987).

Hirsh, Elizabeth A. " 'New Eyes' ": H.D., Modernism, and the Psychoanalysis of Seeing." *Literature and Psychology* 32:1–10 (1986).

Holland, Norman N. "H.D. and the 'Blameless Physician.' " *Contemporary Literature* 10:474–506 (1969).

Kloepfer, Deborah Kelly. "Fishing the Murex Up: Sense and Resonance in H.D.'s *Palimpsest.*" *Contemporary Literature* 27:553–573 (Winter 1986).

Laity, Cassandra. "H.D.'s Romantic Landscapes: The Sexual Politics of the Garden." *Sagetrieb* 6:57–75 (Fall 1987).

Levertov, Denise. "H.D.: An Appreciation." *Poetry* 100:182–186 (June 1962).

Mandel, Charlotte. "Magical Lenses: Poet's Vision Beyond the Naked Eye." In King, pp. 301–317.

Morris, Adalaide. "The Concept of Projection: H.D.'s Visionary Powers." *Contemporary Literature* 25:411–436 (Winter 1984).

———. "A Relay of Power and of Peace: H.D. and the Spirit of the Gift." *Contemporary Literature* 27:493–524 (Winter 1986).

Ostriker, Alicia. *Writing Like a Woman.* Ann Arbor: University of Michigan Press, 1983. Pp. 7–41.

———. "No Rule of Procedure: The Open Poetics of H.D." *Agenda* 25:145–154 (Autumn–Winter 1987–1988). Revised version in Friedman and DuPlessis, *Signets.*

Pondrom, Cyrena N. "H.D. and the Origins of Imagism." *Sagetrieb* 4:73–97 (Spring 1985).

Riddel, Joseph N. "H.D. and the Poetics of 'Spiritual Realism.' " *Contemporary Literature* 10:447–473 (1969).

———. "H.D.'s Scene of Writing: Poetry as (and) Analysis." *Studies in the Literary Imagination* 12:41–59 (Spring 1979).

Silverstein, Louis H. "The H.D. Papers at Yale University." *H.D. Newsletter* 1:7–9 (Spring 1987).

Smith, Paul. "Wounded Woman: H.D.'s Post-Imagist Writing." In *Pound Revised.* London: Croom Helm, 1983. Pp. 110–132.

———. "H.D.'s Identity." *Women's Studies* 10:321–337 (1984).

———. "H.D.'s Flaws." *Iowa Review* 16:77–86 (Fall 1986).

Wallace, Emily Mitchell. "Athene's Owl." *Poesis* 6:98–123 (Winter 1985).

Zajdel, Melody M. "Portrait of an Artist as a Woman: H.D.'s Raymonde Ransome." *Women's Studies* 13:127–134 (1986).

BIBLIOGRAPHIES

Boughn, Michael. "The Bibliographic Record of H.D.'s Contributions to Periodicals." *Sagetrieb* 6:171–194 (Fall 1987).

———. "The Bibliographic Record of Reviews of H.D.'s Works." *H.D. Newsletter* 2:27–47 (Spring 1988).

Bryer, Jackson R., and Pamela Roblyer. "H.D.: A Preliminary Checklist." *Contemporary Literature* 10:632–675 (1969).

Friedman, Susan Stanford. "Selected Bibliography." In *Signets: Reading H.D.* Edited by Susan S. Friedman and Rachel D. Blau. Madison: University of Wisconsin Press, 1990.

Mathis, Mary S., and Michael King. "An Annotated Bibliography of Works about H.D., 1969–1985." In *H.D.: Woman and Poet.* Edited by Michael King. Orono, Me.: National Poetry Foundation, 1986. Pp. 393–511.

The author would like to thank Susan Stanford Friedman and Louis H. Silverstein for their helpful readings of the manuscript of this essay.

ADALAIDE MORRIS

JESSIE FAUSET

1882–1961

WHENEVER JESSIE FAUSET is cited as a writer of the Harlem Renaissance, a predictable response follows: Who is he? Those familiar with the movement know that Jessie was a she, but their knowledge of her tends to be restricted to a handful of generalizations and clichés. Most of these issue from long-standing misinformation about Fauset's supposed background as an Old Philadelphian of wealth and status. (Much of this misinformation is corrected in Carolyn Sylvander's biography of Fauset.)

Born 27 April 1882 in Snow Hill Center Township, New Jersey, Fauset was the seventh child of Redmon Fauset, a minister in the African Methodist Episcopal Church, and of Annie Seamon Fauset. After her mother's death, Fauset's father married Bella Huff. They had three children, including Arthur Huff Fauset, a writer and intellectual who assisted Sylvander in setting the record straight about Fauset's supposed background of privilege. But despite Sylvander's corrections, misinformation about Fauset's life continues to dominate the critical reading of her work.

Reading from life to art, even Fauset's most charitable readers have generally concluded that she was simply an apologist for the black middle class, and that her most important role in the Harlem Renaissance was that of midwife. Langston Hughes's famous statement in his autobiography, *The Big Sea* (1940), might well be said to have served as her epitaph. He groups her with one of three people who "midwifed the so-called New Negro literature into being."

Like midwives throughout history, Fauset played a role reserved for women, in particular for women who failed to conform to their socially assigned roles. As a midwife to the Harlem Renaissance, she played the now depreciated role of one who assists at a birth but is otherwise considered unessential to it.

Yet Fauset's contribution was vital to the Harlem Renaissance as it is popularly understood, despite the movement's dominance by male writers. In *Color, Sex, and Poetry* (1987), Gloria Hull observes that though women certainly participated fully in the movement, broad social factors—most prominently men's negative attitudes toward women and male-formulated aesthetic norms and expectations—worked to exclude and marginalize its women writers. Those norms and expectations served a regulating function that Fauset was able to sidestep, if not ignore.

The *Crisis,* a magazine published by the National Association for the Advancement of Colored People, gave temporary license and support to Fauset's independence during the period from 1919 to 1926, when she was its literary editor. She took the position at the height of the magazine's circulation and during the period of its most intense involvement in the arts. Fauset proved to be an astute and responsive advocate of others' work. As editor she published (some for the first time) those writers who went on to become the most prominent figures of the Harlem movement: Claude McKay, Jean Toomer, Anne Spencer, and, arguably the most famous, Langston Hughes. It was Fauset who accepted Hughes's most anthologized poem, "The Negro Speaks of Rivers." In a 1922 letter to Hughes, following her acceptance of more of his poems, she wrote, "You assuredly have the true poetic touch, the divine afflatus, which will someday carry you far." Her prediction came true: Hughes later won distinction as poet laureate of Harlem and eventually of African Americans everywhere.

Although Hughes was the best-known of the writers she encouraged, Fauset was equally important to the career of Jean Toomer, whose work she considered "marked proof of an art and of a contribution to literature which will be distinctly Negroid and without propaganda." Impressed especially with his poem "Song of the Son," she praised its "studied and practiced" technique and advised him to "read voraciously, not only the moderns but the ancients. Get some translations of the Greek poets. Get together enough French to be able to read the imagist poetry of France."

Fauset's editorial stance had nothing to with pedantry or a dilettantism. Rather, as an unerring editor, she understood the limitations of provincialism on the production of art. Her impatience with narrow conceptions of art was especially evident in her interest in various black literatures. She both translated and reviewed translations of French West Indian writing, appreciating, as only a translator can, that few works bear resetting in another tongue. Her review (1922) of the translation of René Maran's celebrated novel, *Batouala*, is a judicious and nuanced piece of criticism, alert to both the translation's technical achievements and its failings.

Throughout her term as literary editor of the *Crisis*, Fauset strained to encompass the common thread, to see the larger perspective, not only in her views about art and in her advice to younger writers, but also in her political commitments and activities. She traveled to the Second Pan-African Congress, held in London, Brussels, and Paris in 1921, and supported the position of the delegates that the status of blacks in modern society could no longer be seen as a domestic problem of the United States or of any other specific geographical locale; rather, it must be seen as a worldwide problem to be solved within an international frame. Fauset published her reports on the congress in the *Crisis*.

Displaying her wit and talent as an essayist, which are seldom acknowledged, Fauset's first report, "Impressions of the Second Pan-African Congress," ran in the November 1921 issue of the *Crisis* and was followed by "What Europe Thought of the Pan-African Congress" in the December issue. The two pieces form a brilliant study in contrasting representations of the congress—the first, black; the second, white. Fauset published her "impressions" first, casting "what Europe thought" in an uncharacteristic secondary place. Excerpts from "Impressions" display an incisive awareness of the need for blacks from the four corners of the world to close ranks in fighting "the rod of the common oppressor."

Unsparing in her condemnation of that oppressor, Fauset was especially caustic and astute in her observations about Belgium as a colonial power: "Many of Belgium's economic and material interests centre in Africa in the Belgian Congo. Any interference with the natives might result in an interference with the sources from which so many Belgian capitalists drew their prosperity." Visiting the Congo Museum and seeing a storehouse of "illimitable riches," she "was able to envisage what Africa means to Europe, depleted as she has become through the ages by war and famine and plague."

Fauset registers her dismay at the absence of strong criticism of colonial dominion, especially from black Africa. Missing was any "suggestion that this was an international Congress called to define and make intelligible the greatest set of wrongs against human beings that the modern world has known." Between Brussels and Paris she noted "blasted town, ravaged village and plain," ruined in World War I, "whose basic motif had been the rape of Africa."

Arguably one of Fauset's most inspired essays, "Impressions of the Second Pan-African Congress" displays her political astuteness about the shadow of colonial domination and white supremacy. That acuity emerges with even greater clarity in "What Europe Thought of the Pan-African Congress." There, Fauset lets Western arrogance speak for itself. Structured as a series of newspaper reports about the congress, the essay opens with coverage from the London *Christian World* that turns on die-hard myths of superior and inferior races. The report notes: "Every white man present must have been amazed at the revelation of power and ability. . . . Most Europeans must have envied some of the speakers' command of lucid English." Still exposing ideas of absolute racial difference, Fauset turns to the report from the Paris *Petit parisien,* which considered it "extremely fitting that the Congress should be held in Rue Blanche (White Street)," thereby symbolically establishing "an equality between the black race and the white race" and proving that "some Africans have . . . attained to the very highest degree of civilization."

Fauset's interpolated commentary between each newspaper excerpt is measured but pungent, as shown in her preface to the report in the London *Observer:* "No less noted a personage than Sir Harry Johnston, African explorer and writer, remarks. . . ." The essay comes full circle with a concluding statement from *Punch.* Taking a headline from the London *Times,* "No Eternally Inferior Races," *Punch* responded, "No, but in the opinion of our colored brothers, some infernally superior ones."

Fauset displayed both her skill as an essayist and her commitment to geopolitical analysis and criticism in a group of essays based on her travels to France and Algeria in 1925–1926. In contrast with travel narratives, which are often regarded as an ethnocentric form, told from the perspective of a condescending, privileged, and dominating eye / I that fixes the "Other" in its gaze, Fauset sustains a respectful perspective in these travel essays, neither romanticizing and homogenizing those whose experiences she observed, nor exaggerating their differences from her. She shows an especial sensitivity to the differences of class and gender that exist within and between national boundaries.

Her essay "This Way to the Flea Market" is perhaps the best example of Fauset's achievement in the travel narrative form. A lesson in subtlety, it is full of well-placed, politically rich details, beginning with a stop at a small savings bank. Her guide, the father of a friend, instructs her beforehand in the tricks of the bargaining trade at the flea market, tricks essential for "foreigners," who are often exploited by the market's merchants.

The opening positions Fauset in a class having the economic privilege to travel abroad, and thus the leisure to spend a Sunday afternoon at the flea market accompanied by an equally privileged guide. The essay takes a surprising turn after she arrives at the flea market. There "foreigner" meets "foreigner," and the result is connection, not distance and estrangement; identification across lines of class, race, culture, and national boundary. In a remarkably subtle shift in the narrative, Fauset establishes her difference from her male guide, a difference that emphasizes contrasting views of the vagaries of economic circumstances. While he haggles for a long time over a picture of Strasbourg Cathedral, ultimately paying only half the first asking price, Fauset, though intrigued by the haggling, happily pays the full price asked for a beaded table mat. Interestingly, her guide has interposed himself between Fauset and the woman merchant, "but her figure was her first and last."

At this point in the narrative, Fauset fully identifies herself with the woman merchant rather than the male guide, and admires the fact that "the women merchants are the hardest bargainers, seldom if ever yielding." She admits to being glad the woman would not yield: "Her calmness, her determination even to the point of grimness is characteristic of this class." Although Fauset associates this "granite-like quality" with French character more generally, she notices that this "hardness shows nowhere more plainly than in the poor and middle-class French woman," whose exchange with the guide captures opposing positions on "life" and "things" that derive from their different class positions:

> "You know I've got to live, Monsieur."
> "Yes, but you shouldn't try to make all your profit on me."
> "I'm not trying to. . . . It isn't necessary for you to have the mat, but it is necessary for me to make my living. *Il faut vivre, Monsieur.*"

Not only does Fauset identify with the woman merchant in this scene, but she reinforces that connection in the echoes between the merchant's declaration that "one must live," and Fauset's own earlier musings on "life" versus "things." Observing the various items for sale at the flea market, she asks herself, "How can people be encompassed about with all these gee-gaws and yet find time to live?" And while her class privilege affords her such a stance, she understands that selling "things" is the "life" of the poor merchants at the Marché aux Puces. Though she possesses the advantage of class, she has the disadvantage of race, a factor that may explain her affinity to the merchant woman without eliding the differences between them.

Fauset's travel essays reveal just one aspect of a writer with considerable range, political acuity, and deep social commitments. Despite the range of her interests and commitments, however, in considerations of the Harlem Renaissance, Jessie Fauset is grouped invariably and invidiously with the writers classified as "the rear guard," the "traditional," "imitative" writers who, in an effort to earn white critical approval, avoided technical and thematic innovations, retreating instead to the safety of outworn literary conventions. That assessment, generally made on the basis of Fauset's fiction, is far more accurate as a judgment of her poetry. Never collected in a single volume, her poems were published mainly in the *Crisis* and in such important anthologies as James Weldon Johnson's *The Book of American Negro Poetry* (1931).

Though the emphasis in Harlem Renaissance writings was professedly on things "Negro," Fauset's poetry, with few exceptions, was both conventional in form and curiously silent on questions of race. Except for two or three experimental pieces, her roughly two dozen published poems are unremarkable imitations of Western poetic conventions in spirit, form, and theme. Her two predominant themes are nature and unrequited love, both timeworn, "universal" poetic subjects, which she treats with a casual matter-of-factness. Seldom is there a concrete reference to race, gender, or any of the controversial political and social issues of her day that readers might take as evidence of a "black woman's" signature.

If readers look for such a signature merely in the presence and number of references identified narrowly with race and gender, then Fauset's poems will disappoint. In an era when many black writers were celebrating their racial origins and distinctiveness and calling for representation of those origins in the arts, Fauset was writing poetry whose indebtedness to the Western literary tradition is everywhere apparent. Her fascination with the French, for example, is revealed in many of her poem's titles: "La Vie C'est la Vie," one of the most successful and frequently anthologized poems, "Oriflamme," "Rencontre," "Rondeau," "Douce Souvenance," and "Noblesse Oblige."

Critics have been severe in their assessments of Fauset's poetry, especially of its "Western" predilections, impugning in the process her consciousness of and commitment to her race. Viewed from a different perspective, however, her "universal" (read "Western") lyrics of love and nature can be said to make problematic the very idea and category of "Western" seen in opposition to "black." Behind all of Fauset's work, both as editor and as writer, is a sensibility, catholic and global in its reach, that complicates simplistic orthodoxies. For her, "blackness" was not synonymous with "African American" but included black people the world over. Hence, the French references in her poetry are not necessarily evidence of a flight from blackness but, rather, of her awareness of "the French connection" to a number of French-speaking blacks in other parts of the world. As Fauset herself had noted in her translation of Haitian poets, "Both France and the classics are the property of the world."

Arthur Davis's assessment of Fauset's poetry (in *From the Dark Tower*) is, in the end, closest to the mark. In his estimation her lyrics are "light and sophisticated . . . neither good enough to become an impressive part of the canon of New Poetry or [*sic*] bad enough to be overlooked entirely." It is reasonable to conjecture, especially given Fauset's keen editorial eye, that she herself may have held a similarly balanced view of her poetry. In any case, she wrote almost no poems after the mid 1920s. A letter written to Joel Spingarn about that time suggests that she may even have been considering giving up writing altogether.

In a letter to Arthur Spingarn, then vice-president of the NAACP, dated 26 January 1926, asked for his assistance in securing employment. About to end her roughly seven-year stint as literary editor of the *Crisis*, she enumerated her preferences:

1) to be a publisher's reader (if remunerative enough)
2) to be a social secretary in a private family, preferably for a woman
3) to be connected with one of the foundations here in New York.

She concluded the letter, "In the case of publisher's reader, if the question of color should come up, I could of course work at home."

This matter-of-fact letter shows Fauset combining an enterprising spirit with a sober, no-nonsense recognition of the realities of occupational segregation. Her training and credentials, which she listed for Springarn—A.B., A.M., Phi Beta Kappa, and fluent French polished through study at the Sorbonne—did little to dissolve the occupational barriers she confronted throughout her adult life. Upon graduation from Philadelphia High School for Girls in 1900, it was assumed that she would go to college, but as Sylvander notes, "Precedent in Pennsylvania for a Black woman in college was . . . in 1900 invisible." After unsuccessful attempts to gain admission to Bryn Mawr College, Fauset received a scholarship to Cornell University, where she enrolled in 1901. Although Cornell's records are sketchy, it is believed that Fauset was the first black woman to matriculate there. After graduating in 1905, she found that her color kept her from obtaining a teaching position in Philadelphia. She noted in an interview: "When I graduated from training school, I found the high schools barred to me because of my color. Philadelphia, birthplace of Independence and City of Brotherly Love—I have never quite been able to reconcile theory with fact."

As it turned out, Fauset did not become a publisher's reader, at least not in the strictest sense. She did, however, closely monitor publishers' attitudes toward black art as she struggled to write while teaching in the New York public school system. Fauset was particularly alert to the lurking prejudices of publishers against any writing that failed to satisfy the demand for the "different," the "distinct," and the "indigenous" in black art. These were usually code words for what came to be considered a cultural cult of the primitive exotic—in large part, the construction and fantasy of white intellectuals—and Fauset was brave enough to resist it, though that resistance proved difficult to sustain.

When Fauset ventured publication outside the pages of the *Crisis*, she met with censorship and rejected manuscripts because of her surface subject matter: black middle-class life. She battled with the major New York publishing firms, which stifled her creative freedom by prescribing and proscribing her literary province. "White readers just don't expect Negroes to be like this," wrote the first publisher to see and reject the manuscript of *There Is Confusion* (1924), Fauset's first novel. Other publishers followed suit. Only a promised preface by a white writer, Zona Gale, persuaded the Frederick Stokes Company to publish Fauset's third novel, *The Chinaberry Tree* (1931). Fauset criticized publishers for not being " 'better sport[s]' " about work that did not succumb to current fashion and charged them with having "an *idée fixe*." She felt that "they, even more than the public, . . . persist in considering only certain types of Negroes interesting and if an author presents a variant they fear that the public either won't believe in it or won't 'stand for it.' "

The history of criticism of Fauset's work has, in large measure, repeated the assessment of these early publishers. All too frequently, critics have merely read her work as has Arthur P. Davis has: as an attempt to show "white America . . . that, except for superficial differences of color . . . upper-class Negroes [were] just like the better-class whites." Such readings have been produced and reproduced ad infinitum in a powerful example of critical mimesis that revisionist readings of Fauset have done little to dislodge. Misunderstandings of the subtle function of class, race, and color in her work abound. Even her most sympathetic readers still see Fauset's novels as ideologicaly conservative on racial history and class dynamics (Carby), and as unconscious of "her own internalized race prejudice," evident in "a hierarchy based on color" (Zafar, p. 1).

Such readings miss the thematic and ironic complexity, and the stylistic subtlety, apparent in all of Fauset's novels, despite their many stylistic weaknesses. If her works imply "a hierarchy based on color," that hierarchy resides not in the value system implied in the novels themselves but in the social structures and patterns they dramatize and encode. All of Fauset's novels comprehend the extent to which social hierarchies are color-coded, both within and between the races, a coding that interacts with America's basic attitudes toward racial intermixture. Central to this attitude is what is popularly called the "One Drop Rule," captured in the axiom "One drop of black blood makes a Negro."

Fauset quarrels with this pseudoscientific system of racial classification and its use in regulating social mobility by solidifying one's "place" in class and caste. For example, in *The Chinaberry Tree* (1931) Laurentine Strange wants social "respectability," and it is mainly the black society of Red Brook and its evocations of bad blood that ostracize her because she is the "illegitimate" product of a black mother and a white father. When Laurentine explains these "illegitimate" origins to her fiancé, he responds: "What bosh to talk to a physician! Biology transcends society! . . . The facts of life, birth and death are more important than the rules of living, marriage, law, the sanction of the church or of man."

Fauset's explorations of "blood" and biology to make problematic the absurdities of racial classification (and thus social hierarchies) are demonstrated perhaps most interestingly in her first novel, *There Is Confusion* (1924). In form the novel seems appropriately and perhaps unintentionally ironic in that "confusion" inheres in any effort to unravel and separate three slenderly related plot lines, complicated further by too large a canvas of underdeveloped characters. However, seen from another perspective, plot replicates and reinforces theme in this novel whose investigations of miscegenation make tracing clear genealogical lines confusing indeed. Though schematic characterization and excessive sentimentality in dialogue and image weaken the force of the novel, the text sustains the reader's interest in questions of racial or genealogical "purity" and "descent" as a basis of socioeconomic and political "inheritance," or of national citizenship with all the rights and privileges appertaining thereto.

Although *There Is Confusion* dramatizes distinctions of birth and heritage that affect the lives of all its characters, the text centers on how these distinctions figure in the genealogy of Peter Bye. Peter is a product of the racial intermixture during slavery that so entangled black and white bloodlines as to make racial distinctions fictive but powerful constructions of culture, encoding and maintaining unequal relations of class, property, and privilege. In presenting the histories of the black and white Byes who are Peter's ancestors, the novel negates the fiction of biology and "racially" distinct groups, and insists on the role of law and custom in preserving a racially divided society.

Drawing on the weight of religious tradition and biblical authority, the narrative traces Peter's ancestry back to his great-grandfather, Joshua Bye, the slave of Aaron and Dinah Bye, who remained in their service even after his emancipation in 1780. On the occasion of Joshua's marriage to Belle Potter, the white Byes present him with a huge family Bible, on the title page of which is written: "To Joshua and Belle Bye from Aaron and Dinah Bye. 'By their fruit ye shall know them.' " It is left to Peter's grandfather, Isaiah, to decipher this inscription. In a clever literalization of the "biblical" injunction, the narrative inserts, "The white Byes . . . were the possessors of very fine peach-orchards in the neighborhood of what is now know as Bryn Mawr," where Isaiah had been taken as a little boy to pick peaches.

Importantly, it is not Isaiah who interprets the inscription but his white playmate Meriwether, the son of Aaron and Dinah. Meriwether literalizes "By their fruits ye shall know them" and interprets it from his perspective: "It means it shows the kind of stuff you are. . . . You do perhaps know an apple blossom when you see it. . . . In the spring you see that tree covered . . . with apple blossoms. Well, you know it's an apple tree." In an equally literal way Isaiah responds: "But what's that got to do with us? . . . My father hasn't any fruit trees."

Because the narrative places this exchange in the mouths of babes, as it were, its concern with the relationship between economics and power seems less heavy-handed than it might otherwise. Packed into the passage is not only a critique of the relationship between discourse and power (the white Meriwether interprets the text) but also of the role of economics in the construction of a "noble" ancestry and identity. The motto "By their fruits shall ye know them" transcends matters of mere biological reproduction to embrace its connections to commodity production. Thus the text teases out an additional resonance of the biblical script: "*Buy* their fruits [and] ye shall know them." The narrative, then, attempts to establish this legacy that divides the black Byes from the white as the source of racial divisions in twentieth-century Philadelphia.

But, importantly, the novel strains against the pull of that history in its liberal ideas of social reform, ideas inherent in the theme of miscegenation. As Mary Dearborn and others have argued persuasively, miscegenation functions in the cultural imagination of America as a site for questioning and contesting assumptions about identities of race, class, heritage, nation, and gender. In *There Is Confusion* such questioning and contestation occur *within* existing social structures. Those who fall outside those structures through the sheer accident of birth must find a way to defy origins and enter in. In her efforts to become a dancer, Joanna Marshall does just this. The narrative counterposes her drive to transcend the predictions of origins with Peter Bye's passive acquiescence in his. But that should imply no naive and uncritical faith in the Protestant work ethic alone. While the narrative does emphasize the power of individual initiative to overcome the circumstances of birth, that power must work transactively with the greater power of *structural* change.

For example, although Joanna works hard to realize her ambitions to be a dancer, it is only when the District Line Theatre dismantles its "districting lines" and lets her dance that she achieves real success. Reciprocally, the theater's "The Dance of the Nations" pageant has no real "legitimacy" until Joanna is included in its cast. When the white Miss Sharples, one of the theater's directors, takes a chance on Joanna, one structural barrier partly collapses. She invites Joanna because the white woman who dances the "red" and "white" parts of "America" refuses to darken her face in order to represent black dance. When the woman leaves the company altogether, mainly because of Joanna's success, Joanna must dance all three parts of "America." But, because she is unable to pose as a white American, her sister suggests that she perform the dance wearing a mask. "She could then be made as typically American as anyone could wish and no one need know the difference." When Joanna finishes the dance, one member of the audience calls out: "Pull off your mask, America. . . . Let's see your face. . . ."

The ironies of this rich and textured scene proliferate, doubling and redoubling, as Fauset strengthens her critique of the absurdities of color prejudice. Significantly, the passage captures the discursive equation of "America" with "whiteness," which necessitates that Joanna wear a mask to hide her blackness. But, more important, the passage points to one of the signal peculiarities of the American system of biracial classification, which recognizes only two "races"—"black" and "white"—assimilating, in a crowning irony, the Native American "red" into the category of whiteness. That system notwithstanding, the narrative keeps returning to one of its central points: Blackness and whiteness are constructed and inextricably intertwined.

In one of the least successful sections of this novel, this point is repeated with an ideologically interesting twist. On his way to France to fight "the war to make the world safe for democracy," Peter meets the grandson of Meriwether Bye and they trade family stories. In one strained coincidence, Meriwether and Peter end up on the same battlefield, where Meriwether is killed: "The colored man's head had dropped low over the fair one and his black curly hair fell forward straight and stringy, caked in the blood which lay in a well above Meriwether's heart." Despite the heavy-handed sentimentality of the passage, the transgression of racial boundaries implied in this act of touching is suggestive. The white and black "bodily" connection in the world of war points toward a new world order, but only after great conflict.

But while *There Is Confusion* uses genealogical metaphors to telescope and complicate questions of race, in the process it necessarily takes into its purview the effects of origins on class and gender constructions. Maggie, "the true daughter of the Tenderloin," laments that "she had no background" and is obsessed with achieving a "respectable" life. And while the narrative perceives social respectability for its own sake as a shallow ideal, it understands that Maggie's obsession with respectability stems from "colored" Philadelphia society, which is organized more carefully than white Philadelphia society: "One wasn't 'in' in those days unless one were, first, 'an old citizen,' and, second, unless one were eminently respectable." Both here and in the other three Fauset novels, being "in" is decidedly based on color and class.

While the laws and customs governing class arrangements are strict and impenetrable, those governing gender point unmistakably to the fact that women "had the real difficulties to overcome, disabilities of sex and of tradition." Despite Joanna's success as a dancer, the big theatrical trusts refuse to try her: "One had even said frankly: 'We'll try a colored man in a white company but we won't have any colored women.' "

Fauset succumbs to "disabilities" of narrative tradition in her treatment of women, as the novel displays a tendency toward ambivalence, toward unanticipated and abrupt reversals in characterization more in line with cultural norms of femininity. Joanna begins the novel as a "new" career-oriented female who finally and unconvincingly defers to a traditional role as wife and mother, regarding her husband as "the arbiter of her own and her child's destiny, the *fons et origo* of authority." Consistent with popular cultural wisdom, for women, marriage is the most desirable solution to the universal emptiness and alienation that work cannot fill.

Without suggesting that an author's artistic choices must mirror her personal choices or that women must choose marriage over career, it is important to note that while Fauset seemed to succumb to that false opposition in *There Is Confusion,* she avoided it in her life. Given her generation, she defied custom and tradition by remaining single for an unusually long time. She was forty-seven years old when she married Herbert Harris, an insurance broker, in 1929. And even after marriage she insisted upon maintaining an active career as a writer and teacher, though her productivity did decline.

In the three novels that follow *There Is Confusion,* on the other hand, Fauset appears more definite and forthright in exploring nontraditional options for women and in challenging social conventions that work to restrict those options by keeping women's sights riveted on men, marriage, and motherhood. In *Plum Bun* (1929), *The Chinaberry Tree* (1931), and *Comedy: American Style* (1933), women must alter culturally produced fantasies of marriage and construct alternative patterns, even when they do marry. But again Fauset clearly understands that changes in women's status in society cannot be wrought merely through a transformation of consciousness. Like racial barriers, the social barriers against women must be removed. In *Plum Bun,* easily Fauset's best novel, she dramatizes what a formidable obstacle these barriers can be for black women, barriers demanding sober realism rather than fairy-tale illusion.

On its face, *Plum Bun* seems to be just another novel of racial "passing," one of the most popular narrative forms of the Harlem Renaissance. It has all the generic features of the "passing" novel: A mulatto protagonist, seeking to avoid the constraints of color prejudice in America, decides to cross the color line and pass for white, a deception attended with many anxieties and frequently discovered. After learning that life on the "other side" is not without its hardships, the heroine, Angela Murray, develops an appreciation for black life and culture, and returns "home" psychically, if not physically, to the black community.

While *Plum Bun* certainly displays the most salient features of the novel of "passing," to read it simply as such is to miss its complex treatment of the intricacies of gender oppression, as well as the irony and subtlety of its artistic technique. *Plum Bun* is a richly textured and ingeniously designed narrative comprising plots within plots and texts within texts that comment upon one another in intricate combinations. Within this tapestry the "passing" plot constitutes just one thread, albeit an important one, woven into the novel's overarching frame—the bildungsroman, the novel of development.

While the "passing" plot constitutes a major phase in Angela Murray's coming-of-age, in the narrative's configuration it cannot be separated from the marriage plot, which constitutes the structural core of the novel. Angela's obsession with getting married is frustrated by the exigencies of sex-role stereotyping and the limitations of her own romantic assumptions. Although she still plans to marry at the novel's end, it is not because she believes marriage to be "the most desirable end for a woman." Instead, she has attained a hardheaded realism regarding the position of women, particularly women of color, in the United States.

Combining "passing" and marriage as dual plots in a novel of female development serves to underline Fauset's prevailing theme: the unequal power relationships in American society. These two plots could not be more appropriate in a narrative about power, for both "passing" and marriage are attempts—at times naive and fantasy-ridden—by blacks and women to overcome the structural inequalities that disempower them. Both marriage and "passing" are means by which these two disenfranchised groups hope to gain access to power. As the narrative makes clear, their expectations are frequently unfulfilled.

This tension between expectation and fulfillment is introduced in the epigraph that gives the novel its title and that structures its five sections ("Home," "Market," "Plum Bun," "Home Again," and "Market Is Done"):

> To Market, To Market
> To buy a Plum Bun;
> Home again, Home again,
> Market is done.

The fulfilled expectation of the speaker in the nursery rhyme stands in ironic contrast to the foiled expectations of Angela Murray. Further, as Ian McInnes notes astutely:

> If the nursery rhyme epigraph is part of the white male narrative of hope and fulfillment, it is also part of the white male narrative of political and economic opportunism. The only character in the novel who actually buys much of anything, for instance, is Roger Fielding [the wealthy white man Angela hopes to marry]. The verse is thus sexually as well as racially ironic.
> ("Closure and the Fiction of Female Development")

As befits a novel of female development and power asymmetries, the opening of the narrative reads like a classic fairy tale. Fauset begins by describing, largely through her protagonist's eyes, the address on Opal Street in Philadelphia where Angela lives: It is an "unpretentious little street lined with unpretentious little houses, inhabited . . . by unpretentious little people. . . . In one of these houses dwelt a father, a mother and two daughters." Continuing a pattern she began in the novella "The Sleeper Wakes" (1920), Fauset focuses on the powerful role fairy tales play in conditioning women to idealize marriage and romantic love.

Reading fairy tales to Angela and her sister, Virginia, their mother adds, "And they lived happily ever after, just like your father and me." The narrative necessarily gives a racial inflection to the fairy-tale plot, for Angela's mother follows this generic ending with a different and realistic injunction: Angela and her sister must become "schoolteachers and independent" so as to escape the degrading and exploitative conditions she once suffered as a lady's maid. But for much of the narrative this practical imperative, based on the realities of most black women's lives, wars with Angela's frenzied pursuit of a different and dominant cultural fantasy in which women are rescued by wealthy men and secondarily share in their power.

Nowhere is this fantasy more strikingly illustrated than in the following passage:

> She remembered an expression, "free, white and twenty-one"—this was what it meant then, this sense of owning the world. . . . "If I were a man," she said, "I could be president," and laughed at herself for the "if" itself proclaimed a limitation. But that inconsistency bothered her little; she did not want to be a man. *Power*, greatness, authority, these were fitting and proper for men; but there were sweeter, more beautiful gifts for women, and *power* of a certain kind too. Such a *power* she would like to exert in this glittering new world, so full of mysteries and promise. If she could afford it she would have a salon, a drawing-room where men and women . . . should come and pour themselves out to her sympathy and magnetism. To accomplish this she must have money and influence; indeed since she was so young she would need even protection; perhaps it would be better to marry . . . a white man. The thought came to her suddenly out of the void; she had never thought of this possibility before. . . . She knew that men had a better time of it than women, coloured men than coloured women, white men than white women . . . it would be fun, great fun to capture *power* and protection in addition to the freedom and independence which she had so long coveted and which now lay in her hand.
> (pp. 88–89; emphasis added)

This passage vividly captures the novel's central concern with the forms and sources of power, which are gender-, race-, and class-specific. While white men can become president, wielding the power and authority that office affords, women must settle for a secondhand power, experienced vicariously through their husbands. That these husbands must be white underscores the naiveté of such a fantasy for black women. The passage hints, moreover, at what will be a developing connection in the novel: the link between money and power and the white male prerogative of monopolizing both. Angela recognizes these relations of power and fantasizes about enjoying her share by marrying. What she will actually encounter in her relationship with Roger Fielding, a wealthy white man, is a replay of the racial history of concubinage and sexual exploitation. Angela leaves the memory of that history behind her in Philadelphia, and her attempts at fulfillment with Roger in New York—imaged as a contest of wills—glaringly illuminate how unmatched she is.

Ironically, while Angela fights to reach her goal, she fails to realize that Roger is not after marriage but "free love." In other words, their trips to the market are for two radically different commodities. For her the plum is power and influence, attainable only through marriage to a wealthy white man. For him the plum is sex to be bought and consumed. Angela's game play for marriage is Roger's foreplay for sex. Finally and ironically, Angela tries to "buy" in a society that allows her only to "sell," as MacInnes puts it.

Appropriately, the novel's critique of the relations among money, sex, and power gathers force in its core chapters, "Market" and "Plum Bun." Placed next to each other, both chapters are dominated by commercial and sexual imagery. There are repeated references to withholding and giving, terms with both sexual and economic connotations. Martha cautions Angela not to "withhold too much and yet to give very little." The materialist imagery develops in contrast with Angela's perceptions that her "life is rounding out like a fairy tale" and that her relationship with Roger is "the finest flower of chivalry and devotion." She is confident that Roger "loved her and would want to marry her, for it never occurred to her that men bestowed such attentions on a passing fancy."

Angela's relationship with Roger exemplifies Nancy Hartsock's characterization of the commodities exchanged in the courtship market as "sexual gratification and 'firm commitments' (presumably marriage)." To gain his desired end, sex, Roger used his wealth. "Anything . . . that money can buy, I can get and I can give," he tells Angela. This proposition elicits a counterproposition from Angela, who, despite her sexual fastidiousness, considers resorting to the use of the only weapon she has: sex, the power of the "weak." She reasons that "men paid a big price for their desires. Her price would be marriage." Of course, Angela soon discovers her powerlessness to command that price. The novelty of their passion having worn off, Roger ends the relationship.

While Roger's departure fosters in Angela a more mature attitude about male-female relations, it does not destroy the pattern of dependence that her relationship with him encouraged. For a time she convinces herself that, as a woman, she needs the "safety" and "assurance" that marriage putatively affords. It is important, however, that she postpone the fulfillment of that desire. Despite Angela's best efforts to marry first Roger, then Anthony Cross, she is thwarted, for it becomes clear that she must be self-sufficient before entering a relationship with a man.

Angela's self-sufficiency is, significantly, uncovered and sustained by work, and her work becomes empowering. While all of her experiences with power have hitherto been formed by the relational, involving a dialectic of dominance and submission, after her affair with Roger power becomes associated in her mind with individual capacity or the power to act independently. Angela's self-development begins in earnest when she becomes gainfully employed as a designer for a fashion journal while continuing to refine her portrait painting.

Consistent with the romantic conventions on which it draws, the novel ends as Angela is planning to marry. But she has developed an independence and autonomy that need ratification neither from men nor from marriage. She is now ready to enter a marriage in which both partners are "strong individualists, molten and blended in a design which failed to obscure their emphatic personalities."

In concentrating on the social relations of power, in criticizing the norms of female socialization and the sexual double standard, in endorsing female independence beyond traditional definitions of womanhood, *Plum Bun* displays a progressiveness and daring that few critics have noted. Perhaps these features have escaped detection because of Fauset's indirect strategies and narrative disguise. As in so many novels written by women, blacks, and other members of "literary subcultures," indirect strategies and narrative disguise become necessary covers for rebellious and subversive concerns. Such writers often employ literary and social conventions that function as masks behind which lie decidedly unconventional critiques.

Inherently self-reflexive, *Plum Bun,* like the protagonist whose story it tells, is "passing." It passes for another novel of "passing," for a modern fairy tale of age-old concerns. While white skin is Angela's mask, Fauset's deft manipulation of familiar literary genres and conventions is the narrative's mask. Although *Plum Bun* borrows elements from the "passing" novel, the fairy tale, and the women's romance, it eludes classification.

The "passing" plot affords Fauset a subtle vehicle through which to critique the naive act of "passing," and to analyze the paradoxes of color prejudice in America. Because of its literary duplicities, misunderstandings of the function of class, race, and color in Fauset's work abound. All of her novels comprehend the extent to which social hierarchies are color-coded, both within and between the races, a coding that interacts with America's basic attitudes toward racial intermixture.

Plum Bun appeared at the end of a decade in which both lynchings and urban riots were on the rise and in which theories and ideologies of race proliferated. While many of these theories were motivated by a desire to restrict immigration on racial grounds, they were appropriated by agents of white supremacy. Such works as Lothrop Stoddard's *The Rising Tide of Color Against White World Supremacy* (1920), Madison Grant's *The Passing of the Great Race* (1920), Clinton Burr's *America's Race Heritage* (1922), and Albert Wiggam's *The Fruit of the Family Tree* (1926) attempted to define race in strictly biological terms.

In her four novels Fauset challenged the irrationalities of the American attempt to classify races biologically and dramatized race as a cultural construct. The figure of the mulatto who could pass for white exposed the basis of irrationality in racial prejudice. Fauset ended her career as a novelist by dramatizing that irrationality in *Comedy, American Style* (1933). Hugh Gloster is correct in reading the novel as "the most penetrating study of color mania in American fiction."

As in the first three novels, the form of *Comedy: American Style* is its greatest shortcoming. Fauset attempted much in formal innovation but accomplished comparatively little. She used a dramatic structure to divide the novel's sections, just as she did in *Plum Bun.* Her devotion to the theater (she named it her favorite recreation) is undoubtedly the origin of this attempt to incorporate the language and structures of drama into the novel. In this last novel Fauset departs from the bildungsroman pattern that she used to effect in her other three novels, and appropriately so, for Olivia Carey, the central character, does not grow into any awareness but remains enslaved to a rabid complex of racist and sexist assumptions. Even though Olivia's monomaniacal obsession with color is devastating to all around her, "she fascinates one with that hard, glittering frostiness of purpose with which she wrecks and ruins." Olivia is "self-absorbed" and "singleminded." Without compunction, she subjects her family to her willful domination. She is determined to live as a white person and to have her family do so as well, no matter the cost. Her husband and first two children can, but refuse to, pass. Her last child, Oliver, is bronze-colored, and it is on him that Olivia's madness has the most devastating effect. She goes so far as to pass him off as a Filipino servant to her white guests. Learning that his mother considers his "unfortunate color" the only thing separating the family from living as whites, Oliver commits suicide.

Not only does Olivia destroy her daughter and son, but she also destroys herself, although she hasn't the insight to see that she has done so. All of her calculated and deceitful schemes for a grand life have ironically earned her a decidedly mean existence. She is reduced to living alone in France, her resources dwindled to almost nothing. Despite her poverty and loneliness, however, she still keeps up her masquerade as grand lady. The tragedy of Olivia's self-imposed exile is that she has achieved her long-awaited wish—she is recognized and accepted as a white person; but she has purchased that recognition and acceptance at a very precious price.

Comedy: American Style rounds out Fauset's literary career, a career devoted in large part to exposing and delineating what Hugh Gloster calls the effects of "psychopathic Aryanism." To argue, then, as Arthur P. Davis does (in *From the Dark Tower*), that Fauset's novels attempt to show "white America . . . that, except for superficial differences of color . . . upper-class Negroes [were] just like the better-class whites" is to read Fauset's novels as superficially as white supremacists read race. Fauset's use of the "passing" plot makes this clear, for this plot enabled Fauset to attack the system of racial classification that structured and stratified American society. She was alert to the way that system of classification operated in the patronage system and the publishing industry, both of which held fixed ideas about the "proper" subject matter for black writers. That awareness was evident especially in *Plum Bun*.

Although *Plum Bun* is not simply an allegory, it is not unreasonable to suggest that the novel is a response to this prevailing rigidity of patrons and publishers.

It is significant that, early in her artistic career, Angela considers becoming a portrait painter but resists the thought because "she hated the idea of the position in which she would be placed, fearfully placating and flattering possible patrons, hurrying through with an order because she needed the cheque, accepting patronage and condescension." The novel can be said, then, to comment specifically on the Harlem Renaissance and the literary straitjacketing that pervaded the movement, violating many writers' artistic integrity and autonomy.

No examination of the Harlem Renaissance is complete without a consideration of the economics and politics of the literary marketplace at that time, particularly of the complex arrangements that often obtained between black writers and their patrons and publishers. Because these writers were so new to the commercialized arts, "they were necessarily dependent; they had no force or leverage within the publishing or the critical establishments," as Nathan Huggins notes in *Harlem Renaissance.* "Opinion was against black artists," and thus "they needed supporters and advocates, defense and encouragement from those who were supposed to know." The question increasingly became, however, "Whose sensibilities, tastes, and interests were being patronized?" For the most part, it was the white patrons and publishers who demanded what the age as a whole demanded: the treatment of blacks as the wards of primitivism.

Mrs. Rufus Osgood Mason made such a demand on Langston Hughes. She served as his patron for a number of years; the power play in their relationship captures the dynamics that often prevailed between patron and writer during this period.

> Concerning Negroes, [Mrs. Mason] felt that they were America's great link with the primitive, and

> that they had something very precious to give to the Western world. . . . She wanted me to be primitive and know and feel the intuitions of the primitive. But, unfortunately, I did not feel the rhythms of the primitive surging through me, and so I could not live and write as though I did.
> (*The Big Sea*, pp. 316, 325)

Hughes was not the only black writer who felt this pressure. Even those who refused to submit to the pressures toward primitivism debated the issue in literary reviews and symposia throughout the period. Many maintained that the demand for the treatment of primitive exotics was essentially the demand for a depiction of the black "underworld" and thus a desire for control over black representation. One such symposium ran in the *Crisis* between March and November 1926 and was entitled "The Negro in Art: How Shall He Be Portrayed?" The questions posed by the editor, W. E. B. Du Bois, interpreted the publishing industry's demand for the "primitive/exotic" as the demand for the depiction of black sexuality. Du Bois asked a variety of writers—both white and black—to respond to such questions as:

> 6. Is not the continual portrayal of the sordid, foolish and criminal among Negroes convincing the world that this and this alone is really and essentially Negroid, and preventing white artists from knowing any other types and preventing black artists from daring to paint them?
> 7. Is there not a real danger that young colored writers will be tempted to follow the popular trend in portraying Negro character in the underworld rather than seeking to paint the truth about themselves and their own social class?

Fauset responded in the June issue by arguing emphatically that following the popular trend of portraying the black "underworld" was "a grave danger" for black writers. If they followed the crowd, she added, they risked creating "a literary insincerity both insidious and abominable." In choosing not to pander to this aspect of popular taste, Fauset exercised both courage and integrity and remained faithful to her own artistic objectives, which had little currency in a publishing industry obsessed with sensationalism and high profits.

In this book market black writers had few options: they could do the bidding of publishers and patrons or they could encounter great difficulties getting published, as did Fauset.

Despite rejections and difficulties, Fauset refused to satisfy the demands of the publishing establishment. Although she knew that the power to pass judgment on her work rested with the white male literary establishment, she refused to compromise her artistic vision. In the process she took pleasure, at least in *Plum Bun*, in teasing commercial expectations. Although there are no explicitly sexual scenes in the novel, it brims with sexual winks and innuendos. Fauset capitalizes on the multivalent sexual implications of her title. The suggestions in "bun" and "tail" are clear, as are those in Roger's name. Fauset must have heard the classic blues singers of the 1920s—Gertrude "Ma" Rainey and Bessie Smith, for example—and the double entendres of their lyrics gave her an additional lesson in literary duplicity. Perhaps the most common metaphor in these classic blues lyrics is that equating sex with food. Consider the following popular lyric:

> Jelly roll, jelly roll ain't so hard to find,
> There's a baker shop in town bakes it brown
> like mine,
> I got a sweet jelly, a lovin' sweet jelly roll,
> If you taste my jelly it'll satisfy your worried
> soul.

While none of the sexual suggestions of "plum bun" are lost upon Fauset, she bypasses their sensational aspects and offers instead a delicate examination of the politics of sex that extends well beyond the novel. Readers going to the literary market expecting their plum bun —sex and sensationalism—are unfulfilled.

From the beginning of her career, Fauset

insisted that the American publishing system had created a complex of ideologies of race, in fiction and nonfiction alike, that necessitated control by black writers of portrayals of black people. She was skeptical about whether whites could "write evenly on the racial situation in America" and once admitted to an interviewer that she began to write fiction in earnest when T. S. Stribling's novel *Birthright* (1922) failed, in her estimation, to depict blacks authentically. In those times belief in the possibilities of "authentic" representation was strong and widely accepted, and thus Fauset could assert confidently: "Here is an audience waiting to hear the truth about us. Let we who are better qualified to present that truth than any white writer try to do so."

While Fauset had come to accept that most white publishers doubted her qualifications for representing "blackness," ironically most blacks doubted them as well. Her novels were typically regarded as vapidly genteel lace-curtain romances. In one of the most condescending appraisals, in *A Long Way from Home* Claude McKay described Fauset as "prim and dainty as a primrose," and added that "her novels are quite as fastidious and precious."

Unfortunately, responses such as McKay's were all too frequent, stemming primarily from a tendency during and since the Harlem Renaissance to deify the proletarian or "folk" tradition and to demonize the middle class. Wilson J. Moses is one of the few critics to observe with disapproval that this "proletarian/bohemian interpretation" of the art of the movement "has been granted a sort of moral superiority over any other framework of analysis in black literary and intellectual history."

In view of this critical tendency to slight anyone associated with black middle-class existence, Fauset has always been an easy target. She was caught in a shift in black literary aesthetics as well as a shift in African American strategies of social reform. While Fauset's attachment to the priorities of liberal reform struck many readers, then and now, as an insular and thus inadequate strategy of social change, one could say that Fauset chose the terms of her enclosure, swerving away from the finality and fixity of racial classification as well as from the class and caste of gender and genre alike.

It took daring to write in the way that Fauset wrote—against the tide of the era's social and literary currents. That Fauset tried to earn a livelihood as a writer in the first decades of this century, a time when such an attempt was largely anomalous for a black woman, has not been fully appreciated. Like many other writers of the Harlem Renaissance, she labored under severe technical handicaps that could not be easily corrected, given the circumstances under which she wrote. In an interview with Marion Starkey in 1932, Fauset expressed her wish to accumulate an extra one or two thousand dollars "just to see what I really could do if I had my full time and energy to devote to my work."

Fauset never realized her dream, for she spent almost the entirety of her ten-year writing career teaching French in public high schools in order to support herself. Budgeted into an already rigorous schedule, divided unequally between teaching and writing, were editing duties for the *Crisis* and the *Brownies' Book* (a magazine for children), as well as lecture tours, both at home and abroad. Virginia Woolf would have said that Fauset needed sufficient money and "a room of her own." She did not have the luxury that Melville described in his famous "dollars damn me" letter to Hawthorne: "the calm, the coolness the silent grass growing mood in which . . . [one] ought always to compose." Instead, she composed under the most harried of circumstances, believing that "a writer becomes a writer by dint of doing a little every day rather than by waiting for the correct mood, or for uninterrupted leisure." The consequences of this wedging in time for writing were debilitating for both the self and the work.

After her last novel was published in 1933, Fauset disappeared from the literary scene. She was fifty-one years old. Although she lived another twenty-eight years, dying in 1921 of heart failure brought on by hyptertensive heart disease, she published nothing after *Comedy: American Style*. It is reasonable to conclude with Tillie Olsen that "where the claims of creation cannot be primary, the results are atrophy; unfinished work; . . . silences."

Selected Bibliography

PRIMARY WORKS

NOVELS

There Is Confusion. New York: Boni & Liveright. 1924. Reprinted Boston: Northeastern University Press, 1989.

Plum Bun. New York: Frederick A. Stokes, 1929. Reprinted London: Pandora Press, 1985.

The Chinaberry Tree. New York: Frederick A. Stokes, 1931.

Comedy: American Style. New York: Frederick A. Stokes, 1933. Reprinted College Park, Md.: McGrath, 1969.

POETRY

"Douce Souvenance." *Crisis*, May 1920, p. 42.

"Oriflamme." *Crisis*, January 1920, p. 128.

"La Vie C'est la Vie." *Crisis*, July 1922, p. 124.

"Rencontre." *Crisis*, January 1924, p. 122.

ESSAYS

"Impressions of the Second Pan-African Congress." *Crisis*, November 1921, pp. 12–18.

"What Europe Thought of the Pan-African Congress." *Crisis*, December 1921, pp. 60–67.

"This Way to the Flea Market." *Crisis*, February 1925, pp. 161–163.

"The Negro in Art: How Shall He Be Portrayed—A Symposium." *Crisis*, June 1926, pp. 71–72.

SECONDARY WORKS

BIOGRAPHICAL AND CRITICAL STUDIES

Ammons, Elizabeth. "New Literary History: Edith Wharton and Jessie Redmon Fauset." *College Literature* 14:207–218 (1987).

Anderson, Jervis. *This Was Harlem: A Cultural Portrait, 1900–1950*. New York: Farrar, Straus & Giroux, 1982.

Braithwaite, William Stanley. "The Novels of Jessie Fauset." In *The Black Novelist*. Edited by Robert Hemenway. Columbus, Ohio: Charles Merrill, 1970. Pp. 46–54.

Carby, Hazel. *Reconstructing Womanhood: The Emergence of the Afro-American Woman Novelist*. New York: Oxford University Press, 1987.

Christian, Barbara. *Black Women Novelists: The Development of a Tradition, 1892–1976*. Westport, Conn.: Greenwood Press, 1980.

Davis, Arthur Paul. *From the Dark Tower: Major African-American Writers, 1900–1960*. Washington, D.C.: Howard University Press, 1974.

Dearborn, Mary. *Pocahontas's Daughters: Gender and Ethnicity in American Culture*. New York: Oxford University Press, 1986.

Feeney, Joseph J., S.J. "A Sardonic, Unconventional Jessie Fauset: The Double Structure and Double Vision of Her Novels." *CLA Journal* 22:365–382 (June 1979).

———. "Black Childhood as Ironic: A Nursery Rhyme Transformed in Jessie Fauset's Novel *Plum Bun*." *Minority Voices* 4:65–69 (Fall 1980).

Gloster, Hugh. *Negro Voices in American Fiction*. Chapel Hill: University of North Carolina Press, 1948.

Hartsock, Nancy. *Money, Sex and Power: Toward a Feminist Materialism*. New York: Longman, 1983.

Huggins, Nathan I. *Harlem Renaissance*. New York: Oxford University Press, 1971.

Hughes, Langston. *The Big Sea*. New York: Hill & Wang, 1940.

Hull, Gloria. *Color, Sex, and Poetry*. Bloomington: Indiana University Press, 1987.

Johnson, Abby Arthur. "Literary Midwife: Jessie Redmon Fauset and the Harlem Renaissance." *Phylon* 39:143–153 (June 1978).

Lewis, David Levering. *When Harlem Was in Vogue*. New York: Knopf, 1981.

McDowell, Deborah E. "The Neglected Dimension of Jessie Redmon Fauset." *Afro-Americans in New York Life and History* 5:33–49 (July 1981).

MacInnes, Ian. "Closure and the Fiction of Female Development." Unpublished manuscript.

McKay, Claude. *A Long Way from Home*. New York: Furman, 1937. Reprinted New York: Harcourt, Brace, and World, 1970.

Moses, Wilson J. "The Lost World of the Negro, 1895–1919: Black Literary and Intellectual Life Before the 'Renaissance.' " *Black American Literature Forum* 21:61–84 (Spring–Summer 1987).

Sinnette, Elinor D. "The *Brownies' Book:* A Pioneer Publication for Children." *Freedomways*, Winter 1965, pp. 133–142.

Starkey, Marion L. "Jessie Fauset." *Southern Workman*, May 1932, 217–220.

Sylvander, Carolyn Wedin. *Jessie Redmon Fauset, Black American Writer*. Troy, N.Y.: Whitson, 1981. Includes a comprehensive bibliography.

Zafar, Bafia. "Colored People Gettin' More Like W'ite Folks Every Day." Unpublished manuscript.

BIBLIOGRAPHY

Sims, Janet. "Jessie Redmon Fauset, 1885–1961: A Selected Bibliography." *Black American Literature Forum* 14:147–152 (Winter 1980).

DEBORAH E. MCDOWELL

MARY E. WILKINS FREEMAN

1852–1930

MARY E. WILKINS FREEMAN wrote prolifically throughout her adult life, leaving at her death fourteen collections of stories, thirteen novels, eight children's books, several works in collaboration with other writers, a play, several articles, poems for children and adults, and dozens of uncollected stories. Yet despite her popularity and her financial success, which enabled her to support herself by her writing, few of her books remain of critical interest today. Among these, her first two collections, *A Humble Romance* (1887) and *A New England Nun* (1891), and a novel, *Pembroke* (1894), represent her fiction of enduring merit; indeed, many of the stories in *A New England Nun* rival the best in American short fiction and demonstrate Freeman's power as a writer. What happened to the potential that was so evident in her early work? In a letter to literary historian Fred Lewis Pattee (25 September 1919), Freeman expressed her awareness of her own limitations: "I have never bothered to analyze myself, and fear I cannot. I will, however, state one thing. I do know, and have always known, my accomplished work is not the best work of which I am capable, but it is too late now."

Freeman may not have "analyzed" herself directly, but in some of her surviving letters and in her use of autobiographical materials in *Pembroke* and a later novel, *By the Light of the Soul* (1906), she clearly demonstrates the dilemmas that haunted her throughout her adult life and that may perhaps explain why she so rarely realized her power as a writer. The autobiographical source for her best novel, *Pembroke,* identifies Freeman's early expression of her central conflict as her relationship to her own family, and considers the extent to which family history predetermines individual development. Later, in *By the Light of the Soul,* she would characterize this conflict in terms of a woman's choice of spinsterhood or marriage. Yet even in her early fiction, in which she often portrays the lives of unmarried women, Freeman implicitly questions whether a woman who remains unmarried may also develop as a person—and as a writer—or whether a woman must take on a "family" role in order to achieve her developmental potential.

By the time she became a writer, Mary E. Wilkins had suffered a series of devastating losses, losses that contributed to her self-doubt, her fear of social stigma as a woman who remained unmarried until the age of forty-nine, and, most of all, to her sense that, for reasons she could not consciously "analyze," something in both her life and her writing remained undeveloped, leading her to express the belief that what she had accomplished was "not the best work" of which she was capable.

The details of Mary Eleanor Wilkins's early life are easily summarized. Born on 31 October 1852 in Randolph, Massachusetts, she was the second child (but the first to survive infancy) born to Warren Wilkins, a carpenter, and Eleanor Lothrop Wilkins, both of whom had grown up in Randolph. When Freeman was six, her three-year-old brother, Edward, died, and the following year, her mother gave birth to her sister, Anna. Although nineteenth-century families may have learned to accept the death of young children, they nevertheless mourned those deaths. Loss must therefore have already embedded itself in the identity of the Wilkins family before Mary was born, and perhaps she was old enough when Edward died to recall his death later.

Loss continued to characterize the Wilkins

family. In 1867, in the face of a decline in the building trades in Randolph, Warren Wilkins moved his family to Brattleboro, Vermont, in order to open a dry-goods store with a partner. For fifteen-year-old Mary, this meant leaving behind relatives and childhood friends, including Mary John Wales. In 1873, when his business partnership dissolved in a period of economic depression, Warren Wilkins became a carpenter again, but apparently the family's financial situation continued to deteriorate. In 1876 Mary and her parents endured the loss of Anna, who died at the age of seventeen; the following year, their resources shrinking, the family moved into the home of the Tylers, where Eleanor became a housekeeper; according to biographical legend, young Mary E. Wilkins had apparently become romantically interested in the Tylers' son Hanson, an ensign in the navy. Eleanor's early death, in 1880, ended their residence with the Tylers, and perhaps Freeman's frequent contacts with Hanson, and left Freeman at the age of twenty-eight without either sister or mother, and with a pressing need to support herself. Her father's move to Florida in 1882 and his sudden death in April 1883 completed the losses Freeman experienced by the age of thirty that left her the sole survivor of her family. She had graduated from high school in Brattleboro and finished one year at Mount Holyoke College, had taught music for a while, and had then turned to writing as a potential source of income.

Freeman interprets the significance of her losses in *By the Light of the Soul,* the novel that her cousin termed the author's spiritual autobiography. In this novel, the main character, Maria Edgham, experiences the early death of her mother, followed by the death of her father. Freeman writes about this experience: "For some unexplained cause, the sorrow which Maria had passed through had seemed to stop her own emotional development." The language of arrested or "stopped" emotional development appealed to Freeman in her fictional exploration of the significance of losses similar to her own. And although she herself never "analyzed" her failure to accomplish more of her own "best work," we may infer from her treatment of Maria Edgham that she believed she herself had experienced arrested development, both in her life and in her art.

Mary E. Wilkins's earliest fiction identifies family and slowed or arrested development as her particular interests. Although the story has not survived, we know that Freeman received a prize of fifty dollars from the *Boston Sunday Budget* for a story intriguingly titled "A Shadow Family," which appeared on 1 January 1882. Her first significant publication, "Two Old Lovers," appeared in *Harper's Bazaar* on 31 March 1883, less than a month before her father's death. In "Two Old Lovers," later collected in *A Humble Romance,* David Emmons courts Maria Brewster for more than twenty-five years but the two never move into marriage; even on his deathbed, David doesn't actually propose to Maria but says only that he "allers meant to—have asked."

Shortly after she began to publish in *Harper's Bazaar*—five additional stories appeared in 1883—Wilkins moved back to Randolph, Massachusetts, where members of her extended family still lived, and where she began to reside, in 1884, with her childhood friend, Mary John Wales, and her family. Over the years, cousins on both sides of the family would continue to be important connections for Freeman, and she remained close to her paternal grandmother until the latter's death in 1887. Yet it was not relatives but close friends—Mary Wales, and Freeman's editor at *Harper's Bazaar,* Mary Louise Booth—who became the most significant people in her life after her loss of her family.

No letters to Mary Wales appear to have survived, and we therefore know very little about the relationship between Freeman and her childhood friend. Freeman's earliest biographer, Edward Foster, suggests that even as a child, Mary John Wales had served as her friend's protector. Foster characterizes the mature, unmarried Wales as "strong, practical, partly emancipated from the code," and as someone who "delighted in managing the household, mothering Freeman, and sparing her from the minor annoyances of life." Further, according to Foster, Wales provided the encouragement and sympathetic criticism Freeman needed to overcome her self-doubt as a writer. Whatever the emotional configuration of their relationship, the two women were apparently devoted to each other; they lived together for almost twenty years, until Freeman married.

During the years she lived with Mary Wales and her family in Randolph (1884–1901), Freeman began to establish herself as a writer. Like many of her contemporaries, she practiced her craft and published her earliest work for children; her best short stories for children are collected in *The Pot of Gold and Other Stories* (1892). Yet even in her children's fiction, Freeman established her own particular interests. She includes numerous female child heroes, and adult women too make important contributions, as in "The Pumpkin Giant," in which Daphne, the mother of the boy who kills the giant, neutralizes the dead giant's power by inventing pumpkin pie. However, Freeman began fully to reveal her originality and her power in the short stories she wrote for Mary Louise Booth, her editor at *Harper's Bazaar*, during the 1880s, collected in *A Humble Romance* and *A New England Nun*. The fifty-two stories in these two volumes, of which Booth had originally published thirty-eight, remain the source of Freeman's most frequently reprinted fiction, and roughly half form a justifiable basis for her continuing reputation.

Freeman's relationship with Mary Louise Booth, twenty-one years her senior, began in the years immediately following her mother's death, and during the 1880s, when she was publishing her fiction in *Harper's Bazaar*, Booth had exclusive rights to her stories. In later years Freeman would tell an anecdote about her first publication in *Harper's Bazaar* and her earliest contacts with Booth. Apparently Booth's first inclination, when she saw the childish handwriting in which Freeman submitted "Two Old Lovers," was to reject the story, but upon rereading, she accepted it. The author may have appealed subconsciously to Booth as the child the older woman never had; certainly the extant outpourings of love and affection that survive in Freeman's letters to Booth indicate Booth's personal as well as editorial influence on Freeman.

In one letter to Booth, dated 21 April 1885, she alludes to the value she has received from having Booth as her editor and friend:

> I begin to see that there is one beautiful thing which comes from this kind of work, and the thing I have the most need of, I think. One is going to find friends because of it; and when one has no one of their very own, one does need a good many of these, who come next.

In writing as "one who has no one of their very own," Freeman suggests that her position as an orphan informed her relationship with Booth. However, Booth must also have provided support for the adult woman in Freeman, for like Freeman, Booth lived with another woman in a long-term relationship.

Without the editorial courage of Booth, we might not have today the stories collected in *A Humble Romance* and *A New England Nun*. Significantly, most of these stories focus on spinsters or older women, often women living together or for whom women's friendship rather than marriage provides emotional sustenance. In another letter to Booth, dated 17 February 1885, Freeman identifies the subject matter of her fiction as the source of her own self-doubt: "I am on another story with an old woman in it; I only hope people wont tire of my old women. I wonder if there is such a thing, as working a vein so long, that the gold ceases to be gold. . . ." For Booth, fiction about old women and women's friendship would remain "gold," and through her personal as well as editorial commitment to Freeman, she helped inspire Freeman's best work. To Booth, Freeman must have appeared to be not a deviant spinster but another woman who had chosen to live with a woman. As editor, personal friend, and even mother surrogate, Booth gave Freeman the strength to overcome her fear of deviance—and provided for Freeman a sense that she was "normal," not "stopped," in her development as a writer and as an adult woman.

Critics have often categorized the stories that Freeman wrote for *Harper's Bazaar* as local-color fiction in the tradition of Bret Harte or Hamlin Garland; however, we may more accurately describe her as a regionalist, not a local-color writer. By the time Freeman began to write for Mary Louise Booth, her regionalist predecessors and contemporaries—Harriet Beecher Stowe, Alice Cary, Rose Terry Cooke, Celia Thaxter, Mary Noialles Murfree, and Sarah Orne Jewett, among others—had established several formal features of the genre.

In Freeman's best work, as in regionalism, the sketch or short story predominates; place—with its values, idiomatic speech, culinary arts, domestic occupations, and specific references to herbs and flowers—sets a context for the expression of character; visits between women often initiate the sketch or story; and women, usually unmarried women who live alone or with other women, become the central characters in the fiction. In the most striking feature of the genre, regionalist writers "shift the center" of regional perception from the urban to the rural; from the outsider's view—such as that of the itinerant journalist popular in local-color fiction—to the insiders' view; and from the voice of the white male pioneer or adventurer prevalent in American romance fiction to the voice of the rural, aging, poor, and female inhabitant of the region. Such a shift in focus empowers the voices and perspectives of those characters who have experienced powerlessness and disenfranchisement in American society and invisibility in American literature.

Among the group of writers who published their best work in the genre of regionalism, Stowe and Jewett certainly were well known to Freeman, and she and Jewett exchanged correspondence that expressed mutual respect for each other's early work. Freeman also met Jewett in Boston, where Jewett shared the home of Annie Fields, but the acquaintance did not become a personal friendship. Perhaps, in Jewett's Boston circle, Freeman felt keenly her sense of isolating personal difference. She once wrote to editor Kate Upson Clark, in a letter Brent Kendrick dates before August 1892: "I have survived another Boston luncheon. I'm not literary enough for Boston, but I'm awfully afraid I've got to go to a dinner there."

Once again, Mary Louise Booth emerges as Freeman's main critic and supporter, as well as an editor with an affinity for regionalism. She provided an important personal and literary link between Freeman and the origins of regionalism, having known Alice Cary in New York and having frequented the weekly literary gatherings that Alice and her sister Phoebe had hosted before their deaths in the early 1870s. Indeed, Booth displayed a portrait of Alice Cary on the wall of her library in the New York home where Freeman visited Booth and her domestic partner, Anna Wright.

One of Freeman's earliest stories, "A Mistaken Charity." which appeared in *Harper's Bazaar* in May 1883, is an early example of her work in the genre of regionalism and represents one of her best from *A Humble Romance.* Two poor women, one of them nearly blind, Harriet and Charlotte Shattuck, live with independence, poverty, and chinks in their roof rather than accept the town's charity. When a woman named Mrs. Simonds visits their cottage and sees the conditions in which they live, she launches a charitable project to move them to an "Old Ladies' Home," where the sisters feel "totally at variance with their surroundings" and refuse to be transformed from "unpolished old women" into "nice old ladies." Demonstrating a defiant rebellion, they run away from the home and back to the cottage that signifies their ties to region, "with grim humor" hanging the white lace caps that represent their residence in the "home" on the bedposts before they escape.

When Harriet tells her sister, "I guess they'll see as folks ain't goin' to be made to wear caps agin their will in a free kentry," some readers may recall Huck Finn "lightin' out for the territory," for like Huck (who would make his appearance in American literature two years later), the Shattuck sisters will not stand for being "civilized." Yet unlike Huck, they have a "territory" to go to; Freeman offers regionalism as the "territory" for women, a way for women to "stay" in the world, and a way for Charlotte, whose blindness, like the leaky roof, lets in "chinks" of light, to experience vision; she see so many "chinks" when they return home that "they air all runnin' together."

A Humble Romance contains numerous fine stories, but *A New England Nun* records Freeman at her most powerful. "A New England Nun," "A Village Singer," and "The Revolt of 'Mother' " from this collection are often anthologized and likely to be familiar to readers. In each of these stories Freeman presents a woman who defies convention in some way. Louisa Ellis of "A New England Nun" breaks her engagement of many years when her fiancé returns from Australia because she cannot bear to give up control over her life. Candace Whitcomb of "A Village Singer" dies from the intensity of her struggle to make her community aware of the double standard that exists between men and women, and of the discrimination based on age that leads her congregation to replace her as their soprano with a younger woman. And "Mother" in "The Revolt of 'Mother' " moves her family into her husband's new barn during his absence as a way of protesting the inadequacy of the house. This story also demonstrates Freeman's interest in the specific ways her characters act to alter the perceptions of others. Mrs. Penn wants more than empathy and a shift in perception from "Father" when she moves into the barn; she wants real change. And she achieves both by the end of the story; Adoniram Penn weeps when he capitulates to "Mother" and agrees to turn the new barn into a house with windows, partitions, and new furniture.

Perhaps the finest story in *A New England Nun,* the little-known "A Church Mouse," best illustrates Freeman's innovations in the genre of regionalism. In this story, Hetty Fifield moves the sphere of rebellion beyond her own house to involve the entire community of women, transforms the meetinghouse into domestic space, seizes a pulpit of sorts to tell her own story, explicitly raises issues of women's poverty, homelessness, and job discrimination, and lives to triumph over her male oppressors. From the deacon's opening assertion, "I never heard of a woman's bein' saxton," to the closing lines, in which Hetty wakes up on Christmas morning in a legitimized room of her own inside the meetinghouse, Freeman shifts the center of perception to the impoverished and homeless Hetty and demonstrates the power of regionalism to create a literary "home" for women.

Unfortunately for young Mary E. Wilkins, and for her potential to work her own "vein of gold," Mary Louise Booth died on 5 March 1889. Freeman would form friendships with other women editors—Kate Upson Clark, Mary Mapes Dodge, and Eliza Anna Farman Pratt—but none who replaced Mary Louise Booth. After Booth's death, Freeman's literary choices and, by the turn of the century, her decision to marry reflect her inability, without Booth's support, to risk literary difference by remaining a writer of short fiction and to risk the social stigma of spinsterhood. To be fair, among the regionalists, only Sarah Orne Jewett—a woman of substantial independent means—possessed the luxury of not worrying about what would sell, and therefore was to continue to write regionalist short fiction throughout her career, even in her book-length collections of short sketches, *Deephaven* (1877) and *The Country of the Pointed Firs* (1896). Freeman, however, needed to write fiction that would make money, and after Booth's death she began to try to write novels, perhaps in the belief that the novel as a form possessed more literary status and greater financial reward.

Her first attempt at a novel, *Jane Field* (1893), retains her New England village setting, expands a plot that might have been successful in a short story, and contributes to our understanding of Freeman's emotional conflict during this period. In the novel's only plot line, Jane Field passes herself off as her dead sister in order to receive an inheritance that she needs to support her invalid daughter, Lois, but the strain of life as an impostor becomes too great. After confessing her true identity, thereafter, in a refrain she echoes to the book's conclusion, she appears to have lost at least part of her reason, telling everyone she meets, "I ain't Esther Maxwell!" Freeman wrote *Jane Field* as a bridge to the longer novel form and perhaps as a way to release some of her own stress. Insecure in her identity, she may have felt like an impostor as she began, as a woman writer, to assert herself as a novelist.

In her next and best attempt at the novel, *Pembroke* (1894), Freeman examines a moment in her mother's family history and initiates an attempt to find a way, in fiction, to repair her loss of family, including her mother surrogate Mary Louise Booth. According to her biographers, Freeman based the plot of *Pembroke* on the life of her mother's brother Barnabas, who was engaged to marry a woman named Mary Thayer. Barnabas Lothrop and Mary Thayer's father quarreled over politics, the engagement was broken, and the couple never moved into the house that Freeman's maternal grandfather had been building for them. Ten years later, Freeman's mother, Eleanor, and her husband, Warren Wilkins, moved into the house, where the young Mary Ella (she later changed her middle name to Eleanor) was born and lived until the age of fifteen. In life, the formerly engaged couple never married; in *Pembroke*, however, Freeman names her male protagonist Barney Thayer, as if he has not only married Mary Thayer but also taken her name as his own, and the plot of the novel involves numerous attempts to reunite the fictional protagonists Barnabas Thayer and Charlotte Barnard.

In *Pembroke*, Barnabas Thayer leaves after an argument with Charlotte Barnard's father, Cephas, and does not return for ten years (the length of time the Lothrop house stood vacant until Freeman's parents moved in). For both Charlotte and Barney Thayer, life ceases to move forward in the wake of the subsequently broken engagement. Barney stops work on the house into which he had been planning to move with Charlotte, although he begins to inhabit it in its unfinished state, and Charlotte declines another offer of marriage, assumes the role of spinster in the village of Pembroke, and appears older than her years. The word the villagers use to describe both Barney Thayer and Cephas Barnard is "set," and Freeman explores the possibility that some people can become so "set" in their ways that they never change or grow.

Throughout the novel, members of the community enter the world of the Thayers and the Barnards, acting as external agents who try to create the possibility of change for characters who require such outside intervention, although none is so "set" as Barney Thayer. For example, when Charlotte's aunt Sylvia becomes indigent and asks a villager to take her to the poorhouse, the man informs Sylvia's long-estranged lover, Richard Alger, of her plight, and through this action both reverses the estrangement and secures housing for the homeless woman. At another moment, when Barney's sister Rebecca becomes pregnant with her lover's child and her mother, Deborah, forces her to leave home, she runs to the house of a disreputable woman in the community, who shelters her until Barney, the minister, and Rebecca's lover, William, arrive to marry Rebecca against her will. And after Deborah has whipped her invalid younger son, Ephraim, and partly precipitated his death, women from the community, informally serving as what we would term a century later child-welfare workers, go to the house to investigate Ephraim's death.

In *Pembroke,* Freeman explores what has to happen in order to prevent families from simply repeating the patterns of previous generations. Often the families in *Pembroke* do not know that one of their members needs help until an outside agent observes and intervenes, yet these community representatives are alerted only by some character flaw transmitted within the family, what Freeman terms, in referring to the Thayers, their "heart flaw." The families resist the intervention and change, in part, to keep the community from entering their lives: even greater than the fear of change is the fear that the family will require outside help. At the novel's end, an illness that seems fatal brings Charlotte Barnard back to nurse her ex-lover, yet at first Barney remains naively unaware of the consequences: "He had never once dreamed that people might talk disparagingly about" Charlotte when she moves into his house to nurse him. When the minister and one of the deacons call on Charlotte while she is staying at Barney's house, "without overhearing a word, suddenly a knowledge quite foreign to his own imagination seemed to come to him."

In his desire to prevent further intervention by the community, Barney tells Charlotte: "The church—don't—think you ought to—stay here. They are—going to—take it—up. I never—thought of that." As a consequence he is able, ten years after the broken engagement, first to send Charlotte home and then to walk back to Cephas's front door, where he asks to begin again at the point where he first became "set"—and where the novel began. The novel proves capable of healing its own family tragedy, of rewriting a significant aspect of Freeman's mother's history, and perhaps of offering the then Mary E. Wilkins herself hope that it might lie within her power as a writer to intervene and thereby change the shape of her family history.

Although Freeman intervenes artistically in *Pembroke* to change her own family history, the happy ending she provides for Barney Thayer was more elusive in her personal and professional life. Just as lacking in her ability to "analyze" the social position of women as to "analyze" the quality of her own work, she ironically discovered the possibility of individual development and simultaneously sabotaged her potential for growth. Without Booth's courageous support, Wilkins could not resolve the contradictions society creates for the woman interested in personal development. On the one hand, she recognized and applauded a woman's right to personhood; but she also accepted the conventional idea that marriage provides the single path to female development, unable to accept for herself the single state she had earlier so vividly defended for her female characters in the *Harper's Bazaar* stories.

Yet marriage did not offer Freeman a path to development; rather, it restricted her imagination and heightened her sense of insecurity. Her literary career following *Pembroke* demonstrates her turn to conventionality, beginning with *Madelon* (1896), a romance in which her female protagonist struggles to protect the man she loves and, by novel's end, is rewarded by marriage. Alternatively, Freeman wrote novels that did not focus on women as protagonists, such as *Jerome, a Poor Man* (1897). And in moving toward the conventional definition of female development, she abandoned regionalism, with its "vein of gold." As a result, very few of the short stories she wrote during the 1890s and later rank with the best of her early work in the genre.

Twenty years to the day after the young Mary E. Wilkins had published "A Shadow Family," the forty-nine-year-old woman whom the *New York Telegraph* termed "the literary old maid" finally married, moved in with her husband's mother and his unmarried sisters, and apparently attempted to become "unstuck" in her own development. Perhaps here she sought once again to re-create the sense of family she had lost more than twenty years before; perhaps she equally hoped that marriage would re-inspire her writing and produce a new "vein of gold." Yet Freeman did not move directly into marriage; she had broken her engagement to Charles Manning Freeman on several occasions and, as Perry Westbrook notes, began to suffer nightmares during this period and became addicted to sedatives.

Ambivalent about her decision to marry, Freeman must have weighed her friendship with Mary Wales against her fear that others might perceive that relationship as deviant. She may have felt like an "impostor" in the Wales family and may have believed that two women living together formed only "a shadow family," whereas a woman who married, even if, like Freeman herself, she married a womanizer who drank too much, might be able to form a "real" family. In marrying Charles Manning Freeman and moving into the social world the man with medical training occupied in Metuchen, New Jersey, the woman her New Jersey friends knew as "Dolly" would choose social legitimacy over lifelong friendship.

Literary evidence suggests, however, that Freeman's choice did not promote her development as a writer. Far from discovering a second "vein of gold" as the result of her marriage, even in her New England fiction after *Pembroke*—*Jerome, a Poor Man* and *The Portion of Labor* (1901)—she created melodramatic and unbelievable plots. She also proved unable to replace New England with New Jersey as a regional center in *The Debtor* (1905), *"Doc" Gordon* (1906), and *The Butterfly House* (1912). Her biographers unanimously judge all of these novels failures. As nearly as the 1890s she had begun to work in a variety of genres, which suggests increasing lack of direction in her writing. She wrote a play, *Giles Corey, Yeoman* (1893), based on the Salem witch trials, which was performed briefly in Boston and New York in 1893; a series of short stories based on New England's historical past, *Silence and Other Stories* (1898); and a historical novel set in Tidewater Virginia, where she had spent some summers, *The Heart's Highway* (1900).

Freeman continued this pattern of experimentation during her engagement and after her marriage, publishing animal stories (*Understudies*, 1901), ghost stories (*The Wind in the Rose-Bush and Other Stories*, 1903), a collection of mystical sketches (*Six Trees*, 1903), a novel written in serial installments in competition with the British writer Max Pemberton (*The Shoulders of Atlas*, 1908), and a chapter in a novel written in collaboration with twelve authors, including William Dean Howells, Henry James, and Elizabeth Stuart Phelps (*The Whole Family*, 1908). Perry Westbrook rightly terms this the period of Freeman's "literary vaudeville." She demonstrated her ability to try new forms, yet her work failed to develop in any particular direction or to demonstrate consistent power.

Evidence from Freeman's personal life indicates the same anxiety that she could lose her identity. In a letter to a friend dated 11 December 1901, she wonders if she will lose "the old *me*" by marrying. To another friend, a few months after her marriage, Freeman describes herself as "a transplanted spinster." And she fills her letters during the years 1902–1904 with uncharacteristic apologies. To a variety of correspondents, both personal and professional, Freeman repeatedly expresses distress at her long delays in replying, at using the typewriter as a time-saver instead of writing her letters by hand, at inconsistencies and lapses in memory, at vagueness concerning her previous work, at losing things, at trying to get back in touch with people she has lost touch with, at canceling social engagements or previous promises to write an article, and at overall complications in her life. She also waited until May 1904 to instruct her publisher, Harper & Brothers, to use her full name, Mary E. Wilkins Freeman, instead of the

"Mary E. Wilkins" that had continued to identify her as the author of her book published in 1902 and 1903.

If the early years of Freeman's marriage were happy enough, by 1906, with the publication of *By the Light of the Soul,* she had evidently begun a serious reconsideration of her life and her marriage. In her scathing depiction of the emotional shallowness of the novel's Ida Edgham, who marries the protagonist's newly widowed father, she presents an exaggerated version of herself as she had become in the social world of Metuchen. She writes about Ida: "She had wanted a home and a husband; not as some women want them, for the legitimate desire for love and protection, but because she felt a degree of mortification on account of her single estate." Like the fictional Ida, Freeman became preoccupied with household furnishings following her marriage; indeed, the only surviving letter from Charles to his wife-to-be, dated 25 September 1901, concerns furniture for their new house. As late 23 December 1908, Freeman appears to base her enjoyment of marriage on the house rather than on the emotional relationship, writing in a letter to a friend: "We enjoy our new house very much. I wish I were Siamese twins though to run it, and yet wield the pen." In 1909 she hospitalized Charles for alcoholism and the marriage had begun to deteriorate; by the time of Charles's death in 1923, the Freemans were legally separated and living apart.

In *By the Light of the Soul,* the protagonist, Maria Edgham, presents Freeman's more generous, and probably more accurate, self-portrait. Maria spends her life the victim of two events—the death of her mother, which leads her ever after to feel "outside the love of life in which she had hitherto dwelt with confidence," and an improbable but legal "marriage" to a boy named Wollaston Lee, which becomes Maria's greatest mistake in life. The fictional "marriage" comments on Freeman's own emotional history and occurs as an eventual but direct consequence of Maria Edgham's mother's death. When stepmother Ida proves to be neglectful, Ida's child (Maria's half sister), Evelyn, runs away to New York City. Then, after Maria, a friend named Gladys, and Wollaston Lee travel to New York in pursuit of Evelyn, Maria finds herself a dazed bride, ostensibly to protect her reputation when the three friends fear they have missed the last train back to New Jersey and may have to spend the night in a hotel. Using a plot device that is as unbelievable as any she ever conceived—and her novels are replete with such devices—Freeman poignantly conveys her own lack of emotional connection to her marriage, motivated in large part by her desire to save her "reputation" and cease to be the New England spinster.

By linking Maria's unplanned, and thereafter secret and unacknowledged, marriage with the death of a mother, Freeman returns once again, as she did in *Pembroke,* to consider the point of emotional arrest she perceived in her mother's family. In breaking her engagement to Charles on several occasions, Freeman came close to following the family pattern of the old story of Mary Thayer and Freeman's uncle Barnabas Lothrop. Since one of Freeman's motivating forces in her best fiction suggests her desire to break family patterns, she ironically succeeded in repairing her mother's family history by going through with her marriage to Charles, even though, if *By the Light of the Soul* is indeed spiritual autobiography, she spent much of her married life re-examining her decision.

Freeman also re-examines her literary "move" to New Jersey in *By the Light of the Soul.* Maria Edgham experiences her losses in Edgham, New Jersey, but at mid novel she moves back to New England, to a village called Amity, where her mother had grown up. When Maria returns to Amity, Freeman returns to her own "vein of gold"; and her novel situates Maria, to all outward appearances, as a spinster in a New England village. However, at the novel's end, Maria faces the complications of her secret marriage to Wollaston Lee. Freeman brings both Evelyn and Wollaston to Amity, and Evelyn falls in love with the man her sister had secretly married. For a time Maria considers divorce, but she fears the publicity and the newspapers.

Freeman had personally experienced public humiliation when reporters hounded her and expressed their "fatigue" with her series of broken engagements; shortly before her wedding actually took place, the *New Brunswick Home News* ran a story under the headline "Please, Miss Wilkins, Marry Dr. Freeman." To Freeman's credit, in *By the Light of the Soul* she does not, like other writers at the turn of the century, solve her protagonist's emotional problem by killing her or allowing her to commit suicide. Maria expresses the novelist's own dilemma when she thinks, "Elimination and not suicide seemed to her the only course for her to pursue."

Freeman's choice of her character's means of "elimination" creates one of the most bizarre endings in American fiction. Fictionally improbable but emotionally fascinating for what it tells us about Freeman herself, when Maria Edgham finally leaves Amity, destination unspecified, she meets on the train a wealthy dwarf old enough to be her mother; allows this woman, Rosa Blair, to change her surname to Blair and to acknowledge her as her adopted daughter; finds herself "swept off her feet" by the woman; and develops a loving connection based on her view of Rosa Blair as her alter ego: "Here was another woman outside the pale of ordinary life by physical conditions, as she herself was by spiritual ones."

In her protagonist's love and affinity for the dwarf, Freeman comes closest in any of her fiction to accepting her sense of her own deviance. References to love between women abound throughout Freeman's fiction, and when she refers directly to homoerotic connections, she generally aligns herself with her awareness that such bonds were considered socially deviant in the first decade of the twentieth century. In *The Shoulders of Atlas* (1908), for example, she creates two characters with lesbian tendencies, one of whom "adopts" the younger, and in an explicit statement condemning such tendencies, Freeman writes: "Miss Farrel had a jealous dread of [Rose's] forming one of those erotic friendships, which are really diseased love-affairs, with another girl or teacher." Yet at the end of her "spiritual autobiography," *By the Light of the Soul,* Freeman asserts the combined erotic and maternal nurturance of the relationship between Maria Edgham and Rosa Blair as one "solution" to a woman's emotional dilemma.

Perhaps the clearest statement of Freeman's lifelong ambivalence concerning her identity as a married woman but an emotional spinster appears as the chapter she wrote for her "collective novel" with Howells, James, Phelps, and others. Assigned the chapter titled "The Old-Maid Aunt," Freeman apparently offended Howells's sensibilities by portraying the aunt as attractive and as a believable contender in romantic love with her niece, fifteen years her junior, perhaps in simultaneous attempts to modernize the image of the old maid and to return to her earlier empowerment of single women. In her own way, she hoped to create social change for women. In a letter to a friend dated 1 August 1906, she alludes to her conflict with Howells:

> At this minute I can think of a score of women who fifty years ago would have carried out Mr. Howells's idea of the old maid aunt. To-day they look as pretty and as up-to-date as their young nieces—and no pretence about it, either. They really *are.* Their single state is deliberate choice on their own part, and men are at their feet. Single women have caught up with, and passed, old bachelors in the last half of the century.

Perhaps Freeman believed that her renewed defense of single women finally repaired her sense of broken connections, that "the shadow family" had become "the whole family," and that she herself had earned a place among the leading literary figures of her time. She continued to sell her work to the end of her life, and in 1926 she received the Howells Gold Medal for Fiction from the American Academy of Arts and Letters. Later that year, she and Edith Wharton were among the first women to be elected to membership in the National Institute of Arts and Letters. And after her death of a heart attack at home in Metuchen on 13 March 1930, fourteen years after the death of Mary Wales and seven years after the death of Charles, Freeman continued to receive popular acclaim. In 1938, the American Academy of Arts and Letters installed bronze doors at the entrance of its building on West 155th Street in New York City that read, to this day, "Dedicated to the Memory of Mary E. Wilkins Freeman and the Women Writers of America."

Although the inscription has outlasted her reputation, Freeman continues to interest readers, both for the unsurpassed quality of her finest early work in the genre of regionalism and for the lifelong conflict between her emotional connections to women and her desire for acceptance as a married woman. Whether or not she ultimately believed it had been a mistake to choose conventionality, she made no mistake in struggling for a lifetime with the issue. In 1903 she stated cavalierly, to an interviewer from the *New York Herald*, that she expected to find "just as quaint and romantic people" to write about in New Jersey as she ever had in New England. Then she added, "For people are all alike, especially if they happen to be women, whether they live in Massachusetts or Metuchen."

On one level, Freeman's prediction proved inaccurate, for New Jersey did not inspire her writing or supply her with characters for her fiction. However, by bringing her dilemma about status and choice into the public view, she identified the common social ground on which women find themselves "all alike," for all women face the dilemma of single life versus marriage, and all must rebel against marriage, accommodate to it, or find the courage to define their own alternative path to adult female development and emotional fulfillment.

When a female reader a century after Freeman wrote her finest stories discovers her own affinities with Freeman and sympathizes with her conflict, she acknowledges kinship with the writer from Randolph. And thus, in her late-twentieth-century readers, Freeman finds her "whole family" at last.

Selected Bibliography

PRIMARY WORKS

CHILDREN'S LITERATURE

Decorative Plaques: Designs by George F. Barnes, Poems by Mary E. Wilkins. Boston: Lothrop, 1883.

The Cow with Golden Horns and Other Stories. Boston: 1884.

The Adventures of Ann: Stories of Colonial Times. Boston: Lothrop, 1886.

The Pot of Gold and Other Stories. Boston: Lothrop, 1892.

Young Lucretia and Other Stories. New York: Harper & Bros., 1892.

Comfort Pease and Her Gold Ring. New York and Chicago: Fleming H. Revell, 1895.

Once upon a Time and Other Child-Verses. Boston: Lothrop, 1897.

The Green Door. New York: Moffat, Yard, 1910.

ADULT LITERATURE

A Humble Romance, and Other Stories. New York: Harper & Bros., 1887.

A New England Nun and Other Stories. New York: Harper & Bros., 1891.

Giles Corey, Yeoman: A Play. New York: Harper & Bros., 1893.

Jane Field. New York: Harper & Bros., 1893.

Pembroke. New York: Harper & Bros., 1894.

Madelon. New York: Harper & Bros., 1896.

Jerome, a Poor Man. New York: Harper & Bros., 1897.

The People of Our Neighborhood. Philadelphia: Curtis, 1898; New York: Doubleday, McClure, 1898.

Silence and Other Stories. New York: Harper & Bros., 1898.

The Jamesons. Philadelphia: Curtis, 1899; New York: Doubleday, McClure, 1899.

The Heart's Highway: A Romance of Virginia. New York: Doubleday, Page, 1900.

The Love of Parson Lord and Other Stories. New York: Harper & Bros., 1900.

The Portion of Labor. New York: Harper & Bros., 1901.

Understudies. New York: Harper & Bros., 1901.

Six Trees. New York: Harper & Bros., 1903.

The Wind in the Rose-Bush and Other Stories of the Supernatural. New York: Doubleday, Page, 1903.

The Givers. New York: Harper & Bros., 1904.

The Debtor. New York: Harper & Bros., 1905.

By the Light of the Soul. New York: Harper & Bros., 1906.

"Doc" Gordon. New York: Grosset & Dunlap, 1906.

The Fair Lavinia and Others. New York: Harper & Bros., 1907.

"The Old-Maid Aunt." In *The Whole Family: A Novel by Twelve Authors.* New York: Harper & Bros., 1908.

The Shoulders of Atlas. New York: Harper & Bros., 1908.

The Winning Lady and Others. New York: Harper & Bros., 1909.

The Butterfly House. New York: Dodd, Mead, 1912.

The Yates Pride: A Romance. New York: Harper & Bros., 1912.

The Copy-Cat & Other Stories. New York: Harper & Bros., 1914.

An Alabaster Box. New York: Appleton, 1917. Written with Florence Morse Kingsley.

Edgewater People. New York: Harper & Bros., 1918.

The Best Stories of Mary E. Wilkins. New York: Harper & Bros., 1927.

Collected Ghost Stories by Mary E. Wilkins Freeman. Introduction by Edward Wagenknecht. Sauk City, Wis.: Arkham House, 1974.

Selected Stories of Mary E. Wilkins Freeman. Edited by Marjorie Pryse. New York: W. W. Norton, 1983.

CORRESPONDENCE

The Infant Sphinx: Collected Letters of Mary E. Wilkins Freeman. Edited by Brent L. Kendrick. Metuchen, N.J.: Scarecrow Press, 1985.

PAPERS

Sizable collections of Freeman's papers are in the New York Public Library, the library of the American Academy of Arts and Letters, and the libraries of Columbia University, Princeton University, the University of Southern California, and the University of Virginia.

SECONDARY WORKS

BIOGRAPHICAL AND CRITICAL STUDIES

Brand, Alice Glarden. "Mary Wilkins Freeman: Misanthropy as Propaganda." *New England Quarterly* 50:83–100 (March 1977).

Crowley, John W. "Freeman's Yankee Tragedy: 'Amanda and Love.' " *Markham Review* 5:58–60 (Spring 1976).

DeEulis, Marilyn Davis. " 'Her Box of a House': Spatial Restriction as Psychic Signpost in Mary Wilkins Freeman's 'The Revolt of "Mother." ' " *Markham Review* 8:51–52 (Winter 1979).

Foster, Edward. *Mary E. Wilkins Freeman.* New York: Hendricks House, 1956.

Hamblen, Abigail Ann. *The New England Art of Mary E. Wilkins Freeman.* Amherst, Mass.: Green Knight Press, 1966.

Hirsch, David H. "Subdued Meaning in 'A New England Nun.' " *Studies in Short Fiction* 2:124–136 (1965).

Howells, William Dean. "Mr. H. B. Fuller's Jane Marshall, and Miss M. E. Wilkins's Jane Field." In his *Heroines of Fiction.* Vol. 2. New York: Harper & Bros., 1901.

Kendrick, Brent L. "Mary E. Wilkins Freeman." *American Literary Realism* 8:255–257 (Summer 1975). On unpublished dissertations on Freeman.

Koppelman, Susan. "About 'Two Friends' and Mary Eleanor Wilkins Freeman." *American Literary Realism* 21:43–57 (Fall 1988).

"New England in the Short Story." *Atlantic Monthly* 67:845–850 (June 1891).

Pattee, Fred Lewis. "On the Terminal Moraine of New England Puritanism." In his *Sidelights on American Literature.* New York: Century, 1922.

Pryse, Marjorie. "The Humanity of Women in Freeman's 'A Village Singer.' " *Colby Library Quarterly* 19, no. 2:69–77 (June 1983).

———. "An Uncloistered 'New England Nun.' " *Studies in Short Fiction* 20:289–295 (Fall 1983).

———. "Literary Regionalism and the 'General Gender': Time, Place, Myth, and Friendship." *Bennington Review* 16:23–29 (Spring 1984).

Robillard, Douglas. "Mary Wilkins Freeman." In *Supernatural Fiction Writers: Fantasy and Horror*. Edited by E. F. Bleiler. Vol. 2. New York: Scribners, 1985. Pp. 769–773.

Sherman, Sarah W. "The Great Goddess in New England: Mary Wilkins Freeman's 'Christmas Jenny.' " *Studies in Short Fiction* 17:157–164 (Spring 1980).

Thompson, Charles M. "Miss Wilkins: An Idealist in Masquerade." *Atlantic Monthly* 83:665–675 (May 1899).

Toth, Susan A. "Mary Wilkins Freeman's Parable of Wasted Life." *American Literature* 42:564–567 (January 1971).

———. "Defiant Light: A Positive View of Mary Wilkins Freeman." *New England Quarterly* 46:82–93 (March 1973).

Westbrook, Perry D. *Acres of Flint: Writers of Rural New England, 1870–1900*. Washington, D.C.: Scarecrow Press, 1951. Rev. ed., *Acres of Flint: Sarah Orne Jewett and Her Contemporaries*. Metuchen, N.J.: Scarecrow Press, 1981.

———. *Mary Wilkins Freeman*. New York: Twayne, 1967. Rev. ed. Boston: Twayne, 1988.

———. "Mary E. Wilkins Freeman." *American Literary Realism* 2:139–140 (Summer 1969). On criticism of Freeman.

MARJORIE PRYSE

CHARLOTTE PERKINS GILMAN

1860–1935

IN A 1903 poem, "Two Callings," Charlotte Perkins Gilman succinctly joined the "Home" and the "World," two spheres then gender separate: "Home was the World—the World was Home to me!" She managed this integration more easily in her writing than she did in her living. Nevertheless, she left a prodigious record of seventy-five years of accomplishments. She was well recognized during her lifetime: her name appeared on lists of the ten or twelve greatest United States women. Gilman stood at the intellectual helm of the broader women's rights movement during the first two decades of the twentieth century. She was an evolutionary rather than a revolutionary (or Marxist) socialist and feminist—she herself, however, preferred the label "humanist" or "sociologist" to "feminist." By her death in 1935 she had to her credit the equivalent of thirty books: verse, drama, fiction, and polemic. She had delivered so many lectures on ethics, economics, and sociology that she had lost count. Lecture tours—during which she gave sermons and stump speeches, spoke at conventions, and made club appearances—took her to nearly every state in the union, and many Western European countries as well. Yet even with such impressive achievement and recognition, as late in her life as 1917, when she was fifty-eight, Gilman nonetheless wondered whether she had accomplished enough to justify her existence and thought she needed "a few more books."

Although Gilman always concluded with self-justification, again and again in her private writing she questioned the sufficiency of her achievement. Underlying her marked public success ran a dark current of self-doubt. This would ground her soaring mind, once with a depression of several years; thereafter her depression was an intermittent and less severe tax on her energy. A residue of nineteenth-century self-righteous perfectionism cost Gilman substantially. Though we may marvel at her lifework, we must recognize a harshly relentless and unreasonable pattern of self-criticism, apparent even as she records the facts of her birth in her autobiography, *The Living of Charlotte Perkins Gilman* (1935).

She was born Charlotte Anna Perkins in Hartford, Connecticut, on the afternoon of 3 July 1860. Of this birthdate, she bemoaned: "If only I'd been a little bit slower and made it the glorious Fourth! This may be called the *first misplay* in a *long* game that is *full* of them" [emphasis added]. Charlotte had an illustrious and notorious lineage, but also one that bequeathed her conflicting models for womanhood. Her parents were Frederick Beecher Perkins, scion of the noted Beecher family, and Mary A. Fitch Westcott, a descendant of one of Rhode Island's founders. Her father was the grandson of the Calvinist revivalist Lyman Beecher and the first son of Beecher's only child not in public life, his daughter Mary Beecher. Frederick's sister Emily married Edward Everett Hale, author of the utopian *Sybaris and Other Homes* (1869) and a Unitarian minister. Another sister, Katherine, married William C. Gilman; they were the parents of Charlotte's second husband, George Houghton Gilman, who was thus a first cousin.

Frederick was the nephew of Catharine Beecher, Harriet Beecher Stowe, Isabella Beecher Hooker and Henry Ward Beecher. Catharine wrote *Treatise on Domestic Economy, for the Use of Young Ladies at Home and at School* (1841), and with her sister Harriet wrote the even more popular *The American Woman's Home* (1869), an advice book expanding the *Treatise.* Harriet morally galvanized a nation in 1852 with *Uncle Tom's Cabin*, and later scandalized genteel society on both sides of the Atlantic with an exposé of Lord Byron's incest, *Lady Byron Vindicated* (1870). Isabella crusaded for women's emancipation and sided openly with radical feminists against her brother, Henry, an eminent New York preacher who gained notoriety for a sex scandal involving a female parishioner. From the paternal Beecher-Perkins side of her lineage, Charlotte thus received a relentlessly demanding legacy: to take pride in her womanhood—although opposing models existed; to assert courageously her own viewpoint; to be fearless in the face of censure; and to achieve through serving society.

Charlotte's mother, Mary A. Fitch Westcott, brought a more traditionally feminine though comparably independent-minded heritage. She was the frail child of a June-December marriage. Her elderly father, Henry Westcott, a courageous and pacifist Unitarian, practiced incorrigible benevolence at the expense of his family, a pattern of nonsupport that her own husband would follow. As a widower, he took a fifteen-year-old second wife, Mary's spoiled and petted mother, Clarissa Fitch Perkins, who was eighteen when Mary was born. Mary became her father's darling, and since her mother permitted her to accept the attentions of a succession of beaux, Mary came to accept being doted upon as routine.

In 1857, when she was twenty-nine, Mary Westcott married a second cousin, Frederick Beecher Perkins, a linguist, scholar, and professional librarian, who was an intellectual model for their daughter Charlotte. Charlotte was born fourteen months after her brother, Thomas, and two other children died as infants. Frederick subsequently left his family, perhaps because of a physician's warning that Mary could not survive another pregnancy. In 1873, since he had not returned, Mary divorced her husband. That same year Frederick became assistant director of the Boston Public Library, and from 1880 to 1894 he was head of the San Francisco Public Library. Mary died in 1893, and Frederick returned to the East in 1894 to marry his first love, now a widow, Frankie Johnson Beecher, whose family had forced her to break her engagement to him.

The facts of Gilman's precarious childhood can only increase our awe at her achievement. She grew up in a fatherless, intinerant household. Money was constantly in short supply—Frederick supported his family only sporadically. She records in *The Living of Charlotte Perkins Gilman* that the family moved "nineteen times in eighteen years, fourteen of them from one city to another." Though Mary had "a natural genius for teaching little ones," only intermittent employment was available. As a "poor relation" in an upper-class family, she and her children resided in one household, then another. After the divorce, considered a disgrace by the family, she was no longer welcome. In 1873 she went to Providence to care for her dying grandmother and then her dying mother. Having no income, she and the children next lived for a year and a half with a Swedenborgian cooperative-housekeeping group that disbanded in 1876.

Perhaps even harder on Charlotte than these moves was Mary's ill-conceived effort to save her daughter from the suffering she had known: by withholding physical expressions of affection, Mary hoped to suppress the need for it. Charlotte reports that "her caresses were not given unless [Thomas and I] were asleep, or she thought us so." Charlotte knew little tenderness: "Never [any] from anyone, and I did want it."

In addition, her mother feared "what she was led [by a friend with a pre-Freudian mind] to suppose this inner life might become" and forbade Charlotte the fantasy world she "industriously construct[ed]" in her imagination. This world is visible in "The Literary and Artistic Vurks [*sic*] of Princess Charlotte," an unpublished manuscript written when Charlotte was ten. These early unfulfilled yearnings emerge as a child's utopia, especially in the character Elmondine, heroine of "A Fairy Tale," who befriends other women. The tale suggests that female peers are good, older males good but helpless, and older females bad or useless.

A bright child, Charlotte was better able to compensate for her intermittent education—"four years, among seven different institutions, ending when I was fifteen." Although she never shone as a student, she impressed teachers with the fund of knowledge she had gleaned from the wide reading her father sometimes guided. (Throughout her childhood, Charlotte tried to get her father's attention by correspondence: very occasional letters and reading lists were the extent of his response; she knew him personally only during the 1890s.) Charlotte attests in her autobiography to regularly reading the children's magazine *Our Young Folks,* edited by the poet and author Lucy Larcom, as well as novels by the anti-suffragist Adeline Dutton Train Whitney and the pro-suffragist Louisa May Alcott, all three creators of heroines who triumph. Such moral stories, though soon out of fashion, she believed "immensely useful in forming ethical standards." She and her mother together read and wept over sentimental novels, a bonding to each other and an affirming of femaleness, though sentimental heroines often enacted self-defeating female roles. Only partially would Gilman surmount her experience of her mother's "painfully thwarted" life.

During her late teens Charlotte pursued a blend of formal training, self-directed improvement, and gainful employment. In 1878, she attended the Rhode Island School of Design, with her mother's reluctant approval and her father's willingness "to pay the fees." There she gained sufficient skill that in 1883, one of her watercolors was accepted for a juried exhibit. At about this time Charlotte followed self-directed programs of physical culture and spiritual development. She instituted for herself five rules of health, which she conscientiously observed: plenty of good air, exercise, food, and sleep, and as little clothing as possible—this last a stand for "dress reform" against weighty Victorian garments. She found several ways of earning money: giving drawing lessons, selling her floral watercolors, and painting advertising cards for a soap company. A ten-week governess position in Maine in the summer of 1883 pleased her less.

Her attachments were varied. Although Gilman enjoyed the attentions of numerous young men, her closest friends came from a circle of young women: some fellow participants at a women's gymnasium in Providence, some associated with Brown University, some affiliated with Beecher relatives. The deepest emotional tie of these years was to Martha Luther. During the summer of 1881, Charlotte wrot almost daily letters to Martha, an intensely affectionate correspondence that has survived. She asked Martha, "Why in the name of heaven have we so confounded love with passion that it sounds to our century tutored ears either wicked or absurd to name it between women?" Charlotte experienced a profound sense of loss upon Martha's engagement in 1881 and her marriage in 1882 to Charles A. Lane. A letter to Martha in 1890 indicates how hurt Charlotte had been by Martha's marriage. She wrote, "I loved you better than anyone," and admitted to harboring "audacious fancies." Nevertheless, the friendship endured throughout Charlotte's lifetime. Her relationships with women illustrate the positive feelings women felt free to express to each other, as explained by Carroll Smith-Rosenberg in "The Female World of Love and Ritual: Relations Between Women in Nineteenth Century America."

On 12 January 1882, Charlotte met Charles Walter Stetson, a budding artist whom she found "an original: eccentric because unconventional, and well versed in almost everything, I guess!" However, in a letter to Walter dated 20 February, Charlotte acknowledged her resistance: she did not desire to follow the precedent of centuries of women in choosing marriage over a profession, but intended to pursue her goal of sacrificing personal pleasure to doing good and serving the world. By March, Walter noted how "improved" Charlotte now was—far more dependent than formerly! He felt he must stop her from her goal of fame and freedom, that *she* must become less selfish. Yet his own arrogance astounds, especially as he made her refuse a gift copy of Walt Whitman's *Leaves of Grass* because *he* judged it too coarse for her to read.

By May 1882 Walter's self-esteem had been damaged by his learning that his sonnets were "slight." Charlotte had decided in Walter's favor, though she required a delay of their marriage for one year. She feared she could not give her whole self to him—as she stereotypically believed a woman should—because she felt the Beecher call to a larger world service: she was just then determining this to be reform of women's condition in society. Walter, for his part, seemed to pursue her with the assumption that because he loved her, she must of course return the feeling, that his love gave him a right to her. Like so many men of his era, he fondly expected that a wife would inspire and support him in his best work. The primary source for the foregoing material, his diaries for this period, published as *Endure: The Diaries of Charles Walter Stetson,* reveal in yet greater detail how, even in loving a woman, a man thus compromises her life.

Charlotte married Walter on 2 May 1884. One week later she suggested that he pay her for her housekeeping services; he was offended, she then tearful. Another cause for tears was her being "too affectionately expressive": she was to await his initiative. And so the friction between them continued, though she was to claim he was "a devoted husband" in *The Living of Charlotte Perkins Gilman.* On 23 March 1885, Katharine Beecher Stetson was born. She was named for a great-aunt, Catharine Beecher, and a friend, Kate Bucknell, to whom Charlotte had paid summer visits in Ogunquit, Maine, before her marriage. Soon Charlotte lapsed into a serious depression. As an antidote, she decided to winter in California.

In the fall of 1885, she left to visit a girlhood friend—poet and fiction writer Grace Ellery Channing, then living in Pasadena, California—and found that the change of scene led to her recuperation. A return to Walter and Kate in March, however, was followed within a month by the return of her former symptoms. Her 1886 verse "The Answer" expresses her anger at both inequality in the marriage relation and pain experienced, which "had no limit but her power to feel." Charlotte developed a pattern of controlled public expression, which masked her inability to make others aware of her emotional needs, In 1887 she tried the rest cure of a Philadelphia nerve specialist, Dr. Silas Weir Mitchell, but his prescription—"never [to] touch pen, brush, or pencil" as long as she lived—only exacerbated her condition. She ceased to follow his regimen.

With a formal separation from Walter mutually agreed upon, in 1888 Charlotte set out for Pasadena with Kate and settled near the Channings. During 1889 and 1890 Gilman collaborated with Grace Channing on drawing-room comedies exposing the illogic of relations between the sexes. She credited Grace with "sav[ing] what there is of me"; they were to be close friends for over fifty years. Gilman then proceeded to make a living from what by 1896 she saw as her vocation: public speaking, organizing, and writing for a purpose.

Gilman caught the 1890s' popular fever for the Nationalists, a nationwide political party founded to support principles advocated by Edward Bellamy in his 1888 non-Marxist, socialist utopian novel, *Looking Backward, 2000–1887.* One of Gilman's early supporters in these circles was the feminist activist Harriet Howe, thereafter a lifelong friend. With Howe's backing, Gilman quickly became a regular lecturer before Nationalist Club audiences and a writer in support of Nationalist reforms. Club speakers typically addressed such issues as government ownership of transportation and utilities, civil service reform, and public aid to education. Bellamy's key ideas were cooperation and community, as opposed to the then-current belief in Darwinian competition. Enthusiasts, including Gilman, did not question the paternalistic and racist tone of some Nationalist thinking; its ethical intent was what caught their attention.

In April 1890, the *Nationalist* published her satiric "Similar Cases," which was reprinted numerous times. The refrain "You would have to change your nature" satirizes the unthinking ease with which conservatives offer "nature" as an argument against change. With its publication and subsequent favorable critical notice, Gilman began her career as an author. William Dean Howells was among those congratulating her: he claimed "Similar Cases" was the best of its kind since *The Biglow Papers,* satiric verse published in 1848 and 1867 by James Russell Lowell. Of the year 1890 Gilman wrote on New Year's Eve: "My whole literary reputation dates within it—mainly from 'Similar Cases.' Also the dawn of my work as a lecturer."

In August 1890 Gilman wrote her masterpiece, "The Yellow Wallpaper," a brilliant exposé not only of Mitchell's rest-cure treatment but also of patriarchal marriage. The short story provides a rending depiction of a woman driven mad by her environment; her madness is her revenge upon and rebellion against patriarchal confinement. The structure of the story is simple: ten diary entries by a wife, Jane, recording a summer stay at an "ancestral hall" under the care of her husband-physician, John, and a nurse, Jennie, apparently to recover from "temporary nervous depression—a slight hysterical tendency." But the heroine-narrator finds herself confined to a third-floor nursery-playroom with barred windows. Gradually she identifies with the figure of a woman she thinks she sees caught in the wallpaper design.

The short story has received acclaim for its powerful imagery of wallpaper as prison and release, for its heroine who perceives herself as having both an authentic self and a male-constructed self—two selves she learns to "read" as if texts. Recent critics interpret it variously: some consider it a gothic portrayal of a doomed heroine; others see in it a realistic statement about the experience of women in patriarchy. Some stress biographical antecedents; others, literary merit. Charlotte would struggle for two years to locate a publisher. In 1890 Horace Scudder, the editor who rejected the story for publication in the *Atlantic Monthly,* wrote to Gilman, "I could not forgive myself if I made others as miserable as I have made myself [in reading your story]!" And William Dean Howells, who included it in his 1920 *Great American Stories,* called it "terrible and too wholly dire," "too terribly good to be printed." Not until 1892 did Gilman find a publisher for the tale, *New England* magazine.

Never again would Gilman achieve so aesthetically forceful a work; this once she was able to join her public and private expressions in a work of devastating impact. Perhaps because no person in her life was meeting her insistent emotional needs, she had no outlet for her feelings save to harness them to public expression in art. Later she split her emotions from her published work, and let them emerge only in private writing or living.

In the spring of 1891 Charlotte met Adeline E. Knapp, the Dora of her autobiography and the Delle of her diaries, a friend with whom she "sincerely hoped to live continually" and for whom she felt "really passionate love," she wrote in 1899, explaining to her future second husband that letters existed documenting "that I loved her that way." Delle, a reporter for the *San Francisco Call,* was a coworker of Charlotte's in the Pacific Coast Women's Press Association. That September, along with Kate, they set up housekeeping in Oakland, then were joined by Charlotte's mother, who was dying of cancer. This household placed considerable strain upon Charlotte. Determined, however, not to have "failed in every relation in life," she cared for her mother until she died in 1893. Through all this Gilman continued writing, and for once prided herself that "nothing seems to seriously affect my power to write." As her mother died, she was working out her thoughts on the immorality of women's dependence upon men for a living.

Gilman's first book, *In This Our World,* a collection of predominantly satiric verse with a decidedly radical intent, appeared in 1893; it was enlarged and reprinted in 1895. Reviews of her verse were positive. William Dean Howells wrote that "her civic satire is of a form which she has herself invented": her "humor and sarcasm . . . teach by parable."

The public view of her personal life was another matter. In 1894 Gilman's divorce became final. She had remained on good terms with Stetson throughout. Because of the time and energy required to make a living, because she did not wish her daughter to grow up in a fatherless household, and because Stetson had married Grace Channing (with Gilman's best wishes) in 1896, Gilman decided to send Kate to join the Stetsons in New York City. This decision never ceased to pain her; thirty years later, she wrote about it in *The Living of Charlotte Perkins Gilman:* "I have to stop typing and cry as I tell about it." The press scalded her severely for this act. Her own claims of devotion notwithstanding, her correspondence with Kate through the years is strangely formal: letters typically open "Dear Child." Apparently Kate always resented having been sent away by her mother.

During the 1890s Gilman was in touch with such literary notables as poets Ina Coolbirth, Edwin Markham, and Joaquin Miller. She felt that she "took a queer turn and became 'attractive' " to men. She exclaimed in her diary, "Within two days I receive two declarations of love!!!"—presumably from Markham and Eugene Hough, a radical reformer. She found these "hopeless" but "gratifying." Her residence became the location of a salon frequented by a cross section of literary and political people interested in a wide range of issues, including the flagrant abuses of the railroad monopolies of that era.

In the summer of 1894 Gilman moved to San Francisco, where she edited the *Impress,* originally called the *Bulletin,* a publication of the Pacific Coast Women's Press Association. She shared this work with Helen Campbell, a pioneer muckraking journalist who exposed the conditions of wage-earning women in *Prisoners of Poverty* (1887). She became an "adopted mother" to Gilman until about 1912, when poor health curtailed her activities. Campbell contributed a page titled "The Art of Living" to the *Impress.* Gilman provided two series: a literary guessing game called "Studies in Style" and puzzles called "Every-Day Ethical Problems." Although the *Impress* lasted only twenty weeks, it provided an apprenticeship in journalism that would bear fruit from 1909 to 1916 as her own magazine, the *Forerunner.*

Gilman was active in the annual California Women's Congresses. Although these congresses were organized to interest women in improving moral and social conditions, some discussions had clearly feminist and reform intentions. For instance, in 1894 Gilman, Adeline Knapp, and Helen Campbell spoke on socialism, unemployed women, and working women, respectively. In 1895, Gilman met congress speakers Anna Howard Shaw, a feminist minister; Susan B. Anthony, a leader in the movement for women's suffrage; and Jane Addams, founder of Hull House in Chicago, which Gilman soon visited. These congresses appear to have been the catalyst that pushed Gilman into a wider arena. With the support of a nationwide suffrage network, she began to contemplate the possibility of lecture tours.

In 1896 Gilman launched herself as a personage on the national and international stage. She would both earn her way as she traveled and spread ideas to which she was committed. Her itinerary that year included the National

American Woman's Suffrage Association Convention in Washington, D.C., Hull House in Chicago, and the International Socialist and Labour Congress in London. In Washington, Gilman was especially engaged by the debate over Elizabeth Cady Stanton's *Woman's Bible,* a collection of biblical passages concerning women supplemented by feminist interpretations. Stanton argued that woman-affirming religion is essential to women's welfare. Also at this convention Gilman met the social evolutionist and "father of sociology" Lester Frank Ward, who advocated a gynecocentric theory in an 1888 *Forum* article entitled "Our Better Halves." He posited that "the grandest fact in nature is woman"; she, not man, is central to civilization's advance.

Heady with new contacts and ideas, Gilman returned to Hull House, which she used as her base while "at large." She met the accomplished group of women surrounding Jane Addams: Alice Hamilton, physician and scientist; Florence Kelley, lawyer and factory inspector; Julia Lathrop, social researcher and children's advocate; and Ellen Gates Starr, organizer and activist for women workers. Gilman was impressed by Addams's work, and with Helen Campbell would have headed another settlement house, had her mental health not determined otherwise. Mary A. Hill (1980) in *Charlotte Perkins Gilman: The Making of a Radical Feminist, 1860–1896,* suggests that being confronted by several idealizations of motherhood may have triggered a relapse into depression: Stanton's "Heavenly Mother," Ward's "Mother of the Race," and Addams's "Mother of Civilization." In addition, Gilman seems to have required solitude, a room of her own, to maintain a steady sense of self. She resolved incipient depression by moving on.

From spring to midsummer of 1896 Gilman lectured in Eastern and Midwestern cities. Still depressed, yet restless, she embarked for the International Socialist and Labour Congress in London. She spoke in drenching rain on a Hyde Park platform along with the German socialist leader August Bebel and the Fabian socialist and dramatist George Bernard Shaw. Though fascinated by such anarchists as Peter Kropotkin, she was most in agreement with the peaceful revolutionary stance of the Fabians. She also met the utopian author and artisan William Morris; the feminist daughter of Elizabeth Cady Stanton, Harriot Stanton Blatch; and "the distinguished Fabians" Beatrice and Sidney Webb. But depression hit once more and she left England discouraged. Home again, she went directly to the boarding house kept by her stepmother, Frankie Johnson Beecher, only to find that her father had been committed to the Delaware Water Gap Sanitorium. Father and daughter had been reconciled with him during the years after her mother's death, but Gilman could no longer look to Frederick for support. He would die in 1899. She was, however, encouraged by a subsequent invitation from the editor Prestonia Mann Martin to become a contributing editor of the *American Fabian.*

The period until 1900 Gilman labeled "the wander years." She traveled constantly as a lecturer, delivering such speeches as "Our Brains and What Ails Them," "Women and Politics," "The New Motherhood," and "Home: Past, Present, and Future." In the late summer of 1897, while visiting in five different households, she completed the first draft of her masterwork, *Women and Economics: A Study of the Economic Relation Between Men and Women as a Factor in Social Evolution.* She noted in her journal that she needed only seventeen days, on one day writing as many as 3,600 words. In less than six months the book was in an admiring public's hands. "A masterpiece," said Jane Addams; "the only real contribution to economics ever made by a woman," claimed Florence Kelley. The work joins an eminent tradition of polemical writing on behalf of women's rights: the British Mary Wollstonecraft in her 1792 *A Vindication of the Rights of Woman* argued from women's common humanity, reflecting Enlightenment rationalism, while the American Margaret Fuller in her 1845 *Woman in the Nineteenth Century* affirmed women's and men's individualistic differences, in terms of transcendental idealism.

In the 1898 *Women and Economics,* Gilman mustered arguments depending upon both women's commonalities with and differences from men. She showed that economic dependence made woman slaves of men and thereby hindered social evolution. She believed women central to social progress. The tract delineated numerous ills and explained their possible cures. First, she focused upon the subjection of women by men. She decried women's meaningless work, largely limited to domestic servitude in exchange for food and shelter, an arrangement sanctioned by an androcentric church and state. Second, Gilman claimed that women's narrowness of character and atrophied public capacities derived from this condition. For a mercenary marriage—often a woman's sole respectable means of livelihood—she exaggerated sexual and maternal traits. Third, so ignorant a mother could not adequately perform the child-care and homemaking duties to which she was limited. Home and family thereby suffered. Fourth, so excessive was the sexual distinction between women and men that two divergent world views had evolved. Two such individuals could hardly function as equal partners in marriage, hence a double standard existed. Remedies Gilman recommended included economic independence through specialized work. The required training would diversify women's capacities, enable women to perform public service, and lead to general social progress. Improved childcare and improved marriages would also result.

Gilman demonstrated the relationship between women's status and historical conditions. She made apparent the social construction of womanhood and denied that anatomy is destiny, yet she affirmed differences between the sexes. This book undergirds most of her subsequent writing. Though a radical reform tract, it was nonetheless immensely popular and was translated into seven languages. Gilman's knowledge of the main intellectual currents of the time—Social Darwinism, progressivism, democracy, socialism, and the Social Gospel—shaped her thinking, though she herself credited the influence of only two works, Lester Ward's "Our Better Halves" and Sir Patrick Geddes's *The Evolution of Sex* (1889).

About this time Gilman consulted a cousin, George Houghton Gilman, regarding a legal matter. A passionate correspondence ensued: from 1897 to 1900, she wrote twenty-to-thirty-page letters at least twice a week, reviewing her whole life—works, acts, feelings, as well as her judgments upon them. She laid bare conflicts and insecurities that had not abated, contrary to the impression conveyed in her autobiography. She continued to fear the pull of tradition: she implored Houghton to "work out such a plan of living as shall leave me free to move. . . . *I must not* focus on 'home duties'; and entangle myself in them." In the spring of 1899, Gilman sailed for Europe, this time to attend the Quinquennial Congress of the International Council of Women, again in London. Houghton joined her for a portion of this trip.

Gilman was much lionized as the author of *Women and Economics* and, thus, the leading intellectual in the United States' women's-rights movement. The warm reception she received throughout England and Scotland gratified her immensely, and she returned home much encouraged. Immediately she set off on a lecture tour of the Eastern and Midwestern states. Settling in California for the winter, in a Pasadena boarding house with Katharine, she wrote the first of four drafts of *Human Work,* a book that never satisfied her and of which she remarked, "Later thinkers must make it plainer." In the spring of 1900, Gilman made her way east, lecturing as she traveled.

On 11 June 1900, Charlotte quietly married Houghton Gilman in Detroit. Joined by Katharine, the couple moved into a New York City apartment hotel. Secured by husband, daughter, and home, Gilman felt content. Though she argued for innovation, she required a modicum of traditional stasis for her productivity. Finally able to accept support as deserved, she entered the most active phase of her career.

Three nonfiction works appeared before Gilman established the monthly magazine the *Forerunner* in 1909. In *Concerning Children* (1900) she argued for a social motherhood characterized by trained experts providing child care. In *The Home: Its Work and Influence* (1903) she attacked the single-family home as wasteful and isolated; she advocated instead socialized hosework and kitchenless houses, with public kitchens and food delivery services. In *Human Work* (1904) Gilman argued for an organic, sociocentric (communitarian), as opposed to an egocentric (individualistic), theory of society. She was never satisfied, however, with her development of the ideas in *Human Work.*

In addition to a prodigious annual amount of writing, including a contributing editorship with the weekly newspaper the *Woman's Journal* for a portion of 1904, Gilman made several trips abroad. She attended the 1904 International Congress of Women in Berlin, where her reception exceeded even that in London in 1899. After a ten-day sojourn in Italy with Katharine and the Stetsons, Gilman returned home with plans to make a lecture tour the next year that would take her to England, the Netherlands, Germany, Austria, and Hungary. Throughout the decade 1900–1910 Gilman published regularly in such magazines as *Appleton's, Harper's Bazaar,* the *Independent,* the *Saturday Evening Post, Scribner's, Success,* and *Woman's Home Companion.* These essays, along with her lectures, often provided themes for the *Forerunner*'s longer works.

In 1905 Gilman first considered publishing her own magazine as a way to ease her conscience and promote socialism. She found that she was producing far more than she was able to place with publishers. Later told to consider more what editors wanted, she retorted, "If the editors and publishers will not bring out my work, I will!" And so in 1909 the first twenty-eight-page issue of the *Forerunner* appeared. *Charl*otte and Hough*ton* formed the Charlton Company to publish both this monthly magazine and four of its serializations as separate books in 1910 and 1911. Gilman calculated each annual volume to be the equivalent of four books of 36,000 words each. Some of the pieces in the *Forerunner* had first appeared in the *Impress* or another magazine, but for the most part each issue consisted of new works. The magazine was widely distributed in America and abroad by the National American Woman Suffrage Association, the Women's Political Union, and the Socialist Literature Company. The *Forerunner,* in the view of editor Madeleine Stern, is Gilman's "greatest single achievement," unique in combining "a crusade for women's rights and a plea for socialism." It received little critical notice, however, and was a financial drain upon the Gilmans' resources.

With the possible exception of *The Man-Made World; or, Our Androcentric Culture* (1911), which some found comparable to *Women and Economics* in importance, none of the nonfiction serialized in the *Forerunner* repeated the independence of mind exhibited in Gilman's 1898 classic. In *The Man-Made World,* Gilman expounded her gynecocentric theory of sexual differentiation, for which she noted her debt to Lester Ward: men enjoy *both* fatherhood *and* productive work, while women must choose *either* motherhood *or* such work. Society is thus deprived of the traits relegated to women—cooperation, peacefulness, and life orientation—while male domination maintains a society centered upon competition, war, and death orientation, the traits admired in men. The study provided encyclopedic coverage of dress, art, play, religion, education, law and government, and economics.

Subsequent *Forerunner* nonfiction either rehashed former material or joined what had been shorter pieces. "Our Brains and What Ails Them" (1912), a frequent lecture topic; "Humanness" (1913); and "Social Ethics" (1914) are all revisions of *Human Work*. "The Dress of Women" (1915) expanded the 1891 essay "The Dress and the Body," first published in the Nationalist *Pacific Rural Press*. Gilman had antedated Thorstein Veblen's 1899 notion, developed in *The Theory of the Leisure Class*, of women's dress as a display of conspicuous consumption. "Growth and Combat" (1916) pasted together editorials on current issues.

Ironically, the *Forerunner*'s short stories and serialized fiction, given Gilman's estimate that she was better at expository writing, hold greater interest for readers today. Particularly noteworthy are four utopian works. *What Diantha Did* (1909–1910) fictionalizes a solution to problems analyzed in *Women and Economics* and explained in *The Home* and *Human Work*. The heroine, Diantha Bell, demonstrates how a cooked food delivery service and cafeteria can, through specialized labor, relieve women of individual domestic drudgery. Gilman declares her belief in the superiority of professionalized houswork over cooperative schemes of reform. The novel extends the tradition of early-nineteenth-century communitarian (Owenite) socialism to the late-nineteenth-century "grand domestic revolution" of the United States' "material feminists," who wished to professionalize domestic science.

Moving the Mountain (1911) expands what Gilman had begun to envision in 1907 as "A Woman's Utopia"—here seen through the eyes of a male narrator lost for thirty years. He reports changed lives for women, accomplished not by technological but by social and socialist innovations. Gilman reveals a flaw, however, in her willingness to let the ends of an ideal society override the questionable means of violating individual rights.

Herland (1915) wittily recounts the adventures of three men from the United States in search of an all-female country, which they name Herland. They are astonished both to find the women indifferent to their charms as males and to view the sophisticated environment that these women have built. A sequel, *With Her in Ourland* (1916), plods by comparison, as one of the male adventurers and his Herland bride fly over the globe, viewing the devastation of World War I.

Four additional novels were serialized in the *Forerunner*. The reform tract *The Crux* (1911) argues against marriage between a syphilis-infected man and an uninfected woman, the crux of the matter being to avoid committing a biological sin. *Mag-Marjorie* (1912), using the plot from an unpublished play, "The Balsam Fir," written between 1906 and 1910, presents a tale of the fallen woman upraised, as one woman protects and restores another, who is rewarded by a successful career and marriage. *Won Over* (1913), enlarged from the play "Interrupted," written in 1909, depicts a husband won over, perhaps unrealistically easily, by his wife's professional success. Finally, in *Benigna Machiavelli* (1914) the heroine firmly rejects the socialization that "the girl of the period" received; instead, she arranges her household to meet her own and others' needs—but not without Gilman's ease of subverting ends to means.

During the *Forerunner* years, the pace of Gilman's life continued unabated. In 1911 she made a ten-week lecture tour of the United States to raise money for the *Forerunner*. Gilman decided to cease publication of the *Forerunner* at the end of 1916, claiming she had printed what she was compelled to say.

Gilman continued to find ways to make her views known. In 1919 she tried two popular ventures, articles for the *New York Tribune* syndicate and lecturing on the Chautauqua circuit, giving the same talk on successive nights. Although she pronounced herself a failure at both, she continued to give occasional talks to women's club audiences. She participated for a while in the Heterodoxy Club, but wearied of its turn to pacifism and sex psychology. (One of her frequent lectures during the 1920s was "The Falsity of Freud.") She preferred the subjects of the professional women at the Query Club, but she "did not like the smell of tobacco." That suffrage was won in 1920 goes unmarked in *The Living of Charlotte Perkins Gilman,* but Gilman held no illusions about the power of the ballot in the hands of economically dependent women.

In 1922 the Gilmans were ready to leave New York's ethnic mix for Houghton's homestead in Norwich Town, Connecticut. There she wrote *His Religion and Hers: A Study in the Faith of Our Fathers and the Work of Our Mothers* (1923), a corollary to *The Man-Made World* in stressing nature as the basis of sex differences. She believed that men's control of religion had led to an overemphasis upon death; women, because they experience birth and nurture life, would as ministers bring a life-affirming orientation to religion. She saw religion as an ethical and social force, not as a theology. By 1925 Gilman had completed all but the final chapter of *The Living of Charlotte Perkins Gilman.* This is a misleading book: her diaries reveal far more frequent internal angst and uncertainty than she admits. The attitudes toward herself in both diaries and autobiography attest to poor mental health—an excess of self-criticism, superhuman expectations, and a tendency to devalue herself. She concealed anger behind her devotion to social service.

Uneasy about the influx of immigrants, who, she felt, were somehow lesser peoples, Gilman hit upon a new topic in "Progress Through Birth Control" (1927) and "Sex and Race Progress" (1929). Careful selection of partners and limitation of births would lead to peace and progressive race evolution, she believed. (During the 1890s, however, she had been one of the few feminists who did not sanction a literacy test to stem the tide of Eastern European immigrants.) Then, like Candide, she retired to her garden, where with Houghton she grew thirty kinds of vegetables. Around 1929 she wrote a never-published detective novel, "Unpunished"; an angry work, it presents her most villainous male character, who meets murder at the hands of those he has mistreated. With it, Gilman's fiction writing comes full circle, for like her earliest stories this, too, contains elements of the gothic. By 1930 all of her work was out of print.

In 1932 Gilman learned that she had inoperable breast cancer. Houghton died suddenly in May 1934; thereafter she made her home in Pasadena, near Katharine and her family—her husband, the artist Frank Tolles Chamberlin, and their children, Dorothy and Walter. On 17 August 1935, determining that her work was finished, she bathed, went to bed, placed chloroform-soaked cloths over her face, and died peacefully—almost exactly a decade after her prediction in July 1925 that she had ten years left. She left a note asserting, "I have preferred chloroform to cancer."

The death of Charlotte Perkins Gilman was thoroughly consistent with the values by which she had lived. Her act to control her own body and her own life stirred much controversy in newspapers, but those who knew and loved her applauded what they saw as her courage. Praise arrived from diverse quarters. Carrie Chapman Catt, former head of the National American Woman Suffrage Association and mobilizer of the finally successful (though compromised) campaign for suffrage, expressed shock, but remarked: "A woman of her vigor would do exactly that thing to avoid trouble to her daughter . . . and pain to herself. I think she was quite right." The novelist Fanny Hurst believed that Gilman "died as wisely as she lived." Activist Ida Tarbell, while disagreeing with the solution of suicide, noted that she could "see how Mrs. Gilman might have been driven to an extremity." *The Living of Charlotte Perkins Gilman* appeared posthumously in October 1935.

In the September 1936 *Equal Rights,* Hattie Howe wrote of her good friend Charlotte: "Indomitable, valiant, she was never vanquished, she even conquered death. . . . She went resolutely to meet it." Although Gilman in her autobiography does build a case for herself—which Howe has accepted—as the consistently conquering heroine that she was not, her desire thereby was to inspire younger women to follow her in responding to "two callings"—living fully and forcefully as long a possible in a wide arena joining both Home and World.

Selected Bibliography

PRIMARY WORKS

FICTION

The Yellow Wallpaper. New England magazine n.s. 5:647–656 (January 1892). Reprinted Boston: Small, Maynard, 1899. Reprinted with an afterword by Elaine R. Hedges. Old Westbury, N.Y.: Feminist Press, 1973.

What Diantha Did. Forerunner 1 (1909–1910). Reprinted New York: Charlton, 1910.

The Crux. Forerunner 2 (1911). Reprinted New York: Charlton, 1911.

Moving the Mountain. Forerunner 2 (1911). Reprinted New York: Charlton, 1911.

Herland. Forerunner 6 (1915). Reprinted as *Herland: A Lost Feminist Utopian Novel.* Introduction by Ann J. Lane. New York: Pantheon, 1979.

Unpunished. Edited by Shelley Fisher Fishkin, Julien Murphy, and Lillian Robinson. Forthcoming, 1992. Excerpt in *The Charlotte Perkins Gilman Reader,* edited by Ann J. Lane. New York: Pantheon, 1980, pp. 170–177. Typescript, 1929, folder 231, Gilman Papers, Radcliffe College.

DRAMA

"Three Women: A One-Act Play." Success 11:490–491, 522–526 (August 1908). Reprinted in *Images of Women in Literature,* 4th ed. Edited by Mary Anne Ferguson. Boston: Houghton Mifflin, 1986. Pp. 473–488.

VERSE

In This Our World. Boston: Small, Maynard, 1898, 1899. (Earlier, smaller editions had appeared: Oakland, Calif.: McCombs & Vaughn, 1893; San Francisco: J. H. Barry and J. H. Marble, 1895; London: T. Fisher Unwin, 1895.) Reprint of 1899 version New York: Arno Press, 1974.

Suffrage Songs and Verses. New York: Charlton, 1911. Also folder 268, Gilman Papers, Radcliffe College. Reissued in *History of Women: A Comprehensive Microfilm Publication.* New Haven: Research Publications, 1976. Reel 816, no. 6558.

SERIAL

Forerunner 1–7. New York: Charlton, 1909–1916. Reprinted with an introduction by Madeleine B. Stern. New York: Greenwood Press, 1968. Includes, in addition to serializations of works separately listed here, poems, short stories, fables, essays, editorials, plays, one serialized novel, and one serialized work of nonfiction per volume. For each of the 14 issues of vol. 1, the contents appear on the title page; the index for vols. 2–7 appear at the end of the respective volume.

NONFICTION

The Labor Movement. Oakland, Calif.: Alameda County Federation of Trades, 1893. Reissued in *History of Women: A Comprehensive Microfilm Publication.* New Haven: Research Publications, 1976. Reel 943, no. 8563.

Women and Economics: A Study of the Economic Relation Between Men and Women as a Factor in Social Evolution. Boston: Small, Maynard, 1898. Reprinted with an introduction by the editor, Carl N. Degler. New York: Harper & Row, 1966; Source Book Press, 1970.

Concerning Children. Boston: Small, Maynard, 1900.

The Home: Its Work and Influence. New York: McClure, Phillips, 1903. Reprinted with an introduction by William L. O'Neill. Urbana: University of Illinois Press, 1972.

Human Work. New York: McClure, Phillips, 1904.

The Punishment That Educates. Motherhood Leaflets no. 38. Cooperstown, N.Y.: Crist, Scott, and Parshall, 1907.

Women and Social Service. Warren, Ohio: National American Woman Suffrage Association, 1907. Reissued in *History of Women: A Comprehensive Microfilm Publication.* New Haven: Research Publications, 1976. Reel 935, no. 7959.

The Man-Made World; or, Our Androcentric Culture. Forerunner 1 (1909–1910). Reprinted New York: Charlton, 1911; Source Book Press, 1970. Also in the series American Studies. New York: Johnson Reprints, 1971.

Does a Man Support His Wife? New York: National

American Woman Suffrage Association, 1915. With Emmeline Pethick Lawrence.

His Religion and Hers: A Study of the Faith of Our Fathers and the Work of Our Mothers. New York: Century, 1923. Reprinted in the series Pioneers of the Women's Movement. Westport, Conn.: Hyperion Press, 1976.

The Living of Charlotte Perkins Gilman: An Autobiography. With a foreword by Zona Gale. New York: Appleton-Century, 1935. Reprinted New York: Arno Press, 1972; Harper & Row, 1975.

SHORT FICTION

"The Giant Wistaria." *New England* magazine, n.s. 4:480–485 (June 1891). Reprinted in *Legacy* 5:39–43 (Fall 1988).

The Rocking-Chair." *Worthington's Illustrated* magazine 1:453–459 (May 1893). Reprinted in *Boston Budget,* 25 June 1893, p. 10. Also folder 260, Gilman Papers, Radcliffe College.

"A Woman's Utopia." *Times* magazine 1:215–220 (January 1907); 369–376 (February 1907); 498–500 (March 1907); 591–597 (page proofs for April, folder 260, Gilman Papers, Radcliffe College).

SHORT NONFICTION

"The Beauty of a Block." *Independent* 57:67–72 (14 July 1904).

"The Passing of the Home in Great American Cities." *Cosmopolitan* 38:137–147 (December 1904).

"Social Darwinism." *American Journal of Sociology* 12:713–714 (March 1907).

"Why Cooperative Housekeeping Fails." *Harper's Bazaar* 41:625–629 (July 1907).

"A Suggestion on the Negro Problem." *American Journal of Sociology* 14:78–85 (July 1908).

"How Home Conditions React upon the Family." *American Journal of Sociology* 14:592–605 (March 1909).

"The Waste of Private Housekeeping." *Annals of the American Academy of Political and Social Science* 48:91–95 (July 1913).

"Applepieville." *Independent* 103:365, 393–395 (25 September 1920).

"Making Towns Fit to Live In." *Century* 102:361–366 (July 1921).

"Is America Too Hospitable?" *Forum* 70:1983–1989 (October 1923).

"Toward Monogamy." *Nation* 118:671–673 (11 June 1924).

"Progress Through Birth Control." *North American Review* 224:622–629 (December 1927).

"Feminism and Social Progress." In *Problems of Civilization.* Edited by Baker Brownell. New York: Van Nostrand, 1929. Pp. 115–142.

"Sex and Race Progress." In *Sex in Civilization.* Edited by V. F. Calverton and S. D. Schmalhausen. New York: Macaulay, 1929. Pp. 109–123.

"Parasitism and Civilized Vice." In *Woman's Coming of Age.* Edited by S. D. Schmalhausen and V. F. Calverton. New York: Boni & Liveright, 1931. Pp. 110–126.

ANTHOLOGIES

The Charlotte Perkins Gilman Reader: "The Yellow Wallpaper" and Other Fiction. Edited by Ann J. Lane. New York: Pantheon, 1980.

The Yellow Wallpaper and Other Writings. Edited by Lynne Sharon Schwartz. New York: Bantam, 1989.

MANUSCRIPTS AND PAPERS

Arthur and Elizabeth Schlesinger Library on the History of Women in America, Radcliffe College, Cambridge, Massachusetts. Charlotte Perkins Gilman Collection: major depository. Also Grace Channing Stetson Papers.

Houghton Library, Harvard University, Cambridge, Massachusetts. Includes letters to William Dean Howells.

John Hay Library, Brown University, Providence, Rhode Island. Letters to Lester Frank Ward.

Library of Congress, Manuscripts Division, Washington, D.C. Women's movement correspondence.

Rhode Island Historical Society, Providence, Rhode Island. Letters to Martha Luther Lane.

Stowe-Day Foundation, Hartford, Connecticut. Two typescripts; miscellaneous family correspondence.

SECONDARY WORKS

BIBLIOGRAPHICAL AND CRITICAL STUDIES

Allen, Polly Wynn. *Building Domestic Liberty: Charlotte Perkins Gilman's Architectural Feminism.* Amherst: University of Massachusetts Press, 1988.

Bader, Julia. "The Dissolving Vision: Realism in Jewett, Freeman, and Gilman." In *American Realism: New Essays.* Edited by Eric J. Sundquist. Baltimore: Johns Hopkins University Press, 1982.

Bartkowski, Frances. *Feminist Utopias.* Lincoln: University of Nebraska Press, 1989. Ch. 1, on *Herland.*

Bassuk, Ellen L. "The Rest Cure: Repetition or Resolution of Victorian Women's Conflicts?" In *The Female Body in Western Culture: Contemporary Perspectives.* Edited by Susan Rubin Suleiman. Cambridge, Mass.: Harvard University Press, 1986.

Berkin, Carol Ruth. "Private Woman, Public Woman: The Contradictions of Charlotte Perkins Gilman." In *Women of America: A History.* Edited by Carol Ruth Berkin and Mary Beth Norton. Boston: Houghton Mifflin, 1979.

Blamonte, Gloria A. ". . . There Is a Story, If We Could Only Find It": Charlotte Perkins Gilman's 'The Giant Wistaria.' " *Legacy* 5:33–38 (Fall 1988).

Black, Alexander. "The Woman Who Saw It First." *Century* 107:33–42 (November 1923).

Brown, Gillian. "The Empire of Agoraphobia." *Representations* 20:134–157 (Fall 1987).

DeLamotte, Eugenia C. "Male and Female Mysteries in 'The Yellow Wallpaper.' " *Legacy* 5:3–14 (Spring 1988).

Feldstein, Richard. "Reader, Text, and Ambiguous Referentiality in 'The Yellow Wallpaper.' " In *Feminism and Psychoanalysis,* edited by Richard Feldstein and Judith Roof. Ithaca: Cornell University Press, 1989. Pp. 269–279.

Fetterley, Judith. "Reading About Reading: "A Jury of Her Peers,' "The Murders in the Rue Morgue,' and 'The Yellow Wallpaper.' " In *Gender and Reading: Essays on Readers, Texts, and Contexts.* Edited by Elizabeth A. Flynn and Patrocinio P. Schweickart. Baltimore: Johns Hopkins University Press, 1986.

Ford, Karen. " 'The Yellow Wallpaper' and Women's Discourse." *Tulsa Studies in Women's Literature* 4:309–314 (1985).

Fryer, Judith. "From White City to *Herland.*" In her *Felicitous Space: The Imaginative Structures of Edith Wharton and Willa Cather.* Chapel Hill: University of North Carolina Press, 1986.

Gardiner, Judith Kegan. "On Female Identity and Writing by Women." *Critical Inquiry* 8:347–361 (Winter 1981).

Gilbert, Sandra M., and Susan Gubar. *The Madwoman in the Attic: The Woman Writer and the Nineteenth-Century Imagination.* New Haven: Yale University Press, 1979. Pp. 89–92.

———. "Homerule." In *No Man's Land: The Place of the Woman Writer in the Twentieth Century.* Vol. 2, *Sexchanges.* New Haven: Yale University Press, 1989.

Golden, Catherine. "The Writing of 'The Yellow Wallpaper': A Double Palimpsest." *Studies in American Fiction* 17:193–201 (Autumn 1989).

Gornick, Vivian. "Twice Told Tales." *Nation,* 227:278–281 (23 September 1978).

Hayden, Dolores. *The Grand Domestic Revolution: A History of Feminist Designs for American Homes, Neighborhoods, and Cities.* Cambridge, Mass.: MIT Press, 1981. Chs. 9–12.

Hedges, Elaine. " 'Out at Last?': Critics Read 'The Yellow Wallpaper.' " In *"The Yellow Wallpaper": A Casebook,* edited by Catherine Golden. Old Westbury, N.Y.: Feminist Press, 1991.

Herndl, Diane Price. "The Writing Cure: Charlotte Perkins Gilman, Anna O., and 'Hysterical' Writing." *NWSA Journal* 1:52–74 (Autumn 1988).

Hill, Mary Armfield. *Charlotte Perkins Gilman: The Making of a Radical Feminist, 1860–1896.* Philadelphia: Temple University Press, 1980.

———. *Charlotte Perkins Gilman: A Journey from Within.* Philadelphia: Temple University Press, 1990. Correspondence between Charlotte and Houghton.

———, ed. *Endure: The Diaries of Charles Walter Stetson.* Philadelphia: Temple University Press, 1985. Includes paraphrased conversations and direct quotes from Gilman's letters.

Howe, Harriet. "Charlotte Perkins Gilman—As I Knew Her." *Equal Rights* 5:211–216 (5 September 1936).

Howells, W[illiam] D[ean]. "The New Poetry." *North American Review* 168:581–592 (May 1899). See 589–590.

Karpinski, Joanne B. "When the Marriage of True Minds Admits Impediments: Charlotte Perkins Gilman and William Dean Howells." In *Patrons and Protégées: Gender, Friendship, and Writing in Nineteenth-Century America.* Edited by Shirley Marchalonis. New Brunswick, N.J.: Rutgers University Press, 1988.

Kessler, Carol Farley. *Charlotte Perkins Gilman: Progress Toward Utopia.* Chapel Hill: University of North Carolina Press, 1991.

Keyser, Elizabeth. "Looking Backward: From *Herland* to *Gulliver's Travels.*" *Studies in American Fiction* 11:31–46 (Spring 1983).

Kolodny, Annette. "A Map for Rereading: Gender and the Interpretation of Literary Texts." *New Literary History* 11:451–467 (Spring 1980).

Lane, Ann J. *To "Herland" and Beyond: The Life and Work of Charlotte Perkins Gilman.* New York: Pantheon, 1990.

Langley, Juliet A. " 'Audacious Fancies': A Collection of Letters from Charlotte Perkins Gilman to Martha Luther." *Trivia* 6:52–69 (Winter 1985).

MacPike, Loralee. "Environment as Psychopathological Symbolism in 'The Yellow Wallpaper.' " *American Literary Realism* 8:286–288 (Summer 1975).

Magner, Lois N. "Women and the Scientific Idiom: Textual Episodes from Wollstonecraft, Fuller, Gilman, and Firestone." *Signs* 4:61–80 (Autumn 1978).

Meyering, Sheryl L., ed. *Charlotte Perkins Gilman: The Woman and Her Work.* With a foreword by Cathy N. Davidson. Ann Arbor: UMI Research Press, 1989.

Miller, Margaret. "The Ideal Woman in Two Feminist Science-Fiction Utopias." *Science-Fiction Studies* 10: 191–198 (1983).

Nies, Judith. "Charlotte Perkins Gilman." In her *Seven Women: Portraits from the American Radical Tradition.* New York: Viking Press, 1977.

Palmeri, Ann. "Charlotte Perkins Gilman: Forerunner of a Feminist Social Science." In *Discovering Reality: Feminist Perspectives on Epistemology, Metaphysics, Methodology, and Philosophy of Science,* edited by Sandra Harding and Merill B. Hintikka. Boston: D. Reidel, 1983.

Pearce, Lynne, and Sara Mills. "Marxist Feminism: Margaret Atwood, *Surfacing,* and Charlotte Perkins Gilman, 'The Yellow Wallpaper.' " In *Feminist Readings / Feminists Reading,* edited by Sara Mills et al. Charlottesville: University Press of Virginia, 1989. Pp. 208–219.

Pearson, Carol. "Coming Home: Four Feminist Utopias and Patriarchal Experience." In *Future Females: A Critical Anthology.* Edited by Marleen S. Barr. Bowling Green, Ohio: Bowling Green State University Popular Press, 1981.

Poirier, Suzanne. "The Weir Mitchell Rest Cure: Doctor and Patients." *Women's Studies* 10:15–40 (1983).

Potts, Helen Jo. "Charlotte Perkins Gilman: A Humanist Approach to Feminism." Ph.D. dissertation, North Texas State University, 1975.

Scharnhorst, Gary. *Charlotte Perkins Gilman.* Boston: Twayne, 1985.

———. "Making Her Fame: Charlotte Perkins Gilman in California." *California History* 64:192–201, 242–243 (Summer 1985).

Schöpp-Schilling, Beate. " 'The Yellow Wallpaper': A Rediscovered 'Realistic' Story." *American Literary Realism* 8:284–286 (Summer 1975).

Showalter, Elaine. *The Female Malady: Women, Madness, and English Culture, 1830–1980.* New York: Pantheon, 1985.

Smith, Marsha A. "The Disoriented Male Narrator and Societal Conversion: Charlotte Perkins Gilman's Feminist Utopian Vision." *American Transcendental Quarterly* n.s. 3 1:123–133 (March 1989).

Spacks, Patricia Meyer. *The Female Imagination.* 2nd ed. New York: Knopf, 1975. Ch. 6, 7.

Treichler, Paula A. "Escaping the Sentence: Diagnosis and Discourse in 'The Yellow Wallpaper.' " *Tulsa Studies in Women's Literature* 3:61–77 (Spring–Fall 1984).

———. "The Wall Behind 'The Yellow Wallpaper': Response to Carol Neely and Karen Ford." *Tulsa Studies in Women's Literature* 4:323–330 (1985).

Ward, Lester F. "The Past and Future of the Sexes." *Independent* 60:541–545 (March 1906).

Veeder, William. "Who Is Jane? The Intricate Feminism of Charlotte Perkins Gilman." *Arizona Quarterly* 44:40–79 (Autumn 1988).

Winkler, Barbara Scott. *Victorian Daughters: The Lives and Feminism of Charlotte Perkins Gilman and Olive Schreiner.* Ann Arbor: Women's Studies Program, University of Michigan, 1980.

Wood, Ann Douglas. " 'The Fashionable Diseases': Women's Complaints and Their Treatment in Nineteenth-Century America." *Journal of Interdisciplinary History* 4:25–52 (Summer 1973).

BIBLIOGRAPHIES

Moseley, Eva. "Charlotte Perkins Gilman Papers, 1846–1961." Cambridge, Mass.: Arthur and Elizabeth Schlesinger Library on the History of Women in America, Radcliffe College, 1972. Mimeo.

Scharnhorst, Gary. *Charlotte Perkins Gilman: A Bibliography.* Scarecrow Author Bibliographies no. 71. Metuchen, N.J.: Scarecrow Press, 1985.

The Arthur and Elizabeth Schlesinger Library on the History of Women in America: The Manuscript Inventories and the Catalogs of the Manuscripts, Books, and Periodicals. 2nd rev. and enl. ed. Boston: G. K. Hall, 1984.

CAROL FARLEY KESSLER

ELLEN GLASGOW

1873–1945

IN A LETTER to her friend Helen K. Taylor dated 28 March 1941, Ellen Glasgow complains about a reviewer's having written that Glasgow "has lived a thoroughly conventional spinster's life in the big grey, brick, Georgian house." "If this is true," Glasgow wonders, "how does the reviewer know it? And as a matter of verity, the one experience I have never had is the life of a conventional spinster, whatever that is. Or a conventional life of any other nature." But Alfred Kazin in *On Native Grounds* (1942) concurred with the reviewer, commenting that Glasgow "wrote like a dowager." A surface examination reveals that Glasgow did indeed lead a conventional life for a woman of her economic class; and of her nineteen novels, many follow stylistic and thematic precedents set by earlier generations of domestic novelists.

Moreover, Glasgow has been remembered chiefly as a literary personality rather than as an original writer. Even her correspondent and admirer, the influential Agrarian Allen Tate, commented to Glasgow's cousin Stark Young: "The more I think about grand Ellen Glasgow, the more I fall in love with her. None of her books is as grand as she is." As a result, then, both of her perceived conventionality and of her considerable personal charm, a detailed study of Glasgow is absent from many canonized American literary histories. More recent critics, particularly those attuned to theoretical developments in literary study such as feminist criticism, find, however, that Glasgow went, as Linda W. Wagner puts it, "beyond convention," particularly in her best novels, which she wrote while in her fifties. Most serious readers of Glasgow today recognize her transitional position and on that basis claim for her a place in literary history.

Ellen Anderson Glasgow was born on 22 April 1873, the ninth of ten children of Francis Thomas Glasgow and Anne Jane Gholson. Her father, a managing director of the Tredegar Iron Works, which had manufactured munitions for Robert E. Lee's Army of Northern Virginia, had ancestors who had settled the Shenandoah Valley, and her mother claimed Virginia roots traceable to one of the oldest families in the Tidewater. A sickly child, Glasgow was schooled at home by tutors, spending time both at the family's residence in Richmond (after 1899 at 1 West Main Street, said to be haunted by her ghost) and at their nearby 700-acre estate, Jerdone Castle. Julius Rowan Raper (1980) lists her childhood activities as including "story telling, reading, caring for animals, and listening to quarrels between her temperamentally opposed parents." In her autobiography, *The Woman Within* (1954), Glasgow claims that she became a writer when she was seven years old, "but not until I was seven or more, did I begin to pray every night 'O God, let me write books! Please, God, let me write books!' " Glasgow had a black mammy and debuted in Charleston, South Carolina, at the St. Cecilia Ball in 1889: all conventional enough for a woman of her time, place, and class.

Although she never married, she announces in her autobiography: "I have known ecstasy. I have known anguish. I have loved, and I have been loved." In 1907 she was engaged to the Reverend Frank Ilsley Paradise, an Episcopal minister, and in 1917 to Henry W. Anderson, a dashing, successful man-about-town. Glasgow broke both engagements, and attempted suicide after spending the evening with Anderson on 3 July 1918. She reflects in *The Woman Within,* "The obscure instinct that had warned me, in my early life, against marriage, was a sound instinct." Had he been available, however, Glasgow might have married a man she met at the turn of the century who is known only as Gerald B. in her autobiography. She had fallen in love with him at first sight. Following his death seven years after their first meeting, she sought solace in Eastern mysticism.

Glasgow claimed that she lacked "what people call the maternal instinct" and feared passing on her possibly inherited deafness. Perhaps, however, these assertions were attempts to rationalize her childless existence, for she clearly had a deep desire to nurture, as suggested by her relationships to her dogs, particularly her Sealyham, Jeremy, who in illness was attended by a surgeon and who upon his death was embalmed, coffined, and buried, only to be exhumed and buried with Glasgow when she died. Jeremy's passing was clearly one of the greatest tragedies of Glasgow's life. Her adoration, even fetishization, of dogs is exemplified further by her substantial bequest to the Richmond SPCA and her seventy-eight-piece collection of china, porcelain, and pottery dogs, which is housed in Richmond's Valentine Museum. With Anne Virginia Bennett, a nurse who had cared for her father and her sisters Cary and Emily, Glasgow shared a love of dogs and a distaste for men.

Glasgow, then, appeared to be a conventional, if wealthy and eccentric, spinster of the privileged class, traveling, throwing gala parties, pampering her pets, and writing novels. But those novels grew out of a mind that rebelled against intellectual convention, beginning in her early life with her rejection of her father's strict Calvinism. In fact, after her beloved sister Cary died in Richmond in 1911, Glasgow moved to New York, not returning home to live until after her father's death in January 1916. She had first been intellectually challenged by Walter McCormack, Cary's fiancé and Glasgow's mentor, who introduced her to the writings of John Stuart Mill, Herbert Spencer, and Charles Darwin. "Modern sciences and scepticism," Raper (1980) suggests, "afforded the weapons she needed to defend her mind against her father's insistence that she conform to traditional theological authorities."

After Gerald B.'s death, seeking to understand "all the piled up unhappiness of the years, beginning with my delicate and misunderstood childhood," she began a course of reading that included the Neoplatonists, the Stoics, Kant, Schopenhauer, and Spinoza. Later she read the writings of Christ, Buddha, and St. Francis, then Locke, Berkeley, and Hume, and finally Freud. "Intellectual audacity," she wrote to Carl Van Vechten on 3 January 1925, "always appeals to me." In her autobiography she admits, however, that the great thinkers did not save her: "Strangely enough, golf helped me more than philosophy to bear life."

Her deep philosophical bent and her venerable position in the world of letters mark Glasgow as decidedly unconventional. A guiding light of the Southern Literary Renaissance, Glasgow proposed and organized a conference with the title "The Southern Author and His Public," held in Charlottesville, Virginia, on 23 and 24 October 1931. Among the luminaries attending were William Faulkner, Donald Davidson, Caroline Gordon, Allen Tate, James Branch Cabell, and Sherwood Anderson. In the opening address Glasgow discussed the terms "Southern writer" and "truth," lamented the lack of compassion in American literature, and impressed the audience thoroughly with her brilliance and charm. Frederick P. W. McDowell suggests that Glasgow might have achieved "substantial leadership in American letters" had ill health not forced her to resign from the conference organization committee.

The reputation that positioned Glasgow as a guiding light of the Southern Literary Renaissance had resulted, in part, from her clever manipulation of her reviewers. She had made friends and allies of Walter Hines Page, Carl Van Vechten, Allen Tate, Howard Mumford Jones, and Van Wyck Brooks, all powerful men in the academic and publishing worlds, thus ensuring herself good reviews. As recently as 1973, the ever loyal Jones assessed her stylistic development as "one of the wonderful events not merely in the literary history of the South but in the literary history of the United States." She was chosen the sixth female member of the American Academy of Arts and Letters (1938), won the Howells Medal for Fiction (1940), received several honorary doctorates, and was awarded the Pulitzer Prize in 1942 for *In This Our Life*. When, in 1933, *The Sheltered Life* was passed over for the same award in favor of Thomas S. Stribling's *The Store*, Allen Tate wrote to Glasgow that "*The Sheltered Life* is there to make the award ridiculous in the years to come." Her efforts to curry favor with those in power paid off handsomely, and Glasgow enjoyed a degree of success and renown—several of her novels were best-sellers, and all sold well—realized by few conventional spinsters.

Many of the early novels, however, were conventional, following trends in fiction begun in the nineteenth century. As Glasgow herself freely admitted in her autobiography, "I had been brought up in the midst of it [the sentimental tradition]; I was a part of it, or it was a part of me." Proud of this inheritance, she declared to Walter Hines Page in a letter dated 26 June 1908:

> Now personally I have not the slightest objection to being branded as either 'sentimental' or 'emotional,' since it puts me in a very respectable class from Christ to the first sentimentalist who suggested that truth might still prevail though the pursuit of it through the rack and the thumbscrew should be abolished.

Glasgow's two earliest novels, both written before the turn of the century, are set in New York City and deal with naturalism and doomed love. In *The Descendant* (1897), Michael Akershem, the male protagonist, moves from a tiny Southern community to New York, where he makes good editing the *Iconoclast* and falls in love with another Southerner, the emancipated painter Rachel Gavin. As Michael prospers, Rachel suffers, sacrificing her art for her man. Only when Michael kills a man in a business dispute and is imprisoned does Rachel regain her desire to succeed. Both Michael and Rachel are doomed by biology—Glasgow was reading Darwin during the period in which she was writing *The Descendant*.

Because of her gender, Glasgow had difficulty finding a publisher. A friend's brother, who worked at Macmillan, told Glasgow "to stop writing, and go back to the South and have some babies." Although the novel was eventually published anonymously by Harper's, the writer was not satisfied, as she states in her autobiography:

> I wanted an art. I wanted a firm foundation; I wanted a steady control over my ideas and my material. What I understood more and more was that I needed a philosophy of fiction, I needed a technique of working. Above all, I felt the supreme necessity of a prose style so pure and flexible that it could bend without breaking.

Glasgow did not fulfill her desire, however, in her second novel, *Phases of an Inferior Planet* (1898), which continues to work the philosophical themes of Darwinian determinism by presenting incompatible male and female protagonists, an intellectual and an artist, respectively, whose marriage collapses.

Glasgow found her characteristic Virginia setting in the novels of her second phase, beginning with *The Voice of the People* (1900), *The Battle-Ground* (1902), and *The Deliverance* (1904). In these novels of love and marriage, Glasgow's women die (in *Voice*) and live, love, and find happiness (in the other two) as a result of their independent streaks. *The Battle-Ground* and *The Deliverance* were written during Glasgow's romance with Gerald B. Glasgow admitted in her 1938 preface to *The Battle-Ground* that the novel is "the work of romantic youth," and in the happy endings of both novels the hero and heroine prepare to spend their lives together.

When Gerald B. died, Glasgow's novels adopted the ironic tone for which she would become celebrated. (Indeed, she later recommended that moribund Southern letters be infused with "blood and irony.") *The Wheel of Life* (1906), set, once again, in New York, concerns a poet-heroine, Laura Wilde, who realizes that she must renounce physical love and art—both romantic myths—in order to attain happiness. *The Ancient Law* (1908) features a male protagonist who, like Laura Wilde, learns that love of mankind transcends personal physical passion. The next novels, *The Romance of a Plain Man* (1909) and *The Miller of Old Church* (1911), feature conventional plots, the first offering a Horatio Alger romance of the self-made man who sacrifices for love; the second, a saga of three families, marriages among them, and changing class structure. The later novel is important, according to Linda W. Wagner, "because it gives [Glasgow] a way to combine the study of class change with the study of woman's role in the custom-bound South" and because here Glasgow deconstructs the traditions of romance, using, among other techniques, the ironic deflation of the ideal man.

Virginia (1913), generally considered the best of Glasgow's earlier novels, introduces the central problem of many women in her later novels: societal expectation and capitulation to Victorian ideals. Glasgow's original intention, as stated in the preface to the Virginia Edition of the novel, had been to present an ironic portrait of her protagonist, but "my irony grew fainter while it yielded at last to sympathetic compassion. By the time I had approached the end, the simple goodness of Virginia's manners had turned a comedy of manners into a tragedy of human fate." Virginia Pendelton begins as a charming young girl who, unfortunately, compromises herself by desiring only to fulfill her socially determined role as a woman. Little by little she loses her personality through her selfless devotion to her husband and children, and eventually loses her husband.

Life and Gabriella (1916) presents another woman constrained by the laws of culture, but Gabriella triumphs after recognizing her husband's infidelity and turning her dependent life around. She is provided at the end with a new man who appreciates her; thus, as Wagner comments, this best-selling novel is "a highly conventional romance, with a highly conventional ending." Glasgow's sometime fiancé, Henry Anderson, apparently collaborated with Glasgow on *The Builders* (1919) and *One Man in His Time* (1922), both political novels presenting stereotyped characters, the former set at the beginning of World War I and the latter set in postwar Richmond. The major conflict portrayed in both is between old and new orders.

Glasgow's next publication was *The Shadowy Third and Other Stories* (1923), a collection featuring stories important for prefiguring the strong women of her major phase; they are pitted against ineffectual, unresponsive, even stupid men. In 1925 Glasgow published *Barren Ground*, a narrative presenting, according to Marcelle Thiébaux, "a new, elemental woman." As Glasgow writes in *The Woman Within:* "It was not until I came to write *Barren Ground* and my later books that I felt an easy grasp of technique, a practiced authority over style and material. I had worked too hard for this to be modest about it." This ground-breaking novel follows the life of Dorinda Oakley, who clearly speaks for Glasgow. Dorinda, who grows up at Old Farm, Pedlar's Mill, Virginia, in the bosom of her hardworking family, falls passionately in love with Jason Greylock, a wealthy neighbor who impregnates her and then jilts her. When Dorinda finds that he has married another woman, she renounces romantic love:

> The world in which she had surrendered her being to love—that world of spring meadows and pure skies—had receded from her so utterly that she could barely remember its outlines. By no effort of the imagination could she recapture the ecstasy. Colours, sounds, scents, she could recall; the pattern of the horizon; evening skies and

> the colour of mignonette; the spangled twilight over the bulrushes; but she could not revive a single wave, a single faint quiver of emotion. Never would it come back again. The area of feeling within her soul was parched and blackened, like an abandoned field after the broomsedge is destroyed. Other things might put forth; but never again that wild beauty.
>
> (p. 169)

Ashamed and despairing, Dorinda takes her fate in hand and, deciding to leave home, relies on the "vein of iron" in her soul:

> [The] unflinching Presbyterian in her blood steeled her against sentimentality. She would meet life standing and she would meet it with her eyes open. . . . The ever-present sense of sin, which made the female mind in mid-Victorian literature resemble a page of the more depressing theology, was entirely absent from her reflections.
>
> (p. 198)

In New York, after losing the child in what Raper (1980) has described as "one of the most convenient collisions between a pedestrian and a moving vehicle in modern fiction," Dorinda makes a success; however, her native landscape calls, and after a crash course in agriculture, she returns to Pedlar's Mill to redeem the land from the proliferating broomsedge.

Dorinda carefully plans her future and works like a man. At first she avoids seeing her former lover, but when she does, she is, as he puts it, "hard as a stone." "Yes," she replies, "I am hard. I'm through with soft things." Later she exults, "Oh, if the women who wanted love could only know the infinite relief of having love over!" Dorinda prospers, becomes a large landowner, and marries (but never consummates the marriage) an old friend, Nathan Pedlar, whom she treats as "a superior hired man." Marriage makes no change whatsoever in Dorinda's life, and she believes that "she had chosen the best substitute for love, which is tolerance." At the end of the novel, a toughened Dorinda, more successful than ever, reflects on her life during a storm. She is tormented by the youth she never had and the belief that "love was the only thing that made life desirable, and love was irrevocably lost to her." She weathers her dark night of the soul:

> The land which she had forgotten was waiting to take her back to its heart. Endurance. Fortitude. The spirit of the land was flowing into her, and her own spirit, strengthened and refreshed, was flowing out again toward life. This was the permanent self, she knew. This was what remained to her after the years had taken their bloom. She would find happiness again. Not the happiness for which she had once longed, but the serenity of mind which is above the conflict of frustrated desires.
>
> (p. 509)

Here, then, in one of the most symbolic of Glasgow's works, is a new kind of heroine, one who triumphs by imposing her will on the solid earth.

Her next novel, *The Romantic Comedians* (1926), presents a surprising departure from the high seriousness of *Barren Ground*. The first of the Queenborough novels, it held a special place for Glasgow. In a letter dated 10 August 1935 to Bessie Zaban Jones, the wife of Howard Mumford Jones, Glasgow boasts, "As a comedy of manners, I feel (why should I pretend to false modesty?) that *The Romantic Comedians* has never been surpassed in the novel form." The plot concerns the wealthy and respected Judge Gamaliel Honeywell, a widower in his sixties, who gets spring fever, falls in love, and marries young Annabel Upchurch; however, neither is happy. The judge attempts to understand his situation:

> His library, his club, his Archaeological Society, his distinguished position in the community, and his church, of which he was a vestryman,—all these solid advantages were unaltered by the moral disturbances through which he had passed. Nevertheless, in his heart, he knew that, though these upheavals had been more painful than pleasant, he dreaded the moment when the effervescence would subside on the dull surface of life. Annabel, like youth itself, was a source of frustrated impulses and fruitless desires, but she

> was also the last thing on earth he would consent to relinquish. Illogical, absurd in the extreme, and unworthy of the judicial mind; yet wanting what was bad for one had been, he acknowledged, the private history of most minds, judicial or otherwise.
>
> (p. 175)

At the end the judge loses Annabel, who protests that she cannot live without love, to a much younger man.

The real triumph of the novel, however, is the judge's sister, Edmonia Bredalbane, who is, according to Raper (1980), "the most extraordinary character Ellen Glasgow ever created." Married four times, Edmonia flouts convention, lives lustily and pragmatically, enjoys herself thoroughly, and refuses to capitulate to empty convention. She has, according to her brother, a carnal spirit. Edmonia objects:

> I've always believed that happiness, any kind of happiness that does not make some one else miserable, is meritorious. . . . At least one important concern is essential to a cheerful life, and I feel sometimes that I have exhausted my interests. After love and travel, there isn't much left except religion and the pleasures of the palate, and of course social reforms, though none of these make any personal appeal to me. If my digestion gives out, I suppose I shall have to turn to the Church . . . that is the only thing I haven't tried; but it has always seemed to me to lack a sense of humor.
>
> (pp. 210–211, 213)

Nowhere else in her fiction does Glasgow create such a delightfully flamboyant woman whose chief interest is the pursuit of pleasure.

Like *The Romantic Comedians, They Stooped to Folly* (1929) features betrayal in male-female relationships and the entanglements of age and youth. As Thiébaux has explained, "The older generation remains repressed and stabilized despite their yearnings; the young are given to acting out their desires." The last Queenborough novel, *The Sheltered Life* (1932), the second of Glasgow's favorite productions (*Barren Ground* is the other), is rated by Howard Mumford Jones as "one of her perfect works." Glasgow explained to Allen Tate in a letter dated 22 September 1932 what she meant by the title: "By the Sheltered Life, I meant the whole civilization man has built to protect himself from reality. As you perceive, I was not concerned with the code of Virginia, but with the conventions of the world we call civilized." She concludes the letter by expressing delight that Tate has understood what the novel was intended to be—"an expression of the tragic vision which is the end of all vision."

For a comedy of manners, the novel is quite tragic, presenting five women characters, each of whom suffers as a result of the restrictions placed on her by society. The action revolves around two of the five: Jenny Blair Archbald, who grows from a nine-year-old individualist who chants, "I'm different. I'm different. . . . I'm alive, alive, alive, and I'm Jenny Blair Archbald," into a dangerous teenage flirt; and Jenny Blair's idol, Eva Birdsong, the ravishingly beautiful, delicate wife of the handsome George Birdsong. Both women are products of a society presided over by men like Jenny Blair's grandfather, David Archbald, who in clinging to traditional gender roles not only suffers himself but also restricts the self-actualization of others, like Eva Birdsong, who is more a model of ideal womanhood than a real woman.

The plot of the novel follows Jenny Blair's increasing infatuation with the ineffectual, philandering George Birdsong and Eva's steady decline, which results from the strain of keeping up a public face. In the last pages Eva catches George and Jenny Blair embracing and shoots her husband. Jenny Blair takes no responsibility for the event, nor does her grandfather expect her to, believing her "a sympathetic little soul." "Remember how young she is, and how innocent," he admonishs an investigating physician. The sheltered life of Queenborough, the beliefs and values of the population as represented by David Archbald, have bred disaster. C. Hugh Holman has concluded: "We can sum up the Queensborough novels as the comedy of the missed delight, the hunger for the unknown timeless instant of joy, the sorrow of the aged for the passing of what Chaucer called 'the blinde lust, the which that may not laste.' "

Glasgow was sixty-two years old when she published her eighteenth novel, *Vein of Iron* (1935), which she thought "all beautiful and wonderful," her "best and biggest and truest novel." This work, she claimed in a letter to a Miss Forbes dated 3 December 1935, "was torn up by the roots from the experience and observation and reflection of a lifetime." Earlier that year, on 8 January, she had written to Bessie Zaban Jones: "No novel has ever meant quite so much to me. It is, I feel sure, my best book, completely realized and created before I put pen to paper. . . . It is long, thoughtful, tragic, but not melancholy (though I like melancholy novels when they are genuine), and saturated through and through with reality."

In *Vein of Iron*, Ada Fincastle McBride recapitulates Dorinda Oakley of *On Barren Ground*. An illegitimately conceived child forces Ada to move from the family farm to Queenborough, where she gets a job and finally marries Ralph McBride, her childhood sweetheart and the father of her child, after his return from the European war. In Ada's father, John Fincastle, who joins the McBride household, Glasgow writes "of the loneliness of the scholar in America." To help with expenses he teaches at a girls' school, even though he is an internationally known philosopher, while Ralph, a once-promising law student, sells cars until an accident incapacitates him. Ada returns to work at a department store, and the family scrapes by until the Depression hits. The residents of the McBrides' neighborhood pull together to help each other in the nightmarish world of want. Ada reflects: "Distraught, chaotic, grotesque, it was an age . . . of cruelty without moral indignation, of catastrophe without courage." The McBride household perseveres, however. The dying John Fincastle uses his last bit of strength to return to the family farm to save the family the cost of transporting his body.

In the end, the McBrides plan to rebuild their rural homestead and become self-sufficient. Ada exclaims, "Oh, Ralph, we have been happy together!" but when her husband hesitates in his response, she realizes that although his cynicism prevents an answer, he nonetheless depends on her: "And even if his flesh had ceased to desire her, or desired her only in flashes, . . . some hunger deeper and more enduring than appetite was still constant and satisfied." Although Raper (1980) calls it "far too sentimental and didactic to do Glasgow justice," *Vein of Iron* presents a feminist vision of triumph, with the self-sufficient woman escaping conventional expectations but retaining an abiding affection for another human being and achieving mastery over her fate.

Glasgow's last novels, *In This Our Life* (1941) and the posthumously published *Beyond Defeat* (1966), are less successful than the works of the 1920s and 1930s. The former, which completed her works chronicling the social history of Virginia, reprises several Glasgow types, including the strong patriarch and the willful daughter, and the theme of the old order confronting the new. Although she believed *Vein of Iron* a better book, Glasgow considered *In This Our Life* a success partly because it was written in bits during her convalescence from severe heart attacks in 1939 and 1940. The novel won the Pulitzer Prize (1941) and became a popular movie starring Bette Davis, Olivia de Havilland, and Dennis Morgan despite a lack of critical enthusiasm. Readers today remain disappointed. Thiébaux, for example, maintains: "The quality of the writing often seems hasty. . . . The sections about love, especially, resemble the more hackneyed examples of popular fiction. Glasgow's besetting problem, that of making her characters more than ideas or representatives of social or moral positions, here is particularly evident." In an attempt to answer her critics, Glasgow began a sequel to *In This Our Life* in July 1942—"So many readers missed the point of that book that I should like to do a less subtle approach," she explained—but this mythic and mystical novel was left unfinished when Glasgow died on 21 November 1945.

In addition to her novels and her short fiction, Glasgow completed other works: a volume of twenty-seven poems, *The Freeman and Other Poems* (1902); a collection of her critical prefaces for the Virginia Edition of her novels entitled *A Certain Measure: An Interpretation and Prose Fiction* (1943); and her autobiography, *The Woman Within* (1954), whose purpose was to "shed some beam of light, however faint, into the troubled darkness of human psychology."

Her own psychology, as suggested by her books and her life, was troubled and dark, suffused with conflict. She was not at all what she appeared to be, as Marion Gause Canby, the wife of Henry Seidel Canby, explained in a letter dated 23 August 1955, which appears as the afterword to *Letters of Ellen Glasgow:*

> Her lifelong research on the "vein of iron," or in clearer words, the tragedy of life on earth, didn't seem to apply to her. . . . And she never had to go against the grain. She was very actually emotionally and intellectually hungry, but her daily life was filled with devoted care. . . . Somehow *The Woman Within* seemed to *me* in many ways a different person from the Ellen I knew.

Glasgow was a woman who could not reconcile belief and feeling: for example, she owed her independence to her father's detested Calvinism, and although a supporter of women's suffrage, she distrusted her own physical appetites (in contrast with most suffrage supporters, who acknowledged and accepted such appetites). A conventional spinster in many ways, she managed to write several novels that defy convention, if not in form, then in character and theme, and that reveal a transitional writer at odds with her era and with herself. Louis D. Rubin, Jr., concludes: "She was, simply, the first really modern Southern novelist, the pioneer who opened up for fictional imagination a whole spectrum of her region's experience that hitherto had been considered inappropriate for depiction in polite letters."

Selected Bibliography

PRIMARY WORKS

NOVELS

The Descendant. New York: Harper & Bros., 1897.

Phases of an Inferior Planet. New York: Harper & Bros., 1898.

The Voice of the People. New York: Doubleday, Page, 1900.

The Deliverance. New York: Doubleday, Page, 1904.

The Wheel of Life. New York: Doubleday, Page, 1906.

The Ancient Law. New York: Doubleday, Page, 1908.

The Romance of a Plain Man. New York: Macmillan, 1909.

The Miller of Old Church. Garden City, N.Y.: Doubleday, Page, 1911.

Virginia. Garden City, N.Y.: Doubleday, Page, 1913.

Life and Gabriella. Garden City, N.Y.: Doubleday, Page, 1916.

The Builders. Garden City, N.Y.: Doubleday, Page, 1919.

One Man in His Time. Garden City, N.Y.: Doubleday, Page, 1922.

Barren Ground. Garden City, N.Y.: Doubleday, Page, 1925.

The Romantic Comedians. Garden City, N.Y.: Doubleday, Page, 1926.

They Stooped to Folly. Garden City, N.Y.: Doubleday, Doran, 1929.

The Sheltered Life. Garden City, N.Y.: Doubleday, Doran, 1932.

Vein of Iron. New York: Harcourt, Brace, 1935.

In This Our Life. New York: Harcourt, Brace, 1941.

Beyond Defeat: An Epilogue to an Era. Edited by Luther Y. Gore. Charlottesville: University Press of Virginia, 1966.

POETRY

The Freeman, and Other Poems. New York: Doubleday, Page, 1902.

COLLECTED SHORT FICTION

The Shadowy Third and Other Stories. Garden City, N.Y.: Doubleday, Page, 1923.

The Collected Stories of Ellen Glasgow. Edited by Richard K. Meeker. Baton Rouge: Louisiana State University Press, 1963.

Ellen Glasgow's Reasonable Doubt: A Collection of Her Writings. Edited by Julius Rowan Raper. Baton Rouge: Louisiana State University Press, 1988.

SPECIAL COLLECTED EDITIONS

The Old Dominion Edition of the Works of Ellen Glasgow. 8 vols. Garden City, N.Y.: Doubleday, Doran, 1929–1933.

The Virginia Edition of the Works of Ellen Glasgow. 12 vols. New York: Scribners, 1938.

COLLECTED PREFACES

A Certain Measure: An Interpretation of Prose Fiction. New York: Harcourt, Brace, 1943.

AUTOBIOGRAPHY

The Woman Within. New York: Harcourt, Brace, 1954.

LETTERS

Letters of Ellen Glasgow. Edited by Blair Rouse. New York: Harcourt, Brace, 1958.

MANUSCRIPTS AND PAPERS

Glasgow's papers and manuscripts are in the Ellen Glasgow Collection, Alderman Library, University of Virginia, Charlottesville, and in the Marjorie Kinnan Rawlings Collection, University of Florida, Gainesville. Correspondence between Glasgow and Allen Tate is at the Princeton University Library.

SECONDARY WORKS

BOOKS

Auchincloss, Louis. *Ellen Glasgow*. University of Minnesota Pamphlets on American Writers, no. 33. Minneapolis: University of Minnesota Press, 1964.

Donovan, Josephine. *After the Fall: The Demeter-Persephone Myth in Wharton, Cather, and Glasgow*. University Park: Pennsylvania State University Press, 1989.

Godbold, E. Stanly, Jr. *Ellen Glasgow and the Woman Within*. Baton Rouge: Louisiana State University Press, 1972.

Holman, C. Hugh. *Three Modes of Southern Fiction: Ellen Glasgow, William Faulkner, Thomas Wolfe*. Athens: University of Georgia Press, 1966.

Inge, M. Thomas, ed. *Ellen Glasgow: Centennial Essays*. Charlottesville: University Press of Virginia, 1976. Contains C. Hugh Holman, "The Comedies of Manners"; Howard Mumford Jones, "Northern Exposure: Southern Style" and "The Earliest Novels"; Edgar E. MacDonald, "An Essay in Bibliography" and "Glasgow, Cabell, and Richmond"; Frederick P. W. McDowell, "The Prewar Novels"; Monique Parent Frazee, "Ellen Glasgow as Feminist"; Blair Rouse, "Ellen Glasgow's Civilized Men"; Louis D. Rubin, Jr., "Introduction"; and Dorothy Scura, "Glasgow and the Southern Renaissance."

McDowell, Frederick P. W. *Ellen Glasgow and the Ironic Art of Fiction*. Madison: University of Wisconsin Press, 1960. The bibliography includes information on uncollected works.

Parent Frazee, Monique. *Ellen Glasgow: Romancière*. Paris: A. G. Nizet, 1962.

Raper, Julius Rowan. *Without Shelter: The Early Career of Ellen Glasgow*. Baton Rouge: Louisiana State University Press, 1971. The bibliography includes information on uncollected works.

———. *From the Sunken Garden: The Fiction of Ellen Glasgow, 1916–1945*. Baton Rouge: Louisiana State University Press, 1980.

Rouse, Blair. *Ellen Glasgow*. New York: Twayne, 1962.

Rubin, Louis D., Jr. *No Place on Earth: Ellen Glasgow, James Branch Cabell, and Richmond-in-Virginia*. Austin: University of Texas Press, 1959.

Santas, Joan Foster. *Ellen Glasgow's American Dream*. Charlottesville: University Press of Virginia, 1965.

Thiébaux, Marcelle. *Ellen Glasgow*. New York: Frederick Ungar, 1982.

Wagner, Linda W. *Ellen Glasgow: Beyond Convention*. Austin: University of Texas Press, 1982. The bibliography includes information on uncollected works.

ARTICLES

Anderson, Mary Castiglie. "Cultural Archetype and the Female Hero: Nature and Will in Ellen Glasgow's *Barren Ground*." *Modern Fiction Studies* 28: 383–393 (1982).

Atteberry, Phillip D. "Ellen Glasgow and the Sentimental Novel of Virginia." *Southern Quarterly* 23, no. 4:5–14 (1985).

Bond, Tonette L. "Pastoral Transformations in *Barren Ground*." *Mississippi Quarterly* 32:565–576 (1979).
Bunselmeyer, J. E. "Ellen Glasgow's 'Flexible' Style." *Centennial Review* 28:112–128 (1984).
Caldwell, Ellen M. "Ellen Glasgow and the Southern Agrarians." *American Literature* 56:203–213 (1984).
Fryer, Sarah. " 'Love Has Passed Along the Way': Passion and Accident in *The Sheltered Life*." *Southern Quarterly* 23, no. 4:27–36 (1985).
Kish, Dorothy. "Toward a Perfect Place: Setting in the Early Novels of Ellen Glasgow." *Mississippi Quarterly* 31:33–44 (1977–1978).
Lesser, Wayne. "The Problematics of Regionalism and the Dilemma of Glasgow's *Barren Ground*." *Southern Literary Journal* 11, no. 2:3–21 (1979).
MacDonald, Edgar. "A Finger on the Pulse of Life: Ellen Glasgow's Search for Style." *Mississippi Quarterly* 31:45–56 (1977–1978).
Payne, Ladell. "Ellen Glasgow's *Vein of Iron:* Vanity, Irony, Idiocy." *Mississippi Quarterly* 31:57–65 (1977–1978).
Raper, Julius Rowan. "Ambivalence Toward Authority: A Look at Ellen Glasgow's Library, 1890–1906." *Mississippi Quarterly* 31:5–16 (1977–1978).
———. "Invisible Things: The Short Stories of Ellen Glasgow." *Southern Literary Journal* 9, no. 2:66–90 (1977).
Schmidt, Jan Zlotnik. "Ellen Glasgow's Heroic Legends: A Study of *Life and Gabriella, Barren Ground,* and *Vein of Iron*." *Tennessee Studies in Literature* 26:117–141 (1981).
Scura, Dorothy McInnis. "The Southern Lady in the Early Novels of Ellen Glasgow." *Mississippi Quarterly* 31:17–31 (1977–1978).
———. "*Barren Ground:* Ellen Glasgow's Critical Arrival." *Mississippi Quarterly* 32:549–552 (1979).
Seidel, Kathryn Lee. "The Comic Male: Satire in Ellen Glasgow's Queenborough Trilogy." *Southern Quarterly* 23, no. 4:15–26 (1985).
Tuttleton, James W. "Hardy and Ellen Glasgow: *Barren Ground*." *Mississippi Quarterly* 32:577–590 (1979).
Wagner, Linda W. "*Barren Ground*'s Vein of Iron: Dorinda Oakley and Some Concepts of the Heroine in 1925." *Mississippi Quarterly* 32:553–564 (1979).
Wittenberg, Judith B. "The Critical Fortunes of *Barren Ground*." *Mississippi Quarterly* 32:591–609 (1979).

Readers interested in pursuing Glasgow's work should consult the *Ellen Glasgow Newsletter,* published by the Ellen Glasgow Society, Randolph-Macon College, Ashland, Va. 23005.

BIBLIOGRAPHIES

Kelly, William H. *Ellen Glasgow: A Bibliography.* Edited by Oliver Steele. Charlottesville: Bibliographical Society of Virginia, 1964.
MacDonald, Edgar E. "An Essay in Bibliography." In *Ellen Glasgow: Centennial Essays.* Edited by M. Thomas Inge. Charlottesville: University Press of Virginia, 1976. Pp. 191–224.
———. "Ellen Glasgow." In *American Women Writers: Bibliographical Essays.* Edited by Maurice Duke, Jackson R. Bryer, and M. Thomas Inge. Westport, Conn.: Greenwood Press, 1983. Pp. 167–200.
MacDonald, Edgar E., and Tonette Bond Inge, eds. *Ellen Glasgow: A Reference Guide.* Boston: G. K. Hall, 1986.

Glasgow's bibliography is updated annually in the *Ellen Glasgow Newsletter* and the *MLA* (Modern Language Association) *Bibliography.*

CHERYL B. TORSNEY

SUSAN GLASPELL

1876–1948

PLAYWRIGHT AND NOVELIST Susan Glaspell in many ways supplies American literature with a link between early American optimism and modernist despair. Born in her country's centennial year, 1876, she inherited the young nation's hopes and Ralph Waldo Emerson's transcendental faith in the individual's vital relation to spirit. She balanced this solitary mysticism with a sense of the reality and power of society that Benjamin Franklin would have applauded. In her writing Glaspell treats these ostensibly masculine concerns within the quotidian world of domesticity and sentiment, as did her literary mothers, the great writers of nineteenth-century women's fiction. Glaspell, however, was not a transitional anachronism. Before her death in 1948, her work also confronted the harsh conditions of the modern world, such as war, economic inequity, alienation, and class and gender discrimination, while never quite losing its essential faith in humanity and the life force.

Susan Keating Glaspell, the daughter of Elmer S. and Alice Keating Glaspell, was born on 1 July 1876 in Davenport, Iowa, in the American heartland along the Mississippi River, where her ancestors had come as pioneers in the 1830s. She was educated in the local public schools and then, after her high school graduation in 1894, took a job as a reporter on the *Davenport Morning Republican* and was later named society editor for the town's *Weekly Outlook.* Not content with these parochial endeavors, she became a pioneer of sorts in these early years of women's higher education by matriculating at Drake University in Des Moines, Iowa, where she was active in literary circles. After receiving her degree in 1899, she became capitol correspondent and columnist for the *Des Moines Daily News.* After a year she returned to her family in Davenport and continued her literary pursuits. Not satisfied with even these achievements, in 1902 she headed for Chicago, where she did some graduate work at the relatively new but highly respected University of Chicago and was stimulated by the intellectual and artistic ferment of the Chicago Renaissance.

In the busy and challenging years before her thirtieth birthday, Glaspell was also establishing herself as an admired writer of popular fiction with her first novel, *The Glory of the Conquered* (1909), and with the short stories that appeared in such magazines as *Harper's* and *Youth's Companion.* In these stories, many collected in *Lifted Masks* (1912), Glaspell used the urban uproar of Chicago to formulate the themes she would continue to explore in her major works. Many of these fictions seem predictable and sentimental, even trite, but the direction and force of Glaspell's later career are suggested in a few, such as "Contrary to Precedent," which appeared in *Booklovers* magazine in 1904.

The protagonist of "Contrary to Precedent," Mrs. Kramer, has been betrayed many times by her philandering husband, Charlie, and she wants revenge. When she discovers some love letters written to her husband by an idealistic, artistic local girl, Christine Holt, she sees a way to gain recompense for her years of suffering. She cultivates Christine's friendship, but only to make her eventual ultimatum even more brutally shocking: she tells Christine to recall her newly accepted first book from her publishers or she will tell Christine's fiancé, Oscar Fairchild, about the letters. At first Christine elects to recall the book, but later concludes that its publication means too much to her and decides to take her chances with Mrs. Kramer and

Oscar. When Mrs. Kramer confronts Oscar, she finds herself incapable of completing her revenge, since she sees her earlier, happier self in Christine.

This somewhat overwrought plot reveals the techniques, images, and themes of Glaspell's later dramatic masterpieces. In a curious bit of self-reflection, Glaspell has Christine see her situation as "a rather cheap melodramatic play" and wonder if "the scene would be very effective." Glaspell herself attempts a scenic method; instead of editorial moralizing she uses dialogue and gestures, as when Mrs. Kramer's fingers nervously twist a growing vine, suggesting how she would like to warp and destroy the younger woman. The menaced and menacing vine recurs in Glaspell's innovative play *The Verge*.

Such small gestures also prefigure the importance of "trifles" in Glaspell's dramatic masterpiece by that name. Through Christine, Glaspell works out her theory of drama. As she contemplates her life as a play, Christine perceives "the outward commonplaceness of things that were tragic" and believes "[what] she had read in books was wrong. At crucial times people acted just as they did in the commonplace hours—really they acted more so. And that would be a good feature to bring out in the play. The tragedy of the play must be very quiet, very conventional, and commonplace."

Christine's choice between her fiancé and her book introduces Glaspell's major theme, the conflict between the comfort of human love and the challenge of personal integrity. "The primitive woman of her . . ., that essentially human in her heart which called out for love as the thing she could not do without," would recall the book from the publisher, but Christine ultimately chooses the book, which she equates with "her soul, herself." Glaspell's heroines usually make this, the "right," choice, always at the cost of pain and deprivation, but they never pay as much as a woman like Mrs. Kramer, who has numbed "her soul, herself" for a social concept like marital vengeance.

Men are often a source of conflict in Glaspell's work, but in many ways they are not major characters. They are childish: Mrs. Kramer's husband is a good-time Charlie and Christine's fiancé, Oscar, is a "fair child." Men need mothering, and women become the enablers who allow them to function in the world, but Christine selects a progeny that is contrary to precedent when she finds herself "patting the sheets [of her manuscript] as though she were soothing an injured child."

The real conflict in the story is between the women and is resolved by a device that Glaspell uses repeatedly. The older woman's spirit, deadened by years of pain, is resurrected by a younger woman in whom she sees her vanished self, or alter ego. Her soul is revivified, first by the negative emotion of jealousy and then by a vision of sisterhood. As she gazes into the fire, Mrs. Kramer could see "the suffering faces of women, . . . the white hands reached out in imploration, and she could see the open, bleeding hearts," so that, contrary to the precedent of women battling over men, she cannot complete her revenge.

"Contrary to Precedent" also demonstrates how Glaspell's writing uncannily predicts—one might even say writes the script for—her life. Christine views her love letters to Charlie as answering to a higher law than that of matrimony: "You take a girl of my—well, we'll say temperament, though I hate the word, and there comes a time when it's as necessary to write love-letters as it is to breathe." Glaspell herself had confronted the same necessity when she returned to Davenport, where she fell in love with a married man, the neo-transcendentalist and socialist George Cram Cook. For several years she resisted their mutual love, and avoided social opprobrium, by traveling to Chicago, New York, Colorado, and even Paris, but eventually, after his divorce, they were married on 14 April 1913.

George Cram Cook was a member of a wealthy and prominent Davenport family, but local society believed that he, like one of his heroes, Henry David Thoreau, did not live up to his legacy or his Harvard education. After having taught at Stanford and at the University of Iowa, he attempted to live the life of the intellect close to the soil by raising vegetables on a farm owned by his family, a life much like what the New England transcendentalists had essayed at Brook Farm some fifty years earlier. His experiment also failed, and in emulation of another hero, Nietzsche, he courted madness in order to "annihilate self utterly," so that "the great soul of the universe will come in," as Glaspell later wrote in *The Road to the Temple* (1927).

This idealistic extremism was balanced by Cook's passions for baseball, conversation, and drinking. After his life on the farm, two marriages, and two children, Cook was still looking for an ideal community, one that would nourish both the mystical and the social aspects of his personality. When he and Glaspell moved to Provincetown, Massachusetts, in the summer of 1914, they attempted to found such a community, based on an almost religious theory of drama, in the Provincetown Players. They were joined in the years 1914 through 1921 by like-minded souls who included the poet Edna St. Vincent Millay, the revolutionary journalist John Reed, and, especially, Eugene O'Neill, whose towering status in American drama was nurtured by the Provincetown Players. Cook himself remained a Coleridgean figure, best remembered for his talk and inspiration, not his writings or any lasting accomplishments. Glaspell, realizing this, remarked in *The Road to the Temple*, "Sometimes I wish the Provincetown Players had been a magazine."

In contrast, Glaspell's own achievements during these years were both prolific and lasting. They owe much to Cook's philosophy, but the hard work, the craft, and the shape she imposed on Cook's ideas were no one's but her own. Cook influenced her novels by making her question the social order in a more political way, as in her novel of 1911, *The Visioning*, in which she explores socialist theories about the distribution of wealth, the legitimacy of authority, and the plight of working men and women through two women, one privileged and one working-class, who function as alter egos. In *Fidelity* (1915) she further challenges social norms, creating a protagonist who rebels by running off with a married man but whose rebellion ultimately is in leaving him to find herself; once more personal integrity triumphs over the solace of human bonds. In these two novels, the ideas Glaspell absorbed from Cook are imbued with her own sense of the significance of the relations between women and the importance of a woman's solitary soul.

Glaspell's major works during this period, though, are her plays. Between 1914 and 1921 she wrote ten plays that were performed by the Provincetown Players and later published in collected editions. Some are slight comedies, satires of self-important bohemians who pursue the latest intellectual or radical fad into the realm of the ridiculous, such as *Suppressed Desires* (1914), *Tickless Time* (1918), and *Close the Book* (1917), the former two written in collaboration with Cook. Two comedies, however, do explore more serious themes that would become increasingly important in Glaspell's work.

The People (1917) concerns a radical publication by that name which is about to fold because of lack of funds, lack of inspiration, and lack of solidarity among the staff. This dispirited group is reunited by a visit from three representatives of the people, signifying Glaspell's Whitmanesque belief that although intellectuals are needed to articulate humanity's aspirations, intellectuals themselves are sterile, devoid of ideas, without the life force of the people. One representative of the people, The Woman from Idaho, played by Glaspell in the original production, articulates her conviction that the process of forming a higher consciousness, not the success of any social or political movement, is the aim of revolution: "*Seeing*—that's the Social Revolution. . . . The truth that opens from our lives as water opens from the rocks." The Woman from Idaho inspires the Editor with new purpose; she is a woman whose feelings are in touch with the living water of truth, and this truth and her supportive presence allow him to carry on his work in the world.

In another comedy, *Woman's Honor* (1918), Glaspell also confronts the issue of a woman's place in a man's world. Gordon Wallace is about to be sentenced to death because he will not provide the alibi that would save him—it would compromise a woman's honor. When his case is publicized in a newspaper, six women arrive at the jail to supply him with an alibi. They represent a range of women's experience, as their names suggest: The Shielded One, The Motherly One, The Scornful One, The Silly One, The Mercenary One, and the Cheated One.

Although the six women initially fight over the "privilege" of sacrificing their honor for the romantic egoist Wallace, by the end of the play they are more interested in resolving the question of how they all can do away with the limitations woman's honor places on them. As the Scornful One remarks, "Woman's honor is only about one thing, and . . . man's honor is about everything but that thing." Gordon Wallace is thoroughly intimidated by the sight of the united women and declares, "Oh, hell. I'll plead guilty." He believes he is implying that prison or death is preferable to dealing with united, articulate women, but ironically he is also suggesting male guilt for the imprisonment or death of woman's spirit that attends the concept of woman's honor.

The themes of guilt and female solidarity are also raised in the one-act drama generally considered Glaspell's masterpiece, *Trifles* (1916), which she later turned into the short story "A Jury of Her Peers." Two women accompany their husbands and the district attorney to a remote, deserted farmhouse. The men search for clues to prove the guilt of Minnie Foster Wright, who is being held for the murder of her husband, John. Although they are convinced that Mrs. Wright is guilty, they cannot make a case because they are unable to read the domestic "trifles" of the scene of the crime: unwashed pans, a dirty towel, an unfinished quilt, shabby clothes, a broken birdcage, and a dead canary in a decorative box. The district attorney can only conclude that Minnie Wright was "not much of a housekeeper," but the women read the scene differently. They know that the shabby clothes are the result of John Wright's miserliness, that the neglected kitchen signifies Minnie Wright's despair, that the birdcage was broken and the bird's neck wrung by John Wright, who had also killed the song in his young and pretty wife. The women surmise that as Minnie Wright planned to "knot" her quilt, she was inspired to avenge herself by knotting "their own rope" around her husband's neck.

Although the sheriff's wife, Mrs. Peters, is initially reluctant to conceal their deductions because "the law has got to punish crime," she and Mrs. Hale wordlessly decide to remove and conceal the dead bird. They make their decision on the basis of an imaginative identification with Minnie Wright. Mrs. Peters remembers her own desolation after the death of her first child and empathizes with the childless Mrs. Wright. Mrs. Hale elevates this personal concern to the level of gender: "I know how things can be—for women. . . . We live close together and we live far apart. We all go through the same things—it's all just a different kind of the same thing." The two women have also arrived at a conclusion about what true justice is. John "Wright" may have been legally in the right because "he didn't drink, and kept his word," but his constant mean-spiritedness over seeming "trifles" like the canary appear much more wrong to the two women than does Minnie Wright's crime of passion, the last uprising of her free spirit.

Mrs. Hale and Mrs. Peters's revolt is quiet, yet effective, but in two later plays, *The Outside* (1917) and *Verge* (1921), Glaspell creates women who rebel overtly and extremely. In *The Outside,* two women, Mrs. Patrick and her servant, Allie Mayo, live in a remote, abandoned lifesaving station near the outer tip of Cape Cod. Mrs. Patrick is a recluse because of some unspecified betrayal by her husband, and Allie has refused any but minimal communication since the death of her husband at sea twenty years ago. Both women are criticized by the local people for their unwomanly self-reliance, as in the characterization of Mrs. Patrick as "stand-offish, and so doggon *mean.*"

Their retreat from masculine abandonment is disturbed by three men who try to revive a fourth, who has been found drowned on the shore. Although the man dies, the two women are stirred from their spiritual stagnation by the sight of the men's efforts. They discuss their feelings through the symbol of the strange, stunted vegetation that is on the very edge of the woods and protects it from the sand. Mrs. Patrick has watched this vegetation obsessively, in the hope that it would be conquered by the sand, as she herself longs for the burial of her feelings, but Allie Mayo persuades her that these "strange little things" are the necessary beginnings of life and "hold the sand for things behind them. They save a wood that guards a town. . . . where their children live."

These two women see themselves as the brave yet stunted plants that grow on the edge of the civilized world. In *The Verge,* Claire Archer wants to explore that edge, or verge, at first through the growth of new species of plants that she cultivates in her obsessively guarded greenhouse. When one such experimental species, "the Edge Vine," fails, however, she drives her own spirit beyond the verge and into madness. Claire then kills Tom Edgeworthy, the man who failed to be bold enough for her spiritual adventure. In the last lines of the play, she declares her belief that her madness will bring her "nearer, my God, to Thee," although she has succeeded only in destroying her spirit and a human life.

Glaspell is using Cook's earlier experiment in the limits of sanity, as well as his fondness for greenhouses, as the source of Claire's experiment, but Claire, unlike Cook, does become insane. The decisive difference, Glaspell suggests, is that Claire is a woman.

Claire is surrounded by people who want to push her into the appropriate feminine role. She is the scion of a distinguished New England family noted for its conventional and zealous piety. Her husband wants her to be the life of the party, her lover wants her to boost his ego, and the man who understands her spiritually, the mockingly named Tom Edgeworthy, is afraid to lose his solitary independence in a challenging relationship with her. Her sister Adelaide wants Claire to take responsibility for the care of Elizabeth, Claire's debutante daughter by an earlier marriage, although she has not seen Elizabeth for a year and has evinced little interest in her. Claire rejects biological maternity as she equates the conventional Elizabeth with the Edge Vine, which she is savagely uprooting as a failure: "Why did I make you? To get past you!"

The Verge is undoubtedly Glaspell's most profound, radical, and experimental work because she pushes her own themes, along with her protagonist, to the verge. In most of her works, though, Glaspell demonstrates a faith in the future. If the Edge Vine, or a human being, turns back from the brink, something or someone else will profit from that experiment and further the progress of the species, as Glaspell hoped her audience would gain from her writing. She apparently derived this belief in the future collective good from Cook; in her early fiction Glaspell saw the past as encroaching upon the enjoyment of the present, as when, in "Contrary to Precedent," Christine asks, "Were the things of yesterday—the forgotten, the outlived—forever stepping in to put their mark on the things of tomorrow?" But by 1921, in her play *Inheritors,* her heroine chooses prison rather than capitulation, because you must "be the most you can be, so life will be more because you were," and is true to her inheritance from her pioneering forebears.

In most of her later works, however, Glaspell shows her belief in the future through a kind of generalized maternity. Even her early plays and novels are full of childless women who nurture their childish men, other—often younger—women, and the idealism of the human race. In *Bernice* (1919) the title character is childless, despite the fact that "she would have made a wonderful mother." After her death, though, her father, her husband, and her best friend, Margaret, feel Bernice has nurtured them and the future. Margaret declares that Bernice left "a gift to the spirit. A gift sent back through the dark," which was "the beauty of perceiving love."

In Glaspell's later works this love and gift remain somewhat abstract and vague; although she is affirming a faith in the future, she is not actually living it. She and Cook were unable to have children of their own, and she did not find her mental offspring adequate compensation. In *The Road to the Temple,* Glaspell commented: "Women say to one: 'You have your work. Your books are your children, aren't they?' And you look at the diapers airing by the fire, and wonder if they really think you are like that. . . ." In 1922 she was also deprived of the community of artists who had supplied the necessary ferment for her dramatic achievements. Cook, once more the disappointed seeker, decided they should leave what he regarded as the commercialized, Broadway-bound Provincetown Players and begin anew in Greece, a country he idealized. There she also lost Cook, who died in 1924 and, appropriately for this oracular sage, was buried at Delphi.

In two of Glaspell's later works, *The Road to the Temple* (1927) and *Fugitive's Return* (1929), she attempts to come to terms with her series of losses in the first half of the 1920s. *The Road to the Temple* is her biography of Cook, but like *The Education of Henry Adams,* it could be considered a study of the failures and disappointments the idealist meets in the modern world. *The Education,* however, was written by the ironic Adams, who mocked himself as well as the chaotic world; *The Road to the Temple* is written by a woman determined to put the best possible face on what must have been a relationship with a very difficult man.

Much of the book is a chronological compendium of Cook's occasional jottings and sayings, befitting Glaspell's chosen role of Plato to his Socrates. She asserts in *The Road to the Temple* that "things bind us, but he was uncaptured." Unfortunately, she herself seems to have been captured, by her love for him and her need to protect him, as demonstrated in occasional remarks that break through the panegyrics. Glaspell served as Cook's reality principle; "an exasperating thing about him was that his enthusiasms often deprived you of your most righteous resentments." She even found a way to live with his drinking through maternal feelings: one of his hangovers is "a gift—taking care of the man she loves when he has this sweetness as of a newborn soul."

Despite the difficulties of living with an untrammeled idealist, Glaspell felt Cook's loss keenly in a kind of creative drought predicted in her novel *Fugitive's Return.* Her protagonist, Irma Lee Shraeder, becomes mute after the death of her only child and her desertion by her husband. Through a series of coincidences, or fate, she comes to live at Delphi, where she gradually returns to life and communication through sympathetic identification with mistreated animals and women and through the spirit of the place's past. She even is revivified to the point of loving a man—unluckily, one whose first devotion is to a woman who has scorned his love. Irma decides to persevere in her love, a braver, more generous love than conventional monogamy, and "to leave him as he was, loving him for it, even though it withheld from her." She plans to return to America and make a place for him while "in her own vineyard would she labor."

In 1924 Glaspell did return to America to labor in her own vineyard, Cape Cod; and, like Irma, she provided a place in it for a man, the novelist Norman Matson, with whom she would live for the next eight years. Although Irma's words about the man she loves could apply to the freedom that Glaspell felt Cook needed to pursue his idealism, they also could apply to the freedom she gave Matson by not actually marrying him. Indeed, the relationship and the period have an aura of a repetition on a diminished scale. As with Cook, she collaborated with Matson on a play, *The Comic Artist*, produced in 1928. Two of Glaspell's novels, *Brook Evans* (1928) and *Ambrose Holt and Family* (1931), seem like tired recapitulations of her usual themes and techniques. Even her Pulitzer Prize–winning play, *Alison's House* (1930), based on the life of Emily Dickinson, seems like a diminuendo, conventionalized version of the great plays of her middle years. Glaspell's relationship with Matson was also childless, and he left her to marry a younger woman with whom he did have a child.

In another curious repetition, after several years of melancholy, bad health, and financial exigency, Glaspell returned to the theater in 1936. She became head of the Midwest Play Bureau of the Federal Theater Project, a Works Progress Administration program to create jobs for artists and promote American theater. She faced much work, many inflated egos, and constant wrangling, as in the days of the Provincetown Players, but the experience was not nearly as satisfying, and she resigned in 1938. No plays were produced from her own work of these years. Her last three novels seem somewhat formulaic attempts to keep her faith in idealism and the future, despite the Great Depression, World War II, and her own increasing age and infirmity. She died of viral pneumonia in Provincetown on 27 July 1948.

Another great romantic, F. Scott Fitzgerald, remarked that there are no second acts in American lives. If playwright Glaspell's life were regarded as a play, one could say that it had a first act, which was her adventurous and increasingly rebellious youth as student, reporter, and budding writer; a second act, in which her freethinking culminated in the complications of her love for the married Cook; and a third act, which climaxed with her marriage to Cook and their achievements with the Provincetown Players. What the theater and American life have no place for is what could be called either a lengthy denouement or the mellowness of age, experience, and wisdom without intense productivity. These problems are magnified for a woman writer, since women are generally valued for jejune beauty, emotional support of their mates, and childbearing, or judged as honorary men for the quantity of their accomplishments or works.

In her final years Glaspell could conform to neither category, but she had seen beyond these limits in her writing. As Claire states in *The Verge*, after the climax, things "break themselves up into crazy things—into lesser things, and from the pieces—may come one sliver of life with vitality to find the future." For American women playwrights, writers, and readers today, Glaspell's great dramatic works stand as *her* sliver of life, "with vitality to find the future," as they affirm her unwavering, if tempered, optimism.

Selected Bibliography

PRIMARY WORKS

NOVELS

The Glory of the Conquered. New York: Frederick A. Stokes, 1909.

The Visioning. New York: Frederick A. Stokes, 1911.
Fidelity. Boston: Small, Maynard, 1915.
Brook Evans. London: Victor Gollancz, 1928.
Fugitive's Return. New York: Frederick A. Stokes, 1929.
Ambrose Holt and Family. New York: Frederick A. Stokes, 1931.
The Morning Is Near Us. New York: Frederick A. Stokes, 1939.
Norma Ashe. New York: J. B. Lippincott, 1942.
Judd Rankin's Daughter. New York: J. B. Lippincott, 1945.

DRAMA

Plays. Boston: Small, Maynard, 1920. Collects some of her Provincetown plays: *Suppressed Desires* (1914), *Trifles* (1916), *Close the Book* (1917), *The Outside* (1917), *The People* (1917), *Tickless Time* (1918), *Woman's Honor* (1918), and *Bernice* (1919).
Inheritors. Boston: Small, Maynard, 1921.
The Verge. Boston: Small, Maynard, 1922.
The Comic Artist. New York: Frederick A. Stokes, 1927.
Alison's House. New York: Samuel French, 1930.
Plays. Edited by C. W. E. Bigsby. Cambridge and New York: Cambridge University Press, 1987. Includes *Trifles* (1916), *The Outside* (1917), *The Inheritors* (1921), and *The Verge* (1921).

SHORT STORIES

Lifted Masks. New York: Frederick A. Stokes, 1912.

BIOGRAPHY

The Road to the Temple. New York: Frederick A. Stokes, 1927, 1941.

SECONDARY WORKS

BIOGRAPHICAL AND CRITICAL STUDIES

Alkalay-Gut, Karen. " 'A Jury of Her Peers': The Importance of Trifles." *Studies in Short Fiction* 21:1–9 (1984).
Bach, Gerhard. "Susan Glaspell: Provincetown Playwright." *Great Lakes Review* 4:31–43 (1978).
Ben-Zvi, Linda. "Susan Glaspell and Eugene O'Neill: The Imagery of Gender." *Eugene O'Neill Newsletter* 10:22–27 (1986).
Fetterley, Judith. "Reading About Reading: 'A Jury of Her Peers,' 'The Murders in the Rue Morgue,' and 'The Yellow Wallpaper.' " In *Gender and Reading: Essays on Readers, Texts, and Contexts*. Edited by Elizabeth A. Flynn and Patrocinio Schweickart. Baltimore: Johns Hopkins University Press, 1986. pp. 147–164.
Hedges, Elaine. "Small Things Reconsidered: Susan Glaspell's 'A Jury of Her Peers.' " *Women's Studies* 12:89–110 (1986).
Noe, Marcia. "A Critical Biography of Susan Glaspell." Ph.D. diss., University of Iowa, 1976.
———. "Susan Glaspell's Analysis of the Midwestern Character." *Books at Iowa* 27:3–20 (1977).
———. "Region as Metaphor in the Plays of Susan Glaspell." *Western Illinois Regional Studies* 4:77–85 (1981).
Sarlos, Robert Karoly. *Jig Cook and the Provincetown Players: Theatre in Ferment*. Amherst: University of Massachusetts Press, 1982.
Smith, Beverly A. "Women's Work—Trifles? The Skill and Insights of Playwright Susan Glaspell." *International Journal of Women's Studies* 5:172–184 (1982).
Waterman, Arthur E. *Susan Glaspell*. New York: Twayne, 1966.
———. "Susan Glaspell's *The Verge:* An Experiment in Feminism." *Great Lakes Review* 6:17–23 (1979).

BIBLIOGRAPHY

Bach, Gerhard. "Susan Glaspell (1876–1948): A Bibliography of Dramatic Criticism." *Great Lakes Review* 3:1–34 (1977).

VERONICA MAKOWSKY

ELIZABETH HARDWICK

1916–

THERE WAS ONCE, not so long ago, a happy expedient for critics faced with the task of placing writers whose work could not be properly assigned to any single sphere of literary endeavor. The unclassifiable could always be comfortably quartered in the category "man of letters." Fifty years ago, Elizabeth Hardwick might have been called a man of letters, except that she is, of course, a woman, and while there always (or at least for a long time) have been "literary women," the mantle of "letters" has rarely been worn by women, perhaps because the career itself had dwindled into rarity by the time women writers had achieved the kind of authority requisite to taking it up.

One might, then, simply call Elizabeth Hardwick a critic and a novelist, with the recognition that her work in truth belongs somewhere in between, in a space of her own defined by the refusal to place literature in a class apart from life. Hardwick writes criticism with a novelist's attention to character, and fiction with the summarizing intelligence of a critic, addressing us in a voice—lyrical yet skeptical—that is recognizably, inimitably her own.

Elizabeth Hardwick was born on 27 July 1916 in Lexington, Kentucky. Her mother, Mary Ramsey Hardwick, was of Scottish-Irish Presbyterian stock, descended from early settlers. Hardwick's father, who was only fitfully employed, worked as a laborer, a plumber, a seller of furnaces, and a clerk. Eugene Allen Hardwick was, like so many Southerners of his time, intensely political, a passionate reader of newspapers. In Hardwick's autobiographical fiction, *Sleepless Nights,* Elizabeth's father gets up early in the morning with her to "listen on the radio to the fall of Madrid, the signing of the Munich pact. We held hands and wept."

The Hardwicks were a large family—eleven children, a proliferation remarkable even for Kentucky at the turn of the century. Elizabeth, one of the youngest, had older brothers and sisters who were already in college while she was growing up. Describing her childhood in an interview with the *Paris Review,* Hardwick recalled:

> I learned from them [the older brothers and sisters in college]. . . . It was not an intellectual atmosphere, but a stimulating one. Like all writers that I know of, the early days were dominated by a love of reading, just reading, like eating, anything around. . . . I was not aware of any intellectual deprivation and there was none in the general sense. But aren't we all self-educated, and of course our self education never includes all of the things we would like to know or need to know.

When she arrived at the University of Kentucky in the fall of 1934, the range of her reading quite suddenly expanded. It was then that she began reading the newly revived *Partisan Review,* though, as she told the *New York Times Book Review*'s Richard Locke in 1979, "*Reading* scarcely conveys the passion I felt for the political and cultural scenery I found in its pages." She was active politically as well, and by the time she left for New York in 1939, after finishing her master's degree at the University of Kentucky, she had already been a Communist and an ex-Communist, "left variety."

Hardwick identifies the decision to go to New York as "a critical, defining moment . . . in my life." She had received a fellowship to pursue graduate studies at Louisiana State University, "a magical place then, with the *Southern Review* and all sorts of brilliant writers around [Robert Penn Warren, Cleanth Brooks, Katherine Anne Porter]." Only a month before she was to leave for Baton Rouge, she suddenly decided she wanted to go to Columbia instead, even without a fellowship. After two years' immersion in the metaphysical poets, however, she gave up graduate study and began writing stories.

The Ghostly Lover, Hardwick's first novel, was published by Harcourt, Brace in 1945. As the novel opens, a young girl named Marian Coleman, resident of a small Kentucky town, restlessly anticipates the return of her elusive parents: "It had been two years since Marian had seen her mother and father. Now that they were returning, they had no reality. They were like remote ancestors, those raw-boned ghosts whose sins fill you with mystery and dread and whose virtues are an obscure challenge."

The Colemans, Lucy and Ted, are permanently itinerant: leaving two children to be brought up by Lucy's mother, they move from place to place in search of a fresh start so that Ted can "make a success of things."

The relentless movings-on, however, are not the reason Marian and her brother have been left behind. The parents' fascination with each other—uneasy, perplexed, fumbling—precludes all other affections. But there's another reason too: Lucy Coleman, "this woman who was soft, gentle, and compassionate," who was womanly in every other respect, "held her own children very awkwardly." In place of feeling, the mother sends parched bulletins giving the details of her current place of residence, her husband's current plans for a new career.

The curious detachment of Lucy Coleman is mirrored in her own mother (Marian's grandmother), whose self-absorption is if anything more complete:

> Ted and Lucy had been in the house for several days now and the grandmother, had begun to tire of them. She tired of people very quickly, because she had little interest in their problems. There was always noise in the living room now and sometimes when she sat there in the evening and acknowledged the heads turned toward her and saw the smiling faces, a certain feeling of pride was aroused. But this wore off quickly. . . ."

Marian Coleman, held at arm's length by not one but two mothers, can for years think of—long for—little else. She invents "a rich family feeling," and sustains it through "tangible objects," pictures, bits of ribbon, the napkin ring her mother used as a child, stationery from a strange hotel: "Sometimes she was shocked by the passionate avidity of her feeling for any remnant of her parents' lives. . . ."

The dissociations that haunt Marian Coleman's family life are paralleled in her first love affair—with Bruce, whom she meets while awaiting her parents' arrival. Initiating Marian into sexual experience, he becomes yet another of the ghostly lovers (mother, father, grandmother) who hover just beyond knowability. Though he never achieves more than a shadowy existence in the novel, Bruce nevertheless plays a crucial function: he gives Marian the money to go to college in New York. Away from the numbing rituals of home, she is finally able to recognize the urgency of self-definition. She is freed, finally, of "the paralyzing bonds" of invented family feeling, free from the necessity of defining herself through others.

Essentially plotless, *The Ghostly Lover* instead moves through the adumbration of character, exploring the intricate web of strategies through which "intimates" fail to come together:

> Marian did not expect her grandmother to answer. By now she was accustomed to this way of life in which there was never a finale, in which everything was ritualized to the pitch and intensity of a funeral. The endless, unsnipped tatters and threads of life in this house had worked themselves into a fine net and it was impossible to untangle the old omissions.

In retrospect, *The Ghostly Lover* seems oddly prescient, more like a novel of the 1980s than the 1940s. The style no longer feels experimental in the way it must have seemed when the novel was published, but the subject matter—the anaesthetized family connection, the heroine's final push away from marriage—seems utterly contemporary. As there would also be in

Hardwick's later fiction, there is in *The Ghostly Lover* an early version of the critical narrator—in this case, omniscient—who "reads" character and event, commenting, organizing our perceptions, abstracting.

The years immediately following publication of *The Ghostly Lover* were highly productive ones for Hardwick. Philip Rahv, an editor of the *Partisan Review,* had been impressed by her novel and asked her to write for the magazine. She reviewed Richard Wright's *Black Boy* (sympathetically, though with reservations) and contributed a critical essay on the "poor little rich girls" of recent fiction.

In 1946 Hardwick began contributing a regular column, "Fiction Chronicle," to the *Partisan Review,* reviewing James T. Farrell, Eleanor Clark, Eudora Welty, Carson McCullers, Robert Penn Warren, François Mauriac, Jean-Paul Sartre, E. M. Forster, Malcolm Lowry, Kay Boyle, Saul Bellow, Elizabeth Bowen, and William Faulkner.

Hardwick also published a good deal of short fiction during this period, in the *Partisan Review* and elsewhere. Her first published story, "The People on the Roller Coaster," appeared in the *New Mexico Quarterly Review* and was reprinted in *O. Henry Memorial Award Prize Stories of 1945.* Fairly traditional in narrative style and structure, it addresses the central issue of "Southernism" in the 1940s, focusing on an encounter between a pair of gypsies—an albino Negro and his dark-skinned wife—and a genteel Southern white lady, Lavinia Prather, who imagines the fortune-tellers can explain what has come over her colored "girl." Mrs. Prather, who "had always liked Negroes," collapses into a paroxysm of fear at the "unspoken rebellion," the "blankness," that have come between her and the "girl" she depends on.

"The People on the Roller Coaster" was followed by a series of stories in which Hardwick experimented with possibilities of narrative and voice, structure and setting. "The Mysteries of Eleusis" (1946), taking up where *The Ghostly Lover* leaves off, explores "the terror of home" through a disembodied "dreamer" who awakes to become a "she." "She" is to be married that day, though out of what feeling we, and she, are uncertain.

"What We Have Missed," which appeared in *O. Henry Memorial Award Prize Stories of 1946,* returns to the theme of exile, here curiously reversed. An English "lady" is planted by a New York friend (benefactress?) in the territory of a small Kentucky town, distressing the community with her stubborn preference for the local madwoman.

Hardwick introduces a first-person narrator very much like herself in "The Temptations of Dr. Hoffman," also published in 1946. The teller, whose instincts are of a summarizing nature, records her attempts to come to terms with character, to "organize [Dr. Hoffman's] personality," concluding: "I lacked specific details of his experience and even if I had known him forever I could never have felt certain of my abstraction."

In "Evenings at Home" (1948), Hardwick moves still closer to a fictional voice that is indistinguishable from her own "real" voice, reliving the agonies of a visit home, the pain of daughterhood, the flight to exile once more: "I shall leave forever, vanish, change my name, and begin over again in Canada."

In the early stories that came after *The Ghostly Lover,* Hardwick was already beginning to define the theme that would so overwhelmingly inform her later fiction. By the late forties, she had also already begun to move away from the landscape of "Southernness" in which her early writing was framed. Though she respected, even admired, the work of many Southern writers—Allen Tate, Robert Penn Warren, Katherine Anne Porter, Faulkner—she did not wish—emphatically did not wish—to be one herself.

"Southernness is more a decision than a fate," Hardwick later said, "since fine talents are not necessarily under any command of place or feeling. Fidelity to place for subject matter is only the beginning of literary art and is seldom as important as the larger claims of intelligence, contemporaneity, freshness, and awareness of the long, noble challenge of literature itself." Hardwick refused, with a certain ferocity, to be defined by the 'home' from which she had fled: "One may be a Southerner by background and deep experience and yet find himself not a creation of Southernness. Not every creative mind living in the region has found itself engaged by that condition." In her essay "Fictions of America" (1987) Hardwick quotes Julio Cortázar quoting Jacques Vaché writing to André Breton: "Rien ne vous tue un homme comme d'être obligé de representer un pays" (Nothing kills a man faster than being obliged to represent a country).

When she was a young woman in Kentucky, Hardwick once told an interviewer, her great ambition was to become a New York Jewish intellectual. She explained to the *Paris Review:* "What I meant was the enlightenment, a certain deracination which I value, an angular vision, love of learning, cosmopolitanism, a word that practically means Jewish in Soviet lexicography."

In the company of Philip Rahv, Mary McCarthy, F. W. Dupee, Delmore Schwartz, Dwight Macdonald, and others of the *Partisan Review* circle, Hardwick achieved her ambition. By 1948 she had established a reputation as one of the magazine's most feared critics—in a coterie whose critical capacities were not to be underestimated. Remembering her first conversation with Philip Rahv, Hardwick told Richard Locke in 1979: "The name of a respected critic came up and I said something like 'I think he's terrible.' Nothing pleased Rahv so much as a vehement negative, and so he pronounced me 'not as stupid' as he had expected."

In 1948 Hardwick went to Yaddo, the writers' colony near Saratoga, New York, for the summer. She was at the end of her stay when the poet Robert Lowell, whom she had briefly met at the Rahvs' several years before, arrived. They had a number of friends in common, particularly Allen Tate. Lowell was recently divorced from the writer Jean Stafford, whose work had appeared alongside Hardwick's in the *Partisan Review.* Stafford's novel *Boston Adventure* had been published not long before *The Ghostly Lover* had appeared, though the former was a much more unqualified success.

Lowell, thirty-two years old, was rapidly becoming one of the most admired poets of his generation. He was handsome, engaging, stunningly intelligent, and, as Hardwick later said, "unlike anyone I have ever known. . . . He was a very gripping sort of character."

After crossing paths with Lowell for a few days at Yaddo, Hardwick returned to New York, but was persuaded by him to come back in January. In the months that followed, they began a love affair.

Robert Lowell's immense personal attractiveness, his force, speed, and momentum, help explain what happened next, though it seems surprising that both Elizabeth Hardwick and Flannery O'Connor could be persuaded to follow him into a campaign that, as it turned out, was the beginning of Lowell's first nervous breakdown.

A few weeks after Hardwick had rejoined Lowell, FBI agents went to Yaddo to investigate Agnes Smedley, a writer whom they suspected of having had contact with Soviets. Smedley had been a frequent resident at Yaddo and was an old friend of its director, Elizabeth Ames. There was no evidence that Ames was involved in Smedley's political activities (nor indeed any conclusive evidence that Smedley was a spy), but Lowell nevertheless demanded repeatedly that Yaddo's board fire its director. Her Communist sympathies were, he stated, infecting the "body" of Yaddo, "chronically poisoning the whole system." After a careful review of the charges, the board dismissed Lowell's attack.

A few days later, Lowell left Yaddo to visit Allen Tate. After making a scene in a restaurant and shouting obscenities to a crowd, he left the next morning to pay a call on Peter Taylor in Bloomington. There Lowell erupted into full-scale mania, running "about the streets [as he himself later said] crying out against devils and homosexuals." After beating up a policeman, he was put into a straitjacket and moved to Baldpate, an asylum outside Boston.

After witnessing Lowell's mania in Chicago, Allen Tate had written to Hardwick to warn her: "Cal [Lowell] is dangerous, there are definite homicidal implications in his world, particularly toward women and children. . . . You must not let him into your apartment."

Ignoring Tate's admonition, Hardwick hurried to visit Lowell at Baldpate and spent two weeks near the hospital. On 6 July, five days after she had left, Lowell proposed marriage to Hardwick by letter; she accepted, also by letter. Lowell's parents registered their disapproval, echoed by others, but the ceremony nevertheless took place at the end of the month. Lowell spent their honeymoon, Hardwick remembered later, "very self-critical, very tortured about himself, his future, almost on the point of tears." The depression did not lift, and Lowell spent the rest of the year as a patient at the Payne Whitney psychiatric clinic in New York, Jean Stafford's alma mater.

By 1 January 1950 Lowell had recovered sufficiently to take a job teaching writing at the University of Iowa. After a term he and Hardwick decided to go to Italy for a sojourn of indefinite length—as long as their funds held out. They spent the next three years traveling around Europe, resident first in Florence, later in Amsterdam. This relatively happy period came to an end with Lowell's second nervous breakdown, at a conference in Salzburg, Austria.

Hardwick and Lowell returned to Iowa for 1953 and in 1954 moved to Cincinnati, where the university had offered Lowell the chair of its poetry department. By that spring Lowell was entering another manic phase, writing to all his friends that he was divorcing Hardwick to marry an Italian woman he had fallen in love with two years before at the Salzburg conference. His repudiation of Hardwick was humiliatingly public and at first appeared to be thoroughly rational. "[Cal] convinced everybody it was Elizabeth who was going crazy," Flannery O'Connor wrote to a mutual friend.

To Blair Clark, who had been Lowell's friend since adolescence, Hardwick protested:

> I grow more doubtful every day. I am shocked and repelled by what Cal has done to me this time. It is true he doesn't seem to realize emotionally any of the real nature of his conduct . . . the rudeness, the meanness, the stinginess—and on a deeper level he has been of course indescribably cruel. I simply cannot face a life of this. . . . In 4½ years, counting this present breakup, he has had four collapses! Three manic, and one depression. These things take time to come and long after he is out of the hospital there is a period which can only be called "nursing." . . . I knew the possibility of this when I married him, and I have always felt that the joy of his "normal" periods, the lovely time we had, all I've learned from him, the immeasurable things I've derived from our marriage made up for the bad periods. I consider it all a gain of the most precious kind. But he has torn down this time everything we've built up—he has completely exposed to the world all of our sorrows.

By the end of 1954, Lowell had "recovered," and Hardwick had forgiven him. They spent the next five years in Boston, where their daughter, Harriet, was born in 1957. During this period Hardwick continued to produce both essays and stories, but at a much slower rate than in the years after *The Ghostly Lover* was published. The odds against writing must have been considerable: more of Lowell's manic episodes, alternating with sloughs of depression nearly every year; a large house on Marlborough Street to manage, with a suitably large complement of guests; finally, a baby.

Hardwick nevertheless managed to produce another novel: in the spring of 1955 Harcourt, Brace published *The Simple Truth.* The idea for the novel may well have come a few years earlier, during the first stint in Iowa; in 1950 Lowell wrote to a friend that "Elizabeth is moving heaven and earth to enter the Benalek murder trial as an accredited reporter."

The Simple Truth centers on two characters: Joseph Parks, a World War II verteran and a graduate student at the University of Iowa, and Anita Mitchell, the wife of a professor of chemistry. Both are attracted to the murder trial of Rudy Peck, a student accused of murdering his girlfriend. The circumstances of his arrest are fairly damning: Rudy has earlier admitted to worrying over his desire to kill his girlfriend, even consulting a psychiatrist about his homicidal feelings, and on the evening of the murder he freely admits that he was the only person in the room during the time the victim must have been strangled, though he cannot recall doing it himself.

What draws Anita Mitchell and Joseph Parks to the trial is its class element: Rudy is the son of working-class parents and his victim is a rich girl. Her parents regard him as an unsuitable fiancé—because of his social status, rather than the murderous impulses they are not yet aware of—and have tried to break up the love affair, supplying a motive for the killing.

Hardwick is not interested in plot, however; indeed, as in *The Ghostly Lover,* there is hardly any plot to *The Simple Truth* beyond the bare facts of the trial. The novel is, rather, a brilliant dissection of the liberal imagination: as the narrative progresses, we observe Joseph and Anita re-inventing Rudy as a victim. They disregard obvious truths in favor of those that fit their analyses. In the end, when their own liberal views are confirmed by the jury, Joseph and Anita retreat from their earlier positions—baffled and resentful that simpletons like Iowa farmers can have arrived at the same conclusion as they have.

In 1960, Hardwick and Lowell left Boston for New York, where they bought an apartment on West 67th Street, near Central Park West. Hardwick was delighted to return to the literary and intellectual life she had, as a young woman in her twenties, found so exciting. The *Partisan Review* by the early 1960s had dwindled considerably in importance, but Hardwick found a new channel for her writing when in 1963 she helped found the *New York Review of Books.*

Hardwick's story "The Purchase" appeared in *Best American Short Stories* of 1960, but she published no more fiction until the late 1970s. Instead she began to develop a voice in her critical writing. Already apparent in many of the essays collected under the title *A View of My Own* (1962), the critical persona that Hardwick was to make recognizably hers came fully into being in *Seduction and Betrayal* (1974), a second volume of essays.

Refusing the New Criticism, which marked her academic training, she declines in these essays to separate literature from its roots in life. For Hardwick the two are interleaved: she reads life as though it were literature, and literature as though it were life. The character of Hedda Gabler is scrutinized, in *Seduction and Betrayal,* alongside that of Jane Carlyle and Zelda Fitzgerald; Tess, Emma Bovary, Hester Prynne take their place, as though nothing were more natural, next to the "real" tragic heroines—Charlotte and Emily Brontë, Sylvia Plath—who people the narrative of the essays. There is, ironically, more plot in *Seduction and Betrayal* than in Hardwick's novels and stories, but the focus is the same: the perplexing, complex, unanswerable question of why we are what we are—and how.

"Certain fictions have the strong feeling of autobiography even if they are written in the third person," Hardwick once remarked. "It's something a sensitive reader can feel." One feels, similarly, that the preoccupations of *Seduction and Betrayal* have their source in lived experience. Indeed, the essays were written in the four extraordinarily productive years that followed what appeared to be a final betrayal by Lowell.

The discovery of a new love had for a long time been one of the usual features of Lowell's mania, but in the past the obsession had always departed with the illness itself. In 1970, however, Lowell began an affair with the novelist Lady Caroline Blackwood, which outlasted his mania. In 1971 Blackwood gave birth to Lowell's son, and in 1972 he divorced Elizabeth Hardwick to marry Lady Caroline.

Since the late 1950s, when he began writing the "confessional" *Life Studies,* Robert Lowell had been drawing on the details of his life with Hardwick and their daughter, Harriet, in his poetry. But in the two volumes of verse—*For Lizzie and Harriet* and *The Dolphin*—published in 1973, he began incorporating passages from letters Hardwick had actually written him, as well as direct quotes—undisguised—from the transatlantic telephone conversations between them.

Lowell's betrayal, then, was a public one. *Seduction and Betrayal* was, in a sense, Hardwick's response. She chose a form more distanced, cooler, than Lowell's—a form that took its energy from autobiography but stopped short of confession. In essay after essay, Hardwick explores the question of what it means to be a victim, the question of how "damaged" women survive. She does not, however, offer any of the obvious answers: in considering the case of Dorothy Wordsworth, for example, Hardwick dispassionately weighs the pleasures of an ancillary life against its deceptions.

In 1977, on his way home to New York, where he intended to live once again with Hardwick, Robert Lowell died in a taxi. Two years later Elizabeth Hardwick published *Sleepless Nights,* her first long fiction in more than twenty years. The novel, like the essays in *Seduction and Betrayal,* takes its voice from autobiography, but once again resists confession.

The frame of *Sleepless Nights* is that of Hardwick's life: The narrator is a writer named Elizabeth who is born and raised in Kentucky and comes from a large, Presbyterian, Scottish-Irish family. Elizabeth leaves home for graduate school in New York City, then, like Hardwick, moves from Iowa to Florence, Amsterdam, Boston, and finally, to a large artist's flat in New York City on West 67th Street, near Central Park West. But of the story of her life—childhood, marriage, career—we learn practically nothing. Elizabeth's "I" emerges through the lives of others: a homosexual roommate from Kentucky; Billie Holiday; Josette, a maid in Boston.

The narrator is an observer, drawn instinctively, Hardwick herself remarked in the interview with Locke, to "identification with damaged, desperate women on the streets, cleaning women, rotters in midtown hotels, failed persons of all kinds. *C'est moi,* in some sense. . . ." The nature of Elizabeth's "I" is determined by her sex: "After all, 'I' am a woman. . . . Can it be that I am the subject?" Her life, Elizabeth reflects, "hasn't the drama of: I saw the old, white-bearded frigate master on the dock and signed up for the journey."

Elizabeth identifies with women who have lost control of their lives, but she herself is not entirely helpless: she is rescued, at least in part, by her relentlessly ordering intelligence, firmly anchored in the world of literature. She is, in a sense, reading her life, sifting through memory and text.

Describing the limitations and task of current fiction in "The Sense of the Present," one of the final essays in *Bartleby in Manhattan* (1983), Hardwick concludes: "Perhaps we cannot expect a 'novel.' . . . To be *interesting,* each page, each paragraph—that is the burden of fiction. . . ."

Hardwick's acuity of perception renders that burden unfailingly light.

Selected Bibliography

PRIMARY WORKS

NOVELS

The Ghostly Lover. New York: Harcourt, Brace, 1945; reprinted New York: Ecco Press, 1982.

The Simple Truth. New York: Harcourt, Brace, 1955; reprinted New York: Ecco Press, 1982.

Sleepless Nights. New York: Random House, 1979.

SHORT STORIES

"The People on the Roller Coaster." *New Mexico Quarterly Review* 14:444–454 (1944). Reprinted in *O. Henry Memorial Award Prize Stories of 1945.* Edited by Herschel Brickell and Muriel Fuller. New York: Doubleday, 1946.

"Saint Ursula and Her Eleven Thousand Virgins." *Yale Review* 34:524–531 (1945).

"What We Have Missed." In *O. Henry Memorial Award Prize Stories of 1946.* Edited by Herschel Brickell and Muriel Fuller. New York: Doubleday, 1947.

"The Mysteries of Eleusis." *Partisan Review* 12:207–213 (1945). Reprinted in *Best American Short Stories, 1946.* Edited by Martha Foley. Boston: Houghton Mifflin, 1947.

"The Golden Stallion." *Sewanee Review* 54:34–65 (1946). Reprinted in *Best American Short Stories, 1947.* Edited by Martha Foley. Boston: Houghton Mifflin, 1948.

"The Temptations of Dr. Hoffman." *Partisan Review* 13:405–419 (1946).

"Evenings at Home." *Partisan Review* 15:439–448 (1948). Reprinted in *Best American Short Stories, 1949.* Edited by Martha Foley. Boston: Houghton Mifflin, 1950.

"The Friendly Witness." *Partisan Review* 17:340–351 (1950).

"Two Recent Travelers." *Kenyon Review* 15:436–454 (1953).

"Season's Romance." *New Yorker* 32:36–44 (10 March 1956).

"The Oak and the Axe." *New Yorker* 32:49–72 (12 May 1956).

"The Classless Society." *New Yorker* 32:3–52 (19 January 1957). Reprinted in *Stories from the New Yorker, 1950–1960.* New York: Simon & Schuster, 1960.

"The Purchase." *New Yorker* 35:28–62 (30 May 1959). Reprinted in *Best American Short Stories, 1960.* Edited by Martha Foley. Boston: Houghton Mifflin, 1961.

"The Faithful." *New Yorker* 55:36–42 (19 February 1979). Reprinted in *Best American Short Stories, 1980.* Edited by Stanley Elkin and Shannon Ravenel. Boston: Houghton Mifflin, 1981. Chapter 8 of *Sleepless Nights.*

"The Bookseller." *New Yorker* 56:38–45 (15 December 1980). Reprinted in *Best American Short Stories, 1981.* Edited by Hortense Calisher and Shannon Ravenel. Boston: Houghton Mifflin, 1982.

"Back Issues." *New York Review of Books* 28:6 (17 December 1981).

"On the Eve." *New York Review of Books* 30:14 (22 December 1983).

NONFICTION

A View of My Own: Essays in Literature and Society. New York: Farrar, Straus, 1962; reprinted New York: Ecco Press, 1982.

Seduction and Betrayal: Women and Literature. New York: Random House, 1974.

Bartleby in Manhattan and Other Essays. New York: Random House, 1983.

WORKS EDITED BY HARDWICK

The Selected Letters of William James. New York: Farrar, Straus, 1961.

Rediscovered Fiction by American Women: A Personal Selection. New York: Arno Press, 1977. 18 vols., with introductions by Hardwick.

The Best American Essays, 1986. Boston: Houghton Mifflin, 1987. With Robert Atwan.

SECONDARY WORKS

INTERVIEWS

Locke, Richard. "Conversation on a Book." *New York Times Book Review* 84:1, 61–62 (29 April 1979).

Pinckney, Darryl. "Elizabeth Hardwick." In *Writers at Work: The Paris Review Interviews.* Seventh series. Edited by George Plimpton. New York: Viking Penguin, 1986.

ANGELINE GOREAU

FRANCES ELLEN WATKINS HARPER

1825–1911

> O women of America! Into your hands God has pressed one of the sublimest opportunities that ever came into the hands of any race or people. It is yours to create a healthy public sentiment; to demand justice, simple justice, as the right of every race; to brand with everlasting infamy the lawless and brutal cowardice that lynches, burns and tortures your countrymen.
>
> Frances Ellen Watkins Harper (1891)

Poet, lecturer, temperance worker and novelist, in her time Frances Ellen Watkins Harper was, in the words of black abolitionist William Still, "not merely . . . the leading colored poet in the United States, but also . . . one of the ablest advocates of the Underground Rail Road and of the slave." Indeed, Harper, the "Bronze Muse" was the most popular African American poet before Paul Lawrence Dunbar and, as Maryemma Graham has asserted, "a model of ideological and political development and professional commitment." The author of eleven books, including *Iola Leroy: or, Shadows Uplifted* (1892), the second novel known to be published by an African American woman, Harper has long been neglected by the critical literary establishment. However, the recent reexamination and reevaluation of Harper's life and work have established her place in African American literature as a progenitor of the contemporary renaissance of black women's writing and political thought.

Born Frances Ellen Watkins of free parents in Baltimore on 24 September 1825, Harper was nonetheless subjected to the oppression of living in a slave state. Little is known about her father. Her mother died before she was three years old and her childhood was a lonely one. In *Underground Railroad Records,* William Still quotes the poet's adult reflections on her childhood: "Have I yearned for a mother's love? The grave was my robber" (pp. 755–756). Some critics have suggested that living in a slave state and being orphaned at this early age predisposed Harper to identify with the forced separation of the slave family, a scene often depicted in her poetry. Young Frances, an only child, attended a school for free children kept by the Reverend William J. Watkins, her uncle, and was nurtured and cared for by his wife. In this school she studied the classics, rhetoric, the Bible, and the precepts of abolitionism. At the age of thirteen or fourteen she went to work as a housekeeper and seamstress for a bookstore owner and his wife, the Armstrongs. She continued her education in their library, according to Still, "so far as was possible from occasional half-hours of leisure." Her poems and articles were published in local newspapers. Around 1845, her first volume, *Forest Leaves,* appeared. In 1850, Harper left Baltimore for Union Seminary in Columbus, Ohio. She taught classes in embroidery and sewing until 1852 and then departed for Little York, Pennsylvania, where she spent a year teaching fifty-three "unruly children."

She experienced an important "turning point" in Little York, where she saw "the poor, half starved fugitive[s]" moving north on the Underground Railroad. In a letter to a friend she wrote:

> I saw a passenger *per* the underground Rail Road yesterday; did he arrive safely? Notwithstanding the abomination of the nineteenth century—the Fugitive Slave law—men still determine to be free. Notwithstanding all the darkness in which they keep the slaves, it seems that somehow light is dawning upon their minds. These poor

> fugitives are a property that can walk. Just to think that from the rainbow crowned Niagara to the swollen waters of the Mexican Gulf, from the restless murmur of the Atlantic to the ceaseless roar of the Pacific, the poor, half-starved flying fugitive has no resting place for the sole of his foot.

One incident, perhaps more than any other, moved Harper to apply herself to antislavery work:

> About the year 1853, Maryland had enacted a law forbidding free people of color from the North to come into the state on pain of being imprisoned and sold into slavery. A free man who had unwittingly violated this infamous statute had recently been sold into Georgia and had escaped thence by secreting himself behind the wheel house of a boat hound northward; but before he reached the desired haven he was discovered and remanded to slavery. It was reported that he died soon after from the effects of exposure and suffering. . . . Upon that grave I pledged myself to the anti-slavery cause.

Of this singular resolution, she wrote to a friend, "God himself has written upon both my heart and brain a commission to use time, talent and energy in the cause of freedom." In 1854 she moved to Philadelphia, where she made her home at the Underground Railroad station (William Still's house), visited the antislavery office frequently, and became an avid reader of antislavery literature. Thus, Harper continued her primary education in what she called "the fiery furnace" of abolition, not in a formal classroom.

Later she visited the antislavery office in Boston before going on to New Bedford, Massachusetts, "hot-bed of the fugitives," where, in August 1854, she began her public speaking career with an address, "The Education and the Elevation of the Colored Race." The following month she became a lecturer for the Anti-Slavery Society of Maine. During this time she continued to read anti-slavery literature, especially the slave narratives. In a letter dated 20 October 1854, she commented on the power of slave narratives:

> O if Mrs. Stowe has clothed American slavery in the graceful garb of fiction, Solomon Northup comes up from the dark habitation of Southern cruelty where slavery fattens and feasts on human blood with such mournful revelations that one might almost wish for the sake of humanity that the tales of horror which he reveals were not so.

From 1856 to 1859, Harper continued in her role as a public lecturer, speaking in Pennsylvania, New Jersey, New York, Ohio, and Canada and acquiring a wide reputation for her "splendid articulation," her "chaste, pure language," and her abolitionist zeal. She wrote a letter to John Brown that was circulated widely, comforted his wife in her home for the two weeks preceding his execution in 1859, and sent care packages to Brown's comrades as they awaited death by hanging. She also contributed her personal funds to the Underground Railroad.

In 1860, when she was thirty-five years old, she married Fenton Harper, a widower from Cincinnati. The details of this period in Harper's life are sketchy. She and her husband settled near Columbus, Ohio, living quietly on a farm, and for a time it seemed she would retire from public life altogether. A daughter, Mary, was born. After her husband's death in 1864, however, Harper resumed traveling and lecturing, going south among the freed men and women following emancipation. During this time, Still reported in 1871, she developed a special sensitivity to the problems of former slave women, whose "subjugation has not ceased in freedom." Her first tour of the South ended in 1867. Following this tour, Harper returned to Philadelphia for several months before beginning another Southern tour between 1868 and 1871. Her experiences and observations provided much of the raw material for the works she published between 1865 and 1872.

Although most critics agree that Harper was the best-known poet of the antebellum period, many feel that she was "not the most talented or the most promising" and that her poetry relied too extensively on its oral presentation. However, her popularity cannot be dismissed with the simple explanation that "she was on the lecture platform circulating her books among her audiences," as some suggest. Maryemma Graham, in her introduction to *The Complete Poems of Frances E. W. Harper,* refutes this argument: "Because Harper occupied a central position as a black woman in a changing society more than a hundred years ago, her poetry represents the continuity and progression of ideas that brought together the major social movements of her era: anti-slavery, women's suffrage, and temperance." Graham characterizes Harper's poetry as falling into three major groups: those poems written in the years between 1854 and 1864, when she was a lecturer for the Maine Anti-Slavery Society; those written between 1865 and 1872, when she made at least two extensive tours of the South; and those written between 1872 and 1900, when she resided in Philadelphia and held leadership roles in a number of black, civil rights, and women's organizations and temperance societies. After 1900 she published few poems, perhaps a dozen in all.

Harper probably published her first volume of poetry, *Forest Leaves,* in 1845 or 1846, when she was in her early twenties. Although there are no extant copies of *Forest Leaves* and the dates cannot be verified, Graham has found references in historical documents to suggest that Underground Railroad agent William Still helped to circulate this volume before 1854. Considered Harper's most important volume before 1865, *Poems on Miscellaneous Subjects* was composed during the years that she was a lecturer for the Maine Anti-Slavery Society. This volume was originally published in 1854 with a preface by William Lloyd Garrison and was reprinted in approximately twenty subsequent editions. Slavery is the dominant theme in *Poems on Miscellaneous Subjects,* which includes "The Slave Mother," "The Slave Auction," "Eliza Harris," and "The Fugitive's Wife" among other antislavery poems. Such narrative poems, frequently stylistically reminiscent of Longfellow and Whittier, reiterate the concerns of the slave narratives, especially the separation of families. Characteristic in its theme and stanzaic form is "The Slave Mother":

> He is not hers, although she bore
> For him a mother's pains;
> He is not hers, although her blood
> Is coursing through his veins!
>
> He is not hers, for cruel hands
> May rudely tear apart
> The only wreath of household love
> That binds her breaking heart.
>
> . . . .
>
> They tear him from her circling arms,
> Her last and fond embrace.
> Oh! never more may her sad eyes
> Gaze on his mournful face.
>
> No marvel, then, these bitter shrieks
> Disturb the listening air;
> She is a mother, and her heart
> Is breaking in despair.

Both Harper's feminist ideas and her abolitionist convictions are evident in this poem, which challenges the so-called "cult of true womanhood" to recognize the slave mother as a sister and to work to end the cruelty and barbarity of "the peculiar institution" of slavery.

Also in this period between 1854 and 1864, Harper published a short story, "The Two Offers," in the *Anglo-African* (September and October 1859). Probably the first published short story by an African American, "The Two Offers" tells the story of a wealthy white woman who gives up marriage to devote her life to the abolitionist cause. Harper deviates from an otherwise conventional and sentimental tale to have the heroine choose social commitment over romantic happiness. As critic Frances Smith Foster has noted, "Both the protagonist and the themes of this story foreshadow *Iola Leroy.*"

Between 1865 and 1872 Harper made two extensive tours of the South and published three books, all of which drew heavily on her experiences there: *Moses: A Story of the Nile* (1869), *Poems* (1871), and *Sketches of Southern Life* (1872). Critics consider this to be Harper's most productive period and *Moses: A Story of the Nile* to be her best work. Like many of Harper's words, *Moses* was enlarged and reprinted in 1889; it was enlarged again and reprinted as *Idylls of the Bible* in 1901. This forty-page blank-verse biblical allegory was probably inspired by the Emancipation Proclamation in 1863 and Lincoln's assassination in 1865. Although the poem never mentions race, Harper uses the story of the upward movement of Hebrew slaves out of Egypt as a symbol for the freeing of slaves in the American South. Joan R. Sherman praises *Moses*: "The poem's elevated diction, concrete imagery, and formal meter harmoniously blend to magnify the noble adventure of Moses' life and the mysterious grandeur of his death. Mrs. Harper maintains the pace of the long narrative and its tone of reverent admiration with scarcely a pause for moralizing." Harper's stylistic mastery of the poetic form is amply displayed in the following citation:

> Then Moses threw his rod upon the floor,
> And it trembled with a sign of life;
> The dark wood glowed, then changed into a
>   thing
> Of glistening scales and golden rings, and
>   green,
> And brown and purple stripes; a hissing,
>   hateful
> Thing, that glared its fiery eye, and darting
>   forth
> From Moses' side, lay coiled and panting
> At the monarch's feet.

In 1871, Harper published a collection called simply *Poems*. The twenty-six poems in this volume treat themes of death, dying, and immortality, reflecting Harper's psychological preoccupations following the death of her husband in 1864. *Poems* includes some of Harper's best-known verse, including the popular "Bury Me in a Free Land," which first appeared in William Lloyd Garrison's *Liberator* in 1864 and then in Lydia Maria Child's *Freedmen's Book* in 1866 before being published in *Poems*. Harper was ill at the time she wrote "Bury Me in a Free Land," hence her request not to be buried "in a land of slaves":

> I ask no monument, proud and high,
> To arrest the gaze of the passers-by;
> All that my yearning spirit craves,
> Is bury me not in a land of slaves.

"Bury Me in a Free Land" is remarkable among Harper's poems in that the narrator speaks in the first person, seemingly for herself. The power of the poem derives, however, not only from Harper's lived conflict but also from the convention of the deathbed scene and the moral authority of the dying person.

Sketches of Southern Life, a series of poems narrated by Aunt Chloe, is notable for its uses of irony and black folk language. According to J. Saunders Redding, "The language she puts in the mouths of Negro characters has a fine racy, colloquial tang. In these poems she manages to hurdle a barrier by which Dunbar was later to feel himself tripped. The language is not dialect." Redding compliments Harper on her ability to "suit her language to her theme." "In her pieces on slavery," he writes, "she employs short, teethy monosyllables."

Aunt Chloe and Uncle Jacob possess, in the words of Maryemma Graham, "a high degree of political consciousness. They discuss the condition of blacks and the role of education, politics and religion in uplifting the race." Poems like "The Deliverance," Learning to Read," "Church Building," and "The Reunion" demonstrate this acumen, but none perhaps so well as "Aunt Chloe's Politics":

> I've seen 'em honey-fugle round,
>   And talk so awful sweet,
> That you'd think them full of kindness
>   As an egg is full of meat.

Now I don't believe in looking
Honest people in the face,
And saying when you're doing wrong,
That "I haven't sold my race."

When we want to school our children,
If the money isn't there,
Whether white or black have took it,
The loss we all must share.

And this buying up each other
Is something worse than mean,
Though I thinks a heap of voting
I go for voting clean.

The homespun wisdom and mother wit of Aunt Chloe's narration demonstrate the slaves' ability to distinguish and act in their own best interests, advancing the cause of freedom and literacy among their own.

Racial uplift, education, temperance, and women's rights: these are the currents that underlie not only Harper's poetry but also her activities during the 1870s and 1880s. Between 1872 and 1900 Harper lived in Philadelphia and became the first black woman associated with the Woman's Christian Temperance Union (WCTU), the American Woman Suffrage Association, and the National Council of Women. In this context, she campaigned against lynching, discrimination against women in education, and segregation in the women's organizations of which she was a part. After her death, the WCTU recognized Harper by placing her on its Red Letter Calendar in 1922.

Harper's political sentiments were again made clear in a speech called "Duty to the Dependent Races" made to the National Council of Women on 23 February 1891:

> I do not think the mere extension of the ballot a panacea for all the ills of our national life. What we need to-day is not simply more voters but better voters. To-day there are red-handed men in our republic, who walk unwhipped of justice, who richly deserve to exchange the ballot of the freemen for the wristlets of the felon; brutal and cowardly men, who torture, burn, and lynch their fellow-men, men whose defenselessness should be their best defense and their weakness an ensign of protection. More than the changing of institutions, we need the development of a national consciousness, and the upbuilding of a national character. Men may boast of the aristocracy of blood, may glory in the aristocracy of wealth, but there is one aristocracy which must ever outrank them all, and that is the aristocracy of character; and it is the women of a country who help mold its character, and to influence, if not determine its destiny; and in the political future of our nation, woman will not have done what she could if she does not endeavor to have our republic stand foremost among the nations of the earth, wearing sobriety as a crown and righteousness as a garment and girdle.

Maryemma Graham suggests in her biographical article of 1983 that "Harper must have been thinking about her forthcoming novel *Iola Leroy; or, Shadows Uplifted* when she spoke on the 'Duty to Dependent Races' at the National Council. . . . The heroine of Iola Leroy personifies the ideal that Harper had in mind when she spoke."

Harper published *Iola Leroy* in 1892, when she was sixty-seven years old, by then an internationally recognized writer, lecturer, and political activist. Frances Smith Foster argues in her introduction to the 1988 reprint of the novel that Harper's publication of *Iola Leroy* involved considerable risk:

> Unlike the obscure or up-and-coming young writer who in venturing into a new genre risks only continued anonymity or delayed recognition, Frances Harper, at age sixty-seven, had much to lose and little time to regain it. The risk was not simply to her own ego, Harper's gains were considered the gains of her race.

Foster identifies *Iola Leroy* as "probably the best-selling novel by an Afro-American writer prior to the twentieth century." Foster asserts, "Such wide appeal was not accidental. Frances Harper was familiar with both Afro-American literature and the other works that comprise the English literary tradition, and her writings show that she understood the preferences and shared the aesthetic assumptions of her nineteenth-century audiences."

Although *Iola Leroy* reflects the thematic and character development of Harper's earlier short story "The Two Offers," the heroine of *Iola Leroy*, unlike the white protagonist of "The Two Offers," is a woman of African descent fair-skinned enough to pass for white. And, unlike her Caucasian literary predecessor, Janette Alston, who must choose either social commitment or romantic happiness, Iola Leroy finds both.

Iola, in Graham's words, is "a committed young black woman, steeped in her own contradictory racial heritage, who defies convention." She represents, in the view of Vashti Lewis and some others, the archetypal tragic mulatto represented by Harriet Beecher Stowe in *Uncle Tom's Cabin* (1852), William Wells Brown in *Clotel* (1853), and Frank Webb, James Howard, Charles Chestnutt, and Pauline Hopkins in their various fictions. But *Iola Leroy*, the first black novel set in the Reconstruction era, differs from these earlier novels in which "white men do not marry black women who bear their children." In Harper's text, Iola's father, Eugene Leroy, is the uncommon slaveholder who falls in love with one of his slaves, the mulatto Marie, and educates, frees, and marries her. "It was something such as I have seen in old cathedrals, lighting up the beauty of a saintly face," Eugene says, describing Marie's love for him to Alfred, the cousin who will later betray his trust:

> A light which the poet tells was never seen on land or sea. I thought of this beautiful and defenseless girl adrift in the power of a reckless man, who, with all advantages of wealth and education, had trailed his manhood in the dust, and she, with simple childlike faith in the Unseen, seemed to be so good and pure that she commanded my respect and won my heart. In her presence every base and unholy passion died, subdued by the supremacy of her virtue.

Leroy sends Marie to a seminary in the North and offers her freedom and a legitimate marriage, despite the repudiation of his family and the social isolation that follows. Marie is the gentle mistress of his plantation home (an idyllic setting peopled with contented slaves) and the mother of his three beautiful and near-white children, Harry, Iola, and Gracie, who have been told nothing of their racial heritage. All is well until Eugene Leroy dies in a yellow fever epidemic and the faithless cousin, Alfred Lorraine, arrives to take charge of his rich holdings. The children, of course, are shocked to learn of their African heritage, but they are not ashamed of it. Nevertheless, a local judge determines that there is an irregularity in Leroy's manumission of Marie and that their marriage sets a "bad precedent." Marie, Harry, Iola, and Gracie are robbed of their inheritance and "remanded into slavery." Iola is later liberated from slavery by Union troops and becomes a nurse and teacher to the freed blacks. A white physician, Dr. Graham, meets and falls in love with the beautiful quadroon, but she rejects him because of the "insurmountable barrier" of race between them. Iola's refusal on these grounds casts a retrospective judgement on the marriage of her parents. Perhaps she believes that inevitably something would happen to undermine their union. Gracie dies, but Iola is later reunited with her mother and brother. She finds her highest calling as the wife of a "volunteer black" like herself, the blond and brilliant Dr. Latimer.

"A sentimental romance peopled with handsome men and beautiful women," *Iola Leroy* appeals to a "double audience" of white and black Americans, particularly women attracted to a genre that frequently spoke against both racial and sexual oppression: whites identified with Iola and Dr. Latimer because of their Caucasian appearance; women were captivated by the subtext on sexual abuse and blacks by the uplift motif. Like the heroine of "The Two Offers," Iola Leroy must make a choice, but unlike her, Iola is able to make a choice that affirms both love and social commitment. *Iola Leroy* was, in many ways, Harper's answer to the plantation fictions of Thomas Dixon and Thomas Nelson Page, who were, in the words of Vashti Lewis, "openly vicious in the depiction of black people." "To correct this [racist] propaganda," Lewis argues, "black novelists gave their female mulatto characters the attributes of virtue, intelligence and prudence, as well as beauty by idealized white standards."

Although *Iola Leroy* was favorably reviewed in the *A.M.E. Church Review* (1893), the Philadelphia *Public Ledger*, and elsewhere, at least one critic took exception to its "Plantation Negro dialect," most often used by the darker-skinned black characters. Hugh Gloster criticizes Harper for failing to make this dialect "phonetical and natural." Despite the numerous editions and positive reviews, some critics, including Gloster, W. E. B. Du Bois, and Robert Bone, writing after Harper's death in 1911, took essentially patronizing views of Harper's novel. In her introduction, Frances Smith Foster calls the judgment of these critics into question: "In their emphasis on her decorum and integrity instead of the reasons why she was one of the first Afro-American writers whose literature, in Du Bois' own terms, 'gave her fair support,' their own objectivity is questionable." Contemporary black feminist critics like Vashti Lewis and Barbara Christian find *Iola Leroy* flawed, but affirm its importance; the novel, in Christian's words, "delineates the relationship between the images of black women held at-large in society and the novelist's struggle to refute these images." After *Iola Leroy* Harper would go on to publish five collections of poetry: *The Sparrow's Fall and Other Poems* (c. 1894), *Atlanta Offering: Poems* (1895), *Martyr of Alabama and Other Poems* (c. 1895), *Poems* (1895), and *Light Beyond Darkness* (n.d.).

Current critical and scholarly interest in Harper's work is demonstrated by the recent publication of *The Complete Poems of Frances E. W. Harper*, edited by Maryemma Graham, and a new edition of *Iola Leroy; or, Shadows Uplifted*, with an introduction by Frances Foster Smith, both published as part of the Schomburg Library of Nineteenth-Century Black Women Writers. Never before had Harper's complete poems been published. Graham argues, "This edition of Harper's complete poems comes at an appropriate time in the reassessment of her canon. Its publication alone more than justifies the need to restore Harper to her proper social and literary context in the mid-nineteenth-century and to see her development of the genre in which she wrote."

"Critics have accepted Harper's historical significance," Graham asserts, "but have had difficulty with the aggressive link she made between poetry and politics." Because Harper's politics were both racial and sexual, Graham suggests that critics have also had difficulty identifying the tradition in which Harper should be placed, "genteel," "black liberation," or "prefeminist." The answer, perhaps, is all three. Like other black "prefeminists" of Harper's era, such as Anna Julia Cooper, Gertrude Mossell, and Ida B. Wells, Harper took race, not gender, as her point of departure and, in the words of Paula Giddings, "redefined the meaning of what was called 'true womanhood.' " Harper's tools were the lecture, the political essay, the narrative poem, and the sentimental novel, all of which she used to achieve the same purpose, the uplift of the men and women of her race and of women of all races. She pursued this goal tirelessly, seeking new challenges in her full maturity, at an age when she might have rested comfortably on her earlier accomplishments. Even today, Harper's life and work stand as a model of social and artistic commitment that women both black and white might strive to emulate.

Selected Bibliography

PRIMARY WORKS

POETRY

Forest Leaves. n.p., n.d. [ca. 1845].

Poems on Miscellaneous Subjects. Boston: Yerrinton & Sons, 1854; enlarged, Philadelphia: Merrihew &

Son, 1855; enlarged again, Philadelphia: Merrihew & Son, 1871.

Moses: A Story of the Nile. Philadelphia: Merrihew & Son, 1869; enlarged as *Idylls of the Bible,* Philadelphia: Privately printed, 1901.

Poems. Philadelphia: Merrihew & Son, 1871.

Sketches of Southern Life. Philadelphia: Merrihew & Son, 1872; enlarged, 1887.

The Sparrow's Fall and Other Poems. n.p., n.d. [ca. 1894].

Atlanta Offering: Poems. Philadelphia: Privately printed by George S. Ferguson, 1895.

The Martyr of Alabama and Other Poems. n.p., n.d. [ca. 1895].

Light Beyond the Darkness. Chicago: Donohue & Henneberry, n.d.

Poems. Philadelphia: Privately printed by George S. Ferguson, 1895; enlarged, 1898; enlarged again, 1900.

FICTION

"The Two Offers." *Anglo-African* 1:288–292, 311–313 (September–October 1859).

Iola Leroy; or, Shadows Uplifted. Philadelphia: Garrigues Brothers, 1892. Reprinted with an introduction by Frances Smith Foster. New York: Oxford University Press, 1988.

COLLECTED WORKS

Graham, Maryemma, ed. *The Complete Poems of Frances E. W. Harper.* With an introduction by Maryemma Graham. New York: Oxford University Press, 1988.

Foster, Frances Smith, ed. *A Brighter Coming Day: A Frances E. W. Harper Reader.* New York: Feminist Press, 1990.

SECONDARY WORKS

BIOGRAPHICAL AND CRITICAL STUDIES

Bacon, Margaret Hope. " 'One Great Bundle of Humanity': Frances Ellen Watkins Harper (1825–1922)." *Pennsylvania Magazine of History and Biography* 113:21–43 (January 1989).

Barksdale, Richard, and Kenneth Kinnamon. "The Struggle Against Slavery and Racism, 1800–1860: Frances Watkins Harper." In their *Black Writers of America: A Comprehensive Anthology.* New York: Macmillan, 1972.

Bone, Robert. *The Negro Novel in America.* New Haven: Yale University Press, 1965; rev. ed., 1976.

Boyd, Melba Joyce. *Discarded Legacy: A Critical Study of Frances Ellen Watkins Harper.* Jackson: University Press of Mississippi, forthcoming.

Brawley, Benjamin, ed. *Early Negro American Writers.* Chapel Hill: University of North Carolina Press, 1935.

Carby, Hazel V. *Reconstructing Womanhood: The Emergence of the Afro-American Woman Novelist.* New York: Oxford University Press, 1987.

Christian, Barbara. *Black Feminist Criticism: Perspectives on Black Women Writers.* Elmsford, N.Y.: Pergamon, 1985.

———. *Black Women Novelists: The Development of a Tradition, 1892–1976.* Westport, Conn.: Greenwood Press, 1980.

Daniel, Theodora Williams. "The Poems of Frances E. W. Harper, Edited with a Biographical and Critical Introduction and Bibliography." Master's thesis, Howard University, 1937.

[Du Bois, W. E. B.] "Writers." *Crisis* 1:20–21 (April 1911).

Filler, Louis. "Frances Ellen Watkins Harper." In *Notable American Women, 1607–1950: A Biographical Dictionary.* Vol. 2. Cambridge, Mass.: Harvard University Press, 1971.

Frazier. S. Elizabeth. "Some Afro-American Women of Mark." *A.M.E. Church Review* 8:373–386 (1892).

Giddings, Paula. *"When and Where I Enter": The Impact of Black Women on Race and Sex in America.* New York: William Morrow, 1984.

Gloster, Hugh. *Negro Voices in American Fiction.* Chapel Hill: University of North Carolina Press, 1948.

Graham, Maryemma. "Frances Ellen Watkins Harper." In *The Dictionary of Literary Biography.* Vol. 50. Edited by Trudier Harris and Thadious M. Davis. Detroit: Gale Research, 1986.

Hill, Patricia Liggins. " 'Let Me Make the Songs for the People': A Study of Frances Watkins Harper's Poetry." *Black American Literature Forum* 15:60-5 (Summer 1981).

Johnson, H. T. "Negro Literature and Book-Making." *A.M.E. Church Review* 7:199–201 (1890).

Lauter, Paul. "Is Frances Ellen Watkins Harper Good Enough to Teach?" *Legacy* 5:27–32 (Spring 1988).

Lewis, Vashti. "The Near-White Female in Frances Ellen Harper's *Iola Leroy.*" *Phylon* 45:314–322 (1984).

Loewenberg, Bert James, and Ruth Bogin. *Black Women in Nineteenth Century Life: Their Words, Their*

Thoughts, Their Feelings. University Park: Pennsylvania State University Press, 1976.

Love, Alfred H. "Memorial Tribute to Mrs. Frances E. W. Harper." *Peacemaker and Court of Arbitration* 30:118–119 (June–July 1911).

McDowell, Deborah E. " 'The Changing Same': Generational Connections and Black Women Novelists." *New Literacy History* 18:281–302 (Winter 1987).

Pollard, Leslie J. "Frances Harper and the Old People: Two Recently Discovered Poems." *Griot* 4:52–56 (Summer–Winter 1985).

Redding, J. Saunders. *To Make a Poet Black*. Chapel Hill: University of North Carolina Press, 1939.

Review of *Iola Leroy*. *A.M.E. Church Review* 9:416–417 (1893).

Richings, G. F. *Evidences of Progress Among Colored People*. Philadelphia: George S. Ferguson, 1901.

Ridgely, J. V. *Nineteenth-Century Southern Literature*. Lexington: University Press of Kentucky, 1980.

Robinson, William H., Jr., ed. *Early Black American Poets*. Dubuque, Iowa: William C. Brown, 1969.

Scruggs, Lawson A. *Women of Distinction*. Raleigh, N.C.: L. A. Scruggs, 1893.

Sherman, Joan R. *Invisible Poets: Afro-Americans of the Nineteenth Century*. Urbana: University of Illinois, 1974; 2nd ed., 1989.

Sterling, Dorothy. *We Are Your Sisters: Black Women in the Nineteenth Century*. New York: Norton, 1984.

Stetson, Erlene. *Black Sister: Poetry by Black American Women, 1746–1980*. Bloomington: Indiana University Press, 1981.

Still, William. *Still's Underground Railroad Records*. Rev. ed., Philadelphia, 1883.

———. *The Underground Railroad*. Philadelphia: Porter & Coates, 1871.

Walden, Daniel. "Frances Ellen Watkins Harper." In *Dictionary of American Negro Biography*. Edited by Rayford Whittingham Logan. New York: Norton, 1982.

Washington, Mary Helen. *Invented Lives: Narratives of Black Women, 1860–1960*. New York: Doubleday/Anchor, 1988.

White, Newman Ivey, ed. *An Anthology of Verse by American Negroes*. Durham, N.C.: Moore, 1968.

Whiteman, Maxwell. *Frances Ellen Watkins (Harper), 1825–1911: Author, Lecturer, and Abolitionist*. Afro-American History Series, collection 4. Wilmington: Scholarly Resources, n.d.

Whitlow, Roger. *Black American Literature: A Critical History*. Chicago: Nelson Hall, 1973.

Williams, Kenny J. *They Also Spoke: An Essay on Negro Literature in America*. Nashville, Tenn: Townsend, 1970.

JOANNE BRAXTON

LILLIAN HELLMAN

1905–1984

"I WAS BORN in New Orleans to Julia Newhouse from Demopolis, Alabama, who had fallen in love and stayed in love with Max Hellman, whose parents had come to New Orleans in the German 1845–1848 immigration to give birth to him and his two sisters." Lillian Hellman begins her first published memoir, *An Unfinished Woman* (1969), which won a National Book Award, with the fact of her birth, while failing to mention the date, 20 June 1905. How faithfully Hellman chose to represent herself in this and later memoirs became a source of literary gossip and contretemps, and eventually, in the last years of her life, litigation. In her essay "Women and Fiction," Virginia Woolf characterizes her subject as ambiguous and allusive, since it "may allude to women and the fiction that they write, or to women and the fiction written about them." About Lillian Hellman we might augment Woolf's list to encompass the fiction women write about themselves. At Hellman's death in 1984, most discussions of her work debated the accuracy of her best-selling memoirs: *An Unfinished Woman* (1969), *Pentimento* (1973), and *Scoundrel Time* (1976). The drama of vituperation over the factual inconsistencies in Hellman's memoirs conveniently obscured the anger of many of her detractors, most notably Mary McCarthy (as well as Martha Gellhorn and Samuel McCracken), at Hellman's success not only as a writer but as a political organizer. To ignore the scandal created by Hellman's memoirs is to misrepresent her position as an American literary and political figure; however, giving greater attention to the accusations than to her work as a playwright makes Hellman primarily a literary object, a writer whose life preempts the quality and power of her work.

Hellman's childhood granted her the gift of imagination given to those only children surrounded by eccentric, sometimes lonely adults who talk in order to hear themselves remember, forgetting the youth or inexperience of their audience. Lillian Hellman's plays incorporate these odd women out—spinster aunts, immigrant girls, maids—in the life of established families. Often the women seem to come in pairs, like her aunts Jenny and Carrie, whose stories and influence in Lillian Hellman's life all but erase her mother. When not listening to her elders' stories, Hellman cultivated a solitary love in a solitary place: "It was in that [fig] tree that I learned to read, filled with the passions that can only come to the bookish, grasping, very young. . . ."

Her childhood consisted of six months of the year in New York, six months in New Orleans; elderly aunts and an absent father; a black maid whose presence both frightened and comforted; school systems so divergent that she could skip classes in the South and then struggle to catch up in her New York semester; and the paradoxical invisibility and spectacle of being an only child. Attuned by her experience to be an observer rather than a participant, Hellman developed an orneriness more acceptable in the elderly than in the young. She was notorious for her stubborness and her temper. As an observer she kept a "writing book," sketching the portraits of influential adults who would later figure in her memoirs.

After attending New York University and Columbia sporadically in the 1920s, arguing with teachers and avoiding boring classes, Lillian Hellman took a job with Horace Liveright, the publishing wildman who comes to life in Hellman's affectionate, broad portrait in *An Un-*

finished Woman. Hellman was never to stray far from a career that dealt with words, whether as a reader of manuscripts and screenplays, or as a writer of plays, screenplays, and memoirs. Her career took her from New York to Los Angeles, where, in the boredom of being known as mystery writer Dashiell Hammett's new "girl," she began to write her first play.

PLAYS

The tight, three-act form of Hellman's first play, *The Children's Hour* (1934), controlled the inherent melodrama of its subject, two women whose private school is destroyed because of an accusation by one of the students that they are lovers. The play is condensed and careful: the small-town school, the eccentric aunt, the confused girls, the spiteful Mary Tilford. Within the space of three acts, Hellman establishes a world and then allows it to unravel, wither, and die.

Karen Wright and Martha Dobie, the first of many pairs of women characters in Hellman's plays, are somewhere between traditional young women and young female entrepreneurs. As schoolteachers they are engaged in a traditionally female occupation, yet they are schoolteachers who have collaborated to buy a house and establish a private school of their own. The opening scene creates an informal atmosphere, in which Mrs. Lily Mortar tells old stories about her career as an actress. Seven girls make up the class, whose manipulation of the aging Mrs. Mortar's infinite susceptibility to digression is recognizable to any enterprising truant not prepared to answer her Latin questions. Here Mary Tilford is caught by Karen in the first of a series of lies.

The action of the play works in clusters of interaction between an authority figure (Karen) and a child (Mary), two students, or the two teachers. Each interaction develops the plot, placing the characters in situations that challenge their own integrity while demanding a response to the integrity—or lack of it—in others. Mary—who manipulates Mrs. Mortar, exhorts Peggy (another student), avoids Karen, implores her grandmother, and blackmails another student, Rosalie—is a character whose complex and calculated actions and motives dramatize the moral questions the play raises about truth, the act of lying, and the responsibility of believing.

With the exception of Dr. Joseph Cardin, Karen's fiancé, the world of truth and slander is a feminine world: the world of the women who send their girls to school, the girls themselves, and the women who run the school. The power available to these women is limited to influence, gossip, and the education of young girls, while the strictures of class are also forcefully presented. Karen and Martha are dependent upon the wealth of the families whose children attend the school—Mary's grandmother, Amelia Tilford, can, because of her social position, close the school with a mere phone call.

Hellman's dramatic skills entice the "grown-up" audience to join in the emotional games of childhood. In the scene between Mary and her grandmother, we sit forward in our seats, straining to hear the whispered reports of why behavior at the school is "unnatural." In stage directions, Hellman demonstrates Mary's devious talent, the ability to observe her opponent and calculate the effect of her actions. After Amelia Tilford reproaches her for using that "silly" word "unnatural," Hellman adds parenthetically that Mary, "vaguely realizing that she is on the right track, hurries on." The playwright represents the process of slander as a collaborative act, one that requires a willing audience, since Mary's creation grows in proportion to her grandmother's horrified response Theater itself risks the fate of slander, since it too depends upon a willing audience, and the playwright hopes for an intelligent, discerning one.

At the climax of the second act Rosalie ingenuously admits that she did not see Karen and Martha kissing as Mary reported she did, while Mary smoothly interjects with a reminder about Helen's missing bracelet, the one Rosalie has in her possession. Rosalie becomes hysterical, not because she has been traumatized by the sight of her teachers embracing, but because Mary has filled her head with tales of arrest and imprisonment for stealing; she screams and suddenly admits that Mary's story is true after all. The action clarifies for the play's audience who is lying and why, while representing the conflicting, confusing emotions and doubts created in the characters by a talented liar.

The springtime of the first act passes to November by the third act. Over the short time of summer, the school, the women, and the play have aged prematurely. The dialogue is listless, the welcoming, understanding spirit of the first act lost to despair and resignation. Suspicion corrodes, and Karen rejects Joe's offer to flee the country, to make a new life, reminding him that "you're still trying to spare me, still trying to tell yourself that we might be alright again." There is no possibility of "alright" for Martha, who foresees the bleakest of outcomes: "There'll never be any place for us to go. We're bad people. . . . Well, get used to it; we'll be here for a long time. Let's pinch each other sometimes. We can tell whether we're still living." Their death-in-life is intolerable to her, and like an Ibsen heroine, she leaves the stage to shoot herself. Karen's final speech to the repentant Amelia Tilford is the only energy in the final act, for even Martha's shooting seems devoid of power, inevitable within the entropy created by the slander.

The Children's Hour opened in New York and won its unknown playwright immediate success. Throughout the play's performance history, directors questioned whether the subject was lesbianism or whether lesbian love was a convenient social taboo used to illustrate the consequences of slander. (The play was banned in Boston, aptly since the setting is a New England town.) While Hellman vacillated in her own directorial interpretation of the story, she credited the important theme of the play, that of slander and its effects. That Martha admits to a sexual desire for Karen is another of the various outcomes of the strain and pressure of the community and the lie, though early in the play her jealousy of Joe and Karen's engagement is emphasized. Regardless of whether the playwright intended to champion love between women, integrity is on the side of the heroines, and their feelings for each other enhance rather than detract from that integrity.

During the writing of *The Children's Hour,* Hellman's most present influence was her lover, Dashiell Hammett, author of *The Maltese Falcon.* Hellman had Hammett's help, as she recounts it, in writing her first play, and the play's spare, sometimes painfully restrained language echoes Hammett's detective prose. Hellman despised what she referred to as "ladywriter" stories; her first play shows an overwhelming suppression of emotion in a world where slander leads to murder and suicide. While her contemporary Eugene O'Neill could revel in melodramatic language and excess and not be accused of "feminine" prose, Hellman was a woman writing first to a gruff, blunt male whose cutting criticisms often left long days of silence between them, and then to an audience accustomed to male playwrights, since writing for the stage was largely a masculine task. Only later, with the introduction of Freudian themes, did Hellman find an emotional outlet that could be sanctioned by the male establishment, which understood representations of high emotion as a recognizable component of pathology. At times *The Children's Hour* suffers from the pressure for the language to remain tough; the characters are sometimes admirable, sometimes understandable, but seldom sympathetic. When Martha kills herself, the rage that Karen displays is almost casual, a moral necessity with no basis in real compassion or real loss.

Hollywood, ready to devour new scripts almost as soon as they began successful runs as plays on Broadway, made New York the out-of-town test for the film industry. Hellman's reward for her success with *The Children's Hour* was a contract with producer Samuel Goldwyn.

While writing for the movies she and Hammett drank with other legendary writers then working in Hollywood: William Faulkner, F. Scott Fitzgerald, and John O'Hara. Hellman herself often refers to the damage done by Hammett's and her drinking. Alcohol, the great American social elixir and equalizer, eased the social adjustment of class and reputation between many writers. The degree to which alcohol formed the basis of Hellman and Hammett's relationship to each other and to their writing has been too readily dismissed, as in William Wright's biography *Lillian Hellman: The Image, the Woman:*

> If the term is taken to mean one who drinks too much, Hellman certainly qualified. But if the word signifies physiological and psychological addiction requiring in most cases strenuous therapy and lifelong abstinence in order to break, Hellman did not fit. Self-dramatization can be pejorative as well as flattering, to be sure, but Hellman's exaggeration of her liquor probably stemmed from the same impulse that made her drink heavily: Hammett-worship—and an almost pathetic, somewhat tomboyish eagerness to be admitted to his one-man club. Few would deny that Hammett was an alcoholic, but he too could voluntarily stop from time to time.
>
> (p. 75)

A general failure to acknowledge Hellman's addiction to alcohol—an addiction with grave social and affective consequences—leads Wright to indulge in a kind of condescension to his subject, as if she were unaware of her own "pathetic" impulses. The lives of both Hammett and Hellman carry all the marks of alcoholism, not only how they drank, but how they acted when they did. Their stormy relations were the subject of Hellman's own tales and those of the political and literary world who knew them. Much of the grandness critics assail in Hellman's embellished memoirs may have had its source in the disordered universe of the alcoholic, where self-importance vies for preeminence with self-loathing, producing a characteristic alternation in Hellman's autobiographical writing between a loftiness verging on arrogance and withering self-deprecation.

While still writing screenplays for Goldwyn, Hellman began the draft for her next play, *Days to Come* (1936). Infamous for its position as the famous playwright's second play and first failure, the work actually reads better than a play that closed after only six performances. Perhaps her screenwriting influenced the play's conception and Hellman's execution, for it might have been more plausible as a film: the ambition and scope of the action would be better accommodated by the camera, which could pan in and out of rooms, rest idly on the menace of henchmen, follow Julie on her lonely walks, and perhaps free the tightly bound acts.

The three-act play demands precision and scrupulous editing: too many characters and scenes confuse the delicate process of beginning, middle, and end, while too few make the waltz stilted with the thudding drop of preordained climaxes and expected intervals. *Days to Come* follows an awkward path between the Rodman family, with Andrew as the confused, ineffectually loyal businessman; the workers, represented by Leo Whalen, grudgingly idealistic and wise about the ways of strikebreakers; and the pivotal Julie, the rich woman seeking "something else." All of the elements are intriguing: the breakdown of loyalty to the town, which created the Rodman family's wealth; the strange detached relationship between Andrew and Julie; Henry Ellicott and Cora Rodman's ruthlessness; and the unleashing of violence when Sam Wilkie's outside men take over the house. Yet the play lacks subtlety, producing only a sketch of the characters and an easy ending in which the most vulnerable character is killed and the repentant Andrew, like Amelia Tilford, understands that niceness is no substitute for integrity and determination.

Of her third play Lillian Hellman wrote:

> *The Little Foxes* was the most difficult play I ever wrote. . . . Some of the trouble came because the play has a distant connection to my mother's family and everything I had heard or seen or imagined had formed a giant tangled time-jungle in which I could find no space to walk without tripping over old roots, hearing old voices speak about histories made long before my day.
>
> (*Pentimento*, pp. 171–172)

In writing this play (1939) Hellman sought to recapture the success of *The Children's Hour* while erasing the failure of *Days to Come*. She speaks eloquently in *Pentimento* about the fear that assails the writer when the second work fails, the certainty that the first success was a fluke.

The Little Foxes takes place in the South at the turn of the century. The choice to enter the "time-jungle," to re-create a Southern family whose money comes from opportunism and deceit and whose life is overshadowed by the acquiring of that money, allowed Hellman the now familiar setting of an extended family, the Hubbards, of a memorable vixen, Regina, and of the honorable if ineffectual Horace Giddens.

The play encompasses particular aspects of Southern life rarely portrayed onstage, even by Hellman's contemporary Tennessee Williams: the force and vindictiveness of the family as displayed by Ben Hubbard, Regina's older brother; the presence of that family continually in the life of each sibling; and the vehemence with which the family creates and maintains its image in society so that the weaker members, Birdy and Leo, are used to further the "plot" of the family story to their own ruin. Where Williams often saved brutality for outside influences or absent fathers, Hellman taints most of her characters with a bit of viciousness and a great deal of greed.

Alexandra Giddens, Regina and Horace's daughter, takes on the task of the innocent in the corrupt world created by the Hubbard legacy. Though not openly hostile to her mother at the beginning of the play, she seems always distant from her, neither acknowledging Regina's ruthlessness nor recognizing her mother's self-absorption. She is "Daddy's girl" from the beginning, and her concern for his physical welfare contrasts with Regina's disregard.

While money and its distribution preoccupies the Hubbards, in this play Hellman connects greed with escape. Regina wants to go to Chicago and be in society, Ben wants to create an industry and so change the social status of the family, and Oscar wants to get out of the position of underling to his brother and his sister. Horace Giddens is the unstable element in the plan. He is recuperating in Baltimore from a heart ailment—his time away from the family is a release and an opportunity for reappraisal. If he does not contribute to the financing, the deal cannot go forward.

Thus Leo Hubbard, Birdy and Oscar's son, a recalcitrant employee at his uncle Horace's bank, is persuaded to "borrow" Horace's stock from his safe-deposit box. Of course the stocks will be replaced when the company is successfully stable. And to add to the incestuousness of the already suffocatingly entwined family, Leo is to marry Alexandra. The Hubbard siblings play a three-dimensional board game where the characters who are less conniving find themselves moved around on the surface, occupying whatever place is convenient for their owners.

Horace returns weak and wary to find Regina her unrepentant self, interested in his cooperation without his interference. He is appalled at the notion of Leo and Alexandra marrying and sees the endless cycle of misery the Hubbards call family. The climactic scene of Horace's death, gasping for his medicine while Regina looks at the audience, forever freezes the character of Regina into the woman with no heart, whose relief at her husband's death has already given way to her planning to extort money from her brothers by threatening to expose their theft of the bonds.

Alexandra, echoing Addie, the stock representation of the wise, good black maid, establishes the moral lesson to the worlds participating in *The Little Foxes:* "Addie said, there were people who ate the earth and other people who stood around and watched them do it." Her summation comes at the end of the play, as an interesting challenge to the "watching" audience, those who attend and do not interfere. Alexandra, it is implied, will break the cycle of the Hubbards and leave, as her father enjoined her, before she finds her uncles and her cousins permanent guests at her table, permanent combatants in the contest for supremacy and position.

American artists have often debated the nature of political writing—what it is, who does it, whether it is art. Because Lillian Hellman's plays are created out of discussions of power and economic control—in the family or in the town—the question of whether a piece was political was rendered moot; anything that takes a position about a social issue, almost anything written, is political. Hellman herself, while becoming famous as a playwright, worked for the Screen Writers Guild, traveled to the Soviet Union, and hosted parties where the intent of the evening was to generate lively discussion about forms of government and their uses.

Her power as a proponent of a particular cause, her ability to attract and compel other literary figures and political activists of her time, announced her, when the time came, to those men whose places on the House Un-American Activities Committee (HUAC) allowed them the jurisdiction of judges and the license of muckrakers. Her FBI file was impressive; she had been watched since her union activities began. Her work with the Communist Party and her support of the Soviet government were painstakingly documented.

The enormous influence of Joseph McCarthy, and of Richard Nixon and the House committee, greatly affected the American theater and Hollywood during the 1940s and 1950s. At one point, in order to write for the movies, a scriptwriter had to sign a letter swearing he or she would not be involved in subversive political movements. American interest in the new Communism in the Soviet Union had been at first romantic and primarily intellectual; any thinking citizen found the ideas of the new society compelling enough to consider. So when the committee asked the question "Are you now or have you ever been a member of the Communist party?" even ex–Communist supporters were implicated in the supposed plot to overthrow American democracy. The witch-hunt produced a blacklist of writers whose careers were ruined by their honesty and resulted in years of bitterness between colleagues whose friends had turned "friendly witness" for the committee, naming anyone whom they could remember as having been associated with the Communist party.

Both Hammett (in 1951) and Hellman (in 1952) were called before the committee. Because Hammett refused to testify, answering, "I don't know," he was sent to prison for six months. Hellman also refused to testify, though her decision to write a letter offering to talk about herself but not others persuaded the committee to forgo imprisoning her. The Internal Revenue Service, an American institution advantageously positioned to punish when encouraged by the FBI, hit both writers for what it argued were unpaid taxes, the sudden discovery of heretofore unknown royalties, and so on. The farm Hellman and Hammett occupied was sold; although Hellman later became wealthy again, Hammett never regained his comfortable life.

As in so many countries changed by revolution, the path of ideals veered from the path of practice in the USSR; the news of Stalin's purges was slow to come, and the influence of Communist didactics suppressed any outrage about the reality of what was happening in Germany. In a rare move away from partisan Communist beliefs, Lillian Hellman had openly advocated the work of the underground in Germany in *Watch on the Rhine* (1941).

Set in Washington, D.C., at the home of wealthy Fanny Farrelly, *Watch on the Rhine* combines the best of Hellman's strengths. Now a standard subject of theater for Hellman and most other twentieth-century American playwrights, the family and its tensions form the setting for the play. Hellman, however, situates this family at the crux of issues of global politics. The tough matriarch Fanny Farrelly does not quite control her son, David Farrelly. Their visitors, the count and countess de Brancovis, are parasitic nobility whose visit has continued too long for the Farrellys' liking. Hovering around the set are the French companion Anise and the black servant Joseph. In Hellman's plays the upper class is maintained by the black servants, whose characterization contains the very prejudice that keeps them peripheral: a two-dimensional ignorance of the lives of blacks and a lack of courage on the part of the playwright to allow the characters a life and story of their own.

Into this family returns the prodigal daughter, Sara, her German husband, Kurt Müller, and their children, Bodo, Babette, and Joshua. The count, Teck, is overinterested in the presence of Joshua, suspicious of his wartime activities. Fanny, still outraged at Sara's brazen abandonment of her mother's support, showers the family with the kind of comfort impossible for a German family whose father is a member of the underground. Harold Clurman, director of Hellman's later work *The Autumn Garden* (1951), wisely commented in the *New Republic* that Hellman normally "will not embrace her people. She does not believe that they deserve her (or our) love. Love is present only through the ache of its absence." In *Watch on the Rhine,* though, love *does* become present and Hellman's characters win their author's and their audience's respect, particularly Fanny and the oddly formal, awkward-tongued Bodo. What is present is indeed present through the aching absence of explanation. Sara loves Kurt; the children love their parents; their lives are restricted, interrupted by the constant moving of the hunted, comforted only by the satisfaction of living out an ideal.

Neither Fanny's wealth and the comfort it brings nor the possibility of the family remaining together can keep Kurt from his task of returning to Germany. The twist on this moving if romantic vision is the interference of Teck, whose love of money matches his desire to disrupt the Müllers' world. Marthe, Teck's wife, further encourages his plans to blackmail Kurt with her open attentions to David Farrelly. Yet the number of honorable, or at least potentially honorable, characters outweighs the influence of greed and power in *Watch on the Rhine.* Kurt shoots Teck rather than have him endanger the lives of those incarcerated in Germany for their underground activities, David participates in disposing of the body, and Fanny condones the whole venture, reminding her son that she is "not put together with flour paste." Neither is he, "she is happy to learn."

A plot synopsis of *Watch on the Rhine* does not do justice to the subtlety and liveliness of the dialogue. Fanny's caustic repartee is funny and loving and irritating. The children are the stiff grown-ups they should be in light of their past, while Teck is smarmy but charming. The decision to kill Teck is all Kurt's, but the desire to support him comes thoughtfully and naturally from David and Fanny. Of course the question of culpability is exactly what Hellman would be faced with when she appeared before HUAC. The actions, the reactions, and the responsibility of those engaged in or witnessing political activities had remained deeply important to Hellman's art since *The Children's Hour.*

Between *Watch on the Rhine* and *Another Part of the Forest* (1947), Hellman wrote *The Searching Wind* (1944). Famous only because it was the play that introduced the young Montgomery Clift, *The Searching Wind* was unwieldy and reminiscent of the failure of *Days to Come,* with too many characters and too much confusion for the three-act play to contain.

Henry James in his preface to *The Aspern Papers* writes with macabre cheer of his intent to "bring the bad dead back to life for a second round of badness." *Another Part of the Forest* returns to the stage an earlier manifestation of the Hubbards first introduced in *The Little Foxes.* Indeed, Regina is brought back for a second round of badness, but, in good psychoanalytic fashion, her badness is given a context: the badness of her father.

It is 1880 and Marcus Hubbard has made his money on the misfortune of his neighbors during the Civil War. He is rich, ensconced in a manor house, and universally despised. His sons, Benjamin and Oscar, vie for his money, his daughter, Regina, strokes his ego while she pours his coffee, and his wife, Lavinia, longs to start mission work with the black children who "need" her. A little like *Gone with the Wind,* the opening of the play dallies with Southern cliches—the oversexed young woman wanting the honorable man, John Bagtry, who takes her but does not take her seriously; the black maid returning from church with the odd old white lady who insists on going to the "Negro" church; the youngest son, whose girlfriend is a floozy and the love of his life; the appearance of the father, who renders all stiff and guilty; and the grown children, disguising their hatred or withdrawing from the air of disapproval that Marcus exudes.

Ben Hubbard hates his father. Though not a new theme to American letters, the entrapment of the son by the father he longs to overthrow is further exacerbated by Ben's sister's cloying manipulation of her doting father. Regina has replaced her mother; the incest threatens to engulf the stage, since the act of fornication hardly need be added to what is painfully represented, an emotional ownership that keeps Regina gratefully bound to her sickeningly possessive father. The coffee cup takes on the status of a fetish symbolizing Regina's servitude and thus the supremacy of the man first served by her.

The world of the defeated South, rich in land, poor in cash, arrives in the form of Birdie Bagtry—later in the Hubbard family history the sad, defeated Birdie of *The Little Foxes*—asking Ben to loan her money so that her workers might eat. Ben sees Birdie's naiveté and concocts a scheme to make money, cheat his father, and enslave his brother, promising Birdie $5,000 for the sale of her land. Ben then proposes the deal to his father, suggesting that Marcus give Ben the $10,000 Birdie has asked. Even $10,000 is a ridiculously low sum, and Marcus agrees.

Birdie does not realize the value of her own land, nor the greed of the Hubbards. A cage is being woven in which Birdie will marry Oscar, the stupid, and later, as he ages in *The Little Foxes,* vicious little brother. As the power shifts from Ben to Marcus to Regina to Ben, the consequences of the past trap Marcus. Lavinia dreamily tells her son how his father betrayed his neighbors to the Union troops, an action that led to the acquiring of the Hubbard fortune. Keeping the proof in her Bible, Lavinia becomes the unstable witness who will necessitate the handing over of the business by Marcus to Ben and her own release to pursue her pathetic missionary project.

The close of the play is chilling. Despite the possible reductive Freudian interpretations, *Another Part of the Forest* reveals the limitations of any daughter's or sister's role in her own limited plays for power. Regina—dependent on her father for a wardrobe, the single most influential possession of a Southern girl, and dependent on her lover to meet her in Chicago and marry her—sits down defeated and caught at the side of her brother Ben, pouring his coffee. The image haunts the viewer, the inevitability of a woman being passed on in the incestuous chain of father and brother, petted for a fleeting beauty, treasured for the necessary, if insincere, devotion that establishes the power of the male, sibling or father.

The Autumn Garden (1951) portrays another kind of family, whose summer renters have returned for another year to their boardinghouse on the Gulf of Mexico. Here misplaced adults, childless couples, and immigrants take rooms in a house run by sad, dignified Constance Tuckerman. An old beau, Nicholas Denery, is about to return, joined by his French wife, Nina. Meanwhile Ben Griggs tries to persuade his disbelieving wife of his intention to divorce her, though Rosie Griggs cannot conceive of divorce unless Ben is leaving her for another, the comfort of adultery preferable to the nebulous act of breaking up because the marriage is dead. Edward Crossman, a single middle-aged gentleman, witnesses all that passes before him but engages in none of it. And the Ellises—grandmother Mrs. Mary, mother Carrie, and son Frederick—play out familial guilt and obedience as Frederick longs to travel with the disreputable Mr. Payson, who, it appears, shares Frederick's homosexual preferences. To all of this Hellman adds Sophie Tuckerman. Adopted by her aunt Constance from hard circumstances in Europe, Sophie agrees to marry Frederick, though it is a marriage of convenience only, one that will allow her to return with money to her family.

The house proves a wonderful setting for all the variations on the choices adults make for their lives, and the choices they cannot avoid. Nicholas returns to paint a second portrait of Constance, intending to show his talent by starkly creating a picture of a defeated, prematurely aged woman to place beside the original portrait of his flushed fiancée. Constance slowly comes to despise the man whose memory she has honored, while his wife, Nina, cannot get away from him, no matter how many times he carries on grandiose dalliances and dishonest schemes.

Nicholas interferes out of habit, but his directorial efforts are marred by his own stupidity. His advice is usually off in its timing, its truth, or its relevance. With Nicholas's meddling help, Carrie discovers Mr. Payson's true nature while Frederick is already deciding to call off the venture to Europe; Rosie Griggs schemes to keep her husband in ways that manage to firm his resolve to leave; and Sophie's reputation is ruined by Nick's blundering, drunken collapse in her room.

Like a Chekhov play in its construction, *The Autumn Garden* remains simple in its plot, the characters creating complexity in their dialogue. The unfolding of wisdom and sophistry happens according to who is talking to whom. Again the lives of the inhabitants, as in most of Hellman's work, are watched by a judging society. Sophie's disgrace is carried throughout the town by the servants who note the impropriety of Nick's couch.

Between *The Autumn Garden,* produced a year after her 1952 appearance before HUAC, and the last play Lillian Hellman wrote, *Toys in the Attic,* she translated Jean Anouilh's *L'Alouette* (published in 1956 as *The Lark*) and wrote the libretto for *Candide* (1957), an opera based on Voltaire's story. Hellman, struggling to create a new form for her writing, prefigures in her choice of characters for *Toys in the Attic* the sketches she later created in her memoirs. Anna and Carrie Berniers are taken from memories of her aunts, Jenny and Carrie, and Julian Berniers is based on her father, Max Hellman.

The language of *Toys in the Attic,* freer and less restricted than any in Hellman's preceding plays, indicates either the absence of Hammett's influence (he had been ill for many years and died in 1961) or an ease with the autobiographical writing displayed in her memoirs. The action of the play, as in *The Autumn Garden,* is less eventful than in earlier plays, more incorporated into the workings of small-town successes and failures, of lives lived in the telling of stories, in the amending of dreams. A reader can imagine the young Jason Robards, Jr., in the original Broadway production bounding into the character of Julian, the dashing, truly quixotic young man whose appearance reanimates all those around him.

The odd-women sisters work and live their lives in the hope of a trip to Europe, in the familiar disappointment of their lives bound to their mortgage and their jobs. The weariness at the end of the day is evoked in the first scene; Anna and Carrie's sibling marriage rife with patter, contradiction, and worry about the "boy." Their longing for what they do not have enables them to continue until Julian arrives unannounced and delivers their dreams.

The Southern society represented by Hellman in 1961 does produce surprises. Albertine Prine, Julian's mother-in-law, is accompanied by her companion-cum-chauffeur, Henry. Though the nature of the relationship remains unasserted, it is clear that Mrs. Prine has taken up with Henry, a black man, whose lines in this play are unusually forceful and intelligent about the nature of the white people whom he encounters and the white woman with whom he sleeps. Henry comes closer to having an unappropriated position than any other black character in Hellman's plays.

Many of Hellman's plays hinge on some kind of "deal"—money is inextricably linked to family. In *Toys in the Attic,* Julian has an ex-mistress with whom he has concocted a deal. And when he unexpectedly gains the wealth he hoped for the play takes a fascinating twist: Julian gives the members of his family their wildest dreams. He comes home not impoverished, dependent, and in need of protection, but bearing gifts: tickets to Europe, the paid-off mortgage on the house, new clothes.

Faced with the fulfillment of their dreams, the sisters recoil. They never liked the house, they never wanted to go to Europe. Julian, the hero, no longer needs his aunts' suffocating attentions, and the sisters lose their purpose: "I guess most of us make up things we want, don't get them, and get too old, or too lazy, to make up new ones. Best not to disturb that, Julian. People don't want other people to guess they never know what they wanted in the first place," his mother-in-law, Albertine, reminds him.

When the plot moves inevitably to Julian's ruin, by way of fretting on the part of Lily, his young wife, some balance is restored. But the sisters have been separated by Anna's accusation that Carrie had a physical interest in Julian, that her doting turned to lusting. In the aftermath of revelation, Albertine recognizes that Carrie will eventually tell Julian of Lily's interference and the loss of the deal with his ex-mistress; she knows that Carrie will do anything to re-establish the family threesome—and on that day Albertine will return to take Lily back. Like other Hellman families, the Berniers cannot allow outsiders; they must incorporate and then exclude nonmembers or expel them completely.

MEMOIRS

Nine years after her last play was produced, Lillian Hellman published *An Unfinished Woman* (1969), her first memoir. To an American public accustomed to conferring fame on writers of lives lived among the famous rather than on playwrights, Hellman has become more well known for her autobiographical writing than for her contributions as an American playwright. Thus the scandal caused by accusations made about the accuracy of her memoirs, the first by the writer Mary McCarthy on an evening television talk show, has the power to call into doubt her worth as a writer, as a political figure, and as an artist. The debate incorporates artistic questions about truth and memory, about honor and slander, the very questions debated in most Hellman plays.

The glee with which Martha Gellhorn in her article in the *Paris Review* and subsequently Samuel McCracken in *Commentary* collected inaccuracies or inconsistencies in *An Unfinished Woman* and *Pentimento* (1973) seemed to arouse the public's ready ire for the irascible Hellman. By far the most damaging testimony came from Muriel Gardiner, who critics agree had to be the original "Julia," the woman whom Hellman presents as a childhood friend working for the resistance in Germany; yet Gardiner stated that she never met Lillian Hellman. The film *Julia,* with Vanessa Redgrave and Jane Fonda, celebrated Hellman's work and life and made the charges of falsehood acutely public.

Hellman's intelligence and her powerful rendering of her life coexist in her memoirs with the distorting effects of Southern womanhood, alcoholism, and the obvious work of the dramatist. In the South the distinction between truth and fiction is often erased in favor of image and good breeding. Family stories become legends; the details are fabricated as needed or exaggerated for effect. With the grandiosity of an alcoholic, the flair of a Southern playwright, Hellman portrays her life—the political moments and the love affair with Hammett taking precedence over many other activities and many other love affairs. Although her critics are fair in their questioning of her facts and her romantic appropriation of Muriel Gardiner's story, they deny the sheer lack of concern Hellman had for consistency. If Hellman were really trying to present an unflawed lie, she would have edited the glaring inconsistencies—within the first two memoirs she reports herself as being in three countries at once on the same day—to achieve a seamless narrative.

An Unfinished Woman combines a brief description of Hellman's childhood and early career in publishing with extended descriptions of Hellman's visit to the Soviet Union and Spain, and vignettes about Dorothy Parker and Dashiell Hammett. This style of autobiography, small characterizations of people influential in her life, continued in her next work, *Pentimento.*

Hellman adopts a traditional "feminine" pose, self-deprecation combined with the autobiographical, all-telling "I" of the author. In this form she can diminish and embellish without calling undue attention to her own accomplishments, while manipulating the story to reflect her own sense of the truth. Women writers younger than Hellman would, through the feminist movement's influence, establish a direct autobiographical female voice.

Pentimento continues this style with the emphasis on a single character from Hellman's life. Her uncle Willy, her cousin Bethe, her maid Helen, her friend Julia. Added to these characters is the "character" of the theater. In many ways overdue for those who followed Hellman's career as a playwright, this chapter reminisces about the conception, production, and reception of her plays. That Hellman resists much comment on her own work and that she chooses not to write about the work of others is a singular mark of her style as an author. Stories tell morals, opinions are contained in dialogue, rarely in authorial maxims.

Scoundrel Time (1976) allowed Hellman to comment extensively on the behavior of the American public, the American literary and entertainment community, and American politicians during the House Un-American Activities Committee hearings. What some readers deem her moralizing and sanctimonious certainty about who conducted themselves properly and who did not conflicted with the memories of some involved in the hearings. Hellman scorned what she saw as the cowardice of the American intellectual community, their bowing to the pressure of innuendo and small-mindedness.

In the last years of her life Hellman organized friends and prominent figures for the Committee on Public Justice, a group formed to report on the erosion of First Amendment rights by the CIA and FBI. Throughout Hellman's life she incorporated her energy and her extraordinary circle of friends into powerful political forces.

Hellman died on Martha's Vineyard, Massachussets, on 30 June 1984. Her friend John Hersey gave a moving tribute at her funeral, reminding her admirers and friends that Lillian Hellman was "a finished woman now. I mean 'finished' in its better sense." Lillian Hellman "shone with a high finish of integrity, decency, uprightness" and she gave us "this anger to remember and use in a bad world."

Selected Bibliography

PRIMARY WORKS

PLAYS

The Children's Hour. New York: Knopf, 1934.

Days to Come. New York: Knopf, 1936.

The Little Foxes. New York: Random House, 1939.

Watch on the Rhine. New York: Random House, 1941.

The Searching Wind. New York: Viking, 1944.

Another Part of the Forest. New York: Viking, 1947.

Montserrat. Adaptation of the French play by Emmanuel Roblès. New York: Dramatists Play Service, 1950.

The Autumn Garden. Boston: Little, Brown, 1951.

The Lark. Adaptation of the French play by Jean Anouilh. New York: Random House, 1956.

Candide: A Comic Operetta Based on Voltaire's Satire. Musical score by Leonard Bernstein. Lyrics by Richard Wilbur, John Latouche, and Dorothy Parker. New York: Random House, 1957.

Toys in the Attic. New York: Random House, 1960.

My Mother, My Father, and Me. Based on the novel *How Much?* by Burt Blechman. New York: Random House, 1963.

WORKS EDITED BY HELLMAN

The Selected Letters of Anton Chekhov. Translated by Sidonie Lederer. With an introduction by Lillian Hellman. New York: Farrar, Straus, 1955.

The Big Knockover: Selected Stories and Short Novels of Dashiell Hammett. With an introduction by Lillian Hellman. New York: Random House, 1966.

SCREENPLAYS

The Melody Lingers On. 1934.

Dark Angel. United Artists, 1935.

These Three. Adaptation of *The Children's Hour*. United Artists, 1936.

Dead End. United Artists, 1937. Adaptation of Sidney Kingsley's play by the same name.

The Little Foxes. RKO, 1941. Adaptation of the play by the same name.

Watch on the Rhine. Written by Dashiell Hammett. Edited by Hellman. Warner Brothers, 1942.

The North Star. RKO, 1943.

The Negro Soldier. 1944.

The Searching Wind. Paramount, 1946. Adaptation of the play by the same name.

The Blessing. 1953.

The Chase. 1966.

MEMOIRS

An Unfinished Woman. Boston: Little, Brown, 1969.

Pentimento. Boston: Little, Brown, 1973.

Scoundrel Time. With an introduction by Gary Wills. Boston: Little, Brown, 1976.

NONFICTION

Maybe: A Story. Boston: Little, Brown, 1980.

Eating Together: Recollections and Recipes. With Peter S. Feibleman. Boston: Little, Brown, 1984.

COLLECTED WORKS

Four Plays. New York: Random House, 1942. With an introduction by Hellman. Contains *The Children's Hour, Days to Come, The Little Foxes, Watch on the Rhine*.

Six Plays by Lillian Hellman. New York: Modern Library, 1960. With an introduction by Hellman. Contains *The Children's Hour, Days to Come, The Little Foxes, Watch on the Rhine, Another Part of the Forest, The Autumn Garden*.

The Collected Plays. Boston: Little, Brown, 1972. Contains all of Hellman's plays through 1963.

Three: An Unfinished Woman, Pentimento, Scoundrel Time. With new commentaries by Lillian Hellman. Introduction by Richard Poirier. Boston: Little, Brown, 1979.

SECONDARY WORKS

BIOGRAPHICAL AND CRITICAL STUDIES

Adler, Jacob H. *Lillian Hellman*. Austin, Tex.: Steck-Vaughn, 1969.

———. "The Rose and the Fox: Notes on the Southern Drama." In *South: Modern Southern Literature in its Cultural Setting*. Edited by Louis D. Rubin and Robert D. Jacobs. Garden City, N.Y.: Doubleday, 1961.

———. "Miss Hellman's Two Sisters." *Educational Theatre Journal* 14:112–117 (May 1963).

Broyard, Anatole. "Maybe." *New York Times,* 13 May 1980, sec. 3.

Bryer, Jackson R., ed. *Conversations with Lillian Hellman.* Jackson: University Press of Mississippi, 1986.

Clark, Barrett. "Lillian Hellman." *College English* 6, no. 3:127–133 (October 1944).

Davie, Michael. "Lillian Hellman: Life as Fiction." *Observer,* 9 November 1986.

Dick, Bernard F. *Hellman in Hollywood.* Teaneck, N.J.: Fairleigh Dickinson University Press, 1982.

Emerson, Gloria. "Lillian Hellman: At 66, She's Still Restless." *New York Times,* 7 September 1973.

Falk, Doris V. *Lillian Hellman.* New York: Frederick Ungar, 1978.

Feibleman, Peter. *Lilly: Reminiscences of Lillian Hellman.* New York: William Morrow, 1988.

Felheim, Marvin. "*The Autumn Garden:* Mechanics and Dialectics." *Modern Drama* 3, no. 2:191–195 (September 1960).

Gellhorn, Martha. "On Apocryphism." *Paris Review* 23, no. 79:280–301 (Spring 1981).

Gould, Jean. *Modern American Playwrights.* New York: Dodd, Mead, 1966.

Hersey, John. "Lillian Hellman." *New Republic* 175:25–27 (18 September 1976).

Holmin, Lorena Ross. *The Dramatic Works of Lillian Hellman.* Stockholm: Almquist and Wiskell, 1973.

Knepler, Henry W. "*The Lark:* Translation vs. Adaptation: A Case History." *Modern Drama* 1, no. 1:15–28 (May 1958).

Kramer, Hilton. "The Life and Death of Lillian Hellman." *New Criterion* 3, no. 2:1–6 (October 1984).

Lederer, Katherine. *Lillian Hellman.* Boston: Twayne, 1979.

Luce, William. *Lillian.* New York: Dramatists Play Service, 1987.

Moody, Richard. *Lillian Hellman: Playwright.* New York: Bobbs-Merrill/Pegasus, 1972.

Newman, Robert P. *The Cold War Romance of Lillian Hellman and John Melby.* Chapel Hill: University of North Carolina Press, 1989.

Rollyson, Carl. *Lillian Hellman: Her Legend and Her Legacy.* New York: St. Martin's Press, 1988.

Spacks, Patrica Ann Meyer. *The Female Imagination.* New York: Knopf, 1975.

Triesch, Manfred. *The Lillian Hellman Collection at the University of Texas.* Austin: Humanities Research Center, University of Texas, 1966.

Weales, Gerald. *American Drama Since World War II.* New York: Harcourt, Brace & World, 1962.

Wright, William. *Lillian Hellman: The Image, the Woman.* New York: Simon & Schuster, 1986.

PAT SKANTZE

ZORA NEALE HURSTON

1891–1960

THE MOMENT WHEN Alice Walker reached the graveyard where Zora Neale Hurston lay buried in an unmarked grave has become an organizing image for the understanding of both the African American and the feminist literary traditions. Although Hurston had attained widespread fame as a leading personality—more than as a writer—during the Harlem Renaissance, by the time of her death in 1960 she had fallen into almost total obscurity, sick, financially beleaguered, and unable to find publishers. By 1973, when Walker's quest reached its culmination, Hurston's reputation had been reduced to that of a local colorist remembered primarily for the charming love story *Their Eyes Were Watching God* (1937), which was out of print by the end of the 1970s. Against this backdrop, the story of Hurston's rediscovery might appear to be a cause for unqualified celebration. Certainly she has attained a level of recognition commensurate with the quality of her writing. She is honored as literary grandmother by black women writers, and she is celebrated as a central figure in the African American canon by black male critics. Yet much about Hurston and her work remains only dimly understood. Although she wrote at least a half dozen significant books, she continues to be seen almost solely as the author of *Their Eyes Were Watching God*. Not so much inaccurate as partial, the revised understanding of Hurston continues to simplify the woman quite accurately identified in the phrase Walker had engraved on Hurston's tombstone:

"A GENIUS OF THE SOUTH"

NOVELIST, FOLKLORIST,

ANTHROPOLOGIST

However contradictory they may seem, all images of Hurston contain at least a grain of truth. Hurston forged an idiosyncratic personal aesthetic, blending African American folk culture with elements of avant-garde European-American modernism. Highly aware of the underlying ambiguity of all cultural mythologies —a concern that provides the thematic center of her brilliant but still undervalued novel *Moses, Man of the Mountain* (1939)—Hurston projected a dazzling variety of (modernist) personae and (folk) masks. On the few occasions when she encountered individuals aware of the nuances that both connect and distinguish the two phrasings—she never encountered a sizable group who shared her knowledge—they were almost invariably men who were unable to reconcile her ability with their preconceptions concerning women's creative abilities.

Hurston's vision was firmly grounded in the African American folk culture she participated in as a child growing up in the all-black town of Eatonville, Florida. June Jordan has argued compellingly that Hurston's indifference to "protest literature" reflects the security of this unusually secure black upbringing. Still, she did not grow up ignorant of American racial conflict; the stories and songs she heard in Eatonville expressed a folk wisdom predicated on resistance to white domination. In the introduction to *Mules and Men* (1935), Hurston acknowledges the dialectic between the fundamental strategies of African American expression and white preconceptions of that expression. Assuming the role of an anthropologist-observer, Hurston discusses the difficulties of collecting folklore from her own hometown. Somewhat disingenuously referring to the Eatonville storytellers with the third-person pronoun, Hurston observers that "they are most reluctant at times to reveal that which the soul lives by. And the Negro, in spite of his open-faced laughter, his seeming acquiescence, is particularly evasive." Shifting to the first-person plural, she continues: "You see we are a polite people and we do not say to our questioner, 'Get out of here!' We smile and tell him or her something that satisfies the white person because, knowing so little about us, he doesn't know what he is missing." Hurston concludes with a passage that should caution readers against quick conclusions concerning her own texts: "The theory behind our tactics: 'The white man is always trying to know into somebody else's business. All right, I'll set something outside the door of my mind for him to play with and handle. He can read my writing but he sho' can't read my mind. I'll put this toy in his hand, and he will seize it and go away. Then I'll say my say and sing my song' " (pp. 4–5). A more explicit statement of ironic intention is difficult to imagine. Yet many of Hurston's contemporary readers, like most of her original white audience, continue to approach her with very little awareness of the pervasive presence of African American masking strategies.

One of the few women occupying a prominent role in African American literary life during the 1920s and 1930s, Hurston encountered sexual stereotypes as well, and was repeatedly patronized by her male peers, both white and black. Although Ralph Ellison understood both the folk and modernist traditions, he rejected *Moses, Man of the Mountain* as a literary minstrel show, "a calculated burlesque" that contributes nothing to black fiction. Richard Wright, in his 1937 review of *Their Eyes Were Watching God* for the leftist journal *New Masses,* commented that Hurston had "no desire whatsoever to move in the direction of serious fiction," condemning the "facile sensuality" of her prose.

As a graduate student at Columbia University, Hurston studied with anthropologists Ruth Benedict and Franz Boas, both of whom were instrumental in challenging the positivist understanding of human history as a progression from primitivism (associated with African and, to a lesser extent, Asian cultures) to civilization (defined in thoroughly Eurocentric terms). In addition to "legitimizing" the academic study of African American culture, the new anthropology provided the groundwork for the mythological sensibility of American modernists, including T. S. Eliot and Hilda Doolittle (H. D.). Hurston—like other women modernists, most notably H. D. and Virginia Woolf—emphasized the affirmative potential of myth rather than the unbridgeable gap between contemporaneity and antiquity: *Their Eyes Were Watching God* provides continuing commentary on the protagonist, Janie's, experiences through the Babylonian myth of Ishtar and Tammuz, the Greek myth of Aphrodite and Adonis, and the Egyptian myth of Isis and Osiris.

Hurston's willingness to assume a variety of masks reflects her radically Afrocentric sensibility. Like the African American folk communities she both participated in and studied, Hurston repudiated, usually tacitly, all attempts to impose a controlling theoretical structure on an infinitely complex and ever-changing experience. The Afrocentric sensibility, which views all forms of energy as potentially useful, is manifested in two forms of syncretic religion known in its most visible variation as vodun: *Rada,* the "cool" form, and *Petro,* the "hot" form. Typically understood by Eurocentric commentators in terms of "white" and "black" "magic," *Rada* and *Petro* in fact represent two aspects of a larger system. The point is not to choose either *Rada* (loosely associated with the forces of balance and nonviolence) or *Petro* (loosely associated with the relatively extreme warrior energies), but to know when to employ each. In sharp contrast to the Judeo-Christian vision of a world that delineates good and evil forces, often associated respectively with terms such as "white, male, mind" and "black, female, body," the West African systems view all forms of energy as potentially available both to men and to women, although individuals or groups may develop particular energies more fully in response to the demands of their particular circumstances.

Hurston's "academic" investigations of vodun in the "Hoodoo" section of *Mules and Men* and *Tell My Horse,* along with the essays on black Christianity collected in *The Sanctified Church* (1983), remain the most important of the early works on the persistence of African philosophical concepts in black American culture. More important, an Afrocentric approach to Hurston clarifies, if it does not resolve, persistent questions concerning the way she represented her life in her many autobiographical texts; enriches the understanding of *Their Eyes Were Watching God* by shedding light on stylistic problems involving narrative technique; and acknowledges texts other than *Their Eyes Were Watching God*—particularly *Mules and Men, Moses, Man of the Mountain,* and *Seraph on the Suwanee* (1948)—as engaging, and perhaps major, works in the canon of a writer of infinite variety.

Consistent with the Afrocentrism of Hurston's work are the critical concepts derived from the African American musical tradition: the blues, gospel, and jazz impulses. The influence of jazz and blues on literature has come to be seen in terms not of specific forms but of impulses, processes capable of generating and expressing powerful insights grounded in, but not limited to, the African American experience—which writers like Hurston and Ellison understand as part of a dialectic with European-American history and processes. In the essay "Richard Wright's Blues" Ellison examines the blues as a way of defending one's experience against external attack, describing the blues as "an impulse to keep the painful details and episodes of a brutal experience alive in one's aching consciousness, to finger its jagged grain, and to transcend it, not by the consolation of philosophy but by squeezing from it a near-tragic, near-comic lyricism" (in *Shadow and Act,* New York, 1964). His classic definitions of blues and jazz impulses provide entry into specific aspects of Hurston's writing. Frequently focusing specifically on her experience as a black woman, Hurston created numerous blues texts, including the early short story "Isis" (published as "Drenched in Light" in *Opportunity* 2 [December 1924]), the autobiographical novel *Jonah's Gourd Vine* (1934; the frame story of *Mules and Men*), and *Their Eyes Were Watching God.*

Extending the integrity wrested from the blues process, the jazz impulse—which seeks to expand consciousness through a process of multicultural improvisation—provides an Afrocentric analog for aesthetic processes usually associated with modernism. If the blues assume their deepest significance when they elicit the recognition of individuals within the community (the listener-participants), jazz challenges the potential limitations inherent in the blues process, which may resist new perceptions. Many of Hurston's texts can be related directly to the jazz impulse as defined by Ellison in *Shadow and Act:*

> True jazz is an art of individual assertion within and against the group. Each true jazz moment (as distinct from the uninspired commercial performance) springs from a contest in which each artist challenges all the rest; each solo flight, or improvisation, represents (like the successive canvases of a painter) a definition of his identity: as individual, as member of the collectivity and as a link in the chain of tradition.

Improvising on the familiar African American analogy between the Hebrews in Egypt and the situation of blacks in slavery, *Moses, Man of the Mountain* redefines the tradition to incorporate Hurston's meditations on the metaphysical and psychological complexity of the mythmaking process. An example of Hurston's jazz modernism, *Seraph on the Suwanee* begins as a conventional Freudian analysis of a repressed white woman's psychology, but ultimately subverts the Freudian perspective by juxtaposing it with African American traditions of masking.

While the blues and jazz impulses are well-established frameworks for interpreting the work of black writers from Langston Hughes through Gwendolyn Brooks and Ralph Ellison to Toni Morrison, the equivalent, and in some ways more fundamental, importance of "the gospel impulse" has received less attention, although recent literary critics and historians have begun to recognize that fundamental elements of African American secular culture—the blues and jazz impulses—have their roots in an essentially religious sensibility. Because it developed in the black church—the institutional space furthest removed from the attention and mediation of whites—gospel music provided the African American community with a forum for developing appropriate expressions of its experience with relative autonomy. Grounded in Afrocentric values, the gospel impulse refuses to accept, though it has always felt the effects of, the oppositional structures of the European-American analytical tradition. Entirely aware that most whites, because they accept the validity of binary structures without question, behave as if they are "devils," the gospel impulse, like feminist modernism, maintains a strongly affirmative cast, holding out the possibility of universal salvation. As Hurston's investigations of the black church suggest, the gospel impulse contains the clearest traces of an African sensibility that, while not an absolute alternative to the European-American context that has unquestionably influenced its specific form, certainly keeps alive the concept of difference from and within the white world. On the most fundamental level, this affirmative core of the gospel impulse informs almost every aspect of Hurston's sensibility. Her scholarship—particularly the essays "Characteristics of Negro Expression," "The Sermon," and "Spirituals and Neo-Spirituals," published in Nancy Cunard's 1934 anthology *Negro*—identifies the specific ways in which African expression passed into African American aesthetic forms through the mediation of the black church.

Emphasizing the call-and-response dynamic, Hurston isolated the single most important difference between European-American aesthetics, which typically approach artistic creation as a matter of individual genius, and African American aesthetics, which view creative power in Afrocentric terms as an inevitable and empowering collaboration between artist and audience. The surprising (from a European-American perspective) optimism of most of Hurston's resolutions stems in large part from her gospel-based faith in call and response. However intense the seeming isolation of an individual such as Janie in *Their Eyes Were Watching God* or Arvay Henson in *Seraph on the Suwanee,* it is always possible to survive and triumph by articulating one's experience—issuing a blues call—that elicits the recognition and assent—the gospel response—of an audience, thereby creating a new, jazz, version of reality capable of eliminating or reducing the isolation fundamental to the despair articulated by so many modernists writing in the wake of Eliot.

While Hurston's novels are clearly influenced by the blues, jazz, and gospel impulses, the prose of her formal autobiography, *Dust Tracks on a Road,* seems relatively flat in comparison. Its reception was uniformly unfavorable, and it has frustrated as many readers as it has enlightened. Unreliable as a source of purely factual information, *Dust Tracks on a Road* both seems politically quiescent and reveals almost nothing of the motivations behind Hurston's controversial actions, though it attempts to create a new type of black woman's narrative demanding a specifically public, and decisively autonomous, persona. Hurston presents her life as a self-motivated escape from the forces that would limit her, whether imposed by blacks or whites. Ironically, the original publisher of *Dust Tracks on a Road* eliminated or required substantial revision of three chapters included in the original manuscript. Restored in the 1984 reprint edition, the original version of "My People, My People!" and "Seeing the World as It

Is" reflect a much sharper political awareness than anything included in the first published version.

Because *Dust Tracks on a Road* evades or misrepresents certain facts of Hurston's life—her birthdate is the most famous example—Robert Hemenway's definitive *Zora Neale Hurston: A Literary Biography* (1977) is of inestimable value. The first fully realized biography of an African American woman writer, Hemenway's book does an admirable job of untangling the factual evidence concerning Hurston's life and identifying unresolved biographical issues. Although Hemenway had chosen, largely on the basis of the chronological structure of *Dust Tracks on a Road,* 1901 as Hurston's likely birth date, a subsequently discovered birth certificate verifies the date as 7 January 1891. The difference in those ten years is significant. Although Hurston presented herself as a relatively naive "girl" in her early twenties when she arrived in New York, she had in fact already accumulated a great deal of experience. In addition, the discovery of Hurston's birth date creates a somewhat different image of her childhood experiences.

Hurston's parents were John Hurston, a preacher who served as moderator of the South Florida Baptist Convention, and Lucy Hurston, whom Zora remembered as an image of female strength. Hurston records her youth in relatively pastoral terms, emphasizing the unified consciousness she developed growing up in all-black Eatonville, although her mother Lucy's death while Hurston was in her teens became a recurrent theme in her imaginative re-creations of childhood. Responding to her mother's deathbed instructions, Hurston sought to prevent the adults from carrying out two traditional death-room ceremonies: removing the pillow from the head of the dying (to soften the passing), and covering the clocks and mirrors (to prevent the reflection of the corpse from attaching itself). Against the wishes of both Lucy and Zora, the community carried out both rituals. The conflict, which greatly disturbed Zora, seems to have precipitated the decay of her relationship with her natal community. The tension following her father's remarriage to a woman who was hostile to Zora culminated in her departure from Eatonville, sometime around 1910.

In many ways *Jonah's Gourd Vine* provides more insight into Hurston's childhood than *Dust Tracks on a Road.* Written in a little over two months during 1933, her first novel is autobiographical in terms of character rather than plot. Focusing on the relationship between the black preacher John Pearson and his wife, Lucy Potts, *Jonah's Gourd Vine* reflects Hurston's ambivalent response to her father and the Eatonville community. Throughout the novel, John Pearson speaks in a voice resonant with the rhythms and images of the African American sermon. A nearly verbatim transcription of a sermon Hurston was given by the Reverend C. C. Lovelace, the sermon John delivers when his philandering comes under attack from his congregation, is a masterful performance and a celebration of the profound impression that the power and beauty of the black folk tradition made on Hurston's developing aesthetic consciousness. On the other hand, Hurston cannot simply excuse John's hypocrisy, which contributes directly to the death of Lucy, whose superior social and psychological intelligence provides the foundation of her husband's career. Nor does Hurston present a simplistically affirmative image of the black community. Highlighting the potential limitations of the call-and-response dynamic, Hurston's ironic introduction to John's sermon indicates her awareness that a powerful enough individual voice can manipulate the communal response in a way destructive to individual freedom: "The audience sang with him. They always sang with him well because group singers follow the leader" (p. 269). Although most critics consider the contradiction between John's eloquence and his lack of self-understanding an aesthetic fault, the tension expresses one of

Hurston's dominant feminist themes: the hypocritical divergence of public profession and personal action, condoned in males but condemned in women. Like Hurston's own early life, *Jonah's Gourd Vine* suggests that if a Southern black woman is to reconcile herself with, and draw on, her folk heritage, she must be able to sing her own (blues) song and define her own (jazz) reality.

From the mid 1910s until her 1925 arrival in Harlem, Hurston developed the wide understanding of American cultural psychology that provided the foundation for her public personae. After a period during which she lived with various relatives, Hurston spent over a year traveling with a theatrical troupe—no doubt one source of her dramatic flair—before enrolling in Baltimore's Morgan Academy (the high school division of what is now Morgan State University) in 1917. Subsequently she studied at Howard University, where she compiled an erratic academic record but established important contacts with the black poet and playwright Georgia Douglas Johnson and Alain Locke, probably the most influential scholar-critic of the Harlem Renaissance era. Encouraged by her teachers, Hurston submitted a short story ("Spunk") and a play (*Drenched in Light*) to the 1925 literary competition sponsored by *Opportunity* magazine. Both submissions won prizes, preparing the way for Hurston's move to New York. There she worked as a secretary for white novelist Fannie Hurst while beginning graduate study at Barnard under Boas and Benedict, both affiliated with the anthropology department at Columbia.

Drawing on a decade's more personal experience than her New York associates realized, Hurston used her well-developed understanding of social psychology, complemented by her flashy style of dress and her unmatched storytelling ability, to emerge rapidly as a leading figure in the Harlem Renaissance. Proclaiming herself "the Queen of the Niggerati," Hurston contributed stories and essays to magazines and anthologies, including Locke's influential the *New Negro* (1925) and the short-lived *Fire!!*, intended by its co-editors, Hurston, Langston Hughes, and Wallace Thurman, as the journal of the "radical" younger Renaissance writers. As she was to do throughout her life, Hurston alternately charmed and annoyed black associates. Thurman's novel *Infants of the Spring* includes a thinly-disguised, scathing portrait of Hurston as Sweetie May Carr, a charlatan whose success rests entirely on her willingness to play to white expectations. Nonetheless, Hurston's knowledge of white psychology enabled her to enjoy almost unbroken success in charming white Renaissance figures, including Carl Van Vechten and, crucially, Charlotte Osgood Mason, whom she met in December 1927.

The next five years of Hurston's life revolved around her relationship with her literary patron, Mrs. Mason. Less directly, Hurston's relationship with Mrs. Mason contributed to the fiasco surrounding the folk drama *Mule Bone*, which lead to the irreparable breach of her friendship with Langston Hughes. Sharing an interest in folk materials, the two writers had begun collaborating on the play in 1930. Competing obligations and a growing tension over the role of Hughes's friend Louise Thompson, whom Hurston viewed simply as a secretary, brought the active collaboration to an end with no finished product. But the following year Hughes discovered that a production of *Mule Bone* was scheduled for Cleveland's Karamu House theater, crediting Hurston with sole authorship. Perhaps because of the communal origins of the material, Hurston seems never to have been seriously concerned with the question of plagiarism.

Throughout the period of her financial relationship with Mrs. Mason, which lasted until September 1932, Hurston's energies centered on re-establishing contact with the Southern black culture she had left behind while concentrating on her entry into African American literary life. Already experiencing the tension between her roles as academic expert and member of the folk community, Hurston entered into an agreement with Mrs. Mason that provided her with financial support but compelled her to surrender control of her findings to her patron. This was particularly problematic since Mrs. Mason resisted "creative" use of "scientific" findings, intending instead to use Hurston's research as documentation for her own beliefs concerning the "primitive" nature of black character and culture. As a result, the materials Hurston gathered on several trips to Florida and New Orleans became the source of continuing tension before they were finally published in *Mules and Men* in 1935. Her subsequent trips through both the American South and the Caribbean provided Hurston with the material published in *Tell My Horse* (1938), the first substantial inquiry into vodun undertaken by an African American scholar.

Despite Mrs. Mason's reluctance, both *Mules and Men* and the folk pageant presented under the titles *The Great Day* (1932), *From Sun to Sun* (1933), and *Singing Steel* (1934) are important literary adaptations of the folk materials Hurston both remembered and collected. Structured around a day at a railroad camp, *The Great Day* presents folklore as a crucial part of everyday black life in the South. Well received by audiences in both the North and the South, the pageant was largely responsible for Hurston's short-term employment as a teacher of drama at Bethune-Cookman College and the North Carolina College for Negroes in Durham, where she participated in a workshop directed by the Pulitzer Prize–winning playwright Paul Green. Part autobiographical novel and part folklore anthology, *Mules and Men* presents approximately seventy different examples of African American folklore, including spirituals, sermons, animal tales, and jokes. The core of the book, however, is its portrayal of the African American folk process. Presenting herself alternately as observer and participant, Hurston delineates the problems faced by an educated black woman attempting to re-establish contact with her folk heritage. Demonstrating her ability to speak in a "black" voice and her knowledge of folk traditions, Hurston's protagonist, Zora, gradually overcomes the community's distrust and suspicion.

At times, the characters in *Mules and Men* specify their understanding of the meaning of a particular story; more frequently, they offer another story as implied commentary on the first. As narrator, Zora assumes a similar role, juxtaposing male and female or secular and sacred perspectives to suggest the range of resources available in the tradition as a whole. Dspite her understanding, however, Zora's re-integration assumes, from the perspective of a significant part of the community, what amounts to a white role. Both its complex engagement with the role of women in the folk process and its far-reaching influence make *Mules and Men* an underappreciated classic of the African American tradition.

Written during a seven-week period in 1936 while Hurston was in Haiti to investigate vodun, *Their Eyes Were Watching God* has long been recognized as Hurston's most important contribution to African American literature. Until recently, however, even the novel's defenders viewed it in radically simplified terms. In a generally favorable review of the first edition, black poet-scholar Sterling Brown saw *Their Eyes Were Watching God* as a folk romance, praising Hurston's ear for dialect but questioning her "evasion" of political concerns. Most early academic critics emphasized Hurston's romantic regionalism, identifying Janie's search for "the right man" as Hurston's central concern. Following her unsuccessful attempts to find happiness through sexuality with Johnny Taylor, security with Logan Killicks, and prestige with Joe (Jody) Starks, Janie fulfills her destiny as a woman when she discovers sexual fulfillment, adventure, and true love with Tea Cake. Despite their extreme limitations, such early readings contributed one important element to a fuller understanding of *Their Eyes Were Watching God:* by emphasizing the theme of frustrated desire they recognize the lyrical quality of Hurston's style. Specific clusters of resonant images express the development of Janie's consciousness. Her vision of the pear tree in bloom sounds the theme of developing sexuality later associated with Janie's hair. The images of the mule and the porch—associated loosely with the head rags that restrain Janie's hair (which she burns immediately after Joe's funeral)—represent both social prestige and limitation. Associated with Tea Cake and his imaginary guitar, the image of the horizon represents the fulfillment that Janie seeks.

The problem with the early readings, of course, is that they reduce the meaning of fulfillment to a sexist cliché. During the late 1970s and early 1980s black women readers, including June Jordan, Mary Helen Washington, and Alice Walker, along with white feminist critics such as Missy Dehn Kubitschek, began to focus attention on the usually implicit sexism of interpretations that attributed Janie's success to Tea Cake. Although he does not share the condescending attitude of critics such as Darwin Turner, who conflate Hurston's personality with her aesthetics, Hemenway (1977) expresses a common judgment when he argues that the ending of *Their Eyes Were Watching God* "seems poorly plotted, and the narration shifts awkwardly from first to third person" (p. 233). In fact, both problems can be resolved by placing Janie, redefined as questing heroine, at the center of the novel. Everything in her environment discourages her from setting out on her own to attain the wisdom necessary for the fulfillment of her psyche and her community. Probably the most frequently cited passage in *Their Eyes Were Watching God* is the limiting vision expressed—for historically understandable reasons—by Janie's grandmother. Insisting that Janie choose safety rather than adventure, Nanny says, "De nigger woman is de mule uh de world so fur as Ah can see" (p. 29). Less frequently cited, however, is the final line of Nanny's speech, which articulates the desire ultimately pursued by both Janie and Hurston: "Ah been prayin' fuh it tuh be different wid you" (p. 29).

Recognizing Hurston's desire for change transforms *Their Eyes Were Watching God* into a classic quest story in which Janie encounters a variety of trials, from the traditional patriarchy of Logan to the frustration of human desire in the face of incomprehensible and irresistible forces represented by the hurricane. Returning from her quest, Janie assumes the role of blues singer—recounting her own brutal experiences in a voice testifying to her survival—and of African storyteller, or griot—the repository of communal wisdom and experience. Encouraging Pheoby to pass the story on to the other members of the community, Janie encourages her friend to embark on her own quest: "It's uh known fact, Pheoby, you got tuh *go* there tuh *know* there" (p. 31). Similar readings of *Their Eyes Were Watching God* have quite justifiably resulted in Hurston's belated recognition as a major figure in the feminist literary tradition.

While African American critic Robert Stepto praises Janie's first-person voice but criticizes the third-person sections as a refusal to give Janie ultimate control of her own story, critics building on feminist readings—most notably Michael Awkward, John Callahan, and John Kalb—have demonstrated that the third-person voice in *Their Eyes Were Watching God* is neither "objective" nor static. Rather, it shifts emotional and intellectual distance in response to the particular events Janie recounts. Just as Janie's interaction with Pheoby presents a model of call and response within the text, Hurston's manipulation of the relationship between the vernacular first-person and the relatively formal third-person voices reflects her continuing concern with the problem of how the educated, and to some extent deracinated, black person (Hurston as novelist) can respond most appropriately to the call of the communal experience (Janie as griot).

As Kalb observes, the final passage of the novel resolves this tension stylistically by merging the rhythms and imagery of the vernacular tradition with the standard English diction of Hurston's frame:

> Then Tea Cake came prancing around her where she was and the song of the sigh flew out of the window and lit in the top of the pine trees. Tea Cake, with the sun for a shawl. Of course he wasn't dead. He could never be dead until she herself had finished feeling and thinking. The kiss of his memory made pictures of love and light against the wall. Here was peace. She pulled in her horizon like a great fish-net. Pulled it from around the waist of the world and draped it over her shoulder. So much of life in its meshes! She called in her soul to come and see. (p. 286)

Both the sound and the vision of this passage are profoundly Afrocentric. Hurston assumes a fundamental West African position by asserting that Tea Cake is not dead. Rather, his energies have merged with Janie's; he lives in the voice of the griots—Janie and Hurston—and therefore continues to participate in the African American community, which distinguishes far less sharply than its white equivalent between life and death, male and female, past, present, and future.

Afrocentric concepts also help resolve several difficulties encountered by critics attempting to use *Their Eyes Were Watching God* as support for feminist paradigms derived primarily from Eurocentric materials. Many feminist critics have been bothered by the scene in which, following a temporary estrangement, Janie allows Tea Cake to beat her. Like the scenes in which the community uses physical violence to expel the color-struck Turners from its midst, the beating, from an Afrocentric perspective, represents the use of extreme energies in a time of crisis. Emphasizing that both Janie and Tea Cake are capable of, and willing to use, physical force, Hurston does not encourage the use of violence as a primary response to conflict, but rather she acknowledges its reality—a basic aspect of the blues impulse—and insists that its significance cannot be divorced from its actual context. Repeatedly, she treats violence as part of a process leading to the re-establishment of a balance in which neither "masculine" nor "feminine" energies—understood as profoundly interdependent—must be denied by either men or women. However uncomfortable the beating scene may seem, its presence is not fundamentally inconsistent with Hurston's Afrocentric vision.

Following the publication of *Their Eyes Were Watching God,* Hurston's career entered a period of gradual decline complicated by poor health, increasing financial difficulties, and widespread criticism of both her personal and political life. Recalling the ambivalence and hostility of her Harlem Renaissance associates, much of the personal criticism reflected a double standard concerning "acceptable" behavior for men and women. Hurston, who had been married briefly to her lifelong friend Herbert Sheen in the late 1920s, remarried in 1939. Like the first marriage, her marriage to Albert Price III was short-lived. The fact that Price was nearly a quarter-century younger than Hurston fueled criticism of Hurston as a sexual predator. More damaging was her 1948 arrest on charges—subsequently discredited—that she had committed immoral acts with a ten-year-old boy. Widely publicized in the black press, the charges were among the final events that motivated Hurston's withdrawal from African American literary life during the 1950s.

In addition, Hurston assumed a variety of unpopular political stances. Consistently supporting conservative—sometimes segregationist—political candidates, Hurston questioned the wisdom of the Supreme Court's landmark *Brown* v. *Board of Education* decision in 1954. Hemenway's cogent discussion of her political stance during this period emphasizes three crucial factors: her extreme individualism; her deep suspicion of left-wing politics, which found support in the hysteria of the McCarthy era;

and, most importantly, her belief in the cultural self-sufficiency of the African American community. Like the cultural nationalists of the Black Arts Movement of the 1960s, Hurston saw no benefit in integration into a morally and aesthetically impoverished white middle-class society.

Faced by widespread hostility and lacking any supportive intellectual community, Hurston moved permanently to Florida in late 1949. There she supported herself through manual labor, public assistance, and occasional journalistic writing assignments until her death on 28 January 1960, less than a year after she had suffered a debilitating stroke. Although the final two decades of her life were a time of increasing hardship, Hurston continued to write, publishing numerous journalistic articles and reviews; a half-dozen short stories; *Dust Tracks on a Road;* and two important but still undervalued novels, *Moses, Man of the Mountain* (1939) and *Seraph on the Suwanee* (1948). During the final decade of her life, she worked on several novels, one focusing on the experience of the black bourgeoisie, and a revisionist biography of Herod the Great.

Grounded in both the jazz impulse and experimental modernism, *Moses, Man of the Mountain* and *Seraph on the Suwanee* challenge readers to abandon preconceptions concerning the form and subject matter of African American fiction. If approached with conventional expectations, both novels seem seriously flawed. Typically read as a somewhat simplistic allegory, *Moses, Man of the Mountain* explores the relationship between the African American experience and that of the Hebrews in Egypt. Part political leader and part conjure man, Moses experiences the frustrations of attempting to shape an oppressed and demoralized people into a powerful, self-reliant nation. Unlike the Biblical Moses, however, Hurston's Moses is not by birth a member of the community he leads out of bondage. Rather he is a member of the Egyptian nobility who is transformed first into a Hebrew and then into a Hebrew leader by the mythmaking powers of Miriam and Jethro. The phrase "I AM WHAT I AM" reveals the importance of Hurston's confrontation with the inherently ambiguous substructure of cultural mythology. Drawing on his profound knowledge of the natural and supernatural forces—from an Afrocentric perspective there is no real distinction between the two—Moses uses beliefs, as much as material forces, to restructure political reality.

Anticipating Hurston's political positions of the 1950s, *Moses, Man of the Mountain* suggests that the key to meaningful progress for African Americans lies in a belief in their own power rather than in alteration of their institutional context. Sounding the jazz/modernist theme of the isolation of the artist who redefines the mythology, and therefore the reality, of a community, Hurston summons the rhythms of the gospel preacher in her description of Moses as an artist who gradually assumes power over and responsibility for his own mythology. Like Hurston, he is suspended between cultures, confronting the beauty and terror of self-creation.

Certainly the least understood of her published works, *Seraph on the Suwanee* makes it clear how far Hurston had crossed over into a territory unfamiliar to the vast majority of her potential readers, white or black. Focusing on the relationship between two white Floridians, Jim and Arvay Henson, *Seraph on the Suwanee* has continued to disturb readers who assume that black novelists should write primarily about "the black experience." Application of Freudian psychology to Arvay's repressed sexuality, which contributes to the death of her first son and to a growing estrangement from her sexually vital and culturally adventurous husband, contributes directly to a crucial misreading of the significance of African American traditions in the novel. Highly aware of the use of stereotypical masks to deflect attention away from subversive subtexts, Hurston creates a dense and shifting rhetorical texture that challenges readers to abandon preconceptions concerning the desirability of a unified or theoretically consistent narrative voice. Repeatedly, she presents black characters in the process of altering their behavior in the presence of whites. Over two dozen passages in the novel explicitly state that a character—usually Arvay—has failed to understand a joke. Much of Hurston's positive portrayal of Jim Henson—which has been deeply disturbing to feminist readers—derives precisely from the fact that he is able to interact with his black friends without social or cultural pretensions and therefore can comprehend the "masked" levels of African American humor. Supporting this theme with a radically open style, Hurston implicates her readers in a situation analagous to that of Arvay and Jim. Those who remain unaware of the (culturally, though not necessarily racially, specific) black humor framing the main plot resemble Arvay, who until the final sections is able to see only the conventional white surface of reality. Readers sharing Hurston's awareness of the ways in which the oral tradition encourages a constantly shifting rhetorical perspective will be much more likely to appreciate the metahumor pervading the novel.

Although *Seraph on the Suwanee* includes few pieces of "authentic" folklore, it participates deeply in the folk process, assuming various perspectives to provide a running commentary on the foibles of human behavior. What academic critics typically describe as uncontrolled irony or simply bad writing—writing that does not accept the Jamesian preference for a theoretically consistent aesthetic—is for Hurston the sound of process, understood simultaneously in folk and modernist terms. Read with an emphasis on process and an awareness of the multiple levels of its humor, *Seraph on the Suwanee* metamorphoses into a comic master piece. Far from an artistic failure reflecting Hurston's declining powers, the concluding reconciliation between Jim and Arvay expresses the gospel impulse, the deeply Afrocentric belief that whatever the degree of their apparent discord, competing energies can be restored to harmony.

Hurston permitted no theory—Freudian, Jamesian, Marxist, or feminist—to distract her from this vital process. To accept fixation, as Wanda Coleman (1988) observed in a meditation on the black woman as jazz artist, is to accept death. In *Seraph on the Suwanee,* as in *Their Eyes Were Watching God, Mules and Men,* and *Moses, Man of the Mountain,* Zora Neale Hurston commits her energies to life, to process. Like African American jazz artists from Duke Ellington to Billie Holiday, like literary modernists from H. D. to James Joyce, like the African American women who celebrate her passage, Hurston is still teaching us how to respond to her call.

Selected Bibliography

PRIMARY WORKS

NOVELS

Jonah's Gourd Vine. Philadelphia: J. B. Lippincott, 1934. Reprinted with an introduction by Larry Neal, 1971. Reprinted with a foreword by Rita Dove and an afterword by Henry Louis Gates. New York: Harper & Row, 1990.

Their Eyes Were Watching God. Philadelphia: J. B. Lippincott, 1937. Reprinted Urbana: University of Illinois Press, 1978. Reprinted with a foreword by Mary Helen Washington and an afterword by Henry Louis Gates. New York: Harper & Row, 1990.

Moses, Man of the Mountain. Philadelphia: J. B. Lippincott, 1939. Reprinted Urbana: University of Illinois Press, 1984.

Seraph on the Suwanee. New York: Scribners, 1948.

FOLKLORE

Mules and Men. Philadelphia: J. B. Lippincott, 1935. Reprinted with a foreword by Arnold Rampersad and an afterword by Henry Louis Gates. New York: Harper & Row, 1990.

Tell My Horse. Philadelphia: J. B. Lippincott, 1938. Reprinted with a foreword by Ishmael Reed and an afterword by Henry Louis Gates. New York: Harper & Row, 1990.

AUTOBIOGRAPHY

Dust Tracks on a Road. Philadelphia: J. B. Lippincott, 1942. 2nd ed. Urbana: University of Illinois Press, 1984.

ANTHOLOGIES

I Love Myself When I Am Laughing . . . and Then Again When I Am Looking Mean and Impressive: A Zora Neale Hurston Reader. Edited by Alice Walker. With an introduction by Mary Helen Washington. Old Westbury, N.Y.: Feminist Press, 1979.

The Sanctified Church. Berkeley, Calif.: Turtle Island Foundation, 1983.

Spunk: The Selected Short Stories of Zora Neale Hurston. Berkeley, Calif.: Turtle Island Foundation, 1985.

NONFICTION

Negro: An Anthology. Edited by Nancy Cunard. London: Wishart, 1934. Reprint, edited and abridged by Hugh Ford. New York: Frederick Ungar, 1970. Includes Hurston's essays "Characteristics of Negro Expression," "The Sermon," and "Spirituals and Neo-Spirituals."

SECONDARY WORKS

BIOGRAPHICAL AND CRITICAL STUDIES

Awkward, Michael. *Inspiriting Influences: Tradition, Revision, and Afro-American Women's Novels.* New York: Columbia University Press, 1989.

Baker, Houston. *Blues, Ideology, and Afro-American Literature: A Vernacular Theory.* Chicago: University of Chicago Press, 1984.

Barthold, Bonnie J. *Black Time: Fiction of Africa, the Caribbean, and the United States.* New Haven, Conn.: Yale University Press, 1981.

Bell, Bernard W. *The Afro-American Novel and Its Tradition.* Amherst: University of Massachusetts Press, 1987.

Bone, Robert. *The Negro Novel in America.* Rev. ed. New Haven, Conn.: Yale University Press, 1965.

Brown, Sterling A. "Luck Is a Fortune." *Nation,* 16 October 1937, pp. 409–410.

Callahan, John F. *In the African-American Grain: The Pursuit of Voice in Twentieth-Century Black Fiction.* Urbana: University of Illinois Press, 1988.

Christian, Barbara. *Black Women Novelists: The Development of a Tradition, 1892–1976.* Westport, Conn.: Greenwood Press, 1980.

Cooke, Michael G. *Afro-American Literature in the Twentieth Century: The Achievment of Intimacy.* New Haven, Conn.: Yale University Press, 1984.

Dearborn, Mary. *Pocahontas's Daughters: Gender and Ethnicity in American Culture.* New York: Oxford University Press, 1986.

Dixon, Melvin. *Ride Out the Wilderness: Geography and Identity in Afro-American Literature.* Urbana: University of Illinois Press, 1987.

DuPlessis, Rachel Blau. *Writing Beyond the Ending: Narrative Strategies of Twentieth-Century Women Writers.* Bloomington: Indiana University Press, 1985.

Ellison, Ralph. "Recent Negro Fiction." *New Masses* 40:22–26 (5 August 1941).

Gates, Henry Louis. *The Signifying Monkey: A Theory of Afro-American Literary Criticism.* New York: Oxford University Press, 1988.

Gayle, Addison, Jr. *The Way of the New World: The Black Novel in America.* Garden City, N.Y.: Doubleday/Anchor, 1975.

Hemenway, Robert. *Zora Neale Hurston: A Literary Biography.* Urbana: University of Illinois Press, 1977.

———. "Are You a Flying Lark or a Setting Dove?" In *Afro-American Literature: The Reconstruction of Instruction.* Edited by Robert B. Stepto and Dexter Fisher. New York: Modern Language Association, 1979.

Holloway, Karla F. C. *The Character of the Word: The Texts of Zora Neale Hurston.* Westport, Conn.: Greenwood Press, 1987.

Howard, Lillie P. *Zora Neale Hurston.* Boston: Twayne, 1980.

———. "Zora Neale Hurston." In *Dictionary of Literary Biography: Afro-American Writers from the Harlem Renaissance to 1940.* Vol. 51. Edited by Trudier Harris. Detroit: Bruccoli Clark, 1987.

Hughes, Carl Milton. *The Negro Novelist: 1940–1950.* New York: Citadel Press, 1953.

Jackson, Blyden. "Introduction." In Hurston's *Moses, Man of the Mountain.* Urbana: University of Illinois Press, 1984.

Johnson, Barbara. *A World of Difference.* Baltimore, Md.: Johns Hopkins University Press, 1987.

Jordan, Jennifer. "Feminist Fantasies: Zora Neale Hurston's *Their Eyes Were Watching God.*" *Tulsa Studies in Women's Literature* 7(1):105–117 (Spring 1988).

Jordan, June. "Notes Toward a Black Balancing of Love and Hatred." In her *Civil Wars.* Boston: Beacon Press, 1981.

Kalb, John D. "The Anthropological Narrator of Hurston's *Their Eyes Were Watching God.*" *Studies in American Fiction* 16(2):169–180 (Autumn 1988).

Kubitschek, Missy Dehn. " 'Tuh de Horizon and Back': The Female Quest in *Their Eyes Were Watching God.*" *Black American Literature Forum* 17(3):109–115 (Fall 1983).

McKay, Nellie Y. "Race, Gender, and Cultural Context in Zora Neale Hurston's *Dust Tracks on a Road.*" In *Life/Lines: Theorizing Women's Autobiography.* Edited by Bella Brodski and Celeste M. Schenck. Ithaca, N.Y.: Cornell University Press, 1988.

Pondrom, Cyrena N. "The Role of Myth in Hurston's *Their Eyes Were Watching God.*" *American Literature* 58(2):181–202 (May 1986).

Schraufnagel, Noel. *From Apology to Protest: The Black American Novel.* Deland, Fla.: Everett, Edwards, 1973.

Sheffey, Ruthe T., ed. *A Rainbow Round Her Shoulder: Zora Neale Hurston Symposium Papers.* Baltimore, Md.: Morgan State University Press, 1982.

———. "Zora Neale Hurston's *Moses, Man of the Mountain:* A Fictionalized Manifesto on the Imperatives of Black Leadership." *CLA Journal* 29(2):206–220 (December, 1985).

Stepto, Robert. *From Behind the Veil: A Study of Afro-American Narrative.* Urbana: University of Illinois Press, 1979.

Turner, Darwin. *In a Minor Chord: Three Afro-American Writers and Their Search for Identity.* Carbondale: Southern Illinois University Press, 1971.

Walker, Alice. *In Search of Our Mother's Gardens: Womanist Prose.* New York: Harcourt Brace Jovanovich, 1983.

Walker, S. Jay. "Zora Neale Hurston's *Their Eyes Were Watching God:* Black Novel of Sexism." *Modern Fiction Studies* 20: 519–528 (Winter 1974–1975).

Wall, Cheryl A. "Zora Neale Hurston: Changing Her Own Words." In *American Novelists Revisited: Essays in Feminist Criticism.* Edited by Fritz Fleischmann. Boston: G. K. Hall, 1982. Pp. 371–389.

Washington, Mary Helen. *Invented Lives: Narratives of Black Women, 1860–1960.* Garden City, N.Y.: Doubleday/Anchor, 1987.

Watson, Carol McAlpine. *Prologue: The Novels of Black American Women, 1891–1965.* Westport, Conn.: Greenwood Press, 1985.

Willis, Susan. *Specifying: Black Women Writing the American Experience.* Madison: University of Wisconsin Press, 1987.

Wright, Richard. "Between Laughter and Tears." *New Masses* 25(2):22–25 (5 October 1937).

BIBLIOGRAPHIES

Dance, Daryl C. "Zora Neale Hurston." In *American Women Writers: Bibliographical Essays.* Edited by Maurice Duke, Jackson R. Bryer, and M. Thomas Inge. Westport, Conn.: Greenwood Press, 1983.

Newson, Adele S. *Zora Neale Hurston: A Reference Guide.* Boston: G. K. Hall, 1987.

Werner, Craig. *Black American Women Novelists: An Annotated Bibliography.* Pasadena, Calif.: Salem Press, 1989.

CRAIG WERNER

SARAH ORNE JEWETT

1849–1909

"ONE MAY TRAVEL at home in a most literal sense," declared Sarah Orne Jewett in 1892, "and be always learning history, geography, botany, or biography—whatever one chooses." Coming a generation after Thoreau's more famous assertion "I have travelled a good deal in Concord," Jewett's comment in "Looking Back on Girlhood" (1892) is compelling because of what it suggests about her literary identity and situation. A Victorian lady by numerous accounts, a turn-of-the-century New Woman in many respects, and a local colorist by reputation, Jewett nevertheless retained a New Englander's firm foundation in the literary romanticism of Thoreau, Emerson, and Hawthorne.

Four years after extolling the virtues of traveling widely in a small space, that foundation would be placed on display in a pivotal moment of vision in *The Country of the Pointed Firs* (1896), the work that nearly a century of popular and critical response has embraced as Jewett's masterpiece. A delicately connected series of sketches narrated by a summer visitor to a village on the Maine coast, *Pointed Firs* is vintage Jewett in its deft interweaving of tales of excursions, visits, eccentrics, and elderly women, quiet comedy, and the simple pleasures and inevitable privations of rural life. Early in the narrative the visitor and her gregarious, herb-gathering landlady, Mrs. Todd, sail to Green Island, Mrs. Todd's birthplace and the home of her mother, Mrs. Blackett, and her painfully shy brother, William. Invited by William to explore the scenic highlight of Green Island, "the great ledge," the narrator treks with him over "a piece of rough pasture" through which "ran a huge shape of stone like the great backbone of an enormous creature." She continues:

> At the end, near the woods, we could climb up on it and walk along to the highest point; there above the circle of pointed firs we could look down over all the island, and could see the ocean that circled this and a hundred other bits of island ground, the mainland shore and all the far horizons. It gave a sudden sense of space, for nothing stopped the eye or hedged one in,—that sense of liberty in space and time which great prospects always give.
>
> "There ain't no such view in the world, I expect," said William proudly, and I hastened to speak my heartfelt tribute of praise; it was impossible not to feel as if an untraveled boy had spoken, and yet one loved to have him love his native heath.
>
> (pp. 70–71)

William's reverence for his "native heath" marks the passage as a species of the local-color literature produced chiefly by women writers and showcased by the *Atlantic Monthly* in the latter half of the nineteenth century. Still, the narrator's emphasis on vision—her reaching eye's search for "all the far horizons"—suggests that Jewett shared not only Thoreau's fondness for traveling at home but also Emerson's "eye" for the infinite. Given the preponderance of circles in the passage—"the circle of the pointed firs," "the ocean that circled this and a hundred other bits of island ground"—it seems useful to place Jewett together with Emerson, who titled one of his meditations on the expansiveness of the self "Circles" (1891) and began it thus: "The eye is the first circle; the horizon which it forms is the second; and throughout nature this primary figure is repeated without end."

The point of connecting Jewett to her romantic predecessors is to suggest that, like so many of her wandering narrators and characters, Jewett thoroughly explored all the literary possibilities—forms, genres, schools, tastes—

available to her in the cultural climate of late-nineteenth-century America, England, and Europe. She frequently invoked, for example, a dictum of the French realist Gustave Flaubert that she copied out and pinned up on the back of her writing desk: "*Écrire la vie ordinaire comme on écrit l'histoire*" (One should write of ordinary life as if one were writing history). However, in the early 1880s she complained to her friend and companion, Annie Fields, about William Dean Howells's rejection of one of her favorite stories, "A White Heron," when he was editor of the *Atlantic Monthly:* "Mr. Howells thinks that this age frowns upon the romantic, that it is no use to write romance any more; but dear me, how much of it there is left in every-day life after all. It must be the fault of the writers that such writing is dull."

A romantic realist or a realistic romantic, Jewett gently combs the quotidian to achieve an art whose calm surfaces obscure an undercurrent of power and passion, passions that may be glimpsed in isolated moments of communion or confession. In *Pointed Firs,* she suggests the psychocultural origins of her art of understatement, of repression and rare eruption: "Such is the hidden fire of enthusiasm in the New England nature that, once given an outlet, it shines forth with almost volcanic light and heat."

Whatever fires of enthusiasm may have smoldered within Jewett's own nature, her letters, biographies, and literary history have cultivated a decidedly temperate image of a charming, generous woman who lived and wrote in relative ease. The chief facts of her life are well known, but they are unlikely to satisfy the mdoern predilection for "light and heat." Theodora Sarah Orne Jewett was born on 3 September 1849 in South Berwick, Maine, the second of three daughters of Theodore H. Jewett, a country physician, and Caroline F. Perry, with whose father Dr. Jewett had studied medicine in Exeter, New Hampshire. The family was prosperous and stable, its fortune having been secured by Jewett's paternal grandfather, Captain Theodore F. Jewett, who enjoyed adventure on the sea in his youth and prosperity from it in his maturity, as he moved into shipping, shipbuilding, and the lucrative trade in the West Indies. Crucial as early models of storytelling and as sources of information on the industry that had been the economic lifeblood of her neighborhood, the captain and his colleagues are constantly refigured in Jewett's fiction and fondly recalled in "Looking Back on Girlhood" as robust men and lively raconteurs:

> My young ears were quick to hear the news of a ship's having come into port, and I delighted in the elderly captains, with their sea-tanned faces, who came to report upon their voyages, dining cheerfully and heartily with my grand father, who listened eagerly to their exciting tales of great storms on the Atlantic, and wind that blew them north-about, and good bargains in Havana, or Barbadoes [*sic*], or Havre.
>
> I listened as eagerly as any one; this is the charming way in which I was taught something of a fashion of life already on the wane, and of that subsistence upon sea and forest bounties which is now almost a forgotten thing in may part of New England.
>
> (*Uncollected Short Stories,* pp. 2–3)

Plagued in her youth—and, indeed, all her life—by arthritis and other illnesses, Jewett received a formal education at Miss Rayne's School and the Berwick Academy, but her attendance at both was fitful at best. Insisting somewhat disingenuously that she "had apparently not the slighest desire for learning," she confesses in "Looking Back on Girlhood" that she was prone to "instant drooping if ever I were shut up in school." The large library at home seems to have provoked no such ill effects, however, as her keen "appetite for knowledge" was satisfied by wide and eclectic reading. The bookish Dr. Jewett guided his daughter through the rigors of Laurence Sterne, Henry Fielding, Tobias Smollett, and Miguel de Cervantes, while her mother and grandmother led her into "the pleasant ways" of Jane Austen, George Eliot, and Mrs. Oliphant.

Reared on a literary inheritance both paternal and maternal, Jewett would retain all her life the patterns established in her early reading. Her letters are peppered with references to, on the one hand, Matthew Arnold, Alfred Tennyson, Leo Tolstoy, Ivan Turgenev, William Makepeace Thackeray, Henry Wadsworth Longfellow, John Greenleaf Whittier, and William James, and, on the other, to Harriet Beecher Stowe, Elizabeth Stuart Phelps, George Sand, Dorothy Wordsworth, and the wide circle of women writers and artists who were her most intimate friends. A letter of 1898 lovingly details a visit she and Annie Fields made to Haworth, home of the Brontë sisters, and marvels at their burning "their lights of genius like candles flaring in a cave, . . . shut up, captives and prisoners, in that gloomy old stone house." Jewett's sense of the Brontës' captivity is described in the same terms—"shut up"—as her own youthful confinement in the New England proprieties at Miss Rayne's School and the Berwick Academy. It is thus tempting to see in those childhood illnesses, vague in origin, something of the Brontës' romantic and feminist rebellion against the crippling circumstances of women's lives. Certainly she identified to some degree with their situation, insisting to her artist friend Sarah Wyman Whitman, "Nothing you ever read about them can make you know them until you go there."

For Jewett, though, the salubrious effects of salt air and country rambling more than compensated for the strictures of the schoolhouse. Dr. Jewett supplied his daughter with this "cure"—and it was an unconventional one in a culture that generally prescribed inactivity and confinement for girls and women inclined to be imaginative—by allowing her to accompany him on his rounds, experiences that Jewett always identified as essential in her development as a writer. Following her father about "like an undemanding little dog," she learned early the habits of empathy and observation that would serve her so well as an artist. She noticed that the doctor's "kind heart" and "the charm of his personality" did much to relieve his patients' anxieties; outdoors he would direct her attention "to certain points of interest in the character or surroundings of our acquaintances," to "the simple scenes close at hand."

Jewett's 1884 novel, *A Country Doctor,* pays tribute to the character and influence of her father, although, in a larger sense, her entire career in fiction and the aesthetic that shaped it show the profound and enduring marks of his presence. The doctor's daughter clearly believed that language was curative, and that the intense exchange of storytelling brought the teller and the listener into a deeper relationship with one another and with the world around them. In the mid 1890s, describing the relationship between writer and reader, Jewett even lapses into a doctor's vocabulary, telling Whitman (who functioned for her as an ideal reader):

> You bring something to the reading of a story that the story would go very lame without; but it is those unwritable things that the story holds in its heart, if it has any, that make the true soul of it, and these must be understood, and yet how many a story goes lame for lack of that understanding.
>
> (*The Letters of Sarah Orne Jewett,* ed. Fields, p. 112)

A good reader, it seems, is as much a doctor as a good writer is, saving a story from lameness or even, perhaps, a textual "heart" failure.

Jewett's publishing career straddled two centuries and spanned three and a half decades, and almost from the beginning she had her champions in New England's competitive literary marketplace. Drawn to writing early on—"I was still a child when I began to write down the things I was thinking about," she remarks in "Looking Back on Girlhood"—she placed her first story, "Jenny Garrow's Lovers," in *The Flag of Our Union* (18 January 1868), a Boston weekly, when she was just eighteen. Reticent and uncertain in her literary debut, Jewett experimented initially with pseudonyms (including

Alice Eliot, A. C. Eliot, and Sarah O. Sweet)—"I was very shy about speaking of my work at home"—and with plot and narrative devices that seem awkward and contrived. Publishing under "A. C. Eliot," the novice writer made a claim of kinship with George Eliot and even, acronymically, with *A*cton, *C*urrer, and *E*llis Bell. With its excessively melodramatic plot driven speedily forward by a love triangle, false imprisonment, and the heroine's untimely death, however, "Jenny Garrow's Lovers" suggests that Jewett had not yet realized the imaginative possibilities of "the simple scenes close at hand."

Nearly two years later, in "Mr. Bruce"—her first appearance in the *Atlantic Monthly* (December 1869)—Jewett was still struggling with her materials and her method. A comic rather than a tragic courtship tale, "Mr. Bruce" appropriates the mood of Jane Austen but not her mastery of form, as the story makes confusing use of both epistolary forms and tales within tales. Still, the American setting, the foregrounding of female friendships, and the attention given to storytelling as a social activity mark "Mr. Bruce" as a significant improvement over "Jenny Garrow."

In "The Girl with the Cannon Dresses" (*Riverside Magazine for Young Folks,* August 1870), Jewett published for the first time as "Sarah Jewett" and came closer to the "home" she would travel so widely in her career. Here, the figure of the summer visitor/narrator imbues the story with greater unity and a more confident tone, while the rural setting is credited with restoring the health of the ailing (Jewettian) Alice Channing. A wanderer and a reader, Alice, who describes herself as "'most eighteen," encounters on one of her walks in the woods a child, Dulcidora Bunt, who shares the story of how she came to be wearing a calico dress with an outlandish pattern woven into the material:

> There was the word "Union" in large letters, and the cannons were an inch long, and were represented in the act of going off. They were on wheels, and a man in a red shirt was standing with his back to you; an immense cloud of dark smoke and some very vivid flame were coming out at the mouth.
>
> (*Uncollected Short Stories,* p. 20)

Dulcy's parents, it turns out, don't get on well because her father is a sailor who has always lived along the shore, while her mother is from up-country and has always lived in the woods. On a trip into town, charged with buying Dulcy a new dress, her father purchased instead a whole bolt of the outrageous calico because he "thought it was real kind of odd, and they said it would wear first-rate." Dulcy's mother, who is afraid of guns, hates the material but makes her daughter a series of what she and the community take to calling "cannon dresses."

Dulcy is a spirited tomboy figure who will reappear regularly in Jewett's fiction, and her cannon dresses are an effective symbol of the difficulties of "union"—marital and political—that beset Jewett's culture and her country in the wake of the Civil War. That the cartoon-like image of the red-shirted soldier firing his cannon with his back to the audience is so lightly touched upon and placed in a comic context indicates that Jewett has begun in "Cannon Dresses" to hit her stylistic stride. Eschewing melodrama or overt political commentary, she lays in that image the foundation for what would prove to be an abiding concern: the struggle to communicate across the socially constructed boundaries between genders and regions.

Inaugurated by the success of "Cannon Dresses," the 1870s was a significant decade for Jewett, both personally and artistically. During this period she cemented her relationships with editor Horace Scudder and with Howells, who introduced her to James R. Osgood. This introduction proved fortuitous; his James R. Osgood and Company published her three collections of the 1870s before becoming the Houghton Mifflin Company, which carefully managed her career and published all but one of her remaining major works. (Her flagrantly bad foray into history for young readers, *The Story of the Normans,* was commissioned and published by G. P. Putnam in 1887.) In 1873 "The Shore House" appeared in the *Atlantic Monthly,* the first of the seaside sketches that, with Howells's encouragement, would eventually become the seminovelistic *Deephaven* (1877). In that same year she confessed to Scudder, "I am getting quite ambitious and really feel that writing is my work—my business perhaps; and it is so much better than making a mere amusement of it as I used." The artistic fruits of this decade also included *Play Days* (1878), a collection of children's stories, and *Old Friends and New* (1879), which consisted chiefly of stories that had already been printed in the periodicals.

Jewett's growing sense of professional confidence in the 1870s was accompanied by important changes in her personal life, including, in 1878, the sudden and devastating death of her father. Dr. Jewett's fatal heart attack at the age of sixty-three prompted his middle daughter to write to a friend (22 September 1878), "In that grave all my ambitions and hopes seem sometimes to be buried." At some point in this decade, Jewett became acquainted with the publisher James T. Fields and his wife, the dazzling hostess and social reformer Annie Adams Fields. When her husband's death in 1881 left Fields a young and socially prominent widow, Jewett became her primary companion and the two women entered into what has been variously described as "a Boston marriage" or a lesbian relationship—a stable, long-term domestic partnership that may or may not have been sexual. Such partnerships were fairly common in middle- and upper-middle-class Victorian America, so Jewett and Fields's arrangement would not have been viewed as culturally or socially deviant by their contemporaries.

In any event, Jewett henceforth divided her time between the rural solitude of South Berwick and the rarefied air of literary Boston, drawing sustenance from both worlds and from Fields, who was fifteen years older than Jewett and may have served as the prototype for the older women who so frequently guide younger women in her fiction.

Fields was an adept and vivacious guide—an astute critic, a generous friend, and an indefatigable traveling companion who, on their four trips to Europe, introduced Jewett to a galaxy of literary and cultural stars that included Tennyson, Arnold, Henry James, Rudyard Kipling, and Christina Rossetti. At her graceful home in Boston, Fields presided for sixty years over a parade of visitors whom Willa Cather describes in her essay "148 Charles Street" (1922) as "the aristocracy of letters and art." Further, Cather's glowing tribute to Fields's skills as a hostess suggests that Jewett was not the only "artist" in their household. Cather remarks, for example, upon Fields's "great power to control and organize" "the many strongly specialized and keenly sensitive people in her drawing-room" and on her ability to create "an atmosphere in which one seemed absolutely safe from everything ugly."

Jewett seems to have benefited both personally and artistically from her immersion in Annie's "atmosphere" and to have missed her sorely during the several months each year the two women spent apart to give Jewett time with her family and Fields time for her philanthropy. Letters between them during these absences indicate the intensity of Jewett's feelings for Fields as well as the shifting of her moods and roles in the relationship. She alternately expresses daughterly dependence, playful childishness, and physical longing: "I shall be with you tomorrow, your dear birthday. . . . I am tired of writing things. I want now to paint things, and drive things, and *kiss* things."

Even when Jewett was merely "writing things," the emotional and imaginative centrality women held in her mind remains clear. This is true of most of her major works of fiction, beginning in 1877 with *Deephaven.* Another summer travelogue, this group of sketches is narrated by Helen Denis, who accompanies her friend—"dear Kate Lancaster!"—to the home of Kate's deceased aunt Katharine Brandon, where the two young women set up housekeeping for the summer. Despite occasional lapses into didacticism—generally in tributes to rural and Christian virtues or in attacks on materialism and drunkenness—the *Deephaven* narrative is punctuated by memorable portraits of spry, indomitable, or peculiar women who are the backbone of the community and of the aging sea captains ("ancient mariners," Helen even calls them) who are signs of the town's lost economic power. Mrs. Kew, the lighthouse keeper's wife, and Mrs. Patton, a widow whose late alcoholic husband affords an example (rare in the Jewett canon) of domestic violence, are the stalwart women who make do with limited resources. Mrs Patton, as a loyal friend to Aunt Katharine and a gifted storyteller, supplies Kate with a sympathetic view of her formidable forebear and a valuable link to her female past. "I was afraid of [Aunt Katharine] when I was a little girl," reflects Kate after listening to Mrs. Patton's stories, "but I think if I had grown up sooner, I should have enjoyed her heartily."

Deephaven's resident herbalist is Mrs. Bonny, an ardent Calvinist but a careless housekeeper with a flock of hens and a turkey in her kitchen. Despite her unkempt appearance, the young women are transfixed by her "amazing store of knowledge and tradition" and impressed by the fact that through living alone deep in the woods "she knew all the herbs and trees and the harmless wild creatures who lived among them, by heart." They go to visit her, devout communicants, with "offerings of tobacco." Miss Chauncey, who seems to have arrived in *Deephaven* by way of Hawthorne's *The House of the Seven Gables,* is the insane "last survivor of one of the most aristocratic old colonial families," a family whose fortunes turned, as did the Pyncheons', over a broken promise and a legendary curse. She is harmless in her madness, cared for by her neighbors, and, for Kate and Helen, another crucial link to the past as she reminisces about Kate's great-grandmother.

As the complexities of these characters suggest, the vision of *Deephaven* is not filtered entirely through the "rose-coloured spectacles" that novelist Edith Wharton in *A Backward Glance* (1934) self-servingly accused Jewett and her fellow regionalist, Mary Wilkins Freeman, of donning in their portraits of rural New England. Indeed, the figure of "the Kentucky giantess," whom Helen and Kate see in a circus sideshow, is equal in grotesqueness to anything Wharton's *Ethan Frome* (1911) has to offer. The giantess, far under her advertised weight of 650 pounds, is displayed on a platform, sitting astride two chairs with a large cage of monkeys just beyond. When Mrs. Kew, who has accompanied the young women to the circus, recognizes the giantess as an old acquaintance, the freak is made human, and the tragic details of her story are told: a drunken husband, her own decline, and finally desperation. Mrs. Kew's solicitude and her companions' polite respect momentarily brighten the giantess's day, but as the women walk away, the voice of the circus huckster reaffirms her status as freak and spectacle: "Walk in and see the wonder of the world, ladies and gentlemen,—the largest woman ever seen in America,—the great Kentucky giantess!"

To Wharton's credit, however, the giantess is a remarkable—virtually unique—figure in Jewett's fiction. She is indicative, perhaps, of an ambivalence on the author's part resulting from her struggle to distance herself from a fictional world so similar to her own native region that she felt compelled in a preface to a later edition of *Deephaven* to deny that "Deephaven may . . . be found on the map of New England under another name." Or the giantess may represent a sly attempt to satisfy, as well as parody, the expectations of Jewett's mostly urban readers, who, like Wharton, would suspect that the New England villages were "still grim places," harboring and concealing all manner of mental and physical depravities.

Whatever the case, the giantess does not represent the dominant tone or mood of *Deephaven,* which throughout is sustained by Jewett's characteristic blend of optimism, generosity, compassion, and respect. Like so many of Jewett's narratives, this one is driven not by the progress or advance of "plot" in the novelistic sense but by the expansion of the characters' understanding through observation, experience, and storytelling. To the end, Helen and Kate remain visitors and outsiders, but their shared experience of Deephaven as a place and a community sharpens their perceptions, strengthens their bodies—"We both grew so well and brown and strong"—and deepens their connection to each other such a degree that Kate "laughingly" proposes one evening that she and Helen "should copy the Ladies of Langollen, and remove ourselves from society and its distractions." Facetious though it may be, Kate's proposal is of historical and psychological significance because the Ladies were two Englishwomen of the eighteenth century who eloped with each other in the cause of "romantic friendship." Helen's paeans to the intimacy she and Kate have developed—"We are such good friends that we often were silent for a long time, when mere acquaintances would have felt compelled to talk and try to entertain each other"—suggest that the Ladies would have struck her as an entirely appropriate model for their friendship and perhaps for their lives.

Howells lavishly praised *Deephaven* in the *Atlantic Monthly* (December 1878), pronouncing Jewett's "studies" "vividly localize[d]" and "so refined, so simple, so exquisitely imbued with a true feeling for the ideal within the real." Other reviews were more tempered, and the *New York Times* (April 28) dismissed the book with a caustic "It is by some mistake, doubtless, that it got into print at all." Such grousing notwithstanding, *Deephaven* earned for its author acclaim and status, firmly establishing her as one of the *Atlantic Monthly*'s star contributors. Jewett's other adult collection of the 1870s, *Old Friends and New,* also was well received, though some of the stories contained in it, including "Mr. Bruce," weren't quite up to the level of *Deephaven.* "A Bit of Shore Life" is an unusually bitter commentary—in the mode of the story of the giantess—on the barrenness of rural life and its effects on the human spirit, particularly the spirits of the elderly women whose stories and rituals Jewett generally treats with a respect bordering on awe. Here, however, the visitor/narrator seems both impatient and almost cruelly superior toward such women:

> Their talk is very cheerless, and they have a morbid interest in sicknesses and deaths; they tell each other long stories about such things; they are very forlorn; they dwell persistently upon any troubles they have; and their petty disputes with each other have a tragic hold upon their thoughts, sometimes being handed down from one generation to the next. Is it because their world is so small, and life affords so little amusement and pleasure, and is at best such a dreary round of the dullest housekeeping?
>
> (*Old Friends and New,* pp. 243–244)

More interesting in terms of Jewett's later development are "Lady Ferry" and "A Sorrowful Guest," two tales that betray the author's attraction to the supernatural, her debt to the gothic elements of the Brontës' novels, and her entanglement in the tradition of the American romance that came down to her from Hawthorne and Poe. Her "sorrowful guest," a Mr. Whiston, bears a striking resemblance to Poe's William Wilson and is similarly obsessed with the notion that he is being followed, in this instance by a cousin, Henry Dunster, presumed killed in the Civil War. The suspense and ambiguity of Jewett's study in "monomania" are destroyed when, after Whiston's death, Dunster suddenly reappears and confesses that he had once encountered his cousin under bizarre circumstances in Rio de Janeiro, suggesting a rational basis for Whiston's obsession. Still, Jewett's deployment of the romancer's theme of solipsistic delusion and her revision of it demonstrate her need to situate herself within, and to some extent against, this culturally powerful tradition.

Similarly, in "Lady Ferry," a story Howells rejected for the *Atlantic Monthly*, Jewett indulges in the romancer's play with the boundaries between life and death in her portrayal of the mysterious relationship between a young girl and an aged woman. "My lady in the gable"—as one of the housemaids calls Lady Ferry, referring to the part of the old house she has occupied for years—seems a victim of the family decay that beset Poe's Ushers and Hawthorne's Pyncheons, but she is also an American Bertha Mason, Charlotte Brontë's famous madwoman in the attic. A figure of repressed and concealed female madness (though not entirely—Lady Ferry does entertain visitors in her gable, and she walks in the garden at night), Madam so longs for death that she insists every day that her funeral will be tomorrow and arranges her room accordingly—a conceit similar to the one structuring Emily Dickinson's haunting analysis of the collapse of reason, "I felt a Funeral, in my Brain" (ca. 1861). Again, though, the story collapses when the narrator returns to the house years later only to find Lady Ferry's grave, forcing her to acknowledge the foolishness of her and the community's fantasies that the old woman had been cursed to live forever.

Later, Jewett would grow more adept at incoporating elements of the fabulous or the gothic into her fiction, and her treatment of mental delusions would focus less on individual pathologies than on the community's efforts to accommodate eccentricity—a shift that she would begin to make in the watershed period of the 1880s.

Having served a successful apprenticeship, Jewett enjoyed a bold and prolific decade in the 1880s, marked by formal experimentation and some of her most memorable work. After years of pressure from Howells and Scudder, she finally attempted novel writing, despite her insistence that she knew nothing about plot or drama. "It seems to me," she had told Scudder in 1873, "I can furnish the theatre, & show you the actors, & the scenery, & the audience, but there never is any play!" Her two novels of the 1880s, *A Country Doctor* (1884) and *A Marsh Island* (1885), suggest that plot continued to be a challenge for a writer whose natural inclination was to observation rather than to action. Nevertheless, both demonstrate Jewett's willingness to venture into new territory at this critical point in her career.

A Country Doctor is of particular interest because, in its unapologetic defense of the right of women to have access to the professions, it ranks as the most feminist of Jewett's works. The orphaned and exceptional Nan Prince is raised by the sympathetic Dr. Leslie, whose portrait, as has already been mentioned, is based on Jewett's own father. When Nan announces that she, too, would like to be a doctor, instead of thwarting her ambitions, Dr. Leslie encourages her, teaches her, and attacks his culture's notion that productive labor is improper or unnatural for women: "I don't care whether it's a man's work or a woman's work; if it is hers I'm going to help her the very best way I can." Dr. Leslie also recognizes that her natural self-reliance and her need for work make Nan ill-suited for marriage. By the end of the novel, Nan, who experiences the heady feeling "of a reformer, a radical, and even a political agitator," has recognized this for herself and rejected her suitor, George Gerry, but less on political grounds than on religious ones: she asserts that God has chosen a path other than wife- and motherhood for her. Many have seen in Nan's choice a fictional rendering of Jewett's rejection of traditional heterosexual social arrangements, though it should be noted that the writer's life with Annie Fields involved its own complex web of obligations and distractions from duty—distractions Jewett seems to have welcomed.

A number of Jewett's stories from the 1880s share *A Country Doctor*'s preoccupation with women's hunger for social and economic independence, suggesting that the novel's feminist theme was no idle experiment. In her 1884 collection, *The Mate of the Daylight, and Friends Ashore*, a volume dedicated to Annie Fields, Jewett offers "Tom's Husband," the story of a husband and wife who decide to switch gender roles because both realize she is more suited to running the family factory, while he has a knack for housekeeping. Her 1886 volume, *A White Heron and Other Stories*, features "Farmer Finch," whose heroine, Polly Finch, defies gender rules and roles, takes over her father's failing farm, and transforms it into a profitable commercial venture. "Mary and Martha," from the same collection, focuses on the economic plight of the unmarried woman in a story of two sisters who earn a meager living as seamstresses and are saved from poverty by the gift of a sewing machine. Finally, *The King of Folly Island and Other People* (1888) offers the touching, stubbornly feminist "A Village Shop," a self-conscious parody of *The House of the Seven Gables*, in which the scowling Hepzibah Pyncheon is transformed into the smiling and resourceful Esther Jaffrey, who becomes her family's breadwinner when brother Leonard (a stultified man of letters who seems to parody both Clifford Pyncheon and Hawthorne) proves to be uninterested in earning a living. The story insists, however, that "Miss Jaffrey had not ceased to be a lady because she had begun to keep a shop," a placating gesture Jewett frequently made when she was toying with cultural assumptions about gender.

During this period Jewett also honed her skills in the art of nature writing, earning a place in an American tradition of observation and conservation that includes William Bartram, John James Audubon, and John Muir, as well as Thoreau and Emerson. Her first serious efforts in this area are the five excursion narratives that form the heart of *Country By-Ways* (1881): "River Driftwood," "An October Ride," "From a Mournful Villager," "An Autumn Holiday," and "A Winter Drive." Jewett's strategy in these essays is not to posit a tragic polarization between the forces of nature and culture and to attack culture as irredeemably alien and destructive, as, for example, Thoreau does in *The Maine Woods* (1864). Instead, the youthful persona who roams Jewett's woods freely acknowledges that they are well traveled and full of associations. "The land has all been walked over at one time and another," she remarks in "A Winter Drive," even as she searches for a wild space, those mysterious "parts of the woods where [her superstitious neighbors] would not dare to go alone, and where nobody has ever been." But the signs of human life are everywhere in these domesticated woods, and Jewett's narrator ultimately embraces not wildness but limitation, and advocates sound management of natural resources by viewing the woods as an extended and metaphorical home, that is, community, neighborhood, old houses, and the stories of people who lived in them.

In the most famous of her writings about nature, "A White Heron" (1886), Jewett's young protagonist, Sylvia, climbs a tree and opts finally to protect the rare bird of the title from a visiting ornithologist in search of new specimens for his collection of "stuffed and preserved" birds. Sylvia's heroic climb mimics the flight from human relations in favor of a more transcendent relation with nature that is another staple of American romance fiction from Cooper to Faulkner. The anthologists' fondness for "A White Heron" aside, however, Jewett's respect for nature does not generally result in renunciations like Sylvia's. More typical is the stance of the narrator in "An October Ride," who seems both more deeply attuned to the ambiguities in the division between nature and culture and more generous in her ability to feel "at home" in both worlds:

> The relationship of untamed nature to what is tamed and cultivated is a very curious and subtle thing to me; I do not know if every one feels it so intensely. . . . The life in me is a bit of all life, and where I am happiest is where I find that which is next of kin to me, in friends, or trees, or hills, or seas, or beside a flower, when I turn back more than once to look into its face.

Thus, in "An Autumn Holiday," the narrator's immersion in the effulgence and sensuality of a fall afternoon—"when to breathe the air is like drinking wine, and every touch of the wind against one's face is a caress"—easily gives way to a neighborly call on Miss Polly Marsh and her visiting sister, Mrs. Snow.

In the excursion essays in *Country By-Ways,* the narrator's rhetoric of kinship and friendship blurs the boundary between nature and culture, quietly critiquing the American myth of nature as a sanctuary from both society and technology (a pastoral wish that, as Leo Marx has shown, is constantly balked in American literature by the incursion of "machines" into the "gardens" of fantasy). Jewett might occasionally rage against the coarseness and the excessivenss of American acquisitiveness, but the ethic that shapes most of her nature writing is embodied not in Sylvia's silent defense of the heron but in the gregarious narrator of "An Autumn Holiday," who views every walk as "a tour of exploration and discovery" and sees as much value in the chatter of two elderly sisters at their spinning wheels as she does in a solitary ramble through the fields of her neighborhood.

A final and related preoccupation of Jewett's fiction in the 1880s is not only the theme of companionship but also the use of paired figures—and frequently female figures—to emphasize, as she had first sought to do in *Deephaven,* the values of relatedness and the problematics of identity formation. Moving beyond the girlish adventures of Helen Denis and Kate Lancaster, Jewett begins in this decade a more sophisticated exploration of the boundaries between self and other and the balance between autonomy and intimacy in, for example, the relationships between Polly Marsh and Mrs. Snow ("An Autumn Holiday"), the Dobin sisters ("The Dulham Ladies" in *A White Heron*), Mary and Martha ("Mary and Martha" in *A White Heron*), and Miss Binson and Mrs. Crowe ("Miss Tempy's Watchers" in *The King of Folly Island*). In contrast with "A Sorrowful Guest," Jewett's purpose in these pairs seems not to be to expose the demonic underside or the dangerously fragile ego of a primary character but instead to suggest that identities formed through companionship need not lack stability or integrity. Despite a body of shared knowledge and experience, Jewett suggests in the opening of "Mary and Martha," two selves may remain stubbornly unique and separate: "For all this, they were as different as they could be. Mary was Mary-like—a little too easy and loving-hearted; and Martha was Martha-like—a little too impatient with foolish folks, and forgetting to be affectionate while she tried to be what she called just."

In the peculiar tale of Miss Daniel Gunn, a story related to the narrator by Miss Marsh and Mrs. Snow in "An Autumn Holiday," Jewett offers a male figure whose sense of self is fractured first by the death of his sister Patience and then by a sunstroke. Daniel, a former captain in the militia, takes to dressing up in his sister's clothes in the afternoons, but the story lacks the gothic elements of "A Sorrowful Guest" and focuses instead on the captain's confused but understandable desire to recuperate his lost Patience and on the community's loving efforts to cope with his bizarre behavior. "Freaky" though he may occasionally be, Jewett's cross-dresser is not as freakish as her Kentucky giantess and represents the increasing confidence and generosity of her vision.

Solidifying her status as an American literary star, criticism of Jewett's work throughout the 1880s continued to praise the authenticity and simplicity of her style, though detractors still complained about plotlessness and dullness. Nonetheless, she was poised for a quick start and a steady stream of work in the next decade, which she launched in 1890 with three volumes: *Betty Leicester*, a novel for girls; *Strangers and Wayfarers*, a collection of stories from the periodicals; and *Tales of New England*, reprints of stories from earlier collections. Houghton Mifflin apparently was happy to capitalize on the market value of the lady from Maine, and Jewett obliged, rounding out the decade with three other short-story collections—*A Native of Winby and Other Tales* (1893), *The Life of Nancy* (1895), and *The Queen's Twin and Other Stories* (1899)—in addition, of course, to the triumphant *The Country of the Pointed Firs* (1986). Small wonder, then, that in a letter of 11 November 1894 Jewett sheds her ladylike diffidence and exudes authority in offering professional advice to a novice writer, advice that shrewdly emphasizes what a later generation would describe as "demographics":

> [Writing] is, after all, a business like any other and a writer must go into its market and learn the laws of that, and what I might almost call the *personality* of the different magazines and the line of articles which seems to naturally belong to them. While ones [*sic*] personal experience and knowledge count for almost more than in any other business one can hardly expect at first or as an amateur to *catch hold* at once! any more than he could accomplish much by taking a day or two in the law or at real estate brokerage.
>
> (*Sarah Orne Jewett Letters*, ed. Cary, p. 68)

At her best in this last full decade of literary productivity, Jewett skillfully blends the concerns that emerged throughout her career and so deftly manages the tone or mood of individual works that it is easy to see why F. O. Matthiessen in his *Sarah Orne Jewett* (1929) pronounced her "the daughter of Hawthorne's style." Indeed, "In Dark New England Days" (in *Strangers and Wayfarers*) is a Hawthornesque parable of the repressiveness of New England's past that shows two sisters, Betsey and Hannah Knowles, deprived first by a stern, tyrannical father and then by a thief who breaks into their house and steals a chest full of gold they discovered the night of their father's funeral. In Hannah's public curse of Enoch Holt, the man accused but not convicted of the theft—"Curse your right hand, yours and all the folks' that follow you!"—Jewett evokes the supernatural as a possibility and feels no compulsion to explain away the fact that Holt and two members of his family eventually lose the use of their right arms. The story's most superstitious character, Mrs. Downs, acknowledges that accidents may have played a role in the injuries, but the tale concludes ominously, with Mrs. Downs and her friend Mrs. Forder admiring the beauty of the horizon at sunset when suddenly the figure of Enoch Holt crosses the meadow below "like a malicious black insect."

But Jewett's mastery during this period is most effectively displayed in the stories that more serenely plumb the depths of rural life, focusing on the delicate rituals of communion and separation, friendship between women, struggles for independence and understanding, and even, in "The Passing of Sister Barsett" (in *A Native of Winby*), the comic potential of an offstage character's near death. In this brilliantly executed slice of life, Jewett offers the afternoon encounter of Sarah Ellen Dow, who has been nursing the sickly Sister Barsett—known as "the first to have all the new diseases that's visited this region"—and Mercy Crane, a widowed neighbor. In her reading of Sister Barsett's behavior—"She was herself to the last. . . . I see her put out a thumb an' finger from under the spread an' pinch up a fold of her sister Deckett's dress, to try an' see if 't was all wool. I thought 't wa'n't all wool, myself, an' I know it now by the way she looked"—Miss Dow exposes the semiotic structure of the gendered universe that she, Sister Barsett, and Mercy Crane all inhabit, but her conclusion that her patient had died while she was out of the room proves to be a misinterpretation.

Stopping off at Mrs. Crane's for a cup of tea on her way home from "the house of mourning," Miss Dow confides to her friend about Sister Barsett's hypochondria, her self-righteousness, and her limitations as a housekeeper. When a neighbor arrives to announce that Sister Barsett has revived and is "a-screechin' " for Miss Dow, the stunned woman can do little more than collect her bonnet and trust Mrs. Crane's discretion. In the easy movement of Miss Dow and Mrs. Crane's conversation, the loving attention to the details of their tea, and the sly twist of the ending, Jewett demonstrates in "The Passing of Sister Barsett" how entirely she had made the elusive art of the short story her own. Still, her most enduring achievement would not, strictly speaking, fall within that genre.

Had Jewett's career not been cut short by debilitating head and spinal injuries sustained in a carriage accident in 1902, perhaps *The Country of the Pointed Firs* would not seem such an extraordinary and inevitable convergence of the issues and images, forms and themes that had preoccupied the writer for years. Indeed, in the one collection published after *Pointed Firs, The Queen's Twin,* both the title story and "A Dunnet Shepherdess" return to the Dunnet Landing materials, an exploration that continued into the twentieth century with "The Foreigner," published in the *Atlantic Monthly* in August 1900. The high quality of those stories and her ongoing fascination with the unnamed writer/narrator and the figure of Mrs. Todd suggest that Jewett herself saw her masterpiece not as an ending but as a transition that was still incomplete in 1902. Moreover, her historical novel of 1901, *The Tory Lover,* flawed as it is, indicates that Jewett was still interested in pursuing new fictional directions. Sadly, though, Jewett's fifty-third birthday—the day of the accident—brought that pursuit to an abrupt and permanent halt, as headaches and dizziness made sustained concentration on writing or reading difficult for the rest of her life. "It is strange," she lamented to her old friend Sarah Whitman almost a year after the accident, "how all that strange machinery that writes, seems broken and confused." The tragedy of the accident poignantly underscores the success of *The Country of the Pointed Firs.*

Jewett's success in *Pointed Firs* stems primarily from the evocative power of the narrator's taut lyricism and the volume's subtle interrogation of literary and cultural forms. Like *Deephaven,* this narrative of a summer visit stubbornly refuses to be a "novel" and balks at every turn the reader's desire for climaxes, turning points, and resolutions. Unlike the earlier work, however, *Pointed Firs* lacks neither certainty nor continuity, as Jewett tightly controls a vignette structure that shifts smoothly among all of her favorite moods and modes—the nature study, the friendship sketch, the community portrait, the ode to a sea captain, and the comic or elegiac slice of life. Throughout, she also embeds allusions to crucial American precursor texts. In addition to Emerson's "Circles" and probably *Walden, Pointed Firs* glances back at Poe's *The Narrative of A. Gordon Pym* (1838) in the inset tale, related by Captain Littlepage, of strange adventures in the polar regions; at Hawthorne's "Ethan Brand" (1851) in the story of poor Joanna, who has retreated with a broken heart to Shell-heap Island, believing that she, too, had committed the unpardonable sin; and at Harriet Beecher Stowe's *The Pearl of Orr's Island* (1862) an early example of Maine local color that Jewett had admired in her youth. Many have seen in the central relationship betwee Mrs. Todd and the narrator a New England variation of the Demeter-Persephone myth, but it must also be acknowledged that *Pointed Firs,* as an allusive tapestry of male- and female-authored texts, suggests that Jewett did not see herself as the inhabitant of an exclusively female world of love and literature. Drawn as she was to that world, the doctor's daughter had friends in every house on "the country by-ways" of her literary neighborhood, made her rounds, and learned the healing secrets of doctors and midwives alike.

The figure of the summer visitor is especially apt for the kind of cultural and literary examination Jewett undertakes in *Pointed Firs* because she is free to move from house to house and to report on her findings. Unnamed and underdrawn, the narrator is an excellent recorder of the impressions, events, and encounters that reveal the history and art of the community. But her task is not merely the conservative and "realistic" one of preservation. It is also creative, as she participates in a production of new meanings and new stories that not only preserve the community's past but also contribute in a significant way to its future.

As Mrs. Todd and the narrator prepare to leave Green Island, for example, Mrs. Blackett invites the narrator to sit for a moment and enjoy the view from her favorite rocking chair. Her occupation of the elderly woman's literal space prompts Mrs. Blackett to remark, "I shall like to think o' your settin' here to-day," suggesting that in the future she and her visit will occupy a figurative space in the memory stories that relieve the isolation of life on Green Island. The visitor is, of course, by definition a transient (and this visitor, with her writer's need for privacy, withdraws from society and community on a regular basis), but she strives to achieve a permanent place in Dunnet Landing as one who is remembered and recalled in story. She gathers impressions, but she makes them, too—on Mrs. Todd and Mrs. Blackett, on the normally taciturn fisherman whom she draws into conversation with apparent ease, and upon the great assemblage of Mrs. Todd's relatives at the Bowden family reunion.

Situated near the end of the narrative, the reunion is a psychological and symbolic focal point of *Pointed Firs.* With its emphasis on "the transfiguring powers" of such occasions—the power, for example, to transform a humble New England family into "a company of ancient Greeks going to celebrate a victory"—the reunion sequence displays the narrator's personal transformation from outsider to insider as well as a decisive shift from realism to the romance of "every-day life" Jewett had earlier defended in the case of "A White Heron." Here, the symbolic possibilities of everyday life yield a romance that is not gothic, tragic, or solipsistic (as are the romances of Poe and Hawthorne to which Jewett alludes); "romance" as she defines it in the Bowden reunion sketches is a tale of convergence rather than of collapse, a celebration of the human impulses to gather, to feast, to tell. Thus, the narrator moves beyond mere reportage to a language peppered with religious images that suggest the symbolic import of the occasion, and she is quietly "converted" from feeling like "an adopted Bowden" at the beginning of the day to feeling almost like "a true Bowden" at its end.

When farewells are said, Jewett again emphasizes the importance of the transformation from experience to memory and imagination, as the narrator comments that she "parted from certain new friends as if they were old friends; we were rich with the treasure of a new remembrance." To show how immediate this transformation is, on the ride home Mrs. Todd, Mrs. Blackett, and the narrator begin the new cycle of storytelling by swapping tales about the reunion.

To be "a true Bowden," then, is to recognize that language can provide adequate and loving compensation for loss, absence, separation, or isolation, so the narrator's imminent departure from Dunnet Landing is viewed not as a tragic but as "a natural end." Further, her first-person narrative, *The Country of the Pointed Firs,* is proof that although Dunnet Landing is "lost to sight" as the steamer pulls away from shore, the loss is neither permanent nor complete. Her story is a re-creation that mitigates loss, an invitation to readers to curl up in her rocking chair and enjoy the view. The continuing popularity of Jewett's masterpiece suggests that the view retains its power to captivate.

In the pain and quietness of her final year, Jewett came to know Willa Cather, who at the time was struggling through her own apprenticeship in fiction and journalism, and saw in the New Englander a necessary model for success as a woman writer. In Jewett's fiction she found an aesthetic and structural model for the impressionistic lyricism of her later works, especially *Death Comes for the Archbishop* (1927). Jewett's letters to Cather from this period are a lovely balance of affection and insistence, as she encourages the young writer while urging her to abandon both journalism and the "masquerade" of male narrators in favor of a more "quiet centre of life" and a more authentic voice. Cather twice paid tribute to Jewett's influence: in 1913, when she dedicated her novel *O, Pioneers!* to Jewett's memory, and in 1925, when she prefaced a collection of Jewett's works (which she edited) by ranking *The Country of the Pointed Firs* along with *The Scarlet Letter* and *Huckleberry Finn* as "three American books which have the possibility of a long, long life" because no others "confront time and change so serenely."

Cather's yoking together of three such diverse texts is typically idiosyncratic and not fully explained, but her compliment to Jewett's masterpiece is both sincere and apt. In its serene tone and its freewheeling exploration of a universe of literary texts, *The Country of the Pointed Firs* stands as a testament to its author's faith in the paradoxical possibilities of traveling at home. She traveled widely and she traveled well, and her influence on American traditions of romanticism, regionalism, and women's fiction has proven to be both significant and enduring.

In March 1909, during her last visit to the home of Annie Fields in Boston, Jewett was stricken with apoplexy. She traveled home to South Berwick because she wished to die there, "leaving the lilac bushes still green and growing, and all the chairs in their places." On 24 June she died, quietly, of a cerebral hemorrhage.

Selected Bibliography

PRIMARY WORKS

WORKS FOR ADULTS

Deephaven. Boston: Osgood, 1877. Reprinted with other stories. New Haven: College and University Press, 1966.

Old Friends and New. Boston: Houghton, Osgood, 1879.

Country By-Ways. Boston: Houghton Mifflin, 1881.

A Country Doctor. Boston and New York: Houghton Mifflin, 1884. Reprinted New York: New American Library, 1986.

The Mate of the Daylight, and Friends Ashore. Boston: Houghton Mifflin, 1884.

A Marsh Island. Boston and New York: Houghton Mifflin, 1885.

A White Heron and Other Stories. Boston and New York: Houghton Mifflin, 1886.

The King of Folly Island and Other People. Boston and New York: Houghton Mifflin, 1888.

Strangers and Wayfarers. Boston and New York: Houghton Mifflin, 1890. Reprinted New York: Garrett Press, 1969.

Tales of New England. Boston: Houghton Mifflin, 1890. Reprinted Freeport, N.Y.: Books for Libraries, 1970.

A Native of Winby and Other Tales. Boston and New York: Houghton Mifflin, 1893.

The Life of Nancy. Boston and New York: Houghton Mifflin, 1895.

The Country of the Pointed Firs. Boston and New York: Houghton Mifflin, 1896. Reprinted with other stories. New York: W. W. Norton, 1982.

The Queen's Twin and Other Stories. Boston and New York: Houghton Mifflin, 1899. Reprinted New York: Garrett Press, 1969.

The Tory Lover. Boston and New York: Houghton Mifflin, 1901.

The Best Short Stories of Sarah Orne Jewett. Edited with a preface by Willa Cather. 2 vols. Boston: Houghton Mifflin, 1925.

The Uncollected Short Stories of Sarah Orne Jewett. Edited by Richard Cary. Waterville, Me.: Colby College Press, 1971.

POETRY

Verses. Boston: Merrymount Press, 1916.

WORKS FOR CHILDREN

Play Days: A Book of Stories for Children. Boston: Houghton, Osgood, 1878.

The Story of the Normans, Told Chiefly in Relation to Their Conquest of England. New York and London: G. P. Putnam, 1887.

Betty Leicester: A Story for Girls. Boston and New York: Houghton Mifflin, 1890.

Betty Leicester's English Xmas: A New Chapter of an Old Story. Boston and New York: Dodd, Mead, 1894.

An Empty Purse: A Christmas Story. Boston: Merrymount Press, 1905.

LETTERS

The Letters of Sarah Orne Jewett. Edited by Annie Fields. Boston and New York: Houghton Mifflin, 1911.

Sarah Orne Jewett Letters. Edited by Richard Cary. Waterville, Me.: Colby College Press, 1956; rev. and enl. ed. 1967.

PAPERS

The Houghton Library, Harvard University, has the most extensive collection of unpublished Jewett letters, manuscripts, and journals. The Society for the Preservation of New England Antiquities in Boston and Colby College in Waterville, Maine, also have collections of letters, manuscripts, and memorabilia.

SECONDARY WORKS

BIOGRAPHICAL AND CRITICAL STUDIES

Ammons, Elizabeth. "Going in Circles: The Female Geography of *The Country of the Pointed Firs*." *Studies in the Literary Imagination* 16:83–92 (Autumn 1983).

———. "The Shape of Violence in Jewett's 'A White Heron.' " *Colby Library Quarterly* 22:6–16 (March 1986).

Auchincloss, Louis. "Sarah Orne Jewett." In his *Pioneers and Caretakers: A Study of Nine American Women Novelists*. Minneapolis: University of Minnesota Press, 1965.

Bader, Julia. "The Dissolving Vision: Realism in Jewett, Freeman, and Gilman." In *American Realism: New Essays*. Edited by Eric J. Sundquist. Baltimore: Johns Hopkins University Press, 1982. Pp. 176–198.

———. The 'Rooted' Landscape and the Woman Writer." In *Teaching Women's Literature from a Regional Perspective*. Edited by Leonore Hoffman and Deborah Rosenfelt. New York: Modern Language Association of America, 1982. Pp. 23–30.

Cary, Richard. *Sarah Orne Jewett*. New York: Twayne, 1962.

———, ed. *An Appreciation of Sarah Orne Jewett*. Waterville, Me.: Colby College Press, 1973. Reprints a range of important reviews and scholarly essays from 1885 to 1972.

Cather, Willa. "148 Charles Street." In her *Not Under Forty*. New York: Alfred A. Knopf, 1936.

Donovan, Josephine. "A Woman's Vision of Transcendence: A New Interpretation of the Works of Sarah Orne Jewett." *Massachusetts Review* 21:365–380 (Summer 1980).

———. *Sarah Orne Jewett*. New York: Frederick Ungar, 1981.

———. *New England Local Color Literature: A Women's Tradition*. New York: Frederick Ungar, 1983.

Faderman, Lillian. *Surpassing the Love of Men: Romantic Friendship Between Women from the Renaissance to the Present*. New York: Morrow, 1981.

Frost, John Eldridge. *Sarah Orne Jewett*. Kittery Point, Me.: Gundalow Club, 1960.

Gollin, Rita K. "Annie Adams Fields, 1834–1915." *Legacy* 4:27–36 (Spring 1987).

Jobes, Katherine T. "From Stowe's Eagle Island to Jewett's 'A White Heron.' " *Colby Library Quarterly* 10:515–521 (December 1974).

Matthiessen, F. O. *Sarah Orne Jewett*. Boston and New York: Houghton Mifflin, 1929.

Mobley, Marilyn. "Rituals of Flight and Return: The Ironic Journeys of Sarah Orne Jewett's Female Characters." *Colby Library Quarterly* 22:36–42 (March 1986).

Nagel Gwen L., ed. *Critical Essays on Sarah Orne Jewett*. Boston: G. K. Hall, 1984. Reprints crucial early reviews and more recent critical essays as well as eight original and valuable essays.

Pryse, Marjorie. "Introduction." In *The Country of the Pointed Firs and Other Stories*. Edited by Mary Ellen Chase. New York: W. W. Norton, 1982.

Renza, Louis. *"A White Heron" and the Question of Minor Literature*. Madison: University of Wisconsin Press, 1984.

Sherman, Sarah Way. *Sarah Orne Jewett: An American Persephone*. Hanover, N.H.: University Press of New England, 1989.

Toth, Susan Allen. "Sarah Orne Jewett and Friends: A Community of Interest." *Studies in Short Fiction* 9:233–241 (Summer 1972).

Westbrook, Perry D. *Acres of Flint: Sarah Orne Jewett and Her Contemporaries*. Metuchen, N.J.: Scarecrow Press, 1951; rev. ed., 1981.

Zagarell, Sandra A. "Narrative of Community: The Identification of a Genre." *Signs* 13:498–527 (Spring 1988).

BIBLIOGRAPHIES

Cary, Richard. "Some Bibliographic Ghosts of Sarah Orne Jewett." *Colby Library Quarterly* 8:139–145 (September 1968).

Eichelberger, Clayton L. "Sarah Orne Jewett (1849–1909): A Critical Bibliography of Secondary Comments." *American Literary Realism* 2:189–262 (Fall 1969).

Nagel, Gwen L. "Sarah Orne Jewett: A Reference Guide—An Update." *American Literary Realism* 17:228–263 (Autumn 1984).

Nagel, Gwen L., and James Nagel. *Sarah Orne Jewett: A Reference Guide*. Boston: G. K. Hall, 1978.

Weber, Clara Carter, and Carl J. Weber. *A Bibliography of the Published Writings of Sarah Orne Jewett*. Waterville, Me.: Colby College Press, 1949.

MARILEE LINDEMANN

MAXINE HONG KINGSTON

1940–

MAXINE HONG KINGSTON'S works are many things to many people. They have been championed by feminists, dismissed as evidence of collaboration with a white male publishing establishment by a small but vocal group of Chinese American male authors, honored by literary critics, criticized by sinologists, scrutinized by students of biography and ethnic literature, pirated (and corrupted) in Chinese-language editions, included on reading lists in high school and college courses, and widely read and acclaimed by both Chinese Americans and Americans who are not of Chinese descent. The writer herself has been declared a Living Treasure by the state of Hawaii, for a time her adopted home. Though the body of her work is not large (three major books in thirteen years, as well as numerous periodical pieces), her reputation as an important American writer is well established. She has said of her work (in "Cultural Misreadings"): "I want my audience to include everyone. . . . I do believe in the timelessness and universality of individual vision. . . . I hope my writing has many layers, as human beings have layers."

With the exception of some essays, most of Kingston's published work centers on the experiences of Chinese immigrants and Americans of Chinese descent, though she has expressed dismay at being regarded as the representative of those groups, noting that such a view denies both the uniqueness of the artist's own voice and the diversity of Chinese American writers. Two of her major works, *The Woman Warrior: Memoirs of a Girlhood Among Ghosts* (1976) and *China Men* (1980), draw on her own experiences as the eldest of six children born to educated Chinese immigrants. At one time a scholar and schoolteacher in China, her father, Tom Hong, whose life story figures largely in *China Men,* made his living as a gambling-house manager and laundry owner in Stockton, California, where Kingston grew up. After the early deaths of two children and fifteen years of separation, her mother, Chew Ying Lan ("Brave Orchid"), left her position as physician and midwife in China and joined her husband in America, starting a new family in her late thirties and working in the fields, the canneries, and the family laundry.

Kingston, who was born in Stockton on 27 October 1940, describes her younger self—in her writing and in interviews—as a studious, observant girl who loved books, writing, and stories. Like Wittman Ah Sing, the protagonist of Kingston's novel *Tripmaster Monkey* (1989), she received her A.B. from the University of California, Berkeley, in 1962. In the same year she married Earll Kingston, an actor. After teaching high-school English and mathematics in Hayward, California, Kingston moved in 1967 with her husband and son, Joseph, to Hawaii, where she taught language arts and English as a second language. For a time, beginning in 1977, she was a visiting associate professor of English at the University of Hawaii, Honolulu. She now works exclusively on her writing.

Her first book, *The Woman Warrior,* which was immediately accepted for publication, became an instant critical success and a best-seller. When it first appeared, the memoir was deemed "brilliant" and "astonishingly accomplished," demonstrating "the real meaning of America as melting pot." It won the 1976 National Book Critics Circle award for general nonfiction, and *Time* magazine designated it among the top ten nonfiction books of the 1970s. In 1977 Kingston won the *Mademoiselle* magazine award, in 1978 the Anisfield-Wolf Race Relations Award, and in 1980 a writing fellowship from the National Endowment for the Arts.

Though obviously a mixture of genres—autobiography, myth, family and cultural history, and fiction—this memoir remains the best biographical source on Kingston to date. "The woman warrior" of the title is at once Fa Mu Lan, a mythic figure of superhuman powers who does battle when she is pregnant, Kingston's mother, Brave Orchid, whose own intellectual, physical, and psychic strength often seems fantastic; and Kingston herself, who struggles with the dichotomies of being both American and Chinese. The strong and intelligent daughter of a strong and intelligent mother, she is simultaneously encouraged and discouraged by her family's and her community's conflicting attitudes toward women.

The most captivating figure of the three "warriors" is not Kingston herself, nor Fa Mu Lan, but Kingston's astonishingly resilient mother, whose story is told in the section "Shaman." In China, Kingston's mother was a highly trained doctor and midwife, commanding respect in New Society Village and known among her sister students for her studiousness and for her bravery in fighting off ghosts. Later she enthralled and confused her American children with her gift for "talk-story," an oral tradition that includes anecdote, legend, personal history, and ghost tales. "Before we can leave our parents," Kingston explains, "they stuff our heads like the suitcases which they jam-pack with homemade underwear." She claims to have tapered down the figure of the mother for her book; in real life, according to Kingston, she is even more powerful.

Ironically, the author who is now considered an important voice in American literature once had great difficulty being heard. The problems of finding a voice, of using the right language for a particular situation, of speaking up in order to be understood and recognized were concerns for young Maxine Hong specifically, as well as for Chinese women (on both continents) in general, and for all Chinese immigrants in America, indistinguishable and incomprehensible to the "ghosts" (that is, non-Chinese Americans) who affected their lives. Some of the most moving passages in the memoir depict the author's concerns with speech, silence, and secrets—her own and others'.

The Woman Warrior opens with an admonition from the author's mother: "You must not tell anyone . . . what I am about to tell you." Kingston then reveals the story of "No Name Woman," an aunt in China who drowned herself in the family well along with the newborn offspring of an extramarital affair (or rape). As she must do for many of her stories, Kingston fills great gaps in her family's oral history with what her subject might have done, could have said, must have thought. In an effort to propitiate her aunt's neglected ghost, which haunts Kingston, she devotes the first pages of her first book to her, giving flesh to the skeleton of her tale, substance to her experience, listening to her "secret voice," imagining the "silent birth" scene in which her aunt refuses to divulge the name of her seducer/rapist. At these moments Kingston's memoirs take on the feeling of fiction.

In the midst of her aunt's tale, Kingston includes the first of many autobiographical revelations. She confesses to deliberately eschewing the bound-feet walk once considered to be "Chinese-feminine" and the "loud, public" way of speaking that her Chinese friends and family use to communicate with each other. Attempting to turn herself "American-feminine," she imitates other girls and adopts an inaudible voice. Later, in the concluding section of the book, she almost matter-of-factly reveals that when she was an infant, her mother sliced her frenum (the membrane between the tongue and the bottom of the mouth) to ensure that she would never be tongue-tied, that she would be able to speak many languages freely. Nevertheless, young Maxine Kingston's first few years in public school, when she had to speak English for the first time, rendered her mute. Even after she did speak, she and the other second-grade Chinese American girls were excluded from the class play because their voices were too weak. Even in Chinese school, where the girls chanted together in the classroom and screamed during recess, her voice, though loud, was like "a crippled animal running on broken legs." An influential woman in the Chinese American community warned Mrs. Hong that her daughter would never get married: "She has an ugly voice. She quacks like a pressed duck."

The author's pressed-duck voice comes into play at two crucial moments in this last section, titled "A Song for a Barbarian Reed Pipe." A long, painful passage relates a moment in Kingston's youth when she turns on "the quiet girl," also a daughter of Chinese immigrants, who would read aloud in a whisper at school but would never talk. Like young Maxine, this girl is unathletic, "an automatic walk" in every school baseball game. Unlike Maxine, she is totally passive. When the two are alone in the girls' washroom, Maxine at first coaxes, then taunts and torments her mirror image, demanding and finally—in her pressed-duck voice—tearfully begging the girl to speak. Unsuccessful, the young Kingston then spends the next eighteen months in bed with "a mysterious illness."

After she recuperates, she is consumed with a desire to confess to her mother a carefully constructed list of "over two hundred things" about herself, including her treatment of the quiet girl, in order to relieve feelings of suppression and confusion about her role in the family, in the Chinese American community, and in American society at large. Experiencing this tension as a pain in her throat, she tries to unburden herself to her overworked mother, whispering and quacking in her pressed-duck voice, but her "senseless gabbings" are impatiently silenced. At last, at the family dinner table, her vocal cords "taut to snapping," she accosts her mother, "the champion talker," with accusations of trying to marry her off to a wealthy mentally retarded man, of confusing her with Chinese ghost stories, myths, and legends that seem to be both true and false, of calling her ugly and stupid (when in truth she knows that it is a Chinese habit to describe a loved one with a negative, the opposite of what is true). This adolescent confrontation, which pains her mother, becomes one more of the many sins on Kingston's list, but it enables her to move away from her family, attend college, and "see the world logically, . . . shine floodlights into dark corners: no ghosts." Having once spoken out, she is now outspoken, still subject to the throat pain unless she says what she really thinks.

Because numerous critics have failed to recognize the humor in Kingston's works, she has observed that "when people come to ethnic writing, they have such a reverence for it or are so scared they don't want to laugh." In another story about an aunt, Kingston's persistent mother forces her own frail, elderly sister, newly arrived in the United States, to hunt down her long-absent, Americanized husband and his second wife in order to demand her rights. The ludicrousness of timid Moon Orchid executing her officious sister's directions, combined with the incongruity of applying a Chinese view of life in an American setting, makes one laugh out loud:

> How can you let him get away with this? Bother him. He deserves to be bothered. How dare he marry somebody else when he has you? . . . Oh, how I'd love to be in your place. I could tell him so many things. What scenes I could make. You're so wishy-washy. . . . Make him feel bad about leaving his mother and father. Scare him. Walk right into his house with your suitcase and boxes. Move right into the bedroom. Throw her stuff out of the drawers and put yours in. Say, "I am the first wife, and she is our servant."
> ("At the Western Palace," in *The Woman Warrior*)

When Brave Orchid compels one of her sons to drive them to the office of Moon Orchid's doctor husband, she seriously considers placing her sister in the middle of the street, faking a broken leg in order to attract the doctor's attention. The two elderly Chinese ladies create a spectacle, enacting a domestic drama in the back seat of the car while the frustrated son protests, "This whole thing is ridiculous." On a more poignant note, Moon Orchid ends her days in a California mental institution, suffering from paranoia. A counterbalance to the tragic opening story of Kingston's nameless aunt, this aunt's tale is told in a skillful blend of humor and pathos.

A similar mixture of comedy and tragedy, madness and strength is found in Kingston's second book, *China Men*, a companion piece to *The Woman Warrior* that concentrates on the stories of her father, grandfather, great-grandfathers, and uncles, and other "China Men" who immigrated to the West. Kingston uses a technique similar to that of *The Woman Warrior*, embroidering on family "talk-story," adapting classical myth, and combining the results with factual material. In a section entitled "The Laws," she chronologically encapsulates restrictions imposed on Chinese immigration to the United States from 1868 to 1978. Kingston has been criticized for disrupting the flow of the book by including such statistical, nonliterary material, but the passage serves to educate many of her readers who are undoubtedly unaware of these facts. Elements of Kingston's family history are presented as details from a much larger portrait depicting the suppression, suffering, and courage of all the lonely men who worked in the West to earn money for their families back home or those who preceded their families in immigrating to America.

A theme that appears in *The Woman Warrior* is here taken up again: the silencing of Chinese immigrants. In her first book, Kingston often touches on the circuitous means of communication new Chinese Americans were forced to employ when dealing with "the immigration ghosts" and others:

> Sometimes I hated the ghosts for not letting us talk; sometimes I hated the secrecy of the Chinese. . . . Lie to Americans. Tell them you were born during the San Francisco earthquake. Tell them your birth certificate and your parents were burned up in the fire. Don't report crimes; tell them we have no crimes and no poverty. . . . The Han people won't be pinned down.
>
> ("A Song for a Barbarian Reed Pipe," in *The Woman Warrior*)

The experience of being silenced is most dramatically illustrated in *China Men* by the story of Bak Goong, "Great Grandfather of the Sandalwood Mountains," who spent years clearing Hawaiian land to earn money for his family in China. Like the black slaves of the same period who were toiling in American cotton fields, the Chinese laborers in Hawaii were not allowed to talk as they worked. This "rule of silence" ate at Bak Goong until he tried to relieve his boredom by singing, for which action he was whipped. Sometimes he resorted to releasing tension by cursing as he coughed in the choking dust, sputtering Chinese syllables incomprehensible to the demon bosses.

> It wasn't right that Bak Goong had to save his talking until after work when stories would have made the work easier. He grew the habit of clamping his mouth shut in a line, and the sun baked that expression on him. If he opened his mouth, words might tumble forth like coral out of the surf; spit would spout like lava. He still hacked at the cane while coughing: "Take—that —white—demon. Take—that. . . . Die—snake."
>
> ("Great Grandfather of the Sandalwood Mountains," in *China Men*)

Too many men were committing suicide or becoming ill with clogged lungs, crippled limbs, stomach pains. After suffering from a fever himself, Bak Goong, "the talk addict," diagnosed their common ailment as "congestion from not talking." The next day, rather than furrow the land, the men dug a circle in the earth and took turns shouting into it; greetings to family in China, expressions of homesickness, confessions of infidelities, descriptions of their new surroundings: "They had dug an ear into the world, and were telling the earth their secrets." The demon bosses did not dare interfere. From then on, Bak Goong talked and sang at his work with impunity.

The lives of Kingston's male ancestors comprise a history of Chinese immigration to America, and in the telling of that history, Kingston the former teacher reveals a harsh story rarely taught in classrooms. Grandfather Ah Goong risked his life by dangling in a basket over a ravine in the Sierra Nevada mountains, setting off dynamite to make way for the transcontinental railroad. After years of back-breaking labor, living through intense loneliness and a nine-day strike initiated by the Chinese workers, Ah Goong found himself a victim of "the driving out," a diaspora experienced by Chinese laborers who were no longer wanted once their specific jobs were done. As Ah Goong made his way around the West Coast, decades of his life story unaccounted for, forty thousand China Men were "driven out" of the mines where they worked. White residents of Los Angeles massacred their Chinese neighbors, while other whites sent severed bits of anatomy to prominent members of various Chinatowns as ransom tokens. Chinese men were shot, burned, beaten, imprisoned, and driven out of cities, including Denver, Tacoma, Seattle, Portland, and Boston.

Like Aunt Moon Orchid, a number of China Men in Kingston's extended family and in her community suffered mental anguish. Their stories are another side of the same reality presented in Kingston's chronology of immigration laws. Against these obstacles, the Chinese men in America persisted, establishing citizenship, setting up businesses, and raising their families, but not without paying a price for becoming American ancestors.

Talkative Uncle Bun, a distant relation, began innocently enough by urging the Hong family to eat wheat germ as an antidote to American food and by supporting the Communist revolution in China. Tom Hong pronounced him "Foolish man. . . . Long winded," with dreams that fermented like yeast and mold. Gradually, Uncle Bun began to suffer persecution delusions, suspecting at first that all the American ghosts, including the milk demon and the grocer demon, were trying to poison him for his politics, then accusing the Hongs of robbing his bank account, and finally believing that he would be force-fed garbage as punishment for his communism. A casualty of the clash of two cultures, Uncle Bun "returned" to China (though he may never have been there before) in order to "escape" and was never heard from again.

Another relation, "Mad Sao," was guilt-ridden by letters from his elderly mother in China, urging him to stop caring for his daughters (who should be sold) and return to support her in her old age. The money he sent was never enough; she was starving. After she died, Sao's mother's ghost visited him in America and haunted him into extreme agitation: insomnia, weeping, weight loss, babbling, sleepwalking, tossing food into the air. Neither the ghost nor Mad Sao got any rest until he spent all his savings on a trip to China and laid her to rest in the village cemetery. He then returned to America and his American life, acting "normally" again.

Kingston's father, too, suffered from the strain of adapting to a new world and supporting six American children. He was cheated out of his share of a laundry by three fellow Chinese immigrants and then exploited by a more powerful, well-established member of his own community, experiences not unknown in American immigrant groups. When the gambling house that he managed for his wealthy boss was closed down, "Baba" lost heart, sinking into a depression that made him scream in the night and sit motionless during the day. Only the children's mischievousness finally brought back his "sense of emergency" and shook him into an active life again. He bought his own laundry and a house for his family and planted "trees that take years to fruit." Baba's survival is a testament to the strength of the founding China Men whose descendants are now American men and American women.

Appearing nine years after *China Men,* Kingston's *Tripmaster Monkey: His Fake Book* (1989) took significant leaps in new directions. In 1980 Kingston declared in an essay titled "The Coming Book" that her next book would make "a break from the 'I' stories" she had been writing. She predicted that it would "sound like the Twentieth Century" when read aloud and have a modern "texture . . . like black vinyl." At one point she saw the book as existing "without the aid of Chinese metaphors" and envisioned characters with little sense of Chinese mythology and history.

In *Tripmaster Monkey,* Kingston does move away from autobiography and personal family history. The book is indeed a product of mid- and late-twentieth-century America. Its protagonist, Wittman Ah Sing, is a "modern" American, but the Chinese and Chinese American cultures are as important as in Kingston's earlier work. She continues to deal with China and Chinese immigrants in America, still keeping Chinese myths and legends at the heart of her work, but now those elements are filtered through the occasional observations of an omniscient narrator and the perceptions of a fictional character. *Tripmaster Monkey* differs from its precedents in the dominance of Wittman Ah Sing's egocentric personality, in the density of its intertextual references, deftly combining Eastern and Western literary cultures, and in its increased emphasis on the Americanness of its characters.

Many of Kingston's admirers are slightly startled when the work is described as her first novel, since her two previous works read so much like fiction, but *Tripmaster Monkey,* unlike *The Woman Warrior* and *China Men,* is unmistakably and solely of that genre. The novel is set in San Francisco in the 1960s and follows a few months in the life of poet and playwright Wittman Ah Sing, a fifth-generation Chinese American. A recent graduate of Berkeley, he is very much an American Man and at the same time a descendant of China Men. Not unlike Kingston, Brave Orchid, the "talk addict" grandfather, and Uncle Bun, Wittman (named for the poet Walt) is a master storyteller, a manic talker, a "word-drunk" poet. His egotism, his 1960s political rebelliousness, and his experiments with mind-altering drugs, however, distinguish him from Kingston's previous characters. Reviewers and interviewers have missed the mark in concentrating on the psychedelic facets of Wittman's story, distracted by a predeliction for contrasting Wittman's era with our own. Although *Tripmaster Monkey* does capture the sense of a certain place and time (a brief explanation of anachronisms precedes the text), this is not the only, or even the most important, level on which the novel can be read.

Confronting the daily realities (and fantasies) of being an American male of Chinese ancestry, Ah Sing responds instinctively but intellectually to the vicissitudes of his life with stories borrowed from Chinese culture, Western literature and film, a combination of both, or a tale of his own making. He identifies with the legendary trickster Monkey, known for his cleverness and mischievousness, who is credited with bringing Buddhism to China. On impulse, Wittman reads aloud a passage from Rilke on family, ancestry, and ghosts to his fellow bus passengers. He entertains a beautiful young woman with the story of his own beginnings, "born backstage in vaudeville," the son of a Floradora girl and an emcee, and regales a counselor in an unemployment office with outlandish tales of secret DNA experiments talking place in California laboratories. When Wittman views a film cautioning the unemployed not to bring friends and relatives along to job interviews, he reflects on the American way of doing things and recalls an anecdote:

> An American stands alone. Alienated, tribeless, individual. To be a successful American, leave your tribe, your caravan, your gang, your partner, your village cousins, your refugee family

> that you're making the money for, leave them behind. Do not bring back-up. . . . Wittman got lonely for that tribesman that said to the Peace Corps volunteer, "We don't need a reading class; we've already got a guy who can read." That's the tribe where he wants to belong, and the job he wants, to be reader of the tribe. O right livelihood.
>
> ("A Song for Occupations," in *Tripmaster Monkey*)

Wittman is not meant to be admirable or likable at all times; his male chauvinism and egotism are often unattractive. Some reviewers have taken issue with Wittman's (and, it is presumed, Kingston's) anger, complaining of his "harangues" and "manic monkey talk." On the first page of the novel, Wittman thinks about suicide, conjuring up visions of Hemingway and of Olivier playing Hamlet. In the days that ensue, he gets fired from his job in a department store, avoids looking for a job, marries a blonde for whom he feels an ambiguous love, gets high at parties, and encounters various friends, family members, and strangers, incessantly talking his way through it all. Because of Ah Sing's temperament, and also because the book may fall outside the non-Chinese American public's limited expectations and understanding of Chinese American literature, *Tripmaster Monkey* does not enjoy the same popularity as Kingston's previous works.

His irritating qualities aside, this antagonistic protagonist nevertheless grows on the reader. By the novel's conclusion, Wittman's thoughts have evolved from suicide to committed pacifism—the catalyst has been something of his own creation. Defying all attempts to stereotype or convert him to an acceptable, hyphenated Chinese-American, Ah Sing succeeds in writing and producing a three-day theatrical event depicting myriad Chinese legends, but centering on an epic, "The War of the Three Kingdoms." After the production, Wittman delivers extempore a lengthy monologue, and then realizes that he will never fight in Vietnam or in any other war. As Kingston's other works demonstrate, Chinese history and legend combined with an American present can bring about change and create new identities. Wittman the storyteller has been transformed by his own stories.

Ah Sing's prominence in the novel can also be viewed as Kingston's device for sharing with her readers yet more stories, stories about racism, blindness, ignorance, community, humanity, "inscrutability," "orientalism," and "model minorities." Just as the structure of *The Woman Warrior,* with its nonchronological, cyclical repetition of stories and its blurring of genre boundaries, reflects the polymorphousness of Kingston's young life, so do the intertextual, intercultural references in *Tripmaster Monkey* mirror the fecund turmoil in the poet/protagonist's mind. The book is laden with references to stories and storytellers, Eastern and Western. Shakespeare and MGM, Allen Ginsburg and Joang Fu the singer/storyteller, crowd the pages of this novel about the power of storytelling. In Kingston's hands, intertexuality becomes a tool for re-education, rendering the unfamiliar familiar to the reader unacquainted with Chinese history and folklore. As Wittman and his family and friends "talk-story," we are simultaneously entertained and educated.

Kingston has described "talk-story" as an oral tradition of history, mythology, genealogy, bedtime stories, and how-to stories that have been passed down through generations, an essential part of family and community life. When Western sinologists have "corrected" her for not getting certain Chinese stories right, Kingston in turn has corrected them, explaining that they are trained in the "high" literary tradition and that "talk-story" is actually part of the "low" or "small" Chinese culture. According to Kingston, it is difficult for the children of Chinese immigrants to distinguish whether a story is part of traditional Chinese culture, particular to their village, or created by a family member. As a child, Kingston thought that Dr. Dolittle and Robinson Crusoe were Chinese tales. Kingston's version of talk-story is actually Chinese tradition brought here by immigrants, altered by new influences, and rendered as "American stories."

At least one critic from China has come to realize that Kingston's works are first and foremost what she would have them understood to be, American creations, not simply dutiful replications of Chinese culture. Some American critics have been too quick to emphasize the Chinese in Kingston's Chinese American writing, noting the deviations from what is assumed to be the American norm, rather than recording just how American Kingston and her American-born generation are. It is more than possible to understand the Americanness of Wittman Ah Sing, Kingston, her siblings, cousins, and schoolmates; for a full appreciation of Kingston's contribution to American literature, it is imperative.

Selected Bibliography

PRIMARY WORKS

BOOKS

The Woman Warrior: Memoirs of a Girlhood Among Ghosts. New York: Knopf, 1976.

China Men. New York: Knopf, 1980.

Hawai'i One Summer: 1978. San Francisco: Meadow Press, 1987.

Through the Black Curtain. Berkeley, Calif.: Friends of the Bancroft Library, University of California, 1987.

Tripmaster Monkey: His Fake Book. New York: Knopf, 1989.

ESSAYS AND ARTICLES

"Duck Boy." *New York Times Book Review,* 12 June 1977, pp. 54–58.

"Reservations About China." *MS.* 7, no. 4:67–68 (October 1978).

"San Fransisco's Chinatown: A View from the Other Side of Arnold Genthe's Camera." *American Heritage* 30, no. 1:35–47 (December 1978).

"The Coming Book." In *The Writer on Her Work.* Edited by Janet Sternburg. New York: Norton, 1980.

"Cultural Mis-readings by American Reviewers." In *Asian and Western Writers in Dialogue: New Cultural Identities.* Edited by Guy Amirthanayagam. London: Macmillan, 1982. Pp. 55–65.

"An Imagined Life." *Michigan Quarterly Review* 22:561–570 (Fall 1983).

"A Chinese Garland." *North American Review* 273, no. 3:38–42 (September 1988).

SECONDARY WORKS

BIOGRAPHICAL AND CRITICAL STUDIES

Blinde, Patricia Lin. "The Icicle in the Desert: Perspective and Form in the Works of Two Chinese-American Women Writers." *MELUS* 6, no. 3:51–71 (Fall 1979).

Cheung, King-Kok. " 'Don't Tell': Imposed Silences in *The Color Purple* and *The Woman Warrior.*" *PMLA* 103, no. 2:162–174 (March 1988).

———. *Articulated Silences: Narrative Strategies of Three Asian American Women Writers.* Ithaca, N.Y.: Cornell University Press, 1990.

Chua, Cheng Lok. "Golden Mountain: Chinese Versions of the American Dream in Lin Yutang, Louis Chu, and Maxine Hong Kingston." *Ethnic Groups* 4, no. 1–2:33–59 (1982).

Eakin, Paul John. *Fictions in Autobiography: Studies in the Art of Self-Invention.* Princeton, N.J.: Princeton University Press, 1985.

Fong, Bobby. "Maxine Hong Kingston's Autobiographical Strategy in *The Woman Warrior.*" *Biography* 12, no. 2:116–126 (Spring 1989).

Friedman, Susan Stanford. "Women's Autobiographical Selves: Theory and Practice." In *The Private Self: Theory and Practice of Women's Autobiographical Writings.* Edited by Shari Benstock. Chapel Hill: University of North Carolina Press, 1988.

Garner, Shirley Nelson. "Breaking Silence: *The Woman Warrior.*" *Hurricane Alice* 1, no. 2:5–6 (Fall–Winter 1983–1984).

Holaday, Woon-Ping Chin. "From Ezra Pound to Maxine Hong Kingston: Expressions of Chinese Thought in American Literature." *MELUS* 5, no. 2:15–24 (Summer 1978).

Hunt, Linda. " 'I Could Not Figure Out What Was My Village': Gender vs. Ethnicity in Maxine Hong Kingston's *The Woman Warrior.*" *MELUS* 12, no. 3:5–12 (Fall 1985).

Johnson, Diane. "Anti-Autobiography: Maxine Hong Kingston, Carobeth Laird, and N. Scott Momaday." In *Terrorists and Novelists.* Edited by Diane Johnson. New York: Knopf, 1982. Pp. 3–13.

Juhasz, Suzanne. "Towards a Theory of Form in Feminist Autobiography: Kate Millet's *Flying* and *Sita;* Maxine Hong Kingston's *The Woman Warrior.*" In *Women's Autobiography: Essays in Criticism.* Edited by Estelle C. Jelinek. Bloomington: Indiana University Press, 1980.

———. "Maxine Hong Kingston: Narrative Technique and Female Identity." In *Contemporary American Women Writers.* Edited by Catherine Rainwater and William J. Scheik. Lexington: University Press of Kentucky, 1985. Pp. 173–189.

Li, David Leiwei. "The Naming of a Chinese American 'I': Cross-Cultural Sign/ifications in *The Woman Warrior.*" *Criticism* 30, no. 4:497–515 (Fall 1988).

Ling, Amy. "Thematic Threads in Maxine Hong Kingston's *The Woman Warrior.*" *Tamkang Review: A Quarterly of Comparative Studies Between Chinese and Foreign Literatures* 14, no. 1–4:155–164 (Autumn–Summer 1983–1984).

———. *Between Worlds: Women Writers of Chinese Ancestry.* New York: Pergamon Press, 1990.

Neubauer, Carol E. "Developing Ties to the Past: Photography and Other Sources of Information in Maxine Hong Kingston's *China Men.*" *MELUS* 10, no. 4:17–36 (Winter 1983).

Rabine, Leslie W. "No Lost Paradise: Social Gender and Symbolic Gender in the Writings of Maxine Hong Kingston." *Signs* 12, no. 3:471–492 (Spring 1987).

Rose, Shirley K. "Metaphors and Myths of Cross-Cultural Literacy: Autobiographical Narratives by Maxine Hong Kingston, Richard Rodriguez, and Malcolm X." *MELUS* 14, no. 1:3–15 (Spring 1987).

Rubenstein, Roberta. *Boundaries of the Selif: Gender, Culture, Fiction.* Urbana: University of Illinois Press, 1987.

Sledge, Linda Ching. "Maxine Kingston's *China Men:* The Family Historian as Epic Poet." *MELUS* 7, no. 4:3–22 (1980).

Smith, Sidonie. *A Poetics of Women's Autobiography: Marginality and the Fictions of Self-Representation.* Bloomington: Indiana University Press, 1987.

Wang, Alfred S. "Maxine Hong Kingston's Reclaiming of America: The Birthright of the Chinese American Male." *South Dakota Review* 26, no. 1:18–29 (Spring 1988).

Wang, Veronica. "Reality and Fantasy: The Chinese-American Woman's Quest for Identity." *MELUS* 12, no. 3:23–31 (Fall 1985).

Ya-jie, Zhang. "A Chinese Woman's Response to Maxine Hong Kingston's *The Woman Warrior.*" *MELUS* 13, no. 3–4:103–107 (Fall–Winter 1986).

INTERVIEWS AND RELATED ARTICLES

Brownmiller, Susan. "Susan Brownmiller Talks with Maxine Hong Kingston." *Mademoiselle* 83:149 (March 1977).

Islas, Arturo. "Maxine Hong Kingston." In *Women Writers of the West Coast: Speaking of Their Lives and Careers.* Edited by Marilyn Yalom. Santa Barbara, Calif.: Capra Press, 1983. Pp. 11–19.

Rabinowitz, Paula. "Eccentric Memories: A Conversation with Maxine Hong Kingston." *Michigan Quarterly Review* 26, no. 1:177–187 (Winter 1987).

Salisbury, Harrison E. "On the Literary Road: American Writers in China." *New York Times Book Review,* 20 January 1985, pp. 3, 25.

Thompson, Phyllis Hoge. " 'This Is the Story I Heard': A Conversation with Maxine Hong Kingston and Earll Kingston." *Biography* 6, no. 1:1–12 (Winter 1983).

JESLYN MEDOFF

AMY LOWELL

1874–1925

For me,
You stand poised
in the blue and buoyant air,
Cinctured by bright winds,
Treading the sunlight.
And the waves which precede you
Ripple and stir
The sands at my feet.[1]

OF THESE EIGHT concluding lines of "Venus Transiens," written by Amy Lowell for the woman who shared her life, the critic John Livingston Lowes once said: "If those eight lines were the only fragment left of an unknown poet, we should recognize that the craftsmanship which wrought their cool, controlled, and shining beauty was unique." The Amy Lowell of these poems—intimate, lyrical, sapphic—is the Lowell her close friend D. H. Lawrence nurtured as a poet, the Lowell a perceptive, lone editor in the 1950s represented by centering a collection on the poems she wrote for other women, and the Lowell taught and anthologized by feminist critics since the 1970s. But it is not the Amy Lowell literary historians have left us, nor is it the Lowell who made her famous.

Amy Lowell has had two distinct literary careers, and that fact sets her apart from other women poets who more conventionally wrote in obscurity until acts of sympathetic critical "revisioning" called them back to light. The "anecdotal" Lowell, as I shall call the first, largely because anecdotes about her overpower any real, considered attention to her poetry, was a woman of notorious note during her lifetime: Ezra Pound's "hippopoetess," the American queen of an "Imagism" he disdainfully retitled "Amygism"; one of Hemingway's "Lady Poets with Foot Notes" ("She smoked cigars all right, but her stuff was no good"); and Robert Lowell's literal ancestress yet a target nonetheless ("Remember Amy Lowell, that cigar-chawing, guffawing, senseless and meterless multimillionheiress, heavyweight mascot on a floating fortress"). Robert Lowell touches cruelly here on the three major features—not one of them poetic—making Amy Lowell the stuff of early-twentieth-century legend: her mammoth size, her inherited wealth, and her supposed public smoking of cigars.

This Amy Lowell, according to her first biographers, the sympathetic S. Foster Damon and the more judgmental Horace Gregory, earned her fame from her Boston Brahmin heritage, her eccentic behavior, her extraordinary oratorical powers (as demonstrated in public debates and readings of her long dramatic and narrative poems), her immense literary entourage (Lawrence, Pound, Thomas Hardy, John Gould Fletcher, Harriet Monroe, Vachel Lindsay, Witter Bynner, Edward Arlington Robinson, Sara Teasdale, Elinor Wylie, H. D., and Robert Frost are among those she either encouraged or argued with), and the sheer presence of her personality on the contemporary poetry scene. In the thirteen years between the publication of her first book at the age of thirty-eight and her early death at fifty-one, Amy Lowell lived—in spite of the ridicule and the controversy—a rich and successful *public* literary life.

The anecdotes are legion: She ritually draped all mirrors and stopped clocks, even in hotel rooms while traveling; maintained a maroon limousine and two maroon-liveried chauf-

[1] All verse quotations are from *The Complete Poetical Works of Amy Lowell* (Boston, 1955). These lines are on page 210.

feurs; slept in a custom-made, outsize bed with exactly sixteen down pillows and often held her famous tea parties in her bedroom; required that a whole salt cellar and a large pitcher of water be placed next to her at meals, even meals that she ate at the homes of others; covered her guests' laps with towels to protect them from her seven sheepdogs, maintained on sixty pounds of beef a week until wartime rationing made that impossible; and smoked the famous cigars that were more fiction than fact—not the "big, black" cigars reported in the papers but small, light, elaborately wrapped Manilas (ordering ten thousand of them when the war began). Lowell also organized and paid for an all-women's trip up the Nile by boat, ostensibly to lose weight on a regime of vegetables. When her boat was threatened by a band of marauders, she warded off an attack single-handedly by brandishing her fountain pen. On 12 May 1925 she died at Sevenels, the Lowell estate, her birthplace, of complications following surgery for an umbilical hernia brought on by her having bodily lifted onto the road a buggy driven off it by a thunderstorm.

Lowell's reputation, although colored by her flamboyance, was based on real literary criteria, her own prolific output as well as a certain literary tycoonism made possible by her fabulous wealth. She apparently had a knack for placing herself at the heart of controversy, and a hunger for performance and self-display, as well as the economic means to accomplish both. Lowell was the first woman to give a lecture at Harvard, for example, under the auspices of the Music Department, although it might have helped that her brother was that university's president. She handled poetry—writing, publication, promotion—with the talent of a business entrepreneur. "I made myself a poet," she reportedly said to her rival Harriet Monroe, editor of *Poetry*, "but the Lord made me a business man."

It is a notable fact that the debate over the New Poetry in America, conducted largely between 1913 and 1920, was the result of a competition between two powerful women: Monroe and Lowell, based respectively in Chicago and New York, and their two anthologies, *The New Poetry* and *Some Imagist Poets*. As the self-elected representative of Imagism in America (a London avant-garde movement drawing on late-nineteenth-century French symbolist experimentalism in poetry), Lowell wrote and championed "unrhymed cadence," as she renamed *vers libre:* she fought to get its practitioners published, jockeying for position with Pound as Imagism's spokesperson, establishing a stable of six of her own poets, and, in 1915, presenting the hostile old guard of the Poetry Society of America with its precepts. The success of her second book, *Sword Blades and Poppy Seeds*, marked the beginning of her career as an experimentalist; an amalgam of odd cadences, surrealistic imagery, and verse experiments, the book drew enormous attention her way.

Ironically enough, although Lowell was its champion, she was not Imagism's best representative. Imagism, as it was first formulated in the epigrams of T. E. Hulme and later in the principles of Pound, demanded brevity, musicality, and a concise centering upon the image itself, by either description or analogy. Although Lowell was interested in classical sources and translations from the Chinese, and although she claimed, after reading H. D., that the tenets of Imagism described her own poetic experiments, she was best known for longer narrative and dramatic poetry, which she read with considerable flair. A shipboard reading of "After Hearing a Waltz by Bartók," a dramatic monologue ending with a murder, left her listeners white with fear.

Four of her books, *Men, Women, and Ghosts*, *Can Grande's Castle*, *Legends*, and *East Wind*, containing virtually no personal lyrics, feature dramatic monologues. Lowell's brand of the New Poetry was based on the rhythms of breathing rather than traditional meter; she often called her poems "polyphonic prose," and modeled her poetic rhythms on "the long, flowing cadence of oratorical prose." A onetime would-be actress who was held back by her obesity, Lowell transposed that talent into a different register, traveling around the country on the strength of her reputation as a verbal performer: a graceful lecturer, sharp respondent, brilliant storyteller, and dramatic reader of poetry, she was accustomed to standing-room-only audiences.

This same Amy Lowell left a corpus of some 650 poems and wrote eleven individual books of poetry, three critical works on French and American poets, and one of the most important twentieth-century books on Keats, a two-volume revisionary biography of the poet unsurpassed until Walter Jackson Bate published his own prizewinning biography in 1963. The Keats biography, an exhaustive work of some eleven hundred pages critically acclaimed for its sensitivity to the place of Fanny Brawne in Keats's life, may be the crown of Amy Lowell's career.

She wrote many essays and reviews as well, among them the career-boosting review of Frost's *North of Boston,* and published further literary criticism in the form of *A Critical Fable,* a satire of her poetic contemporaries that took its title from a book written by her forebear James Russell Lowell. She also edited five volumes of poetry and translated from the French and also from the Chinese (in published collaboration with her childhood friend Florence Ayscough). Two selections of her poems exist, as well as *Complete Poetical Works,* introduced by Louis Untermeyer. Remarkably few—only two—lyric poems remain unpublished, testimony to her vigorous poetic entrepreneurialism, for few women poets could promote and place their work as Amy Lowell could. T. S. Eliot called her with good reason "the demon saleswoman of poetry." Although in 1926, a year after her death, she received the Pulitzer Prize for her last, posthumously published volume of verse, *What's o'Clock,* this Amy Lowell was virtually out of print by 1969.

Alongside the reputation of the high priestess of Imagism, another biography has remained to be written: that of a highly competent, affectively satisfied, professionally successful, published woman poet of the early twentieth century. Louis Untermeyer, who representatively claimed that Lowell could never win "permanence as a poet" since she had failed as a person, did not have a language for her successes.

Lowell was born on 9 February 1874 on Sevenels, her life-long home, in Brookline, Massachusetts. Her parents, Augustus and Katherine Bigelow Lawrence Lowell, were devout Episcopalians and wealthy intellectuals, whose extensive library the young Amy diligently explored. After her parents' death, Lowell became mistress of Sevenels in 1900, and began to work seriously as a poet. Turning her patrician birth and financial independence to her own advantage, Lowell gained access to and wielded power in a literary world still closed to women. She made of Sevenels, for example, a major literary salon of early-twentieth-century America.

Most important, Lowell permitted herself to manipulate existing codes of gender as a means of escaping a traumatic adolescence. Her girth, the source of cruel amusement on the part of her detractors, may have had an enabling aspect to it. "The great, rough, masculine strong thing" she felt herself to be did find, eventually, its proper sexual home. Her appearance may have prevented the more conventional matches made at the debutante balls and cotillions of her social group, but she met and "married" nonetheless; that is, she enjoyed both a figurative and literal Boston friendship with Ada Russell, her lover, aide-de-camp, and companion from 1914 until Lowell's death in 1925. "A Decade," the poem that pays tribute to their first ten years together, concludes with the words "I am completely nourished." Her early biographers brushed aside the importance of this relationship in her life, euphemistically referring to "friendship" and consequently ignoring some one hundred lesbian erotic and amatory poems. But Lowell, who shocked audiences as early as 1915 by reading her polyphonic prose-poem "Bath" and the frankly erotic "Venus Transiens," left a rich corpus of lesbian poetry attesting to a life of emotional contentment and poetic productivity. It is this second career, that of the "sapphist" Lowell, that has been chronicled more recently by Jean Gould, Lillian Faderman and other feminist critics of women's poetry.

Lowell's lesbian poems, like those of Sappho, tend to be intimate, lyric, short (and scattered like precious fragments throughout the corpus), in sharp contrast to the narratives and monologues, those ventriloquistic experiments in others' voices, that made her name. Like Sappho's, Lowell's muses were always women, her imagery distinctly feminine and homoerotic. The first of her muses was the actress Eleonora Duse, at whose Boston performance in 1902 Lowell experienced her awakening as a poet ("The effect was something tremendous. What really happened is it revealed me to myself"). Lowell remained inspired by the Duse's example over a period of twenty years, supported her on her last tour of the United States, and eventually wrote a series of exquisite sonnets as well as longer poems in her name.

Lowell's most important muse, however, was the partner who made her work possible. Twenty of Lowell's intimate, erotic lyrics—a record of her courtship of Ada Russell—appeared as early as *Sword Blades,* but the experimental and narrative poems drew the critical notice. The problem seems to have been as much an issue of what she could risk saying directly, as of what her contemporary audience wanted to see. Only D. H. Lawrence, with whom Lowell enjoyed a long, mutually enriching literary friendship, admired these short poems in free verse as written by the real Amy Lowell. In a letter to her he asked for more of her "genuine strong, sound self," full of "restrained, almost bitter Puritan passion. . . . How much nicer, finer, bigger you are, intrinsically, than your poetry is." Lawrence was speaking here of the posed poems, the dramatic monologues and the elusive narratives. He singled out for praise from *Sword Blades* "The Taxi," written outright for Ada Russell:

> When I go away from you
> The world beats dead
> Like a slackened drum.
> I call out for you against the jutted stars
> And shout into the ridges of the wind.
> Streets coming fast,
> One after the other,
> Wedge you away from me,
> And the lamps of the city prick my eyes
> So that I can no longer see your face.
> Why should I leave you,
> To wound myself upon the sharp edges
> of the night?
>
> (p. 43)

"I hate to see you posturing," Lawrence both admonished and encouraged Lowell, "when there is thereby a real person betrayed in you."

Critic Lillian Faderman writes that although Lowell battled against literary censorship, and supported Lawrence and Theodore Dreiser in their attempts to gain publication, she tended herself to tell the truth, but to tell it slant. The taboo against homosexuality may not have been the only element to figure in this strategy. Lowell herself may have had trouble reconciling the self-revealing passion of her lyrics and the modernist impersonality she defended. She therefore may have disguised the lesbian erotics behind the poetry by playing with gender positions, mixing pronouns, giving the impression that a conventional lover-beloved relationship was being described. But other poems are overtly homoerotic, sapphic in their invocation of explicitly feminine forms of sexual pleasure. "Absence," for example, ends with the following anticipation of sexual reunion, oral gratification, and orgasm:

> When you come, it brims
> Red and trembling with blood,
> Heart's blood for your drinking;

> To fill your mouth with love
> And the bittersweet taste of a soul.
> (p. 41)

The most sustained erotic sequence in Lowell's corpus, the forty-three poems of "Two Speak Together," in *Pictures of the Floating World,* is an autobiographical portrait, in poetry, of her sustaining relationship with Russell. Details of their shared life abound, but the heart of the poetry is its unmistakable eroticism. This was not the platonic friendship of the biographers: "Vernal Equinox" ends with the question "Why are you not here to overpower me with your tense and urgent love?" "Opal" calls the beloved "ice and fire," and reveals that "the touch of you burns my hand like snow." "The Weather-Cock Points South" is sapphic in its metaphorical catalog of female genitalia:

> I put your leaves aside,
> One by one:
> The stiff, broad outer leaves;
> The smaller ones,
> Pleasant to touch, veined with purple;
> The glazed inner leaves.
> One by one
> I parted you from your leaves,
> Until you stood up like a white flower
> Swaying slightly in the evening wind.
> (p. 211)

"A Decade," celebrating the lovers' anniversary, is included in this sequence, as are "Penumbra," anticipating the poet's death and her beloved's continued life alone in their house, and the concluding "Frimaire," a nostalgic farewell in advance to the woman who has shared her life—"Many mornings there cannot be now / For us both. Ah, Dear, I love you!" Although a few poems in the series suggest the speaker's anguish, they do so in response to the lover's temporary absence. The tone of "Two Speak Together" is remarkably calm: it remains a record of sustained emotional satisfaction, even happiness. Yet these poems, for the most part, eluded Lowell's critics and biographers, who read her work, in the words of one critic, as a virtual "knell of personal frustration . . . an effort to hide the bare walls of the empty chambers of her heart. . . ." Although Lowell suffered terribly as an adolescent ill-equipped to compete in traditional ways, the poems, taken as a whole, do not bear out the critic's grim diagnosis: the love poems span Lowell's entire corpus, appearing in her first and her last, posthumous book as well.

If Lowell achieved a kind of peace with Russell that is reflected abundantly in her poetry, her relationships with other women were ambivalent. Her competitive sparring with Harriet Monroe over the New Poetry was cause for some amusement among male poets, for example, whereas her relationships with the women she addressed at club luncheons and poetry societies across the country, even her relationships with contemporary women poets such as Sara Teasdale and Grace Hazard Conkling, were mutually enriching. She had a rousing effect on other women writers, representing the ways in which women might enter the literary world, seize and exercise power, and revise inherited forms.

Lowell now stands at the beginning of twentieth-century women's poetry in English, not only for the editors of such a representative anthology as Florence Howe and Ellen Bass's *No More Masks! An Anthology of Poems by Women* (1973), but also for women poets who came after her and for whom she founded a tradition. Margaret Atwood, for example, claims to have been deeply influenced by Lowell's much-anthologized and much-misunderstood "Patterns." But Lowell should also be viewed in company with women poets whose time she shared. Her poetic idolatry of "the tragic, incommunicable lady" who was Eleonora Duse or "the madonna" who was Russell bears comparison with H. D.'s revisionary mythologizing of "the Lady" in her *Trilogy,* a collection that makes similar use of feminine imagery and symbolism. For that matter, no other woman poet so resembles Lowell as her exact contemporary Gertrude Stein, whose choice of gender role, domestic arrangement, and financial means allowed her to live a life of similar integration. Lowell and Stein were born in the same week of the same month of the same year, to chronically ill older mothers unable to care for them, and the resemblances do not end there. Yet a competitive mutual antipathy kept them apart, unwilling to meet, unable to read one another's work.

Lowell's profound need—and her fear—of other women poets comes through in "The Sisters," published in her last volume of poems. The poem is as much a meditation on the distance of poetic ancestresses, "the strange, isolated little family" of women who write poetry, as it is a statement on the possibility of women's poetry at all. Yet Sappho, Mrs. Browning, and Emily Dickinson, singled out for their talent, their isolation, and the repression they suffered, remain curiously unknowable to the speaker, as much as she yearns to call them her sisters. "None of you has any word for me," she writes, feeling "sad and self-distrustful." But while "older sisters" may be "very sobering things," the thought of younger ones is heartening. The poem ends with what turns out to be a prophetic gesture toward the future:

> I only hope that possibly some day
> Some other woman with an itch for writing
> May turn to me as I have turned to you
> And chat with me a brief few minutes.
> (p. 459–460)

A tradition of women poets did not exist when these lines of Amy Lowell were published in 1925, but it was soon to exist, and—as she was never to know—she would be mother of it.

Selected Bibliography

PRIMARY WORKS

POETRY

A Dome of Many-Coloured Glass. Boston: Houghton Mifflin, 1912.

Sword Blades and Poppy Seed. New York: Macmillan, 1914.

Men, Women, and Ghosts. New York: Macmillan, 1916.

Can Grande's Castle. New York: Macmillan, 1918.

Pictures of the Floating World. New York: Macmillan, 1919.

Legends. Boston: Houghton Mifflin, 1921.

Fir-Flower Tablets. Boston: Houghton Mifflin, 1921. Translations of ancient Chinese poetry in collaboration with Florence Ayscough.

A Critical Fable. Boston: Houghton Mifflin, 1922.

What's o'Clock. Boston: Houghton Mifflin, 1925.

East Wind. Boston: Houghton Mifflin, 1926.

Ballads for Sale. Boston: Houghton Mifflin, 1927.

COLLECTIONS OF POETRY

Selected Poems. Edited by John Livingston Lowes. Boston: Houghton Mifflin, 1928.

Complete Poetical Works. Boston: Houghton Mifflin, 1955.

A Shard of Silence: Selected Poems of Amy Lowell. Edited by Glenn Richard Ruihley. New York: Twayne, 1957. Includes a useful introduction.

PROSE

Six French Poets: Studied in Contemporary Literature. New York: Macmillan, 1915.

Tendencies in Modern American Poetry. New York: Macmillan, 1917.

John Keats. 2 vols. Boston: Houghton Mifflin, 1925.

Poetry and Poets. Boston: Houghton Mifflin, 1930.

ANTHOLOGIES

Some Imagist Poets. Boston: Houghton Mifflin, 1915. Includes a preface on Imagism.

Some Imagist Poets. Vol. 2. Boston: Houghton Mifflin, 1916.

Some Imagist Poets. Vol. 3. Boston: Houghton Mifflin, 1917.

A Miscellany of American Poetry. New York: Alfred Harcourt, 1917.

A Miscellany of American Poetry. Vol. 2. New York: Alfred Harcourt, 1918.

CORRESPONDENCE AND PAPERS

Florence Ayscough and Amy Lowell: Correspondence of a Friendship. Edited by Harley Farnsworth MacNair. Chicago: University of Chicago Press, 1945.

The Letters of D. H. Lawrence and Amy Lowell, 1914–1925. Edited by E. Claire Healey and Keith Cushman. Santa Barbara, Calif.: Black Sparrow, 1985.

The Amy Lowell Collection, including letters, memorabilia, first editions of her works, family papers, and her famous library, is held in the Houghton Library at Harvard University.

SECONDARY WORKS

BIOGRAPHICAL AND CRITICAL STUDIES

Bryher, Winifred. *Amy Lowell: A Critical Appreciation.* London: Eyre and Spottiswoode, 1918.

Damon, S. Foster. *Amy Lowell: A Chronicle.* Boston: Houghton Mifflin, 1935.

Drake William: *The First Wave: Women Poets in America, 1915–1945.* New York: Macmillan, 1987. Ch. 3.

Faderman, Lillian. "Warding Off the Watch and Ward Society: Amy Lowell's Treatment of the Lesbian Theme." *Gay Books Bulletin* 1:23–27 (Summer 1979).

Flint, F. Cudworth. *Amy Lowell.* Minneapolis: University of Minnesota Press, 1969.

Francis, Lesley Lee. "A Decade of 'Stirring Times': Robert Frost and Amy Lowell." *New England Quarterly* 59:508–522 (1986).

Gregory, Horace. *Amy Lowell: Portrait of the Poet in Her Time.* New York: Thomas Nelson, 1958.

Gould, Jean. *Amy: The World of Amy Lowell and the Imagist Movement.* New York: Dodd, Mead, 1975.

Heymann, C. David. *American Aristocracy: The Lives and Times of James Russell, Amy, and Robert Lowell.* New York: Dodd, Mead, 1980.

Lowes, John Livingston. "The Poetry of Amy Lowell." *Saturday Review of Literature* 2:169–170, 174–175 (3 October 1925).

Ruihley, Glenn Richard. *The Thorn of a Rose: Amy Lowell Reconsidered.* Hamden, Conn.: Archon Books, 1975.

Wood, Clement. *Amy Lowell.* New York: Harold Vinal, 1926.

BIBLIOGRAPHY

There is at present no single-volume bibliography devoted to Amy Lowell, although an early listing of periodical articles on Lowell may be found in the bibliographical volume (vol. 2) of *Literary History of the United States,* edited by Robert E. Spiller et al., rev. ed. (New York: Macmillan, 1974). Another extensive checklist of early Lowell criticism is Francis Kemp, "Bibliography of Amy Lowell," *Bulletin of Bibliography* 15:8–9, 25–26, 50–53 (1933–1934).

CELESTE M. SCHENCK

MARY McCARTHY

1912–1989

MARY McCARTHY'S LIFE spanned most of the twentieth century, and her work reflects the dramatic shifts in values in American culture during this period of rapid urbanization, bureaucratization, and radicalization of the political consciousness of artists and intellectuals. Like her close friend Hannah Arendt, much of whose work focuses on issues of authority and social justice, McCarthy was deeply concerned with civil rights and social responsibility—issues that implicitly involve the examination of traditional assumptions about gender, race, and class. The extraordinary range of McCarthy's intellectual and aesthetic expertise is evident in her many publications, which include drama reviews, political analysis, cultural criticism, and art and architecture history, as well as numerous novels and short stories.

From her early theater columns for the *Partisan Review* and her collection of autobiographical narratives in *Memories of a Catholic Girlhood* to her astute essays on Hanoi, Vietnam, and the Watergate trials, McCarthy demonstrated that she was an important intellectual whose finely honed prose elicits powerful responses from her readers. Her fiction, which ranges from the collection of interrelated stories in *The Company She Keeps* to the novels *The Groves of Academe, The Group, Birds of America,* and *Cannibals and Missionaries,* is deftly crafted and often emotionally penetrating. Critics, such as the writer of an editorial in *Life* magazine (20 September 1963), who are uncomfortable with McCarthy's incisive political analysis and unsparing satirical fiction have called her "cold, steely, merciless" and described her as a "lady with a switchblade." Despite these responses, which essentially attest to her power, McCarthy was widely respected for her intellectual acumen, her wit, and her courage, as well as her mastery of literary genres.

As her autobiographical *Memories of a Catholic Girlhood* (1957) and *How I Grew* (1987) state, Mary Therese McCarthy's personal life was as multifaceted as her work. Born in Seattle, Washington, on 21 June 1912, she was orphaned at the age of six. She grew up in Minneapolis and Seattle. After graduation from Vassar College, McCarthy lived in New York City and began to write book reviews for the *Nation* and the *New Republic,* as well as the theater chronicle for the *Partisan Review.* She was married four times and had one child with her second husband, Edmund Wilson. Although she experienced financial privation for the first part of her childhood, McCarthy enjoyed considerable comfort in her adolescent years, when she lived with her maternal grandparents in Seattle. As an adult, she also knew both poverty and wealth; she lived in a variety of households, from a cold-water flat in New York City and simple country cottages to an elegant and cosmopolitan apartment in Paris and a spacious country house in Maine. McCarthy also traveled in many countries, including Italy, France, England, Portugal, Greece, Libya, the Soviet Union, and Poland. Despite the stresses and challenges of her personal life and the sometimes hostile response of critics to her work, McCarthy was a survivor rather than a victim; she was unequivocally a writer of extraordinary range and a citizen of the world.

The death of her parents, Roy Winfield McCarthy and Therese (Tess) Preston McCarthy, in the influenza epidemic of 1918 orphaned Mary and her three younger brothers—four-year-old Kevin, three-year-old Preston, and one-year-old Sheridan. The McCarthy family had been in the process of moving from Seattle to Minneapolis, where they were planning to live in a house that had been purchased for them by Roy's parents. Instead the McCarthy children were installed in the house with their great-aunt Margaret Sheridan McCarthy and her new husband, Myers Shriver, who became their guardians.

Mary McCarthy's accounts of her life with the Shrivers make it clear that the children's lives had changed much for the worse. The children were verbally humiliated, arbitrarily deprived of reasonable comforts and entertainments, punished severely, and frequently beaten with a hairbrush or razor strop by Myers. In *Memories of a Catholic Girlhood*, McCarthy also remembered that Margaret fed her charges prunes, cornmeal mush, Wheatena, farina, parsnips, rutabagas, carrots, and boiled potatoes, while she prepared special meals for Myers. Aunt Margaret insisted that the children play outdoors for six hours a day, even on the harshest days of the Midwestern winters. McCarthy recalls that she and her brothers would "simply stand in the snow, crying." Finding comfort in religion, she observes in *Memories of a Catholic Girlhood* that she took refuge "at school, with the nuns, at church, in the sacraments."

After living with the Shrivers for six years, Mary went back to Seattle to stay with her maternal grandparents, Harold and Augusta Preston (her brothers were sent to a boarding school). Harold Preston was a successful and respected lawyer; Augusta Preston was acclaimed for her beauty and fashionable elegance. McCarthy enjoyed a luxurious new life in her grandparents' spacious, comfortable home. The Prestons, concerned that their granddaughter receive an excellent education, sent her to the Sacred Heart Convent for her primary schooling and to the Annie Wright Seminary for high school. McCarthy was an outstanding student: not only had she mastered Latin—she reports that she was enamored of Caesar—she was also an accomplished writer. She won many prizes for her expository essays and wrote several short stories. One of McCarthy's high-school teachers, Dorothy Atkinson, had attended Vassar and inspired her star student to enroll there as well.

As an undergraduate at Vassar from 1929 to 1933, McCarthy was thoroughly absorbed in her literature courses and was particularly influenced by John Dos Passos's *The 42nd Parallel*, which she credits with having stirred her political consciousness. In *How I Grew*, McCarthy states that her childhood reading had been traditional—*Black Beauty*, *The Water Babies*, *Hans Brinker; or, The Silver Skates*, *Heidi*, *Alice in Wonderland*, *Little Women*, and *Jo's Boys*. In high school, she read such requisite texts as *A Tale of Two Cities*, *Huckleberry Finn*, and *Moby-Dick*, as well as a considerable amount of what she calls "trash": *True Story*, *True Confessions*, and movie magazines. At Vassar she read the moderns—Eliot, Pound, Millay, Aiken, and Mencken, as well as Tolstoy, Horace, Walpole, Johnson, Swinburne, Virgil, Spenser, Shakespeare, and Milton.

In her autobiographical memoir *How I Grew* (1987), McCarthy recalls that most of her Vassar professors were "Norman Thomas Socialists," and says that she shared their values. As an undergraduate, however, and for many subsequent years, McCarthy received financial support from both her Preston and McCarthy grandparents (her McCarthy grandparents provided her with stock in Capitol Elevator that paid excellent dividends). This financial security enabled her to marry Harold Johnsrud, an aspiring but impoverished playwright, one week after her graduation—when she was twenty-one. In *How I Grew*, McCarthy confides that on her wedding night she already regretted the marriage. At the time, however, she had little confidence in her own abilities and felt that Johnsrud was intellectually and artistically superior; she thought that his career was more important than hers, even though she was then receiving considerable attention for her incisive and outspoken reviews in the *Nation*. The marriage of

Kay Strong and Harald Peterson in *The Group* is based on the relationship of McCarthy and Johnsrud.

After three years of marriage McCarthy left Johnsrud for John Porter, another undistinguished young man. Joan Gelderman, who has written the most comprehensive biography of McCarthy to date, notes that this affair was chronicled in McCarthy's first short story, "Cruel and Barbarous Treatment." Another brief fling, with a man she met on the train en route to Reno to obtain a divorce from Johnsrud, provided the plot for her short story "The Man in the Brooks Brothers Shirt," published in *Partisan Review* in 1941. McCarthy was always candid about her sexual experiences, unreserved about admitting that she had many affairs and several abortions. Her openness about subjects that had long been taboo caused considerable critical controversy—in fact, the details about obtaining and using a diaphragm in her best-selling novel *The Group* created an international scandal. In this novel McCarthy emphatically rejects Victorian norms of female passionlessness and is not afraid of her own sexuality.

After her first divorce, in 1936, Mary McCarthy lived in a small apartment in Greenwich Village and worked as an editorial assistant for the publisher Covici-Friede. During the Depression era the Village was the center for artists and intellectuals, many of whom thought that President Franklin Delano Roosevelt's New Deal was not sufficiently radical. Among writers like Sherwood Anderson, Erskine Caldwell, John Dos Passos, and Upton Sinclair, there were many debates about the politics of Communism; at the many parties McCarthy attended she heard the arguments between the Stalinists and the anti-Stalinists, with whom McCarthy sided. Her allegiance to Trotsky became part of the narrative of two of her short stories, "The Genial Host" and "Portrait of an Intellectual as a Yale Man," which were later included in *The Company She Keeps* (1942).

During the radical political ferment of the mid 1930s, she began an affair with Philip Rahv, a Ukrainian-born Marxist intellectual. While McCarthy and Rahv were living together, they revived the literary journal *Partisan Review*, which Rahv and William Phillips had founded in 1934. In 1937 the editorial board included Mary McCarthy, Dwight Macdonald, F. W. Dupee, and George Morris; McCarthy was the drama critic as well. In 1938 McCarthy left Rahv to marry Edmund Wilson, who was seventeen years her senior. In addition to having been managing editor of *Vanity Fair* and the *New Republic*, Wilson had written a book on literary modernism, *Axel's Castle* (1931), and was considered a formidable literary critic. As McCarthy observes in *How I Grew*, this marriage was extremely destructive to her self-esteem (Gelderman states that Wilson drank excessively and beat McCarthy); however, he did launch her career as a fiction writer. McCarthy reports that in the first year of their marriage, Wilson insisted that she stay in the study until she had written a short story. The result was "Cruel and Barbarous Treatment," published in the *Southern Review* in 1939. She followed with several related stories collected in *The Company She Keeps*, which, according to Gelderman, sold ten thousand copies when published by Simon and Schuster in 1942. The publication of this volume attracted the attention of the *New Yorker*, and McCarthy was commissioned to become a writer for the magazine.

McCarthy admits she never would have written fiction had it not been for Edmund Wilson. In many respects he was her most important professional mentor; he was a well-established and respected critic and his encouragement was essential for McCarthy's professional development. Their marriage, however, was disastrous. Gelderman observes that McCarthy portrayed her feelings about her relationship to Wilson in the novel *A Charmed Life* (1955): "He casts a long shadow. I don't want to live in it. I feel depreciated by him, like a worm, like a white grub in the ground." Finally, in 1945, McCarthy took their six-year-old son, Reuel, and moved to the Stanhope Hotel in New York City. Gelderman reports that the deposition taken during the divorce proceedings cites "physical and mental humiliation" as her reason for leaving Wilson.

To earn money McCarthy accepted a teaching position at Bard College, but she decided not to accept the position for a second year because teaching interfered with her writing. While at Bard, she became involved with Bowden Broadwater, who worked for the *New Yorker;* he was eight years younger than she and deeply impressed with her talent. When McCarthy and Broadwater married in December 1946, he was extremely supportive of her work, and the fifteen years she was married to him were among the most productive of her career. During this time she published *The Oasis* (1949), *Cast a Cold Eye* (1950), *The Groves of Academe* (1952), *A Charmed Life* (1955), *Sights and Spectacles* (1956), *Venice Observed* (1956), *The Stones of Florence* (1959), and *On the Contrary* (1961). If Wilson was the authoritative but punitive father (in her case, uncle), then Broadwater was the kindred brother.

The post–World War II years in New York City were extremely stimulating for McCarthy. She was active in the formation of the Europe-America Groups of artists and intellectuals of the left. Her novel *The Oasis,* published in 1949, was based on her involvement with these groups, which she later came to feel were based on utopian hopes of forming an international anarchist community. During this time, McCarthy and Hannah Arendt became very close friends; they admired each other immensely and shared their work and lives. Gelderman notes that McCarthy once observed that the expressions on her friend's face were "the motions of the mind exteriorized in action." Arendt's description of McCarthy in a letter of recommendation to the Guggenheim Foundation dated 2 February 1959 provides an arresting and unusual portrait:

> What distinguishes her from other writers . . . is that she reports her findings from the viewpoint and with the amazement of the child who discovered that the Emperor has no clothes. The point is that her impetus springs from the fact that she, like a child and unlike anybody else in society, always begins by believing quite literally what everybody says and thus prepares herself for the finest, most wonderful clothes. Whereupon the Emperor enters—stark naked. This inner tension between expectation and reality, I think, runs like a thread through most of her work since *The Company She Keeps.* It gives her novels and stories a rare dramatic quality which, oddly enough, is often independent of the plot.
>
> (Hannah Arendt Papers, Library of Congress)

After Arendt's death in 1975, McCarthy, whom Arendt had appointed her literary executor, postponed her own work to devote two years to editing and reorganizing Arendt's *The Life of the Mind,* published in two volumes by Harcourt Brace Jovanovich in 1978. In *How I Grew* McCarthy observes that in her own life "not love or marriage so much as friendship has promoted growth." During the thirty-year span of their deeply sustaining friendship both McCarthy and Arendt published extensively, became internationally famous, won many awards, and received numerous honorary degrees. Not only did they treasure their personal and intellectual kinship, they took pleasure in each other's professional accomplishments.

In late December 1959, accompanied by Broadwater and her son, Reuel, McCarthy went to Poland to begin a lecture for the United States Information Agency. During the course of the four-week tour, she fell in love with James West, the public affairs officer for the American embassy in Warsaw who had been arranging her itinerary; he was forty-six and she was forty-seven. Gelderman reports that they had hoped to marry almost immediately; however, two difficult years followed this decision. West had three children, the eldest of whom was only seven. Although Broadwater was upset by McCarthy's decision, he agreed to give her a divorce; West's wife was less cooperative. McCarthy decided to remain in Europe to be with

West, even though (as she wrote to Hannah Arendt) she was distressed by being separated from her books and papers and by not having "a stable place to live." Nevertheless, a disciplined, professional writer, she continued to work. In 1961 West became her fourth and final husband.

After their marriage McCarthy and West moved to Paris, where she completed a novel she had begun in the early 1950s. *The Group,* published in 1963, became a best-seller. The critic Elizabeth Hardwick praised McCarthy for writing the novel "from a woman's point of view, the comedy of Sex." McCarthy's life continued to be personally and intellectually challenging. Gelderman states that McCarthy became an active stepmother to West's three children, who visited during holidays and summer vacations. She also began writing about political issues of international importance. Her books of political and cultural analysis—*Vietnam* (1967), *Hanoi* (1968), *Medina* (1972), *The Seventeenth Degree* (1974), *The Mask of State: Watergate Portraits* (1974)— received widespread attention. During this time she also published two more novels, *Birds of America* (1965) and *Cannibals and Missionaries* (1979); two volumes of literary criticism, *The Writing on the Wall and Other Literary Essays* (1970) and *Ideas and the Novel* (1980); and an autobiographical volume, *How I Grew* (1987). Mary McCarthy died of cancer in New York City on 25 October 1989.

Although McCarthy asserted that she was not a feminist, a feminist sensibility clearly informs all of her writing. From the beginning her work was deeply involved with the politics of gender. Indeed, an important subtext in McCarthy's fiction is the battle of the sexes and the distorted aggression inherent in the traditional masculine role as well as the destructive consequences of feminine passivity; another is the need for psychological autonomy for women. Although the women in McCarthy's novels, essays, and political and personal narratives are often sexually liberated, they also are often bound by Victorian norms of passivity and dependence. Sometimes they are constrained by realistic fears of exploitation or loss of reputation. Lack of adequate economic independence in an age of few opportunities for financial self-sufficiency prevents these women from discarding the dream of the gallant knight who will rescue his princess from life's rigors. Without traditions of female assertion and self-reliance, McCarthy's women founder in confusion; often they do not perceive their options, or are paralyzed by them. Like their nineteenth-century counterparts, they look for salvation in a man: "There was no use talking. *She knew.* The mind was powerless to save her. Only a man . . . ," laments Margaret Sargent in the story "Ghostly Father, I Confess."

A modern woman, Margaret Sargent reappears throughout the short-story collection *The Company She Keeps.* She marries, divorces, lives alone, travels alone, works, has deeply held political convictions, remarries, is psychoanalyzed; nevertheless, she remains dependent on male approbation. In each of her picaresque adventures, Sargent nurtures men who are morally defective, psychologically handicapped, or sexually inept: "All my efforts were bent on keeping Mr. Sheer in a state of grace, and I stood guard over him as fiercely, as protectively and nervously, as if he had been a reformed drunkard. And, like the drunkard's wife, I exuded optimism and respectability," says Margaret Sargent, describing her relationship with her employer, a charlatan who sells fake objets d'art and fails to pay her the salary he owes her. While exposing Mr. Sheer's foibles in "Rogue's Gallery," McCarthy also satirizes Margaret Sargent's egotism and the frustrated need to dominate that is part of redemptive womanhood. Sargent's efforts to attain moral superiority through the salvation of unregenerate men are often foiled. The man in the Brooks Brothers shirt refuses to let her play the romantic heroine whose love transforms the toad into a prince: he persists in his toadlike ways.

Trapped by the scenario of feminine self-abnegation in the name of romantic love, Margaret Sargent can neither recognize her own feelings nor acknowledge her fundamental aversion to her seducer—as with the nameless man in the Brooks Brothers shirt: "The attraction was not sexual, for, as the whiskey went down in the bottle, his face took on a more and more porcine look that became so distasteful to her that she could hardly meet his gaze." In McCarthy's dissection, seduction becomes a charade in which the romantic heroine must adjust every gesture, every facial and vocal nuance, to support her leading man: "She found that she was extending herself to please him. All her gestures grew over-feminine and demonstrative: the lift of her eyebrows was a shade too arch: like a passée belle, she was overplaying herself." Margaret Sargent's self-mockery underscores her powerlessness: "The glow of self-sacrifice illuminated her. . . . Quickly she helped him take off the black dress, and stretched herself out on the berth like a slab of white lamb on an altar." Her self-abnegation is complete as she "waited with some impatience for the man to exhaust himself, for the indignity to be over." False pride, a concern for her performance, eclipse her self-knowledge.

While McCarthy's satiric rendering of Margaret Sargent's sentimentality leads to a restructuring of her protagonist's consciousness, the portraits of the men in *The Company She Keeps* (as in much of her work) are static—masculine egotistical perspectives are ridiculed and scorned. Both Mr. Sheer, the dealer in fake antiques, and Pflaumen (which means "prunes" in German), the genial host who is a silly social middleman, are infantile and self-indulgent, but the Yale man, Jim Barnett, is pernicious. In this barbed portrait, the inflated self-importance of the glamorous, liberal intellectual is punctured, and he hates Margaret Sargent for making him aware of his own limitations:

> He had never been free, but until he had tried to love the girl, he had not known that he was bound. it was self-knowledge she had taught him: she had taught him the cage of his own nature. He had accommodated himself to it, but he could never forgive her. Through her he had lost his primeval ignorance, and he would hate her forever as Adam hates Eve.
>
> (1970 ed., p. 246)

In McCarthy's first reconstruction of her early childhood, *Memories of a Catholic Girlhood* (1957), her portrait of her abusive Uncle Myers reduces him to a brute or beast without intelligence:

> [Myers sits] in a brown leather armchair in the den, wearing a blue work shirt stained with sweat, open at the neck to show an undershirt, and lion-blond, glinting hair on his chest. Below this were workmen's trousers of a brownish-gray material, strain at the buttons and always gaping slightly, just below the belt, to show another glimpse of underwear, of a yellowish white. On his fat head, frequently, with its crest of bronze curly hair, were the earphones of a crystal radio set, which he sometimes, briefly, in a generous mood, fitted over the grateful ears of one of my little brothers.
>
> (1981 ed., p. 56)

McCarthy's text probes and pokes the bodies of her other male characters for evidence of malaise, and she takes great delight in examining the tissue of arrogance exposed by her scalpel. Her description of Professor Mulcahy in *The Groves of Academe* portrays his moral flaccidity: "A tall, soft-bellied, lisping man with a tense, mushroom white face, rimless bifocals, and graying thin red hair, he was intermittently aware of a quality of personal unattractiveness that emanated from him like a miasma; this made him self-pitying, uxorious, and addicted to self-love."

Another portrait of arrogant masculinity is the description in *Vietnam* of Colonel Corson, a Marine commander and pacification officer: "Colonel Corson was playing God and the Devil up there in the hills behind Da Nang. . . . He held the little country of Vietnam—where people wore conical hats and lived in bamboo thickets—like a toy in his hand." This same distortion of proportion occurs in McCarthy's earlier novel *The Oasis* when Taub, standing alone on a mountaintop, thinks of the pastoral scene below as a toy agricultural set. Appropriating the landscape before him, he feels like "Utopia's discoverer and an impresario to Nature."

In *The Mask of State: Watergate Portraits,* McCarthy untangles the threads of a national political scandal as in earlier prose she puzzled through the confused memories of her youth. Instead of satiric portraits of Uncle Myers, the man in the Brooks Brothers shirt, the Yale intellectual, Mr. Sheen, or Mulcahy, there are biting descriptions of Maurice Stans, Jeb Stuart Magruder, John Mitchell, H. R. Haldeman, John Ehrlichman, John Dean, and G. Gordon Liddy. The Watergate group is ridiculed for being as self-indulgent, arrogant, and domineering as any of their fictional counterparts in McCarthy's rogues' gallery. For example, her vivid physical portrait of Ehrlichman recalls her description of apelike Uncle Myers: "Everything about his features and body movements is canted, tilted, slanting, sloping, askew. The arms swing loosely; the left hand with a big seal ring, like a brass knuckle, moves in a sweeping gesture. The broad head is too round—pygmyish."

The Group, published in 1963, became an immediate international best-seller (more than five million copies have been sold since it first appeared). It is a novel about eight classmates who graduate from Vassar in 1933, and whose collective belief in women's rights and social progress cannot dispel the fact that their lives are ultimately dominated by men—fathers, husbands, lovers. Despite their ideals of self-reliance and their faith in the promise of modern life, these new women who hope to combine love and work discover that they are as dependent on men for their economic and social survival as their mothers were. McCarthy notes that the novel begins with the inauguration of Franklin Roosevelt and ends with the inauguration of Dwight Eisenhower, and she says: "It was conceived as a mock chronicle. It's a novel about the idea of progress really, seen in the female sphere; the study of technology in the home, in the playpen, in the bed."

In this novel, progress is based on the promise of technology, which is the province of men: nutrition becomes a matter of recipes and availability of canned goods; sex, a matter of contraception; childbearing and rearing, a matter of methodology. Men even attempt to control the basic female biological functions of conceiving, bearing, and nurturing children. For example, Dick (perhaps too obviously named) deflowers Dottie, orders her to get a diaphragm at the Margaret Sanger clinic, and then decides not to see her again. Instead of being angry, she is alternately grateful to him for having been her lover and guilty about her own lack of previous sexual experience. Priss marries Sloane, who takes charge of the birth and breast-feeding of their child as if directing a play in which she has a walk-on part.

The Group chronicles the lives of the daughters of the professional and upper classes. Although their economic advantages could allow them more autonomy than that available to women from other socioeconomic backgrounds, in reality—the novel implies—they are too often the slaves of fashion or convention, and their understanding of freedom is limited to rebellion against parental codes. The novel contains a series of satiric vignettes that are peppered with details about affairs, clothes, recipes, household furnishings. For example, the description of Kay on her wedding day is a characteristic blend of exquisite fashion detail and caustic wit:

> Kay . . . was wearing a pale-brown thin silk dress with a big white *mousseline de soie* collar and a wide black taffeta hat wreathed with white daisies. . . . With her glowing cheeks, vivid black curly hair, and tawny hazel eyes, she looked like a country lass on some old tinted post card; the seams of her stockings were crooked, and the backs of her black suède shoes had worn spots, where she had rubbed them against each other. Pokey scowled. "Doesn't she know," she lamented, "that black's bad luck for weddings?"
> (1964 ed., p. 11)

McCarthy's ability to use what is thought of as feminine chatter to construct the details of her characters' daily lives gives the novel its power. Many critics have objected to its gossipy, trivial, breathy diction and domestic details, but McCarthy's rendering of the traditionally "feminine" effectively exposes the cultural contradictions and absurdities with which her characters live. Given the fact that during much of their lives they have been confined to the domestic and decorative spheres, it is not surprising that their energies are directed toward etiquette and clothes.

In his essay "The Novel" (in *Prejudices: Third Series*, 1922), H. L. Mencken asserts that women novelists have been hindered by a "lingering ladyism—a childish prudery inherited from their mothers." He concludes that women will succeed in the novel as they "gradually throw off the inhibitions that have hitherto cobwebbed their minds." In *The Group*, McCarthy does shed inhibitions, as she writes about sex, birth control, and childbirth in the context of her protagonists' lives as young matrons, wives, and mothers. This novel narrates modern versions of female sexuality from menarche and defloration to pregnancy, lactation, and menopause.

"If I live to the year 1950," Mencken continues in the same essay, "I expect to see a novel by a woman that will describe a typical marriage under Christianity, from the woman's standpoint. . . . That novel, I venture to predict, will be a cuckoo. . . . It will seem harsh, but it will be true. And, being true, it will be a good novel." Certainly McCarthy's unflinching narrative of Kay's marriage to Harald (which has many autobiographical dimensions) deftly portrays marriage from a female perspective, as does the rendering of Priss's marriage to Sloane. In both cases, shortsighted and overbearing husbands expect these extremely bright and capable women to disregard the validity of their own experiences. The only two women in the group who are not dominated by men are Helena, who is described as sexually androgynous—she looks like a freckled little boy—and Lakey, a lesbian. Moreover, only Lakey emerges in command of her energy and power at the end of the novel. Clearly McCarthy is suggesting that traditional gender roles are based on destructive paradigms of dominance and submission. In this context, only those women who stand outside conventions of femininity and masculinity survive with integrity.

The Group begins with a wedding and ends with a funeral. In the course of the novel free love, adultery, misogyny, divorce, and insanity are confronted squarely—the irony, and sometimes the horror, beneath social surfaces is exposed. In addition to exploring taboo subjects and deflating romantic illusions, the novel exposes the limitations and absurdities of traditional versions of femininity, suggesting new scenarios for marriage, work, friendship, and love. The publication of *The Group* was a pivotal point in McCarthy's career; in this novel she successfully places private lives in an illuminating political context that enables her readers to understand the deeper and more complex truths of the lives of two decades of American women.

In Memories of a Catholic Girlhood, McCarthy analyzes her childhood from both historical and political perspectives. Through her portrait of her grandmother Augusta Preston—who lived during the era of Sigmund Freud—McCarthy re-enters history and analyes the silences in the life of a traditional woman. In narrating her grandmother's life story, McCarthy examines the mythology that sustained her grandmother in her role as a great beauty, an icon to be worshiped: "This body of hers was the cult object around which our household revolved." The cultural assumptions of silent and ornamental femininity that sustained her grandmother's life will destroy the granddaughter's if she does not gain conscious control over them; McCarthy therefore demystifies them in order to defuse their power.

McCarthy emphasizes the ritual quality of Augusta's day: hours spent in her boudoir choosing clothes and applying make-up, hours spent shopping in department stores. Grandmother Preston refuses to be photographed after she is no longer an "imperious, handsome matron," but McCarthy supplies the missing visual details of the aging iconic beauty: "When she perspired, on a warm day, the little beads of sweat on her eagle nose under her nose veil and on her long upper lip would produce a caked look that seemed sad, as though her skin were crying." The detail of the crying skin belies cosmetic artifice and underscores the inexorable fact that beauty is subject to mortality.

The portrait of Rosie Morgenstern Gottstein, Augusta Preston's sister, illustrates an alternative to domesticated ornamentality. Aunt Rosie provides a dramatic contrast to her sister's stately silence: she "was a short, bright, very talkative, opinionated woman, something of a civic activist and something of a Bohemian." McCarthy identifies with her aunt's excitable volubility ("I was the only member of my family—not counting Aunt Rosie—who was excitable") and is heartened to know there are ways to exist other than as the living icon of idealized womanhood. Like Aunt Rosie, McCarthy commits herself to articulating her perceptions.

Another great-aunt, Eva, is depicted with a scorn that matches McCarthy's compassion for Aunt Rosie. Aunt Eva spends the considerable resources of her late husband on a life that is both conventional and mindless: "She was a typical wealthy widow of Jewish high society. She traveled a good deal . . . she gambled, and went to resorts and fashionable hotels in season; when she was in Seattle, she was an habituee of the Jewish country club, where they golfed in the daytime and played bridge for very high stakes at night." The words "typical" and "habituee" link Aunt Eva's life to the ritualized existence of Augusta, but without the imperative or excuse of a husband whose position she must maintain. Like Augusta's life, Eva's is perishable. Although these women's lives are based on the cyclical pattern that society imposes on them, McCarthy's linear narration individualizes them and causes her readers to regret the waste such lives represent.

Having been orphaned as a little girl surely motivated McCarthy to record her experience, especially since her parents left her so little that documented her life. Tess McCarthy left only a few letters, and Roy McCarthy's literary legacy was a disappointment:

> As for the legend that he was a brilliant man, with marked literary gifts, alas, I once saw his diary. It was a record of heights and weights, temperatures and enemas, interspersed with slightly sententious "thoughts," like a schoolboy's; he writes out for himself, laboriously, the definitions of an atheist and an agnostic.
>
> (*Memories of a Catholic Girlhood,* 1974 ed., pp. 11–12)

Perhaps the deprivation of a more personal legacy in fact spurred McCarthy to create her own, and while she might have presented her life as merely a series of episodes underscored by loss and pain, instead she constructed her autobiography as characterized by a series of adventures, periods of emotional learning and growth, and increasing levels of artistic maturity and mastery.

In an interview for the *Paris Review* in 1962, McCarthy observed, "I think I'm really not interested in the quest for the self anymore," adding: "What you feel when you're older, I think, is that . . . you really must *make* the self. . . . I don't mean in the sense of making a mask, a Yeatsian mask. But you finally begin in some sense to make and to choose the self you want." McCarthy's many-chaptered life certainly embodies the modernist tenet of the individual as the locus of authority.

In reconstructing her life in her autobiographical writings and in creating the lives of her fictional characters, McCarthy achieved what few American women writers before her could accomplish; as Alison Lurie observed, in a review of *How I Grew,* Mary McCarthy invented "herself as a totally new type of woman who stood for both sense and sensibility; who was both coolly and professionally intellectual and frankly passionate."

Selected Bibliography

PRIMARY WORKS

FICTION

The Company She Keeps. New York: Simon & Schuster, 1942; New York: Harcourt Brace Jovanovich, 1970.

The Oasis. New York: Random House, 1949.

The Groves of Academe. New York: Harcourt, Brace, 1952.

A Charmed Life. New York: Harcourt, Brace, 1955.

The Group. New York: Harcourt, Brace, and World, 1963; New York: New American Library, 1964.

Birds of America. New York: Harcourt Brace Jovanovich, 1965.

Cannibals and Missionaries. New York: Harcourt Brace Jovanovich, 1979.

The Hounds of Summer and Other Stories. New York: Avon Books, 1981.

NONFICTION

Cast A Cold Eye. New York: Harcourt, Brace, 1950.

Sights and Spectacles, 1937–1956. New York: Farrar, Straus & Cudahy, 1956. Theater chronicles.

Venice Observed. Paris: G. & R. Bernier, 1956.

Memories of a Catholic Girlhood. New York: Harcourt, Brace, 1957; New York: Harcourt Brace Jovanovich, 1974, 1981.

The Stones of Florence. New York: Harcourt, Brace, 1959.

On the Contrary. New York: Farrar, Straus & Cudahy, 1961.

Mary McCarthy's Theatre Chronicles, 1937–1962. New York: Farrar, Straus, 1963.

Vietnam. New York: Harcourt, Brace & World, 1967.

Hanoi. New York: Harcourt, Brace & World, 1968.

The Writing on the Wall and Other Literary Essays. New York: Harcourt Brace Jovanovich, 1970.

Medina. New York: Harcourt Brace Jovanovich, 1972.

The Mask of State: Watergate Portraits. New York: Harcourt Brace Jovanovich, 1974.

The Seventeenth Degree. New York: Harcourt Brace Jovanovich, 1974.

Ideas and the Novel. New York: Harcourt Brace Jovanovich, 1980.

Occasional Prose. New York: Harcourt Brace Jovanovich, 1985.

How I Grew. New York: Harcourt Brace Jovanovich, 1987.

SECONDARY WORKS

BIOGRAPHICAL AND CRITICAL STUDIES:

Gelderman, Carol W. *Mary McCarthy: A Life.* New York: St. Martin's Press, 1988.

Grumbach, Doris, *The Company She Kept.* New York: Coward-McCann, 1967.

Hardy, Willene Schaefer. *Mary McCarthy.* New York: Frederick Ungar, 1981.

Hewitt, Rosalie. "A 'Home Address for the Self': Mary McCarthy's Autobiographical Journey." *Journal for Narrative Technique* 12, no. 2:95–104 (Spring 1982).

Lifson, Martha R. "Allegory of the Secret: Mary McCarthy." *Biography* 4, no. 3:249–267 (Summer 1981).

Lurie, Alison. "Her Achievement." *New York Review of Books,* 11 June 1987, p. 19. Review of *How I Grew.*

Martin, Wendy. "The Satire and Moral Vision of Mary McCarthy." In *Comic Relief: Humor in Contemporary American Literature.* Edited by Sarah Blacher Cohen. Urbana: University of Illinois Press, 1978. Pp. 187–206.

McKenzie, Barbara. *Mary McCarthy.* New York: Twayne, 1966.

Niebuhr, Elizabeth. "The Art of Fiction: Mary McCarthy." *Paris Review* 27:58–94 (Winter–Spring 1962).

Stock, Irvin. *Mary McCarthy.* Minneapolis: University of Minnesota Press, 1968.

Taylor, Gordon O. "The Word for Mirror: Mary McCarthy." In *Chapters of Experience: Studies in Twentieth-Century American Autobiography.* New York: St. Martin's Press, 1983.

BIBLIOGRAPHY

Goldman, Sherli Evans. *Mary McCarthy: A Bibliography.* New York: Harcourt, Brace & World, 1968.

WENDY MARTIN

CARSON McCULLERS

1917–1967

BORN LULA CARSON SMITH in Columbus, Georgia, on 19 February 1917, Carson McCullers was destined for a life of celebrity and success, illness and suffering. The famous 1943 publicity photograph of McCullers as the twenty-three-year-old writer of *The Heart Is a Lonely Hunter*—shoulder-length straight hair, frank gaze, warm smile, hands positioned easily on several stacked copies of the novel—expresses none of the pain, both physical and emotional, evident in her later photographs. The Richard Avedon portrait, taken in 1958, presents the same open-eyed gaze, but it is accompanied by closed, downturned lips, carelessly cropped short hair, and hunched shoulders. The intervening fifteen years of triumph and disappointment had changed the confident, promising young writer into a frail invalid whose best writing lay behind her. Although she strove throughout her life to make sense of the story she lived, by bonding with artists she admired and with others she loved, in the end, she was unable to arrive at a final meaning.

When pregnant with Carson, who dropped the "Lula" while still an eccentric high schooler, Marguerite Smith had premonitions of her firstborn's genius. The mother lavished attention on the young girl, encouraging her artistic development, to the detriment, many report, of her other children, Margarita and Lamar. As Marguerite had expected, Carson excelled, especially in music, practicing the piano as many as eight hours a day. Carson thought she would become a concert pianist, and her master plan was, upon graduation from high school, to leave Columbus for the cosmopolitan North to attend the Juilliard School of Music. Financially strapped as a result of the Depression, her family was unable to afford the tuition, however, without selling a family heirloom, a diamond-and-emerald ring. At the age of seventeen, Carson went to New York, where, after unluckily losing all of her money (Virginia Spencer Carr speculates that she had left her pocketbook on the subway), she took odd jobs and enrolled in writing classes at Columbia and New York University. Despite her turning away from music and toward writing as a career, McCullers remained a ready performer and used music, her first love, as a metaphor and motif in her fiction.

Although she had appeared preoccupied with her music as a young girl, Carson had always written stories and plays. It was in New York, however, that avocation turned into vocation and her writing habits were solidified. Because McCullers became a slow, meticulous writer and reviser, she did not produce a voluminous oeuvre, publishing only four novels, a novella, a play, a dramatic adaptation of one of her novels, a volume of children's verse, and several dozen stories, poems, and essays.

Her first story, "Wunderkind," written in 1936, was published the same year in the prestigious *Story* magazine by McCullers's teacher, and the magazine's editor, Whit Burnett. The autobiographical narrative focuses on Frances, a young girl who realizes that she lacks the fire of genius, unlike the foreigners of her acquaintance, in whom true musical brilliance resides: her piano teacher, Mr. Bilderbach; his friend the violinist, Mr. Lafkowitz; and her contemporary, Heime Israelsky. She plays competently, but without drama and emotion, feeling instead "that the marrows of her bones were hollow and there was no blood left in her. Her heart that had been springing against her chest all afternoon felt suddenly dead. She saw it gray and limp and shriveled at the edges like an oyster." With this epiphany, she loses her identity as a wunderkind and becomes like all the other children playing in the noisy neighborhood.

In the summer of that same year, 1936, Carson met the dashing army corporal James Reeves McCullers, whom she married for the first time in September 1937. They then moved to Charlotte, North Carolina, where Carson wrote *The Heart Is a Lonely Hunter*. Their first months together in what Reeves described as "only a barren little island like thousands of others in America," he working as a credit manager and his young wife writing her first novel, were their best. In two years Carson completed an outline of the novel and a large part of the manuscript, sent them to Houghton Mifflin, and won a fellowship of fifteen hundred dollars to complete the project. In 1939 *The Heart Is a Lonely Hunter* was published, and Reeves and Carson moved from Fayetteville, North Carolina, where they then lived, to New York City, where Carson, alienated from her native region and needing to establish some human connections, found a new home.

Her first novel, like many other first novels, is largely autobiographical. It follows the lives, actually the misfortunes, of five loners in a small Southern town: the adolescent girl Mick Kelly, described as the focus of the narrative in "The Mute," McCullers's sketch of the novel; Biff Brannon, the owner of the ironically named New York Café, who serves, by turns, as both narrator and character; Jake Blount, the carnival roustabout who has come to town to do labor organizing; Dr. Benedict Mady Copeland, the idealistic black general practitioner whose dreams for his race are rejected by his own children; and John Singer, the deaf-mute to whom the others look for understanding and validation.

In her outline for *The Heart Is a Lonely Hunter*, McCullers announces that the novel deals with "the theme of man's revolt against his own inner isolation and his urge to express himself as fully as is possible." With a contrapuntal method in mind, the author contrasts this overarching theme with five counter-themes:

> (1) There is a deep need in man to express himself by creating some unifying principle or God. A personal God created by a man is a reflection of himself and in substance this God is most often inferior to his creator.
>
> (2) In a disorganized society these individual Gods or principles are likely to be chimerical and fantastic.
>
> (3) Each man must express himself in his own way—but this is often denied to him by a wasteful, short-sighted society.
>
> (4) Human beings are innately cooperative, but an unnatural social tradition makes them behave in ways that are not in accord with their deepest nature.
>
> (5) Some men are heroes by nature in that they will give all that is in them without regard to the effort or to the personal returns.
>
> (quoted in Evans, p. 195)

Each of the main characters searches for the "expression and spiritual integration with something greater than themselves" that McCullers explains in the outline. Mick, like young Carson, hunts for an expressive outlet in music, one of her first actions being to scrawl her favorite composer's name, "Motsart," on the wall of a house under construction in her neighborhood. She must abandon music as a creative expression of self when, at the end of the novel, she takes a job at the local Woolworth's to help support her family. Another possible avenue for fulfilling Mick's spiritual aspirations, love, is perverted into meaningless sex, when one summer day she and her longtime friend, Harry Minowitz, fall innocently to lovemaking after skinny-dipping in a creek.

The other characters are equally unsuccessful in their searches for meaning. The sexually frustrated and impotent Biff Brannon feels a strange love for Mick, although he feels nothing on the death of his wife. Jake Blount finds refuge in liquor and rhetoric after having been unable to alter the injustices he has seen in the

South. Benedict Mady Copeland, McCullers writes, "presents the bitter spectacle of the educated Negro in the South." Despite his dedication to raising his race out of poverty and illiteracy, he has had little success, even with his own children, Portia, Hamilton, and Karl Marx, who as powerless blacks in a white world maintain the status quo. Mick, Biff, Jake, and Dr. Copeland all rely on John Singer, the deaf-mute, for spiritual sustenance, while Singer, unbeknownst to the rest, devotes himself to the feeble-minded Anatopolous, whom he visits at the state mental hospital on his vacations. When Singer learns that Anatopolous has died, he commits suicide. All of the main characters isolate themselves from their community, in the manner of Young Goodman Brown or the minister Mr. Hooper, characters from Nathaniel Hawthorne, one of McCullers's early influences.

All five of the major characters are lonely hunters, people trying, with little success, to connect in meaningful ways with others, and suffering as a result. Frances Freeman Paden notes that although Mick, Biff, Jake, Copeland, and Singer seem to be attempting to establish contact with others, they are in fact trying to reach themselves; that because they cannot communicate effectively, they end up abusing themselves in a curiously autistic fashion. Singer's suicide, she concludes, is the final blow to everyone's attempt to integrate with the rest of the community: "Because Singer has served as a mirror for people in the town, his suicide fragments their vision of themselves, forcing them to change the direction of their energies. Blount and Copeland leave town, Kelly abandons her dreams, and Brannon confronts his loneliness." Although it is tempting to read Singer as a Christ figure, he does not suffer for the others' sins as much as he reflects them, and no one is saved. The final impression conveyed by the novel is one of tragic waste, according to Richard M. Cook. David Madden concurs, concluding that "*Hunter* is the most pessimistic book ever written." This novel, however, which melds pleasure and pain in a Keatsian way, brought Carson McCullers to the attention of the international literary community.

Whereas the warm reception accorded *The Heart Is a Lonely Hunter* established Carson in her career, it strained relations with Reeves, who was already insecure, with illusions about his own writing talent. Carson meanwhile basked in the newfound admiration of other artists, falling out of love with Reeves and in love with her new life, which included communal living and the adoration of another woman. That their marriage would break up seemed a foregone conclusion.

As Cook writes: "Like the autobiographical heroines of her novels, [Carson] was always searching for a new, exciting friend, waiting to be invited to a grand occasion, looking for an appreciative audience. Unlike them, she had the uncertain comfort of frequently finding what she was looking for." She found a new reason for living when, in the summer of 1940, on the heels of her recent success, she met Annemarie Clarac-Schwarzenbach, a friend of the Thomas Mann family. Carson wanted to commit herself exclusively to Annemarie, with whom she shared a love of both music and literature; however, the Swiss woman did not reciprocate. This relationship taught McCullers what would become for her a basic truth, according to Virginia Spencer Carr: "That for love to survive, passion must mellow to friendship or to a love and devotion that do not depend upon reciprocity, in which there is nothing hoped for, no fear of rejection, no jealousy."

With the encouragement of George Davis, the editor of *Harper's Bazaar,* McCullers spent the late summer at the Bread Loaf Writers' Conference in Middlebury, Vermont, revising *Reflections in a Golden Eye,* a narrative of army-post life clearly indebted to D. H. Lawrence. Given her success with *Hunter,* Houghton Mifflin wanted to publish this second work as soon as possible. When it was finally published in 1941, however, *Reflections* was condemned by many critics, who considered it gothic pulp, featuring as it does an insane army wife who snips off her nipples with garden shears. Though perhaps more carefully crafted, the novel has none of the charm of *Hunter* and "describes a world where the suffering imposed by isolation is unrelieved by the possibility of human idealism and individual struggle. It is a stark, blank world . . . where life exists on its lowest instinctual level" (Richard Cook).

Upon her return from Bread Loaf, McCullers separated from Reeves and moved into 7 Middaugh Street, a brownstone rented by George Davis. Dubbed February House by Anaïs Nin for the common birthday month of many of the residents, this structure became, according to Rex Reed, "the only important literary salon in America." Among its inhabitants were artists and literary celebrities like Louis MacNeice, Benjamin Britten, Christopher Isherwood, W. H. Auden, Richard Wright, Gypsy Rose Lee, Oliver Smith, and Thomas Mann's son Golo. The excess of life and the surreal atmosphere at February House, however, ravaged McCullers's delicate health—she had had rheumatic fever as a child—and in February 1941, while visiting her family in Columbus, McCullers suffered the first of a series of strokes; nonetheless, by spring she had recuperated sufficiently to return to New York, accompanied by Reeves. In the late spring the now-reconciled Carson and Reeves met the young composer and violinist David Diamond, who fell in love with both McCullerses and encouraged Carson to consider working at the Yaddo writers' colony. Carson spent the summer at Yaddo, finally divorcing Reeves in the late fall of 1941. Her life for the next several years involved visiting the South, working at Yaddo, and anguishing over her various love relationships.

Although during the early 1940s her personal life was in turmoil, McCullers won a Guggenheim Fellowship and wrote, most importantly, *The Ballad of the Sad Café,* and also several essays and short stories, including "The Jockey," which was published in the *New Yorker*. *The Ballad of the Sad Café* tells the story of an Amazon, Miss Amelia, whose toughness is softened—and whose moonshine and manners are improved—by her love for her dwarf, hunchbacked cousin Lymon, who deserts Miss Amelia when her former husband, Marvin Macy, enters the scene. From the start, however, Miss Amelia and Lymon's love had been doomed because of the strange, dissimilar experience of the lover and the beloved, who "come from different countries." As McCullers explains in the story: "The beloved fears and hates the lover, and with the best of reasons. For the lover is forever trying to strip bare his beloved. The lover craves any possible relation with the beloved, even if this experience can cause him only pain."

Like McCullers's other work, this novella seems to derive from her tragic experiences with love: with Reeves, who could not live with Carson; with Annemarie, who could not devote herself exclusively to Carson; and with Diamond, who could not allow either Carson or Reeves to swallow up his own talent. McCullers herself noted the autobiographical element in her fiction: "Everything significant that has happened in my fiction has also happened to me—or it will happen, eventually." *The Ballad of the Sad Café,* according to Oliver Evans, "must be one of the saddest stories in any language—not merely on the surface level of narrative . . . [but] on the level of parable."

The parable can be described as one of spiritual isolation. As McCullers noted about her writing in general in "The Flowering Dream: Notes on Writing":

> Spiritual isolation is the basis of most of my themes. . . . Love and especially love of a person who is incapable of returning or receiving it, is at the heart of my selection of grotesque figures

> to write about—people whose physical incapacity is a symbol of their spiritual incapacity to love or receive love—their spiritual isolation.
>
> (Cook, p. 20)

McCullers's next major work, *The Member of the Wedding,* begun in the fall of 1939 and tentatively titled "The Bride and Her Brother," dramatizes how such spiritual isolation causes Frankie Addams to question her identity. A girl of twelve, Frankie "belonged to no club and was a member of nothing in the world." During the summer in which the novel is set, "Frankie had become an unjoined person who hung around in doorways, and she was afraid." She sees her brother's wedding as her chance to gain an identity, envisioning herself first traveling with the newlyweds on their honeymoon and then living with them far away from her own home. Before the wedding, she tries several names on, first exchanging Frankie for F. Jasmine in an effort to have her name resemble those of her brother Jarvis and his bride Janice, and then using Frances. The black housekeeper, Berenice, objects, telling Frankie that she cannot just change her name, since a name accumulates identity. Berenice's is the voice of truth, and like William Faulkner's Dilsey, she not only endures but also prevails. As the one character who exemplifies connectedness and has had a meaningful, long-term love relationship, with her now-deceased husband, Ludie, Berenice is unfortunate only because in attempting to re-create that relationship, she has married a series of thieves and drunkards.

It is not that human warmth and closeness do not exist in Frankie's world, although her one encounter with a boy close to her own age ends with the threat of rape; it is that love introduces the possibility of disaster. Indeed the novel ends on a tragic note, when John Henry West, Frankie's younger cousin with whom she had snuggled in bed, dies of meningitis. McCullers had been painstaking in her writing of the novel, from its inception in 1939 to its publication in 1946, characterizing her project in "The Vision Shared" as a mixed-genre "lyric tragi-comedy in which the funniness and the grief coexist in the same line." She described her agony in writing *The Member of the Wedding* in a letter to Reeves in 1945: "It's one of those works that the least slip can ruin. Some parts I have worked over and over as many as twenty times. . . . It must be beautifully done. For, like a poem, there is not much excuse for it otherwise." Many think she accomplished her goal artfully.

During the mid 1940s McCullers was intermittently ill with influenza and pleurisy; wrote at Yaddo; worried about Reeves, who had become a company commander in the Second Ranger Battalion; and moved with her sister and mother to Nyack, New York. She remarried Reeves when he was discharged from the service, received another Guggenheim, and spent one summer on Nantucket with Tennessee Williams, who helped her reshape *The Member of the Wedding* into a play. In the later 1940s the McCullerses moved to Europe, where Carson arrived in triumph, only to be flown home in 1947 owing to a debilitating stroke. They continued to travel widely during this period, however, and would often stay in Europe for extended visits. Numerous awards and accolades, including being named one of the best postwar writers in America by *Quick* magazine, were offset by McCullers's precarious health, and she continued to suffer from various illnesses, attempting suicide in 1948. The later 1940s were also marked by a number of separations from and reconciliations with Reeves.

The early 1950s brought more personal anguish and illness despite continued career success, with *The Member of the Wedding* premiering at the Empire Theatre on Broadway, winning numerous awards, and running for 501 performances. After a hiatus of nearly seven years, she began a fourth novel, which became *Clock Without Hands.* By 1953 both Carson and

Reeves, drinking heavily, had reached personal nadirs. Unable to talk Carson into a double suicide, Reeves took his own life after Carson left him in France and moved to the American South. The relationship between husband and wife had always been complex. As Virginia Spencer Carr explains in her biography of McCullers:

> Carson had a will to survive, a will to realize itself that took what it needed and sacrificed whatever obstructed it; whereas Reeves, if not recklessly bent on self-destruction, destroyed as he went along because he never found anything or anyone, other than Carson, who even vicariously fulfilled his insatiable need for identity and fulfillment.
>
> (p. 411)

The mid 1950s were both productive and painful for Carson McCullers. At Yaddo she began her play *The Square Root of Wonderful* and continued working on *Clock Without Hands.* At Key West with Tennessee Williams, she continued revising these manuscripts and began to adapt *The Ballad of the Sad Café* for the stage. Several short stories appeared in *Mademoiselle.* Undercutting the thrill of professional success, however, came personal pain: Carson's health remained unstable, her left arm, paralyzed by a stroke in 1947, becoming more painful and withered; and her beloved mother died unexpectedly. Her mental health was further complicated by severe depression, brought on by the closing of *The Square Root of Wonderful* after only 45 performances.

McCullers was unable to do much writing in the last decade of her life owing to her steadily declining health, although she did write some children's verse and several magazine pieces, and worked on a musical adaptation of *The Ballad of the Sad Café.* During this period McCullers enjoyed the friendship of Marielle Bancou, a New York artist; met her literary heroine, Isak Dinesen; and was cared for by Dr. Mary Mercer, whom Carr calls "her guardian spirit." She gave McCullers in her last years "a love, nurture, and comfort such as she had never known." She began to dress, like Emily Dickinson, in white because, as Carr notes, McCullers was obsessed by "the image of whiteness and its ambivalent connotations [of everything and nothingness]. Soon she was granting interviews dressed in white nightgowns and tennis shoes."

Her last novel, *Clock Without Hands,* was completed on 1 December 1960, and although the novel itself is less satisfying than her earlier long fictions, its completion after ten years of illness and suffering "cannot be regarded as anything other than a moral triumph," according to Oliver Evans. This novel contains the same deep structure as McCullers's earlier work, the action centering on four lonely, alienated characters: J. T. Malone, a middle-aged pharmacist dying of leukemia; Judge Clain, an eighty-five-year-old reactionary segregationist; his orphaned grandson, Jester, who is searching both for his identity and for the reason behind his father's suicide; and Jester's double, Sherman Pew, a black man with blue eyes who affects a Hathaway eye-patch and a five-syllable vocabulary to appear distinguished, serves only "Lord Calvert's, bottled in bond, ninety-eight per cent proof," and keeps a notebook in which he records injuries done the black race. None of these men find love, and although in the end Jester finds a measure of freedom and identity in deciding to become a lawyer, the novel remains profoundly pessimistic.

In her final years, Carson McCullers was bedridden and wheelchair bound. After suffering a heart attack in 1959, she had several surgeries to help her twisted limbs, to repair nerve damage, and to remove her cancerous right breast. In the spring of 1964 McCullers fell, breaking her hip and elbow, which necessitated more surgery. During her convalescence, she ate very little, her friend Jordan Massee noting that "she rarely consumed anything in quantity except bourbon and a chocolate bar of Ex-Lax nightly." She also chain-smoked cigarettes at the rate of one pack every two hours, taking only three or four puffs on each cigarette. On 15 August 1967, McCullers suffered a massive brain hemorrhage and lay comatose for forty-seven days, dying on 28 September. She is buried in Oak Hill Cemetery, in Nyack, New York.

All of Carson McCullers's important novels, the works for which she is best remembered, were written before her thirtieth birthday. Her very first effort, *The Heart Is a Lonely Hunter,* has been rated by David Madden as "among the ten greatest American novels; her other work stands in relation to it as Fitzgerald's other work stands to *The Great Gatsby.*" And although V. S. Pritchett writes that McCullers had "a courageous imagination . . . bold enough to consider the terrible in human nature without loss of nerve, calm dignity or love," others believe she lost her ability to create strong, believable characters toward the end of her career.

Like Edgar Allan Poe, another alienated, dreamy, romantic personality, McCullers is valued more in Europe than she has been in her own country. Some speculate that her reputation has suffered in America because she was never an intellectual. Indeed, McCullers favored a romantic sensibility, like that of many of her favorite writers, such as Tolstoy, Dostoevsky, and Lawrence, and her favorite composers, among them Beethoven, Chopin, Schubert, and Sibelius. She was, finally, as Lawrence Graver characterized her, "a master of bright and melancholy moods," "a lyricist, not a philosopher, an observer of maimed characters, not of contaminated cultures."

In "Look Homeward, Americans," McCullers wrote:

> As often as not, we are homesick most for the places we have never known. All men are lonely. But sometimes it seems to me that we Americans are the loneliest of all. Our hunger for foreign places and new ways has been with us almost like a national disease. Our literature is stamped with a quality of longing and unrest, and our writers have been great wanderers.
>
> (p. 75)

Certainly McCullers herself wandered from New York to Georgia and back and forth across the Atlantic, in an intensely experienced life of illness and hard work, self-destruction and brilliance. The loneliness and restlessness, alienation and pain portrayed in her writing are, as Tennessee Williams wrote in his introduction to *Reflections in a Golden Eye,* "not eclipsed by time but further illumined."

Selected Bibliography

PRIMARY WORKS

The Heart Is a Lonely Hunter. Boston: Houghton Mifflin, 1940.

Reflections in a Golden Eye. Boston: Houghton Mifflin, 1941.

The Member of the Wedding. Boston: Houghton Mifflin, 1946.

The Ballad of the Sad Café: The Novels and Stories of Carson McCullers. Boston: Houghton Mifflin, 1951.

The Member of the Wedding. New York: New Directions, 1951. Play.

The Ballad of the Sad Café and Collected Short Stories. Boston: Houghton Mifflin, 1952, 1955.

The Square Root of Wonderful. New York: Houghton Mifflin, 1958; Dunwoody, Ga.: Norman S. Berg, 1971. Play.

The Square Root of Wonderful. New York: Samuel French, 1959. Acting Version.

Clock Without Hands. Boston: Houghton Mifflin, 1961.

Sweet as a Pickle and Clean as a Pig: Poems. Boston: Houghton Mifflin, 1964.

The Mortgaged Heart. Edited by Margarita G. Smith. Boston: Houghton Mifflin, 1971.

UNCOLLECTED ARTICLES AND STORIES

"Look Homeward, Americans." *Vogue* 96:74–75 (1 December 1940).

"The Devil's Idlers." Review of *Commend the Devil* by Howard Coxe. *Saturday Review* 23:15 (15 March 1941).

"Books I Remember." *Harper's Bazaar* 75:82, 122, 125 (April 1941).

"Love's Not Time's Fool." *Mademoiselle* 16:95, 166–168 (April 1943). Signed "A War Wife."

"Our Heads Are Bowed." *Mademoiselle* 22:131, 229 (November 1945).

"Home for Christmas." *Mademoiselle* 30:53, 129–132 (December 1949).

"The Pestle." *Botteghe Oscure* 11:226–246 (1953); *Mademoiselle* 37:44–45, 114–118 (July 1953).

"Mick." *Literary Cavalcade* 10:16–22, 32 (February 1957.

"Playwright Tells of Pangs." *Philadelphia Inquirer*, 13 October 1957, 1, 5.

"Author's Note." *New York Times Book Review* 66:4 (11 June 1961).

"To Bear the Truth Alone." *Harper's Bazaar* 94:42–43, 93–99 (July 1961).

"The Dark Brilliance of Edward Albee." *Harper's Bazaar* 97:98–99 (January 1963).

"A Note from the Author." *Saturday Evening Post* 236:69 (28 September 1963).

"The March." *Redbook* 128:69, 114–123 (March 1967).

UNCOLLECTED POEMS

"The Twisted Trinity." *Decision*, 2 December 1941, 30.

"The Dual Angel: A Meditation on Origin and Choice." *Botteghe Oscure* 9:213–218 (1952); *Mademoiselle* 35:54–55, 108 (July 1952). Including "Incantation to Lucifer," "Hymen, O Hymen," "Love and the Rind of Time," "The Dual Angel," and "Father, upon Thy Image We Are Spanned."

UNPUBLISHED SHORT STORIES

"The Man Upstairs" and "Hush Little Baby." Both in the McCullers Collection, Humanities Research Center, University of Texas at Austin.

SECONDARY WORKS

BIOGRAPHICAL AND CRITICAL STUDIES

Bloom, Harold, ed. "Introduction." In his *Carson McCullers*. New York: Chelsea House, 1986.

Box, Patricia S. "Androgyny and the Musical Vision: A Study of Two Novels by Carson McCullers." *Southern Quarterly* 16:117–123 (1978).

Carr, Virginia Spencer. "Carson McCullers: Novelist Turned Playwright." *Southern Quarterly* 25:37–51 (1987).

———. *The Lonely Hunter: A Biography of Carson McCullers*. Garden City, N.Y.: Doubleday, 1975.

Cook, Richard M. *Carson McCullers*. New York: Frederick Ungar, 1975.

Dazey, Mary Ann. "Two Voices of the Single Narrator in *The Ballad of the Sad Café*." *Southern Literary Journal* 17:33–40 (1985).

Edmonds, Dale. *Carson McCullers*. Austin: University of Texas Press, 1969.

Evans, Oliver. *The Ballad of Carson McCullers*. New York: Coward-McCann, 1966.

Graver, Lawrence. *Carson McCullers*. Minneapolis: University of Minnesota Press, 1969.

Hassan, Ihab. "The Aesthetics of Love and Pain." In his *Radical Innocence: Studies in the Contemporary American Novel*. Princeton, N.J.: Princeton University Press, 1961. Pp. 205–229.

Madden, David. "Transfixed Among the Self-Inflicted Ruins: Carson McCullers's *The Mortgaged Heart*." *Southern Literary Journal* 5:137–162 (1972).

McDowell, Margaret B. *Carson McCullers*. Boston: Twayne, 1980.

Millichap, Joseph R. "Carson McCullers's Literary Ballad." *Georgia Review* 27:329–339 (1973).

Paden, Frances Freeman. "Autistic Gestures in *The Heart Is a Lonely Hunter*." *Modern Fiction Studies* 28:453–463 (1982).

Perry, Constance M. "Carson McCullers and the Female *Wunderkind*." *Southern Literary Journal* 19:36–45 (1986).

Presley, Delma Eugene. "Carson McCullers and the South." *Georgia Review* 28:19–32 (1974).

Rubin, Louis D., Jr. "Carson McCullers: The Aesthetic of Pain." *Virginia Quarterly Review* 53:265–283 (1977).

Smith, C. Michael. "A Voice in a Fugue: Characters and Musical Structure in *The Heart Is a Lonely Hunter*." *Modern Fiction Studies* 25:258–263 (1979).

BIBLIOGRAPHIES

Bixby, George. "Carson McCullers: A Bibliographical Checklist." *American Book Collector* 5:38–43 (January–February 1984).

Carr, Virginia Spencer, and Joseph R. Millichap. "Carson McCullers." In *American Women Writers: Bibliographical Essays*. Edited by Maurice Duke, Jackson R. Bryer, and M. Thomas Inge. Westport, Conn.: Greenwood Press, 1983. Pp. 297–319.

Shapiro, Adrian M., Jackson R. Bryer, and Kathleen Field. *Carson McCullers: A Descriptive Listing and Annotated Bibliography of Criticism*. New York: Garland, 1980. Supersedes all preceding checklists.

CHERYL B. TORSNEY

EDNA ST. VINCENT MILLAY

1892–1950

One wonders sometime what the critic of literature would do were he left entirely in the dark as to the age, sex, amorous proclivities and political affiliations of the writer whose work he is considering. Fortunately, he does not often find himself in this predicament. For the most part, he is in the enviable position of the graphologist who writes, "Send me a sample of your handwriting, and I will read your character," having just looked one up in *Who's Who,* skimmed through one's recently published autobiography, and had an hour or so's ever-so-interesting conversation with one's most garrulous friend.

The above remarks in Millay's preface to her 1936 translation of Charles Baudelaire's *Flowers of Evil* might be taken as a warning against reading her poetry too exclusively in the context of her life. Poems, not poets, Millay insists, are the proper subject of our attention, for a great poem is almost self-authoring: "The poem is the thing. Is it interesting?—is it beautiful?—is it sublime? Then it was written by nobody. It exists by itself." A prodigious success, bursting into the literary world with a poem she wrote at nineteen, Millay never had a chance to be nobody.

Widely seen as an exemplar of the "new woman" of the 1920s, Millay remained in the public eye throughout most of a productive life. She acted onstage in her own plays. In 1923 she was the first woman to receive the Pulitzer Prize for poetry. Her marriage that year to businessman Eugen Boissevain gave her a partner supportive of her public career. She went on reading tours, made recordings and radio broadcasts, and gave frequent interviews. During an almost thirty-year span, her readers were treated to a regular succession of volumes of poetry, including the much-noticed debut *Renascence and Other Poems* (1917) and the light verse of *A Few Figs from Thistles* (1920), which contains many of the best-known of her poems. This was followed by *Second April* (1921); *The Harp-Weaver and Other Poems* (1923); *The Buck in the Snow* (1928); the sonnet sequence *Fatal Interview* (1931); *Wine from These Grapes* (1934); a verse drama that found its way to the stage, *Conversation at Midnight* (1937); *Huntsman, What Quarry?* (1939); and a series of collections of topical poems during the war years, including works written for radio broadcast.

Harper & Brothers, her publisher from 1923 onward, compiled collections of her sonnets (1941) and lyrics (1943). She published five plays between 1920 and 1932, including the libretto for Deems Taylor's opera *The King's Henchman* (1927), commissioned for the Metropolitan Opera and performed there and on tour with great success. (The published libretto enjoyed eighteen printings in its first year.) Her satirical prose sketches written for the magazines *Vanity Fair* and *Ainslee's* were collected as *Distressing Dialogues* (1924). Millay was often in the limelight for her political views and activities as well. She publicly protested the controversial Sacco-Vanzetti execution of 1927, and she was America's poetic mouthpiece during World War II. By then her poetic reputation had begun to ebb, partly on account of the roughness and haste of the advocacy poetry she churned out during the war, and her next book did not appear until the posthumous collection *Mine the Harvest* (1954). Her last decade, largely spent in relative isolation at Steepletop, near Austerlitz, New York, was marked by illness and stagnation. Millay was unable to write for two years following a nervous breakdown in 1944. Boissevain died in 1949, and the grieving poet plunged back into solitary work at Steepletop. She died there of heart failure on 19 October 1950.

For many years after her death, Millay seemed to have been dropped from serious critical consideration. She was and continues to be subject to the occupational hazards befalling the celebrity: public images of Millay have repeatedly distorted or eclipsed the light by which her poetry is read. As the poet Louise Bogan recognized in a 1939 essay on Millay, these hazards are particularly threatening to a woman poet: "It is a dangerous lot, that of the charming, romantic public poet, especially if it falls to a woman."

This dangerous lot fell to Millay early. From the start, readers paid more attention to her personal proclivities and affiliations than to her poetic ones. "Renascence," her first published poem (not counting juvenilia), appeared in *The Lyric Year,* an anthology of the "best verse" of 1912. Although it did not win first prize, it immediately won vocal defenders. Among "Renascence" enthusiasts were two young contributors to the volume, Arthur Davison Ficke and Witter Bynner, who felt sure that they could deduce the poet's identity from the poem. They praised it to the anthology's editor, Ferdinand Earle, as "a real vision, such as Coleridge might have seen," adding that Earle's biographical note about its author, one "E. St. Vincent Millay," must be a joke: "No sweet young thing of twenty ever ended a poem precisely where this one ends: it takes a brawny male of forty-five to do that." The "brawny male" wrote back to her admirers, averring that she was indeed a woman of twenty, but thanking them for their praise. If being told that she wrote like a man was a mixed blessing, it was also a short-lived one. When the author of "Renascence" was revealed to be a charming young woman not yet twenty-one, her poem began to garner accolades that cast its qualities in the feminine mode. The brawny male's Coleridgean vision became, in the words of one contemporary reviewer, the girl's "untutored simplicity accompanying an indefinable magic."

As Millay's life tends to upstage her work, her early work tends to upstage her later. From the start of her career she was a public figure, and she spent much of her creative life living up to, or living down, her youthful coup. "I'm so tired of hearing about Renascence," she confided in 1922. "I find it's as hard to live down an early triumph as an early indiscretion; if Renascence had been an illegitimate child people couldn't have flung it in my face any oftener" (*Letters,* 166). Readers expected her to continue in the visionary, exuberant manner of her firstborn, and it was hard to keep herself from meeting their expectations. Yet popular acclaim buoyed her, and when in the late 1930s her acclaim dwindled, popular censure angered her. The censure was generally the censure of contrast, charging that the new Millay was not like the old—that is, young. The maturing writer watched with dismay as her early poetry, garnished in the public eye with her youthful legend, became a marketable item. She tried to veto selections for the 1950 *Oxford Book of American Verse,* protesting the tendency of the editors (headed by F. O. Matthiessen) "to include the poems which they think will have the most popular appeal," namely "simple and youthful poems." The advertising copywriter in Millay's 1937 play *Conversation at Midnight* may speak for her when he remarks: " 'The Finest,' 'The Best,' 'The Purest'—what do they mean now?— / Something somebody wants to sell." To understand her poetic achievement, then—both its limits and its strengths—we must learn to tell the story of Millay's life not as the legend of, as John Ciardi dubbed her, "a figure of passionate living," but as the life of a poet.

She was born on 22 February 1892 in Rockland, Maine, first child of Cora Buzzelle Millay and Henry Tolman Millay, a school administrator. While pregnant with what both parents were convinced would be a son, Cora Millay learned that an injured brother was recovering in good hands at St. Vincent's Hospital, and she decided to name the boy Vincent. When her daughter was born, she retained "St. Vincent" as the middle name; in the family circle she was called "Vincent." Throughout her life she rechristened herself for different friends. Millay signed her letters variously "Bincent," "Eddyner," (or, in a joky pairing of archaic formality and slangy dialect, "Thine, Edner"), and, once, "Edna St. Vitus Millstone." Her husband sometimes called her "Vincie"; she was never, not even to the tax collector, "Mrs. Boissevain." Over the light, satirical prose she wrote in the twenties her byline was "Nancy Boyd." ("Bird" in Brooklynese? Vincent Sheean's 1951 memoir documents Millay's fascination and perhaps identification with birds.) Edna St. Vincent Millay's name of many names may have helped to foster the poet's proclivity for role-playing and speaking in a range of voices, and her sense that a mercurial variety is part of identity.

In 1900 Cora Millay divorced her husband, though Henry Millay remained on good terms with the family. A former singer, Cora Millay worked as a practical nurse to support her three daughters, Edna, Kathleen, and Norma. Millay grew up in a frugal but literate, closely-knit female household whose only luxuries were the necessities of good music and books. Her mother gave Millay her first music lessons. Under a professional teacher she then studied piano with serious ambition for three years, until about 1908. The Millay sisters made up songs and jingles for their own entertainment, a natural extension of their mother's encouragement in music and literature. In 1906 *St. Nicholas,* a children's magazine, printed Millay's poem "Forest Trees." By the time she was eighteen—and no longer eligible for membership in the St. Nicholas League for young writers—she had published six poems in the magazine. "The Land of Romance," which she wrote at fourteen, won the magazine's Gold Badge and was reprinted in *Current Literature* alongside the work of established adult poets. At seventeen she won the Cash Prize—*St. Nicholas*'s highest accolade—for "Friends," a pair of witty monologues that shows an early sophistication about the play of power between the sexes. The *St. Nicholas* poems reveal Millay's early metrical skill.

After a few years of transient living with her mother's sisters in various Maine towns, in 1903 Mrs. Millay settled the family in Camden, Maine, on Penobscot Bay. In 1909 Millay graduated from Camden High School, where she wrote for the school newspaper, then lived at home, took odd jobs, and cared for her sisters while her mother's nursing took her out of town. In 1912 she went to Kingman, Maine, where her father was in failing health. There her mother sent her notice of the *Lyric Year* competition, which she had come across in a magazine, and urged her daughter to enter it, as she had earlier encouraged her to send poems to *St. Nicholas.* Millay finished a long visionary poem already in progress, sent it in with the title "Renaissance" (the editor Englished it to "Renascence," with her consent) and also submitted a blank-verse monologue, "Interim."

The famous poem begins with a survey of everything the speaker can see from where she stands. She can inventory the world ("three long mountains and a wood"; "three islands in a bay"), but not possess it. She sees only the limits of her world, "the things that bounded me." No sooner does she, in claustrophic terror, touch the sky at her finger's ends, palpable and too close for comfort, than "Infinity / Came down and settled over me." Crushing the speaker, almost grappling her in a wrestling hold, Infinity then grants her extraordinary powers of perception:

> Whispered to me a word whose sound
> Deafened the air for the worlds around,
> And brought unmuffled to my ears
> The gossiping of friendly spheres,

The creaking of the tented sky,
The ticking of Eternity.

How Infinity's whispered secret alters the speaker's perception shows in her language: from the simplicity of the poem's opening survey of countable mountains, wood, and sea—a crayon-like drawing of the world—and the childlike self-dares ("The sky was not so very tall"), the poem's voice is curiously transmuted into remade idioms ("worlds around" instead of the expected "miles around") as it handles immensities in short lines. Pressed down below the earth by the hand of Infinity, the speaker pleads for a rainstorm fierce enough to wash her grave away. It comes, releasing the poet into "A sense of glad awakening." Reborn, she can hear the grass "whispering" to her: in place of Infinity's enclosing whispered secret word, she finds the simple noise of wind through the grass. The poem ends with the speaker having learned a lesson: that "the sky" is "No higher than the soul is high":

And he whose soul is flat—the sky
Will cave in on him by and by.

The poem ends not with jubilation but admonition. The threat of a crushing power to be resisted only through a sufficiently vibrant imagination would recur in a number of forms in Millay's love poems and political verse.

In a 1912 letter to Ficke (the two became lifelong correspondents, and briefly lovers), Millay denied the influence of Coleridge's "The Rime of the Ancient Mariner" on "Renascence." She further declared to Ficke that "I never get anything from a book. I see things with my own eyes, just as if they were the first eyes that ever saw, and then I set about to tell, as best I can, just what I see." As Millay well knew, this is one of the most traditional claims a poet can make; indeed, it is almost a declaration of poetic vocation. The meter of "Renascence" is rhyming tetrameter couplets, and Millay's ear is plainly full of Andrew Marvell's "To His Coy Mistress," a poem she loved (compare the line "A grave is such a quiet place" with Marvell's "The grave's a fine and private place"). The brash directness of "Renascence" is built from its amalgam of Coleridgean outcries, Marvellean cadences, and observations of the Maine landscape. This is to say not that the poem is derivative, but that it is not an unlettered schoolgirl's spontaneous effusion. It is the work of a young writer who has read a great deal of poetry and absorbed it into her way of seeing with her own eyes. As she notes in a late poem, the astringent Maine landscape was in some degree a blankness the young poet peopled with figures from her reading; the apples in her Maine orchards were "Half Baldwin, half Hesperides."

"Interim," her other (and apparently her preferred) submission to *The Lyric Year,* is largely forgotten. But this pair of poems illustrates the two sides of her childhood that shaped the contours of her poetry. The first is growing up on the Maine coast. From "Renascence" on, regional images abound in Millay's poetry: the rugged shoreline, seabirds, the cold Atlantic's ebb and flow, local wildflowers. The second, exemplified by "Interim," is her wide reading of English poetry, chiefly Shakespeare, Milton, Wordsworth, Coleridge, Keats, Browning, and Tennyson.

More plainly bookish than "Renascence," "Interim" is a dramatic monologue in blank verse. The male speaker mourns the death of a woman by a survey of the things in the room she left behind: a book half-read, the diary he gave her. Coming across the ordinary words of her last diary entry, the speaker sees a new "dignity" in the simple phrase ("I picked the first sweet-pea today") because it was the last she wrote. His grief centers on the crushing power of the simplest words, and he marvels that he

can make
Of ten small words a rope to hang the world!
"I had you and I have you now no more."

The poem might be read as a bitter parable about a struggle between male and female brands of writing. Killing off the little lady who jots notes about sweet-peas, ignorant of the weight her death will bestow on her simple words, Millay releases the male mourner to write in full knowledge of the import of words: his own. Concerns of Millay's own writing are distributed between the mourned woman and the mourning man. "Interim" reflects on the problem of how to reconcile a poetry built from the stockpile of homely, conventional images and largely devoted to traditional forms with the authority and power granted to men's voices in poetry. This would prove to be a particularly vexing issue for Millay, as she stuck to conventions amid the innovation and experimentation of the modern movement in poetry.

Cora Millay's encouragement of her daughter's gifts was crucially seconded by a number of women in education and the arts. At a gathering of Camden summer visitors in 1912, Millay sang and recited her poetry. Among the appreciative crowed was Caroline B. Dow, head of the YWCA National Training School in New York City. She proposed that if Millay applied for a scholarship, Dow would cover the rest of her college expenses. After a semester's preparatory work at Barnard College in New York City, where she was lionized by the literati, including the poet Sara Teasdale, and Jessie B. Rittenhouse, secretary of the newly inaugurated Poetry Society of America, in 1913 Millay, then twenty-one, entered Vassar College. While her studies focused on literature, creative writing, and languages (Latin, Greek, French, Italian, Spanish, and German), she also turned her attention to theater. She wrote and performed in college plays and pageants, inluding two pieces with medieval or fairy-tale settings—a blank-verse drama, *The Princess Marries the Page,* and *Two Slatterns and a King,* a brief "Moral Interlude" in four-beat couplets—and an unperformed prose play, *The Wall of Dominoes,* about a bohemian young woman's struggle to maintain her honor in the milieu of contemporary New York.

After graduation in 1917, Millay's interest in music and theater drew her back to New York. She joined the acting companies of two Greenwich Village theater groups, the Provincetown Players and the Playwrights' Theatre. She wrote and directed a morality play in blank verse, *Aria da Capo,* for the Provincetown Players; it opened on 5 December 1919. This play borrows elements of commedia dell'arte—a feature of other art plays of the period—for a serious indictment of human callousness and cruelty. Exchanges of banter between the harlequin figures Pierrot and Columbine bracket a tragic scene in which the shepherds Corydon and Thyrsis treacherously kill each other out of petty greed. Warmly received as an "antiwar" play, *Aria da Capo* typifies Millay's skill at blending literary modes, and using traditional figures to explore contemporary concerns. It also looks forward to the political commitment of her writing during World War II.

Millay's first book, *Renascence and Other Poems* (1917), includes "Interim" and another monologue, "The Suicide." The book introduces what would become Millay's two dominant modes: the short lyric and the sonnet. The brief poems, many in rhyming stanzas reminiscent of folk ballads, revisit some of the gamut of emotions of the title poem, but also raise some of the concerns about woman's power alluded to in "Interim." Constrasting sketches of women sit side by side in the volume. "Indifference" is spoken by a woman who tearfully surrenders to "Life" but can only wait passively for it. The next poem is "Witch-Wife," whose male speaker grudgingly acknowledges that although his beloved "resign[s]" herself to him, "she never will be all mine." Perhaps a thumbnail portrait of Millay herself, this untameable woman is said to have "learned her hands in a fairy-tale, / And her mouth on a valentine." Her connection to a mixture of old poetic genres is part of her power. Like most of Millay's succeeding collections, *Renascence* closes with a short grouping of sonnets. They demonstrate Millay's early dexterity with both the Petrarchan and Shakespearean patterns. But their formal dutifulness houses a rebellious voice that can break into a sonnet by denying received wisdom ("Time does not bring relief; you all have lied / Who told me time would ease me of my pain!") or rejecting time-worn comparisons ("Thou art not lovelier than lilacs,—no, / Nor honeysuckle"). In *Renascence's* final sonnet we hear a female version of the voice of "Bluebeard," insisting to a meddling lover on the sanctity of a room of her own. While biographers read "Bluebeard" as Millay's response to the radical editor and playwright Floyd Dell's interference in her life, the sonnet itself cautions against such an interpretation. Millay turns Bluebeard's locked room into a poet's private sanctuary, which "alone out of my life I kept / Unto myself, lest any know me quite." Millay's first book, while not yet revealing her full poetic power, illustrates what she could make in that locked room out of love poems and ballads, fairy tales and valentines.

The legend of Millay as bohemian gadabout grew in large part from *A Few Figs from Thistles* (1920), a gathering of lighter poems first brought out by Frank Shay, a Greenwich Village publisher, in his series of chapbooks called "Salvos." The book begins with the famous declaration "My candle burns at both ends." Some of the best-known poems from *Figs* are characterized by the flip bravura of a Dorothy Parker. A woman lightly boasts of her infidelity in "Thursday" and "To the Not Impossible Him," citing the time-worn language of love declarations only to undercut it:

> The fabric of my faithful love
> No power shall dim or ravel
> Whilst I stay here,—but oh, my dear,
> If I should ever travel!

Figs is a compendium of wayward female voices. It is as though the "Witch-Wife" of *Renascence* had been given a chance to speak in such poems as "The Singing-Woman from the Wood's Edge." Even in the poems spoken by more conventional women overpowered by love, the glum sagacity with which these women acknowledge their own time-worn predicament is itself a way of rising above it. The longing woman of "The Philosopher" knows the man is unworthy of her infatuation, too ordinary to earn the woman's endless pining. By ending her lament with an echo of *Othello*, she ranks her own love, however ill-placed and "witless," with the devotion of a tragic hero: "And what am I, that I should love / So wisely and so well?" The five Shakespearean sonnets gathered at the end of *Figs* advocate impulse and Jazz Age rebellion. A woman in love so defiantly declares her faithlessness that she transforms it from the traditionally bemoaned fickleness of women to a bitter concession to the way things are, for "Whether or not we find what we are seeking / Is idle, biologically speaking." Millay would continue to turn the sonnet into a vehicle in which we can hear a woman speaking "biologically," declaring her sexual desire outright, with no guarantees of fidelity. Maxwell Anderson praised the book's "almost flawless sensitiveness to phrase"; another reviewer dubbed the author of *Figs* "an urban pagan and a sophisticated dreamer."

Millay wrote the soberer poems collected in *Second April* at the same time she was writing *A Few Figs from Thistles*. The initial poem, "Spring," her first foray into free verse, sets the volume's tone of a more mature reflection on the exuberance of "Renascence." The ambitious "Ode to Silence," if a bit too full of breathless apostrophes to be entirely persuasive, nonetheless deserves more attention than it has received, for its exploration of the poet torn between the urgency of the "hungry noises" that demand to be written and the pull of Silence, Song's "other sister and my other soul." "Memorial to D. C.," for a Vassar classmate, presages the grace and formal variety of Millay's later elegies, such as the sonnet for Elinor Wylie in *Huntsman, What Quarry?* A longing for the Maine shoreline runs through such shorter poems as "Inland," "Low-Tide," "Ebb," and "Exiled." The twelve love sonnets that close *Second April* combine the cynical voice of the worldly-wise new woman, who knows how short-lived lust can be mistaken for love, with the unabashed declarations of the poet, whose love is fueled by the passions that animated such legendary figures as Lilith, Lesbia, Lucrece, and Helen ("No rose that in a garden ever grew").

Second April appeared while Millay was traveling in Europe on assignment for the magazine *Vanity Fair*. The satirical sketches she wrote at this time, occasionally acerbic underneath their lightness, were later collected under the pseudonym Nancy Boyd in *Distressing Dialogues* (1924). They helped keep Millay financially afloat while she was working on a novel under contract with Horace Liveright. An "unmistakable allegory," it was to be called *Hardigut*, about a land "where people . . . do not eat in public, or discuss food except in inuendos [*sic*] and with ribald laughter" and "where the stomach is never mentioned, and if you have a stomach-ache, you tell people you have a head-ache or writer's cramp" (*Letters*, p. 167). She did not finish the novel. But Millay's invective against sexual hypocrisy and double standards was carried out in her poetry instead.

Her next volume, *The Harp-Weaver and Other Poems*, begins "My heart, being hungry, feeds on food / The fat of heart despise." The metaphor of sexual longing as hunger recurs in "Feast" and "Never May the Fruit Be Plucked." The title poem, which came out separately as a pamphlet earlier in 1923, is a ballad with fairy-tale elements, told in simple four- and six-line stanzas. The poem tells of a poor mother who weaves a kingly wardrobe for her son by playing on a golden harp. Leaving behind a toppling pile of garments, the mother is found frozen to death at the end of the poem. If the poem is a tribute to Cora Millay, as it is often read, it is a somewhat disturbing one, and raises difficult questions about the sacrifices women may be called upon to make in any sort of creation. Many of the best poems in Millay's succeeding volumes arouse similarly disquieting reflections about what it means to be a woman who writes poetry and what relation that poetry can or should have to her life. If Millay is to some degree the child who is royally dowered by a selfless, richly creative mother, she is also the desperate harp-weaver herself.

A less entrapping image of a creature weaving for dear life appears in "The Dragonfly":

> I wound myself in a white cocoon of singing,
> All day long in the brook's uneven bed,
> Measuring out my soul in a mucous thread.

The wording recalls Whitman's comparison of his soul to a spider that "launch'd forth filament . . . out of itself," but with a significant difference. Whitman's spider casts its "gossamer thread" in a vast world, till it catches somewhere to anchor the poet. Millay's dragonfly seems to be "walled in an iron house of silky singing," but it will arise winged and spangling, free of slime and shallows of the pond and "making a song of them." Weaving, in Millay's metaphor, is means of self-transformation, a prelude to metamorphosis, rather than a bridge spun out to connect the soul with its surroundings. The woman poet's challenge, the poem suggests, is to make her sacrifices to avoid entrapments, not to weave them herself. Whereas Whitman can send out his filament to connect himself with the world, Millay must be careful lest the very threads she sends out to the world make it impossible for her to rise above it and make poetry out of it. The woman speaker of "The Concert" refuses to allow her lover to attend a concert with her, lest we "make of music a filigree frame."

A number of Millay's poems suggest that the entire issue of what counts as an authentic anchoring of poetry in the world outside the poet may itself differ for men and women writers. The speaker of "An Ancient Gesture" in *Mine the Harvest*," wiping her tears on her apron, reflects:

> This is an ancient gesture, authentic, antique,
> In the very best tradition, classic, Greek;

Ulysses did this too.
But only as a gesture,—a gesture which implied
To the assembled throng that he was much too moved to speak.
He learned it from Penelope . . .
Penelope, who really cried.

Throughout her career, Millay had to consider whether gestures from "the very best tradition" authenticate a poet's experience or merely ventriloquize another's. To share classical sentiments can be ennobling, as it is for the literate, ardent woman of *Fatal Interview* (xxvi), who declares that "of all alive"

I only, in such utter, ancient way
Do suffer love; in me alone survive
The unregenerate passions of a day
When treacherous queens, with death upon the tread,
Heedless and wilful, took their knights to bed.

But Millay's archaisms and use of traditional genres can make her poetry look oddly retrograde to our eyes. While the experiments of modernism were burgeoning around her, Millay was using the lexicon of Renaissance sonnets and folk balladry. Still, she is arguably closer to T. S. Eliot, Ezra Pound, and William Carlos Williams than we might initially suppose. Like them, Millay uses archaisms deliberately, to set off the contrast between older stabilities and the modern world. Other poets were using current slang and being sexually daring in their poems, but Millay is doing so in sonnets, thereby giving a peculiar textual twist to the contemporary language. The traditional form enhances the shock value of this influx of the raw, the urban, the everyday, and the commercial into the world of poetry. The foil of form allows revisions to be seen. Millay's sonnets may be "Shakespearean" or "Petrarchan," but such labels point to their formal schemes rather than their scope and inflections. Her sonnets partake of the loosening of the sonnet in the English Romantic period, in which she had read deeply and widely. Sounding the coda of each of her books, Millay's sonnets may also be taken together to make a mega-sequence that ties the individual volumes together. Many of Millay's best-known poems are sonnets, such as "What lips my lips have kissed, and where, and why" and "Love is not all: it is not meat nor drink." But Millay deprecated anthologists' "preference . . . to use only love sonnets" (*Letters*, 371). Her sonnets take up many topics, including even geometry ("Euclid alone has looked on Beauty bare").

Millay's major sonnet sequences are "Sonnets from an Ungrafted Tree" (the final section of *The Harp-Weaver*), *Fatal Interview* (1931), and "Epitaph for the Race of Man" (the final section of *Wine from These Grapes*). They illustrate the wide range of concerns she was able to treat in this form. "Sonnets from an Ungrafted Tree" is a sequence of seventeen sonnets, each with an elongated fourteenth line of seven feet. It tells the story of a woman who returns to an isolated New England village to nurse the dying husband she has left or divorced years before, and who is now little more to her than "a strange sleeper on a malignant bed." The emotional background of the story is implied rather than told, as the woman's daily tedium of caretaking mixes with reflections on her past. The sequence is largely devoted to an account of the simple tasks the woman performs: hastily gathering wood in a storm, building a reluctant fire, hiding in the cellar from a deliveryman and neighbors, scrubbing the kitchen. Gradually these tasks come to emblematize the emotional history of the marriage, until by the end, with the man's death, we can piece this unremarkable story together. Millay may have had her own parents' marriage in mind, combined with the period when she attended her dying father at his home. But there are no names in this story of "she" and "he." We learn of a misjudged marriage prompted chiefly by need and loneliness, the slow erosion of passion, the woman's increasing isolation and withdrawal from common fellowship, and the dull pain of her dutiful pity at the man's death. New readers of Millay could well begin with "Sonnets from an Ungrafted Tree," which gives a truer picture of Millay's work than does "Renascence," while rich with the New England color of the earlier poem. The fifty-two sonnets of *Fatal Interview* tell the story of a love affair from the woman's point of view. "Epitaph for Race of Man" narrates in eighteen sonnets the grim tale of the human race's self-destruction, "Being split along the vein by his own kind."

In 1938 Millay accompanied a submission to the magazine *Poetry* with a deprecating note, wishing she had sent poems "less early-Millay in character; poems more concerned with, apparently, things going on in the world outside myself today; poems more, if we may still use that old-fashioned word, 'modern' " (*Letters*, 302). With the advent of war in Europe, Millay's verse turned sharply toward the world outside. Critically regarded as "not poems, posters" and "tragic books from which the last vestige of gift has disappeared," volumes such as *Make Bright the Arrows* (1940) may have done their part for the war effort, but they did nothing to redeem Millay's literary reputation. Except for the posthumously published *Mine the Harvest* (1954), all of Millay's subsequent books were collected editions of earlier work.

Three issues deserve more general discussion: the status and dissemination of Millay's voice, literally and figuratively; the crafting of the individual poem and the arranging of poems into books; and the significance of Millay's status as a woman poet wielding such precise control of poetic form and meter.

Millay praised the author of a 1937 "essay in appreciation" of her work for his "almost infallible understanding of my poetry considered as speech." The responsive reader "knows not only what I am saying, but also under the impulsion of what sort of urge, what sort of temperamental and circumstantial exigency, I am saying it" (Yost, p. 3). Millay's theatrical and musical training shaped the public presentation of the poems as well as their composition. She not only gave many public readings of her work but also performed it over the radio and made recordings of it. This range of public performance of her poems should shape our response to what often seem the intensely private feelings that appear to prompt them, whether heated declarations of love or heart-stricken elegies. The novelist and critic Edmund Wilson, an early admirer of Millay and her work, noted in her reading aloud "her power of imposing herself on others through a medium that unburdened the emotions of solitude. The company hushed and listened as people do to music—her authority was always complete; but her voice, though dramatic, was lonely."

Millay's poetry was also read aloud by a range of voices not her own, in a number of different registers. Throughout her life, others sang her verses—from her sisters at home, to Vassar students singing the words of her Baccalaureate Hymn, to the Metropolitan Opera professionals singing her libretto to *The King's Henchman*. A number of her poems were commissioned for public reading on a particular occasion: Millay read "Invocation to the Muses" at Carnegie Hall for a 1941 ceremony of the National Institute of Arts and Letters. On other occasions, her work was read by voices made famous by Hollywood: Ronald Colman read her "Poem and Prayer for an Invading Army," written in advance for radio broadcast on D-Day (6 June 1944). Paul Muni was the reader for the short-wave broadcast of Millay's *The Murder of Lidice*, written at the behest of the Writers' War Board, in response to the 1942 Nazi massacre of civilians in the Czech village of Lidice.

The formal, declamatory nature of Millay's poetry, even at its most intimate, suggests that it is designed to unburden the emotions of solitude. Millay's work designedly recasts private emotion for public utterance. Elocutionary, eloquent, recitable, her poems are best understood as scripts for an impassioned but public voice, speaking *for* others as well as to them. In that sense they bear only a superficial resemblance to the more colloquial, embittered "confessional" poetry of such later poets as Sylvia Plath or Anne Sexton. Millay's are intimacies pitched for audibility, lyric confessions magnified through declaratory rhetoric into stage whispers, designed to be heard in the last row of the balcony. Or more accurately, they partake of the peculiarly twentieth-century intimacy of thoughts spoken into a microphone.

Millay's exposure as an accomplished reciter of her own poetry no doubt helped to spread the legend of the passionate woman whose emotions fed directly into her verse. Any questions about where this poetry came from seem to be fully answered in the figure of the redheaded woman with the beautiful voice. But Millay's public readings, like her poetry, raise vexing questions about what kind of authority a woman's voice may have in lyric poetry. Beautiful women with musical voices have a long history in lyric poetry—but as the subjects, not the authors. Women are traditionally the muses who inspire poetry, but no muse is expected to take pen to paper and do the writing herself. We can feel the tension of these issues even in such conventional compliments as Wilson's praise of Millay's "lovely and very long throat that gave her the look of a muse, and her reading of her poetry was thrilling" (Wilson, 749).

But the muse's-eye-view may be different. In an offhand verse self-portrait of 1920, Millay lists among her features "A long throat, / Which will someday / be strangled" (*Letters*, p. 99). As a woman cast in the incompatible double role of poet and poet's muse, Millay found her throat constricted. Seeing her poems as merely the biographical outpourings of womanly emotions is as inaccurate as seeing her as a muse. In 1948 Millay turned down a request by Harper and Brothers to issue a collection of love poems to be gathered from her published volumes. Her letter of refusal underscores the publisher's questionable motives: Harper's "proposal" that she compose a foreword confiding " 'when, where, and *under what compulsion*' (the italics are mine) these poems were written, leaves me strangely cold" (*Letters*, p. 348). A woman poet is not simply a woman to be wooed, Millay's protest implies, any more than her love poems are just diary entries that rhyme. It is difficult to reconcile the figure of the woman as muse to a world in which women are no longer (if they ever were) merely the passive inspirers of men's poetry. It is difficult also to reconcile the myth of the muse to the horrors of history in the twentieth century. Millay's 1942 "Invocation to the Muses" begins with a self-consciously orotund call for the "Great Muse of Song:

> . . . And thy vast throat builded for Harmony,
> For the strict monumental pure design,
> And the melodic line"

but soon turns to a remembrance of those "herded into prison camps," where, "Though the great voice be there, no sound from the dry throat across the thickened tongue / Comes forth."

Important as the sound of the poem to the ear was to Millay, she was also concerned with the look of the poem to the eye. The material design of her volumes, from binding to typography, interested her deeply. To write a book was to fashion a fine artifact. She reveled in the fact that *Renascence* was "printed on that beautiful, very rough, very torn-edgy paper." The paper that words were printed on was part of their personality, and Millay, cultivating a beautiful roughness, found herself at odds with "the smooth-browed, bridal-satin periodicals" that occasionally solicited her work (*Letters*, p. 303). Sheer legibility was a pleasure: she writes gratefully to her publisher that "the italics are the least alarming I ever saw."

She did not expect her readers to judge a book by its italics, of course. The crafting of her volumes goes much deeper. Most readers today encounter Millay in the two volumes Harper & Row keeps in print as her *Collected Lyrics* and

Collected Sonnets. (There is also a slightly more inclusive single-volume *Collected Poems*.) But during her lifetime, readers would have watched the Millay canon grow in a series of relatively short volumes every five years or so. Today we may tend to think of her as the author of one or two thick books, but during her lifetime she was in the public eye as the producer of a series of thin ones.

Each volume was assembled with detailed care. Millay designed the succession of poems in individual volumes to suggest both continuity and growth in her poetic career. Desgined shifts of mood, meter, and poetic genre characterize her books: their "torn-edgy" quality is balanced by the closure and poise of the poems. Nearly every collection concludes with a gathering of sonnets. One principle of arrangement was variety, as in her and George Dillon's translation of *Flowers of Evil:* "I've kept in mind the desirability of varying the meter from poem to poem whenever possible; of having no two poems close together repeat each other in any important way" (*Letters*, 264). She had the same eye for variety in the groupings of poems she submitted for magazine publication, advising one editor to include "The Snow Storm" in a gathering of her verses, since "it is a lyric, and otherwise it seems to me there'll be a sort of top-heaviness of those long loose irregular lines that Edna Millay is that way about" (*Letters*, p. 305). In *Conversation at Midnight* she aimed for "differences in metrical style" throughout. Here the variety serves a playwright's purposes, but it points to a larger aim behind Millay's mixtures: there is a similar dramatist's touch for modulated changes in voice, tone, mood, and the ordering of the poems. The emotional modulations as one moves from poem to poem in the individual books is thus part of their crafted design. While individual lyrics can stand alone—and in anthologies frequently do—Millay's volumes benefit from being read in order, cover to cover. Her collections of short poems are not simply compilations, but sequences. In this sense they are cast in the mold of what is arguably her strongest genre: the sonnet sequence.

Similarly, Millay thought of her succeeding volumes of poetry as both echoing and revising previous ones. The title of *Wine from These Grapes* (1934) comes from a poem in *The Buck in the Snow* (1928), the first two lines of which appear as the later book's epigraph: "Wine from these grapes I shall be treading surely / Morning and noon and night until I die." As *Second April* declares a breach with the cheer of "Renascence," and the poet is still rethinking that early effort as late as "The Parsi Woman," from *Mine the Harvest*.

Even an abbreviated sketch of the structure of *Wine from These Grapes* will illustrate Millay's orchestrating of her books. There are five sections. The first deals with nature, the keynote poem focusing on nature's indifference to human grief ("The Return"). Then come two detailed vignettes of autumn landscapes ("October—An Etching" and "Autumn Daybreak"). In the next poem, clinging autumn foliage becomes a surrogate for the poet, refusing to accept change and death. The second section is a numbered sequence of six poems in memory of Cora Millay. The eulogy covers a wide range of metrical styles. There is the blunt staccato of "In the Grave No Flower":

> Here dock and tare.
> But there
> No flower.

And there are long lines that infuse adult grief into the rambling rhetoric of a child:

> To be grown up is to sit at the table with
> people who have died, who neither listen
> nor speak.

The fourth poem of this section employs the ballad stanza of iambic tetrameter rhyming *a b a b*. And there is a sonnet to close the section (as a sonnet sequence will close the whole book).

The third section consists of two poems treating death in reference to literary tradition (chivalric romance in "Aubade," Greek lyric in

"Sappho Crosses the Dark River into Hades"), thus transcending private mourning. The elegiac strain continues in section IV, but in accord with the third section, mourned loss turns to the matter of poetry itself. This passage constitutes a varied elegy to the dip in the poet's own powers, like a falcon that refuses to soar ("On Thought in Harness"). In this section the autumnal landscape of the opening section returns as self-admonition: "When will you learn, my self, to be / A dying leaf on a living tree?" Section V is the sonnet sequence "Epitaph for the Race of Man" (which Millay had begun drafting as early as 1920). The sections are thus self-contained but also resonant with each other. Distributed throughout *Wine* are poems about a creature that takes flight ("The Fledgling," "The Fawn," "On Thought in Harness"). The "reassuring" graveyard glimpsed "From a Train Window" (section I) returns for scrutiny in the grim "Lines for a Grave-Stone" (section IV).

When we reach "Epitaph for the Race of Man," we have already seen a number of epitaphs, and the sequence's protest against war has been sounded earlier in the volume (the acid "Apostrophe to Man," "Conscientious Objector"). The overall trajectory of *Wine from these Grapes* thus is from particular to general: it turns from loss and ruin in the natural landscape, to mourning for an individual grief, through the widening perspective in Section IV, where individual losses figure those shared by the entire "detestable race." But the general retains its particularity: section IV closes with the image of a man on a lonely road at night, all but palpably confronting the specter of his own death, as "the draughty caverns of his breath / Grow visible." The title reflects the book's autumnal, elegaic one, its sense of mulling over the results of a late harvest. The epigraph tells us that it is in a sense her own poetic vintage that the poet is testing.

Millay was a painstaking vintner of her own work. Her career may be seen as a large-scale version of her writing habits. She makes a promise to enclose a new poem in a letter, but breaks it in the postscript, calling the poem "lousy. Perhaps I can delouse it, in which event I will send it" (*Letters*, p. 305). Preparing her books for the press was a similarly arduous series of tasks that Millay inventoried as "the business of cutting, cleaning, polishing; of documenting, of correlating; of fitting into place; the masonry of art." Arthur Ficke often helped her ready each book manuscript for Harper. The one exception to these work habits was the period of writing propagandistic verse. But the poet's self-perfecting habits were even harder to break than to maintain. Millay was concerned about ruining the reputation for poetic precision she had worked so hard to attain; a stickler, she hated even a syllable to be wrong in the poems she really cared about and wrote with full attention and discrimination.

Adept as she was at intricate formal schemes, Millay believed that an elemental part of crafting the poem preceded the handling of the materials. As much as any modernist, she makes no distinction between form and content:

> The shape of the poem is not an extraneous attribute of it: the poem could not conceivably have been written in any other form. When the image of the poem first rises before the suddenly quieted and intensely agitated person who is to write it, its shadowy bulk is already dimly outlined; it is rhymed or unrhymed; it is trimeter, tetrameter, or pentameter; it is free verse, a sonnet, an epic, an ode, a five-act play. To many poets, the physical character of their poem, its rhythm, its rhyme, its music, the way it looks on the page, is quite as important as the thing they wish to say.

In the poetry of late 1970s and 1980s a nascent "new formalism" is discernible; the return of meter and rhyme as options surely makes Millay's work look more timely. But Millay's reputation, and our ability read her work instead of her life, may continue to rest on what we think her technical virtuosity amounts to. This idea of Millay tussling with her muse—or is the "shadowy bulk" an anti-muse?—may seem a bit far-fetched for a poet who turned out a variety of lyric genres with ease: ballads, folk songs, fairy tales, elegies, epitaphs, commemorative poems, blank verse, and tetrameter couplets, among others. But the tussle continues with dismissive estimates of this facility. Floyd Dell claimed that Millay "learned the molds first, into which she later poured her emotions while hot." Dell's comment has an epigrammatic flair that has made it a persistently quoted favorite of Millay's commentators. Dell may be simply borrowing Millay's lines from an early sonnet: "Into the golden vessel of great song / Let us pour all our passion." The sonnet advocates making poetry over making love. Songs of longing are a nobler result of desire than its consummation.

But Dell's remark begs important questions about the function of Millay's poetic form. Even molten-hot emotions cannot simply be poured into poetic molds, nor should we expect them to be. The emotions will, must, be themselves reshaped by the mold of lyric form, as the need for a rhyme may occasion a new idea or image in the process of writing a poem. Emotions may even be prompted by the molds themselves, a reversal that can be ennobling, raising an ordinary love to heroic heights, or artificial, in the manner of teenagers learning to kiss from the movies. Infusing her modern love with classical myth, the speaker of *Fatal Interview* feels an emotion grander than the unworthy beloved alone could prompt. Millay's love poetry often acknowledges that loving by someone else's book can be entrapping, especially for women. In the light of the recognition by feminists that seemingly timeless ideas or conditions of the human heart like "falling in love" are to a large degree constructed by societal norms, the use of traditional poetic conventions becomes something of a political issue. Millay's work raises the question of whether emotions identifiably exist outside of molds, conventions, and structures (poetic and social) imposed from without. Against Dell's formula, much of Millay's poetry acknowledges that, for better or worse, we often feel what poems have taught us to expect to feel. The point is not to costume Millay as a radical thinker ahead of her time. Although she was in some ways exactly that, we have also noted that being so much of her time was both a strength and the bane of her literary career. The point is rather to hold Millay's work up to the light of our time and see what has been heretofore hidden in shadow.

The poet on the verge of starting a poem, "suddenly quieted and intensely agitated," is like the listener to Beethoven savoring the moment of "the tranquil blossom on the tortured stem" ("On Hearing a Symphony of Beethoven"). The "shadowy bulk" of the nascent poem looms all but palpably for her: "I am possessed of a masterful and often a cruel imagination," she claimed. But the wording leaves open the question of who is in charge here. Is a poet so endowed possessed or possessor? Can such a cruelly overmastered poet be master? By Millay's report, she worked "not like a dog, not like a slave; dogs and slaves must be relieved and rested from time to time, otherwise they crack up; like a poet, let's say." Part of this labor is the arduous "masonry of art," but the greater part is the very impulse coercing the architect. Millay's poetry figures the relationship between the poet and her imagination through a range of recurrent metaphors: the imagination can be her prisoner or slave, or she its. To write a sonnet was to "put Chaos into fourteen lines," and tame it to

> the strict confines
> Of this sweet Order, where, in pious rape,
> I hold his essence and amorphous shape,
> Till he with Order mingles and combines.
> ("I Will Put Chaos into Fourteen Lines," from *Mine the Harvest*)

That Millay figures sonnet-writing as a prison rape points to the erotic side of this tussle with the imagination. When biographers tell us that Millay wrote poems when she was in love (and they dutifully tell us with whom), they obscure the fact that for Millay the writing of poetry itself has complex erotic connotations.

Our strongest impression of many Millay poems may be, as her first readers noted, that no one has "ended a poem precisely where this one ends." The closing couplets of her Shakespearean sonnets can be logical summations, flip dismissals, surprising reversals, punch lines, clichéd knots, or elegiac decrescendos. Her focus on skillful endings also reveals a connection between the freedom accorded the new woman and the restriction voluntarily taken on by a writer in old forms. Paradoxically Millay identifies the workings of the sonnet with the ethos of the bohemian life. The sonnet, freighted with restrictions, may seem utterly at odds with Millay's search for freedom. By titling a poem a sonnet, the poet signs a stringent metrical contract from which she cannot waver. But Millay makes this restrictiveness consistent with a philosophy of burning one's candle at both ends, of using one's life up completely. The sonnet can embody metrically, sonorously, and syntactically a kind of perfectly efficient hedonism, culminating in a closure with no residue. At the close of "Thou famished grave, I will not fill thee yet" from *Huntsman, What Quarry?* the poet defiantly tells Death how lives and poems are to be ended:

> I cannot starve thee out: I am thy prey
> And thou shalt have me; but I dare defend
> That I can stave thee off; and I dare say,
> What with the life I lead, the force I spend,
> I'll be but bones and jewels on that day,
> And leave thee hungry even in the end.

The poet "staves off" death by the achieved design of her stanzas. The sonnet's neat ending—fulfilling its metrical and rhyming requirements, leaving nothing formally unsatisfied—suggests the way the poet vows to use up her force completely and leave nothing behind. Not a matter of wanton wastefulness but of almost methodical, tasking exhaustiveness, Millayan freedom is thus aptly emblematized by the seemingly opposite, binding contract any sonnet must be. The sonnet's form provides the formula whereby Millay makes sure that her impulses play themselves out to the full.

One of Millay's best recent commentators, Jan Montefiore, notes that Millay's "themes are smoothed with poetic handling" and tend to be "written in a style which assumes that poetry is timeless" (p. 116). Millay's work, Montefiore plausibly implies, validates a stubborn conservatism while masquerading as daring sallies against the way things are. Does Millay ever take a radical stance? Should we expect her to? Harold Lewis Cook's laudatory "Essay in Appreciation," prefacing Karl Yost's 1937 bibliography, claims that "American literature owes to [her] what amounts to a whole new field of expression for its women writers, the field of unrestricted, unprejudiced discussion of personal relationships, giving to woman a position in literature on a par with that of any man" (p. 54). When in 1927 the League of American Penwomen insulted Elinor Wylie with a rap on the knuckles for her scandalous personal life, Millay wrote a scathing defense, gladly joining Wylie in banishment from the League's "fusty province."

The highly emotional tone of many of Millay's poems tended to make critics see the poems as symptoms rather than as creations. But a critical protocol of the literary world included the need to uphold the belief that emotion is no subsitute for the true stuff of high poetry, ideas. When the feelings take over the ideas, it's time to call in the doctor. In 1934 Horace Gregory diagnosed Millay as infected with "elephantiasis of idea and emotion in poetry." A critical commonplace about her is that although she is technically proficient, less than proficient poems result when she allows her feelings to get the better of her. A reviewer of the 1943 *Collected Lyrics* summed up a prevailing estimate that Millay "has mistaken attitudes for convictions or mere moods for profound truths." But from our perspective today Millay's work can also be read as a constant scrutiny of the ideas and truths that "moods" can reveal.

Millay's play with names persisted to the end, when she was living alone at Steepletop in failing health. In one of her last letters she responds to her friends' protests against her isolation: "They all said, 'But you *must* have *some-*

body with you! You simply *can't* be there without *anybody!*' " She continued to live alone, writing poems (they would be collected in the posthumous *Mine the Harvest*), but to please her anxious friends she "named my nurse Mrs. Somebody-Anybody." This late, playful rechristening was an appropriate one: "In order to help me feed myself properly and take my nasty medicines, I have artfully developed a beautiful case of schizophrenia: The strange case of Miss M. and Mrs. Somebody-Anybody." Millay's life and work pointedly illustrate how, even into this century, the strange case of the woman poet always involves an artful split of personalities. If Millay's life, more flaunted than flamboyant, prevented her from ever being nobody, we are increasingly learning how accurate an account her poems give of the lives of the many women who might be called "Mrs. Somebody-Anybody."

Selected Bibliography

PRIMARY WORKS

POETRY

Renascence and Other Poems. New York: Mitchell Kennerley, 1917.

A Few Figs from Thistles. New York: Mitchell Kennerley, 1920.

Second April. New York: Mitchell Kennerley, 1921. Like its predecessors, this book was published by Harper from 1923 onward.

The Harp-Weaver and Other Poems. New York: Harper & Brothers, 1923.

The Buck in the Snow and Other Poems. New York: Harper & Brothers, 1928.

Edna St. Vincent Millay's Poems Selected for Young People. New York: Harper & Brothers, 1929.

Fatal Interview. New York: Harper & Brothers, 1931.

Wine from These Grapes. New York: Harper & Brothers, 1934.

Conversation at Midnight. New York: Harper & Brothers, 1937.

Huntsman, What Quarry? New York: Harper & Brothers, 1939.

Make Bright the Arrows: 1940 Notebook. New York: Harper & Brothers, 1940.

Collected Sonnets. New York: Harper and Brothers, 1941. The revised edition (1988) has twenty additional sonnets.

The Murder of Lidice. New York: Harper & Brothers, 1942.

Collected Lyrics. New York: Harper & Brothers, 1943.

Mine the Harvest. New York: Harper & Brothers, 1954.

Collected Poems. New York: Harper & Brothers, 1956.

DRAMA

Aria da Capo. First published in *Reedy's Mirror,* 18 March 1920. New York: Mitchell Kennerley, 1921.

The Lamp and the Bell: A Drama in Five Acts. New York: Frank Shay, 1921.

The King's Henchman. New York: Harper & Brothers, 1927.

The Princess Marries the Page. New York: Harper & Brothers, 1932.

PROSE

[Pseudonym Nancy Boyd] *Distressing Dialogues.* New York: Harper & Brothers, 1924

Letters of Edna St. Vincent Millay. Edited by Allan Ross Macdougall. New York: Harper & Brothers, 1952.

TRANSLATIONS

[With George Dillon] Charles Baudelaire, *Flowers of Evil.* New York: Harper & Brothers, 1936.

Emilio Prados, "Llegada" (Journey). In Rolfe Humphries, ed., *And Spain Sings.* New York: Vanguard Press, 1937.

SECONDARY WORKS

BIOGRAPHICAL STUDIES

Dash, Joan. "Edna St. Vincent Millay." In her *A Life of One's Own: Three Gifted Women and the Men They Married.* New York: Harper & Row, 1973.

Drake, William. *The First Wave: Women Poets in America, 1915–1945.* New York: Macmillan, 1987. Ch. 2, 4, 7.

Gurko, Miriam. *Restless Spirit: The Life of Edna St. Vincent Millay.* New York: Thomas Y. Crowell, 1962. Includes bibliography.

Gould, Jean. *The Poet and Her Book: A Biography of Edna St. Vincent Millay.* New York: Dodd, Mead, 1969.

Hahn, Emily. "Mostly About Vincent." *Romantic Rebels: An Informal History of Bohemianism in America.* Boston: Houghton Mifflin, 1967.

Millay, Norma. "The Saga of *Conversation at Midnight* in the Living Theatre." *Tamarack: Journal of the Edna St. Vincent Millay Society*, 3:36–58 (Fall 1985–Winter 1986).

Schwab, Arnold T. "Jeffers and Millay: A Literary Friendship." *Robinson Jeffers Newsletter*, 59:18–33 (September 1981).

Sheean, Vincent. *The Indigo Bunting: A Memoir of Edna St. Vincent Millay*. New York: Harper & Brothers, 1951.

Wilson, Edmund. "Epilogue, 1952: Edna St. Vincent Millay." In his *The Shores of Light: A Literary Chronicle of the Twenties and Thirties*. New York: Farrar, Straus & Young, 1952.

CRITICAL STUDIES

Atkins, Elizabeth. *Edna St. Vincent Millay and Her Times*. Chicago: University of Chicago Press, 1936.

Bogan, Louise. Review of *Huntsman, What Quarry? The New Yorker*, 20 May 1939, pp. 80–82. Repr. as "Unofficial Feminine Laureate" in her *Selected Criticism: Poetry and Prose*. New York: Noonday Press, 1955.

Brittin, Norman A. *Edna St. Vincent Millay*. Boston: Twayne, 1967. Rev. ed., 1982. Includes annotated bibliography.

Clark, Suzanne. "Jouissance and the Sentimental Daughter: Edna St. Vincent Millay." *North Dakota Quarterly*, 54:85–108 (Spring 1986).

———. "The Unwarranted Discourse: Sentimental Community, Modernist Women, and the Case of Millay." *Genre*, 20:133–152 (Summer 1987).

Fairley, Irene R. "Millay in Feminist Perspective: Critical Trends of the 70's." *Tamarack: Journal of the Edna St. Vincent Millay Society*, 1:28–31 (Spring 1981).

Farr, Judith. "Elinor Wylie, Edna St. Vincent Millay, and the Elizabethan Sonnet Tradition." In Maynard Mack and George de Forest Lord, eds., *Poetic Traditions of the English Renaissance*. New Haven: Yale University Press, 1982.

Fried, Debra. "Andromeda Unbound: Gender and Genre in Millay's Sonnets." *Twentieth Century Literature*, 32:1–22 (Spring 1986).

Gray, James. *Edna St. Vincent Millay*. University of Minnesota Pamphlets on American Writers, no. 64. St. Paul: University of Minnesota Press, 1967. Repr. in Leonard Unger, ed., *American Writers*. Vol. 3. New York: Scribners, 1974.

Gould, Jean. "Edna St. Vincent Millay: Saint of the Modern Sonnet." In *Faith of a (Woman) Writer*. Edited by Alice Kessler-Harris and William McBrien. Westport, Conn.: Greenwood Press, 1988.

Jones, Phyllis M. "Amatory Sonnet Sequences and the Female Perspective of Elinor Wylie and Edna St. Vincent Millay." *Women's Studies*, 10:41–61 (1983).

McKee, Mary J. "Millay's *Aria da Capo*: Form and Meaning." *Modern Drama*, 9:165–169 (September 1966).

Montefiore, Jan. "Romantic Transcendence: Edna St. Vincent Millay." In her *Feminism and Poetry: Language, Experience, Identity in Women's Writing*. London: Pandora, 1987.

Patton, John J. "Satiric Fiction in Millay's *Distressing Dialogues*." *Modern Language Studies*, 2:63–67 (Summer 1972).

———. "The Variety of Language in Millay's Verse Plays." *Tamarack: Journal of the Edna St. Vincent Millay Society*, 3:8–16 (Fall 1985–Winter 1986).

Perlmutter, Elizabeth P. "A Doll's Heart: The Girl in the Poetry of Edna St. Vincent Millay and Louise Bogan." *Twentieth Century Literature*, 23:157–179 (1977).

Sprague, Rosemary. "Edna St. Vincent Millay." In her *Imaginary Gardens: A Study of Five American Poets*. Philadelphia: Chilton, 1969.

Stanbrough, Jane. "Edna St. Vincent Millay and the Language of Vulnerability." In Sandra M. Gilbert and Susan Gubar, eds., *Shakespeare's Sisters: Feminist Essays on Women Poets*. Bloomington: Indiana University Press, 1979.

BIBLIOGRAPHIES

Nierman, Judith. *Edna St. Vincent Millay: A Reference Guide*. Boston: G. K. Hall, 1977. Includes writings on Millay, 1918–1973.

Yost, Karl. *A Bibliography of the Works of Edna St. Vincent Millay*. New York: Harper & Brothers, 1937.

JOURNAL

Tamarack: Journal of the Edna St. Vincent Millay Society (1981–). Elizabeth Barnett and John Patton, eds. Steepletop, Austerlitz, New York 12017. Subscribers write to: 8A Chauncy Street, 5, Cambridge, MA 02138.

DEBRA FRIED

MARIANNE MOORE

1887–1972

BY THE TIME Marianne Moore died in 1972, she had become a celebrity—America's beloved poet in the tricorne hat and black cape who was probably better known for some of her interests and public appearances than for her artistic endeavors. For many people, Moore was the famous poet who loved sports, particularly baseball. In her foreword to *A Marianne Moore Reader* she commented on her by then well-established "inordinate interest in animals and athletes":

> They are subjects for art and exemplars of it, are they not? minding their own business. Pangolins, hornbills, pitchers, catchers, do not pry or prey—or prolong the conversation; . . . I don't know how to account for a person who could be indifferent to miracles of dexterity, a certain feat by Don Zimmer—a Dodger at the time—making a backhand catch, of a ball coming hard from behind on the left, fast enough to take his hand off.
>
> (p. xvi)

In a 1964 interview with George Plimpton, we find her comparing "two such battling fielders as Roger Maris and Mickey Mantle [who] have at no time been diminished by internecine jealousies." In 1968 she threw out the first baseball of the season at Yankee Stadium. Later that year she predicted for the *New York Times* that the St. Louis Cardinals would win the World Series. (They did not.)

Even those who had not read with care her "animal" poems—"The Jerboa," "The Plumet Basilisk," "The Frigate Pelican," "The Buffalo," "The Pangolin," "The Paper Nautilus," and "The Wood-Weasel"—may have remembered that she made frequent trips to the circus and the zoo. Four years after Moore died, a photograph of her taken at the Bronx Zoo in 1953 was included in a *Life* magazine special report entitled "Remarkable American Women: 1776–1976." The caption is typical of how Moore was perceived by the end of her life:

> Poet Marianne Moore was skimming nimbly from her thoughts on wine labels to grocery stores to gardening to Goethe to the pyramids, when somebody begged, "Don't jump around so." Moore merely paused: "It isn't jumping around. It's all connected." So it was, by her spanning genius that incorporated steeplejacks, swans, baseball, buffalo, granite and steel, silence and years, everything she encountered—even the Bronx Zoo, below—into poetry that won almost every prize there was to win. Nor was her research limited to places she could reach by subway, her favorite transportation; she espied things in hard-to-get-to places, too, bringing back visions of "imaginary gardens with real toads in them."

Those who applauded Moore in this context may have forgotten, if they ever knew, that her *Collected Poems*, published in 1951, won the Pulitzer Prize, the National Book Award, and, in 1953, the Bollingen Award. It is even less likely that those who read *Life* also read Moore's brilliant, difficult, and two longest high modernist poems: "Marriage" (1923) and "An Octopus" (1924). Moore's public persona suggested an accessibility that was at odds with the intricate demands of her syllabic poetry and exacting prose.

Recognizing the extent to which Moore increasingly courted her visibility in the limelight, we can begin to approach the implications of this persona by considering the celebrated photograph of her, taken by George Platt Lynes, that appeared on the cover of *A Marianne Moore Reader* in 1961. (Moore had her portrait taken many times, often by the most famous photographers of her day: Lynes, Cecil Beaton, Marion Morehouse, Henri Cartier-Bresson, Diane Arbus, and Richard Avedon.) Donning her black cape and tricorne hat and holding her white gloves conspicuously in her lap, Moore embodies decorum, distance, formality, privacy, dignity, and above all a studied self-control. As several of her best critics have pointed out, her willingness to portray herself as a nonthreatening spinster poetess has had deleterious effects on her critical reception. Moore, Taffy Martin maintains, has been treated "as a decorative oddity rather than as an active and perhaps even dangerous force." Charles Tomlinson also notes that some of Moore's critics have reduced her "to the status of a kind of national pet." He also wonders "whether Marianne Moore has not suffered more from lax adulation than almost any other signficant poet of our century."

Until recently many of Moore's critics have focused on her tendency to "armor" herself in her work and life. Both the subjects of her poems and her method of composing them have received scrutiny in this light. Many of her poems make extensive use of quotations from overheard conversations, travel brochures, newspapers, and her eclectic reading. Some of her readers have suggested that she hides behind her elaborate compositions. Randall Jarrell, for example, sees her poetic preoccupation with quotations and armored animals as indicative of her own need to be shielded.

Feminist critics such as Suzanne Juhasz and Alicia Ostriker also perceive Moore as armored; Juhasz maintains that Moore "was so successful in the literary world because she could at once capitalize on and repress different aspects of her femininity." Ostriker reads Moore's work and position in the modernist community primarily in terms of the self-image Moore constructed later in her life: "Yet would a sexual and powerful Marianne Moore have met with the respect accorded the chaste and ladylike, self-effacing spinster in the tricorne? There is no reason to think so."

By examining the archive Moore left, as well as the responses her contemporaries had to her work, critics have begun to reassess Moore's aesthetic in terms other than those provided by her public persona. The record does reveal that Moore was shy, reticent, and reserved; but in her letters she also emerges as deeply ambitious, confident, and outspoken, though (as several critics have recently pointed out) she was equally capable of denying her ambition. These contradictory postures, like her gestures of revealing and concealing herself in her poetry and prose, must be seen as integral to her aesthetic.

Moore's archive, housed at the Rosenbach Museum and Library in Philadelphia, is readily available to scholars. As if certain of her place in literary history, Moore maintained fastidious records of her activities, reading, conversations, and correspondence. In addition to the letters she received, she kept carbon copies of the letters she wrote. These documents, as well as her manuscripts, library, and reading and conversation notebooks, are invaluable for readers who wish to trace Moore's development as a poet and prose stylist.

Born on 15 November 1887 in Kirkwood, a suburb of St. Louis, Missouri, Marianne Craig Moore spent her formative years in her maternal grandfather's home. Her father, John Milton Moore, suffered a nervous breakdown and was institutionalized before Moore was born; she never saw him. Mary Warner Moore took Marianne and her brother, John Warner, to live with her father, the Reverend John Riddle Warner, who was the pastor of Kirkwood Presbyterian Church. When he died in 1894, the family moved to Carlisle, Pennsylvania, where Mrs. Moore taught English at the Metzger Institute.

Moore entered the class of 1909 at Bryn Mawr College; Hilda Doolittle (H. D.) was in her class, though they were not friends at the time. By 1915, however, they were corresponding; an early champion of Moore's, H. D. wrote the first review of Moore's poetry, a short, incisive essay that appeared in the *Egoist* in 1916. In the 1920s Moore reviewed H. D.'s poetry for the *Broom* and the *Dial*.

Moore was told at Bryn Mawr that she

could not major in English because her writing was neither clear nor accessible; she majored instead in "history-politics-economics" and minored in biology. Her biology courses undoubtedly enhanced her ability to see her natural surroundings with a microscopic precision. Her poetry abounds with precise observations: "The diffident / little newt / with white pin-dots on black horizontal spaced- / out bands" in "The Steeple-Jack," the cat in "Peter" whose markings resemble "shadbones regularly set about the mouth / to droop or rise in unison like porcupine-quills," " 'the nine-striped chipmunk / running with unmammal-like agility along a log' " in "An Octopus," the pangolin, "Another armored animal—scale / lapping scale with spruce-cone regularity until they / form the uninterrupted central / tail-row!"

The high point of Moore's college studies seems to have been the course she took with Georgiana Goddard King entitled "Imitative Writing," in which the focus was on seventeenth-century prose writers: Francis Bacon, Thomas Browne, Lancelot Andrewes, Thomas Traherne, Richard Hooker, and Richard Burton. Specific references to these writers abound in Moore's prose; for example, in a 1926 *Dial* "Comment" she meditates on their succinctness, a quality not often remarked upon in writers such as Bacon, Donne, or Browne:

> We attribute to let us say Machiavelli, Sir Francis Bacon, John Donne, Sir Thomas Browne, Doctor Samuel Johnson, a particular kind of verbal effectiveness—a nicety and point, a pride and pith of utterance, which is in a special way different from the admirableness of Wordsworth or of Hawthorne. Suggesting conversation and strengthened by etymology there is a kind of effortless compactness which precludes ornateness, a "fearful felicity," in which, like the pig in the churn, imagination seems to provide its own propulsiveness.
>
> (*Dial* 80:444 [May 1926])

Moore imitates in her own style the qualities she admires in these writers: Johnson's balances are captured in her own—"a nicety and point, a pride and pith of utterance"—and Browne's bravura comes alive in Moore's final metaphor in the passage.

The influence of these seventeenth-century prose writers can also be seen in the notes Moore provided for her poems. When asked by Donald Hall in a 1960 interview if any prose stylists had helped her find her poetic style, Moore replied in the affirmative, and proceeded to quote from two seventeenth-century writers—Browne and Bacon—as well as from Johnson, Edmund Burke, Henry James, and Ezra Pound.

Although Moore wrote both poetry and fiction while in college, in her letters home she sought her family's approval for the poems. She published eight poems and eight short stories in the Bryn Mawr magazine, *Tipyn o'Bob,* between 1907 and 1909 but did not attempt to write fiction again until 1929. In 1933 she wrote to H. S. Latham of the Macmillan Publishing Company that she had been working on a piece of fiction since 1929 but was not sure she would ever finish it. Indeed, Moore never published the work.

During the summer of 1911, Moore and her mother traveled extensively in England and crossed the Channel to Paris. For Moore, the trip was enormously stimulating. Letters home to John Warner refer to a lock of Shelley's hair housed in the Bodleian Library at Oxford, the armor they saw in England, a Whistler exhibition at the Tate Gallery, Assyrian art at the British Museum and the Louvre, and Moore's desire to buy a Japanese print in Paris. Her letters, particularly those to her family, provide an invaluable record of the material Moore would later include in her poetry. Typically she would see something, take heed of it, and return to it later to use in one of her poems. For example, a swan she had seen at Oxford probably inspired the one she wrote about in "Critics and Connoisseurs" (1916).

Moore's reading and conversation notebooks, which she began keeping in 1916, also functioned as repositories where she could hoard material that might later appear in her poetry and prose. For example, quotations from

Henry James's fiction, letters, and memoirs, as well as things said about him, find their way into "Picking and Choosing" (1920), "New York" (1921), "An Octopus" (1924), "Sea Unicorns and Land Unicorns" (1924), and her prose tribute to James, "Henry James as a Characteristic American" (1934). Her manuscript notes for a poem or essay may send a reader back to dozens of her reading notebooks for sources. Her library is also invaluable for reconstructing her trajectory toward a poem or review-essay.

The year 1915 was Moore's last in Carlisle, where she had been living with her mother since graduating from Bryn Mawr in 1909. It proved to be a productive year for her. She saw her poems in print for the first time that spring—two poems appeared in the *Egoist* (April) and five in *Poetry* (May). "To the Soul of 'Progress' "—retitled "To Military Progress" in *Observations* (1924), Moore's second volume of poetry—typifies her best early efforts. Addressing a "you," as she did in other early poems such as "To a Steam Roller" and "To Statecraft Embalmed," Moore indicts military activity by setting up an equivalence between that enterprise and a torso without a head. The crows, who presumably feast on that severed head, become "black minute-men / to revive again, / war / at little cost." They are left ominously at the end of the poem:

> They cry for the lost
>   head
> and seek their prize
> till the evening's sky's
>   red.

In the same year in which Moore first published individual poems, she also sent a manuscript of sixty-four poems to Erskine MacDonald of Malory House, which published a series of modern poets. They were not accepted; but by 1916 we find Moore corresponding with H. D. about placing a volume for her. Some years later this became her first collection of verse, *Poems* (1921); with H. D.'s support on Moore's behalf, it was published by the Egoist Press and paid for by Bryher (Winifred Ellerman). Moore's book was in good company; under Harriet Shaw Weaver's direction, the Egoist Press published work by H. D., T. S. Eliot, Ezra Pound, Robert McAlmon, and James Joyce.

In a 1960 interview conducted by Donald Hall, Moore was asked what her reaction had been to H. D. and Bryher's having published *Poems* without her knowledge and why she had not pursued the task herself. Moore replied:

> To issue my slight product—conspicuously tentative—seemed to me premature. . . . For the chivalry of the undertaking—issuing my verse for me in 1921, certainly in format choicer than in content—I am intensely grateful. . . . Desultory occasional magazine publications seemed to me sufficient and plenty conspicuous.
> ("The Art of Poetry IV: Marianne Moore," *Paris Review* 7, no. 26:48 [Winter 1961])

Moore's self-effacing statements to Hall clearly conflict with her earlier inquiries about placing the manuscript and the eager and persistent ambition she displayed in her letters. There is often a dissonance between what Moore revealed privately and what she publicly chose to say on the subject many years later.

In 1915 she also spent a week in New York City; studies of Moore's development and movement toward high modernism frequently highlight this event. Moore was catapulted out of her isolation by this week-long exposure to prominent artists, photographers, and writers and their work. Several letters to her brother provide the record of her ecounters and the effect they had on her. Alfred Kreymborg, who had accepted some of Moore's poems for *Others,* invited her to dine with him and his wife; while there she saw photographs by Alfred Stieglitz and Edward Steichen. Later in the week she visited Stieglitz at his 291 Gallery; Moore was delighted to see more of his own photographs, issues of *Camera Work,* and the paintings he had collected by Marsden Hartley and Picasso. Stieglitz also arranged for her to meet J. B. Kerfoot, a drama critic for *Life,* whose work she had admired for some time.

Another high point of the week included a

meeting with Guido Bruno, the publisher of *Bruno's Weekly* and *Bruno's Chap Books;* in 1916 he published four of Moore's poems: "Apropos of Mice," "Holes Bored in a Workbag by the Scissors," "In 'Designing a Cloak to Cloak his Designs,' you Wrested From Oblivion, a Coat of Immortality for your own Use," and "The Just Man And." These, like many of Moore's early poems published before 1924, were omitted from her *Complete Poems* (1967; rev. ed. 1981).

Complete Poems, in other words, is not complete. As Moore reminds us in her epigraph to the book, "omissions are not accidents." Therefore, a reader who wishes to study her development will need to recover those poems not included in *Complete Poems.* Also, since Moore revised many of the poems she did include, one is advised to seek out the earlier versions. "Poetry," for example, which was originally twenty-nine lines, became three lines in *Complete Poems,* though Moore preserved the earlier version in the notes to *Complete Poems.* The truncated version of the poem, as Margaret Phelan observes, "reads more like a Girl Scout Oath than a wry comment on the seductions of nongenuine rhymes."

In 1918, after spending two years in Chatham, New Jersey (where John Warner had been pastor of Ogden Memorial Church since 1916), Moore and her mother moved to Greenwich Village. The move was not surprising, given Moore's attachment to the literary and artistic circles of New York City. Around this time, in poems such as "Critics and Connoisseurs" (1916), "Picking and Choosing" (1920), and "Poetry" (1919), Moore began to carve out her complicated responses to writing. The original version of "Poetry" is one of her early attempts to map out her own "place for the genuine." Using long lines, and embedding quotations within her conversational lines, Moore makes a plea for language and speech rhythms not usually found in poetry: "nor is it valid / to discriminate against documents and / school-books'; all these phenomena are important."

T. S. Eliot might have been describing this poem when he wrote in 1923 that Moore's poetry contains "at least three elements: a quite new rhythm, . . . a peculiar and brilliant and rather satirical use of what is not, as material, an 'aristocratic' language at all, but simply the curious jargon produced in America by universal university education, . . . and finally an almost primitive simplicity of phrase."

Complementing Eliot's earlier assessment, Louise Bogan in 1947 commented preceptively on Moore's poetry:

> She is never . . . indifferent to what might strike her contemporaries as either precious or rubbish. Advertisements, travel folders, yesterday's newspaper, the corner movie, the daily shop and street, the fashion magazine, the photograph and the map—these phenomena are gathered into her art with the same care with which she "observes" small mammals, birds, reptiles; or with which she microscopically examines details of human artifacts: "sharkskin, camellia-leaf, orange-peel, semi-eggshell or *sang-de-boeuf* glaze" in Chinese porcelain, for example. Unlike a magpie, she is not attracted by any kind of glittering swag. . . . She is occupied with the set task of imaginatively correlating the world's goods, natural and artificial, as a physician correlates "cases," or a naturalist, specimens.
> ("American to Her Backbone," in Bogan's *A Poet's Alphabet,* ed. Robert Phelps and Ruth Limmer [New York: McGraw-Hill, 1970], p. 307)

But these commentaries came later. In the late 1910s Moore, like so many other Americans, was preoccupied with World War I. Her brother had joined the Navy Chaplains' Corps in 1918; perhaps, as some have speculated, Moore had Warner on her mind when she composed several of her "war poems." "Reinforcements" (1918), which was included in *Poems* (1921) and *Observations* (1924), but deleted from subsequent collections, contains a direct reference to "military progress:"

> The vestibule to experience is not to
> be exalted into epic grandeur. These men are
> going
> to their work with this idea, advancing like a
> school of fish
> through

still water—waiting to change the course or
dismiss
the idea of movement, till forced to. . . .

John Slatin points out that if we read "The Fish" in conjunction with "Reinforcements," as Moore invites us to do by placing them on opposite pages in *Observations,* we will see this poem as a commentary on World War I as well. The men who are "advancing like a school of fish" in "Reinforcements" become the fish who "Wade / through black jade" in "The Fish." We are in wasteland uninhabited by a human presence, yet saturated with human destruction:

. . . one
keeps
adjusting the ash heaps;
opening and shutting itself like

an
injured fan.
The barnacles which encrust the
side
of the wave, cannot hide

The swimming fish become "a turquoise sea / of bodies"; this ominous image announces a destruction that is barely contained by the form of the poem. Finally, however, Moore's patterned syllabic lines and rhymes provide an order against which the desolation and impending wreckage of this world can be controlled.

Not long after her move to New York, in 1920, Moore had her first poems accepted by Scofield Thayer at the *Dial.* In his memoir, *Troubadour,* Alfred Kreymborg claims to have been present on this momentous occasion:

About two in the morning, she read something one could barely hear about "England with its baby rivers and little towns," "Italy with its equal shores." . . . A beautiful poem few of the guests could hear distinctly, but which the mystery man from *The Dial* heard so well, he stole over to her and, after a whispered consultation, induced her to part with it. Marianne was the first of "the old guard" to be accepted by the new magazine.
(1957 ed., p. 260).

A footnote to Kreymborg's anecdote of Moore's work being solicited by the *Dial* might include the fact that Moore had sent the poem to the *Dial* some time before, but had had it rejected.

"England" appeared, along with "Picking and Choosing," in the April issue of the *Dial.* The celebration of America, and things American, in "England" would not have been wasted on those who had seen "Poetry" in 1919:

. . . and America where there
is the little old ramshackle victoria in the south,
where cigars are smoked on the street in the
north;
where there are no proof-readers, no
silkworms, no digressions;

the wild man's land; grassless, linksless,
languageless country in
which letters are written
not in Spanish, not in Greek, not in Latin, not
in shorthand,
but in plain American which cats and dogs can
read!

In 1921, Moore took a part-time job at the Hudson Park branch of the New York Public Library. She worked there until she became editor of the *Dial* in 1925. Louise Bogan, who worked at the same branch in the early 1920s, remembers Moore fondly:

. . . I remember very well, working with her in the winter afternoons, upstairs in that library with its general atmosphere of staleness and city dinginess.—Her hair was then a beautiful shade of red; she wore it in a thick braid. She was continually comparing the small objects with which we worked—mucilage brushes and ink and stamping rubbers—to oddly analogous objects; and she smiled often and seemed happy. . . .
(*What the Woman Lived: Selected Letters of Louise Bogan,* ed. Ruth Limmer [New York: Harcourt Brace Jovanovich, 1973], pp. 238–239)

In 1921 Moore published "New York," a poem that exemplifies her readiness to respond to the economic and historical conditions of her environment. In that year, as her note reminds us, "New York succeeded St. Louis as the center of the wholesale fur trade." The first part of the poem comically calls attention to the gap between "the scholastic philosophy of the wilderness" and the economy of "the beau with the muff":

> It is a far cry from the "queen full of jewels"
> and the beau with the muff,
> from the gilt coach shaped like a perfume-
> bottle,
> to the conjunction of the Monongahela and the
> Allegheny,
> and the scholastic philosophy of the widerness.

This comic dissonance, and the distance it affords Moore, allows her in the remainder of the poem to offer an extended critique of the opposition between the "plunder" that "the wholesale fur trade" of New York promotes and the " 'accessibility to experience' " the city affords:

> It is not the dime-novel exterior,
> Niagara Falls, the calico horses and the war-
> canoe;
> it is not that "if the fur is finer than such as
> one sees others wear,
> one would rather be without it"—
> that estimated in raw meat and berries, we
> could feed the universe;
> it is not the atmosphere of ingenuity,
> the other, the beaver, the puma skins
> without shooting-irons or dogs;
> it is not the plunder,
> but "accessibility to experience."

"Marriage" (1923) was critical of another economy—the institution of marriage. Perhaps prompted by Bryher and McAlmon's sudden elopement in 1921, the poem moves beyond this occasion:

> I wonder what Adam and Eve
> think of it by this time,
> this fire-gilt steel
> alive with goldenness;
> how bright it shows—
> "of circular traditions and impostures,
> committing many spoils,"
> requiring all one's criminal ingenuity
> to avoid!

Soon after the poem begins, Moore constructs a dialogue between Adam and Eve in which they agree, at Adam's urging, to be "alone together." Later a more contemporary couple takes over. Quotations from Sir Francis Bacon, Richard Baxter, *Scientific American*, the *New Republic*, Anthony Trollope, William Hazlitt, Shakespeare's *The Tempest*, Daniel Webster, and Ezra Pound enable Moore to orchestrate her critique of "eternal union" from a calculated and wry distance.

William Carlos WIlliams's reading of "Marriage" in 1925 serves to illuminate much of Moore's poetry up to this time, particularly the effect her mosaic of quotations can have. "A poem such as 'Marriage,' " he maintains, "is an anthology of transit. It is a pleasure that can be held firm only by moving rapidly from one thing to the next. It gives the impression of a passage through." Williams might have been describing "An Octopus" as well. In this poem, Moore's rapid eye takes us at a dizzying pace through a landscape where things are known through partial disclosures. Her celebration of epistemological uncertainty masterfully affirms the power of the glimpse, the half-seen, and the fragment as a structure of knowledge.

The very subject of the poem demands that Moore keep moving her own perspective; the glacier appears to be stationary—"it lies 'in grandeur and in mass' "—and yet is surrounded by the motion of "a sea of shifting snow-dunes." Far from being stationary and predictable, this glacier of "unimagined delicacy" can kill "with the concentric crushing rigor of the python." Even the mountain's seemingly accessible facade becomes inseparable from the forces "which prove it a volcano." Mount Rainier, despite the presence of "Paradise Park," becomes a land mine in its potential for danger. Only an attentive eye can negotiate the dangers while embracing the pleasures of "the passage through."

During the early 1920s Moore also emerged as a perceptive critic of her contemporaries. Her first published essay, "Samuel Butler," appeared in 1916 in William Rose Benét's short-lived magazine the *Chimaera,* and she continued to publish prose up until the last few years before her death. Her subjects were varied, but as with her poetry, her best efforts came early—in the 1920s and 1930s—and usually in the form of reviews of her contemporaries. Her prose contributions to the *Dial*—the reviews, essays, "Briefer Mentions," and "Comments" that she wrote between 1921 and 1929—form a separate chapter in the history of modernism; her reviews of the most difficult writers of her time—Stevens, Eliot, Pound, Williams, Stein, H. D., Auden, Bishop, and Kenneth Burke—give us new insights into her own aesthetic.

In 1918, Moore published reviews of T. S. Eliot's *Prufrock and Other Observations,* Jean de Bosschère's *The Closed Door,* and W. B. Yeats's *The Wild Swans at Coole, Other Verses, and a Play in Verse.* While these do not begin to define her critical practice of imitating in her own prose style some quality of the writer under review, they do suggest that Moore's desire to be a poet was linked from the start with her commitment to the writing of prose.

In 1921 Moore reviewed Eliot's *The Sacred Wood* for the *Dial* and Williams's *Kora in Hell* for *Contact.* Praising Williams's "compression, color, speed, accuracy, and that restraint of instinctive craftsmanship which precludes anything dowdy or labored," Moore concludes:

> But one who sets out to appraise him has temerity, since he speaks derisively of the wish of certain of his best friends to improve his work and, after all, the conflict between the tendency to aesthetic anarchy and the necessity for self imposed discipline must take care of itself.
>
> (*Contact* 4:7 [January–March 1921])

In her review of *The Sacred Wood* Moore also openly challenges Eliot when she defends Swinburne as a critic and as a poet. She then silences, or disguises, this difference at the end of the review, when she uses a quotation from Swinburne to shed light on Eliot's criticism:

> In his opening a door upon the past and indicating what is there, he recalls the comment made by Swinburne upon Hugo:
>
> "Art knows nothing of death; . . . all that ever had life in it, has life in it for ever; those themes only are dead which never were other than dead. No form is obsolete, no subject out of date, if the right man be there to rehandle it."
>
> (*Dial* 70:339 [March 1921])

This particular use of quotation—quoting one person on someone else to reveal something about a third person—became a distinctive characteristic of Moore's critical method of approaching her contemporaries. As she quotes Swinburne on Hugo, Moore momentarily drops out of sight, fusing her own judgment implicitly with Swinburne's and avoiding an overt disagreement with Eliot concerning the value of Swinburne's criticism.

In 1924 Moore reviewed Wallace Stevens's *Harmonium.* "Well Moused, Lion," which appeared in the *Dial,* was one of the most positive reviews that Stevens received. Applauding Stevens's "appetite for color," his "precise diction and verve," and his "positiveness, aplomb, and verbal security," Moore also confronts his "deliberate bearishness."

> One resents the temper of certain of these poems. Mr. Stevens is never inadvertently crude; one is conscious, however, of a deliberate bearishness—a shadow of acrimonious, unprovoked contumely. Despite the sweet-Clementine-will-you-be-mine nonchalance of the Apostrophe to Vincentine, one feels oneself to be in danger of unearthing the ogre and in Last Looks at the Lilacs, a pride in unserviceableness is suggested which makes it a microcosm of cannibalism.
>
> (*Dial* 76:86 [January 1924])

Moore's willingness to censure her contemporaries has received little attention. Most considerations of her criticism stress the extent to which she always praised her subjects. Moore's public persona undoubtedly fueled this perception. A case in point is her self-effacing foreword to *Predilections* (1955)—the only collection of her prose published during her lifetime—in which she implies that she translated only those whose projects she unconditionally admired. A close look at her correspondence and *The Complete Prose* documents that Moore was quite capable—

particularly in her early reviews—of expressing her distaste for a writer under review.

In 1924 Moore received the *Dial* Award for her second volume of poetry, *Observations*. This prestigious award, which included a generous stipend of two thousand dollars, had been given to T. S. Eliot in 1922 for "The Waste Land." Before the decade was over, Cummings (1925), Williams (1926), and Pound (1927) would receive the award.

Although Moore claimed that *Observations* was a reprint of *Poems* (1921) with some new poems, it constituted a major addition to her canon. She deleted four of the poems from her earlier volume, revised many of the poems she did include, and added thirty-three new poems. *Observations* also included fifteen pages of notes directing readers to some of Moore's obscure and unlikely sources for her many quotations, and a long, detailed index.

When Moore became acting editor of the *Dial* in 1925, that magazine was well established. In an essay for *Life and Letters To-day* (December 1940), she recalled some of the writers she had encountered as a subscriber: Yeats, Paul Valéry, D. H. Lawrence, Ford Madox Ford, Cummings, Williams, Stevens, Thomas Mann, Pound, and H. D. She also provided a catalog of some of the artwork that appeared in its pages:

> Among the pictures, as intensives on the text, were three verdure-tapestry-like wood-cuts by Galanis; Rousseau's lion among lotuses; "The Philosophers" by Stuart Davis; Adolph Dehn's "Viennese Coffee House"; and Kuniyoshi's curious "Heifer"—the forehead with a star on it of separate whorled strokes like propeller-fins . . . John Marin, Georgia O'Keeffe, . . . Brancusi, Lachaise, . . . Picasso . . . Cocteau line drawings, and Seurat's Circus.
>
> (*Life and Letters To-day* 27:177 [December 1940])

A close look at the *Dial* as it appeared when Moore was editor shows that she did not alter the character or appearance of the magazine. In fact, Moore will probably be remembered more for the prose she wrote during the years she worked there than for her editorial decisions.

When the *Dial* folded in 1929, Moore and her mother moved from Greenwich Village to Brooklyn. They sought quieter lodgings and wanted to be near John Warner, who was assigned to the Brooklyn Navy Yard. Although Moore did not publish any poems between 1925 and 1932, we do well to remember that by 1925 she had published some of her finest poems, perfected her use of syllabic and free verse, changed the shape of the poetic line, called for a new range of subject matter, and altered the way allusions and quotations had been used in poetry. Her duties at the *Dial* undoubtedly contributed to her silence during this period. Another factor may have been that when the *Dial* folded, she began working on a piece of fiction that we know from her correspondence with Macmillan she did not abandon until sometime after 1933.

By the 1930s Moore enjoyed a unique place among her contemporaries: She was a major poetic voice, an often brilliant champion of her peers' work, and she had been the editor of one of the leading journals of her time. She matched Eliot and Pound in her commitment to arts and letters. Her immersion in modernism and her astute promotion of some of the best work being produced were immediately visible. In October of 1931 Pound wrote to Harriet Monroe at *Poetry*, wondering if Moore might be persuaded to take over as editor:

> It shd. also be possible to get a certain amount of backing for Marianne that wd. *not* be available for the wild and boisterous or cerebral younger males. . . .
>
> I don't know how much she makes at whatever she is doing; someday or other she will presumably need less and have less weight to carry . . . etc. . . .
>
> Idunno 'bout the Chicago pt. of view. Nothing but a definite position wd. I suppose take M. M. to Chicago or move her from one side of 4th Ave. to the other. But Chicago might be inspirationated to BRING one of the best contemporary Amurkun minds into Chicago. After all Marianne wuz born in St. Louis and can be claimed by the West in general.
>
> (*The Selected Letters of Ezra Pound, 1907–1941*, ed. D. D. Paige [New York: New Directions, 1971], pp. 235–236)

Given Moore's position in the literary community, Pound's request was a logical one. The following month, he sent a similar letter to Moore, only to discover that she was not interested in making the move.

Also in 1931 Moore published her first review of Pound's *Cantos* in *Poetry;* it was the longest review *Poetry* had ever printed. Praising *A Draft of XXX Cantos* as "the epic of the farings of a literary mind," she did not hesitate to add her criticism to Eliot's and Williams's:

> T. S. Eliot suspects Mr. Pound's philosophy of being antiquated. W. C. Williams finds his "versification *still* patterned after classic metres"; and, apropos of "feminolatry," is not the view of woman expressed by the Cantos older-fashioned than that of Siam and Abyssinia?
>
> (*Poetry* 39:43–44 [October 1931])

In 1934, Moore met Elizabeth Bishop; they corresponded regularly for the next thirty-six years. Moore initially helped to promote Bishop's early poetry, but frequently asked her to consider making certain revisions. Some of Moore's suggestions were heeded. Many were not.

In 1940, for example, they had a spirited exchange about Bishop's poem "Roosters." Moore objected to the use of the phrase "water closet" and wanted Bishop to change the title from "Roosters" to "Cocks." Bishop remembers this incident in her memoir "Efforts of Affection":

> One long poem, the most ambitious I had up to then attempted, apparently stirred both her and her mother to an immediate flurry of criticism. She telephoned the day after I had mailed it to her, and said that she and her mother had sat up late rewriting it for me. . . . Their version of it arrived in the next mail. . . . My version had rhymed throughout, in rather strict stanzas, but Marianne and her mother's version broke up the stanzas irregularly. Some lines rhymed and some didn't; a few other colloquialisms besides "water closet" had been removed and a Bible reference or two corrected. I obstinately held on to my stanzas and rhymes, but I did make use of a few of the proffered new words.
>
> (Bishop, pp. 55–58)

It may strike some as odd that Mrs. Moore figured so prominently in Moore's correspondence with Bishop. It should be remembered, however, that Marianne consulted family members, particularly her mother, on many literary matters. Bishop recalls that Mrs. Moore's "manner toward Marianne was that of a kindly, self-controlled parent who felt that she had to take a firm line, that her daughter might be given to flightiness or—an equal sin, in her eyes—mistakes in grammar."

Moore frequently talked with her mother about her own poems and those she was reading or reviewing; Mrs. Moore, who was a good match for her daughter, could be quite outspoken in her criticism and assessments. Moore also incorporated her mother's phrases into her poems and reviews; she was even known to quote her mother in letters to her contemporaries: Eliot, H. D., Williams, Pound, and Stevens. And, as Laurence Stapleton points out, "In Distrust of Merits" (1943)—Moore's well-known poem about World War II—draws substantively on her mother's responses to the war.

In 1935 Faber and Faber, at Eliot's suggestion, published Moore's *Selected Poems* with an introduction by Eliot. He asserted, "Miss Moore is . . . one of those few who have done the language some service in my lifetime." And he concluded that "Moore's poems form part of the small body of durable poetry written in our time. . . ."

Between 1932 and 1935 Moore had published over a dozen new poems. Eliot placed ten of these at the beginning of *Selected Poems.* Some of these poems from the 1930s appeared initially, though not in subsequent collections of Moore's work, under a common heading: "The Steeple-Jack," "The Student," and "The Hero," were published in *Poetry* in June 1932 under the title "Part of a Novel, Part of a Poem, Part of a Play"; "The Buffalo" and "Nine Nectarines and Other Porcelain" appeared in *Poetry* in November 1934 under the title "Imperious

Ox, Imperial Dish"; and "Virginia Britannia," "Smooth Gnarled Crape Myrtle," "Bird-Witted," and "Half Deity" were published in *The Pangolin and Other Verse* (1936) under the title "The Old Dominion."

Moore's poems from this period represent a notable departure from her poems of the 1920s. She abandoned her previous use of free verse and adopted stanzas with rhyme patterns. We no longer race to keep up with her eye; the aesthetic of the glimpse or partial disclosure is replaced by a more controlled marshaling of quotations, facts, and assertions; all are offered with a certain dogged conviction of incontrovertibility. We also notice that Moore minimizes her own presence in these poems: She seldom uses "I" to frame her remarks.

Moore's relationship to her "American" landscape has changed as well: she moves from an affirmation of epistemological uncertainty in "An Octopus" to the certainty of elegiac mourning in "Virginia Britannia":

> The live oak's darkening filigree
> of undulating boughs, the etched
> solidity of a cypress indivisible
> from the now agèd English hackberry,
> become with lost identity,
> part of the ground, as sunset flames
> increasingly
> against the leaf-chiseled
> blackening ridge of green. . . .

Many of these poems, particularly the ones that take as their ostensible subject certain animals, have led critics to see Moore as someone whose aesthetic required that she conceal herself. For such readers, Moore becomes "the frigate pelican" who "hides / in the height and in the majestic / display of his art," "the jerboa" who "honors the sand by assuming its color," or "the plumet basilisk . . . alive there / in his basilisk cocoon beneath / the one of living green."

Critics have been divided about the quality of Moore's poetry in the 1940s, 1950s, and 1960s. Bonnie Costello, for example, sees a decline in Moore's poetry after the 1930s, while Laurence Stapleton argues that Moore's later poetry represents an advance. While poems like "Rigorists" (1940) and "Light Is Speech" (1941) suffer from a lack of intensity of purpose, poems like "What Are Years?" (1940) and "In Distrust of Merits" (1943) are as fine as any poems Moore ever wrote. These poems are assertively confrontational in their questions and conclusions: "What is our innocence, / what is our guilt? All are / naked, none is safe." By the 1960s, however, in poems like "Baseball and Writing" and "To Victor Hugo of My Crow Pluto," Moore strives for an unnatural lightness of tone that lends her vision a certain hollowness.

In 1945, at Auden's request, Moore began her translation of La Fontaine's *Fables;* nine years later—after seven revisions—she published *The Fables of La Fontaine* with Viking Press. During the early 1940s she tended her mother, who by 1946 was bedridden; Mrs. Moore died in 1947, leaving Marianne with a deep grief and an uncertain freedom. They had been living together since 1909, when Moore returned from Bryn Mawr.

Moore produced several additional translations in the 1950s. In 1954, the same year her translation of La Fontaine appeared, she wrote a play entitled *The Absentee,* based on Maria Edgeworth's novel of the same title. It was published in 1962. In 1963 she published a translation of three Perrault fairy tales, *Puss in Boots, The Sleeping Beauty,* and *Cinderella.*

By the time her *Collected Poems* appeared in 1951, Moore had received the Helen Haire Levinson Prize from *Poetry* (1932), the Ernest Hartsock Memorial Prize (1935), the Shelley Memorial Award (1940), and a Guggenheim Fellowship (1945), and had been elected to membership in the National Institute of Arts and Letters. She had also adopted the tricorne hat and black cape. One story has it that she purchased the hat in the late 1940s with the request that she be attired so as to look like Washington crossing the Delaware; another story states that she purchased the hat for the National Book Award dinner (1951). What is clear is that Moore carved out an image of herself as an American public poet. And she offered this persona to her audience as she once had offered her poems and essays.

This persona increasingly dominated her public's perception of her. When Moore threw out the first baseball of the season at Yankee Stadium in 1968, it is unlikely that her fans knew that she had been awarded the National Medal for Literature that year. Nor was it probably known, when she died in New York City on 5 February 1972, that she had been awarded sixteen honorary degrees.

Today Marianne Moore's place in the canon of modern American poetry is secure. Lauded and taught with the same frequency that Emily Dickinson is, she is once again the poet's poet who enjoys the same visibility as her contemporaries—H. D., Eliot, Williams, Pound, and Stevens.

Selected Bibliography

PRIMARY WORKS

POETRY

Poems. London: Egoist Press, 1921.

Observations. New York: Dial Press, 1924.

Selected Poems. New York: Macmillan; London: Faber & Faber, 1935.

The Pangolin and Other Verse. London: Brendin, 1936.

What Are Years. New York: Macmillan, 1941.

Nevertheless. New York: Macmillan, 1944.

Like a Bulwark. New York: Viking Press, 1956.

O to Be a Dragon. New York: Viking Press, 1959.

Tell Me, Tell Me: Granite, Steel, and Other Topics. New York: Viking Press, 1966.

TRANSLATION

The Fables of La Fontaine. New York: Viking Press, 1954.

PROSE

Predilections. New York: Viking Press, 1955.

COLLECTIONS

Collected Poems. New York: Macmillan, 1951.

A Marianne Moore Reader. New York: Viking Press, 1961.

The Complete Poems of Marianne Moore. New York: Macmillan and Viking Press, 1967. Rev. ed. New York: Viking Press, 1981.

The Complete Prose of Marianne Moore. Edited by Patricia C. Willis. New York: Viking Press, 1986.

MANUSCRIPTS AND PAPERS

The Rosenbach Museum and Library, Philadelphia. Houses Moore's correspondence, manuscripts, notebooks, and library.

The Collection of American Literature, Beinecke Rare Book and Manuscript Library, Yale University. Houses correspondence and papers associated with Moore's tenure at the *Dial.*

The Henry W. and Albert A. Berg Collection, New York Public Library. Houses additional *Dial* correspondence: Moore's letters to and from James Sibley Watson, Jr.

SECONDARY WORKS

Bishop, Elizabeth. "Efforts of Affection: A Memoir of Marianne Moore." *Vanity Fair* 46, no. 4:44–61 (June 1983).

Blackmur, R. P. "The Method of Marianne Moore." In *The Double-Agent: Essays on Craft and Elucidation.* New York: Arrow, 1935. Pp. 141–171.

Costello, Bonnie. *Marianne Moore: Imaginary Possessions.* Cambridge, Mass.: Harvard University Press, 1981.

Engel, Bernard F. *Marianne Moore.* New York: Twayne, 1964; rev. ed., 1989.

Goodridge, Celeste. *Hints and Disguises: Marianne Moore and Her Contemporaries.* Iowa City: University of Iowa Press, 1989.

Hadas, Pamela White. *Marianne Moore: Poet of Affection.* Syracuse, N.Y.: Syracuse University Press, 1977.

Hall, Donald. *Marianne Moore: The Cage and the Animal.* New York: Western, 1970.

Holley, Margaret. *The Poetry of Marianne Moore: A Study in Voice and Value.* Cambridge and New York: Cambridge University Press, 1987.

Jarrell, Randall. "Her Shield." In his *Poetry and the Age*. New York: Alfred A. Knopf, 1953; New York: Ecco Press, 1980.

Juhasz, Suzanne. *Naked and Fiery Forms: Modern American Poetry by Women—a New Tradition.* New York: Harper Colophon, 1976.

Kalstone, David. "Trial Balances: Elizabeth Bishop and Marianne Moore." *Grand Street* 3: 115–135 (Autumn 1983).

———. *Becoming a Poet: Elizabeth Bishop with Marianne Moore and Robert Lowell.* Edited by Robert Hemenway. New York: Farrar, Straus & Giroux, 1989.

Keller, Lynn. "Words Worth a Thousand Postcards: The Bishop–Moore Correspondence." *American Literature* 55: 405–429 (October 1983).

Marianne Moore Newsletter. Philadelphia, 1977–.

Martin, Taffy. *Marianne Moore: Subversive Modernist.* Austin: University of Texas Press, 1986.

Molesworth, Charles. *Marianne Moore: A Literary Life.* New York: Atheneum, 1990.

Monroe, Harriet. "A Symposium on Marianne Moore." *Poetry* 19: 208–216 (January 1922).

Nitchie, George. *Marianne Moore: An Introduction to the Poetry.* New York: Columbia University Press, 1969.

Ostriker, Alicia S. *Stealing the Language: The Emergence of Women's Poetry in America.* Boston: Beacon Press, 1986.

Phelan, Margaret M. "H. D. and Marianne Moore: Correspondences and Contradictions." Ph.D. diss., Rutgers University, 1987.

Phillips, Elizabeth. *Marianne Moore.* New York: Frederick Ungar, 1982.

Poesis: A Journal of Criticism 6, nos. 3/4 (1985). Special Moore/H. D. issue.

Quarterly Review of Literature 4, no. 2 (1948). Special Marianne Moore issue.

Sagetrieb 6, no. 3 (Winter 1987). Special Marianne Moore issue.

Schweik, Susan. "Writing War Poetry Like a Woman." *Critical Inquiry* 13: 532–556 (Spring 1987).

Schulman, Grace. *Marianne Moore: The Poetry of Engagement.* Urbana and Chicago: University of Illinois Press, 1986.

Slatin, John. *The Savage's Romance: The Poetry of Marianne Moore.* University Park: Pennsylvannia State University Press, 1986.

Stapleton, Laurence. *Marianne Moore: The Poet's Advance.* Princeton: Princeton University Press, 1978.

Steinman, Lisa M. *Made in America: Science, Technology, and American Modernist Poets.* New Haven: Yale University Press, 1987.

Tomlinson, Charles, ed. *Marianne Moore: A Collection of Critical Essays.* Englewood Cliffs, N.J.: Prentice-Hall, 1969.

Twentieth Century Literature 30, nos. 2/3 (1984). Special Marianne Moore issue.

Weatherhead, A. Kingsley. *The Edge of the Image: Marianne Moore, William Carlos Williams and Some Other Poets.* Seattle: University of Washington Press, 1967.

Willis, Patricia C. *Marianne Moore: Vision into Verse.* Philadelphia: The Rosenbach Museum and Library, 1987.

BIBLIOGRAPHIES

Abbott, Craig S. *Marianne Moore: A Descriptive Bibliography.* Pittsburgh: University of Pittsburgh Press, 1977.

———. *Marianne Moore: A Reference Guide.* Boston: G. K. Hall, 1978.

CELESTE GOODRIDGE

TONI MORRISON

1931–

THE MEMORY IS long," Toni Morrison explained in a 1977 interview with Paula Giddings, "beyond the parameters of cognition. I don't want to sound too mystical about it, but I feel like a conduit, I really do. I'm fascinated about what it means to make people remember what I don't even know."

Perhaps no description more aptly characterizes the aim and the merit of the writings of Toni Morrison than her self-described role as "conduit." In all of her works she recalls a time in the historical or mythical past whose meanings and lessons she believes need to be brought forth into the present. For African Americans, distanced first from their African past and now, in a subtle and ironic fallout of integration, distanced from the core African American culture built in the cohesive, segregated communities of the past, Morrison believes providing a means to connect is essential, and her mission as writer is to provide that connection: "I think long and hard about what my novels should do. They should clarify the roles that have become obscured; they ought to identify those things in the past that are useful and those things that are not and they ought to give nourishment."

It is not just historical fact that Morrison wants to render in her novels, but something more than that. For while she carefully researches the historical background of her work, what she wants to ring true is the essence of cultural meaning that lies behind that history: the feelings, the gestures, the values, the memories that inform and surround the actions; the recessed mythical meanings of historical experiences that she believes restore the soul and contain the lessons of survival. That Morrison feels guided by a kind of mysticism in her recollections of that interior life, that she is able to tap recessed strengths, emotions, and understandings that have accompanied events in black life, even those she personally did not experience, and that she is able to make her readers connect so viscerally to the interior feelings surrounding those experiences—to make them, as she says, remember "what she never knew"—is the true measure of her achievement.

Since 1970 Morrison has written five increasingly powerful novels—*The Bluest Eye* (1970), *Sula* (1973), *Song of Solomon* (1977), *Tar Baby* (1981), and *Beloved* (1987)—and has come to be regarded as one of the preeminent writers of our time. She is a member of the American Academy Institute of Arts and Letters and a presidential appointee to the National Council on the Arts. She is the recipient of the Modern Language Association of America Common Wealth Award in Literature, the Sara Lee Corporation Front Runner Award in the Arts, and the Distinguished Writer Award of the American Academy and Institute of Arts and Letters. She has received honorary degrees from Harvard, the University of Pennsylvania, Yale, Dartmouth, Sarah Lawrence, Spelman, and Oberlin.

As a former editor and as a college professor, scholar, and artist, she brings an extraordinary quality of intellectual rigor and artistic perception to her works, and she commands almost unconditional respect from her readers. "I buy a Morrison novel the first day it's put on the shelves," says one of her avid readers. "I trust her totally; I know that even if I don't agree with everything she says, it will be the consummate reading experience: a work written extremely well and about something I need to deal with."

Indeed, all of Morrison's novels have received high critical acclaim. *The Bluest Eye,* still a favorite among many of her readers, garnered remarkably positive reviews for a first novel. *Sula,* with its innovative form and lyrical prose, defined Morrison as a formidable literary talent and was nominated for the 1975 National Book Award. In 1978 *Song of Solomon,* now regarded as an American classic, won the National Book Critics' Circle Award. *Tar Baby,* although it caused some difficulty for readers because of lush language—even for Morrison—and a seemingly overwritten combination of allegory and surrealism, was on the *New York Times* best-seller list for sixteen weeks and led to Morrison's being on the cover of *Newsweek. Beloved,* her latest novel and considered her finest achievement to date, won the Anisfeld Wolf Book Award in Race Relations, the Melcher Book Award, and the 1988 Pulitzer Prize for fiction.

Reviewers marvel at the surrealistic quality of Morrison's work and her penetrating analysis and mythical rendering of black life in America, but mostly they sing the praises of her powerful use of language. Her rich, lyrical prose, her deft characterization, and her flawless ear for dialogue are applauded again and again. Her prose, concludes John Leonard of the *New York Times,* is "so precise, so faithful to speech, and so charged with pain and wonder, the novel becomes poetry."

But Morrison shuns an emphasis on her novels that stresses the poetic. Calling the works "poetic," she believes, has a kind of luxuriating quality about it that does not truly represent her intentions. She explained in a 1981 interview with Thomas LeClair, "The works cannot be only, even merely poetic, or that would defeat my purposes, my audience." The people who validate the book for her, Morrison told Paula Giddings, are not readers from a long literary tradition but the "black people in her books who don't read books. If Pilate put down that geography book and picked up *Solomon,* would she say 'uh huh' or not? If it's all right with her, it's all right with me."

Despite her disclaimer, Morrison is a painstaking wordsmith who rewrites over and over again. Her concern with the accuracy of the language is not a private indulgence in wordplay but an effort to restore and validate the oratory of the black community. Restoring that language, she says, is not about dropping *g*'s and adding *i*'s. It's about respecting the rhythm and the sound of the art of storytelling, about enlarging the meaning and sounds of words, about leaving "open spaces" in the dialogue so that her reader can hear the language and participate in the telling. She wants "to dust off the myths," she says, "clean up the clichés, in order to make them mean what they meant originally." And thus her conscientious concern for the language, while producing beautiful prose on a purely literary level, is really a reflection of extraliterary aims. "I write," she explained to LeClair, "what I have recently begun to call village literature, fiction that is really for the village, for the tribe." She reiterates this conviction in her essay, "Rootedness: The Ancestor as Foundation" (1984): "If anything I do in the way of writing novels isn't about the village or the community; then it's not about anything. I am not interested in indulging myself in some private, closed exercise of my imagination that fulfills only my personal dreams." The best art, she believes, is not just beautiful language and technique. The best art is that which is "irrevocably beautiful and unquestionably political at the same time."

The politics of her writing, the message that Morrison delivers again and again in her fiction, is the strength of the way of life lived by blacks in an earlier time, a time, she says, "when passions were deeper, . . . when, heretical as it sounds, blacks knew who they were." There is a healthy nostalgia in Morrison that compels her to record the triumphs and complexities of that life in a time now lost. There is a conflict now, she believes, between urban, material values of the larger contemporary culture and the values of the traditional black village communities of the past. She believes that the contemporary generation of blacks is being "devoured" in this struggle, and that literature can provide a means of survival:

> There has to be a mode to do what the music did for blacks what we used to be able to do with each other in private and in that civilization that existed underneath the white civilization. I think this accounts for the address of my books. . . . My work bears witness and suggests who the outlaws were, who survived under what circumstance and why, what was legal in the community as opposed to what was legal outside of it. All that is in the fabric of the story in order to do what the music used to do. The music kept us alive—in touch with our spirit—but it's not enough anymore.
>
> (LeClair, p. 26)

That Morrison feels this abiding mission to restore, to recall, to reveal the quality of life that she believes to be characteristic of a stronger, early time when blacks, although more openly oppressed, were more cohesive as a group, has to do with her being a child of the middle generation of African Americans, a generation who was born and raised during the 1930s, 1940s, and 1950s in communities where a core black culture was lived, nurtured, and passed on as a matter of course in everyday life, but who are now living, or seeing children grow up, in a world where a protected core culture no longer exists.

For those of that generation, the social integration and the material gains that came as a result of civil rights legislation have been received with mixed emotions—with an appreciation of what was gained and a painful awareness of what was lost. During those years, Morrison explains in her essay "Rediscovering Black History" (1974), one felt both excitement and a sense of loss: "In the legitimate and necessary drive for better jobs and housing, we abandoned the past and a lot of the truth and sustenance that went with it." And there is a growing fear among this middle generation that the distinctive cultural life they once knew, with its pain, its joy, its strength, its distinctive way of looking at the world, will not be passed on to another generation. As she tells Michael Bandler:

> Maybe I'm a little too romantic about what has been possible for blacks like myself—who grew up in enormous economic duress yet never were degraded by it. But I have to write about it so that young blacks who never were told about the resiliency of those who preceded them can understand that courage and heroism.
>
> (p. 28)

In her novels Morrison tries to incorporate the essentials of that past into her fiction. Her autobiographical recall includes not just the names, places, and events of her past, but the flavor, the values, the spirit, the sustaining intangibles of the life she remembers as she was growing up in the 1930s and 1940s with proud, resourceful parents committed to living their way of life on their own terms.

Born Chloe Anthony Wofford on 18 February 1931 in the small town of Lorain, Ohio, Morrison was the second of George and Ramah Willis Wofford's four children. Both her parents had migrated from the South with their families in the early 1900s. Her maternal grandparents, sharecroppers in Greenville, Alabama, had lost their land in the late 1890s and were never able to get out of debt. In secrecy and defiance, they moved north, looking for a better way of life. Her father's family had been sharecroppers in Georgia, and his painful memories of racial strife left him with a bitter attitude toward whites. She was thus brought up—as many in such migrant families were—with a strong distrust of whites and an understanding that the only tangible or emotional aid on which she could depend would come from her own community. Group loyalty was among the earliest values she was taught as a child. It was, her parents believed, one of the most important lessons that she could learn in order to survive in the harsh racial environment of the 1930s and 1940s.

Morrison grew up in a household where the distinctiveness of black cultural life was richly lived and affirmed on a daily basis. Her maternal grandparents lived with them and provided Morrison with a two-generational sense of African American history and a rich involvement with and respect for their ethnic heritage. Her growing years were filled with the jokes, lore, music, language, and myths of African American culture. Her mother sang to the children, her father told them folktales, and they both told "thrillingly terrifying" ghost stories. It was at their knees that she heard tales of Brer Rabbit and of Africans who could fly; heard the names, the imagery, the rhythm of the language and observed the naming rituals that would become a significant part of her later work as a novelist. Her grandmother played the numbers by decoding dream symbols and had an abiding belief in "signs, visitation, and ways of knowing beyond the five senses. . . . We were intimate with the supernatural," says Morrison. This rich variety of songs, stories, beliefs, and history would later give Morrison's fiction its wonder, its humor, and its depth of understanding of the cultural life of African Americans.

In addition to the love for her own culture so essential to the writing of her stories, Morrison's parents instilled in her a love for reading and self-confidence in her abilities as a woman—both of which would contribute to her success as a writer. Her parents were both educated and taught her at home before she began school. In the first grade, she was the only child who could read. As an adolescent she eagerly read the works of Dostoevsky, Tolstoy, and Austen, and it was her early reading of these writers that taught Morrison how the specificity of one's group culture could be captured in a novel. As she explains to Jean Strouse:

> Those books were not written for a little black girl in Lorain, Ohio, but they were so magnificently done that I got them anyway—they spoke directly to me out of their own specificity. I wasn't thinking of writing then . . . , but when I wrote my first novel years later, I wanted to capture that same specificity about the culture I grew up in.
>
> (p. 54)

By their own example, Morrison's parents set a model for the shared role that men and women could play in a family. While her father often worked at three jobs to provide for his family, role division in the household was not enforced on the basis of gender. "There was comradeship between men and women in the marriages of my grandparents, and of my mother and father," she told Nellie McKay in a 1983 interview. "There were no conflicts of gender in that area. . . . My mother and father did not fight about who was supposed to do what. Each confronted whatever crisis there was." The possibility held out to her by the example of her parents—the absence of typecasting, the desire for individual excellence, an appreciation for literature (written and oral), and an abiding belief in the viability of her own culture—would mark her personality and her success as an artist.

The small Midwestern community where Morrison grew up was important in developing her sensitivity to the cultural ways of black life that would become the subject of her novels. The black community of Lorain was composed mostly of migrants who found jobs there when they fled the South in the early 1900s. Having left the South, most of them for the same reason, they had, no doubt, a strong sense of community, camaraderie, and group defiance. Also, in the 1920s and 1930s, when blacks had not begun to assimilate the ways of the larger culture or forget distinctive cultural ways nurtured in slave communities, there was a stronger connection to traditional ways of doing things. And, because Lorain was a small, Midwestern, working-class community made up of people from various ethnic backgrounds—Greeks, Italians, Irish—Morrison early on became sensitive to the integrity of cultural difference rather than to the inferiority in cultural difference often imposed upon blacks in the South.

The people of Morrison's community formed a cast of rich personalities who have always intrigued her. "People were more interesting then than they are now," she told LeClair. "It seems to me there were more excesses in women and men, and people accepted them as they don't now. In the community where I grew up there was eccentricity and freedom, less conformity in individual habits—but close conformity in terms of the survival of of the village, of the tribe." Thus in all of her novels the eccentrics—the rejected, the orphaned, the deformed, the mentally ill, the evil, the wayward—share center stage with the stable and responsible, so that Morrison is able to probe their separate lives and the roles they served in their communities. Years later, Colette Dowling reported her reflection on the role the folks in her community have in her writing; Morrison said she "wanted to find out who those people [were] and why they lived the way they did; to see the stuff out of which they were made."

After graduating from Lorain High School in 1949, Morrison entered Howard University in Washington, D.C. The years at Howard were important years for her later development as a writer and her deeper understanding of the wider range of black life that extended beyond small towns in the Midwest. Always an avid reader, she majored in English and minored in classics, and was a member of the Howard Repertory Theater. With the theater company she took memorable trips to the South, where she got a firsthand look at Southern black life. What she saw there echoed the stories her father had told her about the poverty and racism he had known when growing up. During these trips, Morrison was also able to see that within the community of blacks there were many similarities between those Southern black communities she visited and the community of blacks she had grown up in, in the Midwest. Thus, early in her life she confirmed something about the shared nature of the cultural life of blacks despite regional differences. It was a commonality she learned to trust and would rely on later in writing her novels.

Except for changing her name to Toni because the students at Howard had problems pronouncing Chloe, the college years presented no more feelings of distance from her community than was normal for any college student. Morrison graduated from Howard in 1953. Later, after receiving her master's degree at Cornell in 1955 and teaching at Texas Southern University from 1955 to 1957, she returned to Howard as an instructor in English.

While at Howard, she met and married Harold Morrison, a Jamaican architect. The couple had two sons, Slade Kevin and Harold Ford. In 1964, after the marriage ended in divorce, Morrison returned to Lorain. A year and a half later she moved to Syracuse, New York, to work as a textbook editor for a subsidiary of Random House. Always buoyed by community and family, Morrison had written only for her own pleasure as a teenager and as a member of a writing group at Howard. In Syracuse, away from a nourishing community, she begin to approach her writing seriously as a way to connect to the way of life she had left behind. Alone in the evenings after the children had gone to bed, she wrote as a way of keeping in touch with her community when, she says, she "had no one to talk to."

Morrison worked on a story that she had begun in her writing group at Howard about a little black girl who wants blue eyes. And while the issue of Anglo-Saxon standards of physical beauty and the problems of growing up black and poor in a society that holds whiteness and middle-class values up as the norm are the major conflicts in this novel, these conflicts, as those in future novels would be, are unraveled against the backdrop of a black community largely sustained by its own cultural values.

In *The Bluest Eye,* while we learn about the failures of the Breedloves, we also learn about the responsibility of the members of the community to avoid excesses that put them "outdoors":

> Outdoors, we knew, was the real terror of life. The threat of being outdoors surfaced frequently in those days. Every possibility of excess was curtailed with it. If somebody ate too much, he could end up outdoors. If somebody used too much coal, he could end up outdoors. People could gamble themselves outdoors, drink themselves outdoors. Sometimes mothers put their sons outdoors. . . .
>
> There is a difference between being put *out* and being put out*doors.* If you are put out, you go somewhere else; if you are outdoors, there is no place to go. The distinction was subtle but final.
>
> (p. 11)

We learn, too, of the shame of having "no people" and how in times of need the community comes to the aid of one of their own without family. We see the protective, albeit disdainful, prostitutes who also take part in raising the community's children. While there are many bad things happening to the Breedlove family—all victims of poverty and racism—they are not the norm for their community. The community, like the one Morrison remembers from her own past, remarks their failure but moves in to offer, as best it can, the love and protection the Breedloves cannot provide for themselves.

This leaving of the community, begun with her move to Syracuse and intensified when she moved to New York, affected Morrison deeply, and in some ways still affects her. It is the classic American story of the young innocent leaving the small town for the big city. But Morrison's moving exacted a heavier price for her because, she believes, even under the best of circumstances, rarely are blacks able to connect culturally, in a comforting way, to the predominantly white group settings they enter:

> If black people are going to to succeed in this culture, they must always leave. There's a terrible price to pay. I could only edit in the place where the editing is being done. I had to make sacrifices. Once you leave home, the things that feed you are not available to you anymore, the life is not available to you anymore. And the American life, the white life—that's certainly not available to you. So you really have to cut yourself off. Still, I can remember that world. I can savor it. I can write about it.
>
> (Dowling, p. 56)

In all of Morrison's novels, as in *The Bluest Eye,* recalling community is a way of keeping in touch, of savoring that community's life and keeping it alive. There are always the strikingly specific "remembered" places in her novels. In *Sula* the entire narrative is cradled in the reflection on a place, a neighborhood with a way of life now past: "In that place, where they tore nightshade and blackberry patches from their roots to make room for the Medallion City Golf course there was once a neighborhood." The Bottom, the separately defined black community of Medallion, contains a memorable array of community characters and places: Time-and-a-Half Pool Hall, Irene's Palace of Cosmetology, Reba's Grill—"where the owner cooked in her hat because she couldn't remember the ingredients without it." There are the Deweys, Tar Baby, Shadrack, and Sula, all accepted as part of the community even if other folks don't understand or totally approve of their ways.

In *Song of Solomon* there is the defiant but cohesive presence of the folks on Not Doctor Street, and the men who still hunt the dogs and the women who walk the streets without purses in Shalimar, Virginia. In *Tar Baby* there is Eloe, where yellow houses have white doors that women open and shout lovingly, "Come on in, you honey, you!"; Eloe, where the comforting presence of "fat black ladies in white dresses minding pie tables in church basements" calls up a hundred memories of hometown heroines; Eloe, "where white wet sheets flapping on a line and the sound of a six-string guitar plucked after supper while children scooped walnuts off the ground" are the sights and sounds of home. And, finally, there is the small community surrounding Bluestone Road in *Beloved,* peopled by Stamp Paid, and Ella, and Lady Jones—all caring neighbors who, though they keep their distance, are at the bidding of Sethe and Denver and ready with patience, with songs, and with love strong enough to exorcise a daughter-ghost destroying its mother.

Always there is a nurturing, distinctive community that surrounds the central conflict in Morrison's novels. Getting to that place, that past time, bringing forth those things she remembers from that past, is Morrison's way not only of passing a view of that life on to others but also of connecting to it herself. And when she does throw characters into conflict, it is always those who find connection and sustenance within that community who survive. In her stories Morrison wants to show the values played out in the interior life of the community. It is the most autobiographical part of her writing: "It's always the place where I start. I may not end up there but it's always the place where I start. Always."

In 1973, after Morrison had moved to New York and become a senior trade-book editor at Random House, she began an editing project that would enlarge her understanding and knowledge of the range of black history and culture. The project was called *The Black Book* (1974). Morrison's name appears nowhere in the book, but she was both originator of the idea and the book's in-house editor. She was so involved in the project that she collected materials from her friends and family to add to the enormous collections of Middleton Harrison, Morris Levitt, Roger Furman, and Ernest Smith, the official editors. The book is a history filled with information about the struggles and the triumphs of African Americans. In explaining her desire to do this kind of book, Morrison says she had gotten tired of histories of black life that focused only on leaders, leaving the everyday heroes to the lumps of statistics. She wanted to bring the lives of those who always got lost in the statistics to the forefront—to create a genuine black history book "that simply recollected life as lived." The book is loosely chronological, moving from slavery to roughly the 1940s. It contains newspaper clippings, bills of sale, sheet music, announcements, dream books, definitions, letters, patents, crafts, photographs, sports files, and other memorabilia taken largely from the collections of its editors, but it also includes an array of contributions from the attics, scrapbooks, and trunks of other supporters of the project.

While working on *The Black Book,* Morrison says, she felt the full range of emotions: horror, shock, intrigue, sadness, but mostly joy in witnessing the life blacks created on their own terms—"the part of our lives that was spent neither on our knees nor hanging from trees." It was a time when blacks didn't need to proclaim that they were black and proud—they just were. The rhetoric of the 1960s, compared with this earlier time, seemed to Morrison to be forced and reactionary. *The Black Book* brought to its pages that other, surer time when, as Henry Louis Gates describes it, blackness was "rendered" rather than "posited." This project became a major resource for Morrison's later novels. It informed her sense of the magnitude of the struggle and of the persistent heroism of blacks in America, and provided historical background that would enrich her later novels. Here were the stories of slavery, root-working, dream interpretations, Father Divine, and Harlem; accounts of the middle passage; and, most significantly for Morrison, the story of Margaret Garner, the slave who killed her child rather than have her return to slavery—the story that became the genesis of her Pulitzer Prize–winning novel, *Beloved.*

After *The Black Book,* the range of historical connection in Morrison's novels became more expansive. In *The Bluest Eye* and *Sula,* Morrison depended mostly on the history of her own life in Ohio. After *The Black Book,* she traveled places in her novels where she had not gone before. She records black life from Ohio to Florida, from New York to Kentucky to the Caribbean; her inclusion of black history, myths, songs, folktales, and ways of life was greater than it had been in the earlier novels. From the myths of first-generation Africans in the New World and the details of the middle passage, to the Harlem of the 1920s, Morrison's voice became larger, her historical depth greater, her awareness of the mythical possibilities of her fiction more revealing. Perhaps no experience had greater impact on the cultural and historical depth of her later novels than this book.

While Morrison's novels are filled with the lore, the humor, the language, the values, and the beliefs of the culture of core black communities of the past, her novels are not just reveries about the "good old days." The point of this recall, she says, is not just to "soak in some warm bath of nostalgia," but to present that life in its ugliness and its beauty—to put characters under duress in order to discover who survives and why. The values that she applauds and finds useful are always presented as a background for those major threats in the society that have caused blacks to distance themselves from or to be removed from the values and traditions of their core ethnic culture: alien standards of beauty, desires for existential selfhood, materialism, success, and slavery itself. The penetrating analysis of these conflicts that Morrison offers has been the most provocative aspect of her fiction. How blacks deal with these issues and whether their resolutions affirm or reject community values are the thematic issues she addresses in her novels.

Morrison's first novel, *The Bluest Eye,* explores the problem of establishing self-worth in a society where one is the victim of both racism and classism. Narrated by nine-year-old Claudia McTeer, the novel details the lives of three young girls and their families, and the way in which they struggle—and sometimes lose their battle—for self-affirmation in a world that sets forth Anglo-Saxon standards of physical beauty and a middle-class life-style as the norm. From school primers to dolls to movies, the girls and their families are inundated with images that deny the beauty and reality of their lives.

The book begins with the words of a grade-school primer, first spaced wide (Here is the house. It is green and white), then closer (Here is the house it is green and white), and finally running together without any spacing (Hereisthehouseitisgreenandwhite) in order to establish the way in which the primer story has been consumed to excess by generations of black children who have lived their lives in direct contrast with the one presented to them as the norm. In varying degrees all the people in the community have felt the effects of racism. Claudia and Frieda McTeer have been fed a steady diet of white baby dolls all their lives. Frieda accepts them but Claudia rebels, tearing their heads off and wondering why the adults love them so:

> "Here," they said, "this is beautiful, and if you are on this day 'worthy' you may have it." I fingered the face, wondered at the single-stroke eyebrows, picked at the pearly teeth stuck like two piano keys between red bowline lips. Traced the turned up nose, poked the glassy blue eyeballs, twisted the yellow hair. I could not love it. (p. 20)

Maureen Peal, their light-skinned classmate, has bathed in unmerited luxury by being nearer physically to the white norm than any of the others: "She enchanted the entire school. When teachers called on her, they smiled encouragingly. Black boys didn't trip her in the halls; white boys didn't stone her, white girls didn't suck their teeth when she was assigned to be their work partner." The adults in the community tacitly accept the norm, instilling it in their children or imposing it upon themselves.

The family who is the focus of the most extreme victimization of this pervasive racism and classism is the Breedloves. The father, Cholly, alienated long ago by a mother who deserted him and a father who rejected him, was raised by his great aunt. As an adolescent he was humiliated into submission when two white men, coming upon him and his girlfriend making love in an open field, forced him to continue under the glare of their flashlights:

> With a violence born of total helplessness, he pulled her dress up, lowered his trousers and underwear. . . . Darlene put her hands over her face as Cholly began to simulate what had gone on before. He could do no more than make-belief. The flashlight made a moon on his behind.
> (p. 117)

Seeking recovery later in his relationship with his wife, Pauline, and in the hope of a better life in the North, Cholly becomes even more alienated and disappointed. He never quite finds the love and respect he seeks. He spends his days resisting debtors, getting drunk, and fighting with his wife, until his need for love and his desperate desire to give love ends in his tragic rape of his daughter.

Pauline Breedlove, suffering from a limp since childhood and wanting to be accepted first by her family and later by the women she meets when she and Cholly move from Kentucky to Ohio, descends to self-abnegation, then to abnegation of her storefront home life, and ultimately of her entire family. Her only pleasure comes from her identification with the movie-screen images of Jean Harlow and Greta Garbo. Pauline finally gives up identifying vicariously with these images when, she bites into a candy bar and loses her front tooth:

> *"I don't believe I ever did get over that. There I was, five months pregnant, trying to look like Jean Harlow and a front tooth gone. Everything went then. Look like I just didn't care no more after that. I let my hair go back, plaited it up and settled down to just being ugly."*
> (p. 98)

Her declaration of ugliness causes her to discredit the value of her own life. She cleans for a white family but leaves her own house in disarray. She comforts the child of the family she works for but scolds her own.

Unlike the McTeers, who survive these same forces of racism and classism, the Breedloves become tragic victims. The result of their victimization is most acutely demonstrated in their daughter, Pecola. Laughed at on the playground, scolded at home—a storefront room that holds the yelling and hating of her parents' fights—and ridiculed by her teachers and classmates for her ugliness, Pecola prays for blue eyes as a solution: "It occurred to Pecola some time ago that if her eyes, those eyes that held the pictures, and knew the sights—if those eyes of hers were different, that is to say, beautiful, she herself would be different." Driven to madness after being raped by her father and the death of the resulting baby, Pecola seeks the powers of a deranged spiritual healer, Elihue Micah Whitcomb (known as Soaphead Church), and finally believes that he has given her blue eyes.

There is much sympathy garnered for the Breedloves, as both willing and forced victims of racism. Morrison criticizes both the larger society that holds up physical standards of beauty as a measure of self-worth and the black community, which endorses them. And while she understands the weakness that causes blacks to buy into beauty as a standard, she points out the ultimate destruction to self and family inherent in accepting values from the outside.

The Bluest Eye was well received and established an early following for Morrison, particularly among black women, who understood so poignantly the issues addressed in the novel. The most powerless victim of racism, classism, and sexism, they believed, was a poor black girl. Morrison's exploration of this problem, which revealed its sources and its effects in personal and emotional ways, affected her readers deeply. Critically, *The Bluest Eye* also established the great potential of Morrison's narrative voice.

The mediating voice of the narrator that she established in this novel has been the source of much analysis by critics. Some suggest that Morrison betrays the voice of her characters, mediating unnecessarily, while others say that the duality of these voices represents Morrison's understanding of the duality of black consciousness—of how blacks must simultaneously see themselves on their own terms and through the eyes of others.

In her second novel, *Sula,* Morrison moves away from the story of the passive victims who cannot achieve self-actualization because of imposed forces that distance them from the values of their own culture. She introduces a "willing pariah"—a woman who consciously chooses to reject the values of her community and actively establish self-definition in terms other than those approved and expected. In the novel two childhood friends, Nel Wright and Sula Peace, find solace in each other's differences as adolescents and are strengthened by their desire to rebel against the wishes of their parents—Nel against the sit-up-straight, nose-pulling ritual inflicted by her mother and Sula against the loose and "sooty" ways of her mother and grandmother. As they grow older, Nel submits to the community's standard of acceptable female behavior. She marries, has children, and cares for the sick and the old of her community, realizing there is little difference between her life and the life of her mother. Sula goes away to college, tries to live an experimental life outside her community, and finally returns to Medallion. Her return does not bring submission, however. Sula openly defies the rules of the community: she comes to church suppers without underwear, she sleeps with Nel's husband, she puts her grandmother in a nursing home, and, worst of all for the people in that community, Sula sleeps with white men. Sula is determined not to be like the women of her community. Her declaration to Nel on her deathbed is a truthful commentary on how she has viewed her life: "I know what every Black woman in this country is doing. . . . Dying. Just like me. But the difference is they dying like a stump. Me, I'm going down like one of those redwoods."

The community ostracizes Sula and keep their distance from her; but despite her defiance of their values, she is not put outside the community. Community members tolerate the eccentrics like Shadrack, the shell-shocked war veteran; the Deweys, the wayward orphans; Tar Baby, the withdrawn drunkard; and Sula. They treat evil the same way they treat grace. They respect its presence: "They let it run its course, fulfill itself and never invented ways either to alter it, annihilate it or . . . prevent its happening again." In the characterization of Sula Morrison makes a significant statement about the nature of evil and its acceptance in the black community, and about the way that unconditional acceptance always acts as a balm for the community members, even for those who desire to rebel against it.

When alienation from the larger society is so possible and so prevalent as it would have been for Sula in 1941, existential, acultural definitions of self are futile. Because of both sexism and racism, even rebellion against the ways of the community can, ironically, be actualized only within the community. In its knowing way the community registers its disapproval of evil but does not seek to annihilate it.

Sula received generally excellent reviews from the critics. They praised Morrison's prose style, her ear for dialogue, and her deft characterization. Some critics, missing the focus and aim of the duress suffered by characters in the novel, chided Morrison for her characterizations of pathetic, unusual, exotic community types. *Sula* was nominated for the National Book Award in 1975 and is frequently analyzed by feminist critics, who see the conflict between self-realization and community allegiance dramatically played out in this novel. Other themes that have been of great interest to feminist critics of this novel are friendships between women, mother-daughter relationships, and the connections between gender and evil.

If Morrison's larger theme was subdued by protests and character delineations in her first two novels, her third novel, *Song of Solomon* (1977), allows for no such ambiguity. It is a triumphant endorsement of knowing and accepting ancestral heritage. Here all the knowledge of *The Black Book,* all the sensitivity to the needs for ancestral connection for the contemporary generation moving rapidly toward a materialistic, upwardly mobile culture, are used by Morrison to create a rich and powerful novel. It is the story of young Milkman Dead and his quest, inadvertent at first, for his identity. The only son in a household of two older sisters and a love-starved mother who nurses him until he is six, Milkman is encouraged by his father to become a successful businessman. His father flaunts his wealth as landlord in the community and forbids any association with his sister, Pilate, an old woman who is an embarrassment to his father. She wears brogans and old quilts, sings songs of her history in an uninhibited contralto, and sells bootleg wine. The other members of her household are her daughter and granddaughter. Pilate is a kind of earth woman in the novel: she has no navel, and lives a life with few of the amenities of modern existence but supported by a knowledge of ancestral history and family love. Her physical oddity caused her early on to give up seeking the approval of others and to create her own criteria for how to live in the world.

Milkman spends his adolescence moving between the middle-class strictures of his father's household and the streetwise culture of his friend Guitar. Guitar initiates Milkman into the man's life of the street, women, and revenge as a means of righting the wrongs of racism. Early in his adulthood Guitar becomes a member of Seven Days, a black vigilante group that takes revenge for each death of a black person caused by racial hatred by inflicting the same kind of death upon a white. Milkman never becomes a member of the group, but his initiation into manhood involves his being challenged by Guitar and his finally rejecting violence as a response to racism.

Despite his father's warning, Milkman finally does meet his aunt Pilate and spends many wondrous afternoons crushing grapes for her bootleg wine, listening to family stories, and falling in love with his cousin Hagar. It is Pilate who offers Milkman the most wholesome avenue toward self-affirmation. She, with her love for her family, her desire to maintain connections with the past, is responsible for the journey into self-discovery that he finally takes.

From the beginning, however, Milkman's journey is made not for self-discovery but for gold, for the material wealth that his father believes will offer him manhood. His father is convinced that an old sack that hangs from the ceiling in Pilate's house contains gold, and he encourages Milkman to steal it. When the sack reveals old bones instead of gold, Milkman journeys to the home place of his father and aunt to rescue the gold he believes must still be there. Instead of finding gold in the caves of Virginia, Milkman finds the myths, the songs, the legends that contain his family history.

Although his journey begins as a quest for money and revenge, it ends in a glorious connection to ancestry revealed to him through the legends of his great-grandfather, Solomon. Milkman answers not only his own submerged questions of belonging but those of his father and his aunt as well. The knowledge of great-grandfather who could fly, and who indeed *did* fly away from the slavery destroying his manhood, empowers Milkman with love, strength, and a triumphant sense of who he is and his own potential for transcendence:

> "He could fly! You hear me? My great-granddaddy could fly! He whipped the water with his fist, then jumped straight up as though he too

> could take off. . . . He didn't need no airplane. He just took off: got fed up. *All the way up.* No more cotton. No more bales! No more orders. . . . He just flew, baby. Lifted . . . up in the sky and flew on home!"
>
> (p. 328)

In *Song of Solomon,* Morrison considers the limitations of two options available to blacks in the wake of the civil rights movement: rapid financial advancement and violent retaliation. She attacks both materialism, represented by Milkman's father, and vigilantism, represented by Guitar and Seven Days. Morrison shows the emptiness of self-definition in economic terms, the shortsightedness of the willful violence of revenge, and the healing and growth possible in individuals when they know and are nourished by the history and culture of their ancestry. The heroes and heroines in this text are not financial kings or outlaws but those who find their solace, their wealth, their sense of joy in community and ancestry: Pilate, the men and women of Shalimar who know and live their history, and finally Milkman himself.

In *Song of Solomon* Morrison moved away from the focus on black women that had been at the center of her first two novels. Heralded for its language, its cultural richness in song, folklore, and myth, its triumphant endorsement of the possibility of renewal and transcendence through ancestral reconnection, *Song of Solomon* became the most celebrated novel by a black writer since Ralph Ellison's *Invisible Man* (1952). In 1977 *Song of Solomon* was chosen as the Book-of-the-Month Club Main Selection, a recognition no novel by a black writer had received since Richard Wright's *Native Son* (1940). It has been printed in five languages and has sold well over three million copies.

Still concerned with the challenges of contemporary post-integration society, and more comfortable now than she had ever been in her role as writer, Morrison completed her fourth novel, *Tar Baby,* in 1981. In *Song of Solomon,* she had been concerned with the effects of materialism on a young black man; this time her concern was its effects on a young black woman. Jadine Childs, the protagonist, is a beautiful, young, Sorbonne-educated model whose schooling has been paid for by the employer of her aunt and uncle.

After receiving her degree, Jadine contemplates marriage to a rich French suitor. Haunted by the implications of cultural betrayal in interracial marriage, she decides to return to her family's island, where she can make a final decision in a supportive environment. Upon her return to the Isle des Chevaliers, where her aunt and uncle are maid and butler in the household of a retired candy manufacturer, Valerian Street, she meets and falls in love with a handsome black fugitive, William Green (called Son). Their love affair is complicated by their different outlooks on life. Son is a man of meager means who cherishes his family and finds his strength in the life of village blacks in his hometown of Eloe, Florida. Jadine is energized by the fast life of the city. Their relationship turns into a romantic Armageddon between the old ways and the new: "One had a past, the other a future, and each one bore the culture to save the race in his hands. Mama-spoiled black man, will you mature with me? Culture-bearing black woman, whose culture are you bearing?" In the novel, Morrison is able to articulate the way in which the larger social and political choices of blacks during the late 1970s manifested themselves on a personal level. She successfully dramatizes many of the issues, but the outcome of this debate is not hopeful. Unable to resolve their differences, Son and Jadine end the romance as individuals understanding more about the value of each other's outlook on life but unable to reconcile these ways into a unifying relationship. Clearly on the side of the past in this novel, Morrison not only sets up a thematic argument against Jadine, pointing out that she is one who has "forgotten her ancient properties," but also unravels the story against a natural landscape so mythically rendered that setting, too, suggests the superiority of that which is timeless, rooted, unshaken by contemporary realities. Clouds, bees, butterflies, trees, ants act as a chorus for the tragedy occurring between the main players, and what they say in the refrain always echoes the enduring connectedness between then and now:

> Only the champion daisy trees were serene. After all, they were part of a rainforest already two thousand years old and scheduled for eternity, so they ignored the men and continued to rock the diamondbacks that slept in their arms. It took the river to persuade them that indeed the world was altered.
>
> (p. 9)

Although *Tar Baby* sold well, it was not as well received by reviewers as her earlier novels had been. Many reviewers felt the novel's innovative allegorical descriptions of the natural landscape were overwritten: "Fog came to that place in wisps sometimes, like the hair of maiden aunts. Hair so thin and pale it went unnoticed until masses of it gathered around the house and threw back one's own reflection from the windows." Some questioned the plausibility of the love affair between Jadine and Son—two so different in outlook and upbringing. But most felt that as a novel of ideas, with all the heady limitations such novels usually have, it addressed these issues with an unusual freshness and energy. Its focus on the complexities of issues of race and class both between and among blacks and whites, its criticism of the effects of integration, its attack on capitalism, and its concern for the generational responsibility of "culture-bearing" made it of great interest to many readers despite its mythical descriptions of the landscape and character. The combination of the artistry and the ideas, however, was the true reflection of the novel's merit.

In 1983 a short story by Morrison, "Recitatif," was published in *Confirmation: An Anthology of African American Women Writers*. The story, which focuses on the complexities of interracial friendship, employs a writing style that does not demonstrate the range and maturity of Morrison by 1983. While clearly a beginning effort, it does bear Morrison's signature thematically and stylistically—nurturing black communities, metonymical characterizations, and an emphasis on the difficult truth that the private unities of interracial friendships cannot survive the public divisions dictated by race.

The story deals with the growing up of eight-year-old Twyla and Roberta, one black and one white, who as roommates in an orphanage become the best of friends. After the girls leave the orphanage, they have their friendship tested on several occasions. Twelve years later Roberta, a heavy-haired hippie and fan of Jimi Hendrix, snubs Twyla when she turns up as her waitress in a Howard Johnson motel. Eight years after that, the girls, now married women, meet in a suburban grocery store—Twyla on a visit to a new mall in an exclusive suburb, Roberta on a neighborhood errand. The eight years have softened Roberta, now a well-off suburban housewife, and Twyla, a happily married woman in a working-class family. This time the women reunite with sisterly nostalgia, and Twyla wonders why Roberta was distant before. It was the "black white thing," Roberta explains. After coffee they separate, promising to keep in touch. The next time they see each other is when Twyla's son, transferred from an inner-city school to a suburban one as the result of a desegregation order, meets an angry mob of suburban housewives—including Roberta—protesting bussing. On opposite sides of the picket line the two friends engage in a sign-waving battle of loyalties. Finally, after Twyla's son's graduation, the two women are able to manage a bittersweet reconciliation.

The story, firmly rooted in the political context of the 1960s and 1970s, demonstrates the way in which the personal really does become political and the separate ways these childhood friends' lives turn as the public constructions of whiteness and blackness are forced upon them. Though the characters are not fully developed and the plot is episodic and unbalanced, the story does include some of Morrison's familiar themes: the emphasis on the value of a nurturing community, the ultimate allegiance to the ethnic community, and the conviction that the alliances of integration are false so long as whites, when their privileged way of life is threatened, are more loyal to caste and class than to enduring friendships. "Recitatif" is hardly mentioned among Morrison's published works, and no other short stories are collected. Clearly, by 1983 Morrison's reputation rested solely on her prolific work as a novelist.

Tar Baby and *Song of Solomon* enjoyed much success. There were more than 570,000 copies of *Song of Solomon* sold by 1979, and the paperback rights were reportedly sold for $315,000. In addition to the National Book Critics' Circle Award for fiction, *Song of Solomon* brought Morrison an American Academy and Institute of Arts and Letters Award and inclusion in the public-television series *Writers in America.* Coming after the astounding success of *Song of Solomon,* the publication of *Tar Baby* was received with great fanfare. The novel appeared on the *New York Times* best-seller list less than a month after its publication. The *Newsweek* cover story and a stunning lineup of promotional tours increased the sales and catapulted Morrison into enduring fame: She was, one reviewer claimed after the publication of *Tar Baby,* the "toast of the literary world." The novels are widely read in college courses, and both have gone into at least six editions and been translated into several languages.

After the success of *Song of Solomon* and *Tar Baby,* Morrison says she was officially able to declare her occupation as "full-time writer." She had been a major force in the publishing world as an editor, overseeing the works of many black writers, including Toni Cade Bambara, Gayle Jones, Andrew Young, and Muhammad Ali. With four novels to her credit, part-time lectureship at Yale, Bard College, Rutgers, and Stanford, and a growing number of literary awards, Morrison was becoming highly sought after in the literary world beyond Random House. Considered by 1984 to be a major American writer in her own right, Morrison left her job as senior editor at Random House and accepted an appointment to the Albert Schweitzer Chair in the Humanities at the State University of New York at Albany. Here she taught a class in creative writing and worked on her next novel.

Also while at Albany, Morrison was commissioned by the New York State Writers' Institute to write a play in honor of the first national observance of the birthday of Martin Luther King, Jr. The play, *Dreaming Emmett,* was based on the 1954 murder of a black youth, Emmett Till, who was killed by a lynch mob in Mississippi for whistling at a white woman. The play analyzes the horror of the case through the young boy's dream recollection of the events leading up to his killing. The play was performed by the Capitol Repertory Theater of Albany on 4 January 1986. In the play, Joseph C. Phillips, as Emmett Till, "directed" a monologic film of his dream. He entered wheeling a cart of props, enveloped by fog, and called forth the characters who were involved in the incident: the white woman, the white men who were acquitted of his murder, and his two black friends, whom he believes knew the truth but were afraid to tell it. Reviewers praised Morrison's language and the innovative stage production, but, beyond an indictment of racism, most felt that on a interpretative level the play did not succeed with the literary and imaginative power they had become accustomed to in her novels. While Morrison has expressed great interest in drama, she has not published the play as a separate work.

In 1987 Morrison published her long-awaited novel *Beloved.* The story is based on the life of Margaret Garner, a Kentucky slave who with her four children escaped to Cincinnati, Ohio. When caught, she tried to kill all of her children and succeeded in killing one by cutting her throat. The case received national attention in the 1850s as abolitionists tried to argue for

Garner's citizenship rights and slave owners wanted to test the validity of the Fugitive Slave Act. Garner was taken back to Kentucky but was never returned to Ohio for trial.

When Morrison read this story while working on *The Black Book,* she was deeply moved by the humanistic and symbolic nature of this story—by its telling reflection of how slavery affected the interior life of the individual and how this one woman was not going to allow the experience to deny her rights of motherhood. Here was a woman, Morrison said, who did a courageous thing: she took the lives of her children into her own hands. This incident proved not only the horror of slavery in denying the rights of motherhood but also the inability of slavery to deny blacks their own moral code. "I am always amazed," says Morrison, "at the way in which bestial treatment did not create a race of beasts." Morrison wanted to know no more about Margaret Garner's life in creating her story; she wanted to depend on a shared, recessed response to both the horror of slavery and the killing of the child. She researched the Underground Railroad and the industrial machinery of slavery, but she wanted to depend on her imagination and shared cultural knowledge to construct the interior life of the characters.

In the novel, after killing her baby, Sethe remains in Cincinnati and returns to her mother-in-law's house after a short jail sentence. After her mother-in-law Baby Suggs dies and her two sons run away out of fear of the baby's ghost, Sethe stays in the house at 124 Bluestone Road with her daughter, Denver. The ghost of the daughter she killed frequents the house often, and the two women become accustomed to its recurring presence. Paul D, from the Sweet Home Plantation, where Sethe had been a slave, escapes and finds her in Cincinnati. He beats away the vengeful ghost that has been manifesting itself in poltergeist fashion, shaking the floor, turning over the furniture, remaining unseen and without flesh. After Paul D drives the ghost away, she returns, this time in the flesh, as a young woman the age the baby girl would have been, and calls herself Beloved. She changes from a sick and weepy stranger in need of food, rest, and shelter, to a haunting but harmless presence asking questions about objects and events no stranger would know about, and finally to a mean, threatening spirit seeking revenge on its killer. Finally Denver must get help for her mother. The women in the community respond guardedly but deliberately, forgiving Sethe for both her deed and her pride as they come to aid in exorcising the destructive presence of Beloved:

> They grouped, murmuring and whispering, but did not step foot in the yard. Denver waved. A few waved back but came no closer. Denver sat back down wondering what was going on. A woman dropped to her knees. Half of the others did likewise. Denver saw lowered heads, but could not hear the lead prayer—only the earnest syllables of agreement that backed it: Yes, yes, yes, oh yes.
>
> (p. 258)

Although the novel is based on events in the life of Margaret Garner, the story moves from the specific return of the ghost of her daughter, wherein it is a working out of the mother's grief and forgiveness, to a more symbolic representation of the memory of the more than sixty million men and women and children who lost their lives to slavery. The ghost who comes to life in this novel provides a way for Morrison to use the supernatural to give voice to those who died at the hand of slavery. They must be remembered and mourned, Morrison believes, by those who have not known the horror of their lives and asked forgiveness by those who took their lives. There have been no stories of the middle passage, says Morrison; it has not been the subject of poems, or songs, or myth. In a 1989 interview, published as "A Bench by the Road" in the *World,* she points out:

> There is no place you or I can go, to think about or not think about, to summon the presences of, or recollect the absences of slaves; nothing that reminds us of the ones who made the journey and of those who did not make it. There is no

> suitable memorial or plaque or wreath or wall or park or skyscraper lobby. There's no 300-foot tower. There's no small bench by the road. There is not even a tree scored, an inital that I can visit or you can visit in Charleston or Savannah or New York or Providence or, better still, on the banks of the Mississippi. And because such a place doesn't exist (that I know of), the book had to.
>
> (p. 4)

Beloved offered Morrison the opportunity not only to address the horror of slavery and the power of motherhood, but also to recall what must have been the horror of the middle passage and offer a testimonial that both mourned and celebrated the singular lives of the individuals who made the journey.

Morrison allows for the full range of moral complexity in this novel. Sethe's act is not explained away—even against the horrifying descriptions of slavery that serve as the background of the novel. Even as Morrison describes in gruesome detail an acceptable justification for Sethe's act, she has Sethe work out her own peace and her repentance with the only one who can judge her actions: the daughter herself. In the context of the horror of slavery revealed in the novel, Sethe did the right thing in saving her daughter from a living death. In the context of her own humanity, however, she took another life, and she pays for this act as she seeks repentance and forgiveness from the ghost of her daughter. "She did the right thing," Morrison has explained, "but she didn't have the right to do it."

It is this amazing quality of humaneness, strength, and endurance given to an individual suffering severe duress that has become Morrison's signature in her characterization. Cholly, Eva, and Guitar are all party to destructive crimes against those they love, but the characters are never portrayed as monstrous or totally evil. *Beloved,* however, is the first work where there is healing and the prospect of a new beginning. For all its sadness, it has a hopeful ending. The characters in Morrison's early novels never really find peace, or seek forgiveness, or have an affirming opportunity for self-realization. When Paul D tells Sethe at the end of the novel, as she still mourns the leaving of even the ghost of her child—whom she has repeatedly called "her best thing"—that it is she, not the ghost, that is her best thing, Sethe is on her way to recovery. She has exorcised the guilt and the grief, and can now begin to live a new life.

The kind of reconciliation that Sethe experiences, Morrison suggests, is the same kind of reconciliation with the slave past that blacks in general must face in order to move forward in contemporary society. They must bring slavery, the starting point of their injustice, back to life, must come to terms with that past, must mourn for those lost ancestors, must finally face the horror and the grief on a personal level before they can let go of the ghost of slavery and move forward into the future with hope and wholeness.

Critical responses to *Beloved* have been almost unanimously positive. The complexity of the issues it forces on an event too often "summarized" away in American history gives the novel its greatest moral and historical merit. The method of the telling and the exceptional artistry of the novel have provided a challenge for its readers. Full of intertwining plots and layered time sequences, of "rememory," as Morrison describes it, the novel keeps readers alert and attentive. The order of revelation, always out of chronological sequence in Morrison's novels, is doubly complicated in this novel by characters "remembering what they were remembering" in a time past. The infanticide that is the cause of the action in the story gives way to the labor of working out symbolic meanings of the ghost's presence and understanding the quests for psychological and moral wholeness it inspires in all the characters. The language is musical—full of the chants, the crescendos, and the major chords that the story demands. As Margaret Atwood concluded in her *New York Times* review: "*Beloved* is written in an anti-minimalist prose that is by turns rich, graceful, eccentric, rough, lyrical, sinuous, colloquial, and very much to the point. All of this together has made the work a tour de force in technical and thematic achievement."

Since *Beloved,* the assured place in the American literary canon enjoyed by Morrison has become a fixed, seasoned, unconditional presence. She has received some of the most prestigious literary awards in the country, and she is much sought after for lectures and interviews by public radio and television, literary journals, arts foundations, and universities. Most recently she was the subject of the highly regarded PBS interview series *A World of Ideas with Bill Moyers.* In May 1990, she was invited to deliver the prestigious Massey Lectures in American Civilization at Harvard University. The critical interest in her work has moved beyond that of students of African American Literature and women's-studies classes. Morrison's works are taught in courses in creative writing, feminist literary theory, and American intellectual history. In 1989 she accepted the Robert F. Goheen Chair in the Humanities at Princeton, where she currently teaches creative writing and lectures in American literature.

The effort to understand and interpret Morrison within a large literary and intellectual context—the canonizing of Morrison—has often brought with it an effort to deracialize her. No black writer, male or female, has become as accepted a part of the American literary canon as Morrison. Reviewers and critics often remark in a complimentary way that she is not just "a black woman writer," having moved beyond what they believe to be the limiting confines of race and gender to larger "universal" issues and studious concerns with craft. When interviewers ask whether she sees herself as a writer or as a black woman writer, Morrison bristles at this distinction. She is surprised, and slightly annoyed, that they are unable to accept her as both at the same time, and that they would suggest by the order of their question that the former is somehow superior to the latter. She is a Black Woman Writer, she answers politely but emphatically. Being a black woman does not limit her vision as a writer, she says; rather, it enhances her vision—it enlarges the way she views the world.

Morrison believes, in fact, that black women, perhaps more than any other group in this society, have the ability to see it whole and to understand the weaknesses, the complexities, and the potential of its humanity. Freed by race from the oppressive dictates of the dubious pedestal of "the cult of true womanhood," forced by necessity to be the ship and the safe harbor for their families, historically misused by white men and depended on by black men, black women, Morrison believes, have been in a position to see the world from the inside out. The angle of vision, then, that they bring to any interpretation of the American scene is more clarifying than any other. "Their knowing is deep," says Morrison; theirs is a composite view. Black women "are the touchstone by which all that is human can be measured." To suggest an apology for the richness of her ordering of the world as a writer through the lens of black womanhood would be, she believes, to diminish herself unnecessarily.

Despite Morrison's insistence on gender and race as informing sources for her craft, feminist critics find her works problematic. With her sympathetic portrayals of what are often considered to be weaknesses in men, with the emphasis in *Song of Solomon* on the interior development of the male protagonist, and with her seeming endorsement of traditional roles in her characterization of women, feminist critics do not fully understand the politics of Morrison's feminism. The best way to explain this divergence is to understand that Morrison is not a political feminist. While she certainly does not advocate submission to patriarchy, she is not interested, she says, in attacking men or devising ways to exchange dominance. Morrison reveals most of the stories of her novels through the eyes of black women and says that in large measure her work involves an exploration of "the evolution of self in black women," but she does not embrace the kind of radical political feminism associated with the women's movement of the 1970s.

Morrison has drawn a larger landscape; she has cast a wider net. She is, in Alice Walker's terms, more "womanist" than "feminist"—"committed to survival and wholeness of entire people, male *and* female." And to the extent that she can be called a feminist at all, she is, like most black women—and in the tradition of black women writers like Zora Neale Hurston, Gwendolyn Brooks, and Paule Marshall—a cultural feminist. And as a cultural feminist she celebrates the strengths of black women despite the racism and sexism leveled against them.

Her panoramic view of black women in an often-quoted passage from *The Bluest Eye* suggests the kind of cultural feminism that Morrison advocates:

> Edging into life from the back door. Becoming. Everybody in the world was in a position to give them orders. White women said, "Do this." White children said, "Give me that." White men said, "Come here." Black men said, "Lay down." The only people they need not take orders from were black children and each other. But they took all of that and re-created it in their own image. They ran the houses of white people, and knew it. When white men beat their men, they cleaned up the blood and went home to receive abuse from the victim. They beat their children with one hand and stole for them with the other. The hands that felled trees also cut umbilical cords; the hands that wrung the necks of chickens and butchered hogs also nudged African violets into bloom; the arms that loaded sheaves, bales, and sacks rocked babies into sleep. They patted biscuits into flaky ovals of innocence—and shrouded the dead. They plowed all day and came home to nestle like plums under the limbs of their men. The legs that straddled a mule's back were the same ones that straddled their men's hips. And the difference was all the difference there was.
>
> (p. 108)

Morrison takes the stereotypes under which black women and black men have suffered, "dusts them off," and develops characters who triumphantly and heroically wear those stereotypes, revealing the essence of the strengths that have been caricatured by ignorance and racism. She explores issues that concern women—physical standards of beauty, the nature of female friendships, male-female relationships; but a solution for black women to the problems raised by these issues comes, Morrison believes, when they reconnect themselves to their cultural sources. For Morrison, the enemy is not maleness but forgetfulness. It is that—forgetfulness—against which she protests in her fiction.

As professor at SUNY and at Princeton, Morrison has begun to engage in more scholarly, academic discourse regarding American literature and her own poetics. Many of the essays she has written on these subjects focus on the nature of her own creative process. Significant in these discussions has been the way in which she has described the importance of memory in her creative process. Memory controls not only what Morrison writes about but also how she writes. She says in "Memory, Creation, and Writing" (1984):

> I depend heavily on the ruse of memory . . . for two reasons. One, because it ignites some process of invention, and two, because I cannot trust the literature and sociology of other people to help me know the truth of my cultural sources. . . . Memory then, no matter how small the pieces remembered, demands my respect, my attention, my trust.
>
> (p. 386)

In Morrison's novels, the construction of characters, scenes, and language is derived from the "remains" of experiences in her own past—the way the women in her community said the name of a woman called Hannah Peace, the woman's half-closed eyes, a purple dress, a quality of forgiveness echoed in the calling of her name. She has a quality of recollection that she admits is extraordinary. She is able to cull what she believes is the shared, cultural, ancestral memory of experiences not specifically her own and make them ring true to her readers. It is important, Morrison believes, to begin this kind of memory-based retrieval because that part of black life which is not sensational, statistical, or extraordinary has so often been discredited. But it is that life, that remembered part of past experience, informed by a recessed code of values, practiced daily and involuntarily, which reveals the cultural essence.

Morrison realizes that memory does not give total access and that she must depend on imagination to give it flesh, but the genesis of a setting, a character, a phrase, she says, lies primarily in memory: the "pieces," the "remains" of an event or experience that linger long after it is past, the colors, smells, sounds, associated feelings. These "pieces," and the ideas and feelings they remind her of, are what she tries to capture in her novels.

Clearly, in her evolution from the personal, searching stages of *The Bluest Eye* and *Sula* to the masterful, assured, prophetic, redemptive stage of *Beloved*, Morrison has come a long way. She has told the story of black life with an uncompromising commitment to the integrity of a black worldview. She has trusted her undocumented sources, the "buried stimuli," the recessed memories—her own and those shared by the culture—and touched a resonant cord. She has moved beyond the "mask" of blackness that blacks have had to assume in this country, and has revealed the self-defined interior of their lives. She has brought to the forefront complex issues in the lives of African Americans and has offered in her stories the questions, the possibilities, and the implications central to their resolution. And she has done so with extraordinary vision, skill, and courage.

As a late-twentieth-century black woman writer charged with the cultural and artistic representation of the life and history of her people, now finally casting off the shackles of slavery and segregation, wherein they were defined in terms other than their own, Morrison has become a kind of literary Moses—stripping away the idols of whiteness and of blackness that have prevented blacks in the United States from knowing themselves, and trying in her works to give them their own true words to live by. Her readers are energized intellectually by where she places the distancing culprits of society; they are moved by the poetry of her language; and they are nurtured and empowered by her trust in memory and her always masterful affirmation of that which they have forgotten or never knew about the rich cultural life of their past.

Selected Bibliography

PRIMARY SOURCES

FICTION

The Bluest Eye. New York: Holt, Rinehart & Winston, 1970.

Sula. New York: Knopf, 1973.

Song of Solomon. New York: Knopf, 1977.

Tar Baby. New York: Knopf, 1981.

"Recitatif." In *Confirmation: An Anthology of African American Women Writers*. Edited by Amiri Baraka and Amina Baraka. New York: Quill, 1983.

Beloved. New York: Knopf, 1987.

NONFICTION

"What the Black Woman Thinks About Women's Lib." *New York Times Magazine*, 22 August 1971, pp. 14–15, 63–64, 66.

"Behind the Making of *The Black Book*." *Black World* 23:86–90 (February 1974).

"Rediscovering Black History." *New York Times Magazine*, 11 August 1974, pp. 14, 16, 18, 20, 22, 24.

"City Limits, Village Values: Concepts of Neighborhood in Black Fiction." In *Literature and the Urban Experience: Essays on the City and Literature*. Edited by Michael C. Jaye and Ann Chalmers Watts. New Brunswick, N.J.: Rutgers University Press, 1981. Pp. 35–43.

"Memory, Creation, and Writing." *Thought* 59:385–390 (December 1984).

"Rootedness: The Ancestor as Foundation." In *Black Women Writers (1950–1980): A Critical Evaluation.*

Edited by Mari Evans. Garden City, N.Y.: Anchor/ Doubleday, 1984. Pp. 339–345.

"A Knowing So Deep." Essence, May 1985, p. 230.

"The Site of Memory." In *Inventing the Truth: The Art and Craft of Memoir*. Edited by William Zinnser. Boston: Houghton Mifflin, 1987. Pp. 103–124.

"Unspeakable Things Unspoken." *Michigan Quarterly Review* 28:1–34 (Winter 1989).

INTERVIEWS

"An Interview with Toni Morrison." With Pepsi Charles. *Nimrod* 1:43–51 (1977).

" 'Intimate Things in Place': A Conversation with Toni Morrison." With Robert Stepto. *Massachusetts Review* 18:473–489 (Autumn 1977).

"The Seams Can't Show: An Interview with Toni Morrison." With Jane Bakerman. *Black American Literature Forum* 12:56–60 (Summer 1978).

" 'The Language Must Not Sweat': A Conversation with Toni Morrison." With Thomas LeClair. *New Republic*, 21 March 1981, 25–29.

"An Interview with Toni Morrison." With Nellie McKay. *Contemporary Literature* 22:413–429 (Winter 1983).

"Toni Morrison." With Claudia Tate. In *Black Women Writers at Work*. Edited by Claudia Tate. New York: Continuum, 1983. Pp. 117–131.

"A Conversation." With Gloria Naylor. *Southern Review* n.s. 21:567–593 (Summer 1985).

"Toni Morrison." With Charles Ruas. In *Conversations with American Writers*. New York: Knopf, 1985. Pp. 215–243.

"In the Realm of Possibility: A Conversation with Toni Morrison." With Marsha Darling. *Women's Review of Books* 5:5–6 (March 1988).

"An Interview with Toni Morrison, Hessian Radio Network, Frankfurt, West Germany." With Rosemarie K. Lester. In *Critical Essays on Toni Morrison*. Edited by Nellie Y. McKay. Boston: G. K. Hall, 1988. Pp. 47–54.

"Interview with Toni Morrison." With Christina Davis. *Présence africaine* 145:141–150 (1988).

"A Bench by the Road." *The World: The Journal of the Unitarian Universalist Association* 3:4–5, 37–40 (January–February 1989).

SECONDARY SOURCES

BIOGRAPHICAL AND CRITICAL STUDIES

Atlas, Marilyn Judith. "A Woman Both Shiny and Brown: Feminine Strength in Toni Morrison's *Song of Solomon*." *Society for the Study of Midwestern Literature Newsletter* 9, no. 3:8–12 (1979).

———. "The Darker Side of Toni Morrison's *Song of Solomon*." *Society for the Study of Midwestern Literature Newsletter* 10, no. 2:1–13 (1980).

Awkward, Michael. *Inspiriting Influences: Tradition, Revision, and Afro-American Women's Novels*. New York: Columbia University Press, 1989.

Bakerman, Jane S. "Failures of Love: Female Initiation in the Novels of Toni Morrison." *American Literature* 52, no. 4:541–563 (January 1981).

Bandler, Michael J. "Novelist Toni Morrison: We Bear Witness." *African Woman*, September–October 1979, pp. 28–29.

Bischoff, Joan. "The Novels of Toni Morrison: Studies in Thwarted Sensitivity." *Studies in Black Literature* 6, no. 3:21–23 (1975).

Blake, Susan L. "Folklore and Community in *Song of Solomon*." *MELUS* 7:77–82 (Fall 1980).

Bruck, Peter. "Returning to One's Roots: The Motif of Searching and Flying in Toni Morrison's *Song of Solomon*." In *The Afro-American Novel Since 1960*. Edited by Peter Bruck and Wolfgang Karrer. Amsterdam: Grüner, 1982. Pp. 289–305.

Butler-Evans, Elliott. *Race, Gender, and Desire: Narrative Strategies in the Fiction of Toni Cade Bambara, Toni Morrison, and Alice Walker*. Philadelphia: Temple University Press, 1989.

Christian, Barbara. "Community and Nature: The Novels of Toni Morrison." *Journal of Ethnic Studies* 7, no. 4:65–78 (Winter 1980).

———. "The Concept of Class in the Novels of Toni Morrison." In her *Black Feminist Criticism: Perspectives on Black Women Writers*. New York: Pergamon Press, 1985. Pp. 71–80.

Clark, Norris. "Flying Black: Toni Morrison's *The Bluest Eye, Sula*, and *Song of Solomon*." *Minority Voices* 4:51–63 (Fall 1980).

Coleman, James. "The Quest for Wholeness in Toni Morrison's *Tar Baby*." *Black American Literature Forum* 20:63–73 (Spring–Summer 1986).

Davis, Christina. "*Beloved:* A Question of Identity." *Présence africaine* 145:151–156 (1988).

Davis, Cynthia A. "Self, Society, and Myth in Toni Morrison's Fiction." *Contemporary Literature* 23:323–342 (Summer 1982).

De Arman, Charles. "Milkman as the Archetypal Hero: Thursday's Child Has Far to Go." *Obsidian* 6:56–59 (Winter 1980).

Denard, Carolyn. "The Convergence of Feminism

and Ethnicity in Toni Morrison's Fiction." In *Critical Essays on Toni Morrison.* Edited by Nellie Y. McKay. Boston: G. K. Hall, 1988. Pp. 171–179.

de Weever, Jacqueline. "The Inverted World of Toni Morrison's *The Bluest Eye* and *Sula.*" *CIA Journal* 22:402–414 (1979).

Dowling, Colette. "The Song of Toni Morrison." *New York Times Magazine,* 20 May 1979, pp. 40–42, 48, 52–55.

Edelberg, Cynthia Dubin. "Morrison's Voices: Formal Education, the Work Ethic, and the Bible." *American Literature* 58:217–237 (May 1986).

Giddings, Paula. "The Triumphant Song of Toni Morrison." *Encore,* 12 December 1977, pp. 26–30.

Harris, A. Leslie. "Myth as Structure in Toni Morrison's *Song of Solomon.*" *MELUS* 7:69–76 (Fall 1980).

Harris, Trudier. "Reconnecting Fragments: Afro-American Folk Tradition in *The Bluest Eye.*" In *Critical Essays on Toni Morrison.* Edited by Nellie Y. McKay. Boston: G. K. Hall, 1988. Pp. 68–76.

Hawthorne, Evelyn. "On Gaining the Double-Vision: *Tar Baby* as Diasporean Novel." *Black American Literature Forum* 22:97–107 (Spring 1988).

Holloway, Karla, and Stephanie Demetrakopoulos. *New Dimensions of Spirituality: A Biracial and Bicultural Reading of the Novels of Toni Morrison.* Westport, Conn.: Greenwood Press, 1987.

House, Elizabeth B. "Artist and the Art of Living: Order and Disorder in Toni Morrison's Fiction." *Modern Fiction Studies* 34:27–44 (Spring 1988).

Hovet, Grace Ann, and Barbara Lounsberry. "Flying as Symbol and Legend in Toni Morrison's *The Bluest Eye, Sula,* and *Song of Solomon.*" *CIA Journal* 27:119–140 (December 1983).

Jones, Bessie, and Audrey L. Vinson. *The World of Toni Morrison: Explorations in Literary Criticism.* New York: Kendall & Hunt, 1985.

Joyce, Joyce Ann. "Structural and Thematic Unity in Toni Morrison's *Song of Solomon.*" *CEA Critic* 49:185–198 (Winter 1986–Summer 1987).

Klotman, Phyllis R. "Dick-and-Jane and the Shirley Temple Sensibility in *The Bluest Eye.*" *Black American Literature Forum* 13:123–125 (Winter 1979).

Lange, Bonnie Shipman. "Toni Morrison's Rainbow Code." *Critique: Studies in Modern Fiction* 24:173–181 (Spring 1983).

Lee, Dorothy H. "The Quest for Self: Triumph and Failure in the Works of Toni Morrison." In *Black Women Writers (1950–1980): A Critical Evaluation.* Edited by Mari Evans. Garden City, N.Y.: Anchor/Doubleday, 1984. Pp. 346–360.

Lepow, Lauren. "Paradise Lost and Found: Dualism and Edenic Myth in Toni Morrison's *Tar Baby.*" *Contemporary Literature* 28:363–377 (1987).

Mason, Theodore O. "The Novelist as Conservator: Stories and Comprehension in Toni Morrison's *Song of Solomon.*" *Contemporary Literature* 29:564–581 (Winter 1988).

McDowell, Deborah E. " 'The Self and the Other': Reading Toni Morrison's *Sula* and the Black Female Text." In *Critical Essays on Toni Morrison.* Edited by Nellie Y. McKay. Boston: G. K. Hall, 1988. Pp. 77–90.

McDowell, Margaret B. "The Black Woman as Artist and Critic: Four Versions." *Kentucky Review* 7:19–41 (Spring 1987).

McKay, Nellie Y., ed. *Critical Essays on Toni Morrison.* Boston: G. K. Hall, 1988.

Miller, Adam. "Breedlove, Peace, and the Dead: Some Observations on the Works of Toni Morrison." *Black Scholar,* March 1978, pp. 47–50.

Mitchell, Leatha S. "Toni Morrison, My Mother, and Me." *In the Memory and Spirit of Frances, Zora, and Lorraine: Essays and Interviews on Black Women and Writing.* Edited by Juliette Bowles. Washington, D.C.: Institute for the Arts and the Humanities, 1979. Pp. 58–60.

Mobley, Marilyn E. "Narrative Dilemma: Jadine as Cultural Orphan in Toni Morrison's *Tar Baby.*" *Southern Review* n.s. 23:761–770 (1987).

Otten, Terry. *The Crime of Innocence in the Fiction of Toni Morrison.* Columbia: University of Missouri Press, 1989.

Parker, Bettye J. "Complexity: Toni Morrison's Women: An Interview Essay." In *Sturdy Black Bridges: Visions of Black Women in Literature.* Edited by Roseann Pope Bell, Bettye J. Parker, and Beverly Guy Sheftall. Garden City, N.Y.: Anchor/Doubleday, 1979. Pp. 251–257.

Randolph, Laura B. "The Magic of Toni Morrison." *Ebony,* July 1988, pp. 100–106.

Reed, Harry. "Toni Morrison, *Song of Solomon,* and Black Cultural Nationalism." *Centennial Review* 32:50–64 (Winter 1988).

Samuels, Wilfrid. "Liminality and the Search for Self in Toni Morrison's *Song of Solmon.*" *Minority Voices* 5:59–68 (Spring–Fall 1981).

———. *Toni Morrison.* Boston: Twayne, 1990.

Sargent, Robert. "A Way of Ordering Experience: A Study of Toni Morrison's *The Bluest Eye* and *Sula.*" In *Faith of a (Woman) Writer.* Edited by Alice Kessler-

Harris and William McBrien. Westport, Conn.: Greenwood Press, 1988. Pp. 229–236.

Strouse, Jean. "Toni Morrison's Black Magic. *Newsweek*, 30 March 1981, pp. 52–57.

Turner, Darwin. "Theme, Characterization, and Style in the Works of Toni Morrison." *Black Women Writers (1950–1980): A Critical Evaluation*. Edited by Mari Evans. Garden City, N.Y.: Anchor/Doubleday, 1984. Pp. 361–369.

Wagner, Linda W. "Toni Morrison: Master of Narrative." In *Contemporary American Women Writers: Narrative Strategies*. Edited by Cathering Rainwater and William J. Scheick. Lexington: University Press of Kentucky, 1985. Pp. 191–207.

Warner, Anne Bradford. "New Myths and Ancient Properties: The Fiction of Toni Morrison." *Hollins Critic* 25:1–11 (June 1988).

Wilkerson, Margaret B. "The Dramatic Voice in Toni Morrison's Novels." In *Critical Essays on Toni Morrison*. Edited by Nellie Y. McKay. Boston: G. K. Hall, 1988. Pp. 179–190.

Willis, Susan. "Eruptions of Funk: Historicizing Toni Morrison." *Black American Literature Forum* 16:34–42 (Spring 1982).

———. *Specifying: Black Women Writing the American Experience*. Madison: University of Wisconsin Press, 1987.

BIBLIOGRAPHIES

Fikes, Robert, Jr. "Echoes from Small-Town Ohio: A Toni Morrison Bibliography." *Obsidian* 5:142–148 (Spring–Summer 1979).

Martin, Curtis. "A Bibliography of Writings by Toni Morrison." In *Contemporary American Women Writers: Narrative Strategies*. Edited by Catherine Rainwater and William J. Scheick. Lexington: University Press of Kentucky, 1985. Pp. 205 207.

Middleton, David L. *Toni Morrison: An Annotated Bibliography*. New York: Garland, 1987.

CAROLYN C. DENARD

ANAÏS NIN
1903–1977

ANAÏS NIN'S LIFE and career followed a cycle of alternately striving for and resisting a sense of self-possession. The theme of integration of self marks nearly everything she wrote—her *Diary* (*The Diary of Anaïs Nin* [1966–1978]) as well as her short stories and novels. In the forty-three years covered by the seven volumes of the published *Diary*, she repeatedly describes this effort; volumes 1 to 4 treat the theme obsessively, often with a sense of desperation. In a February 1932 entry she reveals, "I have always been tormented by the image of multiplicity of selves." A few months later she writes, "I am like a shattered mirror. Each piece has gone off and developed a life of its own."

In the two volumes of the *Diary* covering the 1930s, Nin often characterizes her sense of living in fragments as leading to a crisis in loyalty: "How difficult it is to be 'sincere' when each moment I must choose between five or six souls." Her sense of fragmentation at this time cannot be attributed wholly to her being torn between various loyalties—her husband, Hugh P. Guiler (who used the name Ian Hugo for his engravings and films), her passion for Henry Miller, and her artistic vision and production. Although she subjected herself to several terms of psychoanalysis, she would repeatedly subvert her analysits' efforts to move her toward a sense of integration. She used lies and, more than once, seduction of the analyst at the moment the cure threatened completion. Once the cure seemed about to overtake her, Nin eluded it—out of fear of the very solidified self she had sought. Psychoanalytic teleology would result, in Nin's view, in compromising her imagination.

No matter how well he succeeded in liberating her from some of her fears and guilt, her first analyst, René Allendy, ultimately identified successful treatment with a return to "normal" life, for Nin a form of suffocation. In a March 1933 *Diary* entry, she writes of Allendy, "He used his power to separate me from my artist life, to thrust me again into the stifling, narrow bourgeois life." Although she pursued her quest for a unified self almost obsessively, her stubborn determination to undermine its achievement was just as unrelenting. In fact, it was more compelling, welling up from a deeper and more buried need and directed by impulses for which neither her psychoanalysts, nor she herself, nor her protagonists who dramatized these impulses, had a sure vocabulary.

No doubt one of the sources for her sense of fragmentation is rooted in the various, and sometimes warring, ethnic and national threads woven into her genes and life history. When her husband asked her what she was—"not American, that is certain, not French, not Spanish"—she replied, "That fits my philosophy to perfection—the fact that neither in reality nor in feeling do I belong to any nation." Anaïs Nin is popularly thought of as a French expatriate. But although she was born in the Parisian suburb Neuilly-sur-Seine on 21 February 1903, both her parents were born in Cuba, and Nin held a Cuban passport until the 1950s. Her mother's ancestry was Danish and French, and her father's was Catalan. At the age of eleven Nin was uprooted from a comfortable life in Barcelona with her father, Joaquin Nin, a composer, musician and inveterate philanderer. Her mother, Rosa Culmell, brought Nin and her two brothers, Thorvald and Joaquin, to New York, where the fatherless family was welcomed by the New

York Cuban community. In this community, her mother was regarded as a respected musician; she taught voice.

The fact that Nin was enveloped in a close-knit foreign community and that her mother encouraged her bent for playing "the little philosopher" gave bite to Nin's contempt for American schoolgirl society. To her father's fear that she would turn "American," she responded in a letter to him, "The proof that I am far from turning into an American is that if I had to choose between the football game and a concert—a good concert, naturally—I would choose the concert, so you have nothing to fear." In fact, she dropped out of high school in 1919 and continued her education with tutors and a self-designed reading program. In February 1921, she spent a semester at Columbia, but she left the next fall, she writes, for lack of funds.

The problem Nin laid at the feet of her psychoanalysts was this: how could a woman who felt herself in tatters become a writer? For in the psychoanalytic circles in which Nin traveled as an adult, the solid construction of selfhood was thought to be a prelude to all achievement, particularly artistic. But some instinct advised her that her particular achievements were to be mined in the interstices, in the seams of the socially constructed entity traditionally identified as "the self." After reading Otto Rank's book *Art and Artist*, which argues that the neurotic cannot accept himself, while the truly creative personality not only accepts but glorifies his personality, Nin asks in her *Diary*, "How can I accept a limited definable self when I feel, in me, all possibilities?" She describes herself as feeling more drawn to the "space" than the "core" of self, as willing to accept "mystery," for her a more authentic site from which to launch her particular imagination.

Nin's problematic relation toward traditional definitions of self may also be linked to her problematic relation to all the compelling male authorities in her life, of whom her father was the first. She began writing her diary in 1914 at the age of eleven on the boat to New York "as a diary of a journey, to record everything for my father. It was written for him, and I had intended to send it to him. It was really a letter, so he could follow us into a strange land, know about us." But the diary also had another purpose, according to Nin: "It was also to be an island, in which I could take refuge in an alien land, write French, think my thoughts, hold on to my soul, to myself." Nin wished to inscribe herself and offer this inscription to her father, as a substitute for herself. In order to punish her philandering husband, her mother forbade Nin to send the diary, but Nin kept writing it for her father, who is an obsessive presence in the *Diary*. She never anticipated that not only her father, as she presents him, but the various father substitutes in her life, in the guise of lovers and psychoanalysts, would reject her presentation of herself, her self-inscription. They preferred the Anaïs that *they* inscribed, written by their desire. One young Columbia student-artist bumped into her on a staircase and, in an emblematic gesture, immediately offered to paint her. In this move, he is like many of the men Nin knew and wrote about; he wished to re-create her and possess the woman he imagined, in this case, through the medium of paint.

Nin's father, as perceived through her *Diary* (exclusive of *The Early Diary*, which was published posthumously), is more often a trope for a whirlpool of ideas than a real man. In fact, when the first *Diary* volume came out in 1966, Nin's father had been dead for almost thirty years. In preparing the *Diary* for publication, Nin transformed him, at least in part, into a figure of myth and abstraction. Of the eleven volumes of her published diaries, six were published during her lifetime; the rest appeared posthumously, though she edited volume 7 of her *Diary* before she died of cancer in Los Angeles on 14 January 1977. The final editing of the four volumes of her *Early Diary* was accomplished by her family and friends. Reports concerning the number of original journals vary.

Rupert Pole, her lover during the last years of her life and her literary executor, reports they numbered sixty-nine, but he may be including the typed, partially edited versions of the diaries. In a *Diary* entry in the 1950s, Nin reports eighty volumes. The published volumes 1 to 7 are products of extreme distillation: indeed, nine to ten handwritten diary volumes are mined for a single volume of the *Diary*. Thus the term "editing" is inadequate to describe the relationship of the published books to the original volumes. In the transformation from diaries to *Diary*, Nin made literature. Thus the *Diary*'s father-obsessed narrator is partially a creation of Nin's, just as the father is, to a significant degree, a character.

Even as she wrote the original diaries, Nin fantasized about their publication, so that to some extent there was a self-conscious attempt to produce literary writing from the start. A sense of the diaries as products of artistic manipulation is particularly evident in the *Diary* volumes of the 1930s and 1940s. In reading these volumes, one is acutely aware of confronting literature, literature in the spirit of H. D.'s autobiographical novels.[1] For example, the opening passage of volume 1 of the *Diary* is marked by a deliberate, stately movement from image to image:

> Louveciennes resembles the village where Madame Bovary lived and died. It is old, untouched and unchanged by modern life. It is built on a hill overlooking the Seine. On clear nights one can see Paris. It has an old church dominating a group of small houses, cobblestone streets, and several large properties, manor houses, a castle on the outskirts of the village. One of the properties belonged to Madame du Barry. During the revolution her lover was guillotined and his head thrown over the ivy-covered wall into her garden. This is now the property of Coty.
>
> (p. 3)

By beginning her diary with a comparison between her village and Madame Bovary's, Nin summons the quintessential example of a woman who sacrificed everything for her dreams, suggesting from the first sentence the theme of her own story. Before she begins a description of her house, she also summons Balzac and finally, Proust: "One hears the whistle of the small train from and to Paris. It is a train which looks ancient, as if it were still carrying the personages of Proust's novels to dine in the country." She associates herself with a literary tradition and a literary landscape, and by invoking Proust, with a literary method, thus announcing to her reader the company she intends to keep and the range of her ambition.

Although Nin's impetus for starting the *Diary* was her father, he is only an occasional presence in the four volumes of the *Early Diary*. Even her reunion with her father in 1924 in France after about a decade's separation, as she reports on it in volume 2 of the *Early Diary*, is not treated expansively. A partial explanation for the reduced treatment of the father may be found in the fact that the *Early Diary* was edited by others after Nin's death. Nevertheless, he is certainly not the powerful, phallic patriarch, the object of obsession, he is presented as in the first four volumes of her *Diary*.

The snapshots we see of the real Joaquin Nin, probably most reliably in the *Early Diary* but also to some extent in the others, offer images of an overcritical and inaccessible man. Nin's father approved of very little about her. He did not want a girl, and when she had typhoid fever, he called her ugly. He criticized the style of her long, adolescent letters to him, a criticism she takes very well: "I wish I knew from whom I inherited this chatty pen, since you say that my epistolary style puts you on edge!" After a second reunion, in 1933, he expressed his disapproval of her bohemian ways—her clothes, her friends, her ideas. The young Nin in the first two volumes of the *Early Diary* avoids complaining about her father and tends to idealize him, but occasionally she lifts the self-delusionary veil: "He used to experiment with a cage of white mice (he was studying medicine, etc.), and I remember the mice so very well."

When she learns her father is about to marry a much younger woman, she is bitter. In an *Early Diary* entry for December 1924, she writes, "He met me with tears, to which I could not sincerely respond; he talked to me with a show of emotions I could not feel. . . ." However, the young Nin is also beginning to develop her father as a character. She continues, "Yes, he was Paris—intelligent, insidious, cultured Paris."

In volume 1 of the *Diary,* which chronicles the years 1931–1934, Nin describes the 1933 reunion with her father not only as if it had taken place after twenty-two years, but also as a moment toward which her whole life was propelled. She has transformed autobiographical material into myth. On the eve of the 1933 reunion, she explains:

> My life has been one long strain to create, to make myself interesting, to develop my gifts, to make my father proud of me, a desperate and anxious ascension to efface and destroy a haunting insecurity created by the conviction that my father left because he was disappointed in me, because he did not love me. . . . Always aiming higher, accumulating loves to compensate for the first loss.
>
> (*Diary,* 1:204)

Influenced by the psychoanalysis begun with Allendy in 1932, she parlayed her father into a character who would come to dominate the best of the *Diary* and her early fiction.

In the description of their meeting, the figure of the father is fully resonant as a symbol. She sees him as her double (a theme she also explores in *House of Incest* and *Winter of Artifice*):

> Would my double be my evil double? He incarnated all the dangers of my illusory life, my inventing of situations, my deceptions, my faults. In some way they seemed a caricature of me, because mine seemed motivated by deep feelings, and his by more superficial and worldly aims.
>
> (*Diary,* 1:206–207)

The narrator of the *Diary* struggles with her father-obsessed imagination. She insists that the father, a figure who, in the economy of her psyche, is also God as well as the eroticized father of Freudian romance, must be translated into human terms, must also be seen as a man:

> The old legends knew, perhaps, that in absence the father becomes glorified, deified, eroticized, and this outrage against God the Father has to be atoned for. The human father has to be confronted and recognized as human, as a man who created a child and then, by his absence, left the child fatherless and then Godless.
>
> (1:203)

In *Henry and June,* posthumously published excerpts culled from the unexpurgated diary for 1931–1932, having to do with Nin's affair with Henry Miller and her obsession with his wife June, incest is the name Nin gives to her alliance with male values and male power, particularly in regard to the traditionally male domains of creativity and mysticism:

> I have remained the woman who loves incest. I still practice the most incestuous crimes with a sacred religious fervor. I am the most corrupt of all women. . . . With a madonna face, I still swallow God and sperm, and my orgasm resembles a mystical climax.
>
> (p. 246)

She articulates this alliance with male domains as choosing her father's values and negating her mother's—"a volcanic life hunger . . . , a sensual potency that automatically negates my mother's values."

Nin's critics have tiptoed around the theme of incest in her works. They feel compelled to engage in perfunctory and inconclusive speculations about whether Nin actually went to bed with her father and then quickly drop the embarrassing subject. In fact, the theme of incest has a full and complex development. Nin was undoubtedly influenced by her analysis with Allendy and (later) Otto Rank during the 1930s, when she developed this theme, which speaks not only to woman's relationship to man but also to the woman artist's relationship to traditional forms of expression and to the patriarchy in general.

Nin's presentation of the incest theme in her *Diary* (May 1932) is forthright but also resonant: "I talked [to Allendy] about my father's passion for photography and how he was always photographing me. He liked to take photos of me while I bathed. He always wanted me naked." Yet the lasciviousnes of the scene is not the point. Rather, it is the fact that her father's attention is mediated by the camera and his glasses:

> All his admiration came by way of the camera. His eyes were partly concealed by heavy glasses (he was myopic) and then by the camera lens. Lovely. Lovely. How many times, in how many places, until he left us, did I sit for him for countless pictures. And it was the only time we spent together.
>
> (*Diary*, 1:87)

With the camera, Nin suggests, her father's naked eye does not confront the actual daughter. Rather, through the two lenses he transforms the daughter he called "ugly" into an object shaped to his desire. This perception has many transplantings into her fiction. Of the movie actress in "Stella," a story collected in *Winter of Artifice*, Nin writes, "They courted the face on the screen, the face of translucence, the face of wax on which men found it possible to imprint the image of their fantasy."

In the *House of Incest*, Nin's first published work of fiction, which has been praised for the originality of its surrealistic imagery, incest is a trope for a constellation of ideas having to do with structures enforcing patriarchal values. Incest is a form of self-love, a narcissistic desire for one's double: "If only we could all escape from this house of incest, where we only love ourselves in the other. . . ." The incestuous relationship also blocks creativity, allows no seams through which the new may emerge; the incestuous desire is suffocating and destructive:

> In the house of incest there was a room which could not be found, a room without window, the fortress of their love, a room without windows where the mind and blood coalesced in a union without orgasm and rootless. . . . Their love like the ink of squids, a banquet of poisons.
>
> (p. 52)

The imagery of incest suggests limitation, artistic and other, imposed by the father who allows only repetitions of himself and the world he has constructed in his own image: "I borrowed your visibility and it was through you I made my imprint on the world. I praised my own flame in you." Thus the father also represents cultural constraint. Incest is a strategy to keep the daughter imprisoned in the father's world. It serves the daughter as well in that incest allies her with the father's power, yet it prevents her from choosing other objects of desire—those outside of the father, who represents the dominant culture, represents law and patriarchy. As the term is developed by Nin, one implication of "incest" for the artist is conformity to conventional modes; escaping the father would allow innovation, the formulating of new modes.

In a richly evocative passage, Nin presents images of the double (also an incest image) in which the secret self and the overt self are in lacerating tension. The secret self is described as a repressed self, as "Other," while the speaking "I" describes herself as manipulated by outside forces, a "marionette":

> I am ill with the obstinacy of images, reflections in cracked mirrors. I am a woman with Siamese cat eyes smiling always behind my gravest words, mocking my own intensity. I smile because I listen to the OTHER and I believe the OTHER. I am a marionette pulled by unskilled fingers, pulled apart, inharmoniously dislocated; one arm dead, the other rhapsodizing in mid-air.
>
> (pp. 29–30)

Her emotions are engaged not by the external self but by a hidden self, not by the manifestations of convention but by her sensing of and attraction to the repressed, not by the "talk" obligated by living in society but by its "undercurrents": "I laugh, not when it fits into my talk, but when it fits into the undercurrents of my talk. I want to know what is running underneath thus punctuated by bitter upheavals. The two currents do not meet." The two are helplessly bound together, but each struggles to free herself from the other: "I see two women in me freakishly bound together, like circus twins. I see them tearing away from each other." One half of the double suggests a woman constructed by society, obedient to her father; the other half suggests a woman suppressed in this construction and by such obedience.

Incest suggests the uneasy relationship between the woman and the father as society, as convention, as a patriarchy who is protective of her, but only of those qualities in her that reflect himself. Nin links the suppressed to madness: "There is a fissure in my vision and madness will always rush through." But madness, being outside a normality calibrated by the father, means freedom: "Lean over me, at the bedside of my madness, and let me stand without crutches."

The images of freedom associated with escape from the house of incest increase as the narrative moves to a close and culminate in the image of a dancer who "was listening to a music we could not hear, moved by hallucinations we could not see." Yet the narrative issues are not resolved in this image of freedom. Rather, the last two paragraphs conclude with the impasse that marks most of Nin's writing: the "I" who says "all movement choked me with anguish" stands watching her double, who is "dancing towards daylight." This impasse is variously articulated throughout Nin's work. In "Stella," written at the same time as *House of Incest*, Nin describes a movie character who is able to move according to a script but who is, herself, immobilized: "The woman on the screen went continually forward, carried by her story, led by the plot loaned to her. But Stella, Stella herself was blocked over and over again by inner obstacles." In *Diary* 3 (1939–1944) Nin writes: "All my life, it seems, first with my father, . . . I admired form and discipline and rejected them as interfering with life and nature." She both identified with and could not accommodate herself to the various authorities—particularly artistic and psychoanalytic—with whom she sought her liberation.

The impasse that affects Nin's protagonists and her sense of herself as a writer was nurtured by the series of father figures with whom she associated. Although brilliant men, they based their judgments on available paradigms. Since Nin's writerly instincts drew her toward modes that were outside these paradigms, her relations to these men and the various establishments they represented, particularly the psychoanalytic and the literary avant-garde, were problematic. Ultimately, her struggle was to assert her difference as a woman artist and at the same time win approval from a patriarchy either hostile to or dismissive of that difference. In this Nin resembled the innovative women writers of her generation, including Jane Bowles, H. D., and Jean Rhys, who were also torn between the requirements of feminine expression and the requirements of a literary establishment. For Bowles, this conflict resulted in an almost lifelong writer's block; for Jean Rhys it resulted in a quarter-century's obscurity and discouragement so profound that she stopped publishing for twenty-seven years (1939–1966), while H. D. dealt with this dilemma by excavating female myths and incorporating them into autobiographical works. Although Nin accepted Guiler's financial support, she sought approval for her art, as well as emotional support, from men who were insensitive to the vision she put forward. Several of them, including Edmund Wilson (who wanted to marry Nin), offered to teach her how to write. Wilson, whom she identifies with "the full tyranny of the father, the wall of misunderstanding and lack of intuition of the father," sent her a set of Jane Austen, "hoping," as she writes, "I would learn how to write a novel from reading her!"

Disillusionment with fathers and father figures provides a motif in several of Nin's narratives (and is an element in most of her writing).

Collages (1964) is a set of untitled short narratives or episodes connected by a similarity in tone and mood. The protagonist of one of these is an artist, Renate, who wishes to start a magazine in order to publish the innovative work of her friends. When she advertises for capital, John Wilkes, who describes himself as a twenty-seven year old millionaire, responds. After she investigates him, they begin negotiations, which the story details. Based on his firm promise of cash (backed up by a contract), Renate piles up bills, "but no check came." Then she discovers that he is not a millionaire, after all, but only a millionaire's gardener. Nin concludes with humility: "There was no law to jail a man who swindled one of illusions. . . . The gardener watered other people's dreams. It was not his fault that they grew so big and had to be pruned."

This story, in which a paternal figure turns out to be just an ordinary man who deals in illusions, echoes a pattern in Nin's life. René Allendy, Otto Rank, Henry Miller, and Edmund Wilson, men on whom she depended for a sense of self-worth, ultimately used her to forward their own goals. Nin twice established presses, Editions Siana ("Anaïs" spelled backward) in the 1930s and the Gemor Press in the 1940s, in order to publish her own works rejected by commercial houses, and those of her friends. Both times she personally contributed a great deal of cash and physical labor and ironically sacrificed her own writing in order to nurture the presses and the people depending on them. Éditions Siana was planned jointly with Miller and his friend, the writer Michael Fraenkel, but Fraenkel drew up a list of works the press was to publish and excluded Nin's writings. In the case of the Gemor Press, Gonzalo, a Peruvian coffeehouse revolutionary and bohemian who was to run the press, abandoned it despite the fact that one of Nin's motives in setting up the press was to provide him with a job. Relationships with these men generally deteriorated into that of mother and son. In volume 3 of the *Diary*, she describes the burdens associated with what she calls her "mothering complex":

> The five flights of stairs I have to climb every day when I get home seem to represent my difficulties. Somehow, on these stairs I climb after leaving the press, the fatigue and discouragement of the whole day attacks me. It catches me on the very first step of the worn brown rug. As I climb I think that Gonzalo needs new glasses, where will I get the money? Jacobson's bill for the care of Helba [Gonzalo's wife] is overdue. Henry has to see the ear doctor. He also needs eighteen dollars for new glasses.
>
> (3:205)

Otto Rank, who was Freud's assistant for twenty years before he broke with Freud, believed that women could not be artists. Nin quotes him in her *Diary:* "When the neurotic woman gets cured, she becomes a woman. When the neurotic man gets cured, he becomes an artist. . . . For the moment, you need to become a woman." He insisted that she stop writing her diaries, which he viewed as a Scheherazade phenomenon and as "the last defense against analysis," preventing a cure. His metaphor—Scheherazade—equates successful analysis with death and reveals his desire to see the death of the Nin of the *Diary,* the aspect she withheld from him. The *Diary* became a major issue in the several years of analysis she underwent with him during the 1930s. *House of Incest* and *Winter of Artifice* were written at least partially to satisfy Otto Rank's and also Henry Miller's sense that the diary is not a literary form. To be a writer she would have to write "fiction." But she was not content with just fictionalizing, for as she wrote in her diary, she inscribed herself, something that the very form of fiction prevents:

> *It is the woman who has to speak.* And it is not only the woman Anaïs who has to speak, but I who have to speak for many women. As I discover myself, I feel I am merely one of many, a symbol. . . . The mute ones of the past, the inarticulate, who took refuge behind wordless intuitions; and the women of today, all action, and copies of men. And I, in between. Here [in the diary] lies the personal overflow, the personal

> and feminine overfulness. Feelings that are not for books, not for fiction, not for art.
>
> (*Diary*, 1:289)

Otto Rank fell in love with Nin and convinced her to come with him to New York, which she did in 1934; there she became his assistant and eventually developed her own successful practice as a lay analyst. In fact, Henry Miller joined her in New York and, for a short time, also practiced lay analysis. However, the pressures of her practice and Rank's demand that she translate his numerous works made her flee back to France a year later. She missed her writing. She sums up her relationship to Rank in this way: "I went to Rank to solve my conflict with my father, and only added another father to my life, and another loss."

Even the men of the literary avant-garde wanted her to solve "the problem" of her diary. Lawrence Durrell advised, "You must make the leap outside of the womb, destroy your connections." He urged her to rewrite *Hamlet*, an absurd recommendation to a writer trying to excavate woman's consciousness in a patriarchal society and literary tradition since Hamlet is an exemplary representation of the loyalty owed to the father. Durrell and Miller's concept of art was predicated on the artist's bold declaration "I am God." In answer, Nin writes:

> Woman never had direct communication with God anyway, but only through man, the priest. She never created directly except through man, was never able to create as a woman. But what neither Larry nor Henry understands is that woman's creation far from being like man's must be exactly like her creation of children, that is it must come out of her own blood, englobed by her womb, nourished with her own milk. It must be a human creation, of flesh, it must be different from man's abstractions.
>
> (*Diary*, 2:233)

Yet as her story "Birth" intimates, Nin lacks full confidence in the productions of the womb because of the inadequacy of fathers. "Birth," collected in *Under a Glass Bell* (1944), is based on Nin's experience of giving birth to a stillborn child, an event that she relates in an August 1934 *Diary* entry. In an extraordinary passage, she wishes her child dead because there are no "real" fathers. The account of the incident begins and ends with statements against fathers. Early in the entry, she tells her fetus: "You ought to die in warmth and darkness. You ought to die because in the world there are no real fathers, not in heaven or on earth." After the birth, she writes: "I do not believe in man as father. I do not trust man as father. When I wished this child to die, it was because I felt it would experience the same lack."

The story based on this entry raises the experience to the level of myth. It is a myth of the woman artist who gives birth to a creation of her body, her consciousness, but knows this creation can only be stillborn. The story opens, in fact, with the doctor—a father figure—announcing to the protagonist that "the child . . . is dead," with an authority analogous to those who decreed Nin's diaries unworthy. The dead fetus cannot be born, so the doctor, who has told her she is not made for childbearing, thrusts "a long instrument" into her which "paralyzes" her with pain. The painful (and obviously phallic) implement is ineffective, and the doctor would like to use a more radical method—the knife. However, the protagonist reclaims the birth process, and through ritual-like, soft, circular drumming on her belly, she succeeds: ". . . it is a little girl. It has long eyelashes on its closed eyes, it is perfectly made, and all glistening with the waters of the womb." It is an extraordinarily poignant and tragic story, using a woman's most powerful metaphor through which to grieve for the loss when a woman fails, in the arena of patriarchy, to give life to her expressly womanly imagination. In the story, her creation is female, "perfectly made," and "glistening with the waters of the womb," but dead, a condition Nin has related to the limitations of fathers.[2]

Her vocabulary for masculine and feminine writing is occasionally uncanny, presaging the revisionist Freudian language currently used by feminist literary critics. Traditional writing, she asserts, is constructed by the phallus:

> Henry and Larry tried to lure me out of the womb. They call it objectivity. . . . Man today is like a tree that is withering at the roots. And most women painted and wrote nothing but imitations of phalluses. The world was filled with phalluses, like totem poles, and no womb anywhere.
>
> (*Diary*, 2:235)

Her description of womb writing anticipates the language of those current feminists who call on women to "write the female body."[3] Her tenure in psychoanalysis, as both patient and practitioner, gave her the vocabulary to describe the forces denying her the forms and expression that would accommodate her imagination. She used Freudian insights against the systems that validated these insights:

> Man invented a woman to suit his needs. He disposed of her by identifying her with nature and then paraded his contemptuous domination of nature. But woman is not nature only.
>
> She is the mermaid with her fish-tail dipped in the unconscious. Her creation will be to make articulate this obscure world which dominates man, which he denies being dominated by, but which asserts its domination in destructive proofs of its presence, madness.
>
> (2:235–236)

Here, again, Nin pictures madness as the fissure through which the repressed, which Nin codes as feminine, makes its return.[4] She saw her unique task as a writer to rescue the repressed feminine.

Although Rank, Durrell, and Miller eventually allow that Nin is writing in a new style, a "woman's" style, the admission, though presented as a revelation, has the effect of a dismissal. She has convinced them of her uniqueness, but their acceptance of this argument means she is no longer in their domain; she functions outside their realm, and her work, therefore, is considered not equal to their definitions of the "literary."

Like Dorothy Richardson and Virginia Woolf, Nin felt that the traditional fictional forms could not accommodate a woman's consciousness or the deep structures of her experience. In a July 1945 entry in volume 4 of the *Diary,* she states baldly, "The novel is false. I rebel against it while I write it." In imagining a novel that *would* inscribe women, Nin describes it as culled from her diary. She offers a sketch of it in an entry for August 1944:

> Theme of development of woman in her own terms, not as an imitation of man. This will become in the end the predominant theme of the novel: the effort of woman to find her own psychology, and her own significance, in contradiction to man-made psychology and interpretation. Woman finding her own language, and articulating her own feelings, discovering her own perceptions. Woman's role in the reconstruction of the world.
>
> (4:25)

This sketch was to be fleshed out in *Cities of the Interior,* a five-volume work she conceived of as "a continuous novel." *Cities of the Interior,* first published together in 1959, includes *Ladders to Fire* (1946), *Children of the Albatross* (1947), *The Four-Chambered Heart* (1950), *A Spy in the House of Love* (1954), and *Solar Barque* (1958; also published separately in 1961 as *Seduction of the Minotaur*). The narratives have a common cast of characters—most of them drawn from the diaries—with one or two characters usually dominating a particular volume. Each slender volume concerns a woman's quest for self-possession. Episodic, lyrical, fluid, and dreamy, the prose is informed by a psychoanalytic bordering on a surrealistic intelligence. These two elements—the theme of the woman's search for a way to feel she is a subject in the world and the particular texture of her prose, poetically rendered images that resonate out of the unconscious—are Nin's signature qualities, as typified in the opening paragraph of *The Seduction of the Minotaur:*

> Some voyages have their inception in the blueprint of a dream, some in the urgency of contra-

> dicting a dream. Lillian's recurrent dream of a ship that could not reach the water, that sailed laboriously, pushed by her with great effort, through city streets, had determined her course toward the sea, as if she would give this ship, once and for all, its proper sea bed.
>
> (p. 5)

Lillian, the novel's protagonist, accepts a job in Golconda, a Mexican city, in order to escape her bourgeois life, represented by her husband, Larry. A jazz musican with classical training, she hopes to forget her unhappiness in the colors, warmth, and natural rhythms of the land she knew in childhood. Nin describes Golconda as a dream city of pleasure painted gold by the sun, where sensation determines how one spends the hours and where *logos* is lost in the sound of the waves. The ideas in the narrative are conveyed with forceful, symbolic images and cast in blatantly psychoanalytic terms, so that the prose has the feel of a fable in which meaning is communicated almost without ambiguity, winning its effects through sonority and resonance.

The escape from Larry repeats the dominant pattern in Lillian's life, as Dr. Hernandez, the novel's lay analyst, points out. In rebellion against her dour and punitive father and her restrictive, distant mother, Lillian has cultivated chaos, improvisation, and promiscuity, a behavior pattern that continued into her marriage to a gentle, steady man who could not fulfill Lillian's desires for adventure. In Golconda she discovers what she calls "the mystery of the withheld theme": that only a journey into "the labyrinth of self," where she can face the Minotaur of her fears, has curative powers and can help her break this pattern. *Seduction of the Minotaur*, which is the last volume of *Cities of the Interior*, has the most definitive sense of closure of all the volumes. In the end, Lillian recognizes that Larry's approach to life is the compromise he has made with his own inner demons. Having reached this understanding, Lillian feels ready to reunite with Larry. Yet the narrative's final image, though iterating Lillian's renewed love for Larry, conveys a sense of the provisional and tenuous, a sense that whatever understanding she has arrived at has limited validity; it is not jointly held with Larry, but held only in the single consciousness: "In silence, in mystery, a human being was formed, was exploded, was struck by other passing bodies, was burned, was deserted. And then it was born in the molten love of the one who cared." Thus the loved one is a construct created in the emotional imagination of the lover.

It is toward this discovery that Sabina, the protagonist of *A Spy in the House of Love*, a female Don Juan figure, is navigating. Hoping to achieve freedom and through freedom a clear sense of the boundaries of self, she moves from one lover to another in order to achieve sensual fulfillment without emotional attachment, without becoming part of the other, and in this way define her own boundaries. After a series of lovers, however, she recognizes that each of them has responded to a shadow of her, the shadow created by their desire just as she reconstructs each of her lovers according to her desire. She identifies with the figure in Duchamp's *Nude Descending a Staircase:* "Eight or ten outlines of the same woman, like many multiple exposures of a woman's personality, neatly divided into many layers, walking down the stairs in unison." Rather than achieving freedom by following this male (Don Juan) path to self-definition, she feels fragmented, and at the end, when she weeps over her failure, "there was a complete dissolution of the eyes, features, as if she were losing her essence."

In the final volumes of the *Diary*, this intense and frustrated struggle for self-possession is somewhat muted, at times giving way to the middle-aged Nin, a woman of greater confidence and success. These volumes are less contemplative, and though they are still self-examining, they are more attentive to the external and the practical, shading into a simpler record of people and events. They reveal a more settled

Nin, partially a result of her growing fame and perhaps also a result of rounds of therapy with two women analysts, Martha Jaeger and Inge Bogner, whose approach did not require Nin to sacrifice her diaries or her vision of inscribing woman.

Her *Diary* received much praise for its candid and eloquent revelation of female consciousness and sensuality and propelled her to fame. She received France's Prix Sévigné in 1971 and in 1974 she was admitted to the National Institute of Arts and Letters. In the early 1970s the *Diary* was taken up by numerous women's consciousness-raising groups as documenting the life of a free woman, a model for emotional and sexual liberation. Nin's role as pioneer in depicting women's sexuality was further bolstered in 1977 with the posthumous publication of *Delta of Venus,* a collection of erotica written in the 1940s for a patron.

Diane Wakoski's tribute in a 1973 issue of the *American Poetry Review* offered a new favorable context in which Nin's writing could be evaluated. Wakoski judged Nin "more important . . . in the life of 20th century letters than any other figure than Pound . . . , an *avant garde* figure, a provocative influence, a shaper of the forms of both prose and poetry in the past 40 years." She considers Nin's *Diary,* because of its autobiographical content, as having influenced the self-reflexive tendency in so much experimental work and also as validating narrative and poetic forms that arise from content. Rather than following the "life of the great man" paradigm for autobiographical writing valued by traditional critics, rather than manipulating content to fit a Platonic ideal form, Nin in her *Diary* presents a structure that springs directly from the writer's imagination, a structure organically tied to the content. Thus, according to Wakoski, she offers a more authentic expression of the mediation between experience and imagination than do traditionally formulated works.

Wakoski's essay gives Nin a central place among the literary avant-garde. Certainly Nin's literary stature is at least equal to that of the writers who dominate the *Diary,* many of whom were ambivalent or outright negative about her literary accomplishment—among them, Henry Miller, Lawrence Durrell, Antonin Artaud, Edmund Wilson, and Gore Vidal—and with whom she sometimes compared herself, almost always favorably. Wakoski's effort to draw Nin into the tradition of innovation has, however, been insufficiently accepted and amplified. Moreover, despite Nin's lifelong effort to define a female aesthetic and her activism on behalf of other women experimental writers (see, for instance, *The Novel of the Future,* p. 166), feminist literary criticism has not yet embraced her.

With the death in 1985 of her husband, whose wish to be deleted from her published diaries was obeyed while they both lived, unexpurgated volumes began to appear—particularly *Henry and June* (1986), a collection of passages concerning Henry and June Miller, and *A Literate Passion: Letters of Anaïs Nin and Henry Miller, 1932–53* (1987). Part of the volumes' appeal is undoubtedly voyeuristic, but the intimate window they provide, along with the previously published *Diary,* gives a new name to what has traditionally been thought to belong to the male; with added emphasis, they give *desire* a woman's name.

Like other innovative women writers of her generation—Djuna Barnes and Jane Bowles, for instance—Anaïs Nin lived a daring, experimental life. She modeled for artists, performed as a Spanish dancer, practiced psychoanalysis, owned a press, acted in underground films, moved between continents, and took her lovers from among the most brilliant men of her time, although she remained married from the age of twenty. She knew everyone who would become important in the arts—from Maya Deren, grandmother of avant-garde cinema, to Richard Wright, with whom she had a warm relationship. And although she did not completely recover from her obsession with a solidified sense of self, this ambition was subordinate, in the larger scheme, to the urgency of exploring the territory and borders of feminine consciousness and experience. To that end she produced close to forty published volumes of diaries, novels, short stories, literary criticism, and commentary. In her own words:

> I have lived out everything, and . . . contrary to most creative women of our time I have not imitated man, or become man. . . . I represent, for other women too, the one who wanted to create with, by, and through her femininity.

Selected Bibliography

PRIMARY WORKS

PROSE

House of Incest. Paris: Éditions Siana, 1936; Chicago: Swallow, 1958.

Winter of Artifice. Paris: Obelisk, 1939; Chicago: Swallow, 1945.

Under a Glass Bell. New York: Gemor Press, 1942; Denver: Swallow, 1948.

Ladders to Fire. New York: Dutton, 1946; Chicago: Swallow, 1959.

Children of the Albatross. New York: Dutton, 1947; Athens: Ohio University Press, 1959.

The Four-Chambered Heart. New York: Duell, Sloan, and Pearce, 1950; Athens: Ohio University Press, 1959.

A Spy in the House of Love. New York: British Book Centre, 1954; New York: Bantam, 1968.

Solar Barque. Ann Arbor, Mich.: Edwards, 1958.

Cities of the Interior (Ladders to Fire, Children of the Albatross, The Four-Chambered Heart, A Spy in the House of Love, Solar Barque). Denver: Swallow, 1959; Chicago: Swallow, 1974.

Seduction of the Minotaur. Denver: Swallow, 1961; Athens: Ohio University Press, 1985. Enlarged version of *Solar Barque.*

Collages. London: P. Owen, 1964; Athens: Ohio University Press, 1986.

Anaïs Nin Reader. Edited by Philip K. Jason. New York: Avon, 1973.

Delta of Venus: Erotica. New York: Harcourt Brace Jovanovich, 1977.

Waste of Timelessness and Other Early Stories. Weston, Conn.: Magic Circle, 1977.

Little Birds: Erotica. New York: Harcourt Brace Jovanovich, 1979.

The White Blackbird and Other Writings. Santa Barbara: Capra Press, 1985.

NONFICTION

D. H. Lawrence: An Unprofessional Study. Paris: E. W. Titus, 1932; Denver: Swallow, 1964.

Realism and Reality. New York: Alicat, 1946.

On Writing. Hanover, N.H.: Oliver, 1947.

The Novel of the Future. New York: Collier, 1968; Athens, Ohio: Swallow, 1986.

A Woman Speaks: The Lectures, Seminars, and Interviews of Anaïs Nin. Edited by Evelyn J. Hinz. Chicago: Swallow, 1975.

In Favor of the Sensitive Man, and Other Essays. New York: Harcourt Brace Jovanovich, 1976.

DIARIES

The Diary of Anaïs Nin. Vol. 1, 1931–1934. Vol. 2, 1934–1939. Vol. 3, 1939–1944. Vol. 4, 1944–1947. Vol. 5, 1947–1955. Vol. 6, 1955–1966. Vol. 7, 1966–1974. New York: Harcourt Brace Jovanovich, 1966–1980.

A Photographic Supplement to the Diary of Anaïs Nin. New York: Harcourt Brace Jovanovich, 1974.

Linotte: The Early Diary of Anaïs Nin, 1914–1920. Translated by Jean L. Sherman. New York: Harcourt Brace Jovanovich, 1978.

The Early Diary of Anaïs Nin. Vol. 2, 1920–1923. Vol. 3, 1923–1927. Vol. 4, 1927–1931. New York: Harcourt Brace Jovanovich, 1982–1985.

Henry and June: From the Unexpurgated Diary of Anaïs Nin. San Diego: Harcourt Brace Jovanovich, 1986.

CORRESPONDENCE

A Literate Passion: Letters of Anaïs Nin and Henry Miller. San Diego: Harcourt Brace Jovanovich, 1987.

SECONDARY WORKS

BIOGRAPHICAL AND CRITICAL STUDIES

Andersen, Margret. "Critical Approaches to Anaïs Nin." *Canadian Review of American Studies* 10:255–265 (1979).

Demetrakopoulous, Stephanie A. "Archetypal Constellations of Feminine Consciousness in Nin's first *Diary*." *Mosaic* 10:121–137 (Winter 1978).

Evans, Oliver. *Anaïs Nin*. Carbondale: Southern Illinois University Press, 1968.

Franklin, Benjamin V., and Duane Schneider. *Anaïs Nin: An Introduction*. Athens: Ohio University Press, 1979.

Hinz, Evelyn J. *The Mirror and the Garden: Realism and Reality in the Writings of Anaïs Nin*. Columbus: Ohio State University Libraries, 1971. Rev. ed. New York: Harcourt Brace Jovanovich, 1973.

———. "Recent Nin Criticism: Who's on First?" *Canadian Review of American Studies* 13:373:388 (1982).

Knapp, Bettina. *Anaïs Nin*. New York: Frederick Ungar, 1978.

Scholar, Nancy. *Anaïs Nin*. Boston: Twayne, 1984.

Spencer, Sharon. *Anaïs, Art, and Artists: A Collection of Essays*. Greenwood, Fla.: Penkevill, 1986.

———. *Collage of Dreams: The Writings of Anaïs Nin*. New York: Harcourt Brace Jovanovich, 1981.

———. "Delivering the Woman Artist from the Silence of the Womb: Otto Rank's Influence on Anaïs Nin." *Psychoanalytic Review* 69:111–129 (Spring 1982).

———. "The Music of the Womb: Anaïs Nin's 'Feminine Writing.' " In *Breaking the Sequence: Women's Experimental Fiction*. Edited by Ellen G. Friedman and Miriam Fuchs. Princeton, N.J.: Princeton University Press, 1989. Pp. 161–173.

Wakoski, Diane. "A Tribute to Anaïs Nin." *American Poetry Review* 2:46–47 (1973).

Zaller, Robert, ed. *A Casebook on Anaïs Nin*. New York: New American Library, 1974.

SPECIAL JOURNALS

Anaïs: An International Journal. Los Angeles, 1983– .

Seahorse: The Anaïs Nin / Henry Miller Journal. Columbus, Ohio, 1982– .

BIBLIOGRAPHY

For a bibliography of secondary works see Rose Marie Cutting's *Anaïs Nin: A Reference Guide* (Boston: G. K. Hall, 1978).

NOTES

1. In the 1960s, when Nin was in the midst of editing her *Diary*, she changed the nature of the current record to a "journal," a more pedestrian record of people and events.
2. In *Ladders to Fire* the character Lillian, who is pregnant, tells her fetus that it should die, because "you will not find a father who will lull you and cover you with his greatness and his warmth" (78). She has a miscarriage in her sixth month.
3. See Sharon Spencer, "The Music of the Womb: Anaïs Nin's Feminine Writing," in Ellen G. Friedman and Miriam Fuchs, eds., *Breaking the Sequence: Women's Experimental Fiction* (Princeton, N.J.: Princeton University Press, 1989), pp. 161–73.
4. See Hélène Cixous and Catherine Clément, *The Newly Born Woman*, Betsy Wing, trans. (Minneapolis: University of Minnesota Press, 1986).

ELLEN G. FRIEDMAN

JOYCE CAROL OATES

1938–

> Our conviction is that, as readers, . . . we can lay claim to the writer as he truly "is"; and it seems to us a violation of nature that the writer in person so rarely "is" the person we anticipate.

"DOES THE WRITER exist?" asks Joyce Carol Oates in her essay of the same title. She continues: "Does the writer exist in any significant relationship to his or her work? By approaching the person . . . can one approach the work?" Although Oates asked these questions in a 1984 article about other writers, she may also be directing them at her own reviewers and critics who have had trouble reconciling her slender physical appearance with the violent episodes in her work. Early in her career, Walter Clemons wrote in *Newsweek:* "She is a tall, pale young woman with enormous eyes and a timid, little-girl voice. . . . If you met her at a literary party and failed to catch her name, it might be hard to imagine her reading, much less writing, the unflinching fiction [of] . . . Joyce Carol Oates." Suggestive of the brilliant writer in Henry James's story "The Private Life" (about which she has written) who disappoints his expectant dinner companions by his ordinary conversation, Oates declares to interviewers, "I'm not that interesting." She describes herself as "orderly and observant and scrupulous, and deeply introverted." Even when a critic concedes a congruity between the physical woman and the writer, his description is often aggrandized so that it equals, in the critic's estimation, the largeness of the fiction. Brad Darrach, for instance, paints her melodramatically, as "a strange pale flamingo of a woman with great jewelled eyes and a fate for literature."

More typical, though, are portraits that characterize her as neurasthenic and helpless, descriptions that are absurd to anyone actually acquainted with her. In an article that appeared in the March 1986 issue of *Ms.*, "My Friend, Joyce Carol Oates: An Intimate Portrait," the feminist literary critic Elaine Showalter wrote that "Oates is not particularly gentle, as it happens; she is fast and tough, funny and outspoken, impatient with pomposity and cant." Stuck in the perception that the writer is mismatched with the large, eventful epics that repeatedly pour out of her imagination, some reviewers, particularly in the 1970s, voiced their bewilderment. John Alfred Avant asked, "Could this actually be the creator of the voluptuous Clara in *A Garden of Earthly Delights?* Was this the novelist who set down the violent horrors of *them* and *Wonderland*?" Others strain for metaphors. She is, they have written, "crowded with psychic existences," "a Cassandra bewitched by her private oracle"; she has "violence in the head." "Typical activities in Oates's novels," reads a 1970 *Life* magazine review, "are arson, rape, riot, mental breakdown, murder (plain and fancy, with excursions into patricide, matricide, uxoricide, mass fillicide), and suicide."

Oates responded to such descriptions in a 1981 *New York Times Book Review* article called "Why Is Your Writing So Violent?" She comments on the irony of being asked this same question in Germany, "not many miles from where Adolf Hitler proclaimed the Second World War." She adds: "The question was asked in Liège, in Hamburg, in London, in Detroit, in New York City. It would be asked in China if I went to China. It would be asked in Moscow. In Hiroshima." "The question," she writes, "is always insulting . . . always ignorant . . . always sexist."

Some recent commentators—acknowledging the strides that Oates has made for women writers generally—have reveled in the seeming antithesis between the person and what she does. Victor Strandberg opens his essay on Oates's *You Must Remember This* (1987), in which a major character is a boxer, with an account of Oates's television commentary on the Tyson-Smith fight in 1987:

> In the summer of 1987, television sets across America displayed a scene that might have held thousands of pugilistic enthusiasts immobilized in mid-air. Just before the HBO showing of the Mike Tyson–Bonecrusher Smith title fight, a middle-aged ectomorphic lady with gentle eyes and a soft voice previewed with incontestable professional authority the likely exchanges of left hooks, right crosses, and tooth-loosening uppercuts to the jaw.
> (p. 3)

Although this portrait of incongruity also accommodates sexist stereotyping, at least it recognizes Oates's right to her subject.

> Though frequently denounced and often misunderstood by a somewhat genteel literary community, my writing is, at least in part, an attempt to memorialize my parents' vanished world; my parents' lives. Sometimes directly, sometimes in metaphor.

As many literary biographies demonstrate, the writer does exist in "significant relationship to his or her work," and Joyce Carol Oates is no exception. In fact, she is quite candid in acknowledging the biographical elements of her writing. In a preface to a special edition of *Marya: A Life* (1986), she confesses that not only the setting and some of the experiences of the protagonist but "many of Marya's thoughts and impressions parallel my own at her approximate age." Both in the 1970 *Newsweek* interview with Walter Clemons and in a 1989 *New York Times Magazine* article entitled "My Father, My Fiction," she recalls a scene in *Wonderland* (1971) inspired by a snapshot in the family album:

> My beleaguered young hero Jesse stops his car in Millersport, wanders about my parents' property, happens to see, with a stab of envy, my young mother and me (a child of 3 or 4) swinging in our old wooden swing; and when my father notices Jesse watching he stares at him with a look of hostility. So I envisioned my father as a young man of 27—tall, husky, with black hair, intent on protecting his family against possible intrusion.
> (19 March, p. 84)

Although Jesse (orphaned when his father murdered his whole family and then committed suicide) is at this point in the novel propelled by the ideology of American individualism, the image foreshadows the final Jesse, who exchanges isolation for a commitment to his family. Besieged by requests to confess the biographical sources of her fiction, Oates sometimes baits her audience with a humorous overstatement. "Much of *Bellefleur*," she says of this gothic novel with dozens of improbable events and characters (including a poet whose words drive a mob to murder him and a woman who marries a black bear), "is a diary of my own life, and the lives of people I have known."

The landscapes of her childhood and the experiences of her parents are, in fact, deeply ingrained in Oates's fiction. Poverty and family violence had a hand in shaping her pluralistic vision, in which connectedness and the saving net of family ties are valued. She was born, as she proudly declares, on "Bloomsday," 16 June 1938, in Millersport, New York, in Erie County, the "Eden County" of her early fiction and a landscape to which she returns often in her later works. She is the oldest of three children. Her brother was born in 1943 and her sister, who is autistic, in 1956. (A poem on her sister, "Autistic Child, No Longer Child," is collected in *Invisible Woman* [1982].) She attended a one-room schoolhouse in Millersport, where few people went to school beyond the seventh grade. Like her alter ego Marya, she was the first in her family to go to college. Indeed, she was the first in her family to finish high school. Her parents, Frederic and Caroline Bush Oates, came from a working-class Catholic background. Their ancestry was Hungarian, German, and Irish. Until his retirement, her father, a natural musician, worked in Lockport, New York, as a tool-and-die designer and for many years moonlighted as a sign painter. Oates says that his shadow lies over *You Must Remember This.* The small-town upstate New York setting, her father's fascination with boxing, the time period of the mid 1940s to the mid 1950s, when he was raising a family, his interest in politics, and his struggle against poverty coalesced in the portrait of Lyle Stevick, a middle-aged husband, father, and proprietor of a secondhand furniture store who takes the atom-bomb scare of the 1950s seriously enough to build a fallout shelter for his family.

In "My Father, My Fiction," Oates describes "the malnourished circumstances" of her parents' lives. Frederic Oates quit school because of the Depression, a central symbol of dislocation in her fiction. His father, Joseph Carlton Oates, deserted his family in 1914, when Frederic was two. Twenty-eight years later, in a scene that could have come out of an Oates novel, Joseph confronted his son in a Millersport tavern, not to ask for his forgiveness or for a reconciliation, but with the intention of beating him up. Living twenty miles away without contacting his family, Joseph had heard his son had a grudge against him. One result of his desertion was the poverty of his wife, Blanche Morgenstern, who, like the migrants and urban and rural poor in Oates's early novels, moved from one cheap rental to another. Blanche's own father, Oates's great-grandfather, was a gravedigger who beat his wife and finally committed suicide. The youngest in a large family, Caroline Bush, who still sews "demure" dresses for her famous daughter, was adopted as an infant by an aunt when her father was murdered in a tavern brawl, circumstances that Oates adapts for Marya's early history in *Marya: A Life.*

Oates's parents responded to the convulsive histories of their families and the uncertainty of the times with a determined rootedness and an emphasis on family solidarity, a model Oates employs for saving some of her early protagonists from the effects of the violent dislocations that mark their lives. Her parents have lived on the same plot of land, originally the farm of her mother's family, since their marriage in 1936. Her father belonged to the United Auto Workers union for forty years. From descriptions of her childhood, one gathers she was the favored child, the oldest and very smart, adopted by her father as a companion. Although she was consigned to "woman's work" around the farm—taking care of the Rhode Island reds—he allowed her the privileges of a son, taking her up in small planes (two-seater Piper Cubs, Cessnas, and Stinsons) wearing goggles but not a parachute. He also taught her about boxing and the romance of violence, which flowered in her book *On Boxing* (1987) and in the character of Felix Stevick, the boxer in *You Must Remember This.*

> A woman who writes is a writer by her own definition; but she is a *woman* writer by others' definitions. . . . A writer may be afflicted by any number of demons, real or imagined, but only the (woman) writer is afflicted by her own essential identity.

Oates's privileged relationship with her father, who included her in activities and introduced her to knowledge reserved for males, particularly in the late 1940s and 1950s, when she was growing up, empowered her as a writer who refuses to be restricted in subject matter, style, or production because of her gender. It is in this context that her quarrel with the category "woman writer" should be viewed. In her essay "(Woman) Writer: Theory and Practice," she quotes Virginia Woolf to support her own position concerning this category: " 'A woman's writing is always feminine. . . . The only difficulty lies in defining what we mean by feminine.' " Oates's statements about this category are marked with anger and resistance—anger at finding herself identified as a *woman* writer and consequently being placed in purdah with other women writers, and resistance to the idea that the imagination is gendered: "Is there a distinctly female voice?—or even a conspicuously feminine voice? Or is 'gender' in this sense an ontological category imposed upon us from without, for the convenience of others?" She views the ideal writer's mind as one that transcends cultural gender construction—one that is, in Virginia Woolf's terms, androgynous. The parentheses in the title of her collection of essays *(Woman) Writer: Occasions and Opportunities* (1988) are shorthand not only for the marginal position of women writers in literary history but also for Oates's own hesitancy at being listed under such a rubric. She is only too conscious of the fact that the category still carries a set of assumptions of the kind that have colored judgments of her work throughout her career. For a woman writer who claims everything from menstruation to boxing as her proper field, who writes on Mike Tyson and the Ferrarri Testarossa sports car with the authority of and perhaps more profundity than most seasoned male sports writers, and who publishes in a very democratic range of journals, from a mass-market product like *TV Guide* to the very heady and scholarly *Critical Inquiry*, the category "woman writer"—even when most generously defined —simply feels too constraining.

Despite her misgivings about this category, Oates has brought to life an enormous cast of female characters who come from virtually every station in life. She has perhaps the largest gallery of adolescent girls of any contemporary writer. Her much-anthologized stories "Where Are You Going, Where Have You Been?" and "Four Summers" are celebrated for their resonant and knowing portrayals of adolescent girls as they negotiate their rites of passage. Several of her novels of female growth (including *With Shuddering Fall, them, Childwold,* [1976], *Marya: A Life,* and *You Must Remember This*) linger over the protagonists' critical adolescent years. In the satirical epic *A Bloodsmoor Romance* (1982) she brings to life the five Zinn sisters, whose adolescences presage, in ironically unpredictable ways, their future courses. Oates's fiction in the 1980s became increasingly preoccupied with the place of women in society. *Marya: A Life, Solstice* (1985), and *You Must Remember This* are pioneering explorations of the lives of contemporary women in America. *A Bloodsmoor Romance* and *Mysteries of Winterthurn* (1984) provide chastizing dialogues with nineteenth-century practices, literary and historical, that sanctioned the oppression of women in the name of a higher morality. What marks all of her portraits, no matter what the mode—realism, surrealism, or gothic—is the scrupulous detail of the historical documentation and psychological realism. Executed with historical and psychological complexity, her portraits of women have often been groundbreaking.

Even her early short stories treat outlawed topics related to women from unsettling perspectives. For instance, the flow of menstrual blood determines the climax of "At the Seminary," published in *Upon the Sweeping Flood and Other Stories* in 1966. Although the image of blood is traditionally male, associated with violence and war, in Oates's hands it becomes a female image, representing the processes of nature. The story opens with the Downey family—mother, father, and the combative, overweight daughter, Sally, wearing a yellow dress—driving to the seminary where the son, who is studying to become a priest, is in the throes of an identity crisis. The seminary, a male preserve, is described as sleek, cold, perfectly controlled, built with "great flights of glass" and marble. Oates carefully builds the contrast between the lifeless seminary and the defiant young woman, Sally, who bristles with appetites and emotions. As her family is led through the chapel by an "excessively calm" priest, Sally notes the absence of odors. The statue of Christ appears "frozen, immaculate white, . . . the contours of his body so glib, so perfect, that they seemed to Sally to be but the mocking surfaces of another statue, a fossilized creature caught forever within that crust—the human model for it, suffocated and buried." When Sally realizes she has begun to menstruate, "she slammed down her heel" in a perverse, retributive gesture so that the "blood jerked free," running in a "delicate trickle" down her leg. In response, her parents and the priest "suffer their vision as it swelled deafeningly upon them, their absolute disbelief at what they saw." Her brother stares "at the floor just before her robust feet as if he had seen something that had turned him to stone." Readers are themselves shaken, at first by her act but then into a series of realizations having to do with the threat women's biology poses to male institutions and the denial of natural processes on which these institutions depend. As a result of her act, Sally's brother feels compelled to remain at the seminary to expiate her crime.

A complex and searing commentary on institutionalized religion, the patriarchy's condemnation of women for their very biology, the aspiration for perfect control, and the will to subdue the natural order, the story marshals its images along gender lines. Sally's character and act suggest the disruptive force of the feminine, a force Oates depicts as undeniable and inevitably resurgent even in the face of powerful, repressive patriarchal institutions. Sally's role as embodiment of the subversive feminine is emphasized by the images of the last line, in which the story's weakest patriarch, Mr. Downey, looks at his daughter: "Out of the corner of Mr. Downey's eye her face loomed blank and milky, like a threatening moon he dared not look upon."

A second early story, "The Children," published in 1969, not only interrogates the sanctified image of mother and child, but explores the proposition that children may be perceived as a mother's enemies. Compared with this story by Oates, the resolutions of separation and suicide that settle the conflicts between selfhood and motherhood in Henrik Ibsen's *A Doll's House* and Kate Chopin's *The Awakening* seem idealized and romantic. More consonant with the statistics on child abuse, Oates's story details with obdurate honesty the psychological and sociological exigencies that lead to the shocking conclusion, in which a middle-class husband comes home from work to see his wife, formerly a chemist, beating their daughter with a now-bloodied spoon.

"The Children" is collected in *Marriages and Infidelities* (1972), a volume in which Oates offers revisions of texts by such authors as Joyce, Thoreau, James, and Kafka—thus the "marriages" and "infidelities" of the title. Oates's fiction has, in fact, repeatedly taken the form of interrogations of or dialogues with other works and writers. *Childwold* challenges what she has described as the insular, monastic vision of Nabokov's *Lolita*. *Angel of Light* (1981) is based on the story of the house of Atreus. "The Children" evokes Doris Lessing, whom Oates interviewed in 1973, and particulary her now-classic women's story "To Room Nineteen," though Oates's protagonist is aggressive rather than passive in her violence. "To Room Nineteen" achieves resolution with the female protagonist committing suicide—as does Chopin's novel—after she provides for the care of her children. Having acted with complete responsibility, Lessing's protagonist dies a martyr. Oates's conclusion, however, is strategically open-ended. As with Richard Wright's *Native Son*, Oates's conclusion shocks her readers out of complacency by confronting them with a protagonist with whom they cannot sympathize. The end of the story leaves the married couple facing the implications of the mother's act, dramatically projecting the story beyond the ending so that readers consider not only the forces that drove the protagonist to her act but also its consequences and the implications for the society in which those consequences must be faced.

In *Marriages and Infidelities* Oates commits promiscuous "infidelities" in the volume's "marriages" to well-known texts. By thus appropriating canonical texts, she allies herself with a growing tradition of women revisionists, some of whom call themselves "plagiarists" as do Kathy Acker and the artist Sherry Levine. Through their appropriations, these writers and artists rupture the social subtexts and cultural assumptions shaping the original works and with varying degrees of success attempt to break through to a liberated space. Unlike Joyce in his use of the structure of the *Odyssey* in *Ulysses,* their appropriations are meant to interrogate the original.

Oates's interrogation of Chekhov's "The Lady with the Dog" in her story "The Lady with the Pet Dog" (1972), also collected in *Marriages and Infidelities,* is gentle and honoring. Similar to Jean Rhys's revision of Charlotte Brontë's *Jane Eyre* in *Wide Sargasso Sea,* Oates relocates the plot and characters in the twentieth century and changes the point of view from the man to the woman. The structured moral universe, clear emotional allegiances, and well-defined gender roles Chekhov draws become blurred and complicated with the modern setting and the increased interiority Oates writes into the shifted point of view. In both versions of the story, a married man meets a married woman when they are both on a seashore vacation without their respective spouses. They have an affair that continues after the vacation is over. Although Oates's revision offers an enlarged awareness and an expanded sense of possibility arising from the privileging of the woman's point of view, the twentieth-century woman has little superiority over her nineteenth-century counterpart. The choice is between one man or another: "She lay in his arms [her lover's] while her husband talked to her, miles away, one body fading into another. . . . She thought, pressing her cheek against the back of one of these men." Viewed in conjunction with the original, Oates's revision represents something like an accusation. Women's options, this story suggests, have not fundamentally changed since the nineteenth century.

In other works Oates is more sanguine about the advances of the twentieth century over the nineteenth. *A Bloodsmoor Romance* also follows the interrogatory model of *Wide Sargasso Sea.* As Rhys's work projects a subversive twentieth-century consciousness on the nineteenth-century narrative, thus effecting the rescue of the "madwoman" in *Jane Eyre* from bestiality and from blame, so too does Oates's work liberate six women characters from the straitjacket of nineteenth-century requirements by arming them with twentieth-century access to their own feelings and the daring to act on them. It also suggests Edith Wharton's *The Age of Innocence* in its meditation on the increasing fluidity of America's social structure at the approach of the twentieth century. The tone of Oates's virtuoso work, though, is high hilarity, the mode Swiftian satire, the range encyclopedic, the purpose intellectual guerilla warfare on the sexist texts and subtexts of nineteenth-century society. She has called *A Bloodsmoor Romance* the Ph.D. dissertation she never wrote. It is a virtual dictionary of life in late-nineteenth-century America, covering everything from transcendentalism and the institution of a federal income tax to the formula for antiperspirant.

The novel chronicles the history of the Zinn family during the last twenty years of the nineteenth century—from September 1879, when their adopted daughter, Deirdre, is abducted from the bosom of her family in a mysterious, black "outlaw balloon," to the last stroke of midnight in 1899. Raised on their Aunt Edwina's advice books for young ladies, with titles such as *The Young Lady's Friend: A Compendium of Correct Forms,* the four remaining Zinn sisters at first fervently hope for marriage to a partner of the right class.

It is precisely this plot that Oates imaginatively and variedly subverts with each of the sisters. Although two of the sisters do marry within their class, one sister, Constance Philipa, in the words of the Victorian "lady" narrator, becomes "a bride but not a wife." Her bridegroom, a sinister baron with a name that is nine hundred years old, is involved in ivory and slave trading and has survived three wives. During the wedding ceremony, the baron, finding the wedding band too small, jams it onto Constance Phillipa's finger, an act alerting the reader and presumably Constance Phillipa to what they can expect of his future conduct as a lover and husband. In fact, on the wedding night he attempts to rape his bride, the most efficient method in his experience for performing "the connubial act." However, after he is finished with "his exertions," he discovers it is not Constance Phillipa in bed with him, but a dressmaker's dummy. Constance Phillipa had wisely installed a replacement and then fled in disguise as a man. A second sister, Octavia, whose precocious womanly development required that she wear a corset from the age of ten, marries Reverend Rumford, whose tastes in the marriage bed run to the sadomasochistic. Preceding the marriage, she asks her mother, Prudence, for instruction. Prudence replies: "In the matter of marital relations, my dear daughter . . . it is always best to think *not at all*. . . . For, as the wisdom of the Old Testament instructs us, 'This too shall pass.' " Despite Rumford's perverted sexual habits, including his demanding that Octavia wear a hood and a corset and pull a noose around her neck or his, she does not complain, preferring to gnaw her own shoulder to help her endure the pain rather than risk "the fruits of displeasing one's husband," which commonly include being locked in a room and drugged for female hysteria by a physician in complicity with patriarchal notions of wifely obedience. One night Mr. Rumford orders Octavia to pull the noose "yet tighter" around his neck; she obeys, and his death and her well-earned freedom follow. Malvinia, the prettiest of the Zinn sisters, runs off to the stage and is painted by John Singer Sargent, and courted by Mark Twain, Diamond Jim Brady, Jay Gould, and Grover Cleveland. Samantha, who has played the part of dutiful apprentice to her father, runs off with another apprentice, a man not of her social class. The abducted Deirdre becomes a world-famous spiritualist, associated with the renowned Madame Blavatsky.

Having freed and dispersed the sisters, Oates uses the occasion of the reading of Aunt Edwina's will to reunite them; ironically, they gather under a ceiling covered with scenes from Milton's *Paradise Lost* painted in "rainbow hues." Edwina, a quintessential Victorian hypocrite, has been leading a double life. Her will reveals that the spiritualist Deirdre is her natural child, the result of a secret marriage to Captain Elisha Burlingame, known in the Union army as "the Bull," a gambler and roughneck who subsequently died in a drunken brawl. She leaves her fortune to her daughter, who generously shares it with her sisters and adoptive parents.

Edwina's confession finally awakens Prudence, the mother, to the fact that all of the women around her—her daughters and even the sanctimonious Edwina—violate Victorian standards and follow their inclinations, while she, living within the rigid constraints of exemplary Victorian wife- and motherhood, has allowed her spirit to be broken, enduring not only a subordinate and slavish status in her household but also numerous births, miscarriages, and deaths of infants. Edwina's revelation shakes her out of a compliant somnambulism, so that at the age of seventy-six, using her stored energy, she becomes a leader of the women's suffrage movement.

If Edwina's revelation of her double life is the final blow to Prudence's Victorian values, the penultimate blow is her husband's capitulation to the death and war machine. All through their childhood, the Zinn sisters worshiped their inventor father, John Quincy Zinn, who is well-known enough to be admired by Twain and disparaged by Emerson. Throughout his life, Zinn dreamed of inventing a perpetual-motion machine. Having refused during the long course of his marriage to compromise the noble pursuit of invention by applying for commercial patents, John Quincy Zinn sacrificed the economic security of his family, a sacrifice that his wife Prudence tolerated because of its moral rationale. However, after he is flattered by a zealous journalist who paints him as an "unsung hero," he accepts a fifteen-thousand-dollar honorarium from the United States government to find a "humane" method of execution (but, he is instructed, the method should not be completely painless), resulting in his invention of the electric chair. Thus Prudence's comfort and peace of mind have been sacrificed for an instrument of death. John Quincy Zinn also invents a formula for his longed-for perpetual-motion machine, a formula, it turns out, for the atomic bomb, providing perpetual motion through perpetual detonation. One of Deirdre's "spirit masters" guides her into "accidentally" destroying the formula almost at the moment that the inventor dies.

Despite the patriarch's death and the new century's imminent dawning, Oates drives the narrative to the expected nineteenth-century happy ending: all five sisters do, in the end, marry happily—but none follows convention in choosing her mate. One, Constance Phillipa, is first transformed—*Orlando* style—into a man, Phillip Fox. Another, Deirdre, marries Hassan Agha, Madam Blavatsky's former *chela*. The six women face the new century not only with their freedom and a fortune but also, each of them, with a new mate (Prudence moves in with a childhood friend) to suit her liberated status.

In her productions as a novelist, short-story writer, poet, and dramatist over a quarter-century's span, Oates has, in fact, charted the evolution of the possible for women in her time. Reflective of their eras, Oates's novels and stories of the 1960s and early 1970s reward her female protagonists' attempts to establish independence with various forms of incarceration—whether it is returning to her father's house for Karen in *With Shuddering Fall,* withering in a nursing home for Clara in *A Garden of Earthly Delights* (1967), or catatonia for Maureen in *them.* Or her protagonists find themselves in marriages that, in Oates's subversion of traditional fiction's happy ending for women, are last resorts, as with Maureen's marriage to Jim Randolph in *them,* or, at best, compromises. "He would do," thinks Elena as she contemplates Jack, her future husband, in *Do with Me What You Will* (1973).

In works of the 1980s, Oates's protagonists are defined or resolve their conflicts in ways that are exceptional in the tradition of the novel, a tradition in which women are, as Virginia Woolf wrote, largely represented as lovers of men and in which they are obliged either to marry, go mad, or die. Particularly in the 1980s Oates has successfully taken up the challenge presented by Woolf's observation in *A Room of One's Own* that women characters "almost without exception . . . are shown in their relation to men." (The continuing validity of this observation is confirmed by most fiction, even by women, through 1990.) In pioneering works Oates defines her female protagonists in relation to their work, to their aspirations, or to history, as in the award-winning story "My Warszawa: 1980," which appears in *Last Days* (1984).

Although the story's opening and closing scenes depict the main character's relationship with her lover, this relationship fades into the background as the real drama of the story, the protagonist's growing discovery that she is a Jew, is edged progressively to the foreground. In fact, Judith is a half-Jewish writer who has never "felt" Jewish, attending a conference in Warsaw. As she is escorted from place to place, she comes to identify with the Jews whose absence from Poland speaks to her of that country's guilt. She registers the anti-Semitism, implied and overt, in certain remarks of her hosts. She recalls the "brag" of one official that "today the nation is . . . 97% pure." She broods over a Pole's callous assessment that "the Jewish ghetto wasn't much of a loss architecturally" and a convert's rationalization that the ghetto

Jews "could have saved themselves, the ones who ended up in Ośięcim. But they did not try." Oates moves Judith through a series of such experiences that leave her at the end identified in relation to the tragic history of the Jews. The lover with whom Oates equips her is simply emblematic of her normality, not the scale on which she is weighed. Her identity hinges not on her relationship to him, but on an epiphanal acceptance of her Jewishness. Reminiscent of the heroine in Henry James's *The Awkward Age,* which lies on Judith's night table, it is an acceptance that is dependent upon a loss of innocence. Oates's achievement in representing female identity by way of historical allegiances should not be underestimated; not only is it quite rare in realistic fiction, but it may also mark a real change in the grammar of society.

As "My Warszawa: 1980" exemplifies, Oates's later depictions of American life record a shift in consciousness regarding women. Works of the 1980s particularly show Oates repeatedly experimenting with the architecture of narrative to liberate her female protagonists from serving as creations of male desire. The 1985 novel *Solstice* reflects such a shift. In an unprecedented move Oates defines two women not in relation to men and not even in relation to society, but purely and simply in relation to one another. Although there have been fictional depictions of women's friendships since Woolf tried unsuccessfully "to remember any case in the course of my reading where two women are represented as friends," they are often vehicles to make statements about society or about other issues. In these works, female characters are sequestered in friendships to defend against a hostile, invading force—usually male—that ultimately defines them. In contrast *Solstice* defines two women friends, Monica and Sheila, exclusively in relation to one another. Through death and divorce, the significant men have been eliminated before the events begin. Oates does not replace them with other significant men; neither does she isolate the friends from the inequities of patriarchal culture (Monica discovers that a similarly qualified male colleague was given a more advantageous contract) nor does she protect them from the dangers (including date rape) women risk in living without men. In the words of Monica, as she thinks of the abortion her ex-husband convinced her to have: "It's a man's world. . . . A man's world, *that* world, the fluorescent-lit disinfectant-smelling clinic, populated solely by women." In this work Oates responds to Woolf's plea that women write novels in which they are represented in relation to themselves, that their freedom from a restrictive patriarchy depends on it, and she does so without sentimentalizing.

The presiding myth of *Solstice* is Ariadne's thread, which is also the title of a series of paintings completed by Sheila, who is an artist. In presenting the myth Oates alters it, providing a clue to reading the novel. The narrator says, "Ariadne's thread: the labyrinth as a state of mind, a region of the soul: heroic effort without any Hero at its center." Sheila elaborates, "This is only about Ariadne's thread, this has nothing to do with Theseus." In the myth Ariadne, out of love for Theseus, gives him a ball of string that he is to unravel as he travels through the labyrinth to face the Minotaur so that after the battle he can find his way out. Oates revises the myth to emphasize the woman's saving act, the provision of the thread, rather than the heroic quest to kill the Minotaur and escape the labyrinth. She proposes that the labyrinth—which refers to both the tensions in the relationship between Monica and Sheila and the narrative itself—may be confronted without a hero.

The image reflects how Oates has reformed the economy of the traditional narrative in order to accommodate the foregrounding of women's friendship. As Oates demonstrates, conventional narrative structure must be revised for such foregrounding, for with the conventional elements in play—the hero, quest, or goal to be accomplished, the single climax, and the final resolution—the "story," in representing possibilities for women, is fixed and limited; narrative structure to some extent determines a character's fate. Through her application of a relational rather than a heroic aesthetic in developing her plot, Oates enables her female characters to function as subjects in themselves rather than as constructions of male desire.

Nearly every novel Oates published in the 1980s exercises a different liberating narrative strategy. In the stunning novel *You Must Remember This,* set in the United States in the 1950s, she decenters the narrative, developing a constellation of characters almost equally so that the narrative movement is radial rather than linear. This design allows flexibility in bringing the book to closure—not all of the characters' destinies need to be delineated to give the sense of an ending. Two plot strands are tied up: in a twist on the marriage plot, the culmination of the life of the male protagonist, Felix, a boxer, is represented by his marriage; and in a final, warm image of affirmation, a battered, middle-aged couple make love. But a third strand, concerning the female protagonist, Enid, who has survived a suicide attempt, is not resolved. Her story is left open-ended, a gesture of opportunity and possibility.

In *Unholy Loves* (1979), Oates makes explicit her sense of the coercive relationship between narrative and individual lives, whether fictionalized or real. She iterates the position of Hélène Cixous, advocate of feminine writing, whom Oates quotes in "(Woman) Writer: Theory and Practice": "Language conceals an invisible adversary because it is the language of men and their grammar." Through an alter ego, Brigit Stott—who like Oates is a writer of fiction and a professor—she lectures on the "consciousness" pervading language. This "consciousness" may be read as that element of language and narrative delivering patriarchal values:

> There is a consciousness . . . that permeates language and is somehow given birth by it, and it is always with us, we are never free. . . . The world is filtered through it. There is no world except what is filtered through it. . . . As in old-fashioned novels we are guided by a presence we never see; it is always commenting, interpreting, predicting, directing, passing judgment.
> (*Unholy Loves,* pp. 266–267)

Language manipulates the perception of events—and thus, in a real sense, the events themselves—as palpably as the omniscient narrator in nineteenth-century novels manipulates readers' perception of the characters and plot turns. However, Brigit proposes to subvert this dominating "presence," a plan that applies both to Brigit and to the author inventing a destiny for her female character. Brigit pledges: "I will know the nature of this consciousness, I will know its language. . . . I will set my own in opposition to it . . ." (ellipses in text). Shortly following this pledge, Brigit is released from her writer's block. After emotional and professional paralysis, she is, at the end, relatively hopeful, writing steadily, feeling in control of her life. Thus Oates, in re-choreographing narrative structure, has increased the options for a "happy ending" for the female protagonist, largely limited in canonical fiction to marriage. She fulfills the efforts of Dorothy Richardson who, in the first half of the twentieth century, avoided this ending by continually writing her heroine, Miriam, into new situations; at the time Richardson died, Miriam appeared in thirteen volumes of the still-unfinished novel *Pilgrimage.* By rewriting the happy ending without sacrificing psychological realism, Oates has also recorded a relaxation in the culture's prescriptions for women.

Oates's sense of women's growing autonomy in forging their identities is recorded in the evolution of the image of invisibility in her works over the course of two decades. In the "Afterword" to the collection of poems entitled *Invisible Woman,* she writes:

> The theme of invisibility has haunted me for many years, since earliest girlhood. A woman often feels "invisible" in a public sense precisely because her physical being—her "visibility"—

> figures so prominently in her identity. She is judged as a body, she is "attractive" or "unattractive," while knowing that her deepest self is inward, and secret: knowing, *hoping* that her spiritual essence is a great deal more complex than the casual eye of the observer will allow.
> (p. 99)

Oates's heroines of the early 1970s often think of themselves as "not there," as having no mirror image. An early protagonist, Maureen in *them,* thinks: "A person, a girl imagines the mirror will show no reflection to her. So she does not dare look. . . . [She] has no reflection, no face. A headless body." Some of Oates's female protagonists sink into the vegetative blankness of catatonia, an expression of their missing sense of self. They come into visibility and acquire a sense of self only as reflected in a man's desire, and only temporarily: "It was her fate to be Maureen; that was that. But the Maureen she was in the presence of that man she'd been with . . . did not last. It came to an end." Even fictional characters seem more real to Maureen than she seems to herself: "Maureen, dreaming over them, could feel herself begin to dissolve into nothing, nobody, an eye in a head, a blankness." Elena of *Do with Me What You Will* describes herself as sleeping through her life in "virginal blankness." She fears her mirror image will disappear. When she checks her face in mirrors, "She could see herself [only] faintly." She is so convinced that her identity depends on male construction that she tells Mered Dawe, "Dream me."

As the images of female invisibility in early works are delivered with a sense of inevitability, these images, when they appear in works of the early 1980s, are delivered with blame and acrimony. A number of poems in *Invisible Woman* take this tone. The title is the central point of reference for the statements in the title poem, "Invisible Woman," written in 1981. Here invisibility becomes an image of suppressed identity. Lines such as "what are the tales spun of us / in rooms we leave too quickly—" and "Because you know me, we have never met. / Because you see me, you cannot hear" indict a system in which women, particularly, have little authority over the image others have of them; rather, this image is an invention strangely independent of them. The poem "Baby," written in 1980, describes how women's identities are sacrificed to the roles they play. A gigantic baby filling the speaker's space, using up all her air, is a metaphor for the erosion of a woman's sense of selfhood as she is compelled to fill socially acceptable roles. The refrain "the baby grows" gives the poem a Sylvia Plath–like sense of menace and relentlessness:

> Four walls, a ceiling, and the baby grows.
> Floorboards, blinded windows. Airless air.
> And the baby grows.
> . . . .
> *Love and feed.* Swollen sausages for fingers.
> He grows filling the room, the space. You.
>
> Fat knees cutely dimpled. Ears pink and
> delicate
> as shells. O Love you are enormous,
> clambering
> toward me, filling the room, the space.
> The air glistens. There is no air.
> The baby grows.
> (p. 11)

"A Report to an Academy," written in 1980, two years after Oates accepted an appointment at Princeton University, is a bitter meditation on the fact that a woman's participation in the academy depends on her adoption of patriarchal language, forms, and rituals, on "aping" males. In the poem's opening stanzas, the speaker is pictured literally as an ape in "a three-sided cage" with "no way out." As the poem progresses, the speaker lectures her audience on the inadequate size of the cage: "The ceiling against the nape of my neck, / the narrow sides cutting into my thighs, / the bars raising welts on my hide." Her only option, offered by the fourth and open side of the cage, is to be transformed into one of her captors ("Consequently I became one of you"), which also requires suppressing the feminine in her: "I charmed my captors, I learned their speech, / I grew wonderfully cunning, I now wear a necktie." In a simple, striking image, Oates suggests the hypocrisy that each of the speaker's transactions will now require and, beyond that, the complex effect of such deceit not only on her but on the culture as well:

> The first thing I learned from my captors was
> a frank handshake,
> which I practice every day.
> Will you give me your hand?
>
> (p. 75)

This last line echoes the last line in Plath's "The Applicant," a poem in which a man shops for a wife. After the shopkeeper shows him a "model," she demands, "Will you marry it, marry it, marry it." The image of the hand also echoes Plath's poem. When in "The Applicant" the shopper shows the speaker (who is the shopkeeper) his empty hand, she says:

> Here is a hand
> To fill it and willing
> To bring teacups and roll away headaches
> And do whatever you tell it.
>
> (see Oates's "The Death Throes of Romanticism: The Poetry of Sylvia Plath," in *New Heaven, New Earth,* pp. 111–140)

Plath's poem caricatures the culture's objectification of women, while Oates's poem focuses on the male disguise they must adopt to become visible in the culture.

In the 1986 novel *Marya: A Life,* invisibility is not a woman's fate but a condition to be cured. The novel chronicles the deliberate journey of a woman from invisibility to visibility. Abandoned by her mother, raped from the time she was eight until she was fourteen by her older cousin, tormented by her less intelligent schoolmates, Marya as a schoolgirl escapes, as did Oates's earlier protagonists, to a condition of "not-there-ness," retreating from her physical self. In order to carry out his brutal acts, her cousin Lee dehumanizes her, calling her almost anything but her name: "The Bulldog. . . . Snot-nose. Fuckface. Shithead. And sometimes, with a killing simplicity that commingled pity and contempt and a mild threat, *you.*" Conditioned into invisibility, as an adult she is not convinced that her lover truly loves *her:* "It's just his notion of her, a kind of capsule-sized female in his brain, 'Marya' in this pose, 'Marya' in that. . . ." For another lover, her beauty is reminiscent of "certain baroque madonnas," a "*mater dolorosa*" like that painted by Bartolomé Murillo. She gazes at the mirror, "confronted with a Marya not herself, a fictitious Marya," one constructed by her lover. Her sense of invisibility positions her as the other and sabotages her efforts to constitute herself as a subject. As a professional, she thinks of herself as "genderless." When she works, she "quickly became invisible to herself." As her lovers leave or die, she struggles to recover the tenuous sense of identity they gave her. Unable to suppress her need to find herself and dissatisfied with conventional means of establishing female identity—through men—she searches for her mother. As the narrative ends, she examines a photograph of her mother and finally recognizes herself.

Oates describes *Marya: A Life* as the most "personal" of her novels. "What is most autobiographical about the novel," she writes, "is its inner kernel of emotion—Marya's half-conscious and often despairing quest for her own elusive self." With this work, Oates locates another avenue by which to circumvent traditional narrative solutions. A bildungsroman about the making of an intellectual, *Marya: A Life* follows the fortunes of a single character. As her description suggests, Oates uses the scheme of the quest narrative to develop her story, but the quester, in this case, though extraordinarily intelligent, is not heroic. Moreover, Oates reconfigures the female quest plot, so that rather than the usual resolution of marriage (as in *Jane Eyre,* for instance), Marya's story concludes with her painful reunion with her mother. This reunion does not provide a sense of narrative closure but, as Elaine Showalter notes, provides "a powerful moment of opening." It suggests that claiming the matrilineage as her own, acknowledging allegiance to female forebears, is a way of subverting patriarchal formulas and empowering female identity. Meditating on the autobiographical elements of this novel in "Five Prefaces," Oates writes:

> Whether Marya Knauer's story is in any way my own "story," it became my story during the writing of the novel; and it is my hope that, however obliquely and indirectly, it will strike chords in readers who, like Marya, choose finally not to accept the terms of their own betrayal
> (*[Woman] Writer: Occasions and Opportunities*, p. 378)

Her epigraph to the novel is from William James: "My first act of freedom will be to believe in freedom." Here, freedom is approached by connecting with the largely unknown, because unexplored, heritage of mothers.

Oates's focus on women is a natural outgrowth of her particular vision of America. In the most succinct and profound terms this vision may be characterized as feminine. The generally acknowledged master narrative of American literature is masculinist, a quest narrative frequently envisioned as the transcendence of the ordinary or as the pursuit of the not-yet-civilized. Such quests are often dramatized as an aspiration to self-creation dependent upon escape from the domestic and rejection of the world of real (not idealized) women, of mothers and wives. Oates's fiction invites the reader to view this master narrative with Penelope rather than with Homer.

In her early essays Oates interprets the terms of the American imagination driving this narrative negatively. Intense individualism results in isolation, the aspiration for self-creation often disguises narcissism or megalomania, and the hope for transcendence is fulfilled only in death or in madness. She interprets the heroic stance in which the single male protagonist asserts his will against the external world as nihilistic. In a 1972 essay, entitled "Melville and the Tragedy of Nihilism," that appears in *The Edge of Impossibility: Tragic Forms in Literature*, Oates writes: "The nightmare of *Moby Dick* . . . is not without redemption for us because we are made to understand continually that the quest, whether literal or metaphysical, *need not be taken*." For Oates, the individual who is equal to life does not, like the tragic hero, stand above it. She expresses this idea through Jim Randolph, an English teacher, in her Detroit novel *them:*

> Tragedy had always terrified him with its blunt, raw stops and starts, its elegant language and bloody endings and calm revivals, a sense of apocalypse followed by an ordinary morning. Horatio and Fortinbras playing chess in a drafty, velvet-hung room, yawning and patient, good men left over to fight a good fight, ignorant enough to survive. And there was always a Cassio left over, bruised but energetic, and Kent dazed with the past but optimistic enough to take on the future, the long rise of history
> (pp. 416–417)

The relationship between the heroic American aesthetic and Oates's antiheroic vision of it is similar to the relationship between Percy Bysshe Shelley's admiring view of Prometheus and that of his wife, Mary Shelley. In writing *Frankenstein*, subtitled *The Modern Prometheus*, Mary Shelley challenged Romantic notions of the heroic. Her Prometheus is an overreacher whose attempt to rival God by giving birth to his creature has a bitter yield—the death of everyone he loves by the hand of his creation, his nightmarish Adam, the monster. While Percy Bysshe Shelley regards Prometheus as a heroic rebel, Mary Shelley views this figure with skepticism; she emphasizes the danger in allowing him free rein. And just as Mary Shelley challenges Romantic notions of the heroic with Dr. Frankenstein, Oates posits a variety of modern American Prometheuses to stand as interrogators beside the old—to stand beside Melville's Ahab and Fitzgerald's Gatsby.

With characters such as Shar Rule, Jules Wendall, Jesse Harte, Fitz John Kasch, Nathan

Vickery, and Leah Bellefleur, Oates has invented a gallery of New World Prometheuses, but rather than consecrating their attempts to transcend earthly limits, as is the case in classic American literature, she stresses their inevitable defeat. She renders their aspirations so that they are almost comic in their arrogance, yet ironically reflect the promises implicit in America's dream of itself. In *them* Oates draws a loving portrait of Jules Wendall, a hopeful Detroit slum youth: "What he would like . . . was not to be a saint exactly but to live a secular life parallel to a sacred life, . . . to expand Jules to the limits of his skin and the range of his eyesight." Even more expansively, Jules thinks: "He had not liked Jesus. . . . He, Jules, would be a better man, or at least a cleverer man—why not all the kingdoms of the earth? Why not?" And perhaps the most quintessentially American expression of Jules's conviction that he can substitute himself for the world is his thought that "so long as he owned his own car he could always be in control of his fate—he was fated to nothing. He was a true American. . . . he was second generation to no one. He was his own ancestors." In each case, the delusionary efforts of the Promethean will succumb to the pluralistic universe. The hopes of Jules, at the end of the narrative, are reduced to realistic proportions; he hopes for an ordinary job, an ordinary marriage, an ordinary life. The course of the narrative brings him to the understanding that ordinary life brings with it a saving net of relationships, a context for being.

Oates's works of the 1960s and 1970s offer cautionary tales about pursuing the imperatives of the self. Such novels as *With Shuddering Fall, A Garden of Earthly Delights, Expensive People* (1968), *them, Wonderland, Do with Me What You Will,* and *Childwold* follow the paradigm of American history in that just as America freed itself from mother England, the central characters find themselves loosened from the bonds of family and place. In some of these works the Depression, which deeply affected Oates's own parents, is the prime agent of her protagonists' dislocation. Probably the most ambitious of her early works in this mode is *Wonderland.* The title refers both to the America dreamed of by the first settlers, by European immigrants, and currently by the oppressed of the Third World; and also to a fantasy land, like that in Lewis Carroll's *Alice in Wonderland.* In fact, Carroll's *Wonderland* provides Oates's work not only with its title but also with a good deal of its structure and imagery. In her *Wonderland* Oates chronicles a pilgrimage through symbolic landscapes of American culture and history. During the journey the protagonist, Jesse Hart, is lured into the belief that he has the power of self-creation and complete self-sufficiency until, in order to save the life of his daughter, he is forced to acknowledge the outside world and his own limitations. An act of love pulls him into the necessary balance between self and world.

In the novel's initial events, set in the Depression, Jesse escapes his father's gunfire, which is motivated by his abysmal economic failure and which wipes out his whole family and leaves him an orphan. Thus wrenched from his past, homeless and parentless, Jesse, like the pioneers facing the new continent, begins the task of inventing himself and his world. His subsequent stay at his grandfather's farm represents an encounter with the agrarian ideal, which proves isolationist and solipsistic. As the novel shifts to the World War II period, Jesse is adopted by a megalomaniacal, obese, obsessive, and morphine-addicted surgeon, Dr. Karl Pedersen, a parodic inversion of the Nazi Aryan ideal, as well as a satiric embodiment of the American disposition toward self-deification. Pedersen values freaks, deformity, and obesity because they mark the extraordinary; Jesse, as the sole survivor of his father's murderous act, is part of Pedersen's collection. For Oates, the exaltation of the grotesque is a correlative of the imbalance between self and world promoted in America's master narrative. In subsequent episodes of his pilgrimage, Jesse meets with figures who offer science, Manichaeanism, sensualism, and nihilism as paths to self-apotheosis, but when he is faced with the choice of repeating his father's act by abandoning his daughter or breaking out of his confinement in a narrow egotism by rescuing her, he rescues her. Thus, Oates's American Prometheus, transformed into Everyman, is saved for the world.

Nearly a decade after *Wonderland,* Oates attempted another ambitious allegory of American history in light of its master narrative. The dominant overreacher in *Bellefleur* is a woman named Leah who is obsessed with restoring the Bellefleur estate to the 2,889,500 acres in upstate New York that the original Bellefleur who came to America, Jean-Pierre, accumulated in the 1770s for 7½ cents an acre. Described by Oates as "a critique of America," *Bellefleur* is literally an American gothic, with standard features such as a haunted castle and a vampire. The novel also includes more inventive gothic elements, such as nonreflecting mirrors, mirrors and ponds that draw the gazer into their interiors to disappear forever, dwarfs and cats and children with powers, a giant vulture that snatches a baby from a walled garden, a spider the size of a sparrow, a colony of midgets, a child scientist, a hermaphroditic infant, and a boy who metamorphoses into a dog. This novel is her answer to Brad Darrach, who in 1970 called her "an anachronism: the last of the 19th Century Gothic novelists, the fourth Brontë sister." The quintessentially American cast of *Bellefleur* includes monomaniacs, megalomaniacs, religious fanatics, slave owners, rapists, murderers, and mass murderers. Woven into it are allusions to numerous American texts and characters, including Gatsby, William Faulkner's Snopes family, Nathaniel Hawthorne's "The Artist of the Beautiful," Benjamin Franklin's *Poor Richard's Almanac,* Horatio Alger's heroes, and Henry James's *The American.*

Perhaps the American text suggested most clearly, by *Bellefleur* is Faulkner's *Absalom, Absalom!* An exemplary document of the imperial self, it is, like *Bellefleur,* an American gothic in which a penniless man attempts to wrest a dynasty out of the wilderness. The most distinct legacy the Bellefleur American progenitor leaves to future generations of Bellefleurs is the authority of arrogance. His history has nearly all the elements of the American master narrative: Cast out of Europe, Jean-Pierre has no family or place in the new world. He must start again, re-create himself. To compensate for the loss of the old world, he embarks on a megalomaniacal quest sustained by the dream of an ideal woman. Jean-Pierre, youngest son of the Duc de Bellefleur, is banished by Louis XV for radical ideas and arrives penniless in New York. In a short period he accumulates enough land to propose establishing a sovereignty of his own called Nautauga. Dissatisfied with two real women, a mistress (a logging camp whore) and a wife (a New York aristocrat), both of whom bear his children, he yearns for the ideal woman, imagined as the girl he left behind decades earlier in France. Following logically from the fact that both sets of children, the Varrells and the Bellefleurs, share their father's audacity and pride but live on opposite ends of the economic ladder, they become bitter enemies, and in the next generation the Varrells massacre their Bellefleur half-brother and his children.

Each generation spawns permutations of the American imperial self as incarnated by Jean-Pierre. In addition to several robber barons there is Jedediah, who goes to the mountain certain that God will speak to *him;* there is the mass murderer Jean-Pierre II, for whom Leah gets a pardon only to have him murder again (this time his victims are union organizers); more modestly, there is Emmanuel, whose endless project is to map the ever-shifting landscape of the Bellefleur estate once and for all, to fix reality through cartography; and there is Vernon, who wants to awaken the laborers to their misery through his poetry. Finally, there is Leah, an Amazonian woman whose size is a correlative to her ambition and whose overweening ambition blanks out everything in her world but its object. Jean-Pierre II, chastened by decades of prison life, looks on the spectacle of the Bellefleurs and thinks, "What maddened mind, deranged by unspeakable lust, had imagined all this into being . . . ?"

A judgment on the American dream as well as on the relatives of Jean-Pierre II, this statement is made by someone with an outsider's perspective. In fact, it suggests the well-known positions of real outside observers of American democracy and its imagination. The Frenchman Alexis de Tocqueville, meditating on his visit to the new world in *Democracy in America,* noted how the emphasis on freedom and individualism was translated into egotism. He wrote: "Not only does democracy make every man forget his ancestors, but it hides his descendants and separates his contemporaries from him; it throws him back forever upon himself alone, and threatens in the end to confine him entirely within the solitude of his own heart." D. H. Lawrence in *Studies in Classic American Literature* also describes classic American literature as "begotten by the self, in the self, the self made love." American writers want "paradise," but, writes Lawrence, "there is no paradise." De Tocqueville and Lawrence present irreverent views of the American imagination, interpreting the acts engendered by it as narcissistic. It is an interpretation that Penelope would approve, since all she values—home, hearth, and family—are excluded by this imagination.

Bellefleur, Oates reports in "Five Prefaces," began as an image of a garden. In a tale centered on the American imagination, this image suggests the dream emboldening the plans of the Puritans for a new garden of Eden. However, as the novel proposes, attempts to fulfill this dream often skewed the course of the nation. The ideal was twisted into megalomaniacal visions that divided the nation into slaves and masters, the oppressed and the oppressors. Consequently, the novel ends in harmony with its gothic elements. At the moment Leah is about to fulfill her ambition, a deus ex machina subverts her. Leah's husband, Gideon, sabotages her ambition in kamikaze style when he flies his plane into the manor, killing the principal Bellefleur adults, as well as destroying Bellefleur Manor. A memento mori is woven throughout the text, but at the end death becomes the great democratizer. The children, however, survive the conflagration and are thereby freed from the spell of the Bellefleur ambition. They represent hope for the future: "One by one the Bellefleur children free themselves of their family's curse (or blessing); one by one they disappear into America, to define themselves for themselves." In "Five Prefaces" Oates explains the meaning of this ending: "Our past may weigh heavily upon us but it cannot contain us, let alone shape our future. America is a tale still being told — in many voices—and nowhere near its conclusion."

> This principle, in any case, we must hold if we are to survive as writers, deluded or otherwise: even when all evidence is to the contrary, *we are steadily improving; whatever we are working on at the present time is the best thing we have ever done, and the next book will be even better.* In this sense all writers are quintessentially American—we fear that not to progress is to plunge into the abyss. And we may be right.

Since 1963, when Oates published her first volume, *By the North Gate,* a book of short stories, she has published over seventy volumes of plays, poetry, novels, short stories, and literary and cultural commentary. She has also written screenplays, including one for *You Must Remember This.* She has speculated that none of this might have happened, if in 1961 she had not accidentally discovered her name on the Honor Roll in Martha Foley's *Best American Short Stories.* In that same year, on 23 January, she married Raymond J. Smith, Jr., whom she met at the University of Wisconsin, where she earned her M.A. and he his Ph.D., both in English. Before going to Wisconsin, Oates attended Syracuse University on a scholarship, graduating as class valedictorian and Phi Beta Kappa in 1960. An undergraduate professor of creative writing, Donald A. Dike, to whom her first novel, *With Shuddering Fall* (1964), is dedicated, reports that "about once a term she'd drop a 400-page novel on my desk." She was living in Texas, where Smith had his first academic job, and pursuing a doctorate at Rice University when she saw her story "The Fine White Mist of Winter" on Foley's list. As a result of this encouragement, she dropped her doctoral work and determined to be a writer.

She has been crowned with many literary awards since that first honorable mention. In 1967 she won first place in the O. Henry Prize competition for her story "The Region of Ice." The Guggenheim Foundation, National Academy and Institute of Arts and Letters, of which she is a member, and Lotos Club have honored her. In 1970 Oates won the National Book Award for *them,* a novel in which she herself is a character, an English professor at the University of Detroit (where Oates actually taught from 1961 to 1967) to whom the novel's protagonist, Maureen Wendall, her student, writes. In 1968 she went to the University of Windsor in Ontario, where she taught until she was appointed writer-in-residence at Princeton University in 1978. Since 1986 she has held the Roger S. Berlind Distinguished Professor in the Humanities chair at Princeton. Like Virginia and Leonard Woolf, she and Raymond J. Smith have their own press. In 1989 they celebrated the fifteenth anniversary of the Ontario Review Press, which publishes the distinguished journal the *Ontario Review: A North American Journal of the Arts* and a wide variety of poetry, fiction, and literary criticism.

The landscapes and modes of life Oates has treated are as diverse as the formal strategies she has employed in drawing them. She has ranged over rural, urban, and suburban America in the twentieth century as well as the nineteenth. She has taken on farming, migrant workers, law, science, terrorism, Pentecostal preachers, women's friendship, marriage, academia, cults, politics, race drivers, the occult, adolescence, and patriarchal institutions. In addition to narratives in the modes of realism and post-modernism, she has ventured into the detective genre, the gothic, and the thriller. Her carefully detailed settings often define decades, such as the 1930s in *A Garden of Earthly Delights,* the 1940s in *Wonderland,* the 1950s in *You Must Remember This,* the 1960s in *Do with Me What You Will, Wonderland,* and *Because It Is Bitter, and Because It Is My Heart* (1990), the 1970s in *The Assassins* and *Son of the Morning,* and the 1980s in *American Appetites.*

She is not one writer. She is two. Literally. In 1987 she initiated a series of thrillers under the pseudonym Rosamond Smith. This pseudonym is a feminine version of her husband's name, Raymond Smith, thus cleverly designed to iterate the series' theme of "twins" and "the double." The first three in the series, entitled *Lives of the Twins* (1987), *Soul/Mate* (1989), and *Nemesis* (1990), she explains, use the "thriller" genre as a prismatic lens to look at masculine institutions and explore feminist issues. The formal challenge, she asserts, is to make the narrative progress linearly, impel the plot ever forward, without "layering the prose" as she does in narratives signed "Oates."

In "My Friend, Joyce Carol Oates," Elaine Showalter writes: "She is most decidedly not like other people. In the midst of a quite ordinary conversation about the news or television or the family, Oates often inserts remarks whose philosophical penetration makes the rest of us feel like amoebas in the company of a more highly evolved life form." If some of her contemporaries object to her daring range of subjects and enormous productivity, these same qualities, added to her important narrative innovations and consistent brilliance, give the rest of us a new measure of genius.

Selected Bibliography

PRIMARY WORKS

NOVELS

With Shuddering Fall. New York: Vanguard Press, 1964.

A Garden of Earthly Delights. New York: Vanguard Press, 1967.

Expensive People. New York: Vanguard Press, 1968.

them. New York: Vanguard Press, 1969.

Wonderland. New York: Vanguard Press, 1971.

Do with Me What You Will. New York: Vanguard Press, 1973.

The Assassins: A Book of Hours. New York: Vanguard Press, 1975.

Childwold. New York: Vanguard Press, 1976.

Son of the Morning. New York: Vanguard Press, 1978.

Unholy Loves. New York: Vanguard Press, 1979.

Cybele. Santa Barbara: Black Sparrow Press, 1979.

Bellefleur. New York: E. P. Dutton, 1980.

Angel of Light. New York: E. P. Dutton, 1981.

A Bloodsmoor Romance. New York: E. P. Dutton, 1982.

Mysteries of Winterthurn. New York: E. P. Dutton, 1984.

Solstice. New York: E. P. Dutton, 1985.

Marya: A Life. New York: E. P. Dutton, 1986.

Lives of the Twins (as Rosamond Smith). New York: Simon & Schuster, 1987.

You Must Remember This. New York: E. P. Dutton, 1987.

American Appetites. New York: E. P. Dutton, 1989.

Soul/Mate (as Rosamond Smith). New York: E. P. Dutton, 1989.

In the Desert. New York: E. P. Dutton, 1990.

Because It Is Bitter, and Because It Is My Heart. New York: E. P. Dutton, 1990.

Nemesis (as Rosamond Smith). New York: E. P. Dutton, 1990

SHORT STORIES

By the North Gate. New York: Vanguard Press, 1963.

Upon the Sweeping Flood and Other Stories. New York: Vanguard Press, 1966.

Cupid and Psyche: A Short Story. New York: Albondocani Press, 1970. Reprinted as "The Dreaming Woman" in *The Seduction and Other Stories.*

The Wheel of Love and Other Stories. New York: Vanguard Press, 1970.

Marriages and Infidelities. New York: Vanguard Press, 1972.

The Girl. Cambridge, Mass.: Pomegranate Press, 1974. Reprinted in *The Goddess and Other Women.*

The Goddess and Other Women. New York: Vanguard Press, 1974.

The Hungry Ghosts: Seven Allusive Comedies. Los Angeles: Black Sparrow Press, 1974.

Where Are You Going, Where Have You Been? Stories of Young America. Greenwich, Conn.: Fawcett, 1974.

The Poisoned Kiss and Other Stories from the Portuguese (as Fernandes/Joyce Carol Oates). New York: Vanguard Press, 1975.

The Seduction and Other Stories. Los Angeles: Black Sparrow Press, 1975.

Crossing the Border: Fifteen Tales. New York: Vanguard Press, 1976.

The Triumph of the Spider Monkey. Santa Barbara: Black Sparrow Press, 1976.

Daisy. Santa Barbara: Black Sparrow Press, 1977.

Night-Side: Eighteen Tales. New York: Vanguard Press, 1977.

All the Good People I've Left Behind. Santa Barbara: Black Sparrow Press, 1979.

The Step-Father. Northridge, Calif.: Lord John, 1979.

Queen of the Night. Northridge, Calif.: Lord John, 1979. Reprinted in *A Sentimental Education.*

The Lamb of Abyssalia. Cambridge, Mass.: Pomegranate Press, 1979. Reprinted in *Last Days.*

Night Walks: A Bedside Companion. Princeton, N.J.: Ontario Review Press, 1982.

A Sentimental Education. New York: E. P. Dutton, 1980.

Last Days. New York: E. P. Dutton, 1984.

Wild Saturdays and Other Stories. London: Dent, 1984.

Raven's Wing. New York: E. P. Dutton, 1987.

The Assignation: Stories. New York: Ecco Press, 1988.

POETRY

Women in Love and Other Poems. New York: Albondocani Press, 1968.

Anonymous Sins and Other Poems. Baton Rouge: Louisiana State University Press, 1969.

Love and Its Derangements. Baton Rouge: Louisiana State University Press, 1970.

Wooded Forms. New York: Albondocani Press, 1972. Reprinted in *The Fabulous Beasts.*

Angel Fire. Baton Rouge: Louisiana State University Press, 1973.

Dreaming America and Other Poems. New York: Aloe Editions, 1973.

A Posthumous Sketch. Los Angeles: Black Sparrow Press, 1973. Reprinted in *The Fabulous Beasts.*

The Fabulous Beasts. Baton Rouge: Louisiana State University Press, 1975.

Women Whose Lives Are Food, Men Whose Lives Are Money. Baton Rouge: Louisiana State University Press, 1978.

Celestial Timepiece: Poems. Dallas: Pressworks, 1980.

Nightless Nights: Nine Poems. Concord, N.H.: Ewert, 1981.

Invisible Woman: New and Selected Poems, 1970–1982. Princeton, N.J.: Ontario Review Press, 1982.

The Time Traveler. New York: E. P. Dutton, 1989.

PLAYS

Three Plays. Princeton, N.J.: Ontario Review Press, 1980. Includes *Ontological Proof of My Existence, Miracle Play*, and *The Triumph of the Spider Monkey*.

LITERARY CRITICISM AND COMMENTARY

The Edge of Impossibility: Tragic Forms in Literature. New York: Vanguard Press, 1972.

The Hostile Sun: The Poetry of D. H. Lawrence. Los Angeles: Black Sparrow Press, 1973.

New Heaven, New Earth: The Visionary Experience in Literature. New York: Vanguard Press, 1974.

"On Editing the *Ontario Review*." In *The Art of Literary Publishing: Editors on their Craft*. Edited by Bill Henderson. Wainscott, N.Y.: Pushcart Press, 1980. Pp. 142–150. Written with Raymond Smith.

Contraries: Essays. New York: Oxford University Press, 1981.

"Why Is Your Writing So Violent?" *New York Times Book Review*, 29 March 1981, p. 15.

Contraries: Essays. New York: Oxford University Press, 1981.

The Profane Art: Essays and Reviews. New York: E. P. Dutton, 1983.

"Romance and Anti-Romance: From Brontë's *Jane Eyre* to Rhys's *Wide Sargasso Sea*." *Virginia Quarterly Review* 61:44–58 (1985).

On Boxing. Garden City, N.Y.: Doubleday, 1988.

(Woman) Writer: Occasions and Opportunities. New York: E. P. Dutton, 1988.

Reading the Fights. New York: Henry Holt, 1988. Written with Daniel Halpern.

"My Father, My Fiction." *New York Times Magazine*, 19 March 1989, p. 84.

AS EDITOR

The Best American Short Stories. Boston: Houghton Mifflin, 1979.

First Person Singular: Writers on Their Craft. Princeton, N.J.: Ontario Review Press, 1983.

SECONDARY WORKS

BIOGRAPHICAL AND CRITICAL STUDIES

Allen, Mary I. "The Terrified Women of Joyce Carol Oates." In her *The Necessary Blankness: Women in Major American Fiction of the Sixties*. Urbana: University of Illinois Press, 1976. Pp. 133–159.

Anderson, Sally. "The Poetry of Joyce Carol Oates." *Spirit* 39:22–29 (Fall 1972).

Avant, John Alfred. "An Interview with Joyce Carol Oates." *Library Journal*, 15 November 1972, pp. 3711–3712.

Barza, Steven. "Joyce Carol Oates: Naturalism and the Aberrant Response." *Studies in American Fiction* 7:141–151 (1979).

Bender, Eileen T. "Autonomy and Influence: Joyce Carol Oates's *Marriages and Infidelities*." *Soundings* 58:390–406 (Fall 1975).

———. " 'Paedomorphic' Art: Joyce Carol Oates's *Childwold*." In *Critical Essays on Joyce Carol Oates*. Edited by Linda W. Wagner. Boston: G. K. Hall, 1979. Pp. 117–122.

———. "Between the Categories: Recent Short Fiction by Joyce Carol Oates." *Studies in Short Fiction* 17:415–423 (1980).

———. "The Woman Who Came to Dinner: Dining and Divining a Feminist 'Aesthetic.' " *Women's Studies* 12:315–333 (1986).

———. *Artist in Residence: The Phenomenon of Joyce Carol Oates*. Bloomington: Indiana University Press, 1987.

Bloom, Harold, ed. *Joyce Carol Oates: Modern Critical Views*. Edgemont, Pa.: Chelsea House, 1986.

Brown, Russell M. "Crossing Borders." *Essays in Canadian Writing* 22:154–168 (Summer 1981).

Burwell, Rose Marie. "Joyce Carol Oates and an Old Master." *Critique* 15:48–58 (1973).

———. "The Process of Individuation as Narrative Structure: Joyce Carol Oates's 'Do with Me What You Will.' " *Critique* 17:93–106 (December 1975).

———. "Joyce Carol Oates's First Novel." *Canadian Literature* 73:54–57 (Summer 1977).

———. "*Wonderland*: Paradigm of the Psychohistorical Mode." *Mosaic* 14:1–16 (Summer 1981).

Chell, Cara. "Un-Tricking the Eye: Joyce Carol Oates and the Feminist Ghost Story." *Arizona Quarterly* 41:5–23 (Spring 1985).

Clemons, Walter. "Love and Violence: A Vision of America." *Newsweek*, 11 December 1972.

Coale, Samuel C. "Marriage in Contemporary American Literature: The Mismatched Marriages of Manichean Minds." *Thought: A Review of Culture and Ideas* 58:11–21 (March 1983).

Creighton, Joanne V. "Unliberated Women in Joyce Carol Oates's Fiction." *World Literature Written in English* 17:165–75 (April 1978).

———. "Joyce Carol Oates's Craftsmanship in *The Wheel of Fortune.*" *Studies in Short Fiction* 15:375–384 (Fall 1978).

———. *Joyce Carol Oates.* Boston: Twayne, 1979.

Cunningham, Frank R. "Joyce Carol Oates: The Enclosure of Identity in the Earlier Stories." In *American Women Writing Fiction: Memory, Identity, Family, Space.* Edited by Mickey Pearlman. Lexington: University Press of Kentucky, 1989. Pp. 9–28.

Dalton, Elizabeth. "Joyce Carol Oates: Violence in the Head." *Commentary* 49:75 (June 1970).

Darrach, Brad. "Consumed by a Piranha Complex." *Life,* 11 December 1970, p. 18.

Davenport, Guy. "C'est Magnifique, Mais Ce N'est Pas Daguerre." *Hudson Review* 23:154 (Spring 1970).

Dean, S. L. "Faith and Art: Joyce Carol Oates's *Son of the Morning.*" *Critique* 28:135–147 (Spring 1987).

DeCurtis, Anthony. "The Process of Fictionalization in Joyce Carol Oates's *them.*" *International Fiction Review* 6:121–128 (1979).

Dike, Donald A. "The Aggressive Victim in the Fiction of Joyce Carol Oates." *Greyfriar* 15:13–29 (1974).

Ditsky, John. "The Man on the Quaker Oates Box: Characteristics of Recent Experimental Fiction." *Georgia Review* 26:297–313 (Fall 1972).

Early, Gerald. "The Grace of Slaughter: A Review-Essay of Joyce Carol Oates's *On Boxing.*" *Iowa Review* 18:173–186 (Fall 1988).

Fossum, Robert H. "Only Control: The Novels of Joyce Carol Oates." *Studies in the Novel* 7:285–297 (Summer 1975).

Franks, Lucinda. "The Emergence of Joyce Carol Oates." *New York Times Magazine,* 27 June 1980.

Friedman, Ellen G. "The Journey from the 'I' to the 'Eye': Joyce Carol Oates's *Wonderland.*" *Studies in American Fiction* 8:37–50 (1980).

———. *Joyce Carol Oates.* New York: Frederick Ungar, 1980.

Friedman, Ellen G., and Miriam Fuchs, eds. *Breaking the Sequence: Women's Experimental Fiction.* Princeton, N.J.: Princeton University Press, 1989.

Giles, James R. "The 'Marivaudian Being' Drowns His Children: Dehumanization in Donald Barthelme's 'Robert Kennedy Saved from Drowning' and Joyce Carol Oates's *Wonderland.*" *Southern Humanities Review* 9:63–75 (Winter 1975).

———. "Suffering, Transcendence and Artistic 'Form': Joyce Carol Oates's *them.*" *Arizona Quarterly* 32:213–226 (Autumn 1976).

———. "From Jimmy Gatz to Jules Wendall: A Study of 'Nothing Substantial.' " *Dalhousie Review* 56:718–724 (Winter 1976–1977).

———. "Destructive and Redemptive Order: Joyce Carol Oates's *Marriages and Infidelities* and *The Goddess and Other Women.*" *Ball State University Forum* 22:58–70 (1981).

Godwin, Gail. "An Oates Scrapbook." *North American Review* 256:67–70 (Winter 1971–1972).

Goodman, Charlotte. "Women and Madness in the Fiction of Joyce Carol Oates." *Women and Literature* 5:17–28 (1977).

———. "The Lost Brother, the Twin: Women Novelists and the Male-Female Double Bildungsroman." *Novel: A Forum on Fiction* 17:28–43 (Fall 1983).

Grant, Mary Kathryn. *The Tragic Vision of Joyce Carol Oates.* Durham, N.C.: Duke University Press, 1978.

———. "The Language of Tragedy and Violence." In *Critical Essays on Joyce Carol Oates.* Edited by Linda W. Wagner. Boston: G. K. Hall, 1979. Pp. 61–76.

Higdon, David Leon. " 'Suitable Conclusion': The Two Endings of Oates's *Wonderland.*" *Studies in the Novel* 10:447–453 (1978).

Johnson, Gregg. *Understanding Joyce Carol Oates.* Columbia, S.C.: University of South Carolina Press, 1987.

Karl, Frederick P. *American Fictions, 1940–1980.* New York: Harper & Row, 1983. Pp. 420–422, 546–549.

Kazin, Alfred. *Bright Book of Life: Storytellers from Hemingway to Mailer.* Boston: Little, Brown, 1974.

Keyser, Elizabeth. "*A Bloodsmoor Romance:* Joyce Carol Oates's *Little Women.*" *Women's Studies: An Interdisciplinary Journal* 14:211–223 (1988).

Kuehl, Linda. "An Interview with Joyce Carol Oates." *Commonweal* 91:307–310 (5 December 1969).

Liston, William T. "Her Brother's Keeper." *Southern Humanities Review* 11:195–203 (Spring 1977).

Madden, David. "The Violent World of Joyce Carol Oates." In his *The Poetic Image in Six Genres.* Carbondale: Southern Illinois University Press, 1969. Pp. 26–46.

———. "Upon the Sweeping Flood." In *Critical Essays on Joyce Carol Oates.* Edited by Linda W. Wagner. Boston: G. K. Hall, 1979. Pp. 6–10.

Martin, Carol A. "Art and Myth in Joyce Carol Oates's *The Sacred Marriage.*" *Midwest Quarterly* 28:540–542 (Summer 1987).

Milazzo, Lee, ed. *Conversations with Joyce Carol Oates.* Jackson: University of Mississippi Press, 1989.

Nodelman, Perry. "The Sense of Unending: Joyce Carol Oates's *Bellefleur* as an Experiment in Feminine Storytelling." In *Breaking the Sequence: Women's Experimental Fiction.* Edited by Ellen G. Friedman and Miriam Fuchs. Princeton, N.J.: Princeton University Press, 1989. Pp. 250–264.

Norman, Torborg. *Isolation and Contact: A Study of Character Relationships in Joyce Carol Oates's Short Stories, 1963–1980.* Sweden: University of Göteborg, 1984.

Park, Sue S. "A Study in Counterpoint: Joyce Carol Oates's 'How I Contemplated the World from the Detroit House of Correction and Began My Life Over Again.' " *Modern Fiction Studies* 22:213–224 (Summer 1976).

Petite, Joseph. "The Marriage Cycle of Joyce Carol Oates." *Journal of Evolutionary Psychology* 5:223–236 (August 1984).

Phillips, Robert. "Joyce Carol Oates: The Art of Fiction LXXII." *Paris Review* 20:199–226 (Fall–Winter 1979).

Pickering, Samuel F., Jr. "The Short Stories of Joyce Carol Oates." *Georgia Review* 28:218–226 (Summer 1974).

Pinsker, Sanford. "Isaac Bashevis Singer and Joyce Carol Oates: Some Versions of Gothic." *Southern Review* 9:895–908 (Autumn 1973).

———. "Suburban Molesters: Joyce Carol Oates's *Expensive People.*" *Midwest Quarterly* 19:89–103 (Autumn 1977).

———. "Joyce Carol Oates's *Wonderland:* A Hungering for Personality." *Critique* 20:59–70 (1978).

———. "Joyce Carol Oates and the New Naturalism." *Southern Review* 15:52–63 (1979).

———. "The Blue Collar Apocalypse or Detroit Bridge's Falling Down: Joyce Carol Oates's *them.*" *Descant* 23:35–47 (1979).

Prescott, Peter S. "Everyday Monsters." *Newsweek,* 11 October 1971, p. 96.

Redmon, Anne. "Vision and Risk: New Fiction by Oates and Ozick." *Michigan Quarterly Review* 2:203–213 (Winter 1988).

Schulz, Gretchen, and R. J. R. Rockwood. "In Fairyland, Without a May: Connie's Exploration Inward in Joyce Carol Oates's 'Where Are You Going, Where Have You Been?' " *Literature and Psychology* 30:155–167 (1980).

Showalter, Elaine. "My Friend Joyce Carol Oates: An Intimate Portrait." *Ms.,* March 1986, pp. 44–46.

——— "Joyce Carol Oates's 'The Dead' and Feminist Criticism." In *Faith of a (Woman) Writer.* Edited by Alice Kessler-Harris and William McBrien. Westport, Conn.: Greenwood Press, 1988. Pp. 13–19.

Sjoberg, Leif. "An Interview with Joyce Carol Oates." *Contemporary Literature* 23:267–284 (Summer 1982).

Stegner, Page. "Stone, Berry, Oates—and Other Grist from the Mill." *Southern Review* 5:273–301 (January 1969).

Stevens, Peter. "The Poetry of Joyce Carol Oates." In *Critical Essays on Joyce Carol Oates.* Edited by Linda W. Wagner. Boston: G. K. Hall, 1979. Pp. 123–147.

Stout, Janis P. "Catatonia and Femininity in Oates's *Do with Me What You Will.*" *International Journal of Women's Studies* 6:208–215 (May–June 1983).

Strandberg, Victor. "Sex, Violence, and Philosophy in *You Must Remember This.*" *Studies in American Fiction* 17:3–17 (Spring 1989).

Sullivan, Walter. "Where Have All the Flowers Gone? The Short Story in Search of Itself." *Sewanee Review* 78:531–542 (Summer 1970).

———. "The Artificial Demon: Joyce Carol Oates and the Dimensions of the Real." *Hollins Critic* 9, no. 4:1–12 (December 1972).

———. "Old Age, Death, and Other Modern Landscapes: Good and Indifferent Fables for Our Time." *Sewanee Review* 82:138–147 (1974).

Taylor, Gordon O. "Joyce Carol Oates: Artist in Wonderland." *Southern Review* 10:490–503 (1974).

———. "Joyce 'After' Joyce: Oates's 'The Dead.' " *Southern Review* 19:596–605 (Summer 1983).

Trachtenberg, Stanley. "Desire, Hypocrisy, and Ambition in Academe: Joyce Carol Oates's *Hungry Ghosts.*" In *The American Writer and the University.* Edited by Ben Siegel. Newark: University of Delaware Press, 1989. Pp. 39–53.

Updike, John. "What You Deserve Is What You Get." *New Yorker,* December 1987, pp. 119–123.

Uphaus, Suzanne Henning. "Boundaries: Both Physical and Metaphysical." *Canadian Review of American Studies* 8:236–242 (Fall 1977).

Wagner, Linda W. "Oates: The Changing Shapes of Her Realities." *Great Lakes Review: A Journal of Midwest Culture* 5:15–23 (1979).

———, ed. *Critical Essays on Joyce Carol Oates*. Boston: G. K. Hall, 1979.

———. "Oates's *Cybele*." *Notes on Contemporary Literature* 11:2–8 (November 1981).

Walker, Carolyn. "Fear, Love, and Art in Oates's 'Plot.' " *Critique: Studies in Modern Fiction* 15:59–70 (1973).

Wegs, Joyce M. "Don't You Know Who I Am? The Grotesque in Oates's 'Where Are You Going, Where Have You Been?' " *Journal of Narrative Technique* 5:64–72 (January 1975).

Weinberger, G. J. "Who Is Arnold Friend? The Other Self in Joyce Carol Oates's 'Where Are You Going, Where Have You Been?' " *American Image: A Psychoanalytic Journal for Culture, Science, and the Arts* 45:205–215 (Summer 1988).

Zapf, Hubert. "Aesthetic Experience and Ideological Critique in Joyce Carol Oates's 'Master Race.' " *International Fiction Review* 16:48–55 (Winter 1989).

BIBLIOGRAPHIES

Hiemstra, Anne. "A Bibliography of Writings About Joyce Carol Oates." In *American Women Writing Fiction: Memory, Identity, Family, Space*. Edited by Mickey Pearlman. Lexington: University Press of Kentucky, 1989. Pp. 35–44.

———. "A Bibliography of Writings by Joyce Carol Oates." In *American Women Writing Fiction: Memory, Identity, Family, Space*. Edited by Mickey Pearlman. Lexington: University Press of Kentucky, 1989. Pp. 28–35.

ELLEN G. FRIEDMAN

FLANNERY O'CONNOR

1925–1964

At the beginning of *Wise Blood,* Flannery O'Connor's first novel, the hero is in a paroxysm of mental activity. Hazel Motes looks out the window, then down the aisle of a passenger train as it makes its way through a landscape packed with apocalypse. The sun stands on the edge of the story's canvas, "very red"; it threatens to enter Hazel's world with undisciplined energy. Facing Hazel is an energy that is at once more disciplined and more threatening: O'Connor's quintessential Southern lady, Mrs. Wally Bee Hitchcock.

Like all of O'Connor's middle-class Southern women, Mrs. Hitchcock talks in a voice that is cliché-ridden and sweet as honey. Attempting to evoke a stream of pleasantries, she comments that early evenings are the prettiest times of day and asks Hazel if he doesn't agree. Her manners are impeccable, but as always in an O'Connor story, something is slightly askew. As night descends, the passengers find themselves in a diseased landscape that contains "a few hogs nosing in the furrows," looking "like large spotted stones." Although Mrs. Wally Bee Hitchcock ignores this pimpling of the landscape, O'Connor makes certain that her readers note Mrs. Hitchcock's own scenic oddities: "She was a fat woman with pink collars and cuffs and pear-shaped legs that slanted off the train seat and didn't reach the floor."

As Hazel continues to dart his eyes here and there, Mrs. Hitchcock tries to draw him into her banal Southern world: "I guess you're going home," she says in her best conversational voice. But home is a peculiar place in any O'Connor story. When Hazel refuses to answer, or even move his eyes in Mrs. Hitchcock's pink-cuffed direction, she begins to look him up and down. Although not much over twenty, Hazel seems dislocated and bereft; his broad-brimmed hat is rigid as a country preacher's, and his suit—a "glaring blue"—has the price tag still stapled to its sleeve. Unable to connect with the youth, Mrs. Hitchcock concocts her own story from these details. She decides that Hazel is coming home from the army, and she tries to get a glimpse of the price tag to confirm her sense of Hazel's low origin. Seeing that the suit cost $11.98, she decides, triumphantly, "that that placed him."

Mrs. Hitchcock is just the kind of class-obsessed Southern matriarch that Flannery O'Connor loves to parody. Although some of O'Connor's characters share their author's delight in grotesque narrative as they speak gleefully about tubal pregnancies or plot the macabre details of their own burials, O'Connor's middle-class storytellers all tell the same hackneyed tale: they are preoccupied with the rules for separating and sanctioning the divisions between the South's races, genders, and classes.

In "Revelation," one of O'Connor's final short stories, we meet a grander version of Mrs. Wally Bee Hitchcock. Mrs. Turpin is a large, garrulous woman whose "little bright black eyes" size up the class position of everyone in view. Once again O'Connor invents a backdrop for her story that hints at disease and despair. "Revelation" is set in a doctor's waiting room where ulcerated legs, runny noses, and acne-covered faces are the rule, where plastic ferns do nothing to mask ashtrays filled with bloody cotton wads. Everyone in the doctor's office, even the blond-haired nurse, has exaggerated physical characteristics. The people in this universe are quaint monstrosities; their bodies move like machines, their souls are sluggish as animals.

In "Revelation," O'Connor goes farther than she did in *Wise Blood.* She includes a character who reflects her own passions and biases—a character who stands in for O'Connor herself. While Mrs. Turpin is busy sorting out "the classes of people"—with "the coloreds" on the bottom, "the white-trash" next, followed by the home-owners, and then home- and land-owners, "to which she and Claud belonged"—someone questions the verticality of Mrs. Turpin's placid world view. The perpetrator is Mary Grace, a Southern girl gone North and gone bad, a college student from Wellesley who discovers Mrs. Turpin's hypocrisy at a glance. As Mrs. Turpin exchanges platitudes about cleanliness and godliness with her companions, Mary Grace turns her lower lip inside out and glares at Mrs. Turpin with eyes "fixed like two drills." When Mrs. Turpin continues her self-satisfied commonplaces, finally calling out a "thank you" to Jesus for giving her a meek husband and a passel of property, Mary Grace loses control; she throws a book that hits Mrs. Turpin squarely over the left eye—a blow followed by the shock of greeting Mary Grace's raw face and howling body as the girl's fingers sink into Mrs. Turpin's neck.

Typically for an O'Connor story, this violence becomes the precursor of spiritual grace: "Revelation" is the story of Mrs. Turpin's reformation. Before the wounded matriarch can catch her breath and imagine herself as high-brow victim, she is drawn once again toward the "churning face" of the Wellesley student, who has been wrestled to the floor. "Go back to hell where you came from, you old wart hog," Mary Graces hisses. Her curse becomes Mrs. Turpin's undoing. As Mrs. Turpin's neck throbs from the "little moon-shaped lines" that Mary Grace has left with her fingers, she decides to take this insult seriously; at home in her pig parlor, Mrs. Turpin contemplates her selfish ways. Caught by the crimson rays of the setting sun, she raises her hands in a priestly gesture; she is struck by a dusky hallucination, a fiery vision in which the lowest members of the social hierarchy—"whole companies of white-trash, clean for the first time in their lives, and bands of black niggers in white robes, and battalions of freaks and lunatics"—enter heaven first, while the rich stumble toward perdition, devoid of the armor of respectability as "even their virtues" are "burned away."

While the story turns from Mary Grace's vengeance to its effects on Mrs. Turpin, we can expand our vision of Flannery O'Connor herself by returning to the scene on the floor, where Mary Grace is restrained and medicated. Like O'Connor, Mary Grace is a kind of author: by using her book as a weapon, she authorizes changes in Mrs. Turpin's temperament and body. Her words, like O'Connor's, have a mysterious effect, for Mary Grace is a character at odds with her society—a destroyer and avenger who, like O'Connor, writes a drastic fiction upon Mrs. Turpin's body.

Mary Grace also resembles O'Connor in her bizarre aggressivity. In one of her letters, O'Connor tells an amusing story about herself as a child—a story in which she jousted with angels. She begins this anecdote by noting that while her relations with nuns and priests improved over time, in childhood these relationships were more tempestuous. O'Connor went to a religious school for her early education. At the sisters' hands, she says, "I developed something the Freudians have not named—anti-angel aggression, call it." Between the ages of eight and twelve, O'Connor liked to seclude herself in a locked room

> and with a fierce (and evil) face, whirl around in a circle with my fists knotted, socking the angel. This was the guardian angel with which the Sisters assured us we were all equipped. My dislike of him was poisonous. I'm sure I even kicked at him and landed on the floor. You couldn't hurt an angel but I would have been happy to know I had dirtied his feathers—I conceived of him in feathers.
>
> (*The Habit of Being,* pp. 131–132)

When Mrs. Turpin imagines herself as a benign and angelic gift to the world, Mary Grace launches her attack, much as the young O'Connor boxed with her angel. What Mary Flannery O'Connor and Mary Grace share, in addition to a first name, is a fierce intolerance of hypocrisy and a violent response to paternalism, although for O'Connor as a mature writer this violence takes the form of extraordinary stories meant to have moral impact, to work upon their readers with the same striking design as Mary Grace's physical attack upon Mrs. Turpin.

There is also a more poignant way in which Mary Grace's plight resembles O'Connor's own. In "Revelation," when the college-educated Mary Grace is condemned for her violence, she is not only wrestled to the floor but medicated: held down by the nurse and her mother while a doctor, "kneeling astride her," sinks a long needle into her arm. As she passes out, her anger impotent and cool, Mary Grace's fingers grip her mother's thumb like a baby's. O'Connor herself was the object of a great deal of painful medical attention in the last decade and a half of her life. In the winter of 1950, when she was twenty-five, she came down with disseminated lupus erythematosus, a debilitating and painful autoimmune disease in which the body's defense mechanisms attack the body itself and gradually destroy it from within. Although lupus affects people at different rates, it is a disease that can leave the body in relative peace for long periods, only to attack again fiercely when least expected. O'Connor was familiar with these symptoms, since lupus had killed her father in 1941. The first stages of her own disease were so life-threatening that she required months of extraordinary medical attention before she recovered a portion of her former strength. As she recovered, O'Connor needed daily inoculations of cortisone, which she learned to administer herself. She met the severity of this disease with good cheer and great dignity. Nevertheless, lupus changed her life, and she was forced to spend the rest of her days in her mother's care.

If Mary Grace responds to her medication by wrapping her fingers around her mother's thumb like a baby, O'Connor refused to be so infantilized. She continued to see friends and correspond with them; she arranged her life around her craft—demanding several undisturbed hours for writing every morning. She then accompanied her mother, weather and health permitting, to a formal luncheon at the Sanford House, an elegant restaurant in Milledgeville, Georgia. During the years of her greatest productivity, Flannery's dependence on Regina O'Connor's strength, affection, and organizational skill was absolute. She confided to friends that her only fear, as an adult, was that her mother would die first: "I don't know what I would do without her."

In this affectionate and complex life with her mother, O'Connor's home life was a far cry from the stormy grief of the adolescent Mary Grace. But Mary Grace does capture some of O'Connor's ambivalence about her role as good Southern daughter. Nodding in Mary Grace's direction, Mrs. Turpin and Mary Grace's mother talk about how unpleasant it is to spend time in the company of people with bad dispositions. As Mrs. Turpin begins to chortle about her own good disposition, the daughter makes "a loud, ugly noise through her teeth." Like O'Connor, Mary Grace ventilates her dissatisfaction orally. She hates being the object of conversation and registers her response on her face: "The girl looked as if she would like to hurl them all through the plate glass window." Similarly, O'Connor often arranges violent fates for her characters—especially when these characters are mothers or matriarchs.

What the vexed relation of mother to daughter in "Revelation" also evokes is the fact that Flannery and Regina O'Connor, like Mary Grace and her mother, lived in different mental and emotional worlds. This difference could be trying for both of them. "Regina is getting very literary," O'Connor writes to Sally and Robert Fitzgerald. " 'Who is this Kafka?' she says. 'People ask me.' A German Jew, I says. . . . He wrote a book about a man that turns into a roach. 'Well, I can't tell people *that*,' she says. 'Who is this Evalin Wow?' "

Flannery O'Connor was erudite and college educated; she was not only respected in the literary circles of her time but also well read—versed in philosophy and theology as well as in literature. Regina O'Connor's interests were closer to those of Mrs. Turpin. "Me and Maw are still at the farm and are like to be, I perceive, through the winter," O'Connor wrote to the Fitzgeralds. "She is nuts about it out here, surrounded by the lowing herd and other details, and considers it beneficial to my health." Regina O'Connor was a canny farmer and dairywoman; she was also a Southerner of the old school. Raised in a respected and well-to-do family that was deeply concerned with keeping property values and hierarchies in place, she observed Southern conventions and adhered to the traditional prejudices and etiquette of the white Southern elite. This meant that the pressures on Flannery, even as an invalid, to act the part of a polite Southern lady were immense. As she wrote to Robert Lowell about her mother's response to *Wise Blood:*

> Harcourt sent my book to Evelyn Waugh and his comment was: "If this is really the unaided work of a young lady, it is a remarkable product." My mother was vastly insulted. She put the emphasis on *if* and *lady*. Does he suppose you're not a lady? she says. WHO is he?
>
> (*The Habit of Being,* p. 35)

If O'Connor's adult life was punctuated with more grace and good humor than Mary Grace's, we should note that O'Connor also resembles Mary Grace in her relative affluence, her allotment of material comforts. Although O'Connor was not very worldly, and though her daily problems with her uncooperative body made the spaciousness of the house she inhabited less important, to understand O'Connor fully we must learn something about her heritage. Our most vivid images of this heritage come to us from a former Georgian who was excluded from O'Connor's world: the African American novelist Alice Walker.

In 1952 Flannery O'Connor and Alice Walker lived close to one another in Baldwin County, just minutes apart on the Eatonton-to-Milledgeville road. Their situations could not have been more dissimilar. Although Walker was eight years old and O'Connor twenty-eight, they were separated not so much by age as by differences in racial identity and economic situation. These dissimilarities made a short car ride into a very great distance indeed. By the time Walker reached college age, her family was long gone from O'Connor's neighborhood, but the distance between the two writers had become shorter. Walker read O'Connor indefatigably, and while she later felt ashamed of her passion (since O'Connor had displaced black women writers in her college curriculum), by 1974 Walker was interested, once again, in an integrated literature. In her travels to the South, she decided to visit and compare the two homesteads.

Returning to her family's old sharecropper shack, Walker discovers that even though the house has been abandoned and is rotting away, the yard is still covered with her mother's daffodils. Walker's memories of Baldwin County are bitter. Her school, shabby and segregated, had been the state prison. Its ghosts troubled the children; the second floor bore the marks of a frightening electric chair. Her only good memory is a vision of a faraway field: "It was like a painting by someone who loved tranquillity. In the foreground near the road the green field was used as pasture for black-and-white cows that never seemed to move."

This was Regina O'Connor's farmland, a field still filled with technicolor clover and picturesque cattle. As Alice Walker and her mother sit down in the Holiday Inn that is now across from Andalusia, the large white house where O'Connor and her mother lived, Walker notes that they are the only blacks there; twelve years earlier they would not have been served. They talk about O'Connor's famous collection of peacocks, and Walker's mother argues that peacocks are troublesome, flower-devouring birds.

The daughter defends O'Connor, insisting that she kept peacocks for their unearthly beauty; they are grander than anything man-made, and that is why "this lady liked them."

Here Walker pauses for breath. After rejecting the terms of white Southern culture, she is surprised to find herself using "lady" to describe O'Connor, "since the whole notion of ladyhood is repugnant to me." She imagines O'Connor at a party, making fastidious notes about the evening's absurdities, acting polite while being very bored: "Being white she would automatically have been eligible for ladyhood, but I cannot believe she would ever really have joined."

It is important to realize that, despite O'Connor's reservations about her own ladyhood, this was a status she attained automatically. The Milledgeville townhouse in which she lived as an adolescent had an old and venerable history. In 1820, when Milledgeville was still the capital of Georgia, this house was built to serve as the governor's mansion. In 1886, O'Connor's maternal grandfather, Peter Cline, purchased the grand brick mansion, thereafter known as the Cline House, and it was his home for the twenty-two years he served as mayor of Milledgeville.

Walker reminds us that the high status achieved by these white upper-class men was costly for others. The bricks of this house, and the walls they supported, were made by slave labor. The Cline House was built out of suffering; during O'Connor's lifetime it dominated the landscape in a community that ignored its own contributions to this suffering as best it could.

What was O'Connor's position on race? Although she was a resolute integrationist who recognized the plight of Southern blacks, O'Connor also accepted the most painful of Southern conventions. "No I can't see James Baldwin in Georgia," she wrote to Maryat Lee. "It would cause the greatest trouble and disturbance and disunion. In New York it would be nice to meet him; here it would not." Although O'Connor's stories are filled with disturbance and disunion, she was wary of the tempestuous racial politics of her time. Her letter to Maryat Lee was written in 1959, a time of extraordinary upheaval in the South. Three years earlier African Americans had refused to ride segregated buses in Montgomery, Alabama. Their boycott ended in triumph when the Supreme Court ordered city officials to desegregate. But despite this and other civil rights victories, the South of the 1950s and early 1960s was still ruled by Jim Crow. In 1960 the Greensboro, North Carolina, lunch counter sit-ins ignited a widespread protest movement among black students that had little impact on segregationists. Television networks blacked out the historic speech of the first black presidential staff member, E. Frederick Morrow, so as not to offend the South. In 1961 there were terrifying scenes of cruelty as both black and white Freedom Riders were viciously attacked by white mobs. O'Connor lived in a region that—despite its postwar sophistication, its growing urbanity—thrilled to racist violence and danger. The white Southerners of her era struggled to enforce sharp demarcations between genders, between classes, and, most brutally, between races.

Although O'Connor satirizes this world in her fiction, in public she would not take a stand. "I observe the traditions of the society I feed on—it's only fair," she insists in her letter to Maryat Lee. "Might as well expect a mule to fly as me to see James Baldwin in Georgia. I have read one of his stories and it was a good one."

Despite this uncomfortable side of O'Connor's character, Walker was right to suggest that "ladyhood" was not a status O'Connor embraced. The decision to abide by Southern customs in life did not mean an agreement to abide by them in her writing. O'Connor's fiction refuses to make the reader feel at home in its Southern world.

O'Connor does not share her region's dream of a glamorous Southern past. While Allen Tate insists that Southern literature is always respectfully conscious of the past's endurance in the present, O'Connor's characters are most at risk when they try to recapture the past, when they pay homage to faded plantation glories. In "Everything That Rises Must Converge," a mother and son idealize their family's lost wealth. The mother longs for the plantation house of her youth, its halls still redolent with antebellum fragrance. Her son, Julian, is equally tantalized by what now exists only as memory. He dreams about the old plantation and imagines that he is the only member of his family who can appreciate the "threadbare elegance" of a forgotten era. As the story progresses, the mother and son take on different personae. He is progressive, cynical, and well educated—an integrationist. She is threatened by nonsegregated buses and throws a fit on one of these buses when she sees a black woman wearing a purple-and-green hat just like her own. When she sentimentalizes this woman's son—teasing him in spite of his mother's best efforts to discipline her little boy—Julian's mother becomes the object of attack. She offers the little boy a penny, which the black mother rejects, knocking Julian's mother down in the process and insisting that her child does not take pennies from anyone. As Julian's mother lands on the sidewalk, dazed and weary, Julian rails at her for her racist insolence; then, as she toddles down the street, she has a stroke before his very eyes. The story ends with Julian swept away by currents of grief, on the verge of an unfathomed universe of guilt and sorrow.

In "Everything That Rises Must Converge" the past dominates the present through atavistic patterns of classist and racist superiority. Oddly, the character who seems the most liberal and future-oriented is actually the most backward-looking. Julian's noblesse oblige—his identification with the paternalism of his ancestors—does nothing to stop the prejudice around him; it only hastens the death of his mother. His dreams are dominated by the wide verandas, double stairways, and oak alleys of the antebellum mansion, and O'Connor finds the persistence of these Southern values fatal.

In "A Good Man Is Hard to Find," the dream of the plantation past evokes new fatalities. A grandmother yearns to take her family to see an antebellum mansion with eerie white columns and arbors made for trysts with gallant suitors. As she directs her family on a wild goose chase along abandoned country roads, her stowed-away cat escapes from a basket hidden under her seat, and the family car is wrecked. They are rescued by The Misfit, an escaped convict who speaks like a philosopher-king and has the family shot one by one. The last to go is the grandmother, who, in her crisis of death, speaks her first gentle words. "She was a talker, wasn't she?" says one of the convicts, as he slides down into the ditch "with a yodel." " 'She would of been a good woman,' The Misfit said, 'if it had been somebody there to shoot her every minute of her life.' "

Although this story suggests that only a presentist attitude will save us, O'Connor's vision of the Southern present is equally bleak. Her stories offer stark condemnations of modernity. In "The River," Harry is a boy of four or five who lives in an up-to-date family. His parents drink and smoke to excess; they can understand antiquities only in terms of their cash value. Little Harry is lost in this world. After he has gone down to the river with his fundamentalist sitter and has been baptized, it is too painful to come home to his parents' empty alcohol bottles and burned-out souls. So Harry, who has renamed himself "Bevel" after the baptizing preacher, decides to run away to the river, and there, as he tries to baptize himself again, he drowns.

These are not stories one expects from a demure Southern "lady." How do we account for the disturbing nature of O'Connor's vision? What drives her to write such violent, unsettling prose? If we are shocked by the savagery of her plot lines, O'Connor's relatives were shocked even more. "My uncle Louis [Cline] is always bringing me a message from somebody . . . who has read *Wise Blood*," she commented to the Fitzgeralds. "The last was: ask her why she don't write about some nice people." The Clines were respectable citizens, and all their friends were aghast when they read Flannery's books. One elderly lady asked how a girl from such an excellent background could have heard "all the ugly words wrote into her books—much less learn what they meant."

O'Connor wrote breathtaking prose. Mixed with the colorful twang and cruelty of the rural Georgia vernacular, which she could imitate to perfection, are sentences of overwhelming sophistication and beauty. Her prose plays back and forth between the high, erudite style of the biblical lyric, in which voice seems to emanate from the most visionary moments in the Psalms or the prophets, and a vernacular low style that is violent, arrogant, and unafraid of its own ugliness. The amalgam for these styles is the ironic, detached voice of the narrator, a voice that often erupts into comedy. This combination creates a harsh, absurd fiction of apocalyptic intent that is cleansed of all sentimentality.

Lacking a full-length biography of Flannery O'Connor, it is difficult to pinpoint the moments in her life that inspired this unladylike fiction. Our best sources for O'Connor's biography are memoirs by Sally and Robert Fitzgerald, and Lorine M. Getz's *Flannery O'Connor: Her Life, Library, and Book Reviews* (1980). From Getz and the Fitzgeralds we learn about the dignity and hardship of O'Connor's life and the ways in which she was a kind and loyal friend. We also discover that O'Connor had a marvelous sense of humor, even as a child. The sources of comedy in her fiction are easy to seek, but these sources tell us little about the dark, sadistic side of O'Connor's vision.

O'Connor was not a prankster, but she possessed an iconoclastic imagination and a flair for the unexpected. When she was five, she owned a pet bantam that could walk backward as well as forward. The chicken aroused local interest when it became the subject of Pathé newsreel. An interest became an obsession: O'Connor writes that she had to have more chickens, and she favored fowl "with one green eye and one orange or with overlong necks and crooked combs. I wanted one with three legs or three wings but nothing in that line turned up."

In school, where surrealist chickens were not available, O'Connor turned her absurdist delight elsewhere. She brought tomatoes for her teacher in place of the usual apple and her third-grade teacher was nonplussed when, instead of copying down the exercise "throw the ball to Rover," O'Connor wrote "throw the ball to St. Cecilia." In high school O'Connor's idiosyncrasies became even more marked. Reserved and shy after moving to Milledgeville, she found herself at the center of the town's social whirl. She retired when she could from the spotlight, preferring the company of a pet chicken for whom, with her usual comic bent, she created a fashionable wardrobe.

If O'Connor's stories make us laugh with their twangy, irascible humor, they are also meant to uplift us with their Christian message. To understand the violence behind her fiction, we must grapple with the seriousness of her Roman Catholic faith.

Mary Flannery O'Connor was born on 25 March 1925 in Savannah, Georgia, a city known for its tolerance. Although Georgia's charter forbade the practice of Catholicism, in 1794 Savannah's leaders allowed white Catholic refugees fleeing from Toussaint L'Ouverture's insurrections in Haiti to settle there. Settlers also came from Maryland, and by 1820 the Savannah church was recognized as part of the Catholic see of Baltimore. Although prejudice against Catholics ran high in the South, O'Connor's family found a pleasant home in Savannah, and O'Connor lived there happily until she was thirteen.

Not only did O'Connor grow up in a flourishing city that welcomed Catholics, but her home fronted the Cathedral of St. John the Baptist, built in 1874. She attended parochial school, an experience she transforms in "A Temple of the Holy Ghost." In this story her earthy humor helps to revise the banalities of her faith; the twelve-year-old heroine wonders exactly what it means that her female body is "a Temple of the Holy Ghost." O'Connor gives the girl a peculiar answer: as the story ends, she is blessed by a hermaphrodite's sideshow prophecies rather than by the blundering affections of a "moon-faced" nun.

This story suggests both the orthodoxy and iconoclasm of O'Connor's Catholicism. The little girl in "A Temple of the Holy Ghost" is a bratty sophisticate who is fascinated by freaks but is stunned to learn from her friends that a hermaphrodite is both a man and a woman, just as she is frightened to hear them repeat the hermaphrodite's warning: "God made me thisaway and if you laugh He may strike you the same way." At mass, when "the priest raised the monstrance with the Host shining ivory-colored in the center," the girl suddenly thinks of the tent with the freak in it. The hermaphrodite's scary words dominate her thoughts; they announce the abyss of the sacred: "The freak was saying, 'I don't dispute hit. This is the way He wanted me to be.' " As the story ends, the little girl is transfixed. She looks out the car window and sees the sun as "a huge red ball like an elevated Host drenched in blood." The hermaphrodite beckons to unspeakable mysteries; O'Connor announces that these mysteries pervade the Christian soul and can bestow powers both transcendent and painful.

O'Connor's fiction often culminates in an elaborate vision that comes as a gift to the world from her most grotesque characters. For O'Connor, devout Catholicism and commitment to the grotesque go hand in hand. Drastic measures, as she explains in her posthumously collected essays, *Mystery and Manners* (1969), are necessary for today's Christian writers. The problem is to make modern perversions visible to a nonreligious audience accustomed to seeing perversions as "natural." To achieve this end, O'Connor became increasingly violent in depicting human oddities and transgressions. She argued that any writer who "believes that our life is and will remain essentially mysterious" must always push fiction "outward toward the limits of mystery." For O'Connor, a story's significance begins only when "adequate motivation . . . has been exhausted." The writer who challenges modernity will be interested in spiritual agony rather than in empiricism or enlightenment. This writer "will be interested in what we don't understand rather than in what we do. . . . His way will . . . be the way of distortion."

In pursuit of these spiritual goals, O'Connor twists her characters into stranger and stranger shapes to startle her readers into new modes of vision and action. In "A View of the Woods" a grandfather murders his look-alike granddaughter in a fit of rage. As he looks behind him at "the little motionless figure with its head on the rock," his own monstrosity comes home to him. He suffers a heart attack; his head is filled with terrifying visions of the incommensurability of the modern world and final things, and his eyes come to rest upon a creature both apocalyptic and grotesque: "a huge yellow monster which sat to the side, as stationary as he was, gorging itself on clay."

In *Sacred Groves and Ravaged Gardens* (1985), Louise Westling suggests that this is an unusual event in O'Connor's fiction. Ordinarily the males in O'Connor's stories are aggressive and vengeful, while her women are punished for their dreams of power and property. This state of affairs may reflect the realities of O'Connor's own life. Her passion for storytelling was encouraged by her father's love of good writing. As a child, Flannery left bits of original verse under Edward O'Connor's napkin to be read and praised at dinner. O'Connor suggests that she and her father were alike; he, too, wanted to write, but possessed neither time, money, nor training to realize his dream. Finally, what he lacked most was time. He died when his daughter was only sixteen.

As a result of Edward's poor health, the family left behind his prospering real estate business and Savannah's urbane neighborhoods to settle in Milledgeville under Regina O'Connor's management. Here Flannery confronted the Protestant fundamentalism that became the focus of so much of her fiction; her life also became more agrarian and more matriarchal. Westling suggests that this matriarchy shaped O'Connor's fiction in intriguing ways. Although Flannery had to escape from the role of Southern lady in order to write her grotesque fiction, Regina O'Connor remained a strongly conservative force in her life. As a result, O'Connor's angry daughters are caught in a painful double bind: while they resent their mothers and work toward their downfall, these daughters are also entrenched in their mothers' worlds and forced to acknowledge a feminine partnership.

O'Connor's life in Milledgeville was dominated by a series of new social demands. The chief social event of the spring was the annual garden club tour of homes. With great pomp and solemnity, the Cline house was opened to a public eager to view the upper-class origins of their past—a past, O'Connor explains, "which happened to be in excellent working order and in which I lived." At Peabody Public High School, O'Connor escaped from this past by becoming an artistic polymath, producing paintings, cartoons, poetry, and prose. She wrote short, secret books about her day-to-day family life. "My Relitives" offered funny sketches of uncles and aunts; "Don't Tuch" was the title of her personal journal. Although O'Connor's get-tough spelling seems deliberately humorous, correct spelling was, in fact, hard for her: "It was a source of some small discomfort to these teachers that I could add only with the use of my fingers, confused history with a foreign language, and put ninety percent of my originality into my spelling."

As an English major at Georgia State College for Women (now Women's College of Georgia) in Milledgeville, O'Connor felt that this originality was unappreciated. She changed her major to sociology and entered the determinist world that she learned to parody so beautifully in *The Violent Bear It Away* (1960). Imagining a career in cartooning or writing, she became art editor of the student newspaper and editor of the literary quarterly. She published cartoons in the student paper and submitted numerous cartoons to the *New Yorker*, though none were accepted for publication.

O'Connor's goals became even more ambitious when she was awarded a Rinehart Fellowship to the Writers' Workshop at the University of Iowa in 1945. In honor of the move to Iowa, Mary Flannery O'Connor divested herself of her common first name; she decided that "Mary O'Connor" would be too plain for a famous author, and she became "Flannery O'Connor." At Iowa she began working with Paul Engle, Robert Penn Warren, and Andrew Lytle. Engle found her accent so hard to follow that during their first meeting he asked to put her comments in writing. He later compared O'Connor to John Keats, who spoke with a thick Cockney accent but wrote English sentences as clear and delicious as springwater. O'Connor's dialect was as vivid and difficult as her scribblings were amazing. At this time O'Connor also forged an alliance with Caroline Gordon, a Catholic novelist who was thirty years older than O'Connor and married to Allen Tate. Their relationship flourished; Gordon nourished O'Connor's writing for the rest of her life.

O'Connor's first published story was "The Geranium," a modest but moving account of a dying Southerner displaced in the concrete wilderness of the urban North. Together with "The

Barber," "Wildcat," "The Crop," "The Turkey," and "The Train," she submitted "The Geranium" as a master's thesis dedicated to Paul Engle in June 1947. Although in this early fiction O'Connor is still honing her style, these stories give us a sense of her future direction, especially her interest in portraying bizarre people of differing classes and types from the rural South. She did not publish these stories as a collection within her lifetime, however, and it was not until Robert Giroux collected the complete stories in 1971 that these early tales became accessible to the reading public.

O'Connor's next stories fared somewhat better. At Iowa she was awarded the Rinehart Iowa Prize for a first novel that was to include material from "The Train," "The Peeler," "The Heart of the Park," and "Enoch and the Gorilla." O'Connor spent the winter of 1948 working on this and other projects at Yaddo, a writers' colony in Saratoga Springs, New York, where writers' needs were supplied gratis. Her sponsors enforced a strict work routine that O'Connor was pleased to follow. She acquired a hardworking, loyal agent, Elizabeth McKee, and her stories began to appear regularly in such periodicals as *Mademoiselle* and *Partisan Review*. At Yaddo, O'Connor met Robert Lowell, who introduced her to Robert Giroux and to Robert and Sally Fitzgerald, who became her very dear friends.

After her stay at Yaddo, O'Connor took an apartment in New York City, where she planned to complete *Wise Blood* and enter New York's literary world. But urban life was not for her. In 1949 she moved to Connecticut to live with the Fitzgeralds. The three of them spent many happy evenings together; and O'Connor spent her days writing. Although she had no plans to return to the South to live, many of O'Connor's Connecticut anecdotes focused on Milledgeville and the surrounding area. She plumbed these memories in developing *Wise Blood*, as the novel grew to over a thousand pages.

As *Wise Blood* veered in more existentially violent and theologically shocking directions, the publishers questioned O'Connor's wisdom, claiming that her story line was becoming too narrowly gothic and too parochial. With characteristic panache, O'Connor denounced these criticisms, arguing that the novel's virtues depended upon its limitations: "I am not writing a conventional novel, and I think that the quality of the novel I write will derive precisely from the peculiarity or aloneness, if you will, of the experience I write from." She complained to her agent that the publisher's letters were "addressed to a slightly dim-witted Campfire Girl, and I cannot look with composure on getting a lifetime of others like them." After some urging, Holt, Rinehart, and Company released her from her contract in 1950, and Robert Giroux immediately offered O'Connor a contract. In the wake of her characteristically careful revisions, *Wise Blood* was published in 1952.

According to O'Connor's prospectus, *Wise Blood* describes "an illiterate Tennessean" who "has lost his home through the breakdown of a country community." But Hazel Motes is not the usual modern hero. Although home has a very modern meaning for Hazel, since it reflects neither place nor family, but the need "for some absolute belief which would give him sanctuary in the modern world," Hazel remains atypical in his religious obsessiveness. Searching for sanctuary, Hazel Motes knows only his own "sense of sin and a need for religion." At the end of his compulsive journey—a journey on which he can only search "for God through sin"—Hazel destroys his vision: he blinds himself. This blinding becomes the answer to his demanding religious quest. As he explains this horror to his landlady, "If there's no bottom in your eyes, they hold more." In answer, Hazel's landlady stares at him for a long time, but sees nothing at all. She offers to marry him, sends the police after him when he goes, and is finally left, at his death, peering into the abyss of his vision, sightless, hopeless, looking for light.

Readers were horrified. When they discovered *Wise Blood* amid the consumer-oriented religiosity of the 1950s, O'Connor's spiritualism looked very like atheism; it seemed needlessly harsh and cruel. But her short stories won her a steadfast readership throughout the 1950s, as well as numerous honors and awards. In 1955 O'Connor published her first collection of short stories, *A Good Man Is Hard to Find,* to excellent reviews. In 1960 her second novel, *The Violent Bear It Away,* came into print, and in 1965 her second collection of short stories, *Everything That Rises Must Converge,* was published posthumously. She died in a coma in a hospital in Milledgeville on 3 August 1964. O'Connor kept her sense of humor to the end, reporting to Caroline Gordon Tate that "the doctor says I can't do any work. But he says it's all right for me to write a little fiction." This "little fiction" has met with great results indeed. The complete stories, published in 1971 with an introduction by Robert Giroux, received the National Book Award, and was supplemented in 1979 by Sally Fitzgerald's edition of O'Connor's disarmingly thoughtful and anecdote-filled letters, *The Habit of Being.*

Still, the brevity and kind-spiritedness of O'Connor's life can account only in part for the peculiar violence and perspicacity of her fiction. Her stories are aggressively spiritual, but this aggressiveness is also a direct response to the Southern cult of femininity as this cult meets the hyperbolic division of labor of postwar suburbia. O'Connor's comedy is not only spiritually instructive and entertaining; it also serves to break up and break open a grueling Southern tradition in which women aspire to the pedestaled passivity of beauty queens. O'Connor refused the debutante life; she ridiculed local Georgia beauty contests in her letters: "Miss Gum Spirits of Turpentine has just been elected for the year. This is an election I will always wait for. . . . The other one I look for is Miss North Georgia Chick." Instead of celebrating the belle, O'Connor practices a politics of ugliness in her fiction. Her stories produce a litany of ugly women like Joy-Hulga and Mary Grace, who become conduits for a fierce female rage.

We can add to this politics of ugliness O'Connor's own peculiar aesthetic—an aesthetic that eroticizes pain, that romanticizes torture. Although most critics see the anger and aggression in her stories serving purely religious ends, we should also emphasize O'Connor's private pleasure in acting the part of an Old Testament God toward her erstwhile creations. O'Connor releases an incredible distorting force in her fiction; she writes with a belligerence and sadism unlike any other female author. She seizes, again and again, the opportunity to throw the book at a culture that is both areligious and repressive—a culture in which women are not allowed to be angry, ill-mannered, inventive, intelligent, or visionary. She claims for herself, as woman writer, a litany of aggressive resources, and in so doing, she has expanded our lexicons and challenged our assumptions about femininity with her new and ornery habits of meaning.

Selected Bibliography

PRIMARY WORKS

NOVELS

Wise Blood. New York: Harcourt, Brace, 1952.

The Violent Bear It Away. New York: Farrar, Straus, and Cudahy, 1960.

SHORT STORIES

A Good Man Is Hard to Find. New York: Harcourt, Brace, 1955.

Everything That Rises Must Converge. New York: Farrar, Straus, and Giroux, 1965.

OCCASIONAL WORKS

Dominican Sisters of Our Lady of Perpetual Help Cancer Home. "Introduction." In *A Memoir of Mary Ann.* New York: Farrar, Straus, and Cudahy, 1961. Pp. 3–21.

Mystery and Manners: Occasional Prose. Edited by Sally and Robert Fitzgerald. New York: Farrar, Straus, and Giroux, 1969.

COLLECTIONS

Three by Flannery O'Connor. New York: New American Library, 1964.

The Complete Stories. Edited by Robert Giroux. New York: Farrar, Straus, and Giroux, 1971.

Collected Writings. Edited by Sally Fitzgerald. New York: Library of America, 1988.

LETTERS

The Habit of Being. Edited by Sally Fitzgerald. New York: Random House, 1979.

The Correspondence of Flannery O'Connor and the Brainard Cheneys. Edited by C. Ralph Stevens. Jackson: University Press of Mississippi, 1986.

PAPERS AND MANUSCRIPTS

O'Connor's papers and personal library are in the Flannery O'Connor Collection, Women's College of Georgia, Milledgeville.

SECONDARY WORKS

BIOGRAPHICAL AND CRITICAL STUDIES

Allen, Suzanne. "Memoirs of a Southern Catholic Girlhood: Flannery O'Connor's 'A Temple of the Holy Ghost.' " *Renascence* 31:83–92 (Winter 1979).

Asals, Frederick. *Flannery O'Connor: The Imagination of Extremities.* Athens: University of Georgia Press, 1982.

Baumgaertner, Jill P. *Flannery O'Connor: A Proper Scaring.* Wheaton, Ill.: Harold Shaw, 1988.

Chew, Martha. "Flannery O'Connor's Double-Edged Satire: The Idiot Daughter Versus the Lady Ph.D." *Southern Quarterly* 19:17–25 (Winter 1981).

Cleary, Michael. "Environmental Influences in Flannery O'Connor's Fiction." *Flannery O'Connor Bulletin* 8:20–34 (1979).

Crews, Frederick. "The Power of Flannery O'Connor." *New York Review of Books* 37:49–55 (1990).

Desmond, John F. *Risen Sons: Flannery O'Connor's Vision of History.* Athens: University of Georgia Press, 1987.

Feeley, Kathleen. *Flannery O'Connor: Voice of the Peacock.* New Brunswick, N.J.: Rutgers University Press, 1972.

Fitzgerald, Robert. "Introduction." In O'Connor's *Everything That Rises Must Converge.* New York: Farrar, Straus, and Giroux, 1965.

Fitzgerald, Sally. "Introduction." In *The Habit of Being.* Edited by Sally Fitzgerald. New York: Random House, 1979.

Friedman, Melvin J., and Beverly Lyon Clark. *Critical Essays on Flannery O'Connor.* Boston: G. K. Hall, 1985.

Friedman, Melvin J., and Lewis A. Lawson, eds. *The Added Dimension: The Art and Mind of Flannery O'Connor.* New York: Fordham University Press, 1966.

Gentry, Marshall Bruce. *Flannery O'Connor's Religion of the Grotesque.* Jackson: University Press of Mississippi, 1986.

Getz, Lorine M. *Flannery O'Connor: Her Life, Library, and Book Reviews.* New York: Edwin Mellen Press, 1980.

Giroux, Robert. "Introduction." In *The Complete Stories.* Edited by Robert Giroux. New York: Farrar, Straus, and Giroux, 1971.

Gordon, Caroline. "Flannery O'Connor's *Wise Blood.*" *Critique* 2, no. 2:3–10 (1958).

Hendin, Josephine. *The World of Flannery O'Connor.* Bloomington: Indiana University Press, 1970.

Hyman, Stanley Edgar. *Flannery O'Connor.* Minneapolis: University of Minnesota Press, 1966.

Kahane, Claire. "The Maternal Legacy: The Grotesque Tradition in Flannery O'Connor's Female Gothic." In *The Female Gothic.* Edited by Juliann E. Fleenor. Montreal: Eden Press, 1983.

Katz, Claire. "Flannery O'Connor's Rage of Vision." *American Literature* 46:54–67 (March 1974).

Kessler, Edward. *Flannery O'Connor and the Language of Apocalypse.* Princeton, N.J.: Princeton University Press, 1986.

Love, Betty Boyd. "Recollections of Flannery O'Connor." *Flannery O'Connor Bulletin* 14:44–58 (1985).

May, John R. *The Pruning Word: The Parables of Flannery O'Connor.* Notre Dame, Ind.: University of Notre Dame Press, 1976.

———. "The Methodological Limits of Flannery O'Connor's Critics." *Flannery O'Connor Bulletin* 15:16–28 (1986).

McKenzie, Barbara. *Flannery O'Connor's Georgia.* Athens: University of Georgia Press, 1980.

Nichols, Loxley F. "Shady Talk and Shifty Things." *Flannery O'Connor Bulletin* 14:44–58 (1985).

———. "Flannery O'Connor's 'Intellectual Vaudeville': Masks of Mother and Daughter." *Studies in the Literary Imagination* 20:15–29 (Fall 1987).

Park, Clara Claiborne. "Crippled Laughter: Toward Understanding Flannery O'Connor." *American Scholar* 51:249–257 (1982).

Satterfield, Ben. "*Wise Blood,* Artistic Anemia, and the Hemorrhaging of O'Connor Criticism." *Studies in American Fiction* 17:33–50 (Spring 1989).

Stephens, Martha. *The Question of Flannery O'Connor.* Baton Rouge: Louisiana State University Press, 1973.

Walker, Alice. "Beyond the Peacock: The Reconstruction of Flannery O'Connor." In her *In Search of Our Mothers' Gardens.* New York: Harcourt, Brace, Jovanovich, 1983.

Walters, Dorothy. *Flannery O'Connor.* New York: Twayne, 1973.

Westling, Louise. *Sacred Groves and Ravaged Gardens: The Fiction of Eudora Welty, Carson McCullers, and Flannery O'Connor.* Athens: University of Georgia Press, 1985.

Whitt, Margaret. "Flannery O'Connor's Ladies." *Flannery O'Connor Bulletin* 15:42–50 (1986).

Wood, Ralph C. *The Comedy of Redemption: Christian Faith and Comic Vision in Four American Novelists.* Notre Dame: University of Notre Dame Press, 1988.

Young, Thomas Daniel. "Flannery O'Connor's View of the South: God's Earth and His Universe." *Studies in the Literary Imagination* 20:5–14 (Fall 1987).

BIBLIOGRAPHY

Golden, Robert E., and Mary C. Sullivan. *Flannery O'Connor and Caroline Gordon: A Reference Guide.* Boston: G. K. Hall, 1977.

PATRICIA S. YAEGER

GRACE PALEY

1922–

> I was drawn to the memory of myself—a mere stripling of a girl—the day I learned that the shortest distance between two lines is a great circle.
>
> ("The Floating Truth")

FIRST-GENERATION JEWISH AMERICAN, woman, wife, mother, political activist, storyteller—the order in which these aspects of Grace Paley's identity appear does not suggest a hierarchy of importance, at least not to Paley; rather, it reveals a consciousness developing in time—an evolution of sorts. Her exploration and deepening understanding of these features of her own history made possible and underlie the style and content of her relatively small body of work, which has appeared intermittently since the late 1950s.

Because her stories sound and feel so unusual, interviewers frequently ask Grace Paley to talk about her literary influences, the literary ancestors of her stories. Instead of responding in the expected way—naming James Joyce or Gertrude Stein, innovators in the form of the short story, for example—Paley redefines the terms of the question: the literary to her is not just how language is used in writing, whatever the form; rather, the literary also includes the purely verbal, the way language emerges from the mouths of real people.

Her expansion of the sense of the literary underscores the rich verbal world Paley grew up in. Her parents were Russian Jews who immigrated to the United States in 1905 (they were in their twenties), bringing with them Paley's paternal grandmother and two aunts; the languages of their home were English, Russian, and Yiddish, and because Paley grew up in the Bronx, she also lived in the various idioms and dialects of the street. This rich verbal milieu came to life in the conversations around the kitchen table, on the stoop, and in the neighborhood at large.

While her verbal background finds its expression in the sound, the linguistic realism, of many of Paley's stories, especially the early ones, it is the cultural consciousness implicit within these languages—especially Yiddish and English—that is responsible for the ethos that underpins the stories' narrative point of view. The Goodsides, Paley's family (with the exception of her grandmother, who went to shul every day), were not religious, but they identified themselves as Jews, not as Americans. The dialectic of Jewish and American attitudes forms an almost paradoxical synthesis in the attitudes of a number of her most fully realized characters—a Jewish memory of the past, the consciousness of oppression and the resultant "ancestral grief" bumping up against the American presentness, the ideal of possibility, of change, of upward mobility. For example, in "The Immigrant Story," published in *Enormous Changes at the Last Minute* (1974), we see this dynamic articulated by two characters who appear in a number of Paley's stories, Faith and Jack:

> Jack asked me: Isn't it a terrible thing to grow up in the shadow of another person's sorrow?
>
> I suppose so, I answered. As you know I grew up in the summer sunlight of upward mobility. This leached out a lot of that dark ancestral grief.
>
> (p. 171)

Paley should not be equated absolutely with Faith, but Faith's use of a medical metaphor in this context is important insofar as it suggests Paley's father, Dr. Isaac Goodside, and his influential role as an intermediary in the process of her developing her own cultural identity: his forming a bridge joining the past and the present.

These early influences on her own identity are imaginatively re-created in a number of ways in her first collection of stories, *The Little Disturbances of Man: Stories of Men and Women at Love* (1959). Rose of "Goodbye and Good Luck" and Dorothy Wasserman of "The Contest" both speak in the rich idiom that combines Yiddish and English. But perhaps the story in this volume most clearly relevant to Paley's own youth is "The Loudest Voice."

The central character of this story is Shirley Abramowitz, a school-age girl growing up in Coney Island, the daughter of Jewish immigrants from Russia. Shirley opens her story with a breathtaking and paradoxical evocation of aural experience: "There is a certain place where dumb-waiters boom, doors slam, dishes crash; every window is a mother's mouth bidding the street shut up, go skate somewhere else, come home. My voice is the loudest." The noisiness is the liveliness of her environment in which the inanimate objects seem to take on a life of their own, but her voice is the most lively. The implied connection between life and the production of meaningful sound is almost immediately made explicit when her mother tells the grocer that "if you say to her or to her father 'Ssh,' they say, In the grave it will be quiet.' " Shirley's mother, Clara, in contrast to her father, wants her to stifle the quality that Shirley identifies herself by, that makes her distinctive, and that signifies her being alive. Her mother's attitude suggests that there may be dangers in living, in being identifiably distinctive. Perhaps, from her mother's point of view, it is safer to be quiet.

But because of her robust voice and her constant celebration of language, Shirley has been chosen by her teachers to narrate her school's Christmas pageant. What is an honor to Shirley leads to the central tension in the story, the tension between her parents' conflicting attitudes toward the past, toward cultural identity, and toward acculturation.

Clara has reservations about her daughter's participation in what she sees as an exclusively Christian celebration, while her father, Misha, sees the irony and humor in the situation:

> "Listen," she said sadly, "I'm surprised to see my neighbors making tra-la-la for Christmas."
>
> My father couldn't think of what to say to that. Then he decided: "You're in America! Clara, you wanted to come here. In Palestine the Arabs would be eating you alive. Europe you had pogroms. Argentina is full of Indians. Here you got Christmas. . . . Some joke, ha?"
>
> "Very funny, Misha. What is becoming of you? If we came to a new country a long time ago to run away from tyrants, and instead we fall into a creeping pogrom, that our children learn a lot of lies, so what's the joke? Ach, Misha, your idealism is going away."
>
> (pp. 57–58)

The "creeping pogrom" Clara is afraid of involves Shirley losing her Jewish identity altogether, but to Misha, if idealism means being quiet, living separate from the culture at large and in remembered fear, then he is not idealist. Rather, he has a more liberal imagination. Recognizing that rigidity can be self-defeating, he takes a more inclusive view of history and their particular place in it:

> "Ho! Ho!" my father said. "Christmas. What's the harm? After all, history teaches everyone. We learn from reading this is a holiday from pagan times also, candles, lights, even Chanukah. So we learn it's not altogether Christian. So if they think it's a private holiday, they're only ignorant, not patriotic. What belongs to history, belongs to all men. You want to go back to the Middle Ages? Is it better to shave your head with a secondhand razor? Does it hurt Shirley to learn to speak up? It does not. So maybe someday she won't live between the kitchen and the shop. She's not a fool."
>
> (p. 59)

Misha's point is that a historical imagination includes more than just Jewish and Christian perspectives and events, and that untangling just one thread from the whole cloth of history necessarily limits one's possibilities. Shirley's cultural heritage doesn't necessarily have to limit her future.

This optimism of Shirley's father comes together with the aspect of Jewishness that the young Paley found most appealing: its social tradition of charity, sympathy for and empathy with others. And thus the story ends with Shirley falling asleep, happy because she "had prayed for everybody: my talking family, cousins far away, passersby, and all the lonesome Christians. I expected to be heard. My voice certainly was the loudest."

Like her Shirley Abramowitz, Grace Paley had to "clear my throat" before she could begin to tell her story; but unlike Shirley, who has an assigned narrative to tell (and it is no accident that Shirley is assigned to tell a man's tale), Paley had to discover her own story before she could begin. She had, in short, to discover her individual identity within the context of her cultural heritage and historical moment. In 1938, at the age of sixteen, Paley enrolled at Hunter College; later she took courses at New York University and studied poetry at the New School for Social Research with W. H. Auden, but she was not a particularly successful student. In 1942, with World War II raging, she married Jess Paley, then a soldier and later a motion-picture cameraman. In the early years of their marriage she lived in army camps with the wives of the other soldiers. It was here that she became interested in the lives of women and children who were living apart from men; she recognized herself in this group—a certain class of people having its own interests and characteristic activities—and identified herself as being part of it: she realized that her story *is* the story of these women. These lives—both common *and* important—determined the primary subject of her stories: the lives of ordinary women.

The possibility of living in the more expansive world that Misha envisions for his daughter is not yet possible for the adult women who people the stories of *The Little Disturbances of Man*. In contrast to Paley, the characters of these stories—typical women of the 1950s—have yet to fully recognize the essential separateness of their lives from the lives of their men and to define themselves in terms that are broader than simply caring for the house, their children, and their men before they can achieve personal satisfaction. In this volume, the process toward this realization is undermined by the formulation of the central question that informs these women's lives: "What is man that woman lies down to adore him?" ("A Subject of Childhood"). Until the subject of this question shifts from the nature of men to the nature of women and the shape of their lives these characters will remain frustrated.

Ginny, the narrator of "An Interest in Life," in one such character. After giving her a broom and dustpan for Christmas, Ginny's husband deserts her and their four small children; he feels constricted by the ordinariness of their domestic life—how she looks when she's pregnant and the smell of the diapers of their other small children—and leaves to seek adventure in the army. Searching for a way to survive, Ginny first contacts the Welfare Department, which in turn hounds her brothers-in-law, but getting little help from these sources, she makes a list of her hardships to send to the television show "Strike It Rich." Her former neighbor and soon-to-be lover John Raftery dissuades her from sending it when he tells her that she will be laughed out of the studio because those who make it onto the show "really suffer"; according to John, she is not really suffering, but merely experiencing "the little disturbances of man"—hers really is an ordinary life.

While she looks to John to rescue her, to worry about the emotional development of her sons, she surmises that "all that is really necessary for survival of the fittest, it seems, is an interest in life." This realization is richly ironic because Ginny's thinking that survival lies in the somewhat passive observation of a remarkably limited life does suggest a strength of sorts but not any real heightening of consciousness of the difference between men and women or an evolution in her sense of her own identity. Rather, her stasis is suggested at the end of the story with her imagining, two and a half years later, the return of her husband, their making love and being so happy that she doesn't bother using any form of contraception. She has come full circle, but we cannot help noticing how small that circle is.

But the fittest do survive, and have the potential to thrive, only by adaptation, which is essentially a recognition of and response to the nature of their environment and circumstances. In the two companion stories "The Used-Boy Raisers" and "A Subject of Childhood" (which are grouped together under the title "Two Short Sad Stories from a Long and Happy Life"), Faith Darwin, appropriately named, at least subconsciously recognizes the difference between her life and those of her men but cannot yet respond in a way that satisfies her.

Faith is at the center of both of these stories, not only in the sense that hers is the narrative point of view from which both are told, but also in that her identity as wife, mother, and lover is juxtaposed to the assumptions about these roles that the men who occupy her kitchen, her bed, and her heart act out.

The ostensible subject of "The Used-Boy Raisers" is Faith's two husbands: her first and former, Livid, is the father of her two boys, and her second, Pallid, is their father figure. At the kitchen table, after rejecting the eggs Faith cooked for them, these two "fathers" discuss the boys' education while Faith embroiders in near silence. Their sense of raising children seemingly extends only as far as formal education is concerned. What is so amusingly ironic about these men as they discuss an important aspect of the boys' lives is that they almost immediately lose sight of the issue of education. When Pallid suggests parochial school, the conversation swerves to their antithetical responses to the Catholic church, in which each had been raised. Their histories, rather than education or the boys, become the subject of their conversation.

Faith soon interrupts, changes the subject, and then prepares for the day. It is at this point that the identity of the true "boy raiser" is revealed, as well as the essential difference between mothers and fathers. Her description of her day is telling—

> I made the beds and put the aluminum cot away. Livid would find a hotel by nightfall. I did the dishes and organized the greedy day; dinosaurs in the morning, park in the afternoon, peanut butter in between, and at the end of it all, to reward us for a week of beans endured, a noble rib roast with little onions, dumplings, and pink applesauce.

—juxtaposed as it is with her perception of the lives of Livid and Pallid:

> I must admit that they were clean and neat, rather attractive, shiny men in their thirties, with the grand affairs of the day ahead of them. Dark night, the search for pleasure and oblivion were well ahead. Goodbye, I said, have a nice day. Goodbye, they said once more, and set off in pride on paths which are not my concern.
> (p. 134)

With this the story ends, marking the last the reader will see of these two "fathers" and indirectly but unequivocally making the point about who really raises the children.

If the object of "The Used-Boy Raisers" is to exhibit the unconscious playing-out of roles, "A Subject of Childhood" illustrates the personal costs and benefits of motherhood. Caught between her children and her current lover, Clifford, Faith tries to pacify all of them after they have injured themselves and each other by roughhousing too aggressively. She puts the boys to bed, but Clifford is more petulant. He tells her repeatedly that she's done "a rotten job" raising her kids. What he doesn't realize is that he is not simply criticizing one skill or one aspect of her personality, but is casually dismissing what she sees as her whole existence.

This essential difference between perspectives is the basic problem Paley illustrates in this story and in the volume as a whole. Faith cannot articulate to Clifford why his statements are so devastating, perhaps because she is not yet able to or perhaps because she thinks that he will not be able to understand; instead she heaves a glass ashtray at him, nicking his ear. He abandons the key to her apartment and departs, leaving her alone with her thoughts and her children. Left alone by her lover but not by her younger son, who crawls into her lap and places "his open hand, its fingers stretching wide, across my breast," Faith reflects on her position:

> I closed my eyes and leaned on his dark head. But the sun in its course emerged from among the water towers of downtown office buildings and suddenly shone white and bright on me. Then through the short fat fingers of my son, interred forever, like a black and white barred king in Alcatraz, my heart lit up in stripes.
>
> (p. 145)

This image of love *and* imprisonment solidifies our sense of what Paley has been trying to illustrate in this volume about the complicated emotional dilemma women face being women and mothers.

The fifteen years between the publication of *The Little Disturbances of Man* and her second collection, *Enormous Changes at the Last Minute,* in 1974 were full ones for Grace Paley. She continued to raise her two children, who were by this time nearly adults, became increasingly involved in political causes, both local and national, taught creative writing courses at Columbia and Syracuse universities, divorced Jess Paley, and continued to write. These interests and activities are reflected in *Enormous Changes at the Last Minute* in that the characters—some of whom were introduced in the first collection—are more reflective here about their lives, their connections with others, and the world outside their apartments. The women of this volume discover that the context of their activities extends beyond "the kitchen and the shop," as Misha had hoped for, but that their sphere of activity is characteristically female, organized around and then extending from their activities as mothers.

The concerns of the stories in this collection and in her third book of short stories, *Later the Same Day* (1985), mirror Paley's own personal and artistic development. These stories trace their characters' movement from preoccupation with their individual predicaments, which is necessarily alienating, as we saw in the stories of the first collection, to an awareness of and identification with others. Her argument throughout *Enormous Changes at the Last Minute* is that this conscious identification of women with women is a political position that makes collective action in a broader sphere possible, while in *Later the Same Day* she suggests that this bonding results in relationships—qualitatively different than those women have with men—that endure. Paley's aesthetic principles also spring out of this identification; as her characters become increasingly conscious women they also become increasingly conscious storytellers because they have finally recognized the subject, content, importance, and value not only of their lives but of their life stories. The real—ordinary life, its process and possibilities—becomes realized in art.

Faith Darwin, the put-upon and imprisoned housewife of the first collection, is the character Paley develops in the later volumes to illuminate this process. In "Faith in the Afternoon," in *Enormous Changes at the Last Minute,* we see her still preoccupied with her own unhappiness. But while visiting her parents at the Children of Judea retirement home and hearing from her mother about the lives of the girls, now women, with whom she grew up, Faith haltingly comes to realize that her life is no worse than theirs. This first step toward a consciousness of others is illustrated when the narrator tells us that "for herself and Anita Franklin, Faith bowed her head and wept." She is still weeping alone, but her tears are no longer exclusively for and about herself.

The setting of this story and that of "Faith in a Tree," both occurring outside Faith's apartment, is important. Cooped up in an apartment Faith is not exposed to any perspectives on life and living that might qualify or expand her own limited experience, but by setting these stories outside that enclosed environment, first in the retirement home and then in the park, Paley underscores the importance of perspective and its modulations to the development of character, both real and imagined.

Faith, at this point, is literally up a tree, trying to gain a perspective on her place in the universe, humorously revealing her discombobulated and limited God's-eye view. This quirky narrative, which jumps from Faith's responses to the various women she is with in the park to reflections on their children to her replies to her own children as they interrupt or interject themselves into her remarks, suddenly focuses itself as Faith's attention is arrested by a group of unfamiliar adults who make their way into her field of vision along with their children and their placards protesting the war in Vietnam.

To this point, despite her elevated position, Faith's perspective on motherhood consists only of her own experience and that of her friends. She has not thought about motherhood in more abstract terms until these newcomers, protesting the effect of the war in general and napalm in particular on Vietnamese children, give her pause. When the neighborhood cop, Doug, moves to disperse them, Faith and her friends try to dissuade him, but only half-heartedly in the face of his authority. It is Richard, Faith's nine-year-old son, who acts as their conscience when he screams: "I hate you. I hate your stupid friends. Why didn't you just stand up to that stupid cop and say fuck you," and then reproduces the message of the placards in huge letters on the blacktop with pink chalk. Richard's act jolts her out of her complacency; reflecting historically she says, "I think that is when events turned me around, changing my hairdo, my job uptown, my style of living and telling. . . . Directed out of that sexy playground by my children's heartfelt brains, I thought more and more and everyday about the world." Motherhood is what has motivated her and her friends to act in their local context—in the neighborhood, the park, the PTA. This expansion of Faith's awareness to include the world opens up all sorts of possibilities: to act in a broader sphere, to form new and deepen old friendships, to live responsibly.

In this story, as well as in a number of others in these collections, we see Paley imaginatively re-creating two historical moments that she and her characters were active in: the politicization of women and the feminization of politics. Not only are these interrelated and mutually reinforcing movements re-created in Paley's work, but they also inform her mode of storytelling.

Through these two latest collections, Faith seems to resemble Paley more and more, especially when she begins to develop her identity as a writer and storyteller. How being a woman—thinking and knowing as a woman, experiencing as a woman—affects storytelling is the subject of "A Conversation with My Father" (in *Enormous Changes*). Faith and her father discuss the aesthetic effectiveness of the qualities that differentiate the stories of Faith/Paley from more traditional, male fiction. Faith's father argues for the traditional mode: clearly defined exposition, linear development of plot, and an unequivocal ending in which the conflicts are unmistakably resolved. Faith loathes this way of telling because it doesn't adequately re-create life; to her mind and according to her experience life doesn't work that way; life isn't lived that way.

Her objections to linear plots and decisive conclusions spring from a number of moral principles. According to Faith, here speaking clearly for Paley, that way of telling a story "takes all hope away. Everyone, real or invented, deserves the open destiny of life." Linear plots and immutable conclusions deny the essential quality of life: the possibility of change, of development, of a more inclusive existence. The value Paley places on possibility suggests the responsibility she feels toward her characters; she allows them the same possibilities for good and ill that life affords. But perhaps most important, imagining life into art is a profoundly moral act in that, as one of her characters says, it is a way "to save a few lives."

To save her life and the lives of ordinary women from oblivion, Paley told her stories. She discovered early that a straight line is not the most adequate or satisfying way to live or to tell a tale: it excludes too much. Instead, a circle is a much more realistic metaphor by which to describe lives and shape fiction because it includes more and makes more possible.

This idea of circularity is especially evident in her 1985 collection *Later the Same Day.* Just as Paley's life began in a rich verbal world of conversation and storytelling, this collection ends with a conversation about life and storytelling. "Listening" finishes with Faith's lesbian friend Cassie feeling excluded, as if her life has not been realized, because Faith has not yet told her story. This ending suggests an expansion of Paley's exploration of women's lives to yet another aspect of their experience that remains to be realized in her future work.

Selected Bibliography

PRIMARY WORKS

SHORT STORIES

The Little Disturbances of Man: Stories of Men and Women at Love. Garden City, N.Y.: Doubleday, 1959.

Enormous Changes at the Last Minute. New York: Farrar, Straus & Giroux, 1974.

Later the Same Day. New York: Farrar, Straus & Giroux, 1985.

POETRY

Leaning Forward: Poems. Penobscot, Me.: Granite Press, 1985.

SECONDARY WORKS

BIOGRAPHICAL AND CRITICAL STUDIES

Bibo, Minako. "Faith Darwin as Writer-Heroine: A Study of Grace Paley's Short Stories." *Studies in American Jewish Literature* 7:40–54 (Spring 1988).

Coppula, Kathleen A. "Not for Literary Reasons: The Fiction of Grace Paley." *Mid-American Review* 7:63–72 (1986).

Crawford, John W. "Archetypal Patterns in Grace Paley's 'Runner.' " *Notes on Contemporary Literature* 11:10–12 (September 1981).

DeKoven, Marianne. "Mrs. Hegel-Shtein's Tears." *Partisan Review* 48:217–223 (1981).

Friebert, Stuart. "Kinswomen." *Field: Contemporary Poetry and Poetics* 34:93–102 (Spring 1986).

Gelfant, Blanche. "Grace Paley: Fragments for a Portrait in Collage." *New England Review* 3:276–293 (1980). Reprinted in her *Women Writing in America: Voices in Collage.* Hanover, N.H.: University Press of New England, 1984.

Iannone, Carol. "A Dissent on Grace Paley." *Commentary* 80:54–58 (1985).

Kamel, Rose. "To Aggravate the Conscience: Grace Paley's Loud Voice." *Journal of Ethnic Studies* 11:29–49 (Fall 1981).

Mandel, Dena. "Keeping Up with Faith: Grace Paley's Sturdy American Jewess." *Studies in American Jewish Literature* 3:85–98 (1983).

Schleifer, Ronald. "Grace Paley: Chaste Compactness." In *Contemporary American Women Writers: Narrative Strategies.* Edited by Catherine Rainwater and William J. Scheick. Lexington: University Press of Kentucky, 1985.

Shapiro, Harriet. "Grace Paley: 'Art Is on the Side of the Underdog.' " *Ms.,* May 1974, pp. 43–45.

Sorkin, Adam J. " 'What Are We, Animals?': Grace Paley's World of Talk and Laughter." *Studies in American Jewish Literature* 2:144–154 (1982).

Taylor, Jacqueline. "Grace Paley on Storytelling and

Story Hearing." *Literature in Performance: A Journal of Literary and Performing Art* 7:46–58 (April 1987).

INTERVIEWS

Barthelme, Donald, William Gass, Grace Paley, and Walker Percy. "A Symposium on Fiction." *Shenandoah* 27:3–31 (1976)

Batt, Noelle Rocard. "An Interview with Grace Paley." *Caliban* 25:119–137 (1988).

Friedman, Maya. "An Interview with Grace Paley." *Story Quarterly* 13:32–39 (1981).

Hulley, Kathleen. "Interview with Grace Paley." *Delta* 14:19–40 (May 1982).

Lidoff, Joan. "Clearing Her Throat: An Interview with Grace Paley." *Shenandoah* 32:3–26 (1981).

Marchant, Peter, and Earl Ingersoll. "A Conversation with Grace Paley." *Massachusetts Review* 26:606–614 (Winter 1985).

Perry, Ruth. "Grace Paley." In *Women Writers Talking*. Edited by Janet Todd. New York: Holmes & Meier, 1983.

Saltz, Martha. "Looking at Disparities: An Interview with Grace Paley." *Southwest Review* 72:478–489 (Autumn 1987).

ANNE HIEMSTRA

DOROTHY PARKER

1893–1967

DOROTHY PARKER, POET, dramatist, master of the short story, and ferocious critic, became known as the wittiest woman in America while she was still in her twenties. Both her friends and her enemies found her difficult to capture in a simple bon mot. Beatrice Ames fondly called her "a storm after a rainbow and a rainbow after a storm." Alexander Woollcott described her as "a combination of Little Nell and Lady MacBeth," wearing lace that had "a bottle of vitriol concealed in its folds." Promiscuous, profane, and enormously popular, Parker appropriated many traditionally masculine liberties, and many of the men she emulated found her alarming. Ernest Hemingway viciously noted: "She had a soft side, like blackberry pie. But the bitch was always there, ready to rise with the heat." She rarely failed to offend even those she most often charmed. To Lillian Hellman, Parker was "a tangled fishnet of contradictions." One of Parker's most frequent companions in her final years, Wyatt Cooper, warns: "If you didn't know Dorothy Parker, whatever you think she was like, she wasn't. Even if you did know her, whatever you thought she was like, she probably wasn't."

Parker not only acknowledged her own inconsistencies but brooded on them, tracing her adult miseries to her difficult childhood. Although chronic writer's block prevented her delivery of the autobiography her publishers often requested, she effortlessly chose the title for the unwritten work: *Mongrel,* a reference to her Jewish-Scottish lineage. She was born to J. Henry Rothschild, a New York City businessman (unrelated to the famously wealthy Rothschilds), and Eliza Marston Rothschild, a former schoolteacher, on 22 August 1893, while the family was vacationing in West End, New Jersey. Dorothy, their fourth child, grew up estranged from her siblings by differences in age and temperament. When Eliza died almost five years after Dorothy's birth, she left modest trust funds for her children. Although Parker benefited from the financial resources of her father's successful garment business as well as those of her mother's family, she despised the taint of mercantilism, especially her father's sweatshop profits. After her first divorce, she claimed, "I married to change my name from Rothschild to Parker—that is all there was to it."

One of the more disorienting benefits Parker enjoyed as the daughter of a Jewish businessman was education at the Blessed Sacrament Academy, one of the best Catholic schools in New York City. The school was chosen by Rothschild and his second wife, Eleanor Frances Lewis, a Christian (as Dorothy's mother had been). While the older daughter, Helen, acclimated herself readily enough to the atmosphere of chalk dust, starched uniforms, and moral sanctity, Dorothy failed to thrive. Her classmates did not welcome her, and Parker spent increasing amounts of time alone, even creating a private language for herself, much to her parents' consternation. Bedeviling the nuns and her classmates with equal abandon, she once argued that the Immaculate Conception was nothing more than spontaneous combustion.

In 1907, at the age of fourteen, Parker enrolled at Miss Dana's School in Morristown, New Jersey, a largely Protestant establishment. Her enrollment records claim that her family attended Episcopalian services. Parker did not stay to graduate; while she would in later years admit under duress that she had not completed high school, she would never divulge the particulars of her departure. She returned home after a year to live with her father, widowed for a second time in 1903.

After 1908, Parker followed an autodidactic study program. When her father died in 1913, she found her first job, playing piano in a dance school. New York City was crazy about turkey trots, Castle walks, tangos, and frothy lyrics; light verse such as Edna St. Vincent Millay's was all the rage in publishing. Parker began submitting poems to Franklin Pierce Adams, who printed unsigned verse in his *New York Tribune* column, "The Conning Tower." Although she resented comparisons between her early poems and Millay's, she later admitted to feeling she was following in Millay's footsteps "unhappily in my own horrible sneakers."

Her first identified published verse, "Any Porch," is a slight and cynical satire of the upper-middle-class matrons she had met at summer resorts as a teenager. Printed in *Vanity Fair* in September 1915, it provides an interesting anticipation of her later narrative and poetic techniques. In this poem, Parker adapts the dramatic monologue form, juxtaposing one-sided conversational snippets in which the satirized speakers condemn themselves without the assistance of a judgmental narrative voice:

> "My husband says, often, 'Elise,
> You feel things too deeply, you do—' "
> "Yes, forty a month, if you please,
> Oh, servants impose on *me*, too."
>
> "I don't want the vote for myself,
> But women with property, dear—"
> "I think the poor girl's on the shelf,
> She's talking about her 'career.' "
> (*Vanity Fair*, p. 32; quoted in Meade, p. 302)

Beneath the brittle surface of this poem, Parker seems to be following at least a vague political agenda, arguing for beleaguered husbands, servants, suffragists, and working women. Typically, she champions these groups only by savaging another: upper-middle-class wives. The selectively misogynist shadings of this poem become more articulate in Parker's later work. In her poetry and her short fiction, she concentrated on feminine experiences but often from a distance, deftly and mercilessly satirizing female stereotypes she was desperate to avoid falling into herself. Struggling with a writing project in 1929, Parker prayed daily: "Dear God, please make me stop writing like a woman. For Jesus Christ's sake, amen." She once claimed, apologetically: "It's a terrible thing to say, but I can't think of any good women writers. . . . Of course, calling them women writers is their ruin: they begin to think of themselves that way."

Parker found her first writing job shortly after publishing "Any Porch." While she was delighted to leave the dance studio for the publishing world, composing photo captions for *Vogue* soon bored her. Her boss, editor Frank Crowninshield, remembered her unsuitability for the position:

> Her first caption at *Vogue*, which was designed to explain six photographs showing miscellaneous underwear, indicated that fashion would never become a religion with her. The caption was headed "Brevity is the Soul of Lingerie, as the Petticoat said to the Chemise."
>
> (Frewin, p. 22)

Crowninshield quickly transferred her to *Vanity Fair*, *Vogue*'s sister magazine, where he found more congenial assignments for her, including occasional theater reviews.

Parker's first reviews were fearlessly sarcastic demolitions of lightweight musical comedies. She advised her readers that one play provided an excellent opportunity to knit, and "if you don't knit, bring a book." Even when she praised a show, she did so with tongue in cheek. After viewing a production of Ibsen's *Hedda Gabler*, she wrote:

> I thought Nazimova was consistently wonderful, from the moment of her first, bored entrance to the shot that marked her spectacular final exit. Shots almost always do mark the final exit of Mr. Ibsen's heroines.
>
> I do wish that he had occasionally let the ladies take bichloride of mercury, or turn on the gas, or do something quiet and neat around the

house. I invariably miss most of the lines in the last act of an Ibsen play; I always have my fingers in my ears, waiting for the loud report that means that the heroine has just Passed On.

(*The Portable Dorothy Parker* [1973], pp. 416–417)

Crowninshield continued publishing her poetry, including her memorable "Hate Songs" —free verse compositions in which she lavished vituperation upon large segments of the human race. The opening line of her first effort in this series declares, "I hate Women. They get on my Nerves." She goes on to name various kinds of homemakers as especially loathsome.

"Women: A Hate Song" was followed a few months later by an attack on men. In her article "Why I Haven't Married," published in the October 1916 issue of *Vanity Fair*, Parker lays waste the characters of all the men she has dated. She spares one slightly fictionalized figure, Paul, based upon a handsome Wall Street investment broker from Hartford, Connecticut, Edwin Pond Parker II. Parker preferred beautiful, intellectually inferior men. In "Why I Haven't Married," she describes Paul as "an English-tailored Greek God, just masterful enough to be entertaining, just wicked enough to be exciting, just clever enough to be a good audience." Dorothy found in Eddie Parker the perfect escort for her many social engagements, and the perfect escape from the burden of her father's name. Eddie's Brahmin New England family was not pleased with his choice of a Jewish fiancée. When Dorothy went to Hartford to meet them, Eddie's grandfather gathered the family to pray in the parlor, where he asked God to "grant to the unbeliever in our midst the light to see the error of her ways." When Dorothy and Eddie married on 30 June 1917, the Hartford Parkers were not invited.

The fledgling marriage consisted of weekend trysts when Eddie could get away from the Army; like Ernest Hemingway, e. e. cummings, and John Dos Passos, Eddie had joined the 33rd Ambulance Corps, a group primarily comprising pacifist volunteer alumni of Yale, Harvard, and Princeton. Trying to build a marriage out of stolen moments, Dorothy wavered between swelling patriotic pride in Eddie's enlistment and a festering jealousy of Eddie's fellow soldiers, his imagined girlfriends, the army, and World War I as a whole. This scenario, and Dorothy's complex response, would be repeated with additional complications during World War II when her second husband joined the Army Air Force. Dorothy drew on her experience of both wars to write "The Lovely Leave" (1943), a short story about a couple who repeatedly fail to enjoy their brief reunions:

> She turned, not with an actual shrug, only with the effect of one, and went to the window and looked out, as if casually remarking the weather. She heard the door close loudly and then the grind of the elevator.
>
> When she knew he was gone, she was cool and still no longer. She ran about the little flat, striking her breast and sobbing.
>
> Then she had two months to ponder what had happened, to see how she had wrought the small ugly ruin.
>
> (*The Portable Dorothy Parker* [1973], p. 5)

Several of Eddie's visits were lost in a haze of alcohol. Dorothy had not yet learned to drink, but Eddie was already having problems that worsened after his unit shipped out to Europe.

While he was gone, Dorothy received increasing attention from *Vanity Fair*'s readers. Her miscellaneous pieces on various "women's topics" (permanent waves, women's hobbies) were applauded, although her scathing essay on interior decoration ("Interior Desecration") offended New York City's homosexual decorators and their influential patrons (the same well-to-do, underemployed women satirized in "Any Porch").

When the humorist Robert Benchley was named managing editor of *Vanity Fair* in 1919, he and Parker soon became inseparable friends. Like Parker's, Benchley's sense of humor embraced the morbid. When he introduced Parker to the undertaking magazines *Casket* and *Sunnyside*, she was so pleased that she became a subscriber, and her office walls at *Vanity Fair* were soon decorated with instructive illustrations of embalming techniques. Benchley did not tire of graveyard humor until the next decade, when Dorothy, by then a confirmed alcoholic, began her series of unsuccessful suicide attempts and Benchley quickly ran out of bedside jokes. After her first attempt, he told her, "Snap out of it, Dottie. You might as well live." She later reworked his consolation into a poem, "Résumé":

> Razors pain you;
> Rivers are damp;
> Acids stain you;
> And drugs cause cramp.
> Guns aren't lawful;
> Nooses give;
> Gas smells awful;
> You might as well live.

After her second attempt, Dorothy took to wearing tuberose perfume, the scent recommended by morticians for corpses. A review of the titles Parker chose for her books shows her continuing fascination with death: *Enough Rope* (1926), *Laments for the Living* (1930), *Death and Taxes* (1931), *Here Lies* (1939).

She frequently revised her own epitaph, the most famous being "Here Lies Dorothy Parker. Excuse My Dust!" Composing epitaphs became a kind of parlor game among her friends at the Algonquin Round Table, an informal New York City institution formed in the early 1920s. Parker outlived most of the original members of the Round Table. Suicide and various alcohol-related illnesses would cut short the careers of an appalling number of them; in her last years, Parker described her longevity as an embarrassment as well as a bore.

Early meetings of the group were hilarious affairs. Dorothy first met some of the group's more prominent members at a luncheon celebrating Alexander Woollcott's return from Europe in 1919. Woollcott, a venomously witty man whose meager sex life consisted of a solitary delight in cross-dressing, had been the drama critic for the *New York Times* before the war. Assigned to the Paris office of the army's weekly newspaper, *Stars and Stripes,* Woollcott had developed an unlikely friendship with former private Harold Ross, the newspaper's managing editor, who would go on to create and manage the *New Yorker.* At their first meeting, after Ross had derided the profession of drama critic as effeminate, Woollcott had responded, "You know, you remind me a great deal of my grandfather's coachman." Ross, in turn, thought of Woollcott as "a fat duchess with the emotions of a fish."

Other luminaries present at Woollcott's homecoming included Franklin Pierce Adams, who would help make Parker famous in the following years by printing her less scabrous quips in his column "The Conning Tower." (Parker's friends often lamented the loss to the public of her most inspired jokes, which were too obscene for publication.) Adams had worked on *Stars and Stripes* with Ross and Woollcott. Ruth Hale, a militant feminist who refused to relinquish her maiden name, was also in attendance, with her husband, Heywood Broun, whom she had married while they were war correspondents. The company so enjoyed themselves that someone vaguely proposed that the group lunch together again.

Parker's friends Benchley and Robert Sherwood were quickly assimilated, along with a number of other young journalists. The Algonquin management began seating the burgeoning group at a large, circular table. When their reputation for scandalously amusing conversation began attracting prominent celebrities like H. L. Mencken and H. G. Wells to the luncheons, a cartoonist for the *Brooklyn Eagle* published a caricature of the club meetings and labeled it the Algonquin Round Table.

Although group regulars included several women (besides Parker and Hale, the circle welcomed Ross's wife, journalist Jane Grant, and, when she appeared, author Edna Ferber), the atmosphere at the Round Table was that of an Old Boys' club, varied by frequent flarings of urbanely catty temper. The women held their own. When Noël Coward and Edna Ferber arrived wearing similar double-breasted suits, Coward said sweetly, "Edna, why it's you! You look almost like a man!" Ferber replied, "So do you."

In later years, Ferber most clearly recalled the steel beneath the gaiety at the Round Table jousts:

> Far from boosting one another, they actually were merciless if they disapproved. I have never encountered a more hard-bitten crew. . . . Theirs was a tonic influence, one on the other, and on the world of American letters. . . . The people they could not and would not stand were the bores, hypocrites, sentimentalists and the socially pretentious. . . . Casual, incisive, they had a terrible integrity about their work and a boundless ambition.
>
> (Frewin, pp. 44–45)

It was a combination of integrity, ambition, and unbridled chutzpah that resulted in Parker's dismissal from the staff of *Vanity Fair* in 1920. She had been unsparing in her negative reviews of plays produced by several influential figures, including Florenz Ziegfeld, and she had compounded her offense to Ziegfeld by insulting his wife, actress Billie Burke, whose performing style Parker compared with that of the flamboyant exotic dancer Eva Tanguay. After his forced apology to Burke (Ziegfeld was one of the larger advertisers in *Vanity Fair*), Crowninshield relieved Parker of her duties as drama critic. Parker later recalled that "*Vanity Fair* was a magazine of no opinion, but *I* had opinions."

Although he had a family to support, Benchley resigned to protest Parker's dismissal, and the pair rented a tiny office where they planned to collaborate on free-lance writing projects. "An inch smaller and it would have been adultery," Parker said. By all accounts, their long relationship remained physically (if not emotionally) chaste. When Benchley opened a charge account at Polly Adler's fashionable brothel, where he would play backgammon with the madam for the services of the employees, Parker helped to collect a library of tasteful books for Adler's parlor. She was delighted to drink champagne with a famous madam, and remained friendly with Adler for years.

Parker was no more inclined to celibacy than Benchley was, however, and nearly matched his promiscuity after Eddie left her in 1922. Eddie had returned from the war a stranger to her; he could not keep up with the Algonquin crowd even when he was not under the influence of alcohol. Dorothy reveled in the flashing repartee of the Algonquin and of the speakeasies the Round Table moved to in the evenings. Her best jokes were made at the expense of her sex and herself. Her biographer Marion Meade lists some of the most oft-quoted quips:

> Wicked put-downs seemed to flow effortlessly. Hearing that a friend had hurt her leg while visiting London, she voiced a naughty suspicion: Probably the woman had injured herself while sliding down a barrister.
>
> Wasn't the Yale prom wonderful? she said. If all the girls in attendance were laid end to end, she wouldn't be at all surprised.
>
> At a Halloween party, she hoped they would play ducking for apples. There, but for a typographical error, was the story of her life.
>
> Bidding good night to a friend, she promised to telephone soon, then immediately cracked that the woman spoke eighteen languages but couldn't manage to say no in any of them.
>
> She excelled at punning word games. When asked to use the word horticulture in a sentence, she answered, "You may lead a horticulture, but you can't make her think."
>
> (Meade, p. 82)

Parker polished her prose style in a monthly column of drama reviews for *Ainslee's* magazine, "In Broadway Playhouses." She began contributing poetry and prose pieces to *Life*, and developing certain trademark techniques: surprising twists in the last lines of her poems, and Algonquin-style word games in her prose (she told *Life*'s readers that Avery Hopwood's plays went "from bed to worse"). She continued her early experiments with dialogue, both in poetry and in prose pieces such as "The

Christmas Dinner'' (1922). In ''The Far-Sighted Muse,'' she used typography to delineate her two voices:

> Dark though the clouds, they are silver-lined:
> *(This is the stuff that they like to read.)*
> If Winter comes, Spring is right behind;
> *(This is the stuff that the people need.)*
> Smile, and the World will smile back at you;
> Aim with a grin, and you cannot miss;
> Laugh off your woes, and you won't feel blue.
> *(Poetry pays when it's done like this.)*
> (*Life*, 9 March 1922, p. 3)

She wrote her first book reviews for *Life*, and excoriated selected novelists with the same glee she took in castigating playwrights. Reviewing Kathleen Norris's *The Beloved Woman*, she reassured her readers:

> Remember that the book is by Kathleen Norris, so everything is going to turn out for the best, and there will never be a word that could possibly give pain to any of her readers and make the sales fall off.
> (*Life*, 17 November 1921, p. 22)

The years 1920–1922 were very productive for Parker. In addition to her work for *Ainslee's* and *Life*, she published character sketches, essays, and verse in most of the major popular journals; her name became familiar to a wide audience. When not writing, she was partying with the Round Table, and she began drinking more heavily. Several of her short stories chronicle the New York City nightlife of the 1920s. She shows us a typical evening of speakeasy-hopping in the short dramatic monologue ''Just a Little One'' (1930), as we listen to a narrator becoming increasingly sentimental, jealous, irrational, and finally ridiculous in her drunkenness. ''You Were Perfectly Fine'' (1930) follows a young man's effortful unraveling of the events of the night before, which have left him with a crushing hangover, a new, unlooked-for fiancée, and no memory of what he did to deserve these things.

The Round Table group grew increasingly dependent upon each other's company. In 1922, they began working as well as playing together, staging a musical comedy as a group effort. *No, Siree!*, soon retitled *The Forty-Niners*, written by and starring Algonquin members, opened on Broadway for a very brief run enjoyed more by the players than by the audience. Dorothy began a series of collaborations that season, working with Franklin P. Adams on a book of light verse, *Women I'm Not Married To; Men I'm Not Married To* (1922).

Socially, Parker was at loose ends. Woollcott, a perennial matchmaker, was moved by her plight to introduce her to Charles MacArthur, a young journalist and playwright who later collaborated with Ben Hecht on *The Front Page*. Hecht remembers MacArthur as a ''dashing, mysterious fellow'' with ''a poet's infatuation with death.'' Parker fell deeply in love with MacArthur, only to watch him quickly lose interest in her. When it was clear that the relationship had foundered, she ended an unexpected pregnancy with an abortion. Ten years later, she wrote ''Lady with a Lamp'' (1932), another dramatic monologue, telling—from a safe distance—the story of her abortion. We hear only the voice of a malevolent acquaintance who intrudes into a the sickroom of a woman recovering from an abortion; the woman has come not to comfort but to torment:

> Because after all—well, of course, you never looked sweeter, I don't mean that; but you're—well, you're not getting any younger. . . . Look at the woman he's in love with, and you'll see what kind he is. . . . The minute he had you, he didn't want you any more. That's what he's like. Why, he no more loved you than—
>
> Mona, don't! Mona, stop it! Please, Mona! You mustn't talk like that, you mustn't say such things. You've got to stop crying, you'll be terribly sick. Stop, oh, stop it, oh, please stop! Oh, what am I going to do with her? Mona, dear—Mona! Oh, where in heaven's name is that fool maid?

> *Edie. Oh, Edie! Edie. I think you'd better get Dr. Britton on the telephone, and tell him to come down and give Miss Morrison something to quiet her. I'm afraid she's got herself a little bit upset.*
>
> (*The Portable Dorothy Parker* [1973], p. 253)

Soon after the abortion, Parker slashed her wrists. Her friends rallied around her at the hospital, and she greeted them gaily, waving the pale-blue ribbons she'd tied over her bandages. Convalescing at home, she replaced the blue ribbons with black velvet bands and oversized bows.

Parker resigned from *Ainslee's* and began a number of new poems on such topics as shrouds and decomposing corpses—"Testament," for instance:

> Oh, let it be a night of lyric rain
> And singing breezes, when my bell is tolled.
> . . . .
> Kinder the busy worms than ever love;
> It will be peace to lie there, empty-eyed,
> My bed made secret by the leveling showers,
> My breast replenishing the weeds above.
> And you will say of me, "Then has she died?
> Perhaps I should have sent a spray of flowers."

Early in 1923, Dorothy and Eddie attempted a reconciliation, but did not admit their failure until January 1924. In July, she published the short story "Too Bad," a study of a moribund marriage. She frames her close examination of the marriage with two conversations by outsiders who are shocked to learn that the couple are separating. The gossiping neighbors sound foolish in their opening conversation; after Parker has anatomized the marriage in the central portion of the story, we see that the divorcing couple understand the mechanisms of their estrangement no better than the uninvolved neighbors do. Dorothy and Eddie separated permanently in 1924 and were divorced in 1928. (In 1933, five years after marrying for a second time, he died of an overdose of sleeping powder.)

After Eddie left, Dorothy gave up her apartment and moved into the Algonquin. Writing with uncharacteristic speed, she produced part of a play inspired by Benchley's unconcealed, embarrassingly inappropriate affair with a show girl. She was attempting to explain his behavior to herself as well as to New York society, and found herself with an enormously overlong first act consisting entirely of endless dialogue—interesting material that could not be acted onstage. Collaborating with the experienced playwright Elmer Rice to turn her static conversation into a stageable domestic comedy, she finished the play by summer. It opened under the name *Close Harmony* in December 1924, receiving good reviews but disappointing box office returns.

After extricating herself from a tepid affair with Rice, Parker consoled herself with a series of brief liaisons. One of her fellow Round Tablers, journalist Marc Connelly, described a typical romance:

> She fell in love with some of the goddamnedest terrible people. John What-the-hell-was-his name—society boy with the famous brother, you'd know the name if I could remember it. He and his brother were very, very, very East Hampton. Handsome guy, pretty good tennis player. He was a wealthy mucker and quite a bastard. We were all delighted when she shook him off—he was dandruff. Have you got a list of her beaux? Not a full list? Well, I wouldn't think so.
>
> (Meade, p. 140)

Parker's writing was slowed by her drinking and her overbooked social calendar. In 1924 the exasperated publisher George Palmer Putnam had to threaten to call out the police and fire departments before Parker produced her very late manuscript of Chapter 7 of *Bobbed Hair*, a serialized, collaborative mystery novel written by nineteen prominent writers, including Woollcott. She collaborated with George S. Kaufman on a film script, *Business Is Business*, a short comedy satirizing avaricious commerce. The film was successfully produced, but neither Kaufman nor Parker liked the result—or each other. Kaufman later directed a play by George Oppenheimer, *Here Today* (1932), that involved a most unflatteringly recognizable alcoholic character modeled on Parker.

When Harold Ross established the *New Yorker* in 1925, he assembled an editorial board of impressive names, including Parker's, but Parker's contributions to the magazine were disappointingly erratic. She began seeing a psychiatrist and reduced her drinking with his help, but would not give up the Veronal tablets to which she had become addicted. Depressed in the aftermath of a minor love affair, she used her supply of Veronal in a second suicide attempt. Her hospital room was again filled with encouraging friends; Heywood Broun brought her gin in his hip flask.

Parker's social contacts broadened in the 1920s as her fame increased. She met a number of American expatriates, including Hemingway, F. Scott and Zelda Fitzgerald, Dos Passos, and Gerald and Sara Murphy. Her admiration for Hemingway approached adulation, and her immediate fondness for the Murphys (exempted from her usual complex contempt for the very wealthy) developed into one of the most heartfelt and long-lasting friendships of her life.

Parker became enamored of the European life Hemingway described, and decided to join the expatriates for a working vacation. Traveling with Hemingway and several Algonquinites, in 1926 she took a steamer to France, where the Murphys provided her a cottage in which to work. Her enthusiasm for all things Hemingwayesque was slightly qualified after an unhappy excursion to Spain to watch the bullfights, which revolted her. Perhaps in response to her animal-lover's abhorrence of bullfighting, Hemingway's enthusiasm for Parker curdled into a racist, sexist attack delivered behind her back. At a party in Paris, depressed over his marital situation and seriously considering suicide himself, Hemingway read a poem titled "To a Tragic Poetess—Nothing in her life became her like her almost leaving of it":

> Spaniards pinched
> the Jewish cheeks of your plump ass
> in holy week in Seville
> forgetful of our Lord and His passion.
> Returned, your ass intact, to Paris
> to write more poems for the New Yorker. . . .
> (quoted in Meade, p. 173)

This poem was not published until 1979, and it is not clear how much Parker knew of Hemingway's opinion of her; but her opinion of his work, if not of his hobbies or his ethics, remained untarnished. Among the short stories she published in the *New Yorker* in 1926 is "Oh, He's So Charming," in which an egomaniacal author strongly resembling Hemingway is lampooned. However, reviewing Hemingway's short-story collection *Men Without Women* for the *New Yorker* in 1927, she called him "the greatest living writer of short stories" and praised the collection as "a truly magnificent work." She was apparently plagued by lingering doubts of his affection, however. Her last recorded words, spoken to Beatrice Ames several days before her death in 1967, were "I want you to tell me the truth. Did Ernest really like me?"

Settled somewhat dyspeptically in Paris ("*la belle, la brave, la* raw, *la* rainy"), Parker worked on her first collection of poetry, *Enough Rope* (1926). The poems in this book are related through the theme of death, discussed with sardonic disillusion. The book immediately became a best-seller.

Parker returned to New York just as her book appeared in the stores, and basked in her sudden popularity. She began writing enormously popular book reviews for the *New Yorker* in the column "Constant Reader," slashing authors guilty of sentimentality, commercialism, and dullness. She wrote many of her most famous lines for this column, including her account of reading A. A. Milne's *The House at Pooh Corner:*

> "*The more it snows, tiddely-pom—*"
> " 'Tiddely what?' said Piglet." (He took, as you might say, the very words out of your correspondent's mouth.)

> " 'Pom,' said Pooh. 'I put that in to make it more hummy.' "
>
> And it is that word "hummy," my darlings, that marks the first place in "The House at Pooh Corner" at which Tonstant Weader fwowed up.
>
> ("Far from Well," *New Yorker,* 20 October 1928, p. 98; reprinted in *The Portable Dorothy Parker* [1973], p. 518)

Her second collection of poems, *Sunset Gun* (1928), sold as well as her first, and was soon followed by "Big Blonde" (1929), her longest and possibly her best short story. Hazel Morse, the title character, is a statuesque blond model, a "good sport," popular with men because she never whines. One of her suitors marries her; she relaxes into the marriage, slips out of her "good sport" persona, and occasionally admits, with a slight whine, that she is not always perfectly gay. She loses her husband, who thought he was marrying a female version of "one of the guys," and devolves into a fleshy, coarsened, alcoholic, unsuccessfully suicidal barfly. The story won the O. Henry Award for 1929. Parker included "Big Blonde" in her first collection of stories, *Laments for the Living* (1930), which was received fairly well by the critics. T. S. Matthews wrote of it:

> We recognize her own style: style which is apparently compact of merely reported speech, but which has a bite, nevertheless, as individual and unmistakable as Ring Lardner's or Hemingway's.
>
> ("Curses Not Loud but Deep," *New Republic,* 17 September 1930, p. 133)

With the O. Henry Award, Parker had achieved enough visibility to attract the attention of Hollywood. She was lured to the West Coast by the fabulous salaries Hollywood offered its screenwriters. She endured the inanities of the film industry only three months, however, before fleeing to New York, and left New York almost immediately for Paris, where she planned to write a novel entitled "Sonnets in Suicide; or, The Life of John Knox." John Knox had appeared in *Sunset Gun,* in the poem "Partial Comfort":

> Whose love is given over-well
> Shall look on Helen's face in hell,
> Whilst they whose love is thin and wise
> May view John Knox in paradise.

In Europe she made little progress on her novel. She spent less time writing than struggling with health problems—her own liver disease inconvenienced her, and she spent months helping the Murphys watch their young son dying of tuberculosis in Switzerland. Returning to New York in January 1930, Parker confessed to her friends that the project had overwhelmed her, and that she was "quite incapable of it—I'm a short distance writer." Another trip to Europe did not help; after summering in Switzerland, Italy, and Germany, she again sailed for New York in the fall of 1930, with only a few poems in hand.

By the spring of 1931, although distracted by reviewing duties for the *New Yorker* and *McCall's,* Parker had accumulated enough verses for a third collection, *Death and Taxes.* Several of the poems refer to her latest wretched love affair, an unprecedentedly ugly relationship with a young reporter, John McClain: "Every love's the love before / In a duller dress" ("Summary"). When he left her, she described him as a "male prostitute" and predicted that he would tire of his wealthy new mistress "as soon as he has licked all the gilt off her ass." In February 1932, she tried suicide again, this time with barbiturates.

After her recovery, Parker wrote a number of fine stories. "From the Diary of a New York Lady" (1932), a series of journal entries revealing the diarist's selfishness and vacuity, varies the narrative technique Parker had practiced in "A Telephone Call" (1928), a combination of stream of consciousness and internal monologue in which a jilted woman argues with herself and with God in an attempt to make her long-silent telephone ring. Parker's subtitle for "From the Diary of a New York Lady" sharpens her portrait of upper-class social irresponsibility by placing her self-absorbed diarist in the context of the Depression: "During Days of Horror, Despair, and World Change."

Parker had developed liberal political sympathies at Miss Dana's School, and her work is filled with allusions to controversial topics such as women's suffrage and racial integration. In "Arrangement in Black and White" (1927), a story inspired by black actor Paul Robeson's appearance on the New York social scene, she attacks the racism of those socialites who viewed him as a chic novelty. But she did not become politically active until 1927, when Sacco and Vanzetti had exhausted all legal remedies. Along with many other New York literati (including Dos Passos, Katherine Anne Porter, Upton Sinclair, and Edna St. Vincent Millay), Parker was outraged by the impending execution of the two immigrant anarchists; Benchley also was involved, having found evidence of judicial bias in the trial. On the eve of the execution, Parker went to Boston, where she was arrested for participating in a street protest. A picture of her arrest appeared in the newspapers, and the FBI began a file on her.

Parker's second encounter with political radicalism occurred while she was sailing to Europe with Sara Murphy in 1932. Parker often left her first-class quarters to visit a group of American Communists traveling third-class to the Soviet Union. This group included Mary Mooney, the eighty-four-year-old mother of Tom Mooney, a labor leader who had been imprisoned in San Quentin after a bombing incident; Parker admired Mary Mooney's regal deportment, and wrote a letter praising her to the *New York Sun*. When she tried to obtain a passport to work as a war correspondent during World War II, she was denied permission, partly because of her passing involvement with the controversial Mooneys.

After her return to New York, Parker met a young actor and author, Alan Campbell, Jewish and Scottish like Parker and eleven years her junior. Campbell was stunningly handsome; his beauty and the number of his homosexual friends caused rumors regarding his own sexual orientation. Despite the rumors, Parker and Campbell set up housekeeping in her apartment, where he devotedly attended to organizing her disorderly life. Campbell was gifted with a nurturing nature, and Parker was sorely in need of nurturing. Alan delighted in the Algonquin crowd's sparkle and moved easily among Parker's friends; he published a number of stories in the *New Yorker*.

The Round Table was breaking up in 1932, in part because so many of the members, including Benchley, had moved to Hollywood. Parker and Campbell joined the Hollywood colony in 1933; they married on the way to California, and began working for Paramount Pictures. Both despised Hollywood and their studio bosses; both were frustrated by the Hollywood system of multiple rewrites, which produced films resembling the original scripts only incidentally. But they were a well-matched team and they earned a great deal of money, largely owing to Campbell's stabilizing influence. They were overheard composing dialogue for *Sweethearts*, a sentimental romance:

> "And then what does *he* say?" Alan asked.
>
> Dorothy's answer was soft but audible. "Shit."
>
> "Please don't use that word," Alan muttered. Turning back to his typewriter, he continued, "All right—and then what does *she* say?"
>
> "Shit."
>
> *"Don't use that word!"*
>
> (Meade, p. 290)

As ultimately produced, laundered by the studio machinery, most of their work was forgettable. They contributed dialogue to *Here Is My Heart* (1934), *One Hour Late* (1934), and *Mary Burns, Fugitive* (1935), and worked on screenplay construction and the treatment for *Hands Across the Table* (1935) and *Paris in the Spring* (1935). In 1936, they wrote three joint screenplays, *Three Married Men*, *Lady, Be Careful*, and *Suzy*. Critics dismissed most of these scripts, and lamented the absence of the familiar Parker vitriol. But in 1937, Parker and Campbell were assigned to rewrite an early script for *A Star Is Born*, and their screenplay was nominated for an Academy Award. The *New York Times* called the film "the most accurate mirror ever held before the glittering, tinseled, trivial, generous, cruel, and ecstatic world that is Hollywood. . . . Its script is bright, inventive, and forceful" (quoted in Kinney, pp. 57–58).

Parker became more politically active while living in Hollywood, and her first efforts were against the studio management. In 1936 she became active in the Screen Writers Guild and began writing political pieces favoring unionization for *Screen Guilds* magazine. In her comments on *A Star Is Born,* which she felt demonstrated Hollywood's progression toward cinematic "realism," she echoed the doctrine of the Communist Party. This politicized aesthetic would shape several of the works collected in *Here Lies* (1939), such as "Clothe the Naked," a short story that had been rejected by the *New Yorker.* Socialist realism—a programmed art intended to disrupt the political status quo by depicting its injustice—had no place on the *New Yorker's* agenda, and Parker had no gift for it in any case. "Clothe the Naked" concerns a poor, blind, black child's mistreatment by a white mob, oppressors invisible to the child just as the insidious ideology of the political hegemony is invisible to those who do not know to look for it. For all Parker's "realistic" intentions, however, the story sinks into the same sentimentality she could not tolerate in the work of others.

She had better luck with oblique criticism, as in "Song of the Shirt, 1941," in which she depicts injustice by examining the perpetrators, not the victims. In this story, Mrs. Martindale, a wealthy society matron who cannot sew, volunteers to sew shirts as part of the home effort during World War II. Her commitment to her tony volunteer group is genuine; her commitment to the human race is not. She coldly denies employment to a needy young woman who could assemble the shirts more efficiently. Parker leaves the ever-gracious Mrs. Martindale setting about her self-satisfied, martyred summer project. The story pleased Harold Ross, and he bought it without a qualm. Like *Vanity Fair,* the *New Yorker* subscribed to what Robert Benchley called the Elevated Eyebrow School of Journalism, which, one of Parker's biographers notes, allowed one to "write about practically any subject you wished, no matter how outrageous, so long as you said it in evening clothes."

In 1937, Parker became actively involved in raising funds for the Loyalists in the Spanish Civil War, then visited Spain with Campbell in 1938 and helped Hemingway publicize the Loyalist cause in Hollywood. In 1939, she added the Nazis to her list of political foes, but her speeches against them were variously judged hysterical, insincere, and ill-informed. She was in fact less than perfectly conscientious in researching the numerous political organizations to which she lent her name, an unfortunately habitual lapse that came to light when she was examined by the House Un-American Activities Committee in 1955. Parker and her political ally Lillian Hellman were both dogged by the Committee in the 1950s. Both refused to incriminate their colleagues, yet both escaped imprisonment, possibly because they were women.

Parker's hatred of the Nazis, and her lifelong admiration of men in uniform, prompted Campbell to enlist in the Army Air Force in 1942. Long-festering tensions, a miscarriage, and wartime separation irreparably damaged their marriage. They divorced in 1947, and Parker embarked on a series of increasingly sordid affairs with handsome younger men who helped her drink. She continued to write occasionally, often in collaboration with others: in 1947, the film treatment of *Smash-Up: The Story of a Woman,* which she wrote with Frank Cavett, brought Parker another Academy Award nomination, and a steady job at Twentieth Century–Fox. Writing with Ross Evans, one of her nastier lovers, she produced a successful play, *The Coast of Illyria,* but her debilitating alcoholism was simultaneously eroding her reputation in Hollywood. In 1950, she surprised her friends by remarrying Campbell. His best nurturing efforts were ineffective this time, however. He began drinking as heavily as Parker, and the reconciliation was only fitfully successful.

During one of their separations, Parker collaborated with Arnaud d'Usseau in New York on a play, *Ladies of the Corridor* (1953). Set in a women's hotel in New York City, the play is populated by characters exemplifying Parker's worst fears for herself: alcoholism, age, loneliness, and suicide. After receiving mixed reviews for *Ladies of the Corridor,* Parker and d'Usseau wrote another, *The Ice Age* (1955), the story of a homosexual murdered by his lover. It was never produced.

In 1961, she gave up free-lancing in New York to rejoin Campbell in Hollywood. They worked together for Twentieth Century–Fox, producing nothing particularly memorable. When not too drunk, Parker reviewed books for *Esquire,* but she frequently missed deadlines, despite Campbell's prodding. Between assignments at Fox, they lived on unemployment insurance. Parker was appointed briefly at California State College in Los Angeles, but had no affinity for teaching and failed to attend a third of her classes. She was not often sober, and neither was Campbell. In 1963, Campbell died of an overdose of barbiturates.

Parker published very little new work in the 1960s. In 1964, she moved to New York, where she lived at the Volney Hotel and developed a taste for soap operas. Her attitude towards the fashionable triflings of New York's beau monde remained ambiguous to the end. She was startled but delighted to find herself being cultivated by Gloria Vanderbilt Cooper, who dressed Parker's shrunken figure in a magnificent golden gown for a fete in Parker's honor. Parker died on 7 June 1967. To the surprise of many, she bequeathed what money she had left and her literary estate to Martin Luther King, Jr.

Sympathizing with those who sought intimacy with Parker, her friend Donald Ogden Stewart remarked:

> She was so full of pretense. . . . That doesn't mean she did not hate sham on a high level, but that she could recognize pretense because that was part of her makeup. She would get glimpses of herself doing things that would make her hate herself. . . .
>
> (Keats, p. 62)

As a misogynist woman seeking entry into the predominantly male intellectual circles of New York and Paris, as a self-styled Communist sympathizer seeking the approval of wealthy WASP society, and as an anti-Semitic Jew seeking a separate inner peace, Parker was doomed to a life that would be difficult, at best. But Edmund Wilson's assessment of *Enough Rope* applies to Parker's oeuvre as a whole:

> I believe that, if we admire, as it is fashionable to do, the light verse of Prior and Gay, we should admire Miss Parker also. She writes well: her wit is the wit of her time and place; but it is often as cleanly economic at the same time that it is as flatly brutal as the wit of the age of Pope; and, within its scope, it is a criticism of life.
>
> ("The Muses Out of Work," *New Republic,* 11, May 1927, p. 321)

Selected Bibliography

PRIMARY WORKS

POETRY

Enough Rope. New York: Boni & Liveright, 1926.

Sunset Gun. New York: Boni & Liveright, 1928.

Death and Taxes. New York: Viking, 1931

Not So Deep as a Well. New York: Viking, 1936.

DRAMA

Close Harmony. New York: Samuel French, 1929. With Elmer Rice.

Ladies of the Corridor. New York: Viking, 1954. With Arnaud d'Usseau.

FICTION

Laments for the Living. New York: Viking, 1930.

After Such Pleasures. New York: Viking, 1933.

Here Lies. New York: Viking, 1939.

COLLECTIONS

The Collected Stories of Dorothy Parker. New York: Modern Library, 1942.

The Collected Poetry of Dorothy Parker. New York: Modern Library, 1944.

The Viking Portable Library: Dorothy Parker. New York: Viking, 1944.

The Best of Dorothy Parker. London: Methuen, 1952.

The Portable Dorothy Parker. New York: Viking, 1973. With an introduction by Brendan Gill.

The Penguin Dorothy Parker. New York and Harmondsworth, England: Viking/Penguin, 1977.

CRITICISM

Short Story: A Thematic Anthology. New York: Scribners, 1965. With Frederick B. Shroyer.

Constant Reader. New York: Viking, 1970.

RECORDINGS

An Informal Hour with Dorothy Parker. Spoken Arts 726. 1956.

The World of Dorothy Parker. Verve V-15029. 1962.

SECONDARY WORKS

BIOGRAPHICAL AND CRITICAL STUDIES

Bunkers, Suzanne L. " 'I Am Outraged Womanhood': Dorothy Parker as Feminist and Social Critic." In *Regionalism and the Female Imagination* 4, no. 2:25–34 (1979–1980).

Capron, Marion. "Dorothy Parker." In *Writers at Work: The Paris Review Interviews.* 1st ser. Edited by Malcolm Cowley. New York: Viking, 1957.

Cooper, Wyatt. "Whatever You Think Dorothy Parker Was Like, She Wasn't." *Esquire,* July 1968, pp. 56–57, 61, 110–114.

Crowninshield, Frank. "Crowninshield in the Cub's Den." *Vogue,* 15 September 1944, pp. 162–163, 197–201.

Drennan, Robert E. *The Algonquin Wits.* New York: Citadel Press, 1968.

Frewin, Leslie. *The Late Mrs. Dorothy Parker.* New York: Macmillan, 1986.

Gaines, James R. *Wit's End: Days and Nights of the Algonquin Round Table.* New York: Harcourt Brace Jovanovich, 1977.

Gill, Brendan. "Introduction." In *The Portable Dorothy Parker.* New York: Viking, 1973.

Graham, Sheilah. *The Garden of Allah.* New York: Crown, 1970.

Grant, Jane. *Ross, the "New Yorker," and Me.* New York: Reynal, 1968.

Gray, James. *On Second Thought.* Minneapolis: University of Minnesota Press, 1946.

Guiles, Fred Lawrence. *Hanging on in Paradise.* New York: McGraw-Hill, 1975.

Hecht, Ben. *Letters from Bohemia.* Garden City, N.Y.: Doubleday, 1964.

Hellman, Lillian. *An Unfinished Woman.* Boston: Little, Brown, 1969.

Keats, John. *You Might as Well Live: The Life and Times of Dorothy Parker.* New York: Simon & Schuster, 1970.

Kinney, Arthur. *Dorothy Parker.* Boston: Twayne, 1978.

Maugham, Somerset. "Variations on a Theme." Introduction to *The Viking Portable Library: Dorothy Parker.* New York: Viking, 1944.

Meade, Marion. *Dorothy Parker: What Fresh Hell Is This?* New York: Villard, 1988.

Toth, Emily. "Dorothy Parker, Erica Jong, and the New Feminist Humor." *Regionalism and the Female Imagination* 3, no. 3:70–85 (1977–1978).

Woollcott, Alexander. *While Rome Burns.* New York: Viking, 1934.

GWEN CRANE

SYLVIA PLATH

1932–1963

SYLVIA PLATH'S IS a poetry of extremes, not so much the extremes of light and dark as of darkness itself: "This is the light of the mind, cold and planetary," begins "The Moon and the Yew Tree," a poem from late 1961. "The trees of the mind are black. The light is blue." The extremes of darkness—black, blacker, blackest—also serve as biography, reductive though not far from truth. For Sylvia Plath was constantly making and unmaking both her life—she once attempted, and later committed, suicide—and her work.

Few recent poets have undergone as many literary and biographical postmortems as has Plath. The cult of her personality, and of her poems and prose, has seemed at times to be an industry. The body of work she herself saw into print—*The Colossus* (1962), a volume of poems, and *The Bell Jar* (1971), a pseudonymous novel—is far outweighed by work published posthumously. This imbalance has confused the issue of how Plath wished to present herself to the world: as tragic heroine; as accomplished poet; as author of slick magazine fiction; as dutiful if troubled daughter? She was all of these. What she was not, what she never lived to be, was a writer who matured enough, in both age and achievement, to be merely herself.

Born on 27 October 1932 in the Jamaica Plain district of Boston, Sylvia Plath was the only daughter of Otto Plath, a German immigrant, university professor, and published scientist whose book *Bumblebees and Their Ways* appeared in 1934. Aurelia Schober Plath, Sylvia's mother, was twenty-one years her husband's junior and had been one of his students; after their marriage she was her husband's assistant and typist. Thus theirs was a working home. The late 1920s and the 1930s saw the collapse of the American economy, the Great Depression, and the subsequent hardships suffered by many families. With the influx of Europeans during these difficult years, many Americans looked askance on such immigrants, particularly Germans, many of them holding Germany responsible for World War I.

The family lived under Mr. Plath's domination until he fell ill with what he feared was cancer (then perceived as a disease of the weak) but was in fact diabetes. Chiefly from a refusal to seek treatment until permanent damage had been done, Mr. Plath died shortly after Sylvia's eighth birthday. In spite of her father's death, Plath's childhood seems to have been relatively uncomplicated. "[I was] brought up . . . in the fairy-tale world of Mary Poppins and Winnie-the-Pooh," she once wrote sardonically. Being raised by a single working mother (Mrs. Plath taught German and Spanish at the high school level and then a course for medical secretaries at Boston University) was a situation in which many American children found themselves in the 1940s. Husbands and fathers went off to war, many not to return. Although Otto Plath was neither war hero nor casualty, the coincidence of his Germanic heritage, his death, and World War II contributed to his metamorphosis in "Daddy" (1962), Plath's most famous poem, into "a man in black with a Meinkampf look." The metamorphosis lay years in the future, though its seeds were almost certainly planted with his death.

Preoccupied with Plath's younger brother and the demands of running a household that now included her own parents, Mrs. Plath must have appeared to her daughter as a distant if sometimes beneficent figure. A paradigm of the bright, well-behaved young lady, Plath began at an early age to court her mother's approval and affection, often with small poems and handmade greeting cards. The work of a talented, precocious apprentice, Plath's first poems were published in the *Christian Science Monitor* and her first fiction in *Seventeen*, a magazine for young women. On the strength of these and other accomplishments, she entered Smith College in the fall of 1950.

Plath was one of a generation of women encouraged to move beyond secondary education, though college was rarely considered an end in itself. Most often, college was the means to marriage or to a brief career followed by marriage. An educated woman with no husband seemed suspect, an oddity. Plath's Smith journals are filled with such arguments, and with heated refutations. She wanted desperately to be a writer and less to marry, to lose herself in societal definitions of male-female relationships, afraid that her talents would be dismissed by a husband and thus disappear.

Plath's early poems reflect these concerns. "Female Author," an early sonnet reprinted in an appendix of juvenilia to *The Complete Poems*, is a marriage daydream cynically rendered: "All day she plays at chess with the bones of the world: / Favored . . . she lies on cushions curled / And nibbles an occasional bonbon of sin." Another recounts the tale of Cinderella, the fatherless girl whose one chance for love is spoiled (and not, in the poem, regained) by time. The quantity of Plath's juvenilia is astounding. She once hoped to write a thousand words a day and reportedly relied heavily on a thesaurus for inspiration and guidance. The poems, with their insistence on form and technique, on language as a timepiece that works best when wound to a point shy of breaking, seem almost to belong to another time.

Returning from a month-long student editorship at *Mademoiselle* magazine in the summer of 1953, Plath suffered a nervous breakdown and later attempted suicide. The ambitious, successful young student became that summer a woman whose sense of self failed. "I will have to be cheerful and constructive," she writes in her journal, a sort of pep talk. "I will learn about shopping and cooking, and try to make Mother's vacation happy and good. That in itself would be worthwhile." *I will, I will,* the litany continues. From learning shorthand to writing daily for hours, to reading James Joyce, Plath set goals for herself that she could not meet. The suicide attempt unsuccessful, Plath was hospitalized for psychiatric treatment. A journal entry from February 1956 describes one "shock treatment that went wrong" as "waking to a new world, with no name, being born again, and not a woman." (Plath's experience of electroshock therapy is memorialized in a 1960 poem, "The Hanging Man," and echoed in the fascination of *The Bell Jar*'s heroine with the execution by electrocution of Julius and Ethel Rosenberg, who had been convicted of providing the Soviets with atomic secrets.)

Few writings survive from that summer, if they ever existed. What some readers take for the truth of that time is *The Bell Jar*, a somewhat fictionalized account of this period in Plath's life. But even the "truth" of *The Bell Jar* has been called into question, and a lawsuit in the late 1980s contested the portrayal of one character as a lesbian. Plath herself called the novel a "potboiler," and while the "events" may be autobiographical, they are distorted, much as they are later in the poetry. Never "confessional" in the given sense of the word, Plath's poems are her life transformed into a sort of pagan fable. That Plath has been called a confessional poet stems in part from gossip about her life and in part from Robert Lowell's introduction to *Ariel:* "Everything in these poems is personal, confessional, felt." Although Lowell tempers the claim by writing that "the manner of [Plath's] feeling is controlled hallucination, the autobiography of a fever," the temperance all but vanishes when he states that "her art's immortality is life's disintegration."

In the spring term of 1954, Plath returned

to Smith, and graduated in May of the following year. She had long hoped to pursue graduate work abroad, and was awarded a Fulbright Scholarship to study at Newnham College, Cambridge University. At Cambridge her work began to throw off its undergraduate enthusiasms. "Winter Landscape, with Rooks," written in 1956, is described in her journals as "athletic," by which we can presume she meant the poem's construction, its form: three five-line stanzas, rhymes more slant than not ("ice" and "solace," "frost" and "waste"). The poem is also described as "a psychic landscape"—an example of the pathetic fallacy, which John Ruskin described as a morbid "falseness in all our impressions of external things," most importantly in nature. The pathetic fallacy was a device Plath used in nearly all of her landscape poems, sometimes to great effect. "I am at my best in illogical, sensuous description," she once wrote. The second stanza of "Winter Landscape" begins thus:

> The austere sun descends above the fen,
> an orange cyclops-eye, scorning to look
> longer on this landscape of chagrin.

These lines are characteristic of Plath's poems from the early 1950s. Not only do we find the pathetic fallacy ("this landscape of chagrin") but also the heavens as a demonic timepiece, a device that moves the poem from day to night, from remembered summer to present winter.

Plath's Cambridge studies included continued attempts to publish her work. It had already appeared in *Harper's* and in British magazines and periodicals, but she aimed for the *Atlantic Monthly* and the *New Yorker*. One submission to the latter "was rejected . . . this morning with not so much as a pencil scratch on the black-and-white doom of the printed rejection. . . . Still, the accommodating mind imagines that the poems, sent a week before, must be undergoing detailed scrutiny. I shall no doubt get them back tomorrow. Maybe even with a note."

It was at Cambridge, in the winter of 1956, that Plath met Ted Hughes, the young British poet she would marry that summer. The gossip surrounding the meeting and marriage of Plath and Hughes has often seemed the stuff of supermarket tabloids (and is best left to the gossip mongers). Plath, in her letters and journals, and particularly in her late poems, presents one image of Hughes, the brute with "a black grinning look," an image similar to those she drew of her father, and of most of the men in her life.

The day before meeting Hughes, she wrote, "I'd love to cook and make a house, and surge force into a man's dreams, and write, if he could talk and walk and work and passionately want do his career." Marriage and writing, the delicate balance she had once thought impossible, now seemed more likely. Still, the entry continues, "What I fear most, I think, is the death of the imagination." The day after their meeting, Plath began writing "Pursuit," "a poem . . . about the dark forces of lust . . . dedicated to Ted Hughes." The poem's epigraph, "*Dans le fond des forêts votre image me suit*" (In the depths of the forest, your image follows me), is from Racine, on whom Plath was then writing an academic essay, the theme of which was "passion as destiny." "Pursuit" is unrelenting in its central metaphor: man as beast ("There is a panther stalks me down") and woman as prey, albeit prey whose own hungers rage insatiate ("I hurl my heart to halt his pace, / To quench his thirst I squander blood"). The poem's language is that of the sexual hunt, and closes with a note of expectation and dread: "The panther's tread is on the stairs, / Coming up and up the stairs."

Hughes has remained largely silent on the subject of their life together. Whatever the conceptions and misconceptions about their marriage, he did provide Plath with motivation and discipline. He assigned exercises to be written on a given image or theme, and that is what she began to call many of the poems: exercises. Her poems of this period echo Dylan Thomas, Theodore Roethke, and W. H. Auden. (Plath met Auden while at Smith and "approach[ed] him with a sheaf of . . . poems." His reactions, if he did react, are not in the published journals.) She considered few women poets worthy of emulation, and she viewed her contemporaries, particularly Adrienne Rich, as rivals, and all but dismissed them. Rich was thought "dull"; Isabella Gardner, "facile"; and Elizabeth Bishop, "lesbian and fanciful."

The beginnings of Plath's own lyric strangeness, reminiscent of Emily Dickinson, Edgar Allan Poe, and Christopher Smart, appear in two poems from 1957: "The Thin People" and "All the Dead Dears." They forsake the strangeness of landscape for that of men and women. "The Thin People" seem strangers, unfathomable men and women, "empty of complaint, forever / drinking vinegar from tin cups." They are the Other:

> They are always with us, the thin people
> Meager of dimension as the gray people
>
> On a movie-screen. They
> Are unreal, we say:
>
> It was only in a movie, it was only
> In a war making evil headlines when we
>
> Were small that they famished . . .

These lines invoke newsreels, which Plath might have seen, of the prisoners' release from Nazi concentration camps, the utterly wasted bodies that so haunted the postwar years. If Plath could not yet write of oppressors, the oppressed (and, in some ways, she always counted herself among their number) would have to do.

In "All the Dead Dears," Plath considers the contents of a "fourth-century-A.D." sarcophagus: "the skeletons of a woman, a mouse and a shrew." "How they grip us through thin and thick," she writes, "These barnacle dead." Here the skeletons take on an oceanic significance. The female skeleton is "no kin / Of mine, yet kin she is." In rapt succession, the speaker reels off her own kin: "mother, grandmother, greatgrandmother" and "daft father":

> From the mercury-backed glass,
> Mother, Grandmother, greatgrandmother,
> Reach hag hands to haul me in,
> And an image looms under the fishpond
> surface
> Where the daft father went down . . .

The dead, the ocean, mother and father: she made continued use of these images until they became less image than symbol, each with its own definite sense and spirit.

In June 1957, Plath and Hughes left England for the United States, where she was to teach at Smith College that fall. Before beginning the semester, they took a cottage on Cape Cod, hoping for the time and leisure to write without distraction. Her first manuscript of poems began to take shape. (Constantly revising, Plath titled the manuscript at various times "The Earthenware Head," "Full Fathom Five," and "The Devil of the Stairs," among others—a not uncommon practice for poets with their first books.) Plath was determined to write fiction as well, and her journals are filled with fragments of plot and thumbnail character sketches for the novel that, some years later, would become *The Bell Jar*. Poetry or fiction, Plath believed that her well-being lay in "making stories, poems, novels, of experience: that is why . . . it is good that I have suffered & been to hell, although not to all the hells. I cannot live for life itself: but for the words which stay the flux." (This entry echoes another, more sardonic entry from Plath's 1953 journal: "I can't be satisfied with the colossal job of merely living. Oh, no, I must order life in sonnets and sestinas and provide a verbal reflector for my 60-watt lighted head.") The journals also reveal that Plath continued to battle serious depression.

Teaching left Plath little time to write. She and Hughes decided that, the school year finished, they would move to Boston and try to survive on their writing alone. But there were months still before they could leave the academic life behind, months of hard work and continued self-doubt. Then, a letter from *ART news* "asking for a poem on art and speaking of an 'honorarium' " prompted Plath to begin a series of poems based on paintings. "The Disquieting Muses" (1957), after Giorgio di Chirico's painting of the same name, is the most successful of the series. Unencumbered by what she would later see as a characteristic "machine-like syllabic death-blow," the poem's narrative flows easily. The muses are "the three terrible faceless dressmaker's dummies in classical gowns" of di Chirico's painting; they are also "a twentieth-century version of other sinister trios of women—the Three Fates, the witches in *Macbeth,* de Quincy's sisters of madness": so Plath introduced the poem for a radio broadcast. All three evil, they are also Sleeping Beauty's fairy godmothers:

> Mother, mother, what illbred aunt
> Or what disfigured and unsightly
> Cousin did you so unwisely keep
> Unasked to my christening, that she
> Sent these ladies in her stead
> With heads like darning-eggs to nod
> And nod and nod at foot and head
> And at the left side of my crib?

"Unsightly," "unwisely," "unasked": Plath's explicit negatives prefigure the hammering, implied negatives of "nod / And nod and nod" (not and not and not). Other trios inhabit the poem—the speaker, her mother, and the speaker's brother resemble Plath's own family—and words and phrases are repeated: "Thor is angry: boom boom boom!" and the chantlike "I learned, I learned, I learned elsewhere." Though controlled, the poem seems uncalculated, its final lines oddly opaque: "And this is the kingdom you bore me to, / Mother, mother. But no frown of mine / Will betray the company I keep."

The company Plath kept, her own disquieting muses, was that spring to visit her more often. Reading Robert Graves's *The White Goddess: A Historical Grammar of Poetic Myth,* in which the feminine, matriarchal moon is the poet's true muse, was a watershed. Graves's mythologies led her to studies of African folklore and "a book on demonic possession" over the next year.

"On the Decline of Oracles" (1957), another poem after di Chirico, led to "Full Fathom Five" (1958). Both poems concern a father figure, suggestively Plath's own. But while "On the Decline of Oracles" seems all checks and balances, the range of "Full Fathom Five" seems barely contained:

> All obscurity
> Starts with a danger:
>
> Your dangers are many. I
> Cannot look much but your form suffers
> Some strange injury
>
> And seems to die . . .

The poem concludes: "Father, this thick air is murderous. / I would breathe water." The poem's preoccupations unleashed a set of images that would serve as the origin for other, later poems: The sea, she wrote in her journals, "is a central metaphor for my childhood, my poems and the artist's subconscious, of the father image—relating to my own father, the buried male muse and god-creator risen to be my mate in Ted, to the sea-father Neptune." Plath's muse would always be violently androgynous, asserting in fits and starts now its masculine, now its feminine, aspects.

The "sea change" presaged in "Full Fathom Five" continued with "Lorelei" (1958). If the masculine (father, but also lover) "seems to die" in the sea, it is the feminine (Self, but also mother) that leads it there. The Lorelei are Germanic sirens luring sailors to shipwreck: "They sing / Of a world more full and clear // Than can be." While the moon and the sea are malevolent if dormant, the Lorelei present night's greatest danger. "It is no night to drown in," the poem begins. They offer not solace, "those great goddesses of peace," but the chance for masculine and feminine to become one, for the Self to rejoin its father: "Stone, stone, ferry me down there." The stones suggest a suicide: stones in the pockets of a greatcoat, weights to keep the speaker from rising again to the ocean's surface. The dangers of drowning and "the death-wish involved in the song's beauty," as Plath notes in her journal, are fear and attraction, warning and pull—a battle waged over and again in her work. The repetition of "stone, stone" also suggests, and invokes, the repetition of "Mother, mother" in "The Disquieting Muses" and, in time, the famous repetitions in "Daddy" and "Lady Lazarus" (1962).

In Boston, to make ends meet, Plath worked briefly as a receptionist/clerk at Massachusetts General Hospital, an interlude that figures in the short story "Johnny Panic and the Bible of Dreams." She began as well a course of psychotherapy that helped break the silence she had kept since her suicide attempt five years before. Her journal from this period is largely a record of what she learned about herself in those sessions, many of which seemed to have focused on Plath's ability to write—as "an ordering, a reforming, a relearning and reloving of people and the world as they are, and as they might be." Whatever the benefits of this analysis, it forced Plath to confront a number of hard-won truths about her work. The poems of early 1959 are by and large landscapes or reformations of earlier material: "A fury of frustration, some inhibition [is] keeping me from writing what I really feel." It was also during this time that she began to attend Robert Lowell's poetry workshop at Boston University. Plath's fellow students included George Starbuck and Anne Sexton, who recalls the class in her memoir "The Barfly Ought to Sing." Both Sexton and Starbuck published their first books before Plath had published hers, and Plath's frustrations increased. Attempts at writing and publishing prose were equally daunting. For some time Plath had been at work on a novel, tentatively titled *Falcon Yard*, of which she was greatly uncertain. Its tone, its characters, and even its plot seemed to elude her. A children's book came easier ("I wrote a book yesterday!"), though it, too, met with rejection.

A visit in early March to her father's grave helped to change all this. Some days later she noted: "What good does talking about my father do? It may be a minor catharsis that lasts a day or two, but I don't get insight talking to myself." Still, the visit produced "Electra of Azalea Path" (1959), a poem that seems nothing if not filled with insight: "Small as a doll in my dress of innocence / I lay dreaming your epic, image by image." The poem recounts Plath's visit to the graveyard, with its plastic flowers that bleed in the rain but do not die. Though eventually dropped from the manuscript of *Colossus* (she dismissed it as "too forced and rhetorical"), "Electra on Azalea Path" made possible two other poems: "The Beekeeper's Daughter" and "Man in Black" (both 1959).

Plath saw "Man in Black" as a love poem for Hughes, but also recognized how its images ("the gray sea," "those white stones," "your dead black coat") were similar to those she used in poems for and about her father. "The 'dead black,' she wrote, "may be a transference from the visit to my father's grave." The striking difference in "Man in Black" between lover and father is that the lover unites the elements ("riveting stones, air / All of it, together"). In "The Beekeeper's Daughter," the father has no such power. The redolence of flowers, "peeling back their silks" to entice the bees, becomes "a well of scents almost too dense to breathe in." The similarity between this last line and the closing lines of "Full Fathom Five" is striking: "Father, this thick air is murderous. / I would breathe water.") The lover mends elements, while in the father's world the elements kill.

"The Beekeeper's Daughter" is another poem in which masculine and feminine contest one another. It is the (male) beekeeper who controls the swarm; he is "the maestro of the bees." The bees (the drones, the males) are drawn to the (feminine) flowers, "a garden of mouthings." And yet, the poem's real contest is not masculine-feminine but feminine-feminine, the battle Electra waged for her father's love: "Here is a queenship no mother can contest— / A fruit that's death to the taste: dark flesh, dark parings." The bee-mother is overcome by the bee-daughter:

> Father, bridegroom, in this Easter egg
> Under the coronal of sugar roses
>
> The queen bee marries the winter of your year.

The marriage proves to be uneasy. A bee's season is not winter but spring and summer. The "Easter egg," despite its intimations of resurrection and rebirth, would seem poisonous, a hibernation ending not in marriage or in waking from sleep, but in waking to death.

In the early summer of 1959, Plath and Hughes traveled cross-country. Returning to Boston in August, the two discovered they had been invited for a stay at Yaddo, an artists' colony in Saratoga Springs, New York. It was there that Hughes suggested Plath begin work on a second book of poems and not worry over publication of the first, which had already undergone several incarnations. The idea of a second book seemed to liberate her: "I . . . wrote two poems that pleased me. One a poem to Nicholas, and one the old father-worship subject. But different. Weirder. I see a picture, a weather, in these poems. . . ." Plath, who was then pregnant, believed that her first child would be a boy. Her daughter, Frieda, was born in April 1960.

"The Colossus" (1959), Plath's poem on "the old father-worship subject," is addressed to her father but is less an elegy than an admission that he eludes her still. "I shall never get you put together entirely," the poem begins, "Pieced, glued and properly jointed." It was also an important acknowledgment for Plath that death and its mythologies leave us "none the wiser" for our losses:

> Perhaps you consider yourself an oracle,
> Mouthpiece of the dead, or of some god or
> other.
> Thirty years now I have labored
> To dredge the silt from your throat.
> I am none the wiser.

Like most of Plath's poems, "The Colossus" contains echoes of her earlier work. Here is the animal farm of "Sow" (1957)—"Mule-bray, pig-grunt and bawdy cackles / Proceed from your great lips. / It's worse than a barnyard"—and the classical mythology of "Electra on Azalea Path" (" A blue sky out of the Oresteia / Arches above us"), among others. And yet "The Colossus" is more than the sum of its precedents. What this poem, and others from Yaddo, taught Plath was "not to manipulate the experience but to let it unfold and recreate itself with all the tenuous, peculiar associations the logical mind would short-circuit."

"The Colossus" was followed by "Poem for a Birthday," a long poem in seven sections, only two of which were published in the U.S. edition of *The Colossus:* "Flute Notes from a Reedy Pond" and "The Stones"; the sequence is reprinted whole in *The Complete Poems.* "Poem for a Birthday" allowed Plath to continue writing in the new voice she had found: "different" and "weirder," yes, but also detached and incantatory: "Love is the uniform of my bald nurse. / Love is the bone and sinew of my curse." One critic has suggested that "Poem for a Birthday" is an intricate retelling of Plath's suicide attempt and hospitalization; certainly, it is a poem of death and rebirth. "My heart is a stopped geranium," she writes in the first section; "This is not death, it is something safer," in the fifth. The final section, "The Stones," describes the rebirth, "the city where men are mended." (A clever if malicious pun: Plath's speaker inhabits the city where men not only are healed, made new, but are also men dead, or dead men.) The speaker is a creature of stone; her eye is pried open. Her senses return:

> This is the after-hell: I see the light.
> A wind unstoppers the chamber
> Of the ear, old worrier.
>
> Water mollifies the flint lip.

The poem includes another, implied pun—"old worrier" is very possibly a pun for "old warrior"—and another allusion to her own work—the speaker of "The Colossus" "squat[s] in the cornucopia" of the statue's left ear, "out of the wind." "The city where men are mended," "the city of spare parts," is the hospital (metaphorical or actual) where Plath is reborn, where she "shall be good as new." Or so the last, ironic line promises. Love is the "uniform" of health ("my bald nurse"), but is also "the bone and sinew of my curse." Love has the capacity to heal, though never fully:

> The vase, reconstructed, houses
> The elusive rose.
>
> Ten fingers shape a bowl for shadows.
> My mendings itch.

The alliteration of "vase," "houses," "elusive" and "rose" forces "reconstructed" into particular emphasis; and that emphasis will not let us forget that the vase was once broken. The wound, closed by stitches, by "mendings," reminds its victims of her frailty. It threatens to reopen.

In December 1959, after leaving Yaddo, Plath and Hughes returned to England, where they settled in London. In February 1960, Plath signed a contract with the English publisher Heinemann for a volume of poems, *The Colossus*. The majority of its contents are those poems which Plath had consigned to her first manuscript, "that soggy book," while the remainder were poems written at Yaddo. (U.S. publication of *The Colossus* occurred 1962.) Except for working notes and an occasional extant entry, Plath's post-Yaddo journal either has disappeared or has been destroyed. ("I destroyed it," writes Hughes in the foreword to *The Journals of Sylvia Plath*, "because I did not want her children to read it." A parenthetical aside continues, "In those days I regarded forgetfulness as an essential part of survival.") Other than *The Bell Jar*, which she would presently begin writing in earnest, and a volume of letters written to her mother, comparatively little prose survives from this period until her suicide three years later. What survive are the poems. "You're," a pregnancy poem, and "The Hanging Man," a terse six-line poem about her shock treatments, are the only poems of merit from 1960.

In the fall of 1960, *The Colossus* was published and Plath was once again pregnant. In early February 1961 she miscarried, and she underwent an appendectomy at the end of that month. Between worries about her health and the financial well-being of her marriage, Plath's depression returned. But so did her desire to write. A few days after her miscarriage, she wrote "Morning Song," an evocation of motherhood: "I stumble from bed, cow-heavy and floral / In my Victorian nightgown." The poem seems dedicated to her daughter, not yet one year old, but is also heavy with the pain of recent loss: "The window square / Whitens and swallows its dull stars." The "new statue" of "Morning Song" would, two days later, become a "museum without statues" in "Barren Woman." More and more, Plath was able to shape experience directly into poetry.

The poems Plath wrote from March until October 1961 are important for reasons at once thematic and technical, though only three appear in the *Ariel* that Ted Hughes arranged for publication after her death. They are also literally and figuratively fatter: a great number of the poems are composed of seven-, eight-, or nine-line stanzas of semi-regular line length (usually iambic pentameter). But while the poems grew fat with form, the control Plath exercised over image and voice grew lean—or, rather, precise. Nothing is wasted; nothing is extraneous. Plath's hospitalization for appendicitis provided material for two poems, "In Plaster" and "Tulips," the notes for which have survived as part of "The Inmate" in the published journals. These notes provide one of the clearest examples of how she transformed life into poetry. Significantly different in tone from previous entries, they are more novelistic and less self-absorbed, a sort of warm-up for *The Bell Jar*. A "lady with [a] sour face, chest and arm in plaster," who shared Plath's ward, provided the occasion for "In Plaster." It is unclear (and unimportant, perhaps) if Plath intended herself or the "lady with [a] sour face" for the speaker. What is clear is her fascination with the idea of the double (a thread in her work that dates back to her Smith senior thesis on Dostoevsky), and also with the idea of the fragmented self: "There are two of me now: / This new absolutely white person and the old yellow one." "One of the real saints," this figure in white seems engaged in a battle of wills that the weaker, yellow self fully expects to win. "I'm collecting my strength; one day I shall manage without her." It is not now "thick air" or a garden with its "well of scents" that is murderous, but the Self.

"Tulips," dated the same day as "In Plaster" (March 18), is the stronger poem, if only because it resists easy explications in favor of image (they are all here: stone, sea, the trappings of religion, and the colors white, red, and black) and tone. While both poems are narrative, "Tulips" is an interior monologue. There are not "two of me" but one, and this concentration drives the "I" from one stanza to the next. If there is a division between Self and Other in "Tulips," it lies between the speaker (Self, but also sickness) and the tulips (Other, but also health). "The tulips are too excitable, it is winter here," the poem begins, drawing a line between hospital winter and greenhouse spring. The next three stanzas detail a private history; the speaker's "baggage" is cast off: "I watched my teaset, my bureaus of linens, my books / Sink out of sight, and the water went over my head." And then comes a curious but important line: "I am a nun now, I have never been so pure." Common public and critical perception has centered on Plath's fascination with Judaism. "I think I may well be a Jew," she writes in "Daddy." Otto Plath was neither a Catholic nor a Jew, but a lapsed Lutheran; and neither of Plath's parents seemed overly inclined to impress a religious education upon the children. Whatever the creed, religion was for Plath much like folklore and mythology: a system of symbols and gods. In "Tulips" and other poems, religion (more specifically, Judeo-Christian religion) stands for passive acceptance of fate:

> I didn't want any flowers, I only wanted
> To lie with my hands turned up and be utterly
> empty.
> How free it is, you have no idea how free—
> The peacefulness so big it dazes you,
> And it asks nothing, a name tag, a few
> trinkets.
> It is what the dead close on, finally; I imagine
> them
> Shutting their mouths on it, like a Communion
> tablet.

The "peacefulness" is overcome by the tulips. They are "too red in the first place, they hurt me." Again, the absence of air, the inability to breath, becomes crucial. "The vivid tulips eat my oxygen," their overpowering presence emphasized by Plath's choice of the adjective "vivid" (which, from the Latin, means "full of life"). The flowers next become "dangerous animals . . . opening like the mouth of some great African cat" in a roar of warning. Yet the speaker's response (the poem's final lines) is oddly calm and laced with assent:

> And I am aware of my heart: it opens and
> closes
> Its bowl of red blooms out of sheer love of me
> The water I taste is warm and salt, like the sea,
> And comes from a country far away as health.

The heart is housed in a vase enclosing a liquid that, "like the sea," is "warm and salt." It is not water she tastes but blood, her own unimaginable health.

In the summer of 1961, Plath and Hughes left London for a cottage in Devon. "Blackberrying," a poem from September, is in many ways similar to "Tulips," both formally (its dense stanza structure, its assonance and alliteration) and thematically. Like the tulips, the berries, a "blood sisterhood," mock the speaker: "Theirs is the only voice, protesting, protesting." Certainly, the berries are as carnival and grotesque as were the tulips: "I come to one bush of berries so ripe it is a bush of flies" with "bluegreen bellies." The flies "believe in heaven," but the lane of "berries and bushes" ends at the sea. Although the poem evokes a landscape from Plath's childhood summers on Cape Cod, with its berry bushes, its ocean, what is revealed is not the sea "but a great space / Of white and pewter lights, and a din like silversmiths / Beating and beating an intractable metal." The lights might be sunlight on water; the "beating and beating," the crash of waves. But they are so transformed as to make us forget water and sun, and hear only the jarring cacophony of sound Plath wants us to hear: the *i* of "white," "lights," "din," "silversmiths"; the *b* of "beating and beating" and "intractable" (and also of "blackberries," "bushes," and "bluegreen bellies"); the slant, insistent rhyme of "intractable" with "metal."

The Moon and the Yew Tree," written the following month at the suggestion of Hughes, is, like the earlier "Winter Landscape, with Rooks," a "psychic landscape." The first two lines would make us believe the poem is set in the mind alone, that this pastoral is no more than interior: "This is the light of the mind, cold and planetary. / The trees of the mind are black. The light is blue." Thereafter, we discover that mind and landscape have fused, that everything interior (or psychic) has as its double, its twin, an exterior figure: "The grasses unload their griefs on my feet as if I were God, / Prickling my ankles and murmuring of their humility." The speaker stands just outside her house, "a row of headstones" separating her from "fumy, spiritous mists," from the moon and the yew tree in the distance. This path (house, headstones, mists, tree, moon) seems to paralyze the speaker: "I simply cannot see where there is to get to." She cannot leave the house behind, walk past the headstones and the mist, past the yew (associated with the cross of the Crucifixion and referred to by Robert Graves as the "death-tree") to rejoin the moon. "The moon is no door," writes Plath. "It is a face in its own right, / White as a knuckle and terribly upset." The tone of the poem is "complete despair"—in Christian lore the greatest sin, the belief that God is powerless to redeem. God is powerless, and so is the speaker; thus, the identification of one with the other.

The speaker's stasis is made all the more terrible by her realization that "the moon is my mother." The image should be beneficent, but this mother is "not sweet like Mary. / Her blue garments unloose small bats and owls," themselves messengers of death. "How I would like to believe in tenderness," Plath writes, a tenderness as impossible (though not unimaginable) as redemption:

> How I would like to believe in tenderness—
> The face of the effigy, gentled by candles,
> Bending, on me in particular, its mild eyes.
>
> I have fallen a long way. Clouds are flowering
> Blue and mystical over the face of the stars.
> Inside the church, the saints will be all blue,
> Floating on their delicate feet over the cold
> pews,
> Their hands and faces stiff with holiness.

The vision of tenderness would make forgiveness, redemption, resurrection all possible; but "the moon sees nothing of this" (it sees the vision as "nothing"), and so it ceases to exist.

In a radio broadcast Plath described the yew tree of this poem as "manipulating. . . . I couldn't subdue it." It is true that the image stands "squarely in the middle of [the] poem," and the final line would seem to grant the tree omnipotence: "And the message of the yew tree is blackness—blackness and silence." But the poem is not, as she coyly described it, "a poem about a yew tree." Like "The Beekeeper's Daughter," "The Moon and the Yew Tree" is a poem about the dual contests between masculine (tree) and feminine (moon), and between feminine (moon) and feminine (Self). The latter battle seems the more significant; it is an annihilation of the Self. The battle between masculine and feminine seems more symbolic. The yew stands mute, stonelike, impassive. "Bald and wild," the moon emerges triumphant.

In October 1961, Plath signed a contract for publication of *The Bell Jar*, the novel that fictionalized the events of her *Mademoiselle* internship, her suicide attempt, and her subsequent recovery. Although the novel received mixed reviews when it was published in 1971, its increasing popularity in the years following Plath's death is somewhat problematic. Because of *The Bell Jar*'s status as an "autobiography," its importance as a secondary, albeit unreliable, source for the life has superseded attention to its actual effectiveness as a novel—critical examination, for example, of a protagonist who is a distant, unknowable character whose motivations remain elusive to the reader. There is the very real possibility that had Plath's emotional health not received such notoriety, *The Bell Jar* would have gone the way of most poets' novels: consigned, as a curiosity, to footnotes and to bibliographies.

Plath's son, Nicholas, was born in January, and 1962—unlike the year following Frieda's birth—was productive. Words such as "frenzy" and "fury" have often been applied to the energies with which Plath now devoted herself to poetry. Such words are misleading. Plath was a careful, highly disciplined writer. In his introduction to *The Complete Poems*, Ted Hughes writes, "Her attitude to her verse was artisan-like: if she couldn't get a table out of the material, she was quite happy to get a chair, or even a toy." The poems of 1962 contain an equal number of each: tables, chairs, toys. While the number of poems makes a critical appreciation of each prohibitive here, they can be divided into three major groups: the beekeeping poems; "Daddy," "Lady Lazarus," and their attendant poems; and those written after October, when Plath had separated from Hughes and had begun to make plans for a return to London. (The two notable exceptions to these technically unified and clearly defined groupings are a verse play for radio, "Three Women," and "Berck-Plage," an elegy in seven sections for a Devon neighbor, both of which date from earlier in 1962.)

In June 1962 Plath and Hughes became, like many of the villagers, beekeeepers. However, the beekeeping sequence ("The Bee Meeting," "The Arrival of the Bee Box," "Stings," "The Swarm," and "Wintering") can be traced back to "The Beekeeper's Daughter." Broader and yet more concentrated, the five distinct poems form a single narrative that works on several levels: as a story in itself, as an account of the growing dissolution of the marriage, and as a series of reports from the battle between Self and Other. "The Bee Meeting" continues the black (male) and blue (female) imagery of "The Moon and the Yew Tree" and other poems: "Which is the rector now, is it that man in black? / Which is the midwife, is that her blue coat?" The villagers in their portective garments become indistinct; in their black veils, it is difficult to tell one from another, man from woman. The poem carries intimations of a sacrifice of rite of assimilation: the speaker herself is made to don a black veil. "They are making me one of them," she fears, watching as the villagers go "hunting the queen." It is the dream of a duel between the queen and her "new virgins" that exhausts Plath, leaving her cold; the dream of the bee box, "the long white box in the grove," as something resembling a coffin.

The rite of separating virgin from queen, of preventing "a duel [the virgins] will win inevitably," is taken up in the next poem, "The Arrival of the Bee Box." The speaker's way of averting the duel is to imagine the bees, her "box of maniacs," dead. "I need feed them nothing, I am the owner," she boasts. "Stings" informs us that the bees have not died, that the queen is "old . . . and unqueenly and even shameful," and that the speaker is "in control." She begins to see herself as the queen and unleashes the swarm. The theme of these poems is a coming to power, of the feminine Self asserting its prominence over both masculine and feminine others. "The Swarm" is an extended metaphor: the bees are at war. "The white busts of marshals, admirals, generals / [Worm] themselves into niches." If "The Swarm" is indeed a "war poem," then "Wintering," the final poem, is one of women alone, making do without husbands and fathers (as Plath did as a child), without all the expendable soldiers:

> The bees are all women,
> Maids and the long royal lady.
> They have got rid of the men,
>
> The blunt, clumsy stumblers, the boors.
> Winter is for women—

In the end, the beekeeping sequence earns a hard-won peace. "The bees are flying," Plath writes. "They taste the spring." But the victory proved a burden. A draft of "Elm," a poem from earlier in 1962, includes the memo "stigma (of selfhood)"—and the Self that Plath created (or discovered) in these poems would, over the next months, indeed become a stigma, a burden.

In the poems that followed the bee sequence ("A Secret" and "The Applicant") Plath left peace for black comedy, for the acerbic wit that informs and propels the second group: "Daddy," "Medusa," "Cut," Ariel," "Nick and the Candlestick," and "Lady Lazarus" among them. With "Daddy" and "Medusa," written back-to-back in a sort of dual exorcism, the Self is once again at war.

From its opening line, "Daddy," establishes a nearly metronomic rhythm both dire and merciless. With the simplicity of counting verse ("One, two, buckle my shoe," and so forth), Plath turns the stuff of her childhood, real and imagined, into a burlesque of revenge:

> You do not do, you do not do
> Any more, black shoe
> In which I have lived like a foot
> For thirty years, poor and white:
> Barely daring to breathe or Achoo.

Almost lost in the singsong and deadpan silliness of many of these rhymes is the familiar image from other "father-worship" poems ("Full Fathom Five" and "The Beekeeper's Daughter") that "air is murderous" and breathing often next to impossible. Here, the speaker confesses that she has been too frightened to breathe. And if speech is a kind of breath, she also confesses that "I could hardly speak." The punishment might well have been asphyxiation.

One of the technical qualities that make "Daddy" so visceral is Plath's use of assonance and alliteration, the fierce attention she paid to each sound. Note how the insistent repetition of "Jew" subtly mimics the sound of "an engine, an engine," its insistent whistle:

> I thought every German was you.
> And the language obscene
>
> An engine, an engine
> Chuffing me off like a Jew.
> A Jew to Dachau, Auschwitz, Belsen,
> I began to talk like a Jew.
> I think I may well be a Jew.

Note, too, the subtle rhymes of "obscene" and "engine" and "Belsen."

Plath's radio introduction to "Daddy" is artfully evasive. "Here is a poem spoken by a girl with an Electra complex," she begins. "Her father died while she thought he was God. Her case is complicated by the fact that her father was a Nazi and her mother very possibly part Jewish. In the daughter the two strains marry and paralyse each other—she has to act out the awful little allegory once over before she is free of it." Plath's "awful little allegory" is off base: the father's love is not won. The father is instead killed:

> There's a stake in your fat black heart
> And the villagers never liked you.
> They are dancing and stamping on you.
> They always *knew* it was you.
> Daddy, daddy, you bastard, I'm through.

Plath was anything but through. The poems of October, written at a rate of almost one per day, both shattered and explored her "stasis in darkness." "Ariel," which describes a horse ride in violent imagery, might be seen as a metaphor for the October poems. They act like an "arrow // . . . that flies / Suicidal, at one with the drive / Into the red // Eye, the cauldron of mourning." They range from the tender ("Nick and the Candlestick") to the acidly humorous ("Lady Lazarus").

The blue light of "Nick and the Candlestick," reminiscent of the blue light in "The Moon and the Yew Tree," is the flame in darkness that counters "the cauldron of morning." "I am a miner," Plath writes. "The light burns blue." The flame cools from blue to yellow.

> The candle
> Gulps and recovers its small altitude,
>
> Its yellows hearten.
> O love, how did you get here?

Metaphors of suffocation and drowning are here rendered harmless. The flame that uses oxygen is not a death image but an affirmation of the child (her son, Nicholas):

> You are the one
> Solid the spaces lean on, envious.
> You are the baby in the barn.

The Christlike "baby in the barn" might be said to have raised the spirit of Lazarus, the man Jesus raised from death (John 11), in "Lady Lazarus." Plath's speaker has no need of divine intervention, however. Unlike the broken statue in "The Colossus," but not unlike the "reconstructed" vase in "The Stones," the character of Lady Lazarus is newly fashioned of "spare parts." More important, she is self-made, her flesh and bones the leftovers of atrocities perpetrated by "Daddy": "A sort of walking miracle, my skin / Bright as a Nazi lampshade, / My right foot / A paperweight, / My face a featureless, fine / Jew linen." The life-in-death that is Plath's speaker is also "a smiling woman," a suicidal penitent, a garish chorine.

> The peanut crunching crowd
> Shoves in to see
>
> Them unwrap me hand and foot—
> The big strip tease.
> Gentlemen, ladies
>
> These are my hands,
> My knees.

"Dying," Plath writes, "is an art"—a painful boast. The entire poem is a swagger of pain of sarcasm: "I turn and burn / Do not think I underestimate your great concern." All is destruction. Fire is not here the sweet glow of "Nick and the Candlestick," but that element which reduces everything to "ash, ash." But, like the phoenix, Lady Lazarus promises to rise once more and exact her vengeance:

> Herr God, Herr Lucifer
> Beware
> Beware.
>
> Out of the ash
> I rise with my red hair,
> And I eat men like air.

The story of Sylvia Plath's last months has been told often: her separation from Hughes, the move to London (where the winter was bitterly cold), the illnesses she and her children suffered, her sense of helplessness and isolation (made worse by her lack of a telephone), her suicide (on 11 February). And her last poems, written in January and February 1963, have been taken apart stanza and verse as if they formed an extended suicide note. "The blood jet is poetry," she wrote in "Kindness." "There is no stopping it." These lines alone have fostered the misguided equation of poetry with self-destruction, an equation supported by little though taken as gospel by many. Plath's legacy was for many years the idea that self-destruction is "a Greek necessity." Her poems were mere evidence.

Like T. S. Eliot, Sylvia Plath has gone in and out of fashion. But her more lasting legacy will be the poems, not as evidence of a life but as the visceral, technical marvels they are.

Selected Bibliography

PRIMARY WORKS

POETRY

The Colossus. New York: Alfred A. Knopf, 1962.

Ariel. New York: Harper & Row, 1966.

Crossing the Water. New York: Harper & Row, 1971.

Winter Trees. New York: Harper & Row, 1972.

The Collected Poems. Edited by Ted Hughes. New York: Harper & Row, 1981.

FICTION, SHORT PROSE, LETTERS

The Bell Jar. New York: Harper & Row, 1971.

Letters Home by Sylvia Plath: Correspondence, 1950–1963. Edited by Aurelia S. Plath. New York: Harper & Row, 1975.

Johnny Panic and the Bible of Dreams: Short Stories, Prose, and Diary Excerpts. New York: Harper & Row, 1980.

The Journals of Sylvia Plath. Edited by Frances McCullough and Ted Hughes. New York: Dial Press, 1982.

CHILDREN'S LITERATURE

The Bed Book. New York: Harper & Row, 1976.

PAPERS AND MANUSCRIPTS

Plath's unpublished materials are at the Neilsen Library, Smith College, and at the Lilly Library, Indiana University.

SECONDARY WORKS

BIOGRAPHY

Stevenson, Anne. *Bitter Fame: A Life of Sylvia Plath.* Boston: Houghton Mifflin, 1989.

Wagner-Martin, Linda. *Sylvia Plath: A Biography.* New York: Simon & Schuster, 1987.

CRITICISM

Alexander, Paul, ed. *Ariel Ascending: Writings About Sylvia Plath.* New York: Harper & Row, 1985. See especially Elizabeth Hardwick, "On Sylvia Plath"; Ted Hughes, "Sylvia Plath and Her Journals" (different from his introduction to the *Journals*); Stanley Plumly, "What Ceremony of Words"; and Katha Pollitt, "A Note of Triumph."

Bassett, Susan. *Sylvia Plath.* London: Macmillan, 1987.

Bloom, Harold, ed. *Sylvia Plath.* New York: Chelsea House, 1989.

Broe, Mary Lynn. *Protean Poetic: The Poetry of Sylvia Plath.* Columbia: University of Missouri Press, 1980.

Bundtzen, Lynda K. *Plath's Incarnations: Woman and the Creative Process.* Ann Arbor: University of Michigan Press, 1983.

Hardwick, Elizabeth. "On Sylvia Plath." In her *Seduction and Betrayal: Women and Literature.* New York: Random House, 1974.

Heaney, Seamus. "The Indefatigable Hoof-taps: Sylvia Plath." In his *The Government of the Tongue.* New York: Farrar, Straus & Giroux, 1989.

Holbrook, David. *Sylvia Plath: Poetry and Existence.* London: Athlone, 1976.

Kroll, Judith. *Chapters in a Mythology: The Poetry of Sylvia Plath.* New York: Harper & Row, 1976.

Lane, Gary, ed. *Sylvia Plath: New Views on the Poetry.* Baltimore: Johns Hopkins University Press, 1979.

Matovich, Richard M. *A Concordance to the Collected Poems of Sylvia Plath.* New York: Garland, 1986.

Newman, Charles. *The Art of Sylvia Plath: A Symposium.* Bloomington: Indiana University Press, 1970.

BIBLIOGRAPHY

Lane, Gary, and Maria Stevens. *Sylvia Plath: A Bibliography.* Metuchen, N.J.: Scarecrow Press, 1978.

Tabor, Stephen, comp. *Sylvia Plath: An Analytical Bibliography.* Westport, Conn.: Meckler, 1987.

DAVID CRAIG AUSTIN

KATHERINE ANNE PORTER

1890–1980

KATHERINE ANNE PORTER lived a long life—more than nine decades—that followed the biographical pattern of legendary self-made Americans. Born in a log cabin in the rough-and-ready frontier community of Indian Creek, Texas, she become a best-selling author whose fiction, essays, and reviews were celebrated by America's most demanding critics. Raised in a family with extremely limited financial resources, she died a wealthy woman. While witnessing many of the political, economic, and technological developments that shaped contemporary America, she transformed herself from an impoverished, abused Southern housewife to a self-taught provincial journalist, and went on to create for herself a cosmopolitan life enhanced by her wide network of friends and lovers (including four husbands). Long before her death, she enjoyed international recognition as a gifted writer and urbane citizen of the world.

While still a child, Porter announced to her father that she wanted to "know the world like the palm of my hand." Her fiction demonstrates her acute awareness of the larger world outside southwest Texas, from the rural villages of Mexico to the metropolitan centers of New York City, Washington, D.C., Paris, Berlin, Rome, and London. But her comprehensive vision of the human panorama never overlooks the particular, evocative details that make her characters so vivid to the reader. Eudora Welty, a master of the voluptuously sensual detail in her own fiction, admired Porter's very different narrative technique:

> This artist, writing her stories with a power that stamps them to their last detail on the memory, does so to an extraordinary degree without sensory imagery. . . . Her imagery is as likely as not to belong to a time other than the story's present, and beyond that it always differs from it in nature; it is *memory* imagery coming into the story from memory's remove. It is a distilled, a reformed imagery. . . .
>
> (Eudora Welty, "The Eye of the Story," in *Katherine Anne Porter: A Collection of Critical Essays*, edited by Robert Penn Warren, pp. 72, 75)

Like William Faulkner, Welty, and other writers of the Southern Renaissance in the 1930s and 1940s, Porter was preoccupied with the problematic reconciliation of objective historiography and subjective perception. But while Faulkner was engaged in explorations of regional history in his fiction, Porter concerned herself with the probing of her own past:

> My experiences seem to be simply memory, with continuity, marginal notes, constant revision and comparison of one thing with another. Now and again thousands of memories converge, harmonize, arrange themselves around a central idea in a coherent form, and I write a story.
>
> (Porter, "Notes on Writing," in *Collected Essays*, p. 449)

Her use of the word "memory" implies not a documentary report of past events but a selective use of details, a reworking of facts, and often an imaginative fabrication of events. This highly subjective process informs Porter's descriptions of her life as well as her fiction. In fact, one could say that she fictionalized her life and lived her fiction: insisting for many years that her family was descended from the pioneer Daniel Boone, and claiming his brother Jonathan as one of her great-great-grandfathers, she elaborated this respectable family genealogy in stories like "The Old Order" and "Old Mortality."

Originally named Callie Russell after one of her mother's childhood friends, Porter renamed herself Katherine Anne in honor of her paternal grandmother, Catherine Anne Skaggs Porter, or Aunt Cat, as her grandchildren called her. Katherine's mother, Mary Alice Jones Porter, died of pneumonia complicated by bronchial problems in 1892, soon after giving birth to her fifth child. Katherine, her fourth child (born on 15 May 1890), was not quite two years old. Katherine's father, Harrison Boone Porter, never recovered from the loss of his wife; he held himself and his children responsible for her death and would later tell Katherine that men were "terrible, really terrible."

Harrison Porter sold his farm in Indian Creek and took the children to Kyle, Texas, where his mother raised them with puritanical Methodist rigor. Although the family was painfully cramped in their small house and forced to accept clothes donated by their more affluent neighbors, Aunt Cat demanded the genteel deportment worthy of the descendants of a more gracious Southern past. Katherine feared her grandmother's anger, but later appreciated the emotional stability provided by Aunt Cat, a competent and tough-minded woman who had borne eleven children, lost two as infants, and raised the surviving nine with little help from her husband. Katherine romanticized her memory of her grandmother: "The head of our household was a grandmother, an old matriarch, you know, and a really lovely and beautiful woman, a good soul, and so she didn't do us any harm." One of Aunt Cat's memorable talents was for oral family histories, which she would spin out to distract herself and her family from their reduced circumstances. She taught Katherine not only the skill of surviving in a harsh world but also the art of storytelling.

Most of Porter's female characters are hardy survivors who do not capitulate to adverse circumstances. In "The Jilting of Granny Weatherall," an elderly woman approaches the end of an arduous life with the same strength she brought to all the difficulties she faced as a single woman raising her children alone in an untamed frontier territory. In *Ship of Fools,* Jenny Brown defies her lover's chauvinistic denigration of her artistic talents, choosing to end their relationship rather than to relinquish her very firm sense of self-worth. Each of these characters owes something to Katherine's grandmother. Although Katherine was unsympathetic to modern feminism as an ideology, she observed that most women are trained to give "service to anyone who demands it," and complained that her own work was often interrupted by "just anyone who could jimmy his way into my life."

Long after her grandmother's death in 1901, Porter fictionalized her grief in several of her short stories. In "The Grave," the adolescent Miranda Gay (a character Porter identified as her alter ego and who features in many of Porter's stories) is bereft of her grandmother; gossipy neighbors whisper that "the motherless family was running down, with the Grandmother no longer there to hold it together." Porter generally re-created an idealized version of her biography through her fictional family, which she depicts as genteel, gracious, and educated. Despite straitened financial circumstances, the members of this family live in spacious houses with servants, their large libraries full of Dante, Shakespeare, Milton, Pope, and Dickens. But the neighbors' gossip in "The Grave" is not without foundation. Miranda and her brother are learning about life's extremities—birth, death, and loss—without any assistance from their father.

Porter resented a similar failure in her own father, who was often immobilized by depression and self-pity. After Aunt Cat's death, she remembered, "we started drifting apart. We had lost our core, we had lost our cohesion as a family and we never got it back." As late as 1957, she complained in a letter to her brother Paul that their father was "a terrible example of apathy," blaming him for his "refusal to live" and "to take care of the children left to him." After his mother's death, he repeatedly moved his family around Texas, in 1904 to San Antonio, where Katherine and Gay attended a private Methodist school for a year, and in 1905 to Victoria, where he could not find work and relied upon his daughters to support him by tutoring children in "music, physical culture and dramatic reading."

Joan Givner, who has written the most comprehensive biography of Porter to date, tells us that in Victoria, Porter met John Henry Koontz, a railroad clerk, the son of a wealthy businessman, whom she married (partly in rebellion, and partly in search of emotional and financial stability) in 1906. She was sixteen. The marriage was extremely volatile—Koontz was jealous and sometimes violent. Porter nonetheless stayed with him for seven years. They separated in 1913. When they divorced two years later, Katherine charged him with physical cruelty (claiming that he broke her ankle in 1909), drunkenness, and adultery.

Porter's eagerness to escape the confines of her troubled family and her destructive marriage is voiced by Miranda Gay in the story "Old Mortality":

> She did not want any more ties with this house, she was going to leave it, and she was not going back to her husband's family either. She would have no more bonds that smothered her in love and hatred. She knew now why she had run away to marriage, and she knew that she was going to run away from marriage, and she was not going to stay in any place, with anyone, that threatened to forbid her making her own discoveries, that said "No" to her.
>
> (*The Collected Stories,* p. 220)

Freed from such smothering bonds for the first time, Porter made her first "wild dash into that wilder world" in 1914, when she moved to Chicago. She took with her a suitcase containing more unfinished manuscripts (poetry and prose works-in-progress) than clothes: while Koontz had worked as a traveling salesman, she had used her solitude to begin writing. Her literary ambitions were already shaping her life: "I had to leave Texas because I didn't want to be regarded as a freak. That's what they all thought about women who wanted to write." In other accounts of this period, Porter remembers going to Chicago not to write, but in hopes of becoming a film actress. She had told conflicting stories of working in both fields, sometimes claiming to have worked briefly as a journalist, writing wedding notices and obituaries for a sensationalist Chicago newspaper, and at other times remembering her job as a movie extra, which she had to quit because the long hours on the set in crowd scenes were underpaid and exhausting. Her health began to deteriorate, and she may have suffered her first bout of tuberculosis at this time.

Porter left Chicago in the fall of 1914 to visit her sister Baby in Beaumont, Texas, where Baby was suffering from postpartum depression. Her visit was cut short when she went to Gibsland, Louisiana, to help her pregnant older sister, Gay, who had been abandoned by her husband. Porter proved a resourceful caretaker for Gay and her two children, paying the bills by reciting poetry and singing on the Lyceum Circuit, which combined adult education and popular entertainment.

When Gay's husband unexpectedly returned, Porter continued to work as an entertainer on the provincial theatrical circuit in Texas and Louisiana. Her health had been weakened by her family responsibilities and performance schedule; in 1915, ill and destitute, she was admitted to a charity hospital in Dallas with a diagnosis of tuberculosis. In 1916, her brother Paul arranged for her admission to a sanatorium near San Angelo, Texas, where one of her fellow patients was Kitty Barry Crawford, publisher of the *Fort Worth Critic.* After she was released from the sanatorium, Porter worked for some months at Woodlawn Hospital in Dallas, where she was both a patient and the teacher of a group of tubercular children she formed into a small school, Academy Oaks. When she was well enough to leave the hospital altogether, Crawford hired her to write theater reviews and society columns for the *Fort Worth Critic* in 1917. The next year Crawford, her husband, and Porter spent the summer in Denver, and Porter was hired as a reporter for the *Rocky Mountain News*.

Although Porter had come to Colorado for the beneficial mountain air, she neglected her health, subsisting primarily on coffee, doughnuts, and cigarettes. She again fell ill when the 1918 influenza epidemic swept the country. Porter was admitted to the overcrowded hospital only through Crawford's influence, and so belatedly that she was not expected to survive. Her family made funeral arrangements; her obituary was prepared. An experimental injection of strychnine administered by interns as a last resort saved her life.

Porter once declared in an interview that "everything I ever wrote in the way of fiction is based very securely on something real in life." One of her best short stories, "Pale Horse, Pale Rider," is based on her near death in Denver. The story tells of the love affair between Adam Barclay (a soldier about to be sent into battle) and Miranda Gay, and of Adam's selfless nursing of Miranda during the 1918 epidemic. Adam arranges Miranda's admission to the hospital; when she recovers, she learns that he has contracted the disease and died. Much of the story consists of five dream sequences, which Thomas Walsh has called "the most subjective parts" of the story, because they "reveal the hidden undercurrents of [Miranda's] mind, but they are also the most objective because they enable the reader to understand her in a way that she never understands herself."

Porter always insisted that the story was autobiographical, although her various versions of the real events are inconsistent. In a letter to her sister Gay, she wrote of her guilt over the death of the soldier she fictionalized as Adam Barclay. Porter's critics, many of whom cannot resist the psychological analysis much of her work invites, trace the sources of Porter's (and Miranda's) guilt to her rebellious career ambitions. Jane Flanders notes that Miranda is engaged in a forward flight from human relationships, and that such flights are frequent in Porter's fiction:

> But Miranda will never know the "truth about herself" because she cannot reconcile her need to express her own identity with any acceptable model of mature womanhood; she has never known one. As we may conclude from "Pale Horse, Pale Rider"—the last Miranda story—and from the bulk of her later work, Katherine Anne Porter's own experience was that of the failure of love and the death of the heart.
>
> (Flanders, p. 60)

After leaving the hospital, Porter became drama editor for the *Rocky Mountain News*, writing caustic reviews of the Victorian melodramas popular at the time, as well as reviewing movies, vaudeville, and musicals. Sometime between 1919 and 1920 Porter moved to New York City, seeking more challenging work. The dynamic decade that followed was characterized by dramatic cultural change in America, and an extraordinary shift of values was being expressed in the arts. In her *Collected Essays*, Porter remembers this period vividly:

> I had had time to grow up, to consider, to look again, to begin finding my way a little through the inordinate clutter and noise of my immediate day, in which very literally everything in the world was being pulled apart, torn up, turned wrong side out and upside down; almost no frontiers left unattacked, governments and currencies falling; even the very sexes seemed to be changing back and forth and multiplying weird, unclassifiable genders. And every day, in the arts, as in schemes of government and organized crime, there was, there had to be, something New.
>
> ("Reflections on Willa Cather," in *Collected Essays*, pp. 33–34)

Porter lived alone in Greenwich Village, writing studio publicity for the burgeoning film industry and enjoying her somewhat scandalously independent bohemian life. She published three children's stories in 1920: told in the form of an Eskimo legend, "The Shattered Star" explains the origins of the aurora borealis; "The Faithful

Princess" tells the story of a strong-willed princess who defies the gods in order to marry; "The Magic Earring" describes the daunting journey of a princess who rescues her bridegroom from the kingdom of the wicked fairy queen who has stolen him. All three stories focus on strong, creative, determined young women who must overcome obstacles in order to achieve their desires or demonstrate prowess. She also wrote a story for adults, "The Adventures of Hadji: A Tale of a Turkish Coffee-House," which shows how a misogynic, adulterous husband learns to admire his wife's intelligence.

In addition to publishing her retellings of traditional stories, Porter worked as a ghost writer on an autobiographical novel (*My Chinese Marriage*) by a woman who had married a Chinese student and lived with him in China, where she had three children and became thoroughly acculturated. Investigating foreign cultures at first hand, Porter often visited Mexico throughout the 1920s. She had become interested in folk art when exposed to the Cajun culture of Louisiana; Crawford had encouraged her interest in the folk culture of Mexico. In Greenwich Village, she met several Mexican artists, including Adolpho Best-Maugard, who convinced Pavlova to dance a Mexican ballet when the Diaghilev ballet visited New York. Best-Maugard asked Porter to write the story, and the ballet was triumphantly performed in Mexico City in 1923. Porter accepted a job with *Magazine of Mexico* because it involved traveling to gather material. She was deeply affected by Mexico's vibrant and varied culture, which became the subject matter for her early stories, and she became involved in Mexico's turbid political conflicts, which form the backdrop for her story "Flowering Judas." She described the tense situation in essays published in the *Christian Science Monitor* and *Century* magazine:

> Plots thicken, thin, disintegrate in the space of thirty-six hours. A general was executed today for counterrevolutionary activities. There is fevered discussion in the newspapers as to the best means of stamping out Bolshevism, which is the inclusive term for all forms of radical work.
>
> (*Collected Essays*, p. 399)

When the Mexican government began to suspect that she was a Bolshevik, she fled to the United States, but she would return many times in the following years.

Porter visited the Crawfords in Texas for six months, hoping the relative quiet would allow her to finish some of her perennially incomplete stories; she found new distractions in an amateur theatrical company, however, and returned to New York with no publishable fiction in hand. When she finally finished "María Concepción," it was immediately accepted by *Century* magazine and appeared in 1922. In this story, a Mexican Indian avenges her honor and rebuilds her family after her husband briefly abandons her for another woman. By murdering her husband's lover, she earns the admiration of her village and the right to raise her husband's bastard to replace her own dead baby.

Porter's own romantic life was adventurous, if episodic. In 1922, after a number of insignificant relationships and one wrenchingly unhappy love affair with a married man, she met Charles Sumner Williams, a Harvard graduate and successful businessman who fell deeply in love with her. Although she was fond of Williams, she refused his marriage proposal. Years later, she wrote to a friend that she had been too self-centered to appreciate him. Certainly, most of the men Porter chose as lovers and husbands were far less supportive than Williams. Her next lover was Francisco Aguilera, a fiery, romantic Chilean doctoral student at Yale who was almost twelve years her junior. It was Aguilera who gave Porter the nickname "Miranda," the name of the female protagonist in many of her later stories.

When Aguilera ended their relationship, the disconsolate Porter retreated to rural Connecticut, where she shared a rented farmhouse with friends and began to write in earnest. She worked on several drafts of "Season of Fear," "Holiday," and "Virgin Violeta," slowly transforming her memories of Mexico into coherent tales. Rewriting a tale of seduction she heard from the Nicaraguan poet Salomon de la Selva (whom she described as one of the most evil men she had ever known), Porter developed Violeta into what George Hendrick calls "a prototype of the character of Miranda." Fifteen-year-old Violeta conceives an innocent passion for her older sister's suitor; when his response takes the physical form of a kiss, she is repelled both by the psychological complexities of guilt and by the physicality of sex. The story was published in *Century* Magazine in 1924.

Returning to New York City just as her story was published, Porter began writing book reviews for the *New Republic*, the *New York Herald Tribune*, and the *Nation*. In 1926, at the age of thirty-six, she agreed to marry twenty-five-year-old Ernest Stock, a British interior decorator studying painting at the Art Students' League in New York. The couple moved to an old Connecticut farmhouse where Porter accumulated notes and wrote drafts, but never polished any of her stories sufficiently to submit them for publication. The marriage was not a success. Much later, she would observe that her short story "Rope," a vignette of an acrimonious marriage, was inspired by her frequent quarrels with the humorless Stock, whom she referred to as "Deadly Ernest." Porter's biographer Joan Givner has speculated that Porter compulsively chose to marry younger, inadequate men because they resembled her handsome but weak father.

Back in New York in 1927, without Stock, Porter avoided serious romances and spent more time with a community of women writers (including poets Elinor Wylie and Genevieve Taggard, and novelists Josephine Herbst and Dorothy Day). These women encouraged Porter in her efforts to be more productive. Remembering the puritanical atmosphere of her childhood in a Southern region "poxed with teetotalitarians who seemed to hold that every human activity except breathing was a sin," she decided to write a biography of the New England colonist, Puritan magistrate, and religious leader Cotton Mather. She planned to complete the work for the bicentennial of Mather's death in 1928, and even received a contract and advance from the publisher Boni and Liveright to do so. Although she did research at the Essex Institute in Salem, Massachusetts, and wrote several chapters that were published in journals over the next few years, she never completed the project.

Instead, Porter became embroiled, along with many prominent literary figures and artists, in the attempted vindication of Nicola Sacco and Bartolomeo Vanzetti, two anarchist immigrants who had been sentenced to death for murder in 1921 and whose execution was imminent in 1927. Protesters claimed that the trial had been rigged and the judge was biased. Still involved in her Cotton Mather project, Porter called the Sacco and Vanzetti affair "another and terrible example of an American witch hunt." She was convinced that the two Italian anarchists were the scapegoats of conservative Americans threatened by massive waves of immigration and the rapid social and political changes of the 1920s. She was jailed several times for participating in demonstrations protesting their sentence, and was deeply disturbed when they were executed. She kept elaborate records of her participation in the protests, and after many years and many revisions published a long essay on the subject, *The Never-Ending Wrong* (1977).

While stalled on her research in 1927, Porter resumed writing short stories. An early version of "The Fig Tree" was rejected by *Harper's Bazaar*, but she published "Magic," and placed "The Jilting of Granny Weatherall" in *transition*, an avant-garde magazine of international standing. An extraordinarily compressed story, just over a thousand words, "Magic" is an inverted fairy tale set in a brothel in New Orleans. When one of the prostitutes, Ninette, protests that she has been cheated of her proper pay, the madam kicks the girl in the stomach and smashes a bottle over her head. Ninette crawls off into the night, but the customers demand her return. The madam implores the black cook to use voodoo to locate Ninette. After the cook's incantations over a broth mingling Ninette's fingernails, hair, and face powder, Ninette returns as if nothing had happened. Porter's unconventional subject matter—she is retelling a story she heard from a black maid in New Orleans—shows her increasing confidence in her artistry.

"The Jilting of Granny Weatherall" depicts God as a suitor who fails to claim his elderly bride at the moment of her death. This frequently anthologized story is written in wonderfully evocative language:

> Her heart sank down and down, there was no bottom to death, she couldn't come to the end of it. The blue light from Cornelia's lampshade drew into a tiny point in the center of her brain, it flickered and winked like an eye, quietly it fluttered and dwindled. Granny lay curled down within herself, amazed and watchful, staring at the point of light that was herself; her body was now only a deeper mass of shadow in an endless darkness and this darkness would curl around the light and swallow it up. . . .
>
> For the second time there was no sign. Again no bridegroom. . . . Oh, no, there's nothing more cruel than this—I'll never forgive it. She stretched herself with a deep breath and blew out the light.
>
> (*Collected Stories*, pp. 88–89)

In Granny's dying thoughts, Porter again experiments with the stream-of-consciousness techniques she used to such splendid effect in "Pale Horse, Pale Rider." Analyses of the story frequently observe that Granny remains tough-minded and staunchly independent even as she relinquishes her hold on life.

Back in New York in 1928, Porter took a job as a copy editor for Macaulay and Company, where she met Matthew Josephson, who had recently published a successful biography of Émile Zola. He was very supportive of her writing, and they became lovers, although Porter was distressed to learn that Josephson was married and the father of a small child. They spent long hours talking about literature and art, and with his encouragement, she began concentrating on her unfinished works. When Josephson decided to be her friend rather than her lover, concerned friends—including Josephine Herbst, Andrew Lytle, and Becky Crawford—sent the distraught Porter to Bermuda to recuperate from respiratory problems brought on by the stress of her break-up. The change of scene was effective. Porter was enchanted with the tropical beauty of the island, and several of her stories include descriptions of the landscape and her house there. Shortly after her return to New York at the end of the summer of 1930, she finished her revisions of "The Fig Tree" and completed "Flowering Judas," which was published in *Hound and Horn* that same year and made her literary reputation.

"Flowering Judas" is an elegantly crafted story, set in Mexico, that captures the anxiety of twenty-two-year-old Laura, who came to Mexico as a teacher but has become involved in the effort to subvert the old political order. Although the story focuses on the dangers of revolutionary politics, the descriptions of the landscape create an atmosphere of extraordinary power:

> The moonlight spread a wash of gauzy silver over the clear spaces of the garden, and the shadows were cobalt blue. The scarlet blossoms of the Judas tree were dull purple, and the names of the colors repeated themselves automatically in her mind, while she watched not the boy, but his shadow, fallen like a dark garment across the fountain rim, trailing in the water.
>
> (*Collected Stories*, p. 96)

Porter took the title "Flowering Judas" from T. S. Eliot's "Gerontion":

> In depraved May, dogwood and chestnut,
> flowering judas,
> To be eaten, to be divided, to be drunk
> Among whispers; by Mr. Silvero
> With cressing hands, at Limoges
> Who walked all night in the next room.

Porter's literary allusions in "Flowering Judas" have been linked to Eliot's allusive style: identifying her references and deciphering her symbols became a sort of parlor game in the 1930s and 1940s. M. M. Liberman comments on this passing literary craze:

> The neo-euhemerism of the thirties and forties seems down but by no means out, and the readings of "Flowering Judas" which can serve as paradigms of that era's notorious and, often, hilarious symbol-mongering have, to my knowledge, never been recanted.
>
> (in Harold Bloom, ed., *Modern Critical Views: Katherine Anne Porter*, p. 54)

Evolving critical styles have not diminished the stature of this story, however; it remains a universally acknowledged masterpiece.

Matthew Josephson and several other admirers of Porter's work (including Caroline Gordon, Allen Tate, Edmund Wilson, and Yvor Winters) encouraged Harcourt, Brace to publish a collection of Porter's work, and a limited edition of *Flowering Judas and Other Stories* appeared in 1930. When her health began again to deteriorate, her friends took up a collection to send her to Mexico in April 1930, where she planned to write a novel, "Thieves' Market" a project that went through several permutations and title changes. She never completed it, distracting herself instead with her elaborate network of friends. She went on shopping expeditions, traveled locally, attended and gave numerous dinner parties and receptions, and began an affair with Eugene Dove Pressly, a dour and disapproving twenty-seven-year-old whom she later fictionalized as David Scott in her novel *Ship of Fools*. (To her friends' dismay, she would marry him in 1933.) In 1931, she was awarded a Guggenheim Fellowship and began planning a trip to Europe. Arriving in Mexico with a Guggenheim Fellowship of his own in 1931, the poet Hart Crane became one of her numerous houseguests and, according to her letters, caused her enormous problems. His alcoholic excesses, suicidal rantings, and melodramatic homosexual affairs, inconveniently carried on at all hours, angered Porter until she threw him out. She wrote him a furious letter:

> I have borne to the limit of my patience with brutal behavior, shameless lying, hysterical raving, and the general sordid messiness of people who had not the courage to be as shabby as they wished when sober. . . . Let me alone. This disgusting episode has already gone too far.
>
> (*Letters*, pp. 45–46)

Her rejection of Crane became notorious after he committed suicide the following year. Porter's lack of sympathy for theatrical suicides was widely known; she kept a list of those who had attempted to win her sympathy by suicidal posturings. One anecdote, which Porter repeated herself, told of Elinor Wylie arriving at Porter's door to announce her impending death; Porter was the only person she cared to say good-bye to. Porter replied, "Well, good-bye, Elinor," and closed the door. Wylie survived her passing depression, but their friendship did not.

Despite the distractions she found for herself, Porter did manage to make notes for her story "Hacienda," a work that she began after watching Sergei Eisenstein shoot a film in Mexico. Experimenting with politicized symbolism, she describes the plantation chosen for the filming as redolent with the sickly-sweet smell of pulque, a cheap brew that represents government exploitation and oppression of the Indians, an alcoholic version of Marx's opiate of the masses:

> All over Mexico the Indians would drink the corpse-white liquor, swallow forgetfulness and ease by the riverful, and the money would flow silver-white into the government treasury.
>
> (*Collected Stories*, p. 168)

"Hacienda" would take another three years to finish. After eighteen months in Mexico, Porter had not completed a story, much less a novel.

In August 1931, Porter sailed to Europe on the German ship *Werra* with Pressly. En route, she collected material for *Ship of Fools*, material that would not coalesce into a novel until thirty years later. The relationship between Jenny Brown and David Scott in that novel parallels Porter's relationship with Pressly—a mixture of antagonism and affection. Several passengers on the *Werra* also surface in the novel, among them a "huge fat man with a purple face and watermelon pink shirt [who] . . . roared and sprawled and guzzled beer and sang in a voice that drowned out the brass band"; a hunchbacked man sporting gaudy neckties; and the ship's doctor, "an old Heidelberg student with a grand hooked nose, a fine head, and two sabre scars across his cheek and forehead."

Pressly accompanied Porter to Berlin. The conflict between the Nazis and the Communists was increasingly violent. There were many Nazi marches, parades, and attacks on Jewish shops and synagogues. Porter and Pressly soon quarreled; Pressly departed and Porter stayed on in Berlin, where she soon acquired a sophisticated circle of friends and acquaintances. Herbert Klein, a correspondent for the *Chicago Tribune*, introduced her to members of the Reichstag. As in New York and Mexico, she was a popular guest at dinner parties; at one party she met Hermann Goering, who took her to a nightclub and expressed interest in meeting her again. In 1975 she would report in the *Washington Star* that she had argued with Goering about his definitions of racial purity.

During her stay in Berlin, Porter took copious notes, including her impressions of the boarders at her pension, later incorporated into "The Leaning Tower." After recovering from an acute respiratory infection, which she thought was another bout of tuberculosis, Porter left for Paris, where she renewed her relationship with Pressly, who had been assigned to a diplomatic post in Madrid. She also had an affair with William Harlan Hale, a novelist twenty years her junior whom she had met in Berlin. Her schedule of social events was extraordinarily full. Her literary friends in Paris included Ford Madox Ford, Monroe Wheeler, Sylvia Beach, and Glenway Wescott, who described her striking beauty:

> She has in fact a lovely face, of the utmost distinction in the Southern way; moonflower-pale, never sunburned, perhaps not burnable. She is a small woman with a fine figure . . . Her eyes are large, dark, and lustrous, and they are apt to give one fond glances, or teasing merry looks, or occasionally great flashes of conviction or indignation. Her voice is sweet, a little velvety or husky.
>
> ("Katherine Anne Porter Personally," in Robert Penn Warren, ed., *Katherine Anne Porter: A Collection of Critical Essays*, p. 37)

Between social engagements, Porter followed an uncharacteristically disciplined work schedule. She expanded "Hacienda" to twice its original length; it was published with "Theft," "That Tree," and "The Cracked Looking-Glass" in a new edition of *Flowering Judas and Other Stories* in 1935. "Theft" describes a single woman's growing fears and frustrations, culminating in the theft of her purse; "That Tree" is another story of expatriate life in Mexico; "The Cracked Looking-Glass" creates a moving portrait of a vibrant Irish woman trapped in a marriage to a much older man. In addition, "The Circus" appeared in the *Southern Review;* "The Grave," "That Tree," and "Two Plantation Portraits" were published in the *Virginia Quarterly*.

Although their marriage was becoming increasingly stormy, Porter and Pressly traveled together in 1936 when they returned to the United States, where Pressly wanted to try his hand at journalism. They separated again after the trip home, however; Porter retreated to a quiet inn in Bucks County, Pennsylvania. In an astonishing burst of disciplined creativity, she wrote for long hours every day, producing in rapid succession "Noon Wine," "Old Mortality," and "Pale Horse, Pale Rider," as well as a draft of "Promised Land," a story based on her ocean voyage from Mexico to Germany that would eventually become *Ship of Fools*. This extraordinary output convinced her that she required solitude for her writing, and freedom from the discord of her marriage. She asked Pressly for a divorce, but he insisted upon trying again, and they spent several miserable months together in New York City. The relationship was effectively and mercifully ended in

1937, when Pressly took a diplomatic post in Venezuela. Soon after his departure, Porter began "A Day's Work," a story about family frictions. Dim as Pressly seemed to her friends, she remembered him more kindly than she did her other husbands.

While visiting Houston in the summer of 1937, Porter was invited by Allen Tate and Caroline Gordon to participate in a conference at Olivet College in Michigan. The lively group assembled at the Tates' home included Cleanth Brooks, Robert Lowell, and Albert Erskine, the business manager for the *Southern Review*. The twenty-six-year-old Erskine reminded the forty-seven-year-old Porter of Adam, the beautiful soldier in "Pale Horse, Pale Rider." She promptly fell in love with him and moved to New Orleans, both to avoid Pressly, who had returned to New York City, and to be near Erskine, who worked in Baton Rouge. She interrupted her new affair to visit her family in Houston for Christmas and extended her stay to avoid making a decision about Erskine's marriage proposal. She was grateful to learn, in March 1938, that her Guggenheim had been renewed, allowing her to concentrate on her work. Typically, she persisted in diverting herself from writing by continuing to teach a creative writing class twice a week and, when her divorce from Pressly became final in early April, agreeing to move to Baton Rouge and marry Erskine on 19 April. (Erskine did not discover that Porter was nearly twice his age until their wedding day.) Although the marriage was unhappy from the start, they did not separate until the spring of 1940, when she accepted a coveted invitation to join the artists' colony at Yaddo in upstate New York.

Although she wrote little new material during her marriage to Erskine (her last), three of the stories she worked on in Bucks County were published together in 1939 with the title *Pale Horse, Pale Rider*. In addition to the title story, the volume included "Old Mortality" and "Noon Wine." Each of these three extended stories, which Porter called short novels, centers on the character Miranda Gay. The title "Pale Horse, Pale Rider" is taken from Revelation and refers to the pale horse of death that represents the death of Miranda's lover, Adam—the first man—from influenza. This story, so often anthologized, is exquisitely written: a house is described as "snoring in its sleep"; the first light of morning "strike[s] a sudden blow on the roof." Both "Old Mortality" and "Noon Wine" recreate life in the traditional South and trace Miranda Gay's complex ties to her past. Critics agree in judging "Noon Wine" as one of Porter's finest achievements, and it has received a great deal of critical commentary. Porter later wrote an interesting bit of criticism on the story herself, indulging in the same sort of source-hunting that preoccupied her readers in the 1930s and 1940s:

> This short novel, "Noon Wine," exists so fully and wholly in its own right in my mind, that when I attempt to trace its growth from the beginning, to follow all the clues to their sources in my memory, I am dismayed; because I am confronted with my own life, the whole society in which I was born and brought up, and the facts of it. . . . Yet in this endless remembering which surely must be the main occupation of the writer, events are changed, reshaped, interpreted again and again in different ways, and this is right and natural because it is the intention of the writer to write fiction, after all–real fiction, not a *roman a clef*, or a thinly disguised personal confession which better belongs to the psychoanalyst's seance.
>
> (" 'Noon Wine': The Sources," in Robert Penn Warren, ed., *Katherine Anne Porter: A Collection of Critical Essays*, p. 59)

Perhaps unfortunately, Porter follows this disclaimer with a list of autobiographical sources for the story that to a certain degree validates all the psychoanalytic criticism she tries to dismiss in the opening lines of her essay.

Pale Horse, Pale Rider received excellent reviews in the *New York Times*, the *New York Herald Tribune*, the *Saturday Review of Literature*, and many other journals. All the reviewers praised her powerful style and command of her craft, comparing her favorably with Hawthorne, Flaubert, James, and Hemingway.

The 1930s were Porter's most productive and creative years. During the early 1940s, she lived primarily on publishers' advances for planned work she had not yet begun. After her unproductive stay at Yaddo, during which time she bought a house she could neither afford nor use, Porter moved to Washington, D.C., in 1944. She began an affair with Charles Shannon, a young soldier from Alabama. At the end of her life, she remarked in a conversation with Enrique Hank Lopez that after her first marriage, she "couldn't stand anything to do with sex. I was frigid as a cucumber and never did really get over it altogether." Nevertheless, she described her affair with Shannon as the most passionate of her life:

> I saw him first in his golden glory. . . . I did love his beauty and goldness and savoury sweet-smelling firm body with its light down of golden fur like an infant lion. . . . His health and hardness and sweetness and his endless pleasure in me and my presence and all we did and had and knew together.
>
> (Givner, *A Life,* p. 337)

She continued the affair even after learning that he was married; when the relationship ended, she still believed in romantic love, which she defined as "probably the silliest kind of love there is, but I am glad I had it.

Her next collection of fiction, *The Leaning Tower and Other Stories,* was published and favorably reviewed in 1944. The volume sold 20,000 copies in the first two weeks after publication. The stories selected for this collection include "The Old Order," "The Downward Path to Wisdom," "A Day's Work," and "Holiday," and the title story. "The Old Order" comprises several related short pieces Porter wrote in Paris in the late 1930s, and completes the history of Miranda Gay's search for role models. Jane Kraus DeMouy summarizes this short novel:

> If "The Old Order" is a catalogue of the "giants" of Miranda's childhood who taught her what a woman might be, "Old Mortality" is the story of Miranda's confrontation with the most formidable archetype her society can offer: the Southern belle, a nineteenth-century American manifestation of the virgin love goddess. . . . Miranda is caught between the negative image of one alternative and her own dissatisfying experience of the second.
>
> (DeMouy, pp. 147, 157)

When her affair with Shannon ended in January 1945, Porter needed a change of scene; she accepted a very lucrative offer to work in Hollywood but abandoned screenwriting after less than a year. She stayed in California to work on the formless manuscript of *Ship of Fools.* Porter had become increasingly outspoken against the menace of Nazism and German militarism, and recast the tenor of the narrative so that it became deeply critical of German culture. In a letter to Josephine Herbst, she wrote:

> My book is about the constant endless collusion between good and evil; I believe that human beings are capable of total evil, but no one has ever been totally good: and this gives the edge to evil. I don't offer any solution, I just want to show the principle at work and why none of us has any real alibi in this world.
>
> (Givner, *A Life,* p. 352)

Although Porter accomplished very little on the novel while she was in California, she accepted Wallace Stegner's invitation to teach at Stanford during the academic year 1948–1949. She received an honorary degree from the University of North Carolina at Chapel Hill in 1949. For the next few years, she wrote essays and reviews in New York, leaving the city periodically for lecture tours, occasionally worked at Yaddo, and, at the age of sixty, began a doomed affair with William Goyen, a thirty-five-year-old novelist from Texas. Depressed when the affair ended, she went to Paris in the fall of 1952 as a delegate to the Congress for Cultural Freedom, where she was reunited with her friends Cyril Connolly, Janet Flanner, Stephen Spender, Allen Tate, Virgil Thomson, and Glenway Wescott. She stayed in Paris for six months to work on her collection of essays, *The Days Before,* which was published upon her return to New York City. In 1953–1954, she taught at the University of Michigan, receiving another honorary degree at the end of the academic year. During her recovery from a mild heart attack in the spring of 1954, she worked on her novel.

In many respects, Porter's talent and temperament were not suited to the novel form, which she found unwieldy. In July 1956, she wrote to Glenway Wescott that she was bored with the project, as well as fatigued by the effort of sustaining her focus on a single project:

> I am slogging at this devilish book, and . . . how bored I am with it, because the plan is so finished, there is nothing to do but just type it down to the end, and OH GOD! how I have to beat myself over the head to get started every morning—and even so I am late, and wake every day with my heart sinking, thinking I'll *never* make it. But I must and will, and I shall *never* write another novel, that is flat!
>
> (Givner, *A Life,* p. 407)

After the initial excitement that greeted the long-awaited publication of *Ship of Fools* in 1962, some reviewers complained about the forced and sometimes monotonous pace of the narrative. Porter clearly recognized that *Ship of Fools* did not contain her best writing, and she lamented that there were at least forty short stories she could have been writing instead of the novel. But she had always had difficulty managing her talent; Marianne Moore described her as the world's worst procrastinator, and Porter often carried the ideas for stories in her mind for years before actually writing them down. When she did write, it was with an unusual intensity and concentration suited to literary forms more condensed than the novel. She herself observed:

> I've never made a career of anything, you know, not even of writing. I started out with nothing in the world but a kind of passion, a driving desire. I don't know where it came from, and I don't know why—or why I have been so stubborn about it that nothing could deflect me. But this thing between me and my writing is the strongest bond I have ever had—stronger than any bond or any engagement with any human being or with any other work I've ever done. I really started writing when I was six or seven years old. But I had such a multiplicity of half-talents, too: I wanted to dance, I wanted to play the piano, I sang, I drew. It wasn't really dabbling—I was investigating everything, experimenting in everything.
>
> (Givner, *Conversations,* p. 79)

In the mid 1950s, Porter changed publishers; she felt Harcourt, Brace did not advertise her work widely enough. With a hefty advance from Atlantic, Little, Brown, she moved to Connecticut, where she established a rhythm of "uninterrupted meditation and long hours of steady work" until she had nearly completed her novel. After a brief return to Washington, D.C., where she enjoyed the festivities surrounding John Kennedy's inauguration and indulged in an affair with her forty-nine-year-old Italian eye doctor, she traveled to California to lecture, and then to New York City to see friends, before she moved to a quiet hotel in Pigeon Cove, Massachusetts in June 1961, where she finished her final revisions.

In a prefatory statement, Porter explains that the German ship *Vera* is an allegory for "this world, on its voyage to eternity," concluding "I am a passenger on that ship." The character most resembling Porter in this work is Jenny Brown, the American artist. The other passengers on the *Vera,* which sails from Veracruz, Mexico, to Bremerhaven, Germany, in the late summer of 1931, hold a variety of passports: German, Swiss, Spanish, Cuban, Mexican, and Swedish. These passengers are from every walk of life and political persuasion: doctor, lawyer, priests, faith healer, teacher, families—parents and children—widow and widower, divorcée, garment manufacturer, hotel keeper, chemical engineer, painters, laborers in the Cuban sugar fields, singers, and dancers. The novel explores international tensions as they manifest themselves in the relationships developed on board ship. Perhaps the most obvious is the hostility between Jewish and non-Jewish Germans. But there are other enmities as well: between old and young, healthy and sick, rich and poor. In short, Porter tries to represent the human condition.

One of the most interesting relationships in the novel is that of David Scott and Jenny Brown, two young painters who are lovers and are traveling together for the first time. Theirs is a modern arrangement in which long-term commitments are fiercely avoided. Porter creates an evocative portrait of the psychological complexities—especially for women—of the episodic life.

Some critics of the novel blame this very multiplicity for the novel's failure: They cannot identify a single hero; the multiple subplots are not subordinated to an overarching master plot that focuses the reader's attention on one larger-than-life figure. Her sorrier characters are not tragic; her more successful ones are not epic. Even the Nazi sympathizers seem to fall far short of demonic. But the trivial banality of evil closely examined is precisely Porter's point: the very danger of fascism is founded on its pettiness, its capacity for innocuousness in its domestic form. When one of the German burghers stifles his intimidated wife, or when David Scott scoffs at Jenny Brown's artistic work, we are watching an allegory of World War II in its most elemental, germinal form.

Throughout her life Porter continued to view sexual relationships as inherently paradigmatic of a basic flaw in the human species. In a letter written in 1958, she expands on this idea:

> Men are continually accusing women of trying to castrate them by insulting their maleness, treating it with disrespect, trying to diminish their confidence in their own manhood. I am sure this is true, it is a kind of revenge some women take on some men for whatever reasons they may have. But do you forget that all boys start this kind of thing with all girls very early, and they keep it up very late? I know that when a woman loves a man, she builds him up and supports him. . . . I never knew a man who loved a woman enough for this. He cannot help it, it is his deepest instinct to destroy, quite often subtly, insidiously, but constantly and endlessly, her very center of being, her confidence in herself as woman. It's a great mystery, but there it is. I don't quarrel with it, I just see it and know it is there and try to deal with it.
>
> (*Letters,* p. 549)

Despite the reservations of some critics, *Ship of Fools* made Porter a wealthy woman. She bought jewels, traveled to Rome, and basked in her success. When the novel was made into a movie, she enjoyed the production as well as the profits.

In 1965, Harcourt, Brace, and World published *The Collected Stories of Katherine Anne Porter,* including all the stories in her previous collections as well as "The Fig Tree" and "Holiday." The late story "Holiday" tells of a young writer's visit in the household of a German farming family on the Texas prairie. Again the prose is extraordinarily well crafted, as the following description of spring demonstrates:

> The trees were freshly budded out with pale bloom, the branches were immobile in the thin darkness, but the flower clusters shivered in a soundless dance of delicately woven light. . . . Every tree was budded out, with this living, pulsing fire as fragile and cool as bubbles.
>
> ("Holiday," in *Collected Short Stories,* pp. 419–420)

Porter wrote her first version of "Holiday" not long after she wrote the early tale "María Concepción." In "María Concepción," Porter trains her gaze on a sturdy young matriarch in her first depiction of Mexican folk culture; she uses this same technique to illuminate the immigrant German peasant community in "Holiday." Miranda Gay comes to stay with the Müller family; the Müllers' grotesquely deformed daughter, who is the servant of the household, may be a projection of Miranda's psychological state. In the course of the story, Miranda learns from the family's indestructible matriarch, Mother Müller, that it is possible to accept a cosmos which includes both good and evil, both light and dark. *The Collected Stories* won the National Book Award and the Pulitzer Prize, as well as the Gold Medal for Fiction of the American Academy of Arts and Letters.

With her new wealth, Porter bought a twelve-room house, which she described as "1905 American Stratford-on-Avon," in suburban Washington, D.C. In 1966 she received an honorary degree from the University of Maryland—where she decided to deposit her papers and some of her possessions. Although she was writing very little in these final years, she did go to Cape Canaveral to cover an Apollo moon mission for *Playboy* in 1972.

In the late 1970s, Porter moved to a comfortable apartment near the University of Maryland, and at the age of eighty-seven she hired William Robin Wilkins, a retired naval officer, as her assistant. As her health failed, she drifted into a generalized paranoia, turning against all who had worked with her, including Wilkins. In the fall of 1977 she was declared legally incompetent, and in March 1980 she was installed in a nursing home in Silver Spring, Maryland, where she stayed until her death on 18 September of that year.

In many respects, Katherine Anne Porter was the role model Miranda Gay could not find. She created herself in many versions, inventing chapters of her life as she went. She found living in the twentieth century a great adventure, and she eschewed the sexual and social conventions that she felt confined too many of her contemporaries. Her fiction is as varied as her life. As Glenway Wescott observes, there is very little repetition in Porter's work:

> Katherine Anne, when not hitting high spots, really has preferred not to hit anything at all, at least not anything fictitious. She just keeps turning the pages of her mind until she comes to one that is untouched, to which she then applies a new pen, silvery and needle-sharp.
>
> ("Katherine Anne Porter Personally," in Robert Penn Warren, ed., *Katherine Ann Porter: A Collection of Critical Essays*, p. 52)

Porter's fiction encompasses a remarkable range: she captures the highly textured colors and shapes of the Mexican landscape and the violent emotions that mark the lives of obscure peasants in "María Concepción"; the dark incantations invoking the mysteries of voodoo and folk superstitions that shape the life of a New Orleans prostitute in "Magic"; the lilting cadences of the sexually frustrated Irish housewife in "The Cracked Looking-Glass"; the staccato rhythms of a married couple's argument in "Rope"; the shrill complaints of a spinster in "Theft"; and the sharply etched response of an old woman to her own death in "The Jilting of Granny Weatherall." Even though Porter was only sporadically productive, she labored at her craft:

> I mastered my craft as well as I could. There is a technique, there is a craft, and you have to learn it. Well I did as well as I could with that, but now all in the world I am interested in is telling a story. I have something to tell you that I, for some reason, think is worth telling, and so I want to tell it as clearly and purely and simply as I can. But I had spent fifteen years at least learning to write. I practiced writing in every possible way that I could. I wrote a pastiche of other people, imitating Dr. Johnson and Laurence Sterne, and Petrarch and Shakespeare's sonnets, and then I tried writing my own way. I spent fifteen years learning to trust myself: that's what it comes to.
>
> (Givner, *Conversations*, p. 91)

Selected Bibliography

PRIMARY WORKS

FICTION

Pale Horse, Pale Rider. New York: Harcourt, Brace, 1939.

Flowering Judas and Other Stories. New York: Harcourt, Brace, 1935.

The Leaning Tower and Other Stories. New York: Harcourt, Brace, 1944.

Ship of Fools. Boston: Little, Brown, 1962.

The Collected Stories of Katherine Anne Porter. New York: Harcourt, Brace, and World, 1965.

ESSAYS AND OTHER WORKS

The Collected Essays and Occasional Writings of Katherine Anne Porter. New York: Delacorte Press, 1970.

The Never-Ending Wrong. Boston: Little, Brown, 1977.

The Letters of Katherine Anne Porter. Edited by Isabel Bayley. New York: Atlantic Monthly, 1990.

SECONDARY WORKS

BIOGRAPHICAL AND CRITICAL STUDIES

Barnes, Daniel R., and Madeline T. Barnes. "The Secret Sin of Granny Weatherall." *Renascence* 21:162–165 (Spring 1969).

Bloom, Harold, ed. *Modern Critical Views: Katherine Anne Porter*. New York: Chelsea House, 1986.

Bluefarb, Sam. "Loss of Innocence in 'Flowering Judas.' " *CLA Journal* 7:256–262 (March 1964).

Brooks, Cleanth. "The Southern Temper." In his *A Shaping Joy: Studies in the Writer's Craft*. London: Methuen, 1971. Pp. 198–214.

DeMouy, Jane Krause. *Katherine Anne Porter's Women: The Eye of Her Fiction*. Austin: University of Texas Press, 1983.

Fetterley, Judith. "The Struggle for Authenticity: Growing up Female in the Old Order." *Kate Chopin Newsletter* 2, no. 2:11–19 (1976).

Flanders, Jane. "Katherine Anne Porter and the Ordeal of Southern Womanhood." *Southern Literary Journal* 9:47–60 (Fall 1976).

Givner, Joan. "The Genesis of *Ship of Fools*." *Southern Literary Journal* 10:14–30 (Fall 1977).

———. *Katherine Anne Porter: A Life*. New York: Simon & Schuster, 1982.

———. *Katherine Anne Porter: Conversations*. Jackson: University Press of Mississippi, 1987.

Gunn, Dewey Wayne. " 'Second Country': Katherine Anne Porter." In his *American and British Writers in Mexico, 1556–1973*. Austin: University of Texas Press, 1969. Pp. 102–122.

Hardy, John Edward. *Katherine Anne Porter*. New York: Frederick Ungar, 1973.

Hartley, Lodwick. "Dark Voyagers: A Study of Katherine Anne Porter's *Ship of Fools*." *University Review* 30:83–94 (Winter 1963).

Hartley, Lodwick, and Core, George, eds. *Katherine Anne Porter: A Critical Symposium*. Athens: University of Georgia Press, 1969.

Hendrick, George. *Katherine Anne Porter*. New York: Twayne, 1965.

Hendrick, Willene, and George Hendrick. *Katherine Anne Porter*. Rev. ed. Boston: Twayne, 1988.

Hennessy, Rosemary. "Katherine Anne Porter's Model for Heroines." *Colorado Quarterly* 25:301–315 (Winter 1977).

Johnson, Shirley E. "Love Attitudes in the Fiction of Katherine Anne Porter." *West Virginia University Philological Papers* 13:82–93 (December 1961).

Liberman, Myron M. *Katherine Anne Porter's Fiction*. Detroit: Wayne State University Press, 1971.

Lopez, Enrique Hank. *Conversations with Katherine Anne Porter, Refugee from Indian Creek*. Boston: Little, Brown, 1981.

Mooney, Harry John, Jr. *The Fiction and Criticism of Katherine Anne Porter*. Pittsburgh: University of Pittsburgh Press, 1957.

Nance, William L. *Katherine Anne Porter and the Art of Rejection*. Chapel Hill: University of North Carolina Press, 1964.

Partridge, Colin. " 'My Familiar Country': An Image of Mexico in the Work of Katherine Anne Porter." *Studies in Short Fiction* 7:597–614 (Fall 1970).

Ruoff, James, and Del Smith. "Katherine Anne Porter on *Ship of Fools*." *College English* 24:396–397 (February 1963).

Schwartz. Edward Greenfield. "The Fictions of Memory." *Southwest Review* 45:204–215 (Summer 1960).

———. "The Way of Dissent: Katherine Anne Porter's Critical Position." *Western Humanities Review* 8:119–130 (Spring 1954).

Thompson, Barbara. "Katherine Anne Porter: An Interview." *Paris Review* 29:87–114 (Winter–Spring 1963). Reprinted in *Writers at Work: The Paris Review Interviews*. 2nd ser. Edited by Malcolm Cowley. New York: Viking, 1963. Pp. 137–163.

Unrue, Darlene Harbour. *Truth and Vision in Katherine Anne Porter's Fiction*. Athens: University of Georgia Press, 1985.

Walsh, Thomas F. "Deep Similarities in 'Noon Wine.' " *Mosaic* 9:83–91 (Fall 1975).

———. "Identifying a Sketch by Katherine Anne Porter." *Journal of Modern Literature* 7:555–561 (1979).

———. "Xochitl: Katherine Anne Porter's Changing Goddess." *American Literature* 52:183–193 (May 1980).

Warren, Robert Penn. "Uncorrupted Consciousness: The Stories of Katherine Anne Porter." *Yale Review* 55:280–290 (Winter 1966).

———, ed. *Katherine Anne Porter: A Collection of Critical Essays*. Englewood Cliffs, N.J.: Prentice-Hall, 1979.

West, Ray B., Jr. *Katherine Anne Porter*. University of Minnesota Pamphlets on American Writers, no.

28. Minneapolis: University of Minnesota Press, 1963.

Wilson, Edmund. "Katherine Anne Porter." *New Yorker*, September 30, 1944, pp. 72–74. Review of *The Leaning Tower*.

BIBLIOGRAPHIES

Kiernan, Robert F. *Katherine Anne Porter and Carson McCullers: A Reference Guide*. Boston: G. K. Hall, 1976.

Schwartz, Edward. "Katherine Anne Porter: A Critical Bibliography." *Bulletin of the New York Public Library* 57:211–247 (May 1953).

Waldrip, Louise, and Shirley Ann Bauer. *A Bibliography of the Works of Katherine Anne Porter and a Bibliography of the Criticism of the Works of Katherine Anne Porter*. Metuchen, N.J.: Scarecrow Press, 1969.

WENDY MARTIN

ADRIENNE RICH

1929–

ADRIENNE RICH IS widely recognized as the preeminent American poet-critic of the post–World War II years. Such claims about living authors are always controversial; in Rich's case her gender and her radical politics make her status even more contested. Still, her powerful and moving poetry and her often chillingly lucid essays have brought her a large popular following, as well as critical acclaim, for her dual role as poet and political spokesperson of the contemporary feminist movement. One of the most passionate and complex statements of the evolution of feminist thought in a time when feminism is challenging and changing virtually every field of endeavor, Rich's work draws on the great tradition of social and political poetry but enriches that tradition with the revolutionary feminist insight that the personal is political. In her poems and essays, her life and the lives of countless other women become the site of social and political analysis. And through this analysis, Rich's poetry breaks the mold of the modernism she was trained in, shattering the confinement of formalism, aestheticism, and universalism to achieve a distinctly postmodern engagement with history, society, and identity.

In the foreword to *The Fact of a Doorframe* (1984), Rich writes: "One task for the nineteen- or twenty-year-old poet who wrote the earliest poems here was to learn that she was neither unique nor universal, but a person in history, a woman and not a man, a white and also Jewish inheritor of a particular Western consciousness, from the making of which most women have been excluded." Rich's career charts her refusal of the dual idealism of the unique, which seeks an authentic self repressed by patriarchal society, and the universal, which seeks a female essentialism.

In its progress Rich's writing and, indeed, her life seem an allegory of American feminism. She began as the privileged daughter, wife, and mother writing carefully constructed formalist poems, became radicalized by the repression of the 1950s and the politics of the 1960s, and turned to writing passionate, experimental, political poems that rage against "the oppressor's language," which will not let her speak herself. Rich emerged in the 1970s as a radical spokesperson for women's rights and lesbian feminism, writing a consciously woman-centered poetry and prose. But in the late 1970s and 1980s, under pressure from those women of color who felt excluded by the white, middle-class biases of the feminist movement, Rich was moved to examine her own complicity in oppression by virtue of her privileged background. In doing so, she had to discover the importance of differences beyond the simple binary of male/female.

In her influential essay "Notes Toward a Politics of Location" (1984), Rich emphasizes the myriad differences "among women, men, places, times, cultures, conditions, classes, movements," finding that she must first locate herself, hold herself accountable for where she is in her particular place, historical moment, and personal history: "I need to understand how a place on a map is also a place in history within which as a woman, a Jew, a lesbian, a feminist I am created and trying to create." Rich's emphasis on "location" keeps her tied to the material world and away from the temptations of philosophical idealism and transcendence that tend to obscure the material conditions of different people's lives. Instead, in her most mature poetry Rich grapples with history and difference, and the webs of knowledge and power in a poetic expression of the most sophisticated critical theory of our time.

Rich was born on 16 May 1929 in Baltimore, Maryland. Her father, Arnold Rich, was Jewish, a shopkeeper's son raised in Birmingham, Alabama, and sent in his teens to a military school in North Carolina that Rich describes in her autobiographical essay "Split at the Root: An Essay on Jewish Identity" (1982) as "a place for training white southern Christian gentlemen." Intense, brilliant, and cultured, he became a doctor at Johns Hopkins University. At Hopkins, where no Jew had ever held a chair in the medical school, his appointment to a professorship of pathology was delayed for years. Nevertheless, Arnold chose to identify himself as a scientist and a deist rather than as a Jew. It was a choice he imposed on his children as well, although, as Rich saw in retrospect, it is not something about which society gives one a choice.

Rich's gentile mother seems to have been as brilliant and independent as Rich's father. Helen Jones was a talented concert pianist and composer who won a scholarship to the Peabody Conservatory in Baltimore and later studied in New York, Paris, and Vienna. After marrying, she gave up her career to devote herself to her family, managing the household and teaching Adrienne and her younger sister, Cynthia, all of their lessons, including music, until they were in the fourth grade.

In *Of Woman Born* (1976) Rich compares her parents with Louisa May Alcott's parents, Bronson and Abigail Alcott, transcendentalists who believed they could raise their children according to "a unique moral and intellectual plan" removed from the determinants of society or history. Rich's charismatic father seized upon his precocious first child and educated her like an elder son:

> My father was an amateur musician, read poetry, adored encyclopedic knowledge. He prowled and pounced over my school papers, insisting I use "grown-up" sources; he criticized my poems for faulty technique and gave me books on rhyme and meter and form. His investment in my intellect was egotistical, tyrannical, opinionated and terribly wearing. He taught me, nevertheless, to believe in hard work, to mistrust easy inspiration, to write and rewrite; to feel that I *was* a person of the book, even though a woman; to take ideas seriously. He made me feel, at a very young age, the power of language and that I could share in it.
>
> (*Blood, Bread, and Poetry*, p. 113)

Rich did take herself seriously as a writer from a very young age, having some of her work published when she was only ten.

Arnold Rich occupies a place of ambivalence for Rich; he is the inspired source of her art but also the cruel patriarch who would make the world, including himself, into an ideal image of intellectual perfection. She sees her first resistance to him as a bodily one, recognizing, perhaps, how impossibly her female, child's body fit into his ideal vision. Early on, she was given to "tics and tantrums" caused, she feels, by her father's perfectionist pressures on her; the crippling arthritis she developed in her early twenties also becomes for her an emblem of her body's resistance to perfection. Rich's need to assert her difference from her father's vision is one seed of her later feminism.

Her first conscious rebellion focused on her Jewishness. In "Split at the Root" Rich describes how, at age sixteen, she slipped off to a theater to watch films of the liberation of the death camps, looking at the evidence of the Holocaust with uncomprehending eyes, knowing that she "was connected to those dead by something—not just mortality but a taboo name, a hated identity." But the connection was vague and tenuous in a house where anti-Semitism had never been discussed, where the belief endured that you could choose to transcend society. Only later did Rich learn that, in spite of her father's disregard of his Jewishness, "according to Nazi logic, my two Jewish grandparents would have made me a *Mischling*, first degree—nonexempt from the Final Solution."

Rich's parents disapproved of her interest in the Holocaust. Though they felt they were encouraging intellectual objectivity, Rich later recognized that they actually encouraged conformity to the anti-Semitism of the dominant culture. Her household respected the norm of "white social christianity," and she was taught Southern manners and female passivity even while she was encouraged to be critical, assertive, and independent. No wonder this alternative world of the intellect came to be associated with the secret Jewishness. From the beginning she felt "split at the root": both Jewish and casually anti-Semitic, educated to conform to stereotypes of feminine behavior and to question, critique, and aggressively challenge the world as it is from the position of a transcendentalist's "unique moral and intellectual" perspective.

When Rich left the South—for good, it turns out—to attend Radcliffe (from which she graduated with honors in 1951), she tried to turn away from the contradictions of her home through both intellectual achievements and associating with Jewish friends. When in 1953 she married Alfred Conrad, a divorced Jew from Brooklyn, her parents refused to attend the wedding. By the time her first child was born, she says, "I was barely in communication with my parents."

But Rich had hardly left her parents behind. Alfred Conrad, seemingly so different from Rich's father in his acceptance of Jewish culture, was also similar in many ways. He, too, was a university professor, teaching economics at Harvard, he, too, had deep, though more conflicting, ambivalences about his heritage, having changed his name to assimilate into the Yankee Protestant culture more easily. Rich, like her mother, pushed aside her own rising career as a poet to be the proper academic wife and mother, having three children before she was thirty.

Even her early poetry was under the spell of her father's perfectionist eye and her family's respectability. Rich's first book, *A Change of World* (1951), was chosen by W. H. Auden for the Yale Younger Poets Award. Auden's rather indirect and patronizing foreword to this book personifies Rich's poems in saying they are "neatly and modestly dressed, speak quietly but do not mumble, respect their elders but are not cowed by them, and do not tell fibs." Indeed, these early poems are beautifully crafted, displaying a wide range of reading and the influence of the modernist masters Robert Frost, Wallace Stevens, William Butler Yeats, and Auden. What Auden misses is the repressed passion, the struggle, so evident to readers today, against the boundaries of life. In her 1971 landmark essay "When We Dead Awaken: Writing as Re-Vision," Rich writes of these poems:

> Looking back at poems I wrote before I was 21, I'm startled because beneath the conscious craft are glimpses of the split I even then experienced between the girl who wrote poems, who defined herself in writing poems, and the girl who was to define herself by her relationships with men. "Aunt Jennifer's Tigers," written while I was a student, looks with deliberate detachment at this split. . . . It was important to me that Aunt Jennifer was a person as distinct from myself as possible—distanced by the formalism of the poem, by its objective, observant tone. . . . In those years formalism was part of the strategy—like asbestos gloves, it allowed me to handle materials I couldn't pick up bare-handed.
>
> (*Adrienne Rich's Poetry*, p. 93)

"Aunt Jennifer's Tigers" contrasts the creative needlework produced by Aunt Jennifer's fingers with "the massive weight of Uncle's wedding band," which "sits heavily upon Aunt Jennifer's hand." As the fingers that metonymically represent Aunt Jennifer's desires remain bounded by the wedding ring, so Rich's feminist awareness remains bounded by the formal demands of her verse:

> When Aunt is dead, her terrified hands will lie
> Still ringed with ordeals she was mastered by.
> The tigers in the panels that she made
> Will go on prancing, proud and unafraid.

The irony of the poem seems diminished by the neat and undisturbed closure; indeed, this ending emphasizes the ability of art to transcend the terror of a woman's life.

Other poems from this volume also view life as difficult and constraining, but they ascribe problems to universal, existential causes rather than social, historical ones. In Rich's lovely "Storm Warnings," "weather abroad" is likened to "weather in the heart"; both are forces of nature that we can only shelter ourselves against, not change: "We can only close the shutters." Again, in the tradition of modernism her ending sets her art against an alien world:

> I draw the curtains as the sky goes black
> And set a match to candles sheathed in glass
> . . . .
> This is our sole defense against the season;
> These are the things that we have learned
> to do
> Who live in troubled regions.

Rich recognizes the trouble in her world, the contradictions in her life and her husband's, and yet, like her parents, tries to see herself as exceptional, and art as a sheltered world—behind the curtains, sheathed in glass—apart from the turbulence of life.

Rich's second book, *The Diamond Cutters and Other Poems,* was published in 1955, in the same month her first child, David, was born. It received wide acclaim, winning the Ridgely Torrence Memorial Award of the Poetry Society of America (1955) and leading to a National Institute of Arts and Letters Award in 1960 and a second Guggenheim Fellowship in 1961 (her first was in 1952). Still, she writes in "When We Dead Awaken," "By the time that book came out I was already dissatisfied with those poems, which seemed to me mere exercises for poems I hadn't written."

Showing the influence of Frost in masterful narrative pieces about domestic life such as "The Perennial Answer" and "Autumn Equinox," the poems in this volume speak of people torn between their desire and their social roles. The erotic passion of women is hinted at but repressed, seemingly by the demands of art as well as of society. The title poem provides Rich's metaphor for the poet; the diamond cutter, by his careful craft, can "liberate" the light of the diamond from the stone, as poems create light from the darkness and pain of our lives. Africa is the unexamined metaphor for that darkness, as diamonds are used as universal symbols of value. When the poem was reprinted in 1984, Rich added this note:

> Thirty years later I have trouble with the informing metaphor of this poem. I was trying, in my twenties, to write about the craft of poetry. . . . The enforced and exploited labor of actual Africans in actual diamond mines was invisible to me, and therefore invisible in the poem, which does not take responsibility for its own metaphor.
>
> (*The Fact of a Doorframe,* p. 329)

For Rich the process of taking responsibility for her metaphors began with trying to understand how supposedly "natural" meanings are political and historical. Nowhere was this process more urgent for her than in her understanding of the roles of woman, mother, and wife. After the births of her second and third sons, Paul (1957) and Jacob (1959), Rich found that the exhausting task of caring for three young children led to frustration, anger, and guilt never associated with her image of mother. In 1960 she felt monstrous in her anger toward her children. She wrote in her diary:

> My children cause me the most exquisite suffering of which I have any experience. It is the suffering of ambivalence: the murderous alternation between bitter resentment and raw-edged nerves, and blissful gratification and tenderness. Sometimes I seem to myself, in my feelings toward these tiny guiltless beings, a monster of selfishness and intolerance. Their voices wear away at my nerves, their constant needs, above all their need for simplicity and patience, fill me

> with despair at my own failures, despair too at my fate, which is to serve a function for which I was not fitted.

Later, in *Of Woman Born* (1976), Rich would write with eloquence about how the isolation of women and children in middle-class America of the 1950s put an impossible burden upon mother and child. But in 1960 Rich blamed herself for failing to meet her "fate," seeing her difference from the ideal as monstrous.

The admission of the monstrous, however it covered over the systemic causes of her problems, was the admission of difference. Rich needed to disengage herself from allegiances to poetic masters and to her father's craft, leading her to a critique of the definitions of woman in the brilliant, angry poems of *Snapshots of a Daughter-in-Law* (1963). The title poem, her first fully feminist poem, is written in ten loosely connected free-verse sections; the force of "snapshots" in the title of the poem indicates how much she was abandoning her idea of poetry as careful craft set against the storms of life. Now there is no refuge in the home, no place for transcendence and self-definition apart from the social forces. In "When We Dead Awaken Writing as Re-Vision" she writes of this poem:

> In the late fifties I was able to write, for the first time, directly about experiencing myself as a woman. The poem was jotted in fragments during children's naps, brief hours in a library, or at 3 a.m. after rising with a wakeful child. . . . Yet I began to feel that my fragments and scraps had a common consciousness and a common theme, one which I would have been very unwilling to put on paper at an earlier time because I had been taught that poetry should be "universal," which meant, of course, non-female. . . . It was an extraordinary relief to write that poem.
>
> (*Adrienne Rich's Poetry*, p. 97)

This poem teems with images of the monstrous and violent consequences of the oppression of women. The repressed mother has a mind "mouldering like wedding-cake," "crumbling to pieces under the knife-edge"; the angry daughter trapped in the kitchen lets "the tap-stream scald her arm, / a match burn to her thumbnail"; the thinking woman "sleeps with monsters"; later, "she shaves her legs until they gleam / like petrified mammoth-tusk"; men label the independent Mary Wollstonecraft "harpy, shrew and whore." The poem uses literary allusion and quotation to indict literature and deny its distance from politics. If, as she says, "Time is male," then so are literature and history. Rich's violence lashes out at women as well as men, at herself as well as others: women are victims but also inevitably perpetrators of the culture that oppresses them.

The final section of the poem provides a way out of this vicious circle, but it, too, is monstrous in a way: the apocalyptic vision of a new woman who would "smash the mould straight off" can only be defined as a strange and monstrous being, part woman, part bird or avenging angel, part boy, part machine:

> Well,
> she's long about her coming, who must be
> more merciless to herself than history.
> Her mind full to the wind, I see her plunge
> breasted and glancing through the currents,
> taking the light upon her
> at least as beautiful as any boy
> or helicopter,
> poised, still coming,
> her fine blades making the air wince
> but her cargo
> no promise then:
> delivered
> palpable
> ours.

Rich's now famous image alludes to a similar one in Simone de Beauvoir's *The Second Sex* and complexly combines irony, war, and sexuality in this powerful, otherworldly vision. The vision aspires to a freedom beyond human knowledge, a vision of woman as Other, a triumph of the imagination that marks a beginning, not an ending, of work to be done. In spite of its bitterness and self-hatred, the poem begins the work of reshaping the world by recovering women's voices in Rich's allusions to de Beauvoir, Wollstonecraft, and Emily Dickinson and by rewriting the male tradition to include women (as she rewrites T. S. Eliot's allusion to Baudelaire's "mon semblable, mon frère" as "ma semblable, ma soeur").

The poems in this volume completely shake off Auden's epitaph of "modest" and instead present bold, disturbing images, particularly of women in domestic situations. Rich's need to get out of the house and, in a figurative sense, out of the house of this culture, is figured in the apocalyptic flying woman of "Snapshots." A similar image of escape informs "The Roofwalker," where she identifies with the builder, the roofwalker, standing on the roof of the unfinished house: "exposed, larger than life, /and due to break my neck." What she wants to rise above is both her own handiwork—"Was it worth while to lay— / with infinite exertion— / a roof I can't live under?"—and something she is a victim of: "A life I didn't choose / chose me." Given her complicity in the building of the unlivable house and home, she must leave behind not just the house but also her clothes and her very identity as female—wife and mother—and be "a naked man fleeing / across the roofs."

The urge to transcend the world remained storng in Rich's most visionary poems for two decades. But it was met with an equally powerfully realism that kept her struggling to find community and protesting the inadequacy of language to represent the reality of women's lives.

The title poem of *Necessities of Life* (1966) defines the poet, but this time as one who turns from all models for her existence, models that "swallowed me like Jonah," to "the bare necessities": "I learned to make myself / unappetizing. Scaly as a dry bulb / thrown into a cellar." This reduction does not lead to finding an authentic voice; instead, she rather comically wants to see herself as a cabbage or an eel, and her inspiration comes from outside:

> . . . I have invitations:
> a curl of mist steams upward
>
> from a field, visible as my breath,
> houses along a road stand waiting
>
> like old women knitting, breathless
> to tell their tales.

Rich's play on "breath" as the etymological root of inspiration, as well as a metonym for speaking, links her poetic project to telling the stories of those who are silent in this culture, the old women who, like Aunt Jennifer, have only their (much undervalued) needlework to speak for them. This feminist project would not be completely realized until 1974, when Rich returned to the house for her tales in the powerful "From an Old House in America." The poems in *Necessities of Life* still generally shun the house and female roles, often imaging the active resistance to these roles as masculine. She praises Emily Dickinson in "I Am in Danger—Sir—" as "you, woman, masculine / in single-mindedness," and her vision of herself as mother is still monstrous: In "Night-Pieces: For a Child" she sees herself as "death's head, sphinx, medusa." But she also expresses moments of great tenderness for her family and of belief in the "difficult, ordinary happiness" that "finds us" in the midst of existential and historical death and despair ("In the Woods").

In 1966 Rich moved with her family to New York City, where Alfred Conrad taught at City College of New York. With all three of her children in school, Rich was able to turn her attention more fully to her own interests. She lectured at Swarthmore College from 1966 to 1968 and was also adjunct professor of writing in the graduate school of Columbia University from 1967 to 1969. She had amassed an impressive number of awards for her work; in addition to two Guggenheim Fellowships she had won two prizes from *Poetry* magazine, and her work was generally respected and praised. She had begun to write essays and reviews and could, it seems, have settled comfortably into the role of the academic poet. Instead, her life and her writing took a radical turn toward a political engagement and profound self-questioning that still distinguish her work.

In 1968 Rich began teaching writing in City College's open admissions and SEEK programs, instituted to provide remedial instruction to freshmen entering City College from substandard ghetto high schools. In "Teaching Language in Open Admissions" (1972) she describes how the "unnerving and seductive" experience of teaching in such a program reinforced her sense of the complicity between language and power. Many of her students who were inarticulate within the bounds of white, middle-class academic work were forceful and articulate intelligences within the bounds of their own cultures. She and many of her colleagues felt neither willing nor able to reconcile these students to an academic way of speaking and writing that, far from objective, was in fact a language full of the biases of race, class, and sex that helped keep them economically disadvantaged. Still, Rich hoped to use the resources of both the language of the status quo and the language of the street, believing that "language can be used as a means of changing reality."

At this time Rich was increasingly involved in protests against the Vietnam war, and her heightened political awareness put pressure on her poetry. The poems in *Leaflets* (1969) achieve a strong, consistent voice, rich with erotic passion, rebellious energy, and political commitment. The language of war, often figured as the Holocaust or as a war between women and men, runs throughout this collection. Increasing in intensity, especially after 1967, many of the poems mirror the violence of the race riots, student demonstrations, and assassinations of 1968. Rich was working in two modes in this book. While she continued to craft images contrasting the oppression of the house to a transcendent freedom in the sky, a dualism beautifully realized in the poem "Orion," she was also working into a much more radical and experimental vision. The title poem finds yet another image for poetry:

> I want to hand you this
> leaflet streaming with rain or tears
> but the words coming clear
> something you might find crushed into your
> hand
> after passing a barricade
> and stuff in your raincoat pocket.
> I want this to reach you
> who told me once that poetry is nothing sacred
> —no more sacred that is
> than other things in your life—

Here, much more clearly than in the quite literary poems of *Snapshots,* Rich desires a poetry not removed from the world but, rather, engaged, active, a part of the political and emotional turmoil of the time. Using the work of Urdu poet Mirza Ghalib (1797–1869) as a model, in the summer of 1968 Rich wrote some of the most formally experimental poems of her career. Her "Ghazals: Homage to Ghalib" consists of seventeen sections, each dated and including at least five thematically unconnected couplets. This form produces cryptic and enigmatic images with almost none of the discursive clarity that marks much of Rich's other verse. Instead, the poems suggest her profound distrust of language as communication yoked to her deep belief in the expressive powers of the poet: "These words are vapor-trails of a plane that has vanished; / by the time I write them out, they are whispering something else."

In "Tear Gas," a powerful, emotionally wrought poem written in 1969 but not collected until 1975 *(Poems Selected and New),* Rich again brings the weight of political acitivty to bear upon her private life and her poetry. In this poem she wants "a word that will shed itself like a tear / onto the page / leaving its stain." This desire for emotional immediacy and physical presence in language indicates her frustration with the inadequacy of language, both in its publicness and in its inevitable split between word and thing. But she is also increasingly aware of the body as a political issue. She connects the demonstrators being teargassed outside Fort Dix, New Jersey, with her memory of a childhood punishment: "Locked in the closet at 4 years old I beat the wall with my body / that act is in me still." What shall be done with bodies—their killing, maiming, imprisonment, or their more subtle disciplining by a culture (as Michel Foucault so eloquently chronicles in *The History of Sexuality)*—becomes the crucial issue for Rich: "The will to change begins in the body not in the mind / My politics is in my body."

This poem foreshadows the politics of the body that would become central to feminism in the 1970s, both in the practical world of political action and in the theoretical writings of French feminists, who speak of writing the body as an alternative to the oppressor's language. But Rich has never believed it is possible to write the body, even metaphorically, given the nature of language and its tie to institutions of power. Instead, after listing a series of images of a more physical, apprehensible language, she says: "but this is not what I mean / these images are not what I mean / . . . I want you to listen / when I speak badly / not in poems but in tears / not my best but my worst." A raw, risky poem that admits the failure of poetry, it nevertheless uses rhetorical resources—short lines, repetition—to touch the reader emotionally in a shameless exposing and manipulation of emotions. This poem, as well as the longer poems in *Leaflets* and in her magnificent next volume, *The Will to Change* (1971), show Rich making the longer poem her own, using it as a vehicle for building emotional intensity and turning meditation into a form of rhetorical action. Siding with the rhetoricians against Plato, she accepts the fact that language is always interested, political. She will want nothing less from poetry than for it to become intertwined with politics and history, a move still resented by readers of poetry for whom a political poem equals propaganda.

In *The Will to Change,* Rich rewrites the figure of Orion, who symbolizes freedom and creativity, as a female, human heroine who fulfills Rich's earlier dream of "smashing the mould straight off." In "Planetarium" she writes of Caroline Herschel, the eighteenth-century astronomer who discovered eight comets but is almost unknown (unlike her famous brother, the astronomer William Herschel). The poem begins with monster images of the woman who fits no categories, "levitating into the night sky / riding the polished lenses." The images of ascension and power ("what we see, we see / and seeing is changing") are not, in this poem, allowed to become transcendent. The woman's body remains in the foreground through direct reference ("she whom the moon ruled / like us"), through the historical references in a factual headnote to the poem, and in quotations from historical documents.

Most important, the final images of the poem combine the body and outer space. The diffusing, confusing, and "untranslatable" forces entwine with a body that absorbs, resists, and translates these forces: "Heartbeat of the pulsar / heart sweating through my body / . . . I am bombarded yet I stand." The breakdown of the dualism between body and world and the many other dualisms implied in that one—self and other, inner and outer, transcendence or freedom and necessity, body and mind—is implied in the feminist principle that the personal is political. The end of the poem breaks down formally, also; the prosaic rhythm and irregular lines turn the final stanza into a paragraph rushing formlessly along. Poetic form itself is questioned, used, and undermined at the same time.

In "The Burning of Paper Instead of Children," Rich again questions the efficacy of langage and of poetry. This magnificently realized poem juxtaposes prose sections with lyrical poetry, probing the various relations between language and power, literature and life. The poem layers images of burning: Daniel Berrigan's burning of draft records in Catonsville, Maryland, to protest the Vietnam war; the use of napalm in Vietnam; Hitler's book burnings; Joan of Arc burning at the stake; sexual desire. While the title indicates her clear devaluing of literature before the demands of life, still the poem presents a great standoff: "this is the oppressor's language / yet I need it to talk to you." The ending of the poem is in prose, abandoning poetic form as it rushes toward an apocalyptic ending: "The burning of a book arouses no sensation in me. I know it hurts to burn. There are flames of napalm in Catonsville, Maryland. I know it hurts to burn. The typewriter is overheated, my mouth is burning, I cannot touch you and this is the oppressor's language." In this poem language is both the problem and the solution, as that final clause rings with despair at the enormity of the problem and her complicity in it, and with the ironic triumph of how much her poem succeeds in making language new. Over and over again, the poems in *The Will to Change* repeat these moments of despair and triumph as Rich focuses on the modes of representation—not only poems but also films, photographs, newsreels—by which we seek knowledge and change.

The year 1970 marked a point of crisis in Rich's life: her marriage broke up, and her husband committed suicide. These two events remain great silences in Rich's work. When Rich finally speaks of her husband in "Sources" (1982), she addresses her own silence and hints at the depth of his despair about life: "I've had a sense of protecting your existence, not using it merely as a theme for poetry or tragic musings; letting you dwell in the minds of those who have reason to miss you, in your way, or their way, not mine." Speaking to him now in a poem about Jewish culture and identity, she writes:

> No person, trying to take responsibility for her or his identity, should have to be so alone. There must be those among whom we can sit down and weep, and still be counted as warriors. (I make up this strange, angry packet for you, threaded with love.) I think you thought there was no such place for you, and perhaps there was none then, and perhaps there is none now; but we will have to make it, we who want an end to suffering, who want to change the laws of history, if we are not to *give ourselves away*.
>
> (xxii)

Alfred Conrad's failure to find community, and his belief that he could make himself new, as Rich's father had believed, is seen by Rich as a tragedy that the women's community will help her avoid.

That her marriage was difficult seems evident from Rich's poetry, which protests her role as wife and mother but also suggests the difficulty of male-female relationships. On the other hand, her poems addressed to her husband remain loving, pained, struggling. But around 1970, Rich's increasing involvement with the women's movement led her to a radical break with her married life: "The passion of debating ideas with women was an erotic passion for me, and the risking of self with women that was necessary in order to win some truth out of the lies of the past was also erotic. The suppressed lesbian I had been carrying in me since adolescence began to stretch her limbs. . . ." Rich's lesbian, woman-centered consciousness gives her radical politics a focus that is reflected in *Diving into the Wreck* (1973). Coinciding as it does with the acceleration of the women's movement in the United States, this book, which concentrates on male violence and on women's anger toward men, established Rich as a leading figure of feminism and won the National Book Award in 1974. Rich refused to accept the award for herself; instead, she accepted it with two other feminist nominees, Audre Lorde and Alice Walker, saying: "We symbolically join here in refusing the terms of patriarchal competition and in declaring that we will share this prize among us, to be used as best we can for women."

"Diving into the Wreck," perhaps Rich's most anthologized piece, is a well-crafted poem that symbolically delves into an androgynous unconscious, thus appealing to readers worried about her rejection of men and poetic beauty. As such, it is somewhat at odds with the scorching anger of other works in the collection, such as "Rape," a poem that in its raw indictment of the pervasiveness of male violence toward women refuses poetic subtlety or complexity.

"Rape" remains a controversial poem, often criticized as a simpleminded and propagandistic condemnation of all men. But neither "Rape" nor the aesthetized vision of "Diving into the Wreck" is quite representative of Rich's poetry; the longer "Phenomenology of Anger" and "Meditations for a Savage Child," in their searching explorations of violence and victimhood, draw on Rich's work from the late 1960s to question both aesthetic form and the possibility of clear political categories.

After *Diving into the Wreck,* Rich began more and more to combine her critique of patriarchy with a positive search for women's community, a search based on both utopian visions and historical understanding of women's lives. In "From an Old House in America" (1974), the house becomes a place of female resistance to male domination, as well as a place revealing America's history of violence toward women. While Rich continues to insist on the historical and cultural forces shaping identity, she also wants to assert the positive force of what she calls "local" power: "my power is brief and local / but I know my power." This local power gives Rich a place to begin, a place of identity from which to speak. But her identity refuses "isolation, the dream / of the frontier woman" and instead reachs out to the community in a final line that echoes John Donne: "Any woman's death diminishes me."

In what may be her most widely read book, *Of Woman Born: Motherhood as Experience and Institution* (1976), Rich uses her experience of motherhood as a place from which to begin a historical critique of the seemingly natural role of mother as a cultural institution constructed to support male control of women. This scholarly work is an impressive example of cultural materialism—an analysis of how identity is shaped by institutions and practices rather than some essential femaleness or even an essential humanness. But because the book was one of the first popular critiques of patriarchal structures and coincided with a rather official declaration of her lesbianism in *Twenty-One Love Poems* (1976), Rich was widely labeled as a man hater and ideologue, an advocate of a female essentialism that defines female qualities as natural and superior to male qualities. But for a poet so suspicious of natural meanings and so aware of the shaping powers of language, society, and history, the essentialist label has never fit comfortably. Rich's clear ethical stance and willingness to speak harsh truths are always combined with a critique of the categories of her own and others' thought, a critique that undermines the idea of ideological purity or separatism.

In this book Rich's final vision of mother love as a model for a non-oppressive and non-hierarchical society is utopian rather than essentialist. Indeed, she warns that "it can be dangerously simplistic to fix upon 'nuturance' as a special strength of women, which need only be released into the larger society to create a new human order." She believes, quoting Susan Sontag, that "there are ways of thinking that we don't know about yet." Like the monstrous flying woman at the end of "Snapshots of a Daughter-in-Law," this formulation reaches out into the unknown, but now Rich keeps herself firmly planted in the historical and material world. This dual movement of being within and without the culture at once allies Rich's thought with many projects of poststructural theorists.

With the publication of Rich's essays on poetry and politics in *On Lies, Secrets, and Silence: Selected Prose, 1966–1978* (1979), the revisionary power of her woman-centered critique emerged more clearly. These essays clarify the dual vision of her poetry: the negative critique of the representations of women, including her own visionary ones, and the affirmative recovery of women's history and voices that may lead us to think in ways we do not yet know. Her perspective is simultaneously inside a history and culture and outside of it; she wants to change prevailing histories and representations while she is constantly critiquing even her language of change. Her vision is always a split one, inside and outside at once, the assimilated Jew, the Southerner/Northerner, the wife/lesbian.

Rich's lesbianism provides a particularly telling perspective on the culture. In the controversial and influential essays "The Meaning of Our Love for Women Is What We Have Constantly to Expand" (1977) and "Compulsory Heterosexuality and Lesbian Existence" (written in 1978 and published in 1980), Rich argues that sexuality, as much as motherhood, is mediated by the culture and that lesbianism is more than just "sexual preference"; it is a challenge to the institution of heterosexuality, which, in its present form, is structured to keep women under male power. Because of its potential subversiveness, lesbian existence has been erased from history, transformed into tales of witches, or simply ignored. As she says in *Twenty-One Love Poems,* "No one has imagined us." Rich's task is to imagine, to place lesbian love within a tradition. But this task faces formidable obstacles from within and from without. In *Twenty-One Love Poems* the struggle to write, especially within a heterosexual tradition of the sonnet sequence, is seen as part of the problem: "What kind of beast would turn its life into words? / . . . when away from you I try to create you in words / am I simply using you?" The relationship eventually founders on this conflict between public and private, but Rich ends the poems with an assertion of her continuing effort to "stake out" a territory in which she can live.

Critics were slow to understand the innovative critical and poetic position Rich was developing. Many mainstream critics, schooled in New Critical principles stressing craft and the autonomy of the poem, disliked political poetry and were even more offended by her critique of patriarchy; some labeled her an ideologue and stopped reading and reviewing her poetry. Many of her feminist supporters discussed her politics to the exclusion of her poetry, especially after her prose work began to appear. Only in the 1980s, when political poetry became important and feminist critiques widespread, did fine critical studies of Rich as an important political poet and feminist theorist begin to appear.

The splendid poems of *The Dream of a Common Language* (1978) and *A Wild Patience Has Taken Me This Far* (1981) continue the project of double vision: affirming and critiquing women's power and place in history. In "Power," Marie Curie's death from radiation sickness becomes a symbol of this dual vision of affirmation and negation:

> She died   a famous woman   denying
> her wounds
> denying
> her wounds   came   from the same source
>   as her power

In "Phantasia for Elvira Shatayev," the leader of a women's climbing team, all of whom died in a storm on Lenin Peak, speaks of the visionary triumph of a community of women striving to climb the mountain, an image of transcendence. But Shatayev speaks from the grave. The final triumphal vision, "*We have dreamed of this / all our lives,*" is words written in a diary "torn from my fingers" by the destroying wind. The choice of the women to strive toward community and achievement is both powerful and ineffective, an inspiration that challenges cultural presuppositions but also a doomed, quixotic mission.

This dual vision is best articulated in "Transcendental Etude" (1977), dedicated to Michelle Cliff, a writer and poet who would become Rich's long-time companion. Here, Rich once again turns to the image of the galaxies as freedom, only to end back in the kitchen she had so bitterly scorned in "Snapshots." The poet understands that "there come times" when we have to

> . . . cut the wires,
> find ourselves in free-fall, as if
> our true home were the undimensional
> solitudes, the rift
> in the Great Nebula.

But this necessary dislocation leads to "the pitch of utter loneliness / where she herself and all creation / seem equally dispersed," an image recalling the fate of the women climbers. Rich connects the need to break away with a recognition that women "were always like this, / rootless, dismembered," because of a historical situation in which women and mothers are repressed, denied, and destroyed. Thus, the breaking away, essential to Rich in so many poems, becomes complicit with a culture that wants to keep women ungrounded, without a base of power, "homesick" for a woman, the mother, her self. Rich's solution is to come back home to a dual subject: *"I am the lover and the loved, / home and wanderer, she who splits / firewood and she who knocks, a stranger."* Rich's new home wants to tremble on the dangerous, shifting margins of representation but also remain enclosed within representations that give us a ground for identity and action. The poem ends with Rich's most extensive paean to the domestic particular:

> Vision begins to happen in such a life
> as if a woman quietly walked away
> from the argument and jargon in a room
> and sitting down in the kitchen, began turning
> in her lap
> bits of yarn, calico and velvet scraps

These lines are followed by a long catalog of particular ordinary things to be woven into the woman's "composition." She is "pulling the tenets of a life together / with no mere will to mastery, / only care for the many-lived, unending / forms in which she finds herself."

This poem may best articulate the tension in the phrase "dream of a common language." The dream of transcending the cultural determinants of language, of communicating immediately in a commonality of women, is countered by a need for the ordinary, rooted, "common" language in history from which action and change can arise. Transcendence of history, place, culture, and discourse is impossible; still, our visions must lead us into uncharted territory. The new, the unsaid, the monstrous can be thought only from within a discourse: "a whole new poetry beginning here," she says, with as much emphasis on "here" as on "new."

Rich developed this mature, complex vision in her poems and prose throughout the 1980s, as well as in the lesbian-feminist journal *Sinister Wisdom,* which she coedited with Michelle Cliff. In the poems of *A Wild Patience Has Taken Me This Far* (1981) she intensifies her use of historical material, focusing on the lives of women in the past and liberally using quotations from their writings. But these historical facts also point up the limitations of any act of revision: "history / is neither your script nor mine," Rich writes of Willa Cather. She tries to imagine Ethel Rosenberg, only to leave her "political in her ways not in mine"; she writes of her admiration for the nineteenth-century women reformers, only to criticize them, and implicitly herself, for their "class privilege" and "partial vision." In the magnificent "Turning the Wheel," Rich speaks of the Indian woman, lost in mythic history, who "stifles in unspeakable loneliness," yet she warns: "look at her closely if you dare / do not assume you know those cheekbones / or those eye-sockets; or that still-bristling hair."

The ability to revise history is limited by Rich's own complicity in the culture she wishes to change; yet this awareness of limitations is joined to an imperative to know. In "The Spirit of Place" the need for lucidity, figured in a crystal-clear night (so like her earlier transcendent images), is entwined with the complex "compost" of history, the obscuring river fog and underground journey. Rich rejects amnesia or nostalgia, both forms of forgetting history, in favor of trying to understand the world "as it is not as we wish it." The struggle to recover history is part of finding a "here" to change from. As she says in "For Memory," "The past is not a husk yet change goes on." Not a husk to be shaken off, nor a permanent mold, the past becomes a key to freedom that is not transcendence of the world:

> Freedom. It isn't once, to walk out
> under the Milky Way, feeling the rivers
> of light, the fields of dark—
> freedom is daily, prose-bound, routine
> remembering. Putting together, inch by inch
> the starry worlds. From all the lost collections.

This assertion of individual agency remains in tension with Rich's uncomfortable sense of her limited vision, a sense that was accentuated in the late 1970s and early 1980s by the attacks on feminism by women of different color, class, and ethnicity as a white, middle-class movement. Her need to understand her own frame of reference led Rich more and more toward her own past in the poems of *Sources* (1983) and *Your Native Land, Your Life* (1986). These poems, along with the essays published in *Blood, Bread, and Poetry* (1986), fully articulate a shift in feminism away from the single difference of male and female to an understanding of the multiple differences of gender, race, class, ethnicity, and sexual preference, each of which shapes the world differently. Rich's essay "Notes Toward a Politics of Location" has been lauded by critics in many fields for its lucid and complex articulation of a clear political focus within the dispersed field of differences that feminism must acknowledge. Rich agonizes over the question "Who is we?" as she contemplates the problem: "You cannot speak for me. I cannot speak for us. Two thoughts: there is no liberation that only knows how to say 'I'; there is no collective movement that speaks for each of us all the way through." "Location" is the term she uses to acknowledge differences and identity, necessity and chance.

The poems of *Your Native Land* (which reprints the poems of *Sources*) explore Rich's location: many reflect upon her move in 1984 from the Northeast to Northern California; others probe her Jewishness, speak to her father, contemplate her racism and Southern roots, and wonder what it means to be North American. These roots can no more be escaped than her body, twisted by the pain of lifelong arthritis. But the particularity of the body is embraced, as she writes in "Contradictions: Tracking Poems":

> The best world is the body's world
> filled with creatures filled with dread
> misshapen so yet the best we have
> our raft among the abstract worlds

The body's world is in history, in places, in discourses, a world we cannot escape or control. In a compelling long poem from this volume, "North American Time," Rich rejects the ideal of the "politically correct" for the confusions of history: "Poetry never stood a chance / of standing outside history." Instead, "Words are found responsible." Her attempt to remain responsible to the profusion of historical fact and event leads her to despair; but the thought of North American amnesia about history (as she says in "Notes Toward a Politics of Location," "I come from a country stuck fast for forty years in the deep-freeze of history") leads her to action. The poem ends with the line "and I start to speak again."

Rich's *Time's Power* (1989) keeps its focus on memory and history in a series of meditative poems. As she says in "Living Memory," recovering the details "bunched, packed, stored / in these cellar holes of memory" is a way to gain knowledge and power, "time's / power, the only just power. . . ." Only through the past can a new future be imagined, can what we don't yet know be called upon. These poems ring with optimism in a troubled world, as she writes of Middle Eastern conflict in "Turning": "the subject is how to break a mold of discourse, / how little by little minds change / but that they do change."

Rich has remained deeply committed to a material world and to women's role in maintaining and bettering that world through the minute, daily tasks of survival. In "Divisions of Labor" she speaks of "the women whose labor remakes the world / each and every morning." The attention to the daily task becomes a remaking, a creative revisioning of the world. In this poem Rich gives us an image for herslf, for the world created by her poetry:

> I have seen a woman sitting
> between the stove and the stars
> her fingers singed from snuffing out the candles
> of pure theory Finger and thumb: both
> scorched:
> I have felt that sacred wax blister my hand

Between the kitchen stove and the galaxies of stars, Rich continues her feminist project of re-visioning the world and embracing its contradictions through unflinching critique and passionate commitment.

Selected Bibliography

PRIMARY WORKS

PLAYS

Ariadne: A Play in Three Acts and Poems. Baltimore: J. H. Furst, 1939.

Not I, But Death: A Play in One Act. Baltimore: J. H. Furst, 1941.

POETRY

A Change of World. New Haven: Yale University Press, 1951; London: Oxford University Press, 1952.

The Diamond Cutters, and Other Poems. New York: Harper & Bros., 1955.

Snapshots of a Daughter-in-Law: Poems, 1954–1962. New York: Harper & Row, 1963; London: Chatto & Windus/Hogarth Press, 1970.

Necessities of Life: Poems, 1962–1965. New York: Norton, 1966.

Selected Poems. London: Chatto & Windus/Hogarth Press, 1967.

Leaflets: Poems, 1965–1968. New York: Norton, 1969; London: Chatto & Windus/Hogarth Press, 1972.

The Will to Change. New York: Norton, 1971; London: Chatto & Windus, 1972.

Diving into the Wreck: Poems, 1971–1972. New York: Norton, 1973.

Poems: Selected and New, 1950–1974. New York: Norton, 1975.

Twenty-One Love Poems. Emeryville, Calif.: Effie's Press, 1976.

Dream of a Common Language: Poems, 1974–1977. New York: Norton, 1978.

A Wild Patience Has Taken Me This Far: Poems, 1978–1981. New York: Norton, 1981.

Sources. Woodside, Calif.: Heyeck Press, 1983.

The Fact of a Doorframe: Poems Selected and New, 1950–1984. New York: Norton, 1984.

Your Native Land, Your Life. New York: Norton, 1986.

Time's Power: Poems, 1985–1988. New York: Norton, 1989.

PROSE

"Teaching Language in Open Admissions." In *The Uses of Literature.* Edited by Monroe Engel. Cambridge: Harvard University Press, 1973. pp. 257–273. Reprinted in *On Lies, Secrets, and Silence.*

Of Woman Born: Motherhood as Experience and Institution. New York: Norton, 1976; London: Virago, 1977.

"The Meaning of Our Love for Women Is What We Have Constantly to Expand." Brooklyn, N.Y.: Out and Out Books, 1977. Pamphlet, reprinted in *On Lies, Secrets, and Silence.*

On Lies, Secrets, and Silence: Selected Prose, 1966–1978. New York: Norton, 1979.

"Compulsory Heterosexuality and Lesbian Existence." *Signs* 5:631–660 (Summer 1980). Reprinted in *Blood, Bread, and Poetry.*

"Split at the Root: An Essay on Jewish Identity." In *Nice Jewish Girls: A Lesbian Anthology.* Edited by Evelyn Torton Beck. Watertown, Mass.: Persephone Press, 1982. Pp. 67–84. Reprinted in *Blood, Bread, and Poetry.*

Blood, Bread, and Poetry: Selected Prose, 1979–1985. New York: Norton, 1986.

SECONDARY WORKS

CRITICAL STUDIES

Altieri, Charles. *Self and Sensibility in Contemporary American Poetry.* Cambridge and New York: Cambridge University Press, 1984.

Bennett, Paula. *My Life, a Loaded Gun: Female Creativity and Feminist Poetics.* Boston: Beacon Press, 1986.

Carruthers, Mary J. "The Re-Vision of the Muse: Adrienne Rich, Audre Lorde, Judy Grahn, Olga Broumas." *Hudson Review* 36:293–322 (Summer 1983).

Christ, Carol P. *Diving Deep and Surfacing: Women Writers and Spiritual Quest.* Boston: Beacon Press, 1980.

Cooper, Jane Roberta, ed. *Reading Adrienne Rich: Reviews and Re-Visions, 1951–81.* Ann Arbor: University of Michigan Press, 1984. Contains useful articles, reviews, and a complete primary and secondary bibliography.

Deane, Patrick. "A Line of Complicity: Baudelaire—T. S. Eliot—Adrienne Rich." *Canadian Review of American Studies* 18:463–481 (Winter 1987).

Des Pres, Terrence. *Praises and Dispraises: Poetry and Politics—the 20th Century*. New York: Viking, 1988.

Diaz-Diocaretz, Myriam. *The Transforming Power of Language: The Poetry of Adrienne Rich*. Utrecht: HES Publishers, 1984.

———. *Translating Poetic Discourse: Questions on Feminist Strategies in Adrienne Rich*. Amsterdam and Philadelphia: John Benjamins, 1985.

DuPlessis, Rachel Blau. "The Critique of Consciousness and Myth in Levertov, Rich, and Rukeyser." In *Shakespeare's Sisters: Feminist Essays on Women Poets*, edited by Sandra M. Gilbert and Susan Gubar. Bloomington: Indiana University Press, 1979. Pp. 280–300.

Erkkila, Betsy. "Dickinson and Rich: Toward a Theory of Female Poetic Influence." *American Literature* 56:541–559 (December 1984).

Farwell, Marilyn R. "Adrienne Rich and an Organic Feminist Criticism." *College English* 39:191–203 (October 1977).

Ferguson, Ann. "Patriarchy, Sexual Identity, and the Sexual Revolution." In "On 'Compulsory Heterosexuality and Lesbian Existence': Defining the Issues." *Signs* 7:158–172 (Autumn 1981).

Flowers, Betty S. "The 'I' in Adrienne Rich: Individuation and the Androgyne Archetype." In *Theory and Practice of Feminist Literary Criticism*. Edited by Gabriela Mora and Karen S. Van Hooft. Ypsilanti, Mich.: Bilingual Press, 1982. Pp. 14–35.

Friedman, Susan Stanford. " 'I Go Where I Love': An Intertextual Study of H. D. and Adrienne Rich." *Signs* 9:228–245 (Winter 1983).

Gelpi, Barbara Charlesworth, and Albert Gelpi, eds. *Adrienne Rich's Poetry: A Norton Critical Edition*. New York: Norton, 1975. Contains selected poems, interviews, reviews, articles, and a bibliography.

Harris, Jeane. "The Emergence of a Feminizing Ethos in Adrienne Rich's Poetry." *Rhetoric Society Quarterly* 18:133–140 (Spring 1988).

Janows, Jill. "Mind-Body Exertions: Imagery in the Poems of Adrienne Rich." *Madog* (Wales) 3:4–18 (Winter 1979).

Juhasz, Suzanne. *Naked and Fiery Forms: Modern American Poetry by Women—a New Tradition*. New York: Harper & Row, 1976.

Kalaidjian, Walter. *Languages of Liberation: The Social Text in Contemporary American Poetry*. New York: Columbia University Press, 1989.

Kalstone, David. *Five Temperaments: Elizabeth Bishop, Robert Lowell, James Merrill, Adrienne Rich, and John Ashbery*. New York: Oxford University Press, 1977.

Kennard, Jean E. "Ourself Behind Ourself: A Theory for Lesbian Readers." In *Gender and Reading: Essays on Readers, Texts, and Contexts*. Edited by Elizabeth A. Flynn and Patrocinio P. Schweickart. Baltimore: Johns Hopkins University Press, 1986.

Keyes, Claire. *The Aesthetics of Power: The Poetry of Adrienne Rich*. Athens: University of Georgia Press, 1986.

Martin, Wendy. *An American Triptych: Anne Bradstreet, Emily Dickinson, Adrienne Rich*. Chapel Hill: University of North Carolina Press, 1984.

Middlebrook, Diane Wood. *Worlds into Words: Understanding Modern Poems*. Stanford, Calif.: Stanford Alumni Association, 1978.

Mohanty, Chandra Talpade. "Feminist Encounters: Locating the Politics of Experience." *Copyright* 1:30–44 (Fall 1987).

Nelson, Cary. *Our Last First Poets: Vision and History in Contemporary American Poetry*. Urbana: University of Illinois Press, 1981.

Ostriker, Alicia. *Writing Like a Woman*. Ann Arbor: University of Michigan Press, 1983.

Stimpson, Catharine. "Adrienne Rich and Lesbian/Feminist Poetry." *Parnassus* 12–13:249–268 (Spring–Winter 1985).

Strine, Mary S. "The Politics of Asking Women's Questions: Voice and Value in the Poetry of Adrienne Rich." *Text and Performance Quarterly* 9:24–41 (January 1989).

Templeton, Alice. "The Dream and the Dialogue: Rich's Feminist Poetics and Gadamer's Hermeneutics." *Tulsa Studies in Women's Literature* 7:283–296 (Fall 1988).

Vendler, Helen. *Part of Nature, Part of Us*. Cambridge, Mass.: Harvard University Press, 1980.

HARRIET DAVIDSON

ANNE SEXTON

1928–1974

ANNE SEXTON WROTE poetry in what she called "language," her term for discourse that bypasses rational thought to express repressed truths that are frequently socially unacceptable. Her first discovery of other users of "language" was in a mental institution to which she had been committed. "I found this girl (very crazy of course) (like me I guess) who talked language. What a relief! I mean, well . . . someone!" she wrote in a letter. But as a poet and not just a patient Sexton moved past the solipsism of the madhouse, "magic talking to itself, / noisy and alone" ("You, Doctor Martin"), to make "language" the source of a body of poetry that thrilled, outraged, charmed, and deeply affected a generation of readers in the 1960s and early 1970s.

Sexton's transformation from suburban housewife into famous poet occurred at a moment in history when American woman were beginning to question anew the gender definitions that the culture had neatly laid out for them. Her quest for identity through language helped inspire many women making similar journeys. Finding words to speak the self, words that did not necessarily parallel the ones the culture offered ready-made, seemed a way toward self-discovery, and was one reason why women's poetry flourished in the late 1960s and early 1970s. Discussions about the cultural construction of gender or of language were not common then; feminism, both academic and political, did not have such a sophisticated vocabulary. Nevertheless, the search for this language and the belief in its potential were very real.

Sexton's idea of a language that would "verbalize the non-verbal," that "has nothing to do with rational thought," was clearly a way to get at truths that the culture did not necessarily recognize. "Put your ear close down to your soul and listen hard," she advised. Her description of what happened when she first read W. D. Snodgrass's "Heart's Needle" emphasizes the power of poetry as a non-analytic, essentially physical experience: "It walked out at me and grew like a bone inside of my heart." This sort of poetry invoked a process of discovery for reader and poet alike. "I think a poem that can do that to people, make them see themselves through yourself, is valid, . . . not unseemly, not too personal, but worth it," she wrote in a letter.

When Anne Sexton killed herself in 1974, she left ten volumes of poetry and essays, as well as unpublished poems and an unpublished play. While many readers have admired her poetry's honesty and vulnerability, its shocking revelations of word as well as experience, there have been others who have found it vulgar, badly written, and tastelessly personal. Sexton remains as controversial as she was during her lifetime. But she has persisted in affecting and influencing readers. The critical and biographical work done since her death attests to that fact. Sexton continues to provoke and engage her readers, and scholars are still trying to define the nature of her contribution and thereby assess its value.

Sexton's status as a woman poet is particularly interesting because the exploration and representation of gender are at the heart of her writing. There is no question in her poetry about the gender of its author; that is what is so alluring and painful about reading it. Her writing, in its very repetitiveness and excess, reveals both the potential or repressed power of authentic female identity and another kind of power—that of a patriarchal system to define the female in its own terms, as something attractively and seductively impotent. The language that Sexton found to express the truth of her psychic reality as it tracks "primitive" or repressed phenomena tells the stories of these two versions of the female self, both incarnated in one woman, Anne Sexton. Particularly in her dual emblems of the poet's persona, the witch (the poet as mother) and the rat (the poet as naughty child), Sexton reveals contradictory functions for poetry itself: it is language in the service of life, or of death.

The "double" female self, as Sexton's poetry inscribes it, takes the following forms. On the one hand there is the woman as culture creates her. This woman seeks identity through the reflected power of others, specifically of males. Fathers, husbands, lovers, doctors, teachers, writers, and God himself—all offer such a woman a piece of their pie if she lets them take her, use her, love her. Her so-called power in these situations is to seduce them into wanting her; she then becomes privy to all that they have and are. In this scenario, other women are clearly peripheral, especially mothers. A girl learns to reject her mother in order to escape the lure of the woman who created her and to cleave in any way that presents itself to the father: one father, all fathers. Anne Sexton writes painfully of a self trapped in bonds such as these.

On the other hand, in another "world," or so it feels, there is a woman who eludes this paradigm. Her identity comes neither from thralldom nor from domination (neither traditionally "female" nor "male") but from and by means of her relationship to others, especially to women, and even more specifically, to her mother and her daughters. In this condition of relatedness she becomes both like and different, connected and individuated. Motherhood is the source and conduit of this version of identity, and of the power that comes from having an identity, because the pre-oedipal relationship between mother and child is the central experience in our culture that is organized in this way. Using "language" to arrive at this place, this knowledge, Sexton sometimes, especially in writing of mothers and daughters, describes a female identity that is nonpatriarchal.

Sexton's poetry bespeaks both kinds of identities because, as is perhaps only "natural," both were hers. Or to put it another way, when her language roots at the truths she knows, it discovers more than one kind. When we read Sexton today, we may find ourselves wanting to pick and choose among these truths. We may well recoil from the poems (and there are so many of them) in which the speaker begs for men's "love" and is rendered helpless by it. As the critic Alicia Ostriker notes: "We may easily find Sexton's addiction to love, her insistence on need, infantile and repellent. She clearly finds it repellent herself, thereby somewhat outflanking us. What must mitigate our judgment is the recognition that we, too, are such addicts, were truth told." And we may respond as powerfully today as when they were first published to the poems in which Sexton, as mother or as daughter, speaks what Ostriker calls a "mothertongue"; these are poems that can cause us to weep in recognition. However, to talk of Sexton's poetry is to acknowledge both these voices and identities, their conflicting presence, as they inform and create her oeuvre.

Sexton's madness cannot be ignored in discussing her art. Although there is a real distinction between being mad and being sane, there is also a relation between these states. Sexton's excessive sensitivity to aspects of existence experienced by the mad and the sane alike provided her with the subject material for her art, sent her into therapy and mental institutions throughout her life, and caused her to kill herself.

Sexton's definition of the artist's role was based on the condition with which her madness was associated: "Creative people must not avoid the pain they get dealt. I say to myself, sometimes repeatedly, 'I've got to get the hell out of this hurt.' . . . But no. Hurt must be examined like the plague." However, the kind of vision that fuels the artist extends further in madness, where it includes as well the inability to protect oneself from what one sees.

Sexton's madness was integrally involved with her art in a particular way, for her writing was encouraged and shaped by psychoanalysis and the therapeutic process. She explicitly connects "language" with madness. "Insanity," she says in a letter, "is surely the root of language." However, it was psychoanalysis that helped her to make use of her madness: as patient, speaking in therapy a specific discourse based in "language," and then as poet, crafting "language" into forms that others could understand.

"Language," however, articulating experience that is not socially sanctioned, is not so choosy about what manner of experience that might be. If "language" is, in Diane Middlebrook's words, "the primitive speech of the buried self," it does not specify *what* self. "Language" can bring to light the child's earliest responses to mother as well as father. Psychic stress has its source in these moments from infancy and childhood, and it is precisely the job of psychoanalysis to return to them and retrieve the spoils. Nonetheless, classic psychoanalysis has a particular perspective on the nature of the self—its proper configuration, what hampers and what aids its development—that reinforces patriarchal definitions of self-identity. That is, although "language" may be impartial, psychoanalysis is not. Therapy works to help the patient develop a "self" that conforms to cultural expectations.

When, for example, Sexton told an interviewer that she had to come home from her trip abroad because "I had, as my psychiatrist said, a 'leaky ego,' " she was referring to the negative connotations her analyst placed on her needing "my husband and my therapist and my children to tell me who I am." Sexton does not question the analyst's interpretation of her experience: "I got sick over there. I lost my sense of self." Self-identity, according to classic psychoanalytic theory, comes from having achieved maximum separation and individuation. The proper self is the self that stands alone.

However, recent feminist psychology has countered this idea with the notion of the "self-in-relation": a self that is formed "by means of continuous psychological connection, in which the presence of the other forms a basic component of one's own experiences of self," in the words of the psychologists Judith Jordan and Janet Surrey. Stressing the necessity of connection, this idea of self locates the sources of self-development in the original, pre-oedipal relationship between mother and infant. Therefore, growth is understood not as a process of achieving autonomy and independence through the breaking of early emotional ties, but rather as an ongoing interaction within the mother-child relationship. Sexton's search for self through "language" brought her to a knowledge of this kind of identity, one that contradicted what she was learning in analysis.

Consequently the role of psychoanalysis in Sexton's art was a complicated one. It fostered her use of a "language" which enabled her to speak the truths of her life in poetry, truths which included important aspects of her female experience that were conventionally devalued and misinterpreted. At the same time psychoanalysis served to teach her an idea about selfhood that emphatically countered these discoveries about female identity. The tenets of psychoanalysis, reinforced by the transference it fostered to yet another powerful father figure, the analyst himself, encouraged her to become a woman according to traditional gender definitions.

It was this patriarchal definition and tradition that finally held sway. Poetry did not save Anne Sexton, as she kept asserting it would, because her poetry itself, more and more, was put in the service of reinforcing her sickness, her neediness, and her powerlessness as a woman.

Anne Sexton, born Anne Gray Harvey on 9 November 1928, grew up and lived her life in suburban Boston. Her mother, Mary Gray Staples Harvey, was the daughter of a newspaper editor in Lewiston, Maine; her father, Ralph Churchill Harvey, was the affluent owner of a woolen firm engaged in interational trade. Anne was the youngest of three sisters; she usually spoke of herself as an unwanted child. Her favorite family member was her unmarried great-aunt, Anna Ladd Dingley, who lived with the Harveys until she was sent to a nursing home when Anne was thirteen.

Sexton attended public and private schools, and the Garland School, a finishing school. She was never considered a good student, although she wrote poetry during this period. In 1948 she eloped with Alfred Muller Sexton II, nicknamed Kayo, who was to be her husband for twenty-five years until she divorced him in November 1973. She was the mother of two daughters, Linda Gray Sexton and Joyce Ladd Sexton. As a bride she put all her energy into becoming a good housewife, but even then madness intervened. "Until diagnosed as mentally ill," writes her biographer, Diane Middlebrook, "Sexton had been regarded by her exasperated family as childish, selfish, incompetent. Her mother-in-law remembered the shock with which she first watched Sexton throwing herself, pounding and screaming, on the floor because she was enraged at being asked to do an errand." Severe depression following the birth of her first child led to her psychiatric hospitalization in 1954. In 1956, on her birthday, she made the first of what were to be many attempts at suicide. For several years thereafter her children were cared for by their grandmothers.

Sexton began writing poetry in earnest in 1956, when she was home from the hospital and her children were not living with their grandparents. After seeing I. A. Richards discussing sonnets, on educational television, she tried to write one herself. Her psychiatrist, Dr. Sidney Martin, also encouraged her to write. "Don't kill yourself," he said. "Your poems might mean something to someone else someday." Thus her career as a poet began; as she later wrote, poetry "gave me a feeling of purpose, a little cause, something to *do* with my life, no matter how rotten I was."

Attending a poetry workshop taught by John Holmes at the Boston Center for Adult Education, starting in 1957, was a major impetus to Sexton's work. There she discovered other poets, notably Maxine Kumin, who was to become her lifelong friend and colleague; there she began to learn about poetry. Holmes himself was a mixed blessing; unintimidating and accessible as a teacher, he was often unenthusiastic about Sexton and her poetry—its uninhibited and personal quality made him cringe. Other classes and workshops—a summer Antioch Writers' Conference in 1958, where she worked with W. D. Snodgrass, whose "Heart's Needle" had inspired her to write of her own deeply personal truths, and Robert Lowell's graduate poetry seminar at Boston University—helped her enormously to strengthen her skills and confidence. "Workshopping" a poem—developing it in response to others' criticism and comments—was a procedure she used with Maxine Kumin all her life.

Sexton's first book, *To Bedlam and Part Way Back,* was published in 1960, a year after her mother and father died. It was followed by *All My Pretty Ones* (1962), *Live or Die* (1966), *Love Poems* (1969), *Transformations* (1971), *The Book of Folly* (1972), and *The Death Notebooks* (1974). Later works, published posthumously, include *The Awful Rowing Toward God* (1975), *45 Mercy Street* (1976), and *Words for Dr. Y: Uncollected Poems with Three Stories* (1978). *The Complete Poems* was published in 1981.

During Sexton's career her fame grew; she received many prizes and awards, beginning with her appointment as a scholar in poetry at the Radcliffe Institute for Independent Study in 1961. A traveling fellowship from the American Academy of Arts and Letters in 1963 took her to Europe with a neighbor as her companion; however, emotional disturbance caused her to return a month early. In 1967 she received the Pulitzer Prize for *Live or Die*. A Guggenheim Fellowship in 1969 enabled her to work on her unpublished play *Mercy Street* in New York. In 1969 she also began teaching a poetry seminar at Boston University, where she was made a full professor in 1972. On 4 October 1974 she committed suicide by carbon monoxide poisoning in the garage of her home.

Throughout her creative period Sexton continued to live the life of a housewife as well as of a poet. In a letter she described it thus:

> I do not live a poet's life. I look and act like a housewife. My daughter says to her friends: "a mother is someone who types all day." But still I cook. But still my desk is a mess of letters to be answered and poems that want to tear their way out of my soul and onto the typewriter keys. At that point I am a lousy cook, a lousy wife, a lousy mother, because I am too busy wrestling with the poem to remember that I am a normal (?) American housewife.
>
> (*Letters*, p. 270)

Even if Sexton had wanted to separate her roles, she could not imagine ways to do so. Role models in the form of women poets who were married mothers were not abundant. Several times she used grant money to pay for child care or cleaning help. But because she lived and worked in this fashion, she demonstrated both the ways in which writing is not distinct from the life of a traditional woman and the ways in which the two roles come into conflict. Writing both belongs to female identity and puts it into question, as Sexton's career as a poet consistently illustrated.

In 1977 Linda Gray Sexton and Lois Ames published *Anne Sexton: A Self-Portrait in Letters.* Sexton's letters, comprising a more informal self-presentation than her poetry, add much to our understanding of her. They reveal her intensity, need, extravagance, humor, charm, generosity, manipulativeness, pain, and fear. Sometimes inspiring, sometimes embarrassing, they are always moving. It is not easy to be with Anne Sexton, for her best and her worst are equally disconcerting.

Sexton's mother-daughter poems are where we find most clearly the expression of the female self-in-relation. In some of these poems she is daughter; in some she is mother; in some she is both. These connections are essential and flexible: a mother is also a daughter; a daughter turns into a mother; a daughter will mother her mother, in time. As early poems like "The Double Image" and late poems like "The Death Baby" insist, all of these are variations on the central relationship between mother and child, and these variations include the connection between life and death. The life that mothers bequeath contains death within it: the death of the mother, the death of the daughter. But that death in turn fosters life, for daughters live on when mothers are dead, to give life to new daughters. Individuality, or differentiation, must always be poised against and understood in terms of this profound connectedness. In this way self-identity is formed.

Sexton's poems reveal these truths, even when she herself might not have recognized them so readily in everyday life. Toward her mother she felt a tangle of emotions—anger, guilt, competition, disappointment, and jealousy—that continued long after her mother's death. Her poems probe deeper to show the source of these feelings in love, yearning, and a sense of abandonment. "I want mother's milk," she wrote late in her life, in the poem "Food": "I want breasts singing like eggplants, / and a mouth above making kisses." But in response to her, "baby all wrapped up in its red howl," her mother "pour[s] salt into my mouth. / [Her] nipples are stitched up like sutures." Despite the fact that Mary Gray's own traditional female socialization made it difficult for her to nurture her child properly, with true empathy and recognition of the child's own self—despite, that is, the truth of Sexton's need and longing—in her poems Sexton discovers a source for her own identity in the very fact of her mother, whose love was real, even if her ability to use it was deficient. "You were mine / after all," she writes about her mother in "The Double Image."

In this important poem the portraits of the dead mother and her suicidal daughter mirror one another, creating nothing less than a "double woman" with "matching smile, matching contour." This sense of connection evokes rage, guilt, and love: rage at her mother for attributing her recently diagnosed cancer to her daughter's suicide attempt; guilt that it might be so.

> Only my mother grew ill.
> She turned from me, as if death were catching,
> as if death transferred,
> as if my dying had eaten inside of her.
>
> (p. 38)[1]

We could see this identification as a crippling thing—Sexton's doctors did—except that it sits at the very heart of this poem addressed not to the mother but to the daughter, Joyce, Sexton's tiny child who had been taken from her while she was recovering from her suicide attempt. Love for the child *and* love for the mother are the poem's cardinal emotions, around which guilt, suffering, and fear hover. Love is what finally enables the speaker to come to life in a very literal way—she recovers from her attempt to kill herself in order to nurture her daughter. The insights of the poem into her relationship with her mother are there to help her get her daughter back.

[1]All quotations of Sexton's poetry, unless otherwise noted, can be found in *The Complete Poems* (Boston: Houghton Mifflin, 1981). All page references are to this edition.

Thus, even though "The Double Image" ends with the wisdom of the doctors—"I, who was never quite sure / about being a girl, needed another / life, another image to remind me. / And this was my worst guilt; you could not cure / nor soothe it. I made you to find me"—we, as readers, are not so convinced that this is such a naughty thing to do. Not when the child is described as "already loved, already loud in the house / of herself"; not when the name is "mother" because for the first three years of her life the child never knew her as such: "You learn my name, / wobbling up the sidewalk, calling and crying. / You call me *mother* and I remember my mother again, / somewhere in greater Boston, dying."

Motherhood gave to Anne Sexton an authenticity and authority that was not hers when she was daughter alone, perhaps because the knowledge of the frailties and failures of her first mother-daughter relationship (as daughter) gave her both the intense desire for and the means to improve her subsequent ones (as mother). Recognizing the child for who she is, someone who is both "me" and "not-me," is a far cry from maternal narcissism, which involves seeing the child as simply an extension of yourself. One does not know what the everyday reality of Sexton's mothering was like, what it felt like to her daughters, but in her poems we experience her as a mother who sees both difference and sameness.

"Darling, life is not in my hands; / life with its terrible changes / will take you, bombs or glands," she writes to her daughter Linda in "The Fortress," evoking difference, as her mother's response "she looked at me / and said I gave her cancer" ("The Double Image") does not. At the same time the sense of likeness in "The Fortress" is strong: "I press down my index finger— / . . . on the brown mole / under your left eye, inherited / from my right cheek." What, then, can a mother do for her child? "I cannot promise very much. / I give you the images I know." The poem concludes: "We laugh and we touch. / I promise you love. Time will not take away that."

That touch is all-important; it is precisely what Sexton as mother uses to bridge the gap between sameness and difference. Sexton recalls that her mother never touched her except to "examine" her. In Sexton's poems to her daughters, the sensual physicality of the imagery is especially memorable. "Little Girl, My String Bean, My Lovely Woman" is emblematic of this kind of poem, as its title alone suggests:

> *Oh, little girl,*
> *my stringbean,*
> *how do you grow?*
> *You grow this way.*
> *You are too many to eat.*
>
> I hear
> as in a dream
> the conversation of the old wives
> speaking of *womanhood.*
> I remember that I heard nothing myself.
> I was alone.
> I waited like a target.
> . . . .
> and someday they will come to you,
> someday, men bare to the waist, young
> Romans
> at noon where they belong,
> . . . .
> But before they enter
> I will have said,
> *Your bones are lovely,*
> and before their strange hands
> there was always this hand that formed.
>
> Oh, darling, let your body in,
> let it tie you in,
> in comfort.
>
> (pp. 146–147)

At the same time, Sexton's maternal understanding extends backward in memory to her own mother, who "died / unrocked, unrocked" ("The Death Baby"). When her mother was dying she could not act upon impulses that made the two roles (mother, daughter) versions of the same kind of love: "To place my head in her lap / or even to take her in my arms somehow / and fondle her twisted gray hair." But in the poem "The Death Baby," these feelings find expression in words, where Sexton's tenderness toward that one ancient antagonist gives her further insight into another relationship that has been with her from the start—"Death, / you lie in my arms like a cherub, / as heavy as bread dough":

> I rock. I rock
> You are my stone child
> with still eyes like marbles.
> There is a death baby
> for each of us.
> We own him.
> His smell is our smell.
>
> (p. 358)

Sexton's sense of herself as a mother is of a person who nurtures with look, touch, care, and "images"—that is, her words themselves, her stories. The poems that she writes are a major part of her maternal gifts; consequently, from her recognition of this role in relation to her own daughters and mother it is not a large step to the concept of the poet as mother, the poet as witch.

Sexton's identification with the figure of the witch had originally to do with her madness: "I have gone out, a possessed witch, / haunting the black air, braver at night" ("Her Kind," 1960). However, by the time she published "Live" in 1966, the association between witch, mother, and writer had been made and the witch's positive power recognized by the poet's daughters:

> I wear an apron.
> My typewriter writes.
> It didn't break the way it warned.
> Even crazy, I'm nice
> as a chocolate bar.
> Even with the witches' gymnastics
> they trust my incalculable city,
> my corruptible bed.
>
> (p. 169)

In *Transformations* (1971), perhaps her finest book, Sexton has the witch emerge as her strongest poetic persona in a sequence of poems whose subject was suggested by her daughter Linda. The witch is the mother, telling her children stories (in this case, Grimm's fairy tales): "The speaker in this case / is a middle-aged witch, me— / . . . ready to tell you a story or two" ("The Gold Key"). Her children are all of us: "Alice, Samuel, Kurt, Eleanor, / Jane, Brian, Maryel, / all of you draw near. / Alice, / at fifty-six do you remember?" And her stories are profoundly maternal, offering to her children revisions of patriarchal myths to reveal the truths that women know.

Sexton's revisions of these tales juxtapose the contemporary with the traditional, the psychoanalytic with the mythic, not simply to create a modern take on an old story but rather to advance a different idea about it. Here "language" serves the purpose of speaking female knowledge, both conscious and unconscious: "Living happily ever after— / a kind of coffin, / a kind of blue funk. / Is it not?" ("The White Snake"). "Happily ever after" is how the old stories end. The word "coffin," however, gives us the perspective of the subject of the story, the princess, suddenly given access to the telling. Her perspective defines the ending, and it is not happy but "living death." The colloquialism of "blue funk" is out of place in the traditional fairy-tale world. It lets us see how contemporary princess brides are still being told to live in the old stories, regardless of what kinds of lies they perpetrate.

All of Sexton's re-interpretations have surprises for us, whether in the startling imagery—"[Rumpelstiltskin] tore himself in two. / Somewhat like a split broiler"; "the virgin is a lovely number: / cheeks as fragile as cigarette paper"—or in the situations themselves. In "Rapunzel," our interest is diverted from the handsome prince to the witch who has locked the girl in a tower. Suddenly we see how that Johnny-come-lately may replace rather than inaugurate "true love," and that the witch had something to protect, something to lose:

> Many a girl
> had an old aunt
> who locked her in the study
> to keep the boys away.
> They would play rummy
> or lie on the couch
> and touch and touch.
>
> (p. 245)

"Briar Rose (Sleeping Beauty)" tells of a girl with unquiet dreams, dreams that Sexton could share with her princess heroine across the centuries:

> It's not the prince at all,
> but my father
> drunkenly bent over my bed,
> circling the abyss like a shark,
> my father thick upon me
> like some sleeping jellyfish.
>
> (p. 294)

The inappropriateness of the imagery to the situation, the way in which the father, conceived of as a deadly, circling shark, turns into a repulsive, comatose jellyfish—heavy, disgusting, and inescapable—makes this version of the incest scene particularly dreadful. And the way in which the sexual act itself is textually repressed, deleted from the discourse, becomes a comment on not only this particular girl's psychological repression of the event but the way in which the culture at large has been guilty of replacing one story with another, one that is deemed more acceptable.

Some critics of Sexton's earlier books had decried their personal, "confessional" nature. Sexton is correct when in a letter she says of the *Transformation* poems that "it would . . . be a lie to say that they weren't about me, because they are just as much about me as my other poetry." However, much of their strength comes from the way in which the personal gets expanded in them so that she comes to tell a tale of her tribe—women. This identity that is at once individual and collective seems a logical poetic extension of her mother-self, "a self-in-relation," formed, we remember, "by means of continuous psychological connection, in which the presence of the other forms a basic component of one's own experiences of self." The mother-witch-poet of *Transformations* is Sexton at her best, because she draws on the stuff of a powerful female identity to speak on behalf of us all. *Transformations* is scary, funny, shocking, clever, and devastating. Each time the cliché turns, we recognize the buried female truths in those patriarchal bedtime stories.

If only the witch had triumphed. She was a power for life as well as truth. But Sexton could not break so completely from the culture's "wisdom"—not when she was imbibing it regularly from the many male authorities in whom she persistently sought to believe: her father, her husband, the male poets who mentored her, her doctors (most of whom were men), and finally, God. As much as these men "loved" her, equally they denigrated her. The only way to teach her was for her to be someone who was ignorant; the only way to cure her was for her to be someone who was sick; the only way to love her was for her to be someone who was needy; and the only way to save her was for her to be someone who had sinned. Poised against the witch as emblem of herself as poet was another—the rat.

The rat is the child of a very bad mother indeed, Eve herself, its birth an "unnatural act" ("Rats Live on No Evil Star"). The rat is "evilest of creatures / with its bellyful of dirt / and . . . two eyes full of poison." The rat takes center stage late in Sexton's oeuvre, as if the witch, once personifying her identity, has been vanquished. Now it is the rat who represents her soul, something clearly to be vilified. In "Rowing," the title poem of *The Awful Rowing Toward God* (1975), salvation is imaged as a door:

> and I will open it
> and I will get rid of the rat inside of me,
> the gnawing pestilential rat.
> God will take it with his two hands
> and embrace it.
>
> (p. 418)

The rat cannot save herself; God must do it for her.

The rat's dilemma is traceable through all of the poems (and they are many) in which Sexton, the bad girl who wants love—as much for her badness as in spite of it—attempts to seduce her many fathers through a bravura that is nonetheless always aware of their power to grant or withhold approval of her naughty charm. "In the long pull, John," she wrote to John Holmes, her first poetry teacher, "where you might be proud of me, you are ashamed of me. I keep pretending not to notice. . . . But then, you remind me of my father."

The poems that Sexton addressed to father figures represent a second major category in her work, running all the way from "You, Doctor Martin" in her first book, *To Bedlam and Part Way Back* (1960), to the painful supplications to God in *The Awful Rowing Toward God* and other poems of the early 1970s. Ralph Churchill Harvey, teaching her to eat oysters, that "father-food," so "moist and plump," at the Union Oyster House in Boston ("The Death of the Fathers"), is the obvious source for her attraction to patriarchal power, but the father figure appears elsewhere in her work in the form of the male psychiatrist. It is useful to focus on these doctor images in order to illuminate more closely the relation between Sexton as daddy's girl and Sexton as poet.

The patient-doctor relationship is set up clearly and centrally in the very first poem of Sexton's very first book, "You, Doctor Martin." Of course she loves him: he is "god of our block, / prince of all the foxes"; his "third eye / moves among us and lights the separate boxes / where we sleep or cry." Of all the crazy women, she is the best, "queen of this summer hotel." She attempts to lure him with her badness, her deviance from conventional femaleness ("Once I was beautiful. Now I am myself") as it is revealed through her lunatic insight—"magic talking to itself." She will trade him the special vision that comes with her madness for just one thing: love and salvation. Other fathers of whom she has made this request have betrayed as well as indulged her: Ralph Harvey, fading "out of sight / like a lost signalman / wagging his lantern / for the train that comes no more" ("The Death of the Fathers"); John Holmes, his fear "like an invisible veil between us" ("For John, Who Begs Me Not to Enquire Further"). But perhaps not the doctor, who, because of his peculiar calling, prizes the very things that have ultimately appalled the others, as the poem "Cripples and Other Stories" reveals:

> Oh the enemas of childhood,
> reeking of outhouses and shame!
> Yet you rock me in your arms
> and whisper my nickname.
> (p. 161)

This poem is addressed to "father-doctor," and it explicitly contrasts the relationship she has with him to her other loves:

> My father didn't know me
> but you kiss me in my fever.
> My mother knew me twice.
> and then I had to leave her.
>
> But those are just two stories
> and I have more to tell
> from the outhouse, the greenhouse
> where you draw me out of hell.
>
> Father, I'm thirty-six
> yet I lie here in your crib.
> I'm getting born again, Adam,
> as you prod me with your rib.
> (pp. 162–163)

The doctor wants her stories. They are of such interest to him, as manifestations of the "language" so valued in the therapeutic process, because they demonstrate how very sick and contemptible she is. The connection between madness, femaleness, infantilism, and pollution is explicitly made, as the poem's imagery yokes outhouse and crib, crazy lady and Eve. Adam, the first man, is not lover and companion to Eve but her father-doctor-savior, poking her with his rib as a doctor would prod a patient with his stethoscope. This doctor's love becomes a version of that first biblical relationship, a manifestation of the paternal power that makes him proud, since he (and only he) can cure her: "You hold me in your arms. / How strange that you're so tender! / Child-woman that I am, / you think that you can mend her." There is a catch to this kind of father-love, even as there was with Ralph Harvey, though his involved a different kind of bargain. The complicity he wrapped her in was sex, as she writes in "The Death of the Fathers":

> You danced with me never saying a word.
> Instead the serpent spoke as you held me
> close.
> The serpent, that mocker, woke up and
> pressed against me
> like a great god and we bent together
> like two lonely swans.
> (p. 324)

Complicity with the doctor required her belief in her madness.

Consequently, Sexton's poetry has functions other than to create life. It can also be used to demonstrate impotent need so that the all-powerful doctor-father will want to keep her alive. But this contract has significant drawbacks. First, it is dependent upon his continued presence; second, it demands her sickness, not recovery—for she is attractive to him only if she is sick. Frequent visits to the doctor are requisite; also necessary, we might surmise, are frequent relapses: major depressions, and of course (the ultimate proof), suicide attempts.

In 1964, when Dr. Martin decided to move his practice to Philadelphia, a hysterical letter to Anne Clarke, a California psychiatrist and friend of Sexton, revealed the extent and nature of the psychiatric patient's dependence upon the doctor:

> Dr. Martin is leaving . . . Christ. I can't. I *mean* I can't . . . eight years of therapy . . . At start me nothing . . . *really* nothing . . . for two years me still nothing . . . and then I start to be something

> and then my mother dies, and then father . . . a large storm . . . then recovery and that slow and trying to both Martin and me . . . I mean "hell" and not just "trying" . . . and I'd come quite far . . . but . . . now . . . if he goes next Sept. . . . I have had it. I can't make it (the intense trust, *the* transference all over AGAIN) . . . Please! Help me! . . . I HAVE GOT TO HAVE SOMEONE.
> (*Anne Sexton: A Self-Portrait in Letters,* p. 229)

For doctors, like lovers, husbands, teachers, and fathers, *do* leave. In each departure there is betrayal, even if someone else can be seduced into taking his place. Until the next betrayal. In *Anne Sexton: A Self-Portrait in Letters* Linda Gray Sexton and Lois Ames write that in her last months

> her friends grew angry and frustrated with her midnight suicide threats, her inability to go to the dentist alone, enter a store alone, mail a letter alone. She required constant service and care, and those closest to her began to set limits in self-protection. Anne saw these limits as unreasonable fences erected by those she loved—the ultimate desertion.
> (p. 389)

The father to whom Sexton turns at last, in her final poems, is God himself. Surely *he* will not abandon her. The poems that became *The Awful Rowing Toward God* were written in two and a half weeks, taking only three days off during that time, as she told an interviewer:

> One for exhaustion and two for a mental hospital. Then out and back to the book. Staying up till three A.M., and getting up again at six. Writing in seizure, practically not stopping; maybe not even drinking; maybe just gobbling my meal and running back in there again. The poems were coming too fast to rewrite.
> (quoted in Coburn, *No Evil Star,* p. 189)

In these poems the rat seeks God. If there had been moments in her writing when she had imagined God as a mother—sometimes as Mary or even "some tribal female who is known but forbidden" ("Somewhere in Africa")—that fantasy no longer works. Rather, in the poem "Is It True?" and other works from her last years, God, the ultimate doctor-father, is pictured offering salvation to the poet, who declaims her essential evil in order to be an appropriate object for his love:

> But the priest understands
> when I tell him that I want to
> pour gasoline over my evil body
> and light it,
> He says, "That's more like it!
> *That* kind of evil!"
> (p. 448)

These poems are, of course, further versions of those stories that she told to the doctor to please him. "A story! a story!" she promises God, and offers him her manic vision of apocalypse. Poetry is again her lure, but it can never be her power, not in this scenario. Power belongs only to the father, never to the daughter. God's power is explicitly revealed in the final poem of the volume, "The Rowing Endeth," when, having moored her boat at the dock of the island called God, she plays a game of poker with him. With a royal straight flush, she thinks she has won; but she is wrong, for "a wild card had been announced / but I had not heard it / being in such a state of awe / when He took out the cards and dealt." That is the point, and the ultimate dilemma. She adores God for his very lack of fairness, his lack of interest in equality, his power over her:

> Dearest dealer,
> I with my royal straight flush,
> love you for your wild card,
> that untamable, eternal, gut-driven *ha-ha*
> and lucky love.
> (p. 474)

When the patriarchy co-opts the poet's gift, the gift of "language," her stories become agents in the perpetuation of the hegemony to which the poet has abased herself. No power here. And no salvation. This kind of poetry is a blueprint for the loss of identity, not for the attainment of it. On the other hand, the witch's stories, the poems of the mother-poet, are both life-affirming and life-enhancing. The mother's primal power to create life manifests itself in words as well as personal relationships, as the "images" she gave to her one daughter, to her many daughters, served and continue to serve as affirmations of our identity as well as her own. These "images," or stories, are ways of naming and of recognizing what they name. Here was power—the power of life and of self-identity—released by "language" into the light of day.

Psychoanalysis created Anne Sexton the poet out of Anne Sexton the madwoman and helped to destroy her. It gave her the tools for a trade—poetry—but at the same time it taught her to put those tools to work in the service of the father. One reason for the inequality of the struggle between the witch and the rat is that Sexton apparently never had an awareness of a real precedent for her role as a mother-poet and hence found insufficient support for her endeavors. Her own mother was associated with things literary in the family mythology, although she wrote nothing other than occasional verse; but her endeavors were the source of a peculiar rivalry between them, especially from her mother's point of view, so that Mary Gray was, in Diane Middlebrook's words, both "censor and precursor." Nevertheless, it was her mother, not her father, who bore the literary mantle in Harvey household; and it is the daughter, with her grandmother's name, Linda Gray Sexton, who has inherited it. It is also significant that Sexton's relationships with the few actual women writers she knew, such as Maxine Kumin, Carolyn Kizer, Tillie Olsen, and Lois Ames, appear to have been exceptionally important to her. But they were few in contrast to the male writers, both in person and on the page, who influenced her ideas about poetry and poets. Masculine authority was dominant if not absolute.

Sexton's lasting significance, however, lies in the fact that at least some of the time she did manage to speak as a mother—to daughter-readers and daughter-writers, including her daughter Linda, and to many other women as well, women who now understand in a more self-conscious fashion the need for a mother as source and model. Sexton's mother-daughter poems are an important legacy in American women's poetry.

Selected Bibliography

PRIMARY WORKS

POETRY

To Bedlam and Part Way Back. Boston: Houghton Mifflin, 1960.

All My Pretty Ones. Boston: Houghton Mifflin, 1962.

Selected Poems. London: Oxford University Press, 1964.

Live or Die. Boston: Houghton Mifflin, 1966.

For the Year of the Insane. Boston: Impressions Workshop, 1967. Broadside illustrated by Barbara Swan.

Poems by Thomas Kinsella, Douglas Livingstone, and Anne Sexton. London: Oxford University Press, 1968. Selection of previously unpublished poems.

Love Poems. Boston: Houghton Mifflin, 1969.

Transformations. Boston: Houghton Mifflin, 1971.

The Book of Folly. Boston: Houghton Mifflin, 1972.

The Death Notebooks. Boston: Houghton Mifflin, 1974.

The Awful Rowing Toward God. Boston: Houghton Mifflin, 1975.

45 Mercy Street. Edited by Linda Gray Sexton. Boston: Houghton Mifflin, 1976.

Words for Dr. Y: Uncollected Poems with Three Stories. Edited by Linda Gray Sexton. Boston: Houghton Mifflin, 1978.

The Complete Poems. Boston: Houghton Mifflin, 1981.

Selected Poems of Anne Sexton. Edited by Diane Wood Middlebrook and Diane Hume George. Boston: Houghton Mifflin, 1988.

PROSE

"Feeling the Grass." *Christian Science Monitor,* 4 June 1959.

Foreword to *The Real Tin Flower: Poems About the World at Nine* by Aliki Barnstone. New York: Crowell-Collier, 1968. Reprinted in "Stories for Free Children." *Ms.*, March 1975.

"Writing Exercises." In *The Whole Word Catalogue 1.* Edited by Rosellen Brown et al. New York: Teachers and Writers, 1972. Written with Robert Clawson.

"Anne Sexton." In *World Authors, 1950–1970.* Edited by John Wakeman. New York: H. W. Wilson, 1975. Autobiographical statement.

Anne Sexton: A Self-Portrait in Letters. Edited by Linda Gray Sexton and Lois Ames. Boston: Houghton Mifflin, 1977.

"Journal of a Living Experiment." In *Journal of a Living Experiment: A Documentary History of The First Ten Years of Teachers and Writers Collaborative.* Edited by Phillip Lopate. New York: Teachers and Writers, 1979.

No Evil Star: Selected Essays, Interviews, and Prose. Edited by Steven E. Colburn. Ann Arbor: University of Michigan Press, 1985.

CHILDREN'S BOOKS
(WRITTEN WITH MAXINE KUMIN)

Eggs of Things. New York: Putnam, 1963.

More Eggs of Things. New York: Putnam, 1964.

Joey and the Birthday Present. New York: McGraw-Hill, 1971.

The Wizard's Tears. New York: McGraw-Hill, 1975.

SECONDARY WORKS

BIOGRAPHICAL AND CRITICAL STUDIES

Colburn, Steven E., ed. *Anne Sexton: Telling the Tale.* Ann Arbor: University of Michigan Press, 1988.

George, Diana Hume. *Oedipus Anne: The Poetry of Anne Sexton.* Urbana: University of Illinois Press, 1987.

———, ed. *Sexton: Selected Criticism.* Urbana: University of Illinois Press, 1988.

Hall, Caroline King Barnard. *Anne Sexton.* Boston: Twayne, 1989.

McClatchy, J. D., ed. *Anne Sexton: The Artist and Her Critics.* Bloomington: Indiana University Press, 1978.

Middlebrook, Diane Wood. *Anne Sexton: A Biography.* Boston: Houghton Mifflin, 1991.

Wagner-Martin, Linda W., ed. *Critical Essays on Anne Sexton.* Boston: G. K. Hall, 1989.

BIBLIOGRAPHY

Northouse, Cameron, and Thomas P. Walsh. *Sylvia Plath and Anne Sexton: A Reference Guide.* Boston: G. K. Hall, 1974.

SUZANNE JUHASZ

SUSAN SONTAG

1933–

ESSAYIST, CRITIC, NOVELIST, screenwriter, polemicist, activist, and film and theater director, Susan Sontag is internationally known for her extraordinary intellectual range and vigor. Born in New York City on 16 January 1933, Sontag was an asthmatic child. She and her younger sister were raised by their widowed mother in Tucson. The family moved to Los Angeles in 1946, after her mother's remarriage to a Captain Sontag, "a handsome, bemedalled and beshrapnelled Army Air Forces ace." She graduated from North Hollywood High School at age fifteen, spent one year at the University of California, Berkeley, and then transferred to the University of Chicago. There she majored in philosophy and graduated in 1951, a year after her marriage (at seventeen) to the sociologist Philip Rieff. In 1952 a son, David, was born; Sontag and Rieff were divorced in 1958.

At Harvard, Sontag earned two master's degrees—one in English (1954) and one in philosophy (1955). She continued her graduate studies at Harvard; St. Anne's College, Oxford; and the Sorbonne. Although she has taught philosophy at Harvard, City College (CUNY), and Sarah Lawrence, English at the University of Connecticut, religion at Columbia, and writing at Rutgers, Sontag has not held a university appointment since the mid 1960s. Nor has she held a salaried position as an editor since a brief stint at *Commentary* in the late 1950s, though her work has appeared in such distinguished journals as *Partisan Review, Harper's, Atlantic Monthly, Commentary,* the *New Yorker,* and the *New York Review of Books.*

In the 1960s Sontag became known both as an astute, sophisticated commentator on modernism and the avant-garde and as an experimental novelist. In *Against Interpretation and Other Essays* (1967) she introduced numerous European (in particular, French) artists, directors, writers, and thinkers to a wide American audience while presenting herself as a critic fearless before the most challenging, rigorous, heterodox, and seemingly unfathomable currents in contemporary arts and letters. Sontag's two novels of the 1960s—*The Benefactor* (1963) and *Death Kit* (1967)—are experiments in assimilating a modernist aesthetic to narrative. In *Trip to Hanoi* (1969), an account of her sojourn as a guest of the Communist regime, Sontag made public her passionate opposition to the Vietnam War. In her second, most eclectic collection of essays, *Styles of Radical Will* (1969), she reprinted *Trip to Hanoi,* together with speculative essays on silence and pornography and incisive critiques of films by Jean-Luc Godard and Ingmar Bergman.

In the late 1960s and early 1970s, Sontag was invited to direct two films in Sweden: *Duet for Cannibals* (1969; filmed in Swedish) and the English-language *Brother Carl* (1971). After she made these films and a third, *Promised Lands* (1974), Sontag's long-standing fascination with photography crystallized into the six essays collected in *On Photography* (1977), which won the National Book Critics' Circle prize for criticism. She discovered that she had breast cancer in 1976 and subsequently wrote *Illness as Metaphor* (1978), a study of the discourse of disease. A collection of short stories, *I, Etcetera,* appeared in 1978. In 1980 Sontag published *Under the Sign of Saturn,* a group of meditative essays on such writers as Walter Benjamin, Antonin Artaud, Elias Canetti, and Roland Barthes. The appearance of *A Susan Sontag Reader* (1982) and Sontag's election to the presidency of the PEN American Center in 1987 are two indications of her high stature in American letters. Throughout the 1980s she continued to produce stories and essays, and in 1989 published what has become her most controversial book, *AIDS and Its Metaphors*.

From this chronological overview, it should be clear that approaching Susan Sontag (to borrow the title of her magisterial essay on Artaud) requires some circumspection. Neither biography nor bibliography does justice to her diverse achievements; grouping her works generically threatens to trivialize her self-conscious, skeptical approach to genre. Approaching Susan Sontag and her work by way of the four personae in which she confronts her audience—the critic, the experimentalist, the breaker of images, and the spiritualist—is much more revealing of her intellectual complexities, though her disparate personae at times render her career a study in contradictions. As she ranges from communism to camp, aesthetics to AIDS, photography to pornography, and speech to silence, her work develops in ever-widening spirals, doubling back on itself as her experience raises new issues, new complexities, and new expectations.

A generalist working in a variety of genres, Sontag returns repeatedly, even obsessively, to a limited number of political and philosophical issues. She writes about ideas viscerally and sensually; about the body impersonally, detachedly. Having chosen a career largely independent of academia, Sontag insists on the making and remaking of canons; "greatness" remains one of her most trusted, if vague, criteria for judgment. In 1982 the author of the pro-Communist *Trip to Hanoi* sent shock waves through the American intellectual establishment by equating Communism and fascism in a public speech on Poland. For a writer who covets her privacy ("I won't appear on television," she told an interviewer. "My life is entirely private"), Sontag is highly visible at international writers' conferences and symposia.

In "Pilgrimage" (1987), a rare autobiographical essay, Sontag sheds some light on her transformation from an adolescent wayfarer in European culture (devouring French and German novels in translation) into a polymath cultural ambassador. She recounts meeting Thomas Mann in California at age fourteen after a school friend, having found Mann in the local phone book under *M*, managed to wangle an invitation to tea. Mann, who "talked like a book review," remarked that "he was always pleased to meet American young people, who showed the vigor and health and fundamentally optimistic temper of this great country." Mortified, the adolescent Sontag realized that he had mistaken her for a representative American teenager. Appallingly, Mann assumed that she had read Hemingway, "the most representative American author"; enamored only of Europe, she had not. Throughout the essay, the mature Sontag suppresses both the patent comedy of this encounter and an ironic view of her own adolescent presumption: after forty years, her embarrassment is virtually unabated. She locates that embarrassment in "the gap between the person and the work," but it seems, rather, to hover over the abyss between America and Europe, which continues to gape at the memoir's end. The mature writer

> still sees a big space ahead, a far horizon. Is this the real world? I still ask myself that, forty years later. . . . Childhood's sense of plenitude was denied me. In compensation, there remains, always, the horizon of plenitude, to which I am borne forward by the delights of admiration.
> (p. 54)

In "Pilgrimage," Sontag's vision of Europe as a complex horizon of limitation and plenitude—a space in which alien traditions might avail to remake the self—takes on a deeply American, even Emersonian, cast. Sontag has acknowledged a profound debt to "that allegorical, surrealist, romantic speculative tradition of American fiction which is not strictly speaking novel writing—Emerson, Poe, Hawthorne, and some of Melville obviously"; "Poe," she adds, "was my Kafka." But disdaining the anti-intellectualism among American writers as "a macho ideal of individualism and being solitary," Sontag identifies instead with the European idea of a writer's community and, more important, with a literary past that has been "sorted out for us, so we only know, for all practical purposes, the great writers of the past."

It is difficult to reconcile Sontag's grateful reception and perpetuation of a tradition of "great writers" with her defense of the avant-garde, the marginal, the abstruse, and the obscure. Indeed, her "Notes on 'Camp' " (1964) first brought her to national attention as a critic demoting "the good-bad axis of ordinary aesthetic judgment" in favor of an unfamiliar and provocative aesthetic. Praising the democratic esprit of camp, the sense that "one can be serious about the frivolous, frivolous about the serious," Sontag's essay prophesied a career in which a keen, sophisticated, widely read intellectual would train her estimable powers on the most subversive sensibilities ever to confront Western culture.

In some measure, of course, Sontag's career bears out this prophecy. But "Notes on 'Camp,' " for all its Wildean, aphoristic freedom, proves to be a far more cautious essay than it might have once appeared. For Sontag carefully inserts her analysis of camp into a survey of three "great creative sensibilities": the moralistic "pantheon of high culture: truth, beauty, and seriousness"; the moralistic and aesthetic sensibility of modernism, "whose goal is . . . overstraining the medium and introducing more and more violent, and unresolvable, subject-matter"; and, finally, the aesthetic of camp, "sensibility of failed seriousness." Sontag's powers and limitations as a critic reside in her refusal to identify her own critical agenda definitively with any one of these three sensibilities.

CRITIC

Whether the "work" under review is a film by Hans-Jürgen Syberberg or American foreign policy, Sontag's critical writings demonstrate thought in action. Defining, describing, discerning, and deciding, she negotiates deftly between minute details of execution or performance and the larger philosophical issues that her observations raise. To decide where her aesthetic criticism ends and her social criticism begins is fruitless; Sontag's early essay "On Style" (1965) initiates an evolving dialogue between aesthetics and ideology that, twenty-five years later, remains at the heart of her criticism. In "On Style," Sontag observes that "the main tradition of criticism in all the arts . . . treats the work of art as *a statement being made in the form of a work of art.*" This tradition, she argues, is rooted in a false distinction between aesthetics and ethics:

> For it is sensibility that nourishes our capacity for moral choice, and prompts our readiness to act. . . . Art performs this "moral" task because the qualities which are instrinsic to the aesthetic experience (disinterestedness, contemplativeness, attentiveness, the awakening of the feelings) and to the aesthetic object (grace, intelligence, expressiveness, energy, sensuousness) are also fundamental constituents of a moral response to life.
>
> (*Against Interpretation,* p. 25)

Leni Riefenstahl's films *Triumph of the Will* and *Olympia,* according to Sontag, "transcend the categories of propaganda or even reportage. . . . Through Riefenstahl's genius as a film-maker, the 'content' has—let us even assume, against her intentions—come to play a purely formal role."

Ten years later, in "Fascinating Fascism" (1975), responding to Riefenstahl's rehabilitation—her "current de-Nazification and vindication as indomitable priestess of the beautiful"—Sontag warns against regarding Rienfenstahl without a historical perspective: "The force of her work [is] precisely in the continuity of its political and aesthetic ideas." Sontag appeals to the historical record, to "facts" that expose "lies": in making *Triumph of the Will* Riefenstahl was hardly a disinterested documentarian of the 1934 Nazi party convention at Nuremberg (as her publicists claim) but, rather, an artistic and political collaborator in an event expressly designed for her camera. The unholy alliance between art and politics in Nazi Germany, where "politics appropriated the rhetoric of art," produced fully evolved "fascist aesthetics," which Sontag articulates brilliantly:

> [Fascist aesthetics] flow from (and justify) a preoccupation with situations of control, submissive behavior, extravagant effort, and the endurance of pain; they endorse two seemingly opposite states, egomania and servitude. The relations of domination and enslavement take the form of a characteristic pageantry: the massing of groups of people; the turning of people into things; the multiplication or replication of things; and the grouping of people/things around an all-powerful, hypnotic leader-figure or force. The fascist dramaturgy centers on the orgiastic transactions between mighty forces and their puppets, uniformly garbed and shown in ever swelling numbers. Its choreography alternates between ceaseless motion and a congealed, static, "virile" posing. Fascist art glorifies surrender, it exalts mindlessness, it glamorizes death.
>
> (*Under the Sign of Saturn,* p. 91)

As a counterpoint to her attack on Riefenstahl, Sontag offers high praise for Syberberg's *Hitler: A Film from Germany* (1979) in her essay "Syberberg's *Hitler*"; Syberberg's "largest moral ambition" is "to understand the past, and thereby to exorcise it."

Whether or not "Fascinating Fascism" transformed Riefenstahl's reputation, it undoubtedly transformed Sontag's own. The youthful, hip, and intellectually bedazzling culture critic had become more temperate, more versatile in her procedures, and, above all, more inclined toward historicism. During the late 1960s Sontag had lamented the burden of history with Yeatsian pathos: "Meaning drowns in a stream of becoming: the senseless and overdocumented rhythm of advent and supersession. The becoming of man is the history of the exhaustion of his possibilities." But during the early 1980s she told an interviewer, "If there's been a real change in my views over the years, it's that I've had to give the historicist approach a more central role in my reaction to things." In both "Fascinating Fascism" and "Syberberg's *Hitler,*" Sontag reinterprets the dialectic between aesthetics and ideology: instead of subverting the accustomed hierarchy of form and content, she analyzes the mutuality of form and *context.*

To turn to Sontag's explicitly political writings over two decades is to find "the historicist demon" gradually gaining power over her critical sensibility. Once again her cultural and political criticism are of a piece: if the former came to focus on the ideology of aesthetics, the latter persistently focuses on the aesthetics of ideology. In *Trip to Hanoi,* Sontag is made uneasy by an unaccountable "gap between ethics and aesthetics" among the "monochromatic" and "monothematic" North Vietnamese:

> And perhaps it's the general tendency of aesthetic consciousness, when developed, to make judgments more complex and more highly qualified, while it's in the very nature of moral consciousness to be simplifying, even simplistic, and to sound—in translation at least—stiff and old-fashioned.
>
> (*Styles of Radical Will,* pp. 217–218)

Gradually and painfully, Sontag comes to see that her dichotomy between aesthetics and ethics is fallacious and patronizing. As Vietnamese culture becomes increasingly legible to her, abstractions such as patriotism, respect, sincerity, virtue, shame, cleanliness, and dirt gain heft and significance. Although Sontag realizes how easily a conservative "cut-rate" ideology of primitivism can pass for a revolutionary politics, she fails to distinguish clearly between the intellectual roots of Vietnamese culture in Confucianism and Buddhism and the ideology of Ho Chi Minh. For her syncretic—and ultimately aesthetic—account of North Vietnam, Sontag pays a price. Unable to decide whether the problem of history, as she quotes Hegel, is indeed a problem of consciousness, or whether "the promiscuous ideal of revolution" remains necessary, she offers neither clear answers nor clear questions.

More successfully than *Trip to Hanoi,* "The

Third World of Women" (1976) assesses the forms and contexts of a political movement. Sontag uses the analogies of racist and colonialist systems, in which political discriminations masquerade as natural distinctions, to decry the conventions of sexual difference: "The 'femininity' of women and the 'masculinity' of men are morally defective and historically obsolete conceptions." For Sontag, any gender identity traceable to sexual identity is specious and oppressive. True, she fails to anticipate a climate in which "difference" has become a feminist watchword, a climate in which mainstream feminists celebrate the distinctive cultural traditions of women. But the premise of her essay—that "liberation means *power*—or it hardly means anything at all"—remains the rallying cry of feminists in the vanguard of political activism.

Sontag's program for feminism is the abolition of "the mystique of 'nature' " through a radical transformation of society and consciousness. To Sontag, such a transformation can be motivated only by a strong, socialistic women's movement; historically, she observes, feminism has never been effectively absorbed by a Marxist agenda or regime. Nor does she suffer gladly the concept of a humanistic transformation that will liberate men as well as women; to Sontag, the liberation of women is a zero-sum game to be played out at the expense of male privilege. Years before the mass media would complacently measure the strides of liberal feminism in the workplace, Sontag prophetically proclaims the limitations of legalistic and economic reformism:

> I would predict that most of the reformist demands will be granted in most countries by the end of the century. My point is that then the struggle will have only begun. The granting of these demands can leave intact all the oppressive and patronizing attitudes that make women into second-class citizens.
>
> (p. 198)

The radical transformation Sontag envisions includes overturning a sexist division of labor (women as consumers, men as producers), instituting subsidized child care, legalizing abortion, advocating a "genuine bisexuality," rethinking the nuclear family by "destroy[ing] the opposition . . . between 'home' and 'the world,' " valuing women's solidarity, and initiating a program of subversive acts (among them whistling at men and "collecting pledges to renounce alimony and giggling"). Despite her identification in this essay with feminism, Sontag has made it abundantly clear elsewhere that feminist issues are not always a priority for her. When Adrienne Rich asked why she failed to explore the feminist implications of fascist aesthetics, Sontag replied acidly:

> Suppose, indeed, that "Nazi Germany was patriarchy in its purest most elemental form." Where do we rate the Kaiser's Germany? Caesarist Rome? Confucian China? Fascist Italy? Victorian England? Ms. Gandhi's India? Macho Latin America? Arab sheikery from Mohammed to Qaddhafi and Faisal? Most of history, alas, is "patriarchal history." So distinctions will have to be made, and it is not possible to keep the feminist thread running through the explanations all the time. . . . If the point is to have meaning some of the time, it can't be made all the time.
> ("Feminism and Fascism: An Exchange," p. 31)

EXPERIMENTALIST

In "On Style," Sontag offers an exquisite appreciation of "the twin aspects" of modernist art "as object and as function, as artifice and as living form of consciousness, as the overcoming or supplementing of reality and as the making explicit of forms of encountering reality, as autonomous individual creation and as dependent historical phenomenon." But when she observes that "art is the objectifying of the will in a thing or performance," she moves toward the more radical aesthetics of modernist experimentalism articulated in "The Pornographic Imagination" (1967). Passing beyond a nostalgia for the objet d'art, she writes:

> One of the tasks art has assumed is making forays into and taking up positions on the frontiers

> of consciousness (often very dangerous to the artist as a person) and reporting back what's there. . . . [The artist's] job is inventing trophies of his experiences—objects and gestures that fascinate and enthrall, not merely (as prescribed by older notions of the artist) edify or entertain. His principal means of fascinating is to advance one step further in the dialectic of outrage. He seeks to make his work repulsive, obscure, inaccessible; in short, to give what is, or seems to be, *not* wanted. But however fierce may be the outrages the artist perpetrates upon his audience, his credentials and spiritual authority ultimately depend on the audience's sense . . . of the outrages he commits upon himself. The exemplary modern artist is a broker in madness.
>
> (*Styles of Radical Will,* p. 45)

Sontag defends the aesthetics of pornography for liberating art from both realism and humanism. In *The Story of O,* for example, she locates a powerful antinomy between humanism and sexual fulfillment. Veering away from the novel's constructions of gender, Sontag concludes, startlingly, that the heroine's dehumanization "is not to be understood as a by-product of her enslavement to René, Sir Stephen, and the other men at Roissy, but as the point of her situation, something she seeks and eventually attains." It is Georges Bataille, according to Sontag, who "understood more clearly than any other writer I know of that what pornography is really about, ultimately, isn't sex but death." Next to Bataille, whose "blasphemies are autonomous," the negativity of Sade appears but a counteridealism, a species of bad faith. Sontag's aesthetics of pornography ends with a strained attempt to resituate pornography—and, implicitly, modernist aesthetics—within the sociopolitical matrix: "the demonic vocabularies" of pornography are demanded by "the traumatic failure of modern capitalist society . . . to satisfy the appetite for exalted self-transcending modes of concentration and seriousness."

Sontag's experimental novels of the 1960s are informed by an aesthetic far closer to that of pornography (as Sontag defines it) than to the novelistic tradition of psychological realism. Her heroes, Hippolyte in *The Benefactor* and Dalton (Diddy) Harron in *Death Kit,* are simultaneously brokers in madness and broken by madness. While neither is an artist in any traditional sense, each composes a life that objectifies the will, violently and perversely. *The Benefactor,* a fictional autobiography, is narrated by the sixty-one-year-old Hippolyte from a place of retirement. While it has deep affinities to Rousseau's *Confessions,* its form is that of the picaresque anti-quest, in this case, an exhaustion of the possibility of certitude. The terrain traversed by Hippolyte, of course, is that of the mind; rejecting the metaphor of a journey, he repeatedly crisscrosses the Rubicon of his dreams. Vivid, erotic, and painful, his dreams (narrated in more detail than the events of his waking life) beg for interpretation. But the more concretely Hippolyte experiences them, the more they defy his interpretative efforts.

In *The Benefactor* Sontag boldly inverts the normative, psychotherapeutic hierarchy of consciousness and unconsciousness: here, dreams interpret waking life by liberating the will into action. Because the dreamed acts have but dreamed consequences, dreams can epitomize freedom. The outrageous, violent acts Hippolyte commits—selling his married lover into slavery during a trip to North Africa, igniting her house while she (supposedly) sleeps—bespeak his resolve to model his waking life on the wisdom of his dreamed life. While Hippolyte occasionally teases an ad hoc existentialism out of his freedom, Sontag makes it clear that he seeks—and achieves—a freedom from himself. Once Hippolyte discovers that "to execute an intention amounts to abolishing a desire," his career as a dreamer gradually consumes the possible grounds for a self.

In the course of this process the reader is placed on increasingly shaky ground. As dreaming becomes the focus of Hippolyte's existence, it becomes impossible to say which acts are dreamed and which are "real." Toward the end Hippolyte proposes several alternative titles for his book and presents a brief narrative of his life (which he may—or may not—have written while confined in a madhouse) pared down to the events of his dreams. In sum, Hippolyte "reads" his own book as a parody of Cartesian rationalism:

> You will remember that at the beginning of this narrative I formulated my researches into myself as a quest for certitude. A great philosopher, the first to make this the goal of his inquiry, found that all he could be entirely certain of was that he existed. He was certain he existed because he thought; denial of this was itself an act of thought. My quest led to the opposite conclusion. Only because I existed—in other words, thought—did the problem of certitude arise. To reach certitude is to learn that one does not exist.
> (p. 250)

"Cleansed and purged of my dreams," Hippolyte spends his retirement as an unpaid nurse in a paupers' hospital—and writing. Ironically, his docile, "posthumous" existence brings forth his most truly objectified act—the writing of his book, the "trophy" of his dangerous existence.

Compared with *The Benefactor, Death Kit* is drab, flat, and crude. Written in the third person, Sontag's second novel lacks the subtlety and urbanity provided by the voice of Hippolyte. For the autobiographer and dreamer, Sontag substitutes an advertising executive; for continental cafés, parks, and villas, she substitutes a hotel, hospital, and factory in a city in upstate New York. Sontag has commented that her first novel uses irony to "recoil from pain." In *Death Kit* she recoils from irony: pain and suffering, rather than existential anxiety, provide the rationale for styling and constructing one's own death. Whereas *The Benefactor* exploits the shimmering, dreamlike resources of first-person narrative to dramatize incertitude, the ascetic *Death Kit* makes concrete a metaphysics of disintegration.

Sontag's strategy is to present the theme of disintegration as a series of visual and visionary failures. Diddy, an employee of a microscope company, becomes preternaturally sensitive to the desiccated texture of his life. At the start of the novel he attempts suicide:

> The customary opaque medium has begun leaking away. The soft interconnected tissue-like days are unstrung. The watery plenum is dehydrated, and what protrudes are jagged, inhuman units. The medium steadily evaporates; the teeming interlocked plenitude is drained of its sustenance. Dies. All that's left is arbitrary and incomprehensible.
> (p. 4)

After sleeping pills have been pumped from his stomach, Diddy embarks on his "posthumous" existence by taking a train bound for a conference in upstate New York. When the train becomes lodged in a tunnel, he ventures into the darkness, where he apparently murders a railroad workman. Shattered and unbelieving, he becomes utterly attached to Hester, a young blind woman in his compartment, whom he believes can confirm his capacity for violence. Diddy is fascinated by Hester's blindness, interpreting it as imprisonment, liberation, instability, and fixedness; Hester, always engimatic, refuses to confirm or deny these beliefs. But the palpable irony of Diddy's dim, self-serving interpretations is flattened by the narrator's predilection for symbolic extrapolations: Diddy sees too closely; Hester, without vision, perceives more. Hester is Diddy's good eye; the murdered workman, Incardona, his bad eye. Diddy even dreams that Hester receives an eye transplant from Incardona. Ultimately, the very strategy that was to make the novel's philosophical problem concrete abstracts it into an overly schematic symbolic structure.

Unlike *The Benefactor,* in which a social reality gradually emerges (Jews are rounded up for death camps, the capital is liberated, and Hippolyte devotes himself to service), *Death Kit* witnesses the demise of a world in which responsible acts are possible. Neither love, marriage, professionalism, nor even pleasure affords Diddy a respite from his own blasted vision. Diddy's chosen destination, finally, is the scene of his crime. With mythic fatalism, Sontag narrates his descent to a museumlike underworld containing galleries of coffins, inscriptions, corpses, and refuse—a variegated, rich, austerely beautiful world in which history becomes meaningful but in which all meanings are supplied by death. While *Death Kit* is a deeply uneven performance, Sontag's memorable phantasmagoria of death remains among her boldest and most accomplished achievements.

Even as Sontag's fictions dramatize the career of the will and the constructed nature of experience, she is unfairly faulted for writing fiction that is inorganic and overly cerebral; her novels and stories prove that intellectualism and originality are indeed compatible. In Sontag's short fictions, eight of which are collected in *I, Etcetera,* the Brechtian revelation of fictive contraptions occurs more swiftly and elegantly than in the novels; perhaps for this reason, her stories have won popular acclaim for their incisive depictions of private *crises de conscience.* In stories such as "Debriefing," "Old Complaints Revisited," "Unguided Tour," and, more recently, "The Way We Live Now," women and men grapple with bereavement, political disillusionment, the failure of love, and AIDS. But if a penchant for psychological realism occasionally tempers Sontag's modernist austerity, it does not compromise her self-consciousness about subjectivity and narrative. In such haunting stories as "American Spirits," reminiscent of the darkest Nathanael West, and "The Dummy," a contemporary *Frankenstein* in a dozen pages, Sontag renders vertiginous cross sections, dissections, and reduplications of the narrative "I." For Sontag, the fictive self—"I, etcetera"—remains a precious, if shabby, conceit.

BREAKER OF IMAGES

In "Against Interpretation" (1964) Sontag takes issue with the mimetic theory of art. To view art as a figuration or image of reality, she argues, is to suppress the sensuous experience generated by art, to privilege content, and to license anxious, relentless acts of interpretation, "the revenge of the intellect upon art." Sontag's early polemic sounds the watchcry of her first volume of essays: "In place of a hermeneutics we need an erotics of art." But within ten years, Sontag would move beyond the context of aesthetics to consider the complex role of images in culture and politics. In three book-length essays—*On Photography, Illness as Metaphor,* and *AIDS and Its Metaphors*—she ponders the history of images, their career in our culture, and the way we live among them.

Sontag's opening account of the ubiquity of photographs in *On Photography* renders her sensitivity to the meanings, uses, and ambiguities of the medium all the more remarkable. The six essays in the volume refract, from a variety of angles, the issue of how photography shapes our perception of history, of reality, and of meaning itself. In the history of photography Sontag discerns two interpenetrating aesthetics. On the one hand, "surrealism lies at the heart of the photographic enterprise," particularly in the camera's ability to make concrete "a reality in the second degree," arbitrary, accidental, and disorderly. On the other hand, American photography from its inception absorbed the democratic aesthetics of Walt Whitman, "a transvaluation of beauty and ugliness, importance and triviality." In the resulting amalgamation of these aesthetics, the moral program of American photography is neutralized; instead of embracing all sectors of society or celebrating the "ineffability of American life," photography levels differences, equating history with the photographic "scatter of evidence." Seen through photographs, faces lose their particularity, bespeaking "the vulnerability of lives heading toward their own destruction."

> While traditional arts of historical consciousness attempt to put the past in order, distinguishing the innovative from the retrograde, the central from the marginal, the relevant from the irrelevant or merely interesting, the photographer's

> approach . . . is unsystematic, indeed, anti-systematic. The photographer's ardor for a subject has no essential relation to its content or value. (p. 77)

Tacitly assuming that it is the historian's responsibility to construct and propound hierarchies of value, Sontag sees photography (despite its archival significance) as a calamity for historical consciousness.

While photography desensitizes us to the meanings of the past, it also makes our sense of reality increasingly complex. Far more than written language, photographs lower "the threshold of what is terrible," rendering us both "there" and "not there": we witness atrocities but are insulated from them. Photographs empty out and disable the present, "antiquing" the world before our eyes. Beyond depersonalization and escapism, Sontag links disaffection and alienation to photography: "In the past, a discontent with reality expressed itself as a longing for *another* world. In modern society, a discontent with reality expresses itself forcefully and most hauntingly by the longing to reproduce *this* one." But the most profound effect of photography is the pervasive confounding of image and reality—*not* by a primitive "sacralizing" of images but by the public's ability (indeed, inclination) to perceive reality as an image. Failing to credit that a saving skepticism about the nature of political "reality" might result, Sontag sketches an alarming scenario in which sinister, capitalist regimes exploit photography to enhance consumption and ensure social control and surveillance.

To Sontag, photography resembles language insofar as it is a medium rather than an art form. Photographs, she insists warily, have no absolute meaning, but take their meaning from context—that is, in relation to the meanings of their accompanying captions, books, frames, and museum exhibitions or inscriptions. Sontag's apprehensions about the instability and exploitation of photographic meanings—about the variety of uses to which the "language" of photographs can be put—reasonate deeply with the concerns of her polemical essay *Illness as Metaphor*. In a preface, Sontag encapsulates her polemic as follows: "My point is that illness is *not* a metaphor, and that the most truthful way of regarding illness—and the healthiest way of being ill—is one most purified of, most resistant to, metaphoric thinking." The strength of *Illness as Metaphor* lies not in Sontag's fantasy of thinking "purified" of metaphor (a fantasy as metaphorical as it is unpersuasive), but in her incisive analysis of the ways in which the discourses of nature and culture converge.

Illness as Metaphor comprises both a cultural history of two diseases—tuberculosis in the nineteenth century and cancer in the twentieth—and a diatribe against the institutionalization of disease metaphors. Sontag begins by contrasting the cultural mythologies of TB and cancer: TB is a disease of transparency and fluidity, cancer of opacity; TB is a disease of time, cancer of space; TB is a disease of poverty, cancer of the bourgoisie; TB affects the passionate personality, cancer the repressed personality; and so on. When historicized, however, the two mythologies appear to be genetically related: in this century "the cluster of metaphors and attitudes formerly attached to TB"—those associated with enlightened self-transcendence and those associated with anguished self-destruction—have been separated and "parceled out" to insanity and cancer, respectively. What the cultural mythologies of TB and cancer reveal, then, is a historical shift from a fascination with the potential of the self to an obsession with the self's limitations and vulnerability.

The less the causality of a disease is understood, Sontag theorizes, the more moralistic will be its attendant mythology. With vehemence, she demystifies the commonplace of a cancer-prone personality type; if anything, such a notion is more, not less, moralistic than the punitive Christian yoking of sin and illness. Offering historical evidence, Sontag demonstrates that ideas of personality-related diseases are contingent and reflective of changing social anxieties. Regrettably, she does not acknowledge that an efficacious anti-cancer activism depends on sober determinations of causality; calling cancer simply "multi-determined," she casts suspicion on all attempts to fix on a cause for cancer. The conversion of cancer into a metaphor, Sontag argues, has been undertaken by a variety of moralistic, paranoid interests: those who fear unbridled economic growth, those who fear alien military aggression, those who fear revolutionary instability, and those who fear "Nature taking revenge on a wicked technocratic world." To Sontag, the metaphor of cancer answers a need for moral severity at a time "when we have a sense of evil but no longer the religious or philosophical language to talk intelligently about evil." Such rhetorical "uses" of cancer, beyond dangerously oversimplifying political realities, oppress cancer patients forced to listen to "their disease's name constantly being dropped as the epitome of evil."

That Sontag identifies herself in *Illness as Metaphor* as a former user of cancer metaphors but not as a former cancer patient is perhaps unsurprising; she wrote the book soon after her own ordeal, in "anxiety about how much time I had left to do any living or writing in." A decade later, commenting on *Illness as Metaphor*, she writes:

> I didn't think it would be useful—and I wanted to be useful—to tell yet one more story in the first person of how someone learned that she or he had cancer, wept, struggled, was comforted, suffered, took courage . . . though mine was also that story. A narrative, it seemed to me, would be less useful than an idea.
>
> (*AIDS and Its Metaphors*, p. 13)

Sontag's similar approach in *AIDS and Its Metaphors*—to consider AIDS as an idea, a cultural myth, a construction—has drawn a barrage of criticism so negative as to surprise Sontag herself (no novice to intellectual controversy). Ironically, the fact that she does *not* have AIDS (and is not in an obvious high-risk group) has been adduced to undermine both her polemic and her historical analysis. Some reviewers charge that she confuses the roles of polemicist and historian; others, that so many metaphors associated with AIDS—particularly those implying its fatality—appear to be apposite. In the journal *October*, D. A. Miller savages the "urbane" Sontag for effacing the anguish, activism, and cultural response of the gay community. On the one hand, Miller's charge that Sontag's book is "opportunistic"—while ungenerous—is understandable. For Sontag, writing on AIDS provides a dubious occasion for returning to concerns broached in her earlier work: the fate of modernism, the capitalist proliferation of oppressive images and metaphors, and the exploitation of disease metaphors by political paranoids. On the other hand, the conventional wisdom that those with AIDS are only served by activism and that writing such a tract is at best tactless, at worst self-serving, bespeaks precisely the moralism that Sontag attributes to the alarmist metaphorization of AIDS.

As she had done for cancer, Sontag hypothesizes a metaphorical genealogy of AIDS: as a microprocess, it evokes the mythology of cancerous "invasion"; as a sexually transmitted disease, it evokes the syphilitic mythology of corruption and pollution. Moreover, to identify AIDS as a plague is to identify it with foreignness, dehumanization, and contamination. Since the term "virus" has become widely metaphorized, AIDS is also associated with insidious viral latency and mutation.

But AIDS differs from diseases such as cancer, TB, syphilis, and cholera. As Sontag points out, AIDS is not a disease but a syndrome conceived by the medical establishment under the Reagan administration. According to her analysis, the three stages of AIDS—HIV infection, AIDS-related complex (ARC), and "full-blown" AIDS—suggest an inevitable, organic process that culminates in death. Sontag detects in this construct "the antiscientific logic of defilement," a dangerous return to "a premodern experience of illness." Such a conception of AIDS, she avers, is inhuman and oppressive to AIDS patients; moreover, it threatens to transform our experience of sexuality from one of "pure presentness (and a creation of the future)" into "a chain of transmissions of the past."

Arguing for a discontinuous reading of these stages (and anticipating the eventual redefinition of AIDS) Sontag reasons that "it is simply too early to conclude . . . that infection will always produce something to die from, or even that everybody who has what is defined as AIDS will die from it." Despite the fact that, as Paul Robinson observes in the *New York Times Book Review,* "there has not been a single known case of recovery," Sontag finds the vigorous international response to AIDS largely irrational: "AIDS occupies such a large part in our awareness because . . . it seems the very model of all the catastrophes privileged populations feel await them." Accordingly, she deems the U.S. government's calls for "mobilization" a capitalist hypocrisy, a bad-faith throwback to an ideal of community that is irreconcilable with capitalist self-interest.

AIDS and Its Metaphors concludes by analyzing the apocalyptic rhetoric surrounding the disease. Sontag uses the analogy of images to warn of a dangerous "bifurcation of reality":

> There is the event and its image. And there is the event and its projection. But as real events often seem to have no more reality for people than images, and to need the confirmation of their images, so our reaction to events in the present seeks confirmation in a mental outline, with appropriate computations, of the event in its projected, ultimate form.
>
> (*Illness as Metaphor and AIDS and its Metaphors,* p. 177)

Whereas photography disables our sense of the present by weakening our consciousness of the past, the metaphorization of AIDS disables our sense of the present by lessening our consciousness of the future. But if, as Sontag insists, "an unparalleled violence . . . is being done to our sense of reality, to our humanity," by the alarmism surrounding AIDS, it does not necessarily follow that "it is highly desirable for a specific dreaded illness to come to seem ordinary." To lump together so-called AIDS frenzy, apocalyptic paranoia, changes in sexual behavior and attitudes, and mobilization and activism as so much irresponsible mythmaking is to fail to make the distinctions by which reasoned action becomes possible. To conclude *AIDS and Its Metaphors* by attacking an apocalyptic, militaristic rhetoric rather than by insisting on the concrete realities of AIDS is, perhaps, to find metaphors utimately more interesting than AIDS.

SPIRITUALIST

"Every era," Sontag writes in "The Aesthetics of Silence" (1967), "has to reinvent the project of 'spirituality' for itself. . . . In the modern era, one of the most active metaphors for the spiritual project is 'art.' " Under the aegis of modernism, "art" becomes an arena of struggle between consciousness and the " 'material' character of art itself." Sontag's allusion here to a Christian rhetoric of spirit and flesh is one of many such displacements of religion in her work: describing art as prophecy, redemption, curse, miracle, paradox, ascesis, ecstasy, a *via negativa* (negative way), and priestly rite and defilement, her language makes vivid "the spiritual project" of modern art. "The Aesthetics of Silence" (in *Styles of Radical Will*) considers modernism as "an exercise in asceticism" whose goal is to redeem the materiality of art by attaining "the unfettered, unselective, total consciousness of 'God.' "

Sontag's own antagonism toward images and metaphors emerges from her realization that "the artist's activity is cursed with mediacy." For Sontag, literal silence is an unrealized—and unrealizable—modernist ideal; the subject of her essay is the modernist *rhetoric* of slience, a critique of language installed in unintelligible, uncommunicative, invisible, inaudible, or unassimilable art. In Ingmar Bergman's *Persona,* for example, the silent Elizabeth induces "spiritual vertigo" in her talkative nurse, Alma; in the end, it is not Alma's humane, healing powers that prevail but "the violence of the spirit." In both of her Swedish-made films—*Duet for Cannibals,* which revolves around the mute Francesca, and *Brother Carl,* which parallels the "voluntary mutism" of the dancer Carl with the involuntary silence of an autistic child—Sontag derives a bracing "dramaturgy of silence" from Bergman's seminal work.

For the writer, however, redeeming the curse of mediacy entails the redemption of language, which, having "fallen" into history, has dragged consciousness along with it. Sontag imagines the transcendence of "this ignominious enslavement to history" in a kind of discourse in which consciousness strives to attain priority over language—or to consume it altogether: "The serious art of our time has moved increasingly toward the most excruciating inflections of consciousness." During the fifteen years between *Against Interpretation* and *Under the Sign of Saturn,* Sontag shifted her focus from written works to the arduous work of writing. With this shift, her essays have become more searching, more passionate, more personal, and more keenly aware of Sontag's own writerly premises: "There's a part of me that identifies with most of the people I write about; it's almost as if I'd invented them, as if they were fantasy projections of part of myself."

In brief, early essays on Cesare Pavese and Simone Weil, Sontag insists on the "exemplary" nature of the artist's suffering, arguing that writers of "acute personal and intellectual extremity" exercise and extend the moral imagination of our culture. In the essays of the Romanian-born philosopher E. M. Cioran, Sontag detects "a passion play of thought"; Cioran's work is "best read as a manual of . . . an atheist spirituality." Ultimately, Cioran's "self-cannibalizing" thought—a dialectic between contempt for intellect and exaltation of mind—delivers him to a mystic's impasse "at the expense of body, feelings, and the capacity for action."

The essays in *Under the Sign of Saturn,* which Sontag has somewhat disingenuously described as "seven portraits in consciousness," are more truly described as modernist hagiographies, the intellectual lives of martyrs to a variety of modernist quests. In the title essay, Sontag meditates on Walter Benjamin's melancholic temperament, its intellectual consequences, and its personal costs. Benjamin, despite his professional, marital, and social difficulties—despite his temperamental morbidity—becomes for Sontag a "hero of will," a "righteous" if "inhuman" martyr to the life of the mind. In the writings of Bulgarian-born Elias Canetti, Sontag finds heroic "refutations of power and death" through "magical thinking and moral clamorousness." Above all, Sontag identifies Canetti's fierce desire to learn everything—a desire to place the world's library inside the mind—as a spiritual striving for immortality.

In her extended essays on two twentieth-century thinkers—"Approaching Artaud" and "Writing Itself: On Roland Barthes" (collected in *A Susan Sontag Reader*)—Sontag provides a diptych of modernist extremes, two antithetical versions of modernism as a spiritual project. Sontag's essay on Artaud centers on his "passion"—not "passion play"—of thought, the agonizing ordeals of consciousness that he made the subject, form, and genre of his writing. What fascinates Sontag is not Artaud's agony but his rhetoric of mental pain, a psychological materialism that merges mind and body. For Sontag, Artaud's sensibility transcends the modernist dualism of consciousness and art by obviating the art object; according to Sontag, Artaud's obsession—his spiritual quest—was to "match 'being' with hyperlucidity, flesh with words." In his writings on theater, Artaud imagines a performance in which thought might fully materialize; "the theater of cruelty" is conceived as a dreamlike, amoral space in which the will fully achieves the freedom to act.

For Sontag, both Artaud's "failure" in his quest and his "madness" inhere in his modern-day Gnosticism, a heterodox sensibility that conjoins libertinism and asceticism; his fantasy of a redeemed body and a redeemed language make up a single dream of liberation. A Gnostic "shaman," Artaud does not "fail"; rather, he achieves "a wisdom that cancels itself out in unintelligibility, loquacity and silence." His madness becomes "a profoundly spiritual exile."

If Sontag's Artaud is an agonist of the mind, her Barthes is the mind's voluptuary. Like Artaud, Barthes collapses mind and matter in the "sensual melodrama of ideas"; reading Barthes, one experiences a "kinetics of consciousness." But whereas Artaud regards both language and matter as tragic, Barthes's sensibility is "post-tragic," erotic, and aesthetic. Artaud's "theatre of cruelty" finds a comic parallel in Barthes's "writing itself," a notion of writing liberated from power, persuasion, and authorial procreation. While the work of both Artaud and Barthes presupposes a politics of radical individualism, Sontag credits Barthes with more political self-consciousness about his own subversions. Whereas the Gnostic Artaud conceives of theater as a higher reality, the aesthetic Barthes regards reality as a mode of theater, eschewing dualism of surface and depth.

Sontag's portrait of Barthes, idiosyncratic and intimate, reveals the notorious systematizer as a man skeptical of systems; the theorist of semiotics as a man in love with language; the tireless reader of the world's signs as "a devout, ingenious student of himself." For Sontag, Barthes's late work suggests his restlessness with the gestures and poses of aestheticism. While Barthes articulated his own obsession with signs as an aesthetics of absence, Sontag prefers to understand it as a quest to discover meaning everywhere, a revolt against finality, limitation, personal loss, and even one's own mortality. "An ideally complex form of consciousness," Barthes's theory of writing reveals "an ecstatic experience of understanding" with which Sontag is in full sympathy.

For nearly three decades Susan Sontag has impressed, provoked, and educated readers with her intellectual reach. The fact that such extreme sensibilities as Artaud's pain and Barthes's pleasure fall within her grasp reveals the acutely compassionate life of her mind. Her mature studies of consciousness—a form she has made her own—bring her own "spiritual strivings" to bear on urgent issues in philosophy, art, and politics. In Sontag's sensitivity to the extreme destinies of mental life, we discover the heightened awareness with which she, at mid-career, explores her own intellectual destiny.

Selected Bibliography

PRIMARY WORKS

NONFICTION

Against Interpretation and Other Essays. New York: Farrar, Straus & Giroux, 1967.

"Introduction." In E. M. Cioran, *The Temptation to Exist.* Translated by Richard Howard. Chicago: Quadrangle, 1968.

Styles of Radical Will. New York: Farrar, Straus & Giroux, 1969.

Trip to Hanoi. New York: Farrar, Straus & Giroux, 1969.

"Feminism and Fascism: An Exchange." *New York Review of Books* 22:31–32 (20 March 1975). With Adrienne Rich.

"The Third World of Women." *Partisan Review* 40:180–206 (1976).

On Photography. New York: Farrar, Straus & Giroux, 1977.

Illness as Metaphor. New York: Farrar, Straus & Giroux, 1978.

Under the Sign of Saturn. New York: Farrar, Straus & Giroux, 1980.

"On Literary Tradition: A Symposium." *Shenandoah* 33:3–46 (1982). With Nadine Gordimer, David Kalstone, James Merrill, William Matthews, Myra Sklarew, Susan Sontag, D. M. Thomas, and Edmund White.

A Susan Sontag Reader. Introduction by Elizabeth Hardwick. New York: Farrar, Straus & Giroux, 1982.

"Communism and the Left." *Nation* 234:229–231 (27 February 1982). Sontag's Town Hall speech on Poland.

"Pilgrimage." *New Yorker* 63:38–54 (21 December 1987).

AIDS and Its Metaphors. New York: Farrar, Straus & Giroux, 1989.

Illness as Metaphor and AIDS and Its Metaphors. New York: Doubleday, 1990.

FICTION

The Benefactor: A Novel. New York: Farrar, Straus & Giroux, 1963.

Death Kit. New York: Farrar, Straus & Giroux, 1967.

I, Etcetera. New York: Farrar, Straus & Giroux, 1978.

"The Way We Live Now." *New Yorker,* 62:42–51 (24 November 1986).

SCREENPLAYS

Duet for Cannibals: A Screenplay (Sandrew Film & Teater AB, Sweden, 1969). New York: Farrar, Straus & Giroux, 1970.

Brother Carl: A Filmscript (Sandrew Film & Teater AB and Svenska Filminstitutet, Sweden, 1971). New York: Farrar, Straus & Giroux, 1974.

EDITED ANTHOLOGIES

Antonin Artaud: Selected Writings. Translated by Helen Weaver. Edited and with an introduction by Susan Sontag. New York: Farrar, Straus & Giroux, 1976.

A Barthes Reader. Edited and with an introduction by Susan Sontag. New York: Hill & Wang, 1982.

SECONDARY WORKS

BIOGRAPHICAL AND CRITICAL STUDIES

Brooks, Peter. "Death as/of Metaphor." *Partisan Review* 46:438–444 (1979).

Copeland, Roger. "The Habits of Consciousness." *Commonweal* 108:83–87 (13 February 1981).

Gilman, Richard. *The Confusion of Realms.* New York: Random House, 1970.

Grenier, Richard. "The Conversion of Susan Sontag." *New Republic* 186:15–19 (14 April 1982).

Kazin, Alfred. *Bright Book of Life: American Novelists and Storytellers from Hemingway to Mailer.* Boston: Little, Brown, 1973.

Miller, D. A. "Sontag's Urbanity." *October* 49:91–101 (Summer 1989).

Nelson, Cary. "Soliciting Self-Knowledge: The Rhetoric of Susan Sontag's Criticism." *Critical Inquiry* 6:707–726 (Summer 1980).

Robinson, Paul. "Against Fatalism." *New York Times Book Review,* 22 January 1989, p. 11.

Ruas, Charles. "Susan Sontag: Past, Present, and Future." *New York Times Book Review,* 24 October 1982, p. 11.

Smith, Sharon. *Women Who Make Movies.* New York: Hopkinson & Blake, 1975.

Solotaroff, Theodore. *The Red Hot Vacuum.* New York: Atheneum, 1970.

"Susan Sontag." In *Contemporary Authors: New Revision Series* 25:419–424 (1989).

"Susan Sontag." In *Contemporary Literary Criticism* 1:322 (1973), 2:413–414 (1974), 10:484–487 (1979), 13:514–519 (1980), and 31:405–419 (1985).

"Susan Sontag." In *Dictionary of Literary Biography* 2:447–451 (1978) and 67:268–275 (1988).

Taylor, Benjamin. "A Centered Voice: Susan Sontag's Short Fiction." *Georgia Review* 34:907–916 (Winter 1980).

Vidal, Gore. *Reflections upon a Sinking Ship.* Boston: Little, Brown, 1969.

ESTHER H. SCHOR

GERTRUDE STEIN

1874–1946

ON READING GERTRUDE STEIN

> So as I say poetry is
> essentially the discovery, the
> love, the passion for the name
> of anything.

I WOULD LIKE TO enter into the world of Gertrude Stein's writing through this statement about poetry from her 1935 essay "Poetry and Grammar," for the presence of "love" and "passion" in her definition may surprise anyone who thinks of Stein's writing as wholly abstract. Her writing can indeed be abstract and hermetic, just as it can at other points be astonishingly lucid and simple; yet throughout all her literary experiments (and all of her writing took the form of experiments, of "discovery"), her love of words, in their infinite variety, urges itself on us. To write about her life without writing about her relationship to language would be impossible, for her life was as much a life with words as it was a life made valuable through love, friendships, cherished pets and objects, and the nuances of landscape.

With this definition of poetry, Stein signifies both her presence within a company of modernist and Romantic writers, and her difference. Like Ralph Waldo Emerson, she desires to make "names" come alive again through surprising us out of our familiarity with them; in this sense, she accepts his call for a new poet, even as she redefines his vision of this poet as representative man (a vision claimed in various forms by many male modernists, including Walt Whitman and Wallace Stevens preeminently). Stein offers a deeply feminist contribution to our thought about language and writing, and about the very language in which we think about writing in relation to the world. She attempts to renegotiate the relation between words and the (loved) world, to create forms of writing that undermine the hierarchies of "subject" over "object" to a far more radical extent than the writing of any of her fellow modernists, and that allow the "object"—especially when this object is the landscape of the female body and the female-to-female relationship—to emerge within the writing in a felt but indirect way.

The question of Stein's feminism is an intricate one, in part because she does not openly assert a feminist position. In her lectures, essays, and autobiographies, she makes no direct or sustained claim for her writing as addressing or redressing women's position (or repression) within culture. Although in *The Geographical History of America* (1936) Stein abruptly states that "in this epoch the important literary thinking is done by a woman," she does not analyze the significance of this claim; as she claims further, "I think nothing about men and women because that has nothing to do with anything." On the surface Stein's politics seem blithely unfeminist, as her famous remark in *The Autobiography of Alice B. Toklas* (1933) appears to confirm: "Not, as Gertrude Stein explained to Marion Walker, that she at all minds the cause of women or any other cause but it does not happen to be her business."

Stein's writings contradict this claim. Her "cause"—if this word can be used of so spontaneous and unprogrammatic a writer—lies in the realm of language and literary form, which come to us marked with various hierarchies and exclusions, and whose markings can be re-marked and in some sense transformed. A growing consensus has arisen among many critics of Stein—including Carolyn Burke, Marianne DeKoven, Pamela Hadas, Lisa Ruddick, Cynthia Secor, Catharine Stimpson, and Linda Watts—that her writing, particularly after about 1910, reveals a feminist concern with gender hierarchy, a system of domination allied with the dominance of certain narrative and linguistic forms over others.

Stein's understanding of language as the major site for transformation bears a resemblance in many ways to recent French feminist thought. The various French feminist projects converge on the idea that language (construed in its largest sense, as the varied system of discourses through which the world becomes constructed) is the primary cultural agency through which the masculine dominates and represses the feminine. To effect a change at all, as many French feminist theorists claim, it is necessary to undermne language from within, or to mark the ways in which language reveals its own undermining. Stein shares with many of these more recent writers—particularly Hélène Cixous and Luce Irigaray—numerous literary strategies: the disruption of conventional grammar, plot, genre, and modes of representation, together with the exploration of plural voices and of a writing attached to the body, particularly the lesbian body. Her erotic writings especially, for example the love poems, plays, and other works from 1910 to 1920, offer a rich area of comparison. In such compositions, she creates a poetics inscribed with a specifically lesbian sexuality; her undoing of conventional form allies itself with her attempt to bring female-to-female relationships into writing.

Stein differs from these theorists, however, in her larger sense of language's possibilities. In much French feminist thought, the potential for genuine transformation remains largely in the form of a wish, or a call for an as yet unimagined new writing. Language, understood as a wholly phallogocentric and monolithic domain, has no place for "woman," who becomes in her essential difference and otherness the figure for all that remains repressed and silenced. The danger here, as many critics have noted, is that the sense of difference between the masculine and the feminine central to gender hierarchy may become simply re-inscribed in new forms.

Stein offers an alternative to this positing of "woman" as the silent other, able to enter language only through appropriating the masculine position or through a nearly unimaginable writing of the female body, in its essential difference. Although Stein too gestures within much of her writing toward a specifically female and lesbian erotics, she often appears to counter the idea that her writing springs from an essential biological difference, especially one that would imply outsidership in relation to language. If the female in Western culture has often been assigned in a philosophic sense a place "outside" the symbolic order, Stein refuses to agree to this assignation. The symbolic order appears in Stein's writing not as an irrefutable law, but as a structure open to transformation. Her playfulness with language—her sense that language can be played with—allows her to make use of symbolic forms in order to create a voice for the unsymbolic, associated with the pre-oedipal intimacy with the mother based on a dialogue of sound and of the body.

Stein catapults us, then, into "a world of words," in William Gass's term, in which gender has been inscribed, even as gender's inscriptions can be mimed, parodied, re-instated, critiqued, loosened, and often erased. The sense of an essence, of a near but absent female presence, remains, linking her writing with that of writers like Cixous and Irigaray; but the movement from her writing to this essence is difficult and uncertain. Her writing poses a knotty contradiction by asking us both to imagine a femaleness just "outside" the writing, and to accept the writing as a place within which gender can become comically undone.

Stein's oeuvre is remarkable for its abundance and variety, as well as for its experimental nature. She wrote daily for almost fifty years, from 1903 until her death from cancer in 1946, accumulating a body of work composed of plays, operas, portraits, novels, essays, poetry, autobiographies, and meditations. All of her writing intended for publication is now published, although during her lifetime she often had to wait for years before seeing pieces published, including her monumental novel *The Making of Americans,* written between 1903 and 1911 but unpublished until 1925, or her myriad early plays and portraits, which found their way finally into the 1922 *Geography and Plays.* After her death, and the placement of all her extant manuscripts and typescripts, notebooks, and correspondence in the Beinecke Rare Book Library at Yale University, Yale University Press brought out eight further volumes of her work, titled with a revealing contradiction *The Unpublished Writings of Gertrude Stein* (1951–1958).

Despite delays in publication, much of Stein's work did find its may into print in her lifetime, both in book form and scattered among French avant-garde journals like *transition* and American magazines like *Camera Work* and *Harper's.* Stein has always had readers, and good ones. Her earliest readers were often, perhaps not surprisingly, writers, painters, or musicians, including Sherwood Anderson, Richard Wright, Ernest Hemingway, Samuel Beckett, Edith Sitwell, Carl Van Vechten, Virgil Thomson (who composed the music for two of Stein's operas, *Four Saints in Three Acts* [1927] and *The Mother of Us All* [1945]), and in more recent times experimental artists or writers like John Ashbery, John Cage, and Susan Howe. Her intimate circle of friends comprised at any one moment an extraordinary range of figures, from Pablo Picasso, Henri Matisse, and Jean Renoir to the young Hemingway, and from journalist-writers like Mildred Aldrich to well-known patrons and muse figures like Mabel Dodge. Stein's influence on the avant-garde of literature, music, and visual art both before World War II and after has been immense, although the history and intricacies of this influence have until now gone largely unexplored within the academy.

Stein's reputation, in this sense, remains much larger among artists and writers themselves than among the majority of the culture or even among academic critics. To make use of the vocabulary she offers in her 1926 essay "Composition as Explanation," she has not yet become "classical," because her art remains to most of us too strange to be accepted, "a thing irritating, annoying stimulating," and it is therefore judged to be without the "beauty" granted to any art that has been "classified" and accepted as classic. Although many critics have made excellent studies of Stein in the last forty years, beginning with Donald Sutherland's groundbreaking critical work in 1951, her importance within the modernist canon generally has remained surprisingly small. It is only now, almost half a century after her death, that literary criticism at large seems to be catching up to her, although her reputation has still not reached the sudden turn of canonical acceptance described in "Composition as Explanation": "For a long time everybody refuses and then almost without a pause everybody accepts."

Although high modernist writing has always appeared to thrive on the notion of its excessiveness, its marginality to mainstream literature and culture, Stein's writing, in its much more startling excessiveness and its more outrageous challenge to interpretation, throws other modernist literature into a more conservative light. Stein refuses to conserve what most modern writers—even writers like James Joyce and Virginia Woolf—wish to conserve: a certain interest in formal coherence, and a sense that, no matter how fragmented the surface of one's art appears to be, the critical effort to be anticipated is one of filling the gaps and finding the meaning toward which the fragments gesture. With Stein, in an abundant variety of forms, this critical effort can certainly take place, up to a point, and to a greater degree than many critics seem to feel; but her writing tends to bring us always to a place from which our habitual critical tools can do no good whatsoever. It is difficult even to interpret her writing with a post-structuralist approach, since in a sense her writing is already deconstructed, its gaps between signifieds and signifiers already cheerfully open and acknowledged, so that one is left wondering what to do next. Her writing acts as a mirror, asking us what we are up to, as critics, and playfully refusing to allow us to continue without confronting the most difficult questions about what we do when we read.

What is both frustrating and exhilarating about Stein's writing, then, is its capacity to elude us, to stay at least ten steps in advance (or to the side) of our most sophisticated critical methods. And maybe it is precisely these methods that Stein hopes to compel us to throw out, as she herself threw out so much in order to create "the modern composition." Her writing, in any case, makes the boundary between the critic and the text unnervingly unclear. To read her with any sense of gratification, one must, in a sense, just take the plunge and allow oneself to swim alongside her various barges and multicolored fish, marking the attempt *as* an attempt, and accepting the full range of one's responses not only to decipherable meaning, but to all the associations and sensations called up through this most visual and aural—and sensual—use of language. Stein's feminism becomes most clear in the metamorphosis she appears to hope for in her readers, *as* readers. No longer masters, we can only read her writing as co-players, opening ourselves up to its manifold pleasures.

TWINNING IN A LANDSCAPE ON THE MARGINS

> She liked to talk and to sing songs and she liked to change places.
>
> *Ida*

> Act so that there is no use in a centre.
>
> *Tender Buttons*

Stein's fascination with whatever is off-center tempts one to think about her life in terms of margins. Born on 3 February 1874 in Allegheny, Pennsylvania (a birthplace of which she later would boast delightedly), the fifth child of Amelia Keyser Stein and Daniel Stein, both middle-class German-Jewish immigrants, Gertrude Stein made her first transatlantic journey at eight months old, to Europe, where she lived in Vienna and Paris until she was five, when her parents returned to America to settle ultimately in Oakland, California. In Protestant America, she remained Jewish and in some sense European; just as in Europe, both as a child and in her twenties, when she returned to Europe for the rest of her life, she remained stubbornly American. Although she writes with ardor about both the United States landscape and the French countryside around Bilignin, where she and Alice Toklas spent their summers from the late 1920s on, she is not in any usual sense a writer about place, a fact that may begin to mark her difference from writers like Willa Cather or Eudora Welty. The south of France held her deep love as a landscape, yet her writing attempts not so much to bring this place into writing, even in her self-defined "romantic" works of the mid to late 1920s like *Four Saints in Three Acts* and *Lucy Church Amiably* (1930), as to make of her writing a new place, a "landscape" in its own right, replete with its own geography and internal movements. Stein's writing, in this sense, can be understood as moving on the margins: between cultures, as between the "real" landscape and the written one.

For Stein, language too becomes interesting when it most clearly plays in border territory. As a child, she spoke German and French (and possibly Yiddish too) in addition to English, although she asserts in *The Autobiography of Alice B. Toklas* that she learned to read first in English, and that English "then as always . . . was her only language." English, however, undergoes a sea change in Stein's hands, as anyone who has glanced at a page of Stein has noted. The man from the Grafton Press who embarrassed himself by coming to this young author with questions about her use of English in *Three Lives* (1909) hit on something important about her sense of language. Mistaken in his speculation that she either was not American or had not "had much experience in writing," he was correct in his perception that her writing contained mistakes.

Stein chose immigrant and African American figures as her heroines in these three early experimental stories precisely because she desired a language apart from the mainstream for her own art. Although Richard Wright and other readers may have been partially right in noting Stein's interest in dialect in "The Good Anna," "Melanctha," and "The Gentle Lena," her preoccupation seems to be more in imagining and appropriating "incorrect" and ungrammatical speech for an art in opposition to the conventional and founded upon "mistakes." In one of her most important essays, "Poetry and Grammar," she elucidate her sense of the liveliness of language as residing in its mistakes: English verbs and adverbs, for instance, "have one very nice quality and that is that they can be so mistaken," in contrast to the more solid and boring nouns and adjectives.

Stein's sense of "English" emerges, in this essay and elsewhere, as an arbitrary and even whimsical set of playing rules, in which the most intriguing event involves the breaking of the rules. English comes to seem, especially in Stein's most experimental writing, curiously foreign and unfamiliar, a situation nurtured by her sense of intense relationship with English as she wrote surrounded by French. In *The Autobiography* she tells us (through the persona of Alice Toklas) how her situation as an American writing in France "has left me more intensely alone with my eyes [since she "feels" a language with her eyes] and my english. I do not know if it would have been possible to have english be so all in all to me otherwise."

This love of mistakes becomes associated in Stein's writing with her lesbianism. From the perspective of the mainstream heterosexual culture, to love sexually another of the same sex is precisely to make a "mistake." Whereas some critics, like Richard Bridgman, have understood Stein's writing as resorting to an abstract and coded language in order to hide her lesbianism, it is possible to make a more positive connection: her lesbianism, in positioning her "outside" the mainstream, in the "margins," became an important element enabling her to create and embrace an increasingly exuberant and unconventional art.

Stein's earliest writing, the novel titled alternately *Q.E.D.* or *Things as They Are* (first published in 1950), appears to have been inspired by her love affair between 1900 and 1903 with a young Bryn Mawr graduate, May Bookstaver. Having left Radcliffe in 1897 (one Latin exam short of receiving her B.A.), Stein had gone to medical school at Johns Hopkins, with the intention of studying the physiological aspects of mental processes. By her last year at Hopkins, beginning to lose interest in her medical study, she became deeply involved in a new, if related, subject for study: an intricate love triangle in which she herself played an at first reluctant but always impassioned role. Drawn to May, she gradually came to understand and to be disturbed by the relationship between May and Mabel Haynes, another Bryn Mawr graduate living in Baltimore. Mabel, as a wealthy Bostonian, held May as a protégée and sexual companion; the financial strings appeared to Stein to be all too clearly attached.

The importance of this early affair emerges in its reappearance in different forms in *Q.E.D.* (based extensively on Stein's experience with May and Mabel), *Fernhurst* (1905; published in 1971), and *Three Lives.* In "Melanctha" the triangle becomes subtly reworked in the relationships between Jane Harden and Melanctha, and Melanctha and Jeff Campbell. The "wisdom" Melanctha gains from Jane and attempts to impart to Jeff is a knowledge at once sexual and linguistic; for Stein's language begins to "wander" away from an ongoing and realistic story line and toward a sensuously repetitive chant, just as Melanctha "wanders" from her father's house into the uncharted depths of passionately errant relationships. "Each One as She May," the subtitle of "Melanctha," marks one of the first encodings of May's name, linking Stein's own passional relation with the possibility of "may" and "might."

Stein, inscribing May into composition after composition as "may," "Mary," "May Mary," "M.," "M. M.," and "marry," retained a strong sense of May (possibly herself) as her muse, long past May Bookstaver's marriage and new existence as May Knoblauch. The two women remained friends for many years. And the intensity of Stein's feelings about this early and sustaining muse may be measured by the trouble opened up in Stein's relation with Alice Toklas when, upon Stein's belated revelation of the *Q.E.D.* manuscript almost forty years after its writing, Toklas understood for the first time the full sexual nature of Stein's earlier involvement.

Perhaps the most important moment in Stein's life, however, was her meeting with Alice Toklas in 1907, described with quiet detail by the persona of Alice at the opening of *The Autobiography*. If Alice Toklas, as Stein has her claim, met in Stein her "genius," then Stein met in Toklas the audience and lover she most needed. From 1909, when Alice finally moved in with Gertrude at the Paris residence Gertrude shared with her brother Leo (the famous salon at 27, rue de Fleurus), until Gertrude's death in 1946, the two women were daily companions. Alice cooked and shopped, and in addition typed all of Gertrude's manuscripts. She became gradually an informal business manager and agent as well, in her correspondence with publishers and her eventual founding of the Plain Editions Press in the late 1920s, created specifically to put Stein's unpublished work into print.

Alice Toklas offered herself to Stein's imagination as a welcome substitute for Stein's older brother Leo. As Stein writes in the autobiography she wrote after *The Autobiography of Alice B. Toklas*, *Everybody's Autobiography*, Leo had always "led in everything." In childhood, Gertrude and Leo had had an intensely close relationship, within an already intensely emotional and isolated family life, directed with an old-fashioned sternness and intrusiveness by their father. For Gertrude, her relationship with Leo was like that of twins; in addition, she felt haunted by the family understanding that she and Leo had been born to fill the places of two children who had died. With Leo, she read books, went to plays and museums, and argued about philosophical issues. When Leo went to Harvard after the death first of their mother and then of their father, and after Gertrude and her older sister Bertha had been placed with relatives in Baltimore, Gertrude soon joined him at "the Harvard Annex"; when Leo went to Johns Hopkins to study biology, Gertrude followed; when Leo went to Europe, Gertrude visited him there and finally set up housekeeping with him.

Together Leo and Gertrude became extremely interested in the new art of the late nineteenth and early twentieth centuries—the art, as Stein later named it, of "the modern composition." For Gertrude, a lifetime of artistic patronage and friendship with artists began in these years. With her brother, and with their pooled independent incomes, she began to buy Japanese prints and the then strange and unfamiliar paintings of Paul Cézanne, Paul Gauguin, Renoir, and (especially after the 1905 Fauve exhibit) Picasso and Matisse. They met Renoir, Picasso, Matisse, and other artists, and began to hold weekly salons at 27, rue de Fleurus. And, along with their older brother Michael and his wife, Sarah, they were among the first to introduce post-impressionist art to the United States.

As Gertrude began to feel that in addition to appreciating and discovering art she could actually create her own written art, her relationship with Leo became more uneasy. Leo responded to her early writing with a hostility that never was to diminish. Desirous of becoming great at something but unable to follow through on the production of any one thing, including at various points painting, the history and criticism of art, philosophy and psychoanalytic thought, Leo must have felt jealous of his younger sister's capacity to consider herself a writer, even at a very early stage, and to continue in her serious ambition. Gaining a sense of independence, she began to listen less to his "explanations" of her work. As she writes in *Everybody's Autobiography:* "Then slowly he began explaining not what I was doing but he was explaining, and explaining well explaining might have been an explanation. Now and then I was not listening. This had never happened to me before."

Gertrude's gradual substitution of Alice for Leo, described obliquely in the abstract and repetitive form of her "participial" style (grounded in words like "coming," "living," and "being") in the intricate windings of *Two,* achieves completion in Stein's first portrait, "Ada," a portrait of Alice Toklas. In this succinct piece, only three pages long, Stein inscribes her own double movement within her first decade of writing: from conventional narrative to an epiphanic, circling, and repetitive form, and from family (brother, father, and mother) to an unidentified, loved and loving "some one." "Telling" and "listening" merge and intertwine—activities foreign to the hierarchical "explaining"—just as the telling of stories mingles with a pungent erotics: "Trembling was all living, living was all loving, some one was then the other one."

The capacity of two "ones" to engage in such doubling suggests a lesbian poetics, which emerges in new forms with the love poems and plays to follow. And it is this possibility (this "may marry") that grounds other forms of intimacy inscribed into Stein's portraits. Twinning, in this sense, becomes a fundamental figure for the relationship between portrait-subject and portraitist, especially as Stein moves away from the more detached and "scientific" portraits embedded in paragraph after paragraph of her thousand-page experimental novel, *The Making of Americans,* to the more intimate and shorter portraits, for example, of Picasso and Matisse, or of the dancer Orta (in "Orta or One Dancing"). The literary portrait becomes for Stein a way of exploring the relationship between the one "telling" and the one being "told" or written about. For Stein, the primary act of the portrait is to open up and articulate a space between two figures. The portrait, in this sense, is always double, marking a twinning (and entwining) movement between writer and subject, in which the question of what is subjective, what is objective, becomes impossible to answer—and becomes so in a way that playfully dissolves such dichotomies.

Stein's portraits, of course, make mischief with our ordinary sense of representation, just as many post-impressionist portraits seem to take pleasure in doing. Her gradual movement away from realism and toward a series of different modes of abstraction, up through the 1920s, can be compared especially to Picasso's development of cubism, just as his later return to the figure, although in pared-down form, suggests a relation to Stein's return, in her later work like *Ida* (1941) and *The World Is Round* (1939), to a new mode of story and character. Stein herself participated quite intimately in Picasso's early struggle when she posed for her own portrait in 1906, during the time she was writing *Three Lives.* This portrait marks a crucial and half-accomplished metamorphosis in Picasso's art: the torso, dressed in realistic detail, and the finely articulated hands, are contradicted by the curiously masklike face, more akin to African masks than to an individual woman's face. It is no surprise that Picasso, unhappy with his attempts to complete the face, finally painted it in the absence of Stein. Like Stein, Picasso understood the power of "the modern composition":

as he said to Alice Toklas about this portrait, "Everybody says that she does not look like it but that does not make any difference, she will."

It is possible that, for Stein, something in the intimacy of sitting for a portrait may have encouraged her own experiments with words. Her sense of Picasso's brushstrokes may have played a part in her attempt to make the words in her own art more like paint, through foregrounding their presence as material and sensual objects—an attempt that blossomed in her richest period of writing, beginning with the *Tender Buttons* (1914) period, around 1912, and continuing up to 1932. And it is possible, in a further sense, that the experience of sitting for a portrait, as she herself meditated on the long and repetitive sentences (pen-strokes) of "Melanctha," led her to think in serious ways about the subjecthood of the portrait's subject. Her own subjects, she may have felt, would have their own life, often a very private life (as in Saint Therese's question in *Four Saints in Three Acts,* "Who settles a private life?"); and it would be up to her to create a form of art suggestive at once of the portraitist's (or writer's) feelings about the subject, and the subject's own inner feelings or essence. A "private life," in this sense, may not be "settled," but it can be glimpsed, however indirectly, through the response (however oblique) of the one "telling," as teller and subject mingle and create the landscape of intimacy that is the writing.

RE-CREATING THE VISIBLE WORLD: POETRY, PLAYS, GRAMMAR (1912–1932)

> Lifting belly is a language. It says island.
> "Lifting Belly"

What began to "bother" Stein around the time of *Tender Buttons* (written between 1910 and 1912) was the difficult problem of "looking." As she writes in "Portraits and Repetition," looking involves "remembering": "looking inevitably carried in its train realizing movements and expression and as such forced me into recognizing resemblances" between the writing and the world written about, which in turn "forced remembering," and a "confusion of present with past and future time." For a writer desirous of creating (in the Emersonian tradition) always in the present tense, to cause "remembering"—to signify something in the world—became an obstruction to genuine writing, which "actually create[s] the thing in itself" rather than "suggesting" it.

Stein's discussion in "Poetry and Grammar" of *Tender Buttons* touches on a further, and less openly stated, reason for her wish to create a writing independent of "looking." She links the noun, as the part of speech most bound to the visible and referential, with an authoritarianism harmful to the objects named: "just naming names is alright when you want to call a roll but is it any good for anything else." As she adds, with a glance at the fascist, military elements coming into power in the mid 1930s, "To be sure in many places in Europe as in America they do like to call rolls." In addition to her attempt, shared by other modernists, to renew the language—to create in her own namings the "thrill" felt in the namings of Homer and Chaucer—Stein desires a language that would make "roll calls" impossible. To identify objects in the world through known names is, Stein quietly argues, to acquiesce in a structure of domination: the domination of the world by words used not to (re-)create but to own and exploit.

To counter this authoritarianism, Stein makes an astonishing and unprecedented leap. She creates a poetics of resistance to nouns and direct naming, even as she builds this poetics precisely around nouns. As she says in "Poetry and Grammar," she attempted to "mean names without naming them," just as Shakespeare created a Forest of Arden "without mentioning the things that make a forest": "You feel it all but he does not name its names." This attempt is at cross-purposes with an Adamic naming of one-to-one correspondences, filtered through an

Emersonian poetic labor of rediscovering the original and absolute correspondence between word and world. Stein's effort is, quite literally, to make mistakes, with nouns no less than with grammar. What emerges is a sense of nouns and other words glittering with the richness of association they hold within the language, yet placed in such new contexts that, although we catch glimpses of a signified reality, we remain radically uncertain of its dimensions.

Tender Buttons can be read as a prose poem engaged simultaneously in this form of oblique "description" and in a meditation on Stein's re-creation of the scene of description. Rather than becoming a literary still life (of "Objects," "Food," and "Rooms"), this magnificent and frustrating composition asks what is involved in representation: can there be a form of representation that allows "life" to be sensed (and loved) but without being directly named? One gains, throughout *Tender Buttons,* an extraordinary sense of a life lived intricately among different relationships and with different moods, and gestured toward through clusters of named phenomena, from literal objects like mutton and oranges, boxes and tables, to more metaphysical ones like language, space, resignation, and explanation.

Although it is possible to bridge over the shards and to piece together a personal narrative (about Leo and Gertrude and Alice) amid this plethora and confusion of the physical and metaphysical, it is equally possible to confront, at every turn, Stein's desire for another form of reading, one that allows itself to enact a "wedding" with the composition, as in this shard of "Objects": "I hope she has her cow. Bidding a wedding, widening received treading, little leading mention nothing." Who the "she" is, who the "I" is, remain secret; yet the sensual wedding being suggested here (the "widening received treading" intimating the opening up of a vagina, to receive the "treading," the movement—possibly like the sewing movement of a treadle-driven sewing machine—of another) can open out to include us as well, for we are "bid" to join in, to resist trying to "lead," and to allow the composition to "mention nothing"—to refuse to name directly.

This "wedding" between ourselves and the composition is called for further in Stein's most private and ruminative poetry, *Before the Flowers of Friendship Faded Friendship Faded* (a cycle of thirty poems written in 1930 and based on Georges Hugnet's poetry) and especially *Stanzas in Meditation* (first published in 1956), written in 1932, along with *The Autobiography of Alice B. Toklas,* and termed by Ulla Dydo "the other autobiography." As in *Tender Buttons,* a sense of a personal narrative urges itself on us in *Stanzas,* yet remains suggested and elusive. Whereas in *Tender Buttons* Stein brings nouns and adjectives into the foreground, making us wonder toward what reality they gesture, in *Stanzas* pronouns—I, she, they—engage in a quiet and contemplative dance, carefully avoiding most names and nouns completely, and evoking questions about relationship, especially between an audience (often marked as other—"they") and the writing.

The feminism implicit in such poetry emerges in bold colors in Stein's 1927 essay-meditation "Patriarchal Poetry," which can illuminate the later *Stanzas.* Resisting the cataloging of phenomena and the politics and poetics of conventional namings grounded in a (patriarchal) Word, this difficult composition attempts to clear a space for a new form of creation. The abundance of words, out of all ordinary order, suggests a fantastical realm of language before language became allied with the biblical "Let there be": "For before let it before to be before spell to be before to be before. . . ." Within this realm of re-creation and rejuvenation ("Reject rejoice rejuvenate"), a "she" emerges midway through, shyly but powerfully, as an unnamed figure for Stein's writing: "Let her be let her let her let her be let her be let her be let her be shy let her be let her be let her try." What is asked for here ("Let") is an opening up of "letters"—and of the "letter"—to "her": the "letter" now becomes "let her." This new poetic will allow for "her" to be let alone, "never to be what he said." "She" will enter the writing—the letter—not through "an arrangement in a system to pointing," as Stein puts it in *Tender Buttons,* but through a chanting language showing vital connection to an unseen but suggested realm of the female body.

It is difficult, one usually assumes, to be quite so shy about being seen once one moves to the stage. In Stein's numerous plays and operas, however, composed between 1913 and 1946, what is to be seen onstage remains wittily uncertain. The movement from her pages to the theater involves, as any director of Stein's plays must notice, an act of embodiment curiously unencouraged within her language. In her earlier plays especially, like *Sacred Emily* or *Pink Melon Joy,* an astonishing number of elements we rely on in most plays become tossed out: identifiable and named characters, plot, the succession or arc of acts. Such plays often look, on the page, like long poems, and often sound like a sequence of floating voices, sometimes responding to each other and sometimes not. This form allows Stein precisely to "let her be": to open up a space in writing for a suggested but invisible erotics—an erotics in which the eye, linked to militarism and domination (the "Oh say can you see" of the 1915–1917 love poem and play *Lifting Belly,* for instance), cannot find a place.

Stein hoped for her plays to be produced, and a good number have been and continue to be; yet she needed another way of thinking about what would be visible onstage. By the time she wrote *Four Saints in Three Acts* in 1927, an opera with music by Virgil Thomson (first produced with an all-black cast in Hartford, Connecticut, in 1934), she had come to identify the kind of "happening" she desired onstage as "a landscape" rather than "a story." As she writes in her 1935 lecture "Plays," "A landscape does not move nothing really moves in a landscape but things are there." Nothing "really" moves, and yet, as she adds, the movement in *Four Saints* "was like a movement in and out," similar to that of "nuns very busy and in continuous movement but placid as a landscape has to be."

The sacral and ritualistic aspect of such landscape-plays, evident as early as *Sacred Emily* and coming to the force in Stein's writing of the mid 1920s, connects with Stein's presentation of the erotic as a sacral realm. The "acts" in Stein's plays—jumbled up in number, scattered haphazardly throughout—can be understood often as actions at once erotic and sacral, open to the participation of the audience or congregation, just as Stein's much-used pun on "scene"/"seen" raises the question of how much the audience can really "see" of the play, how much remains somehow secret and cloistered.

Stein's preoccupation with the visible, in plays as in the world with which plays play, emerges in other writings of the 1920s, preeminently the difficult but moving experimental novel *Lucy Church Amiably,* subtitled *A Novel of Romantic Beauty and Nature and Which Looks Like an Engraving.* In suggesting how her novel "looks," and in tying its visible presence to an "engraving," Stein raises with pungency the question of her writing's relation to the visible world. One can glimpse obliquely, as with much of Stein's writing, the autobiographical and daily living, just as one can glimpse the actual landscape of Belley, in southern France, a part of the country Stein and Toklas began to visit regularly in 1923. Yet the visible world of cows and sheep and goats stands also as an idyll, within the "engraving" of language, in which the erotic can find a quiet, indirect, and sacred place. As Stein writes in the "Advertisement" at the beginning of the book: "and this makes [the landscape] have a river a gorge an inundation and a remarkable meadowed mass which is whatever they use not to feed but to bed cows." The landscape in *Lucy Church* accumulates phenomena and "happenings" suggestive of a landscape of the female body, protected from encroachment and inhabited only by such saints and other figures as can understand its manifold pleasures.

IDENTITY (1932–1946)

> He said I know you, and he not only said it to Ida but he said it to everybody, he knew Ida he said hell yes he knew Ida.
>
> *Ida*

Much of what Stein writes—arguably all of her writing—has a strong autobiographical dimension, yet it was not until *The Autobiography of Alice B. Toklas* (written in 1932, published in 1933) that Stein made this dimension explicit. Although this autobiography is by no means simple or straightforward, and shows an important alliance with her earlier experiments in floating voices and erotic doublings, it has often been understood in terms simpler than those in which it is presented. Suddenly, to a majority of readers, Gertrude Stein—or at least Alice Toklas as constructed by Gertrude Stein—sounded lucid, even chatty, ready to tell a straightforward narrative grounded in facts and with actual people as characters. She seemed to open the doors to the salon, and to allow her audience to observe the geniuses and saints—all the artists and writers she knew—at close quarters.

This autobiography, in becoming such an immediate popular success in contrast to all of Stein's previous writing, created a crisis in her life. As she writes in *Everybody's Autobiography,* the more personal and revelatory work that followed *The Autobiography of Alice B. Toklas,* "when nothing had any commercial value everything was important and when something began having a commercial value it was upsetting." For the "outside" to "put a value on you" is to lose your "inside," the creative and deeply private realm out of which, she felt, all her experimental writing had emerged. What made this success even more difficult was Stein's sense that this was not her real writing. She had written *The Autobiography* in six weeks, apparently for fun as well as with a half-joking hope that it might be a "best-seller." In appropriating Alice's voice, she quite literally buried her own more difficult and elusive mode of composition, so that the question of whom the audience was now acclaiming came uncomfortably into the foreground. As Stein noted, "after all I do want them to print something else to prove that it was not only that that they wanted but of course they do not."

This situation presented Stein with questions about identity and audience vital to all of her writing during the remaining thirteen years of her life. The sudden presence of an audience—particularly the American audience to whom she delivered her lectures on her first and last return to America in 1934 and 1935—pressed her to attempt explanations of her difficult methods. Published as *Lectures in America* in 1935, these essays remain her most full-bodied elucidation of her oeuvre, immensely valuable to any further interpretation of Stein; yet in contrasting these essays with the more experimental "essays" on grammar in the late 1920s, especially in *How to Write* (1931), one can see how she may have understood the newly elucidating mode as making a sacrifice.

In *The Geographical History of America; or, The Relation of Human Nature to the Human Mind,* Stein attempts to counter this form of sacrifice with a defense of "the human mind": the transcendent realm in which identity, audience, tears, emotions, and mortality cannot enter. The profound anxiety about loss of one's creative inner self becomes in this curiously personal philosophical meditation assuaged by the claim that this innerness remains, untrammeled by the anguish inevitable in the world of flux and of money, where some books become bought for the wrong reasons and some stay unbought for the same wrong reasons.

The anxieties associated in *The Geographical History* with identity become more clearly marked as gender-specific in the novels of this late period, including the "murder mystery"

Blood on the Dining Room Floor, Ida, and *Mrs. Reynolds* (1952), as well as the operas *Dr. Faustus Lights the Lights* and *The Mother of Us All.* As *Blood* suggests, the blood discovered is specifically a woman's, just as its appearance (at least in the title) on "the dining room floor" fits into a larger frame in which the dining room represents the scene of literary consumption and the possible murder of the (female) text by the reader. *Ida,* an obliquely autobiographical novel, presents in fuller detail the dangers of one's being visible to others, leading directly to one's consumption. As a woman, or a woman writer, to win a beauty contest (like the one on Mount Ida, with Paris as judge, or like the "beauty contest" Stein herself had just won with *The Autobiography*) is to allow oneself to become alien to oneself. For Ida (as for *Ida,* the novel) it is imperative to move beyond an audience—composed of husbands and other "officers"—that claims knowledge of one's identity.

The reality of "beauty contests," clearly allied in Stein's mind with the larger and more destructive reality of national contest, became increasingly urgent for Stein as World War II began. In *Mrs. Reynolds,* as in the autobiographical works *Wars I Have Seen* (1945) and *Paris France* (1940), Stein attempts to locate a place in language from which to contemplate war. As in the Great War, Stein and Toklas moved out of Paris, yet the brevity and relative serenity of their sojourn in Mallorca during 1915 and 1916 contrasts with their prolonged stay at their summer home in Bilignin and then at Culoz, within occupied France. Jewish women in a nation occupied by the Germans, they were at great risk, apparently spared deportation only through the efforts of Bernard Faÿ, who held a position of some power within the Vichy government. The act of writing itself—a more pleasurable and more innocent "occupation"—appears to have kept identity's natural "tears" (mentioned but resisted in *Wars*) in abeyance, as Stein labored to keep the trauma of war largely outside her writing, and to evoke on the other hand a community of neighbors and intimate acquaintances who could participate in a language not of contest but of a more authentic communication.

Stein's joy in the liberation, and her gratitude to the American doughboys, celebrated at the end of *Wars I Have Seen,* were to be short-lived; for, after returning late in 1944 to Paris, and after a tour of United States Army bases in Germany, Stein fell ill with cancer of the uterus in July 1946. On 27 July 1946, she died at the American Hospital at Neuilly-sur-Seine. Alice Toklas survived her by twenty years, living on in Paris until her own death in 1967. Yet it is difficult to imagine Stein as dead, when she remains so fresh and alive in her abundant writings. To end a story with death, after the early *Three Lives,* was never Stein's style. It is more appropriate to allow Stein's own words from *Ida* to resist any attempt at closure:

> Her life never began again because it was always there.
> And now it was astonishing that it was always there. Yes it was.
> Ida
> Yes it was.

Selected Bibliography

PRIMARY WORKS

Three Lives: Stories of the Good Anna, Melanctha, and the Gentle Lena. New York: Grafton Press, 1909; New York: Modern Library, 1933.

Tender Buttons: Objects, Food, Rooms. New York: Claire-Marie, 1914. See also *Selected Writings of Gertrude Stein.*

Geography and Plays. Boston: Four Seas Company, 1922.

The Making of Americans. Paris: Contact Editions, 1925; New York: Something Else Press, 1973.

An Acquaintance with Description. London: Seizin Press, 1929.

Composition as Explanation. London: Hogarth Press, 1926.

Useful Knowledge. New York: Payson & Clarke, 1928; London: John Lane, 1929.

Lucy Church Amiably. Paris: Plain Edition, 1930.

Before the Flowers of Friendship Faded Friendship Faded. Paris: Plain Edition, 1931.

How to Write. Paris: Plain Edition, 1931.

Opera and Plays. Paris: Plain Edition, 1932.

Matisse, Picasso, and Gertrude Stein, with Two Shorter Stories. Paris: Plain Edition, 1933.

The Autobiography of Alice B. Toklas. New York: Harcourt, Brace, 1933; New York: Random House, 1936; London: Penguin Books, 1966. See also *Selected Writings of Gertrude Stein: Portraits and Prayers*. New York: Random House, 1934.

Lectures in America. New York: Random House, 1935; Boston: Beacon Press, 1957.

Narration: Four Lectures by Gertrude Stein. Chicago: University of Chicago Press, 1935. Introduction by Thornton Wilder.

The Geographical History of America; or, The Relation of Human Nature to the Human Mind. New York: Random House, 1936. Introduction by Thornton Wilder.

Everybody's Autobiography. New York: Random House, 1937; London and Toronto: William Heinemann, 1938.

Picasso. Paris: Librairie Floury, 1938 (in French and English); London: Scribners, 1939.

The World Is Round. London: Batsford, 1939, New York: William R. Scott, 1939.

Paris France. New York: Scribners, 1940; London: Batsford, 1940.

What Are Masterpieces. Los Angeles: Conference Press, 1940. Foreword by Robert Bartlett Haas.

Ida: A Novel. New York: Random House, 1941.

Wars I Have Seen. New York: Random House, 1945; London: Batsford, 1945.

Brewsie and Willie. New York: Random House, 1946.

POSTHUMOUS PUBLICATIONS

Four in America. New Haven: Yale University Press, 1947. Introduction by Thornton Wilder.

The Gertrude Stein First Reader and Three Plays. Dublin and London: M. Fridberg, 1946; Boston: Houghton Mifflin, 1948.

Last Operas and Plays. Edited and with an introduction by Carl Van Vechten. New York: Rinehart, 1949.

Things as They Are [*Q.E.D.*]. Pawlet, Vt.: Banyan Press, 1950.

The Yale Edition of the Unpublished Writings of Gertrude Stein. 8 vols. New Haven, Conn.: Yale University Press, 1951–1958. Comprises the following volumes:

Two: Gertrude Stein and Her Brother, and Other Early Portraits, 1908–12. Published 1951. Foreword by Janet Flanner.

Mrs. Reynolds, and Five Earlier Novelettes, 1931–42. Published 1952. Foreword by Lloyd Frankenberg.

Bee Time Vine, and Other Pieces, 1913–1927. Published 1953. Introduction by Virgil Thomson.

As Fine as Melanctha, 1914–1930. Published 1954. Foreword by Natalie Clifford Barney.

Painted Lace, and Other Pieces, 1914–37. Published 1955. Introduction by Daniel-Henry Kahnweiler.

Stanzas in Meditation, and Other Poems, 1929–33. Published 1956. Preface by Donald Sutherland.

Alphabets and Birthdays. Published 1957. Introduction by Donald Gallup.

A Novel of Thank You. Published 1958. Introduction by Carl Van Vechten.

ANTHOLOGIES

Gertrude Stein. 3 vols. Edited by Catharine R. Stimpson and Harriet Scott Chessman. New York: Library of America, 1993.

Look at Me Now and Here I Am: Writings and Lectures, 1911–1945, by Gertrude Stein. Edited by Patricia Meyerowitz, with an introduction by Elizabeth Sprigge. London: Peter Owen, 1967.

Selected Writings of Gertrude Stein. Edited, with an introduction and notes, by Carl Van Vechten. New York: Random House, 1946.

The Yale Gertrude Stein: Selections. Edited, with an introduction, by Richard Kostelanetz. New Haven, Conn.: Yale University Press, 1980. Contains a useful bibliography of Stein's writings.

SECONDARY WORKS

BIOGRAPHICAL AND CRITICAL STUDIES

Barry, Ellen E. "On Reading Gertrude Stein." *Genders* 5:1–21 (July 1989).

Bridgman, Richard. *Gertrude Stein in Pieces*. New York: Oxford University Press, 1970. Contains a valuable bibliography of secondary sources on Stein up to 1970.

Burke, Carolyn. "Gertrude Stein, the Cone Sisters, and the Puzzle of Female Friendship." *Critical Inquiry* 8, no. 3:543–564 (Spring 1982).

Chessman, Harriet Scott. *The Public Is Invited to Dance: Representation, The Body, and Dialogue in Gertrude Stein.* Stanford, Calif.: Stanford University Press, 1989.

DeKoven, Marianne. *A Different Language: Gertrude Stein's Experimental Writing.* Madison: University of Wisconsin Press, 1983.

Doane, Janice Louise. *Silence and Narrative: The Early Novels of Gertrude Stein.* Westport, Conn.: Greenwood Press, 1986.

DuPlessis, Rachel Blau. "Woolfenstein." In *Breaking the Sequence: Women's Experimental Fiction.* Edited by Ellen G. Friedman and Miriam Fuchs. Princeton, N.J.: Princeton University Press, 1989.

Dydo, Ulla. "Must Horses Drink; or, 'Any Language Is Funny If You Don't Understand It.' " *Tulsa Studies in Women's Literature* 4, no. 2:272–280 (Fall 1985).

———. "*Stanzas in Meditation:* The Other Autobiography." *Chicago Review* 35, no. 2:4–20 (Winter 1985).

Fifer, Elizabeth. " 'Is Flesh Advisable?' The Interior Theater of Gertrude Stein." *Signs* 4, no. 3:472–483 (Spring 1979).

Gass, William H. "Gertrude Stein and the Geography of the Sentence." In his *The World Within the Word: Essays.* New York: Knopf, 1978. Pp. 63–123.

———. "Gertrude Stein: Her Escape from Protective Language." In his *Fiction and the Figures of Life.* New York: Knopf, 1970. Pp. 79–96.

Gibbs, Anna. "Hélène Cixous and Gertrude Stein: New Directions in Feminist Criticism." *Meanjin* 38: 281–293 (1979).

Hoffman, Michael J., ed. *Critical Essays on Gertrude Stein.* Boston: G. K. Hall, 1986.

Mellow, James. *Charmed Circle: Gertrude Stein and Company.* New York: Praeger, 1974.

Mizejewski, Linda. "Gertrude Stein: The Pattern Moves, and the Woman Behind Shakes It." *Women's Studies: An Interdisciplinary Journal* 13, nos. 1–2:33–47 (1986).

Neuman, Shirley, and Ira B. Nadel. *Gertrude Stein and the Making of Literature.* Boston: Northeastern University Press, 1988.

Perloff, Majorie. "Poetry as Word-System: The Art of Gertrude Stein." In her *The Poetics of Indeterminacy: Rimbaud to Cage.* Princeton, N.J.: Princeton University Press, 1981. Pp. 67–108.

Ruddick, Lisa. " 'Melanctha' and the Psychology of William James." *Modern Fiction Studies* 28, no. 4: 545–556 (Winter 1982–1983).

———. "A Rosy Charm: Gertrude Stein and the Repressed Feminine." In Hoffman. Pp. 225–240.

———. "William James and the Modernism of Gertrude Stein." In *Modernism Reconsidered.* Edited by Robert Kiely and John Hildebidle. Cambridge, Mass.: Harvard University Press, 1983. Pp. 47–63.

Schmitz, Neil. *Of Huck and Alice: Humorous Writing in American Literature.* Minneapolis: University of Minnesota Press, 1983.

Secor, Cynthia. "Gertrude Stein: The Complex Force of Her Femininity." In *Women, the Arts, and the 1920s in Paris and New York.* Edited by Kenneth W. Wheeler and Virginia Lee Lussier. New Brunswick, N.J.: Transaction Books, 1982. Pp. 27–35.

Steiner, Wendy. *Exact Resemblance to Exact Resemblance: The Literary Portraiture of Gertrude Stein.* New Haven, Conn.: Yale University Press, 1978.

Stimpson, Catharine R. "Gertrice/Altrude: Stein, Toklas, and the Paradox of the Happy Marriage." In *Mothering the Mind: Twelve Studies of Writers and Their Silent Partners.* Edited by Ruth Perry and Martine Watson Brownley. New York: Holmes & Meier, 1984. Pp. 122–139.

———. "Gertrude Stein and the Transposition of Gender." In *The Poetics of Gender.* Edited by Nancy K. Miller. New York: Columbia University Press, 1986. Pp. 1–18.

———. "Gertrude Stein: Humanism and Its Freaks." *boundary,* Spring–Fall 1984.

———. "The Mind, the Body, and Gertrude Stein." *Critical Inquiry* 3, no. 3:489–506 (Spring 1977).

Toklas, Alice B. *Staying on Alone: Letters of Alice B. Toklas.* Edited by Edward Burns. New York: Liveright, 1982.

Walker, Jayne L. *The Making of a Modernist: Gertrude Stein from "Three Lives" to "Tender Buttons."* Amherst, Mass.: University of Massachusetts Press, 1984.

Watts, Linda. " 'The Moment of Recognition': A Feminist Approach to Religious and Artistic Creation in the Writings of Gertrude Stein." Ph.D. diss., Yale University, 1989.

Weinstein, Norman. *Gertrude Stein and the Literature of the Modern Consciousness.* New York: Frederick Ungar, 1970.

BIBLIOGRAPHY

Bridgman, Richard. "Key to the *Yale Catalogue,* Part 4." In *Gertrude Stein in Pieces.* New York: Oxford University Press, 1970.

HARRIET SCOTT CHESSMAN

ANNE TYLER

1941–

ANNE TYLER DOES not teach, lecture, or travel on book-promotion tours. In 1977 she told Marguerite Michaels that she neither expected nor desired fame. She has since become a best-selling author, but continues to avoid the notion of a wide readership: "I try to think as little as possible about critical reception, since the only way I can happily write a book is to pretend that no one but me will ever read it."

The books Tyler has written with this strategy have brought her enormous critical acclaim: in 1977, the year her seventh novel, *Earthly Possessions,* was published, she received the American Academy and Institute of Arts and Letters Award in Literature; in 1981 *Morgan's Passing* (1980) was nominated for the National Book Critics Circle Award, and in 1982 *Dinner at the Homesick Restaurant* (1982) was nominated for the Pulitzer Prize. *The Accidental Tourist* (1985) won her the National Book Critics Circle Award for fiction for 1985; four years later the novel was made into an Academy Award–winning film. Her next novel, *Breathing Lessons* (1988), won the Pulitzer Prize.

Tyler does grant interviews, but when given a choice, she would rather answer questions by mail: "I find that letter-answering can be scheduled at two A.M., if that's where my free time falls, while interviews at two A.M. are often difficult to arrange," she told Marguerite Michaels. In Tyler's schedule, her family and her writing have priority. She lives with her husband, Iranian psychiatrist and author Taghi Modarressi, and their children in a Baltimore home that she not only refuses to sell but hates to leave even for shopping excursions. She prefers buying her clothes from mail-order catalogs. Since the births of her daughters Tezh (in 1965) and Mitra (in 1967), Tyler has written her novels between and around her family activities.

Tyler's exclusive involvement with her family has provoked comparisons with her fictional characters. She has repeatedly responded to such critical speculation about the autobiographical in her work by claiming that writing is, for her,

> simply a way of living other lives. . . . Just about everything I've written has been based upon "what if." What if I led such-and-such a life instead of the one I do lead? What if that person I see standing at the bus stop were to go home and find out such-and-such had happened?
>
> (Brown [1983], pp. 10–11)

Her own childhood was peripatetic and unorthodox, offering her little experience of the claustrophobically conventional family traditions she examines so intimately in her fiction. Born in Minneapolis, Minnesota, on 25 October 1941, she spent most of her childhood in the South, where her parents, Lloyd Tyler, a chemist, and his wife, Phyllis Mahon Tyler, moved their family through a series of experimental communes. Tyler observes that this background has made her view "the normal world with a certain amount of distance and surprise, which can sometimes be helpful to a writer." She populates her novels with characters who yearn to escape from their families, a desire that contrasts with her own youthful experiences: "I did spend much of my older childhood and adolescence as a semi-outsider—a Northerner, commune-reared, looking wistfully at large Southern families around me. . . . I never knew anyone who ran away from home."

Tyler did not go far from home until after receiving her B.A. in 1961 from Duke University. She continued her studies in Russian at Columbia University for a year, then returned to work in Duke University's library as the Russian bibliographer from 1962 to 1963. After her marriage in 1963, she moved to Montreal, where she was assistant to the librarian at McGill University's law library from 1964 to 1965.

Tyler had been writing for some years before quitting work to juggle her domestic and literary projects. As an undergraduate she studied with Reynolds Price, who recognized her talent and recommended her to his own literary agent, Diarmuid Russell. Her undergraduate efforts in the short-story genre proved difficult to place with publishers, and her first novel, completed before graduation, was universally rejected and consigned to oblivion. Her first published novel, *If Morning Ever Comes* (1964), nearly met the same fate. She wrote the book to pass the time during six months of unemployment immediately following her marriage. She left the unfinished manuscript on a plane, recovered it only by chance, and disowned it soon after it was published. Tyler finds her first two published novels boring, but both *If Morning Ever Comes* and *The Tin Can Tree* (1965) introduce her readers to themes she has developed throughout her writing career.

Reviews of *If Morning Ever Comes* were laudatory, with qualifications. The novel records one week in the life of Ben Joe Hawkes as he struggles to place himself properly in his family of six women, and finally admits to himself that the "unchanging world of women" would continue to "exist solid and untouched no matter where he was." Julian Gloag's 1964 review noted censoriously that Ben Joe "is hardly better defined at the end than he is at the beginning"; Gloag found Tyler's "niceness of observation" too "absolutely feminine" not to compromise Ben Joe's masculine identity. More recent readers, however, have praised Tyler's egalitarian treatment of her male characters. While her women are frequently eccentric, baffled by adversity, and alarmingly defenseless, both inside and outside the confines of their extended families, her men are perhaps even more vulnerable, sensitive, and perennially confused by life than are the supposedly scatterbrained women they love.

The complex and unfathomed love holding even fractious families together is one of the motifs that run through all of Tyler's novels, including *Breathing Lessons* (1988), which details the events of a single day in the marriage of Ira and Maggie Moran. While driving to the funeral of an old friend, they quarrel; Maggie finally leaves the car and walks away, somewhat giddily wondering whether she is walking into another kind of life, but Ira coaxes her back to the car with surprising ease. At the wake a few hours later, they offend their widowed hostess by spontaneously making love in the master bedroom. Despite the unevenness of their relationship, Ira thinks of his marriage as an institution "steady as a tree; not even he could tell how wide and deep the roots went." At privileged moments, he looks at his troublesome parents and sisters with the same insight:

> He had known then what the true waste was; Lord, yes. It was not his having to support these people but his failure to notice how he loved them. He loved even his worn-down, defeated father, even the memory of his poor mother who had always been so pretty and never realized it because anytime she approached a mirror she had her mouth drawn up lopsided with shyness. But then the feeling had faded (probably the very next instant . . .) and he forgot what he had learned. And no doubt he would forget again. . . .
>
> (p. 175)

All of Tyler's novels involve runaway wives, husbands, fathers, mothers, and children. Although emotional forces motivating her runaways are less clearly defined in her first two novels, variations on Ira's lesson draw all of Tyler's runaways home again, if only briefly. The power of familial affection becomes increasingly convincing in her later works. This conviction grows out of Tyler's own fondness for her characters:

> My people wander around my study until the novel is done. It's one reason I'm very careful not to write about people I don't like. If I find somebody creeping in that I'm not really fond of, I usually take him out. I end a book at the point where I feel that I'm going to know forever what their lives are like. You know what Charlotte [in *Earthly Possessions* (1977)] is doing now. I build a house for them and then I move to the next house.
>
> (Michaels, p. 43)

The stasis Tyler describes here has drawn some criticism from those readers who do not welcome the idea of predictable lives. Millicent Bell describes the communities in Tyler's second novel, *The Tin Can Tree,* as "stagnant": "Life, this young writer seems to be saying, achieves its once-and-for-all shape and then the camera clicks. This view . . . does not make for that sense of development which is the true novel's motive force" But Bell misses one of Tyler's most oft-repeated points: Things do not really change much, in the end. Families usually survive, changed but recognizable, living on through minor quarrels like Maggie and Ira's in *Breathing Lessons,* and through incomprehensible cataclysms, like the death of six-year-old Janie Rose Pike in *The Tin Can Tree.*

In *The Tin Can Tree,* Janie Rose's meaningless death in a tractor accident shocks her family, almost knocking them permanently off the steady-state course Tyler feels she must achieve for her characters before she concludes her novels. Janie Rose's parents cannot move beyond their grief to continue with their lives; they begin to neglect their remaining child, Simon, who must come to terms with the family's loss without his parents' help. While his grieving parents turn increasingly inward, leaving their son suddenly outside the innermost family circle, Simon unsuccessfully promotes the integration of a new family member. Joan, a nurturing, ordering niece who helps reunite the ravaged Pike family, is engaged to James Green, a photographer and part-time worker in the tobacco fields who shares the Pikes' three-family dwelling. James's brother, Ansel, thwarts their marriage, in part by constantly reminding the other characters of Janie Rose's absence. Joan decides to leave; after failing to convince her to stay, Simon leaves as well, but runs only as far away as the next town. When Simon is fetched home, he finds that his absence has jolted his parents into remembering his existence and the need to resume their relationship with him. Fleeing by bus, Joan changes her mind before her absence is noticed and returns in time to join the celebration of Simon's retrieval, but Ansel's equivocal welcome suggests that her future role in the family will remain perpetually marginal. The family seems destined to continue much as it did before Janie Rose's death.

James Green, simultaneously failing to establish a family of his own and to establish himself as a photographer, is one of the many artists and craftsmen who figure in Tyler's works. His being a photographer in *The Tin Can Tree* indicates Tyler's particular concern with the relationship between photographic techniques and writing, an interest that makes Millicent Bell's use of photography metaphors to critique Tyler's fiction especially apt. Tyler's interest in photography grew in part from her enthusiasm for the work of Eudora Welty, an enthusiasm that she shared with Reynolds Price at Duke University and that extends beyond Welty's fiction to the photographic chronicle Welty made of the South during the Depression. Like Welty, Tyler focuses on brief spots of time—a day, a week—that illuminate a whole family history. Her use of flashbacks to enhance her family portraits has become more richly intricate and effective with each work. Her novels end when she has created a perfectly strung necklace of such illuminating moments and fastened the end of her tale to its beginning. Her narratives borrow a detailed precision from her favorite photographers, and her experiments with varying points of view owe as much to cinematography as to Faulkner. Tyler's study is filled with photography books that she keeps "just to sink into. To fill up on when I feel empty." On her wall hangs a picture of her grandfather playing a cello in a barn loft—a photograph that appears unchanged in *Searching for Caleb* (1976).

Tyler describes the composition process in photographic terms: "Sometimes a book will start with a picture that pops into my mind and I ask myself questions about it and if I put all the answers together I've got a novel." This was the case when she began writing *A Slipping-Down Life* (1970), an uncharacteristically bizarre tale. Although Tyler's characters are often odd, they are usually benign—only in *A Slipping-Down Life* does she create a shocking grotesque in the tradition of such Southern writers as Sherwood Anderson and Flannery O'Connor. After reading a newspaper story about a Texas girl who carved the name "Elvis" into the skin of her forehead, Tyler used the mental picture of the Elvis fanatic to create the character Evie Decker. Evie is a passive, overweight wallflower who briefly startles her small town by inscribing the name of Drumstrings Casey, a local musician, across her forehead with nail scissors—magnifying the absurdity of her act by forgetting to write backward as she looks at her mirror reflection. She is pleased with her self-willed disfigurement, pleased to have done something to change her too-sensible life, no matter what the consequences: "Impulse is the clue. . . . Taking something into my own hands for once. . . . If I had started acting like this a long time ago my whole life might've been different." But her life is not changed. Her friends' shocked response is short-lived, as is her marriage to Casey, and she ends as she began, leading a colorless life in her father's house, no longer noticing the inscription when she faces her mirror.

Tyler often dwells upon the problem of self-determination. Her characters attempt to define themselves and direct their own destinies either by obsessively controlling their immediate material environment or by radically rejecting such compulsions in their parents. In *The Clock Winder* (1972), Elizabeth Abbott worries that she cannot escape repetitions of the past, that "life might be . . . a cycle of seasons, with childhood recurring over and over like that cold rainy period in February." Attempting to step out of that cycle, she becomes (like several other Tyler characters) a handyman, hiring herself out to a wonderfully incompetent widow, Mrs. Emerson, who cannot properly look after the collection of clocks bequeathed her by her husband. Mrs. Emerson hires Elizabeth to wind the clocks, and help run the household; Elizabeth is soon indispensable to the entire Emerson family. Unable to disentangle herself from Mrs. Emerson's two smitten sons, she runs away to become a companion to an elderly man, but the Emersons soon woo her back. She has escaped her own family only to find herself recruited into a new one, leaving one unwilled fate only to encounter another. The Abbott and Emerson families function in similarly inexplicable, inexorable ways, although at different social levels; Elizabeth, finally married to an Emerson and the mother of Emerson children, has merely continued the family cycles she sought to escape.

As an organizing, controlling repair person who succeeds in governing only small-scale, concrete situations, Elizabeth anticipates the characters Macon and Rose in *The Accidental Tourist*. Macon is an author-*cum*-amateur-handyman who recommends plumbing repair as the ultimate demonstration of manly competence, and writes books instructing businessmen on efficient, orderly travel arrangements. He also organizes his wife's daily life for her, until she surprises him by asking for a divorce—a request he finds he cannot argue away with logically ordered reason. His sister Rose repairs plumbing for the neighbors on her street; she also alphabetizes all the groceries in her cupboard. But she fails to order her life in relation to the larger world. When she turns from her family to outsiders, she has difficulty forming any human connections strong enough to save her from spinsterhood.

Tyler characters who cannot control their own lives often become pseudo playwrights and stage managers, attempting to direct the lives of others. In *Dinner at the Homesick Restaurant* (1982), Ezra Tull is one of Tyler's most poignantly failed scenarists. To set the stage for a family dinner, he reorganizes the spaces of a frigidly formal restaurant, transforming it into a welcoming haven of familial warmth. Attempting to open communications between his mother and her children, and to create an atmosphere in which the family will, for once, see the dinner through to its end, Ezra impulsively demolishes the wall between the kitchen and dining room. He succeeds only in inadvertently exposing the plumbing pipes and electrical wires behind the wall—an image Tyler uses variously to suggest both lines of communication and claustrophobic enclosure. Tyler's stage managers are all domestic artists of sorts, and each discovers that families resist the fiat of artistic design, that human lives move along stubbornly illogical and disorderly paths.

Tyler's most detailed portrait of the artist at work appears in *Celestial Navigation* (1974), a work she admits is more closely autobiographical than her other novels. Jeremy Pauling is a middle-aged collage artist whose mother's pampering has aggravated his agoraphobia into a dissociative pathology more like autism. After his mother's death, he must descend from the upper floors of her Baltimore boarding house and remember how to engage with other human beings. In the novel's early scenes he never speaks for himself; the various female relatives who have cared for him (particularly his chillingly efficient older sister, Amanda) speak for him, defining him as authors define their fictional characters.

In Jeremy's clumsy courtship of Mary Tell, one of the boarders, he makes his first attempts to take independent action, to define his own future. When he braves the outside world for a terrifying walk with Mary to a store two blocks away, the outing seems to him equivalent to "slaying dragons"; he collapses, nauseated, outside the store and proposes to her from his seated position on the sidewalk. Mary eventually accepts, although the two will wait ten years for her divorce to become final, living together in the boarding house and producing five children in the meantime. Mary is another of Tyler's runaway wives.

Despite his experience as pseudo husband and father, Jeremy remains distanced from the world outside, clinging instead to his boarding house as an island of refuge. He is disoriented in space outdoors, and disoriented in time indoors. As one of his friends observes, Jeremy moves through his indistinct days and nights guided only by celestial navigation, rather than by a plan of his own devising. His organizational faculties are quite exhausted by his artistic endeavors; the rest of his life is shaped by outside influences, or their absence. When his long-awaited wedding day arrives, Jeremy is caught up in his art. In the absence of a reminder, he forgets the time of the ceremony, and Mary leaves him.

Whether or not Tyler intended the comparison, *Celestial Navigation* comprises an updated, reorganized rendition of Kate Chopin's *The Awakening*. Mary combines the strongest qualities of Chopin's domestic goddess Adèle Ratignolle and the rebellious Edna Pontellier. Like Adele, she revels in maternity: "Motherhood is what I was made for, and pregnancy is my natural state." She flourishes in the society of other women, having lived "in a world made up of women. My mother and Guy's, the neighbor women who gave me their old baby furniture and their bits of advice—women formed a circle that I sank into." But, like Edna Pontellier, Mary finds men problematic, and the women's circle she idealizes acquires a defiant misanthropy when men have disappointed her: "Women should never leave any vacant spots for the men to fill; they should form an unbroken circle on their own and enclose each child within it." Abandoning Jeremy to hermetic reclusion in his boarding-house "island," she takes their children and, again like Edna Pontellier, escapes to the shore, where she finds refuge in a shack near a boatyard. Jeremy's attempts to pull the family back together fail. Tyler leaves him alone with his art in his decaying boarding house, where his collages have acquired a new, sculptural dimension but his daily activities closely resemble the life he led before Mary's arrival. While Mary seems to fuse Edna Pontellier and Adèle Ratignolle, Jeremy finally resembles, oddly, Chopin's Madame Reisz, the spinsterish pianist who cannot combine art and marriage.

Tyler has admitted to identifying with Jeremy, whose creation prompted her to examine her own "tendency to turn more and more inward." She also has echoed Jeremy's fantasies of impulsiveness. Jeremy dreams of suddenly escaping his life, of driving forever and possibly settling in "a small, bare, whitewashed cubicle possibly in a desert" where he would be completely alone and his art would be very different. Tyler says:

> Living alone is the start of one of my favorite fantasies. But the end of it is when I realize that, having got everything arranged exactly to my liking and all distraction dispensed with, I would probably look around me and ask, "Why was it I imagined I wanted this?"
>
> (Brown [1983], p. 13)

Tyler and Jeremy also have in common a technique of artfully layering and overlapping colorful bits and pieces to bring order to a chaos of disparate details and images—whereas Jeremy collects collage pieces, Tyler collects unrelated details of character or action that she preserves on index cards:

> It seems to me that very often the way I begin a novel is that I have these index cards—say a hundred. They are things that at one time or another I thought I would like to explore, maybe a conversation I've overheard on a bus that I wondered where it was going or what did it really mean. At every fifth card or so a little click will go in my mind and I think "boy that would be fun" and I start to expand on it and then I set the card aside. At the end I have maybe 10 cards, and they are such disparate things that the problem is how on earth am I going to get them all into one framework? I have to think a month before I can figure it out.
>
> (Michaels, pp. 42–43)

Just as Tyler broods over her index cards and arranges her characters' futures with them, so Justine Peck in *Searching for Caleb* (1976) broods over the cards she uses for telling fortunes, worrying that she, too, is arranging the futures of those who consult her. Her regular customers trust her talent, following her from town to town as she follows her husband, Duncan, a wandering jack-of-all-trades and inventor.

Duncan is Justine's cousin as well as her husband, and their marriage distressed the stable, predictable, primordially bourgeois Peck family. The Pecks have been immovably fixed in Baltimore for generations, the men succeeding each other in the family business and the women running perfectly ordered households. Duncan's professional instability and Justine's haphazard domestic habits defy almost all of the Peck family traditions. With each move, they discard more of the home furnishings foisted upon them when they married. Duncan delights in new places, new projects; Justine only gradually learns to share his enthusiasm:

> Sometimes he remembered that she had not always been this way, though he couldn't put his finger on just when she had changed. Then he wondered if she only *pretended* to be happy, for his sake. Or if she were deliberately cutting across her own grain, like an acrophobe who takes up sky diving.
>
> (p. 147)

But "her own grain," the Peck genetic code, is not purely conventional. Two older Pecks, her grandmother Margaret and later her uncle Caleb, began an alternative Peck tradition of forward flight from the family mansion. Justine's hybrid heritage painfully conjoins a longing for the stability of her childhood with a need to escape from that stability. She spends much of the novel helping her grandfather look for his brother Caleb. In their retracing of Caleb's steps, Tyler has metaphorically inscribed a search for freedom, paradoxically qualified by their efforts to return Caleb to the family confines. Like other Tyler characters, Justine, her grandfather, and her uncle are homesick for an intolerable home.

In her depiction of travelers Tyler brilliantly illustrates this tension between her characters' contrary urges toward flight and retreat. Like Justine and Duncan, like the reluctant adventurer Macon in *The Accidental Tourist,* many of Tyler's characters manage to travel widely without ever entirely leaving home. Motoring excursions combine confinement and movement; Tyler's car interiors are like drawing rooms on wheels, and her car trips occasion dramatic dialogues and intensifications of long-brewing disputes, followed by crises, resolutions, and, usually, return trips to a remarkably unchanged homelife.

Tyler treats this topic most exhaustively in *Earthly Possessions* (1977). Charlotte Emory, middle-aged, frustrated, and determined to run away from her home in Clarion, Maryland, is taken hostage by Jake Simms, a hoodlum bungling his first bank robbery. The novel follows Jake and Charlotte on an uneasy car trip to Florida. On the way, the unlikely pair reveal unexpected common traits, until they seem to form an ad hoc family unit: like abused siblings, both are emotionally handicapped, claustrophobic, and fearful of commitment. Both speak of being "locked" into personae others have created for them. But Charlotte gains an unprecedented perspective on her life in Clarion while viewing it from several states away. When she returns home unharmed, her husband suggests that they take a trip together. Charlotte responds: "We have been traveling for years, traveled all our lives, we are traveling still. We couldn't stay in one place if we tried."

Earthly Possessions was not as well received by the critics as Tyler's other books, perhaps because its sense of despair overwhelms the humor and irony of the fast-moving narrative. Tyler thinks of it as "the work of somebody entering middle age, beginning to notice how the bags and baggage of the past are weighing her down, and how much she values them." Like her characters, Tyler chafes against ties to a past she does not wish to discard.

If we accept Tyler's claim that she writes "simply as a way of living other lives" and not as self-portraiture, we must, paradoxically, find another portrait of the author in the protagonist of *Morgan's Passing* (1980). Morgan Gower is a middle-aged hardware store manager, professionally allied with Tyler's plumbers and handymen—characters driven to interrupt, repair, and reform other people's lives. He is a dreamy eccentric who goes beyond imagining lives to realize his dreams as an imposter dressed in various guises and traveling under fictional identities: he becomes, among other things, a street priest, a French immigrant, a doctor, and, significantly, an artist. Like Jeremy Pauling in *Celestial Navigation,* Morgan is a reflection of his maker. Tyler remarks that Morgan's situation "probably is not unrelated to being a writer: the inveterate imposter, who is unable to stop himself from stepping into other people's worlds."

As the novel opens, Morgan has just convinced a young couple, Leon and Emily Meredith, that he is a doctor and can help them as they rush to the hospital for the birth of their first child. Failing to arrive there in time, he delivers the child himself. After playing such an important part in others' lives, he has difficulty returning to his own. He shadows the couple for several years and eventually insinuates himself into their family, abandoning his wife to replace Leon in Emily's bed. When Emily becomes pregnant, he welcomes his new responsibilities:

> An assignment had been given him. Someone's life, a small set of lives, had been placed in the palm of his hand. Maybe he would never have any more purpose than this: to accept the assignment gracefully, lovingly, and do the best he could with it.
>
> (p. 246)

Eventually, having appropriated Leon's name as well as his wife, Morgan also appropriates his profession: he becomes a puppeteer, working with Emily at local carnivals and children's parties. Once he learns to dramatize his fantasies in the puppet theater, where a small set of *fictional* lives rests in the palm of the puppeteer's hand, he no longer feels the need to adopt new identities. After all his experiments with exotic personae, Morgan comes to admire Emily's ability to wear the same hairstyle and clothes year after year. He concludes "that there is some virtue in the trivial, the commonplace, where the ordinary triumphs." When the ordinary has triumphed in Morgan's life and his future becomes predictably happy, Tyler concludes her novel.

Tyler paints a darker picture of family life in *Dinner at the Homesick Restaurant*, a best-seller in 1982 and 1983 that some critics have read as Tyler's version of William Faulkner's *As I Lay Dying*. This tightly constructed novel, more disturbing than most of Tyler's work, begins with Pearl Tull on her deathbed and concludes with her wake. In between, Tyler reviews Pearl's life as an insecure single parent abandoned by her traveling-salesman husband, Beck Tull. She manages her home quite well without him (she is much handier with household repairs than Beck ever was) but struggles to pay the rent, and the financial strain takes its toll, indirectly, on her children. Pearl occasionally succumbs to feelings of helplessness, thinking, "How scary to have everyone depend on me." Her children are the center of her life, but her love for them does not prevent her from verbally abusing them in sudden outbursts of hysterical cruelty.

As adults, her children cannot avoid repeating their parents' mistakes. Cody, the elder son, is most visibly scarred by his father's absence and his mother's abuse. Although he travels as a businessman, like his father, Cody does not leave his family alone as his father did. His wife and son accompany him, setting up temporary households wherever he needs them. By insisting on a movable family, Cody guarantees that his wife and son will never miss him as he missed his own father, but he denies them the opportunity to establish a permanent home where they might settle into a community among friends and neighbors. He is rather daunting company for them, and he is all the company they have. Authoritarian elements in his personality are compounded by a temper that matches his mother's: in a fit of jealousy, screaming within his son's hearing, Cody accuses his wife of adultery, naming his own brother as her lover and his own son as the offspring of their imagined illicit union.

This pattern of impassioned, uncontrolled violence is recapitulated when Cody's sister, Jenny, overworked as a divorced mother attending medical school, abuses her own daughter and then realizes that "certain things were doomed to continue, generation after generation." To avoid perpetuating her mother's violence, she withholds some essential part of herself from her children. When she remarries, her stepchildren know her as gay, tolerant, funny, and not entirely present. She must absent herself, just as her father did: "She was learning how to make it through life on a slant. She was trying to lose her intensity."

Jenny succeeds to the extent that her stepchildren never see any traces of sorrow or anger in her. One of her stepsons has difficulty recognizing her in a childhood photo: "Why, it's like a . . . concentration camp person, a victim,

Anne Frank! It's terrible! It's so sad!" While critics have often commented on Tyler's refusal to address political issues in her work, she is clearly addressing them here. The family dynamics she describes in *Dinner at the Homesick Restaurant* are those of fascism, scaled down to domestic drama.

Ezra, Pearl's favorite child, remembers his mother as only rarely a termagant, but always as a "non-feeder." Jenny compensates for her mother's failure to nurture her children by becoming a pediatrician; Ezra similarly chooses a career in a reactionary response to his childhood memories: he becomes a restaurateur. He is a mediator in his family, determined to "fix" their splintered relationships just as Pearl used to fix broken windows and stairs in their house. His ambitions in this undertaking diminish over the years to a single, eternally frustrated desire: he wants his family to complete a meal in his restaurant without quarreling. Pearl dies before Ezra manages to stage this event for her, but the novel ends with the promise of a successful family dinner that includes his prodigal father, who has returned for Pearl's funeral.

Having examined the violence latent within the family, in *Dinner at the Homesick Restaurant,* Tyler proceeded to study the demise of a family strained by its encounter with evil in the outside world in *The Accidental Tourist.* She begins her story after Sarah and Macon Leary's only son, Ethan, has died in a holdup at a fast-food restaurant. Macon is compulsively systematic; during his first year of grieving he numbly continues his rituals of efficiency, waiting for his pain to lift. After his wife's unexpected departure, and a household accident that leaves his leg in a cast, Macon rejoins his two divorced brothers and his unmarried sister, Rose, at home, where he can "settle down safe among the people he'd started out with." The neurotically reclusive Learys form a peculiarly idiosyncratic but unified middle-aged group whose behavior reinforces their past and dictates their future. Their rejection of the world outside their insular hermitage is not quite complete. They refuse to answer the phone but do not have it disconnected, and while it rings, they seem to enjoy guessing who might be silly enough to try to call them. They tend to get lost on even the shortest errands, but they do not stop going outside altogether, as Jeremy did in *Celestial Navigation.*

This incomplete isolation allows Macon to embark on a new relationship with Muriel Pritchett, a dog trainer whose eccentricities equal those of the Learys in degree, if not in kind. She not only believes wholeheartedly in using the telephone, but believes in using it to chat about highly personal matters with perfect strangers. She greets life with the same enthusiasm that the Learys turn to shutting the world out.

Still unprepared to commit himself to Muriel, Macon returns to his wife after a year's separation. But, in a plot turn uncharacteristic of Tyler, their marriage has not survived the loss of their son. Both are changed: Sarah has learned to live without Macon's organizational guidance, and Macon has learned the limits of his ability to shape his own life, let alone anyone else's. He realizes that no matter how frightening an unscripted, uncontrolled life may be, it is the only kind of life available. He returns to Muriel, who offers him an opportunity to escape the confines of his self-deluding, phobic family.

In *Breathing Lessons,* (1988), Maggie Moran shares Muriel's outgoing exuberance. Her generosity extends her family to include friends and chance acquaintances. But, as she sometimes realizes, all the warmth and affection she offers to anyone entering her company is really offered to her husband. When Maggie falls in love with strays and strangers, she is falling in love with whatever there is in them that reminds her of Ira Moran:

> Why, Mr. Gabriel was just another Ira, was all. He had Ira's craggy face and Ira's dignity, his aloofness, that could still to this day exert a phys-

> ical pull on her. He was even supporting that unmarried sister, she would bet, just as Ira supported *his* sisters and his deadbeat father: a sign of a noble nature, some might say. All Mr. Gabriel was, in fact, was Maggie's attempt to find an earlier version of Ira. She'd wanted the version she had known at the start of their marriage, before she'd begun disappointing him.
>
> (pp. 45–46)

She has disappointed him, she thinks, by aging into a clownish maladroit:

> Compared to Ira she talked too much and laughed too much and cried too much. Even ate too much! Drank too much! Behaved so sloppily and mawkishly!
>
> She'd been so intent on not turning into mother, she had gone and turned into her father.
>
> (p. 78)

All the characters in *Breathing Lessons,* like those in Tyler's earlier novels, anxiously rebel against parental influence. Maggie's daughter, Daisy, single-mindedly, remorselessly heading for an Ivy League college, rejects her mother's bourgeois tastes. Maggie remembers her daughter's response to a tuna casserole Maggie offered at supper:

> Daisy just sat there and studied me for the longest time, . . . with this kind of . . . fascinated expression on her face, and then she said, "Mom? Was there a certain conscious point in your life when you decided to settle for being ordinary?"
>
> (p. 30)

But Ira does not think Maggie is either ordinary or disappointing. After many years of marriage, he looks back on her arrival in his life as "a wonderful gift." He is jealous of the expense of spirit Maggie offers to strangers, resentful even of their own children:

> For weren't Jesse and Daisy also outsiders—interrupting their most private moments, wedging between the two of them? (Hard to believe that some people had children to hold a marriage *together.*)
>
> (p. 148)

In *Breathing Lessons,* Tyler shows us the extraordinary interior of an apparently ordinary marriage, one that has endured and will continue, seemingly, beyond the end of the novel. The Morans are flawed: they are sometimes "lonely and tired and lacking in hope." Ira has acknowledged that "his son had not turned out well and his daughter didn't think much of him, and he still couldn't figure out where he had gone wrong." He is appalled by the finality of his life, and by Maggie's seemingly careless tendency to live her life as if it were a rehearsal for some real life to be lived at a later date. And Maggie is dismayed by her vision of endless rehearsals of a repeated plot. After failing to reunite her son and his ex-wife, she has "a sudden view of her life as circular. It forever repeated itself, and it was entirely lacking in hope." Despite moments of despair, however, Maggie and Ira always restore each other, drawing strength and hope from their flawed, perhaps too-exclusive union. In the novel's last lines, Maggie watches Ira concentrating on a card game: "She felt a little stir of something like a flush, a sort of inner buoyancy, and she lifted her face to kiss the warm blade of his cheekbone." Tyler can end the Morans' story at this point, because her readers can now "know forever what their lives are like."

Questioned about literary models, Tyler lists Gabriel García Márquez, Joyce Carol Oates, and Eudora Welty among her favorite authors. This unlikely grouping reflects the difficulty of placing Tyler in any particular literary tradition. She is not precisely a feminist, not overtly political, and despite setting all her novels in Baltimore, she resists categorization as a regional writer. Sarah English has remarked on this resistance:

> Like the great Southern writers, [Tyler] is centrally occupied with the survival of the past in the present, but for her the past is not moonlight-and-magnolias romance or miscegenation or incest or racism or violence (black people play mostly peripheral roles in her fiction). The past in her work is never antebellum; the furthest back she has gone, in *Searching for Caleb,* is Baltimore in the 1880s. Instead, in Tyler's work the

past is one's mother, grandmother, and aunts. . . .

(English, p. 187)

Where other Southern writers, such as Faulkner or Katherine Anne Porter, examine the larger cultural history of the South, or focus, like Flannery O'Connor, on the interior landscape of the Southern psyche, Tyler has chosen the American family as her region, and her comments on other aspects of American life appear only in the context of the family drama. Her work can be compared with Kate Chopin's feminist writings or the grotesqueries and tragicomedies of the Southern Renaissance, but only in its many differences as well as its similarities. She considers topics that have concerned other twentieth-century writers, even such disparate authors as Vladimir Nabokov (who romanticizes plumbing in *Ada*) and Milan Kundera (who worries about unrehearsed lives in *The Unbearable Lightness of Being*). But Tyler does not associate closely with other writers, explaining in one interview that there are not many writers living in her immediate neighborhood. Although she has written many book reviews, she tends to ignore the advice of her own reviewers. While absorbing influences from various literary schools, she subscribes to none, and continues to chart her own literary course.

Selected Bibliography

PRIMARY WORKS

NOVELS

If Morning Ever Comes. New York: Knopf, 1964.
The Tin Can Tree. New York: Knopf, 1965.
A Slipping-Down Life. New York: Knopf, 1970.
The Clock Winder. New York: Knopf, 1972.
Celestial Navigation. New York: Knopf, 1974.
Searching for Caleb. New York: Knopf, 1976.
Earthly Possessions. New York: Knopf, 1977.
Morgan's Passing. New York: Knopf, 1980.
Dinner at the Homesick Restaurant. New York: Knopf, 1982.
The Accidental Tourist. New York: Knopf, 1985.
Breathing Lessons. New York: Knopf, 1988.

ARTICLES

"Youth Talks About Youth: 'Will This Seem Ridiculous?' " *Vogue,* 1 February 1965, pp. 85, 206.
"Because I Want More Than One Life." *Washington Post,* 15 August 1976, Sect. G, pp. 1, 7.
"Trouble in the Boys' Club: The Trials of Marvin Mandel." *New Republic,* 30 July 1977, pp. 16–19.
"Chocolates in the Afternoon and Other Temptations of a Novelist." *Washington Post Book World,* 4 December 1977, Sect. E, p. 3.
"Writers' Writers: Gabriel Garcia Marquez." *New York Times Book Review,* 4 December 1977, p. 70.
"My Summer." *New York Times Book Review,* 4 June 1978, pp. 35–36.
Untitled article on the author's favorite books of 1978, *Washington Post Book World,* 3 December 1978, Sect. E, pp. 1, 4.
"Please Don't Call It Persia." *New York Times Book Review,* 18 February 1979, pp. 3, 34–36.
"Still Just Writing." In *The Writer on Her Work: Contemporary Women Writers Reflect on Their Art and Situation.* Edited by Janet Sternburg. New York: Norton, 1980. Pp. 3–16.
"A Visit with Eudora Welty." *New York Times Book Review,* 2 November 1980, pp. 33–34.
"Symposium: Books That Gave Me Pleasure." *New York Times Book Review,* 5 December 1982, p. 9.
"Why I Still Treasure 'The Little House.' " *New York Times Book Review,* 9 November 1986, p. 56.
"Classics? Bah, Humbug: A Symposium." *New York Times Book Review,* 4 December 1988, p. 51.

SECONDARY WORKS

BIOGRAPHICAL AND CRITICAL STUDIES

Bell, Millicent. "*Tobacco Road* Updated." *New York Times Book Review,* 21 November 1965, p. 77.
Betts, Doris. "The Fiction of Anne Tyler." *Southern Quarterly* 21, no. 4:23–37 (Summer 1983). Reprinted in *Women Writers of the Contemporary South.* Edited by Peggy Whitman Prenshaw. Jackson: University Press of Mississippi, 1984. Pp. 23–37.
Binding, Paul. "Anne Tyler." In his *Separate Country: A Literary Journey Through the American South.* New York and London: Paddington Press, 1979. Pp.

198–209. 2nd ed. Jackson: University Press of Mississippi, 1988. Pp. 171–181.

Brock, Dorothy Faye Sala. "Anne Tyler's Treatment of Managing Women." Ph.D. diss., North Texas State University, 1985.

Brooks, Mary Ellen. "Anne Tyler." In *Dictionary of Literary Biography*. Vol. 6. Edited by James E. Kibler, Jr. Detroit: Gale Research, 1980. Pp. 336–344.

Brown, Laurie. "Interviews with Seven Contemporary Writers." *Southern Quarterly* 21, no. 4:3–22 (Summer 1983). Reprinted in *Women Writers of the Contemporary South*. Edited by Peggy Whitman Prenshaw. Jackson: University Press of Mississippi, 1984. Pp. 3–22.

Dunstan, Angus Michael. "The Missing Guest: Dinner Parties in British and American Literature." Ph.D. diss,. University of California, Santa Barbara, 1986.

Elkins, Mary J. "*Dinner at the Homesick Restaurant:* Anne Tyler and the Faulkner Connection." *Atlantis* 10, no. 2:93–105 (Spring 1985).

English, Sarah. "Anne Tyler" and "An Interview with Anne Taylor." In *Dictionary of Literary Biography Yearbook, 1982*. Edited by Richard Ziegfeld. Detroit: Gale Research, 1983. Pp. 187–193 and 193–194, respectively.

Gibson, Mary Ellis. "Family as Fate: The Novels of Anne Tyler." *Southern Literary Journal* 15, no. 3:47–58 (Fall 1983).

Gloag, Julian. "Home Was Full of Women." *Saturday Review*, 26 December 1964, pp. 37–38. Review of *If Morning Ever Comes*.

Gullette, Margaret Morganroth. "The Tears (and Joys) Are in the Things: Adulthood in Anne Tyler's Novels." *New England Review and Bread Loaf Quarterly* 7, no. 3:323–334 (Spring 1985).

Jones, Anne G. "Home at Last, and Homesick Again: The Ten Novels of Anne Tyler." *Hollins Critic* 23, no. 2:1–14 (April 1986).

Lamb, Wendy. "An Interview with Anne Tyler." *Iowa Journal of Literary Studies* 3, no. 1–2:59–64 (1981).

Michaels, Marguerite. "Anne Tyler, Writer 8:50 to 3:30." *New York Times Book Review*, 8 May 1977, pp. 13, 42–43.

Nesanovich, Stella Ann. "The Individual in the Family: A Critical Introduction to the Novels of Anne Tyler." Ph.D. diss., Louisiana State University, 1979.

Robertson, Mary F. "Anne Tyler: Medusa Points and Contact Points." In *Contemporary American Women Writers: Narrative Strategies*. Edited by Catherine Rainwater and William J. Scheick. Lexington: University Press of Kentucky, 1985. Pp. 119–142.

Shelton, Frank W. "The Necessary Balance: Distance and Sympathy in the Novels of Anne Tyler." *Southern Review* 20, no. 4:851–860 (Autumn 1984).

Voelker, Joseph. *Art and the Accidental in Anne Tyler*. Columbia: University of Missouri Press, 1989.

BIBLIOGRAPHIES

Gardiner, Elaine, and Catherine Rainwater. "Bibliography of Writings by Anne Tyler." In *Contemporary American Women Writers: Narrative Strategies*. Edited by Catherine Rainwater and William J. Scheick. Lexington: University Press of Kentucky, 1985. Pp. 142–152.

Nesanovich, Stella Ann. "An Anne Tyler Checklist, 1959–1980." *Bulletin of Bibliography* 38, no. 2:53–64 (April–June 1981).

Zahlan, Anne R. "Anne Tyler (1941–)." In *Fifty Southern Writers After 1900: A Bio-Bibliographical Sourcebook*. Edited by Joseph M. Flora and Robert A. Bain. Westport, Conn.: Greenwood Press, 1987. Pp. 492–504.

GWEN CRANE

ALICE WALKER

1944–

THE THEMATIC POWER and stylistic versatility of Alice Walker's rather voluminous canon—four novels, two collections of short stories, two volumes of prose, five books of poetry, and numerous essays—is indeed impressive. So widely discussed, anthologized, and translated are her works that both they and she seem omnipresent. Her characters, dramatic situations, and generic forms in the novels, for example, engage numerous narrative strategies: social realism, gothic realism, folk epistolary, and mythical history. Yet these novels, like all of Walker's works, are related by their anecdotal format and their depiction of what Walker insists is a fundamental human responsibility: to improve the quality of one's relationships with other people and ultimately with all life on the planet.

In an early interview Walker suggests that the main character in her first novel, *The Third Life of Grange Copeland* (1970), is an ideal fulfillment of this responsibility. "To him," she explains, "the greatest value a person can attain is full humanity, which is a state of oneness with all things." Throughout her writing Walker repeatedly relates art to what she considers the all-important process of self-improvement. In fact, the most striking and consistent feature of her work is that it manifests a rigorous critical attitude about her own life. Although the allusive presence of self-reflection in much of her work may invite interpretations, posing as literary scholarship, of the writer's personality, readers should be wary: such works are often imaginative reconstructions of experience, not factual, personal histories.

Born on 9 February 1944 to Willie Lee Walker, a sharecropper, and Minnie Lou Grant Walker, Alice Walker grew up in rural Eatonton, Georgia, the youngest of eight children. She attended segregated public schools and, like many of her characters, encountered rundown conditions and worn surplus textbooks. Walker's desire to inscribe her own presence among generations of those whom she esteems as just plain black folks living in a world unjustly dominated by many racist white people no doubt helped to propel the very shy and solitary Walker through high school, where she distinguished herself by winning scholarships to Spelman College (1961) and to Sarah Lawrence (1963).

The summer before her graduation in 1965 from Sarah Lawrence, Walker traveled to Africa, and "returned to school healthy and brown, and loaded down with sculptures and orange fabric—and pregnant." She recalls the suicidal despair she experienced while seeking an illegal abortion. During her week of recuperation after the abortion, she wrote almost all the poems that appear in her first book, *Once* (1968). Her candid revelation of this intensely private, personal, and painful experience as the genesis of that first book is an early indication of her courageous commitment to critical self-revelation in her work. In *Once* Walker also establishes concise, anecdotal free verse as her poetic style, as the poem "The Democratic Order: Such Things in Twenty Years I Understood" illustrates:

> My father
> (back blistered)
> beat me
> because I
> could not
> stop crying.
> He'd had
> enough "fuss"
> he said
> for one damn
> voting day.

In the late 1960s Walker returned to Georgia to work with the voter registration drive of the civil rights movement, a movement that had incited white retaliation—bombings, murders, and other forms of terrorism—especially during the 1960s. By the time of her active involvement, racial discrimination was under legal assault: schools were being desegregated, housing discrimination was declared illegal, public accommodations were to become available to all, irrespective of race. Walker's experiences during this period inform much of her subsequent work.

In 1967 Walker married Melvyn Leventhal, a white civil rights lawyer; they moved to Jackson, Mississippi, where she was a teacher and writer-in-residence at Jackson State College and Tougaloo College during the academic years 1968–1969 and 1970–1971, respectively. Her only child, Rebecca, was born in 1969, three days after she had finished *The Third Life of Grange Copeland*. By that time, as Walker emphatically affirms in "One Child of One's Own," she was undoubtedly a writer:

> Write I did, night and day, *something*, and it was not even a choice. . . . When I didn't write I thought of making bombs and throwing them. Of shooting racists. Of doing away—as painlessly and neatly as possible . . . with myself. Writing saved me from the sin and *inconvenience* of violence.
>
> (*In Search of Our Mothers' Gardens*, p. 369)

In 1977 Walker moved to San Francisco, after she and her husband divorced. Walker continues to reside in Northern California, with her companion of ten years, Robert Allen.

Walker's growing reputation as a writer brought a grant from the National Endowment for the Arts (1969), a Radcliffe Institute Fellowship (1971–1973), the Rosenthal Foundation Award (1974), presented annually by the American Academy and Institute of Arts and Letters, and a Guggenheim Fellowship (1977).

When Walker's *The Third Life of Grange Copeland* appeared in 1970, it joined Maya Angelou's *I Know Why the Caged Bird Sings*, Paule Marshall's *The Chosen Place, the Timeless People*, Louise Meriwether's *Daddy Was a Numbers Runner*, and Toni Morrison's *The Bluest Eye*, all of which dramatize the consequences of race and gender in the lives of black girls and women. Part of what scholars have called the Second Black Renaissance, these works are only a very small sample of the novels written by black women during that decade; the production of black women is considerable in the other genres as well.

Rendered in an indelible social realism as vivid as the red Georgia clay, *The Third Life of Grange Copeland* dramatizes the tragic consequences of a distinct form of racial oppression—sharecropping. Sullen reserve, brooding silence, and violent quarrels dominate the lives of Grange Copeland, his wife, Margaret, and their son, Brownfield. Seeking relief, Grange abandons his family; Margaret eventually commits suicide, leaving Brownfield to construct a life based on impoverished self-esteem. Brownfield marries an ambitious young schoolteacher, Mem, in the hope that he can chart a new future for himself. When Grange returns, he finds that poverty, racism, and hopelessness have destroyed Brownfield's humanity. Of Brownfield's three daughters only the youngest, Ruth, is saved from a life of degradation. Grange rescues her and carefully maps out a way for her to become a woman with a productive future.

At one point in the story Brownfield tells Mem that "[he] ought to make [her] call [him] Mister. . . . A woman as black and ugly as [Mem] ought to call a man Mister." He repeatedly tells Mem that she is black and ugly, as if physical appearance makes her (and later Celie) deserving of abusive treatment. Brownfield's desire to assert male prerogative with the appellation "Mister" foreshadows Celie's acceptance (in *The Color Purple*) of her menial role, evident by her inability to refer to her cruel and dominating husband by his given name; she calls him "Mister." In the racial context of slavery, "Master" would have been the prescribed title. Brownfield's appropriation of "Mister" in an intraracial context underscores the fact that Mem and later Celie find their lives circumscribed by sexist oppression as virulent as slavery.

The novel utilizes the conventions of literary realism to depict the material and emotional conditions of the Copelands' lives. Walker has us witness the impact of poverty on their minds and bodies, hear them express their frustrations, and share their exhaustion from hard physical labor that offers virtually no reward. Although Walker's narrative strategies here dramatize how extreme despair erupts into domestic violence, the lives of her characters are not determined entirely by social and economic conditions; her characters have the fundamental human responsibility of improving themselves and their relationships—they have the ability to change, and change for the better.

Walker consciously began searching for black female artistic models in the early 1970s, developing a course, which she taught at Wellesley College in 1972–1973, devoted specifically to such black women writers as Jessie Fauset, Nella Larsen, Ann Petry, Paule Marshall, Gwendolyn Brooks, Phillis Wheatley, and Zora Neale Hurston. Walker's particular admiration for Hurston's life and work, and especially *Their Eyes Were Watching God* (1937), engendered her long-term commitment to restoring Hurston's work to literary prominence. She edited a collection of Hurston's works, *I Love Myself When I Am Laughing . . . and Then Again When I Am Looking Mean and Impressive* (1979), and on one dramatic occasion passed herself off as Hurston's illegitimate niece in order to facilitate the marking of Hurston's grave in Eatonville, Florida (her birthplace), with a headstone in 1973. The importance of Hurston's life and work to Walker's writing has prompted many literary scholars to trace Hurston's continued influence on Walker's writing as well as to explore issues of influence in the works of many other black writers. Walker's personal recovery of Hurston and of other late-nineteenth- and early-twentieth-century black women writers—along with the growing literary presence of such contemporary writers and critics as Toni Morrison, Paule Marshall, Toni Cade Bambara, Maya Angelou, and others—no doubt significantly contributed to the academic institutionalization of the culture of African American women.

During the women's movement of the early 1970s, which had awakened the public to sexism and moved that word into popular currency, Walker began to grapple with reflecting that sexism in her work. Her collection of short stories *In Love and Trouble* (1973), as the title suggests, depicts a series of black women largely involved in destructive relationships with men, made more emphatic by Walker's experimentation with narrative perspectives. In "Roselily," for example, she traces the history and expectations of the title character by recalling her conscious thoughts, simultaneously narrating the basic event of the story, a marriage ceremony. Another story, "Really, Doesn't Crime Pay?" evolves as journal entries. Both narrative methods are effective for rendering extreme psychological distress. Indeed, many of the characters go mad. Some go mad quietly, as does the young wife in "Really, Doesn't Crime Pay?" who exhausts her husband with domestic obsequiousness:

> I wait, beautiful and perfect in every limb. . . . Lying unresisting on his bed like a drowned body washed to shore. But he is not happy. For he knows now that I intend to do nothing but say yes until he is completely exhausted.
>
> (*In Love and Trouble*, pp. 22–23)

Some go mad violently, as does Mrs. Jerome Franklin Washington III in "Her Sweet Jerome," screaming in engulfing flames, from a fire she has set.

However, a few of the women have the courage to define and subsequently act on their own convictions rather than capitulate to intimidation by those who are better educated, or have more money or power. In "Everyday Use," for example, Mama learns to appreciate the ordinary daughter she has taken for granted in favor of another daughter whose scholarship have invited her to a world larger than the family's dusty, rural yard:

> I [Mama] did something I never had done before: hugged Maggie to me, then dragged her on into the room, snatched the quilts out of Miss Wangero's [Maggie's sister's] hands and dumped them into Maggie's lap.
>
> (p. 58)

By insisting that the quilts be used as bedcovers, thus refusing to make them objects of excessive reverence, Mama re-invigorates specifically the custom of quiltmaking and generally all black cultural practices. She ensures the continuation of quilting not only as a tradition but also, and more importantly, as the reproduction of her culture through Maggie. Hence, Mama's choice alerts the reader to the danger inherent in fetishizing products of a living culture by transforming them into artifacts to be hoarded.

In her collection of poems *Revolutionary Petunias,* also published in 1973, Walker similarly examines the alienation between the educated older daughter and those she left behind in "For My Sister Molly Who in the Fifties." Relying on terse anecdotes in free-verse relief, Walker has the speaker—a younger unnamed sibling, like Maggie—recall in one stanza that Molly ". . . FOUND ANOTHER WORLD / Another life . . . And frowned away / Our sloppishness." The poem questions how we define education and progress, and what values we attach to their acquisition.

Walker's second novel, *Meridian* (1976), records Meridian Hill's pilgrimage not so much to a place as to a level of spiritual well-being. In this novel Walker abandons the chronological realism of the first novel and presents instead a series of small, nonlinear, often grotesque anecdotes about Meridian's experiences, such as her attempt to mother Wild Child and her sexual exploits with an undertaker in a mortuary establishment. In contrast with the cogent argument about the violent consequences of economic exploitation in Walker's first novel, *Meridian* requires that the reader participate in constructing the motives for the characters' actions—the gothic aspects of the novel serve as clues for determining the sources of the obsessive guilt, spiritual longing, and social crises that direct their lives.

Set in the early 1960s, the novel focuses on Meridian, a black high school dropout of seventeen, a deserted wife and mother. Desperately seeking relief from her dead-end life, she decides to return to high school and join the local branch of the civil rights movement. Her life takes a drastic turn when she wins a scholarship to the elite Saxon College for black women in Atlanta, puts her child up for adoption; and, as a consequence of both decisions, consigns herself "to penitence, for life." Walker examines the importance of the civil rights movement in redefining racial and sexual customs by dramatizing the relationships between Meridian and her small circle of friends—white and black, male and female. At the novel's close Meridian is ready "to return to the world cleansed of sickness."

The poetry collection *Good Night, Willie Lee, I'll See You in the Morning* (1979) and the short-story volume *You Can't Keep a Good Woman Down* (1981) followed the publication of *Meridian* in rapid succession. (Many of the poems and stories from both collections had been published previously.) Both works repeat the theme of healing oneself of past guilt so as to face the future with courage.

The poems in *Good Night, Willie Lee, I'll See You in the Morning* typify Walker's poetic style: poignant, emotionally charged, free-verse narratives of people, events, and experiences. They are more judgmental, ellipsis often replaced by commentary that cuts quickly to honest perception. Writing this kind of verse, as Walker suggests in "Confession," deliberately places the self in danger:

> All winter long
> . . . .
> I have told everyone
> the truth:
> The truth is killing me.

In the title poem of the collection, the speaker, who seems to be Walker herself, quiets her own ambivalent feelings about her father in the calming assurance of the mother's final farewell:

> Looking down into my father's
> dead face
> for the last time
> my mother said . . .
> . . . with *civility*
> "Good night, Willie Lee, I'll see you
> in the morning."

Against what seem to be many painful recollections, the mother professes the meaning of their life together in the magnanimity of unquestioning belief and healing self-affirmation, and Walker's evocation of the mother's voice and demeanor in this eulogy represent the courage to accept the past without reservation.

Unlike the first collection of short stories, *You Can't Keep a Good Woman Down* (1981) clearly signals black female celebration rather than predicament, and marks a transition in Walker's broadening vision for the potential lives of her black heroines. "Advancing Luna—and Ida B. Wells" is reminiscent of *Meridian*, while "Source" prefigures *The Temple of My Familiar* (1989).

"Advancing Luna—and Ida B. Wells" recalls the dilemma that the narrator, a young black woman, encounters when she learns that her good friend Luna, a young white woman, had been raped by Freddie Pye, a black man, while she worked in the civil rights movement. Race and gender complicate the narrator's response because each demands a different set of feelings, a different allegiance. That response is represented as an imaginary dialogue between the narrator and Ida B. Wells, a late-nineteenth-century black newspaperwoman who vigilantly protested lynching (especially of black males charged with raping white women). Just when the narrator thinks she has resolved the problem and can terminate the imaginary dialogue, she sees Luna and Freddy together again under troublesome circumstances. Ultimately, the narrator fails to resolve the dilemma satisfactorily and settles instead on three opposing, ideologically aligned explanations for the rape and Freddy's return; none is convincing. The problematic closure underscores the difficulty of relying on pat explanations to give meaning to human interactions.

Whereas "Advancing Luna . . ." probes the relationship of a young black woman and a white woman, "Source" examines the friendship between two young black women. Anastasia Green comes from an upper-middle-class background; she looks white but is culturally Southern and black. Irene is also Southern and visibly black. She is afraid that achieving success will cause her to abandon a life of social commitment and subsequently transform her into an ordinary bourgeois woman whose ambition is subsumed in wearing designer clothing. During the years immediately following college, Anastasia has several identity crises and crosses the color line in a variety of ways. During that same period Irene, fearful of becoming that ordinary, bourgeois black woman, dedicates herself to working in a Southern antipoverty program. Years later the woman meet again and discover that each has always embodied aspects of character that the other has sought. Anastasia appropriates the fervor with which Irene claims her identity as a black woman in order to embrace her own racially indefinite background, while Irene finally sees Anastasia's absolute refusal to let her middle-class background make her ordinary and socially uncommitted. Hence, each woman learns to rely on the convictions of the other in order to fortify her own.

The Color Purple (1982), Walker's third novel and winner of both the Pulitzer Prize and the American Book Award in 1983, employs the narrative structure of the epistolary novel. Rather than adhere to the European androcentric literary convention of the epistolary novel by placing authorial control of a woman's life (as depicted in her letters) in the hands of a man, Walker gives Celie the task of telling her own story through her letters. As critics insist, Walker rewrites the tradition of the epistolary novel, and her revisionist activity has clear political implications, especially given the battle between racial and sexual ideologies and personal convictions foregrounded in the novel.

The novel evolves as Celie, a fourteen-year-old black girl, confides in God through letters about what has happened to her. She has been raped by a man whom she assumes to be her father. (He is actually her stepfather.) He takes the two children she has borne him away from her and marries her off to a widower, who requires that she tend his house, fields, and four unruly children, as well as be available to him for sex. Celie seems the epitome of Hurston's mule, her symbol of black women's historic oppression. Moreover, her life reads like a slave narrative in which gender, rather than race, qualifies the condition of enslavement. As if her plight were not severe enough, the widower beats her:

> He beat me like he beat the children. Cept he don't never hardly beat them. He say, Celie, git the belt. The children be outside the room peeking through the cracks. It all I can do not to cry. I make myself wood. I say to myself, Celie, you a tree.
>
> (p. 22)

Later he brings his mistress, Shug Avery, home for Celie to nurse back to health. Instead of becoming rivals, as patriarchal codes dictate, Celie and Shug become intimate friends, and the novel ultimately negates (or deconstructs) the presumed value of the male-centered nuclear family and constructs the female-centered extended family as the domestic ideal.

While sales of four million copies and the Steven Spielberg–directed film *The Color Purple* transformed the novel into a controversial media event, some of Walker's readers have contended that Walker exploited the racist stereotype of the violent black male and sensationalized black lesbianism. Others have contended that Walker's authentic rendering of black folk speech transcends stereotype or caricature, and that the success of the novel and the motion picture was an occasion for celebrating sisterhood among black women. They have applauded, even defended, the novel, claiming that Celie's self-affirmation is inspirational and that black domestic violence is a most legitimate subject for literary treatment. Walker's focus on negative social behavior, they have argued, does not detract from her belief in the beauty and the power of the individual or the group, but instead reveals her willingness to experiment boldly with ways of depicting her vision.

Three characters from *The Color Purple*—Miss Celie, Shug Avery, and Celie's daughter Olivia—reappear throughout the recollections of Fanny, Miss Celie's granddaughter, in Walker's novel of ideas, *The Temple of My Familiar* (1989). *The Temple* dramatizes the social issues raised in Walker's first feminist or "womanist" collection of essays, *In Search of Our Mother's Gardens* (1983), and in *Living by the Word* (1988), protesting the rights of animals, exhorting the protection of the land, affirming the divine in all things, healing familial estrangement, and, of course, eradicating racial and sexual oppression—and, like the earlier novels, is anecdotal. The numerous story fragments evolve primarily as conversations among the six principal characters, who are paired in marriage. Two couples live in Northern California; they are multiracial and middle-class, entering the crisis of self-examination that comes in mid-life. The third is an elderly black couple who live in Baltimore.

In this very risky novel, Walker abandons the critique of rural, Southern black folks and moves her characters to the West Coast, placing the story in a culturally plural, academic context where characters learn critical self-reflection on futon mats during luxurious almond oil massages.

At the beginning of the story, the death of Suwelo's great-uncle Rafe in Baltimore grants him a temporary reprieve from his troubled marriage to Fanny, a college administrator, and from his dissatisfying career as a history teacher. A very popular singer, Arveyda, also has recently separated from his wife, Carlotta, a women's studies professor; he is traveling in Central America with Carlotta's mother, Zedé, with whom he has recently had an brief affair. The old couple, Miss Lissie and Mr. Hal, are the impetus for the characters' reform. Experimenting with novelistic form by blurring the distinction between fiction and essay, legend and history, fantastic vision and realistic fact, Walker uses the complicated plot of intricate relationships to expand the critical scope of her examination of Western civilization, especially its imperialist, patriarchal values.

What unifies this unusual novel are the central characters' interlinked struggles to liberate themselves from the stultifying effects of the traditional values underpinning Western civilization, values that can be summarized as the pressumed manifest destiny of white males to exploit all women, nonwhite men, the land, animals, and natural resources. Through Miss Lissie's recollections, Walker recalls centuries of such exploitation. Her dream memories allow us to travel back to the dawn of history in order to re-create such events as living among apelike humans, the destruction of prehistoric matriarchal tribes, the displacement of female mythos by male legend, and the advent of Christianity. Counterbalanced with these larger memories are Lissie's more recent personal memories—her transportation across the Atlantic in a slave ship, numerous experiences as an American slave, and the destruction of American Indian nations.

Miss Lissie preserves her most suppressed dream memory for Suwelo on a tape recording to be heard after her death. In this story she recalls a time of paradise, like the biblical Garden of Eden, when she was a male child living in a female tribe with his mother. The mother had a large lion as her familiar: "In these days of which I am speaking, people met other animals in much the same way people today meet each other. . . . The women alone had familiars." The boy's blissful existence ends when a female friend causes him to see that he is different: "All I could think of was hiding myself—my kinky but pale yellow hair . . . my pebble-colored eyes, and my skin that had no color at all." In outwardly directed self-contempt he chases her away, killing her serpent familiar, which tries to protect her. This dream memory evokes prehistoric tribal lore and biblical verse to rewrite the original sin that causes the fall from grace, not simply for humankind but for all life.

Cast against Miss Lissie's reconstruction of history are the painful efforts of the two other couples—Suwelo and Fanny, Arveyda and Carlotta—to accept their past lives and to base their relationships on trust rather than possession. By the end of the novel the two couples are temporarily realigned as they self-consciously work to retrieve a small version of the utopian tribal community. Like *The Color Purple*, *The Temple of My Familiar* celebrates the possibility of happiness restored with the reconfiguration of the family as open, extended, and loving, and with the characterization of individuals who are not afraid to abandon social prescriptions for honest relationships.

Whether exploring racial or sexual dynamics, Walker has, in all her works, maintained that individuals are responsible for their own growth, their self-improvement, and the enhancement of all their relationships. In "These Days," the final poem in her collection *Horses Make a Landscape Look More Beautiful* (1984),

Walker reasserts her vital belief that "surely the earth can be saved / by all the people / who insist / on love." Walker's works invigorate, challenge, and delight us; they also pain, anger, scare, and dare us to remember that she ". . . would give / to the human race / only hope."

Selected Bibliography

PRIMARY WORKS

POETRY

Once: Poems. New York: Harcourt, Brace, and World, 1968.

Five Poems. Detroit: Broadside Press, 1972.

Revolutionary Petunias and Other Poems. New York: Harcourt Brace Jovanovich, 1973.

Good Night, Willie Lee, I'll See You in the Morning. New York: Dial Press, 1979.

Horses Make a Landscape Look More Beautiful: Poems. San Diego: Harcourt Brace Jovanovich, 1984.

NOVELS

The Third Life of Grange Copeland. New York: Harcourt Brace Jovanovich, 1970.

Meridian. New York: Harcourt Brace Jovanovich, 1976.

The Color Purple. New York: Harcourt Brace Jovanovich, 1982.

The Temple of My Familiar. San Diego: Harcourt Brace Jovanovich, 1989.

SHORT-STORY COLLECTIONS

In Love and Trouble: Stories of Black Women. New York: Harcourt Brace Jovanovich, 1973.

You Can't Keep a Good Woman Down. New York: Harcourt Brace Jovanovich, 1981.

CHILDREN'S LITERATURE

Langston Hughes, American Poet. New York: Harper & Row, 1974.

To Hell with Dying. San Diego: Harcourt Brace Jovanovich, 1988.

EDITED ANTHOLOGY

I Love Myself When I Am Laughing . . . and Then Again When I Am Looking Mean and Impressive: A Zora Neale Hurston Reader. Edited by Walker. Introduction by Mary Helen Washington. Old Westbury, N.Y.: Feminist Press, 1979.

ESSAYS AND OTHER PROSE

In Search of Our Mothers' Gardens: Womanist Prose. San Diego: Harcourt Brace Jovanovich, 1983.

Living by the Word: Selected Writings, 1973–1987. San Diego: Harcourt Brace Jovanovich, 1988.

INDIVIDUAL SHORT STORIES

"Cuddling." *Essence* 16, no. 3:74–76, 110, 114 (July 1985).

"Kindred Spirits." *Esquire* 104:106–111 (August 1985).

"Olive Oil." *Ms.* 14:35–36, 78 (August 1985).

INDIVIDUAL ESSAYS

"Porn at Home." *Ms.* 8:67, 69–70, 75–76 (February 1980).

"Not Only Will Your Teachers Appear, They Will Cook New Food for You." *Mendocino County,* September 1, 1986.

SECONDARY WORKS

BIOGRAPHICAL AND CRITICAL STUDIES

Awkward, Michael. "*The Color Purple* and the Achievement of (Comm)unity." In his *Inspiriting Influences: Tradition, Revision, and Afro-American Women's Novels.* New York: Columbia University Press, 1989. Pp. 135–164.

Babb, Valerie. "*The Color Purple:* Writing to Undo What Writing Has Done." *Phylon* 47, no. 2:107–116 (June 1986).

Baker, Houston A., Jr., and Charlotte Pierce-Baker. "Patches: Quilts and Community in Alice Walker's 'Everyday Use.' " *Southern Review* 21, no. 3:706–720 (Summer 1985).

Bloom, Harold, ed. *Alice Walker.* New York: Chelsea House, 1989.

Bobo, Jacqueline. "Sifting Through the Controversy: Reading *The Color Purple.*" *Callaloo* 12, no. 2:332–342 (1989).

Bradley, David. "Novelist Alice Walker Telling the Black Woman's Story." *New York Times Magazine,* 8 January 1984, pp. 24–36.

Brown, Joseph A., S.J. " 'All Saints Should Walk Away': The Mystical Pilgrimage of *Meridian.*" *Callaloo* 12, no. 2:310–320 (1989).

Butler, Robert James. "Making a Way Out of No Way: The Open Journey in Alice Walker's *The Third Life of Grange Copeland.*" *Black American Literature Forum* 22, no. 1:65–80 (Spring 1988).

Byerman, Keith. *Fingering the Jagged Grain: Tradition and Form in Recent Black Fiction*. Athens: University of Georgia Press, 1985. Pp. 128–170.

———. "Desire and Alice Walker: The Quest for a Womanist Narrative." *Callaloo* 12, no. 2:321–331 (1989).

Cheung, King-Kok. "Don't Tell: Imposed Silences in *The Color Purple* and *The Woman Warrior*." *PMLA* 103:162–174 (1988).

Christian, Barbara. "Alice Walker: The Black Woman Artist as Wayward." In *Black Women Writers, 1950–1980: A Critical Evaluation*. Edited by Mari Evans. Garden City, N.Y.: Anchor-Doubleday, 1984. Pp. 457–477. Reprinted in Bloom.

Coleman, Viralene J. "Miss Celie's Song." *Publications of the Arkansas Philological Association* 11, no. 1:27–34 (Spring 1985).

Davis, Thadious. "Alice Walker's Celebration of Self in Southern Generations." *Southern Quarterly* 21, no. 4:39–53 (Summer 1983). Reprinted in Bloom.

DeVeaux, Alexis. "Alice Walker." *Essence* 20, no. 5:56–58, 120, 122, 124 (September 1989).

El Saffar, Ruth. "Alice Walker's *The Color Purple*." *International Fiction Review* 12, no. 1:11–17 (Winter 1985).

Erickson, Peter. " 'Cast Out Alone / to Heal / and Re-Create / Ourselves': Family-Based Identity in the Work of Alice Walker." *CLA Journal* 23:71–94 (1979). Reprinted in Bloom.

Fifer, Elizabeth. "The Dialect and Letters of *The Color Purple*." In *Contemporary American Women Writers: Narrative Strategies*. Edited by Catherine Rainwater and William J. Scheick. Lexington: University Press of Kentucky, 1985. Pp. 155–171.

Fontenot, Chester J. "Alice Walker: 'The Diary of an African Nun' and Du Bois' Double Consciousness." *Journal of Afro-American Issues* 5: 192–196. (1977). Reprinted in *Sturdy Black Bridges: Visions of Black Women in Literature*. Edited by Roseanne P. Bell, Bettye J. Parker, and Beverly Guy-Sheftall. Garden City, N.Y.: Anchor-Doubleday, 1979. Pp. 150–156.

Freeman, Alma S. "Zora Neale Hurston and Alice Walker: A Spiritual Kinship." *Sage* 2, no. 1:37–40 (Spring 1985).

Froula, Christine. "The Daughter's Seduction: Sexual Violence and Literary History." *Signs* 11:621–644. (1986).

Gates, Henry Louis, Jr. "Color Me Zora: Alice Walker's (Re)Writing of the Speakerly Text." In his *Signifying Monkey: A Theory of Afro-American Literary Criticism*. New York: Oxford University Press, 1988. Pp. 239–258.

Harris, Trudier. "On *The Color Purple*, Stereotypes, and Silence." *Black American Literature Forum* 18, no. 4:155–161 (Winter 1984).

———. "From Victimization to Free Enterprise: Alice Walker's *The Color Purple*." *Studies in American Fiction* 14, no. 1:1–17 (Spring 1986).

Hellenbrand, Harold. "Speech, After Silence: Alice Walker's *The Third Life of Grange Copeland*." *Black American Literature Forum* 20, no. 1–2:113–128 (Spring–Summer 1986).

Henderson, Mae G. "*The Color Purple:* Revisions and Redefinitions." *Sage* 2, no. 1:14–18 (Spring 1985). Reprinted in Bloom.

Hernton, Calvin C. "Who's Afraid of Alice Walker? *The Color Purple* as Slave Narrative." In his *The Sexual Mountain and Black Women Writers: Adventures in Sex, Literature, and Real Life*. New York: Anchor-Doubleday, 1987. Pp. 1–36.

Hiers, John T. "Creation Theology in Alice Walker's *The Color Purple*." *Notes on Contemporary Literature* 14, no. 4:2–3 (September 1984).

Hogue, W. Lawrence. "History, the Feminist Discourse, and Alice Walker's *The Third Life of Grange Copeland*." *MELUS* 12, no. 2:45–62 (Summer 1985).

Kane, Patricia. "The Prodigal Daughter in Alice Walker's Everyday Use.' " *Notes on Contemporary Literature* 15, no. 2:7 (March 1985).

Kirschner, Susan. "Alice Walker's Nonfictional Prose: A Checklist, 1966–1984." *Black American Literature Forum* 18, no. 4:162–163 (Winter 1984).

Lenhart, Georgann. "Inspired Purple?" *Notes on Contemporary Literature* 14, no. 3:2–3 (1984).

Mason, Theodore O., Jr. "Alice Walker's *The Third Life of Grange Copeland:* The Dynamics of Enclosure." *Callaloo* 12, no. 2:297–309 (1989).

McDowell, Deborah E. " 'The Changing Same': Generational Connections and Black Women Novelists." *New Literary History* 18:281–302 (Winter 1987). Reprinted in Bloom.

Nadel, Alan. "Reading the Body: Alice Walker's *Meridian* and the Archeology of Self." *Modern Fiction Studies* 34:55–68 (1988).

O'Brien, John. "Alice Walker." In *Interviews with Black Writers*. Edited by John O'Brien. New York: Liveright, 1973. Pp. 185–211.

Parker-Smith, Bettye J. "Alice Walker's Women: In Search of Some Peace of Mind." In *Black Woman*

Writers, 1950–1980: A Critical Evaluation. Edited by Mari Evans. Garden City, N.Y.: Anchor-Doubleday, 1984. Pp. 478–493.

Robinson, Daniel. "Problems in Form: Alice Walker's *The Color Purple*." *Notes on Contemporary Literature* 16, no. 1:2 (January 1986).

Royster, Philip M. "In Search of Our Father's Arms: Alice Walker's Persona of the Alienated Darling." *Black American Literature Forum* 20, no. 4:347–370 (Winter 1986).

Sadoff, Diane F. "Black Matrilineage: The Case of Alice Walker and Zora Neale Hurston." *Signs* 11, no. 1:4–26 (Autumn 1985). Reprinted in Bloom.

Shelton, Frank W. "Alienation and Integration in Alice Walker's *The Color Purple*." *CLA Journal* 28, no. 4:382–392 (June 1985).

Stade, George. "Womanist Fiction and Male Characters." *Partisan Review* 52, no. 3:264–270 (1985).

Stein, Karen F. "*Meridian:* Alice Walker's Critique of Revolution." *Black American Literature Forum* 20, no. 1–2:129–141 (Spring–Summer 1986).

Tavormina, M. Teresa. "Dressing the Spirit: Clothworking and Language in *The Color Purple*." *Journal of Narrative Technique* 16, no. 3:220–230 (Fall 1986).

Tate, Claudia. "Alice Walker." In *Black Women Writers at Work*. Edited by Claudia Tate. New York: Continuum, 1983. Pp. 175–187.

Tucker, Lindsey. "Alice Walker's *The Color Purple:* Emergent Woman, Emergent Text." *Black American Literature Forum* 22. no 1 (Spring 1988), 81–98

Wade-Gayles, Gloria. *No Crystal Stair: Visions of Race and Sex in Black Women's Fiction*. New York: Pilgrim, 1984. Pp. 102–114, 199–215.

Wall, Wendy. "Lettered Bodies and Corporeal Texts in *The Color Purple*." *Studies in American Fiction* 16:83–97 (1988).

Washington, Mary Helen. "I Sign My Mother's Name: Alice Walker, Dorothy West, Paule Marshall." In *Mothering the Mind: Twelve Studies of Writers and Their Silent Partners*. Edited by Ruth Perry and Martine Watson Brownley. New York: Holmes and Meir, 1984. Pp. 142–163.

Willis, Susan. "Alice Walker's Women." *New Orleans Review* 12, no. 1:33–41 (Spring 1985). Also in her *Specifying: Black Women Writing the American Experience*. Madison: University of Wisconsin Press, 1987. Pp. 110–128. Reprinted in Bloom.

Wilson, Sharon. "A Conversation with Alice Walker." *Kalliope: A Journal of Women's Art* 6, no. 2:37–45 (1984).

BIBLIOGRAPHIES

Banks, Erma Davis, and Keith Byerman. *Alice Walker: An Annotated Bibliography*. New York: Garland, 1989.

Byerman, Keith, and Erma Banks. "Alice Walker: A Selected Bibliography, 1968–1988." *Callaloo* 12, no. 2:343–345 (1989).

Pratt, Louis H., and Darnell D. Pratt. *Alice Malsenior Walker: An Annotated Bibliography, 1968–1986*. Westport, Conn.: Meckler, 1988.

CLAUDIA TATE

EUDORA WELTY

1909–

AT THE CLOSE of her 1956 essay "Place in Fiction," Eudora Welty seems to imagine a hostile reader who might interpret her advice to write" where you have put down roots" as an advocation of "regional" writing. " 'Regional,' " she writes, "is a careless term, as well as a condescending one." In the essay's opening remarks she dismisses this "term of the day" as meaning little, "like most terms used to pin down a novel." Framing her essay in this way, Welty clearly recognizes the potential threat of the term "regional" as a negative if ill-conceived judgment. This threat seems to inform her concluding statement that "the challenge to writers today is not to disown any part of our heritage." She insists that "regional" is "an outsider's term; it has no meaning for the insider who is doing the writing, because as far as he knows he is simply writing about life." In 1972, Welty asserted that she didn't "mind being called a regional writer," insisting, "I just think of myself as writing about human beings and I happen to live in a region, as do we all, so I write about what I know—it's the same case for any writer living anywhere. I also happen to love my particular region."

Welty's sensitivity and even defensiveness may well be understood in light of the tendency of reviewers to praise her by reassuring readers that she is more than a regionalist. Indeed twenty-four years after she stated her position about place, major reviews of her 1980 *Collected Stories* included the seemingly obligatory praise that she was not to be dismissed as a regional writer. Such remarks followed a decade of feminist scholarship in which one could find scholars pointing to Henry James's recognition of Mary Wilkins Freeman's work as evidence that she was "more than a simple regionalist," or the introduction to a new edition of Kate Chopin's *The Awakening* attributing that author's twentieth-century obscurity to the designation of her work as regional. Such backhanded compliments usually go on to praise the work of writers such as Welty as being "universal." Masking anxiety about the representation of cultural difference and reflecting a particularly "American" concern with aesthetic and literary nationalism, this use of "universal" may strike Southern writers as provincial as well as condescending.

Mary Austin shrewdly put Edith Wharton in her place by describing *The House of Mirth* as Wharton's regional novel. What critic has sought to reassure readers that Henry James's *The Bostonians* was universal and not merely regional? Welty writes in "Place in Fiction" that "Jane Austen, Emily Brontë, Thomas Hardy, Cervantes, Turgenev, the authors of the books of the Old Testament, all confine themselves to regions, great or small—but are they regional? Then who from the start of time has not been so?" Yet beyond these anxieties about critical prejudices, Welty places herself in a Southern tradition. The South, she has said, "endows me, and it enables me." As a regionalist and as perhaps the greatest living American author, Welty must be recognized as an unmistakably Southern writer as well as a writer for whom place is a generative factor.

According to Welty, "The Southerner is a talker by nature, but not only a talker—we are used to an audience. We are used to a listener and that does something to our narrative style." Speaking as a Southerner and not merely as a writer, Welty has said:

> We in the South have grown up being narrators. We have lived in a place—that's the word, Place—where storytelling is a way of life. . . .

> So, when Southerners write, they are doing what comes naturally. Their stories have been a part of their lives, and maybe they do tell them more convincingly, more freely, as some say, but if that's so, it has happened because the writer has been a part of The Place.
>
> (Prenshaw [1984], pp. 142–143)

Welty's fiction comes from a region that has a long tradition of oral performance. The emphasis on voice—the oral and storytelling voice, not just accent—is a major characteristic of the region, and Southern literature often turns on the power of story and the way in which the story itself is the motive in life as well as art. Beyond this narrative tradition, or perhaps because of it, Welty also writes in a tradition of an unusually powerful line of Southern authors: Mark Twain, Kate Chopin, William Faulkner, Zora Neale Hurston, Richard Wright, Katherine Anne Porter, Flannery O'Connor, Carson McCullers, Robert Penn Warren, and Walker Percy, to name a few. Twain and Faulkner are arguably the most important of these writers for Welty, although it is significant in imagining the possibilities available to Welty that so many of the best Southern writers have been women.

Heir to both a powerful tradition of oral narrative and a powerful tradition of Southern literature, Eudora Alice Welty was born in Jackson, Mississippi, on 13 April 1909, the oldest child of three and the only daughter of Christian Webb Welty and Chestina Andrews. Along with her brothers, Edward and Walter, Eudora Welty was a first-generation Mississippian. She has joked that the only suffering she knew in her childhood was caused by "my father's being from Ohio, a Yankee." Christian Welty's ancestors were Swiss German farmers who had settled in Pennsylvania and southern Ohio prior to the Revolutionary War. Early in the century, Christian Welty took a summer job with a lumber company in West Virginia, where he met Chestina Andrews, the oldest child and only daughter in a family with five sons. The Andrews family lived on top of a mountain above the Queen's Shoals of the Elk River.

Welty's maternal grandfather, Edward Raboteau (Ned) Andrews, came from Virginia and a family of teachers, preachers, and lawyers. He attended Trinity College (later Duke University), where he founded a literary society; he later worked as a photographer and journalist in Virginia. Ned Andrews became a country lawyer known for his dramatic style; he once saved an unfortunate fortune-teller who, having predicted an early death, was accused of her client's murder. Welty's grandmother, Eudora Carden Andrews, the daughter of a minister, had been in West Virginia from the time before it was a state. She stayed close to her daughter even after her marriage; mother and daughter wrote to each other daily, although the letters from West Virginia were often continued from day to day because of the difficulty of getting them down from the mountain and onto the train.

Both of Eudora Welty's parents shared a love of music and reading. Chestina Andrews taught school to earn money to go to Marshall College in the summers; she earned her degree and later showed her daughter "the notebook she still kept with its diagrams" of *Paradise Lost.* When, as a child, Chestina Andrews was asked by her parents to cut her heavy, waist-length hair for health reasons, she refused a bribe of gold earrings and agreed only after being offered a full set of the novels of Charles Dickens (brought in a barrel from Baltimore). Welty writes that her mother, who "read Dickens in the spirit in which she would have eloped with him," once ran into a burning house on crutches to rescue her precious novels. She also read Sir Walter Scott, Robert Louis Stevenson, John Galsworthy, Charlotte Brontë, Edith Wharton, and Thomas Mann. For most of his life, Welty's father worked for the Lamar Life Insurance Company, eventually becoming its president. Welty recalls him as a gentle-tempered man who "had no interest in ancient history—only the future, he said, should count"; he "never happened to tell us a single family story." She writes that "he was not a lover of fiction, because fiction is not true, and for that flaw it was forever inferior to fact." Although Welty and her brothers went to Sunday school, she was aware that her family was different in a number of ways from those of her friends. The Weltys did not go to church or say grace at the table. The same mother who like a scholar would consult a concordance while reading the Bible also kept a flour-dusted copy of Darwin's *The Origin of Species* in the pantry to read while she was baking bread.

In her memoir, *One Writer's Beginnings,* Welty describes a childhood in which books, reading, and listening were a major part of life. "I am a writer who came of a sheltered life," she writes, alluding to the title of a novel by Ellen Glasgow, adding: "A sheltered life can be a daring life as well. For all serious daring starts from within." Welty recounts that when she was five, since she could read and had been vaccinated, her mother arranged for her to enter Jefferson Davis Grammar School in the middle of the school year. A year or two later, she was taken out of school and put to bed for several months because of an ailment the doctor diagnosed as "fast-beating heart." From her parents' bed she watched the school (which was across the street from their house) and read storybooks. She describes the experience of falling asleep in the bed and listening to her parents talk as they sat in their rockers: "What was thus dramatically made a present of to me was the secure sense of the hidden observer."

From an early age, at her mother's request, she was given a library card, which entitled her to borrow two books a day. In addition to reading, Welty's education and initiation into the art of fiction came from listening to the stories and storytellers around her: "Long before I wrote stories, I listened for stories. Listening *for* them is something more acute than listening *to* them." Her fiction-loving mother shunned gossip and refused to repeat neighbors' stories she believed to be lies; but Welty listened to the tales of women such as Fannie, "an old black sewing woman" who was "like an author," as well as those of a friend of her mother's whose "accounts" were filled with "dialogue" ("I said," "He said") and *"scenes."* She recounts: "My ear told me it was dramatic. Often she said, 'The crisis had come!' "

After graduating from Central High School in 1925 at the age of sixteen, Welty attended Mississippi State College for Women in Columbus, two hundred miles north of Jackson. There she met women from all of the regions of Mississippi. In an interview she described this experience as her "first exposure to people from across the state," and one can imagine that part of her training as a writer came from the revelation of what she called these "different voices! There was the difference in the way the people from the hill country spoke and those from the Delta." Welty describes how she would "sit up at night and just listen to the voices coming down the hall" to see if she could "tell what part of the state the girls were from by their different voices." Here she became a reporter and a humorist for the school newspaper. For an April Fool's issue Welty wrote an editorial that (in reference to the crowded living conditions that placed as many as six students in a single dormitory room) "lamented that five of our freshman class drowned when the water rose, but by this Act of God, it went on, there was that much more room now for the rest of us." Welty later learned that H. L. Mencken had offered this to readers of the *American Mercury* as an example of Bible Belt thinking.

Katherine Anne Porter described "the typical collection of books" that a family such as Welty's would have had "at arm's reach," suggesting that Welty read "the ancient Greek and Roman poetry, history and fable, Shakespeare, Milton, Dante, the eighteenth-century English and the nineteenth-century French novelists, with a dash of Tolstoy and Dostoievsky, before she realized what she was reading. Yet Welty writes that she arrived at college "unprepared for the immediacy of poetry." The first book she purchased from the college bookstore was *In April Once*, by the Mississippi poet William Alexander Percy. After two years at MSCW, Welty transferred to the University of Wisconsin at Madison (her father believd that "the big Middle Western universities were the most progressive"), where she studied English literature. She describes how she discovered Willian Butler Yeats (who would be a major influence on her work), citing in her autobiography a description of her own experience that she later put in the mouth of a fictional character: "I happened to discover Yeats. . . . I read 'Sailing to Byzantium,' standing up in the stacks, read it by the light of falling snow. It semed to me that if I could stir, if I could move to take the next step, I could go out into the poem the way I could go out into that snow."

After receiving a B.A. from the University of Wisconsin in 1929, Welty studied advertising for a year at the Columbia University School of Business in New York (where, she recalls, she went to the Thalia and "every little foreign film place in New York"). Unable to find full-time work in New York because of the Depression, Welty returned to Jackson in 1931. Her father died in the same year. She continued to work in advertising and copywriting, but (she told an interviewer) she "quit advertising because it was too much like sticking pins into people to make them buy things that they didn't need or really much want." According to Ruth Vande Kieft, her first job in Jackson "was a part-time job with radio station WJDX—the first in Mississippi and a venture initiated by her father's insurance company—at which she earned sixty-five dollars a month for writing scripts and being generally useful at assorted tasks (among which, she said, was cleaning the canary bird cage)." Welty recounts: "I used to write everything that was said over a small-town radio station—and to keep the job wrote myself a lot of fan letters each week." She also wrote a society column about Jackson for the *Memphis Commercial-Appeal*. In 1933 she took a job as "Junior Publicity Agent" for the Works Progress Administration, which let her go "all over the state with a camera" and gave her "an honorable reason to talk to people in all sorts of jobs." She held this job until 1936, when she began to work for the Mississippi Advertising Commission, helping to draw tourists and industry to the state.

During the 1930s, Welty made visits by train to New York City, carrying a portfolio of her photographs and a sheaf of her stories. Welty recalls having more hopes about the responses to the photographs and more doubts about the stories. In 1936, the same year in which she published her first story, an exhibition of her photographs of Mississippi blacks was shown at the Lugene Gallery in New York. A selection of these photographs was published in 1971 in *One Time, One Place: Mississippi in the Depression*. A larger collection of the more than twelve hundred negatives and prints that she took during the 1930s appeared in the 1989 book *Photographs*.

In New York she stayed at the Barbizon Hotel for Women yet went dancing in Harlem. She also participated in the most exiciting aspects of New York City's cultural life. Welty recalls being present

> at the opening of the Mercury Theater, during the WPA days. I remember seeing the opening of the black *Macbeth*, which was put on in Harlem, directed by Orson Welles. The play's location was changed from Scotland to Jamaica. . . . Hecate was played by a black man dancing on a drum without any clothes on.
>
> (Prenshaw [1984], p. 218)

In 1944 she returned to New York for several months to work at the *New York Times Book Review*, during which time she wrote some reviews under the pseudonym "Michael Ravenna." Robert Van Gelder recalled of her "reviews of World War II battlefield reports from North Africa, Europe, and the South Pacific" that when "a churlish *Times* Sunday editor suggested that a lady reviewer from the Deep South might not be the most authoritative critic for the accounts of World War II's far-flung campaigns, she switched to a pseudonym." Welty, however, claimed that this "was a mischievous figment of imagination on the part of Nash Burger of Jackson," explaining that when the staff couldn't get other people to write reviews, "we would do them and sign them."

Welty published what she later called her "first good story," "Death of a Traveling Salesman," in 1936. She recounts in *One Writer's Beginnings* that the story had its origin in a remark a Jackson neighbor (himself "a traveling man") had heard on a trip to North Mississippi: "He's gone to borry some fire." The primal spirit of such a quest conveyed by these words—with their "lyrical and mythological and dramatic overtones"—caught Welty's imagination, and the story "began spontaneously." Faulkner claimed that *The Sound and the Fury* had its source in the image of a little girl's muddy drawers as she climbed a tree, and he described the origin of *Light in August* as a momentary vision of the back of a pregnant woman at dusk as she walked down a road. Similarly, Welty recounts that the sight of a woman "bent on an errand" first led her to imagine Phoenix Jackson, the elderly black woman in "A Worn Path" who is on an errand to get medicine for her grandson. For Welty, however, the inspiration and the genesis of fiction more often originate in language, some scrap of a spoken word. It was the image of the woman joined with a sentence spoken on the same road by a figure who might or might not have been the same person—"I was too old at the Surrender"—that inspired the character in "A Worn Path."

With the acceptance of "Death of a Traveling Salesman" by *Manuscript*, Welty became a published author. In the years that followed, Welty published in little magazines such as *Prairie Schooner* and *Accent*; she found her most receptive audience in the editors of the newly founded *Southern Review*. There she was read and encouraged by Robert Penn Warren, Albert Erskine, and Cleanth Brooks. Other early supporters were Ford Madox Ford and Katherine Anne Porter. Welty subsequently published six stories in the *Southern Review* but had trouble getting published in "national" magazines. Eventually she was discovered in Jackson by Doubleday editor John Woodburn, who was on a trip south looking for talent; he recommended her to the aspiring literary agent Diarmuid Russell (son of the Irish poet A. E. Russell), who placed "A Worn Path" and "Why I Live at the P.O." in the *Atlantic Monthly* in 1941. Cleanth Brooks describes this moment (with some irony) as Welty's real "discovery" since one "couldn't be discovered in the South" or by the *Southern Review*. That same year Russell sold Welty's first collection, *A Curtain of Green*, to Woodburn and Doubleday, despite a reluctance on the part of New York publishing houses to publish collections of short stories. Furthermore, as Welty has remarked, "for Doubleday to publish a book of short stories by an unknown writer was really extraordinary in those days. Or, maybe, at anytime for anyone to." Published in 1941, *A Curtain of Green* contains seventeen stories, written over six years, that vary widely in subject and form. In the same year Welty won her first O. Henry Award, second prize for "A Worn Path"; she would win first prize in the following year for "The Wide Net."

Welty's subsequent career has been steady and successful. She has published six collections of short stories, four novels, a book of essays and criticism, two books of photography, a fairy tale, a children's book, and an autobiography. Her awards and honors include the O. Henry Award (1941, 1942, 1943, 1951); two Guggenheim Fellowships (1942–1943 and 1949–1950); an award of the American Academy of Arts and Letters (1944); election to the National Institute of Arts and Letters (1952); the William Dean Howells Medal of the American Academy of Arts and Letters (1955, for *The Ponder Heart*); the Edward McDowell Medal (for *Losing Battles,* 1970); election to American Academy of Arts and Letters (1971); the National Institute of Arts and Letters Gold Medal (1972); the Pulitzer Prize (for *The Optimist's Daughter,* 1973); and the National Medal of Literature and the Medal of Freedom Award (1980). Welty has lectured widely as well as given readings of her work. The William E. Massey Sr. Lectures in the History of American Civilization that she delivered at Harvard in 1983 were published the following year as *One Writer's Beginnings.* She has received numerous honorary degrees. She has continued to live and write in Jackson.

When it was first published in 1941, *A Curtain of Green* contained an introduction by Katherine Anne Porter, whom Welty had met in Baton Rouge through the editors of the *Southern Review.* Although it prefaces Welty's first book, this introduction still offers an insightful portrait of Welty as a short-story writer. Speaking of the modest and unassuming young writer who referred to herself as being "underfoot locally" in Jackson, Porter wrote that Welty did not need to "follow a war and smell death to feel herself alive: she knows about death already." In contrast to herself, perhaps, Porter added: "She shall not need even to live in New York to feel that she is having the kind of experience, the sense of 'life' proper to a serious author." Commenting on the "extraordinary range of mood, pace, tone, and variety of material" in Welty's first volume, Porter found within the diversity three different types of stories: comic stories that are highly oral, stories that combine "an objective reporting with great perception of mental or emotional states," and interior narratives that are imbued with poetry and mystery.

Welty is perhaps most popularly known for those stories in which, in Porter's words, "the spirit is satire and the key grim comedy." These stories, which include "Why I Live at the P.O." and "Petrified Man," are among the pieces of fiction that Welty describes as having been written "by ear." After "Petrified Man," a story Porter calls "a fine clinical study of vulgarity," had been rejected by a number of magazines, Welty actually burned the manuscript. When the editors of the *Southern Review* changed their minds and requested the story back, since Welty had it "by ear" she was able to write it again from memory.

The type of story that Porter describes as a combination of reporting and psychological perception include "Clytie," "Old Mr. Marblehall," "The Hitch-Hikers," and "Powerhouse." "Powerhouse," inspired by hearing and seeing Fats Waller perform in Jackson, is one of the rare stories that Welty admits to having composed in the passion of the moment. It is strongly influenced by the music, the rhythms of which are embodied in the voices of the story. The same Welty who was criticized in a review of her first novel for being the daughter of the president of a life-insurance company and a member of the Junior League was censored by the *Atlantic Monthly* when it published "Powerhouse." Welty's quotation of the African American musical idiom apparently was too much for them; she had to change the song that she had chosen to conclude the story and substitute "Somebody Loves You, I Wonder Who" for the more pungent lyrics of "Hold Tight" as sung by Fats Waller: "fooly racky sacky want some seafood, Mama!"

The kind of Welty story in *A Curtain of Green* that Porter states a preference for is that "where external act and the internal voiceless life of the human imagination almost meet and mingle on the mysterious threshold between dream and walking, one reality refusing to admit or confirm the existence of the other, yet both conspiring toward the same end." "Death of a Traveling Salesman" and "A Curtain of Green" are located in the mysterious region that Porter prophetically names as Welty's "most familiar territory." In the decade that followed, this territory would be the location for most of Welty's work. Literally set in the Natchez Trace or the Delta, it demarcates the dreamworld of *The Robber Bridegroom, The Wide Net, Delta Wedding*, and *The Golden Apples*.

The stories in Welty's second collection, *The Wide Net* (1943), were written within the space of a year. Early readers found the stories too poetic, too mystical, even inaccessible. Robert Penn Warren, however, in what has become the most famous description of these stories, found them to be about "love and separateness," the important tragedy that Welty made the center of her next book and first novel, *Delta Wedding* (1947). The opening sentence of "First Love" (the story that begins *The Wide Net*) introduces the world of metamorphosis and transfiguration that will follow: "Whatever happened, it happened in extraordinary times, in a season of dreams." The story is set in the past of the Mississippi winter in which Aaron Burr, in a historical episode that is veiled in mystery, dreamed his dream of empire. Aware of the impossibility of knowing Burr's words, Welty tells her story from the perspective of a deaf child, an orphaned bootblack whose deafness becomes a metaphor for the struggle that all the characters in *The Wide Net* experience in reading the world and people around them.

In the title story, as William Wallace and his friends drag a river because he fears that his pregnant wife has drowned herself, we learn about the distance that separates the experience of men and women. As he dives to the bottom of the riverbed, William Wallace goes through the motions of a baptism and a type of birth and in doing so learns about the experience of his pregnant wife. Like Dante, William Wallace with his guide Virgil finds himself in the course of his guest. Like the hero in the the epic of Gilgamesh, who dives deeply to bring up the plant of everlasting life, William Wallace sees "the green ribbon of plant" slip from his grasp. Unlike Orpheus, William Wallace finds his wife back home after his visit to the underworld. The wise doctor who owns the net and speaks in proverbs already has declared: "The excursion is the same when you go looking for your sorrow as when you go looking for your joy."

"A Still Moment," like "First Love," is set in the historical past of the Natchez Trace. A story that Welty found to be one of her favorites when she reread her work in preparation for the publication of her *Collected Stories*, "A Still Moment" takes place in the year 1811. Three famous historical figures who were all in Mississippi at the same time are brought together for an imagined meeting at dusk along the Natchez Trace: the evangelist Lorenzo Dow, the murderer and bandit James Murrell, and the naturalist and artist John James Audubon. As each character focuses on a different vision of a single "snowy heron," Welty reflects on the distance between art and nature and the relation between life stories and death. Audubon thinks:

> He knew that the best he could make would be, after it was apart from his hand, a dead thing and not a live thing, never the essence, only a sum of parts; and that it would always meet with a stranger's sight, and never be one with the beauty in any other man's head in the world.

Paradoxically, perhaps, the hallucinatory visions of "A Still Moment" and "First Love" take place within the context of Welty's attempts to imagine actual historical persons or events. She drew on diaries, letters, and sermons in "A Still Moment," and her travels throughout the regions of Mississippi as a photographer for the WPA included archival research into the flamboyant narratives and legends of Mississippi history. The study of the legends and traditions of the Natchez Trace in her subsequent job with the Mississippi Advertising Commission also contributed to the composition of *The Robber Bridegroom*, "a fairy tale of the Natchez Trace" that Welty wrote in the midst of writing the stories contained in *The Wide Net*, in response to a request for a longer piece of fiction from her publisher. In this 1942 novella, set in the late eighteenth century, Welty tells the story of the intimate relation between robbers, bridegrooms, and planters, combining German fairy-tale motifs and American folk culture with both imaginary and historical characters. After reading this playful work, Faulkner wrote to Welty offering his compliments and asking if there were anything he could do for her in Hollywood.

Calling herself "a short story writer naturally," Welty is conscious of "never [having] intended to write a novel." She names "the long short story" as her "favorite form" and she claims that "every single one of my novels came about accidentally." *Delta Wedding*, according to Welty, began when she sent a short story called "The Delta Cousins" to Diarmuid Russell and he wrote back, "This is chapter two of a novel." Welty's first novel describes the extended Fairchild family as its many members and relatives have gathered together for a wedding. Welty was criticized for her choice of topic, faulted for having written a novel about the Old South and what remained of Southern plantation society in the Mississippi Delta country of the early 1920s. John Crowe Ransom warned that the novel would be perceived as "nostalgic for a way of life that already had passed beyond recognition."

Criticized in the national press for not writing a work of social criticism dealing with the problems of the South, Welty was defended by readers who argued that *Delta Wedding* was not intended to be about "the South"; it was rather a book-length extension of the epistemological, aesthetic, and psychological concerns of *The Wide Net*. Published in 1946, immediately after World War II, it is set in 1923, at a time when there was no flood, crop failure, or Depression to intrude upon the story of family relationships. Taking place just before the mechanization of cotton production, *Delta Wedding* is in many ways a historical novel that depicts a particular remnant of plantation society. Welty seems to have placed her novel before social and labor relations were irrevocably altered. Furthermore, as Barbara Ladd has argued, it is important to recognize the depth and complexity of Welty's treatment of black characters in *Delta Wedding*, and not to underestimate the ways in which they undermine or question the world of a white Delta family.

Criticism that Welty or her fiction should more explicitly address the political problems of the day—voiced both in print and in anonymous midnight telephone calls—led Welty to write an essay in 1965 entitled "Must the Novelist Crusade?" A defense in part of Faulkner, whose relevance had been questioned because he was "after all, only a white Mississippian," the essay asserts that "writing fiction is an interior affair" and defends the private truths of fiction that shows "life where it is lived." In an interview in 1973, Welty stated:

> Fiction is one thing; journalism's another. . . . Just because an author chooses not to crusade doesn't mean he has no conscience. . . . All my life I've been opposed to such things as racism and injustice and cruelty. Back when the civil rights movement was heating up, I used to get midnight phone calls from strangers, demanding to know why I was sitting down here, allowing such awful things to go on, and why I didn't make amends for my shortcomings by writing something that would teach those devils a lesson.
>
> (Prenshaw [1984], p. 151)

If Welty refused to be didactic, however, her subtle and detailed representations of the Southern folk, black as well as white, are not without lessons. In this context it is worth noting that the photographs she took during the Depression provide one of the most important documentary resources available today about black life in Mississippi during the early 1930s.

Welty's story of a Delta wedding is a story of "the wall of family" that stands against the outside world—even, as Ruth Vande Kieft points out, the outside "Southern world" that includes Memphis, small-town Virginia, the

Mississippi hills, and the state capital of Jackson. Welty's novels and her longer works of fiction (a category that includes *The Golden Apples*) typically tell the story of characters who struggle with the meaning of their own lives in relation to what is often the overpowering story of family and the identity that resides in family legend and tradition. The events described in Welty's novels, all of which might be said to have begun as short stories, typically elapse over brief periods of time ranging from a few hours to several weeks; yet their focus on highly charged ritualistic occasions (a wedding, the aftermath of a trial for murder, a family reunion, a funeral) extends over generations as the events of the present are transformed by the remembering of the past and the events of the past are revised or seen again through acts of retelling.

An exception to Welty's adherence to her version of the classical unities is *The Golden Apples,* a story cycle that spans two decades as it depicts Virgie Rainey and other characters in different periods of their lives. In the retrospection of these related stories, Welty represents several characters over a period of forty years, roughly the years from Welty's birth in 1909 to the time of the publication of the book in 1949. The "made-up Delta town" of Morgana is named for "*Fata Morgana*—the illusory shape, the mirage that comes over the sea." "All Delta places have names after people," Welty has explained, "so it was suitable to call it Morgana after some Morgans. My population might not have known there was such a thing as *Fata Morgana,* but illusions weren't unknown to them, all the same—coming in over the cottonfields." Like *Delta Wedding,* which had its origin in a story about a young girl's sexual initiation, *The Golden Apples* had its beginning in "June Recital," a story of sexual initiation that originally was titled "The Golden Apples" and that Welty once in an apparent slip of the tongue referred to as "Wedding Day." Like the longer works of fiction that follow it—*The Ponder Heart, Losing Battles,* and *The Optimist's Daughter*—*The Golden Apples* is concerned with death: "The Wanderers" concludes the volume with the story of the death and funeral of Virgie Rainey's mother.

Speaking of *The Golden Apples,* the book she has described as being "in a way closest to my heart of all my books," Welty recalls:

> I did not realize until I'd written half of these stories that all these people really did live in Morgana. So I was showing different phases of it, different aspects. They were all under the same compulsion. It was a marvelous moment with me when I realized that a story I'd written really was about a character from an earlier story. My subconscious mind, I guess, had been working on the same lines all the time. Everything slid into place like a jigsaw puzzle. . . . I loved it because I felt I could get deeper into all the people through using a number of stories and different times in their life than I could hope to do in using one story.
>
> (Prenshaw [1984], p. 332)

Despite these connections, Welty resists efforts to call *The Golden Apples* a novel on the grounds that each piece, although related to the others, stands alone as a story complete in itself. Unlike the sketches that make up Sarah Orne Jewett's story cycle *The Country of the Pointed Firs* (1927), which can be read as a novel because of their essential interdependence, the stories of *The Golden Apples* have, in Welty's words, "independent lives. They don't have to be connected, but I think by being connected there's something additional coming from them as a group with a meaning of its own." Read separately, for example, "June Recital" is arguably the finest story that Welty has written. Yet "June Recital" is even more powerful when read next to the profound account of female identity that is told in the concluding story, "The Wanderers."

During the 1950s, Welty for the most part wrote individual stories. In 1955 a group of loosely related stories that are all set outside of Mississippi were gathered in a collection called *The Bride of the Innisfallen.* These stories take place on the way to the Bayou country outside of New Orleans, Ireland, Naples, and even on Circe's island; the times range from the era of Odysseus to the Civil War to the present. Each story explores a foreign world from the perspective of a stranger. These characters are, in the opening words of first story of the volume, "No Place for You, My Love," both "strangers to each other" and "strangers to the place." The only longer work of fiction Welty published in this decade appeared in 1954. *The Ponder Heart* is a book-length monologue spoken by Edna Earle Ponder, the proprietress of the Beulah Hotel in Clay, Mississippi. Edna Earle's monologue is addressed to a stranger seated on a couch in the hotel, and the speaker tells the story of how she became estranged from the townsfolk who used to be her audience. One of Welty's most humorous pieces, the novel was dramatized and produced on Broadway in 1956.

The Ponder Heart and *Losing Battles* (1970), Welty's shortest and longest novels, are separated by fifteen years. During these years Welty was preoccupied with the illness and subsequent death of her mother. "I didn't write it in a normal way," Welty said of *Losing Battles*, "because I had private things at home." (She also wrote the first version of *The Optimist's Daughter* during this time; published in the *New Yorker* in 1969, it would win the Pulitzer Prize when revised as a novel in 1972.) Begun as a story about a father's return from the state "pen" at Parchman, *Losing Battles* contains the voices of some thirty-five characters who are attending a family reunion celebrating the ninetieth birthday of Granny Vaughn in the late 1930s. Like *The Ponder Heart*, the novel makes use of oral narrative and a dramatic structure. Welty described the importance of the novel's location in the hill country of northern Mississippi as a place that would allow "a chorus of voices, everybody talking and carrying on at once. I wanted to try something completely vocal and dramatized. Those people are natural talkers and storytellers."

Welty explains her technique in this extensive narrative experiment as an attempt to write

> a whole novel completely without going inside the minds of my characters, which is the way I do in most of my writing. I didn't tell how anyone thought—I tried to show it by speech and action. I was deliberately trying to see if I could convey the same thing by speech and outward appearance, as I used to do by going inside people's minds.
>
> (Prenshaw [1984), p. 293)

In its range and scope *Losing Battles* is the most Faulknerian of Welty's works; the map and the cast of characters that serves as a family genealogy, as well as its exploration of the significance of acts of storytelling, recall *Absalom, Absalom!* However, despite these and other similarities, *Losing Battles* also displays Welty's difference from Faulkner. In *Absalom, Absalom!* all of the voices "sound like father," whereas in *Losing Battles* (as in much of Welty's work) each character speaks in his or her own voice to tell the collective story of a family and that family's relation to the story of its place.

The Optimist's Daughter was written before Welty completed *Losing Battles*. Described by Welty as "in form a long story, though it undertakes the scope of a novel," it was first published in story form in the *New Yorker* in 1969 and finally published in its revised form in 1972. Welty has referred to it as "an interior story of what went on in a young widow's mind in response to grief and loss and her adjustment to facing up to it"; the novel, which Welty dedicated to her mother, Chestina Andrews Welty ("For C.A.W."), was written following the deaths of both her mother and her youngest brother in the same week. Laurel McKelva Hand, an artist whose husband has been killed in World War II, returns home to Mount Salus, Mississippi, after her father, Judge McKelva, has died following an operation for an eye ailment; his problems with his vision began when he thought he could see behind himself. After the death of his first wife, Laurel's mother, the judge had married a woman from a lower class, and much of the action of the novel involves the tension between the two women and their vastly different styles of mourning.

Although these particular details of plot do not correspond directly to Welty's life, *The Optimist's Daughter* is her most autobiographical book besides *One Writer's Beginnings.* She has referred to Laurel's memories of going to visit her mother's family in West Virginia as her own "literal memory," by which she means "the physical memory of how it looked—the shoals, the mountains—and how it sounded; the memory of the entire setting." In describing the "transposition" of her own feelings and experience in her fiction in an 1978 interview, Welty gives the account of the death of the father in *The Optimist's Daughter* as an example of how her own experience of the death of her father has been "altered" and "transmuted" in the "entirely different" death of the judge in the novel. She mentions that her mother, like Laurel's father, had "operations on her eyes" and "did die within my recent experience."

The 1984 publication of *One Writer's Beginnings* revealed that *The Optimist's Daughter* also represents the story of the death of Welty's own mother's father. The story recalled by Laurel about how her mother at the age of fifteen had taken her dying father across an ice-filled river to get the hospital in Baltimore contains all the essential details of the story about Chestina Andrews's attempt to save her own father that is recounted in *One Writer's Beginnings;* indeed, the dialogue in the two versions is virtually identical. Welty honors her mother by inscribing this story in *The Optimist's Daughter.* Her decision to render the spoken words of the story her mother had told her—how it sounded—with relatively little transposition in her novel suggests the sanctity of this story of death for Welty. Such a story has cultural as well as personal significance; unlike other stories, which become embellished over the years, stories that convey last words and the moment of death tend to remain intact.

Welty has gone to some lengths to assert that although her fiction may be "very personal" it is not autobiographical. She insists that "your private life should be kept private. . . . They'd have a hard time trying to find something about me. . . . It's best to burn letters, but at least I've never kept diaries or journals." *The Golden Apples* is prefaced with the unusual disclaimer that "the characters . . . and their situations are products of the author's imagination and are not intended to portray real people or real situations"—which apparently moved Katherine Anne Porter to write in her copy of the book, "All right honey, we shorely believes you!"

Welty explains that although she writes "out of emotional experience," this "is not necessarily out of factual experience." She continues: "What I do is translate something that's happened to me into dramatic terms. . . . I couldn't write about any important emotional thing if I hadn't experience it." Although she doesn't "deliberately avoid being autobiographical," Welty explains that in writing she must "invent the things that best show my feelings about my own experience or about life. . . . I do much better with invented characters who can better carry out, act out, my feelings." Characters, she has said, "are really conceptions of my own. . . . I endow them with things I have observed, dreamed or understood but no one represents a real person."

"Except for what's personal," Welty has remarked, "there is really so little to tell, and that little lacking in excitement and drama in the way of the world." Welty's work is clearly personal in this sense, but to fully understand its autobiographical dimensions one has to understand how her fiction is about questions of biography, identity, family, memory, and the significance of telling one's story. Within the powerful tradition of family that Welty represents, the lines between autobiography and biography, between individual and family, form a crossroads where "our separate journeys converge"—what Welty calls in *One Writer's Beginnings* the "meeting points" that are "the charged dramatic fields of fiction." In a world where family is the source of identity, autobiographies must begin long before a particular individual is born. For Southerners this is more than a genealogical account; it is an account of living memory. Harry Crews's memoir, *A Childhood: The Biography of a Place* (1978), opens with his first memory: a scene that took place ten years before he was born. Welty's memoir, *One Writer's Beginnings,* tells about her childhood and her origins as a writer but to a great extent recounts the life stories of her parents and grandparents. Her autobiography, personal yet still private, is also the biography of place and family. In the last pages she writes: "I glimpse our whole family life as if it were freed of that clock time which spaces us apart so inhibitingly, divides young and old, keeps our living through the same experiences at separate distances."

Welty's fiction is most deeply autobiographical, however, in its consistent concern with female identity, the relation between mothers and daughters, and the story of the woman artist. Several of Welty's fictions take the form of first-person monologues spoken by women; these pieces often are comic, such as *The Ponder Heart,* "Why I Live at the P.O.," and "Shower of Gold." As Louise Westling and others have suggested, in each of Welty's longer works of fiction there is a beloved male character who is the focal point of attention: George of *Delta Wedding,* King MacLain of *The Golden Apples,* Uncle Daniel of *The Ponder Heart,* Jack of *Losing Battles,* and Judge McKelva of *The Optimist's Daughter.* With the exception of Jack, who assumed a larger role than Welty originally anticipated, they are for the most part mysterious heroes who speak relatively little in the narrative yet stir the imagination of the female characters with their actions. However, the narrative point of view of these works tends to reside in female characters. One of the few stories Welty wrote in the first-person narration of a male character is "Where Is the Voice Coming From?," her uncannily accurate attempt to imagine the psyche of the murderer of Medgar Evers. "I really cannot envision my telling something from the male viewpoint," Welty commented; yet in this case, she explained, "somehow, this was more than a man; he was a murderer. Now, does that make me more of a murderer than a man?" One could imagine that the nine-year-old motherless girl who arrives at the beginning of *Delta Wedding* is at least partly a transposition of the story of her own father, whose mother died when he was seven, translated from the male to the female point of view.

Welty has described the Delta as "very much of a matriarchy," but indeed all of her novels take place in a world that has women at its center. In the motherless girl who begins *Delta Wedding,* in Edna Earle Ponder of *The Ponder Heart,* in the grieving widow and orphaned daughter of *The Optimist's Daughter,* Welty has focused on bereft and in many ways isolated female characters who must puzzle over the meaning of loss, family, and consolation. The most powerful pattern of female identity that emerges in Welty's fiction might be seen in the story of mothers and daughters that is told in *The Golden Apples* and *Losing Battles.* In these works Welty portrays reluctant daughters who desire to escape from the bounds of family yet in ritualized scenes must come to terms with the meaning of their mothers' lives—and by implication, the meaning of women's lives. Both Virgie Rainey of *The Golden Apples* and Gloria Short of *Losing Battles* are placed between two mothers who represent two possible alternatives for female identity. In each work there is a teacher who represents the call of art (the piano teacher Miss Eckhart and the schoolteacher Miss Mortimer) and a biological mother who represents the body and physical desire (Miss Katie Rainey and Rachel Sojourner). In these works, the reluctant daughter who figures the potential female artist gains what Katherine Anne Porter in another context calls "blood knowledge."

In *Losing Battles,* Gloria Short is forcibly re-membered into the family clan. Her initial stance as an in-law recalls other outsiders in Welty's fiction who make "the wall of family" visible by their resistance to it. Gloria in particular recalls Robbie Reid of *Delta Wedding,* who insists rather hopelessly in relation to the Fairchild clan: "I didn't *marry into* them! I married George!" *Losing Battles* tells the story of the Beechams, an upland family, by telling the story of their reunion. In perhaps the most violent scene in all of Welty's work, Gloria is forced to eat watermelon by her female relatives. This episode recalls a quieter scene from a reunion in Jewett's *The Country of the Pointed Firs* in which the narrator (an outsider, the writer who ultimately tells the family story) is ritually included into the family by being served a piece of pie that literally bears the family name. Jewett's story, which attributes the popularity of reunions to the unsettling events of the Civil War, recalls the more painful history of "reunion" for the South. In Welty's novel, "reunion" describes not only a family gathering but a narrative process that (like "reunion" for Mississippi) is enacted through a scene of violence. In Welty's novel, Gloria Short is thrown to the ground by women who encircle her and with "hands robbed of sex" force chunks of seed-filled melon down "her little red lane" as they try to make her say the family name.

Forced to eat "the blood heat" of the melon, Gloria is pressed to "say Beecham." The women of the family demand that she eat words: "say who's a Beecham! Then swallow it!" In Welty's colloquial joke, Gloria may indeed be made to say "uncle." While the women here are ostensibly forcing the orphan Gloria to submit to their version of her life's story, which names her husband's uncle as her father, by forcing her to "say Beecham" they would force her to say the name of the mother: her husband's mother, Beulah Beecham Renfro. Welty underlines this point by having Miss Beulah lift Gloria from the ground as she announces: "Gloria Beecham Renfro. . . . Get up and join your family, for a change." Although Gloria resists the idea that she is a Beecham on the inside, this is proven by the existence of her daughter, Lady May, who in this instance is what Welty elsewhere has described as "reality and symbol in one." Remembering Gloria's recent pregnancy, the young girl Elvie imagines the consequences of the Beecham women's implanting of seeds. Gloria may again become Beecham on the inside since "if she swallows them seeds she'll only grow another Tom Watson melon inside her stomach." As she eats symbols in a struggle over names, Gloria enacts a ritual of blood, family, and fertility.

Welty creates the character of a daughter who, so to speak, has family forcibly shoved down her throat. Caught between two mothers—the schoolteacher Miss Julia Mortimer, who represents the written word and the life of the mind (asexual reproduction), and the fox-headed Rachel Sojourner, who sews but can't read or cipher and represents bodily generation—Gloria is claimed by Miss Beulah, the next matriarch of the clan. The significance of blood relation to Gloria's role as the listener/teller of the family story is declared by Uncle Noah Webster (who is named, of course, for the author of the dictionary): "he smacked Gloria's cheek with a last big kiss that smelled of watermelon" and declares: "Gloria, this has been a story on us all that never will be allowed to be forgotten. . . . Long after you're an old lady without much further stretch to go, sitting back in the same rocking chair Granny's got her little self in now, you'll be hearing it told to Lady May and all her hovering brood."

In *The Golden Apples,* published more than twenty years before *Losing Battles,* the heroine also chooses between mothers: the piano teacher (Miss Eckhart) and the biological mother (Miss Katie). Virgie Rainey is described with her

> fingers set, after coming back, set half-closed; the strength in her hands she used up to type in the office but most consciously to pull the udders of the succeeding cows, as if she would hunt, hunt, hunt daily for the blindness that lay inside the beast, inside where she could have a real and living wall for beating on, a solid prison to get out of, the most real stupidity of flesh, a mindless and careless and calling body, to respond flesh

> for flesh, anguish for anguish. And if, as she dreamed one winter night, a new piano she touched had turned, after the one pristine moment, into a calling cow, it was by her own desire.
> (p. 235)

Welty's own mother bought a cow and sent her only daughter to deliver milk so they could afford to buy an upright Steinway piano. "While I sat on the piano stool practicing my scales," she writes in *One Writer's Beginnings*, "I imagined my mother sitting on her stool in the cowshed, her fingers just as rhythmically pulling the teats of Daisy." Beyond this association between mother, milk, cows, and pianos, however, the significance of Virgic Rainey's dream images lies in their reunion of the two halves of her life: her different mothers, the milk of art and the milk of nature.

In "June Recital," the second story of *The Golden Apples*, Cassie recalls Virgie Rainey at age thirteen standing up after her performance of Beethoven with a "red sash drawn around under the arms of a starched white swiss dress"; she recalls how "the red of the sash was all over the front of her waist, she was wet and stained as if she had been stabbed in the heart." At the end of "The Wanderers," in another image of division and dismemberment, Virgie recalls a picture that Miss Eckhart "hung over the dictionary" that "showed Perseus with the head of the Medusa. . . . Cutting off the Medusa's head was the heroic act, perhaps, that made visible a horror in life, that was once the horror in love, Virgie thought—the separateness." Just before her death Virgie Rainey's mother Miss Katie senses the appropriateness of the division of her own body by a stroke and sees herself as a model for all women:

> Whereas, there was a simple line down through her own body now, dividing it in half; there should be one in every woman's body—it would need to be the long way, not the cross way—that was too easy—making each of them a side to feel and know, and a side to stop it, to be waited on, finally.
> (p. 207)

With a still body that must be waited on by a living body, Miss Katie in her self-division becomes a literal embodiment of memory, the necessity that the living remember the dead. Having had a stroke, Miss Katie has escaped the fate of the Medusa; she has not been divided "the cross way" in the traditional cut of the mind/body split. The living body waits on the still body, the present waits on and remembers the past, a past that is dead if it is not served.

At the time of her death Miss Katie is also doubled in another sense; having literally forgotten herself, she thinks that she is her own daughter and she contemplates the impending death of her mother—that is, herself. As she dies, she remembers herself: "Mistake. Never Virgie at all. It was me, the bride—with more than they guessed. Why, Virgie, go away, it was me." Despite these figures of divided women, however, in "The Wanderers," the final story, Welty emphasizes Virgie's resistance to self-division, her efforts toward wholeness. After Miss Katie's death, Virgie seems separate from her mother for the first time. In a scene that enters into dialogue with a tradition of writers as diverse as George Eliot, Willa Cather, and Kate Chopin (each of whom has written fictions of female identity in which women who have given up a life of art or teaching for sexuality are threatened with drowning), Virgie goes swimming. Instead of drowning, on the day of her mother's death, Virgie is allowed a temporary regression into a watery world. Undivided as she sees "her waist disappear into the reflectionless water," Virgie seems re-membered by the water: "All was one warmth, air, water, and her own body. All seemed one weight, one matter. . . . She felt this matter a translucent one, the river, herself, the sky all vessels which the sun filled." Here she senses the effluvia of the river as the passage of time and "the ribbons of grass and mud . . . leave her, like suggestions and withdrawals of some bondage that might have been dear, now dismembering and losing itself." In the end, as Virgie is left "all to herself," the narrative asks (with profound Faulknerian skepticism): "Was she that? Could she ever be, would she be, where she was going?" Welty suggests a story of identity in which Virgie Rainey cannot be "all to herself," cannot be all one, cannot be severed from the past or past relationships.

Although the mothers in both *Losing Battles* and *The Golden Apples* represent choices, neither is chosen in an act of final definition. Rather, both mothers are remembered. Each reluctant daughter looks for the graves of her two mothers. To choose the life of either the bodily mother or the artistic mother would mean that Gloria or Virgie would be cut crossways at the neck. What Welty offers in her repeated images of the divided woman is perhaps an odd figure for the possibility of wholeness where wholeness may come in halves at some later moment when, in a reformulation of a question asked in *The Golden Apples*, "daughters *forgive* mothers (with mothers under their heel)." Wholeness in Welty's view may come only after the knowledge of death, in the remembering that, in Welty's words, "acquires the power of an art." She continues, in discussing "memory and the life of the past" in Faulkner:

> Remembering is done through the blood, it is a bequeathment, it takes account of what happens before a man is born as if he were there taking part. It is a physical absorption through the living body, it is a spiritual heritage. It is also a life's work.

In her autobiography, Welty dramatizes an act of remembering through the blood that tells a story about mothers and daughters, focusing on the moment before death. It is, in a sense, a story about what she describes at the end of *One Writer's Beginnings* as "the wonderful word *confluence,* which of itself exists as a reality and a symbol in one. It is the only kind of symbol that for me as a writer has any weight, testifying to the pattern, one of the chief patterns, of human experience." In describing this word, this pattern of experience, Welty cites the closing of *The Optimist's Daughter,* in which the daughter describes "the confluence of the waters" of the Ohio and the Mississippi rivers, a "confluence" in which she and her then living husband take part. *One Writer's Beginnings* contains a scene of deadly confluence in which "the separate journeys" of Welty and her mother "converge." This is the scene in which the twenty-two-year-old Welty is present in the hospital as her mother tries to save her father's life with a blood transfusion.

Welty watches, knowing that in the mind of her mother—"whose strongest habit of thought was association"—is the memory of a time that she had faced death and her husband had saved her life by giving her champagne: "This time, *she* would save *his* life, as he'd saved hers so long ago." However, as Welty's mother lies on a cot next to her husband, Welty sees the poetic argument fail. As the mother's blood flows directly into the father's body, his "face turned dusky red." In this instance the mystery of blood caused death. In trying to save her husband, Welty's mother is repeating more than one story; and consequently Welty herself in this scene of her life is repeating the story of her own mother's life, when the young Chestina Andrews took *her* father across an icy river and by train to Johns Hopkins Hospital in an effort to save his life. In this family story, which is repeated in the fiction of *The Optimist's Daughter,* she did not see him die but is the only one there to tell the story, the story of her father's death. Eudora Welty *might* have been present to see this story rewritten, but what she saw instead was a fatal confluence—in which she, like her mother, is unable to prevent her father's death and is left to tell the story. Welty repeats the story of her mother's life as Chestina Andrews Welty also unwittingly repeats her own story in failing to save the life of her husband. Trying to repeat the story of her life, Welty's mother repeats the wrong story, and her daughter finds that she must repeat it as well. In the version of this moment represented in *The Optimist's*

Daughter, Laurel understands what she and her mother share: "Neither of us saved our fathers."

As she watches, Welty is more than a literary figure. She is a literal figure: "symbol and reality in one." An emblem of life, the literal embodiment of her parents' joined blood, she witnesses a deadly version of a primal scene in which the joining of her parents—the mixing of her parents' blood—causes death rather than life. This convergence, this confluence, memorialized by the daughter who embodies one form of transfusion, suggests the profound sources of Welty's vision in her critical insight: "Remembering is done through the blood." Having lived "through the same experiences at separate distances," whether present in the same time and space or not, Welty offers an interpretation of the life's work that acquires the power of an art. It is this transposition of memory and blood that Welty translates into dramatic terms in her fiction.

In an interview Welty called Virgie's piano teacher, Miss Eckhart, "a very mysterious character." In *One Writer's Beginnings,* noting, "It was not my intention—it never was—to invent a character who should speak for me, the author, in person," she acknowledges that Miss Eckhart turned out to be such a persona, "a character with whom I came to feel oddly in touch." She writes:

> As I looked longer and longer for the origins of this passionate and strange character, at last I realized that Miss Eckhart came from me. There wasn't any resemblance in her outward identity: I am not musical, not a teacher, nor foreign in birth; not humorless or ridiculed or missing out in love; nor have I yet let the world around me slip from my recognition. But none of that counts. What counts is only what lies at the solitary core. She derived from what I already knew for myself, even felf I had always known. What I have put into her is my passion for my own life work, my own art. Exposing yourself to risk is a truth Miss Eckhart and I had in common. What animates and possesses me is what drives Miss Eckhart, the love of her art and the love of giving it, the desire to give it until there is no more left. (p. 101)

In the final chapter of *One Writer's Beginnings,* entitled "Finding a Voice," Welty explains: "Not in Miss Eckhart as she stands solidly and almost opaquely in the surround of her story, but in the making of her character out of my most inward and most deeply feeling self, I would say I have found my voice in my fiction." Perhaps in the future the reading public will know more about the details of Eudora Welty's biography: whom she loved, her crises and triumphs, her silences, the personal facts of a private life. However, the lessons of such mysterious and luminously opaque characters as the artist and teacher Miss Eckhart always will instruct us in the acts of remembering and imagination that make up both Welty's life story and the stories of our own lives.

Selected Bibliography

PRIMARY WORKS

NOVELS

The Robber Bridegroom. New York: Doubleday, Doran, 1942.

Delta Wedding. New York: Harcourt, Brace & World, 1946.

The Golden Apples. New York: Harcourt, Brace, & World 1949.

The Ponder Heart. New York: Harcourt, Brace & World, 1954.

Losing Battles. New York: Random House, 1970.

The Optimist's Daughter. New York: Random House, 1972.

SHORT STORIES

A Curtain of Green and Other Stories. New York: Doubleday, Doran, 1941.

The Wide Net and Other Stories. New York: Harcourt, Brace & World, 1943.

The Bride of the Innisfallen and Other Stories. New York: Harcourt, Brace & World, 1955.

Thirteen Stories. New York: Harcourt Brace Jovanovich, 1965.

The Collected Stories of Eudora Welty. New York: Harcourt Brace Jovanovich, 1980.

NONFICTION

One Time, One Place: Mississippi in the Depression—Snapshot Album. New York: Random House, 1971.

The Eye of the Story: Selected Essays and Reviews. New York: Random House, 1978.

One Writer's Beginnings. Cambridge, Mass.: Harvard University Press, 1984.

Photographs. Jackson: University Press of Mississippi, 1989. Introduction by Reynolds Price.

MANUSCRIPTS AND PAPERS

Marrs, Suzanne. *The Welty Collection: A Guide to the Eudora Welty Manuscripts and Documents at the Mississippi Department of Archives and History.* Jackson: University Press of Mississippi, 1988.

SECONDARY WORKS

BIOGRAPHICAL AND CRITICAL STUDIES

Aargione, Nancy D. "Portrait of an Assassin: Eudora Welty's 'Where Is the Voice Coming From?' " *Southern Literary Journal* 20:74–88 (Fall 1987).

Blackwell, Louise. "Eudora Welty: Proverbs and Proverbial Phrases in *The Golden Apples.*" *Southern Folklore Quarterly* 30:332–341 (December 1966).

Bloom, Harold, ed. *Eudora Welty.* New York: Chelsea House, 1986.

Bryant, J. A., Jr. *Eudora Welty.* University of Minnesota Pamphlets on American Writers, no. 66. Minneapolis: University of Minnesota Press, 1968.

Davis, Charles E. "The South in Eudora Welty's Fiction: A Changing World." *Studies in American Fiction* 3:199–209 (1976).

Delta 5 (November 1977). Special issue on Welty.

Desmond, John F., ed. *A Still Moment: Essays on the Art of Eudora Welty.* Metuchen, N.J.: Scarecrow Press, 1978.

Devlin, Albert J. *Eudora Welty's Chronicle: A Story of Mississippi Life.* Jackson: University Press of Mississippi, 1983.

———, ed. *Welty: A Life in Literature.* Jackson: University Press of Mississippi, 1987.

Dollarhide, Louis, and Anne J. Abadie, eds. *Eudora Welty: A Form of Thanks.* Jackson: University Press of Mississippi, 1979.

Eudora Welty Newsletter. Toledo, Ohio. 1977– .

Howard, Zelma Turner. *The Rhetoric of Eudora Welty's Short Stories.* Jackson: University and College Press of Mississippi, 1973.

Kreyling, Michael. *Eudora Welty's Achievement of Order.* Baton Rouge: Louisiana State University Press, 1980.

———. "Modernism in Welty's *A Curtain of Green and Other Stories.*" *Southern Quarterly* 20:40–53 (Summer 1982).

Ladd, Barbara. " 'Coming Through': The Black Initiate in *Delta Wedding.*" *Mississippi Quarterly* 41:541–551 (Fall 1988).

Mann, C. "Eudora Welty, Photographer." *History of Photography* 6:145–149 (April 1982).

Manning, Carol S. *With Ears Opening Like Morning Glories: Eudora Welty and the Love of Storytelling.* Westport, Conn.: Greenwood Press, 1985.

Manz-Kunz, Marie Antoinette. *Eudora Welty: Aspects of Reality in Her Short Fiction* (Bern: Francke Verlag, 1971).

Marrs, Suzanne. "The Metaphor of Race in Eudora Welty's Fiction." *Southern Review* 22:697–707 (Autumn 1986).

Moreland, Richard C. "Community and Vision in Eudora Welty." *Southern Review* n.s. 18:84–99 (Winter 1982).

Morris, Harry C. "Eudora Welty's Use of Mythology." *Shenandoah* 6, no. 2:34–40 (Spring 1955).

Mississippi Quarterly 26 (Fall 1973). Special issue on Welty.

Mississippi Quarterly 39 (Fall 1986). Fiftieth-year celebration of publication of Welty's first story.

Prenshaw, Peggy Whitman, ed. *Eudora Welty: Critical Essays.* Jackson: University Press of Mississippi, 1979.

———. *Conversations with Eudora Welty.* Jackson: University Press of Mississippi, 1984.

Rubin, Louis D., Jr. "Art and Artistry in Morgana, Mississippi." *Mississippi Review* 4:101–116 (Summer 1981).

Shenandoah 20 (Spring 1969). Special issue on Welty.

Spacks, Patricia Meyer. *Gossip.* New York: Knopf, 1985.

Sprengnether, Madelon. "*Delta Wedding* and the Kore Complex." *Southern Quarterly* 25:120–130 (Winter 1987).

Tiegreen, Helen Hurt. "Mothers, Daughters and One Writer's Revisions." *Mississippi Quarterly* 39:605–626 (Fall 1986).

Trouard, Dawn, ed. *Eudora Welty: Eye of the Storyteller.* Kent, Ohio: Kent State University Press, 1989.

Turner, W. Craig, and Lee Emling Harding. *Critical Essays on Eudora Welty.* Boston: Hall, 1989.

Vande Kieft, Ruth M. *Eudora Welty.* New York: Twayne, 1962. Rev. ed. 1987.

Warren, Robert Penn. "Love and Separateness in Eudora Welty." *Selected Essays.* New York: Random House, 1958.

Westling, Louise. *Sacred Groves and Ravaged Gardens: The Fiction of Eudora Welty, Carson McCullers, and Flannery O'Connor*. Athens: University of Georgia Press, 1985.

———. "The Loving Observer of *One Time, One Place*." *Mississippi Quarterly* 39:587–604 (Fall 1986).

———. *Eudora Welty*. London: Macmillan, 1989.

Yaeger, Patricia S. "The Case of the Dangling Signifier: Phallic Imagery in Welty's *'Moon Lake.'* " *Twentieth-Century Literature* 28:431–452 (Winter 1982).

———. " 'Because a Fire Was in My Head': Eudora Welty and the Dialogic Imagination." *PMLA* 99: 955–973 (October 1984).

BIBLIOGRAPHIES

Gross, Seymour L. "Eudora Welty: A Bibliography of Criticism and Comment." Secretary's News Sheet, Bibliography Society, University of Virginia, no. 45 (April 1960).

McHaney, Pearl Amelia. *A Eudora Welty Checklist, 1973–1986*. In *Welty: A Life in Literature*. Edited by Albert J. Devlin. Jackson: University Press of Mississippi, 1983. Pp. 266–302.

Polk, Noel. *A Eudora Welty Checklist, 1936–1972*. In *Welty: A Life in Literature*. Edited by Albert J. Devlin. Jackson: University Press of Mississippi, 1983. Pp. 238–265.

Swearingen, Bethany C. *Eudora Welty: A Critical Bibliography, 1936–1958*. Jackson: University Press of Mississippi, 1984.

Thompson, Victor H. *Eudora Welty: A Reference Guide*. Boston: G. K. Hall, 1976.

Eudora Welty Newsletter. 1977– . Contains updated checklists of works by and about Welty.

CANDACE WAID

EDITH WHARTON

1862–1937

BORN INTO A genteel and socially secure family that could trace its ancestry back through English and Dutch patricians of New York, Edith Wharton would seem to be the very definition of the society writer, especially when one examines the many photographs of her that present the viewer with an immaculately coiffed and gowned woman who looks at the camera with a decidely superior air. Yet Edith Wharton in many ways was a rebel, even an outcast, and her many novels and tales passionately endorse the struggle to forge one's identity outside accepted social boundaries.

Edith Newbold Jones was born in New York City on 24 January 1862 to the socialites George Frederic and Lucretia Rhinelander Jones. She had two much older brothers, and thus she was essentially an only child; like many only children she seems to have used her imagination to produce fictions that would serve as an antidote to loneliness. More than six years of her childhood were spent abroad, where she began her mastery of European languages.

Edith's aloof and socially obsessed mother greeted her twelve-year-old daughter's tale about a hostess caught with a messy drawing room by a caller with the icy comment "Drawing rooms are always tidy." Nevertheless, Mrs. Jones saw to it that Edith's adolescent poems were privately published (under the title *Verses*) in 1878 and hired excellent tutors to instruct her in carefully selected literature and the foreign languages. In 1877 Edith's novella *Fast and Loose*, a tale of doomed young love, was completed (but not published) under the nom de plume "David Olivieri." In 1879 William Dean Howells, acting on the recommendation of Henry Wadsworth Longfellow, published one of Wharton's poems in the *Atlantic Monthly*.

Even at age seventy-five, Wharton was still bemoaning "how pitiful a provision was made for the life of the imagination behind those uniform brownstone facades" of her childhood. The fashionable homes in Washington Square and on Fifth Avenue were bastions of tradition but not necessarily of culture. They featured good food, fine wines, elegant clothing, the teachings of the Episcopal church; however, the great books in the libraries often went unread, and European diversions such as music and art were not part of the fashionable life until much later. Although Wharton, a voracious reader, begged forbidden books from her tutors and traveled widely with her parents, she essentially was trained to think of herself as an ornament of society, much like her heroine Lily Bart (indeed, *The House of Mirth* was originally to be called *A Moment's Ornament*).

All young girls were expected to make a debut, marry, and become involved in polite societal functions. Shy and attractive but not pretty, Edith seems to have been shaken in 1882 by her broken engagement to Harry Stevens; her fiancé was reported by the *Newport Daily News* to have dropped her because "Miss Jones is an ambitious authoress, and it is said that, in the eyes of Mr. Stevens, ambition is a grievous fault." This perhaps led her to accept the suit of Edward Wharton (known as Teddy), her brother's friend and thirteen years her senior. A handsome, athletic man who shared her interest in pets, gardens, and society, he had beautiful manners, a Harvard degree, a modest income, and the Bostonian's ease in elegant company. They were married on 29 April 1885 and moved into a cottage on her mother's estate in Newport, but annually spent February through June in Europe. Eventually they bought a home on

Park Avenue, and Edith employed the Boston architect Ogden Codman to remodel it. After suffering a nervous breakdown, she once again turned to writing as a release, collaborating in 1896 with Codman on the first American book on home design, *The Decoration of Houses* (published in 1897). She suffered another paralyzing depression the following year, which she attempted to cure by undergoing the notorious "total rest" Weir-Mitchell treatment.

The 1897 breakdown no doubt occurred because of Wharton's growing sense of marital entrapment. She had begun to realize how uncomfortable Teddy was in intellectual areas, and their sexual relationship seems initially to have been traumatic, and soon after, nonexistent. To make matters worse, Edith was judged a failure in Boston, her husband's home, and in New York as well, because people thought she was too intelligent to be fashionable.

Hints of her unhappiness surfaced in one of Wharton's first stories, "The Fullness of Life" (1891), which depicts a woman in conversation with the Spirit of Life as she enters eternity. She confesses that her marriage had always been lacking: "His boots creaked and he always slammed the door . . . and he never read anything but railway novels and the sporting advertisements in the paper—and—in short, we never understood each other." Increasingly, husbands such as this one appear in Wharton's fiction, dominating a much stronger and almost always more intelligent wife.

Wharton put up with this situation because she had been reared in a society that did not tolerate divorce. In the early years of the marriage, however, there were definitely compensations, especially in their shared love for travel. In 1901 she and Teddy began to build a magnificent home, the Mount, in Lenox, Massachusetts, which was the scene of fabled house parties. Wharton's beloved Henry James, whom she met in in 1887 but really came to know in 1900, was a visitor when in America, taking long motor trips with the Whartons across the Berkshire Hills, a prefiguring of their European jaunts in Edith's chauffeured cars. Wharton was an insatiable traveler; like Alexander the Great, she was always in search of new worlds to conquer—fist with Teddy, later with male friends such as Walter Berry, Bernard Berenson, Howard Sturgis, Gaillard Lapsley, and, of course, James.

As close as Wharton was to James, her relationship with Berry was more intense and longer-lasting. She had known him before her marriage, and may have been in love with him even then. Certainly, however, he had much to do with her attitude toward fiction; his pithy observation "It is easy to see superficial resemblances between things. It takes a first-rate mind to percieve the differences underneath" because one of her critical touchstones. Wharton began a lifelong tutelage with him when he assisted with *The Decoration* of *Houses.*

This literary triumph encouraged Wharton to write stories, and in 1899 she published a collection under the title *The Greater Inclination.* Several of the tales significantly dissected unhappy marriages; "The Other Two" masterfully describes the destruction of a woman as she transforms herself, like a well-worn shoe, to accommodate the needs of three successive husbands. Critical and public success greeted the new book, and Wharton's career as a writer began. More important, Wharton observed that until *The Greater Inclination* appeared, she had no "real personality" of her own.

In Wharton's day, her short stories enchanted the public with a mix of drama and manners and a gradual unfolding of facts that frequently inverted the reader's initial understanding of the narrative. Some of the best, such as "Mrs. Manstey's View," "The Fullness of Life," "The Rembrandt," "Bunner Sisters," and "The Other Two," were written early in her career (before 1904). In *The Writing of Fiction* (1925) she codified what was already present in her fiction as early as 1899:

> Drama, situation, is made out of the conflicts thus produced between social order and individual appetites, and the art of rendering life in fic-

> tion can never, in the last analysis, be anything, or need to be anything, but the disengaging of crucial moments from the welter of existence. . . . There must be . . . some moral standard, some explicit awareness of the eternal struggle between man's contending impulses, if the tales embodying them are fix the attention and hold the memory.
>
> (p. 14)

True to her philosophy, Wharton again and again used this formula for her fictions. She seems to have decided that the world was a place where dichotomy reigned, both in morals and in nature. The characters in her works are often failures because they cannot cope with this ambivalence. She wrote of the struggle of the heart from her own experiences, first as a shy debutante, then as a socially disparaged "bohemian" New York writer, and later as an unhappy wife and thwarted lover, and self-exiled expatriate. She also wrote that in novels "no conclusion can be right which is not latent in the first page," and, deeply influenced by Darwinian science, she seemed to believe this was true of people and characters as well.

The Greater Inclination was followed in 1900 by the novella *The Touchstone,* a moving story of a young man who had an affair with a famous writer, now dead, whose letters to him are now worth money (an ironic prophecy: Wharton's lover sold her letters to him long after her death). Her first novel was *The Valley of Decision* (1902), a long, derivative, but scrupulously researched drama of ecclesiastic and political intrigue in *settecento* Italy. The book echoed both Wharton's search for identity and the trauma of the twentieth century's birth into modernism. *Valley* sold well and garnered glowing reviews, but literary success meant little to Wharton's social standing in New York. Among her friends it caused puzzlement and embarrassment, and in her own family:

> None of my relations ever spoke to me of my books, either to praise or blame—they simply ignored them. . . . The subject was avoided as if it were a kind of family disgrace. . . . At first I had felt this indifference acutely; but now I no longer cared, for my recognition as a writer had transformed my life. I had made my own friends and my books were beginning to serve as an introduction to my fellow writers.
>
> (*A Backward Glance,* p. 144)

As a consequence, Wharton eventually moved to Paris, where she met her greatest friends and wrote many of her greatest books. Once settled on the rue de Varenne, where she lived for thirteen years, she began to write of her former life. Old New York feared change, and change was coming in with the industrial fortunes of "the lords of Pittsburgh" and their ilk. Her satire turned both ways, attacking both the old order and the new.

Why did Edith Wharton choose to write about the society that she rejected, at least partly, because it had rejected her? She did so in an attempt to adhere to the essential rules that she recognized in writing: first, an author should deal only with what is within her reach, and second, the novelist's subject is valuable only to the degree that she sees it. The society she knew had imprisoned her in a suffocating world of trivia; it had also burdened her with an unhappy marriage. Yet it had taught her to appreciate beauty, order, and tradition. If she was to write of it in any meaningful way, her subject must be one that expressed her own experience. And for Wharton, as has become increasingly evident since the 1970s, as more biographical data has surfaced, that experience was one of repeated frustration and loss. Pondering how to justify the treatment of society while writing *The House of Mirth* (1905), she wondered:

> In what aspect could a society of irresponsible pleasure-seekers be said to have, on the "old woe of the world," any deeper bearing that the people composing such a society could guess? The answer was that a frivolous society can acquire dramatic significance only through what its frivolity destroys.
>
> (*A Backward Glance,* p. 207)

Furthermore, Wharton felt the modern novel had been born from the union of the French psychological novel and the English narrative of manners; Henry James had shown what both genres could do with American materials. She also saw that Honoré de Balzac and Jane Austen had described social worlds as limited as the one she came from, and that they had similarly dramatized those worlds by revealing their power to destroy. Edmund Wilson puts it another way: "Her tragic heroines and heroes . . . are passionate or imaginative spirits, hungry for emotional and intellectual experience, who find themselves locked into a small closed system, and either destroy themselves by beating their heads against their prison or suffer a living death in resigning themselves to it."

Lily Bart, heroine of *House of Mirth,* born into a world of wealth, is taught by her mother to despise anything that is "dingy." By the time she is twenty-nine, her naturally moral nature is a complement to her radiant but waning beauty, and her father's bankruptcy has taught her to marshal her assets. Financial ruin has brought about the death of both parents, which forces Lily to rely on the beneficence of her puritanical and eccentric Aunt Peniston and the social favors of wealthy friends. She spends long periods of time visiting the great country and town houses of the rich and powerful, seeking the only security she can hope for: a wealthy marriage. Her halfhearted pursuit of the boring but wealthy Percy Gryce involves pretending she understands the Americana he collects; her greatest social triumph comes during an evening of *tableaux-vivants,* when she poses frozen on a stage, depicting Reynolds' portrait of Mrs. Lloyd. Society will accept Lily only if she "freezes" herself into accepted poses and roles—but doing so "Bart"-ers away the "Lily" of the self.

Wai-chee Dimock is one of several critics who have commented tellingly on the debasing commodification of women in this business-obsessed culture. Lily, for most of the book, tries to find a buyer for her beauty but ruins her chances by periodically rebelling, albeit weakly, against the system. This reading somewhat ignores, however, the novel's equally strong fixation on chance. As Lily observes, "Society is a revolving body which is apt to be judged according to its place in each man's heaven"; latent in the metaphor one finds the wheel of fortune. In fact the novel opens with a chance encounter between Lily and Lawrence Selden in Grand Central Station: "What luck! . . . How nice of you to come to my rescue!" He responds joyfully that to do so is his mission in life, and asks what form the rescue is to take. Here the central theme emerges. Often meeting by chance, and magnetically attracted to each other, Selden, a well-born lawyer of modest means, and Lily remain star-crossed lovers, doomed to tragedy because neither can move the other to action and because their moments of insight never coincide. Like the novels of E. M. Forster, those of Wharton are frequently about missed connections, and none more so than this one.

Selden appeals to Lily because of his apparent moral sense and refinement, but fearing poverty, she rejects him and his proposed "republic of the spirit," a lofty moral and metaphysical realm. And he has reservations about her; acting as Wharton's surrogate, he wonders: Despite her "fine glaze of beauty . . . was it not possible that the material was fine but that circumstance had fashioned it into a futile shape? . . . She was so evidently the victim of the civilization which had produced her, that the links of her bracelet seemed like manacles chaining her to her fate." Indeed, near the end of the book, when asked what began her misfortunes, Lily replies, "In my cradle, I suppose, in the way I was brought up and the things I was taught to care for." It is Selden's fate to see her for what she is, to urge her to aspire to higher values, but to fail to rescue her because of his own fear of involvement. Lily says to him, "Why do you make the things I have chosen seem hateful to me, if you have nothing to give me instead?" Eventually, we learn Selden is a moral fraud; he's been having an affair with Bertha Dorset, the wealthy, predatory, and vindictive villain of the novel. He succeeds as a moral catalyst, however, for he brings out the finer instincts that eventually destroy Lily physically but save her morally.

We watch in fascinated horror as Lily becomes compromised by a series of predatory men, such as Simon Rosedale and Gus Trenor, who offer her protection and/or money for decreasingly veiled terms. They seize on her tendency to vacillate in the face of decision, and as a result—and because she will not surrender her virginity—she finds herself banished from a series of social worlds, each cruder and more predatory than the above it. Louis Auchincloss feels that "Lily's beauty is the light in which each of her different groups would like to shine, but when they find that it illuminates their ugliness they want to put it out, . . . a beauty that is the haunting symbol of what society might be—and isn't."

The determinist themes are reinforced throughout the novel by Darwinian terms. Selden sees Lily as "a higher species . . . that must have cost a great deal to make," and she can look on an ugly charwoman scrubbing Selden's stairs as "a creature." Outside Selden's house she meets the social climbing Rosedale, who is described in primitive terms, with his "screwed-up" eyelids and "glossy" look, which make Lily shiver. Nevertheless, his animal cunning and powerful drive to make money contrast in both positive and negative ways with Selden's aristocratic dilettantism. Wharton shows through Rosedale that "lower forms" like the nouveau riche are capable of advancement if they are provided with a society that is careless about its barriers, but we eventually see moral possibilities in him as well. Lily fails to "connect" with him, too; like Selden, another would-be savior, in the end Rosedale paradoxically cannot risk his recently hard-won social position to help such "damaged goods" as Lily has become.

Wharton brings her themes together in a brilliant juxtaposition of scenes. Lily's poor working-class friend Gerty Farish, alone in her cozy but drab apartment, muses on the glamorous life Lily must lead, even as Lily flees from the advances of Gus Trenor, who reveals that the returns on "investments" he has made for her were really gifts for which she is obliged to provide sexual favors. Fleeing, Lily feels the Furies she has read about in Aeschylus pursuing her: "She was alone in a place of darkness and pollution. Alone!" At this moment Lily loses the support of Gus, his wife's friendship, and Selden's confidence, as he sees her leave the Trenors' house, apparently compromised. The scene also begins the Dreiserian theme of the individual lost and alone in a great city, which gains momentum as Lily's doom approaches near the end of the book.

At this juncture, Lily is temporarily saved by Bertha Dorset's invitation to join her yachting party in Europe, but that setting proves to be a social duplicate of the one in New York. Worse, Lily makes the same mistakes, winning European male attention coveted by Bertha, yet never following through on her successes. The desperation of Lily's situation becomes clear to Selden as he watches her:

> A subtle change had passed over the quality of her beauty. Then it had had a transparency through which the fluctuations of the spirit were sometimes tragically visible; now its impenetrable surface suggested a process of crystallization. . . .
>
> She was on the edge of something, . . . on the brink of a chasm, with one graceful foot advanced to assert her unconsciousness that the ground was failing her.
>
> (1963 ed., pp. 185, 186)

Bertha's expulsion of Lily from the yacht for supposed involvement with George Dorset covers Bertha's own adultery. Her cruelty is duplicated by Judy Trenor and Carry Fisher, thus demonstrating that married women have greater freedom than Lily, who, as a single woman, must represent the myth of purity that stands for all women.

As always, moral and financial factors are intertwined. When news of what has happened on the yacht reaches Aunt Peniston, she virtually disinherits Lily, leaving her only ten thousand dollars. Lily sums up the moral-financial aspect of her situation succinctly: "What is truth? Where a woman is concerned, it's the story that's easiest to believe. In this case it's a great deal easier to believe Bertha Dorset's story than mine, because she has a big house and an opera box, and it's convenient to be on good terms with her."

Paradoxically, Lily has acquired letters written by Bertha that document the latter's affair with Selden, but her fine moral nature causes her to destroy them rather than stoop to the level of her enemies. Her moral victory is all the more costly in that she loses Rosedale as a result, for he will marry her only if she will blackmail Bertha. Elaine Showalter tellingly notes that Lily is caught in the historical transition from a supportive nineteenth-century feminine culture based in love and ritual to a new world of gender definition where women's roles are more dependent on relations with men (certainly this was true for Wharton herself as intellectual and author), and Lily's betrayal by her high-society friends speaks to this issue.

The remainder of the book reads like a parody of the first part. The increasing vulgarity of Lily's subsequent "houses" lets in more and more cold air and isolation, twin forces that conspire to make this "orchid" droop. As she moves into the social set of Sam and Mattie Gormer, she sees that it is

> only a flamboyant copy of her own world, a caricature approximating the real thing as the "society play" approaches the manners of the drawing-room. . . . The difference lay in a hundred shades of aspect and manner, from the pattern of the men's waistcoats to the inflexion of the women's voices.
>
> (1963 ed., p. 228)

Within this new world Lily zigzags across the continent with nouveau riche revelers, going from the Adirondacks to Alaska. Eventually she descends to the bottom level of the "house," the overheated and overstuffed hotel world of Norma Hatch and her circle. Norma's appearance places her on the lower end of the Darwinian scale: Her "large-eyed prettiness had the fixity of something impaled and shown under glass. . . . Lily had the odd sense of being behind the social tapestry, on the side where the threads were knotted and the loose ends hung." At Selden's urging she leaves this realm, only to find no means of support other than trimming hats in a fashionable shop. Scorned by the other women, who know her story, and resented by the employer, who sees her incompetence, she takes lonely walks home among the dreary New York tenements.

The last great scene in the novel is set in Selden's room, where Lily served afternoon tea in the first chapter. Now, however, "the gathering dusk" echoes Lily's life. Having been dismissed from her job, she has no road open but dishonor or death. She tells Selden that his love has sustained her and that the old Lily Bart is gone:

> I have tried hard—but life is difficult, and I am a very useless person. . . . I was just a screw or a cog in the great machine I called life. . . . What can one do when one finds that one only fits into one hole? One must get back to it or be thrown out into the rubbish heap.
>
> (1963 ed., p. 302)

Her only release from pain becomes the druggist's bottle, and she dies (is it suicide? we don't know) from an overdose of chloral.

One of Lily's last acts is to write out a check to Charles Augustus Trenor for the amount she owes him. This is the first time we learn Trenor's full name, and the word his initials spell and his imperial middle name are both emblematic of the society that has destroyed Lily. Selden finds the check when he comes, too late, to propose to Lily. Shortly before this scene, we have glimpsed Lily holding Nettie Struther's baby—a symbol of her own infant-like helplessness—in a tenement kitchen, feeling instinctively the possibilities of "the continuity of life" that others seem to be able to create out of nothing, even though this "house" has "the frail, audacious permanence of a bird's nest built on the edge of a cliff." The scene speaks of motherhood, but also of the possibilities of sisterhood, in Lily's bonding with working-class women.

The House of Mirth, crucial in Wharton's career, establishes many of her major themes and motifs. In its careful structure and symbolism, it reveals how much she had learned about her craft. Its imagery, concerned with fate, Furies, light, darkness, beauty, Darwinian nature, economic determinism, a social realm in transition, and, above all, a circumscribed role for women, points to themes she would employ throughout her career. A key element of all her succeeding work, however, is missing: the Strindbergian hell of an unhappy marriage. Her next great novels, *Ethan Frome* (1911) and *The Custom of the Country* (1913), would dramatically limn the contours of this lifelong preoccupation.

Wharton's life on the rue de Varenne lasted until the noise and crowds of postwar Paris drove her into residence in the French countryside. She gradually met important members of the *faubourg* society (initially through the author Paul Bourget), and eventually attracted a salon that included Rosa de Fitz-James, Anna de Noailles, Jean Cocteau, Bernard Berenson, Jacques-Émile Blanche, and Kenneth Clark. With the exception of Vernon Lee, she did not mix socially with lesbian writers in salon circles such as those of Natalie Barney and Gertrude Stein; and although she admired his writing, she never met Proust.

Between *House* and *Custom,* Wharton published *The Fruit of the Tree* and *Madame de Treymes* (both 1907). *Fruit* was an attempt at the novel of reform, and also touched on euthanasia. Although an interesting and rewarding book in many ways—especially in its depiction of the heroine, Justine Brent, and her marriage to a weak man—it ultimately lacks the power and scope of Wharton's greater works for the simple reason that she did not know this subject well. *Madame de Treymes* is a Jamesian tale of Americans in Paris, and seems indebted in particular to his novels *The American* and *The Ambassadors.* One of the key early lines is indicative of Wharton's interest in the novel of manners: "Durham, indeed, was beginning to find that one of the charms of a sophisticated society is that it lends point and perspective to the slightest contact between the sexes."

Fanny de Malrive's unhappy marriage echoes Wharton's, and her plan to divorce could be seen as a fictional rehearsal for the author—but this is even more true of the title figure's marriage. Mme. de Treymes asks the American Durham, who wants to marry Fanny, "You have heard horrors of me? When are they not said of a woman who is married unhappily?" The novel involves a sinister French family much like the Bellegardes of *The American,* and a young boy who is their heir and pawn. At the end, Durham renounces a future with Fanny that can be purchased only by giving up her son to the French family.

This outcry aganist matrimonial imprisonment immediately preceded Wharton's initial contact with Morton Fullerton (1907), which blossomed into a passionate affair that lasted at least four years, providing her with the most intense physical fulfillment of her life. Fullerton, a protégé of James, was a dissolute but fascinating man of forty-two who had had affairs with both women and men. Wharton's attraction to him represented the release of what she called "the wild woodland woman" in her personality, an element in keeping with her philosophical interests and her very American determination to find freedom. In the last year of her life she wrote to Bernard Berenson, "How thankful I am to remember that, whether as to people or to places and occasions, I've *always* known the gods the moment I met them." If Fullerton was a god, he was a cruel one. His treatment of Wharton alternated between passionate attention and total neglect, causing her to beg him (more than once) to subside into mere friendship, which he eventually did. In 1908 she wrote to him about "the way you've spent your emotional life, while I've—bien malgré moi—hoarded mine, is what puts the great gulf between us, and sets us not only on opposite shores, but at helplessly distant points of our respective shores."

Fullerton's influence on Wharton's work was tremendous, beginning with *Ethan Frome* (1911), one of Wharton's best-written pieces, a tale of an unhappy marriage set in rural, wintry New England. Imprisoned by his marriage to the embittered invalid Zeena, Ethan finds release but then despair in his hopeless love for Mattie Silver. Their attempt to kill themselves in a sled crash results in Ethan's disfigurement and Mattie's transformation into a permanent duplicate of Zeena for Ethan to serve. The stark tale unfolds along carefully crafted lines, via the unusual (for Wharton) device of an unnamed narrator. Ethan and Mattie's suicidal ride echoes Wharton's sentiments during the anguish of her affair with Fullerton; she wrote to him: "When I heard that the motor [her own car, being sent to Hâvre in 1908] . . . had run into a tree and been smashed . . . I felt the wish that I had been in it, and smashed with it, and nothing left of all this disquiet but a 'coeur arreté.' "

The Reef (1912) stands alone among Wharton's novels as an essay into Jamesian psychological depth, handled from a tightly controlled point of view. Furthermore, the author dared to insert overtly sexual material; the story focuses on a brief affair and its unintended results. George Darrow, on his way to woo a woman he once loved, the now widowed Anna Leath, dallies with Sophy Viner in Paris and later (rather incredibly) finds her installed as governess in Anna's house. Worse, Anna's stepson Owen is engaged to Sophy. The contrast between the two women is finely drawn and full of sexual subtleties, with Anna representing societal sexual repression and Sophy the modern liberated woman. As Elizabeth Ammons notes, the submerged imagery presents Anna as a sleeping (Leath/Lethe) beauty waiting, literally in a chateau, for the sexual kiss of her prince. Once again, however, renunciation rules at the conclusion, after the prince is revealed as a fraud; both engagements are broken, and Sophy travels to India. The mysteries of human sexuality are thematically central, but perhaps not as fully explored as the book initially seems to promise. Anna Leath and Sophy Viner might be seen as the two halves of Edith Wharton's identity after her affair with Fullerton, halves existing uneasily with one another. The book's integrity is compromised, moreover (as is a later novel, *The Mother's Recompense* [1925]), by reliance on coincidence.

A third type of woman dominates Wharton's next novel, *The Custom of the Country* (1913), in some ways her most successful work, in that it draws on all her strengths as a novelist, especially as satirist and social chronicler. The novel's power may stem from improvements in Wharton's personal life. The exhilarating but painful affair with Fullerton had wound down, and Wharton finally separated from an increasingly unstable Teddy in 1911, after learning of his infidelity and his embezzlement of her money (they divorced in 1913). The Mount was sold, and Edith settled permanently in France, perhaps because she felt her divorce had made her unwelcome in America.

Acceptance in Parisian society led Wharton to draw transatlantic lines of social comparison. As in *The House of Mirth, Custom* is filled with penetrating satire, acute observations of the new Gilded Age, forcefully drawn characters, and international settings charged with a new power and direction. Having decided to leave the world of her youth perhaps made her view it more kindly, for here members of Old New York gain our sympathy as Undine Spragg ravages them. The only child of a doting self-made industrialist, named after a hair-curler he patented, the Midwestern Undine arrives in New York intent on learning the forms (but not the content) of polite society. In many ways Undine is a Lily Bart transformed from victim to predator. She uses her sexuality to advantage in marrying four times, but she is personally indifferent to sex. Undine, as amoral as Lily was moral, is rootless; from the very beginning, during her childhood in Apex, she maneuvers her parents into a gypsy-like life, moving ever onward in an attempt to find a richer social milieu. The summer watering places lead inevitably to New York and the gilded hotel where we find her:

> Undine was fiercely independent and yet passionately imitative. She wanted to surprise every one by her dash and originality, but she could not help modelling herself on the last person she met, and the confusion of ideals thus produced caused her much perturbation when she had to choose between two courses.
>
> (1956 ed., p. 19)

This novel takes Wharton's continuing saga of Old New York and the Invaders much further than *The House of Mirth.* In *House,* in the late 1800s, the vulgar nouveaux riches were just beginning to make inroads into society. In *Custom* the action takes place well into the new century, when the old crowd had virtually capitulated to the sorties of the Invaders, a fact strongly underlined when Undine caps her early career with marriage to the scion of an Old New York family, Ralph Marvell, another of Wharton's noble but effete dilettantes. Ralph, blind to his cousin Clare's love, not only marries Undine but earlier has unknowingly precipitated Clare's marriage to the vulgar Peter Van Degen. The terms of this new equation mean a shift in Wharton's point of view, for she hated the Invaders. Her own class may have ceased to be creative, but it still had the redeeming qualities of taste and morality—qualities Undine and her crowd lack. They can learn fashion, but they can only mimic morality. Undine, in dress, surroundings, houses, trips, conversation, and lifestyle, has not one original idea. Her only creativity lies in manipulating others, and even in this she is somewhat imitative, for her methods closely approximate the business dealings of her father and the other unscrupulous financiers of the period.

Custom also represents a rather sour retrospective of Wharton's own life. Peter Van Degen offers some advice to Undine after her painfully illuminating and boring honeymoon with Ralph Marvell: "Ah, there's the secret of domestic happiness. Marry somebody who likes all the things you don't, and make love to somebody who likes all the things you do." This is exactly what Peter and Undine eventually do, and it is what we come to feel Ralph and Clare should do as well. They cannot, however, because they are members of "the Aborigines," the anthropological term Ralph uses to describe Old New York.

The novel, written after the collapse of both Wharton's marriage and her affair with Fullerton, slights romance, tragedy, and pathos (although all of these are present) to feature a hard-edged social comedy. We are alerted to this new emphasis by the setting and tone of the first chapters, which are faithful to Wharton's dictum that conclusions should be latent in the first pages. The Hotel Stentorian is the very embodiment of the new Gilded Age. Gilt, mirrors, overstuffed upholstery and people, uneatable but exotic food, and slavish imitation are all hallmarks of fakery and pretension.

The first sentence in the book, uttered by Undine's mother, Mrs. Spragg (who is affectionately called "Loot" by her husband), is repeated by the reader throughout the course of the novel: "Undine Spragg—how can you?" Mrs. Heeny, a shrewd masseuse who acts as a Greek chorus and social tutor to Undine, alerts us to her student's real nature when she says, "I never met with a lovelier form," making the first of many references to Undine's harsh but striking beauty—all form and no content.

If Lily Bart's beauty is transparent, Undine's is opaque. Whereas Lily is always an agent of light that must be extinguished by the forces of darkness, Undine is a creature of glaring light, a blinding, raw force of primitive beauty. She surrounds herself with light and mirrors, echoing the narcissistic society she craves, which inhabits hotels named the Nouveau Luxe and the Incandescent. This light, however, is false; Undine loves glaring light because it draws attention to the mask of her beauty. It blinds men to her real personality; indeed, in many ways she is a Medusa figure. Undine's animal restlessness and constant movement emerge from her linkage with powerful verbs that connote a natural force to be reckoned with rather than a beautiful ornament, like Lily, to be admired. Undine "possessed," "threw," "suddenly shifted," "crump[led] the note and toss[ed] it with a contemptuous gesture," "snapped," "flashed back," "eyes dart[ed] warnings," "swept round"; "She [is] always doubling and twisting on herself." Undine's tigerlike pacing, however, is not really indicative of impatience with enclosure, but of an eagerness for prey. While Lily Bart yearns for freedom from the gilt cage of society, Undine longs to get in so she can feed. Images of penetration emanate from her, even as images of enclosure surround Lily.

From Mrs. Heeny—who, from the lower classes herself, makes a comfortable living by preying on the weaknesses and foibles of the rich, manipulating people with her hands and her conversation—Undine learns two of the maxims that sustain her throughout her campaigns: "If you go too fast you sometimes have to rip out the whole seam," and "Go steady, Undine, and you'll get anywheres." Combining Mrs. Heeny's advice with her father's example, Undine always coaxes, barters, and trades to get what she wants. At the end of their honeymoon, in Paris, she agrees not to return to America on Peter Van Degen's notorious yacht only if Ralph agrees to a longer stay in Europe, and to luxurious accommodations on the voyage home.

Once again Wharton employs Darwinian imagery to good effect: Observing Peter Van Degen, Undine notices "his bulging eyes, . . . saurian head, with eye-lids as thick as lips and lips as thick as ear-lobes," yet finds him "vaguely agreeable"—as well she might, since in many ways he is her counterpart; he has mated with Clare as Caliban would have with Miranda, in order to raise himself socially. He prefers Undine, though, for he responds to crudely drawn beauty rather than refinement.

Ralph Marvell is the equivalent of Selden in *The House of Mirth,* but with a difference: he does get involved, albeit in the wrong way. Like Selden, he is a dilettante, full of taste but unable to create. He eschews business but is forced to work to support Undine's extravagance. His romantic image of himself as Perseus rescuing the innocent Undine from the monster of society again equates him to Selden, but Marvell soon learns that Undine is the Medusa. He differs from Selden in that he does not function as the author's representative but does provide the feeling and texture of the old society in his musings:

> He was fond of describing Washington Square as the "Reservation," and of prophesying that before long its inhabitants would be exhibited at ethnological shows, pathetically engaged in the exercise of their primitive industries.
>
> Small, cautious, middle-class, had been the ideals of aboriginal New York; but it suddenly struck the young man that they were singularly coherent and respectable as contrasted with the chaos of indiscriminate appetites which made up its modern tendencies.
>
> (1956 ed., p. 74)

Undine's monstrousness extends to the world of maternity; when she learns she is pregnant, she wails because she will lose her figure as well as time in society. Here we contrast the penultimate image of Lily Bart with Nettie Struther's baby. We also note at this juncture that Wharton is not as concerned with a unified time scheme as in earlier books; after the above scene, four years go by in a page—Undine, posing for a portrait, hasn't changed, and is off to Europe after hounding her father and Ralph for money. Her boy, whose birthday she forgets, is left at home with the Marvells.

In Europe, the empty activities of the nouveaux riches seem more like celebrations of wealth than amusements. During Undine's sojourn she meets husband number three, the French aristocrat Raymond de Chelles, but before she can concentrate on him, Wharton has her divorce Ralph for Peter Van Degen, with whom she lives for two months. Van Degen refuses to marry her, however, for he learns of her cruel refusal to go to Ralph when he is desperately ill.

Before she marries de Chelles, Undine demands custody of her son in hopes of gaining money from Ralph's family that will cover the cost of annulling the marriage. Ralph tries to raise the money through speculation and, when this fails, commits suicide. Ralph's position between the Aborigines and the new world of wealth has crushed him, just as Lily Bart's tenuous position crushes her.

Undine soon learns she has duplicated her mistake of marrying Ralph by marrying de Chelles. Like Ralph, he is heir to a tradition and family leadership, and Undine is expected to take her place with other women doing needlework at the ancestral château, aptly named, as far as Undine is concerned, Saint Désert. The de Chelles, however, unlike Old New Yorkers, engage in politics, land management, and family affairs; and Raymond stands up to Undine, refusing to let her sell the family tapestries to finance a spring sojourn in Paris.

Undine, ever adapting, finds her escape through remarrying Elmer Moffatt. The tapestries they buy for their vulgar new home are from Saint Désert; Raymond de Chelles has lost his money through the misfortunes of his profligate brother, Hubert. It may seem that once again sacred traditions and artifacts are bought by and placed in the hands of barbarians who cannot understand them (this act parallels Undine's resetting of Ralph's family's jewelry), but one of the interesting notes sounded here is Elmer's growing aesthetic and moral faculties (echoing Rosedale's development), in contrast with Undine's continued vulgarity. For this American woman, all must be made new, or else meshed with the new in order to provide a vulgar imitation of the ideal. Before she leaves de Chelles, he bitterly denounces all she stands for:

> You're all alike. . . . You come among us speaking our language and not knowing what we mean; wanting the things we want, and not knowing why we want them; aping our weaknesses, exaggerating our follies, ignoring or ridiculing all we care about. . . . You come from . . . towns as flimsy as paper, where the streets haven't had time to be named, and the buildings are demolished before they're dry, and the people are as proud of changing as we are of holding to what we have—and we're fools enough to imagine that because you copy our ways and pick up our slang you understand anything about the things that make life decent and honourable for us!
>
> (1956 ed., p. 545)

This speech by a Frenchman could just as well be that of an Aborigine in New York speaking to an Invader from Apex. It is a damning portrait of the social climber, the nouveau riche, the uncaring and unfeeling.

The irony of the final scene owes much of its force to the fact that it is seen through the eyes of Ralph's son, Paul. Deprived of his own father and then "the French father" he also loved, he is frightened of Moffat, although it is obvious Elmer likes the boy. Paul's loneliness and neglect underline Undine's vulgarity, egotism, coarseness, and lack of feeling.

Custom further develops the tapestry of *The House of Mirth* into a vast panorama that covers two continents. It enables Wharton to deal with more complex people and a greater variety of situations. The minor figures are more fully drawn, and the contrasts and interactions among the characters are revealing and ironic in a fuller sense. Missing, however, is the note of tenderness apparent in Lily and Selden's love.

The acid flows to every corner of this book as Ralph perishes and Undine succeeds. The Old New York that was dying in *The House of Mirth* is buried in this book. Its survivors must become predators along with the Invaders or perish. To this extent, the book is extreme in its pessimism.

We should note, however, that Undine's predicaments are presented in such a way as to permit us to see her as a victim. As Mr. Bowen notes:

> The average American looks down on his wife. . . . How much does he let her share in the real business of life? . . . All my sympathy's with them, . . . when I see their fallacious little attempts to trick out the leavings tossed them by the preoccupied male—the money and the motors and the clothes—and pretend to themselves and each other that *that's* what really constitutes life.
>
> (1956 ed., pp. 205, 206, 208)

A slight gleam of hope is noted in the greater continuity of European civilization, which de Chelles represents.

World War I traumatized Wharton. She served the French Republic as an administrator and fund-raiser for refugee work, for which she was made chevalier of the Legion of Honor in 1916. These experiences solidified her commitment to France as well, and after the war she set up two elegant residences, the Pavillon Colombe at St. Brice-sous Forêt, near Paris, and Ste. Claire at Hyères in southern France, which were her homes for the remainder of her life.

Perhaps as a release from pressing wartime realities, she wrote one of her best books, *Summer* (1917). Set in rural New England, she called it "the hot *Ethan*," and it burns with youthful desire and sexuality. It is the bildungsroman of Charity Royall, the frustrated young ward of North Dormer's most important citizen, the noble but defeated Lawyer Royall, who rescued Charity as a child from a barbarous mountain community. Lonely and drunk one night, he forces his way into her room, only to be scornfully rejected.

Charity's developing sexuality finds a more likely outlet in a passionate affair with a visiting architecture student, Lucius Harney, that is conducted in an airy deserted house in the woods. Their love first ignites in a magnificently rendered scene on the Fourth of July, when Charity and Lucius are watching the fireworks in the nearby town of Nettleton. Significantly, Charity is spotted and called a whore by the drunken Royall, who is on the arm of an actual prostitute, Julia Hawes. When Charity, pregnant with Lucius's child, learns he is engaged to a society belle, Annabel Balch, she refuses to tell him of her condition and releases him from their relationship. Scorning the solution of abortion, she seeks shelter where she can, returning to the mountain she left as a small girl, only to find her depraved mother dead and herself surrounded by an equally degenerate community. For once in Wharton's work, a would-be rescuer (Lawyer Royall) succeeds; he marries Charity and forbears to consummate their relationship on their first night together.

In this story Wharton seems to be reliving the passionate affair she experienced in middle age, but she also limns the inevitable accommodations young people must make in maturity. Some feminist critics have read the book as a tragedy, but such an interpretation fails to take into account the careful development of lawyer Royall, the altered perception of Royall that Charity experiences (as does the reader), and the powerful "Old Home Week" scene, which depicts the community's homecoming festivities. Royall, as the town's leading figure, orates a strong case for the virtues of life in North Dormer, as well as the need to recognize and accept one's limitations. The refrain "Come Home" really means a return to the self, and he speaks for himself while appealing to Charity. The writing throughout the book is perhaps Wharton's finest; nature, the psychological intricacies of her characters, the unfolding drama of sexual awakening—all are sensitively and beautifully rendered, largely through Charity's shifting point of view, which helps make the ending bittersweet.

The passion of this book and the netherworld of the mountain have parallels in Wharton's impressive travel book, *In Morocco,* based on her visit to that country in 1971, after reading her friend André Gide's *The Immoralist* (which is partly set in North Africa). The exotic settings and customs she saw—including ritual sacrifices, harems, and casbahs—fascinated and repelled her, leading to a far-ranging assessment of feminine rights and values. The war brought forth some of Wharton's weaker writing as well: a short novel about a soldier, *The Marne* (1918), and an overwrought tale of a father's grief at losing his son, *A Son at the Front* (1923). A nonfiction work, *French Ways and Their Meaning* (1919), however, offers an inspiring tribute to the French culture, including an instructive commentary on the advantages French women enjoy over their American counterparts, and an indictment of America's failure to respect its own past.

Wharton's final masterwork, *The Age of Innocence* (1920), was generated by these works and their themes. Set in the early 1870s, it takes a kinder, more mature look at the culture that produced Wharton. She was perhaps waxing nostalgic as she took in the tremendous changes wrought by the war, especially in Paris, with its gathering of writers, cubist artists, and revolutionary musicians, accompanied by crowding, factories, noisy traffic, and pollution. Moreover, she was still grieving over Henry James's death in 1916 and the more recent passing of Egerton Winthrop and Howard Sturgis. "The new intensity of vision" all these events produced helped conjure extraordinarily detailed memories of the 1870s; Wharton shows us period interiors in great scenes like the ball at the Beaufort mansion. The types of carriages used, the antiquated social cards and calling practices, the gardenias that gentlemen wore—they are all here, providing a gracious and ordered picture of a world that was content with itself. Wharton thus cast herself back in the mode of chronicler, as in her first novel, but this time, ironically, of her own era.

As R. W. B. Lewis notes, many of the portraits here were based on people Wharton had known during the period; indeed, she seems to be wondering what might have happened to her if she had, like Archer, acceded to the standards of "the tribe." Similarly, May Welland, Archer's bride, could be the matron of convention Wharton might have been.

The hero, Old New Yorker Newland Archer, is fictional brother to Lawrence Selden and Ralph Marvell. The novel also provides a kind of summary Wharton surrogate in Ellen Olenska, the expatriate European who, like her predecessors Fanny de Malrive *(Madame de Treymes),* Anna Leath *(The Reef),* and Undine Spragg, has had an unhappy marriage to a European. She is considering divorce, which scandalizes "the tribe." Ellen, much like Miriam in Nathaniel Hawthorne's *The Marble Faun,* represents Europe, sophistication, and beauty, but also sexual mystery and tragedy, especially in her marriage to a corrupt, offstage foreigner. She seems to be the perfect mate for the intellectually and culturally aspirant (and possibly sexually frustrated) Archer, but he is already virtually engaged to the seemingly simple and pure May Welland. Once again, missed connections emerge as a theme.

The term "Aborigine" is clarified in this novel, amplifying Marvell's use of it in *Custom.* The tribal imagery of the book is communicated in the opening scene, which contains the seeds of what will develop. We see Archer at the opera—specifically, *Faust*—at the Academy of Music, which soon will be supplanted by the Metropolitan Opera. On Monday and Friday evenings there are tribal gatherings. Archer spies May in a box with her cousin, the unhappy and separated Ellen. While fuming at May's generous public display of support, he hears the cries of the soprano—"M'ama . . . non M'ama . . . M'ama!"—to a diminutive

Faust. They prefigure the burning question Archer will have to ask about his relation to May and Ellen and his willingness to strike a Faustian pose in order to win the latter. Initially, Archer is clearly conventional; his idea of a honeymoon by an Italian lake where he will read *Faust* to May is an echo of the Sienese honeymoon of Ralph and Undine. His allegiance to male tribal values—"he instinctively felt that . . . it would be troublesome—and also rather bad form—to strike out for himself"—changes over the course of the novel through his love for Ellen, who shows him the real meaning of the credos he mouths to her.

Although "the tribe" would never approve of Archer's love for Ellen, they ironically ensure its development by urging him to become her attorney, pointing out her relationship to May. His love for Ellen develops from visits to her somewhat foreign but pleasant rooms, where she succinctly skewers his false images of Old New York families.

Symbolism and detail are used to great advantage in *The Age of Innocence,* as in Wharton's brilliant portrait of an afternoon archery meet at Newport. May, an excellent archer, like the goddess Diana, also exhibits Diana's chastity; she is the "innocent" member of the triangle. Her marksmanship is also a fitting symbol of her success in keeping her man; revealing her pregnancy to Ellen scores a hit in that it pinions Archer into his marriage once and for all. Newland bears the name "Archer," but his aim is poor; caught between the real and the ideal, he cannot focus on the only target society will give him, marriage to May. Eventually, May's torn and muddy wedding dress comes to be a symbol of her stained marriage, and of the way that even innocent parties may be tarnished by propinquity to sin (here recalling Hilda's fate in *The Marble Faun*).

Long after Ellen leaves permanently for Europe, Archer's thoughts are with her, preventing any sort of meaningful salvage of uxorial love. He makes peace with society's "death-in-life" sentence for him, however, because he cannot achieve personal freedom by trampling on others. Newland's traditional morality—or is it a failure of nerve?—has caused him to lose his aim, just like "the wooden cupid [on the summerhouse at the stud farm] who had lost his bow and arrow but continued to take ineffectual aim. . . . A grizzled Newfoundland dozing before the door seemed as ineffectual a guardian as the arrowless Cupid."

Ironically, Archer has given Ellen strength for renunciation, not unlike the spiritual gift Durham offers in *Madame de Treymes:*

> You had felt the world outside tugging . . . with its golden hands—and yet you hated the things it asks of one; you hated happiness bought by disloyalty and cruelty and indifference. That was what I'd never known before—and it's better than anything I've known. . . . when I turn back into myself now I'm like a child going at night into a room where there's always a light.
>
> (*The Age of Innocence,* p. 172)

This highly spiritual scene stands in contrast with the harshness of the anthropological elements; tribal imagery is more extensive here than in any other Wharton text, and has a brutal aspect. May's farewell dinner for Ellen is "the tribal rally around a kinswoman about to be eliminated from the tribe." Geological terms are used, too, reflecting Wharton's lifelong fascination with science. The van der Luytens are associated with coldness, ice, "bodies caught in glaciers," which suggests both the mastodons helpless before a new era and the death-in-life that Archer will experience.

Eventually, however, Archer finds some solace. He achieves a good public career, dabbles in politics, and enjoys the friendship of Theodore Roosevelt (a personal friend of Wharton's). The greatest loser in the triangle could be May, for she gains Archer but loses his love. In the poignant closing scene between the widowed Archer and his son, Dallas, Dallas reveals May's knowledge of the love between Archer and Ellen: "Yes: the day before she died. It was when she sent for me alone—you remember? She said she knew we were safe with you, and always would be, because once, when she asked you to, you'd given up the thing you most wanted." The news stirs Archer deeply. Although Dallas has arranged a meeting for him with Ellen, Archer knows he cannot see Ellen now, as to do so would cheapen the renunciation that marks three lives. He asks Dallas to tell Ellen, "I'm old-fashioned: that's enough."

The scene occurs in Wharton's old Paris neighborhood, where she perhaps came to Archer's conclusion: that, after all, there was good in the old ways. At the same time, the reader cannot help being skeptical of Archer's love—might not his admitted dilettantism extend to his feeling for Ellen as well? His lack of courage—especially when weighed against that of his fictional predecessors in Wharton's oeuvre—somewhat contradicts Ellen's high opinion of him. In earlier versions of the novel, in fact, Archer runs away with Ellen, but Wharton was unable to work out a satisfactory relationship for them, perhaps deciding, as James did about Christopher Newman and Claire De Cintre in *The American*, that the union would have been a disaster.

The book may well be a tribute to Wharton's long (but probably platonic) relationship with Walter Berry, who had deeply influenced both her taste and her literary career. In *A Backward Glance* she wrote:

> Meanwhile I found a momentary escape in going back to my childish memories of a long-vanished America, and wrote "The Age of Innocence." I showed it chapter by chapter to Walter Berry; and when he had finished reading it he said: "Yes; it's good. But of course you and I are the only people who will ever read it. We are the last people left who can remember New York and Newport as they were then, and nobody else will be interested."
>
> (p. 369)

Berry, of course, was wrong. The novel turned out to be one of her most popular and honored works, garnering the 1921 Pulitzer Prize.

Wharton's late novels—1922 to 1937—have frequently been dismissed, but recent appraisals suggest that this opinion is shifting. Certainly *The Mother's Recompense* (1925), *Twilight Sleep* (1927), *The Children* (1928), and especially *The Buccaneers* (published unfinished after her death) offer some of the most affecting writing she ever did, and even the flawed duo *Hudson River Bracketed* (1929) and *The Gods Arrive* (1932) present some riveting issues and memorable characters amid a welter of poorly informed satire and generally slack writing. The short fiction of this period was more distinguished, including masterpieces such as "A Bottle of Perrier," "Roman Fever," and "After Holbein," and some of her best ghost stories, especially "All Souls" and "Pomegranate Seed." There was the fine four-volume *Old New York* (1924), highlighted by *The Old Maid*, which later became a distinguished play and film, and *False Dawn*, a lovely story about an ardent collector of art without honor in his own country.

Perhaps because they were initially intended for magazine serialization (and therefore had a more popular audience in mind), the later novels fail to approach the stature of those written before 1922. The language also seems inappropriate at times, possibly because Wharton had been living abroad so long. The only truly forgettable late novel, *The Glimpses of the Moon* (a 1922 best-seller, later a film with dialogue by F. Scott Fitzgerald), offers a weak portrayal of Nick and Susy Lansing, who marry as part of a scheme to roam European high society in search of truly wealthy mates, only to realize at the end that they love each other.

The Mother's Recompense, by contrast, is emerging as a novel of distinction, largely because it best represents what R. W. B. Lewis has called Wharton's late series of dramas about parents and children, but also because Kate Clephane and the moral dilemma she faces are expertly and sympathetically drawn. A woman who deserted her infant daughter, Anne, and her pompous husband (now dead) years earlier for a wealthy man, whom she also left, Kate has spent the ensuing years in shabby exile in various European watering spots. The only bright spot was a brief affair with a much younger man, Chris Fenno (who bears obvious parallels to Morton Fullerton).

Now grown, and in command of her dead father's fortune, Anne sends for her mother to join her in New York, where Kate enjoys brief happiness and toys with the idea of marriage to an old family friend, Fred Landers. Her peace is shattered, however, by the revelation that Anne has met and fallen in love with Chris. Eventually Kate must ask herself if maternal concern or jealousy is motivating her campaign to thwart the marriage, which she eventually permits, withdrawing, in a typical Wharton renunciation, to Europe once again, and spurning marriage with Fred.

The novel rehearses many Whartonian concerns—divorce, women's needs, social opprobrium, the life of a woman alone—and also examines tellingly the demands of motherhood once one's child reaches maturity.

If the book has faults, they lie in the singularly one-dimensional, almost unattractive nature of the daughter, the difficulties involved for the reader in taking Chris Fenno seriously, and plot reliance on an unlikely coincidence.

Twilight Sleep features a May-December relationship between Dexter Manford and his stepson's wife (echoing the near-incest theme of *Summer*) but essentially is a comedy of manners, in some ways Wharton's version of *Babbitt.* Pauline Manford, the central figure, emblemizes the busy but empty and superficial lives of "modern" American women of the upper class; in her furious social activity that leads nowhere, she resembles the more overtly comic and redoubtable heroine of E. F. Benson's *Lucia* novels. Pauline neglects her children (who represent Wharton's idea of "the lost generation"), avoids problems, and pursues ways to restore her youth. While this kind of richly satirical material seems ideal for Wharton, the overly episodic structure (no doubt planned for serial magazine readers) makes novelistic unity impossible, and the serious themes become fragmented. Ironically, this Babbitt-like novel replaced Sinclair Lewis's *Elmer Gantry* at the top of the best-seller lists.

Relationships between the generations are examined again in *The Children.* Set in Venice, it concerns the seven Wheater children (the progeny of four marriages) and their relationship with Martin Boyne, a bachelor whose attempt to help the children work out a way to stay together culminates in a plan for the middle-aged Boyne to marry the oldest child, the teenage Judith. The novel has many comic moments in its initial chapters but deepens into almost tragic dimensions as it progresses, possibly because the book's composition was interrupted by the drawn-out death of Wharton's beloved Walter Berry. The novel ends in renunciation when Boyne realizes that marriage to Judith is impossible and that his love for her makes marriage to his longtime love, Rose Sellars, out of the question as well. The novel was enormously successful and earned Wharton a great deal of money, and although it is more modest in scope than her major works, it deserves a wider audience.

Wharton's last published novels, *Hudson River Bracketed* and its sequel, *The Gods Arrive,* represent an unfortunate return to cramped writing and clumsy, even cruel, satire. Vance Weston, the writer-hero of these two books, in some ways reflects Wharton, but so does the more perceptive Halo Spear, whom he victimizes. The savage depiction of Midwesterners provides little more than crude caricature, and the reader finds it hard to believe in the genius of Vance Weston, who all too frequently appears to be an undereducated and callow cad, certainly unworthy of Halo Spear's love. Still, as in William Faulkner's *Mosquitoes,* the discussions of art and culture and the portrayal of

Vance mastering literary craft are compelling, and offer insight into Wharton's sense of her vocation.

It is heartening to find an amazing revitalization of Wharton's literary powers in the last year of her life, reflected in her unfinished novel, *The Buccaneers,* published posthumously with an afterword by Wharton's close friend Gaillard Lapsley. Initially set, like *The Age of Innocence,* in Old New York and Saratoga during the 1870s, this is Wharton's positive and rousing tribute to the American girl. In the portrayal of Laura Testvalley, the mentor of a bevy of beauties who take the English social world by storm under her guidance, it is also a kind of summary of the possibilities of femininity for women of all ages. Laura's protégé, Nan St. George, carries off the ultimate trophy husband, the Duke of Tintagel, but eventually leaves him for a Guards officer, Guy Thwarte. In a final drama of renunciation, Laura yields her only hope of security to further Nan's elopement. One sees Wharton coming full circle as a writer, for her juvenile novella's central characters were the doomed English lovers Georgie and Guy; this time, they have a happy end.

It would be fine to think of Wharton's last years solely in this positive manner, but they were saddened by the death, one by one, of her literary friends, her servants, and members of her family, most of whom seemed to be members of a lost world that existed before the war. With an eye to her own death and her future reputation, Wharton set down her artistic theories in *The Writing of Fiction* (1925), and her personal memories and views on life in *A Backward Glance* (1934), published three years before her death. It is remarkably reticent about her marriage, never mentions Morton Fullerton or her divorce, and eulogizes Berry in rhapsodic language. There are fine and moving portrayals of Henry James and her other literary friends, and many illuminating comments about her craft—including, along with praise for the man, reservations about James's art. Increasingly the book relies on anecdote and is concerned with a defense of Wharton's art, pointing out her literary experiments, her brave assaults on Victorian prudery, and the overall career trajectory that obviously gave her much retrospective pride. To some extent the rather stuffy and cautious tone may be due to the fact that Wharton had decided to leave more scandalous revelations in the Yale archives, along with a note "to my biographer." Perhaps *A Backward Glance* was meant to be read alongside the future biography, with a third, mediating view intended for the reader.

Wharton's reputation declined after her death at Pavillon Colombe on 11 April 1937, especially after the publication of her supposed friend Percy Lubbock's less than appreciative account of her life (1947), which depicted her as a grand and rather frosty society matron and an inferior disciple of Henry James. This mode of approach dominated discussion of Wharton's work until 1975, when R. W. B. Lewis's monumental Pulitzer Prize–winning biography, which drew on the shocking materials in Yale's archives, appeared. Lewis found evidence of the passionate and adulterous affair with Fullerton, revealing letters, and, perhaps most amazingly, a fragment of a pornographic tale concerning father-daughter incest ("Beatrice Palmato").

Wharton criticism had to be re-imagined after the biography, and it was. Cynthia Griffin Wolff's perceptive analysis of Wharton's oeuvre, *A Feast of Words,* began a psychoanalytic linkage of Wharton's life and aesthetic, one that has been deepened and complicated by more overtly feminist critics such as Elizabeth Ammons and Elaine Showalter, among others. Wharton conferences have been held at the Mount, which has been restored, and the Edith Wharton Society has been issuing a *Newsletter* for some years.

Clearly, Wharton is emerging as one of the most important American writers; we now see that throughout her career she was fascinated, as most great writers have been, by the tension that exists in America between the needs of democracy and of individualism, and the dramatic situations that develop when seismic encounters between these two realms create catastrophe. Simultaneously, although it is often forgotten, Edith Wharton possessed a tremendously comic vision of life that usefully balanced her sense of fated, individualistic tragedy. She excelled in the comedy of manners and social satire, and all of her best books draw much of their strength from this resource, especially her powerful sense of irony and her ability to create believable comic dialogue.

It would be wrong, however, to pigeonhole Wharton as a novelist of manners, as is often done. Her vast oeuvre ranges fearlessly across the spectrum of American culture, sometimes in areas she knew little about, but always with a penetrating eye, a devastating wit, and a abundance of compassion. Her feminine protagonists offer unusually compelling and widely varying illustrations of the difficulty of finding fulfillment as a woman in America, a country whose rapid changes frequently brought only new modes of oppression for its women. Wharton's keen sense of the special literary and personal difficulties facing a female author (she was profoundly moved by the histories of George Eliot and George Sand) gave her depictions of frustrated women a special urgency.

Wharton was almost as effective, however, with her male protagonists (especially Newland Archer and Ethan Frome), and her best novels go beyond gender issues, the comedy of manners, and other categories; they are, *au fond*, quests for identity, in the classical American tradition. Her characters struggle with society and each other, but ultimately arrive at a knowledge of who they are—and, frequently, who they might have been—through a final conflict with their own souls. As such, they eloquently chart the course of what Wharton called "the eternal struggle between man's contending impulses."

Selected Bibliography

PRIMARY WORKS

NONFICTION

The Decoration of Houses. New York: Scribners, 1897; reprinted New York: Arno Press, 1975. Written with Ogden Codman, Jr.

Italian Villas and Their Gardens. New York: Century, 1904.

Italian Backgrounds. New York: Scribners, 1905.

A Motor-Flight Through France. New York: Scribners, 1908.

Fighting France, from Dunkerque to Belfort. New York: Scribners, 1915.

In Morocco. New York: Scribners, 1920.

The Writing of Fiction. New York: Scribners, 1925.

A Backward Glance. New York: Appleton-Century, 1934.

The Letters of Edith Wharton. Edited by R. W. B. Lewis and Nancy Lewis. New York: Scribners, 1988.

NOVELS AND NOVELLAS

The Touchstone. New York: Scribners, 1900.

The Valley of Decision. 2 vols. New York: Scribners, 1902.

Sanctuary. New York: Scribners, 1903.

The House of Mirth. New York: Scribners, 1905. Edited and with an introduction by R. W. B. Lewis. Boston: Houghton Mifflin, 1963.

The Fruit of the Tree. New York: Scribners, 1907.

Madame de Treymes. New York: Scribners, 1907.

Ethan Frome. New York: Scribners, 1911.

The Reef. New York: Appleton, 1912.

The Custom of the Country. New York: Scribners, 1913. Reprinted with an introduction by Blake Nevius. New York: Scribners, 1956.

Summer. New York: Appleton, 1917.

The Age of Innocence. New York: Appleton, 1920.

The Glimpses of the Moon. New York: Appleton, 1922.

A Son at the Front. New York: Scribners, 1923.

Old New York. 4 vols. New York: Appleton, 1924.

The Mother's Recompense. New York: Appleton, 1925.

Twilight Sleep. New York: Appleton, 1927.

The Children. New York: Appleton, 1928.

Hudson River Bracketed. New York: Appleton, 1929.

The Gods Arrive. New York: Appleton, 1932.

The Buccaneers. New York: Appleton-Century, 1938.

Fast and Loose (as David Olivieri). Edited and with an introduction by Viola Hopkins Winner. Charlottesville: University of Virginia Press, 1977.

Novels. Edited by R. W. B. Lewis. New York: Library of America, 1985. Contains *The House of Mirth, The Reef, The Custom of the Country*, and *The Age of Innocence*.

Novellas and Other Writings. Edited by Cynthia Griffin Woolf. New York: Library of America, 1990. Contains *Madame de Treymes, Ethan Frome, Summer, Old New York, The Mother's Recompense*, and *A Backward Glance*.

POETRY

Verses. Newport: C. E. Hammett, Jr., 1878. Published anonymously.

Artemis to Acteon and Other Verse. New York: Scribners, 1909.

SHORT STORIES

The Greater Inclination. New York: Scribners, 1899.

Crucial Instances. New York: Scribners, 1901.

The Descent of Man and Other Stories. New York: Scribners, 1904.

The Hermit and the Wild Woman and Other Stories. New York: Scribners, 1908.

Tales of Men and Ghosts. New York: Scribners, 1910.

Xingu and Other Stories. New York: Scribners, 1916.

Here and Beyond. New York: Appleton, 1926.

Certain People. New York: Appleton, 1930.

Human Nature. New York: Appleton, 1933.

The World Over. New York: Appleton-Century, 1936.

Ghosts. New York: Appleton-Century, 1937.

The Collected Short Stories of Edith Wharton. Edited by R. W. B. Lewis. 2 vols. New York: Scribners, 1968.

SECONDARY WORKS

BIOGRAPHICAL AND CRITICAL STUDIES

Ammons, Elizabeth. *Edith Wharton's Argument with America*. Athens: University of Georgia Press, 1980.

Auchincloss, Louis. *Edith Wharton: A Woman in Her Time*. New York: Viking, 1971.

Bell, Millicent. *Edith Wharton and Henry James: The Story of Their Friendship*. New York: Braziller, 1965.

Benstock, Shari. *Women of the Left Bank: Paris, 1900–1940*. Austin: University of Texas Press, 1986.

Bloom, Harold, ed. *Edith Wharton: Modern Critical Views*. New York: Chelsea House, 1986.

Dimock, Wai-chee. "Debasing Exchange: Edith Wharton's *The House of Mirth*." In *Edith Wharton: Modern Critical Views*. Edited by Harold Bloom. New York: Chelsea House, 1986. Pp. 123–137.

Fetterly, Judith. "The Temptation to Be a Beautiful Object: Double Standard and Double Bind in *The House of Mirth*." *Studies in American Fiction* 5:199–211 (1977).

Fryer, Judith. *Felicitous Space: The Imaginative Structures of Edith Wharton and Willa Cather*. Chapel Hill: University of North Carolina Press, 1986.

Gilbert, Sandra M., and Susan Gubar. *No Man's Land: The Place of the Woman Writer in the Twentieth Century*. Vol. 2, *Sexchanges*. New Haven: Yale University Press, 1989.

Gimbel, Wendy. *Edith Wharton: Orphancy and Survival*. New York: Praeger, 1984.

Goodman, Susan. *Edith Wharton's Women: Friends and Rivals*. Hanover, N.H.: University Press of New England, 1990.

Howe, Irving, ed. *Edith Wharton: A Collection of Critical Essays*. Englewood Cliffs, N.J.: Prentice-Hall, 1962.

Kaplan, Amy. "Edith Wharton's Profession of Authorship." *ELH* 53:433–457 (Summer 1986).

Lawson, Richard H. *Edith Wharton*. New York: Frederick Ungar, 1977.

Lewis, R. W. B. *Edith Wharton: A Biography*. New York: Harper & Row, 1975.

Lindberg, Gary H. *Edith Wharton and the Novel of Manners*. Charlottesville: University of Virginia Press, 1975.

Lidoff, Joan. "Another Sleeping Beauty: Narcissism in *The House of Mirth*." In *American Realism: New Essays*. Edited by Eric J. Sundquist. Baltimore: Johns Hopkins University Press, 1980. Pp. 238–258.

Lubbock, Percy. *Portrait of Edith Wharton*. New York: Appleton-Century, 1947.

McDowell, Margaret B. *Edith Wharton*. Boston: Twayne, 1976.

Nevius, Blake. *Edith Wharton: A Study of Her Fiction*. Berkeley: University of California Press, 1953.

Ozick, Cynthia. "Justice (Again) to Edith Wharton." *Commentary* 62:48–57 (October 1976).

Peterman, Michael Alan. "The Post-War Novels of Edith Wharton, 1917–1938." *Dissertation Abstracts International* 39:4248-A (January 1979).

Rae, Catherine M. *Edith Wharton's New York Quartet*. Lanham, Md.: University Press of America, 1984.

Raphael, Lev. *Edith Wharton's Prisoners of Shame: A New Perspective on Her Fiction*. Ann Arbor: University of Michigan Press, 1990.

Schriber, Mary Suzanne. *Gender and the Writer's Imagination: From Cooper to Wharton*. Lexington: University Press of Kentucky, 1987.

Showalter, Elaine. "The Death of the Lady (Novelist): Wharton's *House of Mirth*." In *Edith Wharton: Modern Critical Views*. Edited by Harold Bloom. New York: Chelsea House, 1986. Pp. 139–154.

Stein, Allen F. "Wharton's *Blithedale:* A New Reading of *The Fruit of the Tree*." *American Literary Realism* 12:330–337 (Autumn 1979).

Tintner, Adeline R. "Mothers, Daughters, and Incest in the Late Novels of Edith Wharton." In *The Lost Tradition: Mothers and Daughters in Literature*. Edited by Cathy N. Davidson and E. M. Broner. New York: Frederick Ungar, 1980. Pp. 147–156.

Walton, Geoffrey. *Edith Wharton: A Critical Interpretation*. Rutherford, N.J.: Fairleigh Dickinson University Press, 1970; 2nd ed., rev., 1982.

Wershoven, *The Female Intruder in the Novels of Edith Wharton*. Rutherford, N.J.: Fairleigh Dickinson University Press, 1982.

Wilson, Edmund. "Justice to Edith Wharton." In *Edith Wharton: A Collection of Critical Essays*. Edited by Irving Howe. Englewood Cliffs, N.J.: Prentice-Hall, 1962. Pp. 19–31.

Wolff, Cynthia Griffin. *A Feast of Words: The Triumph of Edith Wharton*. New York: Oxford University Press, 1977.

BIBLIOGRAPHIES

Bendixen, Alfred. "Wharton Studies, 1986–1987: A Bibliographic Essay." *Edith Wharton Newsletter* 5, no. 1:5–10 (Spring 1988).

———, ed. "A Guide to Wharton Criticism, 1974–1983." *Edith Wharton Newsletter* 2, no. 2:1–8 (Fall 1985).

Lauer, Kristin O. *Edith Wharton: An Annotated Secondary Bibliography*. New York: Garland, 1990.

Springer, Marlene. *Edith Wharton and Kate Chopin: A Reference Guide*. Boston: G. K. Hall, 1976.

Springer, Marlene, and Joan Gilson. "Edith Wharton: A Reference Guide Updated." *Resources for American Literary Study* 14, nos. 1–2:85–111 (1984).

JOHN LOWE

CONTRIBUTORS

David Craig Austin. Poet and writer. ELIZABETH BISHOP; SYLVIA PLATH

Joanne M. Braxton. Frances L. and Edwin L. Cummings Professor of American Studies and English, the College of William and Mary. Author of *Sometimes I Think of Maryland* (poetry); *Black Women Writing Autobiography: A Tradition Within a Tradition;* co-editor of *Wild Women in the Whirlwind: Afra-American Culture and the Contemporary Literary Renaissance.* FRANCES ELLEN WATKINS HARPER; MAYA ANGELOU

Deborah Carlin. Assistant Professor of English, University of Massachusetts, Amherst. Author of *Cather, Canon and the Politics of Reading* and various articles on nineteenth- and twentieth-century American fiction. WILLA CATHER

Harriet Scott Chessman. Associate Professor of English, Yale University. Author of *The Public Is Invited to Dance: Representation, The Body, and Dialogue in Gertrude Stein* and co-editor with Catharine R. Stimpson of three volumes of the writings of Gertrude Stein in the Library of America. GERTRUDE STEIN

Gwen Crane. Lecturer in English, Princeton University. Has worked as a medical editor and book reviewer. Currently writing a book on literary representations of the Inquisition. DOROTHY PARKER; ANNE TYLER

Harriet Davidson. Associate Professor of English and Comparative Literature, Rutgers University. Author of *T. S. Eliot and Hermeneutics: Absence and Interpretation in "The Waste Land"* and articles on contemporary poetry and contemporary theory. ADRIENNE RICH

Carolyn C. Denard. Assistant Professor of American Literature, Georgia State University. Author of "The Convergence of Feminism and Ethnicity in the Fiction of Toni Morrison" in *Critical Essays on Toni Morrison*, edited by Nellie McKay, and *Tar Women and Magical Men: Heroism in Toni Morrison's Fiction.* TONI MORRISON

Wai-chee Dimock. Associate Professor of Literature, University of California, San Diego. Author of articles on Edith Wharton and Kate Chopin and of *Empire for Liberty: Melville and the Poetics of Individualism.* KATE CHOPIN

Debra Fried. Associate Professor of English, Cornell University. Author of articles on American poetry and film. EDNA ST. VINCENT MILLAY

Ellen G. Friedman. Professor of English and Director of Women's Studies, Trenton State College. Author of *Joyce Carol Oates* and numerous articles on American and women's literature. Contributing editor of *Breaking the Sequence: Women's Experimental Fiction* (with Miriam Fuchs) and *Joan Didion: Essays and Conversations.* JOYCE CAROL OATES; ANAÏS NIN

Celeste Goodridge. Assistant Professor of English, Bowdoin College. Author of *Hints and Disguises: Marianne Moore and Her Contemporaries.* MARIANNE MOORE

Angeline Goreau. Writer. Author of *Reconstructing Aphra: A Social Biography of Aphra Behn; The Whole Duty of a Woman: Female Writers in Seventeenth-Century England;* and articles on history and literature. Editor and introducer of Anne Bronte, *Agnes Grey.* ELIZABETH HARDWICK

Janet Gray. Poet; Teaching Assistant in English, Princeton University. Author of *To Pull Out the Peachboy; Flaming Tail out of the Ground Near Your Farm; The Purse;* and *A Hundred Flowers.* LOUISE BOGAN

Anne Hiemstra. Adjunct Associate Professor of English, Iona College. Currently completing her dissertation on the poetry of Robert Browning at Columbia University. GRACE PALEY

Suzanne Juhasz. Professor of English, University of Colorado, Boulder. Author of *Metaphor and the Poetry of Williams, Pound, and Stevens; Naked and Fiery Forms: Modern American Poetry by Women, A New Tradition; The Undiscovered Continent: Emily Dickinson and the Space of the Mind;* and *Facilitating Environments: Jane Austen and Women's Romance Fiction.* Editor of *Feminist Critics Read Emily Dickinson* and, with Cristanne Miller, *Emily Dickinson: A Celebration for Readers.* EMILY DICKINSON, ANNE SEXTON

Carol Farley Kessler. Associate Professor of English, American Studies, and Women's Studies, Penn State University. Author of *Elizabeth Stuart Phelps;* editor of *Daring to Dream: Utopian Stories by United States Women 1836–1919* and *The Story of Avis* by Elizabeth Stuart Phelps (1877). Forthcoming publications include

Charlotte Perkins Gilman: Progress Toward Utopia and a revised edition of *Daring to Dream*. CHARLOTTE PERKINS GILMAN

Marilee Lindemann. Instructor of English, Howard University. Author of a dissertation, "Women Writers and the American Romance: Studies in Jewett and Cather" (Rutgers University, 1991), and articles on Willa Cather and contemporary women's fiction; contributor to *Engendering the Word: Feminist Essays in Psychosexual Poetics*. SARAH ORNE JEWETT

John Lowe. Assistant Professor of English, Louisiana State University. Author of articles in *The Harlem Renaissance Re-examined*, edited by Victor Kramer; *American Quarterly; Studies in American Indian Literature; Journal of the Short Story in English;* and several other journals. Editor of *Redefining Southern Culture;* co-editor with Jefferson Humphries of *The Future of Southern Letters*. EDITH WHARTON

Veronica Makowsky. Associate Professor of English, Louisiana State University. Author of *Caroline Gordon: A Biography*. Editor of R. P. Blackmur's *Henry Adams* and *Studies in Henry James*. Co-editor of *The Henry James Review*. Author of articles on Blackmur, Stark Young, Caroline Gordon, and Walker Percy. SUSAN GLASPELL

Wendy Martin. Chair of the Department of English and Professor of American Literature and American Studies at Claremont Graduate School. Author of *An American Triptych: The Lives and Work of Anne Bradstreet, Emily Dickinson and Adrienne Rich*. Editor of *An American Sisterhood: Feminist Writings from Colonial Times to the Present*. Editor of *We Are the Stories We Tell: Best Short Fiction by North American Women Writers 1945 to the Present*. Editor of *Women's Studies: An Interdisciplinary Journal*. MARY McCARTHY; KATHERINE ANNE PORTER

Deborah E. McDowell. Associate Professor of English, University of Virginia. Author of numerous articles and reviews and co-editor with Arnold Rampersad of *Slavery and the Literary Imagination*. Author of *"The Changing Same": Generational Connections and Black Women Novelists* and general editor of the Beacon Press Black Women Writers Series. JESSIE FAUSET

Nellie Y. McKay. Professor of American and Afro-American Literature, University of Wisconsin, Madison. Publications include *Jean Toomer, Artist: A Study of His Literary Life and Work* and articles on Afro-American and American fiction and autobiography. Editor of *Critical Essays on Toni Morrison*. GWENDOLYN BROOKS

Jeslyn Medoff. Graduate student, English, Rutgers University. Co-editor of *Kissing the Rod: An Anthology of Seventeenth-century Women's Verse*. Contributor to *British Women Writers: A Critical Reference Guide*. Author of articles on Elizabeth Bowen, Sarah Fye Egerton, Willa Cather, and other British and American women writers. MAXINE HONG KINGSTON

Adalaide Morris. Professor of English, University of Iowa. Author of *Wallace Stevens: Imagination and Faith* and essays on the poetry of Dickinson, Rich, H.D., and the American literary canon. Co-editor of *Extended Outlooks: The Iowa Review Collection of Contemporary Women Writers;* editor of H.D. centennial issue of the *Iowa Review*. HILDA DOOLITTLE

Marjorie Pryse. Associate Professor of English and psychotherapist. Consultant on curriculum inclusion at State University of New York at Plattsburgh. Publications include: *The Mark and the Knowledge: Social Stigma in Classic American Fiction; Conjuring: Black Women, Fiction, and Literary Tradition;* and numerous articles on American fiction. MARY E. WILKINS FREEMAN

Celeste M. Schenck. Associate Professor of English, Barnard College. Author of *Mourning and Panegyric: The Poetics of Pastoral Ceremony;* co-editor of *Life/Lines: Theorizing Women's Autobiography*. Editor of *Reading Women Writing*, a series of feminist criticism from Cornell University Press; founder and director of *Women Poets at Barnard*, annual poetry contest, prize and book series. AMY LOWELL

Esther H. Schor. Assistant Professor of English, Princeton University; Director, Mellon Seminar on Gender and Feminist Theory. Co-editor (with Pat C. Hoy and Robert DiYanni) of *Women's Voices: Visions and Perspectives;* co-editor (with Audrey Fisch and Anne Mellor) of *The Other Mary Shelley: Beyond "Frankenstein"*; author of essays on nineteenth-century British literature and women writers; poems published in *Times Literary Supplement* and the *Yale Review*. SUSAN SONTAG

Pat A. Skantze. Teacher and writer. Currently completing a doctoral dissertation at Columbia University on gender, performance, and print in seventeenth-century drama. LILLIAN HELLMAN

Claudia Tate. Professor of American and African-American Literatures, George Washington University. Editor of *Black Women Writers at Work* and *The Works of Katherine D. Tillman;* author of *Domestic Allegories of Black Political Desire;* and numerous articles on African American literary culture. ALICE WALKER

Cheryl B. Torsney. Associate Professor of English, West Virginia University. Author of *Constance Fenimore Woolson: The Grief Artistry.* Editor of *Critical Essays on Constance Fenimore Woolson.* Author of articles on Henry James, literary theory, and American fiction. ELLEN GLASGOW; CARSON McCULLERS

Candace Waid. Assistant Professor of English and American Studies, Yale University. Author of *Edith Wharton's Letters from the Underworld: Fictions of Women and Writing.* Edited and introduced Edith Wharton, *The Muse's Tragedy and Other Stories;* author of introduction to Edith Wharton, *The Custom of the Country.* EUDORA WELTY

Craig Werner. Professor of Afro-American Culture, University of Wisconsin, Madison. Author of *Paradoxical Resolutions: American Fiction Since James Joyce; Adrienne Rich: The Poet and Her Critics;* and *Black Women Novelists: An Annotated Bibliography.* ZORA NEALE HURSTON

Patricia Yaeger. Associate Professor of English, University of Michigan, Ann Arbor. Publications include *Honey-Mad Women: Emancipating Strategies in Women's Writing* and essays on Kate Chopin, Flannery O'Connor, Eudora Welty, Charlotte Brontë, and critical theory. Co-editor of *Refiguring the Father: New Feminist Readings of Patriarchy.* FLANNERY O'CONNOR

Joan Zseleczky. Editor. Eight of her books have won professional awards, including three from the Professional and Scholarly Publishing Group of the Association of American Publishers. Managing Editor, *European Writers, Dictionary of Scientific Biography, Supplement II, Modern American Women Writers,* and *African American Writers,* among others. Currently originating new works in special reference at Garland Publishing. JOAN DIDION

INDEX

Arabic numbers printed in bold-face type refer to extended treatment of a subject.